James "Athenian" Stuart, 1713–1788

The Rediscovery of Antiquity

JAMES "ATHENIAN" STUART
1713–1788
THE REDISCOVERY OF ANTIQUITY

SUSAN WEBER SOROS, EDITOR

Published for The Bard Graduate Center for Studies in the Decorative Arts, Design, and Culture, New York, by
Yale University Press, New Haven and London

For Mark

This catalogue is published in conjunction with the exhibition
"James 'Athenian' Stuart, 1713-1788: The Rediscovery of Antiquity,"
held at The Bard Graduate Center for Studies in the Decorative Arts, Design and Culture
from November 16, 2006 through February 11, 2007.

Exhibition tour: Victoria and Albert Museum, London
March 15 through June 24, 2007

Exhibition curator and catalogue editor: Susan Weber Soros
Project coordinators: Catherine Arbuthnott, London;
Michelle Hargrave and Olga Valle Tetkowski, New York
Catalogue production: Sally Salvesen, London
Editor: Martina D'Alton

Director of Exhibitions and Executive Editor, Exhibition Catalogues,
Bard Graduate Center: Nina Stritzler-Levine

Library of Congress Control number: 2006934327
ISBN: 0-300-11713-2

Catalogue and jacket design: Michael Shroyer
Printed and bound: CS Graphics, Singapore

Front cover (detail of fig. 2-10): James Stuart. View of the west end of the Temple of
Minerva Polias and Caryatid Porch of the Erectheon, Athens, 1750s-60s. Gouache. Stuart is
shown sketching in the foreground. RIBA Library Drawings Collection, London, SD
145/6. *Checklist no. 29.*

Frontispiece: Attributed to Philip Jean. Portrait miniature of James Stuart, ca. 1778.
Watercolor and body color on ivory. National Portrait Gallery, London, NPG 55a.
Checklist no. 203.

Endpapers: Map of Greece. Engraving. From *Antiquities of Athens*, vol. 3 (1794): foldout.
Checklist no. 90.

Support for "James 'Athenian' Stuart, 1713–1788:
The Rediscovery of Antiquity"
has been generously provided by
Jan and Warren Adelson,
Constance and Harvey Krueger,
The Graham Foundation for Advanced Studies in the Fine Arts,
The Samuel H. Kress Foundation,
and Martin P. Levy.

CONTENTS

ABOUT THE AUTHORS

Catherine Arbuthnott

Consulting curator of exhibitions at the Bard Graduate Center; author of books on nineteenth-century British designers, including *E. W. Godwin: Aesthetic Movement Architect and Designer* (contributing author, 1999) and *Thomas Jeckyll: Architect and Designer, 1827–1881* (co-curator and co-author with Susan Weber Soros, 2003).

Geoffrey Beard

Former Director of the Visual Arts Centre at the University of Lancaster, co-founder of the Furniture History Society, and former editor of *Furniture History* (1965–74); author of numerous books and articles on British craftsmen and interior decoration in country houses, including *Craftsmen and Interior Decoration in England, 1660–1820* (1981), *Stucco and Decorative Plasterwork in Europe* (1982), and *Upholsterers and Interior Furnishing in England, 1530–1840* (1997).

Barry Bergdoll

Professor and Chair of the Department of Art History, Columbia University; exhibition curator and author of many books on modern European architectural history, particularly in France and Germany between 1750 and 1900, including *Léon Vaudoyer: Historicism in the Age of Industry* (1994), *Karl Friedrich Schinkel: An Architecture for Prussia* (1994), *European Architecture, 1750–1890* (2000), *Mies in Berlin* (2001), and *Fragments: Architecture and the Unfinished: Essays Presented to Robin Middleton* (co-editor with Werner Oechslin, 2006).

Kerry Bristol

Lecturer and Director of the Centre for Architecture and Material Culture, University of Leeds, School of Fine Art, History of Art and Cultural Studies; author of "James 'Athenian' Stuart (1713–1788) and the Genesis of the Greek Revival in British Architecture," Ph.D. diss., Courtauld Institute of Art, London (1997), and numerous articles on Stuart, including "The Painted Rooms of 'Athenian' Stuart," *Georgian Group Journal* (2000).

Julius Bryant

Keeper of the Word and Image Department, The Victoria and Albert Museum, London; editor of *Collections Review*; author of numerous articles and catalogues on English country houses, including *Marble Hill: The Design and Use of a Palladian Estate* (1986), *The Landscape of Kenwood* (with Carol Colson, 1990), and *London's Country House Collections* (1993).

Christopher Eimer

Dealer in medals and related works of art; author of *British Commemorative Medals and Their Values* (1987), *Medallic Portraits of the Duke of Wellington* (1994), and *The Pingo Family and Medal Making in Eighteenth-Century Britain* (1998).

Richard Hewlings

Senior Properties Historian, English Heritage, and member of the Faculty of Architecture and History of Art, University of Cambridge; honorary editor, *The Georgian Group Journal*; author of numerous articles on English historical properties, including "Belsay Hall and the Personality of Sir Charles Monck" in *Late Georgian Classicism: Papers Given at The Georgian Group Symposium, 1987* (1988), and "The Link Room at Chiswick House: Lord Burlington as Antiquarian," *Apollo* (1995).

Alexander Marr

Lecturer in Art History, The University of St. Andrews, Scotland; author of books and articles on the relationship between mathematics, material culture, and the book in the Late Renaissance, as well as the history of gardens and designed landscapes in the eighteenth century, including "William Beckford and the Landscape Garden" in *William Beckford: 1760–1844: An Eye for the Magnificent* (2001), and *Mutio Oddi* (forthcoming).

Frank Salmon
Assistant Director for Academic Activities, Paul Mellon Centre for Studies in British Art, London; Adjunct Associate Professor of the History of Art, Yale University, New Haven; Chairman of the Faculty of Archaeology, History, and Letters of the British School, Rome (beginning 2007); author of books and articles on the architectural and archaeological interchange between Britain and Italy in the eighteenth and nineteenth centuries, including *Building on Ruins: The Rediscovery of Rome and English Architecture* (2000).

Michael Snodin
Co-curator of International Baroque Exhibitions, The Victoria and Albert Museum, London; President, International Confederation of Architectural Museums; editor and contributing author of many books on Western ornament and architecture, including *European Ornament: A Social History since 1450* (with Maurice Howard, 1996) and *Sir William Chambers, Architect to George III* (with John Harris, 1996).

Susan Weber Soros
Founder and Director of the Bard Graduate Center; curator of exhibitions and author of books on nineteenth-century decorative arts, including *The Secular Furniture of E. W. Godwin* (1999), *E. W. Godwin: Aesthetic Movement Architect and Designer, 1827–1881* (editor and contributing author, 1999), *Thomas Jeckyll: Architect and Designer* (with Catherine Arbuthnott, 2003), and *Castellani and Italian Archaeological Jewelry* (co-editor with Stefanie Walker, and contributing author, 2004).

M. G. Sullivan
Department of Western Art, Ashmolean Museum, University of Oxford; assistant editor of the *Gunnis Dictionary of British Sculptors, 1660–1851* (forthcoming); author of "Rapin, Hume and the Identity of the Historian in Eighteenth-Century England," *History of European Ideas* (2002), and various entries in the *New Oxford Dictionary of National Biography* (2004).

David Watkin
Professor of the History of Architecture at the University of Cambridge; Vice-Chairman of The Georgian Group; author of numerous publications on architectural history from the eighteenth through the twentieth century, including *Neoclassical and Nineteenth Century Architecture* (with Robin Middleton, 1980), *The English Vision: The Picturesque in Architecture, Landscape, and Garden Design* (1982), *Athenian Stuart: Pioneer of the Greek Revival* (1982), and *Morality and Architecture Revisited* (2001).

PREFACE

In 1748 James Stuart and Nicholas Revett were not alone in the archaeological bonanza that swept the mid-eighteenth-century culture of the Grand Tour when they set out to document ancient Greek architecture. Their express aim was to influence the practice of modern architecture and design. Over the next three-quarters of a century, as the four volumes of *Antiquities of Athens* slowly appeared, their names would be associated as almost none other with the radical contemporary potential of new knowledge of the ancient world. For over a century their engraved plates would be the standard reference for implementing the reform project of Enlightenment neoclassicism. Theirs was arguably the first great avant-garde project of cultural reform in the history of modern architecture, even as it would set new standards in archaeological site recording, and play a remarkable role in the history of taste.

"Architecture owes all that is perfect to the Greeks," the French Abbé Laugier declared in 1753, even as the two Englishmen were hard at work in Athens, measuring and documenting buildings that many had upheld as standards, even if hardly any western Europeans had seen them at first hand. "There is but one way for the moderns to become great, even inimitable; I mean, by imitating the Greeks," added the German Johann Joachim Winckelmann—who would never set foot in Greece—two years later in his famous *Reflections on the Imitation of the Painting and Sculpture of the Greeks* (1755). A dense theoretic, and polemical, discourse, with European-wide reverberations, was being established. It promoted a return to fundamental architectural truths and to Grecian simplicity as matters of far weightier import than the issues of taste discussed in the London meetings and country house saloons of the members of the Society of Dilettanti, major underwriters of Stuart and Revett's expedition. *Antiquities of Athens* added imagery, measurements, and concrete models to a theoretic sea change and to a historical debate. The dimensions of this debate were hardly imaginable to the two English artist/travelers as they set out on the arduous task of distilling the truth of fourth- and fifth-century Athenian culture from the sediment of later Byzantine and Ottoman culture in modern Athens. By 1762, when the first volume of *Antiquities* finally appeared in London, Greek archaeology had become an instrument of self-conscious artistic reform; along with it, historical knowledge became a medium of cultural critique. What had begun as a project of refined documentation entered the realm of public discussion and debate as another salvo in the debates over the relative merits of Greek vs. Roman culture and over the very nature of Imitation in the arts, one of the first great episodes then of the emerging historicist culture of the late eighteenth century. For the next century European and American architectural theory and practice would be closely entwined with archaeological research and debate. In the 1750s and 1760s archaeological knowledge emerged not only as an essential professional advantage but as an instrument for taking position on the very nature of architecture and the proper course for its development. To what extent James Stuart set out with a foreknowledge of the consequences of his complex project on the Greek mainland, the full meaning of his enterprise became clear once sides began to shape up, and debate became inflamed. Nearly everyone who was anyone in the antiquarian circles of Rome weighed in, from

Piranesi to Stuart's fellow countrymen Robert Adam and Alan Ramsay. It might even be argued that had it not been for the rivalry with the parallel French project of Julien David Le Roy, who scooped Stuart and Revett when he published his *Ruines des plus beaux monuments de la Grèce* in Paris in 1758, Stuart's reputation and career would have been very different. In a strikingly modern way, Stuart was operating in a new hybrid world, with one foot in the elite circles of the Society of Dilettanti, another in the ever greater whirlwind of public debate.

The fragmented nature of James, now "Athenian," Stuart's subsequent career in England has always seemed difficult to reconcile with the zeal he demonstrated in the preface to the first volume of *Antiquities*. Although almost since its inception the book has been seen as a document of a clearly defined, almost visionary, project, Stuart's architectural and design work in the three decades between his return to England and his death in 1788 has seemed contradictory. His designs are grounded as much in the styles he set out to reform—seen, for instance, in the underlying Palladianism of the façade of Lichfield House of 1764—as they are in an unwavering project of distilling new models of purity from distant exemplars. His relatively small oeuvre, particularly in comparison to the avalanche of success that greeted his rival Robert (Bob the "Roman") Adam, seems to point to a rather lackluster initial reception of his project for a Greek Revival, if such was ever his intent. Hardly anywhere was he able to work exclusively on ex novo projects. His practice, with the notable exception of his work at Greenwich, remained largely private and luxurious. A full-blown Greek Revival in English architecture would not emerge until after the Napoleonic Wars and the posthumous publication of the fourth and final volume of *Antiquities* in 1816. Stuart's greatest influence, therefore, was—paradoxically enough—to take place in a cultural, social, and political moment that bore very little relationship to his own.

Stuart's career demands reconsideration, for woven throughout it are the paradoxes of practice in the great century and a half of historicism, still one of the least understood phenomena of modern cultural practice. Stuart's work can be interpreted as a polemical adherence to a single model, or as the inventive eclectic response to a widened field of references. His antiquarianism can be viewed as nostalgic or vanguard, while his relations with patrons and clients were on a cusp between the artist as a radical trendsetter or the craftsman who fulfills the larger vision of aristocratic tastes established in networks such as that of the Society of Dilettanti. It is a career that is still animated by both unresolved research questions and larger issues that provide insight into the roles of model, imitation, and historical knowledge in architectural practice. The present volume, brilliantly brought together by Susan Weber Soros, offers an outpouring of new research, not only on Stuart's career, but also on the social, political, and intellectual context in which his work was created. The book adds a wealth of new information and insights into the achievements and impact of a seminal figure, who until now has been the subject of only one comprehensive, but brief study, David Watkin's *Athenian Stuart, Pioneer of the Greek Revival* (1982). As famous as Stuart's publication has been, and as iconic as his garden follies have been in countless survey texts, it is only with this latest addition to the Bard Graduate Center's combination of fundamental research and public exhibition that this complex personality, whose career was so central to the practices established by the archaeological revolution of the mid-eighteenth century, is fully unearthed.

Barry Bergdoll
Columbia University, New York

Editor's note:
Regarding style and citations in the text and footnotes — In quotations from old texts and original documents such as letters, most misspellings are left, without annotating each word with "sic." For each chapter bibliographic citations are given in full, when they first occur, and in a short form thereafter. There are a few exceptions: *The Antiquities of Athens*, the seminal work by James Stuart and Nicholas Revett, is referred to in the notes simply as *Antiquities* with volume and page information given. The full citation is under "Stuart" in the bibliography. Two other references, which are cited in most of the chapters, are also accorded a short form: David Watkin's early investigation of Stuart, *Athenian Stuart: Pioneer of the Greek Revival* (1982); and Kerry Bristol's unpublished dissertation, "James 'Athenian' Stuart (1713–1788) and the Genesis of the Greek Revival in British Architecture," which is referred to as Bristol, "Stuart and the Genesis of the Greek Revival" (1997). Figure references are keyed to each chapter; the notation "see" indicates illustrations cited out of sequence in the chapter or found elsewhere in the book. "Checklist" numbers at the end of the illustration captions indicate objects displayed in the exhibition and refer the reader to the list at the end of the book for further information on the pictured object.

James Stuart. View of the Tower of the Winds, Athens (Horologium of Andronikos of Cyrrhestes), 1750s–60s. Gouache. RIBA Library Drawings Collection, London, SD 145/3. *Checklist no. 27.*

INTRODUCTION

SUSAN WEBER SOROS

James "Athenian" Stuart (1713–1788): The Rediscovery of Antiquity is the first comprehensive exhibition and publication focusing on the life and career of this major innovator in the development of neoclassicism. Although Stuart was one of the most compelling figures in the history of architecture and design, his contributions remain largely unknown, overshadowed by those of his two leading rivals, Sir William Chambers and Robert Adam.

In 1762 Stuart and his collaborator Nicholas Revett published the long-awaited first volume of *Antiquities of Athens.* This extraordinary work, with its hundreds of measured drawings, helped to shape the European understanding of ancient Greece and its architectural heritage, sparking an interest in antiquity that profoundly affected the history of architecture. More immediately, it contributed to the creation and dissemination of the neoclassical style in England and throughout Europe during the third quarter of the eighteenth century. Three subsequent volumes were completed after Stuart's death, and *Antiquities* was eventually translated into French, German, and Italian. It continued to serve as a principal source well into the nineteenth century. As Stuart himself stated, the primary purpose of the work was to expand the classical repertoire of architects and designers, and to "contribute to the improvement of the Art itself, which at present appears to be founded on too partial and too scanty a system of ancient examples." While best known today for *Antiquities,* Stuart was also an artist in his own right and an architect and designer of interiors, furnishings, paintings, and monumental sculpture.

★ ★ ★

In the long tradition of scholarly discussion and debate, twelve distinguished authors bring together the most recent research on Stuart's life and career in this volume. David Watkin examines Stuart's most enduring achievement, *Antiquities of Athens,* placing it in context and relating it to the creation of what might be called the "myth of Athens." In a later chapter, David Watkin expands on this theme, exploring the ripple effect of *Antiquities.* At the time of the posthumous publication of volume four in 1816, the Greek Revival style was about to dominate British architecture and would eventually spread to other countries, including Scotland, Germany, and the United States, its influence lasting well into the twentieth century.

Catherine Arbuthnott deftly sketches a life of Stuart, drawing from contemporary evidence as well as modern research, especially by Kerry Bristol. Stuart came from humble beginnings, the son of "a mariner of inferior station," yet in an age when British society was especially stratified, he managed to rise to extraordinary heights. Training in the arts, specifically as a painter of fans, then a fashionable accessory and artifact, served as a stepping stone. Like artists before and since, Stuart embarked on a journey of artistic discovery across Europe, with Rome his destination. Frank Salmon writes about this important, formative period of Stuart's life. In Rome, Stuart established himself as an antiquary and made contacts that would later serve him well. He also honed his skills as an early archaeologist, sketching and studying the Obelisk of Pharoah Psammetichus II which was then being excavated. Stuart published his findings in *De Obelisco Caesaris Augusti . . .* (1750). This chapter also details Stuart and Revett's pioneering work in Athens, where they painstakingly measured and sketched the city's ancient buildings and ruins, work that forms the heart of *Antiquities of Athens.* It was a risky business, almost costing Stuart his life.

One of the striking features of Stuart's career is the close-knit patronage circle that he cultivated. Kerry Bristol traces the strands of this "web of patronage," as it spun outward. Through connections made in Italy, Stuart was invited to join the Society of Dilettanti, a somewhat quirky London dining club that also promoted serious scholarship. Most of Stuart's commissions came about through members of the Dilettanti. Stuart belonged to other societies as well, notably what came to be known as the Royal Society of Arts, and these memberships were also useful to him. In a later chapter, Kerry Bristol focuses in depth on Stuart's most important public commission, one that he acquired via a Dilettanti member—the Royal Hospital for Seamen at Greenwich. Detailed analysis of Stuart's contributions to the project provides valuable insight into eighteenth-century architectural practices and public works projects.

Stuart's finest known interior design work centered on a few London town houses, the subject of a chapter by Richard Hewlings. Here, Stuart's intimate knowledge of decoration developed in antiquity was given free rein. The most extraordinary demonstration of his skill was at Spencer House, where Stuart applied accurate Greek and Roman detail to the furnishings and interiors, making it a very early example of neoclassical design. The Painted Room today remains one of the jewels of British neoclassicism. Outside of London, some of Stuart's first architectural projects involved alterations to country houses and villas, and Julius Bryant isolates Stuart's contributions to the known projects. During the eighteenth-century, garden buildings increasingly became an important part of the landscaping of these country estates. Alexander Marr's essay focuses on Stuart's contributions in this area. Taken together, these three chapters correct the conventional view that Stuart's architectural commissions largely consisted of copies of Greek sources. In his designs Stuart revealed an expertise in Roman, Renaissance, and baroque models, as well as Greek.

The eighteenth century also saw a shift in the field of architectural sculpture. M. G. Sullivan explores the relationship between Stuart and the carvers he hired. Once considered merely craftsmen, masons in Great Britain gradually came to be accepted as sculptors of the fine arts, a change influenced by Stuart. Three further chapters concentrate on particular products of Stuart's designs: my own chapter is a study of Stuart's furniture designs, while Michael Snodin writes about Stuart's metalwork, and Christopher Eimer enumerates Stuart's designs for medals. In each of these areas, Stuart developed special working relationships with the craftsmen who executed his designs. The projects often involved true collaboration. In the appendix to this catalogue, Geoffrey Beard has compiled and annotated a list of these eighteenth-century craftsmen, some newly identified.

The objects in the exhibition, many of them photographed especially for this publication, serve as illustrations to the thirteen chapters, along with comparative photographs, from period portraits to engravings. The exhibition objects represent the formation and flowering of Stuart's oeuvre. A separate checklist details materials, measurements, probable dates, and publication history. An illustrated chronology of Stuart's work and a full bibliography of primary and secondary sources also serve as valuable resources for scholars. The chronology allows an assessment of Stuart's various activities at any one moment and reveals the changing nature of his fields of work. The bibliography is the first full bibliography on Stuart to be published.

Acknowledgments

James "Athenian" Stuart (1713–1788): The Rediscovery of Antiquity has been several years in the making and has involved the efforts of a very dedicated group. I would especially like to recognize the extraordinary talent and diligence of my research associate, Catherine Arbuthnott. During the past three years, she has attended to all the organizational and logistical details, guided me through the numerous archives and libraries in Great Britain, and assisted with the photography of Stuart material in Great Britain. This project would not have been possible without her dedication, interest, and insights. Thanks are also due to Michelle Hargrave, research associate at the Bard Graduate Center. She painstakingly did research in New York City's many libraries, made contributions to the appendix, and helped with captions, footnotes, the checklist, and bibliography. My assistants Caroline Stern and Sandra Fell undertook the task of photographic permissions. Michael Erwee provided useful information and help through the archives and museums of Rome. At an important stage in the development of this catalogue, I received critical support from Barry Bergdoll, who also graciously undertook to write the preface to this catalogue, and from Tracy L. Ehrlich and William Rieder.

I am grateful to the authors of the essays that comprise the main part of this catalogue. They have added considerably to the Stuart literature. Kerry Bristol has been especially generous in making available her original research, first presented in her doctoral dissertation. The other authors have been equally collegial. My sincere thanks to: Catherine Arbuthnott, Geoffrey Beard, Julius Bryant, Christopher Eimer, Richard Hewlings, Alexander Marr, Frank Salmon, Michael Snodin, M. G. Sullivan, and David Watkin.

The Victoria and Albert Museum, London, was the major lender to the exhibition, and I am especially grateful to Mark Jones and his staff at the museum, including

Frances Collard, Sarah Medlam, Christopher Wilk, and Oliver Winchester, Department of Furniture and Woodwork; Fiona Leslie, Department of Prints, Drawings, and Paintings; Michael Snodin and Julius Bryant, Word & Image Department; and Roxanne Peters and Elaine Morris, V&A Images. A special note of thanks goes to Charles Hind, Justine Sambrook, Catriona Cornelius, and the Royal Institute of British Architects (RIBA), London, who made their holdings of Stuart gouaches and drawings available for the exhibition. Additional thanks to Poppy Hollman, Linda Lloyd Jones, Mike Malham, David Packer, and Rebecca Wallace.

We would also like to recognize the many other museums, galleries, institutions, and individuals who generously loaned work from their collections or gave us permission to include photographs: Antikensammlung, Staatliche Museen zu Berlin: Ursula Kästner; *Apollo* Magazine, London: Jessica Chaney, Michael Hall; Ashmolean Museum, University of Oxford; Beinecke Rare Book and Manuscript Library, Yale University, New Haven: Julie Clements, Stephen Jones, Sue Moss; Bexley Local Studies and Archives Centre, London: Simon McKeon, Frances Sweeny; Bibliothèque municipale de Besançon: Marie-Hélène Ménie, Marie-Claire Waille; Bibliothèque nationale de France, Paris: Zoubida Zerkane; Bildarchiv Preußischer Kulturbesitz, Berlin: Ulla Harmsen, Sylvia Hoffmann, Kornelia Hurraß, Norbert Ludwig, Elke Schwichtenberg; Birmingham City Archives: David Bishop, Rachel Clare, Samantha Collenette, Paul Hemmings, Corinna Rayner; Bodleian Library, University of Oxford: Bruce Barker-Benfield, Tricia Buckingham, Reginald P. Carr, Melissa Dalziel; John and Rebecca Booth; The Bridgeman Art Library, London: Nick Dunmore, Georgina French, Thomas Haggerty; The British Library, London: Barbara O'Connor, Robert Davies, Maz Karim, Sandra Powlette; British Museum, London: Joe Cribb, Virginia Ennor, Antony Griffiths, Mary Hinton, Janet Larkin, Keith Lowe, Bethan Mogford, Kirstin Munro, Sheila O'Connell, J. Ramkalawn, Janice Reading; Christie's Images, Ltd., London: Stella Calvert-Smith, Angela Minshull, Emma Strouts; Sir Robert Clark of Penicuik Bt.; Durham University Library: Sheila Hingley; Earl Gregg Swem Library, the College of William and Mary, Williamsburg, VA: Stacy Gould; Country Life Picture Library, London: Camilla Costello, Nicole Mendelsohn, Jackie Moss, Lara Platman, Dominic Walters; Courtauld Institute of Art, London (Book Library, Conway Library, Photographic Survey of Private Collections, and Witt Library): Jane Cunningham, Timothy Davies, Geoffrey Fisher, Emma Hayes, Beth S. Taylor; The Devonshire Collection, Chatsworth: Diane Naylor; Downing College, University of Cambridge: Sarah Westwood; École nationale supérieure des beaux-arts, Paris: Françoise Portelance; Edinburgh University Library: Lynda Ardern, Tricia Boyd, Sheila Noble, John Scally; English Heritage / National Monuments Record Centre, Swindon: Natalie Hill, Alyson Rogers, Kirsty Scorer, Neil Stevenson, Lucinda Walker, Emma Whinton, Nigel Wilkins; Sir Nicholas Goodison; Greenwich Heritage Centre, London: Jenny O'Keefe; Guildhall Library, City of London: John Fisher, Alice Powell, Jeremy Smith, Anne Stewart; Fine Arts Museums of San Francisco: Susan Grinols, Robert Johnson; Hunterian Museum, Glasgow University: Donal Bateson, Mungo Campbell, Sally-Anne Coupar, Anne Dulau, James Lafferty-Furphy, Pamela Robertson; Istituto Nazionale per la Grafica, Rome: Serenita Papaldo; Library of Congress, Washington, D.C.: Barbara Moore; London Metropolitan Archives, City of London: Howard Doble, Heather Edwards-Hedley, Bridget Howlett, Hilary Ordman, Elizabeth Scudder; The Metropolitan Museum of Art, New York: Deanna Cross; The National Archives of Scotland, Edinburgh: David J. Brown, George P. MacKenzie; National Library of Ireland, Dublin: Joanna Finegan, Sandra McDermott, Colette O'Flaherty; National Maritime Museum, Greenwich: David Taylor; National Museum of Antiquities (Rijksmuseum van Oudheden), Leiden: Peter Jan Bomhof, M. E. Kleiterp; National Portrait Gallery, London: David McNeff, Tom Morgan, Kathleen Soriano, Helen Trompeteler; The National Trust, UK: David Adshead, Chezzy Brownen, Harvey Edgington, Maggie Gowan, Nikita Hooper, Geoffrey Howarth, Richard L. Kemp, Simon McCormack, Gill Spencer, Arabella Stewart, Alexa Warburton, Lynne Wray; Neumeister Münchener Kunstauktionshaus, Munich: Michael Scheublein; The New York Public Library: Tom Lisanti, Steven Saks; Partridge Fine Arts PLC, London: Lucy Morton; The Paul Mellon Centre for Studies in British Art, London; The Pierpont Morgan Library, New York: Patricia Courtney, Lucy Eldridge, Marilyn Palmeri, Charles E. Pierce, Jr., Eva Soos, Kathleen Stuart; The Royal Collection, Windsor: Caroline de Guitant, Karen Lawson, Sir Hugh Roberts; Royal Commission on the Ancient and Historical Monuments of Wales, Ceredigion: R. A. Griffiths, Peter White; Sheffield Archives: Bob Hale, Robin Wiltshire; Sir John Soane's Museum, London: Stephen Astley, Helen Dorsey, Tim Knox, Susan Palmer; Sotheby's Picture Library, London: Sue Daly, Fergus Lyons; St. George's Chapel Archives and Chapter Library, Windsor: Enid Davies, Eileen Scarff; Staatliche Graphische Sammlung München: Sabine Wölfel, Kurt Zeitler; Staffordshire Record Office: Joanne Cartwright, Thea Randall, Joanna Terry; University of Durham, County Durham: J. Lake; University of Glasgow; The Vatican Museum, Vatican City; Wadsworth Athenaeum Museum, Hartford; Wedgwood Museum, Barlaston, Stoke-on-Trent: June Bonell, Lynn Miller, Gaye Blake Roberts; Robert Weighton Partnership, Stamford; Westminster School, London: Eddie Smith, Douglas Heathcote; William Salt Library, Stafford: Thea Randall.

I am grateful to Lord Rothschild and Earl Spencer for their many kindnesses. I also wish to thank the owners of Stuart buildings and the keepers of those churches and monuments with Stuart commissions who allowed access, provided photographs, and generously helped with this study of Stuart's work: Earl Spencer, Bruce Bailey, Jane Clucas, Edward Crookes, Zainab Desai, Caroline Dwyer, Dawn Griffin, Charlotte Millar, Althorp, Northampton; Rev. John Williams, Linda Watson, St. John the Baptist Church, Ashley; Nancy Lady Bagot, Blithfield Hall, Staffordshire; Rev. Jeanette Gosney, St. Mary the Virgin Church, Braughing; Joy Coupe, Bristol Cathedral; Peter Foord, Anne Wren, Valerie Pitcher, Chislehurst Golf Club, Camden Place; Rev. Prebendary Patrick Tuft, St. Nicholas of Myra Church, Chiswick; James Methuen Campbell, Corsham Court; Rev. C. L. Beevers, Ron Collins, Sid Eagles, St. John the Baptist Church, Eastnor; Forsters LLP, 31 Hill Street, London; Manda Patel, Global Retreat Centre, Nuneham Park, Oxfordshire; Helen Beioley, Valerie Dalgliesh, Tess O'Flynn, Chenoa Bailey, Jeanette Norris, The Greenwich Foundation for the Old Royal Naval College; Lord Cobham, Joyce Purnell, K. Wilkinson, Hagley, Worcestershire; Fiona Walklett, Marc Goodwin, Ingestre Hall Residential Arts Centre; M. Jameel Ltd., Lichfield House, London; Lucinda J. A. Compton, Stewart Gill, Newby Hall, Yorkshire; W. H. C. Gascoigne, Nuneham, Oxfordshire; Rev. Bill Merrington, St. Mary the Virgin Church, Preston-on-Stour; David Wall, Catherine O'Connor, Melissa Brennan, Adnan Muhammad, Caoimhe Allman, Office of Public Works,

Dublin; Rathfarnham Castle, County Dublin; Jenny Allen, David Doehren, Lizzie Nurse, Shugborough, Staffordshire; Jane Rick, Spencer House, London; Julie Firth, Stowe Landscape Gardens, Buckinghamshire; Rev. John Vickerstaff, Sudbury, Derbyshire; George Potiakis, Wimpole Hall; Rev. Neil Brice, St. Andrew's Church, Wimpole; Duncan Jeffery, Westminster Abbey, London; Fitzwilliam Estate Offices, Wentworth, Yorkshire; Rev. David Paskins, John Radford, Wimborne St. Giles, Dorset.

This project has benefited greatly from the contributions of many scholars, as well as curators and dealers, who have shared their valuable insights: David Adshead, The National Trust; Stephen Astley, Drawings Curator, Sir John Soane's Museum, London; Rosemary Baird, Goodwood House; Jonathan Betts, Senior Curator of Horology, the Royal Observatory, National Maritime Museum; Sir Nicholas Goodison; John Hardy, Christie's London; John and Eileen Harris; John Heward; Charles Hind, Royal Institute of British Archictects, Department of Prints and Drawings; Niall Hobhouse; Pat Kirkham, Professor, Bard Graduate Center; Martin P. Levy, H. Blairman & Sons, Ltd.; Harris Lindsay; Peter Linstead-Smith, horologist; Christopher Lloyd, Surveyor of the Queen's Pictures, the Royal Collection, Windsor; James Lomax, Curator, Temple Newsam House, London; Jonathan Marsden, Deputy Surveyor of the Queen's Works of Art, the Royal Collection, Windsor; Lucy Morton, Partridge Fine Arts PLC, London; Richard Pailthorpe; Roger Quarm, Paintings Curator, National Maritime Museum, Greenwich; Sir Hugh Roberts, Director of the Royal Collection, Windsor; Christopher Simon Sykes; Michael Vickers, Professor of Archaeology, University of Oxford.

Librarians and archivists at many institutions and collections provided valuable assistance: *Apollo* Magazine, London; Ashmolean Museum, Oxford (Department of Antiquities); Avery Architectural and Fine Arts Library, Columbia University, New York; Bedfordshire and Luton Archives and Record Service; Beinecke Rare Book and Manuscript Library, Yale University, New Haven; Bexley Local Studies and Archives Centre, Kent; Bibliothèque municipale de Besançon; Bibliothèque nationale de France, Paris; Bildarchiv Preußischer Kulturbesitz, Berlin; Bodleian Library, Oxford (Department of Western Manuscripts); British Museum Archive, London; British Newspaper Library, Colindale; Birmingham City Archives and Central Library (Local Studies Collection); The Bridgeman Art Library, London; Bromley Central Library

(Local Studies Collection); Brook's Club, London; Buckinghamshire County Record Office; Cambridge University Library; Cambridgeshire Collection, Cambridge Central Library; Cambridgeshire Country Records Office; Centre for Kentish Studies, Maidstone; Charleston Museum; Chislehurst Library; Courtauld Institute of Art, London (Book Library, Conway Library, Photographic Survey of Private Collections and Witt Library); The Devonshire Collection, Chatsworth; Country Life Picture Library, London; Downing College, University of Cambridge; East Sussex Record Office; École nationale superieure des beaux-arts, Paris; English Heritage / National Monuments Record Centre, Swindon; Family Records Centre, Islington; Greenwich Heritage Centre, London; Hammersmith and Fulham Libraries (Archives and Local History); Historic Buildings Department, Department of the Environment, Heritage and Local Government, Dublin; Hertfordshire Archives and Local Studies; Irish Architectural Archive, Dublin; Irish Georgian Society, Dublin; Istituto Nazionale per la Grafica, Rome; The Archive Centre, King's College, Cambridge; Library of Congress, Washington, D.C.; London Metropolitan Archives, City of London; Paul Mellon Centre for Studies in British Art, London; National Archives, Kew; Simon Machola, Madlin and Maddson, Chartered Surveyors, Farnham; Ministry of Defence Art Collection, London (Royal Navy Trophy Centre, Admiralty Centre); National Archives of Scotland, Edinburgh; National Museum of Antiquities (Rijksmuseum van Oudheden), Leiden; National Library of Ireland, Dublin (Department of Prints and Drawings); Liverpool Museum (Department of Decorative Art); The Metropolitan Museum of Art, New York (The Thomas J. Watson Library); National Maritime Museum, Greenwich; National Trust Photo Library, Swindon; The New York Public Library; Probate Registry, York; Royal Collection Picture Library, Windsor; Royal Commission on the Ancient and Historical Monuments of Wales, Ceredigion; Royal Institute of British Architects Library (RIBA), London; Royal Library, Windsor; Royal Society of Arts Archive and Library, London; St. George's Chapel Archives and Chapter Library, Windsor; William Salt Library, Stafford; Sheffield Archives; Sheffield City Council; Staffordshire Record Office, Stoke-on-Trent; Syon House, Middlesex; Trevor Carpenter Royal Naval Museum, Portsmouth; Trinity College Library, Dublin; Victoria and Albert Museum, London (Archive of Art and Design, Museum Archive and Registry, National Art Library); Wadsworth Athenaeum Museum, Hartford; Westminster City Library (Archives Centre).

Bruce White traveled throughout the United Kingdom photographing locations and objects for this catalogue. The results are remarkable. The Photography Department at the Victoria and Albert Museum also made a significant contribution to this catalogue. Additional photography was provided by Dirk Bakker, Clive Boursnell, A. F. Kersting, Simon Robertson of Prudence Cuming Associates, and Han Vu. Photographic assistance was provided by Simon Cuff and Matthew Wilson.

Martina D'Alton has done a magnificent job as copyeditor, and designer Michael Shroyer has created a beautiful book. I also want to thank Sally Salvesen at Yale University Press, London, for major support throughout this project. Additional thanks to Carol Liebowitz for the elegant, meticulous typesetting, Enid Zafran and Indexing Partners for indexing, and Joyce Hitchcock for proofreading.

Many individuals at the Bard Graduate Center contributed to the realization of this exhibition and catalogue. Nina Stritzler-Levine of the Exhibition Department provided invaluable support and assistance. Her team included Linda Stubbs, Olga Valle Tetkowski, and Han Vu. Ian Sullivan created an inspired installation. Rebecca Allan originated a marvelous array of public programs with Kate Haley, Rebecca Mitchell, and Corinna Zeltsman. Susan Wall and Brian Keliher of the Development Office skillfully found the necessary funding for this important exhibition. Tim Mulligan and Hollis Barnhart organized a successful press campaign. The library staff under the direction of Heather Topcik answered numerous calls for information. Lorraine Bacalles, director of Finance and Administration, kept the financial aspects of this project in order. The gallery facility is managed by John Donovan and his able staff. Finally, my thanks go to Chandler Small and the Bard Graduate Center security staff for looking after the galleries with great professionalism.

I am especially grateful for the generous contributions to this volume from the Graham Foundation for Advanced Studies in the Fine Arts and the Samuel H. Kress Foundation. Additional support was provided by Jan and Warren Adelson, Constance and Harvey Krueger, and Martin P. Levy.

Fig. 1-1. James Stuart. View of the Temple of Theseus, Athens, 1750s–60s. Gouache. RIBA Library Drawings Collection, London, SD 145/8. *Checklist no. 22.*

STUART AND REVETT:

THE MYTH OF GREECE

AND ITS AFTERLIFE

David Watkin

Despite the recent interest in establishing Stuart's varied artistic oeuvre as a designer of everything from medals to buildings, his most enduring achievement was *Antiquities of Athens* and his contribution to the creation of what we might call "the myth of Athens" (fig. 1-1). If this be so, then those of his contemporaries who regarded him primarily as an interior designer were wrong, while those are right who, from his death until the present day, have hailed him primarily for his project of uncovering Greek architecture. At the same time, he had more than one achievement and was differently viewed at different times by different people. His contribution was not just to design a number of buildings but, through *Antiquities of Athens*, to influence the style of a whole generation of architects in Europe and North America.[1]

An authority on Greek architecture has recently claimed that "it was Stuart and Revett who shaped the modern image of the Parthenon."[2] This bold claim must be set in its historical and intellectual context, in view of the central importance which, rightly or wrongly, has been assigned to the Parthenon since the days of Johann Joachim Winckelmann. As a product of the Enlightenment, which was an essentially European phenomenon,

Stuart's Grecian endeavor will thus be related to contemporary developments in France, Germany, and Italy.[3]

The European Background

Modern art historians sometimes imply that Greek architecture was confined, or at least best expressed in, what we now call Greece. However, in the ancient world there was no sharp distinction between the geographical concept now known as Greece and the rest of Hellas, or the Hellenic world, a cultural concept that included settlements in Magna Graecia (parts of Italy and Sicily) and much of the coast of present-day Asia Minor. The monuments in Italy and Sicily were thus quite as Greek or Hellenic as those in places such as Athens and Corinth. Despite this, it seems that very little was known of Greek architecture in Renaissance Italy.[4] However, during the period when the Acciaiuoli family, dukes of Florence, ruled Athens — from 1388 until its fall to the Ottoman Turks in 1548 — Ciriaco de' Pizzicolli di Ancona (Ciriacus of Ancona), an Italian merchant, man of letters, and traveler, made drawings on visits to the city in 1436 and 1444.[5] It was on the basis of these sketches that the Florentine architect Giuliano da Sangallo (1445 – 1516) made a very inaccurate drawing of the Parthenon, chang-

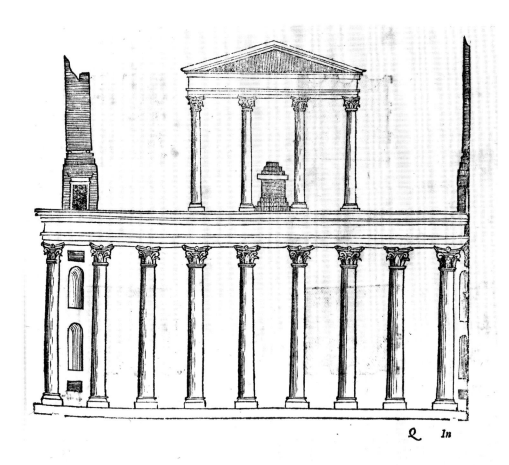

Fig. 1-2. Elevation of a building "composed of one hundred columns." Woodcut. From Sebastiano Serlio, *Tutte l'Opere d'Architettura* (1634): 97. By permission of The British Library, London, 60.e.6.

ing its order from Doric to Composite.[6] This may have inspired the open portico or Ionic temple-front that he embedded into the façade of his Villa Medici at Poggio a Caiano (ca. 1489–97), the first of its kind on any Renaissance villa, and with a figured frieze possibly inspired by that on the Parthenon.[7] Giorgio Vasari stated that Raphael (1483–1520) "kept designers all over Italy, at Pozzuolo, and even in Greece; and he was for ever searching out everything of the good that might help his art."[8] It has thus been suggested that Raphael's fresco of Venus and Amor (1517) in the Loggia of Psyche in the Villa Farnesina, Rome, was influenced by the Aphrodite and Eros on the east frieze of the Parthenon.[9]

In what was probably the most influential architectural treatise of the Renaissance, *L'Architettura* by Sebastiano Serlio, published in seven books with various titles between 1537 and 1575, the author explained that, "although the Greeks were the originators of worthy architecture — as our instructor Vitruvius and also vari-

ous other authors attest . . . those places were so despoiled that there is very little in Greece that can still be seen standing."[10] The one building in Athens to which Serlio referred was in fact Roman, the Library of Hadrian, though he identified it solely as "a building . . . composed of one hundred columns," without mentioning that his account was drawn from the celebrated travel guide, *Description of Hellas*,[11] written by Pausanias in the second century A.D. (fig. 1-2). Nonetheless, Serlio illustrated it with a handsome but necessarily imaginary elevation and plan, while he also provided engravings of a remarkable Roman gateway in Verona featuring fluted baseless Doric columns of Greek form, though with Roman astragals (fig. 1-3).[12]

During the seventeenth century there was greater familiarity than is often thought with conditions in Athens and other parts of Greece. Information was available in a wide variety of sources, including printed travelers' accounts and entries in general works such as books for

Fig. 1-3. Roman arch in Verona. Woodcut.
From Sebastiano Serlio, *Tutte l'Opere
d'Architettura* (1634): facing p. 117. By
permission of The British Library,
London, 60.e.6.

mariners and guides for pilgrims, as well as engraved maps and images. Athens was typically described as fruitful and its inhabitants as healthy, while both Greeks and Turks were commended for their welcome. William Lithgow (1582 – ca. 1645) visited Troy, commissioning an engraving of himself in Turkish dress amid the ruins, and left a brief account of his visit to Athens in 1609.[13] France had a permanent consul in Athens from 1645 to oversee the interests of the French expatriate community and of visitors. Charles-Henri-François Olier, marquis de Nointel (ca. 1630 – 85), collector and diplomat, was in Constantinople from 1670 to 1679, as French ambassador to the Ottoman Empire, with a team of artists and antiquarians to investigate ancient sites. He was allowed access to the Acropolis in 1674 where he employed the artist Jacques Carrey (1646 – 1726) to make the first accurate record of the sculpture on the Parthenon.[14]

These unique drawings were acquired in 1685 by Michel Bégon for his large collection of books, manu-

scripts, engravings, coins, and other material about the ancient world, which he probably made available to interested visitors. They later passed to the Bibliothèque Nationale in Paris, where they were available from 1797. Stuart did not see them, though he observed of Carrey that "two or three of . . . [his] drawings are represented in Montfaucon's Antiquities."[15] A comparison of a drawing by Carrey of Slab XII in the north frieze of the Parthenon with Stuart's engraving of it, has shown that Carrey was "more faithful in many details, especially the chariot wheel, to the original."[16] In his account of the Parthenon, Stuart quoted from *Panathenaica* by Joannes van Meurs (Johannes Meursius, 1579 – 1639),[17] professor of Greek at the University of Leyden, who was one of those responsible for the recovery and consolidation of references to buildings and customs in ancient sources.

Thus, much was known about the Parthenon before a large part of it was destroyed in the explosion of 1687.[18] Indeed, travelers and traders in the Levant in the early

Fig. 1-4. Archway with baseless Doric columns. Engraving. From Roland Fréart de Chambray, *Parallèle de l'Architecture Antique et de la moderne . . .* (1650): 33. By permission of The British Library, London, 560*.e.1.

commissioned drawings of the temples, intending to cover those of the whole of Magna Graecia.[19] However, the views of Paestum were not published until 1784, after his death. In the meantime, Giuseppe M. Pancrazzi published the Greek temples on Sicily in *Antichità Siciliane* (1751). Most of the volume's engravings were dedicated to British Grand Tourists who visited Naples around 1750.[20]

France: Theorists, Travelers, and Architects

A century or so after Serlio, the diplomat, connoisseur, and traveler Roland Fréart de Chambray (1606 – 76) published *Parallèle de l'architecture antique et moderne* (1650), in which he made greater claims for Greek architecture, though still, like Serlio, knowing nothing of it. Nonetheless, he was important for seeing Greek architecture as superior to Roman on the grounds that the latter was necessarily a later copy. This belief was expressed in the full title of his treatise which showed that the first part would contain what he called the "three Greek orders," and the second part, the "Latin" orders, Tuscan and Composite, though this part constituted only 24 of the 109 pages of the whole work (fig. 1-4).

In language worthy of Stuart, who quoted him in the first volume of *Antiquities of Athens*, Fréart de Chambray urged architects to "ascend to the very source of the orders, and to draw images and ideas of great purity from the admirable [Greek] masters who had invented them."[21] He went on to argue that this "is in my opinion the sole remedy for reestablishing the arts in all the primitive splendor from which they have fallen through scorn." Speaking of the orders, he praised "the Greeks who were their inventors and with whom alone they first came to perfection," stressing that "there is nothing worthy of commendation in the world that this divine country has not once produced in the fullness of excellence."[22]

Fréart de Chambray was an early figure in the French rationalist tradition which flowered in the eighteenth-century Enlightenment. Claude Perrault (1613 – 88), physician and amateur architect, was the key figure in the seventeenth century. He was best known for his part in the creation of the east front of the Louvre (1665 – 74) with its giant colonnade, which seemed to his French contemporaries and successors to rival the greatest monuments of antiquity. He also published an influential translation of Vitruvius in the course of which he illustrated the baseless and fluted Doric column more accurately than had Renaissance commentators.[23] However, like

seventeenth century such as Sir Kenelm Digby, Lewes Roberts, and Sir Henry Blount, all published accounts of it. However, for a period of about half a century after 1687, almost no visitors from western Europe recorded their experiences. When they began to return they found the whole Acropolis site cleared and transformed, mainly because of extensive rebuilding of the defenses by the Turks in the earlier eighteenth century.

Serious investigation of Hellenic architecture began in the eighteenth century, though not initially in Athens but in the more easily accessible Italy. The history of the Peloponnesian War and of the Hellenic race by Thucydides was widely known and led to a growing awareness that there were Greek temples on Italian and Sicilian soil, notably at Paestum, Segesta, Selinunte, and Agrigentum. This led to the investigation of Paestum, which began in earnest in 1745 – 50 under Conte Felice Gazzola who

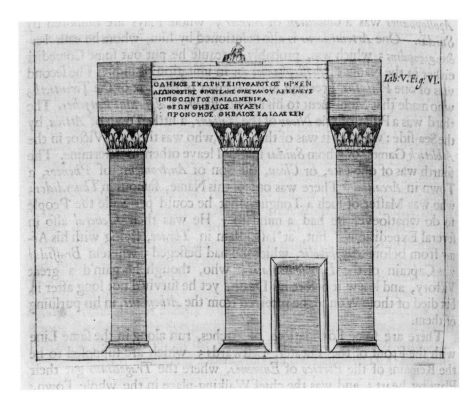

Fréart de Chambray, he had not been able to study at first hand Greek buildings which remained an ideal for French architects until 1750. Until that date, it could scarcely be more than a literary trope. In his monograph on Perrault, Wolfgang Herrmann showed that paying lip-service to the superiority of the Greeks, daring when Fréart de Chambray proposed it in 1650, had by the middle of the next century almost become a cliché, among those who had not been there.[24]

The French Protestant physician Jacob Spon (1647 – 85) and the English gentleman and soldier George Wheler (1650 – 1723) traveled in Turkey, Asia Minor, and Greece, in 1675 – 76. Spon was the first to publish his account of this epoch-making journey under the title, *Voyage d'Italie, de Dalmatie, de Grèce, et du Levant . . .* (1678 – 80). Spon followed this with *Recherches Curieuses d'Antiquités, contenues en plusieurs dissertations . . .* (1683).[25] This contains a striking engraved frontispiece of an assembly of fourteen monuments with the Parthenon, not very accurately depicted, as the central feature. The other thirteen are all Roman, many of them in the south of France in order to demonstrate, improbably, that, as Spon put it in his introduction, France has "as fine pieces as Greece and Italy."

Spon's friend Wheler expressed his gratitude to Spon for having included his name on the title page of *Voyage d'Italie* but was anxious to publish his own version which

he did under the title, *A Journey into Greece . . .* (1682; fig. 1-5).[26] Le Roy and Stuart and Revett referred to these books constantly in their respective works on Greek architecture.[27]

Wheler explained in his preface that he had added to Spon's account new information based on "medals and other Antiquities . . . since sent from Athens to me," a map he had drawn of Achaia, and descriptions of plants. Wheler had been born in Breda in Holland, where his parents had been exiled as Royalists, but he was educated at Lincoln College, Oxford, and was able to undertake a Grand Tour in 1673. He dedicated his *Journey into Greece* to Charles II, explaining in his dedication that Greece was "a Country once Mistress of the Civil World . . . but now a Lamentable Example of the Instability of humane things." In this, he had an agenda which was to support the recent Restoration of the British monarchy by comparing the unhappy political state of present-day Greece to that of England under Cromwell. His praise of the present blessed state of England helped earn him a knighthood from Charles II in 1682.

This point is important because it relates to the Philhellenism, adopted by Stuart and Revett by which the inhabitants of Athens were, rather improbably, regarded as true descendents of the ancient Hellenes and thus worthy of "gaining their Liberty from the Turkish Tyranny."[28]

Fig. 1-6. View of the Propylaeum, Athens. Engraving by Jacques Philippe Le Bas. From Julien-David Le Roy, *Les Ruines des plus beaux monuments de la Grèce* (1758): pl. VI. By permission of The British Library, London, 1899.g.30. *Checklist no. 35.*

Wheler had persuaded himself that the Athenians he met were "more polished, in point of Manners and Conversation" than the inhabitants of other parts of Greece,[29] and, indeed, that the Greek they spoke was itself closer to that of the ancients. Stuart later made very similar parallels. This rosy view was associated with an idealized view of Greece and ancient Greek culture which led Wheler to claim of Athens that it enjoys a "fame so great, that few Cities in the World can dispute Precedence with her," and even that "she still seems triumphant."[30] He went so far as to claim: "As to eminent Monuments of Antiquity, yet remaining at Athens, I dare prefer them before any Place in the World, Rome only excepted." The Parthenon was thus "both for Matter and Art, the most beautiful piece of Antiquity remaining in the World," while the Temple of Theseus (Hephaisteion) was "a Master-piece of architecture, not easie to be parallel'd, much less exceeded by any other."[31]

Jacques Carrey showed his drawings to Spon and Wheler, who also drew extensively on Pausanias's guide to Greece, though they would not have found in his pages so great a eulogy of the Parthenon. Indeed, it has not been pointed out before that the high-pitched praise of Athens and its monuments was due to Wheler and is not found in the account of their journey by Spon, normally seen as the greater scholar. Wheler included crude engravings of the principal monuments of Athens, which were to feature in the publications of Le Roy and of Stuart and Revett: the Parthenon, Temple of Theseus, gateway to the Agora, Choragic Monument of Thrasyllus (see fig. 1-5),

supposed Temple of Jupiter Olympius, Tower of the Winds, Arch of Hadrian, and Aqueduct of Hadrian.

The antiquarian and traveler, Anne-Claude-Philippe de Tubières, comte de Caylus (1692 – 1765), may have inspired and even paid for the great expedition to Greece of Stuart's rival, Julien-David Le Roy (1724 – 1803). However, the main subject of Caylus's monumental work, *Recueil d'antiquités Egyptiennes, Etrusques, Grècques, Romaines et Gauloises* (1752 – 67), was not architecture but everyday objects.[32] Though Caylus was unusual in according a key role to Egyptian culture and artifacts, an opinion that eventually became influential, his immediate impact was greatest in his eulogies of the arts of Greece where, he claimed, "knowledge joined to the most noble elegance brought the arts to their greatest perfection," in contrast to "Roman taste [which] is in general heavy, flabby, without delicacy . . . [so that] almost all the works of any elegance in Rome are due to the Greeks."[33]

In touch with the architect Jacques-Germain Soufflot (1713 – 80) on the subject of Greek vases,[34] Caylus declared that Greece was "the Temple of the Arts"[35] and that "the Greeks seem to me the most pleasing nation which has inhabited the earth."[36] He promoted the *goût grec* in French interior design and furniture, recommending Louis-Joseph Le Lorrain (1715 – 59) as designer of the famous suite of furniture *à la grecque* for Ange-Laurent Lalive de Jully in 1756 (see fig. 10-9).[37] Though such work became fashionable at the time of the return of Le Roy from Athens, it did not in fact incorporate authentic Greek details.

Fig. 1-7. Ruins of the Temple of Mars. Engraving. From Marie-Gabriel-Florent-Auguste de Choiseul-Gouffier, *Voyage pittoresque de la Grèce,* vol. 1 (1782): pl. 99. By permission of The British Library, London, 149.i.6.

When Greece and the eastern Mediterranean were part of the Ottoman Empire, it was not easy to secure a passport for travel from Constantinople. There was access to Greece, however, from several trade links such as Smyrna and the Ionian Islands which were then part of the empire of Venice. Travel inland was not only expensive but also impeded by fear of pestilence and brigands, lack of security, absence of roads, and even the quarantine laws imposed on those returning. Le Roy and Stuart were among those who took the opportunity of visiting Greece when travel became easier during the eighteenth century. After traveling in Greece in 1754, Le Roy announced on his return his intended book on Greek architecture, *Les Ruines des plus beaux monuments de la Grèce* (1758; fig. 1-6).[38] This was based on the "Proposal" by Stuart and Revett, but unlike them Le Roy was not interested in promoting the copying of Greek details in modern buildings. He did not practice as an architect but as an historian, and he established an intellectually impressive history of architectural development, especially of sacred architecture, into which contemporary architecture could take its place. The title of his great work centered on "ruins," making it strikingly different from Stuart and Revett's title, which was devoted to "antiquities." The new response to ruins lay on the cusp between the Enlightenment and the age of sensibility. Indeed, this "challenging issue of ruins, fragments, and unformed architecture is key to understanding not only the form of Le Roy's great folio but also his theories of architecture. His book, in contrast to that of Stuart and Revett, can be seen as a

reflection of newly emerging attitudes to ruins."[39] Le Roy came close to presenting the Hephaisteion as a ruin by showing it invaded by "non-existent brambles,"[40] even though it had survived intact from antiquity and was in use as the main church of Athens. Le Roy and his engraver, Jacques-Philippe Le Bas, also showed its eastern entrance seemingly blocked by a massive boulder, in fact the Areopagus Hill which is half a mile away, while they also repositioned the local stream.

Le Roy was followed in his feeling for ruins by Marie-Gabriel-Auguste-Florent, comte de Choiseul-Gouffier (1742 – 1818), author of *Voyage pittoresque de la Grèce* (1782 – 1822).[41] Choiseul-Gouffier had studied with Abbé Jean-Jacques Barthélemy, author of the *Voyage du jeune Anacharsis* (Paris: 1788), whose scholarship had led him to be regarded as much Athenian as French.[42] Choiseul-Gouffier toured Greece with a large team of artists from 1776, preparing his ambitious *Voyage pittoresque* which contained illustrations of scenery and classical ruins (fig. 1-7), preceded by a discussion of the struggle of Greece for liberty.

One of the most influential of Perrault's rationalist successors was Marc-Antoine Laugier (1713 – 69) who called for a return to a functionalist architecture of post-and-beam construction in his *Essai sur l'architecture* (1753; fig. 1-8). Laugier's radical concept was a development from the notion that the roots of classical architecture lay in the primitive hut, the world of Rousseau's noble savage. Translated into English in 1755 as *An Essay on Architecture* and also into German in various editions in 1756, 1758,

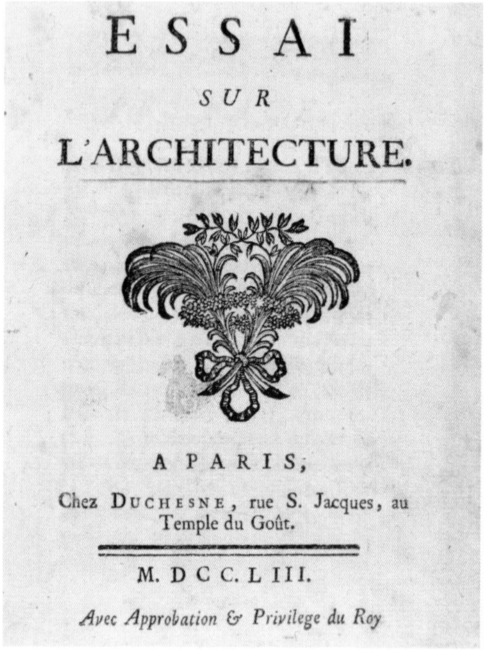
ESSAI

SUR

L'ARCHITECTURE.

A PARIS,

Chez Duchesne, rue S. Jacques, au Temple du Goût.

M. D C C. L III.

Avec Approbation & Privilege du Roy

Fig. 1-8. Title page. From Marc-Antoine Laugier, *Essai sur l'architecture* (1753). Courtesy of the Trustees of The Victoria and Albert Museum, London / National Art Library, 31.NN13.

1768, and 1771, Laugier's widely read book found a parallel in the writings of Francesco Milizia (1725 – 98), the most important architectural theorist of the Enlightenment in Italy. Works such as his *Dizionario delle belle arti del disegno* (1787) promoted only Greek and gothic architecture as truly original and adopted so anti-baroque a tone that they were also of use to the pro-Greek camp.

Laugier was viewed as lending support to those who wished to see a return to the principles of Greek architecture. One of these was the architect Soufflot who visited Paestum in 1750 to see the Doric temples of the Greek colonies called Magna Graecia in 1750. His companions included the engraver Charles-Nicolas Cochin and Gabriel-Pierre-Martin Dumont, who published some of Soufflot's drawings in 1764, a project proposed by Caylus in 1755.[43] Soufflot regarded his masterpiece, the Church of Sainte Geneviève, later the Panthéon, in Paris (begun 1757), as uniting the principles of Greek and Gothic architecture. In early designs for its crypt, Soufflot incorporated lively variants of the Paestum Doric order at the same moment that Stuart built the temple at Hagley with its less adventurous imitation of Greek Doric (see fig. 7-2).[44]

The most influential architectural teacher and theorist in eighteenth-century Europe was Jacques-François Blondel (1705 – 74). His many distinguished pupils included Sir William Chambers, Marie-Joseph Peyre and Charles De Wailly (who were both friends of Chambers), Claude-Nicolas Ledoux, Etienne-Louis Boullée, Jacques Gondoin, Alexandre-Théodore Brongniart, and Jean-François Chalgrin. Blondel published his opinions in his *Cours d'Architecture* (1771 – 77) and many contributions on architecture to Diderot's *Encyclopédie*.[45] Regarding Greece as the cradle of good architecture, he rejected "imitations of Rome," preferring "authentic Doric" to Roman Composite. From 1762 Blondel had been a professor at the French Académie Royale d'Architecture along with Le Roy. In his eulogy of Greece, Blondel may have been influenced by one of the few surveys of architectural history available to him, the chapter on architecture by Charles Rollin (1661 – 1741) in his widely read history of ancient peoples. Rollin declared of architecture in 1737 that "it is to Greece that one attributes if not its invention, then at least its perfection."[46]

England: The Picturesque, Travel, and Archaeology

The pictorial, indeed specifically "Picturesque," character of Choiseul-Gouffier's approach recalls Stuart's principal visual contribution to *Antiquities of Athens,* namely his Picturesque views of the ruins, engraved from his gouache drawings, thirteen of which appeared in the first two volumes (see figs. 3-36, 13-6). This departure from the standard method of depicting ancient architecture, as exemplified in that seminal archaeological work, Antoine Desgodetz's *Édifices antiques de Rome dessinés et mesurés tres exactement* (1682), was the product of the Picturesque tradition, a development of largely British origin.[47] Indeed, Robert Sayer brought out a plagiarized edition of Le Roy's book as *Ruins of Athens* in 1759 in which the views were reunited as Picturesque *capricci.*

A key figure in the Picturesque movement was Joseph Addison (1672 – 1719), a classical scholar and popular essayist whose "Pleasures of the Imagination" (1712), was one of the central documents of eighteenth-century taste and influenced the new art of informal landscape gardening. In a remarkable comparison of the poetry of Homer, Virgil, and Ovid, to landscapes, Addison argued:

> Reading the *Iliad* is like travelling through a Country uninhabited where the Fancy is entertained with a thousand Savage Prospects . . . On

the contrary, the *Aeneid* is like a well ordered Garden . . . But when we are in the *Metamorphosis*, we are walking on enchanted Ground, and see nothing but Scenes of Magick lying round us.[48]

A fresh appreciation of Homer was encouraged by the new sensibility in which natural feelings and passions were increasingly valued. Addison went on to describe how Virgil "in his *Georgics* has given us a Collection of the most delightful Landskips that can be made out of Fields and Woods, Herds of Cattle, and Swarms of Bees."[49] Even the historian Livy was woven into this tradition on the grounds that he "describes every thing in so lively a manner, that his whole History is an admirable Picture . . . his Reader becomes a kind of Spectator, and feels in himself all the variety of Passions which are correspondent to the several Parts of the Relation."[50]

Drawing on the treatise on the Sublime by Longinus of the first century A.D., Addison popularized the word *sublime*, arguing that "*Homer* fills his Readers with Sublime Ideas, and, I believe, has raised the Imagination of all the good Poets that have come after him."[51] Pope, also a great admirer of Longinus, made early use of the word *picturesque* in 1717 in the "Observations" to his enormously popular translation of Homer's *Iliad*. Summing up Book 10 of the *Iliad*, Pope claimed that "the principal Beauty of it . . . is the Liveliness of its Paintings: The Reader sees the most natural Night-Scene in the World. . . . We see the very Colour of the Sky." He also observed that "The marshy spot of Ground where Dolon is killed . . . and the Reeds that are heap'd together to mark the Place, are Circumstances the most Picturesque imaginable."[52] It was precisely on this tradition that "Athenian" Stuart was to draw when he interpreted the monuments of Athens through the medium of Picturesque gouache views in *Antiquities of Athens* from 1762. Though concentrating on sublimity in literature, Longinus had included as Sublime the views from mountaintops.

The opening of new horizons in the eighteenth century, including the exploration of primary sources through travel and archaeology as undertaken by Stuart and Revett, was also heralded in Addison's world view. He believed that "Everything that is *new* or *uncommon* raises a Pleasure in the Imagination, because it fills the Soul with an agreeable Surprize, gratifies its Curiosity, and gives it an Idea of which it was not before possest."[53] Modern

writers and poets "should be very well versed in every thing that is noble and stately in the Production of Art, whether it appears in Painting or Statuary, in the great Works of Architecture which are in their present Glory, or in the Ruins of those which flourished in former Ages."[54]

Addison quoted at length from Fréart de Chambray's *Parallèle de l'architecture antique et moderne* (1650) as an example of the quality of perception.[55] He was also influenced by the philosophy of association of John Locke (1632 – 1704) in his *Essay Concerning Human Understanding*. On a related topic, he paraphrased Locke's *Essay* when he wrote, "I have here supposed that my Reader is acquainted with that great Modern Discovery . . . Namely, that Light and Colours, as apprehended by the Imagination, are only Ideas in the Mind, and not Qualities that have any Existence in Matter."[56]

Addison was also indebted to *An Essay Towards a New Theory of Vision* (1709) by Bishop George Berkeley (1685 – 1753) who himself quoted from Locke's *Essay*.[57] In his *New Theory of Vision*, Berkeley established what might be called the philosophical foundation of the Enlightenment theory of vision, for it was cited by Voltaire, Condillac, and the philosophes. Though it was a complex and sometimes contradictory work, those who wished to could find in it a subjective approach to perception which was akin to Perrault's claim that the rules of proportion in classical architecture were dependent on nothing more than custom and "fantaisie" and were not rooted in divine harmony as had been believed in the Renaissance.

A friend of Lord Burlington and a lecturer in Greek at Trinity College, Dublin, Berkeley traveled in order to widen the basis of his knowledge of Greek history and literature. While on his travels in southern Italy in 1716 – 20, he formed a belief that Mediterranean light was most adapted to an emotionally intense and conceptually lucid perception. He wrote as early as 1718 from Rome:

there is not any one modern building in Rome that pleases me, except the wings of the capitol by Michael Angelo and the colonnade of Berninies before St Peter's. The Church itself I found a thousand faults with, as indeed with every other modern Church here. I forget the little round one in the place where St Peter was beheaded built by Bramante, which is very pretty and built like an ancient temple. This gusto of

Fig. 1-9. View of the Temple of Concord, Selinunte. Engraving by P. Fourdrinier. From John Durant Breval, *Remarks on Several Parts of Europe . . .* , vol. 1 (1738): facing 37. By permission of The British Library, London, 215.f.15.

mine is formed on the remains of antiquity that I have met with on my travels, particularly in Sicily, which convince me that the old Romans were inferior to the Greeks, and that the moderns fall infinitely short of both in the grandeur and simplicity of taste.[58]

After having seen the Doric temples of the Greek colonies on Sicily, he could accept nothing in Rome but the freestanding columns of Bernini and Bramante, and the powerful forms of Michelangelo.

Berkeley's opinions, anticipating those of Stuart, were adopted by John Durant Breval (ca. 1680 – 1738) who visited Sicily in 1725, publishing *Remarks on Several Parts of Europe* (1723 – 28).[59] Educated at Westminster School, London, and a Fellow of Trinity College, Cambridge, from 1702 to 1708, this attractive figure was a poet, playwright, soldier, traveler, and antiquarian. His book, its title doubtless inspired by Addison's *Remarks on Several Parts of Italy* (1705), was the fullest account in English of Italy since Addison's and was also the first to be illustrated, apparently by himself.[60] The revised edition of 1738 contained the first full account of the remains of Greek and Roman buildings in Sicily as well as the first engravings of them ever published.

Breval commented on the nine temples built by Greek settlers at Selinunte in about 580 – 480 B.C., a long period of peace: "The Ruins of amazing Temples, and other publick Structures, have not their Equal, in all likelihood, in our Age, on this Side *Palmyra* or *Egypt*, and are a Demonstration beyond any other that *Europe* affords, how far the Antients exceeded the Moderns, not only in a great Taste of Architecture, but likewise their Skill in Mechanicks, by raising to such an Height such unwieldy and ponderous Bodies."[61]

Breval accurately illustrated the Temple of Concord at Selinunte with its baseless Doric columns (fig. 1-9), writing an account of it in which he made early use of the key aesthetic terms from the mid-eighteenth century — Sublime and Picturesque. He thus claimed of this temple that "I have seen no Ruin in any Part of my Travels that could furnish an Artist in that Stile (such as *Panini* may be now, or *Viviano* [Codazzi] was formerly) with more sublime or Pinturesque ideas."[62] He interpreted their significance as an aid to painters, setting them in the context of Giovanni Paolo Panini (1691 – 1765) and Viviano Codazzi (1604 – 70), who were pioneers of the pictorial architectural paintings known as *vedute*. Breval here also echoed those pioneering figures, Joseph Addison and Alexander Pope.

Richard Pococke (1704 – 65) brings us to Athens itself.[63] Indeed, it has been suggested that the visit of Stuart and Revett to Athens may have been inspired by Stuart's meeting with Pococke in 1740 in Naples at the Three Kings Inn on Pococke's return from Athens.[64] Educated at Corpus Christi College, Oxford, Pococke was a collector and obsessive traveler, who held successive ecclesiastical appointments in Ireland, becoming Bishop of Meath in 1765. He seems to have met the archaeologist Robert Wood in Padua in about 1738 and was painted in Turkish dress in Constantinople by Jean-Etienne Liotard (1702 – 89), a pattern followed by Stuart who depicted himself in Turkish dress in his gouaches of Athens (see figs. 2-10, 1-16).[65]

Pococke's major work, *A Description of the East, and Some Other Countries* (1743 – 45), was widely popular, being translated into French, German, and Dutch.[66] The first volume was devoted exclusively to Egypt while the second volume, dedicated to Philip, Earl of Chesterfield, included Greece, Turkey, and Syria. Pococke provided especially useful plates of the curvaceous temple at Balbec (fig. 1-10),[67] one of the most unusual surviving monuments of antiquity. The plates of this building in Robert Wood's book on Balbec of 1757 have been cited as the source of imitations of it, such as Henry Flitcroft's Temple of Apollo at Stourhead, Wiltshire (ca. 1765), but Pococke's record would have been equally helpful to eighteenth-century architects.

Pococke's detailed descriptions of Egyptian monuments were, and remain, more valuable than those in his much shorter account of Greece. Indeed, his description of Athens, illustrated with eleven plates of buildings, sometimes inaccurate or distorted, is just ten pages long, only two more than he devoted to Balbec. However, he gave an especially valuable account of the temple on the river Ilissus in Athens, describing it as "a beautiful small temple . . . built of very white marble."[68] Its delicate Ionic order was to be widely imitated in the Greek Revival, as in Stuart's church at Nuneham Courtenay (see fig. 7-5), but few records of it were made before its demolition. Pococke also noted "a very beautiful Ionic order" at the Erechtheion and pronounced the so-called Temple of Jupiter Olympius, now known to be the Library of Hadrian, to be "the most magnificent and beautiful piece of architecture in this city."[69] Stuart also devoted much space to this monument, describing its Corinthian columns as forming "one of the most considerable Remains of Athenian Magnificence."[70]

Thus Pococke, like Stuart after him, responded sympathetically to the decorated orders, Ionic and Corinthian, with which he was most familiar. The Parthenon with its Greek Doric could be something of a stumbling block. Pococke wrote of it that "it may be questioned whether

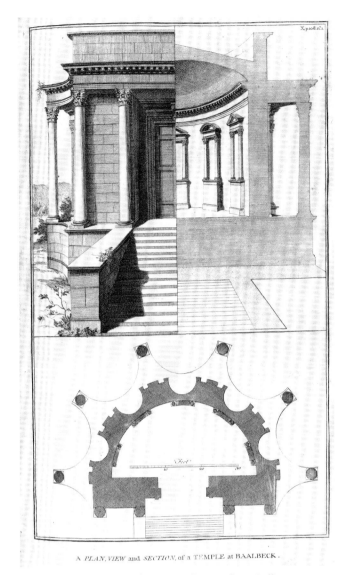

A *PLAN, VIEW* and *SECTION*, of a TEMPLE at BAALBECK.

Fig. 1-10. Plan, view, and section of a temple at Balbec. Engraving. From Richard Pococke, *A Description of the East and Some Other Countries*, vol. 2, pt. 1 (1745): 108, pl. X, no. 1. By permission of The British Library, London, 457.f.9.

the other more beautiful orders were invented when it was built."[71] His sensitive eye, however, took pleasure in its sculptural adornment, and he noted the "most beautiful bas reliefs in the freize," writing that if the sculpture on the Parthenon was "of the same date" as the building itself, it was "a proof that sculpture was in the greatest perfection, when architecture was not arrived at it highest improvements."[72] His understanding of Greek design, shown in this remarkable sensitivity to Greek sculpture, is not necessarily thrown into question by his reaction to the Doric of the Parthenon, which he evidently found

LXX.p.164 N°.2

Fig. 1-11. View of the Choragic Monument of Thrasyllus, Athens. Engraving. From Richard Pococke, *A Description of the East and Some Other Countries,* vol. 2, pt. 2 (1745): 164, pl. LXX, no. 2. By permission of The British Library, London, 457.f.9.

harsh and unsympathetic. After all, ancient Greek architects had themselves found, in Vitruvius's words, "that the Doric order ought not to be used for temples, because faults and incongruities were caused by the laws of its symmetry."[73] This, in the end, is doubtless why the Greek Doric was abandoned in the ancient world.

Pococke responded charmingly to the carved figures of the winds on the Tower of the Winds, suggesting that "the creator of Raphael moving over the elements in his paintings in the Vatican gallery, are something in this taste."[74] Like Stuart, he also provided valuable plates of the now destroyed Choragic Monument of Thrasyllus (fig. 1–11), over the caption "a grotto at Athens," of the so-called Temple of Theseus, and of the Choragic Monument of Lysicrates.

With their faults, these remained the most accurate images of Greek architecture until Richard Dalton (ca. 1713 – 91) published twenty-one engravings of the same buildings in *Antiquities of Greece and Egypt* (1752). Librarian to George III from 1760 to 1791 and Surveyor of the King's Pictures from 1778 to 1791, Dalton was a cicerone, artist, art dealer, and engraver. He was traveling in Italy in 1749 when he accepted the invitation of Lord Charlemont to join his expedition to the Levant as a draftsman.[75] Charlemont was a key patron of Stuart, having subscribed generously to his "Proposal for publishing an Accurate Description of the Antiquities of Athens" in 1748. Engravings, dated April 12, 1751, were made of the drawings of the monuments of Athens which Dalton had produced on his journey with Charlemont. These included four of the Erechtheion and as many as nine of the Parthenon, featuring five of the sculptures in the frieze

Fig. 1-12. A segment of the Parthenon Frieze: "The Basso Relievos on the Frieze of the Inner Portico of the Temple of Minerva." Engraving. From Richard Dalton, *Antiquities and Views in Greece and Egypt* (1752): n.p. By permission of The British Library, London, 149.i.14.(1.).

Fig. 1-13. Views of the Temple of Minerva, Theater of Bacchus, Temple of Jupiter Olympius, Athens, and the Acro Corinth. Engraving. From Johann Bernard Fischer von Erlach, *Entwurff einer historischen Architectur,* book 1 (1725): pl. XIX. By permission of The British Library, London, 648.a.15.

(fig. 1-12), from Dalton's own watercolors. In a remarkable anticipation of Stuart's re-creation of the Choragic Monument of Lysicrates in 1758 for Thomas Anson as a garden ornament at Shugborough (see fig. 7-9), Dalton wrote in 1752 that this monument "would make a very proper Building for the Mount in your Park."[76] Stuart was later to note the accuracy of Dalton's representations of the Tower of the Winds.[77]

Dalton's engravings of Athens had been published without a text, and his second set of engravings (of the monuments of Egypt), announced for publication in 1752, were not published until 1781. Dalton was evidently aware that the quality of his plates and measurements did not match that of those published by Wood and Stuart, for he explained that the reason for the lengthy delay was "the great expectations formed of the Views and Antiquities of Athens, to be then engraved from the drawings of Messrs Stuart and Revett, as also those of Palmyra and Balbec."[78]

Germany: Fischer von Erlach and Winckelmann

The Viennese baroque architect Johann Bernhard Fischer von Erlach (1656 – 1723) published the first comparative history of world architecture, *Entwurff Einer Historischen Architektur* (1721), with a text in German and French. A second edition of 1725 was reprinted with an English translation by Thomas Lediard under the title, *A Plan of Civil and Historical Architecture . . .* (1730). It contained eighty-six double-folio plates, including many reconstructions of ancient buildings, based on scholarly reading, the evidence of ancient authors and coins, and the writings of modern archaeologists and travelers. This revolutionary publication, with its dramatic images of Egyptian, Babylonian, Roman, Chinese, and Islamic buildings, as well as Greek (fig. 1-13), including a not very accurate image of the Parthenon, did not include the customary section on the orders but in a proto-Enlightenment way appeared to concede parity of esteem to the architectural productions of all the great religions and countries of the world.[79]

31

Another key document in the European cultural world in which Stuart moved was *Gedanken über die Nachamung der griechischen Werke in der Mahlerey und Bildhauerkunst* (1755) by Johann Joachim Winckelmann (1717 – 68), a propagandist essay on Greek art of only fifty pages. It is unclear whether Stuart read this at the time, but it was translated by the artist Henry Fuseli (1741 – 1825) in 1765 as *Reflections Concerning the Imitation of the Painting and Sculpture of the Greeks*. There were further translations into English, French, and Italian.[80] Winckelmann's work had an impact almost akin to that of Laugier, though neither of them was ever to visit Greece. Winckelmann had not even been to Rome when he wrote this passionate call to imitate a Greek ideal whose sensuous beauty he knew mainly from casts and engravings of Greco-Roman works. Coining the phrase, "noble simplicity and sedate grandeur,"[81] which became famous as an evocation of Greek art, he claimed on the first page that "there is only one way for the moderns to become great, and perhaps unequalled: I mean, by imitating the ancients."[82] It was a paradox to believe that moderns would become inimitable by emulating the Greeks because, he explained, their work depended on contingent factors, including their temperate climate, political freedom, and customs such as the athletic prowess which improved their physical appearance as could be seen in their sculpture.

In 1759 Winckelmann published a pioneering work on the Greek temples of Sicily, *Anmerkungen über die Baukunst der alten Tempel zu Girgenti in Sizilien*, based on drawings made on the spot in 1757 by the Scottish architect Robert Mylne (1733 – 1811). Stuart inherited Winckelmann's interpretation of Greek architecture as essentially colorless, bathed in an otherworldly light. This was fundamental to Winckelmann's definition of beauty as based on pure form, exclusive of color. "White," Winckelmann argued, "is the colour which reflects the greatest number of rays of light, and consequently is the most easily perceived."[83] Hence, for him, the whiter a body, the more beautiful it was.

Stuart gave copies of *Antiquities of Athens* to the library of the University of Göttingen in the Electorate of Hanover where George III sent three of his sons to be educated in 1785. Among their teachers was the scientist, man of letters, and anglophile Georg Christoph Lichtenberg (1742 – 99), who had been England in 1769 and 1774 – 75 at which time he was taken up by George

III and Queen Charlotte.[84] The plagiarized illustrations of Le Roy that were published by Robert Sayer as *Ruins of Athens* (1759) also aroused interest in Germany, where they appeared in *Ruinen und Uberbleibsel . . .* (1782).[85]

Italy: Piranesi and the Greco-Roman Debate

Winckelmann was far from alone in promoting the Greek cause over the Roman, for other publications in the 1750s included Laugier's *Essai sur l'architecture* (1753), Allan Ramsay's *Dialogue on Taste,* and, above all, Le Roy's *Ruines des plus beaux monuments de la Grèce* (1758).[86] Such works were a cause of alarm to the great engraver of views of ancient and modern Rome, Giovanni Battista Piranesi (1720 – 78). His first published response to the undermining of the supremacy of Rome on which his fame and income depended was *Della Magnificenza ed architettura de' Romani* (1761). He condemned Le Roy's *Ruines* throughout the text of his substantial publication. In the plates of *Della Magnificenza*, Piranesi adopted a satirical device of pinning copies of Le Roy's dry line-engravings of Greek details onto pages crammed with his own representations of rich Roman ornament, heightened with chiaroscuro.[87] The resultant contrast between the Greek and Roman work made Le Roy's criticism of Roman capitals as "pauvres et defectueux," which Piranesi quoted, seem ridiculous (fig. 1-14). Piranesi foolishly stated, however, that the Etruscans, the Tuscan neighbors of the inhabitants of Rome, were earlier in date than the Greeks and had taught the Romans architecture. He claimed that while Etruscan design was severe, that of the Greeks was merely pretty, a fault that the Romans had corrected. Despite Piranesi's error, the nationalist basis of his arguments struck a chord in Italy.

Richard Dalton had been pursued by Piranesi on his return from Greece. This turned out to be a clever coup, for Dalton was prepared to give him some unfavorable opinions of Greek architecture. Piranesi must have been pleased to be able to inform his readers that he had "asked his [Dalton's] opinion about the monuments. He told me with his usual frankness that the Caryatids [on the Erechtheion] were the work of a mediocre mason and that some of the remains of the reliefs on the tympanum of the temple of Minerva were beautiful but that if everything else described by Le Roy were to vanish, lovers of the fine arts would suffer no loss at all."[88]

Piranesi went on to develop his ideas in a strange and fascinating work, *Diverse manière d'adornare i cammini*

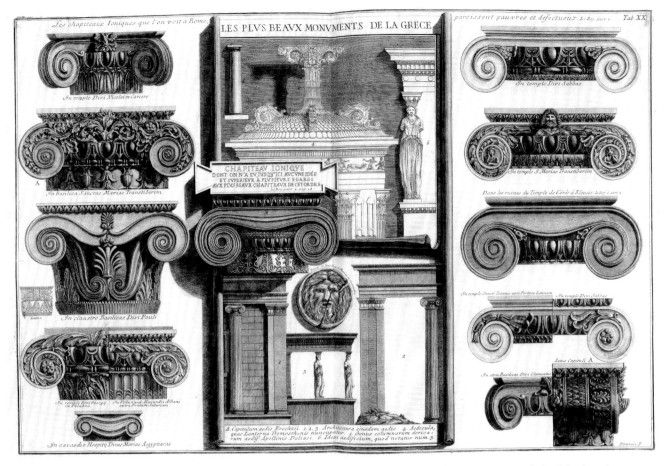

Fig. 1-14. Roman capitals compared with those in Julien-David Le Roy's *Ruines des plus beaux monuments de la Grèce* (1758). Engraving. From Giovanni Battista Piranesi, *Della Magnificenza ed Architettura de'Romani* (1761): pl. XX. By permission of The British Library, London, 744.f.3.

(1769), which he published with texts in Italian, French, and English, the English title being *Divers Manners of Ornamenting Chimneys. . . .*[89] This book was part of the process whereby Piranesi hoped to redeem the appalling state of modern architecture which, he lamented, "having been carried by our ancestors to the highest pitch of perfection, seems now on the decline, and returning again to barbarism."[90] He denied that the Greeks had invented the orders, on the grounds that they were to be found in the Temple of Solomon at Jerusalem.[91] He also criticized Caylus for identifying in *Recueil d'antiquités* "Etruscan" vases as Greek, not Etruscan. However, Piranesi had by now developed a theory of creative and eclectic originality which allowed the modern architect to incorporate Greek forms. He selected the design of chimneypieces as a vehicle for creative novelty because he had not found any in antiquity. They would, therefore, be a good

demonstration of his belief that antique forms can be applied to new building and design types. He probably also saw some professional advantage in the fact that England, whence came most of his clients, was a country always in need of chimneypieces.

Worried by the minimalist implications of Laugier's obsession with the primitive hut, Piranesi also criticized as irrational the hallowed arguments, dating back to Vitruvius, that the origins of the temple lay in timber construction. He condemned Le Roy for upholding this view and produced a series of engravings to illustrate it,[92] though these were so visually compelling that they refuted his position. It is interesting that Piranesi always chose to condemn Le Roy, not Stuart. Perhaps he was reluctant to criticize Stuart because he had far more English clients than French, and his friends included Adam and Chambers who were both powerfully influenced by

Fig. 1-15. View of the Basilica at Paestum. From Giovanni Battista Piranesi, *Différentes vues . . . de l'ancienne ville de Pesto, autrement Possidonia* (1778): pl. III. By permission of The British Library, London, 146.i.18.

him. Piranesi was also proud of his election in 1767 as an honorary member of the Society of Antiquaries of London, of which Stuart had been a Fellow from 1758. Indeed, describing himself as "Socio dell Reale Accademia degli Antiquari di Londra" on the title page of his books, Piranesi elevated the society to a royal status which it has never enjoyed.

Piranesi summed up his anti-Greek position in a memorable passage near the end of *Diverse maniere* in which he refers to the fact that "new pieces are daily dug out of the ruins," thus conveying the excitement of discovery and exploration that characterized this period in many fields of endeavor:

> The law which some people would impose upon us of doing nothing but what is Grecian, is indeed very unjust. Must the Genius of our artists be so basely enslaved to the Grecian manners, as not to dare to take what is beautiful elsewhere, if it be not of Grecian origin? . . . But let us at last shake off this shameful yoak, and if the Egyptians, and Tuscans present to us, in their monuments, beauty, grace, and elegance, let us borrow from their stock, not servilely copying from others . . . by prudently combining the Grecian, the Tuscan, and the Egyptian together, he [the architect] ought to open himself a road to the finding of new ornaments and new manners . . . new pieces are daily dug out of the ruins, and new things present themselves to us, capable of fertilizing, and improving the ideas of an artist, who thinks, and reflects. Rome is certainly the most fruitful magazine of this kind.[93]

The battle was not over. Piranesi himself finally succumbed to the power of Greek Doric architecture in his superb engravings of the temples at Paestum in his *Différentes vues . . . de Pesto* (fig. 1-15), published two months after his death in 1778. Yet in his text he could not bring himself to describe them as Greek, but stressed that their merit derived from their being on Italian soil and thus having Etrusco-Roman, rather than Greek, origins.

Antiquities of Athens

Greece, the "Divine Country"

As early as 1650, Greece was described as a "divine country" by Fréart de Chambray.[94] This climate of opinion, even if based on little actual knowledge of Greek art, spread throughout Europe during the 1750s, virtually assuring a favorable reception of the first volume of Stuart and Revett's *Antiquities of Athens* in 1762. Their preface began with the bold statement that Roman architecture was inferior to Greek and that their book would contribute to a reform of contemporary architecture: "as Greece was the great Mistress of the Arts, and Rome, in this respect, no more than her disciple, it may be presumed, all the most admired Buildings which adorned that imperial City, were but imitations of Grecian Originals." Stuart thus argued that "a performance of this kind might contribute to the improvement of the Art itself, which at present appears to be founded on too partial and too scanty a system of ancient Examples."[95]

In further support of this novel view, it was emphasized that, "of all the countries, which were embellished by the Ancients with magnificent Buildings, Greece appears principally to merit our Attention . . . [because] the most beautiful Orders and Dispositions of Columns were invented in that Country, and the most celebrated Works of Architecture were erected there: to which may be added that the most excellent Treatises on the Art appear to have been written by Grecian Architects."[96] Despite this reference, derived from Vitruvius, to ancient writings on architecture, Stuart himself had virtually nothing to say about the history and theory of architecture, in marked contrast to Le Roy.

The earlier "Proposal" for their publication, which they claimed to have written in 1748, had also begun with a challenging statement, in view of the hegemony of Rome at the time: "No part of Europe, more claims the attention and excites the curiosity of the Lovers of Polite

Literature, than the territory of Attica, and Athens its capital City." They pointed to the "monuments of the good sense and elevated genius of the Athenians, and the most perfect Models of what is excellent in Sculpture and Architecture."[97] Investigation of such monuments involved a certain downgrading of the Romans who "seem not to have equalled the Originals from whence they had borrowed their Taste, either for purity of Design, or delicacy of Execution." Though Rome "borrowed her Arts, and frequently her Artificers from Greece . . . [it is] Athens the Mother of elegance and politeness, whose magnificence scarce yielded to that of Rome, and who but for the beauties of a correct style must be allowed to surpass her; has been almost entirely neglected."[98] Stuart claimed that "Rome never produced many extraordinary Artists of her own," citing as evidence that "when the Roman Authors themselves celebrate any exquisite production of Art, it is the work of Phidias" and his contemporaries.[99]

Current studies of Stuart stress that his ambition was not to replace Roman orders and ornament but to increase the range of sources available to architects by adding Greek models. Though that is true in practice, it is not what the rhetoric of *Antiquities of Athens* primarily suggests, nor how he was seen by contemporaries and successors. He stands or falls by his association with Greece, because as a creator of vibrant classical interiors, he was no rival to architects such as Robert Adam or Charles Cameron, Catherine the Great's architect.

Stuart's central claim was that the result of rescuing the monuments of Greece, which had been "almost entirely neglected," would be that "those Artists who aim at perfection, must be more pleased, and better instructed, the nearer they can approach the Fountain-Head of their Art."[100] The call for a return to primary sources in all fields of endeavor was, of course, in harmony with Rousseau's call for a return to nature. We have seen this anticipated in Fréart de Chambray's call to architects to "ascend to the very source of the orders" of Greece, that "divine country."

Placing Greek architecture, the Parthenon in particular, on a near-divine pinnacle of perfection can be described as the creation of a myth. This is more remarkable given how little is still known about the Parthenon, even its purpose. As a Greek scholar has recently asked, "What was the building as a whole *for*? . . . There were no priests or priestesses attached to the Parthenon, no ancient religious festival or ritual is known to have taken place there, and it did not even have that most basic piece of Greek temple equipment: an altar directly outside its front entrance."[101]

The approach that underlay *Antiquities of Athens* was all the more novel considering that Greek and Roman writers were not themselves given to hailing the Parthenon as representing the summit of architectural achievement. The historian Thucydides, writing in the late fifth century B.C., praised Pericles but failed to mention any of the buildings or the decoration that he commissioned on the Acropolis. Even Vitruvius, writing shortly before 27 B.C. in the sole surviving architectural text to survive from the ancient world, described the Tower of the Winds in Athens but made no reference to the Parthenon other than to mention in passing that Ictinus and Carpion had written a book on it.[102] Vitruvius noted that such monographs on buildings were not unusual. The Parthenon was not included among the Seven Wonders of the World. The historian Plutarch, a Greek living under the Roman Empire and writing around the turn of the first and second centuries A.D., praised the achievement of Pericles in directing the vast program of works on the Acropolis but made it clear that what impressed him most was the remarkable speed with which the works were completed.[103] He also paid full attention to the contemporary political and financial opposition to the controversial project, quoting the resentment of the Athenian allies in the Delian League when their contributions to what they supposed was a common defense budget were used for the purpose of "gilding and bedizening our city . . . like a wanton woman."[104] A scholar has recently written that "for many fifth-century non-Athenians, we may confidently conjecture, the Parthenon was not a monument to the glories of contemporary Hellenic civilisation, but a humiliating reminder of the recent assumption by Athens of a hegemony over them and their own cities."[105]

In the mid-second century A.D., Pausanias, a Greek-speaker from what is now Turkey, wrote an extensive guidebook to Greece, *Description of Hellas*, but had nothing to say about the architecture of the Parthenon. It seems likely that he would have reflected a popular view of its canonic status if that had prevailed at the time. Though he gave fuller accounts of the temples at sites such as Olympia, Delphi, and Bassae, in his account of the Athenian Acropolis, he failed to mention either the sculptured frieze and metope panels of the Parthenon, or the

names of the architects and sculptors involved. The only feature he described was the now-lost colossal cult image of the goddess Athena by Phidias.[106] Like all writers on Greece up to the present day, Stuart relied heavily on the descriptive accounts of Pausanias.

Greece and Liberty, Ancient and Modern

Greece as the mother of arts and the home of liberty had long been familiar rhetoric. The appropriation of the buildings of Hellas was part of the appropriation of Hellenism as a whole and was debated and established in many texts, notably those by historians. In the eighteenth century, the claim for a relation between political freedom and artistic creation was made notably by Winckelmann in 1762 and again by Thomas Major in his book on Paestum of 1768. Le Roy followed their example in 1770 in the second edition of his *Ruines* where he explained that his aim in analysing an unusual combination of buildings of different dates was "to make clear the difference between the buildings erected by a free people, when in their power and brilliance, they gave laws to other peoples, and those produced by the same people when, under the yoke of Rome, they had lost part of their former pride and genius."[107] A literary Philhellenism celebrating the "Harmony of the Ancients and the Modern" and the possibility of regeneration was given one of its clearest and most influential statements by Pierre-Augustin Guys (1722–1801) in his *Voyage Litteraire de la Grèce . . .* (1771).[108]

Stuart now jumped on this bandwagon by announcing in 1787 that his aim in the second volume of *Antiquities of Athens*, devoted to the Acropolis, was to "treat of Buildings erected while the Athenians were a free people, chiefly during the administration of that great statesman Pericles."[109] He also described, somewhat awkwardly, how Greece, "subdued by the Romans, with the loss of her Liberty, that love of Glory likewise, and that sublimity of Spirit which had animated her Artists, as well as her Warriors, her Statesmen, and her Philosophers, and which had formed her peculiar Character, were now extinguished."[110] Stuart's vision of all aspects of Greek achievement as the expression of a total Zeitgeist was to be characteristic of the culturally holistic outlook of Winckelmann.

Following Wheler's account of 1682, Stuart somewhat naively identified the modern inhabitants of Athens, whom he obviously liked, with those of the ancient world. Praising "artful Speakers and busy Politicians," he

Fig. 1-16. James Stuart. View of the Incantada or Propylaea of the Hippodrome, Salonica, 1750s–60s. Gouache. RIBA Library Drawings Collection, London, SD 146/3. *Checklist no. 30.*

noted with pleasure that "the Coffee-House which this species of Men frequent, stands within the precincts of the ancient Poikile." Echoing Wheler's language, he stressed that "the Athenians have perhaps to this day more vivacity, more genius, and a politer address than any other people in the Turkish Dominions. Oppressed as they are at present, they always oppose, with great courage and wonderful sagacity, every addition to their Burden, which an avaricious or cruel Governor may attempt to lay on them."[111] In a charming touch, he noted a church that lacked a bell because, "at present, Bells are not permitted in Athens; the Turks have a great antipathy to them, and generally destroy them." He added that the Greeks "talk, even now of the destruction and prohibition of their Bells, as one of the greatest Mortifications they suffer."[112]

This is a classic statement of Philhellenism, meaning a love of modern Greece and its people, as opposed to Hellenism which denotes interest in the ancient Greeks. Links between the two had become increasingly familiar in travel books and essays about ancient and modern Greece. These attempts to link memories of ancient Greek democracy with the struggle of modern Greeks to overcome the oppression of the Ottoman Empire, found expression in the Greek War of Independence of 1821 – 34.[113]

The Orders: A New Look

Stuart was concerned to point out the seriousness and novelty of his work in providing new information on the orders, the bedrock of classical architecture. He must have enjoyed claiming that the scarcely known temple on the river Ilissus in Athens "may doubtless be reckoned among those Works of Antiquity which best deserve our attention."[114] One of the incidental values of *Antiquities of Athens* was that it provided rare records of buildings that were later demolished: notably the Ilissus temple (see fig. 3-26), destroyed by the Turks around 1778; the Choragic Monument of Thrasyllus (see fig. 10-5), destroyed in 1826 during the Greek War of Independence; and the Incantada at Thessalonika (fig. 1-16), a curiously ornamented work of the late second century A.D., dismantled in the nineteenth century.

Stuart boldly pointed out the inadequacies, as he saw them, of the two most widely consulted studies of classical architecture: Andrea Palladio's *Quattro Libri dell'Architettura* (1570) and Desgodetz's *Édifices antiques de Rome* (1682). Describing how they were "deficient in what relates to the Doric and Ionic, the two most ancient of these Orders,"[115] Stuart complained, with only slight exaggeration, that there was no Doric building in

Palladio's *Quattro Libri*, that Palladio's only Ionic building was the "Temple of Manly Fortune,"[116] and that the only Doric illustrated by Desgodetz was that of the small half-columns of the Theatre of Marcellus. Nonetheless, Stuart followed the techniques of Desgodetz and of seventeenth-century publications in the way in which he chose to depict Greek buildings in engravings. He did, however, add some true line drawings, for example, of the cymas of the capitals in the peristyle of the Parthenon. Fréart de Chambray, indeed, had already included some line drawings showing abstract sections which anticipated eighteenth-century techniques.[117]

Sensitive to criticism, from Winckelmann among others, of the modesty and late date of the buildings in the first volume, Stuart claimed in the second volume that, if subscribers made no demand for further volumes, then at least they "might find in it something interesting on the different Grecian modes of decorating Buildings."[118] He has thus been criticized for being concerned with increasing the stock of decorative motifs rather than advancing knowledge of Greek architecture. However, he would have regarded the orders as the basis of all classical design, while the notion that columns are not ornamental but are necessarily structurally load-bearing and therefore "honest" is a modern rationalist concept that is not borne out by most classical buildings. For once Stuart was in harmony with Sir William Chambers who evidently saw the orders as decorative, for he was to publish his masterly survey of them in a book entitled *Treatise on the Decorative Part of Civil Architecture* (1791), which was the third edition of his *Treatise on Civil Architecture* (1759).

It is ironic that the third volume of *Antiquities of Athens* should contain a long and devastating attack on Chambers for his extreme hostility to Greek architecture.[119] This was written by Willey Reveley (1760 – 99) who had been a pupil of Chambers and his assistant clerk of works at Somerset House from 1782. Reveley had been chosen to edit the third volume after Stuart's death. His qualifications included having accompanied the collector Sir Richard Worsley (1751 – 1805) as architect and draftsman on Worsley's tour of Italy, Greece, and Asia Minor in 1785 – 88.[120]

Le Roy, the Rival

Revett, not Stuart, was responsible for the most important part of *Antiquities of Athens* — the measured drawings of Greek buildings. Stuart's own principal contribu-

tions included the Picturesque gouache views, and these were criticized by Le Roy because, in them, the principal monuments were "choked by subsidiary objects." At the same time, Le Roy complained that Stuart "saw the only merit of a publication on Greek architecture as the provision of scrupulously exact measurements."[121] What lay behind this criticism of the narrowness of scope of *Antiquities of Athens* was its lack of a conceptual framework. Ranging from discussion of the theoretical analyses of Claude Perrault to the relativist philosophy of Montesquieu, Le Roy painted a broad canvas in which he placed Greek temples within the whole context of sacred architecture. He traced this back to the grandeur of Egyptian architecture, through Bramante's basilica of Saint Peter's in Rome, and to modern Paris and the ambitious projects of the 1650s and 1660s for completing the church of the monastery of the Grands Augustins.[122]

This was all part of Le Roy's broad position in which he did not promote a Greek Revival but asked of Greek monuments, "must we imitate them servilely?" His answer was that this would seem to be "a biased approach," arguing that it would be

> better on this subject to look at all the fragments
> of the ancient monuments that one can gather in
> Greece; all those one can find in Asia Minor or
> in Syria, as well as those which still survive in
> Rome; the precepts of Vitruvius on the propor-
> tions of the orders; and finally the feelings of the
> most celebrated architects on these proportions,
> as well as many elements which can aid in the
> composition of the finest possible orders.[123]

This position was close to that of his friend Sir William Chambers to whom he sent copies of the second edition of his *Ruines des plus beaux monuments de la Grèce* in November 1769.[124] Chambers's association with Le Roy may have reinforced his hostility to Stuart.

The Problem of Polychromy

Stuart's understanding of the articulation and ornament of the orders was hampered by his lack of appreciation of the role of color. His sometime assistant, the architect James Gandon, noted of temples that "Stuart frankly acknowledged that the fine blue sky, the constant sunshine, with the bleaching of the stone and marble to a pure white colour . . . contributed to render their appearance truly impressive."[125] The belief, with Winckelmann, in "pure white" had some foundation in Greek philosophy, if not in artistic practice. Plato's notion of truth embodied in the idea could be interpreted as a visible form, drained of color, while Aristotle also envisaged a definite image without color, claiming that "the chalk outline of a portrait will give more pleasure than the most beautiful colours laid on confusedly."[126]

Stuart assumed that the statue of Athena by Phidias in the Parthenon was probably "delicately painted" because Strabo (ca. 64 B.C.–A.D. 19) had claimed that a relative of Phidias had "assisted him in colouring the statue of Jupiter at Elis."[127] For whatever reason, Stuart failed to realize the significance of the traces of color that he had observed at the temple on the Ilissus. He was thus able to publish an engraving, scarcely an inch long, of an anthemion ornament at the temple, noting only that the "upper Fascia of this Architrave, [is] enriched with a painted Ornament, which appears to be as ancient as the Building itself."[128] Similarly, in the account of the Temple of Theseus (Hephaisteion), the painted decorations of doubled anthemion palmettes in the entablature between the antae of the pronaos, or vestibule between the portico and the cella, were included in two plates, yet the text scarcely mentioned them.[129] In his engraving of a palmette ornament in the soffit of the portico of the Parthenon, he chose to depict it in relief though it is in fact painted.[130] Stuart was no different, however, from other eighteenth-century scholars in his lack of understanding of color in Greek architecture.

The Impact of Stuart in the Eighteenth Century

The publication of the first volume of *Antiquities of Athens* in 1762 coincided with that of two other significant works: *Anmerkungen über die Baukunst der Alten* (Remarks on the Architecture of the Ancients) by Winckelmann, and *Emile* by Jean-Jacques Rousseau.[131] Winckelmann argued for a return to primal simplicity, on the grounds that "when decoration in architecture is combined with simplicity the result is beauty: for if a thing is good and beautiful it is what it ought be. So the ornamentation of a building should be in keeping with the general purpose . . . ; the larger the groundwork of a building the less decoration is required." Drawing an analogy with languages, he claimed that "architecture suffered the same fate as the old languages, which became richer when they also

lost their beauty," complaining that "over-lavish decoration probably began under Nero."[132]

Stuart will probably have been aware of the enormously popular writings of Rousseau. Indeed, it has been suggested that in calling on architects to return for inspiration to "the fountain-head of their art," Stuart was "clearly influenced by contemporary theories relating to the nature of cultural development, especially the writings of Rousseau. Stuart was among the first, however, to apply these ideals to architecture, and his remarks reached a wide audience and made a wide and lasting impression."[133] In *Emile*, Rousseau recommended direct speculative inquiry, intellectual curiosity, condemnation of vain knowledge, search for the primary elemental form of things, and return to earth as the source of moral and physical well-being. He also argued that judgment may be formed by way of the sensations. The three books by Stuart, Winckelmann, and Rousseau, though with different tones and aims, have features in common as products of the Enlightenment concern with a return to primary sources.

A characteristic patron from this world was Duke Ernst II of Saxe-Gotha and Altenburg (1745 – 1804), an Enlightenment prince and patron who in 1768 traveled in Holland and England, as well as France where he met Diderot and the Encyclopédistes. Deciding on his return to create a Picturesque English garden at Gotha, near Schloss Friedenstein, he sought advice from his aunt, Augusta, Princess of Wales, George III's mother. He had doubtless seen the remarkable gardens that she had created at Kew, and she sent him John Haverfield (1705 – 84), chief gardener of the royal gardens both at Richmond and Kew. The garden they created during the 1770s at Gotha became one of the most celebrated of its day.[134] One of its novel features was a Greek Doric temple (fig. 1-17), built of stone, which, overlooked by historians of the Greek Revival, was based on the gateway to the Agora in Athens, a Roman building of the first century A.D. Surprisingly, the Agora was given pride of place as the first monument to be described in *Antiquities of Athens*.[135] The temple at Gotha contained a statue of Diana which had been commissioned by the duke from Jean-Antoine Houdon (1741 – 1828), who was noted for his representations of monarchs but also of key Enlightenment and Revolutionary figures such as Diderot, Voltaire, Franklin, and Washington.[136]

It is doubtful whether there was any direct influence from Stuart and Revett on eighteenth-century architec-

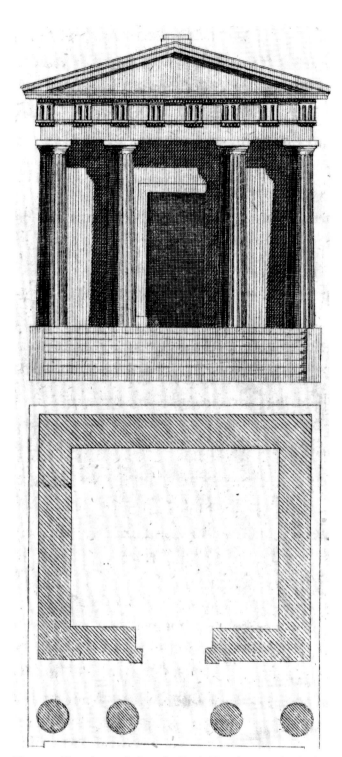

Fig. 1-17. Elevation and plan of a Doric Temple at Gotha, built ca. 1770. Engraving. From Christian Hirschfeld, *Theorie der Gartenkunst*, vol. 2, pt. 4 (1782): 236. By permission of The British Library, London, 34.c.17.

ture in France, where architects would have been more likely to draw on Le Roy as a source. Indeed, one critic, the comte de Saint-Victor, regretted in 1811 that Stuart and Revett's book was "very little known" in France.[137] This statement was made in his reference to the Hôpital de la Charité, Paris, built in the 1760s by Jacques-Denis Antoine (1733 – 1801). In *Description de Paris et de ses édifices* (1806), Jacque Guillaume Legrand and Charles Paul Landon wrote that Antoine's aim had been "to convey an idea of the Propylaea, of which David Le Roy had spoken in his lessons."[138] Like the temple at Gotha, however, the Greek Doric portico of Antoine's design was probably inspired by the gateway to the Agora in Athens, though it featured demi-metopes in the frieze, a Roman not a Greek practice. Saint-Victor in fact complained that it had not been designed in the accurate Doric of Stuart, but it was still singled out by Quatremère de Quincy in 1830 as the first building in the Doric style executed in Paris. Antoine went on to deploy a version of the Ionic of the Erechtheion at the south façade of the Château d'Herces, Eure-et-Loire (ca. 1770) while Charles de Wailly (1730 – 98) adopted the same model for the portico of the Hôtel Voyer d'Argenson, Paris (1762 – 70).[139]

Another early monument with a Greek flavor was the grotto with baseless columns at the Château de Ménars, near Blois, built by Soufflot in 1768 – 69 for the marquis de Marigny with whom Soufflot had visited the temples at Paestum. The late-eighteenth-century pumphouse at Plessis-Chamant, near Senlis, north of Paris, echoing the Tower of the Winds, must have been inspired by Stuart's versions of this monument at Shugborough or at Mount Stewart (see figs. 7-1, 7-26), for it incorporated the side porticoes that are shown in *Antiquities of Athens* (see fig. 7-23) but not in Le Roy's work. The Plessis-Chamant pumphouse was described and illustrated in Alexandre de Laborde's important book on French garden design, published in 1808 with texts in English, French, and German.[140] Claiming that the monument at Plessis-Chamant was "exactly copied from the pretty monument of Athens, known by the name of the Lanthorn of Demosthenes," he argued that "too much encouragement cannot be given for introducing the imitation of the fine monuments of antiquity into gardens." Asking "What finer buildings could be erected?" he pointed out as justification for such practice that "the like monuments embellished the villa of the Emperor Adrian."[141] The architect Jacques-Guillaume Legrand (1753 – 1809) built a similar monu-

Fig. 1-18. "A View of the Three Temples, taken from the East." Engraving. From Thomas Major, *Ruins of Paestum* (1768): pl. II. By permission of The British Library, London, 146.i.16.

ment known as the "Lantern of Diogenes" in the park of Saint-Cloud.[142]

More striking is the vaulted entrance court with fluted baseless Doric columns at the Hôtel de Ville, in Neuchâtel, then a Prussian state in Switzerland. It was built in 1784 – 90 after designs provided by Pierre-Adrien Pâris (1747 – 1819). Jean-Nicolas-Louis Durand (1760 – 1834) adopted columns with flutes only in the necking band of the capital and at the foot of the column for his Maison de la Thuille, Paris (1788).[143] These were derived from the plates of the Temple of Apollo on Delos of the fourth century B.C. in either Stuart or Le Roy, though probably the latter.

In 1768 two works influenced by Stuart were published: *The Ruins of Paestum* by Thomas Major (1720 – 1799; fig. 1-18), issued in simultaneous English and French editions, and *The Grecian Orders of Architecture* by Stephen Riou.[144] Riou's work was fulsomely dedicated to

James Stuart and contained plates engraved by Thomas Major who had provided engravings for Robert Wood's seminal archaeological publications on Palmyra and Balbec in the 1750s. Major had learned the art of engraving at the Académie Royale de Peinture et de Sculpture in Paris under Jacques-Philippe Le Bas who made the engravings for Le Roy's *Ruines*. Le Bas had himself studied under the engraver, draftsman, and theorist Charles-Nicolas Cochin (1715 – 90), who included a remarkably early and accurate depiction of a Greek Doric temple in his red-chalk drawing, *The Wounding of Lycurgus at an Insurrection* (1760), which he exhibited at the Paris Salon of 1761.[145]

Major's *Ruins of Paestum* was principally inspired by Stuart and Revett's *Antiquities of Athens* in its combination of architectural, archaeological, and literary scholarship, illuminating in word and image a classical subject of commanding novelty. Major assembled over two hundred sub-

TO·JAMES·STVART· ESQ. F. R. S.

PAINTER·AND·ARCHITECT·

WHO·THREE·CENTVRIES·

AFTER·THE·REVIVAL·OF·LETTERS·

WAS·THE·FIRST·

TO·EXPLORE·AMONGST·THE·RVINS·OF·ATHENS·

AND·TO·PVBLISH·TO·THE·WORLD·

THE·GENVINE·FORMS·OF·GRECIAN·ARCHITECTVRE·

EXACTLY·DELINEATED·BY·HIS·SKILL·AND·CARE·

ILLVSTRATED·BY·HIS·ERVDITION·

THVS·RESCVING·FROM·THAT·OBLIVION·INTO·WHICH·

THE·CEASELESS·INSVLTS·OF·BARBARIANS·

WOVLD·SOON·HAVE·PLVNGED·THEM·

THE.MOST·EXCELLENT·MODELS·OF·THE·ART·

WHICH·HE·HAS·TRANSMITTED·

WITH·HIS·OWN·REPVTATION·TO·FVTVRE·AGES·

TO·HIM·

THIS·WORK·IS·THEREFORE·INSCRIBED·

BY·THE·AVTHOR·STEPHEN·RIOV.

WHO·VISITING·ATHENS·

IN·THE·TIME·OF·THOSE·RESEARCHES·

WAS·AT·ONCE·AN·EYE·WITNESS·

OF·THE·DILIGENCE·AND·ACCVRACY·

OF·HIS·INVESTIGATIONS·

AND·A·SPECTATOR·

OF·THE·SVRPASSING·ELEGANCE·AND·BEAVTY·

OF·THE·BVILDINGS·

WHICH·ONCE·ADORNED·THAT·CELEBRATED·CITY·

Fig. 1-19. Dedication page. From Stephen Riou, *The Grecian Orders of Architecture . . .* (1768). By permission of The British Library, London, 558★g.36.

scribers to his book, including Soufflot, Le Roy, Abbé Barthélemy, and Gabriel-Pierre-Martin Dumont. Some of the engravings were based on drawings by Soufflot and Le Roy which had been obtained for Major by Riou. In the polemical preface, Greece was claimed as "superior to all ancient nations," "the school of human kind," and "the general centre of illumination of all the rays of true knowledge and wisdom which then lit the world and which embellished it, [and] seem there united."[146] The notion of illumination was deeply embedded in the Enlightenment which saw itself in France as the *siècle des lumières*, in Italy as *illuminismo*, in Germany as *Aufklärung*. Major's book on Paestum also argued that "in the

short space of less than a century, the Greeks arrived at the highest degree of perfection in painting, sculpture and architecture: and this century can in that respect be called the golden age." This was the language of Stuart, based on suggestions in Plutarch, while the text also followed Stuart in adopting the political interpretation of Winckelmann. Since "liberty is the foster-mother of the arts," Greek art was perfect because it was produced in a republic. This led him to a questioning of the traditional view linking culture with climate, so that "to compare the ancient Greeks and their republican government with the Greeks living today under Turkish rule, you would take them for different peoples who did not live in the same climate: so much is the difference between spirits formed under liberty and those who stagnate in slavery."[147]

Stephen Riou (1720 – 80), was a soldier and architect and the son of a Huguenot. He had studied architecture at the Protestant University of Geneva, where he wrote a polemical treatise on architecture. Riou's passionate belief in the Greek Doric order for modern architecture earned him the disapproval of Chambers. An essentially European figure, he knew Soufflot, Le Roy, and other French architects, who subscribed to his book, including Conte Felice Gazzola, and Pierre-Louis Moreau-Desproux. He was also in Rome in the early 1750s and "was witness during this time to the birth of the neo-classical style in French rather than English circles."[148] He traveled in Paestum, Greece, and Asia Minor, meeting Stuart in Athens and again in Smyrna in May to June 1753 when Stuart and Revett were on their way home from Athens.

Riou's *Grecian Orders of Architecture* (1768) was one of the most elegantly designed books of the Greek Revival, a masterpiece of classical typography and layout (fig. 1-19). In contrast, Winckelmann's *Anmerkungen über die Geschichte der Kunst des Alterthums* (Remarks on the History of the Art of the Ancients), published within a few months of *Grecian Orders*, is printed in Gothic black letter so that, despite its Enlightenment subject matter, it seems to have stepped out of the dark ages.[149]

Riou's almost excessively enthusiastic dedication of his book to Stuart, making no reference to Revett or Le Roy, reads:

To James Stuart, Esq. FSA, painter and architect, who three centuries after the revival of letters was the first to explore amongst the ruins of Athens and to publish to the world the genuine forms of

Grecian architecture, exactly delineated by his skill and care, illustrated by his erudition, thus rescuing from that oblivion into which the ceaseless insults of the barbarians would soon have plunged them, the most excellent models of the art which he has transmitted with his own reputation to future ages. To him this work is inscribed by the author Stephen Riou who, visiting Athens in the time of those researches, was at once an eye witness of the diligence and accuracy of his investigations and a spectator of the surpassing elegance and beauty of the buildings which once adorned that celebrated city.[150]

Riou's plates were aimed at the practicing architect, not the archaeologist, so that they do not depict ancient buildings but provide details of the orders, with modular measurements, for contemporary use. Referring in his preface to the work of Fréart de Chambray, Winckelmann, Le Roy, as well as of Stuart and Revett, Riou pointed out that he had borrowed from Le Roy the idea of taking the measurements of the Greek orders "to make a modulary division of all their components parts for practical uses."[151] The origin of a modular technique in this form lay with Perrault, but Le Roy adopted it to only a limited extent.[152] Stuart was also reluctant to adopt modules because, as he explained, he had given "the Measures and all these Buildings in English Feet and Inches . . . forbearing to mention Modules, as they necessarily imply a System, and perhaps too frequently incline an Author to adopt one." Stuart was, however, certain that any architect could use his measurements to "form whatever kind of Module, or modulary division he best fancies."[153] Nonetheless, in applying a modular system, Riou took his measurements from Stuart, regarding them as more accurate than those of Le Roy.

Having no wish to encourage a Greek Revival, Le Roy had recommended a broader base of sources, as Riou noted.[154] Riou, and probably Stuart, shared this view, though with some reservations. Riou, for example, believed that "the addition of a base to the Doric shaft is a downright innovation against the most deliberate intention of the ancients," so that it was akin to what he, like Fréart de Chambray, referred to as the "Tuscan and Composite" orders of the Romans. Riou thus argued of the orders that "the three genuine ones . . . are alone sufficient to answer all the purposes in building."[155] He saw himself

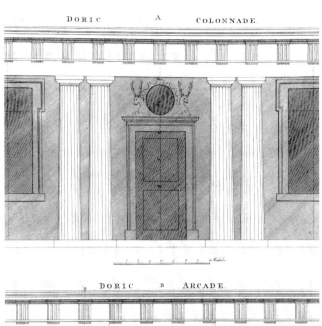

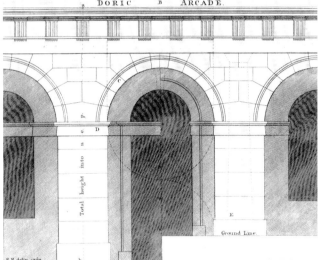

Fig. 1-20. "Doric Colonade; Doric Arcade." Engraving. From Stephen Riou, *The Grecian Orders of Architecture . . .*, pt. 1 (1768): pl. 7. By permission of The British Library, London, 558*g.36.

less as a Greek revivalist than as a restorer of the Doric, Ionic, and Corinthian orders. His plates are thus not confined to Greek models but include, for example, a façade with round arches below a Doric triglyph frieze (pt. 1, pl. VII; fig. 1-20), a Corinthian portico (pt. 1, pl. XIV), and even a triumphal arch (pt. 1, pl. XV). He reserved his chief criticisms for baroque, not ancient Roman, architecture.

His work was well received, but its impact would have been greater if his own designs at the end of the book had been more successful. These include: "The design of a church after an antique temple" (pt. 2, pl. I), which was little more than St. Martin-in-the-Fields with the tower placed at one side as a free-standing campanile, a street of terraced houses, and some clumsy villas.

To understand the hostility of Adam and Chambers to Stuart and the architecture of ancient Greece, we have to imagine ourselves back in the period of the late 1750s when Stuart had the enormous advantage in knowing more about Greek architecture than anyone else in Europe. Adam and Chambers could be forgiven for fearing that a Greek Revival might rise up in the 1750s with Stuart at its head, rather than, as actually happened, in the years after 1815, when all three architects were dead. Adam's denigration of Greece, probably inspired by his association with Piranesi, began early on his Grand Tour. In Rome in 1756, Adam was already condemning Richard Dalton's engravings of the monuments of Athens, made in 1751, the year in which Stuart and Revett began to collect their materials for *Antiquities of Athens*. Adam wrote witheringly of Dalton that "those of true taste esteem him one of the most ignorant of mortals. He went with Lord Charlemont to Greece, Athens &ca., and on his return published a book of the temples &ca. he had seen there which is so infamously stupid and ill done that it quite knocked him on the head and entitled him to that name of Dulton which is generally given him."[156]

Adam therefore conceived the project of publishing his own rival account of Greek architecture, writing to his sister in 1757 that he was considering "taking Clérisseau and my two draftsmen with us, [to Athens, where] we would finish very tolerable work to rival Stuart and Revett's in three months' time and return home laiden with laurels."[157] Adam had also considered making his name as early as 1755 by bringing out a revised edition of Desgodetz's *Édifices antiques de Rome* and in 1756 by publishing works on Hadrian's Villa or the baths of either Diocletian or Caracalla. Instead, he decided on Diocletian's Palace at Spalatro, stopping en route at Pola in Istria in July 1757 to survey the Roman amphitheater. Even here, Stuart and Revett were his rivals, so Adam abandoned measuring this building when he learned that they had already made drawings of it for publication in *Antiquities of Athens*. The keen rivalry between men such as Wood, Stuart, and Adam, is also well conveyed in Adam's explanation of the circumstances in which his book, *Ruins of the Palace of the Emperor Diocletian at Spalatro in Dalmatia* (1763), was published.[158] He recorded that "we were just five weeks at Spalatro and [during] that time four people were constantly at work, which is equal to twenty weeks

of one person. Mr Wood was but 15 days at Palmyra and had but one man to work for him—judge then of the accuracy of such a work!"[159]

The rivalry was unending, for Robert Adam's brother James was still ready in 1760 to prepare "views of Pola . . . with greater exactness and likewise to take the details of that work, lest Stuart should never publish it."[160] Moreover, just as the plates and text of Spalatro were completed in August 1762, the long awaited first volume of Stuart and Revett's *Antiquities of Athens* appeared. Adam thus postponed the publication of his own book on Spalatro for another eighteen months. James Adam was also pleased in Rome in February 1762 to be able to report the poor opinion expressed of "the Athenian Stuart" by John Hinchliffe (1731 – 94), Fellow of Trinity College, Cambridge. Adam recorded Hinchliffe as "saying how he had been disappointed with him and his works: he says he is the most specious discourcer he ever knew, has a superficial knowledge of most things & knows nothing. I thought the character so just I couldn't help inserting it for you."[161] Hinchliffe had studied the orders of architecture under the young George Dance in Rome in 1762 and was also a talented painter.[162] In 1768 he was appointed Master of Trinity College where he employed James Essex to remodel part of Great Court in the Palladian style in 1771 – 74.

In January 1758 Adam returned from Italy to London where he found Stuart and Chambers installed as rivals, both having returned from Italy in 1754 – 55. Adam and Stuart seem to have been particularly aware of the new interest in interior design and furnishing as a vehicle for self-expression. This field had been developing during the eighteenth century, encouraged by writers such as Addison in the *Spectator* and reflected in countless diaries and letters as the century progressed. The intensity of the competition between Stuart and Adam is well demonstrated at Kedleston, Derbyshire. Though Nathaniel Curzon did not inherit this great estate and the Curzon baronetcy until November 1758, he had begun commissioning designs in 1757 for a new house from the Palladian architect Matthew Brettingham (1699 – 1769) and for its interior decoration from Stuart (see figs. 6-30 to 6-33). Adam soon caught sight of Stuart's drawings of about 1757 – 58, writing gleefully to his brother James in December 1758 that "Sir Nathaniel [Curzon] brought me out a Design of the Great Athenians for his Rooms finishing . . . so excessively and ridiculously bad, that [he]

44

immediately saw the folly of them & said so to some people which so offended the proud Grecian, that he has not seen Sr. Nathaniel these 2 years."[163] Though two years was clearly an exaggeration, it is striking that in 1759 Curzon appointed James Paine (1717 – 89), another Palladian designer, as architect of the new house. Having seen off Brettingham and Stuart, Adam now persuaded Curzon that he was the only architect fashionable enough to complete Kedleston. Adam was thus in charge by April 1760, though he was not above cribbing Stuart's designs for the dining room (see fig. 11-18, 11-19).

Adam continued his onslaught against Stuart's "Gusto Greco" when he saw Stuart's work at Spencer House in progress from 1759 – 65. He described this as "pityfulissimo," complaining that the ceilings might well be regarded as "Greek to the teeth but by God they are not handsome."[164] Adam also recalled Paul Sandby telling him that when he was visiting Earl Harcourt at Nuneham Park, Earl De La Warr called in order to see "the room which the Archipelagan Architect had ornamented for him" in about 1760 – 64. According to Sandby and Adam, De La Warr exclaimed, "God damn my blood, my Lord, is this your Grecian architecture? What villainy! What absurdity! If this be Grecian, give me Chinese, give me Gothick! Anything is better than his! For shame, my Lord, pull it down and burn it."[165] It is only fair to note that Adam did not adopt in public the intemperate language which he used in private to condemn Stuart's work, as apparently did Lord De La Warr. Thus, in the preface to his *Works in Architecture,* Adam claimed, seemingly without irony, that "Mr. Stuart, with his usual elegance and taste has contributed greatly towards introducing the true style of antique decoration."[166]

In the meantime, Adam and Chambers had been appointed joint architects to George III in November 1761 at the start of the reign of the young king. Chambers was close to the king, having been his tutor in architecture since 1757, so that he had little difficulty in ensuring that Adam received no important royal commissions, particularly since the king found Adam's work too fussy and expensive for his tastes. Nonetheless, Chambers and Adam, and possibly also Stuart, all worked on the remodeling of Buckingham House for George III as Queen's House in 1762. All three architects successfully sought the permission of the king to dedicate publications to him. The potential value of such marks of approval is demonstrated by James Adam who, referring to the ambition

of his brother Robert to dedicate his work on *Spalatro* to the king and queen confessed in 1761 that "I have taken a sort of dread that the Athenian [Stuart] may have the same project & may be able to execute it through the M[arque]s of R[ockingha]me".[167]

This assumption was correct. Stuart and Revett dedicated the first volume of *Antiquities of Athens* in 1762 to the king. Their dedication expressed the widely felt expectations of royal patronage at the start of the reign in the fulsome language of the day:

> Athens was particularly celebrated for those Arts, which amidst the cares of Government, and the glories of Conquest, Your Majesty deigns to patronize. The fame of Athens and of these remains of her ancient splendor, which we have described, would not sufficiently embolden us thus to approach Your Majesty, did we not behold, in the prospect which our own Country affords, the Arts of Elegance, and those of Empire equally flourishing, under the influence of a Sovereign in whose Mind they are united.

The hostility of Chambers to Stuart was shared with Le Roy and promoted by his friendship with Chambers. In the autumn of 1769, Le Roy visited London where Chambers entertained him and introduced him to leading members of the Royal Academy of Arts.[168] Some time between 1768 and 1771, Chambers prepared notes on Grecian architecture, perhaps for delivery as lectures at the newly founded Royal Academy.[169] These unpublished notes were probably also related to the second edition (1768) of his *Treatise on Civil Architecture* (first published in 1759). Whereas Piranesi had censured Le Roy, whom he perceived as a threat, Chambers, as a friend of Le Roy, criticized his own potential rival, Stuart. In the most intemperate language, he argued that one "might with equal success oppose a Hottentot & a Baboon to the Apollo and the Gladiator as set up the Grecian Architecture against the Roman."[170] In another somewhat offensive parallel, he suggested that "it would be to imagine that a Peasant could set the Fashion of a dress," and went on to argue that "it hath afforded Occasion of Laughter to every intelligent Architect to see with what Pomp the Grecian Antiquities have lately been ushered into the World & what Encomiums have been lavished upon things that in Reality deserve little or no Notice." He dis-

Fig. 1-21. James Wyatt. The Radcliffe Observatory, Woodstock Road, Oxford, from the southwest, 1776–94. Photographed in 1930. © Country Life Picture Library.

missed the Choragic Monument of Lysicrates for being "in Reality not quite so large as one of the Sentry Boxes in Portman Square," comparing it to "a silver Tankard excepting that the Handle is wanting." Despite these shortcomings, "Messrs Steward and Ryvet have given twenty six Plates of this Edifice," though the worst criticism Chambers could make of it was to complain that it "bore a very exact resemblance to the Taste of Boromini." The Tower of the Winds he ridiculed because it "resembles exactly one of the Dove houses usually erected on Gentlemens Estates, excepting that . . . there is no Turret for the Pigeons to creep in & fly out at."[171] He also made a more serious complaint, a version of which he incorporated in the third edition of his *Treatise* (1791):

> How distant the Grecians were from Perfection in Proportions in the Art of Profiling & I may venture to say in the whole Detail of the Decorative Part of Architecture will appear at first Sight to every one whether Ignorant or informed

who unprejudiced compares the Columns, Capitals, Bases Pedestals, Entablatures & Ornaments in the Works of Messrs le Roy, Revet & Stewart and other ingenious travellers with the Antiquities of Rome.[172]

Welcoming its claims to be balanced and "unprejudiced," Horace Walpole had praised an earlier edition of this hugely influential work as the "most sensible book and the most exempt from prejudices that ever was written on that science."[173]

With opposition to Greek architecture from so august a source as Sir William Chambers, the king's architect and a founder member and treasurer of the Royal Academy, it was not surprising that a Greek Revival, even had Stuart sought one, was slow in coming. Yet despite Chambers's ridicule of the Tower of the Winds, an imaginative response to its forms was produced by James Wyatt (1746 – 1813) at the Radcliffe Observatory, Oxford (1776 – 94; fig. 1-21). Though inspired by Stuart and

Fig. 1-22. Nicholas Revett. East
portico of Trafalgar House,
Downton, Wiltshire, ca. 1766.
Undated photograph. English
Heritage / National Monuments
Record A38/1853.

Fig. 1-23. Nicholas Revett. Ayot Saint Lawrence Church, Hertfordshire,
1778–79. Photographed ca. 1970. English Heritage / National Monuments
Record BB78/3224/©Nicholas Cooper.

Fig. 1-24. The Temple of Apollo, Delos. Engraving.
From *Antiquities of Athens,* vol. 3, chap. 10 (1794): pl. I.
Courtesy of the Library, The Bard Graduate Center for
Studies in the Decorative Arts, Design, and Culture,
New York. *Checklist no. 90.*

Revett's engravings of the tower, Wyatt's building was
more original than Stuart's version of the same source at
Shugborough in 1764 (see fig. 7-1). Wyatt also adopted
fluted baseless Doric columns of Greek form, though with
Roman astragals for his gateway at Christ Church,
Oxford (1773 – 83), and at two country houses, Castle
Coole, Ireland (1790 – 97), and Stoke Park, Bucking-
hamshire (ca. 1793 – 97).[174]

In porticoes at Standlynch (now Trafalgar Park),

Wiltshire (ca. 1766; fig. 1-22), and Ayot Saint Lawrence
Church, Hertfordshire (1778 – 79; fig. 1-23), Stuart's former partner, Nicholas Revett (1720 – 1804), adopted the
Greek Doric order with fluting at only the top and bottom of the shafts, for the first time since antiquity, as featured at the Temple of Apollo on the island of Delos (fig.
1-24).[175] The open colonnades flanking Ayot Saint
Lawrence Church are a livelier response to antiquity than
appears in Stuart's executed work. They are an inventive

Fig. 1-26. Nicholas Revett. Portico of West Wycombe Park, High Wycombe, Buckinghamshire, 1771. Photographed in 1950. English Heritage / National Monuments Record AA61/6028.

Fig. 1-27. Temple of Dionysus, Teos. Engraving by J. Basire. From Richard Chandler, William Pars, and Nicholas Revett, *Ionian Antiquities,* vol. 1, chap. 1 (1769): pl. II. By permission of The British Library, London, 745.e.11.

souvenir of the ruined temples that Revett had seen in Greece, even if the overall form is filtered through Palladio.

Another monument on Delos, the Hellenistic stoa of about 212 – 205 B.C., known to Stuart as "the Portico of Philip, King of Macedon," featured widely spaced columns with smooth flutes on their lower third, perhaps to pro-

tect them from the wheels of passing carts. Stuart surprisingly observed, "I have not any where seen a more elegant Doric example, nor any more fitted for the use of profane or private edifices." He recommended it as a model to modern architects "on account of the lightness of its proportions [in which it] differs from all the other examples we have given, and is more suitable for common use."[176] It was not used until Thomas Harrison adopted it for his gateway or propylaeum at Chester Castle, initially conceived in 1785 but not built until 1810 – 22 (fig. 1-25). A subtle but unsung example of this Delian Doric order is the elegant ashlar front of 13 St. John's Street, Salisbury, Wiltshire (ca. 1820), the atelier of William Osmond (1791 – 1875), the statuary and monumental mason who doubtless designed it.[177] Osmond was a friend of the arch Goth, A. W. N. Pugin (1812 – 52), who urged him to "leave your *blisters* [Pugin's term for Osmond's memorial tablets in churches], leave your Doric porticoes, leave all and follow me."[178]

Revett's great portico at West Wycombe Park, Buckinghamshire (fig. 1-26), of 1771 was more powerful than anything by Stuart. It had been inspired by the Ionic Temple of Dionysus (Bacchus) at Teos, built by the Hellenistic architect, Hermogenes, in about 220 – 205 B.C. In 1764 Revett had measured the remains of this vast building which he published in *Ionian Antiquities* (fig. 1-27).[179] On a smaller scale than West Wycombe, though

Fig. 1-28. Henry Holland. Entrance screen and portico, York House, Whitehall, also known as Dover House and Scottish Office, 1787–88. Photographed ca. 1945–80. English Heritage / National Monuments Record AA98/06239.

Fig. 1-29. Portico of the Library of Hadrian. Engraving. From *Antiquities of Athens,* vol. 1, chap. 5 (1762): pl. III. Courtesy of the Library, The Bard Graduate Center for Studies in the Decorative Arts, Design and Culture, New York. *Checklist no. 36.*

equally refined, were the additions to York House, Whitehall (fig. 1-28), built in 1787 – 88 by Henry Holland (1745 – 1806) for the Duke of York, second son of George III. The duke was an architectural patron of some interest who had, for example, subscribed to Riou's *Grecian Orders of Architecture*.[180] Holland evidently raided the *Antiquities of Athens* where, as a model for his entrance portico and screen at York House, he found plates of the

Library of Hadrian (A.D. 132; fig. 1-29), a sumptuous and sophisticated building described by Stuart as "one of the most considerable Remains of Athenian Magnificence."[181] Holland followed this unusual antique model closely with his four-columned portico, flanked by blank rusticated walls fronted with columns, each with its own entablature breaking over it.[182] He exchanged the Corinthian of the original, however, for the lighter Ilissus Ionic, illustrated in the same volume of *Antiquities of Athens*; he further simplified the columns by making them unfluted.

Thomas Harrison, incidentally, adopted the Ilissus Ionic order, though again unfluted, for his Shire Hall, or Court of Justice (1791 – 1801; fig. 1-30), at Chester Castle, to which he gave the semicircular plan of the ancient Roman theater. Soane's master, George Dance (1741 – 1825), also enlivened the staircase hall at his Greek Revival essay, Stratton Park, Hampshire (1803 – 6; fig. 1-31), with a colonnade of unfluted Ilissus Ionic columns. Holland's debt to Stuart and Revett was further demonstrated in his elegant Temple of Liberty at Woburn Abbey (fig. 1-32) for the fifth Duke of Bedford.[183] Built in

1802 – 3 to house busts of the duke's Whig political heroes, this took the form of a temple in the Ilissus Ionic order with a frieze taken from the Choragic Monument of Thrasyllus, again as illustrated in *Antiquities of Athens*. Holland here indulged the luxury of fluting the Ilissus columns, though his Thrasyllan frieze contained only seven laurel wreaths, in contrast to the eleven of his model.

Greek Sculpture

Among Stuart's most important contributions to knowledge of antique art were the engravings of the sculpture on the Parthenon in the second volume of *Antiquities of*

Fig. 1-30. Thomas Harrison. Interior of the Shire Hall, Chester Castle, Cheshire, 1791–1801. Photographed in 1991. English Heritage / National Monuments Record BB93/2008.

Fig. 1-31. George Dance. The staircase hall, Stratton Park, Hampshire, 1803–06. Undated photograph. English Heritage / National Monuments Record AA52/863.

Fig. 1-32. Henry Holland. Temple of Liberty, east end of the sculpture gallery, Woburn Abbey, Bedfordshire, 1802–03. Photographed in 1949. English Heritage / National Monuments Record AA50/113.

Athens, its title page dated 1787 but seemingly not published until January 1790. Of help to Stuart were the drawings made in Athens by William Pars (1742 – 82) who had accompanied Revett and Richard Chandler on the expedition to Greece and Turkey of the Society of Dilettanti in 1764 – 66. The principal impact of the illustrations of sculpture in the *Antiquities of Athens* took place in the nineteenth century (see chap. 9).

Pars's drawings were known to Sir Richard Worsley, the only collector in late-eighteenth-century England to specialize in Greek antiquities.[184] He spent the years 1785 to 1787 in Greece, visiting Athens and the islands as well as the coasts of Asia Minor, accompanied for part of this time by Willey Reveley, editor of the third volume of *Antiquities of Athens.* Recalling the first thrilling sight of the Parthenon in the spring of 1785, Worsley observed that

"the beauty and magnificence of that edifice, on the closest examination, surpassed even my most sanguine expectations."[185] He acquired many antique gems and some fine Greek grave reliefs or *stelae,* publishing them in two lavish folios, the second of which included forty-three engravings of the Parthenon frieze. These were close to those in the second volume of *Antiquities of Athens,* a work that Worsley acknowledged.[186]

Other early reactions to Stuart's publication of Greek sculpture include the remarkable achievement of the ceramics manufacturer, Eleanor Coade (1733 – 1821), who produced variants of the Erechtheion maidens inspired by Stuart's plates. John Soane bought some of these figures for his Consols Transfer Office at the Bank of England (1798 – 99) and for several other works.[187] Coade displayed in her gallery in Lambeth in 1799 a figure of Decelia holding the tripod won by Thrasyllus sur-mounting the Choragic Monument of Thrasyllus in Athens, based on Stuart's engraving of it.[188] The sculptor, John Flaxman (1755 – 1826), a passionate admirer of Winckelmann, is known to have made tracings from *Antiquities of Athens*, buying his own copy in 1796. He had probably already used Stuart's plates of the Tower of the Winds as inspiration for the clinging yet fluttering draperies of the angels in his stunning monument to Mrs. Sarah Morley (died 1784) in Gloucester Cathedral.[189]

In 1790 Flaxman's friend Henry Fuseli, who had trans-lated Winckelmann's *Reflections Concerning the Imitation of the Painting and Sculpture of the Greeks* in 1765, published a lengthy review of the second volume of the *Antiquities of Athens*.[190] A generation younger than Stuart, Fuseli was an extravagant and sometimes visionary romantic classicist whose review was a passionate response to the engravings of the Parthenon frieze. He enthused of them:

> All these, though many of them are little more than wrecks of forms, still more disfigured in the copies, claim the uniform praise due to every work of ancient Greece — of propriety and dig-nity, considered as ornaments; of correctness and style, examined as works of art: but still they have another claim to superiority over modern art, the general composition, notwithstanding a sufficient variety of contrast and action, possesses that simplicity, that parallelism, or continuity of atti-tude and gesture, which produces energy of expression, and through the eye forces itself on the memory of the beholder.[191]

The passionate tone was further heightened in Fuseli's reaction to the representations of the maidens on the cary-atid portico of the Erechtheion of which he wrote: "They may furnish another authentic hint to the modern man of wealth, that in the most classic age of Greece the arts went hand in hand, and that no tyrant architect precluded the sculptor from adding splendour to his structure."[192] This powerful image of the artist as un unbridled roman-tic genius is rather different from the unadventurous phrase with which the engravings of the largest surviving section of the Parthenon frieze were introduced in *Antiquities of Athens*: "the work is admirable, and the sub-ject interesting."[193]

Relief carving in the ancient world generally included additions in metal as well as the application of color, but as with polychromy, there was a general lack of understanding in the eighteenth century of the use of metal additions to sculptural works. The Parthenon frieze contains many drill holes to enable bronze objects to be attached to the carvings of figures and animals. These metallic additions included armor and weapons, wreaths, incense burners, a caduceus or trumpet, sacred baskets, sandal straps, and the bridles and reins of horses.[194] Stuart's only significant reference to metal applications was in a footnote in the course of his quotation from Spon and Wheler's description of the Parthenon. Stuart here noted of Phidias's statue of Athena that "perhaps her Helmet, Buckler, and Aegis, were of gold, or of brass gilt: for we observed this kind of decoration to have been practised in the bass-relievos remaining on the freeze which surrounds the Parthenon, and on that within the Portico of the Temple of Theseus."[195] Neither Stuart nor his contemporaries, however, gave full consideration to the impact of this on the appearance of Greek art and archi-tecture where such bright metallic objects in the Parthenon frieze would have stood out against what is supposed to have been a blue background. All this would not have conformed with Winckelmann's image of Grecian purity. Indeed, even today, in the reconstructions of how the Parthenon frieze might have looked in antiquity in the explanatory gallery that opened in the British Museum in 1998, lost limbs and heads, as well as color, have been added with the aid of computers, but none of the metal.[196]

Stuart and Revett's *Antiquities of Athens*, the most comprehensive presentation of Greek and Hellenistic architecture produced in the eighteenth century, made a major contribution to the creation of the myth of Greece which had begun in the fifteenth century. While some architects derided its message, others, notably Wyatt, Holland, and Soane, none of whom had actually been to Greece, drew inspiration from the plates in *Antiquities of Athens,* as did contemporary carvers and sculptors. Stuart's impact, however, would be far greater in the nineteenth century, when the *Antiquities of Athens* became one of the most influential architectural publications of all time.

1. Based on Stuart's executed buildings alone, without *Antiquities of Athens,* it is unlikely that he could claim a major position.

2. Panayotis Tournikiotis, "The Place of the Parthenon in the History and Theory of Modern Architecture," in *The Parthenon and its Impact in Modern Times,* ed. Panayotis Tournikiotis (Athens: Melissa, 1994): 204.

3. In the opening sections of this chapter, the material is organized by country, but this does not mean that architects and patrons in the various countries saw only books written in their local languages.

4. Robert Weiss, "The Discovery of the Greek World," chap. 10 in *The Renaissance Discovery of Classical Antiquity,* 2nd ed. (Oxford: Blackwell, 1988).

5. See Edward Bodnar, *Cyriacus of Ancona and Athens* (Bruxelles-Berchem: Latomus, 1960): 35 – 40, 50 – 53.

6. Codex Barberini, fol. 28v, Vatican Library. See Beverly Brown and Diana Kleiner, "Giuliano da Sangallo's Drawings after Ciriaco d'Ancona: Transformations of Greek and Roman Antiquities in Athens," *Architectural History* (USA) 43 (December 1983): 321 – 35.

7. A suggestion made by Tassos Tanoulas, "Through the Broken Looking Glass: The Acciaiuoli Palace in the Propylaea Reflected in the Villa of Lorenzo Il Magnifico at Poggio a Caiano," *Bolletino d'arte* (April/June 1997): 25.

8. Vasari, *Lives of the Most Eminent Painters, Sculptors and Architects,* vol. 1 (London: Everyman's Library, 1996): 736.

9. Jenifer Neils, *The Parthenon Frieze* (Cambridge University Press: 2001): 228 – 29.

10. Serlio, *Tutte l'Opere d'Architettura et Prospetiva,* book 1 [1737], trans. and ed. Vaughan Hart and Peter Hicks (New Haven and London: Yale University Press, 1996): 190.

11. Pausanias, *Guide to Greece* [*Description of Hellas*], trans. Peter Levi, rev. ed., vol. 1 (Harmondsworth: Penguin, 1979): 53.

12. Serlio, *Tutte l'Opere* (1996): 230 – 31. Probably of early Augustan date, this building is masked by the Porta dei Leoni and is known largely from Renaissance drawings.

13. William Lithgow, *The Totall Discourse of the Rare Adventures and Painful Peregrinations . . . in Europe, Asia and Affrica* (1632; repr., Glasgow: James MacLehose and Sons, 1906): frontispiece, 66 – 68.

14. See Theodore Bowie and Diether Thimme, eds, *The Carrey Drawings of the Parthenon Sculptures* (Bloomington: Indiana University Press, 1971).

15. *Antiquities,* vol. 2 (ca. 1790): 4, referring to Bernard de Montfaucon, *Antiquité expliquée et représentée en figures,* vol. 3 (Paris, 1724): pl. I.

16. Neils, *Parthenon Frieze* (2001): 4 and figs. 4 – 7.

17. *Antiquities,* vol. 2 (ca. 1790): 1, 8, 13, and 38.

18. William St. Clair, review of *The Ruins of the Most Beautiful Monuments of Greece,* by Julien-David Le Roy, transl. by David Britt, in *Times Literary Supplement* (12 November 2004): 12 – 13. I am indebted to Mr. St. Clair for sending me an advance copy of his review in which he argues that Francis Mallgrave and Robin Middleton (in their introductions to this work) exaggerate the isolation of Greece and Athens in the seventeenth century and first half of the eighteenth.

19. See *La Fortuna di Paestum e la memoria moderna del Dorico, 1750 – 1830,* exh. cat., 2 vols. (New York, National Academy of Design, 1986); and the one-volume summary, Joselita Raspi Serra, ed., *Paestum and the Doric Revival, 1750 – 1830: Essential Outlines of an Approach* (Florence: Centro Di, 1986).

20. See Edward Chaney, *The Evolution of the Grand Tour* (London: Frank Cass, 1998): 29.

21. Fréart de Chambray, *Parallèle de l'architecture antique et moderne* (Paris: Edmé Martin, 1650): 2. Author's translation.

22. Ibid., 3.

23. Perrault, *Les Dix livres d'architecture de Vitruve* (1673; 2nd ed., Paris: Jean Baptiste Coignard, 1684): 113 – 22 and figs. 24, 25, 27. His columns, however, have Roman astragals, and his friezes, Roman demi-metopes.

24. Those writing in praise of Greece in the 1730s and 40s included J.-F. Blondel, A.-F. Frézier, Charles Batteux, and Charles Rollin. See Wolfgang Herrmann, *Laugier and Eighteenth Century French Theory,* Studies in Architecture, vol. 12 (London: Zwemmer, 1962): 26.

25. Spon, *Voyage d'Italie, de Dalmatie, de Grèce, et et du Levant. Faite dans les années 1675 & 1676. Par Jacob Spon & George Wheler,* 4 vols. (Lyons, 1678 – 80); Spon, *Recherches Curieuses d'Antiquités, contenues en plusieurs dissertations, sur des medailles, bas-reliefs, statues, mosaiques, & inscriptions antiques; enrichies d'un grand nombre de figures en taille douce* (Lyon: Thomas Amaulry, 1683).

26. Wheler, *A Journey into Greece* (1682).

27. They continued to be cited by travelers and archaeologists into the nineteenth century. See the seven-page pamphlet by Edward Daniel Clarke, *Critique on the Character and Writings of Sir George Wheler, Knt. as a Traveller* (York: Thomas Wilson and Sons, 1820).

28. Wheler, *A Journey into Greece, by George Wheler Esq; In Company of Dr Spon of Lyons. In Six Books* (London: Cademan, Kettlewell, and Churchill, 1682): 349.

29. Ibid., 356.

30. Ibid., 337.

31. Ibid., 357, 360, 385.

32. Caylus, *Recueil d'antiquités Egyptiennes, Etrusques, Grècques, Romaines et Gauloises,* 7 vols. (Paris, 1752 – 67).

33. Ibid., new ed., vol. 1 (Paris: Desaint and Saillant, 1761): ix, 159. Author's translation.

34. Ibid., vol. 4 (Paris, Tilliard, 1761): 174 – 75.

35. Ibid., vol. 2 (Paris: Duchesne, 1756): 109.

36. Ibid., vol. 5 (Paris: Tilliard, 1762): [127].

37. Svend Eriksen, "Lalive de Jully's Furniture 'à la grecque'," *Burlington Magazine* 103 (August 1961): 340 – 47; and Hugh Roberts, "A Postscript on Lalive de Jully's Furniture 'à la grecque'," *Burlington Magazine* 131 (May 1989): 350 – 53.

38. Le Roy, *Les Ruines des plus beaux monuments de la Grèce* (1758; 2nd ed., Paris: Guerin and Delatour, 1770).

39. Robin Middleton, introduction to Julien-David Le Roy, *The Ruins*

of the Most Beautiful Monuments of Greece, trans. by David Britt (Los Angeles: Getty Publications, 2004): 25.

40. St. Clair, review of *Ruins of the Most Beautiful Monuments of Greece* (2004): 13.

41. Choiseul-Gouffier, *Voyage pittoresque de la Grèce,* 2 vols. (Paris: J. J. Blaise, 1782 – 1822).

42. *The Mark J. Millard Architectural Collection*, vol. 1, *French Books: Sixteenth through Nineteenth Centuries*, intro. and cat. by Dora Wiebenson (Washington: National Gallery of Art, 1993): 114 – 18.

43. See Middleton, introduction to *Ruins* (2004): 10 – 11; and *Soufflot et l'architecture des lumières*, colloquium proceedings (Paris: École Nationale Supérieure des Beaux-Arts, 1986).

44. *Le Panthéon: Symbole des révolutions: de l'église de la nation au temple des grands hommes,* exh. cat. (Paris: Caisse Nationale des Monuments Historiques et des Sites, Paris, 1989): 14 (illus.).

45. Blondel, *Cours d'Architecture*, 9 vols. (Paris: Desaint, 1771 – 77). Denis Diderot and Jean le Rond d'Alembert, *Encylopédie ou dictionnaire raisonné*, 33 vols. (Paris: Briasson, and Amsterdam: Rey, 1751 – 77).

46. Rollin, *Histoire ancienne des Egyptiens, des Carthaginois, des Assyriens, des Babyloniens, des Medes et des Perses, des Macedoniens, des Grecs*, vol. 5 (Paris: Veuve Estienne, 1752): 565. And see Middleton, introduction to *Ruins* (2004): 117 – 18.

47. Desgodetz, *Édifices antiques de Rome dessinés et mesurés tres exactement* (Paris: Jean Baptiste Coignard, 1682).

48. *Spectator*, no. 417 (28 June 1712).

49. Ibid.

50. Ibid., no. 420 (2 July 1712).

51. Ibid., no. 417 (28 June 1712).

52. *The Iliad of Homer. Translated by Mr. Pope*, vol. 3 (London: Bernard Lintott, 1715 – 18): 140.

53. *Spectator*, no. 412 (23 June 1712).

54. Ibid., no. 417 (28 June 1712).

55. Ibid., no. 415 (26 June 1712), quoting from Fréart de Chambray's account of the Doric order (*Parallèle* [1650]: 10 – 11), though relying heavily on Evelyn's translation, which was published in London in 1664.

56. *Spectator*, no. 413 (24 June 1712).

57. See Chaney, *Evolution of the Grand Tour* (1998): 22 – 32, 314 – 76.

58. George Berkeley to Baron Percival of Burton, 28 July 1718, in Berkeley, *Works*, ed. A .A. Luce and T. E. Jessop, vol. 8 (London: Nelson, 1948 – 57): 111.

59. Francis Haskell, *Patrons and Painters,* 2nd ed. (New Haven and London: Yale University Press, 1980): 222, 266, 306 – 7; Breval, *Remarks on Several Parts of Europe, Relating Chiefly to their Antiquities and History*, 2 vols. (1723 – 28; rev. ed., London: 1738).

60. John Ingamells, ed., *A Dictionary of British and Irish Travellers in Italy, 1701 – 1800* (New Haven and London: Yale University Press, 1997): 122.

61. Breval, *Remarks on Several Parts of Europe*, vol. 1 (1738): 37.

62. Ibid.

63. On Spon and Wheler, Chandler, and, briefly, Pococke, see David Constantine, "The Question of Authenticity in Some Early Accounts of Greece," in *Rediscovering Hellenism: The Hellenic Inheritance and the English Imagination*, ed. G. W. Clarke (Cambridge University Press, 1989): 1 – 22.

64. See Michael McCarthy, "'The Dullest Man that Ever Travelled'? A Re-assessment of Richard Pococke," *Apollo* 143 (May 1996): 33.

65. The portrait, painted while Liotard was in Constantinople (1738 – 42), is in the Musée d'Art et d'Histoire, Geneva.

66. Pococke, *A Description of the East, and Some Other Countries*, 2 vols. (London: W. Bowyer, 1743 – 45).

67. Ibid., vol. 2., pt. 1, pls. X – XI.

68. Ibid., 167.

69. Ibid., 163 and 169.

70. *Antiquities*, vol. 1 (1762): [37].

71. Pococke, *Description of the East*, vol. 2 (1743 – 45): 162.

72. Ibid., 163.

73. Vitruvius, *On Architecture*, vol. 2, Loeb Classical Library (London: Heinemann; Cambridge: Harvard University Press, 1983): 218 – 20.

74. Pococke, *Description of the East*, vol. 2 (1743 – 45): 168.

75. Eileen Harris, *British Architectural Books and Writers, 1556 – 1785*, assisted by Nicholas Savage (Cambridge, UK, and New York: Cambridge University Press, 1990): 173 – 75; and Ingamells, *Dictionary of British and Irish Travellers* (1997): 196 – 99.

76. Dalton, *Remarks on XII Historical Designs of Raphael, And The Musaeum Graecum Et Aegyptiacum* (London: M. Cooper 1752): 22. The park referred to is that of Marino House, Dublin, the Irish seat of Lord Charlemont.

77. *Antiquities*, vol. 1 (1762): 19 – 20.

78. Dalton, "The Explanation of a Series of Prints . . ." (1781): 9, cited in E. Harris, *British Architectural Books* (1990): 174.

79. Erlach, *Entwurff einer historischen architektur* (1721; 2nd ed., Leipzig, n.p., 1725): book 1, pl. XIX (Parthenon); 2nd. ed. translated by Thomas Lediard as *A Plan of Civil and Historical Architecture . . .* (London, n.p., 1730).

80. There are no adequate modern translations into English of any of Winckelmann's books and letters, but the best monograph on him in any language is Alex Potts: *Flesh and the Ideal: Winckelmann and the Origins of Art History* (New Haven and London: Yale University Press, 1994).

81. Winckelmann, *Reflections concerning the Imitation of the Painting and Sculpture of the Greeks,* trans. Fuseli (1755), in *Winckelmann: Writings on Art*, ed. David Irwin (London: Phaidon, 1972): 72.

82. *Winckelmann: Writings* (1972): 61.

83. Winckelmann, *The History of Ancient Art*, trans. by G. Henry Lodge, vol. 1 (London: Sampson Low, Marston, Searle and Rivington, 1880 – 81): 308.

84. We know of Stuart's relations with Göttingen from a letter sent from London by Lichtenberg to Christian Gottlieb Heyne, 16 March 1775, cited in *Georg Christoph Lichtenberg: Schriften und Briefe*, ed. Franz

Mautner, vol. 4 (Frankfurt-am-Main, Insel Verlag, 1983): 179. I am indebted to Marcus Köhler for this reference.

85. Sayer, *Ruins of Athens* (London: n.p., 1759); Sayer, *Ruinen und Uberbleibsel von Athen nebst anderen merkwürdigen Altherthüm Griechenlands* (Augsburg, 1782). I am indebted for this information to William St. Clair.

86. Ramsay, "A Dialogue on Taste," *Investigator*, no. 332 (London, 1755); reprinted as a pamphlet in 1762.

87. Piranesi, *Della Magnificenza ed architettura de' Romani* (Rome, 1761): pls. XX, XXXI – XXXV.

88. Ibid., clxxxix – cxci.

89. Piranesi, *Diverse maniere d'adornare i cammini* (Rome: Generoso Salomoni, 1769); the full English title is *Divers Manners of Ornamenting Chimneys and all other parts of Houses taken from the Egyptian, Tuscan, and Grecian architecture with an Apologetical Essay in Defence of the Egyptian and Tuscan architecture.*

90. Ibid., 2.

91. Ibid., 27.

92. Ibid., 30.

93. Ibid., 32 – 33.

94. Fréart de Chambray, *Parallèle* (1650): 3. Author's translation.

95. *Antiquities*, vol. 1 (1762): [i].

96. Ibid., ii.

97. Ibid., v, n. (a).

98. Ibid.

99. Ibid: iv, v.

100. Ibid: v, n.(a).

101. Mary Beard, *The Parthenon* (London: Profile Books, 2002): 45.

102. Vitruvius, *On Architecture*, vol. 2 (1983): 72 – 73.

103. *Plutarch's Lives*, vol. 3, Loeb Classical Library (London: Heinemann; New York, Macmillan, 1915 – 26): 39 – 41.

104. Ibid., 35 – 37.

105. William St. Clair, in an unpublished lecture at a conference on art and imperialism.

106. Pausanias, *Guide to Greece*, vol. 1 (1979): 70.

107. Le Roy, *Ruins* (2004): 205.

108. Guys, *Voyage Litteraire de la Grèce, ou Lettres sur les Grecs Anciens et Modernes, Avec un Parallèle de leur Moeurs*, 2 vols. (1771; 2nd ed., Paris, 1783). For a good account of Guys, see Terence Spencer, *Fair Greece Sad Relic* (London: Weidenfeld and Nicolson, 1954): 214 – 17. For a description of the literary origins of the Philhellenic response to the Greek War of Independence, see William St. Clair, *That Greece Might Still be Free: The Philhellenes in the War of Independence* (New York and London: Oxford University Press, 1972).

109. *Antiquities*, vol. 2 (ca. 1790), advertisement.

110. Ibid., vol. 1 (1762): iv.

111. Ibid., x.

112. Ibid., 41.

113. On this point, see Richard Jenkyns, *The Victorians and Ancient Greece* (Oxford: Blackwell, 1980): 3.

114. *Antiquities*, vol. 1 (1762): chap. 2, p. 7.

115. Ibid., ii.

116. Temple of Fortuna Virilis; see ibid., v, n.(a).

117. Dora Wiebenson and Claire Baines, *The Mark J. Millard Collection*, vol. 1, *French Books: Sixteenth through Nineteenth Centuries* (Washington: National Gallery of Art; New York: Braziller, 1993): 196.

118. *Antiquities*, vol. 2 (ca. 1790), advertisement. Winckelmann's criticism came in a letter to Fuseli, 22 September 1764, in Winckelmann, *Briefe*, ed. Hans Diepolder and Walther Rehm, vol. 3 (Berlin: De Gryter, 1956): 57.

119. *Antiquities*, vol. 3 (1794): x – xviii.

120. Ingamells, *Dictionary of British and Irish Travellers* (1997): 807 – 8, 1018 – 19.

121. Le Roy, *Ruines des plus beaux monuments de la Grèce*, 2nd ed., (Paris: H. F. Guerin and L. F. Delatour, 1770): pt. 1, v – vi. Author's translation.

122. Ibid., 1st ed. (Paris: Guerin and Delatour, 1758): pt. 1, xiv. On the Church of the Grands Augustins, see Piganiol de la Force, *Nouvelle description de la France*, vol. 2 (Paris: Florentin Delaulne, 7 vols., 1722): 455 – 61.

123. Le Roy, *Ruines* (1758): pt. 2, vi – vii. Author's translation.

124. This was despite the fact that the edition is dated 1770. See Middleton, introduction to *Ruins* (2004): 20.

125. Thomas Mulvany, *The Life of James Gandon, Esq.* (Dublin: Hodges and Smith, 1846): 198 – 99.

126. Aristotle, *Poetics*, 1450a – b. For an excellent account of color in antique painting, though not in architecture, see John Gage, *Colour and Culture: Practice and Meaning from Antiquity to Abstraction* (London: Thames and Hudson, 1993): chap. 1.

127. *Antiquities*, vol. 2 (ca. 1790): 4 and 7, referring to Strabo, *Geographica*, I, viii, p. 354.

128. *Antiquities*, vol. 1 (1762): chaps. 2, 10 and pl. VIII, fig. 3.

129. Ibid., vol. 3 (1794): chap. 1, pls. VII, VIII. The palmettes are incorporated into the ornamental head-piece of the chapter and are described as "painted in dark ochre" (p. 10).

130. Ibid., vol. 2 (ca. 1790): pl. VII, fig. 3.

131. Winckelmann, *Anmerkungen über die Baukunst der Alten* (Leipzig: J.G. Dyck, 1762) in *Winckelmann: Writings* (1972). Rousseau, *Emile, ou de l'Education* (Amsterdam: n.p., 1762).

132. Winckelmann, *Remarks* (1762), in *Winckelmann: Writings* (1972): 86 – 87.

133. Joseph Friedman, *Spencer House: Chronicle of a Great London Mansion* (London: Zwemmer 1993): 128.

134. Christian Hirschfeld, *Théorie der Gartenkunst*, vol. 2, pt. 4 (Leipzig: M.G. Weidmanns Erben and Reich, 1782): 236.

135. *Antiquities*, vol. 1 (1762): chap. 1, pl. III.

136. Dated 1776, the statue of Diana is today in the Schloss Museum,

Gotha. See H. H. Arnason, *The Sculpture of Houdon* (London: Phaidon, 1975): 43 – 44, fig. 9.

137. Cited in Dora Wiebenson, *Sources of Greek Revival Architecture* (London: Zwemmer, 1969): 69.

138. Jacque Guillaume Legrand and Charles Paul Landon, *Description de Paris et de ses édifices . . .* (Paris: C. P. Landon, 1806).

139. Monique Mosser and Daniel Rabreau, *Charles de Wailly: peintre architecte dans l'europe des lumières,* exh. cat, Hôtel de Béthune-Sully, Paris (Paris: Caisse nationale des monuments historiques et des sites, 1979): 44 – 45, and Middleton, introduction to *Ruins* (2004): 76.

140. Alexandre de Laborde, *Description des nouveaux jardins de la France et de ces anciens châteaux* (Paris: Delance, 1808): pl. 69.

141. Ibid., 134.

142. Michel Gallet, *Paris Domestic Architecture of the 18th Century* (London: Barrie and Jenkins, 1972): 171.

143. Jean-Charles Krafft, *Recueil des plus jolies maisons de Paris et de ses environs* (Paris, J. L. Scherff, 1809): pls. 33 – 34; and Werner Szambien, *Jean-Nicolas Durand (1760 – 1834): De l'imitation à la norme* (Paris: Picard, 1984): 23 – 26.

144. Major, *The Ruins of Paestum, otherwise Posidonia, in Magna Graecia* (London: T. Major, 1768). For the fullest account of Major's work, see Robin Middleton in *The Mark J. Millard Architectural Collection,* vol. 2, *British Books: Seventeenth through Nineteenth Centuries* (Washington: National Gallery of Art, 1998): 151 – 61. Middleton discusses the authorship of the text, pointing out that it was unlikely to have been by Major who was an engraver, not a scholar, published no other book, and had not visited Paestum. Riou, *The Grecian Orders of Architecture, Delineated and Explained from the Antiquities of Athens. Also The Parallels of the Orders of Palladio Scamozzi and Vignola. To Which Are Added Remarks Concerning Publick and Private Edifices With Designs* (London: J. Dixwell, 1768).

145. Paris, Musée du Louvre, Cabinet des Dessins. On Cochin, *graveur du cabinet du roi* and a member of the Académie Royale de Peinture et de Sculpture, see Christian Michel, *Charles-Nicolas Cochin et l'art des Lumières* (Rome: École Française de Rome, 1993).

146. Major, *Ruins of Paestum* (1768): [vii].

147. Ibid., 24.

148. E. Harris, *British Architectural Books* (1990): 390.

149. Winckelmann, *Anmerkungen über die Geschichte der Kunst des Alterthums* (Dresden: Waltherischen Hof Buchhandlung, 1767).

150. Riou, *Grecian Orders* (1768). Filling a whole page, this is beautifully printed in Trajan capitals without punctuation, like an ancient marble inscription. A few commas have been added here to aid comprehension.

151. Ibid., [i].

152. Perrault, *Ordonnance des cinq espèces de colonnes selon la méthode des anciens* (Paris: Jean Baptiste Coignard, 1683) see also Wolfgang Herrmann, *The Theory of Claude Perrault* (London: Zwemmer, 1973): 96 – 97.

153. *Antiquities,* vol. 1 (1762): vii.

154. Riou, *Grecian Orders* (1768): [iii].

155. Ibid., 25, 4.

156. John Fleming, *Robert Adam and His Circle in Edinburgh and Rome* (London: John Murray, 1962): 223.

157. Ibid., 230.

158. E. Harris, *British Architectural Books* (1990): 76 – 81.

159. Quoted in Fleming, *Robert Adam* (1962): 240.

160. Ibid., 272.

161. Ibid., 368.

162. Ingamells, *Dictionary of British and Irish Travellers* (1997): 500.

163. Leslie Harris, *Robert Adam and Kedleston: The Making of a Neo-Classical Masterpiece,* ed. Gervase Jackson-Stops, exh. cat., Cooper-Hewitt Museum, New York (London: National Trust, 1987): 28.

164. Fleming, *Robert Adam* (1962): 258.

165. Ibid., 259 – 60.

166. Robert Adam and James Adam, *The Works in Architecture of Robert and James Adam,* vol. 1, pt. 1 (London: the authors, 1773): vi.

167. James Adam to William Adam, Florence, 16 February 1761, quoted in Bristol, "Stuart and the Genesis of the Greek Revival" (1997): 47.

168. Middleton, introduction to *Ruins* (2004): 125, where reference is made to the survival of seven letters or drafts of letters from Chambers to Le Roy, and seven from Le Roy to Chambers (RIBA and British Library).

169. MSS Cha.1/1-1/13, British Architectural Library, and CHA/2/1-76, Royal Academy.

170. MSS Cha.1/1-1/13, British Architectural Library. Apollo and the Gladiator were two of the most celebrated ancient sculptures in the Belvedere Court at the Vatican.

171. "Excerpts from the Notes of Sir William Chambers," appendix 3 in *Sources of Greek Revival Architecture* by Dora Wiebenson (London, Zwemmer 1969): 126 – 27. See also Eileen Harris, "Rome v. Greece," in John Harris, *Sir William Chambers* (London: Zwemmer, 1970): 139 – 41.

172. Chambers, *Treatise on the Decorative Part of Civil Architecture,* 3rd ed. (London: Joseph Smeeton, 1791): 19.

173. Horace Walpole, *Anecdotes of Painting in England [1760 – 1765] . . . ,* ed. Ralph N. Wornum, rev. ed., vol. 1 (London: Swan Sonnenschein, Lowrey and Co., 1888): xiv.

174. His source for this hybrid form might have been the gateway at Verona illustrated in Serlio, *Tutte l'Opere* (1996): 230 – 31.

175. *Antiquities,* vol. 3 (1794): chap. 10, pl. I, and Le Roy, *Ruines* (1758): pt. 2, pl. II, fig. 1.

176. *Antiquities,* vol. 3 (1794): chap. 10, pp. 57 – 58, fig. 3.

177. Royal Commission on Historical Monuments, *Ancient and Historical Monuments of the City of Salisbury* (London, HMSO, 1980): 116.

178. Benjamin Ferrey, *Recollections of A. N. Welby Pugin, and his Father, Augustus Pugin* (London: Stanford, 1861): 90 – 91. It is evident from Osmond's monuments in Salisbury Cathedral, which are mostly in the Gothic style, that he took Pugin's advice.

179. Richard Chandler, Nicholas Revett, and William Pars, *Antiquities of Ionia*, vol. 1 (1769, with the title *Ionian Antiquities*; 2nd ed., London: W. Bulmer and W. Nicol, 1821): 1 – 9. Twenty-four drawings for vol. 1 by Revett are in the British Architectural Library; see Jill Lever, ed., *Catalogue of the Drawings Collection of the RIBA*, vol. 10 (Farnborough, Eng.: Gregg International, 1976): 122 – 23. *Antiquities of Ionia* was published in 5 vols., 1769 – 1915.

180. For his architectural interests, see David Watkin, *The Architect King: George III and the Culture of the Enlightenment* (London: Royal Collection, 2004): 197 – 99.

181. *Antiquities*, vol. 1 (1762): chap. 5, [37]. Stuart was unable to identify the building but spent much of his time in this chapter in attacking Le Roy for his identification of it as the Temple of Jupiter Olympius.

182. Dorothy Stroud, *Henry Holland: His Life and Architecture* (London: Country Life, 1966): 92 – 93.

183. Ibid., 111 – 20.

184. Jonathan Scott, *The Pleasures of Antiquity: British Collectors of Greece and Rome* (New Haven and London: Yale University Press: 2003): 155 – 59.

185. Richard Worsley, *Museum Worsleyanum or A Collection of Antique Basso Relievos Bustos Statues and Gems . . .* , vol. 1 (London, [Shakespeare Press, 1798]): 1.

186. Ibid., vol. 2 [ca. 1803]: 57. Both volumes of *Museum Worsleyanum* were printed with publication dates of 1794.

187. Alison Kelly, *Mrs Coade's Stone* (Upton-on-Severn: Self Publishing Association, 1990): 68.

188. *Antiquities*, vol. 2 (ca. 1790): chap. 4, pl. VI.

189. For the plates see ibid., vol. 1 (1762): chap. 3, pls. XII – XIX. For the monument see David Irwin, *John Flaxman, 1755 – 1826: Sculptor, Illustrator, Designer* (London: Cassell, 1979): 12 and pls. 13 and 15.

190. R.R., review of vol. 2 of *Antiquities of Athens*, in *Analytical Review* (8 October 1790): 121 – 30. For the attribution to Fuseli, see David Irwin, *English Neoclassical Art: Studies in Inspiration and Taste* (London: Faber, 1966): 72.

191. R.R., review of vol. 2 of *Antiquities* (1790): 124.

192. Ibid., 127.

193. *Antiquities*, vol. 2 (ca. 1790): chap. 1, p. 12.

194. Neils, *Parthenon Frieze* (2001): 88 – 93.

195. *Antiquities*, vol. 2 (ca. 1790): 2. Later, puzzled by "certain triangular holes" on the architrave of the east portico of the Parthenon, Stuart noted that "It is difficult to assign any use for the holes, unless we suppose that cramps were fixed in them, to support some kind of ornament, probably Festoons; with which the eastern Front, and that only, has been decorated" (ibid., 10).

196. I am grateful to Mr. William St. Clair for pointing this out to me.

Fig. 2-1. Portrait Medallion of James Stuart, after 1777. Made by Wedgwood and Bentley. Jasper with green dip and white relief. The Wedgwood Museum Trust, Barlaston, Staffordshire, no. 4094. *Checklist no. 202.*

CHAPTER 2

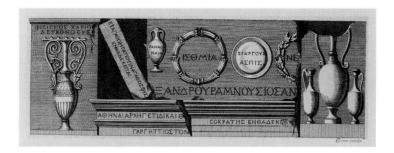

THE LIFE OF JAMES "ATHENIAN" STUART, 1713–1788

CATHERINE ARBUTHNOTT

A round fifteen years before the death of James "Athenian" Stuart, Josiah Wedgwood created a portrait medallion of him, one of many medallions of "Illustrious Moderns" that Wedgwood had produced by 1773. Stuart dressed accordingly: in a formal frock coat and cravat, and wearing a fashionable "tie" wig (fig. 2-1). After his death in 1788 a process of reassessment began, led by family and friends keen to emphasize his achievements and play down his problematic later career. The first posthumous portrait, published by his widow in the second volume of Antiquities of Athens (fig. 2-2) is an idealized one. Stuart wears a toga and his hair is neatly cropped in a Roman style. His wrinkles are minimized, and his bulbous nose reduced to a slight hook. Although it is recognizably Stuart, the blemishes have been removed. His anonymous obituarist performed a similar service in the Gentleman's Magazine in 1788. "Traits for the life of the late Athenian Stuart" focused on inspirational or exemplary aspects of Stuart's life."[1] It reveals more about the values held in high esteem by society of the 1780s than about Stuart's individual personality. The obituarist highlighted Stuart's affection for his family, his self-improvement by study, and his integrity and fortitude, presenting Stuart's career

JAMES STUART Esq. F.R.S.

Fig. 2-2. Portrait of James Stuart. Engraving by C. Knight. From *Antiquities of Athens,* vol. 2 (ca. 1790): frontispiece. Courtesy of the Library, The Bard Graduate Center for Studies in the Decorative Arts, Design, and Culture, New York. *Checklist no. 129.*

Fig. 2-3. View of St. Paul's Cathedral from Ludgate Street, 1804. Engraving by James Sargant Storer, after Frederick Nash. Creed Lane is the narrow alleyway just visible on the right of the picture. Guildhall Library, City of London, Pr.460/PAU(2)ext. q8038261.

made."[5] On a more positive note, architectural historian Dora Wiebenson argued in 1969 that Stuart's outstanding ability to make and keep influential friends was essential to his success.[6] It seems that Stuart's remarkable, wayward personality is central to an understanding of his career.

Surprisingly, the first biography of Stuart was not published until 1816, some twenty-eight years after his death, as a preface to the fourth volume of *Antiquities of Athens*. The publisher, Josiah Taylor, acknowledged that too much information had already been lost forever.[7] Taylor attempted to trace Stuart's surviving friends, and he recorded his conversations with increasing exasperation: "Lord de Grey says he was a Staffordshire man," "Dr Caulder no 13 Lisson Grove informed me that James Stuart . . . was certainly a Scotsman having the accent of that country," and "Mr Caldwall, engraver, knew Stuart well, has no doubt he was *not* a Scotsman, but rather London born (Sir Philip Stephens thinks the same)."[8]

Taylor supplemented his researches on Stuart's life with a "narrative drawn up by a friend of the family," a man named Sheldrake who has never been firmly identified but probably was Timothy Sheldrake, whose father-in-law had been the executor of the will of Stuart's second wife, Elizabeth.[9] Sheldrake's knowledge of Stuart's early life must have been secondhand.[10] Taylor and Sheldrake were forced to fall back on Stuart's obituary in the *Gentleman's Magazine* and a lengthy correction published in the magazine's next issue by a correspondent signing himself "A.H."[11] This was almost certainly the draftsman Anthony Highmore.[12] Highmore, who insisted that his information came from Stuart himself, wrote: "I . . . have often heard him mention that he was born in London in 1713; that his parents lived in Creed-Lane, Ludgate-street; that his father was of Scotland, and his mother from Wales."[13] Highmore had also seen Stuart's coffin being lowered into a vault in the Church of St. Martin in the Fields, with a brass plate carrying the information that he had died on February 2, 1788 "in the 76th year of his age."[14] Although no corroborating evidence has ever been discovered, Highmore's date for Stuart's birth is generally accepted, as is his record of the location and situation of the family. That the information came directly from Stuart does not necessarily mean it can be trusted. Stuart seems to have taken a hand in obscuring his origins. His friend Dr. Caulder was convinced that Stuart had been a foundling, with no knowledge of his parents at all, having "had the above from Stuart's own mouth."[15] Although there are

as a triumph of hard work and perseverance over circumstance.[2] Twentieth-century authors, drawing on contemporary letters that criticized Stuart's idleness and drunkenness, began to rewrite his life as a tale of unfulfilled promise. In 1938 architectural historian Lesley Lawrence noted that "Stuart's dilatoriness and lack of method" were notorious and stated that Stuart "lacked the capacity rather than the opportunity" to be a leader of fashion.[3] About a decade later, diarist and conservationist James Lees-Milne suggested that Stuart might have championed and led a Greek Revival in architectural design but for his laziness and the "increasing depravity of his habits."[4] Lees-Milne placed the blame on Stuart's character, arguing that Stuart had "none of the fibre and initiative of which great leaders of a movement are

clearly dangers in accepting evidence from the recollections of friends of Stuart's in his later life, nonetheless some inferences can be drawn about Stuart's early life, his parents, and schooling, assuming that Anthony Highmore's information is broadly correct.

Stuart's birthplace, Creed Lane, is a small alleyway leading off Ludgate Hill in the City of London. It is only one block from St. Paul's Cathedral, which long dominated the area before high rise buildings (fig. 2-3). None of the prolific diarists, letter writers, and tourists who wrote about eighteenth-century London describe Creed Lane, and no images of it other than early nineteenth-century plans survive. It is frequently mentioned, however, in the proceedings of London's most famous courthouse, the Old Bailey. In these documents Creed Lane was a place where criminals lurked and planned robberies, where evaders of transportation orders attempted to hide, where thieves and pickpockets ran to take cover from pursuit, and, bizarrely, where the dishonest servant of a cornchandler kept 150 rabbits in a cellar.[16] Creed Lane's main landmark was a tavern, which is described in the Old Bailey cases as a haunt of prostitutes and criminals.[17]

Creed Lane and its associated yard, Holyday Yard, were also filled with legitimate businesses. During the course of the eighteenth century, at least thirty book tradesmen, including printers, bookbinders, book and print sellers, book-lock makers, and stationers, were based there.[18] More traded from the nearby streets, particularly St. Paul's Churchyard and Paternoster Lane. This great concentration of printers and print sellers may have been significant in Stuart's early development as an artist: according to his obituarist, "necessity and application were his only instructors."[19] London's print shops have been described as "veritable picture galleries, attracting crowds of window-gazers."[20] Many prints were etched or engraved facsimiles of works by old masters or famous contemporary paintings and will have acquainted Stuart with the rudiments of contemporary visual and artistic culture while he was still a boy. According to his obituarist, "drawing and painting were his earliest occupations."[21]

Nothing is known of Stuart's father except that he was "a mariner of inferior station" and that he died young, leaving his widow and children in "the utmost abyss of penury."[22] Even before his death, the family's finances would have been precarious. Common sailors were among the lower wage earners of the working poor and could expect to earn around £20 per year, less than half the earnings of a tradesman, shopkeeper, artisan, or craftsman, though slightly more than soldiers, laboring men, and out-servants.[23] Common seamen were among the impoverished classes in 1696 who were most likely to require parochial poor relief.[24] Seventy-five years later this was still true when a group of mariners marched in 1768 to demand a pay increase. A sailor's wages were then widely considered only just sufficient to keep a single man.[25] In Creed Lane shared occupancy was common. In almost every Old Bailey case involving residents of the lane or yard, whether as perpetrators, witnesses, or victims, these inhabitants lived with lodgers or were lodgers of others.[26] It was common at this time for whole families of the working poor to live in a single room, making it likely that the Stuart family of six would have lived in one room in a house shared with many other families.[27]

One important piece of information that was not available to Taylor or to Stuart's obituarist in the *Gentleman's Magazine* was that Stuart was identifying himself as a Roman Catholic in 1747.[28] It is possible that he became a convert during his long stay in Italy in the 1740s, but it is more likely that he was born to Catholic parents and privately christened in London. This helps explain the absence of baptismal records for any of the Stuart family, as for most of the eighteenth century, Catholic worship in London was a secretive activity, conducted in private chapels and small missions attached to some of the embassies of the Catholic powers.[29] During the seventeenth century a succession of laws had criminalized Catholic worship, levied fines on people who failed to worship in established Anglican churches, and disbarred Catholics from public life. By 1713 no Catholic could be an executor or doctor, matriculate at university, run a school, sit in parliament, be an office holder in a corporation, or hold any civil, military, or naval office under the crown. Their last wills could be overturned in favor of protestant claimants, and their property was subject to double taxation.[30] If he was poor and Catholic, Stuart was doubly disadvantaged as a youth trying to make his way in the world.

Carrying the Stuart surname, it is significant that Stuart's father named his eldest son after the deposed Catholic King James II and his son James Edward Stuart, known as the "Old Pretender." It seems very likely, (as is argued in chap. 4) that Stuart was a Jacobite, as supporters of the Catholic succession were known. Later in Stuart's life, the name would cause confusion: a letter he wrote in 1747 from Italy was intercepted, and his correspondent, a Dr. Jones in Bath, was hauled in front of the Privy Council on suspicion of being in league with the Pretender."[31]

Education

Poverty will have affected the kind of schooling Stuart received, although Highmore wrote that Stuart's parents "gave their son the best education in their power."[32] A fee-paying grammar school education will probably have been financially out of reach, and being the son of a Scotsman will also have narrowed his options, making it extremely unlikely that he had access to certain kinds of guild or professional education that were available to the children of freemen of the City of London.[33] His Catholicism may also have been a problem, as much of the available free education in early Georgian England was parish based and funded. Stuart was certainly literate, but basic literacy was common in London in the early eighteenth century among all classes, even the very poor.[34] This was partly because city life tended to expose the inhabitants to extensive print media, from handbills and pamphlets to books and newspapers.[35] There were large numbers of newly established charity schools in London and the area surrounding it, but eighteenth-century educators, such as the Society for the Promotion of Christian Knowledge, wished to provide only the most basic reading and writing skills, and religious instruction for the poorer classes, in order to prepare them for a life of useful service.[36] In 1816, writing of Stuart's schooling, Taylor believed it "probable he received but a common education."[37] Stuart's lack of Latin in his early career confirms this. In the eighteenth century the classical languages were still the hallmark of an academic curriculum and a good school. This in turn bolstered Latin as a social signifier.[38] According to his obituarist, Stuart "often confessed that he was first led into the obligation of studying the Latin language by the desire of understanding what was written under prints published after pictures of the ancient masters."[39] Although his curiosity may indeed have been stimulated by the Latin text on prints, Stuart's acquisition of the language may also have been aspirational, a part of the process of leaving behind his origins and reinventing himself as a gentleman.[40]

No information has survived about Stuart's age when his father died, but the resulting change in the fam-

JOSEPH GOUPY,

Engraved by R. Bean, from the Original Picture?

Pub. by C. Dyer, Compton Str.ᵗ Soho.

Fig. 2-4. R. Bean. Portrait of Joseph Goupy, early 18th century. Engraving , possibly after Michael Dahl. National Portrait Gallery London, NPG D2795.

ily's fortunes may coincide with a move they are reported to have made from Creed Lane to the Soho area of London.[41] By the early eighteenth century Soho had become the French quarter of the city, filled with refugee Huguenot artisans and craftsmen who had fled to England after Louis XIV revoked the Edict of Nantes in 1685.[42] Among the later Huguenot immigrants were members of the Goupy family.[43] Stuart's obituarist in the *Gentleman's Magazine* records that he was forced to earn a living for himself and his family "while yet a boy . . . by designing and painting fans for the late Goupee of the Strand."[44] Here is one of the most frustrating gaps in the record. In 1709, by Royal Charter, the lucrative business of fan making became a closed and protected occupation, regulated by the newly formed Worshipful Company of Fanmakers. After that date, by law, the only route into the profession was by apprenticeship, for which parents of apprentices paid a premium.[45] Although a modern estimate suggests that skilled craftsmen could earn above £60 per year, and in London about twice that amount, apprenticeships lasted about seven years during which time only token wages were paid.[46] Under the circumstances it is hard to see how Stuart could have acquired such a position or supported his family until his training was over.

Unfortunately, the early apprentice records of the Worshipful Company of Fanmakers are lost. However, the information that Stuart painted fans as a youth is corroborated by the artist Paul Sandby and by an anecdote relayed by the antiquary, draftsman, and biographer John Thomas Smith: "When Mrs. Nollekens was a girl, Goupy, her father's intimate friend was considered the most eminent of fan-painters; and so fashionable was fan-painting at that time, that the family of Athenian Stuart placed him as a pupil to that artist, conceiving that by so doing they had made his fortune."[47] In this account Stuart's employment is presented as a pupilage rather than as an apprenticeship, probably responding to the distinction that was made between artistic training and craft training and reflecting the social cachet that had come to be attached to the former.[48]

It is not known which "Goupee of the Strand" Stuart worked for. Although there was a little-known fan painter named William Goupy working in London at about the right date,[49] the likeliest Goupy to have been Stuart's master is either Louis Goupy or his nephew Joseph (fig. 2-4), both of whom were widely traveled, and had a demonstrated interest in art education (see chap. 4).[50] It seems possible that "Goupee of the Strand" is a conflation of two or even three Goupys. While Stuart's obituarist believed him to be self-taught as an artist before his apprenticeship began, Stuart will have learned and practiced specific techniques as an apprentice fan painter. In particular he will have become a skilled draftsman and copyist, as some eighteenth-century fans took their composition directly from old master or contemporary paintings and engravings. The ability to copy accurately was highly prized. In 1810 John Gould would remember Joseph Goupy as an artist "celebrated . . . for excellence in copying the works of others."[51] Fan painting of this kind required only limited creativity, but artists engaged in the trade needed ingenuity and adaptive abilities in order to modify rectangular paintings into the semicircular shape required for a fan. Fan painters frequently got around this problem by painting images within vignettes or medallions, which were then surrounded by swags, arabesques, or floral decoration (fig. 2-5).

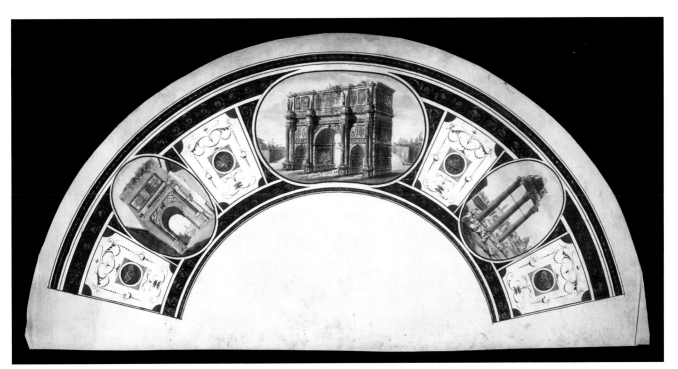

Fig. 2-5. Souvenir fan leaf (unmounted), with views of Rome (from left, Arch of Titus, Arch of Constantine, and the Forum), mid- to late 18th century. Watercolor on skin. Inscribed (signature probably a forgery): "Jose Goupy: 1738 NA." By courtesy of the Trustees of the British Museum, London, Lady Charlotte Schreiber Collection 335; 1891-7-13-719. *Checklist no. 3.*

Fig. 2-6. James Stuart. Self-portrait, ca. 1730–35. Charcoal and wash on tinted paper. RIBA Library Drawings Collection, London, POR/STUA/1. *Checklist no. 1.*

Another significant part of Stuart's artistic education will have been drawing from life. Both Louis and Joseph Goupy had been subscribers to an academy in Great Queen Street founded in 1711 by leading portrait artist Sir Godfrey Kneller.[52] Sir James Thornhill, artist and later father-in-law of William Hogarth, took over the school from Kneller in 1716 before moving on to found a new school at his home in Covent Garden.[53] Although no documentation survives of Stuart's presence among the students, it is possible that he studied life drawing here. There is evidence that he was a member of one of the successor groups to this academy after Thornhill's death in 1734. The publisher, writer, and dealer Algernon Graves wrote of the dispossessed art students that "a few of them (chiefly foreigners), finding themselves without the necessary example of a living model, formed a small society, and established their regular meetings of study in a convenient apartment in Greyhound Court, Arundel Street."[54] The group soon moved to Salisbury Court where, "its chief

promoter was George Michael Moser. . . . He was supported by Marcus Tuscher and by James ('Athenian') Stuart."[55] Moser was a coppersmith and enamel painter by training.[56] It may be significant that at least two artists with whom Stuart is believed to have been associated, Moser and Louis Goupy, who became a portrait painter, made the transition to more prestigious branches of art from beginnings that were highly skilled but artisanal, providing a blueprint for Stuart's own transition from fan painter to portraitist and history painter. Moser would later become the first Keeper of the Royal Academy.[57]

It was probably during his apprenticeship that Stuart drew his reputed self-portrait in charcoal and wash, his earliest known surviving work (fig. 2-6).[58] It is a character study rather than a formal portrait, although a label attached to the back suggests that it was exhibited at some point and won a prize.[59] Stuart's cramped, recoiling pose and averted gaze appear to express shyness and reticence. This may have been a deliberate character statement, but the awkwardness of his posture may also have something to do with the size of the two mirrors he must have used in order to sketch his face in profile. Stuart's clothing in this portrait is particularly revealing. He is wearing lower-class, informal dress of the kind that was characterized by nineteenth-century costume historian Auguste Racinet as "Peasant dress."[60] The key features are the narrow, unornamented cuffs of his jacket. In upper- and middle-class society, wide, folded-over cuffs were worn from the early century through to the 1750s or 1760s.[61] There are signs, however, that the poverty of Stuart's early years had lifted: his close-cropped hair with a slightly longer queue behind strongly suggests that he owned a wig. These were widely worn, even among apprentices and tradesmen, but they were expensive items of dress that could not be afforded by the poor.[62] The absence of the wig in the drawing underlines the intimacy and informality of a self-portrait in which Stuart was making no attempt to identify himself as a gentleman, or to present a social mask. He included only the pen identifying him as an artist.

Journey to Italy, ca. 1740–41

During the eighteenth century, a visit to the ancient centers of Western civilization came to be considered an essential part of a gentleman's general education. Samuel Johnson remarked to Boswell in the 1770s that "a man who has not been in Italy, is always conscious of an inferiority, from his not having seen what it is expected a man should see."[63] Many young artists and architects traveled in the late seventeenth and eighteenth centuries in order to complete their artistic training, acquire polish, and meet potential patrons among the Milordi on their Grand Tour.[64] That Stuart decided to make the trip indicates he had ambitions beyond simply earning a reasonable living as a copyist and fan painter. Encouragement to make the trip may have come from several of the older generation of artists with whom Stuart was in contact in the 1730s. Louis and Joseph Goupy had both visited Italy, Louis Cheron of Kneller's academy had studied in Rome, and Marcus Tuscher of the Salisbury Court academy is recorded as resident in Rome in 1728, and again in 1741.[65]

Stuart was still the main breadwinner of his family, although one of his sisters was by now working as "shop-woman" for his master Goupy, and another may have married well, as her death in Holland in 1750 precipitated correspondence about a legacy.[66] Stuart's obituarist wrote that "the ties of filial and fraternal affection made him protract the journey till he could ensure a certain provision for his mother, and his brother and second sister."[67] Stuart set out on foot for Italy in about 1740–41, at the age of about twenty-seven or twenty-eight, with "a scanty pittance in his pocket."[68]

Whatever provision Stuart had made for his family before leaving, it seems that by 1750 their financial situation had once again deteriorated. Stuart's sister Sarah Teresia begged him to return home. She wrote: "We have no friend, and nobody to rely on but yourself, whom we naturally do expect protection from, therefore pray my Dear Brother, don't be any longer absent, but come and be a means of saving your distressed Family."[69] At this time Stuart had been abroad for about nine years and does not appear to have been a regular correspondent, for Sarah writes of her pleasure at receiving a letter "after a long uncertainty whether you were still alive."[70] From this admittedly limited information, Stuart appears to have been more dutiful than affectionate toward his family. Stuart's obituarists and biographers agree that his early life, when he had "toiled, almost from infancy, for the means of supporting daily existence" for the whole family, had been extremely burdensome.[71] It is not surprising that once he was quit of his responsibilities, he was unwilling personally to assume them again, although he did arrange for an agent to look after his family's interests in Holland.[72] Both sisters, and probably his mother died during his fourteen-year absence from London. Stuart learned of Sarah's death from a letter written by classical scholar Robert Wood which caught up with him while he was in Smyrna in 1753.[73] Stuart's expression of grief was somewhat perfunctory: "the news of my sister's death affects me in the most sensible manner," he wrote, then abandoned the subject to discuss his "highest satisfaction" at seeing one of Wood's engravings of Palmyra.[74]

Stuart began his journey to Italy with a visit to Paris, where he stayed for a while to earn some money "by his ingenuity as an artist."[75] Presumably he also used the time to familiarize himself with the famous art collections of the city and to hone his connoisseurship. Years later, in 1765, Dr. Sleigh recorded, "I had the good fortune to be two or three times in the company of Mr. Stuart at Paris on his return home, and once to go over the Duke of Orleans' collection at the palais-royal with him, where his observations on those noble pictures gave me singular delight."[76] It is probable that from Paris Stuart walked either to Marseilles or to Lyons and then crossed over into Italy via Leghorn or Turin, the usual routes for travelers, possibly stopping off in Florence before heading south.[77]

There is also a tantalizing possibility that he made a detour within northern Italy and became caught up in the war of the Austrian Succession (1740–48). This suggestion stems from Stuart's obituarist who claimed that while in Athens (ca. 1751–54) Stuart had "engaged in the army of the Queen of Hungary, where he served a campaign voluntarily as chief engineer."[78] Maria Theresa was Queen of Hungary until 1745, at which point her husband was elected Holy Roman Emperor and she took the title Empress. If Stuart's military adventure took place at all, it is likely to have been before this date, that is in the missing years in the early 1740s, between his departure from England and his arrival in Rome. Maria Theresa's territories in Italy centered around Milan, and these came under attack by Spanish and Neapolitan forces in 1742.[79] The tale that Stuart was "chief engineer" is highly unlikely, but there may be a grain of truth in the rest of the story, later embellished by Stuart himself or by his obituarist.[80]

Stuart indicated that he had reached Rome in about 1742,[81] although his first documented appearance in the city is not until 1744, when he shared a house in the Salita di San Giuseppe with a James Paxton or Paston (see chap. 3).[82] Taylor noted in 1808 that Stuart's friend Andrew Caldwell believed Stuart "was a Latin Scholar previous to his travelling and that he acquired Greek of the Jesuits at

Fig. 2-7. James McArdell, after James Stuart. Portrait of James Dawkins, ca. 1768. Mezzotint. By courtesy of the Trustees of the British Museum, London, McArdell C.S. 51, II; a.154.Port.o.15. *Checklist no. 32.*

Rome."[83] By the time this information was published by Taylor in 1816, it had become a firm declaration that Stuart studied both Greek and Latin at the Collegio di Propaganda Fide in Rome.[84] With whom he studied painting is not known. At this early stage in his travels, Stuart's main means of support was fan painting. Matthew Nulty, who also subsisted as an itinerant fan painter, noted that Stuart "was his Associate in the same profession."[85] There was a ready market in Italy for Grand Tour souvenir fans that depicted the most famous monuments of the country (see fig. 2-5).[86] By 1745–46 Stuart was earning money from easel paintings commissioned by individual patrons and had also learned enough to begin making a living as an antiquary and cicerone (a connoisseur and guide to the "Curiosities and Antiquities" of Italy).[87] According to another contemporary, Welsh landscape painter Thomas Jones, Nulty himself supplemented his painting with this kind of work, which required a very particular kind of character. By "not being of that oily supple disposition necessary to the Profession & disdain-

ing the little Arts & pretensions to antient Erudition that most of these gentlemen assume—[Nulty] did not find much employment in that Line."[88]

According to Jones, Nulty and Stuart "were both very intimate, & passed through a great Variety of Scenes together—& he used to say that if it were not for fear of giving Offence to that Gentleman, & some other friends, he could have made a very entertaining history of their Adventures."[89] Stuart's gregarious nature may have been his greatest asset when he arrived in Rome. He was evidently likable, lively, and fun to be with. A surviving letter of 1746 to a patron, Jacob Hinde, is filled with flowery phrases expressing Stuart's gratitude and acknowledging his "infinite other obligations," but the letter is light-hearted and friendly, without being servile. (see fig. 3-2).[90] Stuart wrote to amuse his patron, noting that a recent windfall of forty Chequins (gold coins) from Lord Ashburnham had allowed him to "make myself half a Beau, I have been vain enough to buy me a velvet waistco[at] & breeches, besides hat wig coat half a dozen Shirts & many other necessary's."[91] He undoubtedly also made purchases for Hinde, and perhaps for others as well. When Hinde's collection was sold in 1785, it was described as "a Capital well-chosen Collection of Italian, French, Flemish and Dutch pictures, Marble Busto's, Valuable Bronzes, Drawings &c."[92]

In about 1748 Charles Watson-Wentworth, Earl of Malton (see fig. 4-10), arrived in Rome. Stuart must have been introduced to him almost immediately, as in 1749–50 he wrote an illustrated antiquarian treatise in the form of an open letter addressed to Malton.[93] *De Obelisco Caesaris Augusti e Campo Martio nuperrime effosso* was an account of an obelisk that had been excavated from the Campus Martius in Rome in 1748 (see fig. 3-1). Stuart's text was in Latin and Italian. By then he was fluent in both and cited Pliny and Strabo with aplomb. On the first page of the book, Stuart acknowledged the support of the two men who in different ways had prompted the enterprise: Malton, "most noble man" and Cardinal Valenti, "cultivator of the fine arts, and patron." Malton, later Marquess of Rockingham, was a Whig, and militantly loyal to the Protestant Hanoverian dynasty. When he was a schoolboy during the Jacobite uprising of 1745–46, Malton ran away to join the army of the Duke of Cumberland at Culloden.[94] The Pope's secretary of state, Cardinal Silvio Valenti Gonzaga favored the Jacobites (see fig. 4-4).[95] The exiled Pretender lived in Rome. Opinions in the city were dangerously polarized, and each side was spying on English travelers to determine their loyalties. What is remarkable is that by 1748–49 Stuart had a foot in both camps.[96] He obtained subscriptions for his Athenian venture from antiquary and secret agent Baron Stosch, who was the paid spy of the English Government, and from Levantine traveler James Dawkins (fig. 2-7), who funded Bonnie Prince Charlie in exile, went on at least two shady diplomatic missions on his behalf, and only narrowly escaped being arrested for conspiracy.[97] Stuart's Catholicism cannot have been well known in England, for Stuart's architect friend and assistant James Gandon reported that Stuart's *De Obelisco* "procured him the honour of being presented to His Holiness the Pope, a distinction, perhaps, never before conferred on an artist who was a Protestant."[98]

Stuart's politics are impossible to fathom from the record of his diverse contacts and friends at this date. There is some evidence, however, that early Jacobitism gave way to strong Whig affiliations. Gandon recorded that on Stuart's return to London a literary and artistic society met weekly at his house, and "it was generally reported that the political movements of the Rockingham party were arranged at these meetings."[99] The Marquess of Rockingham would become Whig prime minister in 1765–66. Later in life, however, Stuart expressed his incomprehension and contempt of "Political Manouvres & Reconciliations" and urged his friend the radical politician and newspaper editor John Wilkes to attach himself to "any Man, *of any Party*, who will heartily espouse your Cause."[100] Whatever his personal politics, therefore, Stuart was a pragmatist. Robert Adam's brother James suggested in 1761 that Stuart toned down his political radicalism when patronage was at stake, writing that if Stuart was not offered a sinecure by George III, "I shan't be surprised that his Arguments in favour of Democracy increase greatly during this reign."[101]

Journey to Greece, 1750

Stuart's journey to Athens may have had its genesis in a tour he made to Naples early in 1748.[102] In that year Stuart was sharing lodgings in Rome at the Villa Tomati on the via Felice with Nicholas Revett and Gavin Hamilton.[103] The three men were joined on the trip by Brettingham who was newly arrived in Rome.[104] This was a painting tour. Revett detailed the baggage they took in a letter he wrote to his father.[105] It "consisted of a sack, a pair of bags, cloth for painting, umbrellas, portfolios, straw hats, our

Fig. 2-8. William Camden Edwards, after Samuel Provan. Portrait of James Stuart, 1827. Engraving (Provan original, ca. 1748). By courtesy of the Trustees of Sir John Soane's Museum, London, 69/3/4. *Checklist no. 2.*

great coats, a pair of pistols, &c."[106] They took a horse to carry the bags, which quickly acquired a taste for wine and bread. "A good pot companion" Revett noted dryly in a letter to his father. Herculaneum near Naples was a well-known destination on the Grand Tour, but the immediate draw for the four artists may have been the recent discovery of the remains of a Roman town, at first assumed to be Stabiae, and later identified as the city of Pompeii.[107] The combination of archaeological discovery and travel with congenial companions on this Naples trip may have been what suggested the merit of a longer, more ambitious trip to Greece. Additional inspiration may have come from Dawkins, who was planning his own journey to Greece at this time. Dawkins would later provide funding and other assistance to Stuart and Revett.[108]

It seems that it was Revett and Hamilton who first formed the idea of visiting Athens to study and measure the antiquities there, though Stuart's son later disputed this, believing that Stuart was the instigator.[109] As late as September 1749, correspondence about the scheme sug-

Fig. 2-9. James Stuart. View of the Arch of the Sergii (Porta Aurata) at Pola, 1750s–60s. Gouache. RIBA Library Drawings Collection, London, SD 146/8. *Checklist no. 14.*

gests that all four still planned to make the journey.[110] Hamilton helped draw up the first "Proposal" for the scheme but dropped out during the period when Stuart and Revett were attempting to gather support and money.[111] Brettingham also withdrew, perhaps because he was making a good living exporting antiquities on behalf of the Earl of Leicester,[112] and so it was only Stuart and Revett who set out in early 1750 for Venice, on their way to Athens. However, Stuart's friendships with Hamilton and Brettingham were enduring. Hamilton continued to recommend Stuart to his clients,[113] and a portrait of Stuart by Scottish painter Samuel Provan dating from about 1748 or 49 was treasured by the Brettingham family into the nineteenth century. It is now lost, but an engraving survives (fig. 2-8).[114] In it the industrious, impoverished artist of Stuart's early self-portrait has given way to a neatly dressed gentleman gazing into the far distance. Of all the surviving portraits of Stuart, this is the only one that appears deliberately to portray him as a visionary and thinker, perhaps with the extraordinary journey to Athens in mind.

Travel in Greece and the Levant was dangerous. During their famous late-seventeenth-century journeys, Jacob Spon and Sir George Wheler had lost two of their party of four: Sir Giles Eastcourt died of illness near Delphi, and Francis Vernon was captured by corsairs, enslaved, and subsequently murdered.[115] Dawkins's companion John Bouverie was to die in Magnesia in 1750.[116] Stuart and Revett faced storms at sea at Delos, plague at Salonika, and hostility in Athens.[117] Revett survived an attack by pirates, and Stuart an assassination attempt and a serious illness that may have been malaria.[118] Sir James Porter, the British Ambassador to the Sublime Porte had arranged *firmans*, or permissions to travel in Turkish-occupied Greece. In spite of these *firmans*, Stuart and Revett were viewed with considerable suspicion by the local Turkish garrison in Athens. Stuart records that at one point he scaled the steep side of the Acropolis in order to study some columns, but "some Turks in the fortress took umbrage at it, and by dropping down stones from the top of the wall, several of which were very large, and fell very near me, obliged me to a precipitate retreat."[119] Later,

Stuart's obituarist would laud his "natural courage invincible by terror."[120]

Stuart and Revett stayed at the home of the British Consul in Athens, a rapacious Greek named Logotheti. It must have been an uneasy lodging as Stuart disliked Logotheti, and also grew annoyed when several children who were living in the house went through his belongings and "played some tricks with my meridian," the brass instrument that allowed Stuart to calculate latitude and the declination of the sun.[121] Another difficulty was Logotheti's incessant and unreasonable demands for money. Eventually Stuart lost his temper. According to Revett, Stuart "was provoked to knock him down" and then forced to set off for Constantinople in October 1753 to explain his actions.[122] He traveled in the train of the principal Athenian aga, Hadgee Ali.[123] Only a few miles past Salonika, he began to realize that Hadgee Ali had taken a dislike to him. According to an account preserved by Thomas Percy, bishop of Dromore, "Stewart observed, that at every stage it was contrived to put him on a dangerous horse, in order to break his neck."[124] Things soon got considerably worse. They stopped at a village, where Hadgee Ali informed the villagers that Stuart was a "dangerous person, a Magician." Learning that he was going to be killed that night, Stuart tricked his servant and escaped the guard by threatening him with a pair of pistols. He then fled into the fields, pursued by a mob of villagers with flaming torches. At the next village, he feigned madness, "well knowing the veneration with which the Turks regard idiots."[125] What comes across in this account is not only Stuart's bravery, but also his quick-wittedness and ingenuity in a terrifying situation. The vivid detail with which Stuart's tale was remembered by the bishop of Dromore conveys Stuart's retrospective delight in the whole adventure, not to mention his skill as a raconteur. It seems entirely in character that he kept as a souvenir an old Turkish scimitar, which was sold among his effects after his death.[126]

Fig. 2-10. James Stuart. View of the Caryatid Porch, the Erechtheion, the west end of the Temple of Minerva Polias, and the Pandrosium on the Acropolis, Athens, 1750s–60s. Gouache. Stuart is shown sketching in the foreground. RIBA Library Drawings Collection, London, SD 145/6. *Checklist no. 29.*

Stuart and Revett spent around two and a half years in Greece, working on the drawings for *Antiquities of Athens*. They traveled with an assistant called Lowther, about whom nothing is known, though he may be one of the figures that Stuart depicted measuring the arch of the Sergii at Pola while they waited to sail to Athens (fig. 2-9). Revett was responsible for the architectural draftsmanship while Stuart concentrated on drawing the picturesque views that were an expected component of this kind of publication.[127] These views are filled with figures of shepherds, musicians, and women, livestock, men strolling or smoking, and boys at play.[128] In his proposals for *Antiquities of Athens*, Stuart was uncompromisingly disdainful of the Turks, calling them "Barbarians" and "professed enemies to the Arts."[129] The views themselves tell a somewhat different story: Stuart's eye was caught by the colorful non-Western clothing and artifacts of the contemporary Turks, and he delighted in depicting tarbooshes and turbans, caftans and hookahs (fig. 2-10). The accompanying text is detailed enough to demonstrate how intrigued Stuart was with the Turks he met, their families, and their relationships, even though his comments are occasionally barbed. At the Pandrosium, "the Turkish Gentleman smoking a long pipe, is the Disdár Agá, he leans on the shoulder of his son-in-law, Ibrahim Agá, and is looking at our labourers, who are digging to discover the Base, and the steps of the Basement under the Caryatides. He was accustomed to visit us from time to time, to see that we did no mischief to the Building; but in reality, to see that we did not carry off any treasure; for he did not conceive, any other motive could have induced us, to examine so eagerly what was under ground in his Castle. The two Turks in the Pandrosium were placed there by him to watch our proceedings; and give him an account of our discoveries. The little girl leading a lamb, and attended by a negro slave, is the daughter of Ibrahim Agá."[130]

During their stay in Athens, Stuart and Revett were briefly joined by Dawkins and Robert Wood.[131] A gouache painted by Stuart (fig. 2-11), shows Stuart, Revett, and Dawkins admiring the Monument of Philopappus.

Fig. 2-11. James Stuart. View of the Monument of Philopappus, Athens, 1750s–60s. Gouache. Stuart, Revett, and Dawkins form the group to the left. RIBA Library Drawings Collection, London, SD 145/10. *Checklist no. 28.*

Fig. 2-12. James Stuart. View of the Theater of Bacchus, 1750s–60s. Gouache. Nicholas Revett is shown sketching in the foreground. RIBA Library Drawings Collection, London, SD 145/7. *Checklist no. 26.*

Dawkins is wearing a European frock coat, stocking, and hat, while Stuart and Revett are resplendent in flowing Turkish caftans. In other gouache views, Stuart depicts himself and Revett wearing Turkish dress, or at least an adaptation of it that includes Western stockings with yellow embroidered Turkish slippers, a Turkish caftan, and a *kucsma*, a kind of fur-lined hat that the Turks themselves had borrowed from Hungary (fig. 2-12, see fig. 2-10). To Stuart's European audience, the clothing emphasized his and Revett's actual presence in these faraway and exotic places and acted as a guarantor of their expertise without disturbing European preconceptions about the dangerous barbarism of the Turks.

London, ca. 1754–55

Stuart and Revett returned to England in late 1754 or early 1755, after a period of quarantine in Marseilles.[132] By this time it appears that Stuart had no surviving family, and he and Revett went to stay in the London home of James Dawkins in Brook Street, near Hanover Square. They may have remained there for some time, possibly until Dawkins's death in 1757.[133]

Interest in the Athenian venture had built up during his absence, much of it carefully and deliberately set in motion by Stuart and fostered by his friends. For example, Thomas Hollis had met Stuart in Venice before he left for Athens and at Stuart's request sent a copy of the "Proposal" to his tutor Professor Ward conveying with it Stuart's wish to enter into a correspondence, writing that "he would think it an honor, and much to his advantage."[134] Brettingham had continued to promote *Antiquities of Athens*, sending out new proposals from Rome in 1752, and a list in a notebook among the Marquess of Rockingham's papers suggests that he too was actively

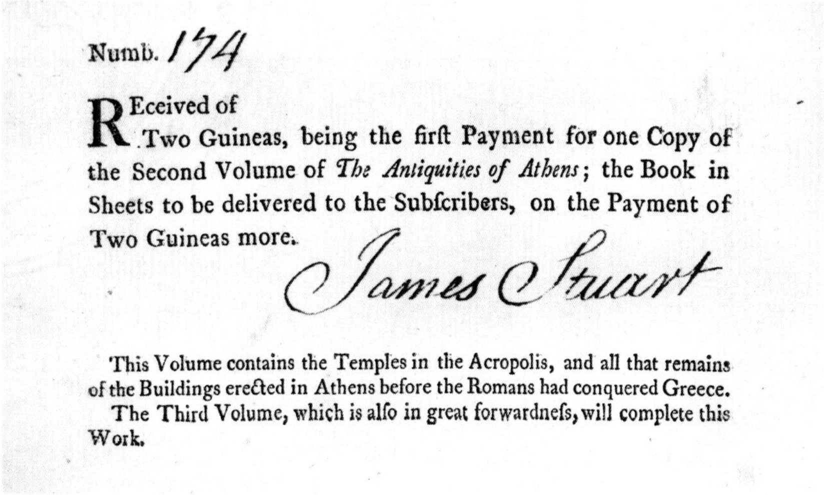

Numb. *174*

Received of
Two Guineas, being the firſt Payment for one Copy of the Second Volume of *The Antiquities of Athens*; the Book in Sheets to be delivered to the Subſcribers, on the Payment of Two Guineas more.

James Stuart

This Volume contains the Temples in the Acropolis, and all that remains of the Buildings erected in Athens before the Romans had conquered Greece. The Third Volume, which is alſo in great forwardneſs, will complete this Work.

Fig. 2-13. Subscription voucher for the second volume of *Antiquities of Athens,* 1773. From the Marquess of Rockingham's notebook, entitled "From Mr Stuart the Athenian," p. 2, Sheffield Archives, Wentworth Woodhouse Muniments R220/3.

gathering subscriptions on Stuart's behalf (fig. 2-13).[135] As a result of this publicity, Stuart's reputation in London was made long before a single volume of *Antiquities of Athens* appeared. In 1758 he was elected to the Society of Antiquaries and also to the Royal Society on the strength of his antiquarian expertise.[136] In 1759 he was given permission to study in the reading room of the British Museum for six months.[137] This was an honor that at this date was only accorded to "Learned and Curious persons" who had managed to prevail upon one of the trustees to vouch for them, which in practice confined access to a limited number of acknowledged scholars and people of rank.[138]

Sir James Porter had realized in 1754 that the next stage of Stuart and Revett's work was "enough to take up some years for the Copper plates."[139] The engraving and preparation of text for the first volume of *Antiquities of Athens* in fact took seven years, partly because Stuart insisted on correcting all his own plates. James Adam wrote, "I am not surpris'd that he [is] slow in giving his designs, for he undertakes a most tedious labor."[140] During this time the reputation of the as yet unfinished *Antiquities of Athens* had grown to the extent that "the very fame of it has blasted the Reputation of these Works of P—a & B—k [Palmyra & Balbec]" by Dawkins and Wood.[141] Inevitably, such great anticipation and excitement about the project began to give way to irritation at the delays as subscribers waited far longer than they had expected for their copies. In 1760 James Adam wrote from Bologna that "even here they begin to think they are never to see the English Athens."[142] When Robert Adam began to worry about delays in the preparation of the copper plates for his own book, *Spalatro*, he wrote that

"people begin to cry out [?] on me as they did on Stuart, so that I am affraid of becoming his appology."[143]

In 1761 Hogarth composed *Five Orders of Perriwigs,* a print satirizing a book that "In about Seventeen Years will be completed" (fig. 2-14). The text on the print mentioned Palmyra and Balbec, and also Rome—the subject of Giovanni Battista Piranesi's book, *Della Magnificenza ed Architettura de' Romani* (1761)—as well as Athens, but there is no doubt that Stuart was the main subject of the lampoon. According to Horace Walpole "the Athenian head was intended for Stewart, but was so like, that Hogarth was forced to cut off the nose."[144] Stuart must have enjoyed the joke because he later pasted his copy of the print onto the fire screen in his parlor and was in the habit of pointing it out to visitors.[145] The delays in publication have contributed greatly, and perhaps unfairly, to Stuart's posthumous reputation as a talented but lazy man. His patroness, the society hostess Elizabeth Montagu (see fig. 4-29), who was later sharply critical of Stuart, gives an alternative picture, describing a "thin & miserable" Stuart in one of her letters of 1762 and noting that he was spending an exhausting eleven hours a day standing over the press.[146]

When Stuart was required for one reason or another after his return to London to name his profession, he identified himself as "History Painter and Architect" or "Painter and Architect."[147] From the evidence of his earliest known architectural commission, which was ongoing in September 1755, nine or ten months after his return from Athens, it seems that Stuart's architectural practice began as a natural extension of his familiar Italian roles of painter and connoisseur. His client was Rockingham, who was in the process of enlarging his country seat, Wentworth Woodhouse, Yorkshire (see fig. 6-6). Stuart planned some minor alterations at the back of the house and the creation of a link corridor, together with some decorative work.[148] This consisted of painted panels for the dining room, which Stuart proposed to execute himself, and the decoration of the grand saloon, about which he wrote: "if I had a Print of the inside of the Grand Saloon I should endeavor to ornament it in the purest taste I can imagine" (see figs. 6-7a,b, 6-8).[149] Stuart and Rockingham also discussed the subjects of panels to be executed by the marine painter Samuel Scott. Stuart suggested "reall Views on the Thames, or Pictures in which those Views are not strictly followed but something Ideal introduced which would be perhaps the best way to procure a good effect in those Pictures."[150] It seems that Stuart's opinions as much as his

designs were the commodity that his patrons sought from him, and many of his activities in the decade after his return from Athens can be interpreted as a deliberate attempt to make a career of the role of connoisseur and arbiter of taste rather than purely to build up a clientele for architectural designs or paintings. Several of Stuart's most loyal and appreciative patrons appear to have used him in this way, calling on his expertise to choose objects and sculptures, to act in acquisitions, and to exercise his taste on their behalf.[151]

Gandon noted that Stuart was "consulted as a truly classical authority upon the subject of architecture."[152] James Harris, when using a composition of Stuart's as the frontispiece of his book, *Hermes, or A Philosophical Inquiry*

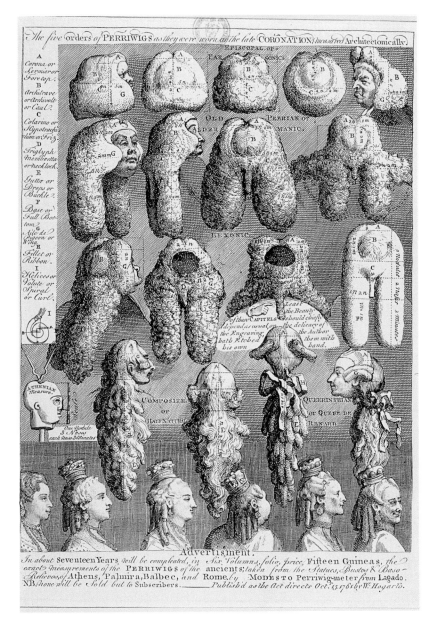

Fig. 2-14. William Hogarth. "The five orders of Perriwigs as they were worn at the late Coronation, measured Architectonically," 1761. Engraving. Guildhall Library, City of London, Hogarth Collection, loc. 64. p543527x. *Checklist no. 33.*

Concerning Universal Grammar (see fig. 4-33), praised Stuart's "taste truly Attic and Simple, which no one possesses more eminently than himself.[153] James Barry, Stuart's assistant in 1765, wrote that "it will be unnecessary to say anything of the depth of his acquaintance in matters of antiquity and literature. The pictures, and every thing of his designing, are distinguished by that unaffected air of the antients, which alone constitutes true taste."[154] One memorandum written in 1766 by Provost Sumner of King's College, Cambridge, makes explicit Stuart's role as an authority, and explains what the college could expect to gain from asking him to review the design of an altarpiece: "that we may have his judgment and character for knowledge in such things—to justify us to the world."[155]

By contrast, Stuart's execution of work, particularly painting, was fairly widely acknowledged to be flawed. Stuart's patron the first Earl of Hardwicke wrote privately in 1763 that Anson was "right to make use of Stewart's Scavoir faire; but I wonder he suffers him to daub his House with his Pencil. . . . He is certainly no painter."[156] Thomas Hollis, writing in his diary about a visit to Wimbledon House in 1759, recorded that he "saw Mrs. Spencer's closet painted in grotesque by Stuart; With the Figures of the Allegro and Pensero [sic] after the divine Milton. Stuart's ideas very fine, his execution indifferent. This easily to be accounted for" (see figs. 6-44, 6-45).[157]

For much of the time that he was working on the plates for *Antiquities of Athens*, Stuart was living only a short distance from Rockingham's London house in Grosvenor Square. In spring 1758 Stuart had moved to 7 Grosvenor Street, Mayfair.[158] Grosvenor Street was described in 1735 as "a spacious well built street, inhabited chiefly by People of Distinction."[159] Previous residents in Stuart's house included Lord Paget, son of the first Earl of Uxbridge who had improved the building in 1731, adding gilt leather panels to one of the rooms, a bathroom, and a greenhouse in the garden.[160] In spite of these amenities, Stuart's new home was smaller and less grand than the houses of many of his neighbors. Its ratable value was £26, considerably less than the £50 of 9 Grosvenor Street, which was occupied by Sir James Peachey, later first Baron Selsey, and was completely overshadowed by the £200 ratable value of the home of the second Baron Conway, later first Earl and first Marquess of Hertford, only seven doors farther up the road at No. 16.[161]

At around the time he moved to Grosvenor Street, Stuart employed a housekeeper named Ann Taylor, and

two years later, on June 9, 1760, they married.[162] Nothing is known of her, except for a brief encomium by Highmore, who recalled in 1788 that she was "a very good woman, by whom [Stuart] had a son, who died at the age of four or five years."[163] Such was Stuart's association with all things Greek that Ann was subsequently declared by Stuart's surviving son, also named James, to have been a "Grecian lady."[164] The marriage was solemnized in the Anglican Church of St. James, Piccadilly. Although this may suggest that Stuart had abandoned his Catholicism, it is in fact inconclusive evidence, as from 1754 marriages had no legal force unless conducted in an Anglican church. Many Catholics thereafter held two ceremonies, one Catholic, one Anglican, in order to fulfill the requirements of the law.[165] The witnesses at the wedding were Ann's mother, Mary Taylor, and a certain John Faber, probably the son of John Faber Jr., a mezzotint engraver. Faber Jr. had been associated with both Kneller and John Vanderbank, who helped establish the first Academy of Art in St. Martin's Lane. Stuart's son John Francis was born in December 1764, and received an Anglican christening at St. James, Piccadilly.[166] Since christenings were not subject to the same legal requirements as marriages, it seems likely that Stuart had abandoned his Catholicism by this date. According to Highmore's chronology, John Francis must have died in about 1768–69, but no record of his death appears in any Westminster parish.[167]

Although he lived conveniently close to Mrs. Montagu in Hill Street, as well as to Rockingham, Stuart had some less congenial neighbors.[168] Across the street at 75 Grosvenor Street was the office of Robert Adam, who disliked Stuart and took every opportunity to ridicule him, at least in private. Adam's published remarks about Stuart were polite.[169] Stuart's move to Grosvenor Street had coincided with a commission to design interiors for Nathaniel Curzon's country seat, Kedleston Hall in Derbyshire.[170] Adam's opinion of Stuart's Kedleston drawings (see figs. 6-30 to 6-33) survives: "They are so excessively & so ridiculously bad. . . . He made a Gallery only 5 feet high so that by that one wou^d think the Modern Greeks diminsh'd in size as well as in Spirit, But forgot that Brittains were taller. . . . His ordinary rooms begger all description however ridiculous, I confess myself unequal to the task. . . . [He] Draws all the Pictures & Colour them in his Drawings But they are So ill done that they move pity rather than contempt."[171]

Adam and his family gleefully collected any detri-

Fig. 2-15. James Stuart. "Ternofaco a fish caught in the sea near Syra," ca. 1751–54. Gouache heightened with white, pen and ink. By courtesy of the Trustees of the British Museum, London, 197*d.4. Checklist no. 13.

mental remarks about Stuart made by the people they met, and shared them by letter, using a bewildering variety of nicknames for Stuart, such as "Glenivot," "the Athenian," and "Atica."[172] Some of the characterizations are simply ill-natured remarks about Stuart's low birth: "He [distinguished line engraver Robert Strange] seems now to have a very propper knowledge of ~~Stuart~~ [crossed out] GlenIviot &c. Rome has open'd his Eyes to many things & he now allows the above Gentleman to be a low Bred scoundrel that has allready got all he deserves & who never will rise higher."[173] Other remarks should be taken more seriously, although the slant given to them is unpleasant. For example James Adam wrote from Rome in 1762, "There is one Hinchlif a shrewd sensible man & one who is very profoundly knowing in a great many things, he was speaking to me of the Athenian one day, . . . he says he is the most specious discourcer he ever knew, has a superficial knowledge of most things & knows nothing."[174]

Though Hinchlif and Adam criticized Stuart's pretensions to "knowledge of most things," this display of learning appears to have been vital to Stuart's reception in society on his return from Athens. In the absence of a large income, Stuart's ability to present himself as a "Learned and Curious person" in the British Museum's parlance, was a shield against attitudes such as that of Robert Strange.[175] As his patron Charles Pratt, Lord Camden later observed, Stuart's social position did not depend on birth.

He had "no rank to sustain, & being a true philosopher he is both above and below the power of fortune."[176] Stuart lived by his ability to manipulate public perception and be seen as a polymath. It is noticeable that he cultivated contacts among those who were in no position to offer him architectural or painting commissions, but whose friendships gave him cultural capital and increased his social prestige and influence. Stuart's list of nominees to the Royal Society reads like a Who's Who of the eighteenth-century artistic, literary, philosophical and scientific worlds, including Adam Smith, Captain James Cook, Josiah Wedgwood, and Sir William Chambers. It also included influential men such as as John Ibbetson, who was secretary to the commissioners of longitude, and to the Admiralty Board.[177]

A list of the contents of Stuart's now missing sketchbooks confirms the breadth of his interests.[178] There are the expected notes on painting and architecture, such as "directions for setting the Pallet to imitate Rubens & Titian," as well as geographical remarks, notes on celestial phenomena, the beginning of an account of the situation of Greek women, the history of Philosophy, Egyptian hieroglyphics, etymologies, poetry, medals, mineral waters, and natural history.[179] One surviving sketchbook page carries a gouache painting of a fish caught in the sea near Syra (Syros), along with copious notes as to its color and the number and size of its spines (fig. 2-15).

Many of these subjects continued to engage Stuart's

Fig. 2-16. James Stuart. Sketches of Athenian coins. Pen and ink, pencil. From Stuart's sketchbook (1751–52): fol. 11. By permission of The British Library, London, Add. Ms. 62,088. *Checklist no. 166.*

interest throughout his life. He presented a paper on Egyptian hieroglyphics to the Royal Society in 1769.[180] In 1773 he exhibited a work depicting one of the strange animal specimens that Captain Cook brought back from his voyages: a "Kongaroo, an animal in New Holland—undescribed by any naturalist."[181] In addition, Stuart's friendships with a significant number of astronomers indicate that his interest in celestial phenomena was more than a passing fancy. Several of his nominees to the Royal Society were astronomers, including two whom he may have first met during his time in Italy.[182] Stuart's society committee memberships also demonstrate how widely he studied. He researched silk production and the making of verdigris, and became involved in the design and striking of medals, having made studies of Greek coinage while on his travels (fig. 2-16; and see chap. 12) as well as becom-

ing something of an authority on antiquarian matters.[183] It was not only serious, weighty subjects that engaged Stuart's curiosity. He and Nulty corresponded about the identity of a mysterious ingredient of a favorite Italian soup of Stuart's, which turned out to be globe artichoke[184]

This wide-ranging curiosity was a mixed blessing. It diverted Stuart's time and attention away from his architectural work but also formed part of his appeal to clients. For example, Mrs. Montagu's wrath at Stuart's failure to "finish the designs he promised me" was averted by an account of "Mexicans and Montezuma." She explained: "Mr Stewart gave me this curious piece this morning. . . . His learning, ingenuity, sagacity and application are surprizing."[185] Stuart's extensive interests enabled him to engage with his architectural clients beyond the purely professional level. His surviving letters to Thomas Anson (see fig. 4-23) are filled with information that had caught Stuart's eye and could be relied upon to interest his patron: an account of a French expedition to the Falkland

Fig. 2-17. William Daniell, after George Dance. Portrait of Nicholas Revett, 1802. Soft-ground etching (Dance original, 1800). National Portrait Gallery, London, NPG 12094.

Fig. 2-18. After Sir Joshua Reynolds.
Portrait of Admiral Sir George Anson,
first Baron Anson, 1755. Oil on canvas.
National Portrait Gallery,
London, NPG 518.

Islands, a recently published translation of a poem writ-ten by the emperor of China, the discovery by the Spanish of a "great Continent to the westward of the Western Coast of Patagonia"[186]

Although Revett's name was to be associated with all four volumes of *Antiquities of Athens*, it was Stuart who acquired the sobriquet "Athenian" and was seen by the Adam brothers as their rival, rather than Revett. Part of the reason may have been that Stuart and Revett parted company before the publication of the first volume.[187] Because Stuart claimed sole responsibility for any errors in the book, he also took the lion's share of the credit.[188] Revett (fig. 2-17, see fig. 4-6) appears to have been a much more retiring character who only capitalized on the success of *Antiquities of Athens* to a limited extent. He became architectural draftsman on Richard Chandler's expedition

to Ionia in 1764, funded by the Society of Dilettanti, and he completed a few architectural works for a handful of patrons.[189] Stuart, by contrast, engaged in tireless self-promotion after he returned from Greece. He was evidently not averse to singing his own praises, thus Hogarth's fictional author of the *Five Orders of Perriwigs* was sarcastically named "Modesto."[190] The network of contacts Stuart constructed on the strength of his book was also never matched by Revett. The growth of this network can be traced through the membership lists of a number of clubs and societies that Stuart joined in the 1750s, especially the Dilettanti, the Royal Society, the Society of Antiquaries, and the Society for the Promotion of Arts, Manufactures and Commerce (SPAC, see chap. 4).[191]

Stuart's earliest and most significant club membership was in the Society of Dilettanti. Co-founded in 1734 by

ure to get a commission to build a screen at the Admiralty in Whitehall was ascribed by James Adam to Admiral George Anson's temporary inattention after the death of his wife. Adam wrote: "I am extremely glad Bob has got the Admiralty affair fix'd. . . . When I first heard of Lady A–n's death I could not help having a Secret satisfaction, at her timely retreat."[194] George Anson (fig. 2-18) was almost certainly responsible for Stuart's acquisition of the post of surveyor to the Greenwich Naval Hospital in 1758, at a salary of £200 per year.[195] Stuart also undertook a variety of work for the Admiralty, including an unexecuted "Lazaretto," or quarantine hospital, near Chatham, designs for a soup tureen (see fig. 11-30), and two Admiralty passes, examples of which survive in the British Museum (figs. 2-19, 2-20).[196]

Though he was extraordinarily good at making and keeping influential friends, Stuart seems to have been ambivalent about the mechanisms of patronage. He expressed a reluctance and distaste for the process, writing to Thomas Anson, "I am become a place hunter in despight of my indifference."[197] A remark of Simon, first Earl Harcourt (see fig. 4-19), implies that this diffidence was not merely an affectation. Harcourt wrote in 1758, "As Stuart is but too apt to neglect his own interest, it is more incumbent upon his friends to think of him."[198] Stuart may indeed have felt a genuine dislike for a system that rewarded contacts rather than merit.[199] All the same he quickly carved out a place in the contemporary British system of patronage, where those high on the social scale had people they protected, who in turn had their own protégés lower down on the scale. Stuart used his influence to benefit his own protégés. James Basire, whom Stuart had employed on the engravings for *Antiquities of Athens*, was hired as engraver to the Society of Antiquaries shortly after Stuart became a fellow.[200] Robert Adam complained in 1758, "That insignificant triffling ignorant puppyish wretch Basire has spoilt me a plate entirely. . . . I suppose Stuart has bribed him, he's quite a sicofantish creature of his."[201] Stuart also used his membership in SPAC to promote the interests of the Pingo family of die and medal makers.[202] In 1769 he wrote a number of letters to Thomas Anson advocating Thomas Pingo for a post at the Royal Mint, indicating that he planned to lobby the Duke of Northumberland on Pingo's behalf.[203]

A few of Stuart's surviving letters show how he made use of his patronage network on his own behalf. In 1764 he asked for Thomas Anson's help in gaining the sinecure

Fig. 2-19. James Stuart. Admiralty Pass, ca. 1764. Engraving by James Basire. By courtesy of the Trustees of the British Museum, London, M.m. 3:-62. *Checklist no. 145.*

the infamous Sir Francis Dashwood and Charles Sackville, Earl of Middlesex, the society was a curiously schizophrenic body that was simultaneously a disreputable dining club for wealthy aristocratic hell-raisers and a serious, influential forum for the promotion of classical scholarship and connoisseurship.[192] Horace Walpole described it as "a club, for which the nominal qualification is having been in Italy, and the real one, being drunk."[193] Individual members of the Dilettanti, such as the Anson brothers, promoted Stuart's interests to the extent that Stuart's fail-

post of Serjeant-Painter to the Office of Works.[204] Stuart wrote: "Mr Hogarth death has vacated a good employment, but I am apprehensive I have applied too late, tho it is not yet disposed of, every body from whom I could hope assistance is out of town. I have wrote to Lord Hyde & to Lord Harcourt, & by the advice of my friend Jenkinson to Ld Bute."[205] The official salary of the Serjeant-Painter was only £10 per year, although the post carried the rights to a percentage of the spending on building works at the royal palaces.[206] Stuart's own estimate was that the office was worth far more. He wrote to Anson that "there is indeed one circumstance which may ruin all, the recommendation of Lord Bute in favor of any of the persons he protects; & as it is a patent place of 400.p Annum, I think there is great danger."[207]

Stuart won the Serjeant-Painter sinecure, but never fully exploited it. Over a period of thirty years in the office, he received a total of £17,949.3.1, of which he would have retained around 5 percent, or £900. His predecessor, Hogarth, was making £400–£900 per year, although about half of this would have been paid to his deputy.[208] Perhaps surprisingly in the light of his impoverished background, Stuart does not seem to have been strongly motivated by money. His failure to make the most of his earning opportunities in this post chimes with comments made by two of his clients. Mrs. Montagu chose him as her architect "on account of his disinterestedness & contempt of money,"[209] while Harcourt noted that the position of clerk of works to Hampton Court Palace "would certainly be most acceptable to Stuart, even perhaps more than some others of a greater value."[210]

The sinecure of Serjeant-Painter, together with Stuart's salary as surveyor to the Greenwich Naval Hospital and his income from architectural commissions, was sufficient to place him in "a state of affluence."[211] A short while after being assured of his appointment as Serjeant-Painter, Stuart began spending heavily on household, library, and studio items. For example in December 1764 he wrote, "I have spent 200£ at least for Pictures this year & I have augmented my number of books Prints & Plaister images."[212] These will have been purchased to decorate Stuart's new London home, in Hollis Street, Westminster, to which he moved after leaving Grosvenor Street in the latter part of 1763. Here he entertained, among others, Wilkes, who took refuge in the house on a brief visit to London from Paris in 1766.[213] In 1763 Wilkes had fled to France to escape arrest for seditious libel. He had been

Fig. 2-20. James Stuart. Admiralty Pass, ca. 1764. Engraving by James Basire. By courtesy of the Trustees of the British Museum, London, M.m.3:-63. *Checklist no. 146.*

tried in absentia in February 1764 and found guilty. Stuart was effectively hiding an outlaw, although this was less dangerous than it might appear because Wilkes had considerable support among the Rockingham Whigs, who were then in power.[214]

In 1767 Stuart moved again. He bought the lease of a substantial house at 35 Leicester Fields, one of London's most fashionable squares (fig. 2-21).[215] The north side of the square was dominated by one of the great houses of London: Leicester House, built in the 1630s for Robert

Fig. 2-21. Thomas Bowles. View of the north side of Leicester Square, London, opposite Stuart's residence, 1753. Engraving by the artist. Guildhall Library, City of London, Main Print Collection Pr.W2/LEI p5403926.

Sidney, second Earl of Leicester.[216] In the eighteenth century this was jokingly known as the "pouting house for princes," when two successive Princes of Wales moved in there after quarrelling with their fathers, most recently Prince Frederick, who "kept a sulky Court there" until his death in 1751.[217] Next to Leicester House was Savile House, where George III lived before his accession to the throne in 1760. This was home of the king's brother, the Duke of York, when Stuart moved to the square.[218]

Stuart would remain in Leicester Fields for the rest of his life, which means he may have been in residence dur-

ing the anti-Catholic Gordon Riots of 1780. Susan Burney gave an eyewitness account of "flames before Saville House that illuminated the whole square" and recorded the arrival of the Horse and Foot guards who managed to prevent the rioters from tearing Savile House down.[219] The crowd went from house to house, demanding that the inhabitants shout "no Popery" to prove their Protestant credentials.[220] Presumably Stuart complied. He will have had a good view from his front windows of the bonfires in Leicester Fields that consumed George Savile's furniture and window frames.[221]

Fig. 2-22. Box once belonging to James Stuart, used to store measuring instruments, n.d. Stained pine, green felt lining. By courtesy of the Trustees of Sir John Soane's Museum, London, X1232. *Checklist no. 34.*

How much Stuart paid for his lease is not recorded, but it will have been considerably less than the £1,650 paid by Sir Joshua Reynolds in 1760 for the lease of No. 47 on the west side of the square.[222] Reynolds's ratable value was £80 to Stuart's £28. After buying the lease, Reynolds spent a further £1,500 to build an extension for a gallery and painting room.[223] Perhaps this inspired Stuart to enlarge his own home to make a display space for his Athenian views.[224] John Thomas Smith, who would later become Keeper of Prints at the British Museum, described a visit to Stuart's house with Nollekens: "Stuart lived on the south side of Leicester-fields; he had built a large room at the back of his house, in which were several of his drawings, particularly those he had made for a continuation of his work."[225] Stuart also had a work room or study, a place of "dust & confusion," according to Mrs. Montagu.[226] This room may have been furnished with some of the items that appear in Stuart's estate sale catalogue of 1791, including a painting table, three mahogany drawing boards, an easel, and a "mahogany table, with 3 drawers for an engraver."[227] Stuart probably also kept six

plaster figures, and "three moulds after the antique" in this room, possibly those he had bought in 1764 for his Hollis Street home.[228] One surviving item from this workroom is Stuart's pine box of measuring instruments, which is preserved in the Sir John Soane Museum, though lacking its contents (fig. 2-22). Inside the lid is a label reading: "Formerly belonged To Poor Stuart."[229]

Stuart's house also contained a library and a parlor, which was "decorated with some of Hogarth's most popular prints."[230] Until his death in 1764, Hogarth lived on the southeast corner of the square, only a few doors down from Stuart's house. When Stuart moved in, Jane Hogarth, James Thornhill's daughter, was still living there.[231] In an engraving by Samuel Rawle of 1805, Hogarth's house is the building on the left, and Stuart's is on the far right (fig. 2-23). Behind Hogarth's house can be seen the spire of the Church of St. Martin in the Fields, where Stuart would marry his second wife, Elizabeth, in 1778 and where he was interred a decade later.[232] Just around the corner in St. Martin's Street lived the musicologist Charles Burney, father of novelist Fanny Burney, and a close friend of

Fig. 2-23. View of Leicester Square, London, ca. 1805. Engraving by Samuel Rawle. Guildhall Library, City of London, Pr. W2/LEI no. p5404529.

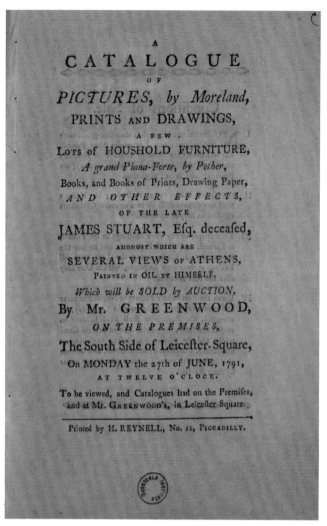

Fig. 2-24. Front cover, "Catalogue of pictures by Moreland, prints and drawings, a few lots of household furniture, a grand piano-forte, by Pether, books, and books of prints, drawing paper, and other effects, of the late James Stuart, Esq. deceased, among which are several views of Athens, painted in oil by himself . . . ," estate sale, Greenwood's, London, 27 June 1791. Book Library, Courtauld Institute of Art, London, Br A 5059 1791/06/27.

Stuart's.[233] Burney was a pallbearer at Stuart's funeral in 1788 and took charge of the education of the Stuart boys afterward.[234] He may have fired Stuart's interest in music, for among the household items sold in Stuart's estate sale of 1791 were not only a harpsichord by master craftsman Jacob Kirckman, but also a grand piano made by George Pether.[235] Although box pianos were fairly common by this date, grand pianos were extremely rare, found in only

a very few wealthy homes.[236] This presumably accounts for its mention on the cover of the 1791 estate sale catalogue (fig. 2-24).

It was at Stuart's house in Leicester Fields that Rockingham and friends may have met for their political meetings, disguised as an artistic and literary society.[237] Stuart also belonged to an informal club that met in the back parlor of a public house called the Feathers which stood on the north side of Leicester Fields.[238] Here, according to Smith, he socialized with a mixed group of artists, antiquaries, writers, and actors.[239] Lacking a record of these meetings, it is only from occasional remarks in letters that the conversational skills and sense of humor that made Stuart such an pleasant companion can be glimpsed: "I should have had the pleasure of writing to you by last Friday's Post, but I dined with your Brother on that Day, who entertained me so very hospitably that I was obliged to be satisfied with drinking some Bumpers to your Health & speedy Return which I frankly assure you did not at all diminish the flavour of his good wine."[240] Stuart's humor was one of his most endearing qualities, according to Highmore, who called him "a great humourist in the most agreeable sense of the word"[241]

At around the time that Stuart moved to Leicester Fields, Reynolds painted his portrait, presumably in his new studio. The two men had been friends for more than a decade, and Stuart's first act on becoming a member of SPAC in 1756 was to nominate Reynolds.[242] The Reynolds portrait of Stuart has vanished, but a proof plate by Samuel William Reynolds gives an idea of the original (fig. 2-25). Stuart is wearing a loose, Turkish or Persian-style robe known in England as a "banyan" and a turbanlike cap. These were highly fashionable articles of informal house dress, and several well-to-do intellectuals of the time had themselves painted "at home" wearing these clothes.[243] However fashionably attired, the fifty-four-year-old Stuart depicted by Reynolds is an anxious-looking, puffy-faced man, showing signs of the sickness that would plague him from the 1760s until his death in 1788.

Stuart's illness was gout, the classic disease of high living. According to Smith, Stuart was "a heavy-looking, man, and his face declared him to be fond of what is called friendly society."[244] Although rich food and alcohol are not the sole causes of gout, overindulgence exacerbates the disease, which is caused by the formation of urate crystals in the sufferer's joints. Gout makes movement excruciatingly painful. It particularly affects the toes and

Fig. 2-25. Attributed to Samuel William Reynolds, after Sir Joshua Reynolds. Portrait of James Stuart, before 1835. Engraving (J. Reynolds original, ca. 1767). Inscribed: "The Athenian Stuart / A Proof never finished." National Portrait Gallery, London, NPG D8967.

Fig. 2-26. James Stuart's hoplite-head seal. From a letter to Philip Yorke, 2nd Earl of Hardwicke, 29 August 1783. By permission of The British Library, London, Add. Ms. 35,621.

Fig. 2-27. James Stuart's Greek-head and dagger seal. From a letter to Thomas Anson, 19 June 1764. Staffordshire Record Office, Stafford, Lichfield Ms. D615/P(S)/1/6/7.

feet and can also cripple the hands. In a letter of 1766 to Philip Yorke, second Earl of Hardwicke, Stuart expressed his anxiety about this prospect: "I am under apprehensions for my right hand, such pain had settled itself on the second joint of my thumb (I mean that farthest from the nail) as to hinder me from writing. . . ."[245] Stuart's first recorded attack of gout was in 1763.[246] It was worse the following year. In September 1764 Stuart wrote: "I have been a Valetudinarian all this summer, my neglect of the gout, or rather, my supposing that it had left me, when it was only a remission of the fit has subjected me to pains in my head, & my stomach, with some returns of it to my feet, so that I have not been free from it in one shape or another, one day since it attacked me."[247] The illness returned in the autumn, and Stuart wrote to Thomas Anson that this attack was particularly severe.[248] Stuart spent the winter of 1765–66 taking the waters at Bath in the hope of alleviating the condition.[249]

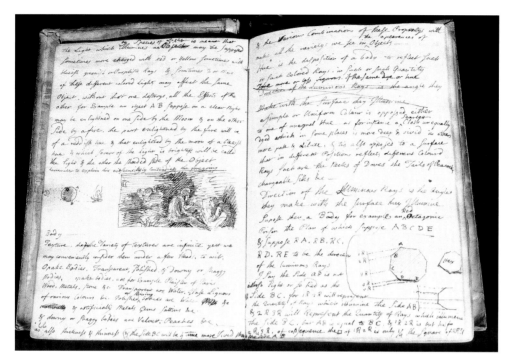

Fig. 2-28. James Stuart. Part of
a treatise on color in painting.
Pen and ink. From Stuart's
sketchbook (ca. 1748–50): fols.
76v–77r. RIBA Library
Drawings Collection, London,
SKB/336/2 [L 3/4].
Checklist no. 8.

Fatigue and anxiety, fevers and colds can also set off attacks of gout. "I am extremely ill with a Cold which is accompanied with a feverish disposition a violent head ache & many gouty Symptoms," he wrote to Anson in 1766.[250] Mrs. Montagu recorded that he was ill again in 1767.[251] He had another bad attack of gout in fall of 1770: "It was late in August when I received my half years Salary for Greenwich Hospital soon after which I was miserably indisposed, & my disorder has terminated in a severe fit of the Gout, which continues notwithstanding the harsh reception I have given it, & all my endeavors to walk it off."[252]

After a while gout damages the joints permanently, so it is likely that Stuart spent the last years of his life with severe arthritis; certainly William Newton thought that he had been "very infirm for some years preceding his death."[253] In a letter of August 1783 to Lord Hardwicke, Stuart may even have been forced to use an amanuensis, possibly his wife, who noted that "he writes with great pain and difficulty."[254] Although this letter is written entirely in the third person, Stuart can be identified as the originator by the use of his Greek hoplite-head seal on the letter (fig. 2-26). He had earlier used the figure of a Greek head with a dagger (fig. 2-27).

In 1816 Josiah Taylor wrote that "if Mr. Stuart had chosen to make a large fortune, he had more favourable opportunities of doing so than most men in his profession; . . . but, having acquired a competence by other means, he soon withdrew from the practice of his profes-

sion to enjoy the society of his friends, and the comforts of his family, in the way that was most congenial to his feelings and habits of life."[255] Taylor was not correct in his judgment that Stuart had retired from architecture, as several major architectural commissions date from the late 1760s and 1770s, including substantial alterations to Sir Sampson Gideon's house Belvedere in Kent (see figs. 6-57, 6-58), the construction of Mrs. Montagu's London house at 22 Portman Square (see fig. 5-87), and also the building of the magnificent chapel at Greenwich Hospital (see fig. 8-1). Also, in spite of Taylor's characterization, Stuart was capable of extraordinary bouts of effort and hard work in some circumstances, such as his eleven-hour working days in the period in which he was striving to complete the first volume of *Antiquities of Athens.*[256] However, there is an underlying truth in Taylor's interpretation of Stuart's career. Even before gout and good living took their toll, Stuart appears to have preferred to avoid work if he could. His friend Caldwell suggested that he spent his afternoons playing skittles.[257]

Stuart became co-chairman of SPAC's Committee of Polite Arts in March 1761—but was castigated for failing to "take an equal share" in the work of the committee.[258] In 1760 he was commissioned by Mrs. Montagu to paint "Zephirs and Zephirettes"[259] in her bedroom (see fig. 5-79), but these were still unfinished two years later, prompting Mrs. Montagu to summon him in July 1762, "with a resolution to pour forth all my indignation upon

Fig. 2-29. James Stuart, "A Design for / The east end of St. Georges Chapel," 1771. Gouache, pen and ink inscriptions. St. George's Chapel Archives and Chapter Library, Windsor, F.21. By permission of the Dean and Canons of Windsor. *Checklist no. 144.*

him."[260] It was another decade before this work was finally complete.[261] Stuart's commission to design interiors at Spencer House began in 1759, but a letter from Lord Villiers to Lady Spencer in 1765 indicates that he was failing to supervise the work: "I called upon Stuart the other morning; he said he was going to St. James's Place immediately. . . . I understood him that he had been several times there lately, and upon enquiry, I learnt of Ben, the porter, that he had never seen him since your ladyship was in town."[262] Examples of Stuart's poor working practices abound. The Greenwich commission was particularly troubled (see chap. 8), leading Stuart's clerk of works, Robert Mylne to characterize him as "a person of a wavering mind and undecided judgment."[263]

In 1788 Stuart's obituarist claimed that "whatever new project he engaged in, he pursued with such avidity, that he seldom quitted it while there was any thing further to be learnt or understood from it."[264] In fact, Stuart was prone to starting things in a rush of enthusiasm and then not completing them. Josiah Taylor's notes on the contents of Stuart's now missing sketchbooks are telling not only for the breadth of his interests, but also for his work habits: "Beginning of a translation of Vitruvius . . . Beginning apparently of a treatise on Architecture . . . Treatise of Architecture: Another beginning—a very empty book. . . . Pola—began Several times—I think the beginning of the volume of Pola is written over one way or another at least 50 times."[265] A surviving sketchbook contains the beginning of a treatise on color in painting (fig. 2-28).

This flaw would sour Stuart's relations with several of his patrons. For example, he accepted the post of portrait painter to the Society of Dilettanti in 1763 "with the usual salary."[266] His first Dilettanti portrait commission, in May 1763, was to paint his deceased patron James Dawkins, but despite repeated promptings from the secretary, the painting was still unfinished five years later.[267] Stuart did paint two portraits of Dawkins, including one that is known only through a mezzotint by James McArdell (see fig. 2-7), but there is no record that the Dilettanti portrait was ever completed.[268] Stuart's failure to complete another commission, to design an altarpiece and east window for St. George's Chapel, Windsor, provoked the chapter to "signify to Mr. Stewart, that unless he bring in his Plan & Estimate for the East Window and altar-Screen, by Midsummer Day next, the Chapter will be under the necessity of applying elsewhere" (fig. 2-29).[269] Stuart became notorious for his lack of application. In one anecdote

recorded by Mrs. Thrale, Stuart is said to have remarked to a gathering of friends that "Painting is my Wife I think, & Architecture my Mistress," whereupon artist Francis Hayman riposted: "What Pity 'tis then Sir, that you have *no living Issue by either!*"[270] A tendency to lie his way out of trouble was also noticed by more than one person. Lord Villiers wrote: "I fancy he sometimes says the thing which is not,"[271] while Mrs. Montagu remarked "Tho he does not mean (I believe) to tell fibs, it is impossible to rely on any thing he says."[272]

Much of the surviving information about Stuart's last years comes from a series of letters written by Mrs. Montagu in which she complains bitterly about Stuart's lack of progress in building her house at Portman Square, a commission that began in 1775 (see chap. 5). Part of the problem was Stuart's inefficiency: orders that were supposed to have been given to workmen never reached them. Designs were "lying in ye dust & confusion of Mr Stuarts study in a very incomplete & unfinishd state."[273] Mrs. Montagu wrote: "I know, by experience, Mr Stuart is apt to forget his promises are not fulfill'd, & talks of designs for chimney pices, & Pillars &c, &c which exist only in his brain, & when I write to ye workmen who are to execute them to know why they are not finishd they answer, they will set about them the moment Mr Stuart gives them the designs."[274] Even before Mrs. Montagu finally lost her patience, she was writing that Stuart was "idle and inattentive"[275] and that he and his assistant Gandon were "so dilatory that they retard every thing instead of forwarding ye business of the House."[276] Mrs. Montagu was, however, a loyal patron to Stuart from 1758 through into the 1780s. Although she became exasperated with his business practices, she always appreciated his artistic abilities, and the disparaging remarks in her letters may have been exaggerated for effect.

In 1780 Mrs. Montagu wrote a long and angry letter to Leonard Smelt in which she accused Stuart of being a liar and also a drunkard:

I have found out that in dealing with Mr Stuart great caution is necessary. I chose him for my Architect on account of his disinterestedness & contempt of money, I did not see how any mischief to my pocket cd arise from these qualities, or indeed with these qualities; but Satan is more cunning than I am, & this sly enemy of human virtue found many assailable & weak places about him, & this said Mr Satan finding at some peephole into ye human Soul, or by observation or external action that what workmen did by bribery of [a] guinea to many Architects could be effected on him by pipes & tobacco & pots of Porter in ale houses & night Cellars, I speak it not on suspicion but certain information that since he began my House he has been for a fortnight together in a most drunken condition with these fellows. Mr Sampson Gideon, for whom he was building a House when I began mine, was obliged to take many precautions to prevent being imposed on by the Workmen whose bills he assented to, about a year & half ago Stuart had by a long uninterrupted State of drunkenness brought himself into such a condition of mind & body as I feard irrecoverable, to this I attribute ye many falsehoods of which I gave him proof by shewing to him his own letters, tho he does not mean (I believe) to tell fibs, it is impossible to rely on any thing he says. It wd be tedious to tell you how often I have been obliged to confront him with ye Workmen whom he blamed for not having executed his orders, & he was then obliged to confess he had forgotten to deliver ye designs. Mr Gandon writes me by this days post that Mr Stuart has put ye design for ye Chimney piece in your room in hand. I wish this may be so, but as he told you he wd send the design to me, & has not done it, I fear he may not have delivered it to ye artists. In business ye strait line is the line of beauty, but Stuart is apt to chuse ye waving line.[277]

Fig. 2-30. Attributed to Philip Jean. Portrait miniature of Elizabeth Stuart, ca. 1778. Watercolor and body color on ivory. National Portrait Gallery, London, NPG 55 b. *Checklist no. 204.*

Mrs. Montagu's account suggests that Stuart may have become an alcoholic. Although it is not uncommon for clients to become irritated by their architects, Mrs. Montagu's accusations of drunkenness gain credence because they are corroborated. Highmore felt obliged to provide an explanation for Stuart's frequent visits to the Feathers in Leicester Square, writing that Stuart did so because he was

> an attentive observer of men and manners; and having learned that there were clubs of artists, &c. held at certain porter-houses in his neighbourhood, belonging to which were some odd geniuses, men of an original turn of thinking and conversation, he would, occasionally, when his evenings were not otherwise engaged, resort for variety to such places, in order to smoke his darling pipe, and listen to their curious debates, &c. At these places he was received with much respect by the company, who thought themselves highly honoured by his presence: and often, on the next day, he would entertain his friends of the higher orders with his pleasant details of what usually passed at such droll assemblies. And where, Mr. Urban, was the harm of all this?[278]

Others were more critical, in particular the anonymous author of a paragraph in a newspaper who censured

Stuart for "spending much of his time in alehouses with low company, &c."[279] Attitudes to drink and drunkenness shifted quite substantially during the century. Early in the century, "Drunkenness was considered a normal and satisfactory condition as much by Defoe or Sir Robert Walpole as it was later by Johnson or Wilkes," but by the 1780s drinking had come to be seen as a vice.[280]

In 1779 "Roger Shanhagan" (an alias for three men, artists Robert Smirke and Robert Watson, and architect William Porden) wrote a criticism about a drawing of Montagu House that Stuart exhibited at the Royal Academy: "If Mr. Stewart had not given so many proofs of his Abilities, we might be justified in asserting that, like many more ingenious men, his studies have more improved the Taste of others than his own. We know not how to account for this falling off, but from his conversion to Epicurianism. Since he resolved to enjoy the pleasures of the passing moment, he seems to have neglected Fame as a Phantom unworthy of being placed in competition with more certain and substantial Good."[281]

"Shanhagan's" accusation of Epicurianism was not only a public suggestion that Stuart was drinking too much, but may also have been a sly reference to an event of the previous year. On August 21, 1778, the sixty-five-year-old Stuart had remarried.[282] His new wife was only sixteen years old. According to the register of marriages at the Church of St. Martin in the Fields, her name was Elizabeth Blacland.[283] Her father, George, had to be present at the wedding in order to give his formal permission, because she was a minor. There are four surviving accounts of Elizabeth Blacland, each slightly different. Highmore thought her surname was Blackstone and believed she was the daughter of a Kentish farmer. His remarks about her character are positive, but unrevealing. She was "a prudent and affectionate mother, to whom this farther testimony of respect is due, that, notwithstanding the disparity of years between her and Mr. S. she made his *latter days* as comfortable and happy as the assiduity and tenderness of an affectionate wife can possibly render those of a fond and truly domesticated husband."[284]

Highmore was in no doubt of their affection for each other, but another account, relayed by Stuart's friend Caldwell to Josiah Taylor, suggests that it was merely convenient for Stuart to choose a wife and that he had first attempted to marry Elizabeth's sister. According to Caldwell, Stuart's "second wife lived with him (as did her sister) in the capacity of a Servant when very young he

offer[ed] her Marriage (which her Sister had previously refused) which she accepting, he sent her to a proper place for Education and when abt 16 years old married her."[285]

Stuart's obituarist also thought that Stuart was considering his comfort in old age: "Mr. Stuart . . . now found himself the master of a very considerable income, which he longed to divide with a companion, to whom his long series of events would be amusing and whose smiles would add comfort to his latter days."[286] This writer also believed that Elizabeth Blacland was from Kent, from the village of Sittingbourne, but thought she was in her twenties when she married.[287]

Perhaps the most revealing of the four accounts, however, is that of Stuart's patron Lord Camden, who was privately relaying gossip by letter rather than preparing information for publication: "Tell Fanny Sir James Stewart, as I hear, for I have not seen him, is again [marry'd]; but this time he has taken a beautifull young virgin of 16, but not of the same rank of females—a Maid servant. What a strange dotage! & yet perhaps he is in the right, being a man individual & an object neither of envy or censure. He pleases himself & hurts nobody, for he has no heir to be disappointed."[288]

Companion portraits of Elizabeth and James Stuart were painted, possibly to celebrate their marriage.[289] Elizabeth is bewitchingly pretty, and the artist, believed to be Philip Jean, has used his subject's sinuous, curling hair and beribboned dress to suggest a restless movement and liveliness (fig. 2-30). Stuart by contrast is still and staid: presenting himself as a respectable, formally dressed, establishment figure (see frontispiece). There is no hint in the portrait that anything is amiss, although from Mrs. Montagu's account, only two months after the wedding, "Stuart had by a long uninterrupted State of drunkenness brought himself into such a condition of mind & body as I feard irrecoverable."[290]

Stuart and Elizabeth had five children in the decade of their marriage. Two daughters, Frances Charlotte and Elizabeth Ann, would outlive Stuart. Frances died young, but Elizabeth Ann survived to see the publication of the fourth and final volume of *Antiquities of Athens* in 1816 and the sale to Jeremiah Harman of her father's gouaches in 1823.[291] Two of Stuart's sons, John George Hardinge and James, would later make use of their father's Admiralty connections and join the navy. John died in the West Indies in 1800 at the age of nineteen, and James, who was born shortly after Stuart's death, would live into the

1860s.[292] Another son, James Stevens Stuart, looked likely to follow Stuart into an artistic or architectural profession. He was, Highmore remarked, "his father's darling" and "'the very image and superscription' of himself, both in body and mind; he manifested a most astonishing turn for drawing, even before he was three years old; and would imitate, with pen or pencil, every thing he saw lying on his father's table. This child . . . died of smallpox towards the latter end of the year 1787: and poor Mr. S's health was observed to decline very rapidly from that time."[293] On February 1, 1788, Stuart "retired to rest at his accustomed hour, 11 o'Clock in his usual health, and was dead at 4 o'Clock the next morning." The cause of death is not known for certain. Years later Stuart's surviving son, James, "was informed by an old servant of the family, who lived to the year 1845, that the cause of his death was gout in the stomach; another informant—paralysis."[294]

According to William Newton, Stuart "left his papers in great confusion and disorder."[295] Inefficient to the end, he had failed to write a will and so died intestate, leaving his pregnant widow to apply for administration of his estate.[296] Apparently she was "unable to settle the affairs of her said Husband the same being very intricate."[297] Not surprisingly she turned for help to her nearest male relative, her sister's husband, Jonathan Bayne, a disastrously bad choice. According to James Stuart Jr., Bayne "fell into loose and dissipated habits, sporting & gambling breaking out into an excess of riot, not to be exceeded; becoming the bousing companion of Moreland the painter, until the sad end of the unhappy man (according to the account of an old servant) was death through madness in a London Workhouse. Thus our affairs went to wreck & ruin."[298] A court case instigated by Elizabeth's friend Richard Papps confirms the story. Bayne appropriated the Stuart wealth and "used frequently to risk and lose divers large Sums of Money in playing and Gaming."[299] By 1796, when Elizabeth Stuart wrote her own will, she no longer trusted Bayne and appointed Papps as executor, asking him to complete the administration of Stuart's estate as well as her own.[300] In fact Papps began to try to sort out the financial mess in 1797, two years before Elizabeth Stuart died. A letter among the Earls of Lichfield papers records that "Mr papp's" attempted to claim an annuity from Thomas Anson's heirs on behalf of Mrs. Stuart.[301]

A writer in the *World* was surprised at the extent of Stuart's wealth, writing that "Athens Stuart, unexpectedly to most people, has died possessed of much property, chiefly on mortgage on new buildings in Marybone."[302] Unfortunately, no inventory or accounting survives, but even after years of theft and mismanagement, when Elizabeth's will was proved in 1804 the estate was still worth £5,000.[303] Stuart's worldly success set the seal on the morality tale presented by his obituarist in the *Gentleman's Magazine* and provided a pleasant coda to the writer's account of Stuart's superhuman achievements: "Raised by his own abilities, and integrity, from the utmost abyss of penury to the most pleasing condition of respectable affluence, without servility, without chicane, without any stratagem, but by the bold efforts of unconquerable perseverance, prudence, and an independent mind! Reader, can we refrain from praise!"[304] Stuart's life seems to display the much more attractive human qualities of humor, curiosity, a talent for friendship, and a sheer joy in designing that was never quite matched by his ability to put his ideas on paper or to execute them efficiently in the round.

Acknowledgments: I have had a great deal of help in the course of writing this chapter. I would particularly like to thank Kerry Bristol for her generosity in sharing some of her original research and making available her transcripts and research notes from several archives. This chapter would have been very difficult to write without reference to her unpublished Ph.D. thesis. I also would like to thank Frank Salmon for insights into Stuart's stay in Italy, and Susan Soros for her encouragement and for many useful suggestions for improving the chapter.—C.A.

1. H. A., "Traits for the life of the late Athenian Stuart," *Gentleman's Magazine* 58 (February 1788): 95–96. "H. A." has never been identified.

2. Ibid.

3. Lesley Lawrence, "Stuart and Revett: Their Literary and Architectural Careers," *Journal of the Warburg Institute* 2 (1938–39): 132, 146.

4. James Lees-Milne, *The Age of Adam* (London: B. T. Batsford, 1947): 51–53.

5. Ibid.

6. Dora Wiebenson, *Sources of Greek Revival Architecture* (London: A. Zwemmer, 1969): 3–4.

7. *Antiquities,* vol. 4 (1816): xxi. This information also appears in James Stuart (Jr.) Memoir, p. 29, Add. Ms. 27,576, BL. Commander James Stuart R.N. was Stuart's posthumous son, born in April 1788. The memoir includes a transcription of the first draft of the biographical preface of *Antiquities*, vol. 4, and added notes, excerpts from obituaries, and other articles. Stuart's son appended his autobiography to the end. British Library dates the manuscript to ca. 1856–60.

8. These quotations are found, respectively, in: page titled "Friends of Jas Stuart," Add. Ms. 22,152, p. 16, BL; Josiah Taylor (attrib.), notes dated 8 June 1808, ibid., 18; and notes dated 20 June 1808, ibid., 18v Joseph Woods was the editor of the fourth volume of *Antiquities*, and the research notes in Ms 22,152 are generally assumed to be his; however, the handwriting of these notes is not the same as that of a letter, Woods to Taylor, 10 April 1815, ibid., 43–43v. The handwriting of the notes does, however, match that of an unsigned draft letter to the editor of the *Gentlemans Magazine* dated July 1809, ibid., 24–24v, BL. From the content of this letter it appears that its author was Josiah Taylor, publisher of *Antiquities*, vol. 4 (1816).

9. *Antiquities,* vol. 4 (1816): iv. Taylor does not name Sheldrake, but in a letter from Stuart's daughter Elizabeth Ann Stuart to Taylor, undated, she refers to the author of the narrative of her father as "Mr. Sheldrake"; Add. Ms. 22,152, p. 41, BL. Sheldrake was christened in St. Martin in the Fields, London, on 15 April. He married Fanny Papps, daughter of Richard Papps, on 29 October 1784 (International Genealogical Index online, on website http://www.familysearch.org).

For Richard Papps as executor of Elizabeth Stuart's will and guardian of the Stuart children, see Papps v. Bayne, C12/1759/6, NA.

10. By the time Timothy Sheldrake was born in 1759, Stuart was already forty-six years old.

11. A. H. [Anthony Highmore], "Further Particulars of the late Athenian Stuart," *Gentleman's Magazine* 58, no. 2 (March 1788): 216–18.

12. In July 1809 Taylor wrote to the editor of *Gentleman's Magazine* asking for the identity of "A. H."; Add. Ms. 22,152, p. 24–24v, BL. Mr. Barnardiston of Sudbury, Suffolk, suggested that A. H. was Highmore in a letter of 13 August 1809. Barnardiston wrote: "I remember he [Highmore] shewed me a vol of Stuart's views, given him by the Author who was his particular friend & this circumstance leads me to think the papers signed A H were by him'" ibid., 31–31v.

13. A. H. [Highmore], "Further Particulars," (1788): 216.

14. Ibid., 217. One of Stuart's obituarists implies he died on Friday, 1 (not 2) February: "On Friday last died, at his house in Leicester Square, at a very advanced age, the celebrated James Stuart, Esq. commonly distinguished by the appellation of 'Athenian Stuart'. We are sorry to add, that he has left the second volume of his *Antiquities of Athens* unfinished, though part of the work is printed, and many of the fine engravings actually executed. The loss which the public has suffered by this event is, we are afraid, *irreparable!*" (*Morning Herald*, no. 2275 [6 February 1788]: 3).

15. "Dr Caulder No. 13 Lisson Grove informed me that James Stuart was a foundling and did not know the place of his birth or quality of his parents . . . Dr C says he had the above from Stuarts own mouth"; Taylor (attrib.), notes, 8 June 1808, Add. Ms. 22,152, p. 18, BL.

16. Proceedings of the Old Bailey are available on www.oldbailey-online.org, which includes a searchable database of cases, such as: no. t17920215-7, John Lewis, Robert Pearce, alias Arnold, theft: housebreaking, 15 February 1792; t17420224-35, John Page, theft with violence: highway robbery, 24 February 1742; t17990911-88, Ambrose King, theft: Simple Grand Larceny, 11 September 1799.

17. Ibid., t17340227-51, John Bracket, alias Braithwaite, killing: murder, 27 February 1734; t17430907-31, Susanna Atkinson, theft: pickpocketing, 7 September 1743.

18. This headcount of booktrade personnel derives from the following sources: Ellic Howe, *List of London Bookbinders, 1648–1815* (London: Bibliographical Society, 1950); H. R. Plomer, *A Dictionary of the Printers and Booksellers who Were at Work in England, Scotland and Ireland from 1726 to 1775* (London: Bibliographical Society, 1932); Old Bailey Proceedings, www.oldbaileyonline.org (the database also records the trades of the complainants, witnesses, and defendants); and Ian Maxted, "The London Book Trades, 1735–1775: A Checklist of Members," Exeter Working Papers in British Book Trade History, EWP03, Devon Library Services, 2001, http://www.devon.gov.uk/etched?_IXP_=1&_IXR=100158. The houses on the west side of Creed Lane and the south side of Ludgate Street backed directly onto Holyday Yard. The sole entrance to the yard was through Creed Lane, and the yard is seen in the Old Bailey cases as an extension to the lane rather than a separate entity.

19. H. A., "Traits" (1788): 95.

20. A. S. Turberville, ed., *Johnson's England: An Account of the Life & Manners of His Age*, vol. 1 (Oxford: Clarendon Press, 1933): 176.

21. H. A. "Traits" (1788): 95.

22. Ibid., 95–96.

23. Gregory King, *Two Tracts*, ed. G. E. Barnett (Baltimore: Johns Hopkins Press, 1936): n.p.; from www.york.ac.uk/depts/maths/histstat/king.htm. Accessed 27 May 2004.

24. Gregory King, *Natural and Political Observations and Conclusions upon the State and Condition of England* (1696), cited in Wilfrid Prest, *Albion Ascendant: English History, 1660–1815* (Oxford University Press, 1998): 165.

25. Liza Picard, *Dr. Johnson's London* (London: Phoenix Press, 2001): 107, citing an unnamed article in *Gentleman's Magazine* (April 1768).

26. For example, Proceedings of the Old Bailey, www.oldbailey-online.org, t17730908-45, John Harwood, theft: Simple Grand Larceny, 8 September 1773, where Harwood is a lodger of paper-stainer John Shearman in Holyday Yard, Creed Lane; t17430907-31, Susanna Atkinson, theft: pickpocketing, 7 September 1743, where Atkinson is one of the lodgers of witness Thomas Kelly; or t17611209-35, Mary, wife of Cowen, theft: petty larceny, 9 December 1762, where Mary Cowen and her husband shared rooms with witness Christopher Clark; and witness Ann Bready also had lodgers. Many other examples can be found in the database.

27. See M. Dorothy George, *London Life in the XVIIIth Century* (London: K. Paul, Trench, Trubner, 1925): 85.

28. The Roman annual "census of souls" recorded the religion of those registered. In 1747, Stuart was living in the Villa Tomati with Nicholas Revett and Gavin Hamilton. In the census they are: "Sign. Jiacobo Stuard Ingles Catol [Catholic] 30 [age 30] Nicola Rivetti Ingles eretico 25 Gavino Hamilton Ingles eretico 20." The ages given are very inaccurate. See "Regisro delle Anime della Parochia di S. Andrea delle Fratte del M. R. Pregugenio Maria Chiarotti . . ." (1747): 18, no. 78, Archivio Storico del Vicariato, Rome.

29. For Catholic worship in eighteenth-century London see Michael Gandy, *Catholic Missions and Registers, 1700–1880*, vol. 1, *London and the Home Counties* (London: Michael Gandy, 1993): 36–43; see also George Rudé, *Hanoverian London: 1714–1808* (Stroud, Gloucestershire, Sutton Publishing, 2003): 111.

30. For Catholic disadvantages see [Arthur Frederic] Basil Williams, *The Whig Supremacy, 1714–1760* (Oxford: Clarendon Press, 1962): 69.

31. Taylor (attrib.), notes dated 21 June 1808, Add. Ms. 22,152 p. 19v, BL. Taylor got this information from Sir Philip Stephens, who had met Dr. Jones in London. This may be the same Dr. Jones who acted as Stuart's medical doctor when Stuart was recovering from the gout in Bath in 1766. See Stuart to Philip Yorke, second Earl of Hardwicke, from Bath, 27 January 1766, Add. Ms. 35,607, p. 233, BL: "Notwithstanding the injunction of my friend Jones who prescribes absolute Idleness to me, I have bestowed some thoughts on your Lordships building. . . . "

32. A. H. [Highmore], "Further Particulars" (1788): 216.

33. For example, the Christ's Hospital school, which specialized in training boys for the navy, confined its free places to freemen's children. For a survey of secondary education in London, including information about Christ's Hospital, see Margaret Bryant, *The London Experience of Secondary Education,* (London and Atlantic Highlands, NJ: Athlone Press, 1986).

34. Eighteenth-century literacy is a subject of some debate. Estimates of its extent tend to use the data from marriage licenses, where the signature of either spouse rather than a mark or "X" is assumed to connote an ability to read and write. In London in the 1750s, some 92 percent of London bridegrooms and 74 percent of their brides were literate by this measure. See Prest, *Albion Ascendant* (1998): 178.

35. Ibid.

36. See Mary Gwladys Jones, *Charity School Movement* (Cambridge University Press, 1938): 18, cited in Williams, *Whig Supremacy* (1962): 141.

37. *Antiquities,* vol.4 (1816): xxi. Also in James Stuart (Jr.) Memoir, p. 30, Add. Ms. 27,576, BL.

38. Prest, *Albion Ascendant* (1998): 176.

39. H. A., "Traits"(1788): 95.

40. For the value of Latin to the upwardly mobile, see Jenny Uglow, *Hogarth: A Life and a World* (New York: Farrar, Strauss and Giroux, 1997): 20. Hogarth's father made a living by teaching Latin to "aspiring young lawyers, doctors, clerks and merchants who wished to toss off a Latin phrase to show their cultured status."

41. Taylor (attrib.), notes dated 21 June 1808, Add. Ms. 22,152, p. 19 v. BL: "Sir P Stephen . . . thinks Stuart was born or passed his youth in the neighbourhood of Soho."

42. The Edict of Nantes had formalized state toleration of the Protestant religion in France. After the revocation of the edict in 1685, some fifty thousand French Protestant families left France for other countries where their religion could be practiced safely. The two greatest concentrations of Huguenot refugees in England were found in Soho and Spitalfields in London. See Maureen A. Waller, *1700: Scenes from London Life* (New York: Four Walls Eight Windows, 2000): 3, 271, 273.

43. See Bruce Robertson and Robert Dance, "Joseph Goupy and the Art of the Copy," *Cleveland Museum Bulletin* 75, no. 10 (December 1988): 356.

44. H. A., "Traits" (1788): 95.

45. Under a law of Charles II, entry to a number of occupations was only legal if accomplished through apprenticeship; however, this law was not always observed. The Royal Charter of the Worshipful Company of Fanmakers was granted in 1709, and it became one of the restricted-entry trades. Details of apprenticeships are only recorded from 1747. See http://www.fanmakers.com/history.htm. For examples of the kinds of premium paid by parents to an apprentice master, see Picard, *Dr. Johnson's London* (2000): 181.

46. Elizabeth Waterman Gilboy, *Wages in Eighteenth-Century England,* Harvard Economic Studies, vol. 45 (Cambridge, Mass.: Harvard University Press, 1934): 220–24, 281.

47. For Paul Sandby see Taylor to James Gandon, 19 August 1809, copy letter, Add. Ms. 22,152, p. 29, BL, which states: "was he a fan painter Mr Sandby says he was." For Nollekens, see John Thomas Smith, *Nollekens and His Times* (London: Turnstile Press, 1949): 10.

48. For the comparative social cachet of fan painting against portraiture, see Edward Croft-Murray's remarks on Louis Goupy, quoting George Vertue: "that affair of Fan painting being not of so much credit, he studied painting in oyl wherein he had success & painted portraits with some reputation for some years"; Edward Croft-Murray, *Decorative Painting in England, 1537–1837,* vol. 2 (London: Country Life Books, 1970): 212.

49. I am grateful to Sheila O'Connell, Assistant Keeper in the Department of Prints and Drawings at the British Museum, for this information. Personal communication, 5 March 2004.

50. For travels, see Croft-Murray, *Decorative Painting* (1970): 211. For teaching, see William Thomas Whitley, *Artists and their Friends in England, 1700–1799* (London and Boston: Medici Society, 1928): 72–74. Whitley describes Louis Goupy as "a well-known teacher." Joseph was "teacher to nearly all the contemporary English Royalties he was for years the most fashionable of drawing masters." Both Goupys subscribed to Sir Godfrey Kneller's Great Queen Street Academy in 1711. Louis was a founder member of the St. Martin's Lane Academy. Joseph was a member of the Virtuosi of St. Luke. See Bristol, "Stuart and the Genesis of the Greek Revival " (1997): 31–33.

51. John Gould, *A Dictionary of Painters, Sculptors, Architects, and Engravers . . .* (London: Gale & Curtis, 1810): 122. Also see Robertson and Dance, "Joseph Goupy" (1988): 354–82.

52. Croft-Murray, *Decorative Painting* (1970): 211–12.

53. Bristol, "Stuart and the Genesis of the Greek Revival" (1997): 32–33.

54. Algernon Graves, "An Account of the Society of Artists of Great Britain . . . " in *The Society of Artists of Great Britain, 1760–1791, the Free Society of Artists, 1761–1783 . . .* (London: George Bell and Sons and Algernon Graves, 1907): 296.

55. Whitley, *Artists and their Friends* (1928): 27. Whitley's source of information was probably the commonplace books of George Vertue, Add. Mss. 23,068-23,074, BL. These notes were made between 1713 and 1754.

56. For biographical notes on Moser, see "George Michael Moser," excerpted from the *Grove Dictionary of Art* (London: Macmillan, 2000), at www.artnet.com/library/05/0598/T059830.asp. Accessed 26 July 2004.

57. Whitley, *Artists and their Friends* (1928): 27.

58. The self-portrait is traditionally ascribed to Stuart, but questions have been raised about the identity of the sitter by Kerry Bristol, among others. However, the face has very strong correspondences with other known portraits of Stuart. I see no reason to doubt the attribution.

59. The drawing was previously in the possession of J. Hawkins, Bignor Park, Sussex, when there was a ticket attached which read "Class 121 S the fourth premium, three guineas." Presented to the RIBA by Joseph Woods, before 1846.

60. "Angleterre XVIIIe et XIXe Siècles: costumes populaires—types de la rue," plate 428 in Auguste Racinet, *Le Costume Historique,* vol. 6 (Paris: Librarie de Firmin-Didot et Cie, 1888): n.p.

61. "Angleterre XVIIIe Siècle: haut dignitaries et types populaires," plate 429 in ibid.

62. For wigs see Waller, *1700* (2000): 163; Picard, *Dr. Johnson's London* (2000): 225–26.

63. James Boswell, *The Life of Samuel Johnson* (New York: Random House, 1952): 633, cited in Brinsley Ford, "The Grand Tour," *Apollo* 114 (December 1981): 390.

64. Ellis Waterhouse, *Painting in Britain, 1530–1790* (London: Penguin Books, 1953): 122. Also see Ford, "Grand Tour" (1981): 390–91, 397.

65. For the Goupys see Croft-Murray, *Decorative Painting in England* (1970): 211–12. For Cheron see Waterhouse, *Painting in Britain* (1953): 90. For Tuscher see "Danmark og Italien: T," in database provided by the Danish Institute at Rome, www.dkinst-rom.dk/dansk/homepage.htm. Accessed 7 June 2004.

66. For a sister as "shop-woman," see H. A., "Traits" (1788): 95. For the legacy see Sarah Teresia Stuart to James Stuart, 14 June 1750, copy letter in James Stuart (Jr) Memoir, pp. 12–14, Add. Ms. 27,576, BL: "We have made shift at last to raise a little money and are determined to set out for Holland in a week's time, to demand the legacies we are entitled to by my Sister's Will. . . . " For correspondence about the legacy, see Sir James Gray to Robert D'Arcy, fourth Earl of Holdernesse, 18 November 1750, Egerton Ms, 3419, pp. 233v to 234, BL.

67. H. A., "Traits" (1788): 95.

68. Ibid. The precise date of Stuart's departure is not known. Lesley Lawrence suggested 1741; see Lawrence, "Stuart and Revett" (1938–39): 129.

69. Sarah Teresia Stuart to James Stuart, 14 June 1750, copy letter in James Stuart (Jr) Memoir, p. 14, Add. Ms. 27,576, BL.

70. Ibid., 12.

71. Ibid., 60; *Antiquities,* vol. 4 (1816): xxiv; H. A. "Traits" (1788): 95, which refers to the "extreme pressure of such a charge."

72. The agent is mentioned in a letter from British Resident at Venice, Sir James Gray to Holdernesse, who was then in the Netherlands: "I beg leave to recommend to your protection Mr Stuart, a very ingenious man who is going from hence to Greece to design the Antiquities of Athens. He has a law suit depending in Holland with the executor of his sister's will. If he has right on his side, I am persuaded, upon his case being made known to your Lordship, which his Agent has orders to do, if it should be necessary, you will be so good as to favour him with your countenance in it." Sir James Gray to Holdernesse, 18 November 1750, Egerton Ms. 3419, pp. 233v –234, BL. I am grateful to Kerry Bristol for drawing my attention to this letter.

73. Stuart to Robert Wood, Smyrna, 30 May 1753, Wentworth Woodhouse Muniments R1-42, Sheffield Archive. This letter was in response to one from Wood informing him of Sarah's death. This second family death has been conflated with that of the sister in Holland, and Stuart is presumed not to have learned of it until receiving Wood's letter in May 1753. See Bristol, "Stuart and the Genesis of the Greek Revival " (1997): 28–29. However, Stuart must have received news of

the first death at least in 1750, as he enlisted the help of Gray and through him, Holdernesse in retrieving the legacy of his other sister in that year Sir James Gray to Holdernesse, 18 November 1750, Egerton Ms. 3419, pp. 233v–34.

74. Stuart to Robert Wood, Smyrna, 30 May 1753, Wentworth Woodhouse Muniments, R1-42, Sheffield Archives.

75. H. A., "Traits" (1788): 95.

76. James Barry, *The Works of James Barry, Esq.*, vol. 1 (London: T. Cadell and W. Davies, 1809): 18–19.

77. For a discussion of the usual routes for Grand Tourists to enter Italy, see Ford, "Grand Tour" (1981): 391–93.

78. H. A., "Traits" (1788): 95–96.

79. See Lesley Lewis, *Connoisseurs and Secret Agents in Eighteenth Century Rome* (London: Chatto and Windus, 1961): 115–16.

80. Taylor believed the story was untrue, see *Antiquities,* vol. 4 (1816): xvii.

81. Stuart writes that the first "Proposal" for *Antiquities of Athens* was drawn up toward the end of 1748, at which time "we were then at Rome, where we had already employed six or seven years in the study of painting"; *Antiquities,* vol. 1 (1762): v.

82. I am grateful to Frank Salmon for this information; personal communication, 17 April 2004.

83. Taylor (attrib.), notes of a conversation with Andrew Caldwell, 20 June 1808, Add Ms 22,152, p. 18v, BL.

84. *Antiquities,* vol. 4 (1816): iv.

85. Nulty's remarks are recorded in A. P. Oppé, ed., "Memoirs of Thomas Jones," Walpole Society annual, vol. 32 (1946–48): 74. This transcription from National Library of Wales, Ms 23,812D, is also available online at www.llgc.org.uk/pencerrig/thjones_s_001.htm.

86. Avril Hart and Emma Taylor, *Fans* (London: V & A Publications, 1998): esp. 57–68.

87. Stuart to Jacob Hinde, 20 March 1746, OSB fc 144, Beinecke Rare Book and Manuscript Library, Yale University Library, transcribed in John Marciari, "Athenian Stuart in Florence," *Burlington Magazine* 140 (September 1998): 614. The letter implies that Stuart was earning money painting and also searching for drawings for the collections of patrons. Stuart mentions that it is "near a year" since he had received a letter from Hinde, so their association began in 1745 or earlier. For general remarks about the profession of antiquary or cicerone, see Ford, "Grand Tour" (1981): 397–98.

88. Oppé, ed., "Memoirs of Thomas Jones" (1946–48): 74.

89. Ibid.

90. Stuart to Jacob Hinde, 20 March 1746, transcribed in Marciari, "Athenian Stuart in Florence" (1998): 614. Hinde paid Stuart a regular stipend through a banker in Leghorn, Houghton Wills. Jacob Hinde was a major London landowner with a country seat at Langham Hall in Essex. He married the daughter and heiress of Thomas Thayer who owned much of Marylebone. (Private Bill Office, Original Acts HL/PO/PB/1/ 1776/16G3n118, House of Lords Record Office). They gave their names to Hinde Street and Thayer Street in London. Hinde was one of the subscribers to the first volume of *Antiquities of Athens.*

He amassed a considerable collection of old master paintings and classical antiquities, some of which were probably acquired for him by Stuart. These were sold in 1785 by Christie's ("A Capital Well-chosen Collection of Italian, French, Flemish and Dutch pictures, Marble Busto's, Valuable Bronzes, Drawings &c.," sale cat., Christie's, London, 28 January 1785).

91. Stuart to Jacob Hinde, 20 March 1746, transcribed in Marciari, "Athenian Stuart in Florence" (September 1998): 614.

92. "A Capital well-chosen Collection," Christie's, 28 January 1785.

93. James Stuart, *De Obeslisco Caesaris Augusti e Campo Martio nuperrime effosso. Epistola Jacobi Stuart Angli ad Carolum Wentworth Comitem de Malton* (Rome, 1750). The engravings are dated 1749.

94. This anecdote is relayed in O.B., "Wentworth Woodhouse, Yorkshire, A Seat of Earl Fitzwilliam," *Country Life* 19 (31 March 1906): 460.

95. See Kerry Bristol's discussion of Cardinals Valenti and Albani, chap. 4, in this volume.

96. Lewis, *Connoisseurs and Secret Agents* (1961): esp. 84, 85, 88, 115, 123, 124, 129, 134, 144.

97. For Baron Stosch's spying activities see ibid., esp. 38–62, 63–116. For Stosch's subscription, see "Names of the Gentlemen who have promised to Subscribe to our Attica," Stuart, "Sketchbook . . . of buildings in N. Italy," RIBA Library Drawings Collection, SKB/336/2 [L 3/4]: 2. Stosch is fifth on the list. For a revealing exchange of letters between Lord Holdernesse and Lord Albermarle about Dawkins' subversive activities in the 1750s, see Andrew Lang, *Pickle the Spy, or the Incognito of Prince Charles,* 3rd ed. (London: Longmans, Green and Co., 1897). Available online from the Project Gutenberg Literary Archive Foundation, at http://www.gutenberg.org/etext/6807.

98. James Gandon [Jr], *The Life of James Gandon Esq.,* (Dublin: Hodges and Smith, 1846): 196.

99. Ibid., 198.

100. Stuart to Wilkes, 15 August 1766, Add. Ms. 30,869, p. 67, BL.

101. James Adam to his mother, 12 January 1761, Clerk of Penicuik Ms GD 18 4882, National Archives of Scotland, Edinburgh.

102. See Eileen Harris, *British Architectural Books and Writers, 1556–1785,* assisted by Nicholas Savage (Cambridge University Press, 1990): 439.

103. "Regisro delle Anime della Parochia di S. Andrea delle Fratte del M. R. Pregugenio Maria Chiarotti . . ." (1748): 18, no. 78, Archivio Storico del Vicariato, Rome. The via Felice is now the via Sistina.

104. Harris, *British Architectural Books,* (1990): 439.

105. Revett to his family (now lost), cited in *Antiquities,* vol. 4 (1816): xxviii–xxix.

106. Ibid.

107. August Mau, *Pompeii, Its Life and Art,* trans. Francis W. Kelsey (New York: Macmillan, 1907): 26–27. Excavations at the site of Pompeii began 30 March 1748 at which time it was believed to be the town of Stabiae. It was only in 1763 that an inscription was found that proved that it was in fact Pompeii.

108. Harris, *British Architectural Books* (1990): 439–40; Bristol, "Stuart and the Genesis of the Greek Revival" (1997): 56–58.

109. *Antiquities,* vol. 4 (1816): xxii. For Stuart's son, see James Stuart (Jr) Memoir, pp. 37–38, 103, Add. Ms. 27,576, BL.

110. Reverend Robert Russel to his son James Russel, 7 September 1749, Add. Ms. 41,169, p. 37, BL.

111. Harris, *British Architectural Books* (1990): 439.

112. See Lewis, *Connoisseurs and Secret Agents* (1961): 151–54.

113. For Hamilton's continuing friendship with Stuart see Bristol, "Stuart and the Genesis of the Greek Revival" (1997): 59. Hamilton recommended to Lord Lansdowne that he consult Stuart on the conversion of a sculpture gallery; see Arthur Hamilton Smith, *A Catalogue of the Ancient Marbles at Lansdowne House, Based on the work of Adolf Michaelis* (London: privately printed, 1889): 64, 67. And he persuaded the Spencers to commission work from Stuart; see Add. Ms. 75,686, BL.

114. For the Brettingham-owned portrait, two prints dating from 1827 are known to survive, one in the National Portrait Gallery, and the other in the collection of the Sir John Soane Museum, London. According to the text on the engraved copy by William Camden Edwards, the original painting was in the possession of Richard Brettingham of Shotford Hall, Norfolk. The original artist was Samuel Provan (misspelled "Proven" on the print), a Scottish painter who was in Rome from 1748. He was a protégé of Dunbar Douglas, fourth Earl of Selkirk and like Gavin Hamilton studied painting in Rome under Agostino Masucci which is how he may have been drawn into Stuart's circle. See Basil Skinner, *Scots in Italy in the 18th Century* (Edinburgh: National Galleries of Scotland, 1966): 29, and notes.

115. Bristol, "Stuart and the Genesis of the Greek Revival" (1997): 80–81.

116. Bouverie died at Guzel Hissar on 19 September 1750. See Nicholas Turner, "John Bouverie as a Collector of Drawings," *Burlington Magazine* 136 (February 1994): 92, 98–99.

117. *Antiquities,* vol. 4 (1816): viii; vol. 3 (1794): 53–54.

118. For the pirates—a Maltese corsair ship—see J. Mordaunt Crook, *The Greek Revival,* rev. ed. (London: John Murray 1995): 14–15. For the assassination attempt see "An Account of the extraordinary escape of James Stewart, Esq., . . ." *European Magazine* 46 (November 1804): 370–71. For Stuart's malarial fever see *Antiquities,* vol. 4 (1816): xvii.

119. *Antiquities,* vol. 2 (ca. 1790): 31.

120. H. A., "Traits" (1788): 95.

121. For the meridian see "Of the Latitude of Athens," dated 28 May 1751, in Stuart's sketchbook, Add. Ms. 62,088, p. 4, BL. For Logotheti, Stuart referred to the man's "insolent rapacity" in *Antiquities,* vol. 2 (ca. 1790): 37.

122. *Antiquities,* vol. 4 (1816): x–xi. It is likely that Stuart will have been tried in the Archbishop's tribunal in Athens before being compelled to journey to Constantinople. For this see Bristol, "Stuart and the Genesis of the Greek Revival" (1997): 98.

123. See Bristol, "Stuart and the Genesis of the Greek Revival" (1997): 98.

124. "Account of the extraordinary escape of James Stewart" (1804): 370.

125. Ibid., 370–71.

126. "Catalogue of pictures by Moreland . . . and other effects, of the late James Stuart . . . ," sale cat., Greenwoods, London, 27 June 1791, p. 4, lot 21, copy in Courtauld Institute Library, Br A 5059 1791/06/27.

127. See Crook, *Greek Revival* (1995): 14–15. Also see Bristol, "Stuart and the Genesis of the Greek Revival" (1997): 111.

128. Stuart's gouache views are now in the RIBA Library Drawings Collection.

129. "Proposals for publishing a new and accurate Description of the Antiquities &c. in the Province of Attica by James Stuart and Nicholas Revett," in *Original Letters of Eminent Literary Men . . .* , ed. Sir Henry Ellis (London: Camden Society, 1843): 383.

130. *Antiquites,* vol. 2 (ca. 1790): 19, pl. II.

131. Crook, *Greek Revival* (1995): 18–19.

132. Bristol, "Stuart and the Genesis of the Greek Revival" (1997): 40, 100.

133. H. A., "Traits" (1788): 96. This information is also relayed in Josiah Taylor (attrib.), notes, Add. Ms. 22,152, pp. 15, 17, 22, BL. An envelope addressed to Stuart and Revett at Dawkins' house in Brook Street survives (Gough Misc. Antiq Fol. 4, no. 172, Bodleian Library), cited in Bristol, "Stuart and the Genesis of the Greek Revival" (1997): 129. The same information is in Lawrence, "Stuart and Revett" (1938–39): 130. This also gives the date of Dawkins's death as 1757. His address in 1755 is given as "James Dawkins Esquire of Hanover square" in nomination papers, EC/1755/18, Archive of the Royal Society; searchable database and facsimiles of nomination papers on website http://www.royalsoc.ac.uk/library. Brook Street leads into Hanover Square.

134. Thomas Hollis to Professor Ward of Gresham College, 26 February 1751, from Venice, in *Original Letters of Eminent Literary Men* (1843): 380–81.

135. For Brettingham distributing proposals, see Harris, *British Architectural Books* (1990): 447 n. 3. For Rockingham, see notebook "From Mr Stuart the Athenian," Wentworth Woodhouse Muniments R220/3, p. 2, Sheffield Archives.

136. For Stuart's nomination to the Society of Antiquaries see Minutebook, 15 June and 7 December 1758, 25 January 1759 (vol. 8, pp. 79, 90, 107), Society of Antiquaries, Egerton Ms. 2381, BL. At this date the Royal Society was England's premier scientific body in the very broadest sense: most branches of knowledge came within its remit, including those now considered arts/humanities. For nomination papers for Stuart, see EC/1758/03, Royal Society; searchable database and facsimiles of nomination papers on website http://www.royalsoc.ac.uk/library/.

137. Standing Committee Minutes, 12 January 1759, Minutes of Meetings C 500, Museum Archive, British Museum.

138. Derek Cash, *Access to Museum Culture, the British Museum from 1753 to 1836* (London: British Museum, 2002): 37, 40–41. Available online at The British Museum, www.thebritishmuseum.ac.uk/researchpublications.

139. Sir James Porter to Rev. Mr. Wetstein, 2 May 1754, Add. Ms. 32,420, pp. 235–36, BL; cited in Bristol, "Stuart and the Genesis of the Greek Revival" (1997): 97.

140. James Adam to Betty Adam, 17 September 1760, Clerk of Penicuik Ms. GD 18 4872, National Archives of Scotland, Edinburgh.

141. Robert Adam to James Adam, 1 November 1757, Clerk of Penicuik Ms GD 18 4843, National Archives of Scotland, Edinburgh.

142. James Adam to Nelly Adam 16 November 1760, Clerk of Penicuik Ms. GD 18 4876, National Archives of Scotland, Edinburgh.

143. Robert Adam to James Adam, 12 January 1762, copy letter, Clerk of Penicuik Ms GD 18 4922, National Archives of Scotland, Edinburgh.

144. Walpole to Mrs. Montagu, 7 November 1761, reprinted in W. S. Lewis, ed., *The Yale Edition of Horace Walpole's Correspondence,* vol. 9 (Oxford University Press, 1983), no. 401.

145. Smith, *Nollekens and His Times* (1949): 19–20. Smith and Nollekens once took shelter in Stuart's house from the rain. Smith noted: "His parlour, where we remained until a shower of rain was over, was decorated with some of Hogarth's most popular prints; and upon a fire-screen he had pasted an impression of the plate called the 'Periwigs'; a print which Mr. Stuart always showed his visitors, as Hogarth's satire upon his first volume of Athenian Antiquities."

146. Mrs. Montagu to Lyttelton, [15 July 1762], Montagu Papers, MO 1414, Henry E. Huntington Library, San Marino, CA, cited in Bristol, "Stuart and the Genesis of the Greek Revival" (1997): 159.

147. Nomination papers for Stuart, EC/1758/03, Archive of the Royal Society; Searchable database and facsimiles of nomination papers on website http://www.royalsoc.ac.uk/library/; Minutebook of the Society of Antiquaries, vol. 8 (18 January 1757 to 20 May 1762): 79, Egerton Ms. 2381, BL.

148. James Stuart to Charles Watson-Wentworth, second Marquess of Rockingham, 28 September 1755, Wentworth Woodhouse Muniments R 1-70, Sheffield Archives.

149. Ibid.

150. Ibid.

151. For example, in 1762–63 Rockingham acquired thirty-six silver and copper medals and four vase candlesticks from Stuart. In 1765 Rockingham paid him £75 for buying and shipping from Rome a bronze lamp and an antique statue of Silenus riding a goat. See David Watkin, *Athenian Stuart: Pioneer of the Greek Revival* (London: George Allen and Unwin, 1982): 32. In 1770 on behalf of Thomas Anson, artist Nicholas Dall consulted Stuart on the subject matter of paintings for Stuart's orangery at Shugborough, Staffordshire; Stuart to Anson, 25 September 1770, Lichfield Ms. D615/P(S)/1/6/28, Staffordshire Record Office, Stafford. In 1770 Mrs. Montagu asked Stuart to help her choose a tea kitchen with a Wedgwood body and ormolu mounts from Boulton and Fothergill; see Kerry Bristol, "22 Portman Square: Mrs. Montagu and her 'Palais de la vieillesse'," *British Art Journal,* 2, no. 3 (Summer 2001): 73. Writing in the 1930s, Lesley Lawrence noted that

Stuart was "regarded as a court of appeal in matters of taste"; Lawrence, "Stuart and Revett," (1938–39): 133.

152. Gandon, *Life of James Gandon* (1846): 197.

153. James Harris, *Hermes: or a Philosophical Inquiry Concerning Universal Grammar,* 2nd ed. (London: John Nourse and Paul Vaillant, 1765): 325.

154. Barry, *Works of James Barry* (1809): 15–16.

155. See Bristol, "Stuart and the Genesis of the Greek Revival" (1997): 169. Undated memorandum in Provost Sumner's hand, probably November 1766, Ms. Altarpiece 1742–1775, p. 9, Muniment Room, King's College, Cambridge.

156. Philip Yorke, first Earl of Hardwicke to Philip Yorke, Viscount Royston, 28 August 1763, Add. Ms. 35,352, p. 413, BL.

157. Bristol, "Stuart and the Genesis of the Greek Revival" (1997): 256, citing the Diary of Thomas Hollis, 3 September 1759, Ms. Eng 1191, Houghton Library, Harvard University.

158. On his election to the Society of Antiquaries on 15 June 1758, Stuart gave his address as 7 Grosvenor Street. Minutebook, 15 June 1758, vol. 8, p. 107, Society of Antiquaries, Egerton Ms. 2381, BL. Stuart first appears in the rate books for the parish of Saint George, Hanover Square, in December 1758. His name is spelled "Stewart" by the recorder; Grosvenor Street ward, 19 December 1758, Poor, Highway and Scavenger rate books, vol. C333, p. 49, St. George, Hanover Square Parish Records, Westminster Archive Centre. Stuart is not registered in the previous volume, vol. C332, dated 11 April 1758. His final appearance in the rate books is in 1763: ibid., 18 April 1763, vol. C338, p. 49.

159. Ben Weinreb and Christopher Hibbert, eds., *The London Encyclopaedia* (London: Macmillan, 1983): 351. Weinreb and Hibbert do not give the full citation or the name of the author of this description of the street in 1735.

160. See F. H. W. Sheppard, ed., *Survey of London,* vol. 40, *The Grosvenor Estate in Mayfair,* pt. 2, *The Buildings* (London: Athlone Press for the Greater London Council, 1980): 35.

161. The ratable value of a property was a notional sum of money, supposed to reflect the amount of income that a landlord could expect to receive if he rented the house, minus expenses. See M. J. Daunton, "House-ownership from Rate Books," in *Urban History Yearbook, 1976* (Leicester: Leicester University Press, 1976): 21–27. For the Grosvenor Street rates for Stuart and his neighbors, see Grosvenor Street ward, 19 December 1758, Poor, Highway and Scavenger rate books, vol. C333, p. 49, St. George, Hanover Square Parish Records, Westminster Archive Centre. Stuart would later nominate Sir James Peachey's son John to the Royal Society, see Archive of the Royal Society, EC/1777/07; searchable database and facsimiles of nomination papers on website http://www.royalsoc.ac.uk/library/.

162. "James Stuart and Ann Taylor," 9 June 1760, Marriages 1760, no. 909, Parish of St. James, Piccadilly, Microfilm MF 31, Westminster Archives Centre. The characterization of Ann Taylor as his housekeeper comes from John Nichols, *Literary Anecdotes of the Eighteenth Century . . . ,* vol. 9 (London: Nichols Son and Bentey, 1817): 146.

163. A. H. [Highmore], "Further Particulars" (1788): 217.

164. James Stuart (Jr) Memoir, Add. Ms. 27,576, p. 100, BL.

165. Michael Gandy, *Catholic Missions and Registers, 1700–1880,* vol. 1, *London and the Home Counties* (London: Michael Gandy, 1993): iv.

166. "February 9 [1765] John Francis Stuart son of James & Ann born Decr. 28 [1764]," "The Register of Births and Baptisms in the Parish of St. James in Westminster in the County of Middlesex," 1 January 1761–30 June 1786, n.p., Parish of St. James, Piccadilly, Westminster Archives Centre.

167. Between 1763, when Stuart left Grosvenor Street, and 1767, when he moved to Leicester Fields, his address was in Hollis Street, in the parish of St. Clement Danes; however, no record of his death appears to survive in the records of any Westminster parish. Stuart did spend considerable periods of time in Bath in the 1760s: possibly his son died outside London.

168. Rockingham's house was at 4 Grosvenor Square. See Sheppard, ed., *Survey of London,* vol. 40, pt. 2 (1980): 121. James Adam refers in 1761 to "the M–s of R–me his only surviving patron" implying that the long delays in publishing *Antiquities of Athens* had reduced Stuart's patrons to this single one. James Adam to William Adam, 16 February 1761, Clerk of Penicuik Ms GD18 4886, National Archives of Scotland, Edinburgh.

169. Adam's office between January 1758 and 1772 was 75 Grosvenor Street (renumbered 76 in 1866). See Sheppard, ed., *Survey of London,* vol. 40, pt. 2 (1980): 56. For Stuart's home at 7 Grosvenor Street see ibid., 35. The numbering of the street is deceptive. Adam's office and Stuart's home were directly opposite each other, see folding map with house numbers in the back of F. H. W. Sheppard, ed., *Survey of London,* vol. 39, *The Grosvenor Estate in Mayfair,* pt. 1, *General History* (London: Athlone Press for the Greater London Council, 1977). For Adam's public praise of Stuart, see the preface to Robert Adam, *Works in Architecture of Robert and James Adam,* vol. 1 (London, 1773): vi, in which he mentions the "elegance and taste" of Stuart's work.

170. Eileen Harris suggests that Stuart's designs may have been intended for old Kedleston Hall, built by Smith of Warwick in 1700, rather than for the new house that was being built from 1759. See Eileen Harris, *The Genius of Robert Adam* (New Haven and London: Paul Mellon Centre and Yale University Press, 2001): 19.

171. Robert Adam to James Adam, 11 December 1758, Clerk of Penicuik Ms. GD 18 4854, National Archives of Scotland, Edinburgh.

172. "Glenivot," in James Adam to Jenny Adam, 2 July 1760, Clerk of Penicuik Ms. GD 18 4862, National Archives of Scotland, Edinburgh; "the Athenian" in James Adam to Betty Adam, 15 July 1760, GD 18 4864; and "Atica" in James Adam to Betty Adam, 25 November 1760, GD 18 4877. Others instances include "proud Grecian" and "Archipelagan Architect" in Robert Adam to James Adam, 11 December 1758, Ms. GD 18 4854; "Your adverse Greek" in James Adam to Robert Adam, 13 August 1760, GD 18 4867; "Your neighbour of Greece" and "Mr S–t" in James Adam to Betty Adam, 17 September 1760, GD 18 4872; "Gleniviot" in James Adam to William Adam, 19 December 1760, GD 18 4879; "Attica" in James Adam to his mother, 12 January 1761, GD 18 4882; "the Athenian" in James Adam to his mother, 16 February 1761, GD 18 4886; "Gleniviot" in James Adam to Peggy Adam, 11 April 1761, GD 18 4893; and "GlenIviot" etc. in James Adam to Peggy Adam,

27 October 1761, GD 18 4913.

173. James Adam to Peggy Adam, 27 October 1761, GD18 4913, ibid.

174. James Adam to Peggy Adam, 20 February 1762, GD18 4927. "Hinchliff" has been identified by David Watkin as John Hinchliffe, Fellow, later Master, of Trinity College Cambridge; see chap. 1 in this volume.

175. Cash, *Access to Museum Culture* (2002): 37, 40–41. Stuart used a similar phrase in *Antiquities of Athens* to describe a particular group of men whom he designated "men of curiosity and learning." See *Antiquities*, vol. 1 (1762): vi n. a.

176. Charles Pratt, first Earl Camden to Robert Stewart, first Marquess of Londonderry, 27 September 1778, Pratt U840 C4/6, Centre for Kentish Studies.

177. Nomination papers for John Ibbetson, EC/1769/09, Archive of the Royal Society; searchable database and facsimiles of nomination papers on website http://www.royalsoc.ac.uk/library/.

178. Taylor (attrib.), "Stuart papers," List of contents of papers acquired by Taylor, Add. Ms. 22,152. pp. 1–12, BL.

179. Rubens and Titian (ibid., 2); Geographical remarks (pp. 6v, 7v); celestial phenomena (pp. 4v, 6v); situation of Greek Women (p. 2); history of philosophy (p. 2); Egyptian hieroglyphics (pp. 4v, 6v); etymologies (p. 6v); poetry (p. 2); medals (p. 6v), mineral waters (p. 6v).

180. Stuart discusses the reception of the paper in a letter, Stuart to Thomas Anson, 17 June 1769, Lichfield Ms. D615/P (S)/1/6/26, Staffordshire Record Office, Stafford: "My dissertation on an egyptian hieroglyphic has met with applause from the Council of the royal society; & will I am told be printed next year." I am grateful to Kerry Bristol for a copy of her transcription of these letters.

181. Graves, *Society of Artists of Great Britain* (1907): 248. This work has not surfaced.

182. Stuart nominated Roger Joseph Boscovich, "Professor of Astronomy in the Roman College now on his travels in London . . . well qualified by his knowledge in Astronomy and other parts of natural Philosophy to be a useful Member" (EC 1760/16, Archive of the Royal Society). He also nominated Giuseppe Toaldo, "Professor of Astronomy in the University of Padua, is known to us, either personally, or by his correspondence, or by the learned works which he has published" (EC1777/11). Other nominees of Stuart's with an interest in astronomy were Alexander Aubert, "a gentleman versed in Astronomy and astronomical observations" (EC 1772/10); Captain James Cook, "a gentleman skilfull in astronomy, and the succesful conductor of two important voyages for the discovery of unknown countries, by which geography and natural history have been greatly advantaged and improved" (EC 1775/27); William Wales, "Master of the Royal Mathematical School in Christs Hospital. A Gentleman deeply skilled in Astronomy, and other branches of mathematical learning, and Author of a restitution of the lost books of Apollonius Pergaeus, concerning determinate Sections. Advantageously known to this Society by his observations, made by their order, [in] the years 1768 and 1769 in Hudsons Bay, on the transit of Venus etc. And since that time, by his appointment to accompany Captn Cook in his late voyage round the World" (EC 1776/18). Searchable database and facsimiles of nomina-

tion papers on website http://www.royalsoc.ac.uk/library/.

183. Stuart delivered his account of silk production on the island of Andros to the Society for the Promotion of Arts, Manufactures and Commerce (SPAC) in August 1756; Minutes of the Society, vol. 1, 4 August and 18 August 1756, RSA. See Bristol, "Stuart and the Genesis of the Greek Revival" (1997): 178; Stuart's letter to the society about silk production, 18 August 1756, PR.GE/110/2/124, RSA. For verdigris see Minutes of the Society, vol. 16 February 1757; and Committee minutes, vol. 121 March 1760, RSA. See Bristol, "Stuart and the Genesis of the Greek Revival" (1997): 180. For antiquarian matters see H. A., "Traits" (1788): 96, where he is described as "an adept in all the remote researches of an antiquary."

184. Stuart mentioned his correspondence with Nulty about a soup called "Gobbi" in Stuart to Anson, undated, Lichfield Ms. D615/P (S)/1/6/9, Staffordshire Record Office, Stafford.

185. Mrs. Montagu to Lord Lyttelton, 15 January 1760, Montagu Papers, MO 1394, Henry E. Huntington Library, San Marino, CA, cited in Bristol, "Stuart and the Genesis of the Greek Revival" (1997): 159.

186. Stuart to Anson, 25 September 1770, Lichfield Ms. D615/P (S)/1/6/28, Staffordshire Record Office, Stafford; Stuart to Anson [June/July 1764], D615/P (S)/1/6/8A.

187. See Lawrence, "Stuart and Revett" (1938–39): 131, 133–34.

188. *Antiquities*, vol. 1 (1762): viii.

189. Lawrence, "Stuart and Revett" (1938–39): 133–34.

190. William Hogarth, *The Five Orders of Perriwigs*, Guildhall Library Print Room, Hogarth Collection loc. 64, no. p543527x.

191. See Bristol, "Stuart and the Genesis of the Greek Revival" (1997): 172.

192. For the Dilettanti see Lionel Cust and Sir Sidney Colvin, *History of the Society of Dilettanti* (London: Macmillan and Co., 1914).

193. Horace Walpole's remarks are quoted in Kerry Bristol, "The Society of Dilettanti, James 'Athenian' Stuart and the Anson family," *Apollo* 152 (August 2000): 46.

194. James Adam to Jenny Adam, 2 July 1760, Clerk of Penicuik Ms. GD 18 4862, National Archives of Scotland, Edinburgh.

195. Bristol, "Stuart and the Genesis of the Greek Revival" (1997): 160–61.

196. "The Admiralty have given me a job that I do not thank them for, the old Passes for the Mediterranean are to be annulled, & I must design the new ones, there are two of them, & what is worse I must next week survey Stangate Creek for the Lazzaretto," Stuart to Anson, 4 September 1764, Lichfield Ms. D615/P(S)/1/6/12, Staffordshire Record Office, Stafford; "I have been obliged to make another drawing of a lazaretto for Lord Egmont . . . I foresee much trouble in that affair whether I engage in the building of it or no. . . . the Admiralty seem to think they have a right to me," Stuart to Anson, ca. September 1764, D615/P(S)/1/6/13.

197. Stuart to Anson, [October or November 1764], Lichfield Ms. D615/P(S)/1/6/16), Staffordshire Record Office, Stafford.

198. Simon, first Earl Harcourt to Rockingham, 4 February 1758, Wentworth Woodhouse Muniments WWM R1-116, Sheffield

Archives. In this letter, Harcourt was attempting to persuade Rockingham "use your interest with Mr. Finch, that Stuart may succeed Mr Wright, as Clerk of the Works at Hampton Court."

199. Stuart's obituarist remarks wrote that "if he could be charged with possessing any partiality, it was to Merit in whomsoever he found it"; H. A., "Traits" (1788): 96.

200. Bristol, "Stuart and the Genesis of the Greek Revival" (1997): 132 n. 376.

201. Robert Adam to James Adam, 25 June 1758, Clerk of Penicuik Ms. GD 18 4850, National Archives of Scotland, Edinburgh.

202. For example see a letter from Thomas Pingo to the SPAC regarding a contract to cut dies for a medal, and Stuart's proposal of Pingo for the contract, 6 July 1758, AD/MA/100/10/406, RSA. See also Christopher Eimer, The Pingo Family and Medal Making in 18th Century Britain (London: British Art Medal Trust, 1998): 21, 25.

203. Stuart to Anson, 17 June 1769, Lichfield Ms. D615/P (S)/1/6/26, Staffordshire Record Office, Stafford; see also Stuart to Anson, 27 May 1769, D615/P (S)1/6/24.

204. The Serjeant-Painter had overall responsibility for painting work connected with the royal palaces, including paintwork to royal barges, coaches, stables etc. Stuart's average annual payment was around £780, of which he would have retained a profit of about £19 per year after his workmen and his deputy had been paid. The post was abolished in July 1782, although Stuart was allowed to retain the salary until his death in 1788. I am grateful to Kerry Bristol for this information. See also Howard Colvin, ed., The History of the King's Works (London: HMSO, 1976): 111.

205. Stuart to Anson, [October or November 1764], Lichfield Ms. D615/P(S)/1/6/16), Staffordshire Record Office, Stafford.

206. Bristol, "Stuart and the Genesis of the Greek Revival" (1997): 200–201.

207. Stuart to Anson, [October or November 1764], Lichfield Ms. D615/P(S)/1/6/18), Staffordshire Record Office, Stafford.

208. See Bristol, "Stuart and the Genesis of the Greek Revival" (1997): 201–3.

209. Mrs. Montagu to Leonard Smelt, 26 April 1780, Montagu Papers, MO 5026, Henry E. Huntington Library, San Marino, CA, cited in Bristol, "22 Portman Square" (2001): 79.

210. Simon, first Earl Harcourt to Rockingham, 4 February 1758, Wentworth Woodhouse Muniments WWM R1-116, Sheffield Archives.

211. James Stuart (Jr.) Memoir, Add. Ms. 27,576, p. 61, BL; Antiquities, vol. 4 (1816): xxiv.

212. Stuart to Anson, 19 December 1764, Lichfield Ms. D615/P(S)/1/6/20, Staffordshire Record Office, Stafford.

213. Stuart to Wilkes, 10 June 1766 (received 24 July 1766), and 24 June 1766 (received 15 August 1766), Correspondence and papers of John Wilkes, M.P., Add. Ms. 30869, pp. 43, 46, 59, 67, BL.

214. See Marjie Bloy, "The Age of George III: John Wilkes (1725–1798)," A Web of English History, at http://ds.dial.pipex.com/town/terrace/adw03/c-eight/people/wilkes.htm. Accessed 17 September 2004. (Site to be moved to http://www.historyhome.co.uk).

215. For remarks about Leicester Fields in the eighteenth century, see George Augustus Sala, ed., Gaslight and Daylight, with some London scenes they shine upon (London: Chapman and Hall, 1859): 176.

216. Weinreb and Hibbert, eds., London Encyclopaedia (1983): 464–65.

217. Sala, ed., Gaslight and Daylight (1859): 176.

218. Weinreb and Hibbert, eds., London Encyclopaedia (1983): 794.

219. For an eyewitness description of the mob in Leicester Fields and the looting of Savile house see Susan Burney to Fanny Burney, 8 June 1780, "Letter Extract 2: The Gordon Riots, St. Martin's Lane, London, 8 June 1780," Susan Burney Letters Project, Humanities Research Centre, University of Nottingham, http://www.nottingham.ac.uk/hrc/projects/burney/letters/gordon.phtml. Accessed 15 July 2004).

220. Ibid.

221. Weinreb and Hibbert, eds., London Encyclopaedia (1983): 794.

222. For Reynolds purchase of the lease and the cost, see Derek B. Hudson, Sir Joshua Reynolds, A Personal Study . . . (London: Geoffrey Bles, 1958): 73.

223. Ibid.

224. Smith, Nollekens and His Times (1949): 19–20.

225. Ibid., 19.

226. Mrs. Montagu to Leonard Smelt, 25 April 1780, Montagu papers, MO 5025, Henry E. Huntington Library, San Marino, CA, cited in Bristol, "Stuart and the Genesis of the Greek Revival" (1997): 322.

227. "Catalogue of pictures by Moreland . . . and other effects, of the late James Stuart . . . ," sale cat., Greenwoods, London, 27 June 1791, p. 3, lots 7, 15, 16, 17, copy in Courtauld Institute Library, Br A 5059 1791/06/27.

228. For the plaster figures and molds, ibid., 4, lot 18. For the 1764 purchase see Stuart to Anson, 19 December 1764, Lichfield Ms. D615/P(S)/1/6/20, Staffordshire Record Office, Stafford.

229. According to Stephen Astley, Curator of Drawings, Soane's Museum, in the earliest inventory of Soane's collection, completed in 1837 (the year of the founder's death), this box is listed as "2 brass measures in a Box, which formerly belonged to Athenian Stuart and Revett." The box is now empty and is identified as that listed from the inscription added to it by Joseph Bonomi (curator, 1861–76).

230. Smith, Nollekens and His Times (1949): 20.

231. See for example Poor Rate F6018, 8 June 1768, Microfilm 1889, Rate Books, Poor Rates, St. Martin in the Fields Parish Records, Westminster Archives Centre. Stuart's house appears on p. 29, Jane Hogarth on p. 40. Her rateable value was £40 to his £28.

232. Register of Marriages, 21 August 1778, St. Martin in the Fields Parish Records, Microfilm MF 42, no.21, p. 106, Westminster Archives Centre. For Stuart's interment, see A. H. [Highmore], "Further Particulars" (1788): 217.

233. The Burney family moved to Sir Isaac Newton's former house, 35 St. Martin's Street, in 1774; see Kate Chisholm, Fanny Burney: Her Life, 1752–1840 (London: Chatto and Windus, 1998): 36.

234. For pallbearers see "On Saturday morning . . . ," *Times,* London (12 February 1788): 3. For the education of Stuart's children, see A. H. [Highmore], "Further Particulars" (1788): 217.

235. "Catalogue of pictures by Moreland . . . and other effects, of the late James Stuart . . . ," sale cat., Greenwoods, London, 27 June 1791, pp. 1, 6, lot 48, copy in Courtauld Institute Library, Br A 5059 1791/06/27. George Pether (fl. 1775–94), London piano and harpsichord maker, had a shop at 16 John Street and 61 Oxford Street; See Martha Novak Clinkscale, *Makers of the Piano,* vol. 1 (Oxford University Press, 1993): 216.

236. See Michael J. Cole, *The Pianoforte in the Classical Era* (Oxford: Clarendon Press, 1998): 116–17.

237. Gandon, *Life of James Gandon* (1846): 198.

238. John Thomas Smith, *A Book for a Rainy Day: or, Recollections of the Events of the Last Sixty-six Years* (London: Richard Bentley, 1845): 88–90; Smith, *Nollekens and His Times* (1949): 20.

239. John Thomas Smith recorded the names of some of the habitués of the Feathers: "For many years the back parlour of 'The Feathers' public-house, which stood on the side of Leicester Fields, had been frequented by artists, and several well known amateurs. Among the former were Stuart, the Athenian traveller; Scott, the marine painter; old Oram, of the Board of Works; Luke Sullivan, the miniature painter, who engraved that inimitable print from Hogarth's picture of the March to Finchley, now in the Foundling Hospital; Captain Grosse, the author of 'Antiquities of England,' 'History of Armour,' &c.; Mr Hearne, the elegant and correct draughtsman of many of England's Antiquities; Nathaniel Smith, my father, &c. The amateurs were Henderson, the actor; Mr. Morris, a silver-smith; Mr. John Ireland, then a watch-maker in Maiden Lane, and since editor of Boydell's edition of Dr. Trusler's work, 'Hogarth Moralized;' and Mr. Baker, of St. Paul's Church-yard, whose collection of Bartolozzi's works was unequalled"; Smith, *Book for a Rainy Day* (1845): 88–90.

240. Stuart to John Wilkes, 10 June 1766, Correspondence and papers of John Wilkes, M.P., Add. Ms. 30869, p. 43, BL.

241. A. H. [Highmore], "Further Particulars" (1788): 217.

242. Bristol, "Stuart and the Genesis of the Greek Revival" (1997): 173. Stuart's membership began on 16 June 1756. He nominated Reynolds on the 18 June.

243. See, e.g., Gilbert Stuart's portrait of William Woollett at work on his engraving of West's *Death of General Wolfe.* The location of the original is not known to me, but a reproduction appears as the frontispiece of Whitley, *Artists and their Friends* (1928). See also William Hogarth, *Self portrait with Pug Dog,* 1745, oil on canvas, Tate Gallery, London, UK.

244. Smith, *Nollekens and His Times* (1949): 20.

245. Stuart to Philip Yorke, second Earl of Hardwicke, 10 January 1766, Add. Ms. 35,607 f. 233, BL.

246. "Other news I heard none yesterday except that Stuart has got the gout . . . ," Lord Villiers to Lady Spencer, 4 May 1763, cited in John Spencer, seventh Earl, "Spencer House—II: St. James's Place, The Residence of Earl Spencer," *Country Life* 60 (6 November 1926): 703.

247. Stuart to Anson, 1 September 1764, Lichfield Ms. D615/P (S)/1/6/11, Staffordshire Record Office, Stafford.

248. Stuart to Anson, 18 September 1764, ibid., D615/P(S)/1/6/14.

249. Letters survive from Stuart to Philip Yorke, second Earl of Hardwicke, addressed from Bath. Stuart to Hardwicke, 10 January 1766 (p. 228); and Stuart to Hardwicke, 27 January 1766 (p. 233), Add. Ms. 35,607, BL. In the letter of 27 January Stuart wrote: "Notwithstanding the injunction of my friend Jones who prescribes absolute Idleness to me, I have bestowed some thoughts on your Lordships building. . . ." Jones is likely to be the Dr. Jones of Bath with whom Stuart had corresponded from Italy in 1742; see Taylor (attrib.), notes dated 21 June 1808, Add. Ms. 22,152, p. 19v, BL.

250. Stuart to Anson, 17 September 1766, Lichfield Ms. D615/P (S)/1/6/21, Staffordshire Record Office, Stafford.

251. Mrs. Montagu to Leonard Smelt, 3 November 1767, Montagu Papers, MO 4994, Henry E. Huntington Library, San Marino, CA, cited in Kerry Bristol, "The Painted Rooms of 'Athenian' Stuart," *Georgian Group Journal* 10 (2000): 169.

252. Stuart to Anson, 25 September 1770, Lichfield Ms. D615/P (S)/1/6/28, Staffordshire Record Office, Stafford.

253. *Antiquities,* vol. 2 (ca. 1790): iii.

254. Stuart to Philip Yorke, second Earl of Hardwicke, 29 August 1783, Add. Ms. 35621, p. 7, BL.

255. James Stuart (Jr.) Memoir, pp. 52–53, Add. Ms. 27,576, BL; *Antiquities,* vol. 4 (1816): xxiii.

256. Mrs. Montagu to Lord Lyttelton, [15 July 1762], Montagu Papers, MO 1414, Henry E. Huntington Library, San Marino, CA, cited in Bristol, "Stuart and the Genesis of the Greek Revival" (1997): 159.

257. Stuart "was in the constant habit of playing at Skittles in the summer afternoons with Caldwell and 2 other friends, after which he constantly went to a Public house to spend the Even. Which C would not do"; Taylor (attrib.), notes of a conversation with Andrew Caldwell, 20 June 1808, Add. Ms. 22,152, pp. 18v–19, BL.

258. Stuart's letter accepting the office of chairman of the Committee of Polite Arts, 27 March 1761, PR.AR/103/10/318. RSA. For Stuart failing to take an equal share in the work of the committee, see Minutes of the Society, vol. 7, 25 November 1761, RSA.

259. Bristol, "Painted Rooms of Athenian Stuart" (2000): 167.

260. Mrs. Montagu to Lord Lyttelton, [15 July 1762], Montagu Papers, MO 1414, Henry E. Huntington Library, San Marino, CA, cited in Bristol, "Stuart and the Genesis of the Greek Revival" (1997): 159.

261. "Mr Steward came here today, & has finish'd yr room," Edward Montagu to Mrs. Montagu, 21 June 1772, Add. Ms. 40,663. p.31, BL.

262. Lord Villiers to Lady Spencer, November 1765, cited in Spencer, "Spencer House—II" (1926): 700.

263. See Bristol, "Stuart and the Genesis of the Greek Revival" (1997): 342, citing ADM 67/12, pp. 46–48, NA.

264. H. A., "Traits" (1788): 96.

265. Taylor (attrib.), "Stuart papers." List of contents of papers acquired by Taylor, Add. Ms. 22,152, pp. 1–12, BL.

266. William Richard Hamilton, *Historical Notices of the Society of Dilettanti* (London: n.p., 1855): 64.

267. Ibid., 65, 105. Stuart was prompted to complete the work in May 1766 and again in January 1768.

268. According to Kerry Bristol (personal communication, 15 December 2005), a gouache portrait by Stuart of James Dawkins is still in the possession of his brother Henry's descendants. The portrait engraved by James McArdell must have been complete before 1765, the year of McArdell's death. In March 1769 Joshua Reynolds was offered the post of Painter to the Society of Dilettanti and accepted; see Minutes, vol. 3, 6 February and 1 May 1763, April and May 1766, 17 January 1768, 5 March 1769, archive of the Society of Dilettanti, Society of Antiquaries, London; Hamilton, *Historical Notices of the Society of Dilettanti* (1855): 64–65; Cust and Colvin, *History of the Society of Dilettanti* (1914): 220–21.

269. Register of Chapter Acts 1748–1773, VI.B.7 483 (447), entry for 12 June 1771, St. George's Chapel Archives, Windsor. There is also an entry for expenses made on the same day that reads, "To Mr. Stuart for his Plan for the Altar & East Window 50..0..0," Audit Book 1767 to 1772, XII.B.8, entry for 12 July 1771.

270. James L. Clifford, *Hester Lynch Piozzi (Mrs. Thrale)* (Oxford, Clarendon Press, 1941): 439.

271. Lord Villiers to Lady Spencer, November 1765, cited in Spencer, "Spencer House—II" (1926): 700.

272. Mrs. Montagu to Leonard Smelt, 26 April [1780], Montagu Papers, MO 5026, Henry E. Huntington Library, San Marino, CA, reprinted in Reginald Blunt, ed., *Mrs. Montagu, "Queen of the Blues," Her Letters and Friendships from 1762 to 1800*, vol. 2 (Boston and New York: Houghton Mifflin, 1923): 83.

273. Mrs. Montagu to Leonard Smelt, 25 April 1780. Montagu Papers, MO 5025, Henry E. Huntington Library, San Marino, CA, cited in Bristol, "Stuart and the Genesis of the Greek Revival" (1997): 322.

274. Mrs. Montagu to Leonard Smelt, 25 April 1780, Montagu Papers, MO 5025, Henry E. Huntington Library, San Marino, CA, cited in Bristol, "22 Portman Square" (2001): 79.

275. Mrs. Montagu to Matthew Boulton, August [1780], Matthew Boulton Papers, Box 330 no. 27. Birmingham City Archives, cited in Bristol, "22 Portman Square" (2001): 76.

276. Mrs. Montagu to Matthew Boulton, 28 September 1780, Matthew Boulton Papers, Box 330, no. 33, Birmingham City Archives, cited in Bristol, "22 Portman Square" (2001): 77.

277. Mrs. Montagu to Leonard Smelt, 26 April [1780], Montagu Papers, MO 5026, Henry E. Huntington Library, San Marino, CA, reprinted in Blunt, ed., *Mrs. Montagu* (1923): 83.

278. A. H. [Highmore], "Further Particulars" (1788): 217.

279. Ibid.

280. Rudé, *Hanoverian London* (2003): 70.

281. Roger Shanhagan, *The Exhibition, or a Second Anticipation, being Remarks on the principal Works to be Exhibited next Month at the Royal Academy* (London: Richardson and Urquhart, 1779): 70.

282. Register of Marriages, 21 August 1778, Microfilm MF 42, no. 21, p. 106, St. Martin in the Fields Parish Records, Westminster Archives Centre.

283. "James Stuart and Elizabeth Blacland a Minor. Both of this Parish by and with the Consent of George Blacland the natural and lawful Father of the said Minor were Married in this Church. . . . ," ibid.

284. A. H. [Highmore], "Further Particulars" (1788): 217.

285. Taylor (attrib.), notes dated 20 June 1808, Add. Ms. 22,152, p. 18v, BL.

286. H. A., "Traits" (1788): 96.

287. Ibid.

288. Camden to Londonderry, 27 September 1778, Pratt U840 C4/6, Centre for Kentish Studies.

289. James Stuart (Jr.) Memoir, p. 10, Add. Ms. 27,576, BL. Stuart Jr. gave these to the National Gallery in November 1858.

290. Mrs. Montagu to Leonard Smelt, 26 April [1780], Montagu Papers, MO 5026, Henry E. Huntington Library, San Marino, CA, reprinted in Blunt, ed., *Mrs. Montagu* (1923): 83.

291. Frances Charlotte Stuart was christened 5 November 1779. Elizabeth Ann was christened 24 July 1783, both at St. Martin in the Fields. This information from Family Search, International Genealogical Index, Church of Jesus Christ of Latter Day Saints, at http://www.familysearch.org. Frances Charlotte's date of death is unknown, but according to James Stuart Jr., she "died of a decline" as a young girl. James Stuart (Jr.) Memoir, p. 64, Add. Ms. 27,576, BL. Elizabeth Ann died in 1832. Her will was proved 21 July 1832. The gouaches had been owned by Dutch merchant Sir Matthew Decker, who kept them in a specially designed "Study, commonly called 'the Athenian Room'" at his house on Richmond Green, London. Decker's heir was his son-in-law Richard, sixth Viscount Fitzwilliam, whose effects would later form the core of the Fitzwilliam Museum in Cambridge. In 1816 the house and contents passed to Viscount Fitzwilliam's cousin, the eleventh Earl of Pembroke, who sold the gouaches by auction. See "Pembroke House: A catalogue of the valuable effects of the above distinguished residence . . . ," sale cat., Squibb and Son, Richmond Green, Surrey, London, 12–21 May 1823. See especially the second day's sale, 13 May, in which the contents of a "Study, commonly called 'The Athenian Room'" were sold, pp. 11–12, lots 5–24. Among the contents of the room were fifteen gouaches by Stuart which were sold to Jeremiah Harman. After Harman's death, the gouaches passed to his wife Mary, who then bequeathed them to her nephew Thomas Howard of Blackheath. In 1873, his executors presented them to the RIBA where they remain today. For the Harman/Howard family relationships, see Elizabeth Howard, "Fragments of Family History," 21 November 1862, *Lord Meade's Budget*, http://www.lordsmeade.freeserve.co.uk/elizhoward-fragments.rtf. Accessed 29 August 2004.

292. For John George Hardinge Stuart's death, see James Stuart (Jr.) Memoir, p. 64, Add. Ms. 27,576, BL. James Stuart Jr. died at his home, 11 Globe Terrace, Stratford, Essex, on 6 September 1867. His will was proved 2 October 1867.

293. A. H. [Highmore], "Further Particulars" (1788): 217.

294. James Stuart (Jr) Memoir, p. 103, Add. Ms. 27,576, BL.

295. *Antiquities*, vol. 2 (ca. 1790): 111.

296. Elizabeth was sworn to administer the estate on 18 February 1788; Wills and Administrations 1788, PROB 6/180, NA.

297. Papps v. Bayne, C 12/1759/6, NA.

298. James Stuart (Jr.) Memoir, pp. 9–10, Add. Ms. 27,576, BL.

299. Papps v. Bayne, C 12/1759/6, NA.

300. Wills and Administrations, PROB 11/1333/805, NA; see also PROB 6/180.

301. "I think Mr Stuart's Annuity must have been settled. it always used to be paid D[dra]ft as near L[ad]y day as possible & as he died in Febry 1788 nothing cou'd have prevented its being paid up to that time, unless from the confused state of Mr Stuarts affairs, it coud not be known who to pay it to with safety . . . they ought to have made their claim for what they thought due of the Ann[ui]ty at a proper time & not have deferred it for so many years, as to lose all right to it. . . . I have a notion the Widow was an odd sort of body & think otherways this wou'd not have been left to rest for 9 years without application," letter dated 14 August 1797, Lichfield Ms., D615/P(S)/2/3, Staffordshire Record Office, Stafford. The letter is addressed from Nuneham, but the writer and addressee are unknown.

302. "Athens Stuart, unexpectedly . . . ," World, no. 359 (22 February 1788): 3. It may be a coincidence that one of the largest landowners in Marylebone at this time was the widow of Stuart's old patron Jacob Hinde; Original Acts HL/PO/PB/1/1776/16G3n118, Private Bill Office, House of Lords Record Office.

303. Wills and Administrations (1804), PROB 6/180, NA. Elizabeth Stuart's will is PROB 11/1333/805. She died in 1799 at the age of thirty-eight. See Bristol, "Stuart and the Genesis of the Greek Revival" (1997): 19.

304. H.A., "Traits" (1788): 96.

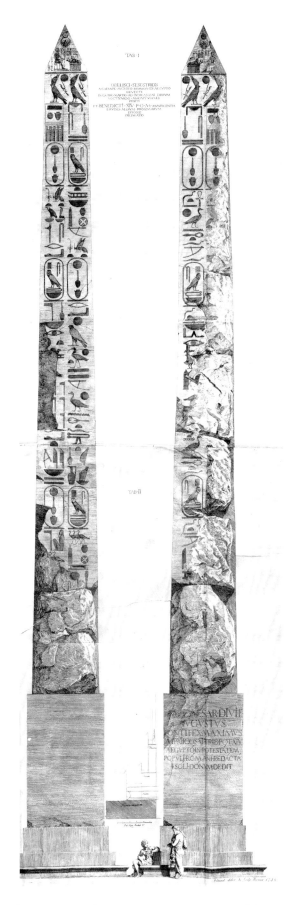

Fig. 3-1. Elevations of the Obelisk of Psammetichus II, 1749. Etching. From James Stuart, *De Obelisco Caesaris Augusti e Campo Martio nuperrime effosso epistola Jacobi Stuart Angli ad Carolam Wentworth Comitem de Malton . . .* (1750): tab. 1. By permission of The British Library, London, 140.h.18. *Checklist no. 9.*

CHAPTER 3

STUART AS ANTIQUARY

AND ARCHAEOLOGIST

IN ITALY AND GREECE

FRANK SALMON

When James Stuart arrived in Italy in the 1740s, evidently traveling on foot, he did so as a humble student of decorative painting. A decade or so later he returned to London as a Fellow of the Society of Dilettanti, with a status that firmly associated him with leading British aristocrats of the day. On his arrival back in England late in 1754 or early in 1755, Stuart's standing depended (as it does largely now) on the scholarly archaeological work he was known to have undertaken in Greece, especially in the city of Athens from which he was to take his sobriquet. However, it was the more fluid world of Grand Tour Italy that had made this dramatic transformation possible, as is indicated by the fact that his election to the Society of Dilettanti had taken place before he even set eyes on Athens.[1] The evidence for Stuart's activities in Italy is, sadly, sparse, although recent discoveries have shed significant new light on this vital early phase of his career. One such discovery has been that of a letter written by Stuart in Florence on March 26, 1746, from which it emerges that he was being maintained in Tuscany in the mid-1740s by a London gentleman named Jacob Hinde and was working as a painter of subject pictures, reproduc-

tive engraver, and fine art expert (or "antiquary," in contemporary terms) for British Grand Tourists.[2] Another hitherto underestimated element in the pre-Grecian phase of Stuart's life is his involvement with the Obelisk of Pharaoh Psammetichus II in Rome (fig. 3-1), which had been brought from Egypt in antiquity and now stands in Piazza Montecitorio in front of the Italian Parliament building. The excavation of this monument in 1748 and subsequent publication of a book about it in 1750, *De Obelisco Caesaris Augusti,* have gone largely unstudied by historians of British antiquarianism or architecture, although Stuart's contribution has been recognized by modern obelisk scholars, one calling it "in a modest way, a landmark in the history of archaeology due to the perspicacity and the methodical instinct of James Stuart."[3] Stuart's formative years in Florence and especially in Rome, then, offer a key to our understanding of his later and more widely recognized work on the monuments of Athens. Moreover, after leaving Rome and prior to arriving in Greece, Stuart and his collaborator Nicholas Revett spent some months studying the Roman architectural remains at the town of Pola in Istria. Although the drawings and notes they produced there were not published until 1816, well after the deaths of both, the studies made at Pola helped establish a *modus operandi* for their subsequent work at Athens and thus also merit some further examination.

Stuart's 1746 letter to Hinde not only reveals the nature of his activities and that he was living in Florence, but also provides a new *terminus a quo* for his presence in Italy. This has previously been given as 1741 or 1742, on the basis of the preface to the first volume of his and Revett's *Antiquities of Athens*, in which Stuart wrote that he had "first drawn up a brief account, of our motives for undertaking this Work" toward the end of 1748 "at Rome, where we had already employed 6 or 7 years in the study of Painting."[4] While the 1746 letter confirms that it was indeed painting that had preoccupied Stuart up until 1748, it also demonstrates that, contrary to the implication of the preface, he had not been living continuously in Rome since the early 1740s.[5] The fact that he was receiving regular quarterly payments from Hinde through the merchant Haughton Wills at Leghorn indicates that Stuart was resident in Tuscany rather than merely passing through. Perhaps, in writing what he did in the preface, Stuart was seeking to suppress the activities he had engaged in earlier in his Italian career, in order to suggest that he had greater familiarity with Rome, as the undoubted capital of European antiquarianism, than was really the case. Or perhaps the use of the plural first person pronoun in the preface may be taken to be ambiguous, in which case the arrival date in Rome of 1742 or 1741 could have been Revett's rather than Stuart's own (Revett definitely had arrived in Rome late in 1742).[6] Such an interpretation would also explain Stuart's lack of precision for a date that might otherwise be thought to have been memorable. This dilemma notwithstanding, Stuart was surely in Italy prior to 1746. The Irish painter-turned-antiquarian Matthew Nulty reported, albeit much later, that he and Stuart had traveled "through a great Variety of Scenes together" in Venice and other cities working as fan painters.[7] Given that Stuart had arrived in Italy with some experience and expertise in fan decorating, this itinerant episode probably came at the start of his Italian years, before his appearance in Florence where he was painting on a grander scale.

If Stuart appeared in Italy prior to his presence in Florence in the spring of 1746, then the first documented instance could be the reference to a Briton named "Giacomo Stuard" in the 1744 annual Roman Eastertide *Stato dell'Anime* census, where he is listed as sharing accommodation in the house of one Signor Taccagni with fellow countryman James Paston ("Giacomo Paston").

Paston is recorded as still resident at this address in 1745, 1746, and 1747, but not Stuart, who would have moved to Florence by 1746.[8] In fact it is possible that Stuart left Rome around Easter 1745, since in May of that year George Edgcumbe, captain of HMS *Kennington*, reported to Horace Mann (the British Resident in Florence) that he had carried a painter by the name of Stuart as a passenger along the Tuscan coastline and that this Stuart had been a friend of the Old Pretender.[9] That Stuart was known as a Catholic when in Italy is clear from the Roman *Stato dell'Anime* censuses of 1748 – 50 where this is recorded.[10] If he harbored distinct Jacobite sympathies, however, then they were not deemed serious by Mann, whose dispatches in 1745 and 1746 comment on those upon whom suspicion was falling and contain frequent references to a man with similar antiquarian interests to Stuart's, John Bouverie (later a companion of Robert Wood and James Dawkins in their 1750 expedition to the Levant).[11] Stuart's position as an artist, as opposed to a gentleman like Bouverie, meant that his political views would have been held to be of less consequence. Moreover, his Catholicism does not seem to have been a significant factor in his career after his return to England, where he was certainly regarded as a Protestant after his death if not before.[12] It seems possible that in these early years Catholicism was more a *religion de convenance,* adopted by a man of Scottish descent with an appropriate name, and deployed in the context of a country where the label *eretico* could be an impediment to the antiquarian career that Stuart — like his initial artistic companion, Nulty — had determined to develop.

Stuart in Florence

The letter to Hinde also shows that in 1746 Stuart had painted a subject picture for his patron and addressee Jacob Hinde, which had led to the commissioning of two more from John Ashburnham, second Earl of Ashburnham, a Grand Tourist then in Florence. It emerges that Lord Ashburnham's tutor, Edward Clarke, had employed Stuart to travel to Bologna in order to examine some drawings that Clarke was considering purchasing. Notwithstanding the lack of references to him in Mann's correspondence, it is extremely likely that Stuart moved in the Resident's circle when in Florence, since he had arrived with a letter of introduction to Mann from Hinde. This connection will have given him ready access to travelers of altogether higher social standing, such as Clarke and Lord Ashburn-

Fig. 3-2. James Stuart. Saint Andrew on the Way to Martyrdom, 1746. Etching. The margins are inscribed with a letter from Stuart to Jacob Hinde, 20 March 1746. Courtesy of The Beinecke Rare Book and Manuscript Library, Yale University, New Haven, OSB fc 144. *Checklist no. 4.*

ham. It is possible, however, that the paths of Stuart and Ashburnham had already crossed in Venice, since Ashburnham had been proposed for the Society of Dilettanti the previous year by James Gray — later Stuart's own proposer. (Clarke had been elected to the Dilettanti much earlier, by 1736.) From the point of view of Stuart's later career, a more important connection than the one he made with a traveling British aristocrat was the intimacy

with British painter and collector Ignazio Hugford, an association suggested in his letter to Hinde. The etching of a scene showing the martyrdom of Saint Andrew, on the margins of which Stuart wrote to Hinde, represented a drawing that was in Hugford's collection and has been attributed to Niccolò Circignani, called "Il Pomarancio" (fig. 3-2).[13]

Hugford was a key figure in the history of Anglo-

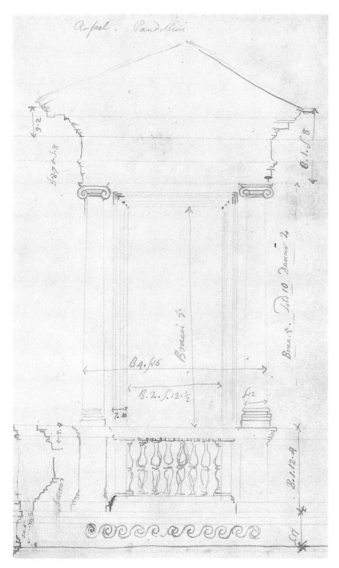

Fig. 3-3. James Stuart. Measured study of a first-floor window of the Palazzo Pandolfini, Florence, Italy, ca. 1746–50. Pen and ink, pencil. RIBA Library Drawings Collection, London, SD 62/21. *Checklist no. 5.*

Florentine cultural relations across the middle of the eighteenth century. Of British parentage, he had trained as a painter specializing in religious subjects and copies, and he also collected and dealt in paintings, prints, and drawings. In the mid-1740s Hugford was preoccupied with painting commissions at Vallombrosa and Badia a Passignano, but his home in Florence was in Via de' Bardi, near Mann's Casa Ambrogi guesthouse and thus in a good position for encounters with British visitors.[14] This was the period when the collection of Francesco Maria Niccolò Gabburri, a Florentine nobleman, diplomat, and connoisseur during

the Grand Dukedom of Gian Gastone de' Medici and the following Regency of the Lorraine Count Emanuel Richecourt, was being dispersed (after his death in 1742). Hugford made important acquisitions from Gabburri's collection, which advanced his standing and skills as a dealer. That Stuart was allowed to make prints of items in Hugford's possession, such as the Pomarancio drawing, for the purpose of sending to his patron as an example of his developing technical skill, suggests a considerable degree of familiarity between the two men. In addition, Stuart's own commission to examine drawings on behalf of Clarke gives evidence of his growing talent as a connoisseur of central Italian Renaissance art, which may well be linked to the tutelage of Hugford.

What is perhaps surprising about Stuart's time in Florence, however, is the lack of any evidence that he participated in the common activity of copying pictures in the Uffizi collection, an important means through which students of painting sought to teach themselves while at the same time hoping to profit through sale of their copies.[15] It is possible that Stuart studied at the Accademia del Disegno, of which Hugford had been a painter-member since 1729, but Hugford's rise to prominence in that institution and with it the number of British who were elected as *Accademici di Merito* did not begin until 1749 (with William Chambers being his first nominee in 1753).[16] It is therefore no surprise that Stuart's name is not to be found among the academy's lists of members, even if his status as an artist had been high enough in 1746. Another moot point about Stuart's time in Florence concerns the question of whether or not his interests in architecture had already begun. The measured study of one *piano nobile* window of Raphael's Palazzo Pandolfini from his sketchbook may be dated to the Florentine period of Stuart's time in Italy because it appears to be the work of a student at a relatively early stage of an architectural career (fig. 3-3). The measurements are given in the Florentine unit of the *braccia* and its subdivisions. Later, Stuart generally measured in the English foot, so in this case the supervisory presence of a local architect may be inferred. The horizontal and vertical elements were ruled in while Stuart was standing on the ground, while the ink profiles and details were added freehand, doubtless from a position on a ladder — a common enough procedure with both modern and ancient buildings in the middle of the eighteenth century. However, a contemporary of Stuart's, probably Anthony Highmore, commented in an

Fig. 3-4. James Stuart. The Finding of Moses, 1747. Etching with aquatint. Istituto Nazionale per la Grafica, Rome, FC 67258.

obituary that Stuart's turn to architecture had occurred later, under the influence of Revett — which might suggest, therefore, that this conversion took place in Rome and that figure 3-3 belongs to a subsequent visit to Florence.[17] What can be said is that, when resident in Florence in the mid-1740s, Stuart was able to paint on a scale grand enough to attract the patronage of a Grand Tourist such as Lord Ashburnham. This development may reflect his proximity to Hugford, as might the considerable competence Stuart showed as a printmaker, using the soft linear technique of etching to reproduce Renaissance drawings (a technique he is unlikely to have acquired earlier, when studying engraving as a pupil of Joseph or Louis Goupy in London; see chap. 2). From the point of view of Stuart's developing career, however, more important still were the growing skills of connoisseurship and perhaps even of scholarship that led a longstanding member of the Society of Dilettanti such as Edward Clarke to lean on his judgment.

Stuart in Rome

Even if Stuart had not lived in Rome prior to his time in Florence, he was certainly resident there by Easter 1748, living on Strada Felice. His two co-tenants were Revett and the painter Gavin Hamilton, the three men being still found at that address in 1749 and 1750.[18] Stuart was already in the city in 1747, however, since that date appears with his signature on an etching after a drawing then thought to be by Raphael in the collection of Cardinal Silvio Valenti Gonzaga (fig. 3-4).[19] At that time, Stuart was probably not yet sharing accommodation with Revett, since his later collaborator is recorded as having been living in Via delle Carozze from 1745 to 1747.[20]

The late 1740s in Rome were a progressive period in the city's history. Under the rule of Prospero Lorenzo Lambertini, Pope Benedict XIV from 1740 to 1758, an intellectual "Catholic Enlightenment" was in progress. The Pope himself corresponded with some of the great philosophical and cultural men of the time: the antiquary and philosopher Lodovico Antonio Muratori, philosopher and art connoisseur Francesco Algarotti, and antiquary and writer Scipione Maffei — and even with Voltaire. In his celebrated, weekly or fortnightly correspondence with the French Cardinal de Tencin, artistic as well as theological and political matters were discussed.[21] Upon the 1747 dismissal of the papal Camerlengo (chamberlain), Annibale Albani, Benedict chose as his successor his trusted Secretary of State, Cardinal Valenti, who had permitted James Stuart to copy the "Raphael" drawing from his collection that same year. Politically conservative, the new Camerlengo was a man of considerable culture, presiding over an administration that was increasingly liberal when it came to accepting non-Vatican, non-Roman, non-Italian, and even non-Catholic interventions in the antiquarian field.[22] In this Valenti was assisted by the Commissario delle Antichità, Ridolfino Venuti, who was responsible for decisions on excavations, papal acquisitions, and export licenses. Venuti had been commissioner since 1744, early in the reign of Benedict XIV, but it was in the late 1740s and early 1750s, when Valenti was Camerlengo, that his real assistance to foreigners — and especially to Anglophones — commenced.[23] These were the years when James Caulfeild, fourth Viscount Charlemont, was in Rome and when Venuti oversaw the younger Matthew Brettingham's exports of sculpture for the Earl of Leicester's Holkham Hall in Norfolk, England, frequently attending the quayside at Ripa to sign off on shipments in exchange for the price of his coach hire or for some wine from Brettingham. They were also the years when the famous antiquities businesses of Gavin Hamilton and Thomas Jenkins were begun. Quite aside from Venuti's standing as one of the great scholars of antiquity of the time, he was no doubt being acknowledged for supporting British interests in the field in 1752 when he was elected a Fellow of the Society of Antiquaries in London.[24] Another Italian of great cultural standing with whom that society chose to affiliate itself was Cardinal Alessandro Albani, who may possibly have been another of Stuart's Roman contacts. After an absence from meetings of almost two years, Stuart reappeared at the society on November 19, 1761, the occasion on which Albani was elected an Honorary Fellow.[25] Albani was no friend of Valenti's, but until the end of the 1740s Stuart's standing as an artist made it easier for him to associate with men of different political camps than would have been the case for a member of the gentry or aristocracy.

As Secretary of State, Valenti was instrumental in implementing Pope Benedict's enlightened decision to establish four academies in Rome to further the study of, respectively: councils, church history, liturgies and rites, and ancient Roman history and antiquities.[26] The last of these institutions, the Accademia della Storia e Antichità Romane, like its three siblings, had fourteen members initially nominated by the Pope. Upon the death of individuals, new members were freely elected by the remaining academicians. The foundation of such an academy represented a significant advance for the study of antiquities. It provided a formal center for antiquarian scholarship outside of the governmental structures of the Curia itself (although Venuti was a member, having been chosen four years before he became Commissario). From the outset the monthly meetings, which took place at the Pope's Quirinal Palace residence, were held in public. Reports of the papers presented appear regularly in the weekly papal newsletter, the *Diario Ordinario*. Many *"persone civili, & erudite,"*[27] attended, along with the academicians, the patron of the institution, Prince Fabrizio Colonna (Gran Contestabile of the Kingdom of Naples in Rome), and the ubiquitous Cardinal Duke of York. The Pope himself was often present too, notably in 1749 (just when Stuart's reputation as an antiquarian was growing in Rome). Stuart's possible association with the academy may be inferred from the fact that, much later, its secretary, Antonio Baldani, was elected to the Society of Antiquaries of London on the same day as Cardinal Albani, a day when Stuart made his surprising reappearance.

Benedict's reign further advanced scholarship through publication of the monthly *Giornale de' Letterati,* which began its life as *Notizie letterarie Oltramontane* in 1742, providing accounts and translations of foreign developments in the arts and sciences. The publishers were the brothers Niccolò and Marco Pagliarini, with Cardinal Valenti becoming patron of the journal after his appointment as Camerlengo.[28] Stuart certainly knew of the *Giornale de' Letterati* as the leading Roman outlet for antiquarian reportage. On March 30, 1753, he and Revett wrote to it from Athens to advertise their forthcoming *Antiquities.* In an exceptional intervention, the Pagliarini brothers added a long editorial note which is translated in full here:

> For proof of Sig. James Stuart's great ability, understanding, excellence in draughtsmanship and in the art of engraving one can turn to an

essay in the work printed by us in Rome in 1750 entitled *Of the Obelisk of Caesar Augustus.* . . . He made precise measurements of all parts of that famous obelisk for his own purposes at the time of its rediscovery when the foundations of the new House of the Lombard Augustinians were being prepared in the Campo Marzio. At the order of the reigning Holy Pope, it was excavated and deposited in the nearby location where it can still be seen. Cardinal Silvio Valenti, Chamberlain, Secretary of State and a great patron of the fine arts and letters, having been offered a dissertation on the monument by Abbate Angelo Bandini, wanted to publish it with appropriate illustrations that would record it accurately. He chose for this purpose Sig. James Stuart, whose ability he knew from having given him permission to engrave for his own studies several drawings and for his Excellency himself an antique bas-relief. Stuart executed these with such diligence and skill that he became known to the public, and no less so for being well-versed in the fine arts of painting, sculpture and architecture as well as in the sciences of geometry and astronomy and in languages, history and classical learning. Stuart not only produced the most precise measurements of that celebrated and singular monument, but also drew and engraved three large copper plates. Moreover, he himself designed and engraved the frieze that shows a view of the Campo Marzio in ancient times and the tailpiece in which the equipment invented by the famous Niccola Zabaglia to lift the obelisk from the earth is represented, surrounded by elegant decoration. Stuart also designed, with great delicacy and taste, the four initial capital letters, with scenes alluding to the monument's history. To add to all this, he gave thought to and analysed the solar function of the obelisk, as described by Pliny, which had become the subject of debate among several of Europe's leading scholars. Stuart dedicated his essay to the Earl of Malton, a fine art lover and one of his patrons, who was in Rome at the same time. It was added to the commentary of Abbate Bandini and, because of its merit and erudition, placed among the other epistles written to Bandini by Europe's most distinguished men of

letters. We printed a few separate copies that can be purchased with the plates, and other images drawn and engraved by the same Stuart.[29]

These comments carry considerable weight. Not only had the Pagliarini brothers published, as a separate entity, Stuart's own essay on the Obelisk of Psammetichus II, but they also became long-standing professional contacts and personal acquaintances, as may be seen from a letter written by Stuart a decade after his return to England.[30] Their description of Stuart in the 1753 *Giornale* as "well-versed in the fine arts of painting, sculpture and architecture as well as in the sciences of geometry and astronomy and in languages, history and classical learning" is at odds with the sour comment, made by the painter James Russel in November 1749, that it was "the opinion of most people" that Stuart (as also Revett and Hamilton) was "not the least vers'd, either in the Latin or Greek languages."[31] The linguistic, humanistic, and scientific skills that are mentioned by the Pagliarini were necessary for admission to papal antiquarian circles and were surely admired within the Accademia della Storia e Antichità Romane. However, Stuart's initial breakthrough to this elevated circle had come through his artistic rather than scholarly skills. Cardinal Valenti had been impressed by Stuart as an artist and allowed him to make copies of artworks in the Valenti collection for his own painterly or graphic education. This is presumably the context for Stuart's etching after a Raphaelesque drawing (see fig. 3-4). The print of an antique bas-relief that the Pagliarini brothers describe as having subsequently been commissioned by Valenti from Stuart does not appear to have survived, but the high degree of finish of a 1748 print made by Stuart of the cinerary urn of Caius Cornelius Zoticus, located in Valenti's gardens, suggests that it was a similar commission (fig. 3-5). This larger-scale work shows a distinct development of the etching technique he used in Florence, which, with the innovative addition of some brown-gray aquatint, had served him well when reproducing Valenti's Raphaelesque drawing (see figs. 3-2, 3-4). To capture the depth of relief of the sculpture on a Roman cinerary urn, something different was required. The range of cross-hatching Stuart deployed and the stippling that he added to the surfaces of the nude human bodies shows his response and, quite conceivably, the impact of his acquaintance with the graphic work of Giovanni Battista Piranesi.

The Pagliarini brothers' editorial note makes it clear

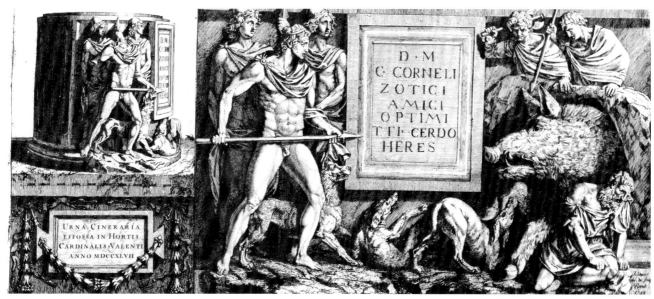

Fig. 3-5. James Stuart. The Cinerary Urn of Caius Cornelius Zoticus, 1748. Etching. Istituto Nazionale per la Grafica, Rome, FC 120901.

that Stuart owed his involvement with the Obelisk of Psammetichus II to Valenti who, having been offered a scholarly treatise on the monument by Angelo Bandini, a young Florentine antiquarian scholar from Cardinal Albani's circle, selected Stuart as the draftsman to produce illustrations that included the elevations (see fig. 3-1).[32] By this time Stuart had already measured the fragments for study purposes, but he had very likely missed the actual rediscovery of the monument, reported in the *Diario Ordinario* on April 6, 1748, probably just after he had left

Rome with Revett, Brettingham, and Hamilton for a planned expedition to Naples.[33] The excavation continued, however, into May and June, and the last piece of the obelisk was not trundled to its temporary home in the vineyard behind the adjacent Palazzo Impresa until the end of August, so Stuart must have returned to Rome to find this the city's most exciting on-going archaeological and antiquarian event.[34] It is intriguing to think of him as potentially one of the onlookers in the well-known view of the excavation given by Giuseppe Vasi (fig. 3-6).

Fig. 3-6. View of the excavation of the Obelisk of Psammetichus II in 1747. Engraving. From Giuseppe Vasi, *Delle magnificenze di Roma antica e moderna . . .* , vol. 2 (1752): opp. p. 12. Courtesy of the Trustees of The Victoria and Albert Museum, London / National Art Library, F.I.9.

Fig. 3-7. View of the extraction of the Obelisk of Psammetichus II in 1747. Etching by Louis Philippe Boitard. From James Russel, *Letters from a Young Painter Abroad to his Friends in England*, vol. 2 (1750): following p. 138. Courtesy of The Paul Mellon Centre for Studies in British Art, London.

Although Vasi was correct in showing that the obelisk had broken into four pieces as it toppled from its base, he depicted the operation at an early stage when the scaffolding itself, devised by the remarkable octogenarian carpenter Niccola Zabaglia, was in process of being constructed. There are ladders up to the trabeated timber structure where the carpenters are still working, and the pulleys necessary for the actual lifting are scarcely in place. According to James Russel, who was an eyewitness and precise chronicler of the events of early summer 1748, Zabaglia began his work on May 10 and completed removal of the four pieces (though the base still remained untouched at this stage) at the end of July, as the *Diario Ordinario*

confirms.[35] Russel's own drawing of the scene, as engraved and published, shows it at a later stage and with greater technical detail than does that of Vasi (fig. 3-7). Here, there are no vertical elements. Instead (doubled) inclined uprights are lashed together with ropes (Russel reported that no nails were used), propped up by additional posts and used to support a pair of cross-beams from which four pulleys are suspended. Each pulley was operated by its own capstan and crew, and a bed of timber was placed under each section of the obelisk as it was raised until it was of sufficient height to be pulled onto a track of boards and rolled into Palazzo Impresa. In Russel's depiction only one of the four capstan crews is visible, two being

Fig. 3-8. View of the extraction of the obelisk from the Campo Marzio. Etching by Jean Barbault. From F. Ficoroni, *Gemmae Antiquae Litteratae, aliaequae rariores* . . . (1757): opp. p. 60. By permission of The British Library, London, 840.i.1.2.

Fig. 3-9. Vignette of Niccola Zabaglia and the machinery he invented to raise the Obelisk of Psammetichus II. Etching by James Stuart. From Angelo Maria Bandini, *De Obelisco Caesaris Augusti e Campi Martii ruderibus nuper eruto commentarius . . .* (1750): opp. p. xxi. By permission of The British Library, London, 138.h.5. *Checklist no. 10.*

located in narrow neighboring streets (indicated by ropes demarcated by the letter *B*) and another obscured behind the scaffolding. All four capstans are shown in the etching by Jean Barbault for Francesco Ficoroni's *Gemmae Antiquae Litteratae* and *Vetera Monumenta,* published in Rome in 1757 (fig. 3-8).[36] Barbault's view appears to show a similar system of inclined posts to that given by Russel, casting doubt on the question of whether the vertical scaffold shown by Vasi ever existed. Barbault, however, had turned the broken monument itself ninety degrees to increase the dramatic effect of the scene, for Russel clearly describes the side of the obelisk with legible hieroglyphs as being that facing the ground. Vasi also showed that the hieroglyphs were not visible from this angle.[37] Stuart's contribution to the documentation of this remarkable event lies in the image of the machinery that appears in *De Obelisco* which, thanks to the Pagliarini brothers' editorial note, can now be securely attributed to him (fig. 3-9).[38] Stuart has schematized the system, to the extent that the four capstans are shown much closer to the scaffolding than can have been the case. The scale of the equipment has also been reduced relative to the figure of Zabaglia, who is seen scratching his head as he contemplates his creation. However, viewing the structure end-on as opposed to taking the angle of Vasi, Russel, and Barbault, Stuart clearly shows the inclined uprights,

props, cross braces, and pulleys. His print adds to the likelihood that Vasi's best-known image of the scaffolding is incorrect in showing vertical elements and that Russel's depiction of the posts as being round in section may not have been correct, for both Stuart and Barbault show the timbers as squared.

A final conclusion that emerges from the Pagliarini brothers' footnote is that it was in Rome that Stuart had met the dedicatee of his essay about the obelisk, Charles Watson-Wentworth, Earl of Malton. This implies that their encounter must have been brief. Malton arrived in Rome from Tuscany in the autumn of 1749 and was introduced to Cardinal Albani before passing quickly on to winter in Naples. He returned to Rome for March and April 1750, but in March Stuart himself left the city for Venice en route to Greece.[39] The date of April 1, 1750, given by Stuart at the end of his very substantial essay on the obelisk was thus a forward one, and since he and Revett were busy preparing for their Greek expedition in late 1749 and early 1750, the research if not the writing was probably well advanced by the time he met Malton. What was the nature of their initial connection? With the usual degree of deference to nobility, the Pagliarini brothers called the earl "a fine art lover and one of [Stuart's] patrons." Joseph Woods later recorded that Malton (as well as Lord Charlemont and James Dawkins)

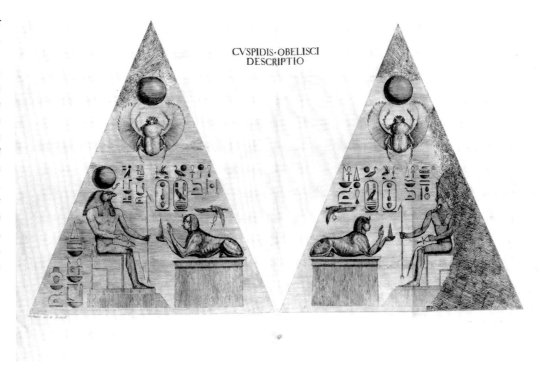

CVSPIDIS·OBELISCI
DESCRIPTIO

Fig. 3-10. Elevations of the top of the Obelisk of Psammetichus II. Etching. From James Stuart, *De Obelisco Caesaris Augusti e Campo Martio nuperrime effosso epistola Jacobi Stuart Angli ad Carolam Wentworth Comitem de Malton . . .* (1750): tab. III. By permission of The British Library, London, 140.h.18. *Checklist no. 9.*

had "liberally assisted" Stuart with money while he was in Rome and subsequently in Athens. Promising to subscribe for ten copies of "our Attica" certainly made Malton the largest initial supporter of the *Antiquities* project (although he later reduced his complement to six copies).[40] The time frame suggests that Stuart's dedication of his essay on the obelisk to Malton was an act of opportunism. The printing of it as a separate entity was probably an enterprising initiative of Stuart's rather than a direct result of Malton's patronage. As the Pagliarini stated, only a "few" copies were printed — a point confirmed by the relative rarity of the volume today. In addition, the dual red-and-black-ink title pages of the Bandini version are missing from Stuart's volume, and, while the typesetting of the text itself is identical, the placement of the images in the latter suggests a relatively cheap production (Stuart's print of Zabaglia, for example, is carelessly inserted over the index on the reverse of page 33).[41] Stuart most likely realized that it would serve a useful purpose back in London for him to have special copies of his erudite work printed by the Pagliarini and dedicated to an English nobleman. Further support for this interpretation emerges from the fact that neither the letter nor the book and its dedication were mentioned in the correspondence Malton and his bear-leader, Colonel Forrester, sent back to his father, the Marquess of Rockingham. Nor, when Malton's Grand Tour acquisitions began arriving in Yorkshire in October

1750, did Rockingham make any reference to Stuart's dedication of the work to his son, even though he commented to Malton that "your books, medals & statues & little pictures etc. are fine and well chose."[42]

De Obelisco Caesaris Augusti

For James Stuart, participation alongside many of Europe's greatest antiquarians in their interpretations of the Obelisk of Psammetichus II in Rome represents a scholarly and social watershed. The obelisk (fig. 3-10), dated from the sixth century B.C., had been brought to Rome from Heliopolis by Emperor Augustus in 10 B.C. In a sense it was the most significant of all Egyptian obelisks in Rome (as well as the fourth largest), for it was erected in the Campus Martius as the "gnonom" or needle of a massive sundial laid out with bronze lines in the pavement over an open area of some 7,000 square meters.[43] The identical inscriptions on the north and south faces of the obelisk's (Roman) red granite base show that Augustus intended the arrangement both as a symbol of the subjugation of Egypt and as an act of worship of the sun. Its importance may be judged from the fact that it became part of the emperor's funerary complex (the "bustum"), along with his mausoleum and the Ara Pacis (when in its original position rather than that it occupies today). In book thirty-six of his *Natural History,* Pliny the Elder described the transport of the obelisk to Rome, the gilt

Excell. V.

Romæ Kalendis Aprilis 1750.

Umil. Addict. Obſeq. Servus
Jacobus Stuart .

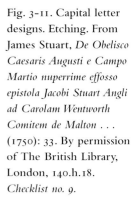

D. V. Ecc.

Roma Aprile 1750.

Umiliſſ. Divotiſſ. Obligatiſſ. St
Giacomo Stu

Fig. 3-11. Capital letter designs. Etching. From James Stuart, *De Obelisco Caesaris Augusti e Campo Martio nuperrime effosso epistola Jacobi Stuart Angli ad Carolam Wentworth Comitem de Malton . . .* (1750): 33. By permission of The British Library, London, 140.h.18. *Checklist no. 9.*

ball placed on top of it to reflect the shadow from the center of the sun and the layout of the sundial below. Owing to subsidence of the soft soil in the Campus Martius, the sundial had already ceased working effectively by the time *Natural History* was dedicated in A.D. 77, and an attempt was made to rectify its malfunctioning shortly afterwards (probably during the reign of Domitian) by raising the obelisk on its base some 1.6 meters. The huge urban area of the sundial was presumably built over and the granite base probably embedded in soil by the end of the first millennium, since the base was undamaged when the obelisk itself fell. The collapse was possibly due to the earthquake that struck Rome in A.D. 849, or, since the shaft was found to have suffered fire damage, it may have fallen when the city was sacked by soldiers of the Norman duke, Robert Guiscard, in 1084.

The Obelisk of Psammetichus II had a long history of partial rediscovery and study prior to the middle of the eighteenth century, culminating in an investigation undertaken at the behest of Pope Alexander VII by Athanasius Kircher in 1666. Kircher found that, although almost completely buried, the base was still in an upright position. Houses had been built on top of the fallen shaft, however, and these would have to be demolished if the monument were to be excavated. Alexander died before any decision had been made on this issue, and it was left to Benedict XIV to press ahead with the excavation in the summer of 1748. Benedict told Cardinal de Tencin on May 15, 1748, that Julius II and Sixtus V had both failed to excavate this obelisk because they balked at buying out the owners of the houses that stood on top of it. After

the Lombard Augustinians paid for the acquisition and demolition of the houses in 1748, Benedict thought he should complete the excavation as a cultural act and "so as not to appear to be a Gothic Pope."[44] As though to set his seal on the project, the Pope came to inspect the site from the windows of neighboring Palazzo Tanari on one of the first days of the excavation.[45] The precocious Bandini, then aged only twenty-two, was ordered to write a short report, which subsequently appeared as an appendix in *De Obelisco Caesaris Augusti* entitled "Notizie per l'obelisco." Based on Kircher's seventeenth-century account, this report doubtless inspired Bandini to begin upon the much more substantive dissertation on the monument that he offered to Valenti for publication some two years later and which appeared under the impress of the Pagliarini brothers.

Bandini's substantial essay in the book, over one hundred pages in length, was remarkable not just of and in itself but because it was accompanied by shorter but still substantive letters dealing with a range of issues raised by the excavation and assessment of the obelisk, written by an international array of scholars.[46] (Strangely, the Commissario delle Antichità, Venuti, was the only major antiquarian figure missing.[47]) Most of these printed letters (which date from July 1748, when the extraction was still ongoing, to March 1749) were presumably commissioned, and some of them were in circulation before Bandini's book appeared in July 1750.[48] A letter by antiquarian Ernesto Freeman, disagreeing with Ruggiero Boscovitch's assessment of the astronomical uses of the obelisk, was printed in the *Giornale de' Letterati* in May 1750 (also published by the Pagliarini). Boscovitch responded in four parts in the *Giornale* in July 1750. Some copies of Bandini's *De Obelisco,* bearing a colophon date of 1751, include Freeman's letter and Boscovitch's riposte as an appendix, placed after the index. Stuart's letter was also a late entrant to the book — situated just after Bandini's original "Notizie per l'obelisco" (1748), which had clearly been intended as the last item. But as Stuart's work is placed before the publishing license and index and as Boscovitch referred to Stuart's essay in his letter, it certainly belongs with the original publication. In fact Stuart was probably acquainted with Boscovitch, who was professor of mathematics at the Collegio di Propaganda Fide in Rome where Stuart is thought to have studied Latin.[49] No doubt Stuart had volunteered his work to Bandini and it was included, as the Pagliarini brothers later stated, because of the merit and ingenuity shown by its author, rather than because of his prior scholarly standing.

That Stuart was familiar with Pliny's account of the Roman history of the obelisk may be seen graphically from the four capital-letter engravings that, thanks to the editorial note of the Pagliarini, can now be assigned to Stuart's hand (fig. 3-11). In the Bandini version of the book the letters *I* and *T* appear on page vii, the first page of the preface, while *C* and *A* appear on page 1, the first page of Bandini's essay. The image associated with the letter *I* shows the obelisk being transported from Egypt to Rome lying on the deck of a great galley. The letter *T* has Roman laborers using a capstan to winch the (unseen) obelisk toward the ramp that will be used to tilt it into its vertical position. A medal of Augustus supported by male and female figures features in letter *C.* The female stands upon a crocodile and presumably represents the Nile, while the male, placed above the she-wolf suckling Romulus and Remus, symbolizes Rome. The letter *A* has a geometer in Rome marking out the first of the pavement lines of the sundial. As is shown by figure 3-11, when Stuart's essay was republished on its own, the letters were printed in a single sequence and were rearranged to read "CITA," thereby achieving a slightly more logical order, with the image of Augustus first, followed by the chronological sequence depicting the obelisk's history in 10 B.C. Also, in Stuart's publication, his view of the Campus Martius was relocated to the title page, having been placed on the first page of Bandini's essay in the full version of the book (fig. 3-12).

By the time that Stuart's essay appeared, two years had

DE OBELISCO
CÆSARIS AUGUSTI
E CAMPO MARTIO NUPERRIME EFFOSSO
EPISTOLA
JACOBI STUART ANGLI
AD
CAROLUM WENTWORTH
COMITEM DE MALTON.

DELL' OBELISCO
DI CESARE AUGUSTO
CAVATO FUORI DA TERRA ULTIMAMENTE NEL CAMPO MARZO
LETTERA
DI GIACOMO STUARD INGLESE
DIRETTA A SUA ECCELLENZA
MILORD CARLO WENTWORTH
CONTE DI MALTON.

ROMÆ MDCCL.
EX TYPOGRAPHIA PALLADIS.
SUPERIORUM FACULTATE.

Fig. 3-12. Title page. From James Stuart, *De Obelisco Caesaris Augusti e Campo Martio nuperrime effosso epistola Jacobi Stuart Angli ad Carolam Wentworth Comitem de Malton . . .* (1750). By permission of The British Library, London, 140.h.18. *Checklist no. 9.*

elapsed since the excavation of the obelisk. These were critical years during which Stuart had transformed himself from painter and graphic artist to true antiquarian man of letters. His text runs to thirty-three pages and amounts to some 16,000 words in each of the two languages in which it was published: Latin and Italian. Stuart's work could have been translated from Latin to Italian or vice versa — but surely not from English to both Latin and Italian. Indeed, there is little reason to doubt his proficiency in both foreign languages. Evidence from his surviving sketchbook indicates that Stuart was fluent in Italian, while the information that he had studied Latin at the Collegio di Propaganda Fide, even if not verified by the college's surviving archives, appears to have derived from someone who knew Stuart personally.[50] Moreover, the Protector of the College at this time was none other

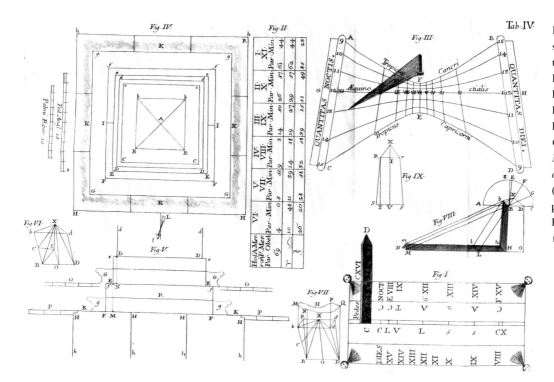

Fig. 3-13. Plan and section of the base of the Obelisk of Psammetichus II. Etching by James Stuart. From Angelo Maria Bandini, *De Obelisco Caesaris Augusti e Campi Martii ruderibus nuper eruto commentarius . . .* (1750): tab IV. By permission of The British Library, London, 138.h.5. *Checklist no. 10.*

than Cardinal Valenti, who could easily have inserted a protégé into the institution's classes.

Stuart's letter describes his efforts to settle the problem of the original gnomic function of the Obelisk of Psammetichus II, whether it had been a solarium (giving the daily hours) or a horologium (indicating seasonal variation in the hours as well). To achieve this it was necessary to determine the exact orientation of the base prior to its removal from the site of its excavation. Stuart assumed that the four sides of the base would have faced the cardinal points of the compass, but his measurements showed this was not the case and that the north face of plinth and pedestal were fifteen degrees from the meridien line. In his illustration (fig. 3-13), the divergence is indicated between the plan and section by an arrow with the lowercase letter *l* for "*levante,*" that is east. Stuart could not have known or guessed the reason for this — which was to enable the tip of the obelisk's shadow to pass over the Ara Pacis on September 23 each year, the date of Augustus's birth.[51] He inferred instead that the obelisk's use as gnomon had postdated its erection. He also excavated around the base and found fragments of the ancient pavement (although none of the inlaid bronze lines). He organized methodical digging and described the various strata he came upon, thereby demonstrating that the entire

pavement and corbeled plinth of base had been raised by about three feet at some point to adjust the functioning of the sundial (now known to have occurred in or around the time of Domitian). Stuart's work has been described fairly as heralding "a new epoch in archaeology, as one of the first efforts to give a systematic account of a methodical excavation and an archaeological description of a monument *in situ.*"[52] The plan of the obelisk's base that appears as plate IV in *De Obelisco Caesaris Augusti* (see fig. 3-13) was prepared by Stuart specifically to illustrate the points of debate in his own essay: none of the other essays in the book make reference to it. He gave a dual scale of Roman *palmi* and English feet, but the measurements had been made in feet, inches, and hundredths of an inch. This is an early indication of the minute degree of accuracy (the "precise measurements" described by the Pagliarini brothers) that Stuart and Revett would later claim for the measurements that they made in Athens. It predates Robert Wood's work at Palmyra and Balbec, which has often been taken as setting a standard that Stuart and Revett sought to emulate.

Stuart's study of the obelisk showed him to be capable of surveying and drawing out a plan, but his other surviving architectural surveys from his time in Rome suggest that he preferred to sketch elevations freehand

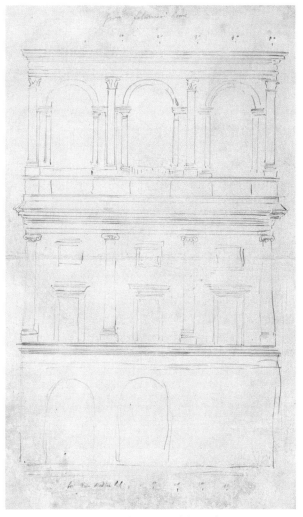

Fig. 3-14. James Stuart. Elevation of the Palazzo
Falconieri, Rome, ca. 1740s. Pen and ink. RIBA Library
Drawings Collection, London, SD 62/22.

Fig. 3-15. Francesco Borromini. The Palazzo Falconieri (south side),
Rome, 1638–41. Photographed in 2006.

rather than to draw them out geometrically. In fact, Stuart probably never did acquire proper skills of architectural draftsmanship.[53] In an elevation of the three loggia-capped bays of Borromini's Palazzo Falconieri, facing the Tiber River, all of the elements, including the horizontal lines of the entablature, were drawn freehand, and the scale (probably in *palmi romani)* was thus of use for general reference only (fig. 3-14). Curiously, in this drawing Stuart has reduced the height of the building by omitting the story that should appear between the arcaded basement and the Ionic *piano nobile* (fig. 3-15), making the sketch of limited utility as a record drawing. It also shows Stuart attempting to "improve" on Borromini's solecistic four stories by reducing them to three, more closely in line

with the rules for the deployment of superimposed orders with which he would have been familiar from British early eighteenth-century practice. Another of his surviving drawings appears to show a revised "elevation" of the same part of Palazzo Falconieri, where this time he ruled and sketched in a Doric frieze between the principal and attic windows of the *piano nobile,* as though seeking to overcome the problem of there being two stories within the one, non-giant order.[54] Such a rule-based approach to architectural design would be in concordance with Stuart's work on the Obelisk of Psammetichus and with the way he applied his architectural understanding to his archaeological work in Athens.

117

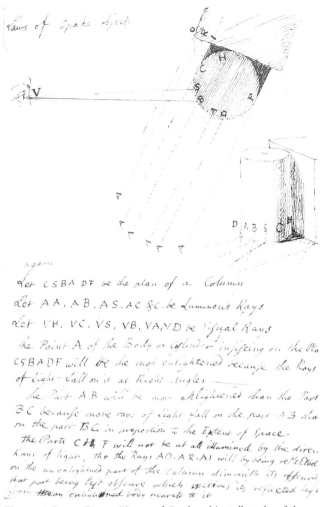

the Point A of the Body or Cylinder insisting on the Pla

Fig. 3-16. James Stuart. "Laws of Opake objects," study of the effects of light on columns. Pen and ink, pencil. From Stuart's sketchbook (ca. 1748–50): fol. 75v. RIBA Library Drawings Collection, London, SKB/336/2 [L 3/4]. *Checklist no. 8.*

Venice and the Pola Expedition

Stuart and Revett left Rome for Venice in March 1750 but were not to set sail for Athens until January 19, 1751. Although the nine intervening months have sometimes been regarded as a time of hiatus and frustration for the two men, they were in fact a formative period for Stuart in a number of respects. His encounter (or perhaps renewed encounter) with the British Resident in Venice, Sir James Gray, may have cemented Stuart's rise to the status of British gentlemanly scholar — evidenced by his nomination for election to the Society of Dilettanti in

1751. These were also months during which, in traveling about the terra firma, Stuart honed skills of architectural design with an eye to English patronage.[55] From the point of view of the present study, however, two aspects of those months merit discussion. The first is the development of the scholarly skills already displayed by Stuart in relation to the Obelisk of Psammetichus II into more abstract, theoretical directions. The second is the trip that he and Revett made for the surprisingly long period of about three months between late July and November 1750 to study the Roman buildings surviving at Pola in Istria. Stuart himself described the Pola expedition as employing "vacant time" but added that he and Revett had used the opportunity to demonstrate "the manner in which we proposed to execute our Athenian work."[56]

Stuart's activities are better documented from this time on than they are before. However, unfortunately, of the fifty-four manuscript books by Stuart handed to Joseph Woods by the publisher Josiah Taylor in the early nineteenth century to aid Woods's production of the fourth volume of *Antiquities of Athens*, only one appears to have survived — a substantial notebook in the library of Edinburgh University. There is also a pocket-size sketchbook by Stuart in the RIBA Library Drawings Collection.[57] Material in both of these volumes dates to 1750 (or from 1750 in the case of the Edinburgh notebook) and concerns Stuart's time in the Veneto and at Pola. Despite the disparity in size, these survivors give a good impression of Stuart's working methods and record keeping. They suggest a wide-ranging and inquiring mind but also one that struggled to synthesize material or to follow through with ambitious literary and philosophical projects. The Edinburgh notebook opens with a title page: "An Exact Description of the Ancient Edifices now existing in Pola by James Stuart Painter & Architect . . . begun August 1750." The text of this "Description" on the first folio contains only one sentence, followed by a map of Pola on the second folio. Notes on the Arch of the Sergii (known as the Porta Aurata in the eighteenth century) and on the two temples at Pola follow on folios 11 and 13 to 14. This fragmentation of the record seems fairly typical of Stuart, who struggled to separate gathering information from shaping it into coherent narrative form. Indeed, Taylor was to comment, as he tried to piece material together for editing in 1816: "I think the beginning of the volume on Pola is written over one way or another at least 50 times," while the actual editor, Woods, observed that a "great

many" of the notebooks he had studied contained memoranda on painting as well as the beginnings of various
essays on architecture, truth, and the absurd.[58] It was
already becoming clear at Pola that the range of Stuart's
interests was inhibiting development of that single-
mindedness necessary to draw ideas into a coherent
whole. In addition his undoubted skills of observation and
acuity in technical analysis did not readily translate into
narrative skills. It might even be inferred from this that the
distinction between the observational Athenian project of
Stuart and Revett and the theoretical Athenian project of
their French rival Julien-David Le Roy was established
before any of them had set foot in Greece.

Joseph Woods's comments on the various "essays" he
found Stuart to have been attempting suggest a man struggling to turn himself to more philosophical and abstract
directions, but the survival of a fragmentary treatise on
painting in the RIBA sketchbook perhaps demonstrates
the grounds on which Stuart felt more comfortable. While
this fragment cannot be dated with certainty, the predom-
inance of Venetian pictures among the examples suggests
a timeframe of spring and early summer 1750, when Stuart
was mainly resident in Venice. Of the various sections and
drafts, only one was worked up to a point of ready comprehension. In it Stuart discussed the effects of light upon
solid bodies, specifically architectural columns. The analytical physics of this study was surely influenced by his
recent and intensive research on the horological function
of the Obelisk of Psammetichus II. This subject dwelled
in Stuart's mind well after his departure from Rome, as
may be seen from several comments on obelisks in the
Edinburgh notebook (not to mention substantial notes on
sundials and eclipses in its early pages).[59] Sketches that
accompany the text of Stuart's treatise draft demonstrate
his understanding of what he defined as the three ways in
which light falls upon an architectural element (fig. 3-16).
In Stuart's analysis, "luminous rays" were those that fell on
the column direct from the light source, while "visual" rays
were those that were not direct but nonetheless percep-
tible to the eye, and "reflected light" came from a lighted
body (the wall, in the example of fig. 3-16) and then
struck an unlighted body or part of the body (in this case
the section of the column marked *C* to *H*). Stuart was also
aware that the effects of these three modes of light perception differed according to the texture of the body on
which the light was falling, a point he demonstrated by
contrasting the "perfectly polished" column of figure 3-

16 with a coarsely finished column, thereby representing
the different effects of light falling upon "shaggy or
Downy Objects."[60]

Stuart's interest in the physics of light can be seen as
part of a developing mathematical inclination that would
move him away from his concern with making measurements for the sake of the survey in itself toward an interest in analysing the results of measurements to elucidate
numerical and geometrical systems. At Pola he may have
joined with Revett in the ostensibly straightforward
process of recording measurements, for in the Edinburgh
notebook there is a page of plans and notes on the Temple
of Rome and Augustus with figures that correspond reasonably closely with the plan of the building as eventually published.[61] By the time the two men reached
Greece, however, it seems that the decision to delegate the
comprehensive collection of measured data to Revett had
been taken. Stuart's notebook increasingly records dimensions not as part of a total record but as the basis of complicated trigonometrical calculations and geometrical
speculations. If Revett thus consolidated his position more
as "architect-archaeologist" during the months at Pola,
then Stuart, in addition to being the scholar struggling to
write erudite treatises, increasingly took the lead as
"topographer-archaeologist." A high proportion of the
images in the RIBA sketchbook are tiny pencil or pen-
and-ink landscape drawings (there are seventeen among
unfilled eighty-five folios). There is little evidence that
Stuart's earlier career as painter and graphic artist had
involved much in the way of landscape studies. A keen
interest in the landscape was one product of his time traveling around the Veneto. At Pola Stuart probably began to
develop topographical views on sheets of paper as large as
could reasonably be held on site, using pen and ink and
then heavily applied gray wash to represent the effects of
light striking or permeating buildings that were the focus
of attention (fig. 3-17).[62] Although the image reproduced
here was not selected by Stuart for further development,
it represents an intermediate stage between his practice of
pen-and-ink sketching and hatching and the production
of the celebrated gouache paintings that would become
the basis of the initial, "actual state" engraved views in
Antiquities of Athens (see fig. 3-25).

Why Stuart adopted gouache for his views and the
question of when he actually executed them can only be
speculated upon. He may have learned to paint in
gouache when studying with Joseph or Louis Goupy in

London, but the technique appears to have lain dormant during his painterly years in Florence and Rome. The Pola expedition, however, would have brought into focus the issue of how the topographical views were to be executed and the evidence of the RIBA sketchbook and his view inside the amphitheater (see fig. 3-17) shows that Stuart traveled with pen, ink, and gray wash readily to hand. In this respect, his technique corresponds with that of Robert Wood's draftsman, Giovanni Borra. Made during Wood's contemporaneous Levantine expedition, Borra's finished pen-and-ink and blue-gray wash views of Palmyra and Balbec were perfectly suited to engraving — and did no more than was necessary for that purpose.[63] Stuart's brightly colored and slightly clumsy gouaches with their busy figurative content are, however, of quite a different nature. The materials needed to produce them and the fact that the opacity of gouache renders the medium more liable to chafing when being transported must cast doubt not just on the idea that they were executed in situ (a doubt confirmed once Stuart reached Greece), but even on the idea that they were executed by Stuart when in the Mediterranean.[64]

Five gouaches survive from Stuart's work at Pola, one of which — the Arch of the Sergii — makes a good case study of his initial approach to the "actual state" view (see fig. 2-9). Not long after Stuart and Revett's visit, the arch was the subject of two further studies, one made in 1782 by Louis-François Cassas, subsequently published in 1802 in *Voyage pittoresque et historique de l'Istrie et de la Dalmatie,* and the other a careful survey by Francesco Monaco for

Giovanni Rinaldo Carli's *Delle Antichità Italiche* of 1788. Then, in the early nineteenth century, Pola was visited by another British architectural student, Thomas Allason, who considered the appearance of its monuments in the fourth volume of *Antiquities of Athens* to be "imperfect and inadequate," failing to afford "just and accurate ideas of them," because their "taste, simplicity, and elegance" could only by shown by "correct views."[65] As published by Allason in his *Picturesque Views of the Antiquities of Pola in Istria* of 1819, the arch can be seen to have been tightly hemmed in on both sides: by dwellings to the right and a high, garden wall to the left (fig. 3-18). Allason's confidence in his views as being more "correct" than Stuart's might have derived from the use of the relatively newly invented camera lucida. However, even allowing for physical changes that must have taken place in the half century after 1750 (and not least because Pola had suffered badly at the hands of Napoleonic troops), Allason's rendition is likely closer than Stuart's to what Stuart must have seen at the site. Both of these images depict the inner side of the arch, that facing the crowded town of Pola rather than the countryside outside the walls. A plan by Cassas (the original of which survives in the British Library) shows the arch with its surrounding architectural contexts in the 1780s (fig. 3-19). Although Cassas reversed the positions of the flanking dwellings and gardens (perhaps with a view to engraving), the houses clearly stood close to the right of the arch, much as shown by Allason rather than by Stuart.[66] Furthermore, across the foreground of Stuart's view lies the low rubble course of a

Fig. 3-17. James Stuart. View of the Amphitheater at Pola, 1750. Pen and ink. By courtesy of the Trustees of the British Museum, London / Department of Greek and Roman Antiquities, Misc. Topography Box.

Fig. 3-18. View of the Arch of the Sergii. Etching. From Thomas Allason, *Picturesque Views of the Antiquities of Pola in Istria* (1819): opp. p. 18. By permission of The British Library, London, 745.e.7.

wall, an oddity that might well be explained as the foot-print of the high wall shown on the left by Allason and in plan by Cassas, visually lowered by Stuart so as to gain the optimal angle of view on the arch. That Stuart increased the picturesque character of the pedestal of the arch itself by showing it as more ruinous than it was in reality emerges when his view is compared to Francesco Monaco's elevation (although Stuart correctly showed the substantial gash toward the top of the second column from the left that can be seen in Monaco's elevation and that was carefully concealed by a tree in Allason's view).[67] In his view Stuart did not show the decoration on the imposts and vault of the arch, nor (in the printed version) the inscriptions that appear on the attic, although these omitted elements were included in the restoration elevations.

The example of Stuart's work at the arch at Pola, then, might give us some reason to be wary of the status of what he later claimed to be topographically exact views of monuments that were the focus of study, at least at this rel-atively early stage of his archaeological career. There is one other factor that might be noted in regard to Stuart's approach to the arch. The text describing the monument in the fourth volume of *Antiquities of Athens,* while writ-ten by Joseph Woods, is a close paraphrase of Stuart's draft as preserved in the Edinburgh notebook. It is clear, there-fore, that it was Stuart and not Woods who completely misdated the arch (which was actually erected around 25

to 10 B.C.) to "the decline of the Empire than near the Augustan age." While he considered the design and workmanship of the arch to be "extremely good" (if lack-ing in "that exquisite taste with which everything of that age is executed"), he could not believe that anyone not of imperial rank could have erected a triumphal arch early in the empire.[68] In other words, a presupposition about Roman architectural and patronal practice (in this case a particularly British presupposition about the nature of the Augustan period) outweighed Stuart's connoisseurly analysis of the surviving fabric. This suggests an historical approach on Stuart's part in which certain fundamentals

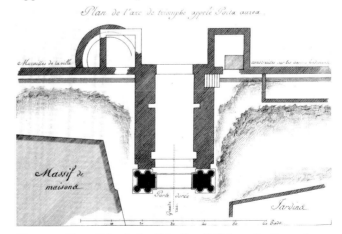

Fig. 3-19. Plan of the Arch of the Sergii, Pola, 1782. Engraving. From Louis-François Cassas and Joseph Lavallée, *Voyage pittoresque et historique de l'Istrie et de la Dalmatie* (1802): pl. 18b (detail). By permission of The British Library, London, 1785.c.3.

were beyond question, an approach which would also affect his work in Athens. Setting these qualifications aside for the present, however, it is clear that Stuart and Revett returned to Venice from Pola in November 1750 with their reputations for accuracy and scholarship enhanced. Thomas Hollis, commenting on Stuart shortly after Stuart's departure for Athens, wrote that he had "particularly distinguished himself in diverse particulars, among others by a Treatise which he wrote upon Obelisques . . . which was thought a very ingenious performance." Hollis continued that Stuart and Revett had sailed for Athens anticipating eight months' work "but as they are men of the greatest accuracy & exactness, & that they may find out more matter than as yet they can be informed of, it is probable it will take up a longer time."[69]

Antiquities of Athens

At the heart of Stuart and Revett's "Proposals" for *Antiquities of Athens,* and in Stuart's preface to the first volume, lay high claims for empirical truth and accuracy — both in terms of the visual record and of the standard of measurement of Greek ruins — as the fundamental objectives of the work. These claims were called into question by some of their own contemporaries, and they have formed the basis of much subsequent deconstruction of the work. Historians, of course, have a duty to look beyond their subjects' statements of intent, but in the case of the history of archaeology they also have to exercise caution in applying today's highly developed scientific standards to situations that occurred when the discipline was in its infancy. In the light of this, some analysis of Stuart's achievements in *Antiquities of Athens* against the background of his Italian years is worthwhile. In what follows an attempt has been made to integrate such manuscript evidence as survives of Stuart's preliminary studies for the published book, since it is arguable that, with a project that preoccupied its author over a period of many years, process may be as important or as informative as final outcome.

It has frequently been suggested that the idea of an expedition to study and record the ancient architecture of Athens was hatched during the visit to Naples of April 1748 undertaken by Brettingham, Hamilton, Revett, and Stuart. Their probable experience in viewing the excavations at Herculaneum and possibly even those just commencing at Pompeii may have been a contributory factor, although this is not likely. Revett described the visit

to Naples in a letter to his father that has landscape and painting as its subjects (not to mention amusing anecdotes about the penchant for wine of the party's horse) but is silent on the matter of antiquities when one might reasonably expect the exact opposite.[70] If the group had actually made a visit in 1748 to the foul-smelling and claustrophobic subterranean passageways of Herculaneum, it would not have been a very architectural experience, nor particularly rewarding from an antiquarian point of view.[71] The objets d'art that had been discovered on the site had been removed and were jealously guarded at the king's Portici villa. By contrast, as we have seen, the party had returned to Rome to find the excavation of the Obelisk of Psammetichus II in full swing, and Stuart had soon become involved in measuring and researching this monument. It is more plausible that the plan to make measured surveys of Greek architecture to match those provided in Antoine Desgodetz's *Édifices antique de Rome* (1682) developed in Rome itself, the capital of the antiquarian world. It was perhaps galvanized by the presence in the city later in 1748 of Lord Charlemont, himself en route for Greece and Asia Minor. Further impetus was provided by the arrival of Robert Wood in 1749 and by the plans he was laying for his expedition to Palmyra and Balbec with James Dawkins and John Bouverie.[72] It was Wood who, in the preface to *The Ruins of Palmyra,* was to use the term "truth" to describe "the principal merit of works of this kind," Stuart's equivalent phrase being "accuracy and fidelity."[73] Wood and Stuart also came to share an understanding of the purpose of the actual-state topographical views that were introduced to architectural surveys of ancient buildings for the first time in their respective works — specifically that these provided "authority for our measures" of surviving fabric and "reasons" for all elements offered in hypothetical restorations.[74]

The absolute nature of statements such as these caused some of Wood's and Stuart's contemporaries to react with scepticism, especially after the appearance of Julien-David Le Roy's *Ruines des plus beaux monuments de la Grèce* in 1758 with its rival texts and alternative measurements, which showed (besides much else) that there could be variation even in the recording of supposedly objective data. Nonetheless, throughout Europe there was acceptance of Stuart and Revett's methods of topographical study, measured survey, and hypothetical restoration as the optimal way of studying the physical remains of ancient buildings. Thanks to this acceptance, their record of Greek architecture — even if criticized in individual detail — held overall legitimacy throughout the nineteenth century (when a number of new English, French, German, and Italian editions and abridgements were published) and well into the twentieth century. It is a measure of their dependability, for example, that when writing the text-book *Greek Architecture* for the Pelican History of Art series in 1957, A. W. Lawrence found that Stuart and Revett's surveys of the Tower of the Winds had not been surpassed and that their study of the order of the Choragic Monument of Lysicrates and their "reliable" surveys of the Ionic temple on the Ilissus River were still of use (although this last monument could not be re-surveyed, having been destroyed by the Turks around 1778).[75] Architectural schools also continued to use *Antiquities of Athens* in teaching Greek orders to students. Only with the decline of the classical tradition of education in the architecture schools, particularly in the post-1945 period, and the coeval rise of academic departments of archaeology in universities, did the process of deconstructing (as opposed to merely modifying) the legitimacy of *Antiquities* begin. A singular moment in that process came with the 1956 publication of an article by an American scholar, Jacob Landy, who, having exposed errors in virtually all areas of Stuart and Revett's operations, suggested that they "were not concerned with as complete a presentation of the facts as they pretended."[76] Landy's individual criticisms were, to varying degrees, justifiable and merit extensive consideration, but his conclusion — that their work was disingenuous (and primarily of use only as a record of remains subsequently lost) — is one that judges them by the standards and methods of twentieth-century archaeological scholarship, suggesting a failure to enter into the contexts in which they had worked two centuries earlier.

It is appropriate to begin an appraisal of *Antiquities of Athens* by considering the literary aspect of the work, not least because the text would become James Stuart's major contribution. Stuart's writing, in Landy's view, "was not objectively descriptive of the actual condition of buildings but was burdened with literary, mythological and historical allusions" — points that were true but that were also entirely consistent with the mindset of a man whose antiquarian skills had been honed in late 1740s Rome.[77] In Rome at that time, where the ruins had been pored over and analysed since the late Middle Ages alongside the numerous verbal descriptions to be found in extant Latin

literature, there was no culture of making objective, quasi-scientific study of Roman architecture before Piranesi made such an effort in *Le antichità romane* (published only in 1756). Rather, to use an archaeological analogy, ruined buildings lay under the strata of the successive textual understandings that had accumulated upon them. This philological approach to architecture was the way Roman buildings were analysed and understood, for example, by the Commissario delle Antichità himself, Venuti, whose *Accurata e succinta descrizione topografica delle antichità di Roma* was finally to appear the year after the first volume of *Antiquities of Athens*. Venuti may represent the scholar-antiquary but, at the other end of the spectrum, even so extraordinary an architect-antiquary as Piranesi was in reality no less encumbered by philological questions in his understanding of ancient Rome, as may readily be seen from the texts and notes of *Le antichità romane* and of his works of the early 1760s, in particular. Stuart had entered fully and vigorously into this world, contending not just with Pliny's account of the functioning of the Obelisk of Psammetichus II but also with Bandini's dissertation and the erudite letters of some if not all of Bandini's fourteen other correspondents on the subject.

Stuart planned for his work in Athens by carefully reading and excising for further attention passages from the texts he thought would enlighten him on questions of architectural fabric. Of foremost importance from a topographical point of view was Pausanias, author of the mid-second-century *Description of Hellas*. Stuart, in fact, began the index of his Edinburgh notebook with "Remarks on Athens from Pausanias," and although the extensive notes he took from this author were placed further on in the notebook, the sudden looseness of the handwriting and ink blots where they do occur suggest that this might have been a task undertaken or begun onboard ship before Stuart physically even set foot in Greece.[78] The Edinburgh notebook also includes notes on Greek architecture taken from Pliny, Strabo, and Thucydides. When Stuart and Revett reached Athens, they found a situation different from that in Rome, inasmuch as there was little local culture relating to the history of the antiquities. To have taken such a situation as a *tabula rasa* and to have studied the monuments in objective isolation, however, would have meant adopting a scientific standpoint not found before the later nineteenth century. Instead, Stuart did what he had trained to do and set to the task of applying texts to buildings. A good example of his

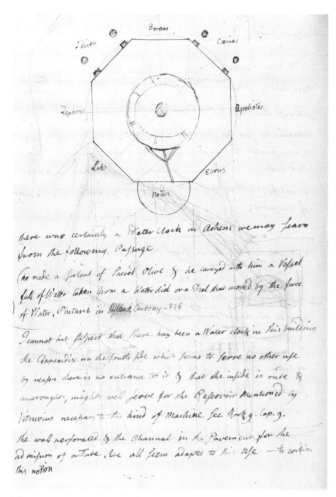

Fig. 3-20. James Stuart. Plan and notes on the Tower of the Winds, Athens. Pen and ink. From Stuart's sketchbook (ca. 1750): fol. 77v. Edinburgh University Library, Laing Mss., La.III.581. *Checklist no. 7.*

working method can be found in his records of the Tower of the Winds, in the Edinburgh notebook (fig. 3-20). Having started with a freehand sketch plan of the building, Stuart moved directly to a quotation from Plutarch's life of Mark Antony: "he carried with him a Vessel full of Water taken from a Water dial or a Dial that moved by the force of Water."[79] Only then did he state that his and Revett's excavation of the tower had revealed the closed chamber which "might well serve for the Reservoir mentioned by Vitruvius necessary for this kind of machine."[80] Stuart was then emboldened to speculate (correctly, in fact) that "I cannot but suspect that there has been a Water clock in this building," but in the process of reaching this conclusion, he had depended on Plutarch's and Vitruvius's texts before the physical excavation. This sequence was reversed, of course, in the way the tower was eventually

presented in the first volume of the *Antiquities,* so that the excavation was described in the text, while Vitruvius was footnoted and followed by a reference to Plutarch.[81]

Stuart's use of Vitruvius is particularly informative. He succumbed to the temptation that had dogged all early modern study of ancient classical architecture until then — relying on the veracity of the Roman writer's architectural history of the Greek world rather than constructing one's own, as his rival Le Roy was to attempt to do. Stuart's experience in Athens actually strengthened his dependence on Vitruvius rather than leading to scepticism. The 1751 "Proposals" for *Antiquities of Athens* stated that the textual explanations of the plates would discuss the buildings "by pointing out the relation they may have to the Doctrine of Vitruvius," but by the time of the 1755 "Proposals," the phrase "pointing out the relation they may have" had been changed to "pointing out their conformity to" the doctrine of Vitruvius, a subtle but significant semantic shift from a hypothetical to a canonical approach.[82] Once the ruined buildings of Athens lay before Stuart's very eyes, his approach to Vitruvius was

Fig. 3-21. James Stuart. Design of a Tuscan temple, after Vitruvius's description. Pen and ink. From Stuart's sketchbook (ca. 1750): fol. 195v. Edinburgh University Library, Laing Mss., La.III.581. *Checklist no. 7.*

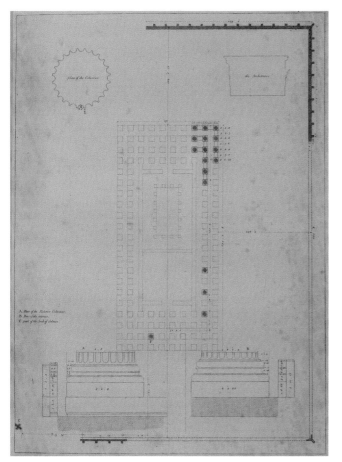

Fig. 3-22. Plan of the Temple of Jupiter Olympius. Engraving. From *Antiquities of Athens,* vol. 2 (ca. 1790): chap. 1, pl. XXXI. Courtesy of the Library, The Bard Graduate Center for Studies in the Decorative Arts, Design, and Culture, New York. *Checklist no. 129.*

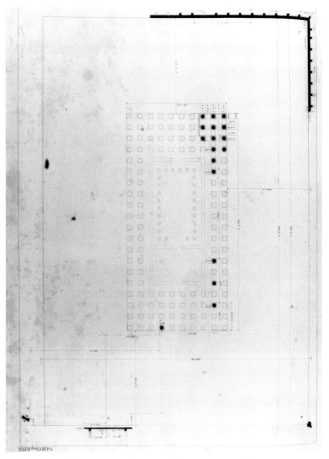

Fig. 3-23. Willey Reveley's Plan of the Temple of Jupiter Olympius (shown upside down for the sake of comparison). Engraving by W. Lowry. From *Antiquities of Athens,* vol. 3 (1794): chap. 2, pl. II. Courtesy of the Library, The Bard Graduate Center for Studies in the Decorative Arts, Design, and Culture, New York. *Checklist no. 90.*

perhaps surprisingly literary as opposed to visual: only at one point in his surviving memoranda — when making a drawing of a Tuscan temple — does he appear to have entered into what, by 1750, was the well-worn Renaissance tradition of attempting to give visual form to Vitruvius's descriptive statements about the history and origins of classical architecture (fig. 3-21). Before quoting from Vitruvius's description of the Tuscan temple, Stuart selected a passage from Book 3 in which the Roman architect had written of generic araeostyle temples, where the intercolumniation forced architects to use timber rather than stone trabeation, producing "splayed, top heavy, low, and sprawling" Tuscan-style buildings.[83] An inference that may be drawn from this is that Stuart's sensibility, as a man trained in the refined antiquarian atmosphere of Rome (and who had evidently not visited

Paestum), was not attuned to the primitive. Writing much later, in the preface to the first volume of *Antiquities,* he commented on the "inferior Elegance" of Tuscan moldings and ornaments and denied that Tuscan temples could have been "noble and magnificent" even in their general appearance and effect.[84]

Stuart's dependence on Vitruvius created difficulties when it came to the preparation of the text of *Antiquities of Athens* in the years between his return to London in 1754/55 and the appearance of the first volume eight years later. Once separated from the physical reality of the objects of study, and confronted after 1758 with Le Roy's work, Stuart's voluminous footnotes suggest that he had been drawn deeper and deeper into the text of Vitruvius. A single but highly significant example of the consequences of this can be found in Stuart's treatment of the great Temple of Jupiter Olympius in Athens (the Olympieion; fig. 3-22). Around 1760, Stuart discovered (from re-reading Thucydides) that the Olympieion could not be identified with the stoa in northern Athens which he (and Le Roy) had taken to be its remains, and which he intended to use in the first volume of *Antiquities of Athens* to exemplify the Corinthian order. Instead the so-called Columns of Hadrian south of the Acropolis were the true remains of the Olympieion. Had he and Revett been apprised of this when they were in Athens they would undoubtedly have attempted fuller study of this monument, although Revett had recorded sufficient measurements to suggest that the building had had twenty columns to each of its flanks (as nineteenth-century excavations would later confirm). According to Vitruvian rules, a temple of such a length should be decastyle at either end, but Stuart knew that Vitruvius had described the Olympieion as an octastyle dipteral temple, a type that should have no more than seventeen columns to each flank (because the lateral colonnades of Greek temples conventionally had double plus one the number of columns found in the end porticoes). Confronted with this difficulty back in London and with no prospect of a verifying return to Athens, Stuart should have had the option either of assuming error of fact on Vitruvius's part or of supposing that rules can sometimes have exceptions (as was, in fact, the case with the Olympieion, which was subsequently shown to have been an unusual octastyle temple with twenty columns to each flank). Instead, he chose a third option and spent the remainder of his life seeking a solution to this problem that would be in "conformity" with the Vitruvian rule. After William Newton, in his 1771 translation of Vitruvius, suggested that the octastyle temple mentioned by the Roman architect might have been one elsewhere in the precinct of the Olympieion rather than being the Olympieion itself, the possibility opened up that the great building could have been decastyle and Stuart could then accept the hard evidence that there were indeed more than seventeen columns to each flank. However, since the Vitruvian rule was that a decastyle temple had to have twenty-one columns to each flank, Stuart fabricated the plan engraved for the second volume of *Antiquities*. He added an extra row of columns in red chalk to Revett's original ink drawing according to the editor of the third volume, Willey Reveley, through whose hands the drawing passed. Stuart's plan, published in the second volume (see fig. 3-22) was accompanied by text

arguing that both the base of the single column marked *F* and its position relative to the imagined enclosure of the entire temple justified his interpretation. Reveley, however, stated that there was "no authority whatever" among Stuart's papers for this reading of the evidence. His own plan (fig. 3-23) duly relocated column *F* in the outer row, thereby removing Stuart's twenty-first column (though still leaving the temple as decastyle).[85]

Once this essentially philological basis of Stuart's methodology is understood, and some of the consequences that flowed from it, his responses to physical remains must be examined. This may, perhaps, be best done in order of archaeological process, through the topographical study, excavation, and recording of data to hypothetical restoration. As in Stuart's work at Pola, the topographical views introducing each monument formed one of the most striking innovations of *Antiquities of Athens* (as of its sister publications, Robert Wood's *Ruins of Palmyra* and *Ruins of Balbec*). In his preface to the first volume, Stuart was quite explicit in stating that "the Views were all finished on the spot; and, in these, preferring Truth to every other consideration, I have taken none of those Liberties with which painters are apt to indulge themselves. . . . Not an object is here embellished by strokes of Fancy, nor is the situation of any one of them changed, excepting only in the View of the Doric Portal where the Fountain on the Fore-ground is somewhat turned from its real position."[86] Scholars have tended to take these claims at face value, perhaps influenced by Stuart's disarming honesty in admitting his single creative intervention with the fountain at the Doric Portico.[87] In the context of eighteenth-century topographical study, however, it is wise to draw a distinction between the perspectival rendition of architectural ruins in the landscape and the painstakingly and necessarily precisely factual objectives of cartography (a form of representation in which Stuart appears to have been extremely proficient).[88] The former must still be recognized as an artistic tradition, notwithstanding Stuart's criticism of the "liberties" taken by painters, and it effectively remained so until the camera lucida in the early nineteenth century introduced the notion of an objective drawing of a building in its spatial setting. Indeed, the scientific potential of the camera lucida, once it did appear, was by no means universally greeted with enthusiasm by architectural students, who were still wedded to the idea that the act of drawing a monument should be an exercise in developing "taste."

Fig. 3-24. James Stuart. Perspective drawing of the Ionic Temple on the Ilissus, 1750–53. Pen and ink. By permission of The British Library, London, Add. Ms. 22,153, p. 2r.

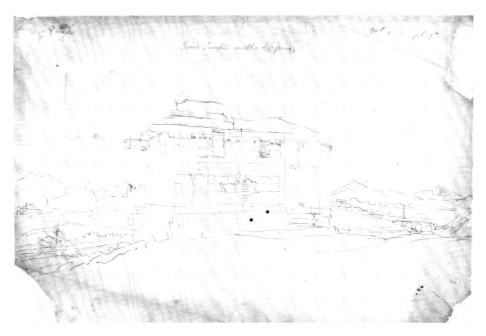

Perhaps the most famous proponent of the camera in the upsurge in travel that followed the Napoleonic Wars was James Hakewill, who traveled in Italy with the express intention of illustrating John Chetwode Eustace's *Picturesque Tour of Italy.* John Soane's pupil, George Basevi, writing from Rome in 1818, commented that Hakewill was "a very vulgar low-bred fellow. . . . I should question if his work took, certainly it will not with those who have been in Italy . . . [his views] are all drawn with a lucida camera, a thing not very creditable to a professed artist, and from its mechanism always unpleasing."[89] Stuart could not have foreseen this debate, of course, but its possible effects have already been analysed above in the comparison of his gouache with Thomas Allason's print of the Arch of the Sergii at Pola, where Allason claimed to have produced the more "correct" view (see figs. 2-9, 3-18).

Stuart's possible creativity with the topography of the arch at Pola does not mean, of course, that he was equally creative when he arrived in Greece. Between production of the views at Pola and doubtless almost all of those executed in Greece came Stuart's renewed encounter with Wood and his party, which took place in Athens in May 1751. Wood was returning from the Levant having completed his surveys of Palmyra and Balbec, and Stuart and Revett had arrived in Athens little more than a month earlier. Given the shared objectives of the two parties and their evident amicability, it is most likely that Wood shared with Stuart and Revett the benefits of the experience he had accumulated and that they discussed the merits of the

"actual state" view that was to become so strategic in their respective publications. Recent analysis of the drawings made by Giovanni Battista Borra as the departure points for Wood's restorations of Palmyra suggests that his images, too, were carefully composed so as to give grounds for full restoration, rather than standing as exact records of what actually lay on the ground.[90] This was, however, a far more subtle process in Borra's case than Stuart's possible exclusion of an awkwardly sited wall at Pola. Perhaps it was a lesson that Stuart learned at that early stage of his Athenian sojourn, for the surviving evidence of Stuart's Greek gouaches supports his later claim not to have changed the "situation" of the monuments under study.[91] There is also evidence to confirm, however, that when Stuart asserted that the views were "all finished on the spot," he was referring to the compositions rather than to the actual gouache paintings. In a volume of papers related to *Antiquities of Athens,* now in the British Library is a drawing by Stuart of the small Ionic temple beside the Ilissus River (fig. 3-24). Clearly this was the on-site sketch that formed the basis of the gouache subsequently engraved by Edward Rooker in the first volume of *Antiquities* (figs. 3-25, 3-26). The sketch was executed only in pen and ink, Stuart never having got as far as laying on the gray wash that would probably have come next, based on his work at Pola (see fig. 3-17). It gives a real sense of the isolation and desolation of the site, so exposed that no rearrangement was necessary to show the surviving elements of the Ionic temple as incorporated into a church (although detail is missing from the left wall of the cella). The gouache thus appears, in topographical terms, to be a fairly faithful working up of the sketch, either carried out back in Stuart's lodgings in Athens or, more likely, back in London some years later.

The most striking difference between Stuart's sketch and his gouache of the temple on the Ilissus is his inclusion in the view of no less a figure than the Turkish governor of Athens, the "Vaiwode," on a hunt with some of his attendants. This imaginary, generic scene was introduced, as Stuart put it, "to represent the Dress and Appearance of the present Inhabitants of Athens."[92] As this implies, the figures serve as a pointer to the historical specificity of the time when Stuart and Revett were in Athens. In a number of other cases where *staffage* was introduced to the gouaches, Stuart presented even more significant subtexts. His view of the Monument of Philopappus, for example, is accompanied by a description of how the figures silhouetted to the left (Revett, Stuart himself, Dawkins, and Wood) were about the drink the coffee that can be seen being made in the foreground (fig. 3-27).[93] The drawing on which this print was based must be one of Stuart's earliest Greek views, and in its precise action and moment of ephemerality, it well represents what has been called "the attestation of presence" in the early history of archaeology, giving evidence not merely of the "reality of the authors' travel experiences but also of the grounding of their architectural authority in

them."[94] That establishment of authority is seen most importantly in Stuart's view of the Erechtheion, where all the personnel are listed in the accompanying text (except for Stuart himself, shown making the drawing at the front right) and an account is given of what they were doing (see fig. 2-10). Stuart noted that "Our labourers . . . are digging to discover the Base, and the steps of the Basement under the Caryatides," but also pointed out that the two Turkish men looking down into the excavation from atop the caryatid portico were part of a constant surveillance team, set up by the commander of the garrison (the Turk with the long pipe in the painting) "to watch our proceedings."[95] Thus, in this single image and accompanying text, Stuart was able to show himself aware of the importance of excavation in the archaeological process while also indicating the hindrances that he and Revett had suffered in pursuit of that objective.

Today, of course, stratified excavation to the ground would be one of the first aims of the classical archaeologist once a proper survey of the building in its extant condition has been conducted. The relatively "little excavation" undertaken by Stuart and Revett was seen pejoratively by Jacob Landy as a clear indication of "their primary interest in surface ornament."[96] In the middle of the eighteenth century, however, excavation for solely architectural purposes (as opposed to in the quest for buried objets d'art) was still a relatively unusual procedure, even in Rome. Almost a century earlier, Desgodetz had

Fig. 3-25. James Stuart. "View of the Temple on the Ilissus," 1750s–60s. Gouache. RIBA Library Drawings Collection, London, SD 145/2. *Checklist no. 23.*

Fig. 3-26. "View of the Temple on the Ilissus." Engraving by Edward Rooker. From *Antiquities of Athens,* vol. 1 (1762): chap. 2, pl. I. Courtesy of the Library, The Bard Graduate Center for Studies in the Decorative Arts, Design, and Culture, New York. *Checklist no. 36.*

made excavations as part of his seminal study of Roman buildings, but his practice can be seen to have been inconsistent, at best, and sometimes so superficial as to have led to publication of error.[97] Stuart well understood the extraordinary potential value of excavation from his study of the base of the Obelisk of Psammetichus II, and it was probably only difficulties of access (perhaps accompanied by shortage of funds) that prevented him from adopting this approach at all of the monuments he and Revett studied in Greece. Stuart's statement, in the preface to the first volume of *Antiquities,* that he and Revett had "carefully examined as low as to the Foundation of every Building that we have copied," with it being "generally necessary to get a great quantity of earth and rubbish removed" may have overstated the case. There is no reason, however, to suspect him of the degree of disingenuousness shown by Robert Adam in exaggerating the extent of his excavations at Split (Spalato) in Dalmatia in

Fig. 3-27. James Stuart. View of the Monument of Philopappus, with Nicholas Revett, Stuart, James Dawkins, and Robert Wood standing in a group on the left. Engraved by Daniel Lerpinière. From *Antiquities of Athens*, vol. 3 (1794): chap. 5, pl. I. Courtesy of the Library, The Bard Graduate Center for Studies in the Decorative Arts, Design, and Culture, New York. *Checklist no. 90.*

1757 to reflect greater scholarly credentials than were perhaps due.[98] Indeed Le Roy — whose objectives little accorded with those of Stuart and Revett — noted before he left Athens in 1755 that "foreigners who travel here are indebted to Messieurs Stuart and Revett. They have revealed treasures hidden underground or in thick walls."[99]

The consequences of the limited opportunities Stuart and Revett had to excavate, especially on and around the Acropolis where the Turks had a garrison, were real enough, as Stuart's unpublished notes reveal. In the case of the Parthenon, for example, he jotted down a reminder to himself that "defects" of measurement were due to "the inequality of the Ground by reason of the Rubbish & which it is difficult to allow exactly for."[100] Where excavations were possible, significant advances were undoubtedly made. At the Tower of the Winds, for example, remote in northern Athens from the Turkish garrison, Stuart commented that "it was necessary to make several considerable Excavations."[101] In fact he and Revett were able to dig down some 15 feet, reaching the original ground level both outside and inside the building (from where Stuart said a volume 2,700 cubic feet of rubble was removed). They thereby established that the entrance had been through a doorcase with fluted columns on the northwest side and that the marble floor was channeled to aid the functioning of a water-clock in the building. The clock's apparatus in the floor was then "faithfully shown" in their plan of the tower, more faithfully in fact than it was by Henry Robinson in making his study of the building in 1943.[102] Stuart and Revett's excavations also revealed sufficient fragments of the entablatures over the doorways to enable fair restoration.

Stuart's private admission of "defects" in the measurements he and Revett had made at the Parthenon leads from the matter of excavation to that of the survey or record drawings they made public in *Antiquities of Athens* and that constituted, in effect, the principal claim to fame of the work. Their model was Desgodetz, whose authority had not yet been called into question in 1740s Rome. Desgodetz had expressed the majority of his measurements in modular form, equating these in some cases with Paris Royal feet, inches, and lines, or *lignes* (unit of measure equal to a twelfth of an inch). Stuart and Revett, however, eschewed modules because, as Stuart explained in the preface to *Antiquities,* modules "necessarily imply a System, and perhaps too frequently incline an author to adopt

one."[103] On the face of it this was a perverse statement because Stuart had an almost biblical respect for Vitruvius's text and, as he well knew, Vitruvius had given the Greek notion of order *(taxis)*, in sympathy with a modular approach, as the very first principle of architectural design.[104] The surviving evidence suggests, however, that the nonmodular approach was adopted by Stuart and Revett from the outset and was not a later rationalization forced upon them by incompleteness in their measurements. The decision to use the modern unit of the English foot — a decision shared, significantly, with Robert Wood — should be seen as part of an Enlightenment project to achieve absolute accuracy by any chosen standard. The elucidation of proportional systems may have acquired greater value in Stuart's mind precisely because the English measurements he and Revett had taken were commensurate with but not identical to the Attic or Roman Attic feet deployed by the original architects of the buildings. As Stuart wrote in the preface to *Antiquities,* any person could "from our Measures form whatever kind of Module, or modulary division he best fancies." That he himself engaged in that practice seems clear both from the numerous calculations in his manuscript notes and from the criticisms aimed at him by Landy, who suggested, for example, that the assumption of symmetry in the stylobate of the Parthenon had led Stuart and Revett to force the dimensions into a set of proportions in the ratio 4:9.[105] Recent studies, however, refocusing on the modular design approach of the Greeks have led to the suggestion that 4:9 was indeed the ratio of column height to stylobate width in the case of the front of the Parthenon.[106]

Stuart and Revett's professed commitment to such absolute standards of measurement can also be seen in the fact that in *Antiquities of Athens* they gave dimensions in feet, inches, and decimal subdivisions of the inch: tenths, hundredths, and even, on occasion, thousandths. Some of their contemporaries were derisory about such minutiae. Lord Charlemont, for example, commented on the imperceptibility to the eye even of the "discrepancies of a few inches" Stuart and Revett had noted with intercolumniations at the Parthenon, and Charlemont proclaimed that the Greeks had "built for the effect, rather than with that minute exactness on which we pride ourselves." "This remark," he continued, "will also serve to show the inutility of those measurements to a hair's breadth upon which Stewart piques himself."[107] These doubts have persisted, with at least one modern scholar

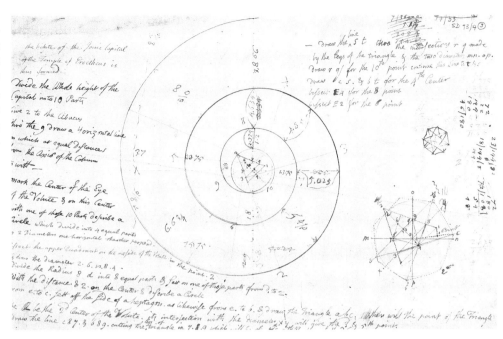

Fig. 3-28. James Stuart. Drawings and calculations for setting out the capital of the Temple of Erechtheus (the east portico of the Erechtheion), 1750–53. Pen and ink. RIBA Library Drawings Collection, London, SD 93/4/3.

stating that "the condition of two-thousand-year-old masonry could hardly have supported such a level of accuracy" as that claimed by Stuart.[108] This is rather to miss the point, however, as the minutest figures were surely produced by mathematical or trigonometrical calculation rather than by physical measurement. Comparisons of Stuart and Revett's dimensions with those made more recently with the benefits of newer instrumentation and technology have pointed to an often impressive degree of accuracy. Even Landy, their sternest critic, felt constrained to admit that their measurements of details were "generally unimpeachable in their accuracy," or "comparatively accurate" in the case of the setting out of the Ionic capital of the temple on the Ilissus River.[109]

Stuart and Revett's measurements were seen by Landy less in terms of an archaeological exercise than of their ulterior purpose of supporting a Greek Revival — "the improvement of the Art itself," as Stuart put it — a good reason (though not the principal one) for the use of English feet and inches.[110] Landy argued that they gave more emphasis to detailed measurements of architectural decoration than they did to the elements of buildings at large, basing his argument on the example of the Ionic temple on the Ilissus where minimal dimensions for the building as a whole were provided by comparison with the immensely detailed rendition of the base, capital, and entablature. In this case, the published information was little more than a reflection of the state in which the remains were to be found — the building in poor condition but

the order relatively well preserved (see fig. 3-24). To judge from the surviving evidence of Stuart's papers, however, he did give almost disproportionate attention to the setting out of Greek Ionic capitals, producing numerous drawings and hugely complicated calculations. There are seven sheets alone in the British Library, for example, on the capitals of the Temple of Minerva Polias (the western cellar and portico of the Erechtheion) and three from the same set at the RIBA of the capitals of the eastern cellar, the Temple of Erechtheus itself (fig. 3-28). These images are an early sign of his personal aesthetic preference for the Greek Ionic order, later reflected in his use of the orders of the Erechtheion, in particular, in his architectural career. Significantly, the only gouache view in which Stuart chose to include an image of himself at work is that showing the Erechtheion (see fig. 2-10), while figure 3-28, which displays the geometry of the capital on the recto, bears on the verso, among the numerous prosaic calculations, a moving and romantic aphorism: "Our imagination is struck/touch'd with the same objects, that light up the Genius of the Poets."[111]

To return, however, to the archaeological value of the measured drawings, Stuart's manuscript notes contain one small but very significant piece of information that enlightens us about his working method in Athens and about the consequent difficulties he encountered when preparing measurements for publication back in London years later. In relation to the Theseion (the Temple of Hephaestus), Stuart recorded in the Edinburgh notebook

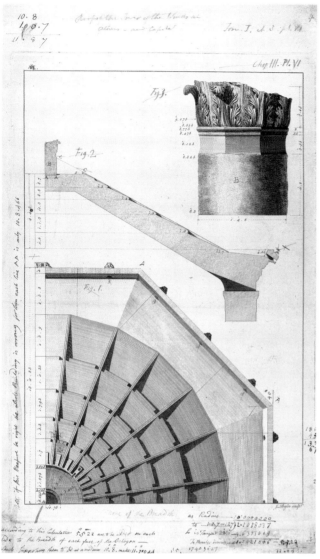

Fig. 3-29. Proof plate for plan of the Tower of the Winds, Athens, late 1750s–early 1760s. Engraving, with pencil, pen and ink notations by James Stuart. By permission of The British Library, London, London, Add. Ms. 22,153, p. 4r.

measurements with a chain as the basis for his mathematical speculations. As a result, when working up the plates for publication years later, there must have been occasions when Stuart had in hand different records of the same dimensions, with his own figures perhaps proving inconsistent with Revett's.

The process of adding measurements onto the plates was by no means a simple one of transcription. Stuart was checking for mathematical consistencies as he worked on the book in London in the later 1750s and early 1760s. This is clear from the fortuitous survival among the British Library papers of the proof for the plan of Tower of the Winds (fig. 3-29), plate VI of chapter 3 in the first volume. Apart from making additions in red ink (to indicate figure numbers and letters needed on the final plate) Stuart wrote along the left margin, where the radius dimension is given as 13 feet, 11 inches and 85 hundredths of an inch: "if this measure is right the whole building is wrong for then each line *AA* is only 10.8.466." At the right foot of the sheet, Stuart continued with a calculation, to seven decimal points, and concluded that: "according to this calculation, 5.522 [5 inches, 522 thousandths] are to be added on each side to the breadth of each face of the octagon — which supposing them to be at a median 10′.8″ makes 11.7.044′."[113] At first reading this note gives the impression that something had gone disastrously

that his measurements had been made "with a Chain," whereas "Revett has since measured it with a Rod which will be more accurate:" this rod was doubtless the brass yardstick made in London for the expedition by John Bird, of which Stuart was sufficiently proud to make mention in the preface to *Antiquities*.[112] From this it can be inferred that the separation of labors agreed upon by Stuart and Revett for their work in Greece had led to an element of independence in their surveying activities — with Stuart recognizing Revett's role as the arbiter of empirical exactitude but nevertheless making his own

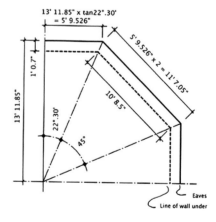

Fig. 3-30. David Yeomans. Trigonometrical drawing of the Tower of the Winds, Athens, 2005. This demonstrates Stuart's dilemma with measurements. Courtesy of the artist.

wrong for five-and-a-half-inch corrections to be needed, but the plate actually amounts to a case study in the problematics of producing a set of measurements of an existing building, a significantly different exercise from the setting out of the building in the first place. In this case the radius 13 feet 11.85 inches is the distance from the center of the building to the outer extremity of the overhanging eaves in the center point of one side of the octagon's plan (see fig. 3-30).[114] Line *AA* on figure 3-29 thus shows the breadth of one side of the tower's roof — but Stuart had no record of the actual figure applicable to this dimension, referring instead to the (inevitably narrower) breadth of the wall, which plate II of the chapter on the Tower of the Winds gives as 10 feet 8 inches (in the case of the two sides with doorways and 10 feet 9.5 inches in the case of the other six sides). Stuart's calculation (bottom right on fig. 3-29) uses the projection of the cornice from the plane of the wall (given on plate V of the chapter as 1 foot 7 hundredths of an inch) and also the tangent 22° 30′, which enabled him to produce the figure of 11 feet 7 inches and 44 thousandths for the breadth of each face of the roof of the octagon. In the plate as finally published, therefore, the line marked *AA* is duly given as 11 feet 7 inches and 5 tenths (the thousandths having been rounded). As figure 3-30 shows, Stuart would have arrived at a closely similar result by a more conventional piece of trigonometry, multiplying the radius of 13 feet 11.85 inches by tangent 22° 30′ (to produce the breadth of half of the roof) and doubling the result. As this single example shows, then, it cannot be assumed that the dimensions given on the plates in *Antiquities of Athens* are those actually measured, and some — perhaps many — of the minutest figures were produced by Stuart by calculation. Most likely he used a table of trigonometrical ratios and worked to the maximum number of significant figures that these gave him, so as to avoid inaccuracies that might have been introduced by rounding figures to levels more believable in the physical contexts of the masonry.

While the division of labors between Stuart and Revett in regard to measuring caused difficulties later for Stuart that could only be resolved by mathematics, the record drawings and subsequent engravings of the sculptural detail of the Greek monuments that forms a large part of *Antiquities of Athens* were the sole preserve of Stuart. Relatively little evidence survives of what Stuart actually did in Athens in terms of on-site work in this respect, but the collections of the British Library and of the British Museum do contain four sheets worked on by Stuart while studying the frieze of the Monument of Lysicrates at first hand (fig. 3-31).[115] One of Stuart's claims to fame is that he was first to correctly identify this frieze, executed 335 − 334 B.C., as showing scenes of a tale told by Ovid of Dionysus and deceitful sailors (the Tyrrhenian "pirates") who, having kidnapped the god with the intention of selling him into slavery, are subsequently transformed into dolphins and jump into the sea as they seek to avoid his chastisements. The sculptor of the monument introduced his own element to the story in the form of silenes (satyrs) who attack the pirates with long flares and other implements of violence. Stuart's drawings show that he drew the small figures in his bold, sweeping hand and that he went to extraordinary lengths, doubtless from a position on a ladder, to record as many coordinates as he could, presumably so as to be able to reproduce the forms of the Greek figures accurately. The drawing in the British Museum was the subject of a study to evaluate Stuart's work in this respect undertaken by Arthur Smith at the end of the nineteenth century. Smith also compared Stuart's drawing (now in the British Library) of a lost relief of Athene and Marsyas with the engraved version that appears in the second volume of *Antiquities* as the tailpiece to the chapter on the Theatre of Bacchus (the Odeion of Herodes). Smith found the drawing to be a good record of Greek figurative sculpture but the engraving to have an "altogether unclassical" plume for Athene's helmet, to have removed Marsyas's tail, to have caricatured the faces of the figures and to have weakened their pose. Smith's conclusion was that Stuart was a "careful draughtsman, accurate in detail, and catching the spirit of the originals, and that he suffered much at the hands of the engravers during his period of infirmity and after his death."[116]

Smith's observations raise two questions: first, what processes were used to translate Stuart's drawings into printed form; and, second, how closely had his drawings actually related to the sculpture of the frieze of the monument in the first place? All but two of the plates of the frieze were engraved by James Basire, whom Stuart had probably met in Rome in 1749 − 50 and who ran a small workshop as one of the leading engravers of later eighteenth-century London. In assessing Basire's role, it is fortunate indeed that one of his proof plates (fig. 3-32) has survived and can be compared with Stuart's on-site work (fig. 3-31) and the plate as finally published (fig. 3-33). The satyr on the left of figure 3-31, for example, is not a full

Fig. 3-31. James Stuart. Figures from the frieze of the Choragic Monument of Lysicrates, Athens, 1750–53. Pencil, pen and ink. By permission of The British Library, London, London, Add. Ms. 22,153, p. 13r.

Fig. 3-32. Proof plate, figures from the frieze of the Choragic Monument of Lysicrates, Athens, late 1750s–early 1760s. Engraving by James Basire. By permission of The British Library, London, London, Add. Ms. 22,153, p. 12r.

profile in Stuart's drawing, and as a consequence of being slightly turned away, the head is small in proportion to the body below. The figure has a short, pointed beard and is apparently shown wearing a cap. In Basire's proof plate the profile has become fuller and the hair and beard have been thickened up (the cap has disappeared). In the plate as finally published, the hair has been made still thicker but with a hairband introduced. The effect of this, when coupled to the progressive building up of the musculature of the torso in the three images, is to make the head too large for the body, while deep setting of the eyes and heavy

shading on the face serves to age the satyr.

A similar developmental sequence may be observed in the case of the figure to the right on figure 3-31 leaning on a tree stump. Stuart's drawing offered no evidence of beard or facial details other than a straight, Winckelmannian nose, yet the figure ended up with full hair, beard, crooked nose, and grin. In fact, Stuart recorded this figure as a young faun (his text makes it clear that he considered all Bacchus's attendants to be fauns, "however of different Ages"), whereas in preparing the plate it was transformed into a fully mature satyr.[117] Without know-

Fig. 3-33. Figures from the frieze of the Choragic Monument of Lysicrates, Athens. Engraving by James Basire. From *Antiquities of Athens,* vol. 1 (1762): chap. 4, pl. XXV. Courtesy of the Library, The Bard Graduate Center for Studies in the Decorative Arts, Design, and Culture, New York. *Checklist no. 36.*

ing whether Basire worked direct from Stuart's on-site drawing, or whether Stuart had prepared intermediate drawings of the figures, we cannot be certain who made these changes, Stuart or his engraver. Despite his reputation, Basire was not without critics. In 1758, for example, Robert Adam described him as a "triffling ignorant puppyish wretch" for producing a plate that was "hard, ill drawn, of a Bad Colour."[118] On the other hand James Adam reported hearing, when in Venice in 1760, that Stuart "corrects all his own plates," thus explaining in part the delay in the appearance of *Antiquities.*[119] Indeed, there is no reason to think that this was not the case, since Stuart had shown himself to be an outstanding reproductive engraver when in Rome, and he would certainly have noticed these changes had Basire introduced them of his own volition. The likely conclusion must be that Stuart had wider concerns in producing the first volume of *Antiquities* or in other areas of his career, or perhaps his aesthetic notions, either of Greek sculpture or of the treatment of satyrs as opposed to human figures, had changed in the years between his studies in Athens and production of the book in London.

How well did Stuart's on-site drawings capture the character of the originals as he saw them in the 1750s? By the eighteenth century these sculptures were already in poor condition. They have subsequently deteriorated further, and casts made for Lord Elgin by 1802, together with drawings by his draftsman Giovanni Battista Lusieri, have, since the late nineteenth century, been taken as the best evidence of their form.[120] Stuart's images have been largely discounted. In the case of the satyr on the right of figures

3-31 to 3-33, although a recent study has stated that the figure (silen 3) did have a wedge-shaped beard, the evidence both of Lusieri's drawing and of the casts makes this inconclusive. The question rests on interpretation of how the crooked left arm meets the chin and accordingly on how the angle of arm and wrist are judged.[121] Stuart does appear to have softened the angle of the wrist, and in reality the distance between wrist and chin is probably too great to allow for Stuart's depiction of the forefinger resting against the lips. Stuart has captured the shoulder blade and breast-bone muscle well in his drawing but missed the distinctive horizontal fold between thorax and abdomen that is still clearly visible today on the monument. All of these features were lost in the disproportionate profusion of musculature of the torso in the proof and final plates. In the case of the satyr on the left (silen 5), shadow evidence in the masonry shows that there was a beard, subsequently broken off but present when the casts were made. Like Stuart, Lusieri gave the figure a hairband, but there seems little evidence for Lusieri's masklike treatment of the facial features.[122] Moreover, the casts suggest that Stuart's drawing captured the relatively lithe legs and torso of this figure better than did Lusieri's. Again, these characteristics were lost in the translation of Stuart's drawing into printed form.

Arthur Smith was broadly correct in his 1892 – 93 article in assessing Stuart as an artist who captured the character of Greek figurative sculpture reasonably well in the 1750s, given the already poor condition of the originals. However, it seems quite possible that Stuart played a part in the subsequent loss of that character in the engrav-

Fig. 3-34. An apobates (right), a seated charioteer, and a marshal (left), from the north frieze of the Parthenon, Athens. Probably engraved by James Newton. From *Antiquities of Athens,* vol. 2 (ca. 1790): chap. 1, pl. XX. Courtesy of the Library, The Bard Graduate Center for Studies in the Decorative Arts, Design, and Culture, New York. *Checklist no. 129.*

ings of James Basire. Smith also suggested that Stuart was not to be depended upon when it came to restoring missing parts of Greek sculpture, taking as an example part of the north frieze of the Parthenon that shows the figure of an apobates to the right of a seated charioteer who is in the process of being crowned by a marshal (fig. 3-34). Stuart's plate suggests that when he saw this part of the frieze, the head and upper left torso of the apobates were sheared off, while the figures of the charioteer and marshal (with his crowning right arm uplifted), and also of the wheel of the chariot, were more or less entire. As the sculpture survives today, the heads of both charioteer and marshal are gone, as is most of the wheel of the chariot. The damage to this part of the frieze had certainly occurred between Stuart's time in Athens and that of Jacques Carrey who, as draftsman to the Marquis de Nointel, had drawn much of the Parthenon sculpture in 1674. In the case of this particular scene, Carrey's drawing shows that while the chariot wheel was already largely lost by the late seventeenth century, all three heads were entire at that time, as was the torso of the apobates, and that the arm of the marshal was extended rather than crooked (fig. 3-35). On the basis of this evidence, it can be seen that Stuart did indeed take considerable liberties in his restoration of the scene: completing the wheel, inventing heads for the charioteer and marshal, and hypothesizing the position of the marshal's arm. Stuart can, however, be exonerated from Smith's accusation that

his restoration of the charioteer's head was not only a fabrication but one that changed the gender of the figure to female. Had Smith looked at Stuart's text as well as at his plate he would have seen that Stuart described "a youth, whom I suppose a Victor in the Chariot race," with a man "about to Crown him."[123] In addition, the wisps of hair that can be seen projecting from the right temple of the charioteer today, not to mention those that appeared on a fragment with the torso and head of the apobates excavated in 1888 – 89, do offer good grounds for Stuart's rendition of a head with curly locks — and actually cast considerable doubt on the veracity of Carrey's drawing at this point (which gives the charioteer close-cropped hair).[124]

The issue of the visual restoration of Greek relief sculpture leads, finally, to the restoration of Greek buildings themselves in *Antiquities of Athens.* Stuart and Revett took a strictly academic approach to restoration, regarding it as an orthographical art and eschewing the use of perspective that crept into Le Roy's work (in his plate of the Propylaea) and even into Robert Wood's.[125] Stuart also claimed, in describing his and Revett's restoration of the Monument of Lysicrates, that they had proceeded "as far as the Remains found on the Spot, will authorize, and no farther."[126] Such a statement appears fully in line with the objective of fidelity that underpinned their work in other respects, but perhaps Stuart's use of the word "authorize" (with its etymological hint of personal creativity) may be

Fig. 3-35. Jacques Carrey. An apobates (right), a seated charioteer, and a marshal (left), from the north frieze of the Parthenon, Athens, 1674. Pencil, colored pencil. Bibliothèque Nationale de France, Paris.

taken to denote his recognition of the fact that any visual restoration of a ruined building requires an act of qualified imagination.

The veracity of Stuart and Revett's restorations naturally depended to an extent on the degree of access they had to buildings, especially where large portions were underground or otherwise encumbered. Thus their restoration of the Doric portico in the Roman agora, which opens the first volume of *Antiquities,* was summarily dismissed as "incorrect" by the archaeologist Henry Robinson in 1943, with no concession being made to the fact that Robinson had been able to study the structure on an isolated site whereas in the 1750s it had been partially incorporated into houses.[127] Stuart and Revett's plan was, in fact, suitably tentative, showing only the part of the structure that survived (only two thirds of the whole, it would later emerge) and indicating what was hypothetical by use of dotted lines (fig. 3-36). The only error of which they can reasonably be accused in this context is that of having misinterpreted the surviving masonry of the architrave, thereby failing to appreciate where the western wall of the Roman agora had intersected with the portico and giving the restored lateral elevation too great a length. Robinson was able to establish this, but he also had the advantage of being able to prove it by undertaking an excavation.

Jacob Landy's principal criticism of Stuart and Revett's restorations was that they had indulged in a process of idealization. As an example of this he gave their north elevation of the Erechtheion, where they regularized masonry and jointing and thus produced fifteen courses of stone above the taller foundation row rather than the existing sixteen.[128] Given, however, that in the parallel case of the Ionic temple on the Ilissus (fig. 3-37) they were evidently correct, to judge from Stuart's topographical view (see fig. 3-24), in showing seven courses of stonework above the taller foundation row, it is clear that there was no consistent "idealization" in this aspect of their work. Difficulties of access on the Acropolis might have caused the discrepancy in the case of the Erechtheion alighted on by Landy. Their restoration of the temple on the Ilissus is actually a model of presentation and reconstruction (except for the introduction of a frieze relief from a fragment found at Athens which they claimed might have come from this temple because its height and depth matched the space). The overall sparseness of the plan and elevation reflects the fact that there was not much evidence for the overall form of the building, while greater attention was given to the (fluted) Ionic order and the *antae* because more fabric survived. Furthermore, the text is explicit about what was present and what was not and, therefore, about what they had supplied. The one element of the building that was suppressed in the restoration was the fact that it was here, as Stuart's text freely admitted, that he and Revett discovered that the architrave had been "enriched with a painted Ornament, which appears to be as ancient as the Building itself."[129] There would, of course, have been no printing mechanism avail-

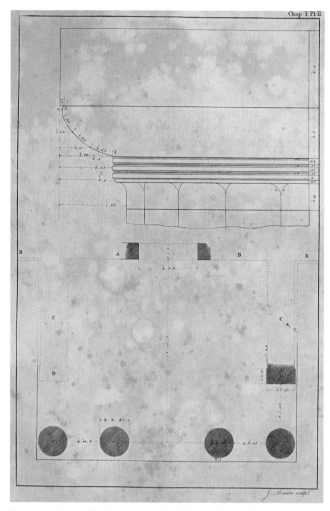

Chap. I Pl. II

Fig. 3-36. Plan of a Doric portico, Athens. Engraving. From
Antiquities of Athens, vol. 1 (1762): chap. 1, pl. II. Courtesy of the
Library, The Bard Graduate Center for Studies in the
Decorative Arts, Design, and Culture, New York.
Checklist no. 36.

able to them had they wished to illustrate the temple as
a building with colored decoration, but there is no escaping the conclusion that Stuart held Winckelmannian views
on the essential whiteness of Greek art and architecture,
for he later reported to James Gandon that he liked the
"bleaching of the stone and marble to a pure white colour"
in Greece, clearly implying that he knew that this was not
how the buildings had been in their original state.[130]

It is less clear that it was Stuart and Revett's sensibil-
ities that were responsible for other oversights laid at their
door by Landy. Foremost among these was their neglect
of the subtleties of Greek design such as entasis, curvature
of the stylobate, the inward inclination of columns and
cella walls, and the outward tilt of entablatures. In some

of these cases, Vitruvius had provided descriptions — he
discussed entasis, for example, in book 3, chapter 3, section 13 — so that Stuart either cannot have understood
what Vitruvius meant or failed to map it onto built examples. In the Theseion (Temple of Hephaestus), however, he
did comment that "the diameters of the columns vary
from 3:3:35 to 3:3:65," but a discrepancy of a mere thirty
hundredths of an inch amounts more to a point of curiosity than to proof of a system of design. Their surveying
instruments might simply not have been sufficient to
enable them to detect such curves and inclinations, or they
were possibly inhibited by presuppositions of perpendic-
ularity.[131] There were also aspects of Greek architecture
that they observed while on site but which were not subsequently incorporated in the text as published. One such
area concerns Greek construction methods, about which
Stuart recorded some comments in his Edinburgh notebook.[132] Although these notes are based on what Vitruvius
said about construction techniques (in book 2, chapter 8,
sections 5 − 6), two small sketches of the first method,
called "Isodamum," show that Stuart appreciated that in
the alternate courses, comprising two stones' thickness, the
stones were "cramped" together. Landy's claim that Stuart
and Revett showed little interest in the technicalities of
Greek building, such as dowels, clamps and *anathyrosis*
(close jointing while blocks' surfaces remained rough), was
thus not entirely fair, based as it was on what Stuart eventually published rather than what he had actually done.[133]
It seems plausible that such technicalities were left out of
Antiquities of Athens because of a decrease of archaeological purpose, as the project moved into the 1760s, at the
expense of increasing architectural appeal. Ancient construction methods would have been of little relevance to
later eighteenth-century building practice.

★ ★ ★

On his return to London late in 1754 or early the following year, Stuart had been faced with the difficulties both
of seeing his Greek archaeological work through to print
and of establishing a career for himself as a practical architect and designer. In producing *Antiquities*, Stuart became
embroiled, after 1758, in refuting what he saw as Le Roy's
claims to primacy in the field of Greek archaeology and
topography and, after 1766, in struggling to gain access to
the additional drawings made by his former collaborator
Revett during a return visit to Athens. This struggle, as
well as Stuart's failure to bring the second volume of

Fig. 3-37. Lateral elevation of the Temple on the Ilissus. Engraving by Edward Rooker. From *Antiquities of Athens,* vol. 1 (1762): chap. 2, pl. IV. Courtesy of the Library, The Bard Graduate Center for Studies in the Decorative Arts, Design, and Culture, New York. *Checklist no. 36.*

Antiquities of Athens to completion before his death in 1788, has been well described in previous accounts. Aside from his continuous work on the Athenian project, Stuart's antiquarian and archaeological interests found a new outlet in his fellowship of the Society of Antiquaries, to which he was nominated for election on June 15, 1758, with the citation:

> A Testimonial was presented & read, recommending Mr James Stuart, of Grosvenor Street, F.R.S. Painter and Architect, to be elected a Member of this Society; of which Honour he is said to be desirous, & from the personal knowledge of the subscribers certified to be a Gentleman exceeding well versed in Antiquities, of which the valuable Collections made by him in his Travels are an undoubted Proof; & they assure themselves from his great Abilities, that he is likely to be a very useful member.[134]

Stuart was duly elected on December 7 and "signed the Books, & was admitted a Fellow" on January 25, 1759, when Horace Walpole and William Stukeley were among those present.[135]

Stuart's involvement with the society (see chap. 4) and the world of the London antiquary must have seemed a very different and, indeed, distinctly less glamorous one from that he had inhabited when in the Mediterranean.

In March 1759, for example, three months after his election, Stuart was in attendance at a meeting when fellows were shown a drawing of an archiepiscopal crozier, "dug up by a Labourer in May 1752, in grubbing a Hedge in the Vicarage Garden at Wesham in Kent," a far cry from the summer of 1748 when he had participated in the study of an obelisk that linked present-day Rome to the historians of the Renaissance, to Pliny, to the Augustan city, and back beyond that to the Heliopolis of Pharaoh Psammetichus II. It was a far cry, too, from the years spent studying the monuments of Athens with Vitruvius and Pausanias in hand.[136] Yet in a real sense, these experiences remained present with Stuart throughout the 1750s and, indeed, for the rest of his life.

The process of writing the text of *Antiquities of Athens* and of preparing the plates was not a static one, in which data collected in the early 1750s was simply drawn together for publication. The work that Stuart carried on was developmental in almost every aspect of the book. His engagement with Vitruvius and other texts was continuous; his "actual state" views moved through the stages of gouache painting and engraving; and his restorations of Greek sculpture took on an aesthetic character of his own devising once no longer before his eyes. Even the measurements, supposedly the most factual element in the entire project, were extended and systematized by mathematical calculation — and this can be seen as less a matter of disingenuousness than of dealing with the problem of recording setting-out dimensions no longer measurable after the fact of a building's construction. Perhaps the only area of the work that Stuart and Revett had undertaken when in Greece that could not be described as subject to subsequent development was that of the excavations they had made. For reasons both temporal and spatial the results of these could not be altered and the problems they created could not be resolved. Seen in this light, Stuart's work seems far removed from the objectives and methodologies of modern-day archaeology. Judged by those standards, his work would indeed be deemed to fall short. When viewed, however, in the light of the antiquar-

ian world of Florence and Rome of the 1740s, where Stuart's connoisseurly and scholarly skills were acquired, a different and more positive appraisal emerges. Stuart's work should be situated on the cusp of a moment in the Enlightenment when the science of archaeology emerged from the broadly philological and artistic approach to the architecture of the ancient world. His presentation of monuments, both in *De Obelisco Caesaris Augusti* and in *Antiquities of Athens,* remains a singular and seminal achievement in the progress of the European archaeological and architectural tradition.

Acknowledgments: For advice and assistance offered during preparation of this chapter, I am very grateful to the following: Catherine Arbuthnott, Kerry Bristol, Paolo Coen, Viccy Coltman, Edward Corp, Michael Erwee, Charles Hind, Tamara Griggs, Ian Jenkins, Jason Kelly, Thorsten Opper, Mark Wilson Jones, and David Yeomans. I must also record (as always) a debt of gratitude to Valerie Scott and the Library of the British School at Rome.

1. Stuart was elected in March 1751, proposed along with his co-worker on *Antiquities of Athens,* Nicholas Revett, by the British Ambassador in Venice, Sir James Gray, whose earlier nominees were almost exclusively aristocratic: the Earl of Holdernesse, the Earl of Ashburnham, Chevalier St. George, Lord Hobart (later Earl of Buckinghamshire), Sir Thomas Sebright, and Thomas Steavens; see Lionel Cust, comp., *History of the Society of Dilettanti* (London: Macmillan, 1898): 77. Much has been made of Stuart as one of the first "artists" the society deigned to elect, but the election might be seen as much as a reflection of Stuart's acceptance into the class of the antiquarian explorer, then a gentlemanly pursuit, on which point see Bruce Redford, "The Measure of Ruins: Dilettanti in the Levant, 1750 – 1770," *Harvard Library Bulletin* 13 (Spring 2002): 5 – 6.

2. Stuart to Jacob Hinde, 20 March 1746, OSB fc 144, Beinecke Rare Book and Manuscript Library, Yale University. See John Marciari, "Athenian Stuart in Florence," *Burlington Magazine* 140 (September 1998): 612 – 14.

3. Erik Iversen, *The Obelisks of Rome,* vol. 1 of *Obelisks in Exile* (Copenhagen: Gad, 1968): 152. See also Edmund Buchner, *Die Sonnenuhr des Augustus: Nachdruck aus RM 1976 und 1980 und Nachtrag über die Ausgrabung* (Mainz am Rhein: Zabern, 1982): 45. Stuart's contribution did not, however, merit mention in Cesare d'Onofrio's standard text on Egyptian obelisks in Rome, *Gli Obelischi di Roma: storia e urbanistica di una città dall' età antica al XX secolo,* 3rd ed. (Rome: Romana società editrice, 1992), even though Stuart's engraved elevation of the monument was reproduced as an illustration (fig. 167) in the first edition of the book (Rome: Cassa di Risparmio, 1965).

4. *Antiquities,* vol. 1 (1762): v.

5. It has been suggested that Stuart may be identified with the "Mr Stewart" who was acting as "governor" to a young Grand Tourist dying of tuberculosis in Naples and Rome in 1740 – 41, and that this Stuart might be the person of that name who appears in the annual Roman Eastertide *Stato dell'Anime* census of 1741, living in Strada Condotti with a Grand Tourist named George Belsches; see Michael McCarthy, "'The Dullest Man that Ever Travelled'?: A Re-assessment of Richard Pococke and of his Portrait by J.-E. Liotard," *Apollo* 143 (May 1996): 28 and 29 n. 21. The surnames Belsches and Stuart also appear together in a list of people encountered by Joseph Spence in Rome during his third Grand Tour in 1739 – 41; see John Ingamells, *A Dictionary of British and Irish Travellers in Italy 1701 – 1800* (New Haven and London: Yale University Press, 1997): 76. The identification is, however, sufficiently problematic as to make it most unlikely.

6. Revett sailed from England for Leghorn on 22 September 1742 and passed straight on to Rome. Cust, *Dilettanti* (1898): 75 – 76.

7. A. P. Oppé, ed., "Memoirs of Thomas Jones," Walpole Society annual, vol. 32 (1946 – 48): 74. It should be noted, however, that this was Jones's 1803 recollection of a conversation with Nulty held in the 1770s, in which Nulty was recalling his life in the 1740s.

8. *Stato dell'Anime*: S. Andrea delle Fratte, left side of the Salita di San Giuseppe, Archivio Vicariato, Rome (notes in Brinsley Ford Archive, Paul Mellon Centre for Studies in British Art, London, and transcriptions for 1745 kindly provided by Edward Corp). The ages of both Paston and Stuart were given as the mid-thirties when Stuart would have been only thirty-one and Paston in his mid-twenties, but errors with age are common enough in the Roman censuses.

9. *Second Report of the Royal Commission on Historical Manuscripts (1871): Papers of the Rt. Hon, the Earl of Mount Edgcumbe* (London, HMSO, 1874): appendix p. 23 (letter dated 8 May 1745). Three days earlier a letter from Edgcumbe to Mann shows that the *Kennington* was off the Italian coast near Pisa. I am grateful to Kerry Bristol for supplying this reference. The Mount Edgcumbe papers were destroyed by German incendiary bombing in 1941. In 1977 a transcript was said to have been made by the nineteenth-century inspector, Alfred Horwood; see *A Companion to the Kraus Reprint of Reports I to IX of the Historical Manuscripts Commission* (Nedeln: Kraus-Thomson Organization Press,

1977): 24. No trace of this can now be found in the Historical Manuscripts Commission papers.

10. *Stato dell'Anime*: S. Andrea delle Fratte, Strada Felice (modern-day Via Sistina) house of Sig. Detti, Archivio Vicariato, Rome (notes in Brinsley Ford Archive, Paul Mellon Centre for Studies in British Art, London). The religion of the "Stuard" recorded in Rome in 1744 was not recorded, making it likely that he was a Catholic, as known Protestants were generally denoted as such. Moreover, "Stuard's" co-resident, Paston, was later listed as a Catholic and was, indeed, paid a salary as a member of the Stuart Court in Rome by the Cardinal Duke of York; see Ingamells, *Dictionary of British and Irish Travellers* (1997): 744 – 45.

11. See SP 98/51, fol. 66r, NA. It is also worth noting that both Mann and Baron Stosch, who reported his spying activities on the Jacobites to Mann, were among the first to signal their support for *Antiquities of Athens;* see "Names of the Gentlemen . . . ," in Stuart, Sketch-book . . . of buildings in N. Italy, SKB/336/2 [L 3/4]: 2, RIBA Library Drawings Collection, London.

12. See *Antiquities,* vol. 4 (1816): xxviii. He is buried in the crypt of St. Martin-in-the-Fields.

13. Marciari, "Athenian Stuart in Florence" (1998): 612 – 14. The source of this drawing was identified by Kerry Bristol; it is in the Staatliche Graphische Sammlung, Munich, inv. no. 2450. There is another copy of the print: FC 120900, Istituto Nazionale per la Grafica, Rome.

14. For Hugford see John Fleming, "The Hugfords of Florence — II," *Connoisseur* 136 (November 1955): 197 – 206; Fabia Borroni Salvadori, "Ignazio Enrico Hugford, Collezionista con la vocazione del mercante," *Annali della Scuola Normale Superiore di Pisa,* 3rd series, 13, no. 4 (1983): 1032; *Dizionario Biografico degli Italiani,* vol. 61, ed. Mario Caravale and Giuseppe Pignatelli (Rome: Istituto della Enciclopedia Italiana, 2003): 745 – 49.

15. See Fabia Borroni Salvadori, "Artisti e viaggiatori agli Uffizi nel Settecento," pt. 1, *Labyrinthos* 4, no. 7/8 (1985): 15 – 16.

16. Hugford became a representative of the painters on the academy's council in 1749, a *conservadoro* in 1756, a *consigliero* in 1757 and finally *provveditore* (secretary, the second most important position after the *luogotenente* or president) in 1762. See Frank Salmon, "British Architects and the Florentine Academy, 1753 – 1794," *Mitteilungen des Kunsthistorischen Institutes in Florenz* 34, no. 1/2 (1990): 210 n.16.

17. See *Gentleman's Magazine* (March 1788): 217.

18. *Stato dell'Anime*: S. Andrea delle Fratte, Strada Felice (modern-day Via Sistina) house of Sig. Detti, Archivio Vicariato, Rome (notes in Brinsley Ford Archive, Paul Mellon Centre for Studies in British Art, London). Stuart's age is given as thirty to thirty-two successively, when in fact he was thirty-six to thirty-eight.

19. Istituto Nazionale per la Grafica, Rome, FC 67258. The unlocated drawing, thought to have been the "gem" of Valenti's collection, is currently attributed to Giovan Francesco Penni. See Simonetta Prosperi Valenti Rodinò, "La Raccolta di grafica," in *Ritratto di una Collezione: Pannini e la Galleria del Cardinale Silvio Valenti Gonzaga,* ed. Raffaella Morselli and Rossella Vodret (Milan: Skira, 2005): 271.

20. Stato dell'Anime: S. Lorenzo in Lucina, Strada Carozze towards the Corso, Archivio Vicariato, Rome.

21. For Benedict XIV the important sources are Ludwig von Pastor, *The History of the Popes from the Close of the Middle Ages,* ed. E. F. Peeler, vols. 35 and 36 (London: Routledge and Kegan Paul, 1961); Emilia Morelli, *Tre Profili: Benedetto XIV, Pasquale Stanislao Mancini, Pietro Roselli,* Quaderni del Risorgimento, 9 (Rome: Edizioni dell'Atteneo, 1955): 3 – 45; and *Enciclopedia dei Papi,* vol. 3 (Rome: Istituto della Enciclopedia Italiana, 2000): 446 – 61.

22. Valenti was said by Horace Mann in 1746 to have been "entirely devoted to the Pretender" (SP 98/51, fol. 141v, NA).

23. For a concise account of Venuti's tenure, achievements, and publications, see Ronald T. Ridley, "To Protect the Monuments: The Papal Antiquarian (1534 – 1870)," *Xenia Antiqua* 1 (1992): 138 – 40. In 1749 Valenti set in place the first proper system for regulating exports of objets d'art through Venuti's office. See Paolo Coen, "Silvio Valenti Gonzaga e il mercato artistico romano del XVIII secolo," in *Ritratto de una Collezione* (2005): 190.

24. "That Il Signior Canonico Rodolfino Venuti deputato sopra la convazione delle Antichita di Roma may become an Honorary Member of this Society; which was immediately put up to the Ballot; and was chosen n[emine] c[ontradicente]"; Minutebook, vol. 7 (14 November 1751 to 23 December 1756), fol. 9 (left), Society of Antiquaries. It should be noted that Venuti's nominators were Walter Bowman and the prominent Fellow and Jacobite, Richard Rawlinson, both of whom had been in Italy in the 1720s and, in Bowman's case, the 1730s too; see Ingamells, *Dictionary of British and Irish Travellers* (1997): 113 – 14 and 801 – 3.

25. Minutebook, vol. 8 (13 January 1757 to 20 May 1762), fol. 357, Society of Antiquaries.

26. Details of the foundation are given in *Notizia delle Accademie erette in Roma per Ordine della Santità di N. Sig. Papa Benedetto Decimoquarto* (Rome: [Giuseppe Collini], 1740). The first twelve topics for discourses in each academy were stipulated at the outset.

27. *Diario Ordinario* 5085 (21 February 1750): 8 – 9.

28. For Valenti and the *Giornale* see Maria Pia Donato, "Profilo intelletuale di Silvio Valenti Gonzaga nella Roma di Benedetto XIV," in *Ritratto di una Collezione* (2005): 81 – 89.

29. *Giornale de' Letterati* (1753): 366 – 67 (author's translation). This document is new to the list of proporals hitherto recognized for *Antiquities of Athens.* See Dora Wiebenson, *Sources of Greek Revival* (London: A. Zwemmer, 1969): chap. 1 and appendix 1, to which the *Giornale de' Letterati* letter should be inserted between entries G1 and H on p. 85. As stated in the letter, the plan for the three volumes differed in certain respects from Stuart's and Revett's 1751 "Proposals" (ibid., 82 – 83), especially for the second volume.

30. In 1766 Stuart wrote to John Nourse to say that he had received a letter from Marco Pagliarini in Rome, stating that Niccolò was shortly to visit England (Laing Mss., La.II.172, Edinburgh University Library). The implication is that Stuart intended to meet and aid his old Roman acquaintance.

31. Add. Ms. 41,169, fol. 40r, BL. In 1816 Joseph Woods recounted that Stuart's (now lost) notebooks contained numerous "extracts from dif-

ferent ancient and modern authors relating to Greece, which Stuart had probably taken the pains to transcribe and translate, in order to make himself completely master of all that had been said concerning the country he visited"; see *Antiquities,* vol. 4 (1816): ii.

32. Stuart himself recorded that Valenti had initially asked him to draw the hieroglyphs; see Stuart, *De Obelisco Caesaris Augusti e Campo Martio Nuperrime Effosso . . .* (Rome: Niccolò et Marco Pagliarini, 1750): lxxiii. For the Bandini version, see Angelo Maria Bandini et al., *De Obelisco Caesaris Augusti e Campi Martii Ruderibus Nuper Eruto Commentarius auctore Angelo Maria Bandinio accedunt CLL. Virorum Epistolae atque Opuscula* (Rome: Pallade, 1750).

33. *Diario Ordinario* 4791 (6 April 1748): 3 – 4. On 2 April, Brettingham had exchanged £20 (receiving 82 scudi), doubtless in preparation for the imminent departure of the group; see John Kenworthy-Browne, "Matthew Brettingham's Rome Account Book, 1747 – 1754," Walpole Society annual, vol. 49 (1983): 54.

34. *Diario Ordinario* 4842 (3 August 1748): 9 – 10.

35. James Russel, *Letters from a Young Painter Abroad to his Friends in England,* vol. 2 (London: W. Russel, 1750): 131 – 47. Russel does not, however, mention Tomasso de Marchis, credited by Iversen with recovery of the obelisk's base; see Iversen, *Obelisks of Rome* (1968): 152.

36. This view was reengraved in Zabaglia, *Castelli e Ponti di Maestro Niccola Zabaglia con alcune ingegnose pratiche e con la descrizione del trasporto dell' Obelisco Vaticano e di altri del Cavaliere Domenico Fontana,* ed. Filippo Maria Renazzi, 2nd ed. (Rome: Crispino Puccinelli, 1824): i. The operation is also described at length therein.

37. D'Onofrio, *Obelischi* (1992): 377 n. 7, states that the Barbault view corresponds less closely to the description given by de Marchis on p. 105 of *De Obelisco* than does that of Vasi, but d'Onofrio was unaware of the evidence provided by Russel.

38. Stuart, *De Obelisco* (1750): 33, verso; Bandini et al., *De Obelisco* (1750/51): facing xxi. The "elegant decoration" of this theatrical image (as it was described by the Pagliarini brothers) includes sea beasts, alluding to the transportation of the obelisk from Egypt to Rome, and a pair of herms experimenting with a capstan and pulley. A version of Stuart's image, without the decoration, was used on the title page of Renazzi's second edition of Zabaglia's *Castelli e Ponti.*

39. These dates are drawn from Malton's correspondence, M2.541, Sheffield Archives. See also Lesley Lewis, *Connoisseurs and Secret Agents in Eighteenth Century Rome* (London: Chatto and Windus, 1961): 174. Stuart gave March 1750 as the date of his departure from Rome in *Antiquities,* vol. 1 (1762): vi.

40. *Antiquities,* vol. 4 (1816): xxiii; "Names of the gentlemen . . . ," in Stuart, Sketchbook . . . of buildings in N. Italy, SKB/336/2 [L 3/4]: 2r, RIBA Library Drawings Collection, London.

41. Woods stated that Stuart's *De Obelisco* was published at the expense of Pope Benedict himself (*Antiquities,* vol. 4 [1816]: iv and xxvii), to whom Stuart is said to have been presented. Given Stuart's position in the circle of Valenti, an audience is quite possible (although it is hardly surprising that there appears to be no record of it). The Pope is not mentioned in Stuart's publication, however, and Woods was probably confusing it with Bandini's, for which the Pope was certainly the dedicatee. If Stuart did receive financial support from the papal court, then it is unlikely he would have mentioned this in a work aimed at creating a reputation for himself in England. Finally, given that no announcement of publication of Stuart's book can be found in the *Diario Ordinario,* it was probably covered by the same papal faculty permitting its publication as Bandini's.

42. Wentworth Woodhouse Muniments, M2.550, Sheffield Archives.

43. My account is indebted to that given by Iversen, *Obelisks of Rome* (1968): 142 – 60.

44. "Per non parere un Papa goto"; see Emilia Morelli, *Le lettere di Benedetto XIV al Card. De Tencin,* vol. 2 (Rome: Edizioni de storia e letteratura, 1965): 51. See also Von Pastor, *History of the Popes,* vol. 35 (1961): 171. The Pope was correct in stating that his predecessors Sixtus V and Julius II had both shown interest in recovering the obelisk, although he omitted to mention the even earlier involvement of Sixtus IV and more recently that of Alexander VII; see Iversen, *Obelisks of Rome* (1968): 145 – 48.

45. *Diario Ordinario* 4803 (4 May 1748): 11.

46. The authors and their residences were (in order of the essays after Bandini's): Giovanni Poleni (Padua), Giovanni Alberto Colombo (Padua), Ruggiero Giuseppe Boscovitch (Rome), Ottaviano Cametti (Florence), Iacopo Marinoni (Vienna), Scipione Maffei (Verona), Lodovico Antonio Muratori (Modena), Gerardo de Bose (Wittemberg), Johann Albert (or Leonhard) Euler (Berlin), Christian Weidlich (Wittemberg), Christian L.B. de Wolff (Halle) and Heinsius (Leipzig). A mathematical dissertation by Giorgio Mulleri followed, then a letter from the Académie royale des inscriptions et Belle-Lettres in Paris, then Bandini's original, Kircher-inspired commentary on the obelisk when first excavated in 1748.

47. Venuti's comments on the obelisk are, in fact, preserved in a manuscript in the Vatican Library (Cod. Vat. 9024, fols. 181r – 184v). These relatively brief comments, addressed as a letter to Cardinal Angelo Querini, Bishop of Brescia, include the draft text (subsequently ameliorated by Pope Benedict himself) for the inscription that still survives on a house adjacent to the site from which the obelisk was extracted.

48. Bandini's book received its papal faculty on 20 June 1750, and its actual appearance was announced in the *Diario Ordinario* 5145 (11 July 1750): 16.

49. *Antiquities,* vol. 4 (1816): iv.

50. See his plan of the amphitheater at Verona annotated in Italian, in Stuart, Sketchbook . . . of buildings in N. Italy, SKB/336/2 [L 3/4]: fol. 22r, RIBA Library Drawings Collection, London. Stuart's Latin studies at the Collegio are mentioned by Woods; see *Antiquities,* vol. 4 (1816): iv. The information evidently had derived from his friend Mr. Sheldrake; see Bristol, "Stuart and the Genesis of the Greek Revival" (1997): 23 – 24. The Latin instructor at the Collegio in this period was a priest from Pistoia named Andrea Nicolai.

51. The Ara Pacis was not systematically excavated until 1903, although fragments of it were discovered in 1859 and others were known from as early as 1568; see Lawrence Richardson, *A New Topographical Dictionary of Ancient Rome* (Baltimore and London: Johns Hopkins University Press, 1992): 287 – 89.

52. Iversen, *Obelisks of Rome* (1968): 153. See also Buchner, *Sonnenuhr des Augustus* (1982): 45 and pls. 16 and 109/2.

53. Bristol, "Stuart and the Genesis of the Greek Revival" [1997]: 122. For an exception, however, see Stuart's evidently measured elevation of the Villa Farnesina, SD 62/23, RIBA Library Drawings Collection, London.

54. SD 62/25, RIBA Library Drawings Collection, London.

55. For the most recent account of Stuart's development as an architect at this time, see Kerry Bristol, "A Newly-Discovered Drawing by James Stuart," *Architectural History* 44 (2001): 39 – 44.

56. *Antiquities,* vol. 1 (1762): vi. According to the Pagliarini brothers writing in 1753, the thirty-four drawings of Pola listed by Stuart and Revett in their 1751 "Proposals" for *Antiquities of Athens* (see Wiebenson, *Sources of Greek Revival Architecture* [1969]: 81 – 82) had been sent to London as a demonstration of how the "great work" on Greek antiquities was to be executed; see *Giornale de' Letterati* (Rome, 1753): 367 – 68.

57. *Antiquities,* vol. 4 (1816): ii. The surviving notebooks are Laing Mss., La.III.581, Edinburgh University Library, and Sketchbook . . . of buildings in N. Italy, SKB/336/2 [L 3/4], RIBA Library Drawings Collection, London. More detailed comments on these notebooks and other Stuart papers that were given to Woods by the publisher Josiah Taylor can be found in Taylor's list in Add. Ms. 22,152: 1r – 8v, BL. Most (but not all) of these papers dated from Stuart's time in the Mediterranean. The volume in Edinburgh is listed as item "S" in Add. Ms. 22,152: 4v, BL, of which Taylor commented "what there is of Pola seems unmanaged."

58. Laing Mss., La.III.581: (a) et seq., Edinburgh University Library. (Revett's name has evidently been torn out of the "Pola" title page.). Add. Ms. 22,152: 5r, BL.

59. Laing Mss., La.III.581: 82r and 198v, Edinburgh University Library. The former notes comprise a short disquisition on the meaning of hieroglyphs which, Stuart argued, would not have formed "memorials of the heroic actions of princes . . . in a Language no body understood but Priests" but must instead have related to the "mathematical or Astronomic" functions of obelisks.

60. Stuart, Sketchbook . . . of buildings in N. Italy, SKB/336/2 [L 3/4]: 73v, RIBA Library Drawings Collection, London.

61. Laing Mss., La.III.581: 14r, Edinburgh University Library; *Antiquities,* vol. 4 (1816): chap. 2, pl. III.

62. A similar drawing, made at the same time can be found in Add. Ms. 22,153: 176, BL. The image of the interior of the amphitheater finally selected for finishing is RIBA Library Drawings Collection, London, SD 146.5.

63. Borra's drawings survive in two bound volumes in the RIBA Library Drawings Collection, London.

64. I owe this suggestion to Charles Hind, who feels that the uniform technique and materials, relatively large size, and probable exhibition purpose of the gouaches suggest that they were executed by Stuart after his return to London. For Stuart's exhibition of many of these images at the Free Society of Artists from 1765 see Algernon Graves, *The Society of Artists of Great Britain 1760 – 1791: The Free Society of Artists 1761 – 1783* (London: Bell and Sons and Algernon Graves, 1907): 247 – 49. Stuart's on-site topographical views, such as that of Mount Parnassus (SD 93/3[3], RIBA Library Drawings Collection, London), subsequently engraved for the fourth volume of the *Antiquities,* appear to have been executed in pen and ink, shaded in pencil but marked up with color notes.

65. Thomas Allason, *Picturesque Views of the Antiquities of Pola in Istria* (London: J. Murray, 1819): 2 – 3.

66. This is also confirmed by two of Cassas's views, which show the dwelling in direct line with the right side of the arch and the walled gardens to the left (Louis-François Cassas and Joseph Lavallée, *Voyage pittoresque et historique de l'Istrie et de la Dalmatie* (Paris: Vilain, 1802), pls. 20 and 21. For an alternative analysis of these views, which does not discuss Stuart's view but which does consider Allason to have indulged in chiaroscuro and picturesque effects, see Gustavo Traversari, *L'Arco dei Sergi* (Padua: CEDAM, 1971): 32 – 33.

67. See Giovanni Rinaldo Carli, *Delle Antichità Italiche* (Milan: Nell'imperial monistero di S. Ambrogio Maggiore, 1788), pt. 1, book 3, facing p. 195.

68. Laing Mss., La.III.581: 11r-v, Edinburgh University Library (see *Antiquities,* vol. 4 [1816]: 15). Woods omitted Stuart's comments on the "very indifferent" workmanship of the arch's figurative and decorative sculpture.

69. Thomas Hollis to Professor Ward, Venice, 26 February 1751, Add. Ms. 27,576: 2r – 3r, BL.

70. Revett's letter was transcribed in full in *Antiquities,* vol. 4 (1816): xxviii – xxix.

71. By April 1748 architectural investigations at Herculaneum had only reached the stage where plans of the still subterranean theater, basilica, and surrounding area could be made; see Christopher Charles Parslow, *Rediscovering Antiquity: Karl Weber and the Excavation of Herculaneum, Pompeii, and Stabiae* (Cambridge: Cambridge University Press, 1995): 47 – 56 and 233 – 41.

72. The date of December 1749 for Wood's presence in Rome on his second visit is a *terminus ante quem* and not a *terminus post quem;* see Ingamells, *Dictionary of British and Irish Travellers* (1997): 1016. We do not know when he actually arrived.

73. Robert Wood, *The Ruins of Palmyra, otherwise Tedmor, in the Desart* (London: the author, 1753): (a)r; *Antiquities,* vol. 1 (1762): vii.

74. Wood, *Ruins of Palmyra* (1753): 35; *Antiquities,* vol. 1 (1762): vi. For other accounts of the genesis of the project, see see J. Mordaunt Crook, *The Greek Revival: Neo-classical Attitudes in British Architecture, 1760 – 1870* (London: Murray, 1972): 13 – 17; Eileen Harris, *British Architectural Books and Writers, 1556 – 1785,* assisted by Nicholas Savage (Cambridge and New York, Cambridge University Press, 1990): 439 – 50; Bristol, "Stuart and the Genesis of the Greek Revival" [1997]: chaps. 2 and 3; Paul W. Nash et al., *Early Printed Books, 1478 – 1840: Catalogue of the British Architectural Library Early Imprints Collection,* vol. 4 (Munich: Saur, 2001): 1993 – 2005. Also see chap. 1, by David Watkin, in this volume.

75. Arnold Walter Lawrence, *Greek Architecture* (Harmondsworth: Penguin Books, 1957): respectively, pls. 133 – 35, 91 and 36, and p. 141. Henry Robinson, in an article of 1943, had noted that Stuart and

Revett's survey of the Tower of the Winds remained the only viable one for scholars, although he considered revision to be "sorely needed"; see Robinson, "The Tower of the Winds and the Roman Market Place," *American Journal of Archaeology* 47 (1943): 291. Far more recently, however, Hermann Kienast has commented that the "illuminating drawings of [Stuart and Revett] leave us with the impression that no questions remain to be asked" (Kienast, "The Tower of the Winds in Athens: Hellenistic or Roman?," in *The Romanization of Athens,* ed. Michael C. Hoff and Susan I. Rotroff [Oxford: Oxbow Books, 1997]: 53).

76. Landy, "Stuart and Revett: Pioneer Archaeologists," *Archaeology* 9 (December 1956): 258. This article resulted from Landy's M.A. dissertation, "Stuart and Revett and their Interpretation of Greek Architecture," Institute of Fine Arts, New York University, 1953.

77. Ibid., 259.

78. Laing Mss., La.III.581: (a)v and 21v – 31r, Edinburgh University Library.

79. Ibid., 77v. Stuart provided the reference "348" for this quotation and chap. 34 of Plutarch's *Antony* does indeed describe its protagonist filling and carrying a vessel. However, the quotation does not seem to be accurate and, furthermore, the water Antony carries is drawn from the Clepsydra — the sacred ebbing well below the Acropolis; see Plutarch, *Life of Antony,* ed. Christopher Pelling (Cambridge University Press, 1988): 75, 210. Stuart had accepted an interpretation by Suidas of clepsydra as a generic term for "an astronomical Instrument, by which the Hours are measured etc." (*Antiquities,* vol. 1 [1762]: 15 n. a).

80. Vitruvius, *The Ten Books of Architecture,* trans. and ed. Ingrid D. Rowland and Thomas Noble Howe (Cambridge and New York: Cambridge University Press, 1999): 117, book 9, chap. 8, section 11 (Stuart gives the reference as book 9, chap. 9, but there is no chapter 9 in that book).

81. *Antiquities,* vol. 1 (1762): 15.

82. *Wiebenson,* Sources of Greek Revival (1969): 80; Harris, *British Architectural Books* (1990): 442 and 447 n. 31.

83. Vitruvius, *Ten Books of Architecture* (1999): 49, book 3, chap. 3, section 5. Stuart's placement of this quotation in chap. 2 of book 3 is careless (and was an error he repeated in *Antiquities,* vol. 1 [1762]: iii, n. e.). The following quotations on fig. 3-21, Vitruvius's opening remarks on the setting out of the Tuscan temple and on the width of its *cellae* or *alae,* come from book 4, chap. 7, sections 1 – 2; see Vitruvius, *Ten Books of Architecture* (1999): 60.

84. *Antiquities,* vol. 1 (1762): iii, n. e.

85. *Antiquities,* vol. 2 (ca. 1790): 14 – 15, and vol. 3 (1794): 16. See Harris, *British Architectural Books* (1990): 443 – 44, for a fuller account of this episode. Stuart's total refusal to acknowledge the evidence for the twenty lateral columns must also be seen in the context of Le Roy's willing acceptance of that fact; see Robin Middleton, introduction to *The Ruins of the Most Beautiful Monuments of Greece* by Julien-David Le Roy, trans. David Britt (Los Angeles: Getty Publications, 2004): 20 and 22.

86. *Antiquities,* vol. 1 (1762): viii.

87. But for a recent reappraisal see Tamara Griggs, "Drawn from Nature: Text and Image in *The Antiquities of Athens* (1762 – 1816)," forthcoming.

88. Edward Kaufman has commented that "if Stuart's sense of historical relationships is ambivalent, his awareness of geographical ones is quite precise"; see Kaufman, "Architecture and Travel in the Age of British Eclecticism," in *Architecture and its Image,* ed. Eve Blau and Edward Kaufman (Montreal: Canadian Centre for Architecture, 1989): 70. A proper study of Stuart as cartographer, which lies beyond the scope of the present chapter, is a *desideratum.*

89. Typescript of George Basevi's letters (ed. Arthur Bolton): 200 – 201, Sir John Soane's Museum, London.

90. See Frank Salmon, *Building on Ruins: The Rediscovery of Rome and English Architecture* (Aldershot, Eng., and Burlington, VT: Ashgate Press, 2000): 41 and figs. 21, 22.

91. For a study of Stuart's Athenian views which concludes that "picturesque" elements were made "incidental to his primary purpose, fidelity to the topographical and architectural reality of the scenes depicted," see Michael McCarthy, "The Image of Greek Architecture, 1748 – 1768" (1991), in *Classical and Gothic: Studies in the History of Art* (Dublin and Portland, OR: Four Courts, 2005): 83 – 90.

92. *Antiquities,* vol. 1 (1762): viii. Kaufman suggests, but does not establish, that Stuart's views were "quite carefully constructed," with characters "systematically deployed . . . not so much to display the ancient monuments as to form a kind of pictorial conspectus of travel themes" (Kaufman, "Architecture and Travel" [1989]: 77). For a study of ethnographic elements in *Antiquities* and other publications related to the Dilettanti see Jason Kelly, *Archaeology and Identity in the British Enlightenment: The Society of Dilettanti, 1732 – 1808* (forthcoming).

93. *Antiquities,* vol. 3 (1794): 37. The gouache of this view was not finished, and the attendants are not included in it (SD 145/10, RIBA Library Drawings Collection, London).

94. Kaufman, "Architecture and Travel" (1989): 65. Redford, "Measure of Ruins" (2002): 16, goes further, considering this image to represent "the primal scene of modern archaeology."

95. *Antiquities,* vol. 2 (ca. 1790): 19.

96. Landy, "Stuart and Revett" (1956): 258.

97. See Salmon, *Building on Ruins* (2000): 35 – 36.

98. *Antiquities,* vol. 1 (1762): vii. For Adam see Iain Gordon Brown, *Monumental Reputation: Robert Adam and the Emperor's Palace* (Edinburgh: National Library of Scotland, 1992): 32 – 33, and Frank Salmon, "Charles Cameron and Nero's Domus Aurea: 'Una Piccola Esplorazione'," *Architectural History* 36 (1993): 86.

99. Le Roy, *Ruins* (2004): 10 (trans. Robin Middleton).

100. Laing Mss., La.III.581: 84v, Edinburgh University Library.

101. *Antiquities,* vol. 1 (1762): 14. Landy praises their work in this case ("Stuart and Revett" [1956]: 258). Redford has interpreted Stuart's words here as an example of "the language of the Royal Society" ("Measure of Ruins" [2002]: 25).

102. This point is made in Joseph Veach Noble and Derek de la Solla Price, "The Water Clock in the Tower of the Winds," *American Journal of Archaeology* 72 (1968): 347.

103. *Antiquities,* vol. 1 (1762): vii.

104.Vitruvius, *Ten Books of Architecture* (1999): 24, book 1, chap. 2, sections 1 – 2.

105. *Antiquities*, vol. 1 (1762): vii; Landy, "Stuart and Revett" (1956): 257.

106. See Gene Waddell, "The Principal Design Methods for Greek Doric Temples and their Modification for the Parthenon," *Architectural History* 45 (2002): 23. See also Mark Wilson Jones, "Doric Measure and Architectural Design 2: A Modular Reading of the Classical Temple," *American Journal of Archaeology* 105 (2001): 675 – 713.

107. Charlemont quoted by Bristol, "Stuart and the Genesis of the Greek Revival" [1997]: 142.

108. Kaufman, "Architecture and Travel" (1989): 74.

109. Landy, "Stuart and Revett" (1956): 254 and 259.

110. *Antiquities*, vol. 1 (1762): i.

111. SD 94/4/3, RIBA Library Drawings Collection, London. SD 94/4/1 offers a seventeen-step guide to the setting out of the Greek Ionic volute. In *Antiquities*, vol. 1 (1762): 2, Stuart offered a long footnote on the shortcomings of the Ionic orders of celebrated Roman buildings.

112. Laing Mss., La.III.581: 73v, Edinburgh University Library; *Antiquities*, vol. 1 (1762): vii. On this and the following page, Stuart publicly paid tribute to Revett's "exactness" and, while stating that he had assisted Revett with a "considerable number" of the measurements, also indicated that there were occasions where he had "measured after him." In 1762 John Bird, under instruction from a Parliamentary Committee established in 1758, produced the yard rule later adopted as the Imperial Standard. It may be inferred, therefore, but cannot be assumed, that the rule Bird constructed for Revett to use in Greece in the early 1750s corresponded with the Imperial Standard.

113. The "median" was necessary because Stuart and Revett's plan of the building (*Antiquities*, vol. 1 [1762], pl. II) showed the breadth of the two sides with doorways was slightly less than that of the other six sides.

114. David Yeomans, to whom I own a great debt of gratitude for bringing his expertise to bear on the problem of fig. 3-29, has pointed out that this "radius" was not in itself a measurable line (it lay in space beneath the pitch of the roof and passed through the outer wall of the building) and thus would have had to have been calculated trigonometrically, probably from measuring down the ridge line of the roof and then converting the sum (based on the pitch of the ridge) to the pitch of the slope between the ridges.

115. The three sheets in Add. Ms. 22,153, BL, are: fol. 9r (*Antiquities*, vol. 1 [1762]: chap. 4, pl. XI); fol. 9v (corresponding with ibid., pl. XIV); and fol. 13r [fig. 3-31 in this volume] (corresponding with ibid., pl. XXV [fig. 3-33 in this volume]); the recto of the one sheet in the Department of Greek and Roman Antiquities, British Museum, corresponds with ibid., pl. VIII and the verso with ibid., pl. XXI.

116. Arthur H. Smith, "Recent Additions to the Sculptures of the Parthenon," *Journal of Hellenic Studies* 13 (1892 – 93): 98 – 99. See Add. Ms. 22,153, fol. 76r, BL, upper image for the Stuart sketch of the now "long missing" Athenian relief with Athene and Marsyas and compare this with the engraved version in *Antiquities*, vol. 2 (ca. 1790): 27.

117. *Antiquities*, vol. 1 (1762): 33 – 34.

118. Robert Adam to James Adam, Edinburgh, 25 June 1758, Clerk of Penicuik Mss. GD 18 4,850, National Archives of Scotland, Edinburgh; cited in Bristol, "Stuart and the Genesis of the Greek Revival" [1997]: 133.

119. James Adam to Betty Adam, Venice, 17 September 1760, Clerk of Penicuik Mss. GD 18 4,872, National Archives of Scotland, Edinburgh; cited in Bristol, "Stuart and the Genesis of the Greek Revival" [1997]: 136, n. 390.

120. See Wolfgang Ehrhardt, "Das Fries des Lysikratesmonuments," *Antike Plastik* 22 (1993), for a recent study that contains photographs of the sculptures in their present state and that makes a comparative study of the Lusieri drawings, the Elgin casts (now belonging to the British Museum) and the casts now in the University of Cambridge Museum of Classical Archaeology.

121. Ibid., 14, figs. 9 – 11 and pl. 7b.

122. Ibid., figs. 12 – 14 and pl. 8a. Lusieri's drawing is overly emphatic in showing the figure in profile. In fact, when the casts are viewed from an oblique angle, both of this satyr's eyes are visible.

123. *Antiquities*, vol. 2 (ca. 1790): 12.

124. See Smith, "Recent Additions" (1892 – 93): 97, fig. 5. Carrey's drawings had been acquired by the Bibliothèque Royale in 1770 but were misshelved until 1797. Stuart thus cannot have known them; see Theodore Bowie and Diether Timme, eds., *The Carrey Drawings of the Parthenon Sculptures* (Bloomington and London: Indiana University Press, 1971): 3.

125. Julien-David Le Roy, *Les Ruines des plus beaux monuments de la Grèce* (Paris: Guerin and Delatour, 1758), pt. 2, pl. 13; for the influence of this plate, see Middleton, introduction to *Ruins* by Le Roy (2004): 141 – 42; Robert Wood, *The Ruins of Balbec, otherwise Heliopolis in Coelosyria* (London: n.p., 1757): pl. 41. On this subject see Frank Salmon, "Perspectival Restoration Drawings in Roman Archaeology and Architectural History," *Antiquaries Journal* 83 (2003): 403.

126. *Antiquities*, vol. 1 (1762): 31. For criticism of their restoration of the monument's substructures, however, see Landy, "Stuart and Revett" (1956): 257 – 58.

127. Robinson, "Tower of the Winds" (1943): 300.

128. *Antiquities*, vol. 2 (ca. 1790): chap. 2, pl. VII; Landy, "Stuart and Revett" (1956): 257 and figs. 6 – 7. It is noteworthy that Le Roy similarly depicted only sixteen rows of masonry in total at the Erechtheion, but that, unlike Stuart and Revett, he also failed to notice the taller nature of the foundation course.

129. *Antiquities*, vol. 1 (1762): 10.

130. Gandon, *The Life of James Gandon, Esq.*, ed. Thomas J. Mulvany (Dublin: Hodges and Smith, 1846): 198 – 99.

131. *Antiquities*, vol. 3 (1794): 7.

132. Laing Mss., La.III.581: 123v – 124r, Edinburgh University Library.

133. Landy, "Stuart and Revett" (1956): 259.

134. Minutebook, vol. 8 (13 January 1757 to 20 May 1762): 79, Society of Antiquaries. Stuart's sponsors were: H. Baker, J. Marsili, J. Hollis, Emanuel Mendes da Costa, J. Parsons, M. Ducane, J. Hunt and D. Wray.

135. Ibid., 90 and 107.

136. Ibid., 136 – 37.

Fig. 4-1. James Stuart and Nicholas Revett. Volume 1 of *Antiquities of Athens,* 1762. Binding designed by Stuart. This copy was once owned by the second Marquess of Rockingham. By permission of The British Library, London, c.160.ee.2. *Checklist no. 37.*

CHAPTER 4

THE SOCIAL WORLD OF

JAMES "ATHENIAN" STUART

KERRY BRISTOL

Since James Stuart's death in 1788, his reputation has rested on *Antiquities of Athens* (fig. 4-1), alongside an oeuvre that includes the first modern use of the baseless Greek Doric order and the earliest surviving "painted room." These works feature in most studies of British architecture, where Stuart is invariably accused of indolence or insobriety, and his works compared unfavorably with those of Robert Adam and Sir William Chambers to whom the torch of neoclassicism is said to have passed by the mid-1760s. Any attempt to measure Stuart against the more obvious professional successes of Adam and Chambers, however, clouds our understanding of the ingenious and often contradictory ways in which Stuart shaped his career. Indeed, Stuart came to practice architecture via a different route than Adam and Chambers, and it was only one of many media in which he exercised his design talents. He relied on the type of old-fashioned patronage circle eschewed by most contemporary architects. He was also a member of clubs and societies that promoted the ideal of the independent artist freed from the clutches of niggardly patrons. From his early training as a fan painter to the opportunities provided by his sojourns in Italy and Greece, Stuart's career development was thus complex and more than a little charmed.

The Early Years and the Beginnings of a Patronage Circle

That Stuart painted fans early in his career is confirmed by several sources.[1] Stuart's early master, identified as "Goupee of the Strand" is most likely an amalgamation of Louis Goupy, the painter who had accompanied Lord Burlington to Italy in 1719, and his nephew Joseph, who resided in the Covent Garden area and had also traveled in Italy (see fig. 2-5). Joseph Goupy commanded large sums for his copies of old masters and was one of the signatories to William Hogarth's petition for the Engravers' Copyright Act (1735). The Goupys subscribed to the Great Queen Street Academy in 1711. Joseph was also a member of the Virtuosi of St. Luke, and Louis became a founder member of the St. Martin's Lane Academy. If little-known today, they moved in circles advantageous to their pupils and were members of organizations at the forefront of efforts to create a market for contemporary British painting.[2] Through the Goupys, Stuart's love of old master paintings was most likely stimulated, and the idea of his traveling abroad probably began to germinate. Fan painting, however, cannot be said to have spurred his interest in antiquity.[3]

By about 1735 Stuart was associated with a school for painting and life drawing opened by George Michael

Fig. 4-2. James Stuart. *Portrait of James Lee*, ca. 1753–54. Oil on canvas. Hunterian Museum and Art Gallery, University of Glasgow, GLAHA 44250. *Checklist no. 31.*

Moser in Salisbury Court.[4] While it is uncertain how long he remained there, his continued interest in this discipline is demonstrated by his notebooks. These were "occupied with remarks on painting," and one sketchbook (RIBA Library Drawings Collection) contains an unfinished treatise on painting which reveals an interest in Rubens, Titian, and Tintoretto.[5]

It is as a painter that one should see Stuart at the beginning of his journey to Italy. At the age of about twenty-seven, he would have been nearly a decade older than most Grand Tourists and British artists abroad, suggesting that his Italian venture was an attempt to salvage an unsuccessful career. It was the right decision, if the murky color and poor handling of anatomy evident in Stuart's portrait of the Smyrna merchant James Lee (exe-

cuted around 1753) are any gauge of his skill (fig. 4-2).[6] One of the advantages of being in Italy in the 1740s was that the number of visitors was relatively small. These travelers formed a closely knit group of the kind impossible to develop back in Britain, and it should be relatively simple to pin down the date of Stuart's arrival. Because he was a Roman Catholic and a suspected Jacobite, however, his early years in Italy are frustratingly elusive. Stuart is likely to have been the painter who "had been a friend of the Pretender" whose presence on board ship off the coast of Tuscany was reported by Captain the Hon. George Edgcumbe in 1745 (see chap. 3).[7]

Stuart continued to ply his trade as a fan painter in Italy, but by March 20, 1746, he was also working as an antiquary. A letter of that date from Stuart in Florence to

148

his patron Jacob Hinde in London reveals that he was about to depart for Bologna to inspect some drawings that Lord Ashburnham's antiquary wanted to purchase and that he had received a commission for two small paintings from Ashburnham similar to a work executed for Hinde.[8] It has not been possible to trace Stuart's paintings. They may have been floral compositions akin to an untraced work sold in 1971 (fig. 4-3). The genre would account for the size and perhaps helps to explain why they await rediscovery.

Although Florence had much to offer, Rome was a better place to find long-term employment. It was there that Stuart was residing by 1747 (see chap. 3).[9] Presumably Stuart continued to work as an antiquary, for his surviving works reveal that he was intimately acquainted with the Grand Tour itinerary: the Capitoline *Antinous* and Medici *Niobids* are mentioned in *Antiquities of Athens*, for example.[10] Stuart benefited greatly from the scholarly atmosphere of Rome during the pontificate of Benedict XIV (1740–58). Crucially, he entered the circle

Fig. 4-4. Pierre Subleyras. *Portrait of Cardinal Silvio Valenti Gonzaga*, ca. 1745. Oil on canvas. Collection of the Palazzo Braschi, Rome.

Fig. 4-3. James Stuart. *Still Life with Flowers, Fan, and Pedestal*, n.d. Oil on canvas. Present location unknown.

of Benedict's Cardinal Secretary of State, Silvio Valenti Gonzaga, the cardinal considered "most favourable to the Jacobite cause" (fig. 4-4).[11] If Stuart had been a Jacobite, as was suspected in 1745, this is most likely how he and Valenti met.

However it came about, the connection with Valenti would have given Stuart privileged access to art collections, architectural works, and archaeological digs. Soon he was plumbing Valenti's collections for his own works (fig. 4-5): an etching of the pedestal of a second-century A.D. Roman cinerary urn was executed shortly after his arrival in Rome, as was an aquatint after a drawing for the Raphael school's "Finding of Moses" in the Vatican Logge (see figs. 3-4, 3-5).[12] This early use of the technique

of aquatint may have been prompted by Stuart's desire to capture the effect of wash on the drawing, as it is the only time that he is known to have used this medium. Richard Mead had given the drawing to the Venetian collector, printseller, and engraver Antonio Maria Zanetti in 1721 and its history was thought to be well documented.[13] Unless Stuart was working from a copy, however, it must have left Zanetti's collection by 1747. Valenti probably acquired the drawing because he held the Logge in high esteem, having already commissioned a complete copy of the decorations in 1745.[14] The aquatint may reflect Valenti's taste rather than Stuart's. It should be noted that the "Finding of Moses" is immediately adjacent to the rinçeau pilaster upon which the Spencers' Painted Room pilasters were based and Valenti played no part in that commission.

Eighteenth-century Rome was an important site of archaeological exploration, and Stuart was one of several artists drawn to the excavation of an obelisk in the Campo Marzo in April 1748. Plans were made to remove the obelisk after Benedict XIV visited the site, the Florentine scholar Angelo Maria Bandini was commissioned to write a history of the monument and, at Valenti's instigation, Stuart engraved the best-preserved sides (see fig. 3-1), eventually publishing his own observations (see chap. 3).[15]

The first "Proposal" for *Antiquities of Athens* was issued in Rome in 1748, when Stuart and Nicholas Revett (fig. 4-6) began to garner support for the project. The scheme had been developed on a trip to Naples that may have been prompted by the recent discovery of Pompeii.[16] A list of potential subscribers that Stuart compiled in Venice in 1750 provides some idea of his circle of acquaintances at this time.[17] Twenty-six of these men were British and Irish visitors to Italy and the resident diplomats in Florence and Venice, only two were Italian, one was an expatriate Prussian, and almost all of the identifiable names were acquaintances that Stuart had made after 1747. Many were associated with his principal English patron, Charles Watson-Wentworth, Lord Malton (later second Marquess of Rockingham). Significantly, James Caulfeild, the future first Earl of Charlemont, follows Rockingham on Stuart's list. Charlemont and Rockingham began a life-long friendship in 1750, shortly after Charlemont's return from a journey to the Levant that had aroused considerable interest.

A biography of James Gandon, Stuart's business partner in the 1770s, suggested that Rockingham had "induced Stuart to embark in the project of exploring Greece, and most munificently assisted him in his prosecution of it."[18] This has been discounted in more recent studies in favor of the Jacobites James Dawkins and John Bouverie, and the classical scholar Robert Wood.[19]

Rockingham's participation should not be dismissed so lightly. Stuart's *De Obelisco Caesaris Augusti*—written at the time the Greek sojourn was planned—was addressed to Rockingham (as Lord Malton), and Lord Leicester hinted that he was involved in the plans to travel to Greece: "I am glad Lord Malton has employed your sons companion in so great a work, wch won't only improve him, but help yr son in his expence . . . yr. son is best judge wh. the uses of accompanying Ld. Malton &c. in his course of seeing the antiquities will be to him and how far he is already master of his business to spare time for yt."[20] It was also to Rockingham that Wood forwarded Stuart's request for financial assistance when he and Revett fled Athens in 1753.[21]

Rockingham's real interests were politics and horses, but he was also a perceptive patron of sculpture, and a noted collector of coins and medals.[22] Stuart described him as "a deep lover of and expert concerning ancient monuments,"[23] around the same time that Rockingham commissioned designs for Wentworth Woodhouse (see fig. 6-6) and annotated a memorandum with a note about the link between the two halves of the building, "vide Stewards drawing done at Rome."[24] His continuing interest in these designs is confirmed by a letter of 28 September 1755.[25]

In what is perhaps the greatest paradox of Stuart's early career, Dawkins and Bouverie do not appear on his list, and it is unlikely that he saw them as potential patrons in 1750. This is surprising as the pair were planning their Levantine journey at the same time. Even more oddly, the names of Dawkins and "James Drake" appear on the following page of Stuart's sketchbook, although Drake's Christian name was William. As Dawkins and Bouverie were not in Venice when Stuart made his list, they most likely met Stuart in late 1749, when all three men were in Rome. It was probably through Dawkins and Bouverie that Stuart met Wood, who was also in Rome in December 1749. Wood had traveled in the Levant in 1742 and 1743, and he could have provided valuable advice, but *De Obelisco Caesaris Augusti* demonstrates that Stuart had committed himself to exhaustive methods of investigation and accurate depiction at least one year earlier.[26] Many questions remain about the closeness of the parties in the 1740s. Dawkins financed an extension of Stuart and Revett's stay in Greece after he met them in Athens in 1751, and shared experiences would have drawn them together in England. Contemporaries perceived Dawkins

Fig. 4-6. *Portrait of Nicholas Revett.* Frontispiece engraving by Isaac Taylor. From *Antiquities of Athens*, vol. 4 (1816). Courtesy of the Library, The Bard Graduate Center for Studies in the Decorative Arts, Design, and Culture, New York. *Checklist no. 11.*

to be a supporter of Revett and it was left to Charlemont to nominate Wood to the Society of Dilettanti in 1763.[27] In any event, it was the support of the Rockingham circle that sent Stuart and Revett to Venice on the first leg of their journey to Athens.

Eighteenth-century Venice was noted for its books, paintings, opera, and theater. In comparison with other places in Italy, however, the city seemed closed. Contact with foreign representatives was discouraged, and while strangers might meet members of the Venetian nobility, they were not commonly admitted to their social gatherings.[28] Fortunately, the British Resident, Sir James Gray, and Consul Joseph Smith were active, cultivated men.

Between 1737 and 1744, owing to what the English felt were "extraordinary distinctions and honours paid to the Pretender's son at Venice" there had been a diplomatic rupture between the two states.[29] Then, in October 1744, Robert D'Arcy, fourth Earl of Holdernesse, arrived as Ambassador Extraordinary. With him came Sir James Gray as Secretary of the Embassy and then as British Resident. Although Holdernesse had left Venice long before Stuart and Revett's arrival, Gray recommended Stuart to his attention, partly because in 1750 Holdernesse was in the Netherlands and in a position to help Stuart in the matter of his deceased sister's will.[30] Gray also nominated the pair for membership in the Society of Dilettanti and garnered subscriptions for their work.[31]

Without the contacts Stuart made in Rome and Venice, the trip to Athens would have been unthinkable. Thanks largely to Cardinal Valenti, the Marquess of Rockingham, and Sir James Gray, in less than a decade he had developed from a minor decorative painter into a highly respected antiquary. He would capitalize on these contacts and others when he returned to London.

Independence: Artists' Societies and Exhibitions, 1755–83

Stuart's patrons had not provided him with adequate funds for the return journey from Athens to London. After he disembarked at Marseilles, he traveled to Paris where he reverted to his old trade of cicerone.[32] The date of his arrival in England remains in doubt, although it must have been some time between October 27, 1754, when he and Revett left quarantine at Marseilles, and April 2, 1755, when their signatures appear on a letter written by a group of artists attempting to form an academy of painting, sculpture, and architecture.[33] Perhaps Stuart's sojourn in Paris was brief, for "Proposals" for *Antiquities of Athens* appeared in London in January 1755. By 1756 he had found lodgings in Lower Grosvenor Street and added that all-important "esquire" after his name.[34]

Stuart returned to London at a time when most artists worked in a range of media in order to earn a living. His years abroad provided him with a certain social cachet. He soon recognized that London's clubs and societies could be used to further his career, providing him with a professional freedom and flexibility unavailable to artists after the foundation of the Royal Academy in 1768. After his Continental sojourn, Stuart now called himself "Painter and Architect" (arousing the ire of Francis Hayman and William Hogarth in the process). Upon his arrival in London, he was absorbed into that group of artists most readily identified with the St. Martin's Lane Academy rather than into the milieu of architects and builders at the Office of Works.[35] After his long absence, St. Martin's Lane would have been an excellent place for Stuart to renew

old acquaintances and make new ones—he became friendly with Joseph and Anthony Highmore and was soon an intimate of Joshua Reynolds—he would also have recognized that the St. Martin's Lane circle was a place to "see and be seen."[36]

By 1755 London's artists were divided over the relative merits of founding a public academy of art. Demands for an academy were hardly new, since the subject had come increasingly to the fore in the years preceding Stuart's return from Greece. Both he and Revett signed the proposal submitted by the St. Martin's Lane group to the Society of Dilettanti in April 1755.[37] This proposal is noteworthy because it represents the point where, after months of negotiation, the artists had made room for nonprofessionals to assist in governing the academy. The Dilettanti met to discuss these proposals and passed three resolutions that, in effect, would have given them a permanent majority of votes.[38] The Dilettanti's secretary, Colonel George Gray was requested to inform the artists that their proposal was approved "as a ground work to proceed upon, tho liable to alterations."[39] The artists declined to accept Dilettanti support. Plans for an academy ground to a halt, as did Stuart's involvement. What he had hoped to gain from these negotiations is unclear. He did not approve of the Royal Academy as it was founded in 1768,[40] and his later support of the Free Society suggests that his vision was of an institution run by artists for artists. Perhaps he saw an opportunity to make his mark among the Dilettanti, with whom he had yet to establish strong connections. Whatever Stuart's motivation, his involvement resulted in increased contact with Lord Holdernesse and Colonel Gray, and that had a profound impact on his architectural career.

The failure to establish an academy coincided with the rise of the Society for the Promotion of Arts, Manufactures and Commerce (now known as the Royal Society of Arts, or RSA), which Stuart joined in June 1756.[41] Evidence of his motives for joining is lacking. As a member of the Dilettanti and the group of artists attempting to found an academy, he must have recognized that the two sides were incompatible. He probably saw the RSA as an alternative. Many artists became members in the 1750s, some because the society looked likely to offer a substitute for aristocratic patronage, others because it represented a convivial atmosphere in which to meet fellow artists.[42] In Stuart's case, Rockingham, Dawkins, and Simon, first Earl Harcourt had become members shortly before his own election, and it is also possible that this prompted him to follow suit.[43]

Recruitment of members was crucial to the society's survival because subscription money made the payment of premiums possible. By nominating nearly fifty men and women for membership, therefore, Stuart made an indirect but substantial contribution to the society's coffers.[44] At the beginning of 1755, there were seventeen subscribing members; by 1764 there were over two thousand members,[45] of whom some 7 percent were Stuart's nominees.

Committee membership was another way in which Stuart contributed to the life of the society. When the RSA was founded, its awards were overseen by ad hoc committees. These were soon regularized and the premiums distributed among committees of Polite Arts, Agriculture, Manufactures, Mechanics, Chemistry, and Colonies and Trade. In the beginning, members had been appointed to the committees. As the membership grew, this practice was abandoned. Instead, two chairmen were elected to each committee, and members chose which meetings they wished to attend. As soon as a committee had established the premiums to be offered that year, the chairmen would report back to the society at large. If their recommendations were accepted, the premiums were advertised in the newspapers, entrants' works received and judged, and the winning entries exhibited in the society's great room.

The Committee Minutes reveal that Stuart served on at least thirty committees and that his activities were wide-ranging and idiosyncratic. He was rarely present at meetings when decisions were made regarding the society's accommodation, for example, nor is there much evidence to suggest that he was involved in the exhibitions of 1760–64. From early in its history, however, the society had had an interest in dyes, pigments, and varnishes, all of which were of interest to painters. Stuart sat on several committees looking into such discoveries.[46] He was also a member of the committee that judged the drawings and paintings competing for premiums. What role he played in choosing the subjects advertised each year is uncertain.

The painting and drawing premiums were highly controversial. At first only children under the age of seventeen were allowed to compete for prizes, a situation that prompted Hogarth to resign on the grounds that it was not children who needed encouragement but professionals whose livelihoods were threatened by the taste for old masters and the work of better-trained immigrants.[47] Ironically, when reforms were implemented, it was under the auspices of a committee that included Reynolds and Stuart, men whose reputations rested upon almost everything that Hogarth despised.[48]

The premium list of 1758 was the first to offer medals for drawings by "Young Gentlemen or Ladies under the age of Twenty" and to those under the age of sixteen.[49] The first recipient was Lady Louisa Greville, and the Minutes record that Stuart was asked to seek confirmation that her drawing of the priory at Warwick was by her own hand.[50] Because Stuart was already acquainted with the Greville family (several of whom he had nominated for membership), his standing within the society and the rapid development of his patronage circle after 1755 probably rendered him a "safe pair of hands" to manage this delicate situation.

In March 1761 Stuart accepted the co-chairmanship of the Committee of Polite Arts.[51] He appears to have reneged on his responsibilities. His co-chairman Thomas Brand always reported back to the society, and when the chairmanships came up for renewal, "Mr. Brand declared a willingness to accept of being Chairman . . . if another Gentleman will take an equal share in the Business."[52] A statement of this nature is unprecedented in the society's minutes and, doubtless smarting from the rebuke, Stuart asked to be excused from the chairmanship in December.[53] Thereafter, his participation declined dramatically. In 1762 he sat on only one committee, in 1763 his name is entirely missing from the minute books, and by 1764 he was in arrears.

By the early 1760s, the more prominent artists were no longer playing a part in the society's affairs. This decline may be linked to the rise of exhibiting societies; most artists who were members of the Free Society were also active in the RSA while the leading members of the Incorporated Society of Artists are "conspicuously absent" from the society's records.[54] In Stuart's case, however, he did not exhibit with the Free Society until after it had severed its connections with the RSA. Other reasons for his departure must be sought. Any suggestion that he was forsaking painting in favor of architecture can be dismissed since he had been appointed portrait painter to the Society of Dilettanti in 1763.[55] He had also lobbied hard to succeed Hogarth as Serjeant-Painter at the Office of Works in 1764.[56] Stuart's widow also sold many of his own paintings, some of which would have post-dated his years in Italy and Greece.[57] A bruised ego may be one reason for Stuart's withdrawal. He may also have been unhappy that he was no longer able to promote his protégés. A week after he declined the chairmanship, a motion was passed stating "that the Chairmen of the several Committees of Premiums shall be chosen from among those Members, who do not profess the Arts, Manufactures, or Branches of Trade, which are the peculiar Objects of those Committees."[58] During the years Stuart served on the Committee of Polite Arts, someone may have noticed that the Pingo family received a disproportionately large number of premiums and that another of Stuart's protégés, the miniature-painter Jeremiah Meyer, was awarded a premium in July 1761.[59] Another spur to Stuart's departure may have been the rupture between the RSA and the Free Society.

The development of the eighteenth century exhibition culture has been the subject of much investigation, but Stuart's role within this has also been overlooked, probably because he allied himself with the Free Society rather than the Incorporated Society of Artists or the Royal Academy. Given his presence at RSA meetings, it is surprising that Stuart was not a member of the committee formed in February 1760 to consider Francis Hayman's request to hold an exhibition in the society's great room, since he was elected to the committee which organized the exhibition.[60] There were no works by Stuart on display in 1760, although Edward Rooker exhibited engravings from *Antiquities of Athens* and Lewis Pingo submitted the society's premium medal, executed after Stuart's design (see fig. 12-1).[61] When Hayman requested permission to hold an exhibition in 1761, the RSA's exhibition committee recommended that his request be granted. Again, Stuart submitted no works for display.[62] He was not a member of the 1762 and 1763 committees. This did not prevent his election to the exhibition committee in 1764.[63] By that date the society had begun to allow nonmember artists to assist in hanging the paintings. The composition of the hanging committee did not meet with the approval of certain other artists, prompting a written protest and the resulting resolution that all artists be removed from the committee.[64]

Unfortunately, the strife did not end there, as questions arose about the management of the money collected from catalogue sales. On March 12, 1764, Jared Leigh spoke on behalf of those artists whose characters had been called into question. After a heated debate, the offending paper was called for and read aloud. This was countered by a formal protest, and by the end of the meeting, the

artists were considered to have "justified themselves from the Insinuations of Mismanagement."[65] Discouraged by this débâcle, the society discontinued its exhibitions. Throughout these undignified squabbles, Stuart's name is markedly absent. As soon as the artists struck out on their own, however, he contributed four gouaches of Athens to the first independent Free Society exhibition and allowed his RSA membership to lapse.

From its inception, the Free Society was run by and for artists, and there was no room for aristocratic patrons to make decisions or hold office. "The Original Plan of the Artist's Society" printed in their 1783 catalogue gives some sense of its organizational structure. This stresses the charitable aims of the society and sets out its statutes: annual election of a president, two vice-presidents, eight ordinary members, and a secretary who made decisions and reported back to the society quarterly; the arrangement of special meetings to organize exhibitions; and the investment of profits in government or other securities. Unfortunately, the society's papers have disappeared, but Stuart appears to have held office on several occasions, including the presidency in 1780.[66] During the eighteen years of the Free Society's independent existence, he exhibited 122 works, submitted works on behalf of Joseph Nollekens when the young sculptor was studying in Rome, and was probably also responsible for encouraging the contributions of one-time exhibitors such as Stephen Riou.

The Free Society's exhibitions began well. Within two years their funds amounted to some £600 and, in spite of decreasing membership as the more renowned artists shifted allegiance to rival societies, their funds remained constant in 1767.[67] Profits dropped in 1768 and rose again in 1769, reflecting the crowds who came to see Henry Benbridge's portrait of the Corsican patriot Pascal Paoli.[68] To take advantage of the opportunity for increased sales, and to make a good showing against the first Royal Academy exhibition, there were also more works on display in 1769 than in previous years. Stuart exhibited only one painting, listed in the catalogue as "Sappho writing an ode which Cupid dictates," but the tone of a letter he wrote Thomas Anson implies that he was involved in the exhibition's organization that year: "Sig-re Paoli has brought much company to our exhibition, all the pictures on sale there . . . have been sold. . . . We shall make a present of 100£ to the Corsicans."[69]

In retrospect, the 1769 exhibition came at a critical

juncture. Clearly Free Society members recognized that exhibitions were social events—implicit in the display of Paoli's portrait was an awareness that viewers would discuss Corsican politics as well as the relative merits of the painting as a work of art. The executive committee was uncertain about the ways in which this could be used to their advantage. Even their catalogues continued to group works by artist's name, long after the Royal Academy had begun to print lists that reflected the arrangement of paintings as they hung on the walls at Somerset House.[70] After 1769 the Free Society's popularity waned. It was a slow process, if one can gauge popularity by personal accounts or reviews in the press. Ultimately Free Society artists could not compete with the stamp of official approval enjoyed by the Royal Academicians.[71] There were no exhibitions in 1777 and 1781, and an apology for the poor quality of the works on display was inserted in the 1782 catalogue, claiming that the exhibition was "hastily collected to avoid the Society from suffering a loss by the Forfeiture of their Room."[72] They ceased to exhibit after 1783.

In the absence of Stuart's papers, it is impossible to tell which, if any, of his works were sold at these exhibitions. Most would not have been available for sale. Eighty-two entries related to *Antiquities of Athens*, two were prints dating from his years in Italy, nine were works by his pupils or models and drawings by others after his own designs, and yet others were illustrations for or after scenes in Andrew Ramsay's *Travels of Cyrus* (1727),[73] John Hawkesworth's account of Captain Cook's first Pacific voyage (1773), and James Harris's *Philological Inquiries* (1781). Conspicuous by their absence are any works related to Stuart's architectural commissions. He could not have hoped or even desired to sell many of the works he exhibited. The Free Society probably represented a better opportunity to publicize his activities as an artist than the exhibition room at his house in Leicester Fields.[74] Evidently neither was an appropriate venue for promoting an architectural career.

Patronage the Old-Fashioned Way

Undeniably, Stuart received fewer architectural commissions than many of his contemporaries. To concentrate on this perceived failure, however, is to overlook the most striking feature of this aspect of his career. His patrons knew each other, corresponded with each other, and vis-

Fig. 4-7. Attributed to James Stuart. Sedan chair for Queen Charlotte, 1763. Made by Samuel Vaughan and Diederich Nicolaus Anderson. Oak, morocco leather, gilt metal, glass, silk. The Royal Collection, RCIN 31182 ©2006 Her Majesty Queen Elizabeth II.

ited each other frequently. This is not to suggest that his patrons were his exclusively—many employed John Carr as executant architect and also commissioned designs from Robert Adam—but rather to highlight Stuart's dependence upon the patronage circle he began to develop in the 1750s. Even the prospect of currying royal favor beyond the commissions he received for a silver throne, (possibly) a sedan chair (fig. 4-7), and the reredos erected in St. George's Chapel, Windsor (see fig. 2-29), seems to have held little appeal for him.[75]

As might be expected of a man who planned to dedicate *Antiquities of Athens* to the Jacobite James Dawkins if a planned dedication to George III fell through,[76]

Fig. 4-8. "Athens." Engraving by William Sharp, after James Stuart. From Ralph Willett, *A Description of the Library at Merly in the County of Dorset* (1785). By permission of The British Library, London, 130.h.1.

Stuart's patrons held a range of political beliefs. Although the majority were Whigs, their allegiances shifted whenever a paying position at court or in government was preferable to a career spent in the wilderness of Opposition. Club membership was something Stuart's patrons held in common. The importance of the Society of Dilettanti in the development of his career has been well documented,[77] but multiple memberships were common and we should be wary of privileging this society at the expense of others. Stuart was also a member of the Royal Society and the Society of Antiquaries, and these clubs were equally suitable venues for meeting potential patrons. The commission to design a monument to Thomas Steavens in the Church of St. Mary the Virgin, Preston-on-Stour, is a case in point (see fig. 9-12). Steavens had been a friend of Lord Charlemont in Italy and was one of the early potential subscribers to *Antiquities of Athens*. After 1750 the trail goes cold. Many years later, when Sarah West of Alscot Park determined to erect a monument to her brother, she turned to the artist most closely associated with the societies of which her husband had

been president—the Royal Society and the Society of Antiquaries—although why she chose to erect a monument to her long-dead brother instead of her recently deceased husband is uncertain.

Another commission that may have resulted from a society membership came from Ralph Willett, a Fellow of the Society of Antiquaries.[78] Willett sought Stuart's advice when designing his own library in 1772, shortly after Stuart had returned to this society after a protracted absence. *A Description of the Library at Merly* (1776; fig. 4-8) and the illustrated edition of 1785 state that the plaster medallion of "Athens" in the ceiling owed its form to "the truly Attick Mr. Stuart."[79]

A further commission that may have resulted from mutual society membership was at Kedleston Hall, the seat of Nathaniel Curzon (fig. 4-9 and see chap. 6). As Curzon had never been on the Grand Tour, it has been assumed that he stood outside Stuart's Dilettanti-based patronage circle and that this accounts for his failure to greet Stuart's proposals with enthusiasm.[80] Curzon was a Fellow of the RSA, however, and served on several of its committees

Fig. 4-9. Arthur Devis. *Portrait of Nathaniel Curzon, first Baron Scarsdale, and his Wife, Caroline,* 1754. Oil on Canvas. Courtesy of Kedleston Hall, The Scarsdale Collection (The National Trust, UK).

with Stuart.[81] The other link is Matthew Brettingham, who helped assemble Curzon's sculpture collection and whose father, Matthew Brettingham the elder, began to build the Kedleston of today.[82]

Italy and Beyond

Stuart's first patron after his return from Greece was Charles Watson-Wentworth, second Marquess of Rockingham (fig. 4-10). Stuart was well known as a Rockingham protégé, and Rockingham's sister Charlotte "continued her friendship to Mr. Stuart's orphan family till the end of her life."[83] Why then did Stuart receive no

large commissions from his mentor? Rockingham was hampered by the realities of Wentworth Woodhouse, the family's Yorkshire seat begun in 1724 by his grandfather as a marker of his inheritance of the Wentworth estate, aggrandized for use as a political power base by his father, and eventually finished only in 1772.[84] Understandably, Rockingham made no plans to replace his father's architect, Henry Flitcroft, when he inherited in 1750. He wisely used a local man, John Carr, as executant architect, even though he had discussed alterations with Stuart when in Italy.

The first Rockingham commission, securely dated to

Fig. 4-10. After Sir Joshua Reynolds. *Portrait of Charles Watson-Wentworth, second Marquess of Rockingham*, ca 1766–68. Oil on canvas. National Portrait Gallery, London, NPG 406.

shortly after Stuart's return from Greece, was for portraits of William III and George II.[85] The bas reliefs in the Marble Hall (see figs. 6-7a, b) and several chimneypieces soon followed; an invoice of 1764 reveals that Stuart designed the "new Statuary enricht Chimney piece, with Sienna marble pillasters" installed in Lady Rockingham's dressing room in 1764 (fig. 4-11).[86] On a visit in 1772, Horace Walpole remarked that "Stewart has given a design of one Chimneypiece but very ugly," which might be the same work or perhaps the chimneypiece similar to those in the great rooms of Lichfield House and Spencer House.[87] From Stuart also came the RSA's "victory" medals (see chap. 12), as well as tripod perfume burners and vase candelabra (see chap. 11), and in 1765 Rockingham paid Stuart £75 for a bronze lamp and a statue of Silenus riding a goat that he had had shipped from Rome.[88]

Loyalty had its rewards. Stuart relied on the marquess to endorse his election to the Royal Society in 1758, and in turn, he acted on Rockingham's behalf at meetings of the Society of Antiquaries.[89] Stuart was proposed for membership in the latter society on the grounds that he was "exceeding well versed in Antiquities, of which the valuable Collections made by him in his Travels are an undoubted Proof."[90] His friends Daniel Wray, William Strahan, John Nourse, and Thomas Hollis were already Fellows, and the group's weekly meetings (held in local taverns until the move to Somerset House in 1781) would have provided Stuart with a learned atmosphere in which to meet friends and make new acquaintances.[91]

Within a year of his election, Stuart's knowledge of the Levant was put to the test identifying Greek coins.[92] In 1762 he was elected to a committee looking into the

Antiquaries' early papers, and in 1763 he proposed John Barnard for fellowship and presented the society with *Antiquities of Athens*.[93] Mysteriously, he then disappears from the minute books until 1770, when he presented the society with *Ionian Antiquities,* nominated Robert Orme, Topham Beauclerk (a close friend of Charlemont), and John Walsh for fellowship, contributed to discussions on ancient inscriptions, and was elected to the society's council.[94]

Antiquarianism did not ignore class barriers, but it could offer a forum for the exchange of information that was sustained by relationships of "equality and deference."[95] That these could be mutually beneficial is demonstrated by Stuart's relationship with Rockingham, a Fellow since 1752. Rather than attend meetings himself, Rockingham used Stuart and, through him, the society to conduct research on objects in his own collection. In 1770, for example, Stuart exhibited a "brass Plate . . . with embossed Figures, & an Inscription . . . round the Rim" that Rockingham had given to a Mr. Rumsey to decipher (unsuccessfully), and in 1774 Stuart presented drawings of a bronze statue of Mars, the owner of which had permitted Rockingham to have sketches made.[96]

Many of Rockingham's friends and allies came to know Stuart and bestowed their patronage accordingly.[97] The earliest of the Rockingham connections was Lord

Fig. 4-12. After Richard Livesay. *Portrait of James Caulfeild, fourth Viscount and later first Earl of Charlemont,* 1784. Oil on canvas. National Portrait Gallery, London, NPG 176.

Fig. 4-11. James Stuart. Chimneypiece, possibly from Lady Rockingham's dressing room, Wentworth Woodhouse, Yorkshire, 1764. Photographed in 1987. English Heritage / National Monuments Record BB93/2947.

Charlemont, whom Stuart had also met in Italy (fig. 4-12). Correspondence between Charlemont and his former tutor Edward Murphy suggests that Stuart received a small commission from Ireland in 1755: "You have the pedestals but I have not as yet an answer from Stewart. . . . In answer to Brown's letter, in which he promises to send off the pedestals by the first good ship, I have sent him an order upon Messrs. Knox and Craghead for £90."[98] Although details were lost in the fire that destroyed Charlemont's papers in 1920, Stuart seems to have been involved in acquiring objects to sit atop the pedestals. Was it for Charlemont that Stuart and Thomas Patch arranged for a shipment of works of art to leave Leghorn for Dublin?[99] Stuart proposed Charlemont for Dilettanti membership and worked with him to plan the Dilettanti-

Fig. 4-13. George Reid
Sarjent. *The Latin Play at
Westminster School*, 1840.
Watercolor. The backdrop
was designed by Stuart
(1758; duplicated in 1808)
showing the Parthenon,
Theseum, and Tower of
the Winds. By permission
of the Governing Body of
Westminster School.
Checklist no. 38.

sponsored voyage that resulted in Richard Chandler's
Ionian Antiquities (1769).[100]

Edmund Burke and his "cousin" William Burke
were also Rockingham connections. Edmund had been
recommended to the marquess by William Fitzherbert and
subsequently became his private secretary during the first
Rockingham administration, when William was
appointed Under-Secretary of State to Henry Seymour
Conway.[101] It may have been the Burkes who introduced
Stuart to Dr. William Markham, another Rockingham
supporter. Markham had been William Burke's headmas-
ter at Westminster School, and he became godfather to
Edmund Burke's son in 1758, the same year that Stuart
designed the stage scenery for the Westminster play (fig.
4-13).[102] Stuart nominated William Burke for membership
in the RSA in 1761 and, at the Burkes' behest, accepted
James Barry into his studio after the young painter arrived
in London in 1764.[103]

Yet another Rockingham connection was Henry
Seymour Conway (fig. 4-14), a career soldier whose first

Fig. 4-14. Isaac Gosset. *Portrait of Henry
Seymour Conway*, 1760. Wax medallion.
National Portrait Gallery, London,
NPG 1757.

Fig. 4-15. James Stuart. The "Grecian Amphitheatre," Park Place, Henley on Thames, Oxfordshire, ca. 1780. Photographed ca. 1900. From an album of the Noble family of Park Place. Private collection.

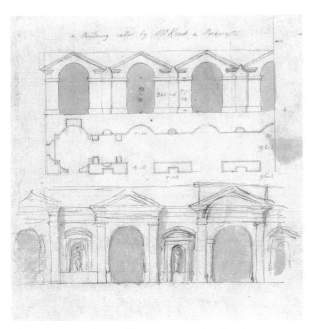

Fig. 4-16. James Stuart. Plan and elevation for the rebuilding of William Kent's Praeneste at Rousham, Oxfordshire, n.d. RIBA Library Drawings Collection, London, SD 62/20.

foray into politics in 1741 had been as Member of Parliament for the Rockingham constituency of Higham Ferrers. He served as Secretary of State for the Southern Department in the first Rockingham administration.[104] Conway broke with Rockingham in 1767 and later returned to the fold, becoming a member of the Cabinet during the second Rockingham administration. He turned to Stuart for the design of a "Grecian amphitheatre" built in the grounds of his Berkshire seat, Park Place.[105] It still survives (fig. 4-15) but is more like the Praeneste at Rousham (fig. 4-16) than a genuine amphitheater.[106]

Finally, the Rockingham connection led to Stuart's involvement with the design of the organ case at Newby Hall (see fig. 10-64), the Yorkshire seat of William Weddell and his wife Elizabeth, the half-sister of Mary, Marchioness of Rockingham.[107] Rockingham was Weddell's political mentor, and they also had artistic interests in common as well as mutual employment of Carr, Adam, and Stuart. Weddell acted as intermediary between Stuart and the poet William Mason in the matter of the monument to Mason's wife, Mary, erected in Bristol Cathedral (fig. 4-

TAKE HOLY EARTH ALL THAT MY SOUL HOLDS DEAR:
TAKE THAT BEST GIFT WHICH HEAV'N SO LATELY GAVE.
TO BRISTOL'S FOUNT I BORE WITH TREMBLING CARE
HER FADED FORM: SHE BOW'D TO TASTE THE WAVE
AND DIED. DOES YOUTH, DOES BEAUTY, READ THE LINE?
DOES SYMPATHETIC FEAR THEIR BREASTS ALARM?
SPEAK, DEAD MARIA, BREATHE A STRAIN DIVINE:
EV'N FROM THE GRAVE THOU SHALT HAVE POWER TO CHARM
BID THEM BE CHASTE, BE INNOCENT, LIKE THEE.
BID THEM IN DUTIES SPHERE AS MEEKLY MOVE;
AND, IF SO FAIR, FROM VANITY AS FREE;
AS FIRM IN FRIENDSHIP AND AS FOND IN LOVE.
TELL THEM, THO 'TIS AN AWFUL THING TO DIE
('TWAS EV'N TO THEE) YET THE DREAD PATH ONCE TROD,
HEAV'N LIFTS ITS EVERLASTING PORTALS HIGH
AND BIDS "THE PURE IN HEART BEHOLD THEIR GOD."

W. MASON.

Fig. 4-17. James Stuart. Monument to Mary Mason, wife of Rev. William Mason, in Bristol Cathedral, ca. 1767. Carving by J. F. Moore. Photographed in 2006. Courtesy of the Dean and Chapter of Bristol Cathedral. *Checklist no. 191.*

17), although it is unclear why an intermediary was needed as Stuart had completed Holdernesse House in London only the year before and Mason was Lord Holdernesse's chaplain.[108]

The Society of Dilettanti

One of Stuart's earliest Dilettanti patrons was Robert D'Arcy, fourth Earl of Holdernesse (fig. 4-18). Holdernesse came from a distinguished Yorkshire family and from 1740 until 1777 was Lord Lieutenant of the North Riding.[109] As an important courtier during the reign of George II, he was assigned to several diplomatic posts, including that of envoy extraordinary to the Venetian Republic, following which Sir James Gray had recommended Stuart to his attention.[110] By the time Stuart had

returned from Greece, Holdernesse was Secretary of State for the Northern Department and a member of the Privy Council alongside Admiral Sir George Anson and Philip Yorke, first Earl of Hardwicke.[111]

The Yorke and D'Arcy families had political interests in Yorkshire and owned borough houses around Richmond. As early as 1721, they had agreed to act together. Later correspondence indicates that their relationship was even closer in the 1750s, in spite of the Yorkes's failure to live up to their side of the bargain by purchasing an agreed number of borough houses.[112] Like many of Stuart's patrons, Holdernesse did not find favor with George III, even if he was cupbearer to Queen Charlotte at the Coronation and carved for her at table. A post office pension and the reversion of the wardenship of the Cinque Ports were his only compensation and he held no further office until his short-lived appointment as Governor to the Prince of Wales and Prince Frederick in 1771.[113]

Holdernesse spent a great part of each year in London, yet he was surprisingly peripatetic until the mid-1760s.[114] He purchased a villa, Sion Hill near Isleworth, in 1755 and began to rebuild it shortly thereafter, possibly with Stuart's assistance,[115] before commissioning Stuart to make designs for 24 Hertford Street, constructed 1761–65 on land that belonged to the Curzon family.[116] Stuart may also have been employed by Holdernesse to update the hall and furnishings at Hornby Castle, the ancient seat of the Conyers family.[117] Major work was undertaken in 1760, with William Mason acting on Holdernesse's behalf, and again in the late 1760s.

Mason was also agent to another of Stuart's early Dilettanti patrons, Simon, first Earl Harcourt (fig. 4-19), who had petitioned Rockingham in 1758 for help in securing him a position at the Board of Works, as Stuart was "too apt to neglect his own interest."[118] In the 1730s, the Duchess of Portland had described Harcourt as "rakish," a description that accords well with his Dilettanti portrait but is at odds with Horace Walpole's assessment of him as a "marvel of pomposity and propriety."[119] Perhaps Harcourt did not age well, as might be anticipated of one who had inherited a large fortune and estates at the age of six, married a woman with a £60,000 dowry, and seldom experienced a career setback from his appointment as Lord of the Bedchamber in 1735 to his retirement as Lord Lieutenant of Ireland in 1777.[120]

The Harcourts' correspondence reveals much about the ways in which Stuart's architectural career developed

Fig. 4-18. George Knapton. *Portrait of Robert D'Arcy, fourth Earl of Holdernesse*, 1752. Oil on canvas. Leeds Museums and Art Galleries (Temple Newsam House), UK.

Fig. 4-19. James McArdell, after Benjamin Wilson. *Portrait of Simon Harcourt, 1st Earl Harcourt*, ca. 1750–65. Mezzotint. National Portrait Gallery, London, NPG. D3224.

in the years after his return from Greece. No architect was mentioned in the letters between Harcourt's children, Elizabeth and George Simon (Viscount Newnham), when the latter was on the Grand Tour with George Villiers (the future Lord Jersey) in 1755–56. It is unlikely to be a coincidence that, at the very moment the Harcourts were planning their villa at Nuneham Courtenay, their son was informing his sister that "I hope my Papa will subscribe to Stuart, Sir James Gray, who corresponds with him and is an excellent judge says he is a most surprising Genius."[121] The fact that Stiff Leadbetter was employed as executant architect and that Harcourt himself was the chief designer has been used to bring Stuart's role at Nuneham Courtenay into question. Picking and choosing motifs from his Athenian drawings and employing a team of local workmen to implement them was the pattern followed by most of Stuart's patrons. It is what one would expect of a London-based designer with little practical building experience.[122] After all, the design of eighteenth-century country houses was invariably controlled by clients. Stuart may also have helped design the stables, the Church of All Saints, and the Temple of Flora (see figs. 7-5, 7-43).[123]

In addition, Stuart appears to have designed a room at Harcourt House, London, since Robert Adam was in

Earl Harcourt's sister Martha was the third wife of George Venables Vernon of Sudbury Hall, Derbyshire. The two families became even closer when Viscount Newnham married his cousin Elizabeth Vernon in 1765, and it is likely that the monument designed by Stuart to Harcourt's niece Catharine Venables Vernon in the neighboring church came about through the Harcourt connection (fig. 4-20).

Another early Dilettanti contact was Colonel George Gray (see fig. 5-4). As secretary to the society, Gray would have known of Stuart as early as 1750 when he was nominated for membership by the colonel's brother, Sir James Gray. This relationship did not begin to bear fruit until around 1758 when the colonel's protégé John Spencer (fig. 4-21) provided Stuart with the commission to redesign the interiors of his Wimbledon villa (see chap. 6).[126]

Stuart's work at Wimbledon was roughly contemporaneous with the commission he received at Spencer House, the town house Spencer began to build shortly after his marriage in 1755. Given the magnificence of Stuart's work here, particularly the celebrated Painted

Fig. 4-20. James Stuart. Monument to the Hon. Catharine Venables Vernon, Church of All Saints, Sudbury, Derbyshire, 1776. Photographed in 2006. *Checklist no. 197.*

the capital when he wrote the well-known outburst that begins: "P. Sandby called here this day & told me he was with Lord Newnham this morning when in came Lord Delaware to the Room which the Archipelagan Architect had ornamented for him" and ends "Christ my Lord Says Delaware Burn this in the meantime not to expose your own Ignorance for it is the most Wretched miserable affair ever was seen by Mortal."[124] DelaWarr was known for his caustic wit but Newnham's agreement with his assessment seems particularly unkind as Stuart had nominated him for RSA membership in 1757.[125]

Fig. 4-21. Thomas Gainsborough. *Portrait of John, First Earl Spencer*, ca. 1763. Oil on canvas. The Althorp Collection.

Room (see, for example, fig. 5-1),[127] it is surprising to discover that Colonel Gray tired of Stuart and may even have contemplated replacing him as early as 1760, when the Adam brothers were watching for signs that they might be able to oust their rival.[128] Ironically, Stuart outlasted Gray's involvement at Spencer House, for it was George Villiers, fourth Earl of Jersey, who oversaw construction from 1763 onwards.[129] Jersey, who served as vicechamberlain in the first Rockingham administration, also seems to have been exasperated by Stuart and no further commissions can be traced through the Spencer connection.

Jersey was not a Dilettanti member but his uncle Thomas Villiers, Baron Hyde, was (fig. 4-22). He had been a member of the society's clubhouse committee and later co-signed the instructions for Chandler's Levantine voyage.[130] He subscribed to *Antiquities of Athens* and supported Stuart when the latter was lobbying to become serjeantpainter.[131] Hyde began to develop the grounds of his seat, The Grove, around 1756 with the "6 column Grecian Doric Portico" that has recently been recognized as one

of Stuart's first architectural commissions, although its exact location and appearance are still unknown.[132] He also commissioned "a Chimney, some medalions & door cases" before 1761 and a cold bath building with "Pillars of Stuart's Ionick" around 1765.[133] Presumably this was the building that Amabel Polwarth, the daughter of Hyde's friend Lord Hardwicke, saw on a visit in June 1782, when she "walk'd in the Evening to the new Ionic Building."[134]

Another Dilettanti who became a patron of Stuart in 1756 was Thomas Anson, elder brother of the famous admiral (fig. 4-23). In the 1720s and 1730s, Thomas Anson had made a Grand Tour that appears to have included parts of the Levant.[135] Although he was Member of Parliament for Lichfield (1747–70) and he and Lords Gower and Stamford had investigated a possible canal route connecting the Trent and the Severn in 1758, Anson preferred antiquarian pursuits.[136] For nearly two decades, he regarded Stuart as an arbiter of taste and presented him with commissions as diverse as garden pavilions at Shugborough (see chap. 7) and alterations to the house that included a *grotteschi*-painted dressing room, the

Fig. 4-22. George Knapton. *Portrait of Thomas Villiers, Baron Hyde and later first Earl of Clarendon*, 1741. Oil on canvas. Courtesy of the Society of Dilettanti, London.

Fig. 4-23. School of John Vanderbank. *Portrait of Thomas Anson*, mid-1730s. Oil on canvas. Courtesy of Shugborough, The Anson Collection (The National Trust, UK).

design and erection of 15 St. James's Square (see chap. 5), a tea-table border and "tripodic tea-kitchen" (see chap. 11), and a medal commemorating Admiral Anson's circumnavigation of the globe (see fig. 12-22).[137] Stuart sometimes acted as Anson's agent in London and was the intermediary when William Woollett wished to engrave a painting in Anson's collection.[138] Anson was also the first Dilettante to be nominated by Stuart to the RSA, where he sat on at least one committee and, through Stuart, proposed that the society award a premium for stucco-making after the stucco on the exterior of Shugborough failed.[139] During Anson's final illness, Josiah Wedgwood acknowledged the pivotal role that he had played in Stuart's career when he informed his business partner Thomas Bentley that "Mr Anson is in a very dangerous way as to his health and I fear cannot live long. . . . Perhaps it may be of some consequence to our friend Mr Stuart to know Mr Anson's situation."[140]

The Midlands

It was almost certainly Anson who introduced Stuart to the Tory Member of Parliament for Staffordshire, Sir William Bagot of Blithfield Hall.[141] Like Shugborough, Blithfield was a perpetual building site, with much of the work carried out by Samuel Wyatt. Sir William also sought the opinions of Roger Newdigate and Nathaniel Curzon.[142] Stuart may have provided designs for a new entrance façade as well as for the orangery (see figs. 7-17, 7-19), the construction of which was supervised by Samuel and Joseph Wyatt in 1769.[143]

Another Anson-related commission was the monument to William Chetwynd, Member of Parliament for Stafford and the brother of Walter Chetwynd of Ingestre, the estate neighboring Shugborough. Chetwynd was a close friend of Thomas Anson and, as Master of the Royal Mint, had given permission for puncheons to be made for Stuart's RSA premium medal and the production of its "victory" medals.[144] Chetwynd was buried in the family vault at Ashley, near Market Drayton in Shropshire, where his daughter Deborah commissioned a monument that was a joint work between Stuart and Wedgwood (fig. 4-24).[145]

Stuart's friendship with Wedgwood has been remarked upon often enough and Stuart was equally close to Thomas Bentley. In the 1770s he became a member of the deist-leaning Club of Thirteen, founded by Bentley, Benjamin Franklin, David Williams, and a Colonel Dawson, which met fortnightly in Covent Garden.[146] Through this club, he became one of the sponsors of the David Williams Chapel in Margaret Street.[147] At Wedgwood's request, Stuart designed a monument to Bentley in 1780–81 (see figs. 9-13, 9-14).[148]

As a member of the Lunar Society, Wedgwood provided an opportunity for Stuart to meet other members of this group and develop his own scientific interests. A letter from Stuart to John Whitehurst was among the papers given to Josiah Taylor in 1809, and a letter to Stuart from Whitehurst regarding experiments made on the weights of metals before and after heating suggests that a reciprocal correspondence existed before Whitehurst became a Fellow of the Royal Society in 1779.[149] Whitehurst was the son of a clockmaker from Congleton. He settled in Derby, where he became renowned as an experimental scientist with wide-ranging interests. Stuart sub-

Fig. 4-24. James Stuart. Monument to William, Lord Chetwynd, Church of St. John the Baptist, Ashley, Staffordshire, 1771–72. Urn by Wedgwood and Bentley, 1772. Photographed in 2006. *Checklist no. 192.*

Fig. 4-25. Artist unknown. *Portrait of George, first Lord Lyttelton of Hagley*, ca. 1756. Oil on canvas. National Portrait Gallery, London, NPG 128.

Fig. 4-26. William Hoare. *Portrait of Richard Grenville, second Earl Temple*, 1760. Oil on canvas. National Portrait Gallery, London, NPG 258.

scribed to his *Inquiry into the Origin and Formation of the Earth* (1778).

Perhaps the first patron to whom Anson introduced Stuart was George, first Lord Lyttelton, of Hagley Hall (fig. 4-25).[150] As he was a nephew of Lord Cobham of Stowe, it was perhaps inevitable that Lyttelton embarked upon a political career at a young age. He was one of the Boy Patriots and an intimate of Frederick, Prince of Wales, in the 1730s and 1740s; a Lord of the Treasury in 1744; and Chancellor of the Exchequer in the Newcastle administration. He resigned the latter post in 1756 and refused all subsequent offers of office, devoting much of his time to literature and to his Hagley estate.[151]

The papers of the first two Earls of Hardwicke reveal close personal and political friendships between the Yorkes, Lytteltons, and Ansons. They visited each other frequently and eagerly discussed any improvements underway, offering encouragement and promoting the work of their favorite architects and craftsmen.[152] And they all had James Stuart in common. At Hagley, he provided paintings of "Flora" and "the Seasons" for the saloon and a

Doric Temple in the grounds (see figs. 6-37, 7-2). Lyttelton was a lifelong enthusiast of the landscape. On his travels, he often linked landscape and architecture with historical events and preferred a variety of emotional experiences within a restricted area.[153] Hagley became a sentimental landscape of the imagination, and many of the monuments were placed to encourage visitors to reflect on the nature of particular individuals or events. Stuart's Doric Temple, reputedly (but erroneously) thought to be modeled on the Theseum in Athens, was located at the head of a valley Lyttelton called his "Vale of Tempe" after the valley in Thessaly where Theseus was reputedly born.

It was most likely Lyttelton who introduced Stuart to his cousin Richard Grenville, Earl Temple (fig. 4-26). Adaptations of Stuart's RSA medals appear on the Grecian Temple at Stowe which Temple had remodeled in the 1750s.[154] Lyttelton, Temple, and his brother-in-law William Pitt were all elected members of the RSA in 1758, and there may be more than a passing relationship between the temple (renamed the Temple of Concord and Victory in 1762) and a premium for a drawing in architecture "of a Temple of Victory, decorated in the purest Stile of Antiquity, with Basso Relievos, Trophies and Tablets for Inscriptions, allusive to the glorious Atchievements of the British Arms during the present War"offered by the society in March 1761, three months before Temple informed Pitt that the revamped temple would include the "victory" medallions (fig. 4-27).[155] Eleven medallions can be identified from medals (see chap. 12). The other five come from a variety of sources, some still unidentified. The portrait medallion of Pitt may stem from the medal Thomas Hollis and Stuart discussed in 1759, although this was never realized,[156] while another, of a flying victory holding a palm, is based on Stuart's proposed design commemorating the victory at Lagos (fig. 4-28 and see fig. 12-14). This design was reused for the Louisbourg Taken and Goree Taken medals (see figs. 12-2, 12-3). Stuart's other unexecuted design for the Lagos medal (see chronology, fig. C6) is also represented at Stowe. This suggests that Temple appropriated Stuart's designs as soon as they were presented to the RSA, or per-

haps Stuart was consulted when the decoration was being planned.[157] Certainly Stuart produced medallions for some of his patrons, notably Lord Hardwicke,[158] and it is probable that he had a hand in those at Stowe, especially as Temple was also a member of the Society of Dilettanti and he had subscribed to *Antiquities of Athens* in 1755.[159]

No doubt Lyttelton was also instrumental in introducing Stuart to George William, sixth Earl of Coventry, Lord of the Bedchamber to George II and George III. Almost immediately after his marriage to Maria Gunning, Coventry had begun to rebuild Croome Court, Worcestershire, consulting Sanderson Miller about the façade and employing James Lovell and Francesco Vassalli for work on the interior at about the same time as they were working at Hagley.[160] Vassalli's bill, dated March 1761, includes a charge for the "Ceiling in ye Salon according to My designe" and "that done before according Mr Stuard designe."[161]

Lyttelton also introduced Stuart to Mrs. Elizabeth Montagu and Stuart returned the compliment by nomi-

Fig. 4-27. James Lovell, after a design by James Stuart. Medallion in the Temple of Concord and Victory at Stowe, Buckinghamshire, 1763. Terracotta, plaster border, lead inscription and ribbon. Inscribed: "LOUISBOURGH." Photographed in 2006. Courtesy of Stowe Landscape Gardens (The National Trust, UK).

Fig. 4-28. James Lovell, after a design by James Stuart. Medallion in the Temple of Concord and Victory at Stowe, Buckinghamshire, 1763. Terracotta, plaster border, lead inscription and ribbon. Inscribed: "GOREE SENEGAL." Photographed in 2006. Courtesy of Stowe Landscape Gardens (The National Trust, UK).

Fig. 4-29. John Raphael Smith, after Sir
Joshua Reynolds. *Portrait of Mrs. Montagu*,
1776. Mezzotint. National Portrait Gallery,
London, NPG D13746.

nating Lyttelton and Mrs. Montagu for RSA membership
in December 1758 (fig. 4-29).[162] By January 1760 Stuart
and Mrs. Montagu were sharing news from Quebec and
within two years she had involved herself in the publication of *Antiquities of Athens*, perhaps by providing financial backing.[163] In return, Stuart painted her a scene from
The Tempest, designed a zephyr-painted bedchamber and
other rooms at 31 Hill Street, and built her new town
house at 22 Portman Square (see chap. 5),[164] where, incidentally, the second Earl Harcourt designed the garden.[165]
In 1770, when Stuart was not active at any of her residences, he even ordered an ormolu tea kitchen with a
Wedgwood Etruscan-ware body for her from Matthew
Boulton.[166]

Mrs. Montagu has a serious claim to be one of Stuart's
most important patrons, but she continues to divide critics. For some, her literary salon provides an archetypal
example of the ways in which women could enter the
public sphere of eighteenth-century Britain, others have
refused to take her literary pretentions seriously.[167]
Unfortunately, it is her correspondence that has fueled
debate about Stuart's sobriety. At this distance in time, it
is unlikely that the issue can be resolved. It is worth noting, however, that Mrs. Montagu's letters can sound shrill
when read in isolation. She also turned to Stuart repeatedly for more than two decades, which is not the behavior of a dissatisfied patron.

The Legal Profession

If clubs, societies, and regional connections played a part
in establishing Stuart's web of patronage, so too did the
legal profession, a prominent member of which was Philip
Yorke, first Earl of Hardwicke, Lord Chancellor during
the Walpole and Newcastle administrations (fig. 4-30).

Fig. 4-30. Studio of Michael Dahl. *Portrait of Philip Yorke, first Earl of Hardwicke*, ca. 1737–43. Oil on canvas. National Portrait Gallery, London, NPG 872.

Although it is debatable whether he really "threw in his lot with the Rockingham Whigs" after his short-lived resignation in 1756,[168] surviving correspondence suggests that the relationship between Rockingham, Hardwicke, and Admiral George Anson was mutually beneficial.[169]

The first Earl and his eldest son Philip Yorke, Viscount Royston, were noted collectors of books and manuscripts. Neither they nor Royston's wife Jemima, Marchioness Grey, were great builders. This did not stop Stuart from visiting frequently, drawing portraits of the Yorke/Grey children and exchanging antiquarian gossip.[170] Careful with money and not admiring Stuart's skills as a painter,[171] the Yorke family sought other patronage outlets. They found it in the form of funerary monuments (see chap. 9).

The first monument was to Catharine Freman Yorke (see fig. 9-5), the first wife of Hardwicke's second son, Charles Yorke. Curiously, it was the first Earl who commissioned the work and paid the sculptor Peter

Scheemakers.[172] It is a substantial memorial for a woman who had been a member of the Yorke family for a mere four years and whose widower remarried with almost indecent haste. The Yorke monuments in St. Andrew's Church, next to Wimpole Hall, spoke more about the creation of a family than of individuals and, should Royston and Marchioness Grey fail to produce a son, Catharine Yorke was the mother of Wimpole's heir-apparent.

The monument must have pleased Royston (now second Earl of Hardwicke) for he turned to Stuart and Scheemakers for a monument to the first Earl and Countess (see fig. 9-6). Stuart's letters to Thomas Anson are full of news about this memorial, suggesting a "design by committee" scenario.[173] His friend Daniel Wray acted as Hardwicke's agent in the matter. Scheemakers supervised the installation of the monument and received £1,100 in three installments between 1764 and 1766, but there are no payments to Stuart recorded at this period in the Earl's bank account.[174] He must have received some remuneration, however, as John Yorke later inquired of his brother: "A Friend of Mine, who has employed Stuart for a *Design of a Monument*, wants to know what would be a proper acknowledgment of his trouble. Can you tell me what you gave him upon such occasions?"[175] Unfortunately, Hardwicke's answer has not survived.

The monuments to Ralph and Agnes Freman at Braughing and Joseph Cocks at Eastnor (see figs. 9-10, 9-15) also resulted from the Yorke connection as Freman was the brother of Catharine Yorke and Cocks was a cousin through the wife of the first Earl.

In spite of their limited interests in architecture, the Yorkes/Greys commissioned the last of Stuart's painted interiors—in the Prospect House or Park Building situated on a rise to the west of Wimpole Hall (see figs. 7-46, 7-47). The project was under discussion by January 1766, but plans were temporarily abandoned, and it was not until November 1773—when Hardwicke's daughter Amabel recorded in her diary that "Mr Stuart came here to design a Building for the Park Hill. Friday th. 19th he went away"—that building began.[176] Payments to Stuart made between May 1774 and May 1777 may relate to this work, which was completed by 1781.[177]

In addition to these commissions, Stuart was also involved in the second Lord Hardwicke's activities at the Society of Antiquaries. The publication of prints of British antiquities had been one of the society's first aims and all Fellows received copies as they came from the press.[178] Production had tapered off by the 1760s, however, and to rectify this situation, Stuart became involved in the production of the society's first large-scale engraving, *Henry VIII and François I on the Field of the Cloth of Gold,* after an anonymous painting at Windsor Castle (fig. 4-31). According to Amabel Polwarth, her father "had first recommended this picture to the Society of Antiquaries."[179] At the meeting held on March 29, 1770, Sir Joseph Ayloffe read a description of the painting, and the following week the president, Jeremiah Milles, reported that permission had been granted to make a copy-drawing.[180] Correspondence between Hardwicke, Ayloffe, and Edward Edwards reveals that the extraordinary time needed to make the drawing had driven the young draftsman to the brink of bankruptcy and embarrassed all concerned when Edwards requested 160 guineas for his work and was offered a paltry 90 guineas instead.[181] The author of this situation was Stuart, who had given Edwards nothing more solid than a small payment up front and vague promises of an unspecified amount to be paid upon delivery of the drawing. Edwards's drawing was eventually engraved by James Basire and published in 1775, the same year it was exhibited at the Free Society.[182]

Since the Yorke brothers had attended Corpus Christi College and their father was High Steward of Cambridge University, it is most likely they who were responsible for Stuart's involvement with plans for a new altar at King's College Chapel (see fig. 2-29).[183] The story begins around late 1758, when Sir James Burroughs was consulted about the altar and his plans were taken to London to seek approval from "those who might be competent judges in such a matter."[184] Popular opinion was unfavorable and those consulted agreed that the altar must be gothic. Stuart was recommended as "the ablest Person we can apply to" for a new design.[185] The matter was discussed again in 1766, when the College Board invited Burroughs's assistant James Essex to submit an estimate.[186] When this proved to be exorbitantly high, it was agreed that Stuart should be consulted again "that we may have his judgement and character for knowledge in such things—to justify us to the world."[187] While declining to submit designs of his own, Stuart apparently expressed reservations because in 1767 James Adam agreed to provide designs. After two abortive submissions, Adam was paid off and Essex built the altarpiece.

A commission not previously associated with the

Fig. 4-31. "Le Champ de Drap d'or. The Interview of Henry VIII, King of England, and the French King, Francis I . . . ," 1774. Engraving by James Basire after a copy by Edward Edwards of the original in Windsor Castle (artist unknown). Courtesy of the Trustees of the Victoria and Albert Museum, London, E.2264-1938.

Fig. 4-32. Artist unknown. *Portrait of James Harris,* 1777. Oil on canvas. National Portrait Gallery, London, NPG 186.

Tour; he became a member of the Society of Dilettanti in 1767.[192] Stuart was commissioned to rebuild Belvedere shortly before 1775, retaining only Gideon senior's reception suite.[193] In most cases the wall treatment would have been restrained so as not to compete with the painting and sculpture collections that Gideon continued to augment, the latter with the guidance of William Petty, second Earl of Shelburne, who may also have had dealings with Stuart at this time.[194]

Another legal contact was James Harris (fig. 4-32), the son of James Harris and his second wife, Elizabeth Ashley Cooper, sister of the third Earl of Shaftesbury. After studying at Wadham College, Oxford, Harris entered Lincoln's Inn and came to know the Yorke family to whom he was related by marriage; the first Earl of Hardwicke's wife, Margaret Cocks, was the younger sister of Catharine, the first wife of James Harris's father.[195] The Harris and Yorke families visited each other regularly and Joseph Yorke was among those who gave an early boost to the political career of Harris's son, the future first Earl of Malmesbury.[196] At his father's death, Harris returned to Salisbury and devoted himself to music and the arts.[197] He represented Christchurch in the House of Commons—where in the early years his fellow Member of Parliament for Christchurch was Sir Thomas Robinson, a kinsman of William Weddell—was a commissioner of the Admiralty in 1762, and in 1763 was promoted to the Treasury, the same year in which he was elected to the Royal Society.[198] After Grenville's ministry fell, he did not hold office again until 1774 when he became Secretary and Comptroller to the Queen. Today, Harris is better known as a scholar of grammar and dialectics. His first publication, "A Dialogue concerning Art," was dedicated to his cousin, Anthony Ashley Cooper, fourth Earl of Shaftesbury. An amended version was dedicated to Lord Lyttelton.[199] His best-known work, *Hermes* (1751), was among the first books to stimulate general interest in the study of language. As a "philosophical and philological consideration of the origins and development of language," it is a development of eighteenth-century debates surrounding "primitivism" and the origins of epic poetry.[200]

After the success of *Hermes,* Harris turned to Stuart for each of his subsequent works published by their mutual friend John Nourse. A precedent for Stuart's involvement with the book trade, if one were needed, was William Kent, who had provided illustrations for some half dozen works.[201] Many artists saw book illustration

Yorkes but one possibly due to their influence was at Belvedere, Kent, the seat of Sampson Gideon, later Lord Eardley. Gideon's father had been one of the new Whig financiers to emerge after the Glorious Revolution and was "the most important underwriter of government loans" in the mid-eighteenth century.[188] He purchased Belvedere in 1751 and, at his death in 1762, left a much "improved" house and grounds, notable artworks, and a fortune of £580,000.[189] Gideon junior entered Lincoln's Inn in the year of his father's death and came to know the Yorke family so well that, after Joseph Yorke declined the seat for Cambridge left vacant in 1770 on the death of Lord Granby, he became the second Earl's chosen candidate.[190] Even his wife Maria Marow Wilmot had Yorke connections. Her father Sir John Eardley Wilmot, Chief Justice of the Common Pleas, was one of the Trustees for Bishop Warburton's Lectures at Lincoln's Inn Chapel, along with Charles Yorke and Lord Mansfield.[191]

Unlike his father, Gideon had been on the Grand

Fig. 4-33. Frontispiece illustration of a Herm. Engraving by James Basire, after James Stuart. From James Harris, *Hermes, or A Philosophical Inquiry Concerning Universal Grammar* (1765). By permission of The British Library, London, 1086.d.4. *Checklist no. 160.*

Fig. 4-34. Frontispiece illustration of the portico of a temple to Ceres. Engraving by Isaac Taylor, after James Stuart. From James Harris, *Philosophical Arrangements* (1775). By permission of The British Library, London, 673.e.23. *Checklist no. 161.*

as a means of keeping the wolf from the door or as personal advertisements. Stuart evidently felt the same way, although his previous foray into the field had not extended beyond arranging the frontispiece to an edition of James Thomson's collected works (1762).[202] His work for Harris was more ambitious, beginning with illustrations for the second edition of *Hermes* (1765; fig. 4-33), dedicated to Lord Hardwicke who had died the previous year. Basire's engraving after Stuart's design depicts a putto representing the "Genius of Man" unveiling Hermes as

the "inventor of letters and regulator of language" while Memory transcribes an inscription on the herm.[203] The explanatory text for the engraving was situated in a chapter explaining elements of language such as syllables. Similarly themed illustrations were provided for *Philosophical Arrangements* (1775; fig. 4-34) and *Philological Inquiries* (1781; fig. 4-35).

Presumably it was through Harris that Stuart received the commission for the monument to Lord Shaftesbury in St. Giles Church at Wimborne St. Giles, Dorset (see fig.

173

Fig. 4-35. Frontispiece illustration of a philosopher and scholars. Engraving by William Sharp, after James Stuart. From James Harris, *Philological Inquiries* (1781). By permission of The British Library, London, 673.e.25. *Checklist no. 162*

9-9). Unlike his more famous father, the fourth Earl played only a minor role in the public arena, although he was a founding member of the RSA.[204] The monument was commissioned by Shaftesbury's second wife, Mary, a daughter of Jacob Bouverie, Viscount Folkestone.

Stuart's final connection with the legal profession was the future first Earl Camden, Charles Pratt, who, as Lord Chief Justice of the Common Pleas, had acquitted the controversial politician John Wilkes on the grounds that general warrants were illegal (fig. 4-36). Pratt had attended King's College, Cambridge, where he would almost certainly have met the Yorke family. Their relationship was not cordial, and Pratt and Charles Yorke were rivals for the position of Attorney General in 1757, and when Pratt received his peerage in 1765 (at Rockingham's behest) and was appointed Lord Chancellor in 1766, Yorke regarded it "as a most humiliating Circumstance to himself."[205] Stuart designed a commemorative medal to celebrate Pratt's Chancellorship (see fig. 12-21), an office he held until 1770, when it was given to Yorke. He retired from political life in 1778 but in 1782 entered the Rockingham ministry as Lord President of the Council. He retained this post (with a hiatus in 1783–84) until his death.

Stuart met Pratt some time before February 1758, when the latter was nominated for RSA membership.[206] As Pratt had the most up-to-date information about progress at Spencer House when Stuart was ill in 1763, their friendship must have been a close one.[207] Indeed it would appear that Stuart had been welcomed into Pratt's extended family circle, as his second son was named John

Fig. 4-36. Nathaniel Dance. *Portrait of Charles Pratt, later first Earl Camden*, 1767-69. Oil on canvas. National Portrait Gallery, London, NPG 336.

Fig. 4-37. Anton Raphael Mengs. *Portrait of Robert Stewart, first Marquess of Londonderry*, n.d. Oil on canvas. Courtesy of Mount Stewart, The Londonderry Collection (The National Trust, UK).

George Hardinge, perhaps after Pratt's brother-in-law, Nicholas Hardinge's son George, and Pratt's own son John.

Camden Place has been much altered, but evidence that Stuart had been responsible for certain interiors can be found in letters between Pratt and his daughters. In 1779 he informed Frances, "I am delighted . . . with the new apartments Stewart is fitting up for our residence. They are spacious & magnificent beyond either my wishes or expectation."[208] Evidently work was still underway the following year, when he wrote his other daughter, Elizabeth:"I perceive you have undertaken the improvement of the place in earnest. . . . I like your Ideas . . .

Tho' with respect to the Glasses I wd not have you be too hasty in making the Change, because perhaps when I come home & we reconsider it together we may both agree but the improvement will not answer the expense. The removal too of the Lanthorn for ye same reason, must be [?] upon, tho' I hate it where it is; but I wish you wd consult with Stuart & Norris about the Bath immediately, for I am determined to execute that building at all events."[209] The "Lanthorn" was a version of the Choragic Monument of Lysicrates that still survives in the grounds (see fig. 7-33). After Stuart's death, Pratt intended that George Dance would bring the second volume of *Antiquities of Athens* to fruition. Elizabeth Stuart, however, had other ideas.[210]

The Pratt connection led to the creation of the Temple of the Winds at Mount Stewart, County Down (see fig. 7-26), the seat of Frances Pratt's husband Robert Stewart, first Marquess of Londonderry (fig. 4-37). In June 1783 Stuart was paid a little over £54 for his designs for the building and furnishings, making this the last of his private architectural commissions.[211] He may also have been responsible for rooms in the big house.

The Admiralty

Stuart was fortunate to enter Admiralty circles at a time of unprecedented growth,[212] and his association with one of the most celebrated naval officers of the century, Admiral Sir George Anson, was to prove highly profitable. Anson had made little mark before 1739, when the War of Jenkins' Ear broke out and British tactics decreed that a fleet under Admiral Edward Vernon would attack Spanish colonies in the Caribbean. Anson's task was to cut off supplies from these colonies. His voyage had little effect on the outcome of the war, and after many adventures, including a gruelling circumnavigation and the loss of every ship except his own, he returned home with £1,000,000 worth of booty, more than enough to secure his promotion and ensure that he became a popular hero.[213] For the next three years, Anson pursued a political career, allying himself at the Admiralty with the Duke of Bedford and the Earl of Sandwich, and with Lord Hardwicke, whose daughter Elizabeth he married in 1748. When France declared war on Britain in 1744 and the war initially turned in French favor, Anson was in a position to push through the reforms for which he is still remembered. By 1747 his successes had ensured that he was raised to the peerage. Following Sandwich's dismissal from the

warding Stuart's name for the post of Surveyor to the Royal Hospital for Seamen at Greenwich.[216] Once established in naval circles, Stuart became the preferred purveyor of small-scale designs such as the Admiralty's Mediterranean passes commissioned in 1764 (see figs. 2-19, 2-20) and silver tureens made by Boulton and Fothergill in 1771 and 1781 (see fig. 11-30).[217] The Adam family correspondence suggests that Stuart might also have designed the screen wall to the Admiralty building in Whitehall in 1760 had not the death of Lady Anson distracted her husband's attention.[218]

Stuart's first Admiralty-related work was the monument erected in Westminster Abbey to George Augustus Howe, General of the British Forces in America (see fig. 9-3).[219] The Court of the Province of Massachusetts Bay paid for the monument. The choice of sculptor was left to the general's brother, Commodore Richard Howe, who had apparently lived in Anson's cabin during the circumnavigation.[220] It is probable that Anson recommended Stuart as a suitable person to design the monument and most likely at this time that Howe subscribed to *Antiquities of Athens*.

Stuart's other monument in Westminster Abbey commemorated Admiral Charles Watson (see fig. 9-4). Watson had commanded the *Princess Louisa* in the 1746 engagements off Cape Finisterre and in the Bay of Biscay under Admiral Anson and was subsequently made Commander-in-Chief of the naval forces in the East Indies. He died following the siege to regain Calcutta. Once again, Anson may have suggested Stuart's services, although Stuart was no stranger to affairs of the East India Company as one of his friends was Robert Orme, the Company's official historian.[221] He also undertook renovations at Warfield House, Berkshire, for John Walsh, an East India merchant.[222]

Via the "Admiralty connection," Stuart also received a commission from Charles Saunders (fig. 4-38), a lieutenant on Anson's circumnavigation. In 1754 Saunders was appointed Treasurer and Receiver General at Greenwich Naval Hospital, comptroller of the navy (at Anson's intervention) in 1755, and a Lord of the Admiralty in 1765 (under Rockingham), reaching the pinnacle as First Lord in 1766.[223] Saunders was mentioned frequently in letters from Stuart to Thomas Anson, and the same sources reveal that Stuart was at work, possibly on the interiors of Saunders's house in Spring Gardens, in 1764.[224]

Another Admiralty-related commission came from Sir Philip Stephens, a Fellow of the Royal Society and Society

Fig. 4-38. Joshua Reynolds. *Portrait of Admiral Sir Charles Saunders*, ca. 1765. Oil on canvas. ©National Maritime Museum, London, BHC 2392.

Admiralty in 1751, Anson became First Lord of the Admiralty.[214]

Although George Anson was elected to the Society of Dilettanti in 1750 and his brother Thomas was an enthusiastic patron of Stuart,[215] Anson never employed him, possibly because work on his seat, Moor Park, was nearing completion when Stuart returned from Athens. However, Stuart proposed dedicating an architectural treatise to the Admiral and Anson was instrumental in for-of Antiquaries, friend of the Anson family, and Secretary to the Admiralty Board 1762–95.[225] In the latter capacity he was the recipient of the tureen that Matthew Boulton dispatched from his Soho manufactory in 1781. The Anson correspondence suggests that Stuart played some role in the construction of Stephens's house at Fulham (see fig. 6-47).[226]

John Montagu, fourth Earl of Sandwich, a protégé of the Duke of Bedford and close friend of Admiral Anson, was also an Admiralty contact (fig. 4-39). Sandwich was First Lord of the Admiralty 1748–51, 1763, and 1771–82; a "monk" of Medmenham; a member of the Society of Dilettanti, Divan and Beefsteak clubs; and a founding member of the Catch Club (formed in 1761 to promote the composition and performance of catches, glees, and canons).[227] Since the Catch Club prize committee met at Sandwich's house, it was probably he who commissioned Stuart to design their prize medal in 1763 (see fig. 12-18).[228]

It was likely that Sandwich had Stuart's scenes of "local color" in *Antiquities of Athens* in mind when he commissioned the illustrations for an "unpublished account of the late Voyage round the World" that Stuart exhibited at the Free Society in 1773.[229] These were intended for the first volume of John Hawkesworth's *Account of the Voyages . . . successively performed by Commodore Byron, Captain Wallis, Captain Carteret and Captain Cook,* published by William Strahan in 1773 to general outrage. It was discovered that the author had denied the existence of divine providence and made radical alterations to the logs and journals of the men concerned, turning them from reliable observers into idealized heroes given to

Fig. 4-39. Joseph Highmore. *Portrait of John Montagu, fourth Earl of Sandwich,* 1740. Oil on canvas. National Portrait Gallery, London, NPG 1977.

Fig. 4-40. "A representation of the interview between Commodore Byron and the Patagonians." Engraving, after James Stuart (attributed). From John Hawkesworth, *An Account of the Voyages . . . Successively Performed by Commodore Byron, Captain Wallis, Captain Carteret and Captain Cook . . . ,* vol. 1 (1773): pl. 23, facing p. 27. By permission of The British Library, London, 455.a.21. *Checklist no. 163.*

Fig. 4-41. "A representation of the attack of Captain Wallis in the Dolphin by the natives of Otaheite." Engraving by Edward Rooker, after James Stuart. Loose page, from John Hawkesworth, *An Account of the Voyages . . .* , vol. 1 (1773): pl. 21. By permission of The British Library, London, Add. Ms. 23,921, fol. 5. *Checklist no. 164.*

philosophical musings on the nature of "primitive" cultures. This did little to stop the book becoming a runaway success, although it tarnished Hawkesworth's reputation and may have hastened his death.[230]

Unfortunately, the name of the artist is seldom given on the plates in Hawkesworth's *Voyages* and one cannot be certain that Stuart's Free Society exhibits were published. It may be significant that, in two cases, the engraver signed his work and both engravers had worked elsewhere for him. "Byron and the Patagonians" (fig. 4-40) is unsigned but is most likely the work of Edward Rooker, who engraved plates for *Antiquities of Athens* and was responsible for "The Natives of Otaheitee attacking the Dolphin frigate" (fig. 4-41).[231] John Hall, who executed plates of the Incantada at Salonika for Stuart, engraved "Interview of the Princess Oberhea and Capt. Wallis in Otaheitee" (fig. 4-42).[232]

Although Cook's first Pacific voyage is well known, the travels of his immediate predecessors are less so. In the first half of the eighteenth century, French activity in the Pacific had been a cause for British concern and became even more so after Charles de Brosses called for enhanced French commitment in the area in *Histoire des Navigations aux Terres Australes* (1756).[233] As First Lord of the Admiralty, Lord Egmont was eager to create new markets for British goods at the conclusion of the Seven Years' War and he sent Commodore John Byron on a secret expedition

to the southern hemisphere in 1764.[234] Byron was tasked to find the (non-existent) Pepys's Island in the South Atlantic, take possession of the Falkland Islands, and search for the Pacific end of the Northwest Passage. He "rediscovered" the Falklands but poor weather forced him to retreat to Port Desire, on the coast of Patagonia, where he had arranged to rendezvous with the *Florida,* a store ship, and he missed the French outpost on the Falklands recently established by Louis-Antoine de Bougainville.[235] While the *Florida* returned home with a letter informing Egmont of British claims to the Falklands, Byron passed through the Strait of Magellan and crossed the Pacific in an attempt to rediscover the Solomon Islands.[236] In fact, he did little more than circumnavigate the globe in record time.

To the general public, however, Byron's voyage was linked with the "giants" of Patagonia first encountered by Magellan's crew in 1520.[237] The Patagonians were the first non-Europeans that Byron's crew met and, as such, they would have been of interest to Hawkesworth's readers. Byron had described the Patagonians as abnormally tall in his letter to Egmont and, after the *Dolphin'*s return in May 1766, polite society could not get enough of "giants."[238] Even the Royal Society was agog and the society's secretary, Dr. Mathew Maty, sent a letter on the subject to M. de La Lande, president of the French Académie de Sciences.[239] French response was swift, suggesting that tales of giants were intended to divert attention from prepara-

Fig. 4-42. "A representation of
the surrender of the island of
Otaheite to Captain Wallis by
the supposed Queen Oberea."
Engraving by John Hall, after
James Stuart (attributed). Loose
page, from John Hawkesworth,
An Account of the Voyages . . . ,
vol. 1 (1773): pl. 22. By
permission of The British
Library, London, Add. Ms.
23,921, fol. 3a. *Checklist no. 165.*

tions to send Samuel Wallis and Philip Carteret to South
America and British plans to exploit a mine there.[240]
Whether or not the government used tales of giants as a
diversionary tactic, they were a gift to any ambitious
author and a depiction of Byron's landing party presenting the Patagonians with beads and other trinkets had
already appeared in an unauthorized account of Byron's
journey published in 1767.[241] Stuart chose to illustrate the
same scene for Hawkesworth's *Voyages.*[242] He may have
done so simply because the episode was one of the few
relating to Byron's voyage with general appeal. The
Patagonians were destined to reappear in the account of
Cook's voyage and Hawkesworth had come down in
favor of their existence as giants.[243]

Although Stuart's approach to recording data in
Greece had drawn on the same observational skills
encouraged by the Royal Society and the navy, he
treated "Byron and the Patagonians" as a history painting,
not an ethnographical study. No visual record had been
made of Cook's subsequent meeting with the Patagonians.
Other drawings, specimens, and artifacts in Joseph Banks's
possession were relatively easy to access.[244] Why did he
ignore this evidence? Did Sandwich tell Stuart what he
wanted and Stuart oblige?

Because the transfer of the Falkland Islands from the
French to the Spanish in 1767 threatened British plans in
the area, Wallis and Carteret's expedition was planned in

haste. The wisdom of such a venture divided the Cabinet
and their voyage failed to win the support that Byron had
enjoyed. Carteret thought he was only going as far as
the Falklands when he and Wallis set sail, but they were
charged with the discovery of the elusive southern continent that Byron thought he had seen. They also carried
instructions from Lord Morton, president of the Royal
Society, to identify a place to observe the transit of Venus
across the sun and a request from Dr. Maty that Carteret
write a report on the height of the Patagonians.[245] It was
Wallis's suggestion that his "discovery," Tahiti, would
make an appropriate location for observing the transit of
Venus, which, of course, was one of the motivations
behind Cook's first voyage to the South Seas.[246]

Stuart's "Natives of Otaheitee attacking the Dolphin
frigate" depicts the moment when, after an initial present
of food, the *Dolphin* had been attacked by a second wave
of canoes. As with "Byron and the Patagonians," this scene
was rendered necessary by Cook's subsequent meeting
with the Tahitians and by his and Wallis's ability to sub-
due the islanders with their superior weaponry in a manner befitting the greatest maritime nation on earth.[247]
Although the image draws on the British tradition of
painting naval battles, Stuart needed to be as accurate as
possible in his depiction of the Tahitians' vessels for it to
be effective (they needed to be *seen* to be inferior to a
British frigate), and he relied on drawings made by Banks's

draftsmen. It is probable that Sydney Parkinson's drawing, "The Tree on One Tree Hill," was the source of some landscape details, and the longhouse derives from Herman Spöring's "Paiheas Longhouse," which also appears in Stuart's third illustration, "Interview of the Princess Oberhea and Capt. Wallis."[248]

An illustration of Wallis's meeting with Oberea was necessary because she reappeared in Hawkesworth's account of Cook's voyage. Tales of licentious Polynesian social customs had already aroused public interest and Stuart had also to meet audience expectation. He must have used the botanical drawings or seen the specimens in Banks's collection—his landscape is clearly intended to be Polynesian, not European—but if he had access to drawings of Polynesians in their native dress, he chose not to use them. Instead, Stuart's figures wear suspiciously classical togas and Levantine turbans suggesting, much as Bougainville had done before him, a parallel between the Golden Age of classical Greece and the "happy innocence" of a Tahitian land of plenty.[249]

Strahan did not publish the fourth illustration that Stuart exhibited at the Free Society, "The Kongaroo, an animal in New Holland—undescribed by any naturalist." Instead, he chose an engraving after the painting George Stubbs exhibited at the Royal Academy in 1773.[250] Parkinson had made only two sketches of kangaroos, neither of which formed the basis for Stubbs's painting. The crew of the *Endeavour* had returned with the skull and skin of an adult male which were subsequently turned over to a taxidermist.[251] The kangaroo was a decidedly curious mammal to European eyes and it is hardly surprising that Stuart and Stubbs were fascinated by it.

Shortly after Cook's return, the Admiralty began to organize a second Pacific expedition, with William Hodges as official painter and John Reinhold Forster and his son George as naturalists, the last two on the recommendation of Daines Barrington.[252] Cook's second circumnavigation lasted from July 1772 until July 1775. Upon his return, he was appointed Fourth Captain at the Royal Naval Hospital. Cook was reluctant to take up this position, interpreting it as an attempt to pension him off,[253] but the appointment brought him into close contact with Stuart. Cook attended Royal Society Club dinners before his election as a Fellow in February 1776, and Stuart was among the signatories supporting his nomination.[254]

Although it has not been recognized previously, Stuart helped the official publication of Cook's second voyage

through the press. Perhaps as a result of a vague suggestion from Barrington, J. R. Forster was convinced that he had been commissioned to write the text, that he would receive all profits from its sale, and that £4,000 and a pension would be forthcoming.[255] He was to be bitterly disappointed. A sharply worded letter to Forster in October 1775 reveals that Sandwich already had doubts about his ability to carry out the work and that it had been decided that Cook would deal with the navigation and Forster with the scientific parts of the publication.[256] The Reverend John Douglas, canon of Windsor, was brought in to assist Cook in writing for the "nicest readers," and Richard Owen Cambridge was engaged to edit Forster's work.[257] In April 1776 Sandwich, Cook, Forster, and Philip Stephens met at the Admiralty and agreed that two volumes would be published, with the authors sharing any profits as well as the cost of paper and printing. The Admiralty would cover the cost of engraving the plates.[258] After repeated wrangling and Forster's refusal to have his work edited, Cook informed Douglas that "if I am to have the whole, the Admiralty I know will forward them [the illustrations] as much as possible. I have leave to remain in Town till this matter is settled, and at the desire of Lord Sandwich, shall join Mr. Stuart with Mr. Strahan to manage the Publication &ca of my book."[259] The affair descended into reams of correspondence between Barrington, Sandwich, and Forster, with one letter from Stuart himself in which he reveals that, on the pretext of needing them for his proposed translations of Cook's account, Forster had appealed to Stuart for certain proof prints and had then attempted to get them fraudulently when access had been denied.[260] Forster had seriously overplayed his hand, but he continued to appeal to Sandwich to reprimand Strahan and Stuart for their behavior long after the final decision to exclude him had been made.[261]

With the publication of Cook's first *Resolution* voyage, Stuart was involved in something "arguably unprecedented among travel books"—a lavishly illustrated work derived largely from "portraits and views drawn in the course of the expedition," instead of descriptions in the text itself.[262] The *et in arcadia ego* component "is considerably stronger in the engravings . . . than in Hodges' original paintings," rather more history painting than landscape or ethnographic study.[263] How much of this was Stuart's doing remains uncertain, although there may be something in the younger Forster's insistence that the engravings were too "Greek" and had strayed from the objective truth of Hodges original paintings.[264]

Stuart played no known role in the official account of Cook's final Pacific voyage but evidently played some part in planning the venture because he invited Thomas Jones to become the official artist-on-board.[265] Curiously, though, he was acting on behalf of the Society of Dilettanti, not the Royal Society or the Admiralty.

★ ★ ★

No all-encompassing conclusion can be reached about Stuart's relationship with his patronage circle. At times, he made a clear distinction between design and execution, and charged accordingly. At other times, and often for the same patron, he involved himself in the process from start to finish and was happy to bend himself to the patron's will. Ultimately, his career sits uncomfortably between the independence offered by the growth of London's bourgeois art market and dependence on the support of an elite group of patrons whose favor he remained content to curry for over three decades. In most cases, the patron became a personal friend and that friendship endured long after the design work had dried up. Perhaps in this area most of all, he was a success.

His club memberships also stood him in good stead. For an artist of Stuart's generation, the advantages of belonging to the Royal Society of Arts, Society of Antiquaries, and the Free Society would have been obvious: they gave him the opportunity to meet other artists, play the patron or promoter, and enhance his reputation as a connoisseur of fine art. The Free Society also provided a charitable outlet and a marketing tool in the form of its annual exhibitions. All would have provided food and drink, an indispensable aspect of eighteenth-century club membership. By the time of Stuart's death, however, his propensity to attend club and society meetings in taverns and alehouses was becoming incomprehensible to the younger generation of artists. Joseph Nollekens refused to join the group that met at The Feathers, and Stuart's obituarist, Anthony Highmore, felt obliged to defend his reputation amid the rumors of insobriety circulating in the months following Stuart's death. Highmore described Stuart as belonging to the "old school" that still attended such gatherings.[266] The old world of clubs and societies, patronage and social connections may have changed, but Stuart had not changed with it.

1. Paul Sandby, J. T. Smith, and Thomas Jones (the latter citing Stuart's friend Matthew Nulty) all noted that Stuart had been a member of that profession. For Sandby, see Taylor to James Gandon, 19 August 1809, copy letter, Add. Ms. 22,152: 29, BL; for Smith see J. T. Smith, *Nollekens and His Times*, vol. 1 (London: Henry Colburn, 1828): 21; for Jones, see A. P. Oppé, ed., "Memoirs of Thomas Jones," Walpole Society annual, vol. 32 (1946–48): 74. See also *Antiquities*, vol. 4 (1816): xxi–xxii; and chap. 2, by Catherine Arbuthnott, in this volume.

2. Add. Ms. 23,082: 34–35, BL; Jean André Rouquet, *The Present State of the Arts in England* (London: J. Nourse, 1755): 42–43; C. Reginald Grundy, "Documents Relating to an Action Brought against Joseph Goupy in 1738," Walpole Society annual, vol. 9 (1920–21): 77–87; Bruce Robertson, "Joseph Goupy and the Art of the Copy," *Bulletin of the Cleveland Museum of Art* 75 (December 1988): 355–82; Ilaria Bignamini, "George Vertue, Art Historian, and Art Institutions in London, 1689–1768: A Study of Clubs and Academies," Walpole Society annual, vol. 54 (1988): 28, 30, 35, 40–41, 69, 91, 97–98. A fan painter named William Goupy also resided in London at about the right time, but nothing else is known of him. *Oxford Dictionary of National Biography in association with The British Academy, from the earliest times to the year 2000*, ed. H. C. G. Matthew and Brian Harrison, vol. 23 (Oxford University Press, 2004): 84–85.

3. Early eighteenth-century fans usually featured characters from the stage, chinoiserie vignettes, scenes from the Old Testament and classical mythology, or copies of famous paintings; see Mary Gostelow, *The Fan* (Dublin: Gill and Macmillan, 1976): 41–42. A fan leaf depicting the Roman Forum and Arches of Constantine and Titus (see fig. 2-5, in this volume), attributed to Joseph Goupy on the basis of a dubious signature, is often cited as a formative influence on Stuart, but this fan leaf—which is Italian, not English—dates from much later than the inscribed "1738." Susan Mayor, personal communication, 9 December 2003.

4. Add. Ms. 23,076: 45, BL; William Thomas Whitley, *Artists and Their Friends in England 1700–1799*, vol. 1 (London and Boston: The Medici Society, 1928): 27.

5. *Antiquities*, vol. 4 (1816): ii; Stuart, "Sketchbook containing preliminary designs; plans, elevations, and details of buildings in N. Italy; topographical views and notes on painting," RIBA Library Drawings Collection, SKB/336/2 [L 3/4]: 63–83. The sketchbook is in fact untitled, but it is listed in the RIBA catalogue with this somewhat inaccurate and anachronistic description.

6. Martin Hopkinson, "A Portrait by James 'Athenian' Stuart," *Burlington Magazine* 132 (November 1990): 794–95.

7. *Second Report of the Royal Commission on Historical Manuscripts, Papers of the Rt. Hon. the Earl of Mount Edgcumbe, at Mount Edgcumbe, Cornwall* (London: H.M.S.O., 1871): appendix, 23.

8. John Marciari, "Athenian Stuart in Florence," *Burlington Magazine* 140 (September 1998): 612–14. Stuart's letter included an etching, *St. Andrew Led to Martyrdom* (see fig. 3-2); in 1998 the source of this etching was identified only as by the artist "Pomarancio." Since then, the original drawing, attributed to Nicolò Circignani, one of three artists known as "Pomarancio," has come to light (Staatliche Graphische Sammlung, Munich, inv. no. 2450), and a comparison of it with Stuart's

etching reveals that he produced a sensitive copy characterized by a light, almost nervous touch. The subject would have been particularly poignant after the failure of the Jacobite rebellion of 1745 and was probably chosen for that reason.

9. John Breval, *Remarks on Several Parts of Europe . . .* , vol. 1, rev. ed. (London: H. Lintot, 1738): 142; Francis Haskell and Nicholas Penny, *Taste and the Antique: The Lure of Classical Sculpture, 1500–1900* (New Haven and London: Yale University Press, 1982): 61, 70; Christopher M. S. Johns, "The Entrepôt of Europe: Rome in the Eighteenth Century," in *Art in Rome in the Eighteenth Century*, ed. Edgar Peters Bowron and Joseph J. Rishel, exh. cat., Philadelphia Museum of Art and Museum of Fine Arts, Houston (London: Merrell; Philadelphia: the Museum; New York: Rizzoli and St. Martins Press, 2000): 19.

10. *Antiquities,* vol. 2 (ca. 1790): 4, 34.

11. See Horace Mann to Thomas Pelham-Holles, first Duke of Newcastle, 23 November 1745, SP 98/50 Secretaries of State: State Papers Foreign, Tuscany, Horace Mann (1745): 309, NA; Basil Skinner, *Scots in Italy in the 18th Century* (Edinburgh: Board of Trustees of the National Galleries of Scotland, 1966): 38.

12. The urn subsequently entered the collection of Lyde Browne and later the Russian royal collection. Xenia Gorbunova, "Classical Sculpture from the Lyde Browne Collection," *Apollo* 100 (December 1974): 460–67; O. Neverov, "The Lyde Browne Collection and the History of Ancient Sculpture in the Hermitage Museum," *American Journal of Archaeology* 88 (1984): 33–42; Nicholas Penny, "Lord Rockingham's Sculpture Collection and the Judgment of Paris by Nollekens," *J. Paul Getty Museum Journal* 19 (1991): 27–28.

13. Peter Ward-Jackson, *Italian Drawings*, vol. 1, Victoria and Albert Museum Catalogues (London: H.M.S.O., 1979): 122.

14. Ludwig Freiherr von Pastor, *The History of the Popes from the Close of the Middle Ages*, vol. 8, ed. R. F. Kerr (London: Paul, Trench, Trübner, and Co., 1908): 317n; Bernice F. Davidson, *Raphael's Bible: A Study of the Vatican Logge* (University Park, PA: College Art Association and Pennsylvania State University Press, 1985): 29, 37.

15. Stuart, *De Obelisco Caesaris Augusti e Campo Martio nuperrime effosso* (Rome: Niccolò and Marco Pagliarini, 1750): 1.

16. Stuart traveled in the company of Hamilton, Revett, and Matthew Brettingham the younger, shortly after the latter's arrival in Rome to purchase sculpture for Lord Leicester. Most sources have assumed that this trip took place in April 1748, but see Gavin Hamilton to Ignazio Hugford, 28 July 1748, in Giovanni Gaetano Bottari, *Raccolta di Lettere sulla Pittura, Scultura ed Architettura*, vol. 5 (Milan: Giovanni Silvestri, 1822): 371–74.

17. "Names of the Gentlemen who have promised to Subscribe our Attica: Lord Malton 10, Lord Charlemount 1, Horace Mann, esq 1, Cardinal Valenti 6, Baron Stosch 1, the Hon. Lewis Watson Esq 1 [Malton's cousin], Thomas Pelham esq 6, John Millbanke 1, Mr. Samuel Ball 2, Capt. Clavering 1 [probably John Clavering], Alexander Inglis of Murdistoun Esqre. 2 [a connection of Gavin Hamilton, who was born at Murdieston House], John Revett of Brandiston Esqre 2, Thomas Humberston Esqre 1, Pagliarini Bookseller at Rome, Mr. Chamier, Roger Kinaston Esqr, Huert Esq [probably William Hewett], Follcort (?) Herbert Esqre, Edward Digby Esqr, ——Vernon Esqr, —

— Crop Esquire, Thomas Stephens Esqre, Hum-y Adams Esqr at Cookham, Berks, —— Smith Esqr his Majesty's Consul at Venice, Sir James Gray Baronet his Majesty's resident Venice, Mr. Hollis, Fred French, Papillon," in Stuart, *Sketchbook . . . of buildings in N. Italy*, RIBA Library Drawings Collection SKB/336/2 [L 3/4]: 2.

18. James Mulvany, *The Life of James Gandon* (Dublin: Hodges and Smith, 1846): 197.

19. Dora Wiebenson, *Sources of Greek Revival Architecture* (London: Zwemmer, 1969): 4.

20. Thomas Coke, first Earl of Leicester, to Matthew Brettingham the elder, n.d., Brettingham Letter 14, Holkham Hall Archives, Holkham Hall, Norfolk, quoted by kind permission of the Earl of Leicester and the Trustees of the Holkham Estate; Ruth Guilding, "Classical Sculpture and the English Interior, 1640–1840: Purpose and Meaning," Ph. D. diss., University of Bristol, 2000, 129.

21. Stuart to Robert Wood, 30 May 1753, Wentworth Woodhouse Muniments R1/42, and Wood to Charles Watson-Wentworth, second Marquess of Rockingham, 26 September 1753, Wentworth Woodhouse Muniments R1/41, Sheffield Archives.

22. R. J. Hopper, "The Second Marquis of Rockingham as a Coin Collector," *Antiquary's Journal* 62 (1982): 316–46; Penny, "Lord Rockingham's Sculpture Collection" (1991): 5–34; Christopher Eimer, *The Pingo Family and Medal Making in Eighteenth-Century Britain* (London: British Art Medal Trust, 1998): 23.

23. Stuart, *De Obelisco Caesaris Augusti* (1750): 1.

24. Wentworth Woodhouse Muniments Misc. 232, Sheffield Archives.

25. Stuart to Rockingham, 28 September 1755, Wentworth Woodhouse Muniments R1/70, Sheffield Archives.

26. This is not to suggest that the Dawkins circle had no influence on *Antiquities of Athens*, or that their subsequent support of Stuart and Revett went unrecognized, but rather that too much emphasis has been placed on the ways in which Stuart's project was influenced by Wood and Dawkins' example. For another view, see Eileen Harris *British Architectural Books and Writers*, assisted by Nicholas Savage (Cambridge University Press, 1990): 440.

27. Add. Ms. 22,152: 17, BL; Lionel Cust and Sidney Colvin, *History of the Society of Dilettanti* (London: Macmillan and Co., 1898): 80, 260; Lesley Lawrence [Lewis], "Stuart and Revett. Their Literary and Architectural Careers," *Journal of the Warburg Institute* 2 (1938–39): 134; Wiebenson, *Sources of Greek Revival Architecture* (1969): 28.

28. John Murray to Robert D'Arcy, fourth Earl of Holdernesse, 1 October 1756 and Holdernesse to Murray, 29 October 1756, Egerton Ms. 3,464: 274, 277–78, BL; Francis Blackburne, *Memoirs of Thomas Hollis*, vol. 1 (London: J. Nichols, 1780): 32–33; Michael Levey, "Introduction to Eighteenth-Century Venetian Art," in *The Glory of Venice: Art in the Eighteenth Century*, ed. Jane Martineau and Andrew Robison (New Haven and London: Yale University Press, 1994): 24.

29. David Bayne Horn, *British Diplomatic Representatives, 1689–1789* (London: The Royal Historical Society, 1932): 84.

30. Sarah Teresia Stuart to James Stuart, 14 June 1750, Add. Ms. 27, 576: 12–16, BL; Sir James Gray to Holdernesse, 18 November 1750, Egerton Ms. 3,419: 233–34, BL. After they met in Athens in 1751, James Dawkins

was given power of attorney to act on Stuart's behalf but it is unknown if the case was ever resolved.

31. *Antiquities*, vol. 1 (1762): vi; Cust and Colvin, *History of the Society of Dilettanti* (1898): 77, 257.

32. Joseph Fenn Sleigh to James Barry, 17 June 1765, quoted in [James Barry], *The Works of James Barry, Esq.* (London: T. Cadell and W. Davies, 1809): 18.

33. *Antiquities*, vol. 4 (1816): xvii; Cust and Colvin, *History of the Society of Dilettanti* (1898): 54.

34. Stuart resided at 7 Grosvenor Street from 1756 until 1763, when he moved to Hollis Street and finally 35 Leicester Fields. Subscription Book 1754-63, Royal Society of Arts (RSA), London; Gough Misc. Antiq. Folio 4, no. 72, Bodleian Library, Oxford; *Survey of London. The Grosvenor Estate in Mayfair. Part II: The Buildings* vol. 40, gen. ed. F. H. W. Sheppard (London: Athlone Press, 1980): 35, 119–21. For Hollis Street, see chap. 2, by Catherine Arbuthnott, in this volume.

35. Stuart's profession was given as "History Painter and Architect" when he joined the Royal Society and as "Painter and Architect" when he became a Fellow of the Society of Antiquaries. According to Hogarth's early biographers, "Stuart being once questioned by Frank Hayman upon his right to assume both these titles, said that 'Poetry was his wife, and Architecture his mistress.' 'You may call them so,' said Hayman, 'but I never heard that you had living issue by either.'" Hogarth's "Five Orders of Perriwigs" was equally scathing about Stuart's abilities. Journal Copy Book, vol. 23: 39 (26 January 1758), 135 (25 May 1758), Royal Society, London; Minutebook, vol. 8: 79 (15 June 1758), Society of Antiquaries, London; John Ireland and John Nichols, *Hogarth's Works: with Life and Anecdotal Descriptions of his Pictures* (London: Chatto and Windus, 1791): 285; Smith, *Nollekens and His Times*, vol. 1 (1828): 38; Bignamini, "George Vertue" (1988): 95–124.

36. Minutes of the Society, vol. 1, 16 June 1756, RSA; Add. Ms. 22,152: 31, BL; Frederick Whiley Hilles, *The Literary Career of Sir Joshua Reynolds* (Cambridge University Press, 1936): 282.

37. Minutes, vol. 2, February, March, and April 1755, archive of the Society of Dilettanti, Society of Antiquaries, London; William Richard Hamilton, *Historical Notices of the Society of Dilettanti* (London: privately printed, 1855): 25–34; Cust and Colvin, *History of the Society of Dilettanti* (1898): 51–54.

38. Minutes, vol. 2, 6 April, 4 May 1755, archive of the Society of Dilettanti; Cust and Colvin, *History of the Society of Dilettanti* (1898): 55.

39. Minutes, vol. 2, 4 May 1755, archive of the Society of Dilettanti.

40. Smith, *Nollekens and His Times*, vol. 1 (1828): 10–11.

41. Minutes of the Society, vol. 1, 16 and 23 June 1756, RSA.

42. The first two artists to join the society after its founder, William Shipley, were Henry Cheere and Richard Dalton. Cheere proposed Hogarth, who became a member on 31 December 1755. The 1760s were the peak years of the society's recruitment of artists. Ronald Paulson, *Hogarth: His Life, Art, and Times* (New Haven and London: Yale University Press, 1971): 214; D. G. C. Allan, "Artists and the Society in the Eighteenth Century," in *The Virtuoso Tribe of Arts and Sciences. Studies in the Eighteenth-Century Work and Membership of the London Society of*

Arts, ed. D. G. C. Allan and John L. Abbott (Athens and London: University of Georgia Press, 1992): 96, 108.

43. Dawkins and Rockingham were not active members, but Harcourt was elected one of the society's vice-presidents in 1758. Minutes of the Society, vol. 3, 1 March 1758, RSA; Rockingham to Edmund Burke, 15 October 1769, in *The Correspondence of Edmund Burke,* vol. 2, ed. L. S. Sutherland (Cambridge University Press, 1960): 94.

44. Stuart's first nominees were Reynolds, John Joshua Kirby (a painter and lecturer on perspective at the St. Martin's Lane Academy), and William Fitzherbert (Member of Parliament for Derby and a friend of Hogarth). For his other nominees, see Kerry Bristol, "James 'Athenian' Stuart and the Society," *Journal of the Royal Society of Arts* 144 (November 1996): 29.

45. [D. G. C. Allan and John L. Abbott], introduction to *Virtuoso Tribe of Arts* (1992): xv.

46. Minutes of the Society, vol. 1, 16 February 1757; Committee Minutes, vol. 1, 21 March 1760, RSA.

47. Henry Trueman Wood, *A History of the Royal Society of Arts* (London: John Murray, 1913): 16, 152; Paulson, *Hogarth* (1971): 218.

48. Committee Minutes, vol. 1, 15 April 1760; and Minutes of the Society, vol. 4, 7 January 1761, RSA; Paulson, *Hogarth* (1971): 219.

49. Wood, *History of the Royal Society of Arts* (1913): 156.

50. Minutes of the Society, vol. 3, 11 January and 6 December 1758, RSA. Louisa was the daughter of Francis Greville, later first Earl of Warwick.

51. Minutes of the Society, vol. 4, 31 March 1761, RSA.

52. Ibid., vol. 7, 25 November 1761.

53. Ibid., 2 December 1761.

54. Allan, "Artists and the Society" (1992): 101.

55. Minutes, vol. 3, 6 February and 1 May 1763, April and May 1766, 17 January 1768, and 5 March 1769, archive of the Society of Dilettanti; Hamilton, *Historical Notices of the Society of Dilettanti* (1855): 64–65; Cust and Colvin, *History of the Society of Dilettanti* (1898): 220–21; Peter Clark, *British Clubs and Societies, 1580–1800: The Origins of an Associational World* (Oxford: Clarendon Press, 2000): 248.

56. Stuart to Thomas Anson, [October or November 1764], Lichfield Ms. D615/P(S)/1/6/16–18, and 1 December 1764, Lichfield Ms. D615/P(S)/1/6/19, Staffordshire County Record Office, Stafford; Work 5/65, NA; Horace Walpole, *Anecdotes of Painting in England; [1760–1795] . . . ,* vol. 5, ed. Frederick Whiley Hilles and Philip B. Daghlian (London: H. Milford, Oxford University Press; New Haven and London: Yale University Press, 1937): 110; Paulson, *Hogarth* (1971): 102–3, 250–52, 509; Howard Montagu Colvin et al., eds., *The History of the King's Works,* vol. 5 (London: H.M.S.O., 1976): 111.

57. "Seven views of Athens, painted by Mr. Stuart," presumably those mentioned on the cover of the sale catalogue, were sold in 1791; see *A Catalogue of Pictures, by Moreland, Prints and Drawings, A Few Lots of Household Furniture, A grand Piano-Forte, by Pether, Books, and Books of Prints, Drawing Paper, and Other Effects, of the Late James Stuart, Esq. deceased, Amongst Which are Several Views of Athens . . . ,* sale cat., Greenwood, Leicester-Square, London, 27 June, 1791. A "Pair of pleas-

ing landscapes and figures," "A landscape, cattle and figures," and a "View of London, by moon-light, and a conflagration, *producing a singular and fine effect*" by Stuart were sold in 1799; see *Catalogue of A Collection of Antient and Modern Pictures, The Genuine Property of Mr. Stuart, Artist and Collector . . . ,* sale cat., Phillips, London, 4 February 1799. Copies of both catalogues in the Courtauld Institute Library, London.

58. Minutes of the Society, vol. 7, 9 December 1761, RSA.

59. Ibid., 15 July 1761.

60. Minutes of the Society, vol. 4, 27 February 1760, and vol. 5, 5 March 1760, RSA; Wood, *History of the Royal Society of Arts* (1913): 228–29.

61. For contributing artists, see Algernon Graves, *The Society of Artists of Great Britain, 1760–1791, The Free Society of Artists, 1761–1783: A Complete Dictionary of Contributors and their Work from the Foundation of the Societies to 1791* (London: George Bell and Sons, 1907).

62. Minutes of the Society, vol. 6, 3 and 31 December 1760, RSA.

63. Minutes of the Society, vol. 7, 3 February 1762 and 24 March 1762, vol. 8, 19 January 1763, vol. 9, 22 February 1764, RSA.

64. Ibid., vol. 9, 7 March 1764; Whitley, *Artists and Their Friends* (1928): 185.

65. Minutes of the Society, vol. 9, 12 March 1764, RSA. The protest was written by Leigh, William Bellers, William Pars, John Williams, Thomas Keyse, James Basire, John Gardnor, and Philip Barraud. Basire was the chief engraver of *Antiquities of Athens.*

66. Samuel Redgrave, *A Dictionary of Artists of the English School . . .* (London: Longmans, Green, and Co., 1874): 398–99.

67. Graves, *Society of Artists* (1907): 336–37.

68. Ibid., 337; Whitley, *Artists and Their Friends* (1928): 188.

69. Stuart to Anson, 27 May 1769, Lichfield Ms. D615/P(S)/1/6/24, Staffordshire Record Office, Stafford. See also Stuart to Anson, 17 June 1769, Lichfield Ms. D615/P(S)/1/6/26.

70. C. S. Matheson, "'A Shilling Well Laid Out': The Royal Academy's Early Public," in *Art on the Line: The Royal Academy Exhibitions at Somerset House, 1780–1836,* ed. David H. Solkin (New Haven and London: Yale University Press, 2001): 42–43.

71. Amabel Yorke invariably recorded that there was "little good" at Free Society exhibitions, even when she herself was an exhibitor, and an entry in Thomas Hollis's diary suggests that this was a common reaction: "At the Exhibition of the Artists at Spring Gardens. A bad one. At the Exhibition of the Artists in Maiden Lane. A worse. Met Mr. Stuart there and had some singular conversation with him." A review of the 1780 exhibition reveals that interest in the Free Society was slight; ten pages were devoted to the Royal Academy, seven pages to the Society of Artists, and a mere three pages to the Free Society, beginning with the statement that the latter was "by far the least shining of the three exhibitions, and will be soon dispatched." Diary of Thomas Hollis, Ms. Eng 1191, 28 April 1766, Houghton Library, Harvard University; Diaries of Lady Amabel Polwarth (née Yorke), Vyner Ms. Acc2299, vol. 1: 137–38 (2 May 1770); vol. 2: 144, 274 (8 May 1771, 10 May 1772), West Yorkshire Archive, Leeds; [Robert Baker], *Observations*

on the Pictures Now in Exhibition at the Royal Academy, Spring Gardens, and Mr Christie's (London: John Bell and G. Riley, 1780): 29–31.

72. Graves, *Society of Artists* (1907): 340.

73. Ramsay was a Scottish Roman Catholic convert who had been tutor to the Pretender's sons in 1724–25. *The Travels of Cyrus* was his most famous work and went into ten editions (some of which were illustrated, but none by Stuart) before the end of the century. The story on which Stuart's exhibited drawing was based is found in book 8, when Cyrus and Eleazer (an "illustrious Hebrew" and favorite of the Babylonian Queen Amytis) encounter King Nabuchodonosor, who had been driven mad as a punishment for idolatry and pride; see Andrew Michael Ramsay, *The Travels of Cyrus. To which is annexed, A Discourse upon the Theology and Mythology of the Pagans*, vol. 2 (London: T. Woodward and J. Peele, 1727): 132–86.

74. Smith, *Nollekens and His Times*, vol. 1 (1828): 38.

75. Diary of Thomas Hollis, 17 September 1761, Ms. Eng 1191, Houghton Library, Harvard University; Register of Chapter Accounts 1748–1773 and Audit Book 1767–1772, XII.B.8., St. George's Chapel Archive, Windsor; W. H. St. John Hope, *Windsor Castle: An Architectural History*, vol. 2 (London: Country Life, 1913): 389–90, 426; Walpole, *Anecdotes of Painting* (1937): 109; Victoria Percy and Gervase Jackson-Stops, "'Exquisite Taste and Tawdry Ornament': The Travel Journals of the 1st Duchess of Northumberland—II," *Country Life* 155 (7 February 1974): 251; David Watkin, *The Architect King: George III and the Culture of the Enlightenment* (London: Royal Collection Publications, 2004): 92–93, 131–33, 145–51; Jane Roberts, ed., *George III and Queen Charlotte. Patronage, Collecting and Court Taste* (London: Royal Collection Publications, 2004): 269.

76. Diary of Thomas Hollis, 24 May 1764, Ms. Eng 1191, Houghton Library, Harvard University; Blackburne, *Memoirs of Thomas Hollis* (1780): 178–79.

77. See, e.g., Lawrence, "Stuart and Revett" (1938–39): 134–35; J. Mordaunt Crook, *The Greek Revival*, 2nd ed. (London: John Murray, 1995): 7, 14–15; Kerry Bristol, "The Society of Dilettanti, James 'Athenian' Stuart and the Anson Family," *Apollo* 152 (July 2000): 46–54.

78. Minutebook, vol. 9: 124, 154 (10 November and 15 December 1763), Society of Antiquaries.

79. Ralph Willett, *A Description of the Library at Merly in the County of Dorset* (London: privately printed, 1785): 29; Tim Knox, "'A Mortifying Lesson to Human Vanity': Ralph Willett's Library at Merly House, Dorset," *Apollo* 152 (July 2000): 43. Another Dorset landowner, Lord Shaftesbury, may have introduced Stuart to Willett, but the latter is not known to have been part of Shaftesbury's circle.

80. Curzon approached Stuart sometime between February 1757, when he purchased Benedetto Luti's *Cain and Abel* and *Christ and Mary Magdalene* that appear in one of Stuart's drawings and December 1758 when Robert Adam wrote his familiar indictment of Stuart's failings as an architect. Robert Adam to James Adam, 11 December 1758, Clerk of Penicuik Ms. GD 18-4854, National Archives of Scotland, Edinburgh; Leslie Harris, *Robert Adam and Kedleston: The Making of a Neo-Classical Masterpiece,* ed. Gervase Jackson-Stops, exh. cat., Kedleston, Derbyshire, and Cooper-Hewitt Museum, New York (London: National Trust, 1987): 27–28; Eileen Harris, *The Genius of*

Robert Adam: His Interiors (New Haven and London: Paul Mellon Centre for Studies in British Art and Yale University Press, 2001): 19–21.

81. See, e.g., Minutes of the Society, vol. 5, 26 March 1760, RSA, when Curzon was chosen to sit on the Drawings Committee.

82. John Kenworthy-Browne, "Designing Around the Statues: Matthew Brettingham's Casts at Kedleston," *Apollo* 137 (April 1993): 248–52.

83. Committee Minutes, vol. 1, 25 October 1758, 1 and 27 November 1758, RSA; James Adam to William Adam, 19 December 1760, Clerk of Penicuik Ms. GD 18-4879, and 16 February 1761, Clerk of Penicuik Ms. GD 18-4886, National Archives of Scotland, Edinburgh; *Antiquities*, vol. 4 (1816): xxiv.

84. Marcus Binney, "Wentworth Woodhouse Revisited—I," *Country Life* 173 (17 March 1983): 624–27; pt. 2 (24 March 1983): 708–11; Binney "Wentworth Woodhouse, Yorkshire," *Country Life* 185 (24 January 1991): 60–63.

85. The latter may have been the equestrian portrait that Arthur Young noticed in the Blue Damask dressing room in 1768 and which was recorded in the State Dining Room in the inventory made at Rockingham's death in 1782. Wentworth Woodhouse Muniments A-1211 and A-1204, 16, Sheffield Archives; Arthur Young, *A Six Months Tour through the North of England . . .*, vol. 1 (London, Salisbury and Edinburgh: W. Strahan, et al., 1770): 253.

86. Vouchers for Works of Art, Wentworth Woodhouse Muniments, Sheffield Archives. The stonemason John Horobin's bill, signed and approved by Stuart, was paid on 28 February 1764. Chimneypieces commissioned by the first marquess had yet to be removed from their boxes when Walpole visited Wentworth Woodhouse in 1756, suggesting that Flitcroft had designed the other chimneypieces itemized in this bill, none of which were called "new." Horace Walpole to Richard Bentley, August 1756, in *The Yale Edition of Horace Walpole's Correspondence*, vol. 35, ed. W. S. Lewis, A. Dayle Wallace, and Robert A. Smith (New Haven and London: Yale University Press, 1973): 267.

87. Horace Walpole, "Journals of Visits to Country Seats," ed. Paget Toynbee, Walpole Society annual, vol. 16 (1927–28): 71; Lawrence, "Stuart and Revett" (1938–39): 140–41.

88. Wentworth Woodhouse Muniments Vouchers for Works of Art and A-1000, 11 June 1762, Sheffield Archives; David Watkin, *Athenian Stuart. Pioneer of the Greek Revival* (London: George Allen and Unwin, 1982): 32.

89. Journal Copy Book, vol. 23: 39, 135 (26 January and 25 May 1758), Royal Society. The certificate in Stuart's favor was signed by Lords Rockingham, Harcourt, and Macclesfield (president of the RSA), William Fauquier, Gowin Knight, Benjamin Wilson, and William Stukeley. Fauquier was a banker and director of the South Sea Company who later became secretary of the Society of Dilettanti. He had been a member of the Dilettanti committee that considered the artists' proposals for an academy of art in 1755. Stuart nominated him for membership in the RSA and, although he never patronized Stuart, their friendship was close. Minutes of the Society, vol. 2, 18 May 1757, RSA.

90. Minute Book, vol. 8: 79 (15 June 1758), 90 (7 December 1758), 107

(25 January 1759), Society of Antiquaries; Egerton Ms. 2,381: 73, 78, BL. Stuart's proposers were Henry Baker, T. Marsili, Thomas Hollis, Emanuel Mendes da Costa, J. Parsons, Matthew Duane, T. Hunt, and Daniel Wray.

91. Wray was deputy teller at the Exchequer under Philip Yorke, Viscount Royston (later second Earl of Hardwicke), who became one of Stuart's most faithful patrons in the 1760s and 1770s. Wray, Stuart, and Edward Langton (Royston's secretary) were among the first eight admissions to the newly opened Reading Room of the British Museum in 1759. Nourse was bookseller to George III and a publisher and importer of French books, especially those devoted to science and mathematics. Strahan was also in the book trade. Hollis was an acquaintance from Italy. Joyce Godber, "The Life of the Marchioness Grey of Wrest Park, 1722–97, and The Travel Journal of her Husband, Philip Yorke, 1744–63," Bedfordshire Historical Record Society annual, vol. 47 (1968): 25; John Feather, "John Nourse and his Authors," *Studies in Bibliography* 34 (1981): 206–27; Louise Lippincott, *Selling Art in Georgian London. The Rise of Arthur Pond* (New Haven and London: Yale University Press, 1983): 28; P. R. Harris, *A History of the British Museum Library, 1753–1973* (London: British Library, 1998): 763.

92. Minutebook, vol. 8 (31 January 1760): 209–10, Society of Antiquaries.

93. Minutebook, vol. 9 (10 and 17 June 1760, 10 February, 19 May 1763): 8–9, 49, 107, Society of Antiquaries; Top. Lond. C.2: 41 (June 1762), Bodleian Library. See also Joan Evans, *A History of the Society of Antiquaries* (Oxford University Press, 1956): 108–10, 140–46.

94. Minutebooks, vol. 11 (18 January, 1 February, 22 March, 23 April 1770): 200, 216, 273, 298; vol. 12 (22 November 1770): 17, Society of Antiquaries.

95. Rosemary Sweet, *Antiquaries. The Discovery of the Past in Eighteenth-Century Britain* (London and New York: Hambledon and London, 2004): 60.

96. Minutebooks, vol. 11 (15 February 1770): 238–40; vol. 13 (17 February 1774): 245, Society of Antiquaries; Top. Lond. C.2: 79, 96, Bodleian Library.

97. For Rockingham's political career, see Paul Langford, *The First Rockingham Administration* (Oxford University Press, 1973) and Warren M. Elofson, *The Rockingham Connection and the Second Founding of the Whig Party, 1768–1773* (Montreal, Kingston, London, and Buffalo: McGill-Queen's University Press, 1996). Rockingham Whigs such as William Fitzherbert feature strongly in Stuart's circle. Minutes of the Society, vol. 1, 17 November 1756, RSA; Journal Copy Book, vol. 24 (1760–63): 349, Royal Society.

98. Edward Murphy to James Caulfeild, first Earl of Charlemont, 19 October 1755, in *Twelfth Report of the Royal Commission on Historical Manuscripts*, vol. 1 (London: H.M.S.O., 1890): appendix, pt. 10, 221, cited in Kerry Bristol, "Rathfarnham Castle and its Place in the Architectural Oeuvre of James 'Athenian' Stuart: A Question of Patronage," in *Lord Charlemont and His Circle*, ed. Michael McCarthy (Dublin and Portland, OR: Four Courts Press, 2001): 115.

99. *Ufficio Sicurtà* filza 60, n.127, Archivio di Stato di Livorno, cited in Elena Lazzarini, "The Trade of Luxury Goods in Livorno and Florence in the Eighteenth Century," in *The Lustrous Trade: Material Culture and the History of Sculpture in England and Italy, c. 1700–c. 1860*, ed. Cinzia Sicca and Alison Yarrington (London and New York: Leicester University Press, 2000): 70, 75 n.12. Frustratingly, no date is given for this shipment.

100. Richard Chandler, *Travels in Asia Minor; or, An account of a Tour Made at the Expense of the Society of Dilettanti* (Oxford: Clarendon Press, 1775): preface; Cust and Colvin, *History of the Society of Dilettanti* (1898): 84–87. The Dilettanti's instructions were signed by Charlemont, Wood, Brand, Fauquier, Stuart, Lord Middlesex, Sir Francis Dashwood, Sir James Gray, and Lord Bessborough.

101. Langford, *First Rockingham Administration* (1973): 274–75; *Oxford Dictionary of National Biography*, vol. 8 (2004): 854.

102. John Markham, *A Naval Career During the Old War . . .*, ed. Sir Clements R. Markham (London: Sampson Low, Marston, Searle, and Rivington, 1883): 14.

103. Minutes of the Society, vol. 7, 2 December 1761, RSA; *The Works of James Barry* (1809): 13–15; *Correspondence of Edmund Burke*, vol. 1, ed. Thomas W. Copeland (1958): 203.

104. Langford, *First Rockingham Administration* (1973): 21.

105. *Picturesque Tour of the River Thames; illustrated by Twenty-Four Coloured Views, A Map, And Vignettes, From Original Drawings Taken on the Spot by William Westall and Samuel Owen* (London: R. Ackermann, 1828): 76–77; Horace Walpole to George Montague, 3 October 1763, in Percy Noble, *Park Place, Berkshire: A Short History of the Place and an Account of the Owners and their Guests* (London: privately printed, 1905): 22, 40–41; David Constantine, *Fields of Fire. A Life of Sir William Hamilton* (London: Phoenix Press, 2002): 2.

106. Giles Worsley, "Out From Adam's Shadow," *Country Life* 186 (14 May 1992): 102. Previously Park Place had belonged to Archibald Hamilton and was the birthplace of his son William who served as Conway's aide-de-camp during the Seven Years' War. During Conway's tenure, Sir William Hamilton was a frequent visitor and it was presumably through Conway that he and Stuart became acquainted; Stuart nominated Hamilton for membership in the RSA in January 1758. After Conway's death, the estate was sold to the first Earl of Malmesbury, the son of yet another Stuart patron, James Harris. See Minutes of the Society, vol. 2, 11 January 1758, RSA; Noble, *Park Place* (1905): 142.

107. John Cornforth, "Newby Hall, North Yorkshire—I," *Country Life* 165 (7 June 1979): 1802–6; pt. 2 (14 June 1979): 1918–21; pt. 3 (21 June 1979): 2006–9.

108. Edward William Harcourt, ed., *The Harcourt Papers*, vol. 7 (Oxford: privately printed, [1880–1905]): 2; Thomas Gray to William Mason, 23 May 1767 and 6 June 1767, in *Correspondence of Thomas Gray*, ed. Paget Toynbee and Leonard Whibley, vol. 3 (Oxford: Clarendon Press, 1935): 957, 963.

109. Giles Worsley, "Hornby Castle, Yorkshire," *Country Life* 183 (29 June 1989): 188.

110. Sarah Teresia Stuart to James Stuart, 14 June 1750, Add. Ms. 27, 576: 12–16, BL; Sir James Gray to Holdernesse, 18 November 1750, Egerton Ms. 3,419: 233–34, BL.

111. Egerton Ms. 3,459, BL; Ian McIntyre, *Joshua Reynolds. The Life and*

Times of the First President of the Royal Academy (London: Allen Lane, 2003): 91–92.

112. Egerton Ms. 3,436: 111–12, BL; Conyers D'Arcy to [Philip Yorke, first Earl of Hardwicke], 31 July 1757, ibid.: 126, and J. Yorke to Holdernesse, 14 April 1759, ibid.: 260.

113. Egerton Mss. 3,495: 3, 146, 385; and 3,496: 2, BL; Worsley, "Hornby Castle" (1989): 188.

114. Holdernesse leased 4 Whitehall Yard from the Crown but sublet this to the Earl of Sandwich and lived instead in Grosvenor Street and then at the Earl of Kildare's house in Arlington Street. Egerton Ms. 3,497: 25, BL.

115. John Harris, "Le Rouge's Sion Hill: A Garden by Brown," *London Gardener or The Gardener's Intelligencer* 5 (1999–2000): 27–28.

116. H. Montgomery Hyde, *Londonderry House and Its Pictures* (London: Cresset Press, 1937); Arthur Oswald, "Londonderry House, Park Lane," *Country Life* 82 (10 July 1937): 38–44.

117. Worsley, "Hornby Castle" (1989): 188–91. See also Young, *Six Months Tour through the North of England*, vol. 2 (1770): 242.

118. Simon, first Earl Harcourt to Rockingham, 4 February 1758, Wentworth Woodhouse Muniments R1-116, Sheffield Archives.

119. Margaret Cavendish, Duchess of Portland, to Catherine Collingwood, 1 December 1735, in *The Autobiography and Correspondence of Mary Granville, Mrs Delany*, ed. Lady Augusta Llanover, vol. 1 (London: Richard Bentley, 1861): 546–47; Mavis Batey, "Nuneham Courtenay: An Oxfordshire Eighteenth-Century Deserted Village," *Oxoniensia* 33 (1968): 110.

120. For biographical information see *Harcourt Papers*, vol. 3 (n. d.): 1–155 and Giles Worsley, "Nuneham Park Revisited—I," *Country Life* 177 (3 January 1985): 16–17.

121. George Simon Harcourt, Viscount Newnham, to Elizabeth Harcourt, [1755], Lee Ms. D/LE/E2/19, Centre for Buckinghamshire Studies, Aylesbury. For the construction and subsequent alteration of Nuneham Park, see chap. 6, by Julius Bryant, in this volume.

122. Only in London did Stuart provide his own team of craftsmen and artisans. On this point, see Kerry Bristol, "A Note on James Stuart and the London Building Trades," *Georgian Group Journal* 13 (2003): 1–11.

123. Lee Ms. D/LE/E2/41, Centre for Buckinghamshire Studies, Aylesbury; *A New Pocket Companion for Oxford: or, Guide through the University*, rev. ed. (Oxford: D. Prince and J. Cooke, 1785): 132; *Harcourt Papers*, vol. 3 (n. d.): 200, and vol. 7 (n. d.): 33, 59–60; Basil F. L. Clarke, *The Building of the Eighteenth-Century Church* (London: S.P.C.K., 1963): 145.

124. Robert Adam to James Adam, 11 December 1758, Clerk of Penicuik Ms. GD18-4854, National Archives of Scotland, Edinburgh.

125. Minutes of the Society, vol. 2, 25 May 1757, RSA.

126. Spencer did not become a member of the Society of Dilettanti until March 1765, and his association with Stuart came about through Colonel Gray, whom Stuart nominated for RSA membership in February 1759. Minutes of the Society, vol. 3, 7 February 1759, RSA; Cust and Colvin, *History of the Society of Dilettanti* (1898): 263. For Wimbledon, see chap.6, by Julius Bryant, in this volume.

127. Then, as now, most visitors commented on the Painted Room. See, for example, Diaries of Amabel Polwarth, Vyner Ms. Acc2299, vol. 2: 273 (7 May 1772), West Yorkshire Archive, Leeds: "Miss Gregory and I in a Mask went with Mrs York, Ldy Beauchamp & Mrs Walker . . . to see Masks at Ldy Spencer's, & the Ds of Argyles . . . Ld Spencers Rooms are singly fitted up by Stuart, the third Room is elegantly painted by him."

128. James Adam to Robert Adam, 5 January 1761, Clerk of Penicuik Ms. GD 18-4881, National Archives of Scotland, Edinburgh.

129. Joseph Friedman, *Spencer House. Chronicle of a Great London Mansion* (London: Zwemmer Press, 1993): 133.

130. Cust and Colvin, *History of the Society of Dilettanti* (1898): 8, 46, 83.

131. Stuart to Anson, [October or November 1764], Lichfield Ms. D615/P(S)/1/6/16, [October or November 1764], ibid., 1/6/17, [October or November 1764], ibid., 1/6/18, Staffordshire Record Office, Stafford.

132. Michael Cousins, "Athenian Stuart's Doric porticoes," *Georgian Group Journal* 14 (2004): 52, 53n18.

133. Thomas Villiers, Lord Hyde, to Philip Yorke, second Earl of Hardwicke, 17 September 1765, Add. Ms. 35,607: 195, BL; Walpole "Journals of Visits to Country Seats" (1927–28): 38.

134. Diaries of Amabel Polwarth, Vyner Ms. Acc2299, vol. 7: 115 (27 June 1782), West Yorkshire Archive, Leeds.

135. James Lees-Milne, "Shugborough, Staffordshire—I. The Park and its Monuments," *Connoisseur* 164 (April 1967): 211; Alastair Laing, "O tempera, o Mores! The Ruin Paintings in the Dining Room at Shugborough," *Apollo* 137 (April 1993): 232 n. 2.

136. Hilary Young, ed., *The Genius of Wedgwood*, exh. cat. (London: Victoria and Albert Museum, 1995): 145, 179–80, 191–92, 194–96, 206; Jenny Uglow, *The Lunar Men: The Friends Who Made the Future, 1730–1810* (London: Faber and Faber, 2002): 109.

137. Philip Yorke, Viscount Royston (later, second Earl of Hardwicke), to Philip Yorke, first Earl of Hardwicke, Add. Ms. 35,352: 413, BL; Lichfield Ms. D615/P(S)/1/6/1-30, Staffordshire Record Office, Stafford. The medal was presented to many of Anson's friends, including Robert Orme, James Harris, William Fauquier, Lord Hyde, and the Yorke family. See James Yorke to Philip Yorke, second Earl of Hardwicke, 7 May 1769, Add. Ms. 35,376: 263, BL; Stuart to Anson, 27 May, 31 May, 17 June and 23 September 1769, Lichfield Ms. D615/P(S)/1/6/22, 24–27, Staffordshire Record Office, Stafford.

138. Stuart to Anson, [June or July 1764], Lichfield Mss. D615/P(S)/1/6/8A; 10 July 1764, D615/P(S)/1/6/9; [before 23 August 1764], D615/P(S)/1/6/10; 4 September 1764, D615/P(S)/1/6/12, Staffordshire Record Office, Stafford.

139. Minutes of the Society, vol. 2, 19 October 1757, and vol. 5, 26 March 1760, RSA. Nathaniel Curzon and Philip Yorke, Viscount Royston, were appointed to the same committee judging drawings and history and landscape paintings. The stucco premium request was recorded in the Minutes of the Society on 19 March 1760 although the reasons behind it were not revealed until the late 1770s, when the Adam brothers were involved in a legal case regarding a patent for exterior stucco. See *Observations on Two Trials at Law respecting Messieurs*

Adam's new-invented Patent-Stucco (London: Fielding and Walker, 1778); *A Reply to Observations on Two Trials at Law, respecting Messieurs Adams's New-Invented Stucco; containing Mr. Wallace's reply to Mr. Dunning with the Summary of the Evidence and Charge to the Jury, as taken down in court* (London: J. Bew, 1778); Frank Kelsall, "Liardet versus Adam," *Architectural History* 27 (1984): 118–26.

140. Josiah Wedgwood to Thomas Bentley, 21 December 1772, in Ann Finer and George Savage, *The Selected Letters of Josiah Wedgwood* (London: Cory, Adams and Mackay, 1965): 140.

141. William, second Lord Bagot, *Memorials of the Bagot Family* (Blithfield: William Hodgetts, 1824): 90; Arthur Oswald, "Blithfield, Staffordshire—I," *Country Life* 116 (28 October 1954): 1492. Anson bequeathed Sir William an extensive collection of coins and medals and appointed him an executor of his will. See Lichfield Ms. exD615/E(L)/69A, Staffordshire Record Office, Stafford.

142. Pennant, *Journey from Chester* (1782): 82; Bagot, *Memorials of the Bagot Family* (1824): 97, 144–46.

143. Oswald, "Blithfield," pt. 1 (1954): 1491–92; ibid., pt. 3 (11 November 1954): 1665.

144. Minutes of the Society, vol. 2, 23 and 30 November 1757, RSA; Christopher Eimer, "The Society's Concern with 'The Medallic Art' in the Eighteenth Century," *RSA Journal* 139 (November 1991): 757.

145. Alison Kelly, *Decorative Wedgwood in Architecture and Furniture* (London: Country Life Ltd., 1965): 42.

146. Elizabeth Meteyard, *The Life of Josiah Wedgwood*, vol. 2 (1866; reprint, Josiah Wedgwood and Sons 1980): 114; Finer and Savage, *Letters of Josiah Wedgwood* (1965): 103; Young, ed., *Genius of Wedgwood* (1995): 18, 35, 68; Uglow, *Lunar Men* (2002): 197, 324, 357–58; *Oxford Dictionary of National Biography*, vol. 59 (2004): 156.

147. Eric Robinson, "R. E. Raspe, Franklin's 'Club of Thirteen' and the Lunar Society," *Annals of Science* 11 (June 1955): 142–44; Uglow, *Lunar Men* (2002): 261–62.

148. Ingrid Roscoe, "Peter Scheemakers and Classical Sculpture in Early Georgian England," Ph. D. diss., University of Leeds, 1990, 169; Uglow, *Lunar Men* (2002): 323–24.

149. Add. Ms. 22,152: 3, BL; "Experiments on Ignited Substances. By Mr. John Whitehurst, in a Letter to James Stuart, Esquire, F.R.S.," *Philosophical Transactions of the Royal Society* 66, pt. 2 (1776): 575–77; Maxwell Craven, *John Whitehurst of Derby, Clockmaker and Scientist, 1773–88* (Ashbourne: Mayfield Books, 1996): 106, 243.

150. The first documented meeting between Stuart and Lyttelton is recorded in George, Lord Lyttelton, to Elizabeth Montagu, 10 October [1758], Montagu Papers MO 1279, Henry E. Huntington Library, San Marino, CA.

151. Arthur T. Bolton, "Hagley Park, Worcestershire," *Country Life* 38 (16 October 1915): 522; Gordon Nares, "Hagley Hall, Worcestershire—I," *Country Life* 122, pt. 1 (19 September 1957): 547.

152. Sanderson Miller designed gothic castles at Hagley for Lyttelton and at Wimpole for the Yorkes, although James Essex eventually executed the latter with much modification. Thomas Anson and the Yorkes were patrons of Thomas Wright, while Lyttelton and Anson used the same plasterer, Francesco Vassalli, as well as the Hitchcox family of masons. In 1749 Philip Yorke and Thomas Anson traveled to Paris to visit Joseph Yorke, who had been appointed to the embassy there, and in 1752 the Ansons and the Yorke/Grey family enjoyed a holiday at Scarborough. Philip Yorke and Jemima Grey's Midlands tour of 1763 is well documented. See Philip Yorke, first Earl of Hardwicke, to Thomas Pelham-Holles, first Duke of Newcastle, 7 February 1759, Add. Ms. 32,888: 17, BL; John Campbell, third Earl of Breadalbane, to Marchioness Grey, 7 August 1763, Lucas Ms. L30/9/17/66, BLARS; Philip Yorke, Viscount Royston (later, second Earl of Hardwicke), to Philip Yorke, first Earl of Hardwicke, 14 August 1763, Add. Ms. 35,352: 403–4, BL; George, first Lord Lyttelton, to Elizabeth Montagu, 8 November 1763, Montagu Papers MO 1317, Henry E. Huntington Library, San Marino, CA; Diaries of Amabel Polwarth, Vyner Ms. Acc2299, vol. 1: 100 (22 February 1770), West Yorkshire Archive, Leeds; *Memoirs and Correspondence of George Lord Lyttelton, from 1734 to 1773*, ed. Robert Phillimore, vol. 2 (London: James Ridgway, 1845): 569; Godber, "Life of the Marchioness Grey" (1968): 47, 52.

153. See, for example, Lyttelton to Archibald Bower, 14 July 1755, Montagu Papers MO 1266, and [July 1755], Montagu Papers 1267; Lyttelton to Elizabeth Montagu, 23 July 1755, Montagu Papers MO 1269, Henry E. Huntington Library, San Marino, CA.

154. Michael Gibbon, "The First Neoclassical Building? Temple of Concord, Stowe, Buckinghamshire," *Country Life* 155 (11 April 1974): 852–53; Jonathan Marsden, "Description of the Garden," in *Stowe Landscape Gardens* (London: National Trust, 1997): 48.

155. Stuart nominated Lyttelton on 6 December 1758, but neither he nor his relatives sat on any of the society's committees. Minutes of the Society, vol. 3, 6 December 1758, and vol. 6, 11 March 1761, RSA; George Clarke, "The Medallions of Concord: An Association Between the Society of Arts and Stowe," *RSA Journal* 129 (August 1981): 612, 613 note 3, 615; Richard Grenville, Earl Temple to William Pitt, 11 June 1761, Chatham Manuscript 30/8/61: 54–55, NA, quoted in Joan Michele Coutu, "Eighteenth-Century British Monuments and the Politics of Empire," Ph. D. diss., University College, London, 1993, 71.

156. Diary of Thomas Hollis, 15 November 1759 and 10 June, 24 June, and 1 July 1762, Ms. Eng 1191, Houghton Library, Harvard University.

157. Clarke, "The Medallions of Concord" (1981): 614.

158. Thomas Anson to Philip Yorke, Viscount Royston (later second Earl of Hardwicke), 15 September [1760], Add. Ms. 35,606: 327–28, BL.

159. Michael McCarthy, "James Lovell and his Sculptures at Stowe," *Burlington Magazine* 115 (April 1973): 229.

160. Lilian Dickins and Mary Stanton, eds., *An Eighteenth-century Correspondence* (London: John Murray, 1910): 288; Anthony Coleridge, "English Furniture Supplied for Croome Court: Robert Adam and the 6th Earl of Coventry," *Apollo* 151 (February 2000): 8–9; E. Harris, *Genius of Robert Adam* (2001): 42.

161. The invoice is quoted in Geoffrey Beard, "Decorators and Furniture Makers at Croome Court," *Furniture History* 29 (1993): 88 and 92.

162. Minutes of the Society, vol. 3, 6 and 13 December 1758, RSA.

163. Elizabeth Montagu to George, Lord Lyttelton, 15 January 1760, Montagu Papers MO 1394, and 15 July 1762, Montagu Papers MO 1414, Henry E. Huntington Library, San Marino, CA.

164. For the Shakespearean painting, see Stuart to Elizabeth Montagu, 14 July 1759, Montagu Papers MO 5135, Henry E. Huntington Library, San Marino, CA. Kerry Bristol, "The Painted Rooms of 'Athenian' Stuart," *The Georgian Group Journal* 10 (2000): 167–69; Kerry Bristol, "22 Portman Square. Mrs. Montagu and her 'Palais de la vieillesse'," *British Art Journal* 2 (Summer 2001): 72–85; Rosemary Baird, "'The Queen of the Bluestockings': Mrs. Montagu's House at 23 Hill Street Rediscovered," *Apollo* 158 (August 2003): 43–49; Rosemary Baird, *Mistress of the House: Great Ladies and Grand Houses, 1670–1830* (London: Weidenfeld and Nicolson, 2003): 169–97.

165. Reginald Blunt, ed., *Mrs Montagu, "Queen of the Blues": Her Letters and Friendships from 1762 to 1800,* vol. 2 (London: Constable and Company, 1923): 61–62.

166. Josiah Wedgwood to Thomas Bentley, 24–26 December 1770, in Nicholas Goodison, *Matthew Boulton: Ormolu,* rev. ed. (London: Christie's, 2002): 49, 418.

167. See, for example, R. Brimley Johnson, *Bluestocking Letters* (London: John Lane, 1926): 24. A more sympathetic view is taken in Deborah Heller, "Bluestocking Salons and the Public Sphere," *Eighteenth-Century Life* 22 (May 1998): 59–82; and Baird, *Mistress of the House* (2003): 63.

168. Godber, "Life of the Marchioness Grey" (1968): 77.

169. See, e.g., Philip Yorke, first Earl of Hardwicke, to Charles Watson-Wentworth, second Marquess of Rockingham, 15 June 1754, Wentworth Woodhouse Muniments R1-58, Sheffield Archives, in which Hardwicke thanks Rockingham for a favor he had done for Viscount Royston (later, second Earl of Hardwicke). A portrait of Anson was listed in the inventory of goods taken at Rockingham's death in 1782. On these points, see John Siddall to Rockingham, 28 October 1761, Wentworth Woodhouse Muniments R1-202; and *Inventory of Household Goods, Plate, Pictures, Statues and Furniture at Wentworth Woodhouse in 1782, and in the house in Grosvenor Square,* Wentworth Woodhouse Muniments A-1204 page 17, Sheffield Archives, Sheffield; Langford, *The First Rockingham Administration* (1973): 5, 284.

170. Elizabeth Anson to Jemima, Marchioness Grey, 26 July 1759, Lucas Ms. L30/9/3/98, and 27 August 1759, /3/108, BLARS; Stuart to Anson, 6 October 1764, Lichfield Ms. D615/P(S)/1/6/15, Staffordshire Record Office, Stafford; Edward Langton to Philip Yorke, second Earl of Hardwicke, 17 August 1765, Add. Ms. 35,607: 191, BL.

171. Philip Yorke, Viscount Royston (later, second Earl of Hardwicke), to Philip Yorke, first Earl of Hardwicke, 22 August 1763, Add. Ms. 35,352: 406–7, and Hardwicke to Royston, 28 August 1763, Add. Ms. 35,352 fol. 413, BL.

172. Stuart to Anson, 19 June 1764, Lichfield Ms. D615/P(S)/1/6/7; [June or July 1764], /1/6/8A; before 23 August 1764, /1/6/9; 4 September 1764, /1/6/12, Staffordshire Record Office, Stafford.

173. Stuart to Anson, 19 June 1764, Lichfield Manuscript D615/P(S)/1/6/7; [June or July 1764], /1/6/8A; before 23 August 1764, /1/6/9, n.d.; 4 September 1764, /1/6/12, Staffordshire Record Office, Stafford.

174. Daniel Wray to Philip Yorke, second Earl of Hardwicke, 30 August 1766, Add. Ms. 35,401: 308, BL; Ingrid Roscoe, "James 'Athenian' Stuart and the Scheemakers Family: A Lucrative Partnership between Architect and Sculptors," *Apollo* 126 (September 1987): 182.

175. John Yorke to Philip Yorke, second Earl of Hardwicke, 10 September 1778, Add. Ms. 35,375: 219, BL.

176. Diaries of Amabel Polwarth, Vyner Ms. Acc2299, vol. 3: 105 (16 November 1773), West Yorkshire Archive, Leeds. Se also Stuart to Philip Yorke, second Earl of Hardwicke, 27 January 1766, Add. Ms. 35,607: 233–34, BL; David Adshead, "A *Modern Italian Loggia* at Wimpole Hall," *Georgian Group Journal* 10 (2000): 150; Bristol, "The Painted Rooms of 'Athenian' Stuart" (2000): 170–71.

177. Elizabeth P. Biddulph, *Charles Philip Yorke, Fourth Earl of Hardwicke, Vice-Admiral, R.N., A Memoir* (London: Smith, Elder, 1910): 164; Adshead, "*Modern Italian Loggia*" (2000): 150, 156.

178. Evans, *History of the Society of Antiquaries* (1956): 57, 85–86.

179. Diaries of Amabel Polwarth, Vyner Ms. Acc2299, vol. 2: 54 (19 January 1771), West Yorkshire Archive, Leeds. See also Minutebook, vol. 12: 89–90, 130–31 (31 January and 7 March 1771), Society of Antiquaries.

180. Minutebook, vol. 11: 283–92, 294–95 (29 March and 5 April 1770), Society of Antiquaries. See also Evans, *History of the Society of Antiquaries* (1956): 160.

181. Joseph Ayloffe to Philip Yorke, second Earl of Hardwicke, 1 February 1771, Add. Ms. 35,609: 304, and Edward Edwards to Hardwicke, 2 February 1771, Add. Ms. 35,609: 305, BL. Edwards eventually accepted 110 guineas.

182. Diaries of Amabel Polwarth, Vyner Ms. Acc2299, vol. 2: 54 (19 January 1771), West Yorkshire Archive, Leeds; Evans, *History of the Society of Antiquaries* (1956): 161; Sweet, *Antiquaries* (2004): 96.

183. Charles Yorke became a member of the council in 1763 and was often consulted about legal matters relating to the university. When the first Earl of Hardwicke died in 1764, Viscount Royston (second Earl of Hardwicke) was appointed high steward in his place; see John Sumner to [Charles Yorke], 12 May 1757, Add. Ms. 35,640: 43; Thomas Chapman to [Charles Yorke], 12 May 1757, Add. Ms. 35,640: 45–46; I. (or J.?) Green to [Charles Yorke], 21 November 1758, Add. Ms. 35,640: 61, BL; James Plumtre to Philip Yorke, Viscount Royston, 5 December 1763, Add. Ms. 35,628: 1, BL; Godber, "Life of the Marchioness Grey" (1968): 46, 74.

184. Allan Doig, "James Adam, James Essex and an Altar-piece for King's College Chapel, Cambridge," *Architectural History* 21 (1978): 79.

185. J. Upton to [Provost John Sumner], 6 March 1759, Ms. Altarpiece 1742–75: 7, Muniment Room, King's College, Cambridge, partly quoted in Doig, "James Adam" (1978): 79. Sumner was provost of King's College from 1756 until 1772 and vice-chancellor of the university 1766–67 and 1770–71.

186. Ms. Altarpiece 1742–75: 17, Muniment Room, King's College, Cambridge.

187. Memorandum in Provost Sumner's hand, 1 November 1766, Ms. Altarpiece 1742–75: 9, Muniment Room, King's College, Cambridge; quoted in Doig, "James Adam" (1978): 79–80.

188. John Brewer, *The Sinews of Power: War, Money and the English State, 1688–1783* (New York: Alfred A. Knopf, 1989): 208.

189. *London and its Environs Described . . .* , vol. 1 (London: R. and J. Dodsley, 1761): 271; Francis Grose, Thomas Astle, and Edward Jeffrey, comps., *Antiquarian Repertory . . .* , vol. 2 (London: F. Blyth, J. Sewell, and T. Evans, 1779): 168; Edward Hasted, *The History and Topographical Survey of the County of Kent,* vol. 2, 2nd ed. (Canterbury: n.p., 1797): 248–49; Brewer, *Sinews of Power* (1989): 209.

190. Diaries of Amabel Polwarth, Vyner Ms. Acc2299, vol. 2: 4 (n.d. November–December 1770), West Yorkshire Archive, Leeds.

191. Hasted, *History and Topographical Survey of the County of Kent* (1797): 249; Joseph Cradock, *Literary and Miscellaneous Memoirs,* vol. 1 (London: J. B. Nichols, 1828): 92; John Harris, *The Parish of Erith in Ancient and Modern Times* (London: Mitchell and Hughes, 1885): 55.

192. *Dictionary of British and Irish Travellers in Italy* (1997): 399.

193. Walter Harrison, *A New and Universal History, Description and Survey of the Cities of London and Westminster, the Borough of Southwark, and their Adjacent Parts* (London: J. Cooke, 1775): 601; George Augustus Walpoole, *The New British Traveller* (London: Alexander Hogg, 1784): 22; Harris, *Parish of Erith* (1885): 55–56; Lawrence, "Stuart and Revett" (1938–39): 142.

194. Gavin Hamilton to William Petty, second Earl of Shelburne, 1 May 1774, 9 February 1775, and 16 April 1775, in *Letters of Gavin Hamilton, edited from the MSS at Lansdowne House (reprinted from the 'Academy'),* ed. Lord Edmond Fitzmaurice (Wiltshire: Devizes, 1879): 33–34, 36.

195. Harris, *The Works of James Harris, Esq. with an account of his life and character, by his son the Earl of Malmesbury* (London: F. Wingrave, 1801): xii, xvii; Clive T. Probyn, *The Sociable Humanist, The Life and Works of James Harris, 1709–1780: Provincial and Metropolitan Culture in Eighteenth-century England* (Oxford: Clarendon Press, 1991): 19–20.

196. See, for example, Diaries of Amabel Polwarth, Vyner Ms. Acc2299, vol. 1: 99 (18 February 1770), West Yorkshire Archive, Leeds; and James Harris to Philip Yorke, Viscount Royston (later, second Earl of Hardwicke), 24 and 28 June 1762, Add. Ms. 35,607: 16–17 and 18, BL.

197. *Works of James Harris,* vol. 1 (1801): xii; Charles Robert Leslie and Tom Taylor, *Life and Times of Sir Joshua Reynolds,* vol. 1 (London: John Murray, 1865): 120, 124, 216; Rosemary Dunhill, "Handel and the Harris Circle," *Hampshire Papers* 8 (December 1995): abstract and 2.

198. For Weddell see Jill Low, "The Art and Architectural Patronage of William Weddell (1736–92) of Newby Hall and His Circle," Ph.D. diss., University of Leeds, 1981, 136.

199. Add. Ms. 18,728, BL, includes a printed copy of "Upon the Rise and Progress of Criticism" amended by James Harris and another version annotated as "corrected and enlarged Octr 1775." The second version is dedicated to Lyttelton, with whom Harris corresponded. See draft letter from James Harris to Lyttelton, 20 December 1769, Add. Ms. 18,729: 1–6, BL.

200. Lois Whitney, "English Primitivistic Theories of Epic Origins," *Modern Philology* 21 (May 1924): 355.

201. Edward Hodnett, *Five Centuries of English Book Illustration* (Aldershot: Scolar Press, 1988): 82.

202. Blackburne, *Memoirs of Thomas Hollis* (1780): 96.

203. James Harris, *Hermes, or, A Philosophical Inquiry Concerning Universal Grammar,* 2nd ed. (London: John Nourse and Paul Vaillant, 1765): 325–26.

204. Allan, "Artists and the Society" (1992): 92; Dunhill, "Handel and the Harris Circle" (1995): 2.

205. Yorke accepted the post of attorney general, but only after he had received "an express Promise from the King's own mouth that he should be Lord Chancellor by the end of next Session"; see Langford, *First Rockingham Administration* (1973): 29.

206. Minutes of the Society, vol. 2, 1 February 1758, RSA.

207. George Villiers, fourth Earl of Jersey, to Georgiana, Countess Spencer [4 May 1763], Add. Ms. 75,669, BL. For evidence of their friendship, see Stuart to Anson, 23 September 1769, Lichfield Manuscript D615/P(S)/1/6/27, Staffordshire Record Office, Stafford; Charles Pratt to Robert Stewart, later first Marquess of Londonderry, 27 September 1778, Ms. U840 C4/6, Centre for Kentish Studies, Maidstone.

208. Charles Pratt to Frances Stewart [1779], Ms. U840 C3/2, Centre for Kentish Studies, Maidstone; Hasted, *The History and Topographical Survey of the County of Kent* (1797): 14; Worsley, "Out From Adam's Shadow" (1992): 101.

209. Charles Pratt to Elizabeth Pratt, 20 September 1780, Ms. U840 C7/8, Centre for Kentish Studies, Maidstone. Presumably "Norris" was Richard Norris junior whose father, Stuart's usual builder in London, had died in 1779.

210. Charles Pratt to Frances Stewart, 23 March 1788, Ms. U840 C3/7, Centre for Kentish Studies, Maidstone.

211. Desmond Fitz-Gerald, "The Temple of the Winds, An Antique Irish Banqueting House," *Connoisseur* 167 (April 1968): 206–9; Gervase Jackson-Stops, "The Temple of the Winds," *Mount Stewart, County Down* (London: National Trust, 1997): 25–29.

212. Daniel A. Baugh, "Maritime Strength and Atlantic Commerce: The Uses of 'a grand marine empire'," in *An Imperial State at War: Britain from 1689 to 1815,* ed. Lawrence Stone (London and New York: Routledge, 1994): 185–223; and Kathleen Wilson, "Empire of Virtue: The Imperial Project and Hanoverian Culture, c.1720–1785," in ibid., 128–64.

213. Philip Saumarez, *Log of the Centurion, Based on the Original Papers of Captain Philip Saumarez . . . 1740–44,* ed. Leo Heaps (London: Hart-Davis, MacGibbon, 1973): 12, 97; Gerald Jordan and Nicholas Rogers, "Admirals as Heroes: Patriotism and Liberty in Hanoverian England," *Journal of British Studies* 28 (July 1989): 202–5.

214. Richard Middleton, "Naval Administration in the age of Pitt and Anson, 1755–1763," in *The British Navy and the Use of Naval Power in the Eighteenth Century,* ed. Jeremy Black and Philip Woodfine (New Jersey: Humanities Press International, 1989): 123.

215. Cust and Colvin, *History of the Society of Dilettanti* (1898): 257.

216. For the treatise, see Add. Ms. 22,152: 4, BL. Stuart was confirmed in the position at Greenwich on 30 May 1758. See Minutes of General Court Meetings, 30 May 1758, ADM 67/10: 337, NA.

217. Stuart to Anson, 4 September 1764, Lichfield Ms. D615/P(S)/

1/6/12, and 18 September 1764, D615/P(S)/1/6/14, Staffordshire Record Office, Stafford; Robert Rowe, *Adam Silver: 1765–1795* (London: Faber and Faber, 1965): 84 and illus. 47.

218. James Adam to Jennifer Adam, 2 July 1760, Clerk of Penicuik Ms. GD 18-4862, National Archives of Scotland, Edinburgh.

219. For a description of the monument in its original location, see E. W. Brayley and J. P. Neale, *The History and Antiquities of the Abbey Church of St. Peter, Westminster,* vol. 2 (London: Hurst, Robinson, 1823): 237.

220. Court Records, the Province of Massachusetts Bay, 1 February 1759, 495; cited in Roscoe, "James 'Athenian' Stuart and the Scheemakers Family" (1987): 178.

221. Ibid., 179. For a description of the monument before it was dismantled, see Brayley and Neale, *Abbey Church of St. Peter* (1823): 214. There are frequent references to Orme in Stuart's letters to Anson. See Stuart to Anson, 27 May 1769, Lichfield Ms. D615/P(S)/1/6/24; 31 May 1769, /1/6/25; 23 September 1769, /1/6/27, Staffordshire Record Office, Stafford.

222. J. Hakewill, *History of Windsor and its Neighbourhood* (London: E. Lloyd, 1813): 290–91. Walsh supported Stuart's application to succeed Hogarth as Serjeant-Painter to the Board of Works in 1764, and Stuart, in turn, was one of the supporting signatories when Walsh was elected a Fellow of the Society of Antiquaries in 1770. Stuart to Anson, [October or November 1764], Lichfield Ms. D615/P(S)/1/6/18, Staffordshire Record Office, Stafford; Minutebook, vol. 12: 17 (22 November 1770), Society of Antiquaries.

223. For Anson's promotion of Saunders, see Admiralty to the Privy Council, 12 November 1755, ADM 3/340, NA; Middleton, "Naval Administration" (1989): 124,n.12. For Saunders at Greenwich, see Greenwich Hospital Various Accounts and Ledgers 1696–1865, e.g., ADM 68/22 1759-1762, NA.

224. Stuart to Anson, [before 23 August 1764], Lichfield Ms. D615/P(S)/1/6/10; 4 September 1764; D615/P(S)/1/6/12; 19 December 1764, D615/P(S)/1/6/20, Staffordshire Record Office, Stafford.

225. Stuart to Anson, [November 1764], Lichfield Ms. D615/P(S)/1/6/18; 19 December 1764, D615/P(S)/1/6/20; 27 May 1769, D615/P(S)/1/6/24, Staffordshire Record Office, Stafford; Stuart to Philip Yorke, second Earl of Hardwicke, 2 August 1783, Add. Ms. 35,621: 7, BL; "Memoirs of the Late Sir Philip Stephens, Bart.," *European Magazine and London Review* 56 (December 1809): 407–9.

226. Stuart to Anson, 23 September 1769, Lichfield Ms. D615/P(S)/1/6/27, Staffordshire Record Office, Stafford.

227. Clark, *British Clubs* (2000): 122.

228. Diary of Thomas Hollis, 20 May 1763 and 24 May 1764, Ms. Eng 1191, Houghton Library, Harvard University. Clark, *British Clubs* (2000): 122, 255.

229. Graves, *Society of Artists* (1907): 248. Stuart knew Joseph Banks, who had accompanied Cook on his first voyage, by February 1774 (when he proposed Banks for Dilettanti membership). Stuart knew James Cook (through the Royal Society as well as via the Admiralty), and he may also have known Hawkesworth personally after the latter had been elected to the RSA on 31 March 1761, but this commission could only have come from Sandwich. See Minutes, vol. 3, 6 February 1774,

archive of the Society of Dilettanti, London; *Antiquities,* vol. 4 (1816): xxiv; George Martelli, *Jemmy Twitcher: A Life of the Fourth Earl of Sandwich, 1718–1792* (London: Jonathan Cape, 1962): 94; John Lawrence Abbott, *John Hawkesworth. Eighteenth-Century Man of Letters* (Madison: University of Wisconsin Press, 1982): 121; Bernard Smith, *European Vision and the South Pacific,* 2nd ed. (New Haven and London: Yale University Press, 1985): 13.

230. See Alexander Dalrymple, *A Letter from Mr. Dalrymple to Dr. Hawkesworth, Occasioned by Some Groundless and Illiberal Imputations in his Account of the late Voyages to the South Seas* (London: J. Nourse, [22 June] 1773); W. H. Pearson, "Hawkesworth's Alterations," *The Journal of Pacific History* 7 (1972): 45–72; Abbott, *John Hawkesworth* (1982): xiv, 137–86, 178–79, 224 n. 42.

231. On Rooker and the difficulties caused by late arrival of his engravings, see Sandwich to David Garrick, 16 April 1773, Ms. SAN/F/36/10, National Maritime Museum; Abbott, *John Hawkesworth* (1982): 151.

232. Hall was the recipient of a premium from the RSA in 1756, where it is probable that he and Stuart met. He exhibited an engraving after Gavin Hamilton's *Dawkins and Wood Discovering Palmyra* (1758) at the Free Society in 1773.

233. Abbott, *John Hawkesworth* (1982): 138.

234. *Byron's Journal of his Circumnavigation, 1764–1766,* ed. Robert E. Gallagher, Hakluyt Society, 2nd series, pt. 2, no. 122 (Cambridge [Eng.]: University Press for the society, 1964): xxxi–xxxii.

235. Ibid., xxxix. For Bougainville, see John Dunmore, *French Explorers in the Pacific,* vol. 1, *The Eighteenth Century* (Oxford: Clarendon Press, 1965): 57–113.

236. *Byron's Journal of his Circumnavigation* (1964): lv, lvii.

237. Helen Wallis, "The Patagonian Giants," appendix to *Byron's Journal of his Circumnavigation* (1964): 185.

238. Ibid., 186–87; *Carteret's Voyage Round the World, 1766–1769,* ed. Helen Wallis, vol. 2, Hakluyt Society, 2nd series, pt. 2, no. 124 (Cambridge University Press for the society, 1965): 323.

239. Wallis, "Patagonian Giants" (1964): 186–87.

240. Ibid.; *Carteret's Voyage* (1965): 322–23.

241. *A Voyage Round the World, In His Majesty's Ship the Dolphin, Commanded by the Honourable Commodore Byron . . . By an Officer on Board the said Ship* (London: printed for J. Newbery and F. Newbery, 1767).

242. The passage to which Stuart's illustration relates is John Hawkesworth et al., *An Account of the Voyages Undertaken by the Order of his Present Majesty for Making Discoveries in the Southern Hemisphere . . . ,* vol. 1 (London: W. Strahan and T. Cadell, 1773): 26–32.

243. Hawkesworth, *Account of the Voyages,* vol. 1 (1773): viii.

244. Alexander Buchan had made field drawings that G. B. Cipriani worked up for Hawkesworth's second volume but no visual record of the actual meeting with the Patagonians was made. Smith, *European Vision* (1985): 34, 36.

245. On these points, see Charles Clarke, "An Account of the Very Tall Men . . . ," *Philosophical Transactions of the Royal Society* 57 (1768): 75–79; "A Letter from *Philip Carteret, Esquire,* Captain of the Swallow Sloop, to *Mathew Maty, M.D. Sec. R.S.* on the Inhabitants of the Coast of

Patagonia," *Philosophical Transactions of the Royal Society* 60 (1771): 20–26; *The Journals of Captain James Cook on His Voyages of Discovery,* ed. J. C. Beaglehole, vol. 1, *The Voyage of the Endeavour 1768–1771,* Hakluyt Society, extra series, no. 34a (Cambridge University Press for the society, 1955): lxxviii; *Byron's Journal of his Circumnavigation* (1964): lxv–lxvii, lxxi; Wallis, "The Patagonian Giants" (1964): 188–89, 195; *Carteret's Voyage Round the World* (1965): 5–6, 14–15, 27, 190, 315–24.

246. Observing the transit of Venus was necessary in order to measure the solar parallax and solve the problem of assessing the distance of the Earth from the Sun. See Lynette Roberts, *The Endeavour: Captain Cook's First Voyage to Australia* (London: Peter Owen, 1954): 13; Pieter van der Merwe, "The Maritime Context, 1768–75," in *William Hodges 1744–1797. The Art of Exploration,* ed. Geoff Quilley and John Bonehill, exh. cat., National Maritime Museum, Greenwich, and Yale Center for British Art, New Haven (New Haven and London: Yale University Press for the museums, 2004): 71–72.

247. Abbott, *John Hawkesworth* (1982): 185; Nicholas Thomas, "Licensed Curiosity: Cook's Pacific Voyages," in *The Cultures of Collecting,* ed. John Elsner and Roger Cardinal (London: Reaktion Books, 1994): 119. For the moment when the Tahitians attacked Wallis's vessels, see Hawkesworth, *An Account of the Voyages,* vol. 1 (1773): 443–44.

248. Rüdiger Joppien and Bernard Smith, *The Art of Captain Cook's Voyages,* vol. 1, *The Voyage of the Endeavour, 1768–1771 . . .* (New Haven and London: Yale University Press for the Paul Mellon Centre for Studies in British Art, 1985): 41. For Spöring, see Averil Lysaght, "Banks's Artists and his *Endeavour* Collecting," in *Captain Cook and the South Pacific,* ed. T. C. Mitchell, British Museum Yearbook, vol. 3 (London: the museum, 1979): 72–73; Wilfrid Blunt, "Sydney Parkinson and his Fellow Artists," *Sydney Parkinson. Artist of Cook's Endeavour Voyage,* ed. D. J. Carr (Canberra: British Museum (Natural History) and Australian National University Press, 1983): 32–33, plate 34.

249. In March 1768 Bougainville's ships had dropped anchor at Tahiti, which he named "New Cythera," unaware that Wallis had claimed the Society Islands for England eight months earlier. An account of his circumnavigation was published in 1771, with an English translation by John Reinhold Forster published in 1772. See also Jack K. Dowling, "Bougainville and Cook," in *Captain James Cook: Image and Impact,* ed. Walter Veit (Melbourne: Hawthorn Press, 1972): 37, 38; Smith, *European Vision* (1985): 42, 46; Joppien and Smith, *The Art of Captain Cook's Voyages* (1985): 22.

250. Averil Lysaght, "Captain Cook's Kangaroo," *New Scientist* 1 (14 March 1957): 17–19.

251. Parkinson's zoological drawings are in the Natural History Museum, London. See Blunt, "Sydney Parkinson and his Fellow Artists" (1983): 37; Alwyne Wheeler, "Animals," in ibid., 202.

252. Barrington was a barrister, naturalist, and Fellow of the Royal Society and Society of Antiquaries. He was also secretary of Greenwich Naval Hospital. Evans, *History of the Society of Antiquaries* (1956): 150–51.

253. J. C. Beaglehole, *The Life of Captain James Cook* (Stanford University Press, 1974): 444–45.

254. Ibid., 450–51.

255. Ibid., 461.

256. John Montagu, fourth Earl of Sandwich to John Reinhold Forster, 28 October 1775, Manuscript SAN/F/36/20, National Maritime Museum, London. See also Beaglehole, *Captain James Cook* (1974): 462.

257. Daines Barrington to John Montagu, fourth Earl of Sandwich, 2 May 1776, Manuscript SAN/F/36/26, National Maritime Museum, London; Beaglehole, *Captain James Cook* (1974): 463–64. Cambridge was a gentleman author and occasional contributor to the periodical *The World.*

258. Beaglehole, *Captain James Cook* (1974): 465.

259. James Cook to John Douglas, 23 June 1776, in ibid., 469. See also James Cook to Sir Joseph Banks, 10 July 1776, Banks Papers Safe 1/68, Mitchell Library, Sydney, in Beaglehole, *Captain James Cook* (1974): 506.

260. Stuart to [John Montagu, fourth Earl of Sandwich], 9 July [1776], Manuscript SAN/F/36/33, National Maritime Museum, London. Extracts of this memorandum were published in Beaglehole, *Captain James Cook* (1974): 469–70, although he did not know the identity of "Stuart." The handwriting of the memorandum is identifiable, however, and there is no doubt that Cook and Sandwich's "Stuart" was James Stuart.

261. John Reinhold Forster to John Montagu, fourth Earl of Sandwich, 2 August 1776, Manuscript SAN/F/36/38; 7 August 1776, Manuscript SAN/F/36/39; 24 February 1777, Manuscript SAN/F/36/42; 28 February 1777, Manuscript SAN/F/36/44, National Maritime Museum, London; Beaglehole, *Captain James Cook* (1974): 469–70.

262. Nicholas Thomas, "Hodges as anthropologist and historian," in *William Hodges* (2004): 27.

263. Smith, *European Vision* (1985): 73–74.

264. Georg Forster and Johann Reinhold Forster, *A Voyage Round the World, in His Britannic Majesty's Sloop Resolution, commanded by Captain J. Cook . . . ,* vol. 1 (London: B. White et al., 1777): 589; reprint in Smith, *European Vision* (1985): 74–75.

265. Oppé, ed., "Memoirs of Thomas Jones" (1946–48): 37; *Thomas Jones (1742–1803). An Artist Rediscovered,* ed. Ann Sumner and Greg Smith (New Haven and London: Yale University Press in association with National Museums and Galleries of Wales, 2003): 40.

266. A. H. [Anthony Highmore], "Further Particulars of the late Athenian Stuart," *Gentleman's Magazine* 58 (March 1788): 216–18; Add. Ms. 22,152: 18–19, BL; Smith, *Nollekens and His Times,* vol. 1 (1828): 38; John Thomas Smith, *A Book for a Rainy Day . . .* (London: Richard Bentley, 1845): 88–89.

Fig. 5-1. James Stuart. The Painted Room, Spencer House, St. James's Place, London, looking toward the bow, ca. 1759–66. Photographed in 2006. ©Spencer House Limited. *Checklist no. 119.*

CHAPTER 5

THE LONDON HOUSES

RICHARD HEWLINGS

Since the Middle Ages, the power of the English governing class was based on agricultural wealth. Although by the eighteenth century that was no longer the case, political power was exercised through control of the membership of Parliament, of which at least the lower house was nominated by the county communities and the parliamentary boroughs. Most of the display that expressed and helped to retain this influence was therefore reserved for their provincial property. However, Parliament and the Law Courts (for Parliament was also a court) sat throughout the winter months, and attention to business in either made it expedient to reside in London concurrently. London alone also offered the opportunity to attend the Royal Court, to which admission was surprisingly easy. After the initial curiosity had been satisfied, attendance at Court was more of an obligation for the ambitious than a pleasure, but a range of other entertainments was devised to make the London season palatable.

London accommodation was thus a necessity. Most of the participants rented houses, or even parts of houses, often a different property each year. Some took houses on long leases. The richest had freehold properties and were able to build their own houses, even though these stood empty throughout the summer. The hospitality offered in the great London houses was part of the entertainment of the season, as was the display that they embodied. The latter offered tantalizing opportunities to luxury tradesmen, including architects. Stuart's reputation put him in a good position to exploit this market, and he was engaged by at least five such clients. They had little in common save great wealth.

Although most members of the aristocracy were far more interested in their country dwellings than their town houses, Stuart was fortunate in being able to procure commissions for interiors as well as complete projects from those few members of the nobility and the aspiring rich who were to build great houses in London. In 1758 he received the commission for an interior at Harcourt House for George Simon, Viscount Newnham, and in the following year for the state rooms of Spencer House for John Spencer, one of the great commissions of the period (fig. 5-1). He executed rooms at 23 Hill Street, London (1759 into the 1770s), for Mrs. Elizabeth Montagu, and he designed interiors at Holdernesse House (1766, later known as Londonderry House), on the corner of Park Lane and Hertford Street for the fourth Earl of Holdernesse. Stuart also built two important London houses: Thomas Anson's house at 15 St. James's Square (1764, later

Fig. 5-2. James Stuart. Design for wall decoration of the Painted Room, Spencer House, London, 1759. Pen and ink, gray wash, watercolor. By courtesy of the Trustees of the British Museum, London, 1955-4-16-13 British Reg PIIIb. *Checklist no. 118.*

known as Lichfield House) and Mrs. Montagu's grander second residence at 22 Portman Square (1781, known as Montagu House). Another London commission was at 45 Harley Street, London, about which nothing is known.[1] In addition, Stuart is believed to have designed parts of two interiors for George III, at Buckingham House (ca. 1763) and at Windsor Castle (ca. 1765–69).

Harcourt House

Stuart's first London commission is a little-known room for George Simon, Viscount Newnham, presumably at Harcourt House, 1 Cavendish Square, in 1758.[2] Newnham was a fellow member of the Society of Dilettanti and a keen supporter of Stuart (see chap. 4). Stuart had already advised on the remodeling of Nuneham Park, Oxon, the country seat of the viscount's father, Simon Harcourt, first Earl Harcourt (see chap. 6). Although there are no known

details, it was a room in the Greek taste according to a letter from Robert Adam in London to his brother James on December 11, 1758. Adam relayed a conversation overheard by the artist Paul Sandby while in Newnham's house:

> P. Sandby called here this day & told me he was with Lord Newnham this morning when in came Lord Delaware to the Room which the Archipelagan Architect had ornamented for him. Upon taking a look of it. . . . He bursts out, God Damn my Blood My Lord is this your Grecian Architecture what villainy what absurdity If this be Grecian, Give me Chinese give me Gothick, Any thing is better than this, For Shame My Lord Pull it down & Burn it . . . not to expose your own ignorance for it is the most Wretched mis-

erable affair ever was seen by Mortal. This dis-course Paul heard with inward satisfaction & could not rest till he had disburthen'd his over-flowings of Joy to me.[3]

Both threatened and spiteful, Adam delighted as usual in any criticism of his rival Stuart.

Spencer House

Stuart's involvement in the commission to build and decorate the most ostentatious private palace in London of its time began in 1759 when he submitted a colored gouache proposal for the decoration of the north wall of the Painted Room (fig. 5-2). His client was John Spencer, created Baron and Viscount Spencer in 1761 and first Earl Spencer in 1765. His extraordinary display was occasioned by a desire to reestablish his dynasty. It was not a new dynasty; the Spencers had established themselves two and a half centuries previously as major landowners in Northamptonshire and Warwickshire. John Spencer, how-ever, was neither a nobleman nor an office-holder; he was the son of the youngest son of the third Earl of Sunder-land, and the earldom still existed, submerged within the dukedom of Marlborough.[4] By an unusual piece of genea-logical engineering, the main line of the Spencer dynasty had been absorbed into a more elevated house and thus effectively suppressed. The engineer was Sarah Churchill, first Duchess of Marlborough, and her achievement was that the Marlborough title passed to her eldest grandson,

John Spencer's uncle, the fifth Earl of Sunderland, while her huge wealth passed to her favorite grandson, John Spencer's father, who died in 1746, when his son was eleven.

At his coming-of-age in 1755, the status of John Spencer (see fig. 4-21), a commoner with wealth greater than many noblemen, was comparable to that of a man who had created his own wealth but had yet to establish a new dynasty. His great-grandmother's egregious bequest was conditional on his not accepting "any pension or any office or employment, civil or military" from the Crown, except the Rangership of Windsor Park.[5] Thus excluded, like a Catholic or dissenter, he was obliged to turn to other methods of dynastic establishment. When he wrote to the Duke of Newcastle to ask for a peerage, he specifically requested that the title should be dynastic, not territorial; so it was that he became Earl Spencer in 1765.[6]

Virtu being a mark of rank in the eighteenth century, as *honor* had been in the sixteenth century, Spencer devoted much of his fortune to Italian travel (1763–64 and 1769–70) and to the acquisition of pictures and antique sculpture.[7] He formed a library and made the acquain-tance of writers.[8] He made gifts to the satirist Laurence Sterne, who showed him the manuscript of *Tristram Shandy* for his approval; he befriended playwright Richard Sheridan; he was a pall bearer at funeral of the celebrated actor David Garrick.[9] He inherited £240,000 in cash,[10] spending £72,000 on land in Northamptonshire alone.[11] He embellished his land at Althorp and Wimbledon and improved his houses at Althorp, Pytchley, and North

Fig. 5-4. George Knapton. *Portrait of Sir George Gray (ca. 1710–1773)*, 1744. Society of Dilettanti, London.

Creake.[12] The construction of an exceptionally ostentatious town house must certainly have been part of this program. Its dynastic nature is made manifest in its great room, an enriched version of the saloon at Althorp, the principal family seat.

John Spencer had no need to marry for money. He married secretly, the day after coming into possession of his fortune, while a ball to celebrate his coming-of-age was being held on the floor below.[13] His eighteen-year-old wife, Georgiana, was the daughter of Stephen Poyntz, a successful Crown servant. She was highly educated; Cardinal Albani, whom they encountered in Rome in 1763, called her the most accomplished woman he had ever met.[14] She was also the embodiment of aristocratic female virtue, and her charitable activities were unmatched by any of her contemporaries.[15] While consistent with dynastic advancement, this aspect of the Spencers' life was not essential to it.

The side elevation of Spencer House faced Green Park and was thus particularly conspicuous (fig. 5-3). Ashlar-fronted, pedimented, and columned, it served as the principal front, rather than merely a side elevation. No street separated the park from the houses on this side, which appeared to have the whole park as their garden and were thus especially fashionable. From Queen Caroline's Library at the south end to Arlington Street at the north, the east side houses were designed either to view or be viewed. Spencer House, in the middle, fell into the latter category.

The site on which Spencer House was to be built was occupied by three houses in St. James's Place, recently built for Lady Burlington to the designs of James Paine, which had to be pulled down.[16] In 1752 a lease of part of the site was granted to the first Lord Montfort, who commissioned designs for a house from John Vardy. However, after Montfort shot himself on January 1, 1755, his son allowed the lease to revert to Lady Burlington.[17] The Spencers were granted the site by Lady Burlington in the autumn of 1755 and took on Montfort's architect Vardy.[18]

Vardy was probably already known to the Spencers. In 1754 he had designed a building for the Duke of Cumberland, to whom John Spencer's father-in-law, Steven Poyntz, had been Governor from 1731.[19] Moreover, John Spencer was a member of the Society of Dilettanti, and Vardy had designed the society's building in 1751.[20] The secretary, treasurer, and founding member of the society was Colonel George Gray, an enthusiastic antiquary and amateur architect (fig. 5-4). Spencer engaged Gray to oversee the construction of the house, even to the extent of approving the designs; many of Vardy's drawings are countersigned by Gray.[21] Gray may also have introduced Stuart to the Spencers. Stuart's membership in the society had been proposed by Gray's brother, Sir James Gray, British Resident in Venice at the time of Stuart's stay there in 1750–51.[22] Stuart's work at Spencer House was confined to the interior, though it is possible that differences between Vardy's drawings and the executed work may owe something to his suggestion. For example, Vardy's north elevation was conceived as part of a longer terrace, but, as built, it was curtailed and altered slightly.[23] Stuart and Vardy overlapped in the date of their work, and in some of the interiors their respective contributions to the design are entangled.

Vardy's signed designs for Spencer House are dated 1755, 1757, 1758, and 1759, and there are others undated (fig. 5-5).[24] He exhibited drawings (now lost) of both

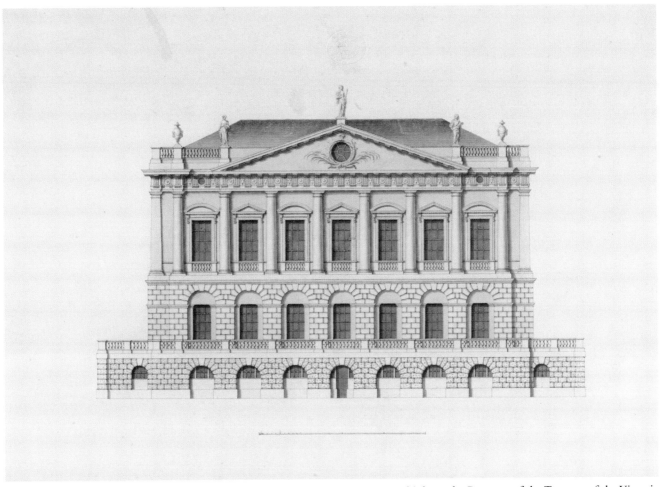

Fig. 5-5. John Vardy. The west elevation of Spencer House, London, 1759. Pen and ink, wash. Courtesy of the Trustees of the Victoria and Albert Museum, London, 3322 (Q.1a).

exteriors and interiors, some of which he described as "executed," at the Society of Artists in 1762 and again in 1763, and he issued a set of signed engravings in 1763.[25] The plates showing Spencer House in Wolfe and Gandon's *Vitruvius Britannicus* (vol. 4, 1767; figs. 5-6, 5-7), also attribute the design to Vardy.[26] There are no known building accounts, but there are payments to Vardy in John Spencer's bank account, running from February 1757 to April 1765, only a month before Vardy's death.[27] By then the house had been occupied for five years, and even the final finish of the state rooms was almost complete.[28]

The payments to Vardy suggest that he had supervisory as well as design responsibilities.[29] They also make it clear that Stuart did not replace or succeed Vardy, at least not until Vardy's death in May 1765.[30] Up to that time,

Stuart's responsibilities must therefore have been complementary. The Spencer bank account records only £250 paid to Stuart, some of which may have covered his work at Wimbledon House (see chap. 6). While Vardy had been responsible for paying tradesmen, Stuart was not. At least seventeen of Vardy's drawings survive (nine of which are signed), plus more signed engravings, but only one of Stuart's survives, unsigned (see fig. 5-2).[31]

Vardy designed Spencer House to stand on a one-story podium at basement level which projected into the royal park. Construction had to await consent from the Ranger of St. James's Park for this, which was granted in spring 1756.[32] By September noted diarist Mrs. Delany saw the ground floor (by which she may have meant the basement) finished.[33] The Spencers moved into the house

199

Fig. 5-6. North or entrance elevation of Spencer House. London. Engraving after a design by John Vardy. From Colen Campbell, continued by James Gandon and John Woolfe, *Vitruvius Britannicus . . .* , vol. 4 (1767): pl. 38. By permission of The British Library, London, 55.j.12.

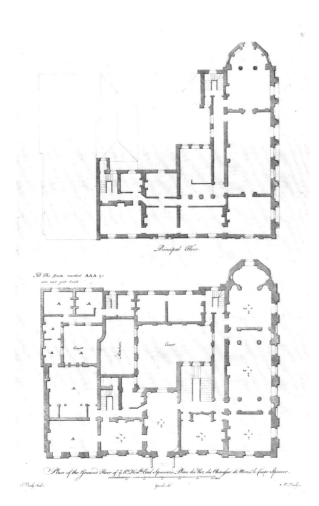

Fig. 5-7. Plan of the ground and first floors of Spencer House. Engraving by M. Darly after a design by John Vardy. From Colen Campbell, continued by James Gandon and John Woolfe, *Vitruvius Britannicus . . .* , vol. 4 (1767): pl. 37. By permission of The British Library, London, 55.j.12.

Fig. 5-8. Antinous relief in the entrance hall, Spencer House. Plaster cast from the 2nd-century original, ca. 1763–64. ©Spencer House Limited.

Fig. 5-9. John Vardy, with additions attributed to James Stuart. The dining room, Spencer House, ca. 1755–60. Photographed in 1996. ©Spencer House Limited.

in 1760.[34] By then the family rooms on the ground floor may have been complete, and perhaps also those on the north elevation, facing St. James's Place. The state rooms on the first floor of the west elevation, facing the park, can only have been empty shells. The central one of these, the great room (see fig. 5-35), was still not plastered in May 1763; its ceiling was finished, ready for gilding, in February 1764.[35] The next room to the south, known as the Painted Room, with Stuart's painted decoration, was unfinished in November 1765.[36] In December Lord Spencer wrote that he believed his house "will be fit to open next Spring."[37]

The decoration of the ground-floor state rooms is usually ascribed to Vardy, yet Stuart may have had some input as some of the proposals illustrated in Vardy's draw-

ings changed in execution. The first of Vardy's rooms, and the entrance to the house, is the vestibule. Here, Stuart was probably responsible for the installation of a cast of the famous relief of Hadrian's favorite, Antinous, supplied by Stuart's friend and former traveling companion Matthew Brettingham (fig. 5-8). The original relief was in the collection of Cardinal Albani in Rome.[38] Stuart had earlier installed an Antinous relief in Wentworth Woodhouse (see fig. 6-10). The largest of the ground-floor interiors was the dining room (in the center of the west side; fig. 5-9), which in execution omits some of the more old-fashioned elements of the original design such as the Palladian over-mantel, the pedimented doorcases, and the mirrors in stucco frames that are shown in Vardy's drawings (fig.

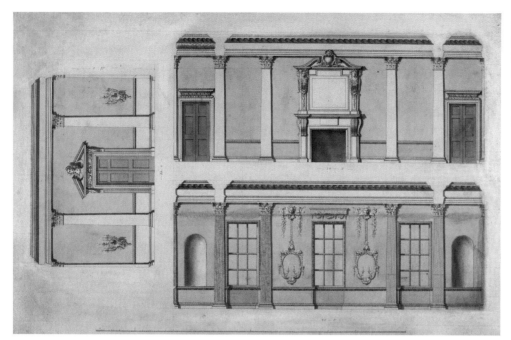

Fig. 5-10. John Vardy. Design for the dining room, Spencer House, 1755. Watercolor, pen and ink, pencil inscription. City of London, London Metropolitan Archives, SC/PZ/WE/02/320.

Fig. 5-11. John Vardy. Design for south wall and alcove in the Palm Room, Spencer House, 1757. Watercolor, pen and ink. Inscribed (verso): "Geo, Gray approved Dec 28th 1757." By courtesy of the Trustees of Sir John Soane's Museum, London, 69/1/2.

5-10).[39] These changes may have been suggested by Stuart, though there is no evidence. Adjoining the dining room at the south end of the west front was Vardy's masterpiece, the Palm Room. The alcove in the Palm Room was executed in a more complex form than that proposed by Vardy's drawing (fig. 5-11); from being an apparently oblong recess with a rectangular window, it was built with a domed vault on pendentives, surrounded by three apses, one of which has a round-arched window (fig. 5-12).[40] The chimneypiece is likely to have been by Stuart as it is stylistically similar to others he designed, and its execution is attributed to Peter Scheemakers, the leading sculptor of the day, with whom Stuart had close professional connections (fig. 5-13).[41]

In the staircase hall, entered from the vestibule, Stuart may have been responsible for the replacement of Vardy's suggested Roman Ionic pilasters with Greek pilasters, with foliage swags between them (fig. 5-14). The anthemion frieze derives from Stuart's drawings of the temple on the Ilissus (see fig. 10-27).[42] The coved ceiling

Fig. 5-12. John Vardy, with additions attributed to James Stuart. The alcove in the Palm Room, Spencer House, 1757–60. Photographed in 1996. ©Spencer House Limited.

Fig. 5-13. Attributed to James Stuart. The chimneypiece in the Palm Room, Spencer House, 1759–66. Carving attributed to the Scheemakers workshop. Photographed in 1996. ©Spencer House Limited.

Fig. 5-14. Attributed to James Stuart. Greek Ionic pilasters with foliage swags in the staircase hall, Spencer House, ca. 1758–66. Photographed in 2006. ©Spencer House Limited.

Fig. 5-15. John Vardy. Sectional drawing of Spencer House, specifying a coved ceiling over the staircase hall, ca. 1758. Pen and ink, wash. Courtesy of the Trustees of the Victoria and Albert Museum, London, 3321 (Q.1 a).

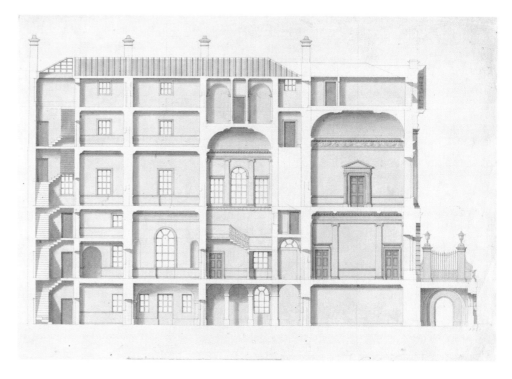

Fig. 5-16. Attributed to James Stuart. Barrel vault ceiling, staircase hall, Spencer House, ca. 1758–66. Photographed before 1995. ©Spencer House Limited.

Fig. 5-17. John Vardy. Drawing of the soffit, or underside of the first-floor landing, staircase hall, Spencer House, 1758. Pencil, pen and ink, gray wash. Courtesy of the Trustees of the Victoria and Albert Museum, London, 3436.198 (A.749).

Fig. 5-18. John Vardy, with minor alterations by James Stuart. The soffit as built, staircase hall, Spencer House, 1758–66. Carved by Thomas Vardy. Photographed in 2006. ©Spencer House Limited.

Fig. 5-19. John Vardy. Frieze below the soffit of the first-floor landing, 1758–66. Ewer and lyre motifs within garlands attributed to James Stuart. Photographed in 2006. ©Spencer House Limited.

that Vardy proposed over the stair (fig. 5-15) was replaced in execution by a barrel vault (fig. 5-16).[43] Vardy intended the soffit of the first-floor stair landing to be supported on elongated consoles (fig. 5-17).[44] In execution, however, these were replaced by tapered brackets with fret-patterned borders (fig. 5-18). In the frieze below Vardy's soffit panels, Stuart probably added the ewer-and-lyre motif surrounded by garlands (fig. 5-19). He had sketched these in Athens near the Theater of Bacchus (see fig. 10-38).[45] Moving up the stairs, Vardy's first-floor plan had a screen of columns at the top of the stairs, which was omitted.[46] Stuart was probably responsible for the rosettes on the imposts of the south wall window (fig. 5-20), which were derived from a fragment of a marble altar he had found on the Isle of Paros (fig. 5-21). Similar rosette decorations can be seen in Stuart's designs for Kedleston Hall (see figs. 6-30 to 6-33).[47]

Stuart is traditionally credited with the design of the interiors of all the principal state rooms on the first floor. However, this wholesale attribution can be challenged. Vardy's section drawing shows the coved ceiling of the great room (the central room of the west front, on the first floor) in a simplified form of what was eventually realized (see fig. 5-15).[48]

Much of the plaster ornament of these first-floor state

Fig. 5-20. Attributed to James Stuart. Rosettes on the imposts beside the Venetian window, south wall, staircase hall, Spencer House, 1758–66. Venetian window designed by John Vardy. Photographed in 2006. ©Spencer House Limited.

206

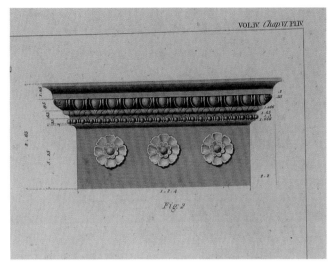

Fig. 5-21. Marble altar on Paros. Engraving. From *Antiquities of Athens,* vol. 4 (1816): chap. 6, pl. IV. Courtesy of the Library, The Bard Graduate Center for Studies in the Decorative Arts, Design, and Culture, New York. *Checklist no. 11.*

Fig. 5-22. James Stuart. Frieze in Lady Spencer's dressing room (also known as Lady Spencer's drawing room and as the Red Drawing Room), Spencer House, 1758–66. Photographed in 2006. ©Spencer House Limited.

Fig. 5-23. James Stuart. Frieze in the Painted Room, Spencer House, 1759–66. Photographed in 2006. ©Spencer House Limited.

Fig. 5-24. James Stuart. Frieze of the doorcase in the Painted Room, Spencer House, 1759–66. Photographed in 2006. ©Spencer House Limited.

rooms, which were completed last, is derived from illustrations in *Antiquities of Athens.* The friezes in Lady Spencer's dressing room, actually a private salon, and the Painted Room (figs. 5-22, 5-23) are taken from an illustration of the Erechtheion (see fig. 10-27).[49] The figure in the relief in the passage outside the great room (see fig. 5-35) is taken from the Incantada at Salonica (see fig. 11-13),[50] and the fluted *cyma recta* friezes of the doorcases in the Painted Room are derived from the same building (fig. 5-24).[51] Some of the carved ornament also came from the book. The marble chimneypiece in the great room (see fig. 5-38) has figures taken from an illustration of the reconstruction of the Choragic Monument of Lysicrates (see fig. 11-12), and its frieze too is taken from the Incantada at Salonica.[52] A band of fret ornament under the over–

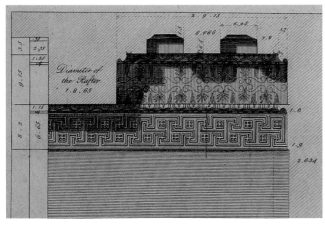

Fig. 5-25. Band of fret ornament from the pronaos of the Temple of Theseus, Athens. Engraving. From *Antiquities of Athens*, vol. 3 (1794): chap. 1, pl. VII. Courtesy of the Library, The Bard Graduate Center for Studies in the Decorative Arts, Design, and Culture, New York. *Checklist no. 90.*

Fig. 5-26. James Stuart. The chimneypiece in Lady Spencer's bedroom, ca. 1758–66. Carving attributed to Peter Scheemakers. Photographed in 1926. ©Country Life Picture Library.

mantel of the Painted Room (see fig. 5-47) came from an illustration of the internal frieze of the Theseion (fig. 5-25).[53] This extensive use of Grecian motifs suggests that Stuart designed these rooms. The plasterers (Thomas Clark and Joseph Rose) and carvers (John Devall, Henry Spang, Joseph Wilton, and Vardy's brother Thomas) must have had access to Stuart's published and unpublished drawings.[54] The presence of ornament at Spencer House that was not in the public domain until the publication of the final three volumes of *Antiquities* (vol. 2, ca. 1790; vol. 3, 1794; vol. 4, 1816) makes it clear that these designs were used with Stuart's agreement, probably even at his instigation. However, all the craftsmen were paid through Vardy, which suggests he too must at least have approved the designs.

On the principal floor, a corridor ran east to west at the head of the stairs. At the eastern end of the corridor, on the St. James's Place elevation, were the private rooms of Lady Spencer. In his travel memoir of 1772, Arthur Young described the furniture of the northeast room, Lady Spencer's bedroom, as "beds and tables very finely carved and inlaid, the former of crimson damask, with coved tops, and elegant."[55] Much of the bedroom suite of furniture survives at Althorp and in the Victoria and Albert Museum (see chap. 10), but little is known of the decoration of the room. The white marble chimneypiece had a central relief medallion in plaster depicting dancing women (fig. 5-26); the same motif appears at Rathfarnham Castle in the staircase anteroom (see fig. 10-67), at Newby Hall on the organ (see fig. 10-66), and as an overdoor in Mrs. Montagu's house at 22 Portman Square (see fig. 5-91).

Next to the bedroom was Lady Spencer's closet, described by Young as "a small dressing-room, very neat; the cornice of the chimney-piece white marble, supported by pillars of Siena."[56] The decoration of this room must be ascribed to Stuart, as it is totally different from Vardy's original designs for "Mrs. Spencers Closet Joyning to the Bedchamber" (fig. 5-27).[57] The chimneypiece, execution attributed to Scheemakers (fig. 5-28), had a decoration of carved urns and a vase linked by floral garlands, reminiscent of the frieze of Mrs. Montagu's bedchamber at 23 Hill Street though this had additional paterae (see fig. 5-80). The room had a foliated, beaded cornice, with egg-and-dart bands that was repeated in the adjoining room, the music room at the head of the staircase.[58]

The music room was the first in the sequence of state rooms on the principal floor. This is the only major room

Fig. 5-27. John Vardy. "A Sketch for Mrs Spencers Closet Joyning to the Bed Chamber Pair of Stairs, Chimney Side, Cove & Ceiling," 1757. Pen and ink, pencil, gray wash. By courtesy of the Trustees of Sir John Soane's Museum, London, 69/1/3.

Fig. 5-28. Attrubuted to James Stuart. The mantelpiece in Lady Spencer's closet, Spencer House, 1758–66. Photographed in 1926. Carving attributed to the Scheemakers workshop. ©Country Life Picture Library.

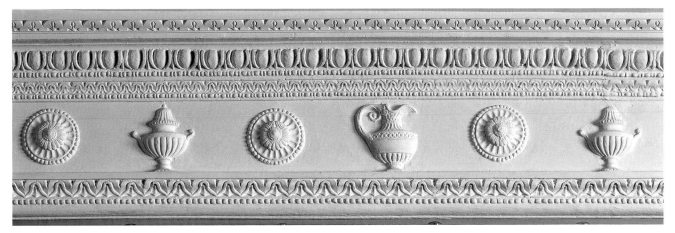

Fig. 5-29. James Stuart. The frieze in the Music Room, Spencer House, ca. 1758–66. Photographed in 2006. ©Spencer House Limited.

Fig. 5-30. James Stuart. Lady Spencer's dressing room, Spencer House, ca. 1758–66. Photographed in 1996. ©Spencer House Limited. *Checklist no. 110.*

of the group to have had its plan altered by Stuart. Vardy had designed a passageway separating the room from the staircase landing, and Stuart removed it, thus enlarging the room.[59] Much of Stuart's decoration was swept away in 1927, but a photograph of 1926 shows the room with its original gilt carved doorcase and chimneypiece of sienna and white marble that was described in 1772 by Arthur Young as "extremely light" (see fig. 10-40).[60] The execution of this chimneypiece is attributed to Scheemakers. The frieze includes a floral garland that picks up the

theme of the pier table and mirror designed for the room by Stuart (see figs. 10-41, 10-42). It has a dentilled cornice with an egg-and-dart band that echoed the cornice of the room. The chair rail was embellished with a scroll of wave-forms that are repeated on the frieze of the elaborate pier table. The frieze in this room is the only survivor of the original scheme. It has an ornament of paterae, ewers, and urns in plaster (fig. 5-29); the urns are similar to those illustrated in *Antiquities of Athens*. There are identical friezes in Holdernesse House and Lichfield House designed by

Stuart (see figs. 5-50, 5-68).[61] The cornice had foliated, beaded, and egg-and-dart bands, a characteristically Stuartian trio of motifs.[62]

The most significant of Lady Spencer's suite of rooms was her dressing room, later known as the Red Drawing Room (fig. 5-30), which better describes its function. This was a reception room, not a private room. Friends would have been received here, and when large parties took place in the house, the doors to the adjoining great room would have stood open. For these doors, and for the doors of all the principal first-floor rooms, Stuart designed gilded brass S-shaped escutcheons (fig. 5-31). These may have been executed by metalworker Diederich Nicolaus Anderson.

Young rhapsodized about Lady Spencer's dressing room, writing that it was "fitted up with great taste; scarce anything can be more beautiful than the mosaic ceiling, the cornices and all the ornaments; the chimneypiece is finely executed. It is of white marble wrought with the utmost taste, and beautifully polished; over the cornice are festoons of the lightest carving, and two eagles, with a very fine basso relieve of carving in the centre; the pictures are disposed with great elegance, and hung up by ribbons of gilt carving in a pretty taste."[63] The chimneypiece was another collaboration between Stuart and Scheemakers.

The "mosaic ceiling" of Lady Spencer's drawing room (fig. 5-32) is very similar to ceilings that Stuart designed for the north drawing room at Holdernesse House and the gilt room at Rathfarnham Castle (see figs. 5-49, 6-54).[64] The design is a modified version of a ceiling in the Baths of Augustus in Rome, illustrated in Montfaucon's *Antiquité Expliquée*, which was published in 1719 (fig. 5-33).[65] In March 1764 Lady Spencer was told by diarist Mrs. Howe that "the ceilings go on very well," but that "none of the compartments in yr dressing room are yet begun."[66] "Compartments" most likely mean the eight roundels within the main lobed circular feature, which, in the ancient ceiling design illustrated by Montfaucon, were filled with painted ornament. Presumably, the roundels at Spencer House were also intended to be painted, and it was that which was not begun in March 1764. However, paint scrapings taken before the restoration of the house contained no evidence of decorative paintwork.[67] The plasterwork was complete by 1764, and the only payments to identifiable plasterers in John Spencer's account were made by Vardy.[68] Here, as at Holdernesse House, the design was paired with a frieze derived from the Erechtheion.

Fig. 5-31. James Stuart. An S-shaped escutcheon from Spencer House, ca. 1758–66. Probably executed by Diederich Nicolaus Anderson. Gilt brass. Now at Althorp, Northampton. Photographed in 2006. The Althorp Collection.

Although the great room, or saloon, had a door leading from Lady Spencer's dressing room, the main entryway for guests after climbing the staircase was via a passageway that led from the first-floor landing. Above the door from the landing was a medallion, the first element of a complex iconographical program of decoration on the theme of music, wine, dance, and conversation. The choice of ornament thus reflected the room's function as a space for entertaining. The medallion held figures in relief representing two dancing bacchantes, one playing the flute and the other holding a cup and ewer (fig. 5-34).

Fig. 5-32. James Stuart. The "mosaic ceiling" of Lady Spencer's dressing room, Spencer House, 1765–66. Photographed in 2006. ©Spencer House Limited. *Checklist no. 112.*

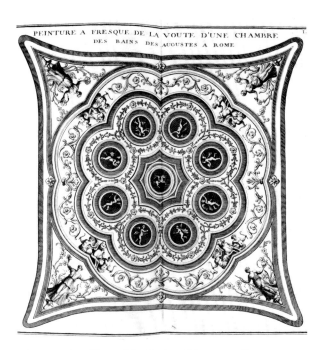

Fig. 5-33. A ceiling of the Baths of Augustus, Rome. Engraving. From Bernard de Montfaucon, *L'Antiquité expliquée et représentée en figures,* vol. 3, supplement (1719): pl. LVIII. By permission of The British Library, London, G11130. *Checklist no. 113.*

Fig. 5-34. James Stuart. Medallion overdoor, staircase hall, above the entrance to the great room, Spencer House, ca. 1758–66. Photographed before 1995. ©Spencer House Limited.

The flute-playing bacchante was taken from a sculpted figure on the Incantada at Salonica, sketched by Stuart and Revett for *Antiquities of Athens* (see fig. 11-13). The source of the other figure is unknown. This composition also occurs in the staircase anteroom at Rathfarnham Castle (see fig. 10-67) and on the organ at Newby Hall (see fig. 10-68).[69]

Once within the great room, guests would have been confronted by the extraordinary coved coffered ceiling, "in mosaic, compartments, green and white and gold; gilt medallions are let into it" (fig. 5-35).[70] The medallions depicted Bacchus with a wine cup, flanked by leopards, framed by foliage and grapes (fig. 5-36). Next was Apollo, the god of music and the arts, supported by griffins from the Spencer crest. These are reminiscent of those in a drawing by Stuart, now in the Pierpont Morgan Library, and used to decorate the Marble Saloon at Wentworth Woodhouse (see figs. 6-7a, b). The Three Graces were the subject of the third medallion, and Venus on her chariot, supported by Hymen, god of marriage, the fourth.

The ceiling was divided into nine parts, its center containing three semidomed circular compartments. The coffering in the cove was derived from the Basilica of Maxentius in Rome.[71] The central dome and the lateral coves were probably inspired by Desgodetz's illustration of the Temple of Concord in Rome (fig. 5-37), which was also the source for the scrolled foliated frieze.[72] Stuart used this frieze again in the central drawing room at Holdernesse House and at Lichfield House (see figs. 5-50, 5-70). The plasterwork for this complex design was expensive: Lord Villiers, another Stuart client, complained that Stuart "has got the gout and the estimate of the plastering work alone of the ceiling intended for your great room amounts to £480."[73] The fact that Villiers linked Stuart's illness to the fate of the plasterwork, however indirectly, does add weight to the contention that Stuart designed the room. Villiers recorded that the ceiling was finished in January 1764, except for the gilding.[74]

The theme of music and wine continued in great room's marble chimneypiece (fig. 5-38), which is almost identical to one Stuart designed for the first-floor front

213

Fig. 5-35. James Stuart. The great room, Spencer House, 1758–64. Photographed in 1996. ©Spencer House Limited. *Checklist no. 117.*

Fig. 5-36. James Stuart. Bacchus medallion from the ceiling of the great room, Spencer House, ca. 1763–64. Photographed before 1995. ©Spencer House Limited.

Fig. 5-37. "Du Temple de la Paix, à Rome."
Engraving. From Antoine Desgodetz, *Les Edifices
antiques de Rome dessinés et mesurés très
exactement . . .* (1682): 109, pl. 2. By permission of
The British Library, London, 679.k.5.

Fig. 5-38. James Stuart. Chimneypiece from the great room, Spencer
House, ca. 1758–66. Carving attributed to the Scheemakers workshop.
Now at Althorp, Northampton. Photographed in 2006. The Althorp
Collection.

Fig. 5-39. Bacchus and
the lion on the frieze
of the Choragic
Monument of
Lysicrates, Athens.
Engraving. From
Antiquities of Athens,
vol. 1 (1762): chap. 4,
pl. X. Courtesy of the
Library, The Bard
Graduate Center for
Studies in the
Decorative Arts,
Design, and Culture,
New York. *Checklist
no. 36.*

Fig. 5-40. James Stuart. Painted panel on the ceiling of the Painted Room, Spencer House, 1764–65. Photographed before 1995. ©Spencer House Limited.

Fig. 5-41. James Stuart. West wall of the Painted Room, Spencer House, 1759–66. Photographed in 2006. ©Spencer House Limited.

room of Lichfield House (see fig. 5-70).[75] It is framed, almost independently of the fireplace architrave, by an aedicule with two fluted pilasters whose capitals are adorned with masks of Apollo, and between them, above the fireplace architrave but below the entablature of the aedicule, is placed a band of bacchanalian figures copied from the Choragic Monument of Lysicrates in Athens (fig. 5-39).

The next room, Stuart's masterpiece of painted decoration and furnishing is one of the most significant surviving interiors of its era (see fig. 5-1). Iconographically, the Painted Room celebrates marriage, specifically the 1755 marriage of John Spencer to Georgiana Poyntz. This was a love match rather than a dynastic and commercial

compact, and the themes of love, marriage, beauty, and romance are explored in the painted and carved decoration. There is little cause to doubt Young's statement that the room was "painted in compartments by Mr. *Steuart*."[76] That was Stuart's trade; in 1764 he became Serjeant Painter in the Office of Works, which was not a sinecure.[77] His predecessors (Thornhill and Hogarth) had actively wielded the brush. In addition, there are no payments in the Spencer bank account to other identifiable decorative painters. However, one of the ceiling panels (fig. 5-40) is virtually identical to one painted by Biagio Rebecca in the drawing room ceiling at Lichfield House.[78] It is likely that Stuart had assistants who may have painted the minor panels such as the grisaille roundels in the bow,

Fig. 5-42. James Stuart. East wall of the Painted Room, Spencer House, 1759–66. Photographed in 2006. ©Spencer House Limited.

Fig. 5-43. James Stuart. Ceiling of the Painted Room, Spencer House, 1759–66. Photographed in 2006. ©Spencer House Limited.

Fig. 5-44. James Stuart. Entablature of the colonnade in the Painted Room, Spencer House, ca. 1759–66. Photographed in 2006. ©Spencer House Limited.

Fig. 5-45. James Stuart. Ceiling of the bow in the Painted Room, Spencer House, 1759–66. Photographed in 2006. ©Spencer House Limited.

or the garlands of flowers in the ceiling, together with the painted ornament that linked the compartments.

The Painted Room is the most densely ornamented room in any London house of that date (figs. 5-41, 5-42). Although the ornament is partly modeled, in wood and in plaster (both remorselessly gilded), the painted decoration on a flat ground is most noteworthy. The concept of the painted decoration is illusionistic in two ways. Firstly, it is based on a *faux* "hang" of forty-three painted

panels set in frames, of which some are actual, some *faux*, and some a combination of both. Secondly, the panels are surrounded by painted ornament which includes lifelike humans and animals set out in patterns. They are stylized, decorative, and generally symmetrical. The subject matter is ancient Greek myth, as represented in the interiors of the buildings of Herculaneum, which Stuart knew through the four-volume *Antichità di Ercolano*, published in 1757.[79] The style, including both the double illusion and

219

Fig. 5-46. James Stuart. North wall of the Painted Room, Spencer House, ca. 1759–66. Photographed in 2006. ©Spencer House Limited.

the subject matter, was ancient Roman, repeatedly used at Herculaneum but also known from previously exposed Roman interiors.

The density is maintained by the ceiling (fig. 5-43). It is divided into nine compartments by a grid of plaster beams, intensely enriched on both soffits and sides. Thirteen of the forty-three painted panels are actually mounted in the ceiling. The four corner compartments have square painted panels in the center, and the four in the middle of the sides have elongated octagonal painted panels; pairs of narrow ribs connect each side of these panels back to the main beams; around the painted sections are arranged plaster panels enclosing swirls of acanthus. The central compartment has a spiral of acanthus leaves, encircled by

a band of Vitruvian scroll, from which lines of husks radiate, separating oval medallions painted with zodiacal signs. The entablature of the colonnade is also heavily enriched, a band of fret on the soffit standing out in relief (fig. 5-44). The ceiling of the bow is also divided by plaster beams, whose soffits are ornamented by bands of laurel leaf. Four of these radiate from a semicircular compartment that butts up to the arch above the colonnade. At the center of the semicircle is a halved boss of pomegranate, from which lotus leaves radiate; further out are two bands of coffering. Outside the semicircle are a band of fluting and a band of fret ornament. Between the radiating beams are five painted panels, surrounded by fronds of acanthus, which fill what space remains (fig. 5-45).

The wall decoration is equally rich, but whereas the ceiling ornament is modeled (around the thirteen painted panels), the walls are painted on a flat ground, at least above the chair rail, which is carved with meander ornament. Stuart's proposal drawing shows a stone-colored ground, but the background is olive green, on which the painted decoration stands out dramatically (see fig. 5-2). The basic arrangement follows the proposal drawing. The two side bays have three painted panels in frames, the two top frames modeled, the lower painted, and backed by a trompe l'oeil cloth festooned from branches of acanthus. The acanthus is arranged in symmetrical arabesques that provide perches for the remaining staffage. Of these, two putti flank the lower panel and two more dance on top of it; standing nymphs are placed on either side of the middle panel, pulling at festoons; incense burners on tripods perch higher up; a putto stands on top of the highest panel, flanked by hippocamps that face him. Only two vases at the bottom stand on terra firma, in the form of the chair rail. Festoons of flowers fill the space between the capitals.

The door is flanked by Roman standards planted in urns (see fig. 5-24). In Stuart's proposal drawing a double-handled urn is on the cornice of the door, flanked by sphinxes facing inward. Shadows on the drawing indicate that these three features were intended to be modeled. Festoons hang between two pouring vases and a patera (see fig. 5-2). Between the capitals of this bay, a *tabula ansata* with the year 1759 in roman numerals is placed in front of two crossed palm branches.

In execution Stuart's design was inevitably modified (fig. 5-46). In the side bays the lowest painted panels were enlarged, displacing the four putti around them. Four Ionic columns with porphyry shafts were added behind the two nymphs, and the incense burners were more securely placed on the outer columns. The putto on the top panel was given a more commanding posture and a torch to hold in each hand. The vases standing on the chair rail were replaced by flying harpies, with putti riding on their wings, and flogging them with twigs. In the central bay the Roman standards were replaced by vases of flowers and morning glory vines climbing canes. Instead of sphinxes above the door, double-handled vases were painted, not modeled. The proposed vase on the chair rail was replaced by an oval painted panel, with garlands of flowers suspended above it and crossed torches below it. There was no *tabula ansata*, perhaps because

Fig. 5-47. James Stuart. Chimneypiece and overmantel in the Painted Room, Spencer House, ca. 1759–66. Carving possibly by the Scheemakers workshop. Photographed in 2006. ©Spencer House Limited.

Stuart did not wish to be reminded of the date, and instead a wreath of roses intertwined with the crossed palm branches was depicted.

Without Stuart's drawing for the other walls, his initial proposals are not known. What he executed, however, repeated some of the motifs established in the north wall. The festoons of flowers and wreaths of roses are continued in alternation around the walls at capital level. The vases of flowers climbing canes reappear on either side of the chimneypiece. The overdoor theme of an oval panel flanked by vases is repeated with variations. The vases are single-handled; the flower garlands above were replaced by palm branches, as were the crossed torches below, where festoons of shells were also added. The sphinxes and the pouring vases that disappeared from the north wall made an appearance in the bow instead. The sphinxes flank circular panels, face outward, have their wings erect, and carry baskets of flowers on their heads. The pouring vases, above festoons of husks, were moved up to the spaces between the column capitals. Candelabra with flower garlands festooned from them stand on the overmantel, flanking the largest of the painted panels, which is rectangular and in a modeled frame. The candelabra are the only motif that does not appear in Stuart's drawing.

Neither the subject matter nor the style was novel. Ancient Roman interiors like this were well known in the Renaissance, at which time they were called *grotesche*. They had first been reproduced by Raphael in the Vatican *stanze* but were not introduced to Britain until 1722–27, when William Kent decorated the ceiling of the Presence Chamber at Kensington Palace in *grotesche*, a word anglicized by John Talman as "grotesk."[80] Kent designed variations at 22 Arlington Street in 1741–50, and at 44 Berkeley Square in 1742–44 (see fig. 5-58). In both projects, the decoration only covered ceilings, and the panels were set into plaster coffering, rather than being surrounded by further illusionistic ornament.[81]

The Painted Room at Spencer House was the first application in Britain of grotesque decoration to walls, not just ceilings. Stuart's application is more successful than Kent's, perhaps in part because Stuart did not have to fit it into an existing room but was able to integrate it with modeled ornament of his own design. Stuart's design for the north wall is annotated with the dimensions of the pilasters. This could have been merely an aide-memoire, but more likely it was for the benefit of Vardy, Gray, Spencer, or the joiner.

The Painted Room was the first of a run of rooms similarly decorated by Robert Adam and James Wyatt, among others, which contemporaries generally called either "Pompeian" or "Etruscan," depending on their prevailing color combinations, rather than "grotesque." None of these rooms show much development—conceptually, iconographically, or stylistically—from the original introduction of the manner by Kent, despite Robert Adam's habitually mendacious claim to have been the first to use this idiom. Nor is the grotesque peculiarly "neoclassical," where that word means characteristic of the late eighteenth century.

The chimneypiece is unique among London chimneypieces of the date (fig. 5-47). The immediate surround is relatively plain—a stone architrave with only the *cyma* enriched by carving. It is set within an aedicule to which it is scarcely related; they are joined only by a raised field above the stone architrave, not a frieze, which is un-modeled but ornamented by a painted copy of the "Aldobran-

dini Wedding,"[82] an ancient Roman fresco owned by the Vatican. The aedicule has a full Composite order entablature resting on the painted field, with a narrow pulvinated frieze. Its span is greater than the fireplace, and at each end it is held by a caryatid term which rises from vertically aligned elongated consoles. The caryatids wear turbans and hold long garlands of flowers; each has one arm raised in front of the frieze, whence their garlands fall, passing behind their shoulders and in front of their lower bodies. Two painted panels, between three terracotta relief panels, set in a row on a plinth enriched with fret ornament, form a sort of overmantel. The room was originally designed by Stuart with a suite of neoclassical gilded furniture. Two torcheres, four mirrors, four sofas with winged lion ends, and six massive armchairs furnished the room (see chap. 10).

The Painted Room is perhaps Stuart's finest surviving work. Spencer House as a whole was almost universally admired by contemporaries. In 1772 Young wrote: "I do not apprehend there is a house in England of its size, better worth the view of the curious in architecture, and the fitting up and furnishing great houses, than Lord Spencer's in St. James's Place. . . . I know not a more beautiful piece of architecture."[83]

In 1788–96 Spencer House was altered by Henry Holland, who combined rooms on the north side and lowered the windows that opened onto the terrace.[84] The house was altered again by Philip Hardwick in 1848, who installed plate glass in the windows, and by Frederick Sang in 1873, who inserted colored marble treads in the stairs.[85] Holland, Hardwick, and Sang redecorated according to the taste of their times, and there was further redecoration in 1924 by W. Turner Lord and Co.[86] Through all these changes, Stuart's ornament was preserved. From 1889 the house was rented out, with short intervals of reoccupation by the Spencers (1914–20 and 1923–26).[87] There were three later periods of major alteration: in 1927 by the Ladies' Army and Navy Club; in 1941 when the seventh earl stripped most of the painted and carved work from the walls in order to preserve it during the Blitz; and in 1956–61 when the British Oxygen Company turned it into a modern office.[88] Then in 1982 Spencer House was leased to the J. Rothschild Group and, after extensive, unprecedented, historical and architectural research, was immaculately restored.[89] In 1991 Stuart's work there was made available for public appreciation for the first time.[90]

Holdernesse House

It is not clear whether Stuart's third London commission was to design a whole house or just to decorate it. It came from Robert D'Arcy, fourth Earl of Holdernesse. His father had married Lady Frederica Schomberg, granddaughter of the famous Marshal Schomberg, and a cousin of George I, who had died in 1722, when his heir was four. Lord Holdernesse was brought up in his mother's paternal home, Schomberg House in Pall Mall, until 1728, when his stepfather became the nineteenth Lord Fitzwalter and the owner of Moulsham Hall, outside Colchester.

For two decades Holdernesse was absorbed by politics rather than building. In his capacity as a Lord of the Bedchamber, Holdernesse had attended George II on the battlefield of Dettingen in 1743. That experience, together with their common ancestry, may have given Holdernesse otherwise undeserved respect from that particularly unimaginative king. This respect was not inherited by George III, who replaced Lord Holdernesse with a much-loved tutor, the Earl of Bute.[91]

Holdernesse was not without some aesthetic sense, however. He was a patron of opera, and Walpole even wrote (although dismissively) of his "passion for directing operas and masquerades."[92] Surprisingly, he shared a mistress, the Comtesse de Boufflers, with David Hume,[93] and he was a patron of the poet William Mason, whom he provided with a living.

It is not certain when Holdernesse began building. It seems to have been after he left office in 1761.[94] The site was 24 Hertford Street, on the south side of the street, at its western extremity, on the corner with Park Lane (fig. 5-48). Its garden occupied the plot to the east of it, so it was freestanding. The new house was largely complete by 1766, when the architect John Carter was able to sketch some of its details.[95] Holdernesse celebrated the opening of his house in 1767, and Mary Coke, who attended the opening, wrote in her diary: "The hangings, chairs and window curtains of the Great Room are of the three coloured damask, but I think the finest I have ever seen. The glasses are magnificent. Four rooms were open, but not many people, three tables at loo."[96] Horace Walpole, however, was not impressed with the house, which he described as "a formal piece of dullness."[97] Holdernesse, a member of the Society of Dilettanti, would often host dinners for fellow members at his new house.

The architect of the house is not known. One of Holdernesse's account books records a payment to Stuart of £50 in 1765,[98] but Holdernesse paid several architects and expensive building tradesmen between 1761 and 1765. He was also embellishing his riverside villa, Sion Hill, at Isleworth,[99] and his paternal inheritance, Hornby Castle, in Yorkshire.[100] The architects in the account book included Lancelot Brown, John Carr, and possibly Stiff Leadbetter, while tradesmen included John Devall, Joseph Rose, Vile and Cobb, and John Adair.[101] The account book

223

Fig. 5-49. James Stuart. North end of the drawing room, Holdernesse House, ca. 1761–66. Altered by Philip and Benjamin Dean Wyatt, 1825–28. Photographed ca. 1937. ©Country Life Picture Library. *Checklist no. 124.*

does not reveal the location of their work. Another account, dated September 1768, records carpenter's work by John Phillips and George Shakespear at Mr. Merry's stables in Park Lane, presumably next to or at least near to Holdernesse House.[102] Because Phillips and Shakespear were architects as well as carpenters, it is possible that they not only built 24 Hertford Street, but designed it as well, leaving only the ornament to Stuart.[103]

That Stuart contributed to the house is certain. John Carter sketched many of the ornamental details of the house in 1766, ascribing them to Stuart.[104] However, a

major rebuilding between 1825 and 1828 by Philip and Benjamin Dean Wyatt left only four rooms on the first floor that can be positively identified as his.[105] They are only known through a series of inadequate photographs taken prior to the demolition of the house in 1964. Two of these rooms were merged to form an enlarged drawing room (figs. 5-49, 5-50); a third adjoining room became the ante-drawing room (its ceiling was photographed in 1962; fig. 5-51), providing a suite of interconnecting rooms along the Park Lane front. The fourth room, the boudoir, survived on the Hertford Street side (fig. 5-52).

Fig. 5-50. James Stuart. Central section of the drawing room, Holdernesse House, ca. 1761–66. Altered by Philip and Benjamin Dean Wyatt, 1825–28. Photographed ca. 1937. ©Country Life Picture Library. *Checklist no. 125.*

The north room (from 1828 the north section of the drawing room; see fig. 5-49) had a deep cove, divided by octagonal panels enclosing painted ornament. The flat central bed of the ceiling had an octagon divided into segments by radial ribs, and the segments had curved faces. Around the octagon were eight circular panels, each concentric with the curved face of the octagon nearest to it, and each encircling another concentric panel in which a painted scene was set. The corners of the ceiling had plasterwork in the form of scrolling foliage. This detail was documented by Carter (fig. 5-53). The overall ceiling design was a favorite of Stuart's, and less complex versions were provided for Lady Spencer's dressing room at Spencer House (see fig. 5-32) and the gilt room at Rathfarnham Castle (see fig. 6-54). The frieze of anthemion ornament that Stuart originally used in Lady Spencer's dressing room (see fig. 5-22) was again deployed in the drawing room at Holdernesse.

The middle room (see fig. 5-50) from 1828 the central section of the drawing room had a flat ceiling. In its center was a shallow dome of elongated octagonal shape, decorated with a painted scene and enclosed by a broad and deep rib, more like a beam. A similar beam, concentric with this, enclosed a much larger area, filled with plaster coffering composed of hexagons, three deep. The outer octagonal beam was not far from the edge of the ceiling, and short beams of the same section spanned the gap

Fig. 5-51. James Stuart. Ceiling of the ante-drawing room, Holdernesse House, ca. 1761–66. Altered by Philip and Benjamin Dean Wyatt, 1825–28. Photographed in 1962. English Heritage / National Monuments Record AA62/7593 (no. 30448).

Fig. 5-52. James Stuart. The boudoir, Holdernesse House, ca. 1761–66. Photographed ca. 1937. © Country Life Picture Library. *Checklist no. 126.*

229

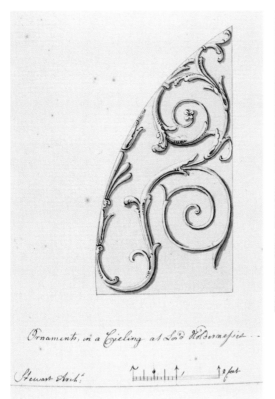

Fig. 5-54. Marble ceiling in the southern shrine of the Temple of the Sun, Palmyra. Engraving. From Robert Wood, *The Ruins of Palmyra . . .* (1753): pl. xix. By permission of The British Library, London, 744.f.16.

Fig. 5-53. John Carter. "Ornaments, in a Cieling [*sic*] at Lord Holdernesses." Pen and ink, ink wash. From a sketchbook, "Drawings made from designs of Flowers and Pateras . . ." (1766): 97. Courtesy of the Trustees of the Victoria and Albert Museum, London, D.386-1890. *Checklist no. 127.*

Fig. 5-55. John Carter. "Ornaments, in a Cieling [*sic*] at Lord Holdernesses." Pen and ink, ink wash. From a sketchbook, "Drawings made from designs of Flowers and Pateras . . ." (1766): 98. Courtesy of the Trustees of the Victoria and Albert Museum, London, D.386-1890. *Checklist no. 127.*

between its corners and the cornice of the walls, leaving rectangular spaces on its cardinal sides and pentagons in the corners, reduced to hexagons by ribs spanning the latter. Painted panels filled the four rectangles, and oval painted panels were set in the four hexagons. The composition of this ceiling was almost identical to Stuart's design for a drawing room ceiling at Lichfield House (see fig. 5-71).[106] These two ceiling designs were derived from the marble ceiling in the southern shrine of the Temple of the Sun at Palmyra as illustrated in Robert Wood's *Ruins of Palmyra* (1753; fig. 5-54).[107] The frieze of foliated scrolls, which was identical to the one he used in the great room at Spencer House (see fig. 5-35), derived from the Temple of Rome and Augustus at Pola, as illustrated in *Antiquities of Athens* (see chap. 10, headpiece).[108]

The boudoir (see fig. 5-52) had another deep cove, divided by square coffering, four squares deep, which was sketched by Carter in 1766 when he visited the house (fig. 5-55). The flat central bed of the ceiling was framed by a broad and deep beamlike rib, forming a large square. At its corners, beams were continued to follow the cove down to the cornice of the walls, leaving residual spaces in the corners which were filled with painted ornament. The flat bed of the ceiling was also filled with painted ornament, although it is difficult to tell whether this was done by Stuart or by the tradesmen of 1822–28. Stuart

Fig. 5-56. John Carter. "An Entablature, at Lord Holdernesses." Pen and ink, ink wash. From a sketchbook, "Drawings made from designs of Flowers and Pateras . . ." (1766): 35. Courtesy of the Trustees of the Victoria and Albert Museum, London, D.386-1890. *Checklist no. 127.*

Fig. 5-57. John Carter. "A Vase, in a Chim[y]: piece, at Lord Holdernesses." Pen and ink, ink wash. From a sketchbook, "Drawings made from designs of Flowers and Pateras . . ." (1766): 9. Courtesy of the Trustees of the Victoria and Albert Museum, London, D.386-1890. *Checklist no. 127.*

designed a similar ceiling for the morning room of Mrs. Montagu's house in Portman Square (see fig. 5-95),[109] and another for an unidentified room at Belvedere (see fig. 6-62). A frieze of anthemion ornaments encircled the room. This was identical to that Stuart provided for the staircase hall in Spencer House, derived from the Temple on the Ilissus illustrated in *Antiquities of Athens* (see fig. 10-27).[110] A corresponding entablature was possibly used in this or another room of the house, as is documented in Carter's sketchbook (fig. 5-56).

In addition to the ceilings and friezes, there were Stuart mantelpieces in these three rooms. For the central section of the drawing room, Stuart created a white marble mantelpiece with jambs and a frieze panel executed in porphyry and acanthus and fluted borders (see fig. 5-50). At the other end of the room, a more elaborate white marble mantelpiece had a frieze with a central winged-cupid figure within a pattern of foliated scrolls ending in

flowers, rosettes, and lions' heads.[111] Scroll-shaped trusses carved with acanthus and husks supported the shelf. Running motifs of egg-and-tongue molding, beading, and acanthus scrolls surrounded the fireplace opening (see fig. 5-49). Stuart designed a similar chimneypiece for the study.[112] In the boudoir, there was a sienna marble chimneypiece with a frieze panel and detatched side columns of poryphry (see fig. 5-52).[113]

Judging from Carter's 1766 sketchbook, there must have been several more Stuart rooms executed in this neoclassical style before the Wyatt remodeling. Carter made twenty-one drawings of details from other rooms in Holdernesse House, more than from any other Stuart project. Aside from those identified for two ceilings and a molding, the sketches indicate that Stuart designed at least one more ceiling, two additional mantelpieces (including one with a carved vase; fig. 5-57), two friezes, four entablatures, seven cornices, two architraves, and three moldings. Unfortunately, insufficient photography of the house before its demolition in 1964 makes it impossible to identify these other rooms.

In common with Spencer House, the Stuart rooms that survived in Holdernesse House to 1964 were decorated with painted panels. But, unlike Spencer House, these panels were not set in an illusionistic painted background and did not appear on the walls. Instead they were set in molded plaster panels on the ceilings alone. As at Spencer House this was an attempt to reproduce Roman painted interior decoration, although in this case it derived from Roman religious buildings, particularly mausolea. Unlike the Spencer House scheme, this was not a novelty. Lord Burlington had also attempted it in the Link Room

at Chiswick House in about 1732, though without painted panels.[114] Kent had achieved it completely at Arlington Street and Berkeley Square (fig. 5-58), and at Holdernesse House, Stuart was following the manner established by Kent.

Lord Holdernesse died in 1778, and his widow, who was Dutch and a considerable heiress, occupied Holdernesse House until her death in 1801.[115] Thereafter it was let, although an adjoining house was built on the site of the garden. Both houses were bought by the third Marquess of Londonderry in 1822, who employed the Wyatts to combine them between 1825 and 1828. Holdernesse House became known as Londonderry House in 1872 and was pulled down in 1964.[116]

Fig. 5-58. William Kent. Saloon at 44 Berkeley Square, London, with painted panels within deeply molded plaster frames, ca. 1742–44. Photographed mid-20th century. City of London, London Metropolitan Archives, Newberry 61121.

Fig. 5-59. James Stuart. Front elevation of Lichfield House, 15 Saint James's Square, London, 1764–66. Photographed in 2006. *Checklist no. 128.*

Lichfield House

The most distinctive of the six London houses for which Stuart provided designs was built for Thomas Anson, a Staffordshire squire who would probably have led a modest life at Shugborough in his native county, had he not been enriched by the fortune of his younger brother. Anson was not interested in public life, devoting his energies instead to travel, estate improvement, and the collection of paintings, ancient sculpture, and medals. Not long after inheriting he was in Spa. In 1724–25 he visited Padua, Rome, Naples, and Florence. In 1734 he was in the Levant. In 1740 he went to Egypt and Syria.[117] He began enlarging the Shugborough property in 1740, putting up ornamental buildings in 1747, and enlarging the house at about the same time.[118] His collection was bought between 1765 and 1771, and the house further enlarged in 1768.[119]

The resources with which to do all this came from his childless younger brother, George, who was created Lord Anson in 1747 and died in 1762. George Anson became as famous as Thomas Anson was obscure. In 1740 he was appointed commodore of a squadron sent to explore the Pacific coast of the Americas. Returning by way of China,

he became the first Englishman since Drake to have circumnavigated the world, and he received a near hysterical welcome on his arrival home in June 1744.

Lord Anson's fortune was inherited by his sixty-six-year-old brother in 1762. It included the house (No. 15) in the northwest part of St. James's Square which the Admiral had bought in 1748.[120] Thomas Anson spent £60,000 of his new money rebuilding it (fig. 5-59). The old house, built in 1673-76, was pulled down in the summer of 1763. A new house on the site had reached first-floor level by June 1764, when Stuart told Anson that "the grand function of wetting [it] was performed . . . [by] upward of 50 [builders] . . . their bellies full of beef pudding and Ale."[121] In October the bricklayer had finished his work to the front elevation and was "going on with the back front."[122] In December the front of the house was being covered.[123] In September 1766 "Rose," probably the famous plasterer Joseph Rose, had been paid in part,[124] and plate glass for the first-floor front windows was under discussion. By the end of that year Thomas Anson was paying rates, and he was presumably in occupation. In this same year John Carter visited, as he had at Holdernesse

Fig. 5-60. John Carter. "Cornice, at Ansons St James Sqr." Pen and ink, ink wash. From a sketchbook, "Drawings made from designs of Flowers and Pateras . . ." (1766): 73. Courtesy of the Trustees of the Victoria and Albert Museum, London, D.386-1890. *Checklist no. 127.*

Fig. 5-61. John Carter. "Entablature, at Anson's St. James. Sqr." Pen and ink, ink wash. From a sketchbook, "Drawings made from designs of Flowers and Pateras . . ." (1766): 36. Courtesy of the Trustees of the Victoria and Albert Museum, London, D.386-1890. *Checklist no. 127.*

House, and sketched designs for cornice and entablature by Stuart (figs. 5-60, 5-61). By April 1768, Anson was entertaining in the house. Lady Shelburne recorded in her diary that she had attended a "breakfast and concert" in honor of Mrs. Montagu at "Mr. Anson's a very fine house, built and ornamented by Mr. Stuart."[125] It may not have been quite complete then, as some payments to the mason were still outstanding in April 1770, and the author of *Critical Observations on the Building and Improvements of London*, published in 1771, remarked "when [it] is compleated according to the plan, the public will be more able do justice to the classic taste which directed it."[126]

This classic taste was shared by Stuart's patron, who was a fellow member of the Society of Dilettanti. Stuart's letters to Anson are full of details relating to the Grecian-inspired designs for the house. He called the Ionic capitals of the giant order on the front elevation "my capitals," and he told Anson that he was "busy designing" them in August 1764; yet for some reason he also had models made by the joiner John Adair.[127] They were copies of the capitals of the portico of Minerva Polias, part of the Erechtheion at Athens, which were not available in published form until about 1790 when the second volume of *Antiquities* appeared (fig. 5-62).[128] Stuart was delighted that his capitals turned out to be "most exactly of the same dimensions with those of the portico of Minerva Polias . . . not a hairsbreath[sic] of difference in their Diameters."[129]

Other details attest to the influence of Athens. The three central first-floor windows of the rear wing, for instance, are linked by a Doric stone pilastrade which composes a widely spaced serliana, a tripartite window with a central arched section and two narrower side sections. The molded archivolt of the central window does not spring from the top of the entablature in the usual way, however, but from the top of the capitals below it, interrupting the entablature rather awkwardly (fig. 5-63). This detail was copied from the Aqueduct of Hadrian at Athens (see fig. 7-7).[130] It also occurs on other buildings with which Stuart was connected: Nuneham Park, Belvedere, the Prospect House at Wimpole, and Montagu House, Portman Square.[131]

Stuart's correspondence with Anson also indicates that he was responsible for the construction. He distributed Anson's money to the principal tradesmen and reported on the progress of the work. His design responsibility, however, is not entirely unchallengeable. The bricklayer

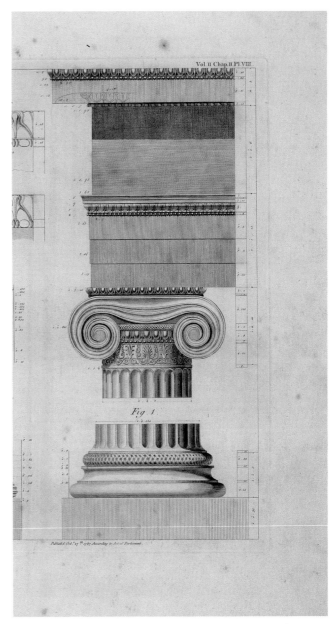

Fig. 5-62. Base, capital and entablature of the portico of Minerva Polias. Engraving. From *Antiquities of Athens*, vol. 2 (ca. 1790): chap. 2, pl. VIII. Courtesy of the Library, The Bard Graduate Center for Studies in the Decorative Arts, Design, and Culture, New York. *Checklist no. 129.*

Richard Norris, who was a surveyor and architect as well, also prepared drawings for the house in November 1764, and Alexander Rouchead, whose experience as mason went back to 1713 when he had worked at Wimpole under Gibbs, was also an architect.[132] Much depended on Rouchead, as he built the entire front elevation, which

Fig. 5-63. The inner courtyard of Lichfield House, showing the central windows of the rear wing. Photographed in 1958. City of London, London Metropolitan Archives, 58/0454.

Fig. 5-64. Front elevation (detail) of Lichfield House, showing the Ionic capitals. City of London, London Metropolitan Archives, 96.0 St Jam 66/5596.

was the first stone façade in the square and the principal advertisement of the building.

The execution of the capitals on this elevation caused Stuart much anxiety ("they must not murder my Capitals the greatest grace and ornament of the building"), and he was relieved that two of the volutes were taken over by Peter Scheemakers (fig. 5-64).[133] "Evans," probably Charles Evans, who later worked for Stuart at 22 Portman Square, was apparently the carpenter, and John Adair, who also worked there, was evidently the joiner. The "Rose" who was paid in 1766 was presumably the same "Mr. Rose" who also billed Thomas Anson's executors in 1773 for plasterwork and is therefore probably Joseph Rose, the leading plasterer. The "Mr. Birimwich" who submitted a bill at the same time for paper hanging was doubtless Thomas Bromwich, a well-known wallpaper manufacturer, and the "Russell" who sent in a bill for painting at the same time may have been Henry Russell, painter at Bagshot Park under James Paine in 1770–72.[134]

The front elevation of 15 St. James's Square (see fig. 5-59) is divided into three "compact" bays; a composition that inspired Adam's similar façade at 20 St. James's Square in 1771–75.[135] No. 15 is arranged into three stories over a basement. This arrangement had been the conven-

tion for London town houses for over a century, but at No. 15 it was executed at unusual expense in Portland stone. In common with the more costly houses of this type, the allusion to ancient architecture was not just implied, but actually expressed. The basement is faced in stone which is vermiculated, as if just wrenched from the quarry. The ground floor, a little more obviously worked, is rusticated, but not otherwise ornamented; its two round-headed windows and doorway to the north are set in unmolded arches. The doorway, altered over the years, has a pair of Roman Doric columns supporting a frieze and cornice. Simple stone surrounds frame the ground-floor windows. The three first-floor windows, by contrast, have architraves, friezes, and even pediments. The three second-floor windows have architraves and a continuous sill band enriched with guilloche molding.

The first and second floors are framed within a tetrastyle temple front resting on the slightly proud ground floor; it has giant fluted Ionic half-columns, which support a full entablature and pediment. The formula was common to Palladian buildings, but the expense of giant half-columns was less usual, and the expense of a pediment was rare. It was actually unprecedented to employ details copied from buildings in ancient Greece, rather than Rome, and it is therefore not surprising that Stuart was so anxious about the effect of capitals which the London public had never seen before. In order to separate the Greek design from the adjoining town houses of the square, Stuart designed a strip of plain walling on either side of the façade. This walling also provided a backdrop for the horizontal moldings that turn back. This was a fairly new idea in house design. It was more usual that the exterior of all terrace houses joined into one architecturally.

The plan was typical of the narrow London town houses of the day (figs. 5-65, 5-66). All the rooms interconnected in a formal plan that was neither innovative nor

unusual. The basement contained the storerooms, wine cellar, kitchen, wash house, and other workrooms. On the ground floor, an entrance hall led through an inner vestibule to a large rectangular staircase hall, which was top lit and rose only to the first floor, a typical stair plan for this period. There were two main ground-floor rooms: a morning room fronting St. James's Square, its ceiling photographed in the 1950s (fig. 5-67) and a dining room. Behind these rooms there was a service hall with a service stair and two small rooms. The first floor had two large rooms (the drawing room and music room) and a small drawing room in the rear. The master bedroom was located

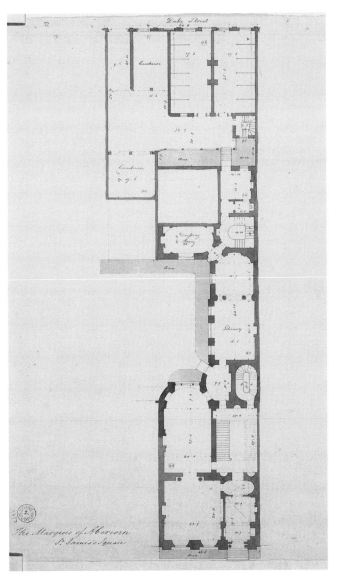

Fig. 5-65. Plan of the ground floor, Lichfield House, 15 Saint James's Square, with proposed alterations for the Marquis of Abercorn, 1809. Pen and ink, ink wash. By courtesy of the Trustees of Sir John Soane's Museum, London, 38/7/2.

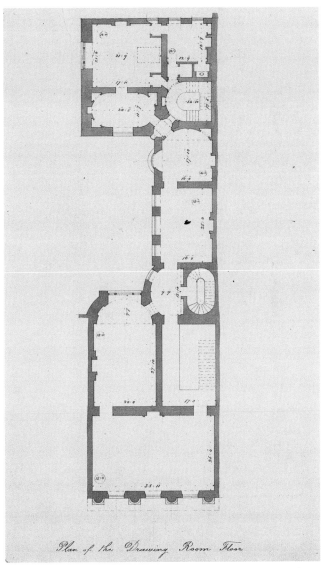

Fig. 5-66. Plan of the principal floor, Lichfield House, 15 Saint James's Square, with proposed alterations for the Marquis of Abercorn, 1809. Pen and ink, color wash, pencil. By courtesy of the Trustees of Sir John Soane's Museum, London, 38/7/4.

Fig. 5-67. James Stuart. Ceiling of the morning room at Lichfield House, 1764–66. Photographed in 1941. English Heritage / National Monuments Record A44/802.

Fig. 5-68. James Stuart. The frieze in the morning room at Lichfield House, looking through into the staircase hall, 1764–66. Photographed in 1941. English Heritage / National Monuments Record A44/819.

Fig. 5-69. James Stuart. Chimneypiece in the main drawing room, principal floor, Lichfield House, 1764–66. Carving attributed to the Scheemakers workshop. Photographed in 1958. City of London, London Metropolitan Archives, 96.0 St Jam 76/11997. *Checklist no. 131.*

behind this small drawing room, but there is no record of its original appearance. The lobby and stairs of the first floor repeated those of the ground floor.[136] The second floor had bedrooms, dressing rooms, and servants' rooms.

Less than thirty years after the house was completed, the elevation was altered by Samuel Wyatt, who added a first-floor stone balcony with copper railings and turned the first-floor windows into French doors.[137] Wyatt also modified the plan of the interior and added a D-shaped bow to the rear of the front wing which "largely destroyed the formal character of Stuart's design."[138] Wyatt then made more extensive internal alterations, with specifications as lavish as Stuart's, making it difficult at times to distinguish the work of the two architects. Some ornament, however,

is identical to Stuart's in other buildings and presumably was his. One example, a frieze of ewers, urns, and paterae in the ground-floor morning room (fig. 5-68), is a repeat of the frieze in the music room at Spencer House (see fig. 5-29). The white marble chimneypiece in the first-floor front room (fig. 5-69) is almost identical to that in the great room at Spencer House, including in particular the distinctive capitals and the figures between them, copied from the Choragic Monument of Lysicrates. At Lichfield House, however, the masks on the capitals are female, rather than Apollonian, and there is no frieze on the entablature of the framing aedicule. The ceiling of the first-floor front room (figs. 5-70, 5-71) is almost identical to the central section of the drawing room at Holdernesse House

Fig. 5-70. James Stuart. Main drawing room, principal floor, Lichfield House, 1764–66. Ceiling panels painted by Biagio Rebecca, 1794. Photographed in 1958. City of London, London Metropolitan Archives, 54/1865.

Fig. 5-71. James Stuart. Main drawing room, principal floor, Lichfield House, 1764–66. Ceiling panels painted by Biagio Rebecca, 1794. Photographed in 1958. City of London, London Metropolitan Archives, 58/0438. *Checklist no. 130.*

(see fig. 5-50), which is particularly remarkable in view of the complexity and density of the ornament at both places. The differences are, first, that the central octagon at Lichfield House is symmetrical, rather than elongated, and, second, that the complete pattern is flanked at Lichfield House by a band of alternating hexagons and lozenges at each end. The ceiling at Lichfield House also recalls the ceiling of the Painted Room at Spencer House (see fig.

5-43), with its gilded scroll arabesques and palm ornament.[139]

The ceiling of the rear first-floor room, or music room, at Lichfield House (figs. 5-72, 5-73) is also comparable to other ceilings designed by Stuart. Its basic pattern is similar to that of the boudoir ceiling at Holdernesse House (see fig. 5-52): a deep cove, surrounding a flat area framed by a broad beamlike rib, which is extended at the corners to follow the cove down to the cornice of the

Fig. 5-72. James Stuart. The music room, Lichfield House, 1764–66. Alterations by Samuel Wyatt, 1791–94. Photographed in 1958. City of London, London Metropolitan Archives, 58/0441. *Checklist no. 132.*

walls. The central flat area of the Lichfield House ceiling, however, is rectangular rather than square. It too encloses a central circular feature, but this is flanked by three rectangular panels at each end. The middle panels have more delicately framed panels within them, connected to the main beams by a pair of thin ribs on each side, a device which also occurs on the ceiling of the Painted Room at Spencer House. Unlike the ceiling at Holdernesse House,

there is no coffering, and the residual spaces are filled by shallow arabesques of thin acanthus fronds, similar to those on the ceiling of the Painted Room at Spencer House. The ceiling's elaborate anthemia are derived from the south adytum of the Temple of the Sun at Palmyra.[140] The music room's white marble chimneypiece (fig. 5-74)— with its eared architrave, egg-and-dart molding around the opening, and pilasters on either side, leading up to carved

241

Fig. 5-73. James Stuart. Ceiling of the music room, Lichfield House, 1764–66. Alterations by Samuel Wyatt, 1791–94. Photographed in 1958. City of London, London Metropolitan Archives, 58/0442.

Fig. 5-74. James Stuart. Chimneypiece in the music room, Lichfield House, 1764–66. Photographed in 1958. City of London, London Metropolitan Archives, 58/0440.

consoles that support the mantel shelf and the wave scroll dado—is also reminiscent of the chimneypieces and doorcases at Spencer House (see figs. 5-9, 5-24) and the Tower of the Winds at Shugborough (see fig. 7-24), both of which derived from the Incantada at Salonica drawn by Stuart for *Antiquities* (see fig. 10-30).[141]

Stuart also designed a garden loggia, as a drawing survives for a three bay pedimented portico intended for the display of sculptures (fig. 5-75). This has been identified as a design for Lichfield house, although the drawing itself gives no indication of the location. If it was for Lichfield house, it was never executed.

Thomas Anson died in 1773, leaving the house to his sister's son, George Adams, who took the surname of Anson. In 1789, George died, leaving the house to his son Thomas, who was created Viscount Anson in 1806. In 1785 George Anson had purchased the house next door, No. 16, and in 1790 his son pulled it down. From 1791 to 1794 the back part of this site was used to enlarge No. 15 according to Samuel Wyatt's designs.[142] Lord Anson died in 1818, and after the second viscount was created Earl of Lichfield in 1831, the house became known as Lichfield House.[143]

Fig. 5-75. James Stuart. Design for a garden loggia, possibly for Lichfield House, n.d. Pencil, pen and ink, color wash. RIBA Library Drawings Collection, London, SD 62/3. *Checklist no. 133.*

Fig. 5-76. Front elevation of 23 Hill Street (now No. 31), London, 1744. Photographed in 2003. By kind permission of Rosemary Baird.

23 Hill Street

Stuart undertook two of his most remarkable London commissions for the society hostess and bluestocking Elizabeth Montagu. Her father, Matthew Robinson, was a cousin of the architect-baronet Sir Thomas Robinson of Rokeby Park, Yorkshire, and had inherited property nearby at West Layton.[144] From the age of six, she had spent long stays with her grandmother and step-grandfather, Dr. Conyers Middleton, in Cambridge. There her tastes were formed, and her precocious linguistic and conversational skills were noted by the "divines, scholars, philosophers, travellers, men of the world who were . . . to be met with at Dr. Middleton's house."[145] Middleton was a friend of the Earl of Oxford, a scholar and bibliophile, whose seat was Wimpole Hall nearby.[146] Through him Elizabeth became a close friend of his daughter, Lady Margaret Cavendish Harley, who married the second

Duke of Portland in 1734. It was this friendship and the consequent stays at Wimpole and the Portland seat at Bulstrode Park, Hampshire, that introduced Elizabeth to the *grande monde.*[147]

In 1742, aged twenty-three, she married Edward Montagu, aged fifty, Member of Parliament for Huntingdon (fifteen miles from Cambridge). Montagu's father had taken the opportunity to acquire church lands in the Bishopric of Durham on favorable terms from his uncle, Lord Crew, the Bishop, and on these he had developed extensive coal-mining interests. He had also acquired more land in Northumberland by two successive marriages, and from his second wife, Edward's mother, he had obtained profitable mining rights at Denton, just west of Newcastle. Edward rented a country house, Sandleford Priory, near Newbury, in Berkshire, but he spent a part of every year in his house near the colliery.

Mrs. Montagu was inordinately famous for her intellectual accomplishments. While her grandfather Conyers Middleton was a classical historian, Elizabeth Montagu became a literary critic, and in her *Essay on the Writings and Genius of Shakespear* (1769), she defended Shakespeare against the criticism of Voltaire and Johnson.[148] Thus, her interests were literary, rather than visual or musical, and her houses are not explicable as those of a *virtuoso.* "I neither find any of the vexation some find in building, nor the great amusement others tell me they experience in it," she wrote in 1774. "Indeed, if it were not that a house must be building before it can be built, I should never have been a builder; I have not had quarter of an hour's pain or pleasure from the operation."[149] The splendor of her houses was only an equivalence of the "service of plate and table plentifully covered" for the benefit of her regular evening literary conversation parties, the English equivalent of Parisian salons. Wraxall's description of her as the "Madame du Deffand of the English capital" acknowledges this.[150] The distinctive feature of her assemblies was that they were presided over by a woman ("brilliant in diamonds, . . . critical in talk"[151]), and that gaming, a pastime of the rich, was forbidden. Her female friends, inexplicably named "the bluestockings," played a leading part in these assemblies.[152] Thus her great wealth was put to house an academy, of a particular kind.

Mrs. Montagu was introduced to Stuart in 1758 by Lord Lyttelton, for whom Stuart was then building a Doric Temple at Hagley, Worcestershire (see fig. 7-2).[153] She disliked the temple, however, writing that all her

Fig. 5-77. Ceiling of the great room at 23 Hill Street. Panels painted by James Stuart, 1766–72. Photographed in 2003. By kind permission of Rosemary Baird.

friends objected to it.[154] Her initial employment of Stuart, therefore, must owe something to Stuart's engaging conversation and manner rather than to her affinity for his work. Conversation was her metier, and Stuart provided it: at their first meeting they discussed her visit to the Vale of Tempe in 1753.[155] In later conversations she found him "amusing and . . . humble," and his "learning, ingenuity, sagacity and application" surprised and delighted her.[156] Lyttelton's decision in 1758 to engage Stuart to paint "a Flora and four pretty little Zephyrs in my drawing room Ceiling" at Hagley (see figs. 6-37, 6-38) may have been what first spurred Mrs. Montagu to employ him as a decorative painter at her London town house at 23 Hill Street (fig. 5-76).[157]

No. 23 (now 31) was a four-bay town house with its principal rooms on the first floor. Mrs. Montagu had begun building the house in 1744, and she proceeded to decorate it up until 1772. She had "a keen flair for the current of fashion,"[158] and her house would include one of the earliest decorative schemes in the Chinese style (1752) which, when it was later replaced by a dressing room by Robert Adam, retained the Chinese style.[159] In 1759, when Mrs. Montagu first employed Stuart, his work was becoming fashionable, and he had an established reputation as an arbiter of taste.

Fig. 5-78. Panel, detail of the great room ceiling. By kind permission of Rosemary Baird. *Checklist no. 135.*

Fig. 5-79. James Stuart. Ceiling of the bedchamber at 23 Hill Street, 1766–72. Photographed in 2003. By kind permission of Rosemary Baird. *Checklist no. 134.*

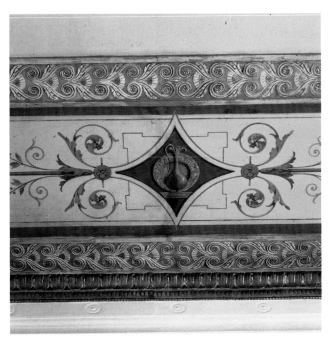

Fig. 5-80. Border decoration, detail of the bedchamber ceiling. By kind permission of Rosemary Baird.

Stuart's first painted subject for the house at Hill Street was Shakespearian, a scene from *The Tempest,* created in 1759, and thus very much within Mrs. Montagu's area of expertise and interest rather than Stuart's.[160] She commissioned further works from him in the 1760s, including the decoration of her bedchamber and the painting of roundels to the ceiling of the great room.[161] In January 1760 she wrote of "designs he promised me,"[162] but it was not until April 1766 that she began "moving towards a contract with Stuart."[163] It took until 1772 for the work to be completed. This long delay is usually ascribed to Stuart's disorganized and dilatory working habits, but the divergence of dates could partly be explained if the work took place in two or even three stages in at least two separate rooms.

Stuart painted the four medallions in the ceiling of the great room (figs. 5-77, 5-78). These were executed in monochrome with a background of terracotta, mimicking antique cameos.[164] The most elaborate of Stuart's decorative schemes at Hill Street was for Mrs. Montagu's bedchamber, overlooking the garden at the rear of the house (figs. 5-79 to 5-81). Stuart designed door frames (fig. 5-82) and the chimneypiece with its central low relief panel that used his favorite tilting-vase motif (fig. 5-83), taken from a sculpted relief panel he had found in Athens

Fig. 5-81. Corner decoration, detail of the bedchamber ceiling. By kind permission of Rosemary Baird.

Fig. 5-82. James Stuart. Doorcase in the bedchamber at 23 Hill Street, 1766–72. Photographed in 2003. By kind permission of Rosemary Baird.

Fig. 5-83. James Stuart. Chimneypiece in the bedchamber at 23 Hill Street, 1766–72. Photographed in 2003. By kind permission of Rosemary Baird. *Checklist no. 136.*

near the Theater of Bacchus (see fig. 10-38). He painted the ceiling on the theme of Aurora, surrounded by eight roundels containing putti.[165] It must have been these to which Mrs. Montagu was referring in November 1767, when she wrote that "Mr Stewart has painted me some of the sweetest Zephirs and Zephirettes in my bedchamber that ever I beheld, but . . . the room will not be finished perhaps till spring."[166]

One oddity of the scheme is that the putti in the roundels appear to represent eight of the twelve signs of the zodiac (figs. 5-84, 5-85), with other signs painted in monochrome in the great room. The zodiac was another

Fig. 5-84. James Stuart. Central section of the bedchamber ceiling, 23 Hill Street, with eight signs of the zodiac, 1766–72. Photographed in 2003. By kind permission of Rosemary Baird.

Fig. 5-85. Painted panel, detail of the bedchamber ceiling, featuring the zodiac sign for Leo. By kind permission of Rosemary Baird.

247

Fig. 5-86. James Stuart. Montagu House, 22 Portman Square, London, ca. 1775–81. Photographed after bombing in 1941. City of London, London Metropolitan Archives, 89.0 Portman 79/6136.

favorite subject of Stuart's. He completed at least two other zodiac ceilings: one in the Painted Room at Spencer House in London and the other in the entrance porch at Rathfarnham Castle near Dublin.[167] He was also responsible for the design of a zodiac case for a John Holmes spring clock for the Council Room at the Royal Hospital for Seamen at Greenwich in 1785.[168]

The incoherence of the division of the zodiac signs between two rooms at Hill Street does not seem in the least characteristic of Stuart, who for example was capable of producing a complicated iconographical scheme celebrating love and marriage in the Painted Room at Spencer House. Mrs. Montagu's reference to "zephirs and zephirettes" (for a painting of Aurora and the zodiac) suggests she may have been responsible for the confusion, particularly if the impulse to employ Stuart in the first place had come from seeing Lord Lyttelton's "Flora and four pretty little Zephyrs"[169] Her willingness to change the direction of the work on a whim is hinted at in a letter of 1767 when she wrote: "I wish that there had been one Zephir quite unfinish'd, & I'd have order'd he sd have been in a *sweeping attitude*, clearing away les feuilles mortis."[170] There was also some difficulty with the subject matter itself. A "Room of Cupidons" was thought unsuit-

able for a woman of Mrs. Montagu's advanced age. Mrs. Delany questioned: "how such a genius, at her age, and so circumstanced could think of painting the walls of her dressing room with bowers of roses and jessamine, entirely inhabited by little cupids in all their wanton ways."[171]

In June 1769 Stuart wrote to Thomas Anson that "Mrs Montagues room is almost finished, if I have no interruption it will be completed next week."[172] Three months later the work was continuing: Stuart wrote: "I have applied as assiduously as was possible to the finishing of Mrs Montagues Room . . . but alas there still remains some work to be done there before all is completed."[173] In June 1772 it was described as finished but for the varnishing, and it was publicly opened in May 1773.[174]

Montagu House

As the coal trade grew through the eighteenth century, Edward Montagu became richer and richer, and by the time of his death in 1775 he had an annual income of £7,000.[175] The Montagus had no children, and therefore this fortune became Elizabeth's, nor was she content to ignore it. She paid close and active attention to her business, constantly corresponded with her managers, and visited the collieries as her husband had done. By the time of her own death in 1800 she had increased her income to £10,000 a year.[176]

Stuart's patron was therefore a very wealthy widow. The same year her husband died, she took a ninety-nine-year lease on a plot in Portman Square, which had been laid out two years earlier.[177] Where Stuart was apparently only a painter and designer of interior details at 23 Hill Street, it is clear that he was the architect of 22 Portman Square (fig. 5-86). Mrs. Montagu reported that she chose Stuart "on account of his disinterestedness & contempt of money."[178] Her letters referred to him as "my architect" and blamed delays on his failing to send his drawings for chimneypieces, columns, and ormolu to the workmen.[179]

Stuart relied on builders such as Richard Norris, who was also an architect and with whom Stuart had worked elsewhere. Norris had built the carcass of 15 St. James's Square (see fig. 5-59). Charles Evans, a carpenter who received regular payments from November 1774 to March 1778, had also been the carpenter at St. James's Square. John Adair, the carver, with payments beginning in October 1774, had made the models of the capitals at St. James's Square.[180] From 1780 at least he was assisted by James Gandon, sometimes described by Mrs. Montagu as

Stuart's assistant, sometimes as his partner, but on one occasion she called them both "my architects."[181] Gandon's responsibilities included at least one drawing for the roof. Norris worked on the project in some capacity until his death in 1779; he was probably the bricklayer, but it may be that he helped Stuart and that Gandon replaced him.[182]

The house that Stuart was to build for Mrs. Montagu occupied most of the block northwest of the square and was freestanding, set back from the street in its own garden, with a carriage sweep up to the door (fig. 5-87). In its isolation and considerable size, it resembled the *hôtels particuliers* of the late seventeenth and early eighteenth centuries, of which the last was Bingley House, Cavendish Square, built in 1725–26.[183] Unlike these, however, Montagu House did not front the square, nor was it even aligned with one side of it. Instead, it was diagonally placed behind the northwest corner. In that respect it reflected the Picturesque sensibility of its own time, and it may also have provided an example for the positioning of the corner houses of Belgrave Square in 1825.

Montagu House was certainly large, with three stories and a front of nine bays, and side elevations clear of encumbering neighbors. Its exterior was very sparingly ornamented (fig. 5-88). The ground-floor windows had plain architraves, and the first-floor windows had molded architraves, while the second-floor windows had none. The central first-floor window was tripartite and had a full entablature with a pediment. The windows at the ends of the first floor were pedimented serlianas. Like that in the rear wing of Lichfield House (see fig. 5-63), the archivolt of the central light rose from a compromise position above the architrave. On the side elevations there were Diocletian windows in the centers of the third story, giving access to the balustraded roofs of the two-story canted bays.

The five central bays broke forward slightly, and the rooms behind them formed a circuit (fig. 5-89).[184] The rooms of parade were on the first floor, which was reached by way of a staircase at the northeast end, rising from a pillared entrance hall. The Ionic three-quarter columns around the walls and screen of freestanding columns were designed by Stuart (fig. 5-90). The fluted frieze of the room is derived from Stuart's drawings of the Incantada at Salonica (see fig. 10-30), and the mosaic tiled floor mimics a Roman mosaic with its bold Greek key and eight-pointed star patterns. Over a doorway in the entrance hall was a medallion derived from a figure on the Incantada at Salonica (fig. 5-91). Stuart was responsible for the design of the wrought iron stair balustrade of ornate scrollwork, which is identical to that he designed for Belvedere at around the same date.[185] The staircase was

Fig. 5-87. James Stuart. Montagu House, 22 Portman Square, London, ca. 1775–81. Photographed in 1894. English Heritage / National Monuments Record 12691A. *Checklist no. 137.*

Fig. 5-88. James Stuart. Rear elevation of Montagu House, ca. 1775–81. Photographed after bombing in 1941. City of London, London Metropolitan Archives, 89.0 79/6328.

Fig. 5-89. Elizabeth Montagu. Sketch plan of 22 Portman Square, London, ca. 1780. Pen and ink. From Mrs. Montagu to Matthew Boulton, 20 August [1780], Birmingham City Archives, Boulton Papers, Ms. 3782/12/93/17.

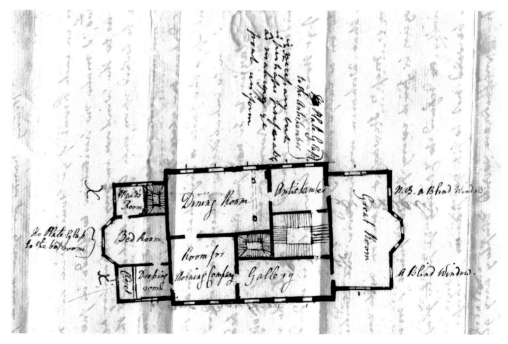

Fig. 5-90. James Stuart. Entrance hall, Montagu House, ca. 1775–81. Photographed in 1894. English Heritage/National Monuments Record BB80/3470. *Checklist no. 138.*

Fig. 5-91. James Stuart. Door in the entrance hall, Montagu House, ca. 1775–81. Photographed in 1941. English Heritage/National Monuments Record BB75/4053.

enclosed and must therefore have been top-lit. It led to an antechamber (later known as the small drawing room) on its northwest side (fig. 5-92). This had semicircular overdoors and an elliptical vault, all painted by Biagio Rebecca and G. B. Cipriani, and the familiar fluted frieze derived from the Incantada.

Thence the circuit led to the dining room in the southwest, reached through a screen with two scagliola columns with capitals of the Ionic order of the Erectheion and supporting a coffered arch.[186] This arrangement was also used by Stuart at Holdernesse House, as detailed in a sketch by John Carter (fig. 5-93).[187] The corresponding pilasters were also derived from the Erectheion (see fig. 5-62). By 1894, when the room was photographed by H. Bedford Lemere, it had become a drawing room (fig. 5-94). The frieze of the room is very similar to those designed by Stuart for Holdernesse House, Lichfield House, and the music room at Spencer house, but it is more elaborate than these, with paterae and floral swags in addition to the vases (see figs. 5-49, 5-68, 5-29).

Southeast of this room was what Mrs. Montagu told

Matthew Boulton was a "Room for Morning Company" (fig. 5-95).[188] The morning room, which Mrs. Montagu was subsequently to cover with feathers, had a ceiling that conformed to others designed by Stuart. It had a deep cove, filled with square coffers. The rib that framed the central flat was extended at the corners to follow the cove down to the corners of the walls. These corners were filled with scrollwork familiar from many other Stuart ceilings, such as those at Belvedere (see fig. 6-62). At the center of the flat of the ceiling was a pattern of intersecting circles.[189] The anthemion frieze was identical to that in the boudoir at Holdernesse House and the staircase hall at Spencer House (see figs. 5-52, 5-19). It was derived from Stuart's drawings of the temple on the Ilissus in *Antiquities of Athens.* To the northeast of this room, and next on the circuit, was the gallery (fig. 5-96), which returned the visitor to the stair. The apsed ends may have been a later addition by Joseph Bonomi, as they do not appear in Mrs. Montagu's plan of 1780.[190] The segmental ceiling was later decorated by Angelica Kauffman, and the Shakespearean subject panels over the doors were painted by Biagio

Fig. 5-92. James Stuart. The small drawing room, or ante-chamber, Montagu House, ca. 1775–81. Photographed in 1894. English Heritage / National Monuments Record BB61/1183 (BL12698).

Rebecca.[191] The chimneypiece (which may also be a later addition) echoes the Greek key mosaic in the entrance hall.

The two end bays of the house held rooms additional to this circuit. The northeast bay contained a single great room on the first floor (fig. 5-97), reached at both ends from the antechamber and the gallery. As completed, to Bonomi's rather than Stuart's design, this had fourteen freestanding scagliola columns and two square-planned pilasters around its walls, although it may be that Stuart had already envisaged this before Bonomi took over. The southwest bay housed Mrs. Montagu's private rooms, reached only from the morning room. The first of these was a dressing room on the southeast side, with a closet

off it. The central room was Mrs. Montagu's bedroom, opening into the canted bay. Southwest of this was her maid's room, reached both from her room and from a back stair. One of these rooms, possibly Mrs. Montagu's bedroom, was photographed before the demolition of the house (fig. 5-98).

Stuart's relationship with Mrs. Montagu ended in an atmosphere of bitterness and recrimination that helped to sour his reputation as an architect. She made frequent complaints of Stuart's dilatoriness and inattention. Surprisingly, therefore, the building work does not seem to have taken unreasonably long. In July 1777 Stuart told Mrs. Montagu that "the floor above the basement

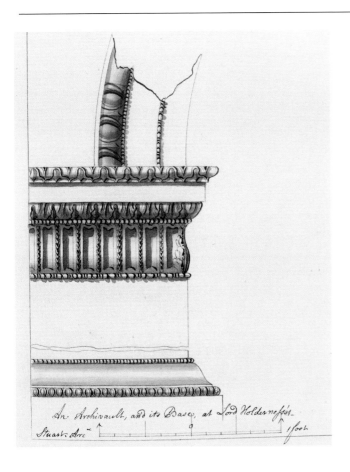

Fig. 5-93. John Carter. "An Archivault, and its Base, at Lord Holdernesses." Pen and ink, ink wash. From a sketchbook, "Drawings made from designs of Flowers and Pateras . . ." (1766): 74. Courtesy of the Trustees of the Victoria and Albert Museum, London, D.386-1890. *Checklist no. 127.*

Fig. 5-94. James Stuart. The drawing room (formerly the dining room), Montagu House, ca. 1775–81. Photographed in 1894. English Heritage / National Monuments Record BB96/754D (BL12696). *Checklist no. 141.*

253

Fig. 5-95. James Stuart. The morning room, Montagu House, ca. 1775–81. Photographed ca. 1915.
©Country Life Picture Library. *Checklist no. 140.*

advances."[192] By November 1779 the attic story was ready for papering, the floors and ceilings of her bedchamber, dressing room, and gallery (all on the first floor) were done, but wet weather had delayed laying floors on the ground floor and inserting the sashes.[193] Mrs. Montagu believed the house to be "almost ready" in November 1780 and proposed moving her furniture from Hill Street. A few months later, in March 1781, she described it as "finished and fit for habitation," but was advised by "the medical people" not "to go into a new house just after the winter damp."[194] By November some of her servants had moved in, and she was "very busy furnishing."[195] Early in December she wrote that she had "changed my mediocre dwelling in Hill Street to my great mansion in Portman Square."[196] Horace Walpole dined there in February 1782 and called it "a noble simple edifice. . . . It is grand, not tawdry, not larded, embroidered, and *pomponné* with shreds and remnants, and *clinquant* like the

Fig. 5-96. James Stuart and Joseph Bonomi. Reception room or gallery, Montagu House, 1775–83. Photographed ca. 1915. ©Country Life Picture Library. *Checklist no. 139.*

Fig. 5-97. James Stuart and Joseph Bonomi. Great room or saloon, Montagu House, 1775–83. Photographed in 1894. English Heritage/ National Monuments Record BL 12693.

Fig. 5-98. James Stuart. Chimneypiece wall in an unidentified room, possibly Mrs. Montagu's bedroom, Montagu House, ca. 1775–81. Photographed in 1941. English Heritage / National Monuments Record BB75/4054

harlequinades of Adam."[197] He would hardly have written that two years later. By then Mrs. Montagu was covering the morning-room walls with feathers, and informing her friends that "any feathers will be very acceptable. The brown tails of partridges are very useful, tho' not so brilliant as some others."[198]

Stuart's evasiveness and his long absences "in ale houses and night Cellars" forced Mrs. Montagu to seek other advice.[199] She was simultaneously employing James Wyatt at Sandleford Priory, and in September 1780 she

asked his advice about Portman Square, but nothing suggests that he gave her any designs. Although Stuart was supposed to place orders for ornament, and he certainly ordered a jasperware frieze from Wedgwood, she found it easier to do so through Matthew Boulton. Boulton ordered ornament from the japanner and modeler Francis Eginton, "mechanical paintings" from his brother John Eginton's firm, Jee, Eginton and Co., and ironwork from a Mr. Shirley, all in Birmingham. Boulton also ordered the "rich doors," and in 1779–80 he conducted a long correspondence with Mrs. Montagu about the contrary merits of plate and crown glass, eventually rejecting Bowles's Vauxhall glass, and recommending George Mackay at the British Plate Glass Manufactory, London, and Robert Honeybourne, at the German Glass Manufactory, Stourbridge.[200]

Stuart's last payment was made on March 12, 1781, nearly a year before the opening party that Walpole attended.[201] Although the great room was not undertaken until 1790, Bonomi's drawings for it are dated 1782, and his first payment was made in July 1783, suggesting that he immediately succeeded Stuart.[202] Some of the luxury tradesmen, such as the painter Robert Smirke (paid in March 1782), the wallpaper manufacturer Thomas Bromwich (paid in April 1782), and the painter G. B. Cipriani (paid in January 1783), may have been introduced by either Stuart or Bonomi. Who suggested the creation of the Feather Room is unknown. It was being considered in 1782 and was made up on framed canvases by Betty Tull, to whom Mrs. Montagu gave over the Octagon Room at Sandleford Priory for "the feather manufactory." It was not opened until 1791.[203]

Mrs. Montagu died at Montagu House in 1800. She left it to her brother's son, Matthew Robinson. The Robinsons remained in occupation until 1874, when Mrs. Montagu's lease expired, and it reverted to the ground landlord, the first Viscount Portman. It was unusual for a ground landlord to find himself in possession of such a palatial and extravagantly decorated private house, and Lord Portman sensibly decided to live in it, adding a *porte-cochère* to the front door.[204] It remained the Portmans' town house until 1941, when it was gutted by an incendiary bomb.[205]

Royal Commissions

Stuart became serjeant painter to the Office of Public Works in 1764, with responsibility for all painting assignments at the royal palaces. Little information has surfaced about the actual work he may have undertaken; but recent research has suggested that he may have contributed to one, possibly two royal interiors at Buckingham House (renamed the Queen's House in about 1762, now Buckingham Palace) and at Windsor Castle.[206] The Saloon at Buckingham House (see fig. 10-63) has a ceiling with coffered coves, a favorite device of Stuart's that appears in several of his London houses, including Montagu House and Holdernesse House (see figs. 5-95, 5-52) However, the ceiling must date from before Stuart's appointment, as the room was complete by 1763 when the Raphael Cartoons were hung there.[207] It is usually considered a collaboration

between Robert Adam, who designed the mantelpiece, and Sir William Chambers, who was certainly responsible for the wall decoration carried out after 1787 when the Cartoons were removed.[208] On stylistic grounds, however, it is possible that Stuart designed the ceiling, although no documentary evidence of this has surfaced.

The second royal interior on which Stuart may have worked is the King's Audience Chamber at Windsor Castle, now known as the Ante-throne Room. The chimneypiece was a close copy of that in the Admiral's study at Greenwich Hospital, designed by Stuart in about 1765-69 (see fig. 8-4), which strongly indicates that Stuart was involved in the decoration of this room. Unfortunately,

Fig. 5-99. "The King's Audience Chamber at Windsor Castle." Hand-colored aquatint, engraved by W. J. Bennett, after a drawing by C. Wild. From W. H. Pyne, *History of Royal Residences . . .* , vol. 1 (1819): pl. 16. Courtesy of the Art and Architecture Collection, Miriam and Ira D. Wallach Division of Art, Prints and Photographs, The New York Public Library, Astor, Lenox and Tilden Foundations.

substantial alterations by Jeffry Wyatville in about 1824–30 swept away any work attributable to Stuart. The eighteenth-century scheme of decoration is only known through a painting of W. H. Pyne, subsequently reproduced in a three-volume work, *Royal Residences* (1819; fig. 5-99).

★ ★ ★

Of Stuart's London houses, Harcourt House is gone, as is 45 Harley Street. The bomb-damaged Montagu House was demolished in 1945,[209] and in 1964 Holdernesse House was swept away. Stuart's scheme at 23 Hill Street, only rediscovered in 2003, lost its chimneypieces to thieves shortly after that. As this book goes to press, Lichfield House is in private hands and is inaccessible to researchers. Only Spencer House has been restored to its former glory and is open to public view. If Spencer House were Stuart's only surviving town house commission, he would still be judged one of the most remarkable designers of the eigh-

teenth century. His suite of first-floor reception rooms was described in 1982 as "the earliest and most important Neoclassical interior in Europe."[210]

Stuart may not have had as many London commissions as his two great rivals, Sir William Chambers and Robert Adam, but he still played an important role in the London building world. Stuart's interiors and facades were discussed in the clubs and societies of London's intellectual circles. His designs were studied and sketched by fellow architects: Adam at Spencer House and John Carter at Lichfield House and Holdernesse House, among others. Stuart wrote to fellow Dilettanti member Thomas Anson during 1764 that "your house is a topic of much conversation among the Connoisseurs in Architecture."[211] These much-discussed buildings, together with the 1762 publication of volume 1 of *Antiquities of Athens,* written with Nicholas Revett, played an influential role in the propagation of neoclassical taste in Georgian England.

1. This house was demolished in the nineteenth century, and there is no record of its appearance. Lesley Lewis, "Stuart and Revett: Their Literary and Architectural Careers," *Journal of the Warburg Institute* 2 (1938–39): 137.

2. Giles Worsley, "Out from Adam's Shadow," *Country Life* 186 (14 May 1992): 102.

3. Robert Adam to James Adam, 11 December 1758, Clerk of Penicuik Mss. GD18-4854, National Archives of Scotland, Edinburgh.

4. George E. Cokayne, *The Complete Peerage, or A History of the House of Lords . . .*, vol. 12, pt. 1 (London: St. Catherine's Press, 1953): 153, 489.

5. Romney Sedgwick, *The House of Commons, 1715–1754*, vol. 2 (London: H.M.S.O, 1970): 433.

6. Joseph Friedman, *Spencer House: Chronicle of a Great London Mansion* (London: Zwemmer, 1993): 36–37, n. 5, citing Add. Ms. 32,915, fol. 115, BL.

7. John Ingamells, *A Dictionary of British and Irish Travellers in Italy 1701–1800* (New Haven and London: Paul Mellon Centre for Studies in British Art, Yale University Press, 1997): 882–84.

8. Friedman, *Spencer House* (1993): 39–40, 43.

9. Ibid., 40.

10. Ibid., 32.

11. Ibid., 37.

12. Ibid., 43.

13. Cokayne, *Complete Peerage . . .* (1953): 153 n. f.

14. Ingamells, *Dictionary of British and Irish Travellers* (1997): 883; Friedman, *Spencer House* (1993): 55.

15. Paul Langford, *Public Life and the Propertied Englishman, 1689–1798* (Oxford: Clarendon Press; New York: Oxford University Press, 1991): 571, 572.

16. Friedman, *Spencer House* (1993): 28, 44; the employment of Paine has not previously appeared in print, but comes from Chatsworth Archives, Lady Burlington's vouchers.

17. Sedgwick, *House of Commons*, vol. 2 (1970): 492–93; Friedman, *Spencer House* (1993): 28.

18. Ibid., 44.

19. Roger White, "John Vardy 1718–65," in Roderick Brown, ed., *The Architectural Outsiders* (London: Waterstone, 1985): 75. For Poyntz, see Philip Woodfine, "Poyntz, Stephen (bap. 1685, d. 1750)," in *Oxford Dictionary of National Biography*, ed. Henry C. G. Matthew and Brian Harrison, vol. 45 (Oxford University Press, 2004): 198–99.

20. Howard Colvin, *Biographical Dictionary of British Architects, 1600–1840*, 3rd ed. (New Haven and London: Yale University Press, 1995): 1010; Friedman, *Spencer House* (1993): 69; White, "John Vardy" (1985): 68.

21. Colvin, *Biographical Dictionary* (1995): 426.

22. Ibid., 938.

23. Friedman, *Spencer House* (1993): 86.

24. For signed drawing see ibid., 67 and 107 (dining room; dated 1755); 122 (dated 1757); and 81 (west elevation, dated 1759); for those dated 1758, see ibid., 67 (dining room), 99 (Palm Room), 102 (anteroom), and 107 (dining room). See also ibid., 89.

25. Ibid., 76, 84, 88 and 189.

26. Ibid., 88.

27. Ibid., 344–45.

28. John, seventh Earl Spencer, "Spencer House—II," *Country Life* 60 (6 November 1926): 700 and 703.

29. £3,636 6s. 10d. was paid for Vardy's own use, and £12,701 11s. 6d. was paid to him to settle bills from named tradesmen.

30. Colvin, *Biographical Dictionary* (1995): 1010.

31. Friedman, *Spencer House* (1993): 68 (proposal drawing).

32. Ibid., 48.

33. Ibid., 188.

34. Spencer, "Spencer House—II," (1926): 700.

35. Ibid., 703.

36. Ibid., 700.

37. Ibid.

38. Friedman, *Spencer House* (1993): 134.

39. Ibid., 67.

40. Ibid., 68.

41. Ibid., 134. Friedman notes that the attribution to Scheemakers was a "tradition already established in the lifetime of the second Earl Spencer," and he cites Thomas Frognall Dibdin, *Bibliotheca Spenceriana . . .*, vol. 3 (London: Longman, Hurst, Rees and Co., 1814–15): 509. For Scheemakers's relationship with Stuart see chap. 9, by Greg Sullivan, in this volume.

42. Friedman, *Spencer House* (1993): 134.

43. Ibid., 89.

44. Ibid., 99.

45. Ibid., 136.

46. Ibid., 88.

47. Ibid., 136.

48. Ibid., 89.

49. Ibid., 141.

50. Ibid., 151.

51. Ibid., 171.

52. Ibid., 150, 152–53.

53. Ibid., 174, 176.

54. Ibid., 186–87, 344–45.

55. Arthur Young, *A Six Weeks Tour through the Southern Counties of England and Wales*, 3rd ed. (London: W. Strahan, W. Nicholl, T. Cadell; Salisbury: B. Collins; Edinburgh: J. Balfour, 1772): 112.

56. Ibid.

57. These Vardy drawings are in the Department of Prints and Drawings, Victoria and Albert Museum, and Sir John Soane's Museum, London.

58. Typescript notes for the restoration of Spencer House (by Joseph

Friedman), n.d., n.p., Red Box file on Spencer House, Department of Furniture and Woodwork, Victoria and Albert Museum, London.

59. Ibid.

60. Young, *Six Weeks Tour* (1772): 112.

61. Kerry Bristol, "James Stuart and the London Building Trades," *Georgian Group Journal* 13 (2003): 2; Friedman, *Spencer House* (1993): 139.

62. Typescript notes, Red Box file on Spencer House, Department of Furniture and Woodwork, Victoria and Albert Museum, London.

63. Young, *Six Weeks Tour* (1772): 112.

64. Bristol, "Stuart and the London Building Trades" (2003): 4–5.

65. Friedman, *Spencer House* (1993): 141–42.

66. Ibid., 133.

67. Typescript notes, Red Box file on Spencer House, Department of Furniture and Woodwork, Victoria and Albert Museum, London.

68. Friedman, *Spencer House* (1993): 344–45. The payments are to Joseph Rose on 23 December 1758 and 17 February 1759, and to Thomas Clark on 25 May 1759.

69. Ibid.

70. Young, *Six Weeks Tour* (1772): 113.

71. Friedman, *Spencer House* (1993): 151.

72. Though Stuart will have seen the original building during his stay in Rome; see Antoine Desgodets [Desgodetz], *Les Édifices antiques de Rome, dessinés et mesurés très exactement* (Paris: J. B. Cognard, 1682): 109, fig. 20.

73. Lord Villiers to Lady Spencer, 4 May 1763, cited in Typescript notes, Red Box file on Spencer House, Department of Furniture and Woodwork, Victoria and Albert Museum, London.

74. Lord Villers to Lady Spencer, 1 February 1764, "called the other day in St. James's Place and had the pleasure to find that the ceiling in the Great Room quite finished and ready for the gilders." Cited in ibid.

75. Bristol, "Stuart and the London Building Trades" (2003): 2.

76. Young, *Six Weeks Tour* (1772): 114.

77. Colvin, *Biographical Dictionary* (1995): 939.

78. Friedman, *Spencer House* (1993): 187.

79. John Wilton-Ely, "Pompeian and Etruscan Tastes . . . ," in *The Functioning and Fashioning of the British Country House*, ed. Gervase Jackson-Stops, Studies in the History of Art, vol. 25 (Washington, D.C.: National Gallery of Art; Hanover, NH: University Press of New England, 1989), 51–73.

80. Ibid.

81. David Watkin et al., *A House in Town: 22 Arlington Street, Its Owners and Builders,* ed. Peter Campbell (London: B. T. Batsford, 1984): opposite 112; Mark Girouard, "44 Berkeley Square, London," *Country Life* 132 (27 December 1962): 1651.

82. Friedman, *Spencer House* (1993): 175.

83. Young, *Six Weeks Tour* (1772): 114.

84. Friedman, *Spencer House* (1993): 218.

85. Ibid., 238, 245.

86. Ibid., 268.

87. Ibid., 249, 263, 264–6, 263, 279, 289.

88. Ibid., 273, 275, 279.

89. Ibid., 292–339, 350–51.

90. Gervase Jackson-Stops, "Spencer House, London," *Country Life* 184 (29 November 1990), 42–47; Elizabeth Lambert, "The Rebirth of Spencer House," *Architectural Digest* 48 (February 1991): 134–43, 200, 202; Stephen Jones, "Roman Taste and Greek Gusto: The Society of Dilettanti and the Building of Spencer House, London," *Antiques* (June 1992): 968–77; Giles Worsley, "Spencer House, London," *Country Life* 186 (24/31 December 1992): 38–41.

91. H. M. Scott, "D'Arcy, Robert fourth earl of Holdernesse (1718–1778)," in *Oxford Dictionary of National Biography,* vol. 15 (Oxford University Press, 2004): 132–34.

92. Ibid.

93. John Harris, "Sion Hill: A Postscript," *London Gardener, or Gardener's Intelligencer* 6 (2000–2001): 81.

94. In 1751 Holdernesse paid rates for 13 Hanover Square (Egerton Ms. 3497, BL); from 1752 he paid rates for a house on the west side of Arlington Street, while his house in Privy Garden, Whitehall, was let to Lord Sandwich (MD 6610/3, Sheffield Archives). Sandwich, who wanted to be released from his tenancy, tried to persuade Holdernesse to rebuild on that site at the end of April 1761; at that moment, six weeks after his dismissal from office, he was presumably not committed to another site; see Bristol, "Stuart and the Genesis of the Greek Revival" (1997): 307 n. 946; Bristol, "Stuart and the London Building Trades" (2003): 10, n. 9.

95. Arthur Oswald, "Londonderry House, Park Lane," *Country Life* 82 (10 July 1937): 42. He may not have moved in then, however, as he paid rates on the Arlington Street house until 1768 (MD 6610/3, Sheffield Archives). Carter sketchbook, "Drawings—made from designs of Flowers & Pateras for Ceilings. . . . Collected chiefly from Noblemen's Houses" (1766), Victoria and Albert Museum, Prints and Drawings, D.386-1890 pressmark 93.D.4.

96. Coke, *The Letters and Journals of Lady Mary Coke,* vol. 2, ed. Hon. J. A. Home (Edinburgh: David Douglas, 1889–96): 15]; quoted in Christopher Simon Sykes, *Private Palaces: Life in the Great London Houses* (New York: Viking, 1986): 185.

97. Quoted in David Pearce, *London's Mansions* (London: B. T. Batsford 1986): 158, fig. 115 cap.

98. Egerton Ms. 3497, fol. 64, BL.

99. John Harris, "Le Rouge's Sion Hill: A Garden by Brown," *London Gardener, or Gardener's Intelligencer* 5 (1999–2000): 24–28; J. Harris, "Sion Hill" (2000–2001): 81; Giles Worsley, "Stuart at Sion," *Country Life* 184 (4 October 1990): 187.

100. Giles Worsley, "Hornby Castle, Yorkshire," *Country Life* 183 (29 June 1989): 188–93.

101. Egerton Ms. 3497, passim, BL.

102. MD 6610/5, Sheffield Archives. Miss Ruth Harman has kindly informed me that Phillips and Shakespeare had previously worked at Holdernesse's house in Arlington Street from 1758 to 1766 (MD 6610/3),

at his wine vaults in Bolton Row in 1765 (MD 6610/6), and at Sion Hill between 1760 and 1769 (MD 6610/1).

103. Colvin, *Biographical Dictionary* (1995): 751, 859–60; Bristol, "Stuart and the Genesis of the Greek Revival" (1997): 64. Holdernesse had first heard of Stuart in 1750, when ambassador to the Netherlands. In that year Sir James Gray, British Resident in Venice, wrote to Holderness seeking his assistance for Stuart on a family matter. In his letter, Gray described Stuart as "a very ingenious man."

104. Oswald, "Londonderry House" (1937): 42. Carter sketchbook, "Drawings made from designs of Flowers and Pateras for Ceiling . . . collected Chiefly from Noblemens Houses" (1766), Victoria and Albert Museum, Prints and Drawings, D.386-1890 pressmark 93.D.4.

105. Oswald, "Londonderry House" (1937): 38, 42–44.

106. David Watkin, *Athenian Stuart: Pioneer of the Greek Revival* (London: George Allen and Unwin, 1982): 42.

107. Ibid., fig. 45 cap.

108. Friedman, *Spencer House* (1993): 148.

109. Watkin, *Athenian Stuart* (1982): 42.

110. Ibid., 134.

111. H. Clifford Smith, "A Catalogue and Valued Inventory of the Furniture and Works of Art, Londonderry House, Park Lane," typescript (1939): 146, copy in the National Art Library, Victoria and Albert Museum, London.

112. Ibid., 148.

113. Ibid., 147.

114. Richard Hewlings, "The Link Room at Chiswick House: Lord Burlington as Antiquarian," *Apollo* 141 (January 1995): 28–29.

115. Scott, "D'Arcy, Robert" (2004): 132, 134.

116. Oswald, "Londonderry House" (1937): 38; Bristol, "Stuart and the Genesis of the Greek Revival" (1997): 308.

117. Sedgwick, *House of Commons*, vol. 2 (1970): 415-16; Ingamells, *Dictionary of British and Irish Travellers* (1997): 21.

118. Philip Yorke, "Memorandum of a Journey into Staffordshire 1748," in *The Marchioness Grey of West Park,* ed. Joyce Godber, Bedfordshire Historical Record Society annual, vol. 47 (1968): 137.

119. James Lees-Milne, "Shugborough, Staffordshire—I," *Connoisseur* 164 (April 1967): 211–15; Bristol, "Stuart and the Genesis of the Greek Revival" (1997): 270–72.

120. F. H. W. Sheppard, ed., *Survey of London*, vol. 29 (London: Athlone Press for the Greater London Council, 1960): 142.

121. Ibid., 143.

122. Bristol, "Stuart and the Genesis of the Greek Revival" (1997): 292.

123. Sheppard, ed., *Survey of London* (1960): 143.

124. Bristol, "Stuart and the Genesis of the Greek Revival" (1997): 298, n.910.

125. Sheppard, ed., *Survey of London* (1960): 143.

126. Ibid.

127. Bristol, "Stuart and the Genesis of the Greek Revival" (1997): 288; Sheppard, ed., *Survey of London* (1960): 143.

128. Sheppard, ed., *Survey of London* (1960): 143; Eileen Harris, *British Architectural Books and Writers, 1556–1785* (Cambridge, UK, and New York: Cambridge University Press, 1990): 446.

129. Sheppard, ed., *Survey of London* (1960): 143.

130. Ibid., 148.

131. Giles Worsley, "The First Greek Revival Architecture," *Burlington Magazine* 127 (April 1985): 226–29.

132. Bristol, "Stuart and the London Building Trades" (2003): 7; Terry Friedman, *James Gibbs* (New Haven and London: Paul Mellon Centre for Studies in British Art and Yale University Press, 1984): 295; Colvin, *Biographical Dictionary* (1995): 835–36.

133. Sheppard, ed., *Survey of London* (1960): 143; Bristol, "Stuart and the Genesis of the Greek Revival" (1997): 288.

134. Bristol, "Stuart and the Genesis of the Greek Revival" (1997): 288, 297. For Bromwich, see Geoffrey Beard and Christopher Gilbert, eds., *Dictionary of English Furniture Makers, 1660–1840* (Leeds: Furniture History Society and W. S. Maney and Son, 1986): 110; and E. A. Entwistle, "Eighteenth Century London Paperstainers-Thomas Bromwich at the Golden Lyon on Ludgate Hill," *Connoisseur* (November 1952): 106–10. For Russell, see Peter Leach, "The Life and Work of James Paine," Ph.D. diss., University of Oxford, 1975, 225.

135. Watkin, *Athenian Stuart* (1982): 43.

136. Bristol, "Stuart and the Genesis of the Greek Revival" (1997): 295–96.

137. Sheppard, ed., *Survey of London* (1960): 148–49.

138. Pearce, *London's Mansions* (1986): 86; Sheppard, ed., *Survey of London* (1960): 142.

139. Pearce, *London's Mansions* (1986): 86.

140. Bristol, "Stuart and the Genesis of the Greek Revival" (1997): 296.

141. *Antiquities,* vol. 3 (1797): chap. 9, pl. 3.

142. Sheppard, ed., *Survey of London* (1960): 148.

143. Ibid., 153–54.

144. Cokayne, *Complete Peerage . . .* , vol. 11 (1953): 71.

145. Barbara Brandon Schnorrenburg, "Montagu, Elizabeth (1718–1800)," in *The Oxford Dictionary of National Biography,* vol. 38 (Oxford University Press, 2004): 721; John A. Dussinger, "Middleton, Conyers (1683–1750)," in ibid., 53.

146. Dussinger, "Middleton, Conyers" (2004): 53.

147. Schnorrenburg, "Montagu, Elizabeth" (2004): 721.

148. Ibid., 720–25.

149. Mrs. Montagu to Mrs. Robinson, 29 December 1779, Add. Ms. 40,663, pp. 96–98, BL.

150. Chancellor, *Private Palaces* (1908): 331.

151. Ibid., 332.

152. Ibid., 331; Schnorrenburg, "Montagu, Elizabeth" (2004): 722.

153. Lyttelton to Mrs. Montagu, 21 October 1758, Montagu Papers MO 1280, Henry E. Huntington Library, San Marino, California; cited in Kerry Bristol, "22 Portman Square: Mrs. Montagu and her 'Palais de la vieillesse'," *British Art Journal* 2 (Summer 2001): 72.

154. Lyttelton to Mrs. Montagu, 19 January 1759, ibid., MO 1495; cited in Bristol, "22 Portman Square" (2001): 72.

155. Lyttelton to Mrs. Montagu, 21 October 1758, ibid., MO 1280; cited in Bristol, "22 Portman Square" (2001): 72.

156. Mrs. Montagu to Lyttelton, 15 January 1760, ibid., MO 1394; cited in Bristol, "Stuart and the Genesis of the Greek Revival" (1997): 159.

157. Lyttelton to Mrs. Montagu, October 1758, ibid., MO 1280; cited in Bristol, "22 Portman Square" (2001): 72.

158. Arthur T. Bolton, "James Stuart at Portman House and Spencer House," *Country Life* 37 supplement (1 May 1915): 7★.

159. Rosemary Baird, "'The Queen of the Bluestockings': Mrs Montagu's House at 23 Hill Street Rediscovered," *Apollo* 158 (August 2003): 45.

160. Stuart to Mrs Montagu 14 July 1759, Montagu Papers, MO 5135, Henry E. Huntington Library, San Marino, California; Mrs. Montagu to Lyttelton, 15 January 1760, ibid., MO 1394; cited in Bristol, "22 Portman Square" (2001): 72.

161. There is some argument about the date of the commission; Kerry Bristol suggests that it was begun in 1760 and completed 1772; see Bristol, "22 Portman Square" (2001): 72; Rosemary Baird suggests Stuart began work in 1766; see Baird, "'Queen of the Bluestockings'" (2003): 48.

162. Mrs. Montagu to Lord Lyttelton, 15 January 1760, Montagu Papers, MO 1394, Henry E. Huntington Library, San Marino, California; cited in Bristol, "Stuart and the Genesis of the Greek Revival" (1997): 159.

163. Baird's phrase, citing Mrs. Montagu to Mr. Montagu, 21 April 1766, ibid., MO 2603, in "'Queen of the Bluestockings'" (2003): 48.

164. Baird, "'Queen of the Bluestockings'" (2003): 48–49.

165. The identification of the central figure as Aurora is made by Baird in "'Queen of the Bluestockings',", (2003): 48.

166. Mrs. Montagu to Leonard Smelt, 3 November 1767, Montagu Papers, MO 4994, Henry E. Huntington Library, San Marino, California; cited in Kerry Bristol, "The Painted Rooms of 'Athenian' Stuart," *Georgian Group Journal* 10 (2000): 169.

167. For Rathfarnham, see Samuel Lewis, *A Topographical Dictionary of Ireland . . .*, vol. 2 (London: S. Lewis & Co., 1837). Lewis writes: "the entrance to the house from the terrace on which it stands is by a portico of eight Doric columns which support a dome painted in fresco with the signs of the zodiac."

168. See John Cooke and John Maule, *An Historical Account of the Royal Hospital for Seamen at Greenwich* (London: the authors, 1789). Cooke and Maule mention the spring clock "ornamented with the signs of the zodiac, beautifully carved and gilt, from a design of the late Mr. Stuart, when Surveyor of the Hospital." The clock is now lost. Thanks are due to horologist Peter Linstead-Smith for information about Holmes.

169. Lyttelton to Mrs. Montagu, October 1758, Montagu Papers, MO 1280, Henry E. Huntington Library, San Marino, California; cited in Bristol, "22 Portman Place" (2001): 72.

170. Mrs. Montagu to Leonard Smelt, 3 November 1767, ibid., MO 4994; cited in Bristol, "22 Portman Place" (2001): 72.

171. E. Beresford Chancellor, *Private Palaces of London, Past and Present* (London: Kegan Paul, Trench, Trübner, 1908): 331–32.

172. Stuart to Anson 17 June 1769, Lichfield Ms. D615/P(S)/1/6/26, Staffordshire Record Office.

173. Stuart to Anson, 23 September 1769, ibid., D615/P(S)/1/6/27.

174. Kerry Bristol, "The Painted Rooms of 'Athenian' Stuart," *Georgian Group Journal* 10 (2000): 164–74.

175. Chancellor, *Private Palaces* (1908): 326.

176. Schnorrenburg, "Montagu, Elizabeth" (2004): 723.

177. Bristol, "22 Portman Square" (2001): 73; Bolton, "James Stuart at Portman House"(1915): 8★.

178. Mrs. Montagu to Leonard Smelt, 25 April 1780, Montagu Papers, MO 5026, Henry E. Huntington Library, San Marino, California; cited in Bristol, "22 Portman Place" (2001): 79.

179. For example see Mrs. Montagu to Leonard Smelt, 25 April 1780, ibid., MO 5025: "I know, by experience, Mr Stuart is apt to forget his promises are not fulfill'd, & talks of designs for chimneypieces, & Pillars &c, &c which exist only in his brain, & when I write to ye workmen who are to execute them to know why they are not finishd they answer, they will set about them the moment Mr Stuart gives them the designs. I wrote a most indignant letter to Mr Egginton at Birmingham to know why some orders which my architect had given them more than a twelvemonth before were unexecuted, he answerd that he had not received thse orders, & behold ye designs were lying in ye dust & confusion of Mr Stuarts study in a very incomplete & unfinished state. Has he given Evans the Carpenters head workman such directions for the Pillars as will enable him to finish them. Why does he not send me ye designs for ye chimneypiece in that room?" Cited in Bristol, "22 Portman Place" (2001): 78–79.

180. Bristol, "Stuart and the London Building Trades" (2003): 8.

181. For Gandon as Stuart's assistant see Mrs. Montagu to Matthew Boulton, August [1780], Boulton Papers, Ms. Box 330, no. 27, Birmingham City Archives; cited in Bristol, "22 Portman Place" (2001): 76. For Stuart and Gandon as "my architects" see ibid., Ms. Box 330, no. 19; cited in Bristol, "22 Portman Place" (2001): 72.

182. Bristol, "22 Portman Square" (2001): 78–80.

183. Leicester House (1635), Bedford House (1638–40), Clarendon House (1664–67), Berkeley House (1665), Burlington House (1667–68), Montagu House (Bloomsbury) (1675–79), Monmouth House (1681), Buckingham House (1702–5), Powis House (1713), Chandos House (1720), Harcourt House (ca. 1725), or Bingley House (1725–26).

184. Bristol, "22 Portman Square" (2001): 76, figs. 4 (Mrs. Montagu's sketch plan, dated 20 August 1780 and sent to Matthew Boulton) and 5 (survey plan, dated 1872) provide the information from which the following description is taken.

185. Watkin, *Athenian Stuart* (1982): 47.

186. Ibid., 49.

187. John Carter, "An Archivault, and its Base, at Lord Holdernesses; Stuart Archt.," in "Drawings—made from designs of Flowers & Pateras for Ceilings. . . . Collected chiefly from Noblemen's Houses" (1766):

74, Victoria and Albert Museum, Prints and Drawings, D.386-1890 pressmark 93.D.4. This correspondence between the two screens was noted by Watkin, *Athenian Stuart* (1982): 49.

188. This is what Mrs. Montagu wrote on her sketch plan of the room, in Mrs. Montagu to Matthew Boulton, 20 August [1780], Boulton Papers, Ms. 3782/12/93/17, Birmingham City Archives.

189. See Watkin, *Athenian Stuart* (1982): 48—"The elaborate ceiling is a familiar Adam pattern of intersecting circles."

190. Sketch plan in Mrs. Montagu to Matthew Boulton, 20 August [1780], Boulton Papers Ms. 3782/12/93/17, Birmingham City Archives.

191. Watkin, *Athenian Stuart* (1982): 49.

192. Bristol, "Stuart and the Genesis of the Greek Revival" (1997): 320 n. 982.

193. Bristol, "22 Portman Square" (2001): 74.

194. Cited in ibid.

195. Ibid.

196. Ibid., 81.

197. Ibid.

198. Ibid., 82.

199. Ibid., 78—80.

200. Ibid., 74—78.

201. Ibid., 80 and n. 63.

202. Ibid., 80.

203. Ibid., 81—82.

204. Chancellor, *Private Palaces* (1908): 334.

205. Bristol, "22 Portman Square" (2001): 83.

206. Worsley, "Out from Adam's Shadow" (1993): 101—2.

207. John Harris and Michael Snodin, eds., *Sir William Chambers Architect to George III* (New Haven and London: Yale University Press in association with the Courtauld Gallery, Courtauld Institute of Art, London, 1996): 48.

208. Ibid.

209. Bristol, "22 Portman Square" (2001): 83.

210. Geraldine Norman, "Trust hopes to take over Spencer House," *Times* [London] (20 December 1982): 2.

211. Stuart to Anson, "About Sept. 1764" [date penciled at top of page], Lichfield Ms. D615/P(S)/1/6/12, Staffordshire Record Office.

Fig. 6-1. James Stuart. Design for the decoration of a closet, Wimbledon Park, Surrey, ca. 1758. Pen and ink, colored washes. RIBA Library Drawings Collection, London, SD 62/6 (1). *Checklist no. 67.*

CHAPTER 6

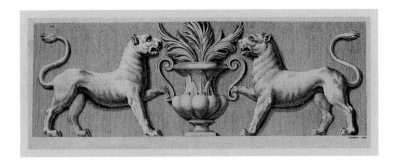

"THE PUREST TASTE" — JAMES "ATHENIAN" STUART'S WORK IN VILLAS AND COUNTRY HOUSES

JULIUS BRYANT

Stuart's architectural career has traditionally been judged by considering two examples of his work: the state rooms he created on the first floor of Spencer House and a group of unexecuted designs for Kedleston Hall (see figs. 6-30 to 6-33). Both have served to illustrate comparisons between Stuart and Robert Adam, between "the Athenian" and "Bob the Roman," in which Stuart's promise is seen as unfulfilled due to his shortcomings as a practical architect and his weakness for drink. A richer understanding of Stuart's contribution to eighteenth-century architecture requires a wider range of examples; the true extent of his work for country houses, and more specifically villas, has been emerging since the 1980s thanks to new research.[1] While no great "lost" commissions have come to light, the pattern of projects for remodelings and refurbishments provides further evidence of Stuart's versatility and helps locate his most significant interests and influence.

Stuart's profession was not that of a practical architect, managing a drawing office and team of workmen, like Adam and Chambers. More like William Kent, Stuart was a painter-turned-polymath, someone who in Rome, in Grand Tourist circles, could be readily identified as a cicerone, a personal trainer-in-taste to an aspirant gentle-man connoisseur (see chap. 3). Both Stuart and Kent lightened their scholarship with charm, as amusing, gregarious characters. Like Kent, Stuart had to find a new line on his eventual return to London, after about thirteen years abroad. Unlike Kent, he was also an antiquary, one who staked his reputation on the accuracy of his survey of Greek buildings. He turned his hand to the arrangement of art collections he had helped to form, and hence to the redecoration and remodeling of interiors. Stuart's eventual profession, from fan-painter-turned-cicerone to architectural decorator, depended on the support of the Grand Tour alumni, the circle institutionalized as the Society of Dilettanti (see chap. 4). In an expanding and competitive London where ambitious architects, painters, sculptors, and other specialists sought to establish their trades as professions outside the old city with its guild system, Stuart's profession could afford to continue undefined, safe at first under the private patronage of the Dilettanti network. The legacy is still with us today, for his professional heirs are not businessmen architects but those versatile consultants, from John Fowler to David Mlinaric, whose eye for color, textures, composition, and the use of collections can make all the difference to other people's buildings. It is from this professional perspective that Stuart's work in country houses makes most sense.

Fig. 6-2. James Stuart. Sketch of a landscape with buildings, ca. 1748–50. Pen and pencil. From Stuart's sketchbook (ca. 1748–50): fol. 13. RIBA Library Drawings Collection, London, SKB/336/2 [L 3/4]. *Checklist no. 8.*

When Stuart returned from Athens in 1755 his greatest market asset beyond his social set of potential patrons was the promise of the fruits of his researches with Nicholas Revett. The traditional explanation for the seven-year delay in publishing *Antiquities of Athens* (1762) is his "natural dilatoriness" and his need to revise the entire text to counter a rival book, Le Roy's *Ruines des plus beaux Monuments de la Grèce,* which appeared in 1758 (see chap. 1).[2] But if Stuart can be credited with some business sense, it would be his shrewdness to secure commissions prepublication, to capitalize on the exclusivity of his design sources before they became widely known and available through engravings. The great expectations of a new vocabulary of design, one that was to be nothing less than the "true style," gave Stuart the means to make his clients members of an artistic avant-garde. Many of his more original designs outside London date from before *Antiquities* appeared, and this may be the reason why. Of course the fact that he undertook these commissions while he was writing, editing, correcting plates, and designing bindings will have contributed to the delay in producing *Antiquities.*

The earliest evidence of Stuart's interest in the architecture of country houses and villas lies in one of his two surviving notebooks (see figs. 3-3, 3-21). His dual interests are immediately apparent as it was begun from both ends; one end is devoted to elevations and plans of buildings, and of buildings in landscape settings (fig. 6-2), while the other end contains a first draft of a treatise on the Venetian

school of painters, in which Giorgione, Titian, and Tintoretto are praised.[3] In the preface to *Antiquities,* Stuart explains the origins of the book in 1748 when he and Revett "were then at Rome, where we had already employed 6 or 7 years in the study of Painting."[4] The "Proposals" for *Antiquities of Athens,* published in Rome in 1748, offered far more than the prospect of measured outlines of Athenian buildings, and confirm Stuart's interests beyond those of a budding architect or architectural historian. He held the belief that Greek art was not a style of choice but rather "perfection" itself. Criticizing the inadequacy of travelers' written accounts he set out the scope of his project:

> For the best verbal descriptions cannot be supposed to convey so adequate an Idea, of the magnificence and elegance of Buildings; the fine form, expression, or proportion of Sculptures; the beauty and variety of a Country, or the exact Scene of any celebrated Action, as may be formed from drawings made on the spot, with diligence and fidelity, by the hand of an Artist.[5]

Architects are not addressed as the intended sponsors or audience for the project; rather, he tempts "those Gentlemen who are lovers of the Arts; and . . . those Artists who aim at perfection," for they "must be more pleased, and better instructed, the nearer they can approach the Fountain-Head of their Art."[6]

Stuart's only known design for a country house is an

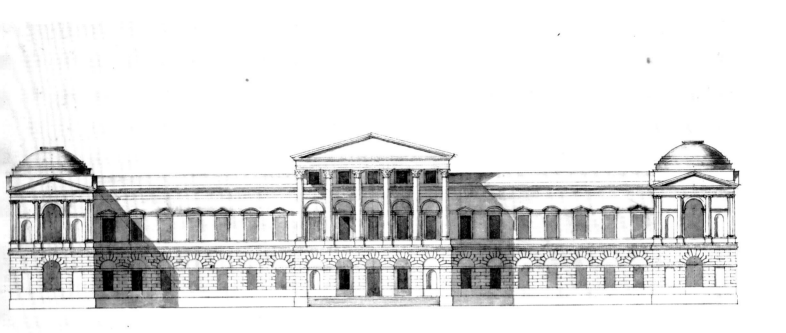

Fig. 6-3. James Stuart. Design for a country house, ca. 1750s. Pen and ink. The Bodleian Library, University of Oxford, Gough Misc. Antiq. Fol. 4, no. 22.

Fig 6-4. James Stuart. Sketch for part elevation of a country house, ca. 1748–50. Pen and pencil, ink wash. From Stuart's sketchbook (ca. 1748–50): fol. 60. RIBA Library Drawings Collection, London, SKB/336/2 [L 3/4]. *Checklist no. 8.*

ambitious elevation, thought to date from around 1750, now in the Bodleian Library, Oxford (fig. 6-3).[7] It shows a twenty-five bay building in the Palladian tradition, based on a series of drawings made in Stuart's sketchbook while he was in Venice, preparing to sail for Athens (fig. 6-4), and on two related drawings, also now in the RIBA collections at the Victoria and Albert Museum.[8] Six other sketchbook drawings relate to Francesco Maria Preti's Villa Pisani, which Stuart saw under construction at Stra between March and July 1750 (fig. 6-5).[9] Potential sources closer to home

for Stuart's design for a country house include Colen Campbell's Wanstead House and William Kent's designs for the Houses of Parliament. It is likely to have been drawn by Stuart for Charles Watson-Wentworth, second Marquess of Rockingham who arrived in Rome on the Grand Tour in 1749 (see fig. 4-10).[10] His support of Stuart must date from that time as he funded Stuart's first archaeological publication, *De Obelisco Caesaris Augusti* (1750; see chap. 3). As Lord Malton (he succeeded his father in 1750, when he was twenty, after he returned to England) he is

Fig. 6-5. James Stuart. "Prospettiva di Pisani," sketch of the garden front of the Villa Pisani, Stra, ca. 1748–50. Pen and pencil. From Stuart's sketchbook (ca. 1748–50): fol. 50r. RIBA Library Drawings Collection, London, SKB/336/2 [L 3/4]. *Checklist no. 8.*

the first on the list in Stuart's sketchbook of "Names of the Gentleman who have promised to subscribe our Attica."[11] Stuart may have made the design not as a proposal for a new façade for Wentworth Woodhouse but rather as a presentation drawing in its own right, one that Rockingham could show to his friends, as an example of the service that Stuart could provide on his return to England.

Wentworth Woodhouse

On September 28, 1755, months after his return, Stuart wrote to Rockingham asking to be sent the plan of Wentworth Woodhouse.[12] Rockingham may have interested Stuart in the dilemma of the vast double-fronted house when they were in Rome. The baroque west front, built 1725 – 28, had been superseded around 1734 by the Palladian east front, the longest country house façade in England (fig. 6-6). Both had been commissioned by the

Fig. 6-6. Ralph Tunnicliffe and Henry Flitcroft. East front of Wentworth Woodhouse, Yorkshire, principally 1730–39 (completed 1772). Additions by John Carr, 1782–84. Photographed in 1987. English Heritage / National Monuments Record 87/1905 89415.

Fig. 6-7a. The great hall, also called the Grand Saloon or Marble Saloon, Wentworth Woodhouse, Yorkshire, view from the southeast. Ornament designed by James Stuart, ca. 1755–68. Photographed in 1987. English Heritage / National Monuments Record BB93/2854. *Checklist no. 41.*

Fig. 6-7b. James Stuart. Bas reliefs in the great hall, Wentworth Woodhouse, Yorkshire, ca. 1755–68. Photographed in 1906. ©Country Life Picture Collection.

same patron but with no planned internal connection between them; indeed, they are almost a story apart in levels. Stuart's earliest known architectural commission was to modify the floor plan, an aspect of country house architecture he did not return to again. He wrote seeking the plan "in order to make those changes I mediate in the back of it next the Garden, & the Connexion between it & the new hall."[13] The offer may have been a necessary preliminary to the exercise of his greater gifts as a painter and designer of two-dimensional ornaments. He continues the letter by asking for "the Size of the three Pannels in the new dining Room that I may make Sketches for the Pictures to be Painted in them, & if I had a Print of the inside of the Grand Saloon that I should endeavour to ornament it in the purest taste I can imagine"[14]

The grand saloon (or great hall, as Rockingham called it) is a vast room measuring sixty feet square and forty feet high. It provides the setting for the eight marble copies of antique sculptures that Rockingham commissioned in Rome (fig. 6-7a).[15] The fifteen bas-relief stucco panels over the niches in the saloon were in place by 1768 when they were admired by diarist Arthur Young (fig. 6-7b).[16] A drawing by Stuart showing griffins flanking a floral sway may be a design for one of the panels (fig. 6-8).[17] Architecturally the grand saloon is an homage to Palladio via the Queen's House at Greenwich, but both lacked

Fig. 6-8. James Stuart. Overmantel bas relief of griffins in the great hall, Wentworth Woodhouse, Yorkshire, ca. 1755–68. Photographed in 1987. English Heritage / National Monuments Record BB93/2855.

relief sculpture. One precedent for Stuart's panels was the garden front of the Villa Medici in Rome but he may also have had in mind William Kent's Stone Hall at Houghton (fig. 6-9).[18] There, between 1726 and 1730, Michael Rysbrack supplied a series of bas-reliefs designed by Kent, exemplifying classical virtues in an iconographical program of overdoors based on antique reliefs Kent knew from engravings in Montfaucon's *L'Antiquité Éxpliquée* (1719 – 24) and Bellori's *Veteres Arcus Augustorum* (1690).[19]

In Stuart's "Proposal" for *Antiquities of Athens*, sculpture had been promised as well as views, plans, and elevations of buildings. Stuart offered "exact delineations of the Statues and Basso-relievos with which those Buildings are decorated. These sculptures we imagine will be extremely curious, as well on account of their workmanship, as of the subjects they represent."[20] In the proposed contents for the first two volumes, the phrase "enriched with Sculptures" occurs four times. The commitment to sculpture is also reiterated in *Antiquities* itself, where the penultimate paragraph opens:

Fig. 6-9. William Kent. The Stone Hall at Houghton Hall, Norfolk, ca. 1726–30. Bas reliefs sculpted by Michael Rysbrack. Photographed in 1951. English Heritage / National Monuments Record CC52/763.

I must likewise answer for whatever faults have been committed, either in delineating the Sculptures, or painting the Views, which are engraven in this Work: my utmost diligence however has been used, to render them faithful Representations of the Originals. The Sculptures were, for the most part, measured with the same care and exactness that was bestowed on the Architecture.[21]

In the fifteen panels for the grand saloon at Wentworth Woodhouse, Stuart gave his patron a tantalizing foretaste of *Antiquities* but kept them symmetrical and shallow (see figs. 6-7a, b). At the border between decorative plasterwork and sculpture, the panels look forward to an austere linear "true" style, one associated with the archaic origins of art; by comparison, Rysbrack's look back to the plasticity of the baroque.

Stuart also installed a plaster cast of Cardinal Albani's celebrated bas-relief of Emperor Hadrian's favorite, Antinous, in the hall of the baroque west side of Wentworth Woodhouse (fig. 6-10). One of the most prized masterpieces of antique sculpture, the original relief had been excavated in Hadrian's Villa in 1735 and was installed as an overmantel in a room designed around it in the Villa Albani on the outskirts of Rome in October 1762. Rockingham's cast would have been highly topical.[22] Further sculptural enrichments to the house included a chimneypiece or chimneypieces. In 1772 Horace Walpole noted "Stewart has given a design of one Chimneypiece but very ugly."[23] This may have been the "new Statuary enricht Chimney piece, with Sienna marble pilasters" made for Lady Rockingham's dressing room in 1764 by the master mason John Horobin, who was also paid for installing three more, apparently older chimneypieces.[24] A chimneypiece in the first-floor long gallery of the house has been ascribed to Stuart (fig. 6-11).[25] Another in a first-floor room at the west end of the house seems more promising (see fig. 4-11). The three paintings for the panels in the dining room no longer survive, but as Arthur Young described in 1770 "pannels, inclosing in wreaths four medallions,"[26] these were either painted medallions or plaster substitutes. Rockingham must have been satisfied with Stuart's contribution for he described him in 1773 as "my Friend Stuart — (whom I call the Athenian . . .) . . . the Father of all the Geniuses in architecture & Elegant designs which now exist here."[27]

Fig. 6-10. Antinous relief in the west entrance hall, Wentworth Woodhouse, Yorkshire. Plaster cast from the 2nd-century original, ca. 1762. Photographed in 1987. English Heritage / National Monuments Record BB93/2910.

Fig. 6-11. Attributed to James Stuart. Chimneypiece on the south wall of the long gallery, Wentworth Woodhouse, Yorkshire, late 1750s–early 1760s. Photographed in 1987. English Heritage / National Monuments Record BB93/2931. *Checklist no. 42.*

271

Fig. 6-12. Moses Griffith. *The West Front of Shugborough, Staffordshire*, 1769. Watercolor. Courtesy of Shugborough, The Anson Collection, SHUG.P.66 (The National Trust, UK). *Checklist no. 43.*

Shugborough

Stuart's client, Thomas Anson came closest to being to Stuart what Lord Burlington had been to William Kent: patron, benefactor, friend, collaborator, and tireless promoter of his work (see fig. 4-23). In 1740 Anson had traveled beyond the traditional frontiers of the Grand Tour and had visited Alexandria and Cairo (and possibly Greece); while Member of Parliament for Lichfield from 1747, he became friends with Dr. Seward, Josiah Wedgwood, and Matthew Boulton. Between 1765 and 1771 he formed a great art collection of 120 paintings and 100 sculptures, together with medals, through Joseph Nollekens, then in Rome, and the British Consul in Leghorn, Sir John Dick.[28] Stuart met his most important patron around 1756. At Shugborough, Anson introduced Stuart to skilled craftsmen and the practicalities of construction, for he had been employing workmen there for nearly fifteen years. Stuart thus met the sculptor Peter Scheemakers, with whom he would collaborate on church monuments (see chap. 9) and made contacts with Anson's neighbors as an architect and designer. For Shugborough, Stuart re-created some of the engravings in the first and third volumes of *Antiquities of Athens* (1762, 1794) as landmarks in the park (see figs. 7-1, 7-9). A founder-member of the Society of Dilettanti, Anson was a subscriber to *Antiquities*. He also gave Stuart his first great opportunity to shine in London when, in 1763, he commissioned him to design his town house, 15 St. James's Square (1763 – 66; see chap. 5).

The main house at Shugborough dated from the seventeenth century but had been enlarged by 1748 with two new wings and single-story links; the additions are attributed to Thomas Wright.[29] Anson probably commissioned Stuart to add the extra story to each link corridor to provide bedrooms and dressing rooms after 1762, as recorded in a view by Moses Griffith (fig. 6-12). He may also have commissioned him to supply furniture for the new rooms (see chap. 10). The house inventory made after Anson's death in 1773 records next to his bedchamber "Mr. Stewarts Painting Room."[30] The earliest reference known to Stuart working inside the main house is in a letter from Philip, Viscount Royston to his father, Philip Yorke, first Earl of Hardwicke, written at Shugborough on August 22, 1763. He described how his host had added:

> Appartments wch are fitted up & furnished with all the Elegance & ornaments wch the Arts of Italy & the Magnificence of China can afford. . . . I do not admire Stewart's Paintings in the Vestibule; they are hard, have no keeping, & the colouring is [illegible] I have not hinted this to Mr Anson.[31]

As William Kent had done, Stuart was persevering with his ambitions as a painter, using commissions for interiors to provide sufficient space for his art. Six days later Hardwicke replied:

Fig. 6-13. James Stuart. Cresting on the parapet on the west side of Shugborough, Staffordshire, ca. 1765–69. Courtesy of Shugborough (The National Trust, UK).

Fig. 6-14. Title-page vignette of Etruscan acroterion, with butting goats heads. Engraving. From Giovanni Battista Piranesi, *Osservazione di Gio. Battista Piranesi . . . E parere su l'architettura, con una prefazione ad un nuovo trattato della introduzione e del progresso delle belle arti in Europa ne'tempi antichi* (1765): 17. Courtesy of the Art and Architecture Collection, Miriam and Ira D. Wallach Division of Arts, Prints and Photographs, The New York Public Library, Astor, Lenox and Tilden Foundations.

the Owner of Shugborough will go on to comb, dress, & improve it, in the manner you represent. He has all the means of doing it in his hands. He had always Tast. . . . In Designs for Sculpture, He is I believe in the right to make use of Stewart's Scavoir-faire; but I wonder He suffers him to daub his House with his Pencil. . . . He is certainly no Painter.[32]

The painted "Vestibule" may have been the dressing room next to Anson's bedchamber. Outside, the parapet cresting featured anthemion and butting goat's heads (fig. 6-13) taken from an engraving in Giovanni Battista Piranesi's *Osservazione di Geo Battista Piranesi sopra la lettre de M. Mariette . . . E Parere su l'Architettura, con una Prefzione ad uno nuovo Trattato della Introduzione e del progresso delle Belle Arti in Europa ne' tempi antichi* (1764 – 65; fig. 6-14). Stuart's interest in Piranese is shown in a 1764 letter to Anson, in which he discussed Piranesi's work: "I have got Piranesi's Book at last. they are fine impressions — & contain many curious fragments of Ornament."[33] The house was remodeled from 1789 for Anson's heir, Thomas Anson II, by Samuel Wyatt, who gave Shugborough a plainer neoclassical exterior, replacing Stuart's cresting on the wings with a balustraded parapet.

Nuneham Park

In 1756 one of the founder-members of the Society of Dilettanti, Simon, first Earl Harcourt, began a new villa at

273

Fig. 6-15. Paul Sandby. *Nuneham Park from the River* (detail), ca. 1760. Oil on canvas. Private collection.

Nuneham Courtenay (figs. 6-15, 6-16), one that would afford a fine prospect of the domes and spires of the Oxford skyline, as if looking across to Rome from the campagna. As a villa, rather than a great country house, Nuneham Park was among the first of a new generation of small Palladian houses in the country.[34] It quotes from Lord Burlington's Chiswick House. Harcourt's original choice of executant architect to realize his designs was Stiff Leadbetter, but by September 1756 he had he turned to Stuart, probably to design all the main rooms.[35] The villa is the only surviving example of the simpler style of Stuart's early country house commissions.

In February 1756, four months after Stuart returned from Greece, Lady Harcourt wrote to Lord Newnham: "I have been entertained lately by a sight of some drawings of Mr Stewart's of the remains of Grecian Antiquities."[36] In December 1756 Harcourt wrote to Thomas Worsley that he had "boldly adventured to follow a design of an old building which I have seen among Mr. Stuart's drawings of Athens."[37] Stuart's sketches for *Antiquities of Athens* were thus exclusively available to the supporters of his trip to Greece, prior to publication, to keep them in the vanguard of taste. The drawing for the screen marking the reservoir of the Aqueduct of Hadrian at Athens was used for the four Venetian windows of the villa (figs. 6-17, 6-18). Harcourt went even further in choosing Greek Ionic capitals, in place of the Roman Ionic capitals on the original. These windows thus became the first example of the Greek Ionic order in England and, indeed, the first direct quotation from ancient Greece in English architecture.[38]

Fig. 6-16. Simon, first Earl Harcourt, with James Stuart. Garden front of Nuneham Park, Oxfordshire, ca. 1756–58. Photographed in 2006.

Fig. 6-17. Simon, first Earl Harcourt, with James Stuart. Venetian window at Nuneham Park, Oxfordshire, ca. 1756–58. Design adapted from drawings by Stuart for *Antiquities of Athens*. Photographed in 2006.

Fig. 6-18. Screen marking the reservoir of the aqueduct of Hadrian at Athens. Engraving. From *Antiquities of Athens*, vol. 3 (1794): chap. 4, pl. II. Courtesy of the Library, the Bard Graduate Center for Studies in the Decorative Arts, Design, and Culture, New York. *Checklist no. 90.*

Fig. 6-19. Attributed to James Stuart. The great drawing room, Nuneham Park, Oxfordshire, ca. 1756–64. Photographed in 1913. ©Country Life Picture Library.

Fig. 6-20. Attributed to James Stuart. The octagonal salon, Nuneham Park, Oxfordshire, ca. 1756–64. Photographed in 1913. ©Country Life Picture Library.

Fig. 6-21. Ionic capital, detail from a plate depicting the base, capital, and entablature of the portico of Minerva Polias. From *Antiquities of Athens*, vol. 2 (ca. 1790): chap. 2, pl. VIII. Courtesy of the Library, The Bard Graduate Center for Studies in the Decorative Arts, Design, and Culture, New York. *Checklist no. 129.*

277

Fig. 6-22. Attributed to James Stuart. The dining room, Nuneham Park, Oxfordshire, ca. 1756–64. Photographed in 2006. *Checklist no. 46.*

Inside the house Stuart contributed to the synthesis of Greek, Roman, and Renaissance decoration.[39] The great drawing room (fig. 6-19) has been identified as "arguably the first neo-classical interior in England."[40] The interiors were remodeled by Lancelot Brown, working with Henry Holland, from 1781, but the original hall and octagonal salon (fig. 6-20) were probably designed by Stuart. His ceiling for the drawing room survives and is based on the ceiling of Inigo Jones's Banqueting House in Whitehall. The window frames with Ionic capitals would have appeared strikingly archaic; they were copied from the engraving in *Antiquities of Athens* of the portico of the temple of Minerva Polias, one of three temples that form the Erechtheion (fig. 6-21). The walls were left plain but Stuart may have specified the reframing of the paintings in twenty-nine "Carlomarats" to provide visual structure to the hang, which was then mostly of landscape paintings.[41]

In the dining room only the window frames and chimneypiece survive in situ (fig. 6-22).[42] The design is identical to the chimneypiece included in Stuart's proposals for Wimbledon House (see fig. 6-42). Flanking the central garlanded urn are motifs symbolic of Dionysus, the crossed thrysae wreathed in vines, paired with Cupid's crossed flaming torches, between paterae that would have been recognized as the libation dishes of Ceres. The frieze derives from a drawing of the Choragic Monument of Thrasyllus that would be engraved for the much-anticipated *Antiquities of Athens* (vol. 2, ca. 1790; see fig. 10-5), while the lion-masked uprights are from Roman furniture (see fig. 10-36). A drawing of the Nuneham Park chimneypiece has recently surfaced, annotated "Stewart — Lord Harcourt" (fig. 6-23). The lack of variation between the design and execution in marble suggests the use of a master-mason without great artistic ambitions of his own, such as John Deval the elder who specialized in

Fig. 6-23. James Stuart. Design for a chimneypiece for Nuneham Park, ca. 1756–64. Inscribed "Stewart-Lord Harcourt." Gray ink and wash. ©Christie's Images Limited 2004.

chimneypieces (fig. 6-24). The hall chimneypiece was probably designed by Stuart,[43] as it relates to a drawing by him for a Doric fireplace with an Ionic overmantel (figs. 6-25, 6-26). A design for another chimneypiece (fig. 6-27) may be for one in the king's bedchamber.[44]

Today Nuneham Park may seem relatively conventional but, like Stuart's reliefs for Wentworth Woodhouse, seen in context it illustrates his strikingly austere aesthetic.

The importance of the marble chimneypiece to the neoclassical interior has yet to be appreciated fully.[45] Framing the source of light and heat, providing the immediate background to the favored place in which to stand, the chimneypiece (and not the painted masterpiece hung as the overmantel) was the focal point of the finest saloon. In providing this exclusive quotation from the *gusto Greco*, in preference to the conventional pictorial central bas-

Fig. 6-24. James Stuart. Chimneypiece in the dining room at Nuneham Park, Oxfordshire, ca. 1756–64. Photographed in 2006. *Checklist no. 47.*

Fig. 6-25. Attributed to James Stuart. Chimneypiece in the hall at Nuneham Park, Oxfordshire, ca. 1756–64. Photographed in 2006.

Fig. 6-26. James Stuart. Design for a chimneypiece, overmantel, and fire grate with lions' heads, late 1750s–early 1760s. Pen and ink, graphite, gray wash. The Pierpont Morgan Library, New York, Bequest of Junius S. Morgan and Gift of Henry S. Morgan, 1966.10: 37. *Checklist. no. 69.*

relief (as employed, for example, by the leading supplier of chimneypieces, Sir Henry Cheere), Stuart integrated the chimneypiece with the room at large. Stuart's chimneypieces for Nuneham are modest in scale to suit the smaller interiors of the villa, but the one in the great drawing room must have seemed particularly restrained. This approach would have been a challenge to Joseph Wilton who returned from Italy in 1755 with William Chambers and was appointed Statuary to his Majesty in 1761. In his *Treatise on Civil Architecture* (1759) Chambers spoke out in favor of architects giving up chimneypieces to sculptors:

> England is at present possess'd of many able sculptors, whose chief employment being to execute magnificent Chimney-pieces, now happily much in vogue, it may be said that in this particular we surpass all other nations.[46]

Chambers may have been writing in reply to the architect Isaac Ware, who had himself designed a grand chimneypiece in the early 1750s for Chesterfield House in Mayfair. In his *Complete Body of Architecture* (1756), Ware traced the origins of "Grecian" caryatid fire surrounds to Scamozzi and Vitruvius but warned of the risks of the current fashion for elaborate figurative sculptural chimneypieces where "every defect will be seen as well as every beauty."[47] Wilton continued the fashion in the pair he designed for the gallery of Northumberland House in the Strand, a room completed by James Paine between 1753 and 1757. Also in contrast to the severely architectural vocabulary of Stuart's design, with its scroll brackets resting on slim fluted lion monopodia, is the massive seven-foot-high caryatid chimneypiece completed in 1756 by Michael Rysbrack for the Red Drawing Room at Hopetoun, a room that is a key example of Robert Adam's early work (fig. 6-28). Robert Adam may have taken from Stuart's example the ambition to design domestic sculpture, such as chimneypieces, as part of a complete decorative scheme.[48] Stuart could, however, design a caryatid chimneypiece when the scheme demanded it, as in the Painted Room at Spencer House (see fig. 5-47).

Fig. 6-27. James Stuart, Design for a chimneypiece for Nuneham Park, ca. 1756. Pen and ink, watercolor. RIBA Library Drawings Collection, London, SD104/31. *Checklist no. 48.*

Fig. 6-28. Robert Adam. Caryatid chimneypiece in the Red Drawing Room, Hopetoun, South Queensferry, Scotland. Executed by Michael Rysbrack, 1756. Photographed second half of the 20th century. RIBA Library Photographs Collection, London, MHGB1765.

Kedleston Hall

After *Antiquities of Athens* and Spencer House, Stuart's best-known surviving work is the set of proposals for the interior of Kedleston Hall that he produced around 1757 – 58 for Sir Nathaniel Curzon (see fig. 4–9). Despite being shelved by Stuart's client, the proposals had great influence; indeed, they could be said to represent the most influential room never to have been built in Georgian England.[49] The principal reason for their status today is the place of Kedleston Hall in the early career of Robert Adam, and the quiet interest the ambitious young Scottish architect evidently took in Stuart's designs, while mocking them to gain the commission for himself. Adam, however, did not persuade Curzon to reject them, and Stuart along with them, as is traditionally stated. Moreover, they should not be seen as designs for a room, but rather as a set of presentation drawings for the arrangement of a collection. They were intended to woo a client but were not taken forward.

Curzon was aged twenty-eight when he succeeded his father as Member of Parliament for Derbyshire and took over the family seat in 1754. By the time his father died in 1758, he had formed a collection of paintings and planned to build a new house, inspired by the example of Holkham in Norfolk. [50] The architect and builder of Holkham, Matthew Brettingham, visited Kedleston in December 1758. Curzon had probably consulted Stuart the year before, in seeking someone who could collaborate with Brettingham in the way that Kent had undertaken the interiors of Holkham and Houghton in Norfolk. Brettingham may have recommended Stuart to Curzon for Stuart had traveled in Italy with his son, Matthew Brettingham the Younger (see chap. 2).

Like Holkham and Houghton, the new Kedleston was based on the Villa Mocenigo, a house that was never built but was published in the second book of Andrea Palladio's *Quattro Libri* (1570).[51] As at Holkham and Houghton, it was conceived both to receive major guests crucial to the patron's political career and to house a collection of old master paintings and statues with which to impress visitors. Curzon had not been on the Grand Tour to Rome and thus did not qualify for membership of the Society of Dilettanti, unlike so many of Stuart's patrons. This may have left him relatively vulnerable to the influence of others who had formed their taste abroad, particularly at a time when the tides of taste were turning. He began his collection in 1749 on a month-long trip

to France, Belgium, and Holland. As well as inheriting his father's paintings and sculptures, he purchased twenty-six pictures in Italy via William Wilkins in 1758, and three masterpieces were acquired in 1757 at the sale of the art dealer William Kent (not the artist-architect of the same name).[52] Curzon also commissioned paintings from Gavin Hamilton, Zuccarelli, and Nathaniel Hone.[53]

Brettingham began the construction of the family pavilion in 1759, but within months he was succeeded by James Paine.[54] However, in December 1758 Curzon had met Robert Adam in London. Adam had returned from Italy in January 1758 and showed Curzon his latest drawings. Adam's own version of what ensued is given in his letter to his brother James:

> every new Drawing he Saw made him grieve at his previous Engagement with Brittingham, He carried me home (to Audley Square) in his Chariot about 3 and kept me to 4 Seeing said Britt' designs; And asked my opinion; I proposed alterations & desired he might call them his own fancys.[55]

Adam returned days later to meet Curzon and his wife and over two hours convinced them to commission him to design the grounds "with full powers as to Temples Bridges Seats and Cascades."[56] Adam's charm offensive did not stop there:

> Sir Nathaniel brought me out a design of the Great Athenians for his Rooms finishing, which he beg'd me for God Sake not to mention to any Body. They are so excessively & so ridiculously bad, that Mr Curson immediately saw the folly of them and Said so to Some people which so offended the proud Grecian that he has not Seen Sr. Nathaniel these 2 Years, And he says he keeps the Drawings Sacred in Self defence. He made a Gallery only 5 feet high so that by that one woud think the Modern Greeks diminish'd in size as well as in Spirit, But forgot that Brittains were taller. Then he advances his columns in his great Hall so much as only to leave 14 feet of space which you know was making a narrow Passage of it; His ordinary Rooms beggar all description however ridiculous, I confess myself unequal to the task, Tables of 2 foot Sqr. In a Room of 50

foot long, with belts of Stone and great Pannels & Roses & festoon & figures all Ramm'd in wherever there was a hole to be got for them. & he wanted to fitt frames for Sir Nat's Pictures but not having, or rather I suppose not being willing to confine his great Genius to the sizes of the pictures, he Cutts 3 foot off the length of the best pictures and 2 foot off the height of others to make them answer, & Draws all the Pictures & Colour them in his Drawings But they are So ill done they move pity rather than contempt.[57]

Evidently Stuart's proposals had already been shelved by Curzon, who did not know where to turn and what to do next, and had kept Stuart's drawings "Sacred in Self defence." He had previously rejected interior designs by another, unidentified architect (perhaps Brettingham) before he went to Stuart.[58] Adam did not oust "the Great

Athenian," for he was already off the scene,[59] but he did prey on the social insecurities of an aspiring gentleman of taste in a way that Stuart's clientele among the Society of Dilettanti might have been able to close ranks and resist.

Today, in the light of Adam's career from 1760 as a designer of complete interiors,[60] and in view of the many colored drawings produced by him and his office (following Stuart's example), it may be difficult to see how Stuart's designs could have seemed so shocking that Curzon hid them in a drawer to defend his reputation. As colored presentation drawings offering specific proposals for hanging paintings, they follow the format of William Kent's designs for Houghton Hall of 1725.[61] Kent's designs entered the art market in 1749 (the year after his death), but if Stuart did not see them he would have known Kent's elevations of the interior of Chiswick House as engraved for Kent's *Designs of Inigo Jones, with some Additional Designs* (1727).[62] Kent's designs, however,

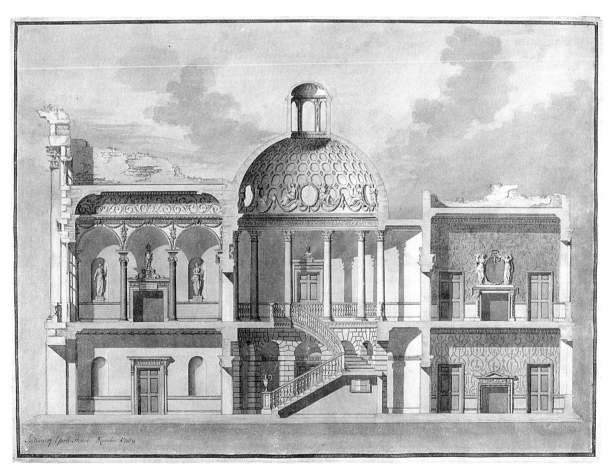

Fig. 6-29. William Chambers. Sectional drawing of York House, Pall Mall, showing proposed interior decoration, 1759. Pen and ink, color wash. RIBA Library Drawings Collection, London, SC 68/10.

Fig. 6-30. James Stuart. Design for the decoration of a window wall of a state room, Kedleston Hall, Derbyshire, 1757–58. Pen and ink, color wash, pencil inscriptions. Courtesy of Kedleston Hall, The Scarsdale Collection, KED/231/10/3 (The National Trust, UK). *Checklist no. 49.*

included neither furniture (other than a single console table) nor sculpture. William Chambers's sectional drawing for York House in Pall Mall of 1759 (fig. 6-29) shows that Stuart was not alone in producing colored interior designs in the late 1750s, before Adam. Chambers may have been responding to Continental examples, but his decorative scheme is confined to patterned wall colors and an impressive range of sculpture.[63]

Curzon must have known Kent's work at Holkham, for the house had been inherited by his close friend and neighbor Lord Leicester.[64] He would have seen Stuart as Brettingham's collaborator, rather than as an architect in his own right, as Adam had trained to be. Like Kent, Stuart had begun as a painter but was able to develop the genre of architectural presentation drawings for complete interiors to new levels of detail and aesthetic finish, probably thanks to his years of experience as a fan painter.

It is not certain whether all four designs are for a sin-

gle room.[65] Indeed, Adam's reference to "his ordinary Rooms" and the "Columns in his great Hall" and the "Gallery only 5 feet high" suggests that there are more drawings to be found. Stuart's "Room of 50 foot long" was a two-story gallery for Curzon's finest paintings and sculpture (fig. 6-30). It may have been in or adjoining the house built around 1700 by Francis Smith of Warwick for Curzon's grandfather. Curzon would have been encouraged to commission schemes by his father who was also a collector. The room is well lit by nine tall windows over two stories (an annotation explains that the upper windows are taller than the lower) and is entered through a glazed double door beneath a lunette (see fig. 6-30).

Facing the entrance and dominating the room is *The Triumph of Bacchus with Ariadne* by Luca Giordano (fig. 6-31). The painting was purchased in 1757, along with the pair of paintings by Benedetto Luti that are shown on an end wall (fig. 6-34), and this may have prompted Curzon

Fig. 6-31. James Stuart. Design for the decoration of the chimneypiece wall of a state room, Kedleston Hall, Derbyshire, 1757–58. Pen and ink, watercolor, pencil. Courtesy of Kedleston Hall, The Scarsdale Collection, KED/1/10-4 (The National Trust, UK). *Checklist no. 50.*

Fig. 6-32. James Stuart. Design for the decoration of the end wall of a state room, Kedleston Hall, Derbyshire, 1757–58. Pen and ink, watercolor, gray wash. Courtesy of Kedleston Hall, The Scarsdale Collection, KED/1/10-1 (The National Trust, UK). *Checklist no. 52.*

Fig. 6-33. James Stuart. Design for the decoration of the end wall of a state room, Kedleston Hall, Derbyshire, 1757–58. Pen and ink, watercolor, pencil. Courtesy of Kedleston Hall, The Scarsdale Collection, KED/1/10-2 (The National Trust, UK). *Checklist no. 51.*

to commission the scheme from Stuart after his architect failed to find a suitable setting for them. The overmantel, *Diogenes with his Lantern*, was formerly attributed to Luca Giordano but is now ascribed to Giocchino Assereto. All four paintings hang at Kedleston today. The scheme also includes two paintings by Claude, one by Feti, and a landscape by Artois (the latter purchased in 1756 at the sale of the architect James Gibbs). Stuart's scheme is, essentially, a celebration of Giordano. As such it is also a reminder that at this stage Stuart was more a decorative painter of the late baroque, in the tradition of Kent, and an expert

adviser to collectors of paintings, than a pioneer architect of the Greek Revival. Giordano was admired at this time for his absorption of the best of Veronese, Titian, and Rubens (artists praised by Stuart in the draft treatise in his sketchbook) and his influence on painters such as Sebastiano Ricci (who Burlington employed about 1713 – 14, before he met Kent).[66]

Following Kent's example at Chiswick, Stuart proposed inserting one of his own paintings between the paintings by Luti. It was based on the frieze of the Choragic Monument of Lysicrates, showing Dionysus.

The decorative detail of the room similarly extends the subject of Giordano's *Triumph of Bacchus,* as the paintings appear to hang from swags looped through rings held by leopard masks (his chariot was drawn by leopards). Beneath the paintings on the end wall, in a niche, the large item of furniture may be an organ, its case decorated with dancers and bacchantes (see fig. 10-64). The theme of beauty and connoisseurship is underlined by Stuart's design for overdoors which appear to depict the Judgment of Paris.

The fourth design (fig. 6-33), showing the sideboard recess, may be an alternative proposal for the same end wall as it lies beneath an overlay showing the three paintings and a large item of furniture. Consequently the same overdoors depicting Paris now flank a proposed double portrait of Curzon and his wife; here the patron is admiring his choice of the modern-day Venus through this flattering allusion. Again, Stuart must have hoped to paint this himself.[67] The painting's frame is decorated above with amorini. Given the consistent iconography of the room it seems likely that this state room was intended to double as gallery and dining room.

Looking closely at Luti's *Christ and Mary Magdalene in the House of Simon* (on the left in Stuart's scheme) it is tempting to speculate that this was considered suitable for a dining room as it includes in the background a fine formal display of baroque plate (fig. 6-34), one that may have inspired Curzon's own collection, as assembled on his sideboard to answer it. Beneath the sideboard stands the plain Sicilian jasper urn that the sculptor Richard Hayward had sent from Rome in 1757 (see figs. 10-7, 10-8). To either side stand urns on pedestals decorated with griffins copied from a tripod now in the Capitoline Museum, Rome (see figs. 10-6, 11-8).

Adam may not have been exaggerating when he wrote to his brother that paintings would have to be trimmed to fit Stuart's strictly symmetrical hang (something he must have been told by Curzon). Burlington and Kent had enlarged and reduced lesser paintings to create pendants and to fit the architectural spaces at Chiswick House when the collection was moved there from Burlington House in 1729. However, it is just as likely that Curzon leapt to this assumption on the basis of Stuart's drawings having given him the wrong dimensions for the paintings.

A selection from Curzon's collection of statuary and busts fills the facing wall. The installation seems to have

Fig. 6-34. Benedetto Luti. *Christ and Mary Magdalene in the House of Simon,* n.d. Oil on canvas. Courtesy of Kedleston Hall, The Scarsdale Collection (The National Trust, UK).

been planned more around the paintings than around the sculpture. Curzon formed his collection of plaster casts, comprising twenty-six busts and twenty-one statues, between 1756 and 1758, mostly through Brettingham, John Cheere, Richard Hayward, and Joseph Wilton.[68] However, he only shows six statues and four casts in his drawing, and this further suggests the absence of another installation scheme by Stuart. The remaining busts in par-

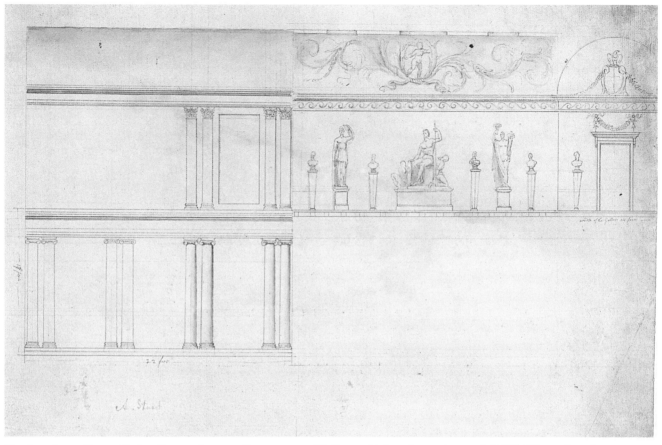

Fig. 6-35. James Stuart. Design for a sculpture gallery, ca. 1755–88. Pen and ink, color wash, pencil. RIBA Library Drawings Collection, London, SD 62/13. *Checklist no. 107.*

ticular would have been acquired to stand on bookcases in a library and on deep cornices above doorcases.

On the window wall the statues and busts stand in shadow against the piers, as Adam noted, the "figures all Ramm'd in wherever there was a hole."[69] At night the busts would have been badly lit from above and behind from candlelight reflected in plain oval pier glasses. Pride of place on this wall, flanking the entrance, is given to a statue of Bacchus (possibly intended to represent the cast in the collection after Sansovino's masterpiece, misdrawn from memory) and *Saint Susanna* by Duquesnoy. The statues in the corners of both long walls seem cramped and would have intruded into the doorways. An unidentified design by Stuart for a sculpture gallery above a colonnade, top-lit through a decorated barrel vault, shows a more sympathetic interest in the challenge of

arranging statuary on pedestals and plinths indoors (fig. 6-35). The central group does not link it to Kedleston, however, and appears to be a modern work, perhaps of Stuart's own design.

The strangest feature of Stuart's design for Curzon is the set of tentlike canopies over the windows and organ case (the latter presumably to serve as a dustcover; see fig. 6-32). If these were intended as pelmets to cover the pulley boards for festoon curtains, the curtains are missing. With the upper windows left bare this wall would have presented an impractically cold façade when the fireplace and candles were lit at night.

The chimneypiece is strikingly austere given the fashion of the day. It is the same design that Stuart realized in the dining room at Nuneham Park, with its wreaths and lion masks quoting the Choragic Monument of Thrasyllus.

It is simply dressed with a pair of Grecian sphinxes (presumably bronzes, as Wedgwood was not to manufacture them in basaltware until 1769). Comparison with the caryatid chimneypiece that Adam designed in 1760 for the drawing room at Kedleston reveals the distance between them (fig. 6-36).[70] The Greek tripod incense-burners on the chimneypiece, like the tripod candelabra on the pier tables and tripod ornament above the overdoors, all derive from Stuart's reconstruction of the tripod on the Choragic Monument of Lysicrates (see fig. 11-12) Curzon may have taken fright at Stuart's set of presentation drawings, but he did subscribe to *Antiquities of Athens* in which the reconstruction was published. The featuring of such motifs would have given Curzon's finest interior the social cachet of being ahead of fashionable taste, but it was not to be.

Compared to his work at Wentworth Woodhouse, Shugborough, and Nuneham, the interior at Kedleston would have been Stuart's most complete installation to date, in a room in which he sheds the bulk and plasticity of ornament of the English neo-Palladians. Adam learned from the designs he scorned not only how to seduce a prospective client with color, detail, and comprehensive design, but also how to hang paintings.[71] Adam won Curzon's confidence and took over the decoration and furnishing of the interiors as well as the more immediate concerns of the architectural design of the new house at large, succeeding James Paine. But Stuart's contribution was recognized by his contemporaries. His tripod was given center stage in Adam's design for the sideboard niche, flanked by vases that he may also have designed (see fig. 11-19). When George Montagu visited Kedleston in September 1766, as he wrote to Horace Walpole, he admired "where Adam and Stewart have showed all their Roman and Palmira skill."[72]

Fig. 6-36. Robert Adam. Caryatid chimneypiece in the drawing room, Kedleston Hall, Derbyshire, 1760. Photographed in 2006. Courtesy of Kedleston Hall (The National Trust, UK).

Fig. 6-37. Painted ceiling of the Tapestry Room, Hagley Hall, Worcestershire, 1758–59. Corner vignettes of "zephyrs" by James Stuart; central panel attributed to Giovanni Battista Cipriani. Photographed in 2006. *Checklist no. 63.*

Fig. 6-38. James Stuart. One of the four "zephyrs," detail of the painted ceiling of the Tapestry Room, Hagley Hall, Worcestershire, 1758–59. Photographed in 2006. *Checklist no. 64.*

Hagley Hall

This is the point at which accounts of Stuart's career traditionally move to Spencer House (begun about 1759) and Montagu House (begun about 1775), where they close with him ending his days in alcoholic disarray, as immortalized in the irate letters of Mrs. Montagu, who assumed she was hiring a practical architect.[73] Stuart had other irons in the fire, however, in houses outside London, and Curzon's bewildered response to his set of drawings did not stop Stuart from finding work elsewhere. In October 1758 he was busy at Hagley Hall in Worcestershire where he had come not as a pioneer and champion of the *gusto Greco* but as a decorative painter who could turn his hand to ceilings in the rococo taste (figs. 6-37, 6-38). His patron, George, first Lord Lyttleton, was pleased to report to Mrs. Montagu:

He has engaged to paint me a Flora and four pretty little Zephyrs in my drawing room Ceiling which is ornamented with Flowers in Stucco, but has Spaces left for these Pictures. He thinks all my Stucco Work is very well done.[74]

Decorative painting was one way of finding more prestigious work. In October 1758 Stuart visited Hagley with his most supportive patron, Thomas Anson of Shugborough, and by January 19, 1759, he had been paid for a design for a Greek Doric temple for Lord Lyttelton's park (see chap. 7).

Fig. 6-39. "Principal Front of Wimbledon House, in Surry, the Seat of the Right Honble Earl Spencer." Engraved by T. White. From Colen Campbell, continued by James Gandon and John Woolfe, *Vitruvius Britannicus . . .* , vol. 5 (1771): pl. 21. By permission of The British Library, London, 55.i.13.

Fig. 6-40. "Plan of the Principal Floor / Plan of the Ground Floor of Wimbledon in Surry the seat of the Rt Honble Earl Spencer." Engraved by T. White. From Colen Campbell, continued by James Gandon and John Woolfe, *Vitruvius Britannicus . . .* , vol. 5 (1771): pl. 20. By permission of The British Library, London, 55.i.13.

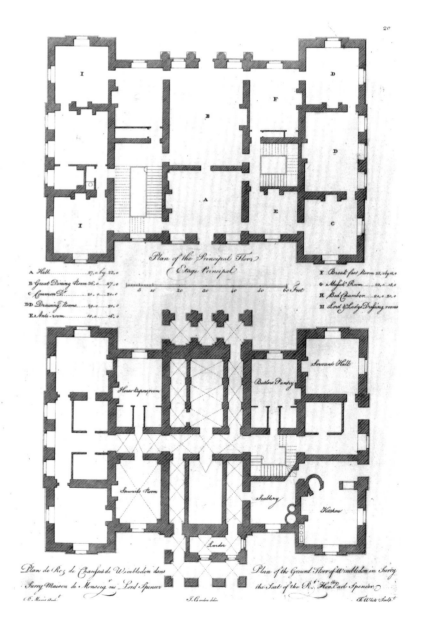

Wimbledon Park

Stuart's prize commission of about 1758 was for
Wimbledon Park in Surrey for John Spencer. The
Palladian villa had been designed by Henry Herbert, ninth
Earl of Pembroke, and built by Roger Morris between
1732 and 1737 for Sarah, Duchess of Marlborough (fig. 6-
39). The same team of "architect earl" and builder had previously created Marble Hill in Twickenham for Henrietta
Howard, retired mistress of George II.[75] This Thames-side
villa now provides the best idea of the kind of interior
architectural decoration that Stuart replaced. For Spencer,
Stuart produced designs for the remodeling of the hall and
dining room, and for a new closet for Lady Spencer. In
1765 Stuart's patron was created first Earl Spencer and
elected a member of the Society of Dilettanti. He
employed John Vardy to build Spencer House between
1756 and 1765, under the supervision of the secretary of
the Society of Dilettanti, Colonel George Gray, and it was

probably Gray who introduced Spencer to Stuart. Wimbledon House may have been their trial run. It was destroyed
by fire in 1785 and was rebuilt by Henry Holland in 1800,
but at least four of Stuart's presentation drawings survive.
Read in conjunction with the floor plans published in
Vitruvius Britannicus (1771), the drawings include rooms
that can be identified and related (fig. 6-40).[76]

The plans reveal that the hall stood on the principal
floor at the top of the stairs and had a blind door to the
right of the chimneypiece. This is shown in Stuart's design
balancing the open door to the left (fig. 6-41). In the same
way, Lord Pembroke had used two blind doors in the great
room at Marble Hill to create symmetry and the illusion
of adjacent suites.[77] This would have been the first room
that visitors entered, for on the ground floor the entrance
led only through a corridor to the stairs; consequently, it
had to be imposing within the confines of a villa. While
commanding views to one side over the gardens, the hall

Fig. 6-41. James Stuart. Design for the decoration of the chimney wall in the hall, Wimbledon Park, Surrey, 1758. Pen and ink,
pencil, and gray wash. RIBA Library Drawings Collection, London, SD 62/5 (1). *Checklist no. 65.*

Fig. 6-42. James Stuart. Design for the decoration of the chimney wall of the great dining room, Wimbledon Park, Surrey, ca. 1758. Pen and ink, color washes. RIBA Library Drawings Collection, London, SD 62/5 (2). *Checklist no. 66.*

also served as the antechamber to the great dining room (fig. 6-42). The shadows in the drawing cast by the chimneypiece and vases came from a strong raking light from the left, perhaps to suggest the intense contrast of light and shadow of architecture when seen under Grecian skies. Compared to his seductive vision for the great saloon at Kedleston, Stuart's drawings for Wimbledon are more like sketches; presumably he already knew he had the commission.

The Grecian character of the hall is established by the Doric triglyph cornices that relate the raised chimneypiece to the doors, and by the cornice frieze, which is a favorite motif of Stuart's, adapted from the necking of the columns of the Temple of Minerva Polias (see fig. 5-6). Flanking the fireplace in niches are large sculptural vases. In their prominence these vases anticipate the gift to Georgiana Spencer in 1764 – 65 from Cardinal Albani of a copy of an antique alabaster vase that she admired at the Villa Albani.[78] Other vases in the room may have included a collection of antique cinerary urns, such as would form the staple stock of the Grand Tour souvenir shop that Giovanni Battista Piranesi opened in Rome in 1761.[79] From their shape it seems more likely, however, that these

vases were to be manufactured, presumably by Josiah Wedgwood. If so, they anticipate Adam's use of decorative vases in his interiors and the general vase-mania to which Piranesi contributed.[80] However, Stuart may also be ahead of Wedgwood, for Wedgwood was producing ornamental creamware by 1762, and his London showroom was only established in 1765 (the year he was granted by Queen Charlotte the title Potter to Her Majesty). Stuart could have been introduced to Wedgwood by his friend Thomas Anson and so helped to create his market by finding a place for decorative vases in designed interiors. The pairs of vases on the door cornices are also to be found in Stuart's proposals for Kedleston (see figs. 6 - 32, 6-36) and as painted decoration above doors at Spencer House (see fig. 5-46).

The mood of archaic austerity is lightened by the overdoors and overmantel. The annotations reveal that they present the classic imagery of English villa decoration: Dionysus and Ceres, in allusion to the benefits of wine and the harvest, over the doors, with the overmantel devoted to "Mercury & Fortune" celebrating the rewards of commerce. As these roundels are not colored, they were probably plaster medallions rather than paintings. They reflect Stuart's interests as a collector of medals and, from 1757, as a designer for this medium (see chap. 12).

In its prominent location, the recumbent figure on the chimneypiece is almost unprecedented in English domestic sculpture. It may be a small model for an effigy on a monument, here reused to underline the character of an English villa as a place of retreat and relaxation. Stuart's own designs for monuments, most to be made by Peter and Thomas Scheemakers, date from 1759 into the 1770s (see chap. 8). Stuart may have known the tetrastyle hall at Marble Hill where a statuette of Shakespeare (modeled by Peter Scheemakers after a design by Kent) crowned the tall chimneypiece.[81] Alternatively, the position may have been intended for a modern "ideal" sculpture. Stuart had joined the Society for the Promotion of Arts, Manufactures and Commerce in June 1756 and served on several of its committees. In 1759 the society awarded the first premium for a model in clay. The recipient, Joseph Nollekens, had been apprenticed to Peter Scheemakers in 1750.[82] Nollekens left for Rome the year he won the prize, and according to his pupil John Thomas Smith:

> Mr. Nollekens, from the year 1761 to the time he left Rome, consigned several of his productions to his friend *Athenian* Stuart, who had undertaken, in consequence of an early intimacy, to see them placed in the best of the exhibitions in London. . . . [83]

In scale the recumbent figure in Stuart's drawing anticipates the sculpture *Boy on a Dolphin* by Nollekens, which Lord Spencer probably purchased from his studio in Rome in 1764.[84] Stuart's interest in promoting Nollekens through placing his sculptures in London exhibitions, and through introducing him to his major client, Thomas Anson,[85] is in contrast to Adam's use of lesser sculptors such as John Deval and Michael Spang to execute his designs for chimneypieces and overmantels. Stuart's influence on modern British sculpture was acknowledged by the Royal Academy's first professor of sculpture, John Flaxman, when he paid tribute to the sculptor Thomas Banks in 1805, writing that "his constant attention to the Admiranda and Stuart's Athens had initiated him in the Greek style and composition."[86]

An unassigned design by Stuart for a chimneypiece and overmantel (see fig. 6-26) may have been a more ambitious alternative option for the hall at Wimbledon. The Doric frieze is enriched with metopes of paired figures in bas-relief, as on the Parthenon.[87] If this was Stuart's intended allusion, it may be the first instance of artistic interest in the Parthenon's sculptures in England, long before the "Elgin Marbles" went on display at the British Museum in 1817.[88] Stuart had originally intended to publish the Parthenon in the first volume of *Antiquities,* but the sculptures did not appear until the second volume (ca. 1790) and the fourth (1816). An alternative source for the triglyph and metope frieze is an even older building, in the Agora in Athens, the Theseion, which has a Parian marble frieze of metopes representing the Labors of Hercules, the exploits of Theseus, and, like the Parthenon, the battle of the Athenians and the Lapiths against the Centaurs (fig. 6-43). It was published in the third volume of *Antiquities* (1794) and is best known in England as the

Fig. 6-43. James Stuart. The Temple of Theseus, or the Theseion, Athens. Engraving. From *Antiquities of Athens*, vol. 3 (1794): chap. 1, pl. III. Courtesy of the Library, The Bard Graduate Center for Studies in the Decorative Arts, Design, and Culture, New York. *Checklist no. 90.*

Fig. 6-44. James Stuart. Design for the decoration of a closet with bookcase, Wimbledon Park, Surrey, ca. 1758. Pen and ink, color washes. RIBA Library Drawings Collection, London, SD 62/6 (2). *Checklist no. 68.*

source of a landmark of the Greek Revival, William Wilkins's Grange Park in Hampshire (built 1804 – 9, see fig. 13-4).

In Stuart's chimneypiece design, the use of a low-relief sculpture as the overmantel (the depth of shadow and lack of color indicate that it is not a painting) has a precedent in the overmantel at Kensington Palace, which shows a Roman marriage, designed by Kent and carved by Rysbrack. Commissioned in 1723 – 24 it was the first relief overmantel in England.[89] A more immediate precedent, however, may have been the Antinous relief that would be installed as an overmantel in the Villa Albani between in October 1762, a cast of which Stuart had used at Wentworth Woodhouse (see fig. 6-10). Spencer also installed the cast of Antinous, which he had received from Albani himself, above the chimneypiece in the entrance hall at Spencer House (see fig. 5-8).[90] The relief in Stuart's design is not readily identifiable as an ancient work, and it may have been intended as an opportunity for a sculp-

tor such as Scheemakers or Nollekens. Modern sculpture was a subject of discussion among Stuart's patrons. In August 1763 Anson's nephew, Philip, Viscount Royston, wrote to his father, the first Earl of Hardwicke, describing the recent improvements at Shugborough and praising the Shepherd's Monument (1762 – 63; see fig. 7-36): "I shd not omit to mention the *Bas Relief* from Poussin's Arcadia Picture, the most elegant Peice of modern Sculpture I ever beheld, & does great honer to Scheemaker's Chisel."[91]

From the sculptural *gusto Greco* of the hall at Wimbledon, guests passed into the more colorful great dining room where full-length portraits of the hosts flank a favorite masterpiece, a view of the Roman campagna by Dughet or even Claude (see fig. 6-42). The simple arrangement of paintings recalls Kent's hang for the Duke of Grafton's dining room, as published in Isaac Ware's *Designs of Inigo Jones* in 1731.[92] As in the Kedleston designs, the paintings hang from leopard masks; these recur in the new chimneypiece to Stuart's design. In contrast to the Doric triglyph door architraves of the hall, for the great dining room, Stuart proposed using the curved fluted frieze of the colonnade of the Incantada at Salonica (Thessalonike), a building of the late second century A.D. (illustrated in *Antiquities of Athens*, vol. 3, 1794; see fig. 10-30). He used the same source at Spencer House for his doors on the east wall of the Painted Room, which he decorated from around 1759 (see fig. 5-42). The door to the right led to the music room which may have been the subject of the two designs for a room with a coved ceiling (fig. 6-44, and see fig. 6-1).

The secure early dating for at least some of Stuart's work at Wimbledon comes from a note made by Thomas Hollis in his journal on September 3, 1759:

> Dined at Wimbledon. Saw Mr. Spencer's. . . . Some fine paintings there, tapestry, jars etc. Saw Mrs. Spencer's closet painted in grotesque by Stuart; With the Figures of The Allegro and Pensero [so] after the divine Milton. Stuart's ideas very fine, his execution indifferent.[93]

The reference to Mrs. Spencer's closet as painted "in grotesque" refers to the ancient Roman style of domestic decoration that had been revived by Raphael and other Renaissance artists in the Vatican *loggie*, Villa Madama and Caprarola, and introduced to England in the 1720s by

William Kent for ceilings at Kensington Palace and Rousham. It became more popular after the discovery of Pompeii in 1748 and the republication of Pietro Santi Bartoli's *Picturae Antiquae* in 1750. Adam soon made it his own, as a colorful alternative to the neo-Palladian approach to interiors based on ancient Roman public buildings. Stuart's sketches for Wimbledon give little evidence of him being in this way one step ahead of Adam (thanks to Kent) once again, although the sketch for the painted doors of the bookcase in Lady Spencer's closet may indicate that they were to be painted *alla grotesca*. A design by Stuart survives for a window surround decorated in this taste (fig. 6-45). It has previously been identified with the great saloon at Kedleston but the Greek key molding of the chair rail is inconsistent with that room. The cornice frieze shows it was not for Wimbledon either.[94]

Hollis's reference to "jars" must refer to the vases in the sketches of the hall and dining room where they stand on the mantelpieces and door cornices and flank the hall chimneypieces in niches. Five more elegant vases crown the bookcase in the closet, making a total of twenty "jars" in the drawings. In the Painted Room at Spencer House, the vases over the doors are painted on to the walls (see fig. 5-42), but at Wimbledon, in Stuart's sketches, they were real, for they cast shadows. Like the *grotesque* painted decoration, such extensive use of vases at Wimbledon may have been inspired by the discoveries at Herculaneum, which Stuart possibly visited in 1748, and also at Pompeii, which Stuart may have seen in the very early stages of its excavation (see chap. 3). He also owned related publications, such as *Le antichità di Ercolano eposte*, available from 1757.[95] Horace Walpole visited Wimbledon House in 1751 but felt the need to see the changes for he was back around 1758. With his waspish wit he noted: "A closet, ornamented and painted by Mr Stewart. The ornaments in a good antique taste. A Hymen, the Allegro & Penseroso, on the ceiling and in compartments, villainously painted."[96]

From the inscriptions on the picture frames (*Allegro*; *Penseroso*) these designs can be identified with Lady Spencer's new closet. It must have been almost a shrine to Stuart's aspirations as a painter, and perhaps there lay his true ambitions. Given its loss, the best idea of its appearance today is found in the Painted Room at Spencer House (see chap. 5). Adam was to make a speciality of such intimate decorated "closets," as the fine lady's answer to the *studiolo* of the gentleman of taste.

Sion Hill and Hornby Castle

Like Wimbledon Park, Sion Hill in Brentford was another villa where Stuart worked while employed on the same patron's London town house. It was purchased in 1755 by Robert D'Arcy, fourth Earl of Holdernesse, for whom Stuart designed interiors for Holdernesse House (later known as Londonderry House; demolished 1964) between about 1761 and 1766 (see chap. 5). The only known evidence of the work at Sion Hill is a comment by the

Fig. 6-45. James Stuart. Design for the wall of a painted room with coved recess, ca. 1757–58. Pencil, pen, and yellow-gray washes. RIBA Library Drawings Collection, London, SD 62/1. *Checklist no. 62.*

Fig. 6-46. Attributed to James Stuart. The great hall, Hornby Castle, Yorkshire, ca. 1760s. Photographed in 1906. ©Country Life Picture Library. *Checklist no. 70.*

Duchess of Northumberland in her diary that a "chimney piece was designed by Stuart."[97] She later noted that it was painted by him. A subscriber to Stuart's *Antiquities of Athens* and a member of the Society of Dilettanti, Holdernesse also erected a Choragic Monument of Lysicrates in his gardens at Sion Hill (see fig. 7-34). The house had been demolished by 1840. Holdernesse appears to have engaged Stuart for his Yorkshire seat, Hornby Castle, to redecorate the great hall between around 1760 and 1765, for there the chimneypiece frieze uses one of his favorite motifs, derived from the Incantada at Salonica (fig. 6-46).[98]

Stuart's design for a chimneypiece for Nuneham (see fig. 6-27) does not correspond directly with the duchess's description but gives some idea of the lost one from Sion Hill, which comprised yellow marble columns in front of a dark gray slab of marble supporting a carved cornice of great width.[99] It may have been included among payments made by Holdernesse beginning in 1755 to the mason John Deval the Elder, who specialized in chimneypieces.[100] An unassigned chimneypiece design (see fig. 10-65) shows the use of a deep mantelpiece for a modern sculpture of Venus and Cupid.

Fig. 6-47. View of a house in Fulham remodeled for Sir Philip Stephens. Color engraving. From Daniel Lysons, *Environs of London,* vol. 2, pt. 2 [ca. 1790]: 366. Courtesy of Guildhall Library, City of London.

Other Commissions

There are a number of commissions by Stuart where the documentation is so thin that only the barest description of the work he undertook can be given. Stuart is known to have designed a ceiling for Croome Court, Worcestershire, for George William, sixth Earl of Coventry, but the only record of it is a bill for plasterwork by Francesco Vassalli presented in 1761. Vassalli charged £47.15.0 for the "Ceiling in ye Salon according to My designe" and a further £22.5.0 for "That done before according to Mr. Stuard designe."[101] The room to which Stuart's ceiling belonged is unknown. Even less is known of the alterations Stuart made to Warfield Park, Bracknell, Berkshire for East India merchant John Walsh. The work, which took place between about 1775 and 1780, may have been substantial.[102]

In 1765 Stuart designed a Doric garden temple for The Grove, Watford, for the Hon. Thomas Villiers, Baron Hyde of Hindon (see chap. 7). The opportunity seems to have been taken to modernize the interior trim of the house even though it had been built recently by Matthew Brettingham, between 1754 and 1761. Horace Walpole noted "A Chimney, Some medallions & door cases, by Stewart; nothing extraordinary."[103] The house was substantially altered in the 1780s by the architect Robert Taylor, and these alterations by Stuart were swept away.

Another example of Stuart's readiness to suggest minor adjustments (further research may prove them to have been more substantial) is his involvement in a house built for Sir Philip Stephens at Fulham (fig. 6-47). This may have been the villa later known as Ranelagh House (built from around 1764 and demolished in 1892) or the one later known as Little Mulgrave House (demolished 1894), both of which belonged to Stephens.[104] On September 23, 1769, Stuart wrote to Thomas Anson, "Mr Stephens is finishing a house at Fulham the Carcase of which he bought with the rest of Sr Francis Goslings estate there, I have given him some hints about the Completing it."[105] Stuart appears to be presenting himself here purely as an advisor, in his role of authority and arbiter of taste rather than designer or executant architect.

Corsham Court

The carved decoration on a chimneypiece in the Cabinet Room at Corsham Court is derived from part of the frieze of the Choragic Monument of Lysicrates (fig. 6-48). Although this implies Stuart's involvement in the commission for Paul Methuen, in fact he appears not to have had any direct connection with the work. The sculptor of the piece is not certain but is likely to have been either Peter Scheemakers or his former pupil Prince Hoare. Both undertook documented work at Corsham in the 1760s, and both were familiar with Stuart's work, particularly Scheemakers, with whom Stuart established a long and fruitful working relationship (see chap. 9). The Corsham chimneypiece demonstrates how Stuart's design ideas could be transmitted by his subcontractors and achieve a wider audience than the immediate narrow circle of

Fig. 6-48. James Stuart. Chimneypiece in the Cabinet Room at Corsham Court, Wiltshire, 1760s. Execution attributed to Peter Scheemakers or Prince Hoare. Photographed in 2006.

patrons with whom he was directly associated.[106] The Ingestre orangery (see fig. 7-18), which is a direct close of the building at Blithfield commissioned from Stuart by Sir William Bagot (see fig. 7-19), provides a further example of Stuart's subcontractors independently replicating his designs in new locations (see chap. 7).

Rathfarnham Castle

Stuart is not known to have visited Ireland, but at Rathfarnham Castle near Dublin, built by Archbishop Loftus at the end of the sixteenth century, interiors were executed to his designs (fig. 6-49).[107] Stuart was probably commissioned in 1769 by the castle's owner, Henry Loftus, first Earl of Ely. However, Ely may not have engaged Stuart to implement his designs, or if he did he soon replaced him. In January 1771 William Chambers wrote to Ely about problems with the workmen at Rathfarnham, where the redecoration was completed by 1783.[108] In 1769 Lady Shelburne noted that some of the rooms were being decorated "after Designs of Mr Stuarts," which have been attributed to Stuart on stylistic grounds.[109] These include the saloon on the principal floor (fig. 6-50). As at Montagu House, Angelica Kauffman is

Fig. 6-49. Gabriel Beranger, "Rathfarnham Castle, 2M from Dublin," 1774. Watercolor. Prints and Drawings Collection, National Library of Ireland, Dublin, ET 1958 TX 83.

traditionally credited with executing inset paintings. However, in both houses these would probably have been mechanical reproductions from the thirty or so sketch designs she sold to Matthew Boulton from 1776.[110] These were replaced in the early twentieth century with paintings with religious themes, but an early photograph shows the room with its original panels (fig. 6-51). The morning room, adjoining the saloon, has a ceiling and frieze nearly identical to those used by Stuart in the morning room at Lichfield House, 15 St. James's Square (fig. 6-52; see fig. 5-68).

On the first floor, Stuart may have designed the ceiling of the breakfast room, which is devoted to the Four Seasons (fig. 6-53), the coved ceiling of the Gilt Room, which is decorated with symbols of the Greek gods (fig. 6-54). As examples of Stuart's late style they could not be more different from his early ceiling in the great drawing room at Nuneham Park and reveal his response to the colorful intricate geometry of Robert Adam. The anteroom may also be attributed to Stuart from the large medallions, which Stuart also used at Spencer House, Montagu House, and on the organ at Newby Hall (see figs. 5-34, 5-36, 5-91, 10-65, 10-66, 10-68). This room had long been

Fig. 6-50. James Stuart. Drawing room or saloon on the principal floor, Rathfarnham Castle, County Dublin, Eire, ca. 1769. Photographed in 2006. Courtesy of OPW, Dublin, and Rathfarnham Castle. *Checklist no. 79.*

Fig. 6-51. James Stuart. Drawing room or saloon on the principal floor, Rathfarnham Castle, County Dublin, Eire, ca. 1769. Photographed ca. 1913. From Georgian Society, *Records of Eighteenth-Century Domestic Architecture and Decoration in Dublin*, vol. 5 (1913): pl. 84. By permission of The British Library, London, Ac.4890.b.

Fig. 6-52. James Stuart. Ceiling in a room, probably a morning room, on the principal floor, Rathfarnham Castle, County Dublin, Eire, ca. 1769. Photographed in 2006. Courtesy of OPW, Dublin, and Rathfarnham Castle. *Checklist no. 82.*

Fig. 6-53. James Stuart. Ceiling of the breakfast room, or boudoir, Rathfarnham Castle, County Dublin, Eire, ca. 1769. Photographed in 2006. Courtesy of OPW, Dublin, and Rathfarnham Castle. *Checklist no. 81.*

Fig. 6-54. James Stuart. Ceiling in the Gilt Room, Rathfarnham Castle, County Dublin, Eire, ca. 1769. Photographed in 2006. Courtesy of OPW, Dublin, and Rathfarnham Castle. *Checklist no. 80.*

Fig. 6-55. Attributed to James Stuart. Ceiling in the staircase anteroom, Rathfarnham Castle, County Dublin, Eire, ca. 1769. Photographed in 2006. Courtesy of OPW, Dublin, and Rathfarnham Castle.

Fig. 6-56. James Stuart. Chimneypiece with Apollo mask and sunburst, Belvedere, Erith, Kent, ca. 1764–80. Photographed in 1943. English Heritage / National Monuments Record A43/7148.

attributed to Sir William Chambers on account of the ceiling decorated with an Apollo mask and sunburst (fig. 6-55), a motif that Chambers used at the Casino at Marino. However, this motif was not unique to Chambers. Stuart designed a fireplace using the Apollo mask and sunburst for Belvedere, Erith, Kent (fig. 6-56). Stuart may also have been responsible for the entrance porch to Rathfarnham, now demolished. This was described in 1837 by topographer Samuel Lewis: "the entrance to the house from the terrace on which it stands is by a portico of eight Doric columns which support a dome painted in fresco with the signs of the zodiac."[111]

Belvedere, Erith, Kent

The modifications that Stuart made to Belvedere from about 1764 for Sir Sampson Gideon, Bt., later Lord Eardley, were exceptional in Stuart's contribution to country house architecture in being structural. Other than the additions to the wings at Shugborough, his contribution had been confined to designing garden buildings, interior remodelings, and the display of collections. The rebuilding of Belvedere reveals his growing confidence and increased stature as an architect after his work on London houses. Belvedere has been called "Stuart's one complete country house" (fig. 6-57).[112] This was also the only country house mentioned in Joseph Woods's biographical

Fig. 6-57. R. Godfrey. *Belvedere The Seat of Sr. Sampson Gideon Bart.* 1777. Hand-colored engraving. Courtesy of Bexley Local Studies and Archive Centre, Bexleyheath. *Checklist no. 73.*

Fig. 6-58. James Stuart. The front elevation of Belvedere House, Erith, Kent, ca. 1764–80. Photographed in 1937. English Heritage / National Monuments Record C37/756. *Checklist no. 74.*

Fig. 6-59. James Stuart. The Venetian window on the north-court elevation of Belvedere House, Erith, Kent, ca. 1764–80. Photographed in 1943. English Heritage / National Monuments Record A43/7136.

Fig. 6-60. James Stuart. Chimneypiece formerly in the anteroom to the dining room, Belvedere House, Erith, Kent, ca. 1780s. Plaques by Josiah Wedgwood. Photographed in 2005. Private collection. *Checklist no. 75.*

introduction to volume four of *Antiquities of Athens* (1816). Unfortunately, it was demolished between 1959 and 1961.

From photographs Belvedere resembles Stuart's Montagu House (about 1776 – 82) both in elevation and interior decoration (fig. 6-58, see fig. 5-88). With its plain brick elevations broken on the entrance façade by Diocletian windows above canted bays (fig. 6-59), it is in the villa tradition of Ware, Paine, and Carr of York.[113] It was probably completed in the 1790s by Joseph Bonomi and the decorator P. M. Borgnis. The extent of Stuart's own work is unclear, but the interiors provide evidence of his use of manufactured decoration, if not on the scale of the Adam brothers. The thirteen inset paintings in the dining room ceiling, traditionally attributed to Angela

Kauffman, were probably mechanical reproductions supplied by Boulton. Boulton also supplied die-stamped pewter decoration for walls, doors, and chimneypieces at Belvedere, some of which was salvaged by the dealers T. Crowther in 1961. A finely carved pine chimneypiece formerly in the anteroom to the dining room, probably supplied in the late 1780s, is decorated with plaques of Wedgwood green and lilac jasper ware (fig. 6-60).[114] Such use of manufactured ornament is consistent with Adam's increasing means of diversifying his family's business and maintaining costs while enriching interiors, but with Stuart it also may indicate a parting from his best craftsmen.

The commission to rebuild Belvedere predates Montagu House by nearly a decade.[115] His experience at Belvedere may have encouraged Mrs. Montagu to take on Stuart as a practical architect in preference to Adam. In 1779, however, the reliable builder Richard Norris, who had been a great help to Stuart at Belvedere, had died. As Mrs. Montagu wrote in 1780, nearly five years after she embarked on her project:

> since he began my house he has been for a fortnight in the most drunken condition with these fellows. Sr Sampson Gideon for whom he was building a house when I began mine, was obliged to take many precautions to prevent being imposed on by the workmen whose bills he assented to.[116]

On the basis of this remark it has been assumed that Stuart began Belvedere around 1775, shortly before Mrs Montagu leased her site in Portman Square in that year, but this late date is unlikely. By then Stuart was already struggling to finish Belvedere, his first and last commission to rebuild a villa from the ground up.[117] The long delays during construction, alluded to by Mrs. Montagu in her letter, may be the source of a tradition that "after the skeleton of the house was completed, two or three years were allowed to elapse before the doors, windows and other woodwork was put in."[118]

In spite of the difficulties, Belvedere was described by Dr. Waagen in 1857 as "one of the most pleasing country seats . . . in England, which is no small praise in a land which surpasses all others in the number and beauty of its country residences."[119] Six staterooms and one private room were listed by Waagen — drawing room, billiard

Fig. 6-61. James Stuart. The dining room, Belvedere House, Erith, Kent, ca. 1764–80. Photographed in 1937. English Heritage / National Monuments Record BB99/06823. *Checklist no. 76.*

Fig. 6-62. James Stuart. Coved ceiling cornice in an unidentified room at Belvedere House, Erith, Kent, ca. 1764–80. Photographed in 1937. English Heritage / National Monuments Record C37/752. *Checklist no. 78.*

Fig. 6-63. James Stuart. Fireplace wall of an unidentified room, possibly later the billiard room, Belvedere House, Erith, Kent, ca. 1764–80. Photographed in 1937. English Heritage / National Monuments Record C37/754.

Fig. 6-64. James Stuart. Ceiling of an unidentified room, possibly later the billiard room, Belvedere House, Erith, Kent, ca. 1764–80. Photographed in 1943. English Heritage / National Monuments Record A43/7147.
Checklist no. 77.

Fig. 6-65. Robert Nixon. "Camden Place, Kent," 1794. Engraved by J. Ellis. From Daniel Lysons, *Environs of London,* vol. 4, pt. 2 [ca. 1790]: 346. Courtesy of Guildhall Library, City of London.

room, library, anteroom to dining room, dining room, gallery, private room — however, when the rooms were photographed in 1937 and 1943 only the dining room suite had retained its original function (fig. 6-61). Photographs survive of a variety of unidentified rooms. One has a deep coved cornice very similar to that in the Gilt Room at Rathfarnham (fig. 6-62). Its size indicates this may have been the private room, or possibly this is the ceiling of the anteroom to the dining room. Another room with an elaborate plasterwork ceiling has a frieze of urns, foliage swags, and rosettes, a theme that is picked up on the chimneypiece and two inbuilt bookcases (figs. 6-63, 6-64). This may possibly have been the billiard room described by Waagen in 1857, although it was probably not used as that in Stuart's day, and by 1937 it was in use as an office.

Camden Place, Chislehurst, Kent
The last known country house commission of Stuart's career was Camden Place in Kent. The legend of Stuart as a man who squandered his talents and succumbed to

drink and alienated his clients, as immortalized by Mrs. Montagu, is belied by the remarks of Stuart's client in 1779. Charles Pratt, later first Earl Camden, wrote to Frances Stewart: "I am delighted . . . with the new apartments Stewart is fitting up for our residence. They are spacious & magnificent beyond either my wishes or expectation."[120] Pratt had the sense not to let his wife Elizabeth liaise solely with Stuart, but with the builder as well, for as he wrote to her on September 20, 1780:

> I perceive you have undertaken the improvement
> of the place in earnest . . . I like your Ideas, & am
> sure I shall be pleased with the Execution: . . . but
> I wish you wd consult with Stuart & Norris
> about the Bath immediately, for I am determined
> to execute that building at all events.[121]

The reference to Norris reveals that Stuart's builder had been succeeded by his son, Richard Norris the Younger. Camden Place survives as the Chislehurst Golf Club and is much altered since Stuart's day (fig. 6-65).[122] In the lit-

Fig. 6-66. James Stuart. Ceiling in the little dining room, Camden Place, Kent, ca. 1779–80. Photographed in 2006. Courtesy of The Chislehurst Golf Club, Kent. *Checklist no. 83.*

tle dining room there is a ceiling of rinceau-vine-like decoration derived from an antique source and medallions (fig. 6-66), and elsewhere chimneypieces and moldings appear to be original.[123] In the grounds stands a version of the Choragic Monument of Lysicrates (see fig. 7-33).

Like Wimbledon House, Nuneham Park, Sion Hill, Belvedere, and even Rathfarnham Castle, Camden Place was a villa, a compact house for hospitality within easy reach of a large town, and not a rambling ancestral seat full of heirlooms set in a vast agricultural estate. Villas offered the very latest in fashionable taste, in architecture, sculpture, furniture, and even paintings. Beyond the London town houses for which he is best known, Stuart found employment as a decorator of villas, modifying them as fashion statements. In so doing he provided one of the most transient forms of architecture. For country houses, with the exception of panels and chimneypieces for Wentworth Woodhouse and the second story to the link corridors at Shugborough, his known commissions were confined to designs, garden features, and painted decoration. At the risk of reading too much into the fragmentary surviving evidence, both in designs and on site, Stuart's work outside central London seems simpler and less ornate than his town houses and thus provides a balance to our understanding of him in terms of his celebrated interiors at Montagu House and Spencer House. The usual claim for Stuart that he designed interiors as entities, from architectural fittings to furniture and furnishings, is not confirmed by the evidence for his work outside London.

The main significance of Stuart's work beyond London lay in demonstrating how older houses (even those built just a generation earlier) could become fashionable without major structural alterations. As a pioneer of neoclassicism, he extended the available vocabulary of ornament by introducing motifs from Athenian art and architecture and by developing opportunities to locate modern sculpture in the domestic interior. However, the traditional role given to Stuart by his patrons and admirers, and by historians, as the champion of a new style, does not stand up to scrutiny, as he seems content to draw upon the example of Palladio, the English neo-Palladians, and even the neo-Romans, Piranesi and Adam. Stuart did not confine his sources to the fruits of his field research as much as his most fashion-conscious patrons and later advocates of the Greek Revival might have wished. Surveys of his known commissions that seek to trace a history of style have found a more archaeological treatment of interiors around 1760, compared to the more inventive decorative geometry of the 1770s that stops short of Adam's "filigree toy-work" (as William Chambers's characterized it).[124] An ingredient of the greater plasticity of his earlier designs that seems to have been overlooked is his interest in modern sculpture. Stuart's contribution as a designer of church monuments is well documented, but his interests in locating modern sculpture beyond the confines of the conventional caryatid chimneypiece becomes apparent when one looks beyond the familiar examples.

Through his success as a designer, Stuart showed how erudite quotations from Athenian buildings could be employed in diverse ways and media, combined with painted grotesque decoration and earlier architectural features. To the eclectic taste of his age, he brought a gift for synthesis. Most of all, he paved the way for Adam's self-proclaimed "revolution" in design by generating a desire for change, through his publications, conversation, and commissions. In an age of specialization and professionalization, Stuart may have been out of step, by continuing as a versatile decorator in the tradition of William Kent, but he may also be seen as forging an alternative path, one more familiar to interior designers today. Like Adam, he was no slave to antiquarian erudition but was an artist at heart who valued individual genius above professional custom and practice. Unlike Adam, he lacked the ambition to establish a distinctive style of his own. There may be no "Stuart Style," but without his example the opportunities for creativity in design in the later Georgian interior might never have been realized.

Acknowledgments: The writer wishes to thank Kerry Bristol, for kindly sharing her unpublished Ph.D. dissertation on Stuart and the genesis of Greek Revival architecture, and Catherine Arbuthnott, for contributing her own primary research, undertaken on behalf of the Bard Graduate Center's project. — J.B.

1. David Watkin, *Athenian Stuart, Pioneer of the Greek Revival* (London: George Allen and Unwin, 1982); Giles Worsley, "Nuneham Park Revisited — I," *Country Life* 177 (3 January 1985): 16 – 19; Worsley, "Hornby Castle, Yorkshire," *Country Life* 183 (29 June 1989): 188 – 93; Kerry Bristol "The Painted Rooms of 'Athenian' Stuart," *Georgian Group Journal* 10 (2000): 164 – 74; Bristol, "The Society of Dilettanti, James 'Athenian' Stuart and the Anson Family," *Apollo* 152 (July 2000): 46 – 54; Worsley, "Out from Adam's Shadow," *Country Life* 186 (14 May 1992): 100 – 103.

2. Howard Colvin, *A Biographical Dictionary of British Architecture, 1600–1800,* 3rd ed. (New Haven and London: Yale University Press, 1995): 939. Other reasons for his delay include his need to raise further funds and his attention to detail in correcting the engravers' plates himself.

3. Stuart, "Sketchbook . . . of buildings in North Italy," RIBA Drawings Collection SKB/336/2 [L3/4]: 63 – 80 (treatise on painting); Stuart's other surviving notebook was among those given to Woods by Taylor to use in preparing vol. 4 of *Antiquities*: Laing Mss., La.III.581, Edinburgh University Library.

4. *Antiquities,* vol. 1 (1762): v.

5. The 1748 "Proposals" were reprinted in full in *Antiquities,* vol. 1 (1762): v n. a.

6. Ibid.

7. See Kerry Bristol, "A Newly-Discovered Drawing by James Stuart," *Architectural History* 44 (2001): 39 – 44.

8. Ibid., 42. Stuart, "Sketchbook . . . of buildings in North Italy," RIBA Drawings Collection SKB/336/2 [L3/4]. For the two loose drawings, see John Harris, "Newly Acquired Designs by James Stuart in the British Architectural Library, Drawings Collection," *Architectural History* 22 (1979): nos. 22b and 26b.

9. Margaret Richardson, ed., *Catalogue of the Drawings of the Royal Institute of British Architects,* vol. S (Farnborough, UK: Gregg International, 1976): 124. In all, thirteen drawings in the sketchbook relate to the Villa Pisani.

10. Bristol, "Newly-Discovered Drawing" (2001): 43.

11. The list of names is in Stuart, "Sketchbook . . . of buildings in North Italy, RIBA Drawings Collection SKB/336/2 [L3/4]: 2.

12. Stuart to the Marquess of Rockingham, 28 September 1755, Wentworth Woodhouse Muniments R1/70, Sheffield Archives.

13. Ibid.

14. Ibid.

15. Marble was preferred to plaster casts, conveying greater prestige to the owner; see Johnathan Scott, *The Pleasures of Antiquity: British Collections of Greece and Rome* (New Haven and London: Yale University Press, 2003): 117.

16. Arthur Young, *A Six Months Tour through the North of England,* vol. 1 (London: W. Strahan, 1770): 281: "very elegant relievo's in panels, from designs of Mr Stewart."

17. Angelica Kauffman album, p. 23, Pierpont Morgan Library, 1966.10:39 (this page has been removed from the album and is stored separately, sharing an accession number). See Watkin, *Athenian Stuart* (1982): 54 and fig. 78, described as "perhaps related to a design for a medal." Watkin writes: "It seems that Rockingham intended these panels to be painted" (p. 32), but the letter of 28 September 1755 only refers to painted panels for the new dining room and painted overdoors for the "Saloon of the Center house." Rockingham collected coins and medals and these may have influenced the design of the panels. For the Rockingham – Stuart friendship see chap. 4, by Kerry Bristol, in this volume.

18. See Francis Haskell and Nicholas Penny, *Taste and the Antique: The Lure of Classical Sculpture, 1500 – 1900* (New Haven and London: Yale University Press, 1982): 24 – 25; Malcolm Baker, "Sculpture for Palladian Interiors: Rysbrack's Reliefs and their Setting," in Katherine Eustace, ed., *Michael Rysbrack: Sculptor, 1694 – 1770,* exh. cat. (Bristol: City of Bristol Museum and Art Gallery, 1982): 35 – 41.

19. Baker, "Sculpture for Palladian Interiors" (1982): 35 – 41.

20. "Proposals," 1748, reprinted in *Antiquities,* vol. 1 (1762): v n. a.

21. Ibid., 8. In the original "Proposal," vol. 3 was to be devoted to statues and bas reliefs.

22. For Cardinal Albani see Haskell and Penny, *Taste and the Antique* (1982): 64 – 67, 144 – 46; the installation design by Albani's architect, Carlo Marchioni, is shown (ibid., fig 34, Cooper-Hewitt Museum, New York). Another copy of the Antinous relief would later be installed in the vestibule at Spencer House (see fig. 5-8 in this volume). Friedman dates the design to ca. 1756 and proposes that the Spencers "themselves conceived the idea" of installing a cast of the Antinous in the entrance hall at Spencer House in 1763, but evidently Stuart and Rockingham had the idea first; see Joseph Friedman, *Spencer House: Chronicle of a Great London Mansion* (London: Zwemmer, 1993): 92. It seems strange that Stuart and Rockingham did not place it in the grand saloon at Wentworth Woodhouse. As the room has two chimneypieces, they may have lacked a suitable relief to stand opposite. The scheme was only completed in 1826 with two overmantel reliefs by John Gibson: *The Hours Leading Forth the Horses of the Sun* and *Phaeton driving the Chariot of the Sun* (still in situ).

23. Paget Toynbee, ed., "Walpole's Journals of Visits to Country Seats," Walpole Society annual, vol. 16 (1927 – 28): 71.

24. Invoice from Horobin, "Masons works done for the most Honourable the Marquis of Rockingham by the order of James Stuart Esqr.," Wentworth Woodhouse Muniments, Vouchers for Works of Art, Sheffield Archives. Also see Bristol, "Stuart and the Genesis of the Greek Revival" (1997): 240 – 41 n. 731.

25. Marcus Binney, "Wentworth Woodhouse Revisited — II," *Country Life* 173 (24 March 1983): 710.

26. Young, *Six Months* (1770): 734.

27. Rockingham to Sir Charles Knowles (draft), 23 June 1773, Wentworth Woodhouse Muniments R1/1432, Sheffield Archives.

28. For Anson see Bristol, "Society of Dilettanti" (2000): 46 – 54; and see chap. 4 by Kerry Bristol, in this volume. For John Dick, the lists of antiques bought by Anson, and correspondence regarding the collection see Joseph Nollekens to Anson, 26 July, 30 October, 1 November 1765; 21 January, 9 December 1767, 19 April 1768, Lichfield Ms. SCRO D615/P (S)/1/6/1-6, Staffordshire Record Office.

29. The attributions are made on stylistic grounds; see Eileen Harris, "A Flair for the Grandiose: The Architecture of Thomas Wright — II," *Country Life* 150 (2 September 1971): 546 – 50. See also John Martin Robinson, *Shugborough* (London: National Trust, 1989): 27.

30. Inventory of the contents of Shugborough, ca. 1773, Lichfield Ms. D615/E(H) 10, Staffordshire Record Office. See also Bristol "Painted Rooms" (2000): 169. Stuart wrote to Anson: "The drawings for the bed Chamber at Shugborough are just finished"; he also complained that "the insolence of your people is insupportable"; see Stuart to Anson, 17 September 1766, Lichfield Ms. D615/P(S)/1/6/21.

31. Philip, Viscount Royston, to Philip Yorke, first Earl of Hardwicke, 22 August 1763, Hardwicke Papers, Add. Ms. 35,352 fol. 406, BL. Bristol notes that the room "was probably similar to his Painted Room at Spencer House"; see Bristol, "Society of Dilettanti" (2000): 48.

32. Philip Yorke, first Earl of Hardwicke to Philip, Viscount Royston,

27 August 1763, Hardwicke Papers, Add. Ms. 35,352 fol. 413, BL.

33. Stuart to Anson, 18 September 1764, Lichfield Ms. D615/P(S)/1/6/14, Staffordshire Record Office.

34. See Worsley, "Nuneham Park," pt. 1 (1985): 16.

35. Bristol cites Lady Harcourt to Viscount Newnham, 10 September 1756, in which she writes: "Stewart, who I mentioned to you in former letters, paid us a visit last week at Newnham"; see Bristol, "Stuart and the Genesis of the Greek Revival" (1997): 243. Worsley notes that "it seems very likely that Lord Harcourt called him in to fit up all the main rooms . . . in 1757 or 1758"; Worsley, "Nuneham Park," pt. 1 (1985): 19.

36. Quoted in Worsley, "Nuneham Park," pt. 1 (1985): 18.

37. Quoted in ibid.

38. Ibid.

39. Worsley, "Nuneham Park," pt. 1 (1985): 18.

40. Francis Russell, "The Hanging and Display of Pictures, 1700 – 1850," in Gervase Jackson-Stops, ed., *The Fashioning and Functioning of the British Country House,* Studies in the History of Art, vol. 25 (Washington: National Gallery of Art; Hanover, NH: University Press of New England, 1989): 141.

41. Carlomarat, or "Maretta frame," was a type of picture frame named after the seventeenth-century painter Carlo Maratti. It became the standard choice for old master paintings purchased on the Grand Tour.

42. William Mason to Horace Walpole, Nuneham, 14 July 1782: "We are here in a most chaotic state, and dine as if among the ruins of Palmyra, with a broken frieze of Stuart's in one corner, and a French moulding (I know not its name) which is to be its substitute in another"; Horace Walpole, *The Yale Edition of Horace Walpole's Correspondence,* vol. 29, *Horace Walpole's Correspondence with William Mason,* ed. W. S. Lewis, Grover Cronin Jr., and Charles H. Bennett (New Haven and London, Yale University Press, 1955): 268.

43. As noted in Worsley "Nuneham Park," pt. 1 (1985): 19.

44. Ibid., 18.

45. The best introduction is Alastair Laing, "The Eighteenth-Century Chimneypiece," in Jackson-Stops, ed., *Fashioning and Functioning of the British Country House* (1989): 241 – 51.

46. William Chambers, *A Treatise on Civil Architecture* (London: printed for the author by J. Haberkorn, 1759): 77 – 78.

47. Isaac Ware, *A Complete Body of Architecture: Adorned with Plans and Elevations* (London: T. Osborne and J. Shipton, 1756): bk. 6, "Of Chimneypieces."

48. For the importance of chimneypieces as domestic showplaces for "modern" sculpture see Julius Bryant *Thomas Banks (1735 – 1805), Britain's First Modern Sculptor,* exh. cat., (London: Sir John Soane's Museum, 2005): cat. nos. 52, 53. For his portrait by Francis Hayman in 1760, Wilton chose to show himself as a designer of a giant telamonic chimneypiece that is dominated by a pair of caryatids for the gallery of Northumberland House. Carved by Benjamin Carter, it is now in the Victoria & Albert Museum, as is the portrait.

49. "Stuart's plans . . . embody the first expressions of neo-Classicism in English interior design"; see John Hardy and Helena Hayward,

"Kedleston Hall, Derbyshire — II," *Country Life* 163 (2 February 1978): 262 – 66.

50. Leslie Harris, *Robert Adam and Kedleston: The Making of a Neo-Classical Masterpiece,* ed. Gervase Jackson-Stops, exh. cat., Cooper-Hewitt Museum, New York (London: National Trust, 1987); L. Harris, "The Picture Collection at Kedleston Hall," *Connoisseur* 198 (July 1978): 208 – 17; Francis Russell, "Securing the Future," *Country Life* 171 (23 July 1987): 96 – 99.

51. See Eileen Harris, *The Genius of Robert Adam: His Interiors* (London and New Haven: Paul Mellon Centre for Studies in British Art and Yale University Press, 2001): 19 – 21. See also Leslie Harris, "Kedleston and the Curzons" in *Robert Adam and Kedleston Hall: The Making of a Neo-classical Masterpiece* (London: National Trust, 1987): 9 – 12.

52. Nicholas Antram, Gervase Jackson-Stops, and Alastair Laing, *Kedleston Hall* (London: National Trust, 1988): 28.

53. L. Harris, "Kedleston and the Curzons" (1987): 12.

54. Ibid., 10 – 11.

55. Robert Adam to James Adam, 11 December 1758, Clerk of Penicuik Ms. GD. 18 4854, National Archives of Scotland, Edinburgh.

56. Ibid.

57. Ibid.

58. See E. Harris, *Genius of Robert Adam* (2001): 19.

59. Watkin (*Athenian Stuart* [1982]) describes "Adam's victory over Stuart" (p. 30) and how he "ousted Stuart from Kedleston" (p. 40) as if they were both tendering for the same commission.

60. Eileen Harris has noted, in response to claims for Stuart as ahead in this service, that Adam designed furniture and chimneypieces for Kedleston and Croome in 1760; see E. Harris, *Genius of Robert Adam* (2001): 336 n. 82.

61. See Andrew Moore, ed., *Houghton Hall: The Prime Minister, the Empress and the Heritage,* exh. cat., Norwich Castle Museum and the Iveagh Bequest, Kenwood (London: Philip Wilson; Wappinger Falls, NY: Antique Collectors' Club, 1996): cat. nos. 38, 39.

62. See John Harris, *The Palladian Revival. Lord Burlington, His Villa and Garden at Chiswick,* exh. cat., Canadian Centre for Architecture, Montreal, et al. (New Haven and London: in association with Yale University Press, 1994): 148, cat 50.

63. John Fowler and John Cornforth, *English Decoration in the 18th Century,* 2nd ed. (London: Barrie and Jenkins: 1978): 26 – 27, where Stuart's designs for Kedleston are dated to 1757.

64. Russell, "Hanging and Display" (1989): 141. Russell notes Leslie Harris's suggestion that Curzon took Holkham "as his *point de depart.*"

65. *As noted by* L. Harris, *Robert Adam and Kedleston Hall* (1987): 27 – 28.

66. James Stuart, "Sketchbook . . . of buildings in North Italy," SKB/336/2 [L3/4], RIBA Drawings Collection. The treatise on painting is pp. 63 – 80.

67. In 1750 Curzon had married the seventeen-year-old Lady Caroline Colyear, daughter of the second Earl of Portmore. This is the only aspect of the scheme that Curzon adopted, but he commissioned the double portrait from Nathaniel Hone by 1761. Stuart's composition may have indirectly inspired Gainsborough's masterpiece, *The Morning Walk* (National Gallery, London). Stuart painted portraits of George II and William III for the Whig Club, York.

68. John Kenworthy-Browne, "Designing around the Statues: Matthew Brettingham's Casts at Kedleston," *Apollo* 137 (April 1993): 248 – 52; Kenworthy-Browne notes that the Brettinghams supplied the Roman casts and Wilton the Florentine casts.

69. Robert Adam to James Adam, 11 December 1758, Clerk of Penicuik Ms. GD 18 4854, National Archives of Scotland, Edinburgh.

70. Adam designed a similar caryatid chimneypiece in 1760 for Hatchlands, Surrey, where it remains.

71. Russell, "Hanging and Display" (1989): 144. Russell notes: "It was at Kedleston that Adam paid most attention to the hanging of pictures."

72. Horace Walpole, *The Yale Edition of Horace Walpole's Correspondence,* vol. 10, *Horace Walpole's Correspondence with George Montagu,* ed. W. S. Lewis and Ralph S. Brown Jr. (New Haven: Yale University Press; London: H. MIlford, Oxford University Press, 1941): 230.

73. See Kerry Bristol, "22 Portman Square: Mrs. Montagu and her 'Palais de la vieillesse'," *British Art Journal* 2 (Summer 2001): 72 – 85.

74. Lyttelton to Mrs. Montagu, Hagley, October 1758, Montagu Papers MO 1280, 21, Henry E. Huntington Library, San Marino, California, cited in Bristol, "Stuart and the Genesis of the Greek Revival" (1997): 301. The paintings may have impressed Mrs. Montagu as well; by the summer of 1762 she had commissioned Stuart to paint her bedchamber in her London house at Hill Street, with what she called "Zephirs and Zephirettes." The work was still unfinished in November 1767 (MO 4994). At Hagley, as at Kedleston, Stuart's opinion may have been sought on the arrangement of sculptures for five plaster casts of statues, including Sansovino's *Bacchus.* These were sent from Florence to Hagley in 1756, a year before Joseph Wilton sent four, also including a cast of the Sansovino, from Florence to Kedleston; see Kenworthy-Browne "Designing Around the Statues" (1993): 251.

75. For this collaboration see Julius Bryant, *Marble Hill, Twickenham* (London, English Heritage 2002); and Bryant, *Mrs Howard, A Woman of Reason,* exh. cat., Marble Hill House, Twickenham (London: English Heritage, 1988).

76. Colen Campbell, with James Gandon and John Woolfe, *Vitruvius Britannicus: or, The British Architect . . . ,* vol. 5 (London: n.p., 1771), pl. 20, pp. 4, 20, 21, 22.

77. Bryant, *Marble Hill* (2002): 9 – 12.

78. See Friedman, *Spencer House* (1993): 92 n. 23.

79. For Piranesi's vases see Scott, *Pleasures of Antiquity* (2003): 104 – 7; Andrew Wilton and Ilaria Bignamini, eds., *Grand Tour: The Lure of Italy in the Eighteenth Century,* exh. cat. (London: Tate Gallery 1996): cat. no. 154 – 55.

80. Stuart also had a supplier of vases in artificial stone: they crown the skyline of the orangery built for Shugborough in 1764. They may have been made by the builder Webb, who was likely the maker of the urns on the triumphal arch at Shugborough. Stuart writes of "Webb's opinion of the Greenhouse . . . I will send him the drawings for the Vases in a week or 10 days" (Stuart to Anson, 19 June 1764, Lichfield Ms.

D615/P(S)/1/6/7, Staffordshire Record Office); "The Vases which you are pleased to mention for the Arch may be wrought by Webb" (Stuart to Anson, n.d., Lichfield Ms. D615/P(S)/1/6/9); "I will call on the artificial Stoneman tomorrow" (Stuart to Anson, 23 September 1769, Lichfield Ms. D615/P(S)/1/6/27). For another letter about vases see Stuart to Anson, "June or July 1764," Lichfield Mss. D615/P(S)/1/6/8A. For Stuart and Wedgwood in the 1770s, see Alison Kelly, *Decorative Wedgwood in Architecture and Furniture* (London: Country Life, 1965): 26, 74 – 75.

81. Bryant, *Mrs Howard* (1988): cat. no. 29.

82. John Thomas Smith, *Nollekens and His Times* (1828; rev. ed., London: Turnstile Press, 1949): 4 – 5.

83. Ibid., 5. Stuart's involvement in the society declined from 1761 when he resigned as co-chairman of the Committee of Polite Arts.

84. Seymour Howard, "Boy on a Dolphin: Nollekens and Cavaceppi," *Art Bulletin* 46 (June 1964): 177 – 89.

85. Nollekens's marble sculpture, *Castor and Pollux* (Victoria & Albert Museum), a copy from a cast of the original, was made for Anson in 1767 in Rome.

86. John Flaxman, *Lectures on Sculpture* (1829; new ed., London: Bell and Sons, 1889): 295; see also chap. 9, by G. Sullivan, in this volume.

87. For Stuart's drawings of the metopes on the Parthenon, see *Antiquities,* vol. 2 (ca. 1790), chap. 2, esp. pls. VI, X – XII. For the drawings of the Parthenon made in 1674 by Jacques Carrey (Cabinet des medailles, Bibliothèque Nationale de France), see chap. 3, by F. Salmon, in this volume.

88. The carved metopes are prominent in a watercolor painted by William Pars in 1766, now in the British Museum; see D. E. L. Haynes, *An Historical Guide to the Sculptures of the Parthenon* (London: British Museum, 1971): 8.

89. See John Cornforth, *Early Georgian Interiors* (New Haven and London: Yale University Press, 2004): 141.

90. See Friedman, *Spencer House* (1993): 92, 94 – 95 (illus.), figs. 48 – 50.

91. Philip, Viscount Royston, to Philip Yorke, first Earl of Hardwicke, August 1763, Add. Ms. 35,352, BL.

92. See Cornforth, *Early Georgian Interiors* (2004): 146.

93. Diary of Thomas Hollis, 3 September 1759, MS Eng 1191, Houghton Library, Harvard University; quoted in Bristol, "Stuart and the Genesis of the Greek Revival" (1997): 255 – 56.

94. J. Harris, "Newly Acquired Designs" (1979): 73 no. 16a.

95. For Stuart's collection of books, see "Catalogue of pictures by Moreland . . . and other effects, of the late James Stuart . . . ," sale cat., Greenwoods, London, 27 June 1791; copy in Courtauld Institute Library, Br A 5059 1791/06/27. Stuart's copy of *Le antichità di Ercolano eposte* was lot 39, described as "Pictures of Herculaneum."

96. Toynbee, ed., "Walpole's Journals of Visits to Country Seats" (1927 – 28): 15.

97. See Victoria Percy and Gervase Jackson-Stops, "'Exquisite Taste and Tawdry Ornament': The Travel Journals of the 1st Duchess of Northumberland — II," *Country Life* 155 (7 February 1974): 250. The remark was probably made between 1755 and 1763, but the article gives

it as in 1752. See also Giles Worsley, "Stuart at Sion," *Country Life* 184 (4 October 1990): 187.

98. Worsley, "Hornby Castle" (1989): 191. He also cites the pier table as "a classic example of Stuart furniture design."

99. J. Harris, "Newly Acquired Designs (1979): 77.

100. Cited by Worsley, "Hornby Castle" (1989): 189.

101. Builders bills no. 18, March 1761, Croome Archives, Croome Estate Office. See E. Harris, *Genius of Robert Adam* (2001): 42. According to Harris, "'Athenian' Stuart's presence at Croome (noted by Geoffrey Beard but overlooked by architectural historians) can probably be dated to around 1759, when he was working at Hagley for Coventry's close friend and arbiter of taste, Lord Lyttelton. Regardless of what he did and why it was redone by Vassalli, the fact of Stuart's being at Croome is important in itself as the first sign of Coventry's avant-garde interest in the rising neo-classical style." See also Beard, "Decorators and Furniture Makers at Croome Court," *Furniture History* 29 (1993): 88 – 113.

102. James Hakewill, *The History of Windsor and Its Neighbourhood* (London: E. Lloyd, 1813): 290 – 91.

103. Toynbee, ed., "Walpole's Journals of Visits to Country Seats" (1927 – 28): 38.

104. Charles James Feret, *Fulham Old and New . . . ,* vol. 3 (London: Leadenhall Press; New York: Charles Scribner's Sons, 1900): 234 – 39.

105. Stuart to Anson, 23 September 1769, Lichfield Ms. D615/P(S)/1/6/27, Staffordshire Record Office.

106. In 1763 Methuen commissioned Peter Scheemakers to supply a caryatid chimneypiece (now in the Picture Gallery at Corsham Court) for £325; he also paid him for another, costing £100, by 1766. Scheemakers's former pupil, Prince Hoare (d. 1769) was paid £242 for chimneypieces in the library, bedroom, and dressing-room at Corsham Court between 1760 and 1762, and for others by 1765. See M. I. Webb, "Chimney-pieces by Scheemakers," *Country Life* 121 (14 March 1957): 491 – 92. See also chap. 4, by K. Bristol, in this volume.

107. Edward McParland, "Rathfarnham Castle, Co. Dublin," *Country Life* 172 (9 September 1982): 734 – 37, 737; G. Madden "Rathfarnham Castle," *Irish Arts Review* 4, no. 1 (1987): 22 – 26; Kerry Bristol, "Rathfarnham Castle in the Architectural Oeuvre of James 'Athenian' Stuart: A Question of Patronage," in M. McCarthy, ed., *Lord Charlemont and His Circle* (Dublin and Portland, Oregon: Four Courts, 2001): 113 – 22; and Edward McParland, review of *Lord Charlemont and His Circle,* in *Apollo* 157 (January 2003): 56.

108. A. P. W. Malcolmson, "A House Divided: The Loftus Family, Earls and Marquesses of Ely, c. 1600 – c. 1900," in David Dickson and Cormac Ó'Gráda, eds., *Refiguring Ireland: Essays in Honour of L. M. Cullen* (Dublin: Lilliput Press, 2003): 184 – 224. See also Worsley, "Out from Adam's Shadow" (1992): 100 – 103.

109. Lady Shelburne cited by E. McParland in "Rathfarnham Castle" (1982): 737. The attribution to Stuart was first made by John Cornforth as noted in ibid.

110. Eric Robinson and Keith Thompson, "Matthew Boulton's Mechanical Paintings," *Burlington Magazine* 112 (August 1970): 497 – 507; for Kauffmann's mechanical paintings see also Julius Bryant,

Kenwood: Paintings in the Iveagh Bequest (New Haven and London: Yale University Press, 2003): 146 – 49, cat. no. 30.

111. See Samuel Lewis, *A Topographical Dictionary of Ireland . . .* , vol. 2 (London: S. Lewis and Co., 1837).

112. Joseph Burke, *English Art, 1714 – 1800* (Oxford: Clarendon, 1976): 323. The date of the commission is uncertain but Stuart's work is cited in 1775 in Walter Harrison, *A New and Universal History, Description and Survey of the Cities of London and Westminster, the Borough of Southwark, and their adjacent parts* (London: J. Cooke, 1775): 601.

113. Stuart had previously used the Diocletian window at Nuneham Park for the church (where it derives from Burlington's Chiswick) and in the stables; he would use it again at Montagu House.

114. Kelly, *Decorative Wedgwood* (1965): 65 – 66, 75, figs. 25, 26.

115. The rebuilding has been dated to 1764, the year after the death of Sampson Gideon Senior; see John A. Pritchard, *A History of Erith*, Pt. 5, *Belvedere and Bostall,* 2nd ed. (London: Borough of Bexley Libraries and Museums Department, 1994): 8.

116. Reginald Blunt, ed., *Mrs Montagu, "Queen of the Blues," Her Letters and Friendships from 1762 to 1800,* vol. 2 (London: Constable and Company, 1923): 83.

117. Only one fine room was saved from the old house; the Gold Room, or Gilt Room.

118. H. Strickland, "Belvedere As It Was," *Erith Times, Belvedere and Abbey Wood Chronicle,* 26 January 1912, extract in "Erith Borough Council Correspondence: Belvedere House, 1947 – 1960," Bexley Libraries and Archives service LAER/DA/7/7/23.

119. Dr. Waagen, *Galleries and cabinets of art in Great Britain, being an account of more than forty collections of paintings, drawings, sculptures, Mss &c. &c. visited in 1854 and 1856, and now for the first time described . . .* (London: John Murray, 1857): 275.

120. Charles Pratt to Frances Stewart [1779] Ms. U840 C3/2, Centre for Kentish Studies. See also Ms. U840 C7/8; Add. Mss. 27,576 f.21, BL; and Worsley, "Out from Adam's Shadow" (1992): 100 – 103. Worsley notes: "Hasted's History and Topographical survey of the County of Kent, published in 1778, describes the 'great additions and improvements as well to the house itself as the grounds about it' he had made since 1770.'"

121. Charles Pratt to Elizabeth Pratt, 20 September 1780, MS U840 C7/8, Centre for Kentish Studies.

122. Thanks are due to the club secretary, Mr Peter Ford, and to the assistant secretary, Anne Wren, for kindly providing access for Catherine Arbuthnott.

123. Worsley, "Out from Adam's Shadow" (1992): 100 – 103.

124. William Chambers, *Treatise on the Decorative Part of Civil Architecture,* 3rd ed. (London: Joseph Smeeton, 1791): 132.

Fig. 7-1. James Stuart. The Tower of the Winds, Shugborough, Staffordshire, 1764–65. Photographed in 2006. Courtesy of Shugborough (The National Trust, UK). *Checklist no. 92.*

CHAPTER 7

THE GARDEN BUILDINGS

ALEXANDER MARR

Landscape architecture occupies a significant position in James Stuart's architectural oeuvre.[1] Of the relatively few architectural commissions that Stuart received between his return from Greece in about 1755 and his death in 1788, at least one third were garden buildings (fig. 7-1).[2] These ranged from single, picturesquely sited monuments, such as the early Doric Temple at Hagley, Worcestershire (about 1758; fig. 7-2), to whole suites of evocative garden buildings, such as those built at Shugborough, Staffordshire, for Thomas Anson throughout the 1750s and 1760s (fig. 7-3), derived mostly from Stuart's drawings for *Antiquities of Athens*.

Not all of Stuart's garden buildings were simple, straightforward copies of ancient Greek exemplars.[3] Stuart designed a park building for Wimpole Hall described at the time as a "Modern Italian Loggia" (fig. 7-4),[4] while his involvement with the design of the Church of All Saints at Nuneham Courtenay resulted in a building that is "more Roman than Greek in style" (fig. 7-5).[5] Indeed, the Triumphal Arch at Shugborough, which he based on a drawing for *Antiquities of Athens,* was essentially Roman, deriving from the Arch of Hadrian, a Roman monument in a Greek location, aptly described as "in a stylistically somewhat Baroque taste" (figs. 7-6,

Fig. 7-2. James Stuart. The Doric Temple at Hagley, Worcestershire, 1758–59. Photographed in 2006. Courtesy of the Viscount Cobham. *Checklist no. 84.*

7-7).[6] This eclecticism is entirely consistent with Stuart's architectural work as a whole. Far from wishing to introduce into English architecture a strict, authentically Greek style, Stuart was apparently quite content to take

Fig. 7-3. Nicholas Thomas Dall. *Shugborough and the Park from the East,* ca. 1768–69. Oil on canvas. Courtesy of Shugborough, The Anson Collection, SHUG.P.16 (The National Trust, UK). *Checklist no. 85.*

Fig. 7-4. Daniel Lerpiniere. Prospect House, or Hill House, Wimpole Hall, Cambridgeshire, 1778. Engraving. By permission of The British Library, London, King George III Topographical Collection, K. Top vol. 8 pl. 83A. *Checklist no. 101.*

Fig. 7-5. Simon, first Earl Harcourt, with James Stuart. The Church of All Saints, Nuneham Park, Oxfordshire, 1764. Photographed in 2006. Courtesy of Brahma Kumaris: The Global Retreat Centre. *Checklist no. 96.*

Fig. 7-6. James Stuart. The Triumphal Arch (facing east) in the park at Shugborough, Staffordshire, ca. 1764. Photographed in 2006. Courtesy of Shugborough (The National Trust, UK). *Checklist no. 89.*

Fig. 7-7. Southeast elevation of the Arch of Hadrian. Engraving. From *Antiquities of Athens,* vol. 3 (1794): chap. 3, pl. IV. Courtesy of the Library, The Bard Graduate Center for Studies in the Decorative Arts, Design, and Culture, New York. *Checklist no. 90.*

Fig. 7-8. Sanderson Miller. The Ruined Castle at Hagley, Worcestershire, 1747–48. Photographed in 2006. Courtesy of the Viscount Cobham.

Roman, Italian Renaissance, and baroque buildings as his models.[7]

In the case of Stuart's sources for garden buildings the question of authenticity is paramount. Some of Stuart's patrons believed that the monuments he had designed for their parks were authentically Greek—a novel and highly desirable addition to a mid-eighteenth-century British landscape. For example, in 1758 Lord Lyttelton wrote to Mrs. Montagu that the Doric Temple Stuart was creating for him at Hagley was "a true Attick building."[8]

Authenticity was certainly an important consideration when it came to commissioning and appraising landscape buildings in the second half of the eighteenth century. British antiquary Horace Walpole famously remarked of Sanderson Miller's ruined castle at Hagley that it had the "true rust of the Baron's Wars" (fig. 7-8) while travel writer and topographical author Thomas Pennant described the Chinese House at Shugborough as "a true pattern of the architecture of that nation, taken in the country by the skilful pencil of Sir Percy Brett: not a mongrel invention of British carpenters."[9] These two examples present two distinct, but complementary, types of authenticity. The ruined castle could claim to be authentic because it made use of genuine medieval windows from the nearby Halesowen Abbey; the Chinese House, meanwhile, was based upon first-hand experience of genuine Chinese architecture.[10] This latter type of authenticity is especially applicable to Stuart's architectural work, which is surrounded by a rhetoric of witness similar to that appended to the Chinese House. For eighteenth-century patrons, the truly "Attick" nature of structures such as the Hagley Temple lay in the fact that their designer had been to Greece, studied the architecture there intensely, and made numerous drawings of the monuments on-site.

Yet when it came to designing garden buildings, Stuart not only adapted his drawings of ancient monuments but also, in some cases, employed architectural elements that were not authentically Greek, even though they might appear so at first glance. For example, Stuart's Doric Temple at Hagley, trumpeted by many as the first example of the true Greek Doric in British architecture, was in fact filtered through Vitruvius's reconstruction of that order.[11] The Theseion at Athens, on which Stuart's temple was based, uses a diameter-to-height ratio for the columns of 1:6. Stuart, however, follows Vitruvius with a ratio of 1:7. Stuart's patrons may be forgiven, however, for believing that their architect's designs were "Attick" through and through. Greece was not yet a routine destination of the Grand Tourist, and knowledge of what actually constituted Greek architecture was slight. Furthermore, the alterations Stuart made in order to turn ancient Greek monuments into eighteenth-century garden buildings were minor. His patrons were probably not concerned that their park buildings should be totally and authentically Greek, down to the minutest measurement. Rather, they were perfectly content with structures that appeared, to all intents and purposes, to be faithful copies of the drawings for *Antiquities*, championed by Stuart and Revett for their first-hand pedigree, accuracy, and comprehensiveness. These edifices would be instantly recognizable to anyone familiar with Stuart's drawings for *Antiquities* or with the printed volumes published from 1762 onward.

In fact much of the cachet in having Stuart design a garden building revolved around exclusivity. Once the first volume of *Antiquities* had been published, anyone could copy the engravings therein. Yet prior to this event, Stuart alone was able to grant access to his portfolio of drawings, and because the publication of subsequent volumes was much delayed he was able to maintain this exclusivity for certain monuments, such as the Arch of Hadrian, published eventually in volume three (1794; see fig. 7-7).

The significance of Stuart's Athenian drawings leads to a further notable point about his garden buildings—the majority were commissioned by members of the Society of Dilettanti. Stuart was elected to the society in 1751 and this provided him with a group of patrons eager for the fruits of his Greek sojourn. This tight-knit circle of friends and acquaintances enabled Stuart to practice architecture, for "without the patronage of certain members of the Society, it is conceivable that he would not have developed

Fig. 7-9. James Stuart. Choragic Monument of Lysicrates, also known as the Lanthorn of Demosthenes, Shugborough, Staffordshire, 1764–69. Undated photograph. Courtesy of Shugborough (The National Trust, UK). *Checklist no. 93.*

his architectural practice at all" (see chap. 4).[12] Members of the society could, with some justification, claim privileged access to Stuart's portfolio of drawings; the society partly funded the publication of the later volumes, while individual Dilettanti members had financially supported Stuart and Revett's work from the outset.

Although Stuart's drawings may have motivated members of the society to commission garden buildings from him, Stuart likely had little control over where the buildings were placed. This is made apparent from the extant correspondence between Stuart and his most important Dilettanti patron, Thomas Anson, concerning the copy of the Lanthorn of Demosthenes for Shugborough Park (fig. 7-9). In June 1764 Stuart wrote to Anson: "I cannot figure to myself where the lanthorn of

Fig. 7-10. Obelisk and Stuart's Doric Temple, in the park at Hagley, Worcestershire. Photographed in 2006. Courtesy of the Viscount Cobham.

Demosthenes can be placed to more advantage than on the spot you showed me near the Ladies seat, I long to know the spot."[13] Anson had clearly chosen the site, and although Stuart approved of the location, he was powerless to influence the situation of the monument further.

Despite this example of Stuart's lack of involvement in the positioning of one of his garden buildings, the importance of their location cannot be stressed enough. Stuart's garden buildings were, with a few exceptions, built with the significance of views firmly in mind. Of course, the period during which Stuart was designing landscape architecture marked the development of the vogue for the Picturesque in Britain, an aesthetic to which prospects and vistas were vital, spurred on largely by the fashion for the landscape paintings of the French classical landscape painters Claude Lorrain and Nicolas Poussin, experience of Continental landscape on the Grand Tour, and an ever-increasing awareness of the variety prevalent in British scenery.[14] In most cases Stuart's garden buildings clearly indicate a response to this emerging sensitivity to certain types of landscape and the arrangement of carefully determined views. Notably, the views to *and* from his garden buildings were often considered to be of equal worth. For example, the Greek Doric Temple at Hagley was "built with as much an eye for the views from it as for those towards it" (fig. 7-10).[15]

George, first Lord Lyttelton, began remodeling Hagley Hall in 1751, and it seems that Stuart was first employed there as a decorative painter. In October 1758 Lyttelton wrote to the society hostess and bluestocking Mrs. Montagu that Stuart had "engaged to paint me a Flora and four pretty little Zephyrs in my drawing room Ceiling"[16] The zephyrs survive today in the ceiling of what is now known as the Tapestry Room (see fig. 6-37). At around the same time, Lyttelton commissioned Stuart to construct the elegant Doric hexastyle temple for his "deliciously rococo" park.[17]

Richard Pococke, author of celebrated travel books, visited Hagley twice, in 1751 and 1756, and provides us with an engaging description of the landscape into which Stuart's temple was placed:

> Sr Thomas Lyttelton's house at Hagley is situated near the western foot of a hill, which rises greatly and is improved into a park, round which there is a plantation of trees, and a shady walk; in the middle is wood and lawn, and on the south side a wood called the Hermitage . . . A very

small stream runs from the hill . . . and on the brow of the hill are three or four clumps of trees and seats for repose, as well as to enjoy the prospect, which is very extensive, taking in a great tract of country, as, to the south the Morven Hills, and the country beyond Gloucester, to the west the Clee hills and the mountains of Wales beyond them, as well as to the north-west, and of the Rekin that way.[18]

When Pococke first visited Hagley, Miller's ruined castle, "seen in different views from many parts of the lawns and wood," had already been erected, as had "the rustick building the rotondo . . . which is seen through a fine visto which in some places meets at the top, and forms a sort of Gothic arch."[19] Clearly, views of garden buildings were an important consideration for Lyttelton's landscape improvements. By 1751 the park also boasted the Prince's Pillar (so-called "because it was presented to Mr. Lyttelton by the late prince of Wales"), an obelisk, grotto, and cascade, as well as urns dedicated to the memory of British poet Alexander Pope, and seats commemorating poets James Thomson (who had composed verses on Hagley) and John Milton. Lyttelton was clearly a man of sensibility, and the park he created was a landscape of association, its varied buildings summoning up a host of pleasing sensations and melancholy thoughts, transporting the viewer to the dark and ruinous Middle Ages or to the pagan splendor of ancient Rome.[20]

It is unsurprising, therefore, that Lyttelton should have added a "Greek" temple to a park that already featured "Roman" and "Medieval" buildings. He may have been quoting partly from the landscape iconography of Stowe, Buckinghamshire, one of the most famous gardens in England, where gothic and classical buildings were juxtaposed for associative effect. The majority of the scheme at Stowe had been created by Lyttelton's uncle, Sir Richard Temple, Viscount Cobham, whose "Grecian temple set in an English Vale of Tempe" is echoed at Hagley.[21] Stowe's Grecian temple was continued under the direction of Lyttelton's cousin, Earl Temple, who renamed it the Temple of Concord and Victory, and filled it with sixteen plaster medallions, several of which are based on designs by Stuart for commemorative medals (fig. 7-11; see figs. 4-27, 4-28).[22] Some understanding of Lyttelton's motives in commissioning Stuart's Doric Temple at Hagley can be gleaned from a letter to Mrs. Montagu of 1758:

Fig. 7-11. James Lovell, after a design by James Stuart. Medallion in the Temple of Concord and Victory at Stowe, Buckinghamshire, 1763. Terracotta, plaster, lead inscription and ribbon, wood. Inscribed: "MARTINIQUE &C." Photographed in 2006. Courtesy of Stowe Landscape Gardens (The National Trust, UK). *Checklist no. 177.*

Mr Anson and Mr Steward who were with me last Week are true lovers of Hagley, but their Delight in it was disturbed by a blustering Wind, which gave them colds and a little chill[d] their Imagination itself. Yet Steward seems almost as fond of my Vale, as of the Thessala Tempe, which I believe you heard him describe when I brought him to see you. Nor could the East Wind deterr him from mounting the Hills. He is going to embellish one of them with a true Attick building, a Portico of six Pillars, which will make a fine Object to my new House, and command a most beautiful View of the Country.[23]

It is clear from this passage that the Doric Temple was conceived as an eye-catching object to be viewed from the house and grounds, as well as marking a spot that pro-

Fig. 7-12. Artist unknown. View of Hagley Hall, Worcester, showing the Obelisk and Stuart's Doric Temple, 19th century. Engraving. English Heritage / National Monuments Record © Bill Drummond.

vided sweeping views of the surrounding countryside. Its prominent situation on a hill to the north of the park fulfilled both aims admirably (fig. 7-12). Lyttelton's reference in the letter to his "Vale" and the comparison with the "Thessala Tempe" may also be related to the design of Stuart's temple. "Tempe" is a literary term deriving from the valley in Thessaly, traditionally noted for its beauty, and the term literally means "a beautiful valley, a delightful rural spot."[24] Stuart's building referred back to the Greek Doric order of the Theseion in Athens, and as such appropriately invoked the Arcadian image of beautiful Thesaly, a Greek vale dotted with simple, unadorned Doric temples.[25] In fact, this was not only a literary conceit of Lyttelton's but also (as indicated by Lyttelton's letter quoted above) a personal recollection of Stuart's. Stuart visited the original Vale of Tempe, which he described at length in a letter published in volume four of *Antiquities*:

> On entering Larissa, we had to ford a pretty wide river, of which we saw no more until we came to the entrance of the Vale of Tempe, where it

appears about as large as the Arno at Florence, but somewhat more rapid; however it does not flow with equal velocity, nor observe an equal breadth in its course through the valley: for it is sometimes broad and perfectly gentle, and every where keeps nearer to Ossa than to Olympus. The rocks which border this valley on both sides are perpendicular to a great height, and have many caverns in them. The tops of the precipices on each side are beautifully fringed with trees. The greatest breadth is no where a quarter of a mile, and generally much less than half that space. Between the river and the foot of Olympus are several large clumps of trees, which I took to be oaks, and all the ground between the mountains and the river was covered on both sides with shrubs, beneath which the ground was clothed thick with a great variety of herbage. Beautiful as this vale is, it was entirely deserted; we neither saw a habitation, nor met a living creature in it . . .[26]

According to Lyttelton's son, Stuart was paid 25 pounds "for the plan" of the temple, a large sum for a small building, although he was apparently not involved in its actual construction.[27] A letter written by Lyttelton to Sanderson Miller in March 1759 reveals that the designer of the ruined castle oversaw the building work:

I thank you for your visit to Hagley, which will, I am sure, be of very great use to forward the Workmen and prevent blunders . . . Hitchcox, I hope, has your orders at Hagley about the Cottage, which should be built as soon as ever they can get the Materials from the old House, and so should the walls of Mr. Stuart's Dorick Portico. A Plan for that, as I understand, was left with Hitchcox by Mr. Stuart . . . I don't know whether Mr. Stuart has yet sent the Drawings for the Capitals, Freize, &c. of the Dorick Building; but I believe Hitchcox has one for all the plain and solid parts. The Bricks which it is to be lined with should be carried from the Old House at

such times as the carts can be conveniently spared.[28]

The process Lyttelton describes is not unique in Stuart's architectural career. For several of his garden buildings, Stuart submitted a set of designs (often based on his drawings for *Antiquities,* which the patron, usually a member of the Society of Dilettanti, had already perused). These were then passed to another architect or supervisor to implement.

Although there is no documentary evidence to support the attribution, Stuart almost certainly created a near-identical Doric Temple for Lyttelton's close friend Thomas Anson at Shugborough, Staffordshire (fig. 7-13). He also designed a "Doric Portico" at The Grove, Watford, for Thomas Villiers, first Lord Hyde, who was connected to Anson and Stuart's Dilettanti patrons through his friendship with Viscount Royston (later the second Earl of Hardwicke), Anson's brother-in-law. There is a case for considering the "Portico" he designed for The Grove as the first Greek Revival building in Britain. The principal

Fig. 7-13. James Stuart. The Doric Temple in the park at Shugborough, Staffordshire, 1760. Photographed in 2006. Courtesy of Shugborough (The National Trust, UK). *Checklist no. 88.*

Fig. 7-14. Thomas Baskerville. "Temple of Pan at Grove Herts / Lord Clarendens Grounds," n.d. Pen and ink, gray wash. By permission of The British Library, London, Add. Ms 9063, fo.224.

evidence for Stuart's work at The Grove derives from an entry in Sanderson Miller's diary, dated September 21, 1756:

> Up before 6. writing account of expences etc. Wrote to Dr Leigh. Rode after breakfast with Mr Bucknall to Lord Hyde's. His lordship, Lady Hyde and Lady Mary Capel showed me the house at the Grove. Two very good rooms etc. Lord Hyde walked with us round the park, and to the gardens, where we met Lady Hyde. Seeing Mr Stewart's 6 column Grecian Doric Portico.[29]

Only two of the architectural features known to have existed at the Grove potentially fit Miller's description: the so-called Temple of Pan, a peripteral Doric temple with six columns, and a "seat built in the Tuscan order," recorded in Webb's *Excursions* of 1812.[30] There are obvious problems in unequivocally identifying either as Stuart's "Doric Portico." There is no visual record of the building described by Webb, making it impossible to compare this structure to Stuart's known garden buildings in the Greek style. Although there exists an undated drawing by Thomas Baskerville of the Temple of Pan (fig.

7-14), this structure was described by Lady Annabel Yorke in 1776 as a "pretty new building," yet Stuart's "Portico" would have been at least twenty years old at that date.[31] Regardless, whatever kind of building Stuart created for The Grove, it had been erected at least five years earlier than the better-known Temple at Hagley. In fact, Lord Hyde continued to champion the Greek style, as in September 1765 he wrote to Earl of Hardwicke of his plans to build a cold bath, which housed a therapeutic bath, at The Grove, explaining: "I should rather the Building was of stone than of wood, & the Pillars of Stuart's Ionick. If it is of Brick & the Columns of Wood, w'h will undoubtedly be much cheaper, it must afterwards be stuccoed or roughcast."[32]

At the same time that Lord Hyde was contemplating the design of his cold bath, Thomas Anson was busy embellishing the grounds of Shugborough, his Staffordshire estate, with a variety of exquisite garden buildings. Although Stuart's Doric Temple at Hagley was not greeted with universal approbation, it is likely that this building influenced Lyttelton's Dilettanti friend Anson to commission a similar monument.[33] Stuart was in the process of designing a Doric Temple from as early as May

Fig. 7-15. Nicholas Thomas Dall. View of the orangery designed by Stuart and the ruins attributed to Thomas Wright at Shugborough, Staffordshire, ca. 1768–75. Watercolor. Courtesy of Shugborough, The Anson Collection, SHUG.P.68 (The National Trust, UK). *Checklist no. 87.*

1760, when Elizabeth Anson wrote to her husband: "Mr Stewart desires to be informed of the *number & size* of your Dorick columns; having made the Drawing of your Portico, which he wants to make the Scale before he sends it." The Shugborough Temple is just one of several garden buildings that Stuart designed or altered for Anson between 1756 and the late 1760s. Like Hagley, the grounds of Shugborough had already been extensively remodeled before Stuart began work there. In addition to the Chinese House, mentioned above, Anson had commissioned an evocative set of Ruins from Thomas Wright, in about 1749 (fig. 7-15), a Palladian bridge, and an obelisk.[34]

Writing in *The Journey from Chester to London* (1782), Thomas Pennant described the "Vale of Shugborough" in the following terms:

> From the middle is a view, of very uncommon beauty, of a small vale, varied with almost every thing that nature or art could give to render it delicious; rich meadows, watered by the *Trent* and *Sow.* . . . The boundary on one side, is a cultivated slope; on the other, the lofty front of Cannock Wood, clothed with heath, or shaded

with old oaks, scattered over its glowing bloom by the free hand of nature.

> It is more difficult to enumerate the works of art dispersed over this *Elysium*; they epitomize those of so many places . . . the genuine architecture of China, in all its extravagance; the dawning of the Grecian . . . [in] the chaste buildings of *Athens* . . .[35]

A member of the Society of Dilettanti, Whig Member of Parliament, and subscriber to the first volume of *Antiquities*, Thomas Anson ranks among Stuart's most important patrons. Fortunately, some twenty letters from Stuart to Anson have survived, revealing that Anson regarded Stuart as "an arbiter of taste".[36] Stuart was employed extensively on the house (although little of his work remains; see chap. 6) and advised Anson on commissions and purchases for his substantial collection of sculptures and paintings. He also created a series of garden buildings that helped to transform the park at Shugborough into "the *locus classicus* of early neo-Classicism and the serious Greek Revival."[37] His first garden building at Shugborough was the orangery, or

Fig. 7-16. John Chessell Buckler. *The Conservatory at Shugborough, Staffordshire*, 1842. Sepia. Courtesy of the Trustees of the William Salt Library, Staffordshire, SV-IV.295 (45/8221).

"greenhouse," demolished in the first half of the nineteenth century (see fig. 7-15).[38] A painting by artist Moses Griffith (see fig. 6-12) shows that it stood at a right angle to the west facade of the house, next to Wright's ruins, and comprised a long colonnaded structure, surmounted by a baluster, with tall niches at each end. Although begun in 1756, the orangery was not finished until 1764, when John Webb was instructed to complete the final decorative details by placing vases "alternately on the Green house, in the manner which the Drawing already in his possession directs."[39] As at Hagley, the orangery (fig. 7-16) was designed by Stuart but constructed by a team of workmen already in the patron's employ. Several of Anson's most prized sculptures were displayed in the building, along with a large painting of the Temple of Minerva Polias by

the Danish painter Nicholas Thomas Dall, apparently commissioned through Stuart, who wrote to Anson in 1770:

> Mr Dall has shown me the designs for the pictures in the green-house & library. The Subject for the Green house is a view of the temple of Minerva Polias with the Caryatides, on the principal ground, & in the distance he has introduced what remains of the Odeum of Pericles, both of them subjects engraved for my second volume.
>
> They compose admirably well, & will have in my opinion a great & a pleasing effect; We agree that this will be executed in oil, as it will then be secure from the moist effluvia of the Orange trees.

Fig. 7-17. Samuel and Joseph Wyatt, after designs by James Stuart. The Orangery at Blithfield Hall, Staffordshire, 1769. Photographed in 2006. Courtesy of Nancy, Lady Bagot. *Checklist no. 98.*

Fig. 7-18. Samuel and Joseph Wyatt, after designs by James Stuart. The Orangery at Ingestre, Staffordshire, ca. 1770s. Photographed in 2006. Courtesy of Ingestre Hall Residential Arts Centre.

The Waterfall, with the scenery accompanying it, he has contrived with great ingenuity, I think it will have a wonderful effect, it must astonish & delight every spectator.[40]

Stuart designed a second orangery some ten years later for Anson's Staffordshire neighbor Sir William Bagot, at Blithfield (fig. 7-17). Similar to the arrangement at Shugborough, Stuart was responsible for the design but supervision was awarded to builders chosen by the owner. In this case, it was the team of Samuel and Joseph Wyatt who had an independent relationship with Sir William and worked on a new family room and drawing room for the Manor House.[41] According to *Memorials of the Bagot Family*, the orangery was built for the first lord "by Mr. Samuel Wyatt, from the designs and under the

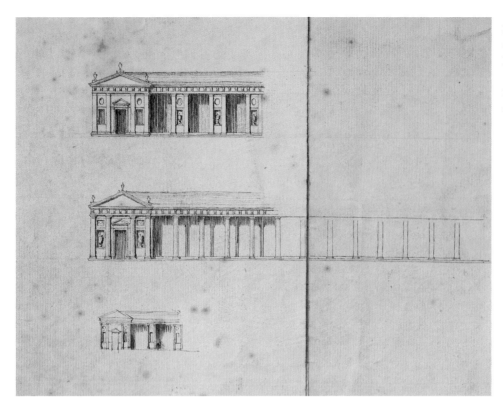

Fig. 7-19. James Stuart. Two designs for an orangery for Blithfield Hall, Staffordshire, ca. 1769. Pen and ink, pencil. Neither design is as executed. Courtesy of Nancy, Lady Bagot. *Checklist no. 97.*

direction of Athenian Stuart."[42] The Wyatts would later independently reuse Stuart's design and build another nearly identical orangery on the neighboring estate of Ingestre which belonged to the Chetwynd family (fig. 7-18). The Blithfield orangery faces the north front of the estate, and its west end adjoins a corner of the churchyard. It is an Athenian-style building with a temple structure at either end, and a Doric colonnade. The temple facades have a pair of niches and pilasters on either side of a central doorway with a fluted frieze above. There is a small, oval, tile-lined underground room under the east end pavilion of the orangery which may have been a cool room, or ice room. A pair of sketch designs still in the collection of the family show that Stuart had initially proposed an even more Greek-inspired building with triglyphs in the frieze and double pairs of pilasters on either side of the central doorways (fig. 7-19).

Unlike the Blithfield orangery, the Shugborough example is more French than Greek in feeling, suggesting that Stuart was not employed by Anson solely for his unique knowledge of Greek architecture.[43] However, throughout the 1760s Stuart, in close collaboration with Anson, created a series of monuments that have rightly been referred to as a "remarkable three-dimensional expression of the *Antiquities of Athens.*"[44]

Fig. 7-20. James Stuart. The Triumphal Arch, Shugborough, Staffordshire, ca. 1764. Photographed in 2006. Courtesy of Shugborough (The National Trust, UK).

The earliest of these buildings was the Triumphal Arch (fig. 7-20 and see fig. 7-6), prominently situated on a high point in the park to the southwest of the house and clearly visible from a long distance, as can be seen in one of Dall's oil paintings of the park and its monuments (see fig. 7-3). Work on this structure probably began towards the end of 1761, when John Hooper, a master-mason from Woodstock, submitted an estimate for construction: "An estimate of the triumphant arch Mr. Stuart delivered to me John Hooper, Woodstock. . . . As to the Ods of prises of the mouldings of the same sorts is because some are Scurculor (circular) and some straight . . . £282.14.1."[45] This monument was originally intended as a copy of the Arch of Hadrian at Athens, although the finished version differs somewhat from the original. The shafts of the columns flanking the end pilasters, missing from the original, have been added, as have the freestanding columns supporting the upper story. The picturesque ruin published in volume three of *Antiquities* has been made whole again. However, it is situated in a similarly pastoral setting to the original.[46] A further alteration is the curvature of the arch, which has been lowered so as not to break through the entablature, although it is not clear whether this amendment was of Stuart's or Anson's devising.

Following the death of Thomas Anson's brother, Admiral George Anson, further modifications were made to the Shugborough Arch.[47] On a visit to Shugborough in August 1763, Marchioness Grey reported that:

> We have been this Morning through a very Stormy Wind on one of the Neighbouring Hills that commands a very fine Prospect, & on which is erected a triumphal Arch out of Mr. Stuart's Athenian Designs, & under his Direction. A most beautiful structure that has been long begun, but will now I understand (by a Drawing *Shewn* but not *Mention'd*,) be applied to a different purpose from what could be first intended.[48]

The "different purpose" was that the arch should now serve as a memorial to the admiral, the first commemorative elements being the addition of vases to the outer ends of the entablature in July 1764.[49] Further additions included the prominent sarcophagi, portrait busts, and the naval trophy (called by Stuart an "Aplustra") carved by Peter Scheemakers (fig. 7-21).[50] The arch was eventually completed in 1769 when two medallions, common fea-

Fig. 7-21. Cenotaphs on the upper stage of the Triumphal Arch, Shugborough.

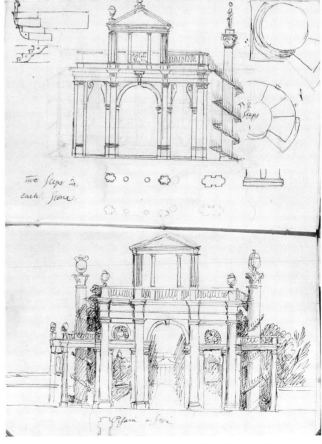

Fig. 7-22. James Stuart. Gateway of the Villa Pisani at Stra. From Stuart's sketchbook (ca. 1748–50): fols. 8v–9r. RIBA Library Drawings Collection, London, SKB/336/2 [L 3/4]. *Checklist no. 8.*

Fig. 7-23. The Horologium of Andronikos Cyrrhestes in Athens. From *Antiquities of Athens,* vol. 1 (1762): chap. 3, pl. 3. Courtesy of the Library, The Bard Graduate Center for Studies in the Decorative Arts, Design, and Culture, New York. *Checklist no. 36.*

tures on Roman monuments, were inserted into the spandrels. The overall effect of the Shugborough triumphal arch is reminiscent of the gateway at the Villa Pisani, drawn by Stuart in his Italian sketchbook in about 1750 (fig. 7-22).[51] Although the original inspiration for the triumphal arch was an Athenian memorial (and not even a Greek one at that), the eventual garden building was a mixture of styles, from the ancient to the modern.

The triumphal arch is an example of a monument in Athens with which the patron could only have been familiar through Stuart's drawings, as it was not published until 1794, in the third volume of *Antiquities.* However, following the publication of volume one in 1762, Anson commissioned two buildings copied from monuments that appeared in that book: the Tower of the Winds and the Choragic Monument of Lysicrates.[52] The Tower of

the Winds (see fig. 7-1), based on the Horologium of Andronikos Cyrrhestes in Athens (fig. 7-23), was probably begun in 1764 and completed in 1765 when the plumbers James and Thomas Warreley inscribed their names on the lead work of the roof.[53] The Shugborough version differs only slightly from the original in that windows were incorporated into its sides to allow light to flow into the banqueting room upstairs, which features a magnificent domed and lozenge-coffered ceiling done, according to Sir John Parnell, "in the manner of Nero's Pallace" (fig. 7-24).[54] Again, this clearly shows that Stuart was happy to mingle Greek and Roman sources in a single building and that he was perfectly willing to sacrifice complete authenticity for practical or aesthetic reasons.

Stuart's engraving of the original building shows sculpted reliefs of the winds in the frieze panels around the tops of the walls which are absent in the Shugborough version as it now stands. Curiously, however, they appear in Moses Griffith's watercolor of the monument, engraved for Pennant's *Journey* (fig. 7-25).[55] These probably formed part of the garden building at the time, possibly made from stucco or even painted in *trompe l'oeil.* This engraving also shows the delightful setting of the building shortly after it was erected, surrounded entirely by water and reached on either side by a pair of "Chinese Chippendale" bridges. Parnell, however, was unimpressed, writing that it was "the most massive and least striking of any . . . situate in the water without any Island and . . . unnatural and Disagreeable," while British explorer and naturalist Joseph Banks, who visited Shugborough in 1767, found the tower "no better than an octagonal pigeon house".[56] The Tower of the Winds did, of course, prove to be one of the most popular monuments of *Antiquities,* serving as the model for Wyatt's Radcliffe Observatory in Oxford (see fig. 1-21), as well as a banqueting house by Stuart for Mount Stewart, County Down, Northern Ireland, which commands magnificent views over Strangford Lough (fig. 7-26), and, ironically, an octagonal pigeon house designed by James Wyatt for Badger Hall in 1780.[57]

The Temple of the Winds that Stuart designed at Mount Stewart differs somewhat from the Shugborough example. Commissioned by Stuart's Irish patron, Robert Stewart (created Baron Londonderry in 1789 and a marquis in 1816), the earliest printed mention of the temple appears in the first edition of *The Post Chaise Companion* (1786), which states: "a little further north is Mount Stewart where the Rt. Hon. Robert Stewart is building

Fig. 7-24. James Stuart. Interior of the upper room of the Tower of the Winds, Shugborough, showing the domed ceiling. 1764–65. Photographed in 2006. Courtesy of Shugborough (The National Trust, UK).

Fig. 7-25. "The Temple of the Winds at Shugborough." Engraving by James Fittler after a watercolor by Moses Griffiths. From Thomas Pennant, *The Journey from Chester to London* (1782): pl. V. Courtesy of the Library, The Bard Graduate Center for Studies in the Decorative Arts, Design and Culture, New York. *Checklist no. 91.*

Fig. 7-26. James Stuart. Temple of the Winds, Mount Stewart, County Down, ca. 1782–83. Photographed ca. 1980. Courtesy of Mount Stewart (The National Trust, UK). *Checklist no. 103.*

Fig. 7-27. James Stuart. Stairwell and coffered dome in the Temple of the Winds, Mount Stewart, ca. 1782–83. Photographed ca. 1980. Courtesy of Mount Stewart (The National Trust, UK). *Checklist no. 105.*

Fig. 7-28. James Stuart. Upper room of the Temple of the Winds, Mount Stewart, ca. 1782–83. Plasterwork by William Fitzgerald; marquetry floor by John Ferguson. Photographed ca. 1980. Courtesy of Mount Stewart (The National Trust, UK). *Checklist no. 104.*

Fig. 7-29. Artist unknown. *View over Strangford Lough, County Down,* 19th century. Oil on canvas. Courtesy of Mount Stewart (The National Trust, UK).

a very magnificent seat, and has erected on a hill near the lough, a temple to the winds, designed after the celebrated model at Athens."[58] Construction started around 1780 and by March of that year Lord Camden had procured a wooden model of the Temple, which he intended to send to Dublin "with the first ship that sails."[59] The building may have been largely complete by 1781, when the young Castlereagh (then Stewart) nearly drowned in Strangford Lough.[60] However, the extensive accounts for the temple continue until 1785, although by this date the exterior may have been finished with work continuing on the elaborate interior. This features a splendid, coffered dome above the staircase (fig. 7-27, comparable to that at Shugborough) and, in the main first-floor room, a finely pat-

terned, inlaid floor and delicately modeled ceiling (fig. 7-28).[61] Both interior and exterior were largely constructed from local materials. In his description of the temple in the *Topographical Dictionary* (1837), noted traveler and topographer Samuel Lewis commented favorably on the use of "stone from the quarries of Scrabo, and the floors, which are of bog fir, found in the peat moss on the estate [which] are, for beauty of material and design, unequalled by anything in the country."[62]

The Mount Stewart Temple of the Winds was conceived as a fine banqueting house (an underground tunnel links the temple to a wine cellar and scullery nearby), taking maximum advantage of the views afforded by its commanding position overlooking the lough (fig. 7-29).

As with so many of Stuart's garden buildings, the abiding significance of views in both positioning and design is evident. The Mount Stewart temple even has small, elegant balconies, the better to appreciate the vista when the winds are not too fierce. These balconies are the most striking difference between the Mount Stewart and Shugborough towers (fig. 7-30).[63] Thomas Anson's building, like the original, features pediments over the porticoes (fig. 7-31). Furthermore, the Mount Stewart version features three, rather than two porticoes and the apsidal projection hous-

ing the staircase is taller and more prominent than that of the Athenian original.

Stuart was clearly responsible for the design, if not the execution, of the Mount Stewart temple. In June 1783 he was paid £50 for "Temple at Mount Stewart for cost of Plan & Designs for furnishing it."[64] There is no evidence Stuart ever visited Ireland to oversee the work. However, Lewis notes that the Temple of the Winds at Mount Stewart was "erected under the personal superintendence of J. Stewart Esq. whose skill and taste in Grecian archi-

Fig. 7-30. Portico with balcony, the Temple of the Winds, Mount Stewart. Courtesy of Mount Stewart (The National Trust, UK).

Fig. 7-31. Portico with pediment, the Tower of the Winds, Shugborough. Courtesy of Shugborough (The National Trust, UK).

Fig. 7-32. The Choragic Monument of Lysicrates. Engraving. From *Antiquities of Athens,* vol. 1 (1762): chap. 4, pl. III. Courtesy of the Library, The Bard Graduate Center for Studies in the Decorative Arts, Design, and Culture, New York. *Checklist no. 36.*

tecture have procured for him the appellation of the Athenian Stewart."[65] It seems likely that Lewis, who was writing more than fifty years after the completion of the temple, was mistaken in asserting that Stewart oversaw the work. It is more probable, and certainly more consistent with his working practices, that Stuart merely provided his patron with designs, leaving the implementation to local workmen.

Another Shugborough monument as popular as the Tower of the Winds was a replica of the Choragic Monument of Lysicrates, which Stuart created for Anson on a knoll overlooking the river Sow (see fig. 7-9). The Choragic Monument was one of the most imitated buildings of *Antiquities of Athens* (fig. 7-32). It was "remorselessly copied and adapted" by British architects in the late eighteenth and early nineteenth centuries.[66] Indeed, Stuart himself

Fig. 7-33. James Stuart. The Choragic Monument at Camden Place, Kent, 1779–80. Photographed in 2006. Courtesy of the Chislehurst Golf Club, Kent. *Checklist no. 102.*

338

designed at least two, and probably three, versions of it. In addition to the one at Shugborough, Stuart devised a Choragic Monument for Charles Pratt at Camden Place, Kent, probably built in 1779 (fig. 7-33), where he also advised on the design for a cold bath (now demolished) that Pratt was planning shortly after the erection of the monument.[67] A Choragic Monument illustrated in the second book of French publisher George Louis Le Rouge's *Detail des nouveaux jardins à la mode* (1776) and labeled as a "Tour de Diogene à Kew," is possibly a Stuart building devised for Sion Hill, Middlesex, and incorrectly labeled by Le Rouge (fig. 7-34).[68]

In volume one of *Antiquities*, Stuart explains how the Choragic Monument was commonly referred to as the Lanthorn of Demosthenes, supposedly built as a place of quiet study; as such, the Shugborough version was christened the "Dark Lanthorn" while that at Camden Place, in an abbreviated version, was referred to simply as the "Lanthorn."[69] While the choice of site at Shugborough was Anson's, Stuart was clearly anxious that his building should be complemented by a fine location, writing to his patron in 1764: "Pray is the place for the Lanthorn of Demosthenes any where by the canal, & near the fine Clump of Trees just at the angle, pardon my inquisitiveness, I can't help thinking about it."[70] The control Anson exercised over the site of the Lanthorn at Shugborough was not replicated at Camden Place. Pratt's assertion that he detested the location of his Choragic Monument—"I hate it where it is"—and his desire to move it from its location in 1780 suggests that Stuart may have been responsible for its original position.[71]

Stuart's version of the Choragic Monument at Shugborough, like that at Camden Place, is exceedingly close to the original, although it lacks the Athenian monument's square base and sculptural frieze. As Stuart noted after his discovery of an inscription on the original, the fourth-century structure was erected by Lysicrates of Kikyana to commemorate a victory by the boys of Akamantis in a dramatic contest. From his examination of the Athenian original, Stuart deduced that it must have once supported a bronze tripod. He published his own hypothetical reconstruction—an elaborate affair supported by dolphins—in *Antiquities* (see fig. 11-12).[72] Anson commissioned Matthew Boulton, of the Soho Works in Harmondsworth, to cast the tripod in his foundry.[73] As Stuart noted in September 1769: "The tripod is in great forwardness, I think it will be best to have

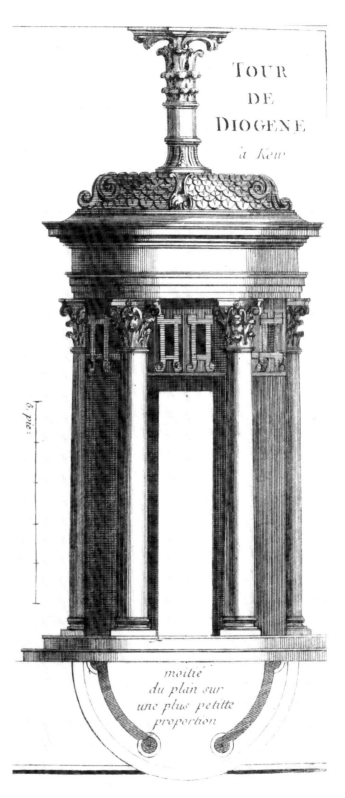

Fig. 7-34. The Choragic Monument of Lysicrates probably in the garden of Sion Hill, Kew. Engraving. From George Louis Le Rouge, *Détails des nouveaux Jardins à la mode et Jardins Anglo-Chinois . . .* , vol. 1, book 2 (1776–87): pl. 3. By permission of The British Library, London, 34.f.11. *Checklist no. 94.*

Fig. 7-35. Josiah Wedgwood and Thomas Bentley. Covered dish depicting garden buildings at Shugborough, 1774. Earthenware. Courtesy of Shugborough, The Anson Collection (The National Trust, UK). *Checklist no. 86.*

it cast at Birmingham, my friend Mr Boulton will execute it there, better & cheaper far than it can be done in London."[74]

The large bowl apparently proved too much of a challenge for the Soho works, as Josiah Wedgwood gleefully explained in a letter to Thomas Bentley in December, 1770:

> I forgot to tell you that Mr Boulton was making an immense large Tripod for Mr Anson to finish the top of Demosthenes Lanthorn, building there from Mr. Stewart's design. The legs were cast & weigh'd about 5 cwt. but they [the workmen] stagger'd at the bowl, & did not know which way to set about it; a Council of the workmen was call'd & every method of performing this wonderful work canvass'd over. They concluded by shaking their heads, & ended where they begun. I then could hold no longer but told them very gravely they were all wrong, they had totally mistaken their Talents & their metals; such great works should not be attempted in Copper or in Brass. They must call in some able Potter to

their assistance, and the works might be completed. Would you think it? they took me at my word & I have got a fine jobb upon my hands in consequence of a little harmless boasting. Mr. Stewart said he knew Mr. Anson would glory in having the Arts of Soho & Etruria united in his Tripod, & that it would be a feather in our Caps which that good gentleman would delight in taking every opportunity to shew to our advantage. So this matter stands at present, but Mr. Boulton, Dr. Darwin, and I are to dine with Mr. Anson on New-Year's Day & shall talk the matter over again.[75]

Wedgwood finished his version of the bowl in April 1771 when he wrote to Stuart asking for instructions about the gilding, although it is unclear whether it was ever actually erected.[76] The present tripod is a fiberglass copy, installed by the National Trust as part of their restoration of the park monuments. Wedgwood must have been impressed with the landscape scheme at Shugborough, as he would later use the garden buildings of the park as the subjects decorating a covered Queensware dish, very similar to the Green Frog service, a 944-piece dinner and dessert service created by Wedgwood and Bentley for Catherine the Great, Empress of Russia. It was designed to show off the best of English landscape and building (fig. 7-35).

Stuart may have contributed to three other monuments in the park at Shugborough: the Shepherd's Monument, Cat's Monument, and the Colonnade. The Shepherd's Monument seems to be composed of elements designed separately by Thomas Wright and Stuart in about 1755 (fig. 7-36).[77] A drawing by Stuart of a rough-hewn column similar to those flanking the monument (fig. 7-37) has led to the suggestion that these were added by Stuart, to whom the Greek Doric aedicule, rustic spandrels bordering Wright's arch, and marble frame around the relief, which is by Scheemakers, are also ascribed.[78] As for the so-called Cat's Monument, dedicated to Anson's

Fig. 7-36. The Shepherd's Monument, Shugborough, Staffordshire, ca. 1755. Arch attributed to Thomas Wright; aedicule, spandrels, and marble frame surrounding relief attributed to James Stuart; relief executed by Peter Scheemakers. Photographed in 2006. Courtesy of Shugborough (The National Trust, UK).

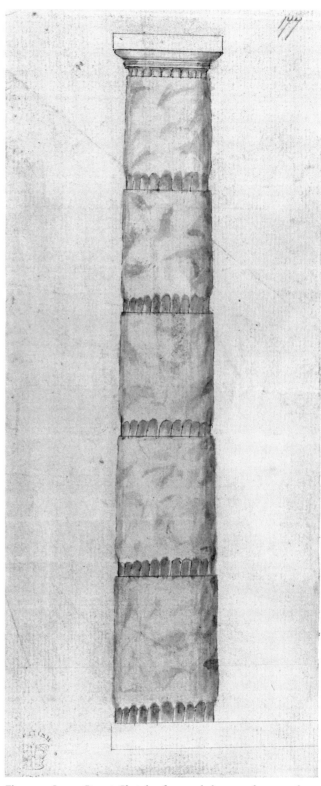

Fig. 7-37. James Stuart. Sketch of a rough-hewn column, n.d. Pen and ink, wash. By permission of The British Library, London, Add. Ms. 22,153 fol. 177.

Fig. 7-38. The Cat's Monument, Shugborough, Staffordshire, ca. 1755–62. Pedestal plaque attributed to James Stuart. Photographed in 2006. Courtesy of Shugborough (The National Trust, UK).

(at least in terms of landscape architecture), he was responsible for a number of other notable garden buildings throughout Britain. He was involved with the design of the Church of All Saints in the park at Nuneham Courtenay (see fig. 7-5), the seat of Simon, first Earl Harcourt, president of the Society of Dilettanti. Although a functioning church, All Saints (completed in 1764) was essentially conceived as a garden ornament, set at the end of a terrace walk, and perhaps inspired by the pictures of Claude or Poussin owned by the earl.[81] Paul Sandby's engraving of the surprise vista of the church certainly depicts it in this picturesque manner (fig. 7-41). According to Horace Walpole, it was "the principal feature in one of the most beautiful landscapes in the world."[82] Yet the extent to which Stuart was actually involved is unclear. The second Earl Harcourt wrote that the church was "erected at the sole expense of the late Earl Harcourt, who himself gave the original design, which received a very slight alteration from Stuart."[83] Harcourt probably chose the Greek Ionic capitals used on the portico from the temple on the Ilissus, which was among Stuart's drawings.[84] It has been suggested that Stuart possibly added the small semicircular porch.[85] This porch provided the entrance to the building, for it served the dual purposes of church and garden ornament.

His involvement may have been somewhat greater than this, however. A surviving drawing by Stuart of an elevation and section of a church can be tentatively asso-

last surviving Persian cat (fig. 7-38), Stuart was probably responsible for the artificial stone slab of addorsed griffins (fig. 7-39). This is ascribed to Stuart on the basis of its similarity to his reliefs in the great hall at Wentworth Woodhouse (see figs. 6-7b, 6-8), an assertion supported by the evidence of a drawing by Stuart, now in the Pierpont Morgan Library, New York, of an urn flanked by comparable griffins (see checklist no. 39).[79] It may be that Stuart also designed the Colonnade (situated on the opposite side of the river to Wright's ruins), destroyed in a flood in 1795 (fig. 7-40). However, this structure (based on the portico of the Temple of Saturn in Rome) has also been attributed to Wright.[80]

Although Shugborough saw Stuart at his most prolific

Fig. 7-39. Pedestal plaque on the Cat's Monument, ca. 1755–62. Courtesy of Shugborough (The National Trust, UK).

Fig. 7-40. Nicholas Thomas Dall. *The West Front of Shugborough, Staffordshire*, 1768. Watercolor. Courtesy of Shugborough, The Anson Collection (The National Trust, UK). *Checklist no. 87a.*

ciated with the church (fig. 7-42). There are certain similarities in the general layout of the building, but there are also sufficient differences to suggest that the drawing is, at best, a very early proposal. Most strikingly, the portico shown in the drawing, the "severer Doric of the Forum Augustus as published by le Roy in 1758," is rather different from the Greek Ionic of the church as built and features six rather than four columns.[86] The dome of the constructed church is more compact than the drawing and the small, semicircular porches are open rather than closed. The Church of All Saints appears to have been influenced by Lord Burlington's villa at Chiswick, an influence that is not overtly apparent in the drawing.

In addition to Stuart's possible involvement with the design of All Saints, the Temple of Flora at Nuneham is sometimes attributed to him (fig. 7-43). This building was described by the second earl as based on "a design of a Doric portico at Athens." There is, however, no documentary evidence to support either this or the suggestion, occasionally made, that he designed the stables there also.[87]

Another somewhat insecure attribution is that of the "Grecian Ruin" at Park Place, Remenham, Henley on Thames.[88] There is a longstanding tradition that Stuart was responsible for this structure which was built in about 1780 at the head of a valley overlooking the Thames. The

client was General Henry Seymour Conway, a close political associate of the Marquess of Rockingham (see chap. 4). The building was described by Percy Noble, one of the subsequent owners of Park Place as "a good imitation of a Grecian amphitheatre, with a grand colonnade falling into decay" (fig. 7-44).[89] The building still stands, but has lost its upper story since it was photographed in about 1900 (see fig. 4-15).

A more secure attribution is the park building, or "Prospect House," at Wimpole Hall, Cambridgeshire, which, it seems, was intended to augment another ruined castle by Sanderson Miller.[90] Hardwicke, Stuart's patron, explained: "I am, as a companion to this antique, engraving a modern Italian loggia, which I have set up at Wimpole under the auspices of Mr. Stewart."[91] The earl clearly appreciated the pleasing play of contrasts between the associations prompted by buildings representing "ancient and modern times."[92] Stuart almost certainly received the commission through his friendship with Anson, whose inlaws, the Yorkes, were beginning to embellish their park in the mid-1760s.[93] A letter from Stuart to Philip Yorke, second Earl of Hardwicke, shows that Stuart had begun to turn his thoughts to the Wimpole park building by January 1766:

343

Notwithstanding the injunction of my friend
Jones who prescribes absolute Idleness to me, I
have bestowed some thoughts on your Lordship's
building, before I proceed I shall be glad to know
the length & breadth proposed for the Room
above the Stairs & the Porticos below, 60 in
length & 15 in breadth will make a fine Spas-
segio—for the Portico—a noble walk in al weath-
ers, & a noble object from all the country in view
of it.[94]

There is no doubt that the Prospect House was in large
part conceived, like the Doric Temple at Hagley, for its
superb views (fig. 7-45).

In addition to Stuart's comments, correspondence of
1781 between the Countess of St. Germans, and her aunt,
Lady Beauchamp, described the position of the building:
"Her Ladyship was so kind as to take us yesterday morning to see the new park building, which is very pretty. It
commands a fine and extensive prospect and is seen at a
great distance."[95] James Plumtree, who visited Wimpole in
1800, provides a full and complementary account of the
Prospect House, although by the time he saw it the building had already fallen into "desolation and ruin." Like the
Countess of St. Germans, Plumtree commented favorably
on the fine views afforded by the building's location, writing in *A Journal of a Tour to the Source of the River Cam*:

Fig. 7-42. James Stuart. Elevation and section for a
church, possibly a preliminary design for the Church
of All Saints, Nuneham Park, Oxfordshire, ca. 1764.
Pen and ink, gray wash. RIBA Library Drawings
Collection, London, SD 62/4. *Checklist no. 95.*

We proceeded up to the Pavilion on the hill and were much pleased with the rich and extended prospect before us. It was not sufficiently clear to see the distance to advantage but we now had a morning and a better view of nearly the same tract that we saw from Arrington church the former evening. The church itself was a good object on the left, and the fine trees on the slope of the hill on which we stood made a good foreground. But the pavilion itself was a scene of desolation and ruin. It had been built about twenty-five years and cost about £1,500 building. When finished it was one of the most elegant buildings I ever remember. The tea-room was simple and elegant; the little room on the left was a rare specimen of painting, of Etruscan figures in colours. It was done by Stewart and cost £700. What the inside is now we did not see, but we could discern from the outside that the blinds were falling to pieces. The pillars which supported the centre were rotting away and the building supported by very rough props. A railing of posts and wire, which formerly extended all round it, and kept off the cattle, was removed, and the pavement and steps torn up, and the place made a shelter for

Fig. 7-43. The Temple of Flora, Nuneham Park, Oxfordshire, ca. 1771–72. Possibly designed by James Stuart. Photographed in 2006. Courtesy of Brahma Kumaris: The Global Retreat Centre.

Fig. 7-44. John Chessler Buckler. *Ruins of the Roman Amphitheatre at Park Place, near Henley*, 1826. Pencil. From an album of Buckler views, vol. 1, p. 231. By permission of The British Library, London, Add. Ms. 36,356.

Fig. 7-45. Henry Reginald Yorke. *View from Hill House,* [Prospect House], *Wimpole Park,* 1836. Watercolor. ©Christie's Images Limited, 1989.

deer and sheep, whose dung sadly spoiled the place. The stucco, which covered the outside, and gave the appearance of stone, was falling off. . . ."[96]

Two of Stuart's drawings for the park building survive: an elevation of the south facade and a section. The elevation (fig. 7-46), which depicts a two-story building with an Ionic portico below and a Serlian window above, corresponds closely to the park building as constructed although the arrangement of the arch differs slightly in the finished version.[97] The design of this building is not overwhelmingly Greek—the use of Italian Renaissance motifs highlights yet again the flexibility and eclecticism of Stuart's approach to architectural design. The section (fig. 7-47) suggests that the ground floor may have been used for displaying sculpture. It shows a classically draped figure in an apsidal niche to the right of the central doorway, which is surmounted by a bust flanked by urns. The second floor had a tea room with "Etruscan colours." Although the building pleased the earl who had it engraved (see fig. 7-4), not all his visitors were as enthusiastic. For example, Lord Torrington called it the "ugly summerhouse." Architect Humphrey Repton, who decried its inadequate foundations and "the absurdity of

building a room on columns" remodeled it into a gardener's cottage. He filled in the open ground-floor bay and moved the Ionic columns to make a balcony at first-floor level (fig. 7-48). The building was demolished in the late nineteenth-century.[98]

★ ★ ★

Stuart's garden buildings were all created through close collaboration between the architect and his patrons, who were, for the most part, well informed about the latest developments in the study of ancient art and architecture. To some extent the tastes of Stuart's patrons may have been molded by discussions with the "Athenian." The relationship he and his patrons shared was informal, and the design process of his garden buildings appears to have been a dialogue between enthusiastic antiquarians, in particular between fellow members of the Society of Dilettanti. Like Anson, Stuart's other patrons may have considered him to be an arbiter of taste. Casual conversations on walks through the parks that Stuart was to embellish, where the discussion doubtless included prospects, ancient architecture, and the Greek ideal, were almost certainly as important to the design process as the formal submission of drawings and contractual negotia-

Fig. 7-46. James Stuart. Elevation of the south front of Prospect House, Wimpole, Cambridgeshire, ca. 1775. Pen and ink, gray wash. RIBA Library Drawings Collection, London, SD 62/7 (1). *Checklist no. 99.*

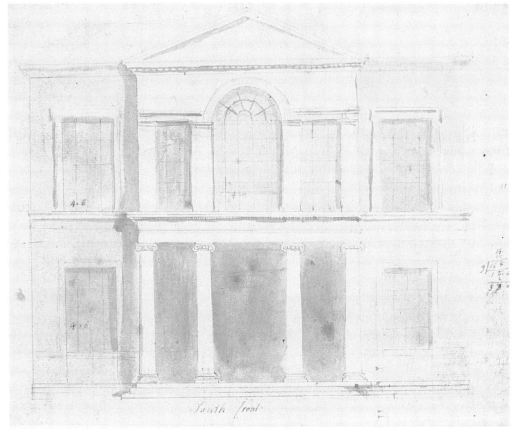

Fig. 7-47. James Stuart. North-to-south section of Prospect House, Wimpole, Cambridgeshire, ca. 1775. Pen and ink, gray wash. RIBA Library Drawings Collection, London, SD 62/7 (2). *Checklist no. 100.*

Fig. 7-48. Humphrey Repton. Prospect House, Wimpole, Cambridgeshire, 1801. Wash drawing. From the Wimpole *Red Book*. Courtesy of Wimpole Hall, The Bambridge Collection (The National Trust, UK).

tions. Furthermore, Stuart's garden buildings were not restricted to copies of Athenian monuments. The orangery at Shugborough and the park building at Wimpole attest to his trademark eclecticism, both far removed from the type of Greek Revival that he was subsequently, and somewhat unfairly, said to have initiated. Indeed, the park building at Wimpole was "a whimsical product of its age,

not a scholarly essay derived from ancient exemplar."[99] Furthermore, after a visit to Shugborough in 1769, Sir John Parnell commented on the "mixture of fine pieces of antiquity with the garden."[100] Thus the available evidence suggests that both Stuart and his patrons delighted in variety in garden buildings as much as in the diversity of the landscape itself.

Acknowledgments: I would like to thank Kerry Bristol for generously making available her Ph.D. thesis and Catherine Arbuthnott for her assistance with the research for and writing of this article. I am particularly grateful to Maureen MaGuire for a delightful visit to Mount Stewart.—A.M.

1. Christopher Hussey's articles in *Country Life*, cited throughout this essay, were instrumental in bringing Stuart's garden buildings to greater prominence. David Watkin devotes an entire chapter to Stuart's landscape architecture in *Athenian Stuart: Pioneer of the Greek Revival* (London: George Allen and Unwin, 1982): 23–30. More recently, Kerry Bristol has provided an invaluable assessment of Stuart's landscape architecture; see Bristol, "Stuart and the Genesis of the Greek Revival" (1997).

2. Bristol has estimated that Stuart received about twenty-eight architectural commissions "some of them small," although this number can probably now be revised upwards slightly. See Bristol, "Stuart and the Genesis of the Greek Revival" (1997): 233 n. 719. At least fifteen garden buildings can be reliably attributed in whole or in part to Stuart, while a further five structures may plausibly be associated with him. I consider the following to be secure attributions—Blithfield House: orangery, or "greenhouse"; Camden Place: Choragic Monument of Lysicrates and Cold Bath; The Grove: Doric Temple; Hagley Hall: Doric Temple; Mount Stewart: Temple of the Winds; Shugborough: Orangery, Doric Temple, Triumphal Arch, Tower of the Winds, Choragic Monument of Lysicrates; Wimpole: Park Building or "Prospect House." I consider the following to be convincing attributions, in whole or in part, although documentation is lacking—Nuneham Courtenay: Church of all Saints; Park Place: Ionic Ruin/Amphitheater; The Grove: Cold Bath. The following are occasionally, though not always convincingly, associated with Stuart—Nuneham Courtenay: Temple of Flora; Shugborough: bas relief on Cat's Monument, Colonnade [behind the Ruins], and alterations to the Shepherd's Monument; Kenwood House: bridge. Regarding the bridge at Kenwood, Richard Hewlings has noted that one of Repton's "Red Books" for remodeling the park refers to "Stuart's Bridge" (Hewlings, personal communication, via Catherine Arbuthnott). A design by Stuart for a garden loggia for Lichfield House, St James' Square, London, survives in the RIBA Drawings Collection, SD 62/3; it was probably not executed. A drawing by Stuart of a three-bay loggia in the same collection (SD 62/12) may have been intended for a park or garden. London art dealer Bill Drummond believes that a drawing of a gothic folly in his possession may be by Stuart. Given Stuart's famous abhorrence of gothic this seems unlikely, though not impossible. Unfortunately it has not been possible to view the drawing concerned.

3. Giles Worsley, "Out from Adam's Shadow," *Country Life* 186 (14 May 1992): 103; Bristol, "Stuart and the Genesis of the Greek Revival" (1997): 234.

4. Second Earl of Hardwicke to the Earl of Dartmouth, 18 February 1788, Mss. Dartmouth, Report 15, appendix I, 1896, 238–39, Historic Manuscripts Commission; quoted in David Adshead, "A Modern Italian Loggia at Wimpole," *Georgian Group Journal* 10 (2000): 152.

5. Jennifer Sherwood and Nikolaus Pevsner, *Oxfordshire,* The Buildings of England (Harmondsworth: Penguin, 1974): 725.

6. Watkin, *Athenian Stuart* (1982): 25.

7. His interest in Renaissance and Baroque architecture is amply attested to by drawings in his sketchbook of ca.1748–50; see Stuart, "Sketchbook . . . of buildings in N. Italy," RIBA Library Drawings Collection, SKB/336/2 [L 3/4].

8. Lyttelton to Mrs. Montagu, Hagley, 21 October 1758, Montagu Papers, MO 1280, Henry E. Huntington Library, San Marino California; quoted in Bristol, "Stuart and the Genesis of the Greek Revival" (1997): 303.

9. Walpole to Bentley, September 1753, quoted in G. Nares, "Hagley Hall, Worcestershire—I," *Country Life* 122 (19 September 1957): 548; Thomas Pennant, *The Journey from Chester to London* (London: B. White, 1782): 69. Miller also designed a Ruined Castle for Wimpole, Cambridgeshire, on which see Gervase Jackson-Stops, *An English Arcadia 1600–1990: Designs for Gardens and Buildings in the Care of the National Trust* (London: National Trust, 1991): 86–88.

10. The reuse of the Halesowen windows is noted in Watkin, *Athenian Stuart* (1982): 25.

11. See Michael Bevington, "The Development of the Classical Revival at Stowe," *Architectura* 21, no. 2 (1991): 162.

12. Kerry Bristol, "The Society of Dilettanti, James 'Athenian' Stuart and the Anson Family," *Apollo* 152 (July 2000): 47. For the history of the Society see Lionel Cust and Sir Sidney Colvin, *History of the Society of Dilettanti* (1898; reprint, London: Macmillian, 1914).

13. Stuart to Anson, June 1764, Lichfield Ms. D615/P(s)/1/6/7, Staffordshire Record Office.

14. For the emergence of the Picturesque in Britain see e.g. Malcolm Andrews, *The Search for the Picturesque: Landscape Aesthetics and Tourism in Britain, 1760–1800* (Stanford University Press, 1989). For the relevance of the Picturesque to landscape design and garden buildings see e.g. David Watkin, *The English Vision: The Picturesque in Architecture, Landscape and Garden Design* (New York: Harper and Row, 1982).

15. Watkin, *Athenian Stuart* (1982): 23.

16. Lyttelton to Mrs Montagu, Hagley, 21 October 1758, Montagu Papers, MO 1280, Henry E. Huntington Library, San Marino, California; quoted in Bristol, "Stuart and the Genesis of the Greek Revival" (1997): 301.

17. Watkin, *Athenian Stuart* (1982): 23.

18. Richard Pococke, *The Travels through England of Dr Richard Pococke, Successively Bishop of Meath and Ossory during 1750, 1751, and Later Years,* ed. J. J. Cartwright, vol. 1 (London: Westminster, printed for the Camden Society, 1888): 223–24.

19. Ibid., 225–26. Miller's Ruined Castle was built 1747–48, the Ionic Rotunda was designed by John Pitt and begun in 1747. Both projects were initiated by George Lyttelton, who began to develop the park in the early 1740s, on which see Nares, "Hagley Hall—I" (1957): 458–59.

20. Bristol, "Stuart and the Genesis of the Greek Revival" (1997): 305. See pp. 302–7 for a detailed account of Hagley Park and its meaning. Bristol observes: "Lyttelton was a lifelong enthusiast of the landscape, both at home and abroad. On his travels, he often equated landscape and architecture with history, especially when visiting castles and cathedrals

and he preferred a variety of emotional experiences within a restricted area. . . . The gardens at Hagley reflect this love of topographical variety . . . Hagley was a sentimental garden of the imagination."

21. George Clarke, "Grecian Taste and Gothic Virtue: Lord Cobham's Gardening Programme and its Iconography," *Apollo* 97 (June 1973): 571.

22. George Clarke, "The Medallions of Concord: An Association between the Society of Arts and Stowe," *Journal of the Royal Society of Arts* 129 (August 1981):612–14.

23. Lyttleton to Mrs. Montagu, Hagley, 21 October 1758, Montagu Papers, MO 1280, Henry E. Huntington Library, San Marino, California; quoted in Bristol, "Stuart and the Genesis of the Greek Revival" (1997): 301.

24. William Little, ed., *New Shorter Oxford English Dictionary on Historical Principles,* 4th rev. ed. (Oxford: Clarendon Press, 1993): 3242.

25. This effect was noted even before the erection of Stuart's temple. Upon revisiting Hagley in 1756, Pococke remarked: "Hagley is greatly improved since I saw it. A very fine house with four fronts of freestone, and a tour on each angle, rising higher than the rest of the building, have a fine effect, and as it is seen through the trees from different parts, appears like what we may imagine one of the Greek and Roman palaces to have been . . ."; see Pococke, *Travels,* vol. 2 (1888): 233.

26. *Antiquities,* vol. 4 (1816): 12.

27. Bristol, "Stuart and the Genesis of the Greek Revival" (1997): 304. The building was apparently paid for by Lyttelton's half-brother, Admiral Thomas Smith. See also Nares, "Hagley Hall—I" (1957): 549.

28. Lyttelton to Miller, Hill Street, 17 March 1759, CR 125B/365, Warwickshire County Record Office, Warwick; quoted in Bristol, "Stuart and the Genesis of the Greek Revival" (1997): 303.

29. The transcript as it appears here was expanded from Miller's highly abbreviated diary entries by Michael Cousins in his article "Athenian Stuart's Doric Porticoes," *Georgian Group Journal* 14 (2004): 52. The original is "Diary of Sanderson Miller," 21 September 1756, pp. 29–30, CR 1382/32, Warwickshire County Record Office, Warwick: "Up bef.6. writg. Acct. of Expences &c. wr to Dr Leigh rode aft. Bft w. Mr Bucknl. to L.d Hide's. His Lp L.y H. & Ly Mary Capel shewed me the Hse at ye Grove 2. Very good Rooms &c. L.d H. w.d w.us round the Park & to ye Garden where we met Ly. H. seeing Mr Stewarts 6 Coln. Greecn. Doric Portico."

30. Cousins, "Athenian Stuart's Doric Porticoes" (2004): 52. Daniel Carless Webb, *Observations and Remarks during Four Excursions Made to Various Parts of Great Britain . . .* (London, Allen and Co., 1812): 164–65.

31. See Cousins, "Athenian Stuart's Doric Porticoes" (2004): 52. Cousins also notes that it seems unlikely that Sanderson Miller would have described a peripteral temple as a "portico."

32. Lord Hyde to second Earl of Hardwicke, 17 September 1765, Add. Ms. 35,607, fol. 195 recto, BL.

33. Lyttelton's son wrote of it to Mrs Montagu: "As for the Building, which you say all your Friends object to, my Papa is resolved to build he says that many People of good taste like it very much & as he has paid Mr Steward 25 pund for the plan, & has got all the Materials ready, he will not change the design." Thomas Lyttelton to Mrs. Montagu,

19 January 1759, Montagu Papers, MO 1495, Henry E. Huntington Library, San Marino, California; Bristol, "Stuart and the Genesis of the Greek Revival" (1997): 304.

34. Studies of the park at Shugborough, including Stuart's work there, are numerous. See e.g. Christopher Hussey, "Shugborough, Staffordshire," pts. 1 and 2, *Country Life* 115 (25 February 1954): 510–13; (4 March 1954): 590–93, Hussey, "Classical Landscape Park: Shugborough, Staffordshire," pts. 1 and 2, *Country Life* 115 (15 April 1954): 1126–29; (22 April 1954): 1220–23; Hussey, *English Country Houses,* vol. 2, *Mid Georgian, 1760–1800* (Woodbridge: Country Life, 1984): 79–85; Eileen Harris, "A Flair for the Grandiose: The Architecture of Thomas Wright—II," *Country Life* 150 (2 September 1971): 546–50; Bristol, "Stuart and the Genesis of the Greek Revival" (1997): 276–88.

35. Pennant, *Journey from Chester* (1782): 67.

36. Bristol, "Society of Dilettanti" (2000): 47.

37. John Martin Robinson, *Shugborough* (London: National Trust, 1989): 20.

38. Both Alastair Laing and John Martin Robinson claim that the orangery was demolished in around 1855, although Christopher Hussey suggests a date of about 1790. See Alastair Laing, "O Tempera, O Mores! The Ruin Paintings in the Dining Room at Shugborough," *Apollo* 137 (April 1993): 228; Robinson, *Shugborough* (1989): 22; Hussey, "Shugborough—I" (1954): 510.

39. Stuart to Anson, 10 July 1764, Lichfield MS D615/P(S)/1/6/9, Staffordshire Record Office.

40. Stuart to Anson, 25 September 1770, ibid., 1/6/28. The picture seems to have been destroyed when the orangery was demolished. Nothing is known about the paintings in the library. They were sold in 1842. For more information see Laing, "O Tempera, O Mores" (1993): 226, 232 n. 3.

41. Arthur Oswald, "Blithfield, Staffordshire—I," *Country Life* 116 (28 October 1954): 1491.

42. William Lord Bagot, *Memorials of the Bagot Family* (Blithfield: William Hodgetts, 1824): 90.

43. Jackson-Stops, *English Arcadia* (1991): 92.

44. Watkin, *Athenian Stuart* (1982): 25.

45. Hussey, "Classical Landscape Park—II" (1954): 1221. The estimate was submitted in November 1761.

46. Watkin, *Athenian Stuart* (1982): fig. 8, caption.

47. It has been suggested that Admiral Anson supported financially Thomas Anson's improvements at Shugborough, as before inheriting a fortune on his brother's death Thomas had only modest funds at his disposal. See e.g. Hussey, "Classical Landscape Park—II" (1954): 1221.

48. Marchioness Grey to Catherine Talbot, Shugborough, 24 August 1763, Lucas Ms. L30/9a/8/121-123, Bedfordshire and Luton Archives and Records Service. See also James Lees-Milne, "Shugborough, Staffordshire—I: The Park and Its Monuments," *Connoisseur* 164 (April 1967): 214.

49. The work was assigned to John Webb. See Bristol, "Stuart and the Genesis of the Greek Revival" (1997): 282.

50. On the addition of these elements, which derive ultimately from

both Roman and Greek models, see e.g. ibid., 282–83. For Schee-makers' association with Stuart see Ingrid Roscoe, "James 'Athenian' Stuart and the Scheemakers Family: A Lucrative Partnership between Architect and Sculptors," *Apollo* 126 (September 1987): 178–84.

51. Bristol also notes that the medallions must have "formed an inte-gral part of [the triumphal arch's] design from early on as the mould-ings were not altered to accommodate them." See Bristol, "Stuart and the Genesis of the Greek Revival" (1997): 283–84. Watkin observes that Stuart was "evidently impressed by [the Villa Pisani's] large hexastyle portico and a number of his sketches consist of proposals for a palace with domed end pavilions inspired by this building." Watkin, *Athenian Stuart* (1982): 17–18.

52. It is notable that Pennant refers to both the chap. and tab. number in the *Antiquities* when referring to the Shugborough versions of these monuments; see Pennant, *Journey from Chester* (1782): 67.

53. Robinson, *Shugborough* (1989): 32.

54. Parnell's diary (1769): 63, LSE Library Misc. 38, University of London, quoted in Bristol, "Society of Dilettanti" (2000): 49–50. The lower room, converted into a dairy by Samuel Wyatt in 1803, originally housed casts of the Furietti Centaurs obtained through Nollekens in 1765.

55. On this drawing see Jackson-Stops, *English Arcadia* (1991): 90.

56. See Lees-Milne, "Shugborough, Staffordshire—I" (1967): 215. Parnell's diary (1769): 63, LSE Library Misc. 38, University of London.

57. The design of the pigeon house is reproduced in J. Mordaunt-Crook, *The Greek Revival,* RIBA Drawings series (Feltham: Country Life Books, 1968): 12.

58. Desmond Fitzgerald, *The Temple of the Winds, Mount Stewart: A Historical Note* (Belfast: Committee for Ireland, National Trust, 1966): 7–9. See also Fitzgerald, "The Temple of the Winds: An Antique Irish Banqueting House," *Connoisseur* 167 (April 1968): 206–9; Gervase Jackson-Stops, "Mount Stewart, Co. Down—I: Property of The National Trust," *Country Life* 167 (6 March 1980): 646–49.

59. Jackson-Stops, "Mount Stewart—I" (1980): 647.

60. Fitzgerald, "Temple of the Winds" (1968): 208. We know that build-ing work was being undertaken at Mount Stewart in 1781 as an adver-tisement for a bricklayer for the estate appeared in the *Belfast Newsletter* of that year.

61. Jackson-Stops, "Mount Stewart—I" (1980): 648. Workmen listed in the accounts are: Robert Orram and Michael Campbell (masons), David McBlain (stone-carver), John Ferguson (carpenter), and William Fitzgerald (plasterer).

62. Fitzgerald, "Temple of the Winds" (1968): 208.

63. Fitzgerald, *Temple of the Winds* (1966): 9.

64. Cited in Jackson-Stops, "Mount Stewart—I" (1980): 647.

65. Fitzgerald, "Temple of the Winds" (1968): 208. It is not altogether clear how Stuart came to receive the commission, but he may have been introduced to Stewart by Dr. Percy, Bishop of Dromore in County Down, who knew the architect personally. Alternatively, as Fitzgerald suggests, he may have met Stewart through Lord Claremont, "Ireland's most important cognoscente, who was a friend of Londonderry."

66. Hugh Honour, "Adaptations from Athens," *Country Life* 123 (22 May 1958): 1120. Stuart and Revett included twenty-six engravings of the monument in *Antiquities,* which no doubt contributed to its pop-ularity. Built examples range from Robert Burns's Cenotaph at Alloway, Ayrshire, to a hexagonal version of the Choragic Monument used for the tower of Saint Pancras Church, London.

67. In 1780 Pratt wrote a letter explaining his wish that Elizabeth Pratt should "consult with Stewart & Norris [the builder] about the Bath immediately, for I am determined to execute that building at all events"; Charles Pratt to Elizabeth Pratt, 20 September 1780, Pratt Mss. U840 C7/8, Centre for Kentish Studies, Maidstone. The cold bath is described in an inventory of 1798 as: "Wood building covered with slates . . . the landing all round the bath paved with Portland Stone . . . Six stone steps go down into bath—two ropes and three rows of small chain round. Entrance pediment front and rear columns to support ditto." See William M. Mitchell, *Chislehurst Golf Club: 100 Years of Golf at Camden Place* (Droitwich, Eng.: Grant Books and Chislehurst Golf Club, 1994): 98 n. 4. Pratt's desire to consult Stuart on the design of the cold bath suggests that he may have been involved with the design of Lord Hyde's earlier cold bath at The Grove.

68. See John Harris, "Le Rouge's Sion Hill: A Garden by Brown," *London Gardener, or The Gardener's Intelligencer* 5 (1999–2000): 24–28.

69. Robinson, *Shugborough* (1989): 26.

70. Stuart to Anson, 19 June 1764, Lichfield MS D615/P(S)/1/6/7, Staffordshire Record Office, Stafford; quoted in Watkin, *Athenian Stuart* (1982): 26.

71. Charles Pratt to Elizabeth Pratt, 20 September 1780, Ms. U840 C7/8, Centre for Kentish Studies, Maidstone.

72. On Stuart's tripod designs in general see Nicholas Goodison, "Mr Stuart's Tripod," *Burlington Magazine* 114 (October 1972): 695–704.

73. As Robinson notes, "Tripods were associated from the earliest Classical times with wealth, honour, hospitality, and victory," qualities that Anson would have considered entirely appropriate for his Country Seat; see Robinson, *Shugborough* (1989): 26. Unfortunately, the monument was widely disparaged. Horace Walpole referred to it is a "fly cage" and William Chambers compared it to a sentry box in Portman Square. See Bristol, "Stuart and the Genesis of the Greek Revival" (1997): 287–88.

74. Stuart to Anson, 23 September 1769, Lichfield Ms. D6/5/P(S)/1/6/27, Staffordshire Record Office.

75. Wedgwood to Bentley, 24–26 December 1770, Wedgwood Archives, Barlaston; quoted in Robinson, *Shugborough* (1989): 26–27. See also Eliza Meteyard, *The Life of Josiah Wedgwood,* vol. 2 (London: Hurst and Blackett, 1866): 222–23.

76. Alison Kelly has suggested that the tripod may not have been installed because "possibly the gilding was not a success"; see Kelly, *Decorative Wedgwood in Architecture and Furniture* (London: Country Life, 1965): 105.

77. For the attribution to Wright see E. Harris, "A Flair for the Grandiose" (1971): 548. The Shepherd's Monument was certainly in place by 1756 as it is described by Anna Seward in her poem on Shugborough; see Robinson, *Shugborough* (1989): 31.

78. See e.g. Watkin, *Athenian Stuart* (1982): 28; Bristol, "Stuart and the Genesis of the Greek Revival" (1997): 278. It is conceivable, of course, that Stuart's drawing is a record of the monument rather than a design for it. Eileen Harris affirms that the Greek Doric aedicule and the marble frame surrounding Scheemakers's relief are by Stuart. See E. Harris, "Cracking the Poussin Code," *Apollo* 163 (May 2006): 29–30.

79. The drawing is included in an album attributed to Angelica Kauffman: Pierpont Morgan Library, New York, 1966.0.39.

80. See Jackson-Stops, *English Arcadia* (1991): 92.

81. See Mavis Batey, "Nuneham Park, Oxfordshire—I: The Creation of a Landscape," *Country Life* 144 (5 September 1968): 540–42.

82. Ibid., 542. Horace Walpole, *The Yale Edition of Horace Walpole's Correspondence,* vol. 29, *Horace Walpole's Correspondence with William Mason,* ed. W. S. Lewis, Grover Cronin Jr., and Charles H. Bennett (New Haven and London: Yale University Press, 1955): 85.

83. Edward William Harcourt, ed., *The Harcourt Papers,* vol. 3 (Oxford: James Parker Co., 1880–1905): 200. This is repeated in John Preston Neale, *Views of the Seats of Noblemen and Gentlemen in England, Wales, Scotland, and Ireland,* vol. 3 (London: Sherwood, Neely and Jones and Thomas Moule, 1820): n.p.

84. Bristol, "Stuart and the Genesis of the Greek Revival" (1997): 248.

85. Batey, "Nuneham Park—I" (1968): 542. Bristol has noted, however, that the "play of light through the Diocletian windows . . . is reminiscent of one of Stuart's favourite Palladian buildings, the Redentore in Venice"; Bristol, "Stuart and the Genesis of the Greek Revival" (1997): 248–49.

86. John Harris, "Newly-Acquired Designs by James Stuart in the British Architectural Library, Drawings Collection," *Architectural History* 22 (1979): 74.

87. See Giles Worsley, "Nuneham Park Revisited—II," *Country Life* 177 (10 January 1985): 65; Bristol, "Stuart and the Genesis of the Greek Revival" (1997): 250.

88. Daniel Lysons and Samuel Lysons, *Magna Britannia; being a concise topographical account of the several counties of Great Britain,* vol. 1, *Bedfordshire, Berkshire, Buckinghamshire* (London: T. Cadell and W. Davies, 1806).

89. Percy Noble, *Park Place, Berkshire: A Short History of the Place and an Account of the Owners and their Guests* (London: F. Calder Turner, 1905): 41.

90. As Adshead notes, in an exemplary study of the Park Building, this structure went by many names, including "palladian building," "hill house," and "belvedere"; see Adshead, "Modern Italian Loggia" (2000): 150.

91. Lord Hardwicke to the Earl of Dartmouth, 18 February 1788, Mss. Dartmouth, Report 15, appendix I, 1896, 238–39, Historic Manuscripts Commission; quoted in Adshead, "Modern Italian Loggia" (2000): 152.

92. Ibid.

93. The Yorkes regularly visited Shugborough and would certainly have been familiar with Stuart's work there. See Bristol, "Society of Dilettanti" (2000): 50; Adshead, "Modern Italian Loggia" (2000): 152. On the park at Wimpole see e.g. Gervase Jackson-Stops, "Exquisite Contrivances: The Park and Gardens at Wimpole—I," *Country Life* 166 (6 September 1979): 658–61; Dorothy Stroud, "The Charms of Natural Landscape—II: The Park and Gardens at Wimpole," *Country Life* 166 (13 September 1979): 758–62.

94. Stuart to Philip Yorke, second Earl of Hardwicke, Bath, 27 January 1766, Add. Ms. 35,607 fol. 234r, BL; quoted in Adshead, "Modern Italian Loggia" (2000): 150.

95. Quoted in Elizabeth Philippa Yorke Biddulph, *Charles Philip Yorke, Fourth Earl of Hardwicke, Vice Admiral. R.N., A Memoir by his Daughter, the Lady Biddulph of Ledbury* (London: Smith, Elder and Co., 1910): 2. An idea of the fine view is provided by fig. 7-45; *British Drawings and Watercolours including Architectural Drawings,* sale cat., Christies, London, 19 December 1989, lot. 134.

96. W. B. Trevilyan and James Plumtree, "Journal of a Tour to the Source of the River Cam made in July 1800," typescript transcription in Cambridgeshire Collection, Cambridge Central Library. See also Bristol, "Stuart and the Genesis of the Greek Revival" (1997): 315–16.

97. See Bristol, "Stuart and the Genesis of the Greek Revival" (1997): 314–15. Adshead has suggested that the engraving of the Park Building may be after a lost drawing by Stuart, noting that "the same image, identical in composition at least, was included by Josiah Wedgwood and Thomas Bentley in the 944-piece dinner and dessert service which they made for Catherine the Great . . . completed and delivered during the second part of 1774, suggesting that the Park Building had probably been built by that date"; see Adshead, "Modern Italian Loggia" (2000): 152.

98. Jackson-Stops, "Exquisite Contrivances" (1979): 760.

99. Adshead, "Modern Italian Loggia" (2000): 156.

100. Parnell's diary (1769): 59, LSE Library Misc., University of London; quoted in Bristol, "Society of Dilettanti" (2000): 48.

Fig. 8-1. James Stuart, assisted by Robert Mylne and William Newton. Interior of the chapel of the Royal Hospital for Seamen at Greenwich, looking toward the altar, 1779–89. Photographed in 2006. Courtesy of the Greenwich Foundation. *Checklist no. 155.*

JAMES STUART, THE ADMIRALTY, AND THE ROYAL HOSPITAL FOR SEAMEN AT GREENWICH, 1758–88

KERRY BRISTOL

Until the recent restoration of Spencer House in London, James Stuart's best-known architectural work was at the Royal Hospital for Seamen at Greenwich (fig. 8-1). This was the second substantial charitable military institution to be founded in England in the last quarter of the seventeenth century, after the army's Royal Hospital at Chelsea. The motives for building both hospitals were "philanthropic and patriotic, as concern for war veterans had been growing since . . . the 1650s," and they were funded by royal and government grants, gifts, donations, and levies on the wages of soldiers at Chelsea, seamen in the case of Greenwich.[1] Neither institution was intended primarily for the care of the sick, but rather to house disabled veterans (volunteers, not men pressed into service), who would otherwise have been homeless or destitute.[2] The plight of sailors, in particular, was to become increasingly obvious in the eighteenth century when it was recognized that the rigors of a maritime existence ensured that the lives of seamen were shorter than their land-based compatriots.[3]

By the time Stuart became surveyor in 1758, the hospital at Greenwich was nearing completion. It was already one of the most celebrated monuments of British

architecture (fig. 8-2), with four blocks, known as King Charles, Queen Anne, Queen Mary, and King William, designed and/or erected by some of Britain's finest architects—John Webb, Sir Christopher Wren, Nicholas Hawksmoor, John James, Sir John Vanbrugh, and Colen Campbell. A history of the institution, written by the hospital's chaplains John Cooke and John Maule, was published in 1789 (see figs. 8-8, 8-38). Available at the hospital's chapel and at several London booksellers, it became the standard source for guides to the site for more than a century.[4]

At the time of his appointment, Stuart had recently embarked upon a new career designing garden buildings and updating the interiors of a small number of town and country houses. This was hardly adequate training for the role of surveyor, but appointments at Greenwich had often been politically or personally motivated.[5] The case of James Stuart is no exception. He owed his office to Admiral Sir George Anson, who, through his naval abilities and political connections, had been promoted to First Lord of the Admiralty, a position that gave him the opportunity to forward the careers of his favorites, be they seamen or artists.[6] With the Greenwich complex nearing completion, Anson most likely saw the surveyorship as a means of giving Stuart a guaranteed income of £200 per

Fig. 8-2. The Royal Hospital for Seamen at Greenwich (now known as Greenwich Hospital), viewed from the river. King Charles Block (right); Queen Anne Block (left). Behind these are the King William (right) and Queen Mary (left) blocks. Photographed in 2006.

annum rather than as an opportunity for him to flex his architectural muscles. It was to be a sinecure in the true sense of the word. Stuart's thoughts on the matter have not survived. It is unlikely, however, that he was disappointed by the apparent lack of new building opportunities at Greenwich. The surveyorship was a prestigious position, perhaps made more poignant because his father was reputedly a Scottish mariner and, of course, because the hospital was a tangible reminder of naval supremacy achieved within the context of British, Protestant political "freedom" or "liberty" as this was understood in the early- to mid-eighteenth century.[7] The surveyorship also thrust Stuart into the heart of a complex administrative infrastructure, which he was able to turn to his advantage.

Naval Administration

Although the seeds had been sown in the seventeenth century, Britain's real rise to naval dominance occurred after 1688 when a program of expansion was initiated. Naval manpower doubled in size, the number of ships nearly tripled, and there was a rapid increase of naval dockyards. This, coupled with an increase in trade goods to and from distant colonies and a refined policy of naval support for the merchant marine, allowed Britain to become the dominant sea power in Europe in the first half of the eighteenth century. By this time several government departments had assumed responsibility for naval management.[8] The most prominent of these was the Admiralty

Board run by seven commissioners whose offices were at Whitehall, in a building designed by Thomas Ripley, the master carpenter who had replaced Colen Campbell as Surveyor of the Royal Naval Hospital in 1729.[9]

A seafaring background was not a prerequisite for a Lord of the Admiralty. The inclusion of one or two naval officers among their number was common nonetheless for much of the century. What really distinguished the Admiralty Board's membership from those of the other naval administrative bodies was the fact that the commissioners were political appointees and thus vulnerable to changes in government.[10] As First Lords of the Admiralty, Stuart's patrons George Anson and John Montagu, fourth Earl of Sandwich, both fell foul of party politics. Their resignations did not affect Stuart's work at Greenwich.[11]

The Admiralty Board's primary role was as liaison between the flag officers, other branches of naval administration, and government (the commissioners represented the navy in parliament). It also dealt with the appointment, promotion, pay, and so on of officers, and it informed government of the navy's fiscal and supply needs on the basis of information provided by subsidiary boards, who received their funds directly from the treasury. The Admiralty Board was not a policy-making body but, as a member of the Cabinet, the First Lord of the Admiralty did contribute to the formulation of naval strategy and operations, even if any such orders came via the Secretary of State for the Southern Department, not the

Admiralty Board.[12] If the work of the Admiralty Board was "routine, almost trivial in nature," with the signatures of only three commissioners regarded as quorate, the tasks were many and onerous for the First Lord, whose presence was required at most meetings, and for the Admiralty secretary, who was authorized to "sign any urgent documents that would then be properly dealt with at the next meeting."[13] For much of the second half of the century, the post of secretary was held by Sir Philip Stephens, a close friend of Stuart who figures in much of his surviving correspondence with Admiral Anson's brother, Thomas. This suggests that Stuart's connection with the Admiralty Board was much more than a relationship of convenience or one brought about solely by virtue of his surveyorship at Greenwich, even if it had begun that way. Since the Admiralty Secretary was also the only man unlikely to lose his position with a change of administration, Stuart was well-placed to cultivate a "sympathetic ear" when his competence and altruistic motives came under intense scrutiny in the 1770s and 1780s.

The other administrative department with which Stuart had contact was the Navy Board housed near Tower Hill. Its membership was comprised of treasurer, surveyor, comptroller, and clerk of the acts, as well as a host of lesser officers who, because theirs were not political appointments akin to those on the Admiralty Board, were able to provide continuity as they went about their business.[14] The responsibilities of the Navy Board's commissioners fell into three major areas: maintenance of the fleet and dockyards, including the purchase of stores and leasing of transport vessels; controlling expenditure and auditing accounts; and monitoring the health and well-being of all mariners through the commissioners of the Sick and Hurt Board and the commissioners of the Victualling Board.[15]

Like any large organization, however, the Royal Navy had many administrative anomalies. Only one is relevant here—the constitution and appointment of the Royal Hospital's board of directors. Although the Navy Board looked after most of the navy's architectural needs, and the Sick and Hurt Board had responsibility for the welfare of men expected to return to active duty, the hospital constituted a quasi-independent authority answerable directly to the Admiralty.[16] An eight-strong council, all of whom were meant to be naval men, was responsible for the day-to-day running of the hospital, while a board of twenty-five directors took responsibility for wider-rang-

ing issues and policies.[17] Originally the two bodies were separate entities. By mid-century certain men sat on both bodies. In Stuart's day the hospital was run by a combination of retired seamen (temporarily "retired" or otherwise) and professional administrators, such as Charles Saunders, another Anson protégé (and future First Lord of the Admiralty), who was the hospital's treasurer and receiver general in the 1760s, and James Cook, who was appointed fourth captain in 1775.[18]

One of the roles of the surveyor was to act as a director of the hospital. Stuart was expected to contribute to discussions on all aspects of hospital business at the quarterly General Court meetings held at the Admiralty and the monthly or fortnightly hospital board meetings held either at Salter's Hall in the City of London or on the hospital premises. The evidence suggests that Stuart took his General Court responsibilities seriously as he was present at seventy-four of ninety-three meetings held during his surveyorship.[19] This, of course, brought him into repeated contact with the First Lord of the Admiralty and is surely why he received a large number of Admiralty-related commissions. Only in later years did his attendance become sporadic, particularly between December 1779 and August 1783, dates that coincide with a decline in his health and the trouble-ridden final stages of construction on Mrs. Montagu's house in Portman Square (see chap. 5).

Architect-builders often took part in hospital management.[20] One under-explored facet of Stuart's involvement with the Royal Naval Hospital was the role he played in strengthening its financial situation by visiting the Derwentwater estate in the mid-1770s. This is a minor incident in the long history of the hospital but one that reveals much about Stuart and his relationship with his fellow directors.

As with many grandiose building schemes, then as now, the hospital's finances were uncertain in the early years. The royal endowment of £2,000 per annum soon fell into arrears and mandatory contributions from the sailors themselves (navy and merchant marine) were hampered by the War of the Spanish Succession (1702–13), when the merchant marine often found itself unable to sail, and the Royal Navy was unable to pay its own men. Sixpence a month could not be deducted from wages that had not yet been paid.[21] In 1719 the institution became a beneficiary of the Greenwich estate of Robert Osboldston. In 1735 it also began receiving rent and profits from Lord Radcliffe's Derwentwater estate. The financial situation started to look more stable, although satisfactory management of the Derwentwater estate was frustratingly difficult to achieve. Stuart was eventually asked to develop strategies and solutions.[22] The survey he undertook with his fellow director Thomas Hicks took over seven weeks to complete (23 July to 14 September 1774) and was extremely thorough. This was no fly-by-night visit made by someone unprepared or unwilling to act in the hospital's best interests. Stuart and Hicks found themselves working from plans of the estate made in 1736. They informed the hospital's board of directors that this had put them to "great difficulties," costing them valuable time when it was discovered that many fences had been moved without authorization and the land divided and subdivided, resulting in "much delay, confusion & embarrassment" during their visit.[23] Their recommendations were sensible, affordable, and forward thinking. Stuart's efficiency and conscientious attention to detail at this time must have been foremost in the other directors' minds when claims to the contrary were made in Captain Thomas Baillie's blistering attack on the hospital's administration in 1778.

As a captain of the hospital from 1761 to 1774 and Lieutenant Governor thereafter, Baillie had become increasingly angry that Lord Sandwich filled posts with his protégés, too many of whom were landmen instead of mariners.[24] He accused the hospital administrators of having lost sight of the institution's original aims. In addition to charges made against a host of other men, Baillie objected most strenuously to a potential conflict of interest between Stuart's position as a director and his role as surveyor. He claimed that he "never attends, except to take his seat at the Board of Directors, (where he sometimes has the honor to preside) to espouse the estimate, given in by his Clerk, of what is called Necessary Works, amounting to large sums; which is presented almost every board-day, and ordered as a thing of course."[25] Baillie then went on to recommend the abolition of either the post of surveyor or clerk of works on the grounds that no major building work was underway.

Although Baillie was careful to cite as many instances as possible of what he thought were unnecessary alterations to the fabric of the hospital and opportunities where Stuart may have approved estimates without due care and attention, each example was systematically examined and disproved in the subsequent internal enquiry. The investigating team, whose report was also published, made spe-

cial reference to the "much-injured Character of Mr. *Stuart*" and noted that he "always attends . . . at the Hospital, when his presence is necessary; and, at the Board of Directors, when his Health, and other Avocations, will admit; and there are few who are more regular or constant in their Attendance than he is."[26] This would appear to corroborate the evidence presented in Stuart's letters to Thomas Anson, particularly those in which he mentions extraordinary visits to Greenwich in the 1760s.[27] This efficiency is at odds with Baillie's claims and the popular perception that Stuart's business practices were shambolic.

The resolution may lie in the phrase "when his presence is necessary" and Baillie's surprise that the surveyor "espouse[d] the estimate[s], given in by his Clerk . . . which is . . . ordered as a thing of course." Baillie was a naval man who became steeped in the original charter of the hospital. Although he was fundamentally honest and well meaning, he may not have known that the flexible day-to-day system within which Stuart worked was of relatively recent devising. After the design of the hospital had been more or less completed, instructions no longer came to the surveyor from the hospital board. Instead they flowed in the opposite direction. Stuart, like all surveyors since Vanbrugh, was expected to "point out what was needed and then take directions" while his clerk of works provided the necessary written reports.[28] In the case of Vanbrugh, the surveyor's duties had been "chiefly administrative." It was for this reason that he attended board meetings.[29] Vanbrugh provided few, if any, designs for Greenwich Hospital; Hawksmoor seems never to have stopped. Half a century later, the evidence suggests that Stuart took the design lead on certain occasions. On others he was content to give his seal of approval to what his clerk of works proposed. Indeed the General Court Minutes reveal that Stuart was both proactive and reactive. If the distribution of work between the surveyor and clerk of works was based on personal preference and decisions were made behind the scenes, then it is hardly surprising that Baillie was confused. The minutes also reveal that, while work was undertaken throughout Stuart's surveyorship, the 1770s were particularly full of minor yet time-consuming tasks. This may have led to what Baillie saw as a duplication of responsibilities between the surveyor and clerk of works.

Much of the work undertaken during Stuart's surveyorship fell into three categories. The first was devoted to refining existing structures to make them visually coherent,

Fig. 8-3. The southwest pavilion of the King Charles Block, as rebuilt by Stuart in 1769–74. Photographed in 2006. Courtesy of the Greenwich Foundation. *Checklist no. 151.*

including such projects as extending and reconstructing in stone Wren's brick southwestern pavilion of the King Charles block (fig. 8-3) so that it matched the south façade of Queen Anne, and removing Ripley's pediment on the west front of the east range of the Queen Mary block.[30] A secondary category concerned alterations to various staff apartments, another bugbear of Baillie's.[31] In the governor's apartment in the southeast pavilion of the King Charles block, for example, two chimneypieces and a ceiling are very likely by Stuart (fig. 8-4).[32] There were also alterations to accommodate the growing number of

Fig. 8-4. Attributed to James Stuart. Chimneypiece in the Admiral's Study (formerly the council room of the Governor's apartment) in the northeast part of the King Charles Block, ca. 1769–74. Photographed in 2006. Courtesy of the Greenwich Foundation. *Checklist no. 150.*

pensioners, about which Baillie was curiously silent.[33] These included refitting the dining room in King Charles and constructing an underground passageway between Charles and William to link the dining areas with the kitchens.[34] The third category, perhaps more "engineering" than "architecture" as these disciplines are understood today, included creating an extension to the Thames-side terrace and river wall, constructing a new wharf, and enlarging the embankment.[35] Stuart was also responsible for such mundane tasks as examining drawings for an engine to draw water into the hospital's brewhouse and arranging the annual dusting.[36] When Sir James Thornhill's Painted Hall was discovered to be "in a very bad condition for want of cleaning and reparation," Stuart recommended that "Mr. Devis" perform the work.[37] Baillie had been particularly scathing about Stuart's handling of this task and accused him of corruption. These charges were not accepted by the investigating panel.[38] Ironically, an entry in Joseph Farington's diary suggests that Baillie may not have missed the mark and that the restoration of the ceiling had actually been detrimental to it. Farington visited Greenwich in 1813 and commented on the decision "to refresh the cieling, a mere ill advised job, sd. [Benjamin] West. Stuart, who traveled to Athens having then the care of it. Buckets of oil, sd. West, were passed over it, which blackened the surface & very much injured the purity of the colour."[39] At this distance in time it is difficult to determine how many of these tasks would have been left in the hands of the clerk of works. It is probably safe to assume that some agreement was reached that left Stuart free to concentrate on the major works discussed below.

Fig. 8-5. James Stuart. Elevation of the infirmary, the Royal Hospital for Seamen at Greenwich, ca. 1760–63. Pen and ink, color wash. Inscribed: "A Design, not proposed, being a study for the Plan to be fixed on." National Maritime Museum, London, Manuscript ART II, fol. 41.

The Infirmary

The Royal Hospital for Seamen at Greenwich was not intended for the care of the sick but from its inception it must have been apparent that its elderly and infirm constituency would require medical care as well as alms. The desirability of a separate building for this purpose had been recognized long before Stuart was appointed surveyor. With funding uncertain and the main buildings still to be completed, the best the hospital could provide was a temporary ward in the King William block to separate those with infectious diseases or infirmities too extensive to be cared for in the residential wards.[40] By 1713 overcrowding prompted the creation of another temporary sick ward in the north part of the Queen Anne block.[41] In 1723 and again in 1728, Hawksmoor had prepared plans for a separate infirmary. Adequate funds could not be found, nor were they available when Ripley presented his proposals in 1747.[42] The idea lay dormant until 1760 when a potential influx of pensioners created by the Seven Years' War may have brought matters to a head. At the end of the war, when it was discovered that the navy treasury owed the hospital nearly £80,000, it was finally possible to develop the waste ground to the west of the King William block.[43] In June 1763 Stuart was requested to present his plans, budget, and timetable to the General Court, which he did promptly, submitting an estimate of £18,489.6s.4d on August 25. His proposal was "thought a very proper one for the purpose." Work was ordered to begin immediately.[44]

What the board minutes do not reveal is that Stuart's proposals were radically simplified to meet the Admiralty's stipulation that the building "be as plain & as little expensive as the Nature of it will admit."[45] Although Stuart had made no attempt to match his infirmary to the existing baroque structure, architectural splendor still came at too high a price. He prepared at least four designs before the final version was reached. The first of these, annotated "A Design not proposed being a study for the Plan to be fixed on," was considerably more complex than the accepted façade, with an interlocking pediment over the three-story central bays, and three-story, three-bay end pavilions with central windows featuring Kentian splayed surrounds (fig. 8-5). Another version was even more complex, with a Diocletian window in the central pediment and Diocletian windows and serlianas within relieving arches in the end pavilions (fig. 8-6). The final courtyard scheme retained the end pavilions but substituted pyramidal roofs for the pediments as used in neo-Palladian country houses such as Hagley Hall, the seat of George, Lord Lyttelton, a close friend of the Anson brothers and an early patron of Stuart (figs. 8-7, 8-8).[46] In deriving from a domestic model, it shares much with the fifty-odd new hospitals and asylums constructed in England during the eighteenth century.[47]

Fig. 8-6. James Stuart. Elevation of the infirmary, the Royal Hospital for Seamen at Greenwich, ca. 1760–63. Pen and ink, color wash. Inscribed: "East and West Front." National Maritime Museum, London, Manuscript ART II, fol. 42.

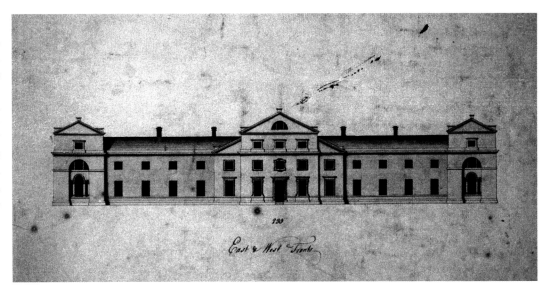

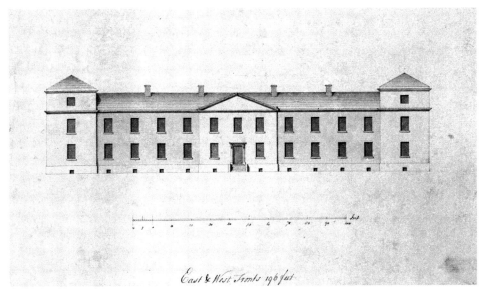

Fig. 8-7. James Stuart. Elevation of the infirmary, the Royal Hospital for Seamen at Greenwich, ca. 1760–63. Pen and ink, color wash, pencil. Inscribed: "East & West Fronts." National Maritime Museum, London, Manuscript ART II, fol. 39.

Fig. 8-8. "Elevation of the East-front of the Infirmary." Engraving by J. Newton. From John Cooke and John Maule, *An Historical Account of the Royal Hospital for Seamen at Greenwich* (1789). Courtesy of the Library, The Bard Graduate Center for Studies in the Decorative Arts, Design, and Culture, New York. *Checklist no. 149.*

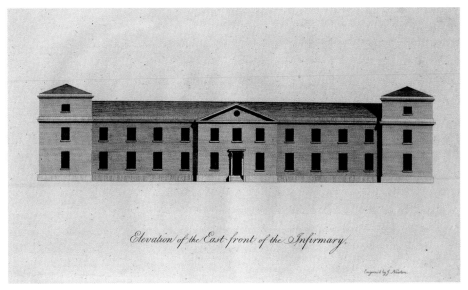

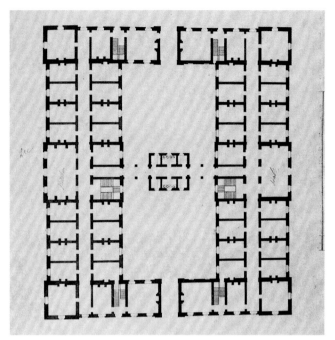

Fig. 8-9. Draftsman unknown, after a design by James Stuart. Plan of the infirmary, Royal Hospital for Seamen at Greenwich, ca. 1760–63. Pen and ink, pencil. Inscribed: "by a Clerk probably." National Maritime Museum, London, Manuscript ART II, fol. 37.

In devising a plan for the new infirmary (fig. 8-9), Stuart was faced with a *tabula rasa*. Separate infirmaries were not a feature of military hospitals. There were no precedents for him to follow. Even the newly built hospitals at Haslar near Gosport and Stonehouse near Plymouth, although setting "new standards of hygiene and care," were far too large to be appropriate models for the more modest needs of Greenwich.[48] Bearing in mind the century's obsession with "miasmata," or "bad airs," which were thought to cause as well as spread illnesses,[49] Stuart's solution was to design a two-story quadrangular building linked by corridors, and a small block for "wash places and water closets." The building was to be divided into two principal parts—one for patients under the care of the physician and the other for those whose cases required the attendance of a surgeon.[50]

In the physicians' half of the building was a two-story entrance hall, while a kitchen and chapel were located in the back, or surgeon's half. Rather than arranging the beds in a large room or rooms (a plan type Baillie appears to have preferred for its enhanced capacity to accommodate patients[51]), Stuart devised a scheme of sixty-four small rooms or cells that would accommodate 256 patients.

These were arranged along a spine corridor and heated by fireplaces in the party wall. The dispensary, surgery, and staff apartments were placed in the corners.[52] Each cell contained four beds, which afforded the patients some privacy and relative quiet as well as "the separation of . . . cases by condition," and was lit and ventilated by sash windows, openings above the door, and "two apertures high in the wall."[53] In this Stuart was influenced by Hawksmoor's plan of 1728, although "both adhere, in general terms, to the planning of Greenwich's residential blocks."[54]

According to the hospital's official eighteenth-century historians, Cooke and Maule, the new infirmary was designed by Stuart and "completed under the direction of Mr. Robinson then Clerk of the Works."[55] This was William Robinson, who had trained under Ripley and been appointed clerk of works in 1746. He was a well-seasoned builder with many years of experience in official posts. He and Stuart worked well together. Robinson remained clerk until his sudden death in October 1775, after which Robert Mylne was appointed in his stead.

Although Robinson was left in charge of day-to-day building operations, Stuart did not neglect his responsibilities. He was a frequent visitor to the site. During the summer of 1764, there was a shortage of bricks, as Stuart wrote to Thomas Anson, "Greenwich goes on pretty well but we want Bricks which are at present a very scarce Commodity."[56] By September of that year, when Stuart ruefully informed Anson that the only comedy he had seen lately "was laying the first stone of the Infirmary," work was well underway.[57] The infirmary was noted as "pretty far advanced" in the board minutes of August 25, 1766.[58] A final allowance of £235 was requested to finish the building in 1769.[59]

In view of the subsequent legal battles involving Stuart's competence as surveyor, it should be noted that at no time was any dissatisfaction with the cost or speed of erection of the new infirmary recorded in the hospital's minutes nor was any dissatisfaction expressed with Stuart's work until Baillie rushed into print in 1778:

> The Architect of the new Infirmary, who, instead of constructing it, as originally intended, principally for the sick and helpless Pensioners, built it rather as a Palace for Officers, than an Infirmary for the Sick: the natural consequence of which is, that there is not room sufficient for the helpless Men; all of whom were intended to be there

placed under the immediate care and inspection of the Physician, Surgeon, &c.

The inside of this costly building, which was intended to stand for ages, is already falling to pieces; but this latter defect is easily conceived; for the Contracting Joiner is not only himself a Freeholder of *Huntingdonshire*; but as he is a man of some property there, he raises Officers of the house to that dignity, by splitting his votes, and selling them Forty-shilling Freeholds.[60]

"Huntingdonshire" is a reference to Lord Sandwich and his seat, Hinchingbrooke, located in that county.

Baillie's charge may sound more like sour grapes from a bitter man than a genuine failure on Stuart's part. It must have alarmed the Admiralty and the Royal Naval Hospital's board of directors for it became the first charge refuted by their investigation committee:

The Charges against the Surveyor, of not construct- ing the Infirmary as originally intended, and build- ing it rather as a Palace for Officers; of not making sufficient Room for the Helpless *who were intended to be placed there*; and of the Inside of that costly Building, which was intended to stand for Ages, being already falling to Pieces, *are void of Foundation*: For it appears that the Building was constructed according to the original Plan approved by a General Court; that the late Lieutenant-Governor *Boys* acquainted the Surveyor, by Letter, that it was unnecessary to enlarge it on Account of the Helpless, as their Wards in the Hospital had been lately very much improved; that the Inside of the Infirmary (notwithstanding the great Hurry with which it was fitted up) is in no worse State than any other Work of the same Standing would be; and that the Building is so far from falling to Pieces, that there is no Appearance of Settlement or Decay in any Part of it, except one Place in the Middle of the Inner Court, set apart for Necessaries and Sinks; the Floor of which is damaged, and the Walls discoloured, through the Carelessness of the Persons appointed to clean the Wards, who instead of trundling their Mops in the Places provided for that Purpose, have made a Practice of doing it in the Middle of the Room.[61]

So much for Baillie.

Fig. 8-10. Thomas Ripley. Chapel in the Queen Mary Building, Royal Hospital for Seamen at Greenwich, 1746–51. Destroyed by fire, January 2, 1779. Engraving by T. Malton and G. Bickham. Courtesy of the Greenwich Heritage Centre.

The Chapel

Without doubt Stuart's most important work at Greenwich Naval Hospital is the chapel in the northwest pavilion of the Queen Mary block. Rebuilding was nec- essary after Ripley's chapel was destroyed in a fire that began in a nearby tailor's shop on January 2, 1779 (fig. 8-10). Early nineteenth-century proponents of the Greek revival regarded the chapel as Stuart's masterwork. They looked to Stuart as a figurehead and found the chapel displayed "so characteristic a magnificence [that it] should be con- sulted and adopted in all ecclesiastical structures, that may be hereafter erected upon the Grecian model."[62] By the early twentieth century, the chapel had fallen from favor and was described as "a somewhat tame and over-orna- mented piece, which is commonly described as 'in the Adam style,' whereas it lacks the distinctive touch and point of the original."[63] Its critical rehabilitation has been slow (figs. 8-11, 8-12; see fig. 8-1).[64]

On January 19 Stuart and his colleagues on the hos- pital board informed the Admiralty that they had visited the chapel to determine the extent of the damage and were ready to submit an estimate for the repair. Stuart and his clerk of works, Robert Mylne, presented their report. The board concluded that the chapel and adjacent wards should be rebuilt with all dispatch. Thornhill's Painted Hall

Fig. 8-11. James Stuart, assisted by Robert Mylne and William Newton. Interior of the chapel of the Royal Hospital for Seamen at Greenwich, looking toward the organ, 1779–89. Photographed in 2006. Courtesy of the Greenwich Foundation. *Checklist no. 156.*

was ordered to be fitted up as a chapel. A reward of £500 was offered to anyone who could discover the identity of the person who may have set the fire.[65] Soon after this display of harmony, however, the relationship between Stuart and Mylne deteriorated. Mylne was a well-trained, "plain-speaking" Scot who held a number of important surveyorships elsewhere; Stuart was a gregarious polymath who relied heavily on others to make his architectural dreams a reality.[66] The previous year Stuart had defended Mylne from Baillie's charge that the position of clerk of works be abolished on the grounds that it was a "Useless Office,"[67] but opposites do not always attract. Soon Mylne could barely contain his scorn for the ailing Stuart when he informed John Ibbetson, secretary to the hospital board, that certain work Stuart had ordered was unnecessary, adding: "If Mr Surveyor had done me the honour to have asked a single question on these points, and the situation of the work done in Repairing the Infirmary, and the Expences thereof, I should have submitted these particulars to his consideration, which I beg maybe veiwed seriously."[68] Until matters came to a head in 1782, however, the board was pleased with the progress made in repairing the damaged parts of the hospital. Mylne was awarded an extra two shillings per diem table money and a further £60 a year to defray the expense of employing a clerk, backdated to January 1, 1779. It was even recommended that he receive a bonus when repair of the fire-damaged area was completed.[69]

The hospital's priority was to rehouse its pensioners as quickly as possible, and only when this task was accomplished could work on the chapel begin in earnest. Consequently, it was not until the spring of 1781 that Stuart recommended that the board employ many of the men then at work on Somerset House, explaining that they had "been trained up to perform works of great elegance under the most eminent architects," and "we have no reason to doubt, that they would acquit themselves as well in the execution of the designs from which they are to finish the Chapel, as they have done in that high finished building."[70]

As the largest new public building of its era, Somerset House was the subject of considerable interest within architectural circles and the craftsmen involved were a natural choice for Greenwich. The complex was erected from 1776 to provide new accommodation for the Navy Board (which moved there in 1780), for government revenue offices such as the Salt and Tax Offices, and for head-

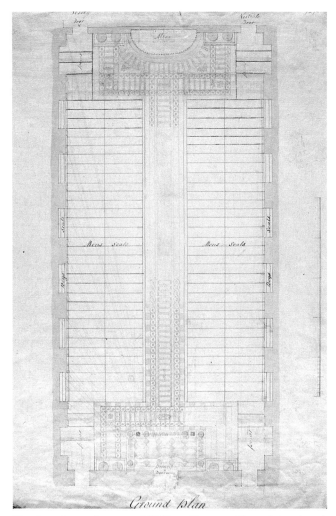

Fig. 8-12. James Stuart and William Newton. Plan of the chapel (drafted by Newton), Royal Hospital for Seamen at Greenwich, ca. 1782–89. Pencil, pen and ink, color wash. RIBA Library Drawings Collection, London, SC 61/1 (2).

quarters for the Royal Society, the Society of Antiquaries, and the Royal Academy of Arts.[71] Of these, the primary concern was for the Navy Board. Much of the decorative scheme had (or was to have) a naval theme that was equally appropriate for the Royal Naval Hospital. Stuart's undated letter on the Somerset House men concluded that "it is impossible properly to conduct this work if we proceed in our accustomed manner by advertising for Tenders, & entring into Contracts. We therefore reccomend the fair & usual method which was adopted on similar occasions, which is, by measuring the quantities, & valuing the materials."[72] This suggests that, to attract craftsmen at the top of their field, the hospital would need to abide by the increasingly unpopular (and frequently

Fig. 8-13. James Stuart, probably assisted by William Newton. Contract drawing for the interior elevation of the south wall (not as built) of the chapel, Royal Hospital for Seamen at Greenwich, signed "received" by Robert Mylne, 1782. Pencil and watercolor, ink inscriptions. RIBA Library Drawings Collection, London, SB 62/4 (2). *Checklist no. 153.*

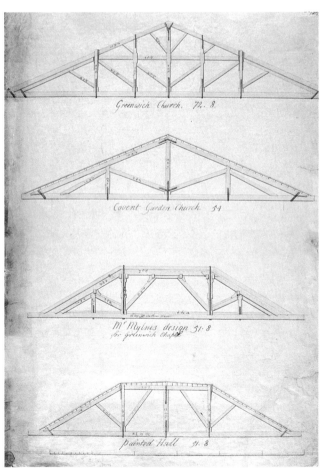

Fig. 8-14. William Newton. Survey drawings of roof trusses and of Robert Mylne's 1782 design for the chapel of the Royal Hospital for Seamen at Greenwich, ca. 1782–89. Pen and ink, color wash. RIBA Library Drawings Collection, London, SB 62/5(16).

more expensive) means of measuring rather than agreeing to a set fee or payment by piece.[73] It is a clear statement that Stuart wanted to employ the best of the best for what was becoming more than a simple reinstatement of Ripley's original scheme.

Initially work was concentrated on the dome and entrance vestibule. By March 1782 Stuart was able to present the Court with "Designs for fitting up the Inside of the Chapel" as well as a model of the roof prepared to designs by Mylne (whose early training as a carpenter was put to good use), and these were "ordered . . . to be proceeded upon and completed as soon as possible" (figs. 8-13, 8-14).[74] Soon the surveyor's office was plagued by problems and work ground to a halt. A major concern was the supply of materials because the Navy Board, which regulated the purchase of stores and controlled expenditure for all branches of the navy, refused to provide timber on the grounds that they did not have enough of certain sizes and what they did have was needed for shipbuilding. This was a constant lament throughout the century but one of great relevance during the American War of Independence.[75] Stuart and Mylne "could by no means approve or recommend the Navy Boards proposition of substituting Dantzic Fir." They had to find another source of oak for the roof, which they accordingly did, "owing to the Civility" of Lord Sandwich's friend, William Wells, one of the hospital's directors and a leading merchant shipbuilder.[76] The new supply was unseasoned, and work slowed while it dried.

In all likelihood Stuart was also incapacitated by gout.

Fig. 8-15. James Stuart. Design for the base of a Corinthian column for the chapel of the Royal Hospital for Seamen at Greenwich, 1782. Pen and ink. Annotations by Robert Mylne on verso. RIBA Library Drawings Collection, London, SC 47/9 (5).

Fig. 8-16. Base of columns at the east end of the chapel of the Royal Hospital for Seamen at Greenwich. Photographed in 1943. Warburg Institute, London, W.60.

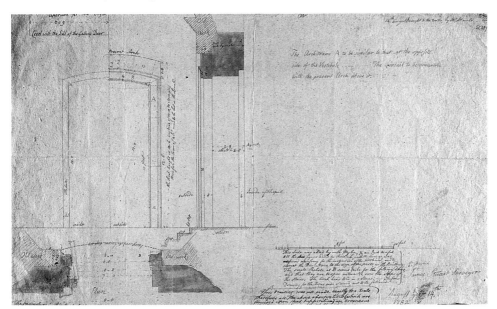

Fig. 8-17. James Stuart. Plan, elevation, and section of a new door below the gallery in the chapel of the Royal Hospital for Seamen at Greenwich, 1782. Pencil, pen and ink, gray wash. Annotations by Robert Mylne on verso. RIBA Library Drawings Collection, London, SC 47/9 (6).

His alcohol consumption had grown to alarming levels in the late 1770s. By 1783 the gout in his thumb had become so painful that he was almost unable to write.[77] Drawing would now be out of the question. At a meeting held on May 11, 1782, he was urged to finish the copies he was making of certain drawings so that the originals could be sent to the proper officers.[78] A sharply worded letter from Mylne dating from July of the same year suggests that Stuart did not always supply drawings promptly, nor were they accurate when he did provide them. For what was to follow, Mylne's letter confirms that Stuart was the controlling force behind the design of the chapel and that

when he failed to provide drawings, work "[stood] still in many parts."[79]

That there were problems with the accuracy of Stuart's work can be corroborated. On March 22, 1782, one full-scale drawing for a Corinthian base for the paired columns on either side of the altar was signed and dated by Stuart but was annotated on the verso, "The Pedestal 7.9 in the Surveyors drawing altered to 7.6 by the Clerk of Works Mr Mylne" (figs. 8-15, 8-16). According to annotations on a section of the west door of the chapel (fig. 8-17), Stuart had given it to the mason John Devall who was to deliver it to the clerk of the cheque, Stephen John

Maule, with instructions to return it to the clerk of works. The drawing was signed by Stuart on August 14, 1782. It was heavily annotated by Mylne later the same day:

> This Scale was added by R. Mylne. 1/2 an Inch to a foot. All the figures added in Red ink, with the lines &c. was found necessary for the instruction of the Workmen, and to correct the Dimentions to the size of the parts in the Building. The small Rebate at B seems to be for the folding Doors, and that they are to open outwards over the Steps of the Stairs. The Arch head to be in 3 Stones—The former Drawing for the Doorcase of Wood, not to be followed. . . . This drawing was not made exactly to a Scale therefore all the above observations (which are founded upon that Supposition) are erroneous the figures only to be followed.

Such inaccuracies must have obstructed work considerably and served to enrage a volatile clerk of works not known for his tolerance. Mylne had already begun to prepare his case against Stuart in 1781 by claiming that "after the fire, all the business of rebuilding a large part of the hospital fell immediately to my single lot to perform" and noting that in three years everything but the chapel and cupola had been restored at a cost of £18,000, several thousand pounds less than the original estimate.[80] His conclusion suggests that he had had enough: "In so far as the business of Surveying even; the contriving, concerting, foreseeing measures to be taken; and making all the necessary Drawings; as well as the directing of the said Works, (nothing of all which belongs [to] me to perform) has been duly, studiously, and diligently executed by me."[81]

As this letter suggests, Mylne had grown to resent Stuart's authority and was no longer willing to make allowances for Stuart's vagaries or ignorance of construction methods. In short the practical implementation of Stuart's ideas fell heavily on Mylne's shoulders. This, of course, was the primary reason why a clerk of works or deputy surveyor was employed on most large-scale building projects.[82] One can sympathize with Mylne's plight. When instructions arrived on site, they came in the form of general drawings (which Mylne was expressly forbidden to use) or faulty detail drawings and, whenever Mylne had taken the initiative and advanced the works, Stuart stepped in with a reprimand.

Their relationship continued to deteriorate. On September 3, 1782, a special meeting of the hospital's General Court was held with only one item on the agenda: Stuart versus Mylne. Those present at the meeting were Admiral Augustus Keppel, recently raised to the peerage as Viscount Keppel and now First Lord of the Admiralty; the other Lords of the Admiralty, Sir Robert Harland, Charles Brett, Richard Hopkins, and John Jeffreys Pratt (the son of Stuart's patron Earl Camden); the secretary to the Admiralty, Philip Stephens; Captain Hartwell (Lieutenant Governor of the Royal Naval Hospital); William Eden (auditor); and Stuart, Thomas Hicks, J. T. Savary, William Allen, and Josiah Hardy as directors of the hospital. The "jury" was already stacked against Mylne.

Stuart made many charges against Mylne: Mylne had falsified drawings given to the mason; Mylne was ill-behaved toward him and most of the other officers of the hospital; Mylne's "vindictive Temper had determined him to deform and spoil the Chapel and sacrifice every thing to the pleasure he would feel in ruining his (the Surveyor's) reputation"; and Mylne had a "fixt and rooted" hatred of Stuart because he would not resign the post of surveyor to Mylne "nor make him an Allowance of £50 per annum which he had demanded with menaces."[83] Stuart also blamed Mylne for the slow rebuilding of the chapel and cupola and suggested that further delay would result because they could not work together. Two of Mylne's letters were read, "representing the want of some drawings, commenting upon others, and holding up the Surveyor as a person of a wavering mind and undecided judgment."[84] The letters were taken in and the meeting adjourned.

Had Stuart been less popular with the hospital's board of directors or the Admiralty Board (to whom he had previously demonstrated that he could build on time and to budget) he would most likely have lost his sinecure or, at the very least, been told to let Mylne "get on with it." Unsurprisingly, the directors did not take kindly to Mylne's attack on Stuart. The board was exceptionally quick to accept that Mylne had never enjoyed the support of his subordinates. A mere week after the special meeting, "Letters from many of the Principal Officers of the Hospital and Others, as also a paper signed by the greatest part of the Artificers under contract with the Hospital were read, complaining, and most of them in the strongest terms, of ill Treatment which they had received from the Clerk of the Works."[85] Mylne was dismissed from his post

Fig. 8-18. James Stuart, assisted by Robert Mylne and William Newton. South wall of the chapel of the Royal Hospital for Seamen at Greenwich, 1779–89. Photographed in 2006. Courtesy of the Greenwich Foundation.

on September 10. He then placed the case in the hands of his solicitors, suing for money he believed he was owed. At the same time the hospital launched a counter-suit for the return of drawings in Mylne's possession.[86] The directors had "some time since permitted the Surveyor to employ as his assistant" William Newton, who was now appointed in Mylne's place. Mylne was eventually paid off.[87] This sequence of events set a dangerous precedent when Newton, snubbed in his attempts to succeed Stuart as surveyor in 1788, began to make his own claims of authorship.

Newton had trained in the London office of Stuart's old friend Matthew Brettingham, and if not there, then he would have met Stuart when he exhibited at the 1760 and 1761 exhibitions held in conjunction with the Royal Society of Arts.[88] No doubt it was at Stuart's behest that Newton also exhibited with the Free Society of Artists in 1783. It was to Newton that Stuart's widow turned as she struggled to publish volume two of *Antiquities of Athens*. Interestingly, Newton was not Stuart's first choice to succeed Mylne, although he was employed at Greenwich at least as early as February 1782.[89] It seems that Stuart had offered the position to Charles White, whom he had known for some twenty years. Accordingly, White made three drawings of "Sections of the Chapel from a Sketch,

which were presented to His Majesty, and I make no doubt also to the Hon-ble Board, and as I understood from Mr Stuart highly approved."[90] When Mylne was dismissed, however, Stuart informed White that he could not make him clerk of the works because "a Mr Newton had great Interest with the Board," but White could have a subordinate position. According to White, "in order to engage me to accept of it, he assured me that he meant to Resign, as soon as the Chapel should be finished, & added that Mr Newton would succeed him, and I of course should succeed Mr Newton."[91] On this assumption, White accepted the position. The relationship between White and Newton was fraught with difficulties (Newton apparently considered White "an eyesore"). White was dismissed in 1784.

With Newton's arrival at Greenwich came a fresh burst of activity at the chapel and a rethinking of its ornament, as a comparison of the approved 1782 elevation of the south wall which the existing structure demonstrates (fig. 8-18; see fig. 8-13). Unlike Ripley's modest design, the rebuilt chapel was destined to become one of the hospital's main attractions. The porter showed it to all visitors along with Thornhill's Painted Hall. Then, as now, visitors entered via an octangular vestibule with niches in which are placed Coade-stone statues of Faith, Hope, Charity,

Fig. 8-19. James Stuart. Vestibule of
the chapel of the Royal Hospital for
Seamen at Greenwich, 1779–89.
Statues of Faith, Hope, Charity, and
Meekness by Benjamin West;
sculpted by John Bacon.
Photographed in 2006. Courtesy of
the Greenwich Foundation.

Fig. 8-20. James Stuart,
assisted by Robert Mylne and
William Newton. Great door
and organ gallery at the west
end of the chapel of the
Royal Hospital for Seamen at
Greenwich, 1781–89.
Photographed in 1943.
Warburg Institute,
London, W.76.

Fig. 8-21. James Stuart, drafted by
William Newton. Design for a
ceiling for the chapel of the Royal
Hospital for Seamen at
Greenwich, ca. 1784. Pen and ink,
pencil, gray wash. RIBA Library
Drawings Collection, London,
SC 47/12 (5).

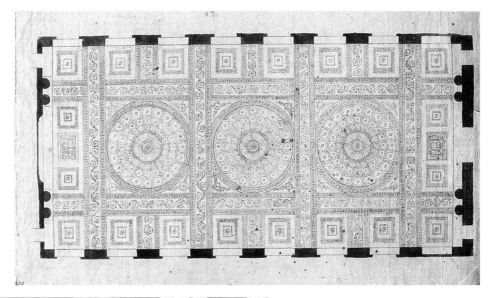

Fig. 8-22. James Stuart. Ceiling of the
chapel of the Royal Hospital for
Seamen at Greenwich, ca. 1784–88.
Photographed in 2006. Courtesy of
the Greenwich Foundation.

and Meekness executed by John Bacon to the designs of
Benjamin West (fig. 8-19).[92] From there, one ascends a
flight of fourteen steps and passes through the great door
(fig. 8-20), above which is an appropriate inscription taken
from Psalm 107: "Let them give thanks whom the Lord
hath redeemed, and delivered from the hand of the
enemy." The visitor then enters the chapel itself by passing under Samuel Green's organ and a magnificent organ
gallery supported by six Ionic columns derived from the
Erechtheion, one of Stuart's favorite Athenian buildings
(see fig. 6-21). The real eye-catcher is the elaborately ornamented ceiling (fig. 8-21). It is organized around three

concentric rings of hexagonal coffers of a type Stuart had
used to more sculptural effect in the Spencer House great
room (although there, of course, the coffers are octagonal and lozenge shaped; see fig. 5-35) and in the drawing
room of Rathfarnham Castle, County Dublin, as remodeled by Stuart in the late 1760s (where the coffers are
octagonal, square, and trapezoid; see fig. 6-50). At
Rathfarnham his handling of ornament begins to reflect
the shallower relief favored by the second generation of
neoclassical architects. Framing the coffered medallions are
rich bands of *rinçeau* and shallow square coffers of equally
elaborate design (figs. 8-22, 8-23).[93] The floor is composed

Fig. 8-23. Detail of the ceiling, showing bands of rinceau and square coffers. Photographed in 2006. Courtesy of the Greenwich Foundation.

Fig. 8-24. James Stuart and William Newton. Paved marble floor of the chapel of the Royal Hospital for Seamen, Greenwich, ca. 1788–89. Photographed in 2006. Courtesy of the Greenwich Foundation.

of rich guilloche bands and medallions of white and black marble (fig. 8-24). To either side of the chapel are galleries that originally contained pews for the hospital's officers and their families,[94] beneath which are cantilevers and fluted Ionic pilasters whose entablature is decorated with marine ornaments (figs. 8-25 to 8-27). Above the galleries are Corinthian pilasters, between which are chiaroscuro paintings of the Apostles and Evangelists and the doors through which the officers passed to take their seats. The major difference between then and now is the location and appearance of the pulpit (fig. 8-28; see fig. 10-78). Originally it was of the triple-deck variety and placed directly in front of the altar to meet the liturgical needs of a service whose emphasis lay in the delivery of a sermon instead of reception of the Eucharist. The reader's desk and clerk's desk were removed in 1952, leaving a pulpit which is based on the Choragic Monument of Lysicrates and decorated with alto-relievos of scenes from the Acts of the Apostles executed by Eleanor Coade after designs by Benjamin West.[95] It now stands to the south of its original location. The original altar was reached by means of three black marble steps and was surrounded by a railing featuring vines and ears of wheat as symbols of the Eucharist. The altar itself was a semi-oval slab of stat-

Fig. 8-25. James Stuart and William Newton. The south gallery of the chapel of the Royal Hospital for Seamen, Greenwich, 1782–89. Photographed in 1943. Warburg Institute, London, W.47.

Fig. 8-26. James Stuart. Pews of the south gallery (detail), 1782–89. Photographed in 1943. Warburg Institute, London, W.64.

Fig. 8-27. James Stuart. Brackets supporting the south gallery (detail), 1786–88. Photographed in 1943. Warburg Institute, London, W.96.

Fig. 8-28. Interior of the chapel of the Royal Hospital for Seamen at Greenwich, showing the original triple-decker pulpit, mid-nineteenth century. Etching by Edward Hopley, after Mrs. R. B. B. Hopley. National Maritime Museum, London, Greenwich PAH 3281. *Checklist no. 158.*

373

Fig. 8-29. Benjamin West. *The Preservation of Saint Paul from Shipwreck on the Island of Melita [Malta],* installed 1789. Oil on canvas. Altarpiece for the east end of the chapel of the Royal Hospital for Seamen, Greenwich. Photographed in 1943. Warburg Institute, London, W.62.

Fig. 8-30. James Stuart and William Newton. Design for the gallery doors of the chapel of the Royal Hospital for Seamen at Greenwich, 1782–89. Pen and ink, pencil. RIBA Library Drawings Collection, London, SC 61/2 (18).

uary marble supported by six cherubim and standing on a white marble step.[96] Above is West's altarpiece, *The Preservation of St. Paul from Shipwreck on the Island of Melita* (Malta), set in a rich gilded frame whose ornament derives from the Erechtheion capitals (fig. 8-29). It is flanked by paired Corinthian columns and marble angels carrying the cross and emblems of the Eucharist in the spandrels. Nestling in the segment above is a chiaroscuro painting of the Ascension by Biagio Rebecca after West, serving "as the climax to the series of paintings devoted to the life of Christ that run beneath the galleries."[97] Throughout the chapel, an iconographic program devoted to themes of rescue and redemption has been skillfully interwoven into a decorative scheme of naval- and antique-inspired ornament.

Is the chapel a masterwork of neoclassical design greater than the sum of its individual contributions? Today the answer would surely be a resounding "Yes," although it must have seemed a curious anachronism by

the time of its completion. By 1789 the character of classically inspired architecture had changed dramatically. Stuart did not introduce "the newest ideas of decoration into a setting representative of the grandest tradition," as was once claimed. New ideas were not adopted at Greenwich in the 1780s.[98] The younger generation of architects was inspired by the form as well as the ornament of antiquity—Joseph Bonomi's gallery at Packington Hall, Warwickshire, constructed from 1785, being an excellent example. This was an approach that Stuart found incomprehensible. Instead, the robust decorative motifs that he had introduced in his domestic commissions of the 1750s and 1760s were reused in the new chapel with little or no compunction.

Perhaps because the new chapel had, and continues to have, a high profile, the case for and against Stuart (or Newton) as the chief designer has been made at regular intervals since the end of the nineteenth century.[99] The reality is more complex. A comparison between Ripley's

Fig. 8-31. James Stuart and William Newton. Gallery door of the chapel of the Royal Hospital for Seamen at Greenwich, 1782–89. Photographed in 1943. Warburg Institute, London, W.92.

Fig. 8-32. James Stuart and William Newton. Design for plasterwork above the ground-floor windows of the chapel of the Royal Hospital for Seamen at Greenwich, 1786. Pen and ink, pencil, color wash. RIBA Library Drawings Collection, London, SC 61/2 (28).

Fig. 8-33. James Stuart and William Newton. Plasterwork above the ground-floor windows of the chapel of the Royal Hospital for Seamen at Greenwich, 1786–88. Photographed in 1943. Warburg Institute, London, W.95.

chapel and its replacement, for example, shows that the cantilevered galleries and paired columns on either side of the altar relied on what had gone before. The ornament above the gallery doors and the ground floor windows (figs. 8-30 to 8-33) is akin to a design usually identified as a proposal by Stuart for Kedleston Hall in 1757–58 (see fig. 6-30). The ceiling bears a certain resemblance to those of the Spencer House great room and the drawing room at Rathfarnham Castle (see figs. 5-35, 6-50). The use of medallions, in this case painted grisailles, is also typical of Stuart. Since one proposal for the gallery soffits used the winged putti terminating in scrolled acanthus which Stuart had used at Nuneham Park, Lichfield House, and Holdernesse House, it is reasonable to attribute these to him even if the drawings are not in his hand (fig. 8-34).

375

Fig. 8-34. James Stuart and William Newton. Design for plasterwork for the chapel of the Royal Hospital for Seamen at Greenwich, 1782–89. Pen and ink, pencil. RIBA Library Drawings Collection, London, SC 61/2 (24).

The decision to base the pulpit on the Choragic Monument of Lysicrates was most likely made by Stuart, who had constructed versions as garden monuments at Shugborough, Camden Place, and possibly Sion Hill (see figs. 7-9, 7-33, 7-34). An early design for the organ gallery, however, with capitals inspired by those of the Tower of the Winds loosely resembles the baldacchino in Newton's unexecuted designs for St. Mary's, Battersea of 1774–75,[100] even if the substitution of the Ionic order of the Erechtheion was made at Stuart's insistence (figs. 8-35 to 8-37). The iconographic program was determined by the hospital's chaplains, Cooke and Maule, and neither the surveyor nor the clerk of works was expected to contribute to this area.[101] Ultimately the chapel will continue to confound those who seek to prove definitive authorship.[102]

The controversy is not one of recent devising. It began in the years immediately following the deaths of Stuart and Newton, when the claims of Newton's executors began to cloud Stuart's role. According to Newton's *Short account of the progress of restoring the Chapel & Dome of Greenwich Hospital*, those works still "in hand" when Stuart died in February 1788 were the pulpit, the altar and its railing, the marble paving, "the Great Marble doorcase arrived & working," the organ gallery, the boys' seats in the window recesses, joiners' work and presses for the vestry, all the mahogany doors, "the Medalion & other Orna-

Fig. 8-35. James Stuart and William Newton. Design for a capital of a pilaster for the chapel of the Royal Hospital for Seamen at Greenwich, 1782–89. Pen and ink, pencil, gray wash. RIBA Library Drawings Collection, London, SC 53/1 (1).

Fig. 8-36. James Stuart, probably assisted by William Newton. Contract drawing, with flap closed to show the interior decoration of the east end of the chapel of the Royal Hospital for Seamen at Greenwich, signed "received" by Robert Mylne, 1782. Pen and ink, color wash. RIBA Library Drawings Collection, London, SB 62/4 (1). *Checklist no. 152.*

Fig. 8-37. James Stuart, probably assisted by William Newton. Contract drawing, with flap open to show the interior decoration of the west end of the chapel of the Royal Hospital for Seamen at Greenwich, signed "received" by Robert Mylne, 1782. Pen and ink, color wash. RIBA Library Drawings Collection, London, SB 62/4 (1). *Checklist no. 152.*

ments over the Altar," the "Great Picture for the Altarpiece," and the paintings over the tower windows.[103] The inclusion of West's altarpiece, finished in 1789,[104] suggests that at this stage Newton was not laying claim to the design of these items, but rather was attempting to demonstrate the speed and efficiency with which he could complete the chapel if he was appointed surveyor. This is also suggested by his "Works remaining to be done," a sig-

nificantly smaller list on the same sheet of paper: the soffit and cornice under the organ gallery, the paintings in the recesses between the upper windows, and the painting of the whole chapel. Perhaps to defend himself from any suggestion of tardiness, this account is annotated: "It is to be observed that the greater part of the aforesaid works are of a kind & in a style not in common use So that every thing was to be Studied & Invented, not only the Designs

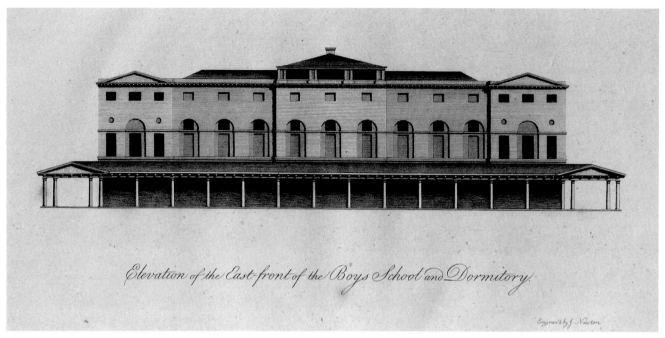

Fig. 8-38. "Elevation of the East-front of the Boys School and Dormitory." Engraving by J. Newton. From John Cooke and John Maule, *An Historical Account of the Royal Hospital for Seamen at Greenwich* (1789). Courtesy of the Library, The Bard Graduate Center for Studies in the Decorative Arts, Design, and Culture, New York. *Checklist no. 159.*

of the several parts and Members, but even in many Cases the Methods of executing them."[105]

In spite of Newton's claim that he was best suited to succeed Stuart as surveyor, he was bypassed in favor of Sir Robert Taylor, who was appointed on February 22, 1788. Taylor died in October of that year and was succeeded in turn by John Yenn.[106] On Yenn's appointment, Newton informed Benjamin West of his intention to present a memorandum to the hospital board stating his claims to the surveyorship by giving a summary of his career and referring to the "Age & Infirmity of the late Mr Stuart" which had necessitated his assistance "in all the duty of Surveyor," and threatening to resign "as it will be displeasing to me to be placed under a younger man & perhaps I may say less eminant in the profession than myself."[107] No doubt mindful of Mylne's successful claim against the Admiralty and exasperated that he had been overlooked twice in one year, Newton also prepared a list of grievances, including claims that he had received no extra payment for drawings and work that Stuart should have done.[108]

Newton died in July 1790, and the board's minutes do not suggest that he submitted his claims before his death.

The papers supporting his claim to be recognized as the designer of the chapel appear to have been collected by his executors in an attempt to obtain payment for the extraordinary services of the recently deceased clerk of works. Newton's brother James may have been responsible for the ambiguous wording of the obituary in which William is credited as the "architect of the newly-erected part of Greenwich-hospital."[109] It was certainly James Newton who published the rebuttal to Cooke and Maule's official history of Greenwich Hospital (1789) in the preface to his brother's translation of *The Architecture of M. Vitruvius Pollio* (1791) in which William claimed the whole of the design of the chapel for himself, except the ceiling, the altarpiece frame, and the balusters used in the side galleries: "These, with the carving of some stone mouldings taken from Greek examples in his Antiquities of Athens were all that he [Stuart] determined. The Whole of the remainder were of my designing or my selecting, where the Antique has been selected."[110]

After an unsuccessful appeal to the hospital board, which Newton's brother described as "ungenerous and unjust" since "the bodily infirmities of Mr. Stuart that prevented his attention to business, were well known to every

Director, and his incapacity to make those Designs equally well known to every Artist," James Newton changed tack.[111] In concert with Robert Smirke, another of his brother's executors, he contacted a number of craftsmen and asked the leading question: "Are you not of Opinion, not withstanding Mr Stewart was the regular surveyor of the hospital, but owing to his advanced age or infirmities incapable of performing the duties of that office, that the designs for the Chapel & publick School were almost wholly if not intirely of the invention, solution & arrangement of the late Clerk of Works Mr Willm Newton?"[112] Unfortunately, only two responses have been preserved, making it impossible to determine if they are representative or, indeed, accurate. John Devall was cautious, revealing little beyond hearsay,[113] but John Bacon had no hesitation in attributing the design of the chapel to Newton because "having been with Mr Newton frequently when he was drawing various parts of it, and, indeed, in some particulars having been consulted by him, I can speak with more confidence on the subject. Those parts of that Building which I was honored with the commands of the Board to execute, Mr Stuart never saw while they were in considerable forwardness; there may have been *some* exceptions, but I am perswaded, what I understood to be the general Opinion, that Mr Newton made the principal part of the Designs for the Chapel, is founded in fact."[114] Bacon's statement should not be dismissed out of hand. His condemnation of Stuart must be tempered by the knowledge that he was also an executor of Newton's will and his involvement at Greenwich occurred late in the restoration of the chapel.[115]

Presumably the "particulars" about which Newton had consulted Bacon were the angels in the spandrels above the altar, installed in 1786. These had been executed without Stuart's approval and brought a rebuke from the board to Newton, whereupon he offered to resign.[116] Bacon is certainly biased. His claim that the surveyor did not visit the building site often enough is substantiated by Stuart's ignorance of the angels until after they were in place. Bacon also seems to claim that Newton executed drawings that he felt should have been Stuart's responsibility. Regardless of the normal duties expected of an executant architect, Stuart required his clerks of works to possess a high level of proficiency in draftsmanship, precisely so that they could execute drawings from his sketches. This was one of the tasks Charles White had been expected to perform when Stuart had considered appointing him in Mylne's place. Although this appears to have been an unusual requirement, Newton must have been aware of it when he accepted the post.

Much of the problem of determining responsibility for the design of the chapel stems from Stuart's business practices. Here, as elsewhere he left the practical side of building to the clerk of works; Robert Mylne and William Newton executed most of the working drawings and may even have been responsible for the general drawings submitted to the board.[117] Did Stuart also relinquish aesthetic control? In this context, it is worth remembering the precedent set by Hawksmoor, who not only prepared Wren's drawings but, after his appointment as clerk of works in 1698, was paid £50 per year for "drawing and designing," and even attended directors' meetings in Wren's place after his appointment as deputy surveyor in 1705.[118] Should we question Wren's importance in the overall design of his masterwork, even where Hawksmoor has been credited with the design of the west range of the King William block and the base block of Queen Anne Court?

There can be no doubt that the role of clerk of works at Greenwich Hospital was a difficult one. Stuart had allowed, even expected, Mylne to prepare drawings, and he gave his tacit support to the board in their decision to pay Mylne for these drawings in 1782. That the universally unpopular Mylne had been paid for drawings, while Newton's executors' claims were rejected, suggests that James Newton and Robert Smirke had significantly overstepped the mark. Indeed, so keen were the board to downplay Newton's role that they even rejected a claim for £100 for "Designing & doing the Surveyor's part to the new Boys School from the beginning to the end of the Building," a claim that was almost certainly justified.[119] The interior of the Boys' School has been altered. The engraving published by Cooke and Maule (fig. 8-38) reveals that the exterior is completely unlike Stuart's work, not least because it was fronted by a Tuscan colonnade, an order that Stuart never used.

In the final analysis, the design and construction of the chapel at the Royal Naval Hospital at Greenwich shows Stuart at his best and his worst. Its construction history is a catalogue of confusion, inefficiency, personal conflict, and blatant political favoritism, yet to split the hairs of its design is to lose sight of the beauty that makes the chapel one of the outstanding interiors of Stuart's—and Newton's—career.

1. Christopher Chalklin, *English Counties and Public Building, 1650–1830* (London: Hambledon Press, 1998): 4–5.

2. Daniel A. Baugh, *British Naval Administration in the Age of Walpole* (Princeton University Press, 1965): 230.

3. On this point see Margarette Lincoln, *Representing the Royal Navy: British Sea Power, 1750–1815* (Aldershot: Ashgate in association with the National Maritime Museum, 2002): 175, citing Gilbert Blane, *A Short Account of the Most Effectual Means of Preserving the Health of Seamen, particularly in the Royal Navy* (London: n. p., 1780): 7.

4. John Cooke and John Maule, *An Historical Account of the Royal Hospital for Seamen at Greenwich* (London: the authors, 1789). For a comprehensive history of the hospital, see John Bold, *Greenwich: An Architectural History of the Royal Hospital for Seamen and the Queen's House* (New Haven and London: Yale University Press for the Paul Mellon Centre for Studies in British Art in association with English Heritage, 2000): 95–248.

5. Stuart's predecessor, Thomas Ripley, was Robert Walpole's executant architect at Houghton Hall, Norfolk, and acquired a number of sinecures through his illustrious patron, including the surveyorship at Greenwich in 1729. See Alan Mackley, "Clerks of the Works," *Georgian Group Journal* 8 (1998): 159. The promotion of Vanbrugh over the more experienced Hawksmoor is too well known to warrant retelling here.

6. Simon Harcourt, first Earl Harcourt, to Charles Watson Wentworth, second Marquess of Rockingham, 4 February 1758, Wentworth Woodhouse Muniments R1-116, Sheffield Archives, Sheffield; Minutes of General Court Meetings, 30 May 1758, 337, NA.

7. On hospitals, tourism, and the British context, see Christine Stevenson, *Medicine and Magnificence: British Hospital and Asylum Architecture, 1660–1815* (New Haven and London: Yale University Press for The Paul Mellon Centre for Studies in British Art, 2000): 62–105, esp. 67, 71–86.

8. On these points, see Daniel A. Baugh, "Maritime Strength and Atlantic Commerce: The Uses of 'a grand marine empire'," in *An Imperial State at War: Britain from 1689 to 1815*, ed. Lawrence Stone (London and New York: Routledge, 1994): 185–223; Kathleen Wilson, "Empire of Virtue: The Imperial Project and Hanoverian Culture, c. 1720–1785," in ibid., 128–64; and H.V. Bowen, *War and British Society, 1688–1815* (Cambridge University Press, 1998).

9. For Ripley's Admiralty building, see Geoffrey Jules Marcus, *Heart of Oak: A Survey of British Sea Power in the Georgian Era* (London, New York, and Toronto: Oxford University Press, 1975): 156–57.

10. Richard Middleton, "Pitt, Anson and the Admiralty, 1756–1761," *History* 55 (1970): 189–91; Clive Wilkinson, *The British Navy and the State in the 18th Century* (Woodbridge: The Boydell Press in association with the National Maritime Museum, 2004): 12.

11. On Anson and Sandwich, see, e.g., J. M. Haas, "The Pursuit of Political Success in Eighteenth-Century England: Sandwich, 1740–1771," *Bulletin of the Institute of Historical Research* 43 (1970): 59 and 64.

12. Wilkinson, *British Navy* (2004): 20–23, esp. fig. 2.2.

13. Ibid., 16.

14. Baugh, *British Naval Administration* (1965): 32–33, 37–38; Wilkinson, *British Navy* (2004): 18.

15. Baugh, *British Naval Administration* (1965): 35; Wilkinson, *British Navy* (2004): 21.

16. Ian Friel, *Maritime History of Britain and Ireland, c. 400–2001* (London: British Museum Press, 2003): 141–42. The navy was one of the three government departments prominent in architecture in the eighteenth century. The others were the Office of Royal Works and the Board of Ordnance. For the hospital's relationship with the Admiralty, see Baugh, *British Naval Administration* (1965): 63.

17. The council comprised a governor, lieutenant governor, captain, three lieutenants, one or more chaplains, a steward, and a surgeon. Until 1747, when a proper superannuation scheme for flag officers and captains was introduced, the hospital board had been a means of providing an unofficial pension for those too aged to see active duty. Cooke and Maule, *Historical Account* (1789): 61; Baugh, *British Naval Administration* (1965): 106, 135.

18. Greenwich Hospital Various Accounts and Ledgers 1759–1762, ADM 68/22, NA; J. C. Beaglehole, *The Life of Captain James Cook* (Stanford University Press, 1974): 444–45.

19. See Minutes of General Court Meetings, ADM 67/10-12, NA.

20. Stevenson, *Medicine and Magnificence* (2000): 109–10.

21. Bold, *Greenwich* (2000): 97.

22. Ibid., 97, 158.

23. Thomas Hicks to the directors of Greenwich Hospital, 25 January 1775, 10–11, ADM 79/57, NA. See also Minutes of General Court Meetings, 2 March 1775, 172, ADM 67/11, and Journal of the proceedings of James Stuart and Thomas Hicks Esqrs, . . . on a Visitation of the Derwentwater Estate . . . , per Jno Ibbetson Secy, 1–2, ADM 79/57, NA.

24. See Nicholas A. M. Rodger, *The Insatiable Earl: A Life of John Montagu, Fourth Earl of Sandwich, 1718–1792* (London: Harper-Collins, 1993): 250.

25. Thomas Baillie, *The Case of the Royal Hospital for Seamen, at Greenwich . . .* (London: n. p., 1778): 26.

26. *State of Facts Relative to Greenwich Hospital* (n.p., [1779]): 9.

27. See, e.g., Stuart to Anson, [before 23 August 1764], Lichfield Ms. D615/P(S)/1/6/10, and Stuart to Anson, 6 October 1764, Lichfield Ms. D615/P(S)/1/6/15, Staffordshire Record Office, Stafford.

28. Bold, *Greenwich* (2000): 142.

29. Kerry Downes, *Sir John Vanbrugh, A Biography* (London: Sidgwick and Jackson, 1987): 373–74.

30. Minutes of General Court Meetings, 22 June 1769, 56–57, ADM 67/11, NA; Cooke and Maule, *Historical Account* (1789): 35; Bold, *Greenwich* (2000): 167.

31. *State of Facts Relative to Greenwich Hospital* ([1779]): 6–10.

32. Giles Worsley, "Out From Adam's Shadow," *Country Life* 186 (14 May 1992): 101.

33. Minutes of General Court Meetings, 16 December 1775, 189, ADM 67/11, NA.

34. Bold, *Greenwich* (2000): 167, 170.

35. Ibid., 104, 167.

36. For remarks on the engine drawings see Stuart to the Admiralty Board, 28 September 1782, Letters from Surveyors, Architects, and others as to Works, ADM 65/106, NA.

37. Minutes of General Court Meetings, 27 January 1777, 218, ADM 67/11, NA; Bold, *Greenwich* (2000): 153. This could have been the portrait painter Arthur Devis or his half-brother Anthony.

38. Baillie, *Case of the Royal Hospital* (1778): 10–11; *State of Facts relative to Greenwich Hospital* ([1779]): 2–3.

39. *The Diary of Joseph Farington*, ed. Kathryn Cave, 12 (New Haven and London: Yale University Press for the Paul Mellon Centre for Studies in British Art, 1983): 4413.

40. Bold, *Greenwich* (2000): 108, 207.

41. Ibid., 142, 156.

42. Various proposals for a separate infirmary can be found in Mss. ART I and ART III, National Maritime Museum, Greenwich. See also Bold, *Greenwich* (2000): 166, 207–208.

43. Minutes of General Court Meetings, 25 August 1763, 384–85, ADM 67/10, NA; Bold, *Greenwich* (2000): 166, 208.

44. Minutes of General Court Meetings, 25 August 1763, 384–85, ADM 67/10, NA. See also Bold, *Greenwich* (2000): 166.

45. Minutes of General Court Meetings, 3 June 1763, 377–78, ADM 67/10, NA.

46. Bold, *Greenwich* (2000): 209.

47. Stevenson, *Medicine and Magnificence* (2000): 9.

48. Bowen, *War and British Society* (1998): 36–37. See also Bold, *Greenwich* (2000): 100, 206; Stevenson, *Medicine and Magnificence* (2000): 176–85.

49. On this point, see Stevenson, *Medicine and Magnificence* (2000): 158–63, who notes that sick people were popularly believed to breathe contagions.

50. Cooke and Maule, *Historical Account* (1789): 117; Bold, *Greenwich* (2000): 209.

51. Baillie, *Case of the Royal Hospital* (1778): 9.

52. Cooke and Maule, *Historical Account* (1789): 117; Bold, *Greenwich* (2000): 210.

53. Bold, *Greenwich* (2000): 211.

54. Stevenson, *Medicine and Magnificence* (2000): 228. See also Bold, *Greenwich* (2000): 208.

55. Cooke and Maule, *Historical Account* (1789): 117. Cooke also served as a director and would have known Stuart well.

56. Stuart to Anson, 19 June 1764, Lichfield Ms. D615/P(S)/1/6/7, Staffordshire Record Office, Stafford.

57. Stuart to Anson, 4 September 1764, Lichfield Ms. D615/P(S)/1/6/12, Staffordshire Record Office, Stafford.

58. Minutes of General Court Meetings, 25 August 1766, 426, ADM 67/10, NA.

59. Ibid., 22 June 1769, 54, ADM 67/11, NA.

60. Baillie, *Case of the Royal Hospital* (1778): 9.

61. *State of Facts relative to Greenwich Hospital* ([1779]): 1–2.

62. James Dallaway, *Anecdotes of the Arts in England . . .* (London: Cadell and Davies, 1800): 154–55.

63. Arthur T. Bolton, "James Stuart at Portman House and Spencer House," *Country Life* 37, no. 956 supplement (1 May 1915): 6★. Bolton's acceptance of Stuart's work as demonstrating the "purity and chasteness," of the ancient Greeks led him to overlook the same qualities he admired in Robert Adam, namely the ability "to combine elements derived from a very wide field."

64. Even now, the carefully researched article that Lesley Lewis published in 1947 has provided the framework for all subsequent discussions of Stuart's work at Greenwich, even where conclusions have differed; see Lewis, "The Architects of the Chapel at Greenwich Hospital," *Art Bulletin* 29 (1947): 260–67. The following account is indebted to her work.

65. Minutes of General Court Meetings, 19 January 1779, 254–55, ADM 67/11, NA; Bold, *Greenwich* (2000): 173.

66. On the basis of Mylne's earlier successes in Rome (where he received the Concorso Clementino for architecture from the Accademia di San Luca, 1758) and London (where he won competition to build Blackfriars Bridge, 1760), he had every reason to anticipate a long and illustrious career. By the time he was appointed Robinson's successor at Greenwich in 1775, Mylne was already architect of the City of London Lying-In Hospital, surveyor to the New River Company, and surveyor (or architect) to St. Paul's and Canterbury Cathedrals. It is unclear why he accepted the subordinate post, although he may have been attracted to the comfortable accommodation it provided in a convenient location. On this point see Roger Woodley, "Robert Mylne (1733–1811): The Bridge between Architecture and Engineering," Ph. D. diss., Courtauld Institute of Art, University of London (1998): 136.

67. Baillie, *Case of the Royal Hospital* (1778): memorial, 5; *State of Facts relative to Greenwich Hospital* (1779): 26–31. Mylne had attempted to sue for libel but was denied redress in the Court of King's Bench because the Admiralty (with Sandwich as First Lord) decided that the case was within their jurisdiction. Stuart defended Mylne at the resulting hearing in April 1779.

68. Mylne to John Ibbetson, 12 November 1779, Letters from Surveyors, Architects, and others as to Works, ADM 65/106, NA.

69. Minutes of General Court Meetings, 4 July 1781, 10, ADM 67/12, NA.

70. Stuart to [?], n.d., Letters from Surveyors, Architects, and others as to Works, ADM 65/106, NA. For the Somerset House craftsmen, see John Newman, *Somerset House* (London: Scala Books, 1990): 88. The men employed at Greenwich were John Groves (bricklayer), John Devall (mason), Samuel Wyatt (carpenter), William Clark for Mrs. Martha Palmer (Smith), John Papworth (plasterer), Charles Catton (painter), Richard Lawrence (carver), George Holroyd and Jeremiah Devall (plumbers), William Bent (ironmonger), and James Arrow (joiner). Bent, Papworth, and Lawrence do not appear in the Somerset House records. The workmen already employed at Greenwich were

unhappy with this turn of events, although they ultimately lost their case. These disagreements were not settled until 1783. Minutes of General Court Meetings, 28 August 1783, 75–76, ADM 67/12, NA.

71. Newman, *Somerset House* (1990): 4.

72. Stuart to [?], n.d., Letters from Surveyors, Architects, and others as to Works, ADM 65/106, NA.

73. On the ways in which craftsmen and architects were paid, see James Ayres, *Building the Georgian City* (New Haven and London: Yale University Press for the Paul Mellon Centre for Studies in British Art, 1998): 5–6, 35, 37.

74. Minutes of General Court Meetings, 14 March 1782, 32, ADM 67/12, NA. William Newton's drawing (fig. 8-14) assigned design credit to Mylne. See also David Yeomans, *The Architect and the Carpenter,* exh. cat. (London: RIBA Heinz Gallery, 1992): 45; Bold, *Greenwich* (2000): 119.

75. On this point, see, e.g., Bernard Pool, *Navy Board Contracts, 1660–1832* (London: Longmans, 1966): 87–94, where demands for new and refurbished ships at this time are discussed. Shortly after Lord Sandwich returned to the Admiralty, a House of Commons committee was set up (March 1771) to consider ways in which the navy could be supplied with quality timber from domestic sources. No adequate means were found.

76. Minutes of General Court Meetings, 22 December 1782, 23, ADM 67/12, NA. See also Ms. New/1/1/6, RIBA, British Architectural Library; and Bold, *Greenwich* (2000): 174. For Wells, see Pool, *Navy Board Contracts* (1966): 88.

77. Roger Shanagan, [Robert Smirke, and William Porden], *"The Exhibition" or a Second Anticipation, Being Remarks on the Principal Works to be Exhibited Next Month at the Royal Academy . . .* (London: Richardson and Urquhart, 1779): 69–70; Mrs. Montagu to Leonard Smelt, 26 April [1780], Montagu Papers, MO 5026, Henry E. Huntington Library, San Marino, California; Stuart to Philip Yorke, second Earl of Hardwicke, 2 August 1783, Add. Ms. 35,621, fol. 7, BL; John Thomas Smith, *Nollekens and His Times* (London: Turnstile Press, 1949): 38.

78. "At a Meeting at Greenwich Hospital 11 May 1782," Letters from Surveyors, Architects, and others as to Works, ADM 65/106, NA.

79. Mylne to Stuart, 6 July 1782, Letters from Surveyors, Architects, and others as to Works, ADM 65/106, NA. See also Woodley, *Robert Mylne* (1998): 19.

80. Mylne to John Ibbetson, 15 December 1781, Letters from Surveyors, Architects, and others as to Works, ADM 65/106, NA.

81. Ibid.

82. On this point, see Mackley, "Clerks of the Works" (1998): 157–66, esp. 157.

83. Minutes of General Court Meetings, 3 September 1782, 46–48, ADM 67/12, NA. See also Bold, *Greenwich* (2000): 175.

84. Minutes of General Court Meetings, 3 September 1782, 46–48, ADM 67/12, NA.

85. Minutes of General Court Meetings, 10 September 1782, 49–50, ADM 67/12, NA.

86. A. and J. Farrer to T. Everest, 16 August 1783, Solicitor's Letters from

1780 to 1785 inclusive, ADM 65/100, NA. See also Lewis, "Architects of the Chapel," (1947): 262; and Bold, *Greenwich* (2000): 174–75.

87. Minutes of General Court Meetings, 10 September 1782, 50, and 7 April 1784, 82-83, ADM 67/12, NA. See also Stuart to John Ibbetson, 12 September 1782, Letters from Surveyors, Architects, and others as to Works, ADM 65/106, NA; copy letter from John Ibbetson to Stuart, 12 September 1782, Manuscript New/1/8/8(i), RIBA, British Architectural Library, London; and Lewis, "Architects of the Chapel" (1947): 262.

88. Howard Montagu Colvin, *Biographical Dictionary of British Architects, 1600–1840,* 3rd ed. (New Haven and London: Yale University Press, 1995): 702.

89. Manuscripts New/1/8/2(i) and New/1/8/8(i), RIBA, British Architectural Library, London.

90. Memorial of Charles White to the Governors and Directors of the Royal Hospital at Greenwich, 17 February 1784, Letters from Surveyors, Architects, and others as to Works, ADM 65/106, NA.

91. Ibid.

92. Cooke and Maule, *Historical Account* (1789): 100; Bold, *Greenwich* (2000): 176.

93. The surviving drawings for the ceiling, which may have accompanied the estimate Stuart presented to the board in December 1784, appear to be in Newton's hand. See Minutes of General Court Meetings, 24 December 1784, 102, ADM 67/12, NA. Bold, *Greenwich* (2000): 174, notes that alterations to the window-heads, which were made in order to replace the original flat, compartmented ceiling, are still visible.

94. Cooke and Maule, *Historical Account* (1789): 102.

95. Ibid., 106–107. An estimate of about £100 for carving the pulpit was submitted by Richard Lawrence to John Ibbetson on 19 August 1786. Ms. New/1/1/9, RIBA, British Architectural Library. The subjects of the medallions on the pulpit and reader's desk were submitted to the Admiralty Board by Cooke and Maule on 27 February 1788. John Cooke and John Maule to John Ibbetson, 27 February 1788, Ms. New/1/1/15, RIBA, British Architectural Library.

96. Cooke and Maule, *Historical Account* (1789): 103.

97. Ibid., 105. West put himself forward for the painting above the altar-piece and proposed four possible themes. Three are unrecorded. The fourth was *Saint Paul Shipwrecked on the Island of Malta.* Minutes of General Court Meetings, 16 November 1781, 14–15, ADM 67/12, NA; Bold, *Greenwich* (2000): 173.

98. Lesley Lewis, "Greece and Rome at Greenwich," *Architectural Review* 109 (January 1951): 18.

99. Wyatt Papworth, "William Newton and the Chapel of Greenwich Hospital," *RIBA Journal* 27–28 (27 August 1891): 417; and Lewis, "Architects of the Chapel" (1947): 260–67 have come down in favor of Newton. Worsley, "Out From Adam's Shadow" (1992): 101, suggests otherwise.

100. Lewis, "Greece and Rome at Greenwich," (1951): 18; David Watkin, *Athenian Stuart: Pioneer of the Greek Revival* (London: George Allen and Unwin, 1982): 53.

101. Cooke and Maule proposed the subjects for the paintings in the

vestibule and chapel, which were then approved by the Admiralty Board. The grisailles over the lower range of windows represent events in the life of Christ. On the south side, four of the paintings are by Theodore De Bruyn and four by Charles Catton. The paintings on the north side are by Milburne and Biagio Rebecca. The apostles and evangelists in the recesses between the upper windows, and the prophets Isaiah, Jeremiah, Moses, and David in the roundels above the gallery doors, are by Rebecca after designs by Benjamin West. See John Cooke and John Maule to John Ibbetson, 27 February 1788, Ms. New/1/1/15, RIBA, British Architectural Library, London, and Cooke and Maule, *Historical Account* (1789): 107.

102. This is also the conclusion reached in Bold, *Greenwich* (2000): 175.

103. Ms. New/1/7/2, RIBA, British Architectural Library. See also Lewis, "Architects of the Chapel" (1947): 263–64.

104. William Newton to John Ibbetson, 26 August 1789, Letters from Surveyors, Architects, and others as to Works, ADM 65/106, NA.

105. Ms. New/1/7/2(ii), RIBA, British Architectural Library.

106. Minutes of General Court Meetings, 22 February and 30 October 1788, 162–63, ADM 67/12, NA. See also Lewis, "Architects of the Chapel" (1947): 263–64.

107. William Newton to Benjamin West, 23 October 1788, Ms. New/1/1/19, RIBA, British Architectural Library; Papworth, "William Newton" (1891): 417.

108. Ms. New/1/8/8, RIBA, British Architectural Library. Newton instructed his brother to claim £900–1000 if he were to die. See "Memorandum by James Newton by the Direction of his late Brother Wm Newton then Clerk of the Works at Greenwich Hospital," 24 April 1790, Ms. New/1/8/1, RIBA, British Architectural Library; and Lewis, "Architects of the Chapel" (1947): 264.

109. "Obituary of Considerable Persons," *Gentleman's Magazine* 60, pt. 2 (August 1790): 766.

110. *The Architecture of M. Vitruvius Pollio,* trans. William Newton, ed. James Newton, vol. 2 (London: James Newton, 1791): advertisement.

111. Ms. New/1/8/8(ii), RIBA, British Architectural Library.

112. Ms. New/1/8/2(ii), RIBA, British Architectural Library. The draft letter is in James Newton's hand, but the responses were addressed to Robert Smirke.

113. John Devall to Robert Smirke, 2 December 1791, Ms. New/1/8/12, RIBA, British Architectural Library: "The Part of the Chapel in Which I was concerned was very forward when Mr Newton was appointed Clerk of the Works. But after that Time I conceived the finishing was from Designs of Mr Newtons."

114. Ms. New/1/8/11, RIBA, British Architectural Library.

115. J. Howard to the commissioners and governors of the hospital and to John Ibbetson (the secretary), 30 May 1795, Letters from Surveyors, Architects, and others as to Works, ADM 65/106, NA.

116. Ibid.

117. This is suggested in Lewis, "Architects of the Chapel" (1947): 264–65.

118. Bold, *Greenwich* (2000): 112.

119. The dispute that arose between Newton and Charles White over the Boys' School suggests that Stuart's involvement with the school's construction was minimal (his signature on a rough estimate for its building, dated 8 March 1783) and, with the exception of Cooke and Maule, *Historical Account* (1789): 127, all sources agree that Stuart had no hand in the design of the new school. See Charles White to the governors and directors of the Royal Hospital at Greenwich, 2 June 1784, and William Newton to John Ibbetson, 3 July 1784, Letters from Surveyors, Architects, and others as to Works, ADM 65/106, NA; Mss. New/1/2/1, New/1/2/3, New/1/2/4, and New/1/8/9, RIBA, British Architectural Library; Lewis, "Architects of the Chapel at Greenwich Hospital" (1947): 263; Bold, *Greenwich* (2000): 107, 225; Friel, *Maritime History of Britain* (2003): 191.

Fig. 9-1. James Stuart. Monument to Admiral Charles Watson (detail of fig. 9-4), Westminster Abbey, London, 1760–63. Sculpted by Peter Scheemakers. Photographed in 2006. Courtesy of the Dean and Chapter of Westminster. *Checklist no. 187.*

STUART AND THE CHANGING RELATIONSHIP BETWEEN ARCHITECTS AND SCULPTORS IN EIGHTEENTH-CENTURY BRITAIN

M. G. SULLIVAN

James "Athenian" Stuart returned from Greece to establish his diverse practice at a crucial moment in the formation of the sculptural profession. It was the mid-1750s, and his principal collaborators, who carved monuments and architectural decoration to his designs, identified themselves as either "masons" or "statuaries." By the time of Stuart's death in 1788, however, those who produced three-dimensional work based on designs from *Antiquities of Athens* did so without his personal supervision and identified themselves as "sculptors." This perceptual shift, from masons to sculptors, was due in no small part to James Stuart.

Stuart's early collaborations with "statuaries" and mason-carvers came at a time in which Stuart was a member of an established and elevated profession, but his collaborators operated within a professional field less defined, apparently less elevated, and more diverse. During Stuart's professional lifetime this situation was to change, as the first professional and noted "sculptors" emerged from the first British art institutions. Stuart and Revett's

great work, *Antiquities of Athens*, helped to place premium knowledge of the ancient world in the hands of such sculptors, and in so doing helped to elevate some practitioners to the status of liberal artists. The direct collaborations of Stuart with the "statuaries" of his time (fig. 9-1), and his indirect collaborations with the "sculptors" of the future, are of considerable significance in our comprehension of the changing relationship between architects and sculptors in the eighteenth century.

Architects and Carvers

The establishment of "Architecture" as a lucrative profession was begrudgingly recognized in 1749 by George Vertue, an engraver. In his notebooks, Vertue "had to own" that this new class of builder, concerned solely with the design and supervision of works, had in recent years "made greater fortunes than any other branch of Art whatsoever."[1] But if it troubled Vertue, it must have been a source of more immediate and direct concern for many carvers whose practice was increasingly affected in economic terms by the intercession of this self-

Fig. 9-2. Robert Pyle. Architect Henry Keene (seated, center left) and his associates meeting in the Guildhall, High Wycombe, 1760. Oil on canvas. Photographed in 1945. Present location unknown.

consciously learned intermediary. In the first half of the eighteenth-century, several patrons looked to architects such as William Kent or James Gibbs, rather than to the executant, to provide fashionable and tasteful designs for their funerary monuments. The roles that the architect took on as his own—the production of designs and the supervision of their realization—were, however, previously part of the daily job for many carver's workshops. John Nost, for instance, whose workshop produced numerous important monuments, was a skilled and distinctive designer-draftsman, but he seems not to have made a fortune comparable to the parvenu "architects," and saw no significant achievement of social status, his profession being described simply as "carver" in his will.[2]

The rise of the professional architect in the first half of the eighteenth century was not accompanied by a comparable rise in the status of the carver. As the architect established a distinct professional identity, made considerable fortunes, and gained social status (expressed, for example, by the commission of portrait busts[3]), those who produced sculpture did not, and presumably could not, adopt a comparable Italianate artistic identity. This prevailed despite the fact that the sophistication of their practice may have warranted the epithet of "sculptor." Although Arnold Quellin, for example, produced inno-

vative works such as the monument to the influential politician Thomas Thynne in Westminster Abbey, with its remarkable relief of Thynne's assassination (apparently cut to Quellin's own design), he went to his own grave designating himself as merely a "stone carver."[4] For practitioners such as William and Edward Stanton, sculpture was but one part of a diverse and seasonally affected masonry/carving business.[5] Each described himself as "mason," and their successful business, which included a large number of monuments with one or more full-size statues, earned them status and recognition within the Masons' Company.[6]

The division between the role of the designer-architect and the executant (a classical division between the "liberal artist" and the "mechanic," or between *inventio* and *executio*) was to affect the profits of carvers' workshops. In 1723 Vertue recorded the increasing mistreatment of the carver Michael Rysbrack by the architect James Gibbs, who supplied the designs for eight of Rysbrack's funeral monuments. Rysbrack was a skilled and innovative draftsman and designer, but the union with Gibbs left him at a considerable financial disadvantage. Gibbs gave Rysbrack "no more than 35 pounds for each statue," while he himself received "upwards of a hundred pounds for each."[7]

If Rysbrack was to suffer an exploitative relationship

as a result of the increasing professionalization of architecture and its focus on the primacy of the design and the division of designer and executant, other carvers were able to use the new conditions to their pecuniary advantage. Thomas Carter founded a successful workshop principally providing architectural decoration. Working first as a carver on building projects under the direction of the architects John Wilkins, Isaac Ware, and Charles Carne, Carter built an extensive business employing over forty men. Under Carter's brother, Benjamin, the workshop specialized increasingly in the supply of high-quality chimneypieces, which incorporated caryatid figures and tablets with figurative or decorative designs drawn from antiquity. Robert Adam turned to the workshop for bespoke or ready-made chimneypieces.[8]

Benjamin Carter himself became part of a team of craftsmen working for the architect Henry Keene. Under Keene, Carter executed three chimneypieces in 1757 for the London house of Thomas Bridges at 18 Cavendish Street. The surviving receipts demonstrate the full control that Keene possessed.[9] From the contract to the final work, he supervised every detail, right down to the polishing. This economic and artistic control was given a visual and ideological form in a conversation-piece commissioned from the painter Robert Pyle as a gift to Keene in 1760 (fig. 9-2). It shows Keene, seated beside a plan for an unknown building, while around him are grouped all his working associates, including Benjamin Carter and the mason Thomas Gayfere. These two men appear to be engaged in some kind of dispute, as they face each other sternly, while leaning over the backs of their chairs. At the center of the composition is the plan, the design that is at the heart of the architectural enterprise. Keene sits proprietarily beside it, in a gentlemanly pose.[10]

Carter gained a good fortune from his business, which was ably continued by his partner and distant relative, Thomas Carter II, who died in 1795 leaving bequests totaling more than £4,000 and a good deal of property.[11] The Carters were the sculptors of choice for Robert Adam also, and their workshop provided piecework for a good many young sculptors, such as Louis-François Roubiliac and John Deare. Yet this success did not bring social distinction with some of the patrons, who felt that a gentleman should not interact with anyone below the architect in the chain of production. When the architect Richard Bentley suggested that Horace Walpole should "traffic with [Benjamin] Carter" directly in connection

with the choice of marbles for Strawberry Hill in 1763, Walpole retorted angrily, "Do you think I can turn broker, and factor, and I don't know what?"[12]

For other sculptors, carving was the first step on the social ladder, which led ultimately to becoming an architect. One of Carter's many young employees, Peter Vangelder, who began his career carving figures and foliage for Carter's monuments and chimneypieces, subsequently executed designs for Robert Adam on his own account.[13] In 1775 he married Martha Evans, daughter of the architect Charles Evans, with whom he subsequently worked at 20 Upper Grosvenor Street, London, and at Badminton Church, Gloucestershire. In the 1780s and 1790s, he became a building-contractor himself, building properties in London's Bedford Square, Riding House Lane, and Devonshire Place.[14]

Perhaps the most notable graduate from sculpture to architecture was Sir Robert Taylor, who trained in the workshop of Sir Henry Cheere, made a trip to Rome in the early 1740s, and executed a number of notable commissions, including a relief on the pediment of Mansion House, the official residence of the Lord Mayor of London. Joseph Farington later described Taylor's Rome visit as a means to gaining "more pretension in his profession."[15] Taylor introduced a variety of Continental influences into his polychrome monuments and rococo chimneypieces.[16] Clearly, Taylor viewed his talents as too great to remain a sculptor, and by the late 1760s he had turned increasingly to architecture, designing Palladian villas for a clientele in the City of London. The graduation to gentleman-architect was certainly lucrative. By 1768 he possessed a fortune of £40,000 and a number of well-paying and notable surveyorships. He was knighted in 1782 and left enough money in his will to endow an institute in Oxford for the study of modern languages.[17]

Taylor was not the only convert. William Tyler was a sculptor and one of the founder-members of the Royal Academy in 1769. Although he had produced monuments and chimneypieces to the designs of Adam, Keene, and William Chambers, by 1772 he was "as poor as could be."[18] In the 1780s he turned increasingly to architecture and worked as a land agent for the Duke of Gloucester. By the end of his life, he owned several properties and left shares and bequests worth nearly £3,500.[19]

The establishment of the professional architect was both a hindrance and a blessing for carvers working in Britain. While it had led in some cases to exploitation and a belittling of the craft, the establishment of one artistic profession based on design and knowledge offered the possibility that carvers could, under some circumstances, also upgrade their status from a branch of masonry to a liberal art. Rysbrack and Roubiliac, who designated themselves "statuary" in contradistinction to those carvers who continued to work within the masonry business, such as John Malcott, both possessed a broad knowledge of antique, French, and Italian design and had attained an amount of popular recognition through the shrewd use of advertising.[20] If the social status of the "statuary" was not yet equal to that of the architect, there were definite signs that the profession was beginning to adapt to changing ideological conditions. Another "statuary" who was able to use the status of the architect for the advancement of his own business was Peter Scheemakers,[21] with whom Stuart made his most productive alliance on his return to England.

Stuart and the Statuaries

Stuart and Peter Scheemakers collaborated on four substantial funeral monuments between 1759 and 1766. Those dedicated to Brigadier-General George Augustus, Viscount Howe (1759 – 62) and to Admiral Charles Watson (1760 – 63) are in Westminster Abbey (figs. 9-3, 9-4). Those to Catharine Yorke (1761 – 62) and to Lord Chancellor Philip, first Earl of Hardwicke (1764 – 66) are at Wimpole, Cambridgeshire (figs. 9-5, 9-6). Stuart's relationship with Scheemakers's workshop was more in the nature of collaboration, mutually beneficial, with varying degrees of control over the artistic outcomes.[22] The resultant works occasionally incorporate details from Stuart's drawings of Greek remains, and in the case of the Watson monument, there developed a novel form of classicizing orientalism. Yet the complexities of the working relationship suggest that the Scheemakers workshop was no mechanical executant of Stuart's designs. The collaboration thus illustrates how, despite the raised status of the architect, and Stuart's own fame among the Dilettanti, the input of the statuary was just as significant.

Peter Scheemakers was an Antwerp-born statuary who came to England around 1720 and established one of the most lucrative London workshops of the period. Collaboration had been a notable feature of most Flemish artists' workshops since the Renaissance,[23] and sculptors such as Arnold Quellin from Antwerp and John Nost from Mechelen continued this practice in London in the late seventeenth and early eighteenth centuries. Working in temporary and often familial allegiance with ironworkers, painters, and other sculptors, these networks of craftsmen were able to assist each other in the production of work and the garnering of contracts.[24] Scheemakers was no exception. After his arrival in England, he worked with the statuaries Laurent Delvaux and Denis Plumier on a number of monuments, as well as assisting Francis Bird on work for St. Paul's Cathedral.

In 1740 Scheemakers collaborated with the architect and all-rounder William Kent on the monument to William Shakespeare in Westminster Abbey. Kent supplied the design, although there was little radical about the standing contrapposto statue, which Scheemakers executed. Kent was responsible to the Committee of Taste created to oversee the erection of the monument. With his royal connections and pretensions to connoisseurial authority, Kent was a useful ambassador in a learned and aristocratic domain that the foreign sculptor was unlikely to be able to enter in his own voice. This work proved to be Scheemakers's most famous, and the collaboration with Kent continued with the monument to General Monck, also in Westminster Abbey. It seems likely that in 1759, when Scheemakers entered into his partnership with Stuart, he saw similar benefits.

Stuart's relationship with Admiral Anson led to the commission for the Howe monument from Howe's son, with funding by the Court of the Province of Massachusetts Bay. But if Stuart was responsible for gaining the commission, there is little sign of a Greek stamp on the final work (see fig. 9-3), which consisted of a single grieving Virtue with a Massachusetts Bay shield and a skull. Two lions peer out from beneath the large inscription slab. The female figure was based on the classical Roman figure of Cleopatra, which, although not used previously in funerary monuments, was already a relatively familiar design in British ornamental sculpture. Lead Cleopatras were even being mass-produced by Hyde Park Corner workshops (an example dating to 1756 is at Stourhead), and before 1728 Scheemakers himself had executed a marble Cleopatra statuette as a companion to a figure of Ariadne by Delvaux.

The monument to Admiral Watson, who had died at the siege of Calcutta in 1757, was commissioned by the East India Company in 1760 (see fig. 9-4). Stuart provided the design and subcontracted the work to Scheemakers in

THE PROVINCE OF MASSACHUSETS BAY IN NEW ENGLAND
BY AN ORDER OF THE GREAT AND GENERAL COURT
BEARING DATE FEBУ 1ST 1759, CAUSED THIS MONUMENT TO
BE ERECTED TO THE MEMORY OF GEORGE AUGUSTUS LORD
VISCOUNT HOWE BRIGADIER GENERAL OF HIS MAJESTY'S
FORCES IN AMERICA WHO WAS SLAIN JULY THE 6TH 1758,
ON THE MARCH TO TICONDEROGA, IN THE 34TH YEAR
OF HIS AGE: IN TESTIMONY OF THE SENSE THEY HAD OF HIS
SERVICES AND MILITARY VIRTUES AND OF THE AFFECTION
THEIR OFFICERS AND SOLDIERS BORE TO HIS COMMAND.
HE LIVED RESPECTED AND BELOVED; THE PUBLICK REGRETTED
HIS LOSS, TO HIS FAMILY IT IS IRREPARABLE.

Fig. 9-3. James Stuart. Monument to Brigadier-General George Augustus, third Viscount Howe, Westminster Abbey, London, 1759–62. Sculpted by Peter Scheemakers. Photographed in 2006. Courtesy of the Dean and Chapter of Westminster. *Checklist no. 186.*

Fig. 9-4. James Stuart. Monument to Admiral Charles Watson, Westminster Abbey, 1760–63. Sculpted by Peter Scheemakers. Partly dismantled and reinstalled in 1957. Photographed in 2006. Courtesy of the Dean and Chapter of Westminster. *Checklist no. 187.*

November of that year. Scheemakers had previously executed the monument to Watson's uncle, Admiral Wager, which may have led to his employment on the commission.[25] Stuart was to supervise the work and approve its completion and installation. He also acted as interpreter of the work's meaning. He supplied a lengthy analysis of the monument's iconography, in which an admiral, clad *all'antica*, offers a palm branch to a kneeling personification of free Calcutta, while a moustachioed Ghereah captive glowers on. Set against the backdrop of four palm trees, the work is a remarkable piece of theatrical alle-

gory. A toga-wearing admiral and a vaguely orientalized Roman slave are set against large banners with the legend CHANDERNAGORE TAKEN, GHEREAH TAKEN, CALCUTTA FREED. This is used to bridge the gap between the predominantly classical symbolism and the events of an alien land that was beyond the limits of the iconographical language of funeral sculpture.

The monument to the Earl of Hardwicke at Wimpole is perhaps the only monument jointly produced by Scheemakers and Stuart that carries the distinct impress of Stuart's pioneering Hellenism (see fig. 9-6). The two

Fig. 9-5. James Stuart. Monument to Catharine Yorke (née Freman), Chicheley Chapel, St. Andrew's Church, Wimpole, Cambridgeshire, 1761–62. Sculpted by Peter Scheemakers. Photographed in 2006. *Checklist no. 188.*

Fig. 9-6. James Stuart. Monument to the first Earl and Countess of Hardwicke, Chicheley Chapel, St. Andrew's Church, Wimpole, Cambridgeshire, 1764–66. Sculpted by Peter Scheemakers with Thomas Scheemakers. Photographed in 2006. *Checklist no. 190.*

had previously produced a monument at Wimpole to Catharine Yorke, commissioned by the earl (see fig. 9-5). This work, which has a portrait medallion and one putto extinguishing the torch of life while two others festoon an urn, has elements in common with the monumental work of Sir Robert Taylor. The Hardwicke monument, however, which was designed and executed after the publication of the first volume of *Antiquities of Athens* in 1762, gives a central position to a sarcophagus, decorated with lion's feet and strigil marking, which is based on a Greek prototype that Stuart saw at Scopolo. The original, "which serves at present as a cistern, or rather as a watering trough,"[26] appeared in *Antiquities of Athens* (fig. 9-7). Several members of the Yorke family were subscribers to Stuart's book, and therefore must have understood and approved the allusion. Yet even with this direct reference to the source of Stuart's own fame, the monument is still predominantly composed of elements from the familiar language of monumental sculpture. On either side of the sarcophagus are standing statues, one of Minerva with a caduceus (an unfamiliar attribute, for which Stuart claimed antique authority), and the other of Pudicitia, personification of modesty. On the stereobata, putti make laurel crowns to place on the chancellor's mace. It has been noted that the drawings of the monument, delivered to the duke, were in Scheemakers's rather than Stuart's hand (fig. 9-8). Furthermore, only Scheemakers appears to have received payment for the work.[27] Therefore, although

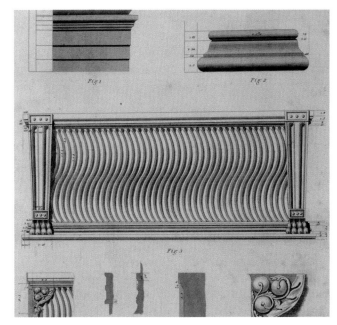

Fig. 9-7. Sarcophagus at Scopolo. Engraving. From *Antiquities of Athens*, vol. 4 (1816): chap. 6, pl. VI. Courtesy of the Library, The Bard Graduate Center for Studies in the Decorative Arts, Design, and Culture, New York. *Checklist no. 11.*

Stuart played a prominent role in its conception and design, he seems not to have exercised a tight control over the progress of the commission, much of which was handled by Scheemakers.

At Shugborough, Stuart and Scheemakers sometimes

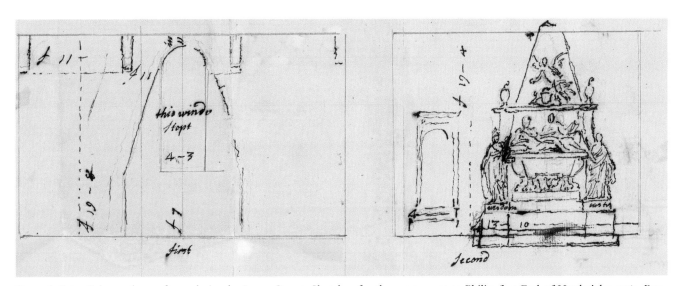

Fig. 9-8. Peter Scheemakers, after a design by James Stuart. Sketches for the monument to Philip, first Earl of Hardwicke, 1764. Pen and ink. Staffordshire Record Office D615/PS/1/6/8b. Reproduced by courtesy of the late Earl of Lichfield. *Checklist no. 189.*

worked together, sometimes separately. Scheemakers executed the additional decoration of a commemorative nature for Stuart's Triumphal Arch (see fig. 7-21), based on the Arch of Theseus or Hadrian in Athens, which changed the arch into something distinct from its prototype. He executed two sarcophagi, a column, and medallions in memory of Lord Anson, and Stuart handled the payments from Anson to Scheemakers. Stuart also seems to have worked in some sort of supervisory capacity on the relief for the Shepherd's Monument (see fig. 7-36), a copy of Poussin's canvas, *Et in Arcadia Ego*. Yet Scheemakers also dealt more directly with Anson, supplying chimney-pieces, busts, and other ornaments. His bill for these and other services, with its barely legible English (including £63 for "ciminy pies" and £3 for repairs to "two sarcoficus") gives some indication of why, in a period of politeness and aristocratic patronage, it was important for Scheemakers to have the mediation of the eloquent Stuart on larger works.[28]

The alliance with Stuart was advertised and exploited by Scheemakers. The Watson monument was very prominently signed "JAMES STUART INV PETER SCHEEMAKERS SCULP" (see figs. 9-1, 9-4), and Scheemakers exhibited the models of the three figures at the Free Society exhibition in 1765. Scheemakers also reused Stuart's designs, such as the chimneypiece relief of Bacchus and the Tyrrhenian Pirates (see fig. 5-69), executed under Stuart's supervision for 15 St. James's Square, and at Corsham Court (see fig. 6-48) where Stuart was not involved. Scheemakers was one of the most successful sculptors of eighteenth-century London, and unlike his contemporaries, he was always in employment. His shrewd collaboration with the most feted architect-connoisseur of the day gives some indication of the reason why.

Thomas Scheemakers

Thomas Scheemakers, Peter's only son, was trained in his father's studio and became one of the principal carvers of the works signed by his father and Stuart. After Peter Scheemakers's return to Antwerp in 1771, the family connection with Stuart was continued, albeit with Stuart apparently taking less of a role, possibly not even supplying the finished designs for monuments that appeared under their joint names.[29] From an early stage in his career, Thomas Scheemakers, or more likely his father, took care to advertise the connection between the boy and the architect, hoping to establish the family

workshop for the next generation. Peter Scheemakers passed the business entirely into his son's hands before his return to Antwerp, as there is no mention of the workshop in his will, which was drafted in June of 1771.[30] The six monumental works signed by Thomas Scheemakers and James Stuart, while perfectly pleasing and competent, show little sign of extensive innovation beyond the works of the first partnership. In fact Stuart's involvement may have been simply providing "contacts and contracts."[31]

The first publicly announced collaboration between Thomas Scheemakers and James Stuart was recorded in the catalogue of the Free Society of Artists exhibition in London in 1765. Thomas exhibited two bas-reliefs of dancing nymphs and a figure of Bacchus at this show, explicitly labeled as designed by James Stuart. In 1770 Thomas exhibited "two sea-horses" designed by the same.[32] None of these works appears to have survived. It was not until 1771 that the two first signed a monument together. The wall-monument to the fourth Earl of Shaftesbury at Wimborne Saint Giles, Dorset, has an *all'antica* bust of the deceased on a socle placed on a sarcophagus, while to either side stand two winged putti. Two simple flaming classical vases make a nod toward neoclassicism (fig. 9-9). Following his father's propensity to reuse designs, whether his own or not, Thomas included these vases once again in a monument to Jemmet and Elizabeth Raymond at Kintbury, Berkshire, where Stuart was not involved.

Stuart was responsible for winning the contract for the monument to Ralph Freman at Braughing, Hertfordshire, which was erected by Freman's nephew, Philip Yorke. It is an impure combination of motifs drawn from the language of funerary sculpture and supplemented by fresh allusions to Stuart's classical studies (fig. 9-10). At the center of the work is a polychrome sarcophagus in a niche, surmounted by two languid putti holding a coat of arms. A double portrait of Freman and his wife, Agnes, in classical garb is attached to the front, while on the adjoining walls are medallion portraits of Ralph Freman and his wife, Elizabeth, as well as William Freman and his wife, Catharina. Sarcophagi and putti had been a staple of monumental sculpture for the best part of fifty years in England. The use of gaudy polychromy was practically exhausted as a novelty by Sir Henry Cheere, and the additional motifs of crossed palm branches in a laurel crown had been regularly used in the works of Sir Robert Taylor

Fig. 9-9. James Stuart. Monument to Anthony Ashley Cooper, fourth Earl of Shaftesbury, St. Giles's Church, Wimborne St. Giles, Dorset, 1771. Sculpted by Thomas Scheemakers. Damaged by fire, 1908; repaired under the direction of Sir Ninian Comper. Photographed in 2006. *Checklist no. 193.*

Fig. 9-10. James Stuart. Monument to Ralph Freman, Church of St. Mary the Virgin, Braughing, Hertfordshire, ca. 1773. Sculpted by Thomas Scheemakers. Photographed in 2006. *Checklist no. 194.*

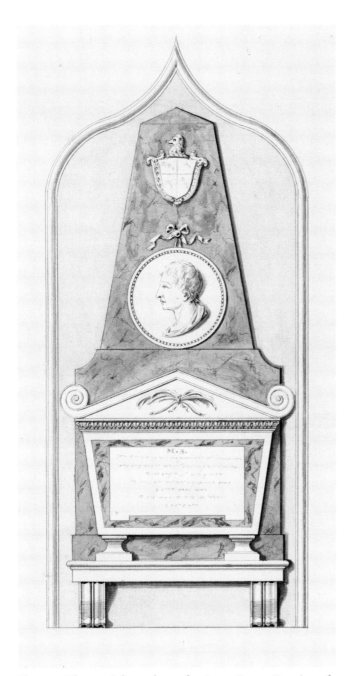

Fig. 9-11. Thomas Scheemakers, after James Stuart. Drawing of a variant of the monument to Thomas Steavens, Church of St. Mary the Virgin, Preston-on-Stour, Warwickshire, ca. 1773. Pen and ink, watercolor wash. By courtesy of the Trustees of The Victoria and Albert Museum, London, 8408.14 (Box H.13). *Checklist no. 195.*

Fig. 9-12. James Stuart. Monument to Thomas Steavens, Church of St. Mary the Virgin, Preston-on-Stour, Warwickshire, ca. 1773. Sculpted by Thomas Scheemakers. Photographed in 2006. *Checklist no. 196.*

and others. Only in some parts of the decoration are there signs that Stuart contributed to the admixture. The sarcophagus follows the design of that at Scopolo (without the strigil carving), with its scrolled lid (see fig. 9-7). A tiny band of simple beading and a stern, plain pedestal with undecorated waisted feet give only an inkling of Greek austerity.

The design of this sarcophagus was reused for the monument to Thomas Steavens at Preston-on-Stour, Warwickshire (figs. 9-11, 9-12), and a far purer version of the Scopolo sarcophagus, replete with strigil decoration and lion's feet, was used for the monument to Josiah Wedgwood's partner, Thomas Bentley, in Chiswick (fig. 9-13). The fact that a drawing for this monument exists in

397

Fig. 9-13. James Stuart. Monument to Thomas Bentley, Church of St. Nicholas of Myra, Chiswick, London, 1781. Sculpted by Thomas Scheemakers. Photographed in 2006. *Checklist no. 200.*

Fig. 9-14. Thomas Scheemakers, after a design by James Stuart. Drawing of a monument to Thomas Bentley in Church of St. Nicholas of Myra, Chiswick, London, ca. 1780. Pen and ink, watercolor wash. By courtesy of the Trustees of The Victoria and Albert Museum, London, 8408.9a (Box H.10, formerly in album 93.B.23). *Checklist no. 201.*

Fig. 9-15. James Stuart. Monument to Joseph Cocks, Church of St. John the Baptist, Eastnor, Herefordshire, 1778. Sculpted by Thomas Scheemakers. Photographed in 2006. *Checklist no. 198.*

Thomas Scheemakers's hand in the Victoria and Albert Museum (fig. 9-14) suggests that Stuart's involvement need not have been extensive.[33] The simple reuse of elements shows little attempt to generate new and interesting forms of composition and decoration, and Thomas was perfectly capable of handling such a commission, from drawing to execution. The design of the whole of the Freman monument was repeated for the memorial to Joseph Cocks (fig. 9-15), another distant relative of the Yorke's, at Eastnor, Herefordshire; it incorporates some

additional Greek key decoration.

One of the last works signed by the pair offers a variation on the repeated sarcophagus decorations, but, again, there is little sign of a revolution in monumental design. The wall-monument to another member of the Cocks family, Mary, at Eastnor (fig. 9-16), shows a Bible-holding figure of Hope in classical garb, mourning beside an urn, while a putto extinguishes a torch. Behind the scene is a carved curtain of drapery held at the sides by two scrolled pins.

Fig. 9-16. James Stuart. Monument to Mary Cocks, Church of St. John the Baptist, Eastnor, Herefordshire, ca. 1779. Sculpted by Thomas Scheemakers. Photographed in 2006. *Checklist no. 199.*

Although trained in the family workshop tradition, Thomas Scheemakers also studied at the Royal Academy (RA) schools in 1772, three years after their foundation. He would have been a relatively mature student in a relatively young institution, but he was not the only semi-established sculptor to realize that the RA provided new opportunities. Not only could a student enjoy access to life and anatomy studies, but the academy could be used to make important artistic connections. The sculptor John Bacon was twenty-nine when he enrolled at the RA schools in 1769, while Edward Burch, a gem-engraver, was thirty-nine. Unlike his father, Thomas Scheemakers had the option early in life of bringing his name before an art-viewing public via the exhibitions held for the first time in Britain in the 1760s. Throughout the 1770s he exhibited at the Free Society, advertising his connection with Stuart in 1774 by exhibiting a "sketch" (presumably a terracotta) for an unidentified monument "designed by Stuart."[34] Alongside this design he exhibited a model of the portrait that was to feature on the same monument.

The finished work is likely to have been either the Shaftesbury or the Freman monument, and from the point of view of artistic identity the exhibition is significant. Scheemakers not only publicized his connection with Stuart but also asserted his independent identity as a sculptor in the exhibited portrait, which is not credited to Stuart and is thus likely to have been his own creation, rather than coming from a drawing by Stuart.[35]

In 1782 Scheemakers exhibited for the first time at the Royal Academy, predictably with a "model of a monument from a design of Mr Stuart."[36] By this date the partnership was, however, largely over. Scheemakers went on to produce and exhibit many more monuments, including that to Anthony, Lord Feversham (erected 1784) at Downton, Wiltshire, which is signed Scheemakers "invt. et Ft," thus announcing the sculptor's ability to produce his own designs. That work is unambitious, but his funerary monument to Mary Russell, with its crisp relief of the subject teaching music to children, is notably sentimental. Scheemakers also received the commission for the monument to the writer and society hostess Lady Mary Wortley Montagu in Lichfield Cathedral, showing a grieving classical female leaning on a fluted, decorated vase. The inscription slab records her rather questionable, but ultimately successful, decision to test the efficacy of smallpox innoculation on her own children. This work, like a number of Scheemakers's other solo efforts, has elements of classical decoration, including fluting on the vase and paterae on the brackets. There is little to suggest, however, that the association with Stuart left the indelible imprint of Greek classicism on the sculptor's designs.

Indeed, given Stuart's status as a pioneering advocate of the primacy of the Greek style, it is notable just how little impact this program had on the monuments produced to his designs by the Scheemakers workshop. One conclusion could be that the strength of the language and economics of British monumental sculpture was such that the expectations of patrons and public would simply not permit wholly revolutionary changes in the appearance of these very works, which were of major personal, family, and social significance. (This is to assume that Stuart intended to revolutionize monumental sculpture, a supposition not necessarily borne out by the amount of intervention he had in the production process). Another conclusion is that Stuart provided little more than a valuable association for the workshop of Peter and Thomas Scheemakers, who could add one or two of Stuart's Greek motifs to the language of monumental sculpture, in which they were well versed, and translate a couple of designs into several executed works.

The changes that Stuart made to the practice of monumental sculpture through his collaboration with Peter and Thomas Scheemakers were negligible. The same cannot be said, however, of the influence of the illustrations to *Antiquities of Athens*, which were to have a profound and significant effect on the practice of sculpture in the fifty-year period after publication of the first volume. By educating sculptors in the art of the classical world, these illustrations were to assist in raising the sculptor's status to liberal artist.

Stuart and the Sculptors: The Influence of *Antiquities of Athens*

The major British sculptors influenced by *Antiquities of Athens* appear not to have entered directly into any contractual relationship with Stuart himself. Their sculptural designs, however, incorporated three-dimensional mani-

festations of Stuart and Revett's published illustrations, ranging from tiny pieces of foliage decoration to a wholesale reproduction of a Greek temple. The relationship of ownership to creative and professional identity is of considerable interest, as it demonstrates the loose nature of Stuart's control over the designs that he publicized and made available.[37] The use of Greek motifs also demonstrates the increasing freedom that textual proliferation gave to sculptors, whose professional identity was bolstered by their access to the higher reaches of classical taste, without the need to enter into actual working collaboration with architects and other tastemakers.

Perhaps the most notable sculptor to incorporate the influence of Stuart into his work was Joseph Nollekens, the London-born son of an Antwerp painter. Nollekens and Stuart may have met through a number of connections, as the sculptor was apprenticed to Peter Scheemakers in the 1750s and won a premium in 1759 from the Society of Arts in which Stuart took a close interest. In 1762 Nollekens moved to Rome, where he remained until 1770. It was common for British sculptors not only to execute original commissions in Italy, but also to act as antiquities restorers, dealers, and copyists, and Nollekens apparently made "considerable sums of money" at these pursuits.[38] By 1765 he was supplying antiquities through his agent, James Stuart, to Admiral Anson. He furnished an Adonis and a cast of Castor and Pollux, which was subsequently followed by a commission for a carved marble replica, made by Nollekens.[39] Stuart probably also secured the patronage of Lord Rockingham, who had bought an ancient statuette from Stuart, and who commissioned from Nollekens a remarkable group of the Judgment of Paris to be juxtaposed with a restored antiquity at Rockingham House.[40] Nollekens also entrusted Stuart with the installation of his own busts at the Society of Arts exhibition in London. This included his bust of Laurence Sterne, which the sculptor sent to Stuart from Rome in 1767.

Although Stuart and Nollekens were business associates, and possibly friends, they never collaborated on a work of sculpture. It has been suggested that the inclusion of columns of the "Delian" Doric order on the monument to the Three Captains (William Bayne, William Blair, and Lord Robert Manners) in Westminster Abbey may have originated with Stuart, whose drawings of the order were subsequently published in the second volume of *Antiquities of Athens* in about 1790.[41] It was not until after Stuart's death, however, that Nollekens produced his

Fig. 9-17. Joseph Nollekens. Monument to William Weddell, Ripon Cathedral, Yorkshire, after 1789. Photographed after 1960. RIBA Library Photographs Collection.

most recognizably Stuartian scheme. For the tomb of William Weddell, who died in 1789, at Ripon Cathedral, Nollekens carved a replica of the Choragic Monument of Lysicrates as a demirotunda, to act as a canopy for a bust of the deceased (fig. 9-17).[42]

Nollekens, like Joseph Wilton, was one of a class of sculptors (then a relatively recent phenomenon) who regarded themselves as members of a particular kind of cognoscenti.[43] Both had made the visit to Rome and were Italian-speaking, knowledgeable on antiquities, and artistically creative. They did not regard themselves as artisans,

nor were they reliant on the intercession of an architect to win commissions or to explain their iconography to well-heeled patrons. Although Nollekens gained from a personal relationship with Stuart, he was unlikely to feel the benefits of a collaborative working alliance, in the same way as had Thomas Scheemakers. Indeed, those who did work with Stuart at this time, with the possible exception of Scheemakers, were not highly regarded sculptors with pretensions to the status of liberal artist. John Horobin (who executed chimneypieces for Stuart at Wentworth Woodhouse) had only recently set up his masonry firm in Windmill Street, Piccadilly, having received his freedom from the Masons' Company in June 1764.[44] Alexander Rouchead of Oxford Row, who worked on Stuart's prized capitals at 15 St. James's Square, was a former master of the Masons' Company.[45] Stuart, in fact, had asked Peter Scheemakers to take the volutes into his special care for fear of the masons ruining them.[46]

For Nollekens, the use of a Stuartian scheme was probably a demonstration of his *own* knowledge, his *own* access to the world of letters and sophisticated taste. Although not a subscriber, Nollekens possessed an edition of the *Antiquities of Athens*, which was among his large library of learned works sold upon his death.[47] Ownership of the work was not a common phenomenon. The book was published by subscription, in five-hundred copies, and its subscribers were principally aristocrats and men of letters rather than practicing artists.[48] The version in the British Library, bound in gold-tooled red morocco, shows how prized as library volumes these works were (see fig. 4-1). Unlike other folio works, such as Rapin's *History of England* (1742), *Antiquities of Athens* was not quickly converted into smaller, more affordable texts by enterprising booksellers.[49] Indeed, it was not until 1837 that an affordable octavo edition was published, in London and Leicester. Sculptors who owned and appreciated *Antiquities of Athens* were therefore limited to a select few, and the possession of this knowledge was a significant social and artistic marker.

Two sculptors who did subscribe to the first volume of *Antiquities of Athens* were Richard Hayward and Prince Hoare. Hayward has sometimes been seen merely as the last of the British mason-sculptors, active within the Masons' Company all his life.[50] Were this the case he would be a curious anomaly among the subscribers. In fact Hayward, despite his allegiance to the Masons' Company, was a far more complex figure. Trained under Sir Henry

Cheere (another subscriber), he was also the owner of a significant estate in Bulkington, Warwickshire, as well as a dealer in books and antiquities and a collector of old master paintings, including works allegedly by Correggio and Poussin. His collection of British sale catalogues and his list of British visitors to Rome, begun during his own time in Rome in the 1750s and updated through contacts, are indispensable sources for historians of British sculpture. He no doubt knew Stuart, since he served on the Fine Arts Committee of the Society of Arts, and as a learned, moneyed artist with a business interest in the development of a taste for the antique, he was a very suitable subscriber to the first volume.[51]

Hayward's monumental sculpture incorporated a range of motifs from Italian Renaissance religious painting (such as his retable of the Last Supper in Bulkington Church) to figures drawn from Roubiliac's oeuvre (such as the crumbling pyramid on the monument to Charles Jennens at Nether Whitacre, Warwickshire). It is of little surprise to see that Hayward's learned eclecticism was also expanded to include Greek-style decoration in the 1780s.

Fig. 9-18. Richard Hayward. Monument to William Wragg, Westminster Abbey, London, 1779. Undated photograph.

Fig. 9-19. Richard Hayward. Pedestal decoration on the monument to Norborne, Baron de Botetourt, College of William and Mary, Williamsburg, Virginia, after 1770. Photographed in 2006. Image courtesy of the University Archives, Earl Gregg Swem Library, the College of William and Mary, Williamsburg, Virginia.

This can be seen in the heavy Greek decoration on the monuments to the Phillipps family at Shepshed, Leicestershire, and in the recurring key patterns and dolphins on the monument to William Wragg in Westminster Abbey of 1779 (fig. 9-18). There is also rich palmette decoration on the pedestal of America's oldest surviving public monument, that to Norborne Berkeley, Baron de Botetourt at the College of William and Mary in Williamsburg, Virginia (fig. 9-19).

Prince Hoare, a Bath sculptor, was, like Hayward, a sophisticated and moneyed practitioner. He was trained in the workshop of Peter Scheemakers and may have known Stuart through this connection. In 1750 George Vertue described the young Hoare as "a tall handsom agreeable person, and somewhat skill'd in music" who "bids fair for a great man."[52] Hoare was a member of the Accademia del

Fig. 9-20. Prince Hoare. Monument to Lord Trevor, St. Owen's Church, Bromham, Bedfordshire, after 1764. Undated photograph.

Disegno in Florence, a collector of antiquities, and a favored sculptor in Bath society.[53] In 1751 he married an heiress—Miss Coulthurst, of Melksham, Wiltshire—with a fortune of £6,000.[54] Hoare was, again like Hayward, a sculptor with social aspirations and status. His monumental work is a typically broad combination of iconographical elements, and into this mixture he added doses of

neoclassicism, for instance on the monument to Lord Trevor at Bromham, Bedfordshire (fig. 9-20).

For the next generation of sculptors, access to *Antiquities of Athens* was an important part of artistic education, although the price pushed the publication beyond the pocket of some aspiring sculptors. John Flaxman, whose father had worked alongside Peter Scheemakers at Shugborough, could not afford to buy a copy until 1796, when he was forty-one years old and relatively established. Before that date he referred only to tracings that he had made from the illustrations. Flaxman then handed on these tracings to his young pupil Thomas Hayley, who was presumably also unable to afford a copy.[55] The influence of Stuart and Revett's *Antiquities of Athens* on Flaxman was extensive and is certainly to be found in the incorporation of Greek decoration on the bulk of Flaxman's monuments. The minimal, linear engravings by William Pars in the first volume of *Antiquities of Athens* probably also influenced Flaxman's celebrated illustrations to Homer, Dante, and Aeschylus (1792 – 95).

The angels on Flaxman's monument to Sarah Morley in Gloucester Cathedral are no doubt derived from the flying figures on the Temple of the Winds,[56] although a more faithful copy was produced by the sculptor John Bacon between 1792 and 1794. Bacon's figures of the winds were fittingly employed for the Radcliffe Observatory in Oxford and cut from local stone.[57] Around the same time, in 1793, Eleanor Coade was producing (almost massproducing) artificial stone columns loosely based upon the caryatids of the Erectheion taken from Stuart and Revett's designs. Examples are at Anglesey Abbey.[58] One of the key modelers for Coade was John Charles Felix Rossi, who was subsequently to produce the towering caryatids for St. Pancras Church, London (1819 – 22; see fig. 13-5). These, however, were based not on engravings, but rather on the original caryatids, which were then in London as a result of Lord Elgin's purchase of the Parthenon marbles. In 1816 an enterprising bookseller issued a separate quarto edition of Stuart's engravings of the Parthenon marbles, appended to the Parliamentary report into the purchase of the marbles, thus adding an extra topical twist to Stuart's engravings.

It is unlikely that Stuart would ever have had any protection against this unlicensed use of his designs, although given his desire to influence the modern practice of architecture he was unlikely to complain about such use.[59] The borrowing of his designs without the need for his direct

Fig. 9-21. Frontispiece. Engraving by C. Grignion after William Hogarth. From *A Catalogue of the Paintings, Sculptures, Models, Drawings, Engravings, &C. now Exhibiting in the Great Room Belonging to the Society for the Encouragement of Arts, Manufactures, and Commerce in the Strand* (1761). By permission of The British Library, London, 58.f.7.

intervention began soon after the publication of his illustrations. In 1765 the drawings of Bacchus and the Tyrrhenian Pirates from the Choragic Monument of Lysicrates were used as the model for a chimneypiece tablet at Corsham Court (see fig. 6-48), carved by Peter Scheemakers under the direction not of Stuart but of Lancelot "Capability" Brown, one of the original subscribers to the *Antiquities of Athens*. The design was also employed in 1776 for the south portico of Stowe House, Buckinghamshire, carved by James Lovell, again apparently without Stuart's intercession. The figure of Bacchus and the Panther was also modeled by John Hackwood for a

basaltware relief issued by Wedgwood about the same time.[60] There was no copyright protection to inhibit the piracy of Stuart's designs, a problem shared by the Glasgow-born sculptor John Henning the Elder, among others.

After the arrival of the Parthenon marbles in England in 1811, Henning spent twelve years producing slate intaglios in which he reproduced the whole of the frieze in minute detail. In 1823 he issued bas-reliefs from these molds in plaster which were sold as a set for 30 guineas. Soon after their appearance, the works were used by other firms in London, Paris, and Vienna as the basis for molds

Fig. 9-22. Richard Westmacott
the Younger. Bas-relief,
Chatsworth, Derbyshire, 19th
century. Photographed in 1982.
Devonshire Collection,
Chatsworth. By permission of
the Duke of Devonshire and the
Trustees of the Chatsworth
Settlement.

from which thousands of pirated copies were produced. By 1830 Henning was reduced to attempting to sell his sets for £8, and complaining bitterly in published articles and private correspondence about the lack of a law to give him copyright protection for his work. Henning explained that the law was lacking because his works were considered to be copies, based on the Greek original. Hence these pirated reproductions were simply seen as copies of copies. This must also have been the case with copies which Scheemakers, Lovell, and others made after Stuart.[61]

Freedom from "The Long-Established Tyranny"

Stuart's career, and the influence of his magnum opus on the practice of sculpture, coincides with the most significant period in the formation of the professional identity of the "sculptor" in Britain. The period from 1759 to the middle of the nineteenth-century saw ideo-

logical and material articulations of the desire to establish a sculptural profession based upon the independent thoughts and designs of sculptors, whose chief work was to be the conception, supervision, and completion of their own work of art. For writers on the new profession, a cornerstone of this ideal was freedom from reliance either on the business or the designs of the architect.

The foundation of the Society of Artists in 1759, by a small group that included some of the leading artists of the day, marked an important moment in the professionalization of the arts.[62] Although its members, and many of the exhibitors at their subsequent exhibitions, comprised craftsmen working in a variety of media, there was nevertheless an ideological commitment to the notion that the visual arts were made up of three distinct and definable fields—painting, sculpture, and architecture. This was expressed most clearly in the Society of Artists catalogue frontispiece of 1761, in which Britannia is seen watering three intertwined but distinct trees (fig. 9-21). The sculptural arts, however, more closely resembled a rhizome than a tree at this time: under the aegis of "sculpture" was a vast array of practices, from carving and designing portrait busts and monuments to casting, polishing, and masonry work. More significantly, some domains rightly belonging to sculpture, such as the original design of sculptural works, were sometimes taken on by architects.

The foundation of the Royal Academy in 1769, which required one to be elected as a painter, sculptor, or architect, had tangible effects on the demarcation of the sculptural profession.[63] Training not only in modeling, but also in principles of design and, later, in the history of sculpture, gave pupils access to the kind of prized learning that had earlier allowed architects and dilettantes to assume the roles of designer for carvers. Among the early RA trainees were Thomas Banks and John Flaxman, who for the rest of their lives explicitly identified their profession as "sculptor."[64] Aspects of this self-identification included their recognized knowledge of antiquity (through visits to Rome and the use of such works as Stuart and Revett's *Antiquities of Athens*) and the execution of their own designs. Banks, indeed, appears never in his adult life to have executed a third party's design. His output was small by comparison with some of his contemporaries but intensely thoughtful and self-consciously innovative. His political radicalism, bound up with his interest in antiquities, similarly affected his output.[65]

One vital component in the establishment of professional (or any) identity is the creation of a lineage or history. The early nineteenth century saw some of the first efforts to formulate the history of sculpture in the light of its professionalization. John Flaxman's lectures on the history of sculpture, researched in pitiless detail, were first delivered in 1810. Allan Cunningham, who trained as a sculptor under Sir Francis Chantrey, gives some indication of the ideology of the professional in his *Lives of the Most Eminent British Painters, Sculptors, and Architects* (1829 – 33).[66] For Cunningham the essence of the sculptor's art was the freedom to pursue an individual creativity. His ire was directed toward two forces that he presented as shackling the development of the sculptor's art: manufacturing and obeisance to architects. One less-than-flattering portrait was of Bacon, whose connections with the manufacturing industry led, in Cunningham's opinion, to a shallow populist form of mass-produced work. This, coupled with John Bacon's pious conservatism, polluted his sculptural work.

In his life of Joseph Wilton, Cunningham casts the sculptor as a hero principally for his resistance to the "long-established tyranny" of the architect.[67] For centuries the sculptural art had submitted to the direction of the architects, and in the previous century they had exploited the impecuniousness of immigrant sculptors. Cunningham lamented that "the names of Kent, Gibbs and Chambers appear upon our public monuments as inventors of the designs, while the artists who executed them are mentioned as mere modelling tools or chisels, which moved as they were directed by these architectural lords-paramount. Rysbrack, Scheemakers, and even Roubiliac, were fain to submit to the tyranny."[68] The might of these men, in truth, made it difficult not to submit, but Wilton, who was possessed of a diverse Continental training and an independent fortune "resisted, and claimed the right of inventing his own designs."[69] Cunningham had chosen a complex figure to cast in this role, however, as Wilton executed a good deal of decorative work for the buildings of his close friend William Chambers. Cunningham excuses this as a token of the close friendship of the two men, but the retrogression may have had some influence on Cunningham's final verdict that Wilton was an artist of "little original merit."[70]

J. T. Smith, whose life of Nollekens was the first substantial biography of a British sculptor, expressed disdain for Nicholas Read for his desertion of sculpture for the building trades. Read had trained under Roubiliac but unlike his master, identified himself in his will as "sculptor."[71] Trading on his master's reputation, Read was able to build up a substantial business. Smith, however, later noted the increasing focus of Read's business not on sculpture but on "the trade of purchasing old houses, fitting them up, and then letting them at an immense increase of rent."[72] For sculptors such as Rossi who were schooled in the ideology of the independent sculptor, there were acute dangers in aiming to produce only the purest forms of sculpture when the patronage for such works in England was profoundly limited. His financial problems and the necessary reliance on architectural sculpture and modeling for manufacturers surely occasioned Rossi's public and private ranting on the subject.[73]

One notably eloquent summary of the struggle to establish the sculptor as a respected professional artist appeared in two articles in the *Builder* in June 1861 and January 1871.[74] The author of the first, Richard Westmacott the Younger, was in a privileged position to understand the transformation. Westmacott belonged to the third generation of a family of carvers and sculptors, whose founder, Richard Westmacott the Elder, had run a diverse mason-statuary business, designing and executing chimneypieces and carving monuments to the designs of the architect James Wyatt. Of Richard the Elder's sons, Henry continued the commercial business, executing architectural carving, among other masonry work, while the eldest son, Richard (later Sir Richard) Westmacott, became one of the most distinguished and scholarly sculptors in British history.[75] Sir Richard had been sent to Italy at an early age, where he formed a lifelong friendship with Antonio Canova. He returned to England in 1796, made a good marriage, and through his family connections with Wyatt, became a successful contender for a host of public commissions occasioned by an outpouring of sentimental triumphalism at the end of the Napoleonic Wars. He had a vast and acknowledged expertise of the art of antiquity, which he passed on to his own son, Richard the Younger, who was sent to Rome in 1818.

Richard the Younger executed a range of ideal works, including a marble relief for Chatsworth, based on figures from Stuart and Revett's *Antiquities of Athens* (fig. 9-22). His article in the *Builder* began with the assertion that "the character and position of the true sculptor" had "long been misunderstood," partially through the "absence of united action" among the acknowledged masters and also because sculptural practice was too diverse. In a reference to the sprawling diversity of many workshops, Westmacott stated that there are "many branches of the art, all of value and importance in their respective classes of sculpture" which were unfortunately "comprehended in the general term."[76]

In the second article, apparently an unsigned editorial, the *Builder* sketched a pitiful history of British sculpture, intended to galvanize modern sculptors to "understand the difficulties which surrounded the art" in the interests of preventing its regression. (This was clearly a feared possibility at the time).[77] Having been characterized by "extreme rudeness" in the medieval period, according to the article, sculpture entered a new period of depravity with the workshop of "foreigners," most notably Roubiliac. Sculpture was saved only by the influence of Flaxman and Canova and by an improved knowledge of Greek and Roman arts. "It must always be remembered," the article went on, "that art is of very late growth in England; and that it makes our progress the more remarkable. While Italy and France were producing, as far back as the fifteenth and sixteenth century, artists of great ability, this country could not boast any native sculptor, of even small pretension, until the end of the eighteenth century."[78]

These two articles and Cunningham's *Lives*, although different in some regards, constitute an important formulation of a vital mythical and self-affirming history of the British "sculptor." This figure was an ideal professional figure whose existence had been achieved through a process of distillation and who could once again disappear should the purity of his profession return to menial diversity. The British form of this ideal figure was devised in the mid-eighteenth century and derived from ancient, French, and Italian models. The following decades saw attempts to actively integrate its conceptual purity into the diversity of the existing carver or statuary's practices. Part of the struggle consisted in the demarcation of the boundaries of sculpture and architecture, which under different terminology had previously been intertwined. Also significant was the need to place the learning of the ancient world into the hands of the sculptor, rather than allowing more educated interlopers to direct their art. Stuart and Revett's extraordinary publication, *Antiquities of Athens,* went a long way toward fulfilling this need.

Acknowledgments: The study of the professional relationship between architects and sculptors in eighteenth-century Britain has largely been inaugurated by Ingrid Roscoe and Malcolm Baker, and their work has helped to shape this essay. I would like to offer my fondest thanks to Dr. Roscoe, for whom I have worked for several years on *The Biographical Dictionary of Sculptors in Britain, 1660 – 1851* (New Haven and London: Yale University Press, forthcoming [2007]), and without whose encouragement and support this essay would not have been written. Appropriately, given the subject matter, the essay was initially a collaborative venture with Dr. Baker, whose influence can, to my eyes, be noted on every page. In the event the execution has been mine, although the general design is at least jointly his. My thanks also to Alicia Weisberg-Roberts, Marjorie Trusted, and Lucy Cutler, who read the manuscript, and always helped.—M.G.S.

1. Quoted in Malcolm Baker, "Portrait Busts of Architects in Eighteenth-Century Britain" in *Figured in Marble: The Making and Viewing of Eighteenth-Century Sculpture* (London: V&A Publications, 2000): 95.

2. Nost's drawing for the monument to the Duke of Buccleuch at Durisdeer is in the Bodleian and was published in John Physick, *Designs for English Sculpture, 1680 – 1860* (London: HMSO, 1969): 18. Will of John Nost, proved in 1710, AM/PW 1710/89, London Metropolitan Archives. Kent produced designs for ten monuments before 1750, Gibbs thirteen.

3. See Baker, "Portrait Busts" (2000).

4. Will of Arnold Quellin (d. 1686), PROB 11/384/332, NA.

5. Mason-carvers produced carving work during the winter months, when the weather did not permit building projects; Baker, "Portrait Busts" (2000): 97.

6. Wills of William (d. 1705) and Edward Stanton (d. 1734), PROB 11/483/152-3 and 11/665/368, NA. Both became Masters of the Masons' Company during their careers.

7. George Vertue, "Vertue—III, Note-books," Walpole Society annual, vol. 22 (1933 – 34): 17.

8. See Eileen Harris, *The Genius of Robert Adam: His Interiors* (New Haven: Paul Mellon Centre for Studies in British Art / Yale University Press, 2001), passim.

9. "Plans etc Cavendish Square House by Henry Keen for Thomas Bridges," 85/223-264: 245, 252, 262, London Metropolitan Archives.

10. H. Clifford Smith, "Henry Keene: A Georgian Architect," *Country Life* 97 (30 March 1945): 556 – 57.

11. Will of Thomas Carter, 'mason,' PROB 11/1257/153, NA.

12. *The Yale Edition of Horace Walpole's Correspondence,* vol. 35, ed. W. S. Lewis, A. Dayle Wallace, and Robert A. Smith (New Haven: Yale University Press, 1973): 231.

13. John Deare wrote to his father in June 1776 that Vangelder had carved a "large figure" for Carter, which was currently in the shop, and he was "considered one of the best hands in London at foliage." Quoted in John Thomas Smith, *Nollekens and His Times,* vol. 2 (London: Henry Coburn, 1828): 306. The identity of the figure is not recorded,

although a possibility is the monumental, melancholic statue of Chaloner Chute for the Vyne, Hampshire, payments for which (to Carter) date from late 1775. At the same time, Vangelder was also working with Robert Adam on the monument to the Duchess of Montagu at Warkton, Northants. As the work is signed "PM van Gelder inv et sc" parts of the design were certainly his own.

14. Family search, International Genealogical Index, http://www.family search.org, accessed in 2005. Accounts for the Building of Badminton Church, Beaufort Papers, 1783 – 85, QA 2/5/2-4 and D2700/RA2/1/ 19-20, Gloucestershire Record Office; Rupert Gunnis, *Dictionary of British Sculptors, 1660 – 1851,* rev. ed. (London: Murrays Book Sales, 1968): 407 – 8.

15. Joseph Farington, *The Diary of Joseph Farington,* vol. 16, ed. Kathryn Cave (New Haven: Paul Mellon Centre for Studies in British Art / Yale University Press, 1984): 5744.

16. Malcolm Baker, "Sculpture," in *Rococo, Art and Design in Hogarth's England,* ed. Michael Snodin, exh. cat., Victoria and Albert Museum (London: Trefoil, 1984): 277 – 309.

17. Ibid.; Marcus Binney, *Sir Robert Taylor: From Rococo to Neoclassicism* (London: Allen and Unwin, 1984).

18. William Chambers's Letter-Books, Add. MSS 41133, BL.

19. Will of William Tyler, PROB 11/1363/619, NA.

20. Wills of Michael Rysbrack, Louis François Roubiliac, and John Mallcott "stone mason," PROB 11/954/224, 11/872/213, 11/2126/13, NA. For Roubiliac's career see David Bindman and Malcolm Baker, *Roubiliac and the Eighteenth-Century Monument: Sculpture as Theatre* (New Haven: Paul Mellon Centre for Studies in British Art / Yale University Press, 1995). For the life and work of Rysbrack see Katharine Eustace, *Michael Rysbrack: Sculptor, 1694 – 1770,* exh. cat., Bristol Art Gallery (Bristol: City of Bristol Museum and Art Gallery, 1982); and Marjorie Isabel Webb, *Michael Rysbrack: Sculptor* (London: Country Life, 1954). For the relationship between the Masons' Company and the development of commercial workshops, see Matthew Craske, "Contacts and Contracts: Sir Henry Cheere and the Formation of a New Commercial World of Sculpture in Mid-Eighteenth-Century London," in *The Lustrous Trade: Material Culture and the History of Sculpture in England and Italy, c. 1700 – c.1860,* ed. Cinzia Sicca and Alison Yarrington (London and New York: Leicester University Press, 2000): 95 – 113.

21. As described in his will, PROB 11/1082/177, NA.

22. Ingrid Roscoe, "James 'Athenian' Stuart and the Scheemakers Family: A Lucrative Partnership between Architect and Sculptors," *Apollo* 126 (September 1987): 178 – 84; and Roscoe, "Peter Scheemakers, Business Conduct and Workshop Practice with Catalogue Raisonné," Walpole Society annual, vol. 61 (1999): 163 – 304, on which most of the following section relies.

23. For importance of collaboration in Antwerp workshops see Elizabeth Honig, "The Beholder as a Work of Art: A Study in the Location of Value in Seventeenth Century Flemish Painting," *Nederlands Kunsthistorisch Jaarbook* 46 (1995): 252 – 97.

24. I am presently preparing an article on the Nost workshop and its relations with the neighboring Portugal Row workshops at Hyde Park Corner; Sullivan, "Female Inheritance, Workshop Collaboration and

Strategies for Survival: The Nost Family Workshop (1676 – 1780)" (forthcoming).

25. Roscoe, "James 'Athenian' Stuart and the Scheemakers" (1987): 179.

26. Stuart and Revett, *Antiquities of Athens*, vol. 1 (1762): 35.

27. Roscoe, "James 'Athenian' Stuart and the Scheemakers" (1987): 182.

28. For a transcription of the bill, see ibid., 181.

29. Ibid., 22. A sheaf of hand-colored designs for their monuments exist in Thomas Scheemakers hand in the Victoria and Albert Museum 8458-1878.

30. Will of Peter Scheemakers, PROB 11/1082/177, NA.

31. Craske, "Contacts and Contracts" (2000): 95 – 113; see also Roscoe, "James 'Athenian' Stuart and the Scheemakers" (1987): 184.

32. Algernon Graves, *The Society of Artists of Great Britain, 1760 – 1791, The Free Society of Artists, 1761 – 1783: A Complete Dictionary of Contributors and their Work from the Foundation of the Societies to 1791* (London: G. Bell, 1907): 227.

33. For Thomas Scheemakers's hand-colored designs: V&A 8458-1878.

34. Graves, *Society of Artists* (1907): 227.

35. Ibid.

36. Algernon Graves, *The Royal Academy Of Arts: A Complete Dictionary of Contributors and Their Work from Its Foundation in 1769 to 1904*, vol. 7 (London: H. Graves, 1905 – 6): 42.

37. It is also, coincidentally, an interesting illustration of the effects of textual proliferation and authorship on the creation of artistic identities. "Book history" has become a lively area of eighteenth-century European history in recent years and supplies a significant alternative to the more narrow focus on "texts." See Robert Darnton, "What is the History of Books," *Daedalus* (Summer 1982): 65 – 83; Roger Chartier, *The Order of Books: Readers, Authors and Libraries in Europe between the Fourteenth and the Eighteenth Centuries*, trans. Lydia G. Cochrane (Cambridge: Polity Press, 1994); Gilles Deleuze and Félix Guattari, *A Thousand Plateaus: Capitalism and Schizophrenia*, trans. Brian Massumi (London: Athlone Press, 1988), esp. chap. 1, "Rhizome."

38. "Account of Joseph Nollikins," *European Magazine and London Review* 13 (June 1788): 387.

39. V&A A.59 – 1940. Nollekens correspondence, D615/P(S)1/6/55, Staffordshire Record Office. Entry for "Nollekens" in *Ingamells* (1997): 709, written by John Kenworthy-Browne; and Kenworthy-Browne, "Joseph Nollekens: The Years in Rome," *Country Life* 165 (7 June 1979): 1844 – 48; (14 June 1979): 1930 – 31.

40. Nicholas Penny, "Lord Rockingham's Sculpture Collection and The Judgement of Paris by Nollekens," *John Paul Getty Museum Journal* 19 (1991): 5 – 34.

41. John Kenworthy-Browne, "Monument to Three Captains (in Westminster Abbey)," *Country Life* 161 (27 January 1977): 180 – 82.

42. David Watkin, *Athenian Stuart: Pioneer of the Greek Revival* (London: George Allen and Unwin, 1982): 27.

43. His pretensions were savagely and repeatedly ridiculed in the venomous two-volume biography by his embittered former student, John Thomas Smith, in *Nollekens and His Times* (1828).

44. Thomas Mortimer, *The Universal Director . . .* (London: J. Coote, 1763): 49; Masons' Company List of Freemen 1677 – 1795, Guildhall Library, MS 5308: 31.

45. Edward Conder Jr., *Records of the Hole Crafte and Fellowship of Masons . . .* (London: Swan, Sonnenschein; New York: Macmillan, 1894): 296.

46. Roscoe, "James 'Athenian' Stuart and the Scheemakers" (1987): 181.

47. *Catalogue of the Library of the late Joseph Nollekens . . . which will be sold by auction by Mr Evans, 93 Pall Mall, London*, sale cat., 18 – 19 December 1823, lot 342, copy in British Museum Prints and Drawing. *Antiquities of Athens*, vols. 1 and 2, original edition of 1762, sold for £11. My special thanks to John Kenworthy-Browne, who very kindly supplied me with a photocopy of the catalogue and answered my questions about Nollekens and Stuart.

48. Watkin, *Athenian Stuart* (1982): 21.

49. For the sale of Rapin's *History of England* by British booksellers, see M. G. Sullivan, "Rapin, Hume and the Identity of the Historian in Eighteenth Century England," in *History of European Ideas*, vol. 28 (Oxford and New York: Pergamon, 2002): 145 – 62.

50. Gunnis, *Dictionary of British Sculptors* (1968): 195.

51. *A Catalogue of the Genuine Stock in Trade of Mr Richard Hayward, Statuary . . .* , sale cat., Smith [auctioneer], London, 4 – 6 November 1800; copy in the Courtauld Book Library, Lugt 6152A. Hayward's large portfolio of "Stuart's Athens" was among the "Books on Architecture" in the sale. For Hayward's list of visitors to Rome and collection of sales catalogues, see A.5.9.Sc, British Museum; see also Deeds of Lease and Release between Richard and Mary Hayward to transfer property in Weston in Arden to Christopher Horsnaile the Younger, 1748 – 49, CR2973/4-6, Warwickshire Record Office; John Lord, "Richard Hayward: An Early and Some Later Commissions," *Church Monuments* 12 (1997): 67 – 76; and Craske, "Contacts and Contracts" (2000): 103.

52. Vertue, "Note-books" (1933 – 34): 152.

53. Will of Prince Hoare, 1769, PROB 11/952, NA.

54. *Gentleman's Magazine* (1751): 284, quoted in Gunnis, *Dictionary of British Sculptors* (1968), 203 – 4; see also the entry for "Hoare" in Ingrid Roscoe, M. G. Sullivan, and Emma Hardy, *The Biographical Dictionary of Sculptors in Britain, 1660 – 1851*, ed. Ingrid Roscoe (New Haven and London: Yale University Press, forthcoming [2007]).

55. Rupert Gunnis and Margaret Dickens Whinney, *The Collection Of Models By John Flaxman, R.A., At University College London* (London: Athlone, 1967): 4.

56. This connection has been made by David Watkin; see Watkin, *Athenian Stuart* (1982): 21; and chap. 1, by David Watkin, in this volume.

57. Ann Cox-Johnson, *John Bacon R.A., 1740 – 1799*, St. Marylebone Society publication, no. 4 (London: the Society, 1961): 28.

58. Alison Kelly, *Mrs Coade's Stone* (Upton-upon-Severn: Self Publishing Association, 1990), passim.

59. *Antiquities of Athens*, vol. 1 (1762), i.

60. Michael McCarthy, "James Lovell and His Sculptures at Stowe," *Burlington Magazine* 115 (April 1973): 220 – 32.

61. John Malden, *John Henning, 1771 – 1851— ". . . A Very Ingenious*

Modeller . . ." (Paisley: Renfrew District Council, Museum and Art Galleries, 1977), passim; John Henning the Elder to David Murray, 10 December 1847, 384 Misc D.97, Marylebone Public Library.

62. "The Papers of the Society of Artists of Great Britain," Walpole Society annual, vol. 6 (1917 – 18): 113 – 30.

63. Although in practice this meant some obfuscation. Francesco Bartolozzi, an engraver, was elected as a painter.

64. Wills of Thomas Banks (d. 1805) and John Flaxman (d. 1826), PROB 11/1421/324, 11/1720/129, NA.

65. Banks was arrested under suspicion of treason in 1794 as a result of his membership of the a member of the Society for Constitutional Information. He wore his hair short in Roman style as an expression of his allegiance to democratic ideals, and he was also a key iconographer of British radicalism during the period. He modeled portraits of numerous members of the Society for Constitutional Information, including Felix Vaughan, Dr John Warner, and Lord Daer, and his sale included works, probably by him, of the radicals Thomas Holcroft and Mary While. See Christina and David Bewley, *Gentleman Radical: A Life Of John Horne Tooke, 1736 – 1812* (London: Tauris Academic Studies, 1998); and Charles Francis Bell, ed., *Annals Of Thomas Banks, Sculptor, Royal Academician . . .* (Cambridge University Press, 1938).

66. Allan Cunningham, *Lives of the Most Eminent British Painters, Sculptors and Architects*, 6 vols. (London: J. Murray, 1829 – 33).

67. Ibid., vol. 3, 712.

68. Ibid., vol. 3, 79.

69. Baker, *Figured in Marble* (2000): 26 – 27; for the relationship see Joan Coutu, "William Chambers and Joseph Wilton," in *Sir William Chambers, Architect To George III*, ed. John Harris and Michael Snodin, exh. cat., Courtauld Institute of Art Gallery, London (London and New Haven: Yale University Press with the Gallery, 1996): 175 – 85.

70. Cunningham, *Lives*, vol. 3, 71 – 72, 79, 81.

71. Will of Nicholas Read (d. 1787), PROB 11/1155/294, NA.

72. Smith, *Nollekens*, vol. 2 (1828): 240 – 41.

73. See Farington, *Diary*, passim. The best example of Rossi's martyred self-presentation as a true sculptor of poetic work in an age of unenlightened patronage is the preface to the sale of his studio contents; Robins [auctioneer], London, *Catalogue of the Splendid Collection of . . . Charles Rossi . . .* , sale cat., 3 – 4 March 1835, copy in the National Art Library, Victoria and Albert Museum, 23L.

74. Richard Westmacott, "An Address to British Sculptors," *Builder* 19 (29 June 1861): 438.

75. Will of Richard Westmacott (the elder), PROB 11/1483, 253-4, NA; for the career of Sir Richard Westmacott see Marie Busco, *Sir Richard Westmacott, Sculptor* (Cambridge and New York: Cambridge University Press, 1994).

76. Westmacott, "Address" (1861): 438.

77. "Sculpture in England," *Builder* (7 January 1871): 1 – 3.

78. Ibid., 3.

Fig. 10-1. James Stuart. Armchair for the Painted Room, Spencer House, London, 1759–66. Probably carved by Thomas Vardy. Carved and gilt limewood, silk damask upholstery (not original). Courtesy of Spencer House and the Trustees of The Victoria and Albert Museum, London, W.8-1977. *Checklist no. 120.*

JAMES "ATHENIAN" STUART AND

FURNITURE DESIGN

SUSAN WEBER SOROS

lthough best known today as a "pioneer" of the Greek-revival style in architecture,[1] James "Athenian" Stuart, architect, designer, archaeologist, and painter, played a critical role in the development of neoclassical furniture and decoration in the third quarter of the eighteenth century in England. He in fact may have been more successful at adapting his knowledge of archaeological architecture and design to furniture and decoration than to architecture.[2] Stuart's furniture output may have been relatively small compared with that of his two main rivals, Sir William Chambers and Robert Adam, yet his sketches and surviving pieces represent some of the earliest and most innovative neoclassical designs of the day (fig. 10-1). They were part of unified schemes of decoration in which all objects were under the creative control of the architect, an approach to design he shared with Chambers and Adam. Too often studied as a precursor of what was to come in terms of "archaeologically correct" neoclassicism, particularly *le goût grec*, Stuart is here seen as a designer in his own right and of his own time, discovering the delights of ancient furniture, interiors, and architecture through a variety of means, and attempting to weave his understanding into contemporary furniture

for which there were often no classical precedents. It is all too easy to label many of Stuart's designs as "transitional," between the rococo style that was popular in Europe from 1740 to the 1760s and the neoclassical style that fully flowered in Britain by the 1760s. "Transitional" is a very broad term, however, and only goes so far in aiding our understanding of an extremely fertile and multilayered period in the interchange of evolving design languages and concepts between Rome, Athens, Paris, and London, the main cities where neoclassical design developed from the 1740s through the 1760s.

Writing in 1773 in the preface to *The Works in Architecture of Robert and James Adam*, Robert Adam noted: "Mr. Stuart, with his usual elegance and taste has contributed greatly toward introducing the true style of antique decoration."[3] Neither Stuart's work, however, nor that of Adam can be described as representing "the true style of antique decoration." Although Stuart described his work as looking back to classical antiquity "in the hope to discover the principles on which the ancients proceeded,"[4] his furniture and interiors were the result of a creative synthesis of ancient models and decoration with contemporary English and French forms. This was not unusual in terms of neoclassical design. There was little precedent within Greco-Roman specimens for convenient modern

Fig. 10-2. James Stuart. Sketch of the
Capella Pellegrini, S. Bernardino, Verona.
From Stuart's sketchbook (ca. 1748–50):
fol. 26r. RIBA Library Drawings
Collection, London, SKB/336/2 [L3/4].
Checklist no. 8.

furniture and interiors of a type suitable for the British
aristocracy and wealthy citizens.

Ancient furniture was limited to a few fundamental
forms: chair, stool, couch, table, and chest, with the addition of bookcases and wardrobes during the Hellenistic
time.[5] Upholstery as known today did not exist, and loose
pillows and cushions were used instead for comfort. In
addition, few actual specimens of ancient furniture survived, with the exception of some examples in bronze and
marble. Other items were mostly known from literary
sources, vase and fresco paintings, and marble reliefs. In
order to create neoclassical high-style pieces appropriate

to the customs of his wealthy patrons, therefore, Stuart
adapted and borrowed motifs and elements of ancient furniture from the few remaining specimens and from two-
dimensional sources, resulting in what has been described
as "brilliant permutations and combinations."[6]

Given his lowly family background, it was most
unlikely that Stuart would enter and succeed in the
rarified world of the antiquary. He was apprenticed in the
studio of a fan painter, very likely Louis or Joseph
Goupy, and learned the basics of painting and engraving.
He also developed an interest in classical art and architecture, and in about 1742 he set out for Rome to make a

firsthand study of the surviving artifacts of the ancient world as well as of the neoclassicism of the Renaissance period. Although the earliest documentary evidence of Stuart in Rome is dated 1744 (see chap. 3), Stuart himself suggests that he was in the city by about 1741 or 1742. He writes that when the first "Proposal" for *Antiquities of Athens* was drawn up toward the end of 1748, at which time "he was then at Rome, where he had already employed six or seven years in the study of painting."[7] Stuart's knowledge of ancient furniture almost certainly stemmed from this first visit to Rome, where he studied painting, architecture, and classical languages in the hope of obtaining a reputation as a classical scholar. Working as a painter and cicerone, or guide, to English travelers to support himself, he sketched some of what he saw. An extant sketchbook, now in the RIBA Library Drawings Collection, includes studies of grotesques, details of windows from palazzi, floor pavements, and Roman sculp-

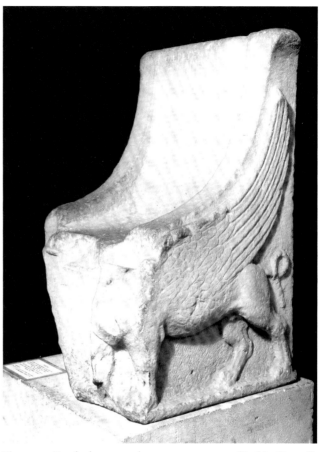

Fig. 10-4. Greek throne, 2nd to 1st century B.C. Marble. Part of the Arundel collection presented to the University of Oxford in 1755. The Ashmolean Museum of Art and Archaeology, Oxford, Michaelis 87.

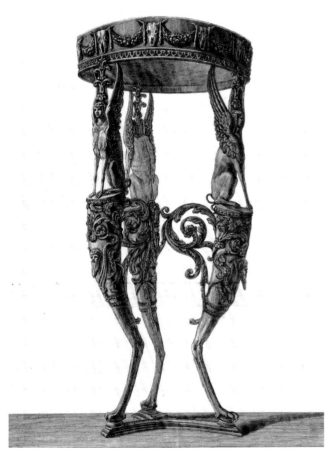

Fig. 10-3. Roman bronze tripod from the Temple of Isis, Pompeii. Etching. From Giovanni Battista Piranesi, *Vasi, Candelabri, Cippi, Sarcofagi, Tripodi . . .* , vol. 2 (1778): pl. 44. By permission of The British Library, London, 147.i.15.

Fig. 10-5. Front elevation of the Choragic Monument of Thrasyllus. Engraving. From *Antiquities of Athens*, vol. 2 (ca. 1790): chap. 4, pl. III. Courtesy of the Library, The Bard Graduate Center for Studies in the Decorative Arts, Design, and Culture, New York. *Checklist no. 129.*

tures, as well as architectural motifs (fig. 10-2). It is not known how much ancient furniture Stuart actually saw in Rome, but he probably was aware of the marble thrones on public view (see fig. 10-36) and of other pieces in contemporary Italian collections.

When he traveled elsewhere in Italy, however, he very likely gained access to recently excavated examples. In 1748 he visited Naples with three companions, all of whom were to make a significant mark on British art and design in one way or another—Nicholas Revett, an English artist and architectural draftsman, Gavin Hamilton, a Scottish painter and art dealer, and Matthew Brettingham the younger, an English art dealer, son of the architect Matthew Brettingham whose prestigious commissions included Holkham Hall. This trip very likely included visits to the excavations at Herculaneum and Pompeii, although those at the latter were in the earliest stages. Both sites would reveal much about architecture and decoration, and over the next decades they yielded many bronze

Fig. 10-6. Roman tripod with three griffins, Hadrianic period (A.D. 117–138). Marble. Capitoline Museums, Rome, MC1964.

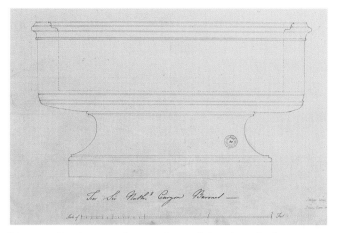

Fig. 10-7. Draftsman unknown. Record drawing of a "Jasper Wine Cooler," or cistern, for the dining room at Kedleston Hall, Derbyshire, ca. 1760. Pen and ink. By courtesy of the Trustees of Sir John Soane's Museum, London, Adam vol. 25, no. 80.

furniture specimens of the ancient world (fig. 10-3). In addition, in 1751 he and Revett took a trip to Greece that resulted in *Antiquities of Athens* (first volume, 1762), establishing their credentials as arbiters of neoclassical taste in the "Greek style."

In the mid-1700s, however, there were other sources available to those interested in antiquities. Collections of ancient objects in Great Britain, such as the marbles presented by the Earl of Arundel to the University of Oxford in 1755 (fig. 10-4), may have supplied examples for study in the 1750s and 1760s, when Stuart was designing furniture for his largest commissions.[8] The encyclopedic seventeenth- and eighteenth-century volumes of Pietro Santi Bartoli (*Admiranda Romanarum antiquitatium*; 1693), the comte de Caylus (*Recueil d'antiquités Egyptiennes, Etrusques, Grècques, Romaines et Gauloises;* 1752–67), and Bernard de Montfaucon (*Antiquité éxpliquée et représentée en figures;* 1724) provided valuable images for the design-

Fig. 10-8. James Stuart. Cistern, or wine cooler, for the dining room at Kedleston Hall, Derbyshire, 1757–58. Sculpted by Richard Hayward. Sicilian jasper. Courtesy of Kedleston Hall, The Scarsdale Collection (The National Trust, UK).

Fig. 10-9. Louis-Joseph Le Lorrain. *Bureau plat* for the Cabinet Flamand, Paris, ca. 1757. Gilt-bronze mounts by Philippe Caffieri. Ebony-veneered oak, ormolu, leather. Musée Condé, Chantilly, OA357.

ers of the eighteenth century. Engraved drawings and illustrated books published in several languages also provided ancient Greek and Roman prototypes and decorative motifs. Stuart was by then an avid antiquary. A list of items in his library at the time of his death in 1788 reveals that he studied the ancient texts of Vitruvius and Thucydides, the Renaissance architectural treatises of Andrea Palladio and Leon Battista Alberti, and the works of contemporary antiquaries such as Giovanni Battista Piranesi and Julien-David LeRoy.[9]

Kedleston Hall, Derbyshire

Stuart's earliest known furniture designs fused neoclassical motifs learned in Italy and Greece with contemporary rococo and neoclassical French taste. Four drawings of 1757–58 for the decoration of a state room for Nathaniel Curzon at Kedleston Hall, Derbyshire, illustrate this point well. To complement Curzon's enormous collection of Italian seicento paintings and copies of antique statues, Stuart designed a pair of console tables with a straight, fluted frieze of classical architectural derivation for the two-storied great saloon (see fig. 6-30). The tables' slender, tapering legs end in a simplified form of the French vase-shaped or peg-top foot that would become popular in Louis XVI furniture ten years later. There were Continental precedents for the marbletops. A tripod candelabrum of neoclassical style was to be placed in the center of each console table (see fig. 11-8). These candelabra derived from the low relief frieze of tripods in the intercolumniations of the Choragic Monument of Lysicrates in Athens, or the Lanthorn of Demosthenes, as it was also known. This monument was illustrated in the first volume of *Antiquities of Athens* (see fig. 7-32). A pair of plain gilt, oval mirrors was to hang over the console tables, which were to be flanked by tripod pedestals with scrolling feet

of baroque form. Busts were to sit on these pedestals.

A set of four large-scale "transitional" armchairs, with rococo-style balloon backs and neoclassical straight, turned legs, flanks the mantelpiece (see fig. 6-31). The chairs were to be upholstered in damask woven with a pattern of palm leaves and wreaths. The mantelpiece itself is decorated with wreath decoration taken from the Choragic Monument of Thrasyllus, also published in *Antiquities of Athens* (fig. 10-5), and with lion monopodia of a type used in ancient thrones and tables. Stuart used similar elements for the mantelpiece he designed for Nuneham Park, Oxfordshire, in 1760 (see fig. 6-27).[10] A low, metal fire grate was to be fashioned of openwork Greek frets.

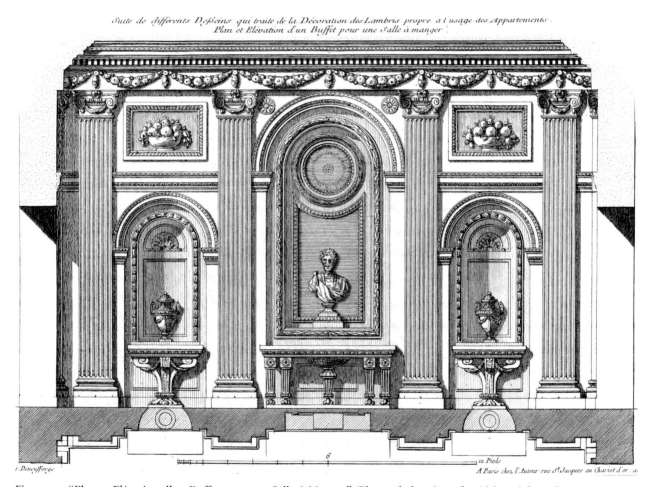

Fig. 10-10. "Plan et Elévation d'un Buffet pour une Salle à Manger" (Plan and elevation of a sideboard for a dining room). Engraving. From J. F. de Neufforge, *Recueil élémentaire d'Architecture . . .* , vol. 1 (1757): 61, pl. 1. By permission of The British Library, London, 558*f.1.

419

Fig. 10-11. James Stuart. Design for a pedestal, late 1740s–early 1750s. Pen and gray wash. From an Album of Drawings for Interior Decoration, Ornament and Architecture, p. 4. The Pierpont Morgan Library, New York, 1966.10:12. Bequest of Junius S. Morgan and Gift of Henry S. Morgan.

Fig. 10-12. James Stuart. Design for a pedestal, late 1740s–early 1750s. Pen and gray wash. From an Album of Drawings for Interior Decoration, Ornament and Architecture, p. 4. The Pierpont Morgan Library, New York, 1966.10:13. Bequest of Junius S. Morgan and Gift of Henry S. Morgan.

Fig. 10-13. "Table, Escritoire, Armoire, Torchere, Gaines . . ." ([Designs for] table, writing desk, armoire, torchere, pedestals . . .). Engraving. From J. F. de Neufforge, *Recueil élémentaire d'Architecture. . . . ,* vol. 5 (1757–68): 348, pl. 6. By permission of The British Library, London, 558*f.3.

The niche at the opposite end of the room housed a neoclassical sideboard table, flanked by scroll-footed pedestals surmounted by silver wine fountains (see fig. 6-33). Above the sideboard hung a painting of Curzon and his wife. Stuart derived the tripod pedestals with their addorsed sphinxes from a classical tripod with griffins in the Capitoline Museum in Rome (fig. 10-6) and later adapted the same tripods for his torchères for the Painted Room of Spencer House (see fig. 10-21). The sideboard table had a deep fluted frieze derived from classical archi-tecture and classical garlands attached to its apron. The four straight, tapered legs ended in French peg feet. In addition to the tripod candelabrum (see fig. 11-1) and other metalwork, the only Stuart design from this commission to be executed was a large Sicilian jasper cistern (figs. 10-7, 10-8), which was placed below a table designed by Robert Adam. The cistern was meant to imitate the *labrum* (marble baths) found in the apse of an ancient Roman *caldarium*.[11] It was made in Rome after Stuart's design by the sculptor Richard Hayward in January 1758.[12]

A fourth design shows a recess with a templelike structure, with colonnade and entablature and large urn placed on a pedestal (see fig. 6-32). This recess was made to accommodate a large organ, such as the one he designed ten years later for Newby Hall (see fig. 10-62).

Curzon's decision not to use Stuart's ideas created a rift between patron and designer, which was exploited by Robert Adam. In 1758 Adam wrote to his brother James that "Sir Nathaniel brought me out a Design of the Great Athenians for his Rooms finishing . . . so excessively & so ridiculously bad, that [he] immediately saw the folly of them & said so to some people which so offended the proud Grecian, that he has not seen Sir Nathaniel these 2 years." Adam goes on to ridicule one particular design for a wall, with its "tables of 2 feet sqr. In a Room 50 foot long with belts of Stone & great pannels of Roses & festoons & figures all Ramm'd in wherever there was a hole to be got for them." According to Adam, Stuart also proposed cropping paintings to achieve a greater unity of effect within the interior schemes: "[he] wanted to fitt frames for Sir Nathaniel's pictures but not having or rather I suppose, not being willing to confine his great genius to the sizes of the pictures, he cutts 3 foot off the length of the best pictures and 2 foot off the height of others to make them answer and draws all the pictures and colours them in his drawings. But they move pity rather than contempt."[13]

Despite Adam's acerbic remarks, Stuart's designs for Kedleston Hall represent some of the earliest neoclassical interiors in England. Among Adam's drawings at the Soane Museum is a sketch of a table and mirrors incorporating several details of Stuart's unexecuted Kedleston designs. Clearly Stuart's work influenced Adam's own designs for the project, including the gold and white sideboard suite on which Stuart's tripod was displayed (see fig. 11-9).[14]

In addition to their classical precedents, Stuart's designs for Kedleston reveal knowledge of contemporary French neoclassical decoration. During his sojourn in the Eternal City (ca. 1742–50), Stuart must have come into contact with the group of French painters, sculptors, and architects studying at the Acadèmie de France in Rome, in the Palazzo Mancini on the Corso. During the 1740s, a critical decade in terms of the development of neoclassicism, the Acadèmie de France was "a melting pot for neo-classic ideas."[15] The curriculum emphasized direct contact with ancient art. Stuart's time in Rome overlapped

with such innovators of the *style antique* as Joseph Le Lorrain and E. A. M. Peittot, both of whom were architects and designers, the painter Joseph-Marie Vien, and the sculptor J. F. Saly.[16] The group's revolutionary neoclassical designs, many of which were created and published while Stuart was still in Rome, must have stimulated his imagination.

When Stuart stopped in Paris on his way home to London in 1755, he probably visited French collections and even met with *goût grec* practitioners, notably Le Lorrain, the most prominent, who was already designing furniture *à la grecque* by 1754.[17] Le Lorrain's suite of monumental neoclassical furniture was adorned with gilt-bronze ornament derived from classical architectural sources. Commissioned in 1756 by the collector Ange-Laurent Lalive de Jully, for his Cabinet Flamand, a room in antique style, the furniture was probably not completed by the time of Stuart's visit. Even so, Paris was already the center of the growing taste for furniture and interiors in the new antique style. The suite's rectilinear ebony *bureau plat* and accompanying *cartonnier* (fig. 10-9), now in the Musée Condé, Chantilly, with ornament of Greek frets, Vitruvian scrolls, ropelike garlands, lion masks, and fluted legs ending in lion's-paw feet, would be numbered among the most celebrated examples of neoclassical taste in Paris. All of the motifs used in this suite became hallmarks of the French *goût grec*.

Similar French designs in the *style antique* were available at that time in illustrated books such as J. F. de Neufforge's *Receuil elementaire d'Architecture* (first section published in 1757). Stuart appears to have known this source well. Comparison of the design of the Kedleston sideboards with a Neufforge illustration (fig. 10-10) reveals that the fluted frieze, triple-fluted tapered legs, and the hanging pendant garlands adapted by Stuart in his designs for console tables are all in evidence in the Neufforge designs. Two early Stuart drawings, now in the Pierpont Morgan Library (figs. 10-11, 10-12), for a pair of pedestals also show unmistakable affinities to the French neoclassical designs created by Neufforge. The heavy pendant swags, carved flutes, bold Vitruvian scroll frieze, and central lion mask of the Stuart pedestals are characteristics of Neufforge's engravings (fig. 10-13). Stuart may also have been influenced by French furniture brought to England in relatively small quantities during the Seven Years' War, often by English collectors and Grand Tourists, and in greater quantity after the end of the war in 1763.[18]

Fig. 10-14. John Vardy. Side table for the dining room of Spencer House, London, ca. 1755–58. Probably carved by Thomas Vardy. Carved and gilt pine, marble top. Courtesy of Spencer House and the Trustees of The Victoria and Albert Museum, London, W. 7-1974.

Spencer House, London

The designs of the British Palladian architect and designer John Vardy also influenced Stuart. Vardy, a follower of William Kent, had been Stuart's predecessor as architect and designer at Spencer House from 1756 to 1758. Although Stuart superseded Vardy as the main designer of the first-floor rooms, Vardy continued to act as executant architect at Spencer House until his death in May 1765. Stuart continued the general classical character of Vardy's work but brought more archaeologically correct elements to the interiors. Part of the challenge for Stuart was to understand the work of Vardy in such a way that the new room designs would not appear to be piecemeal and would not lose their harmony of effect. Vardy's furniture for Spencer House included many of the same classical details that Stuart had incorporated into his own early furniture.

Vardy, however, had not studied classical specimens first-hand in Rome but rather drew his forms and ornaments from illustrated books and engravings, many dating to the Renaissance. His designs show a considerable knowledge of Greco-Roman prototypes. His sideboard for the dining room at Spencer House (fig. 10-14), for example, is based on a Renaissance study of such specimens as a design for a basin from the school of Andrea Mantegna (fig. 10-15). It looks back to a table with griffin monopodia and a large central mask.[19] The lion monopodium, mask of Bacchus, anthemion-and-palmette frieze, and trailing grape vines are all classical references that reappear in Stuart's early furniture. A shared engraved source may be at work here, but more likely Stuart was influenced by Vardy's furniture designs.

Other Vardy works show an understanding of con-

423

Fig. 10-15. School of Andrea Mantegna. Design for a fountain, 2nd half of the 15th century. Pen and ink, color wash. By courtesy of the Trustees of the British Museum, London, 1910-2-12-32, Italian Roy XV.

temporary French rococo style, particularly certain seat furniture that must have influenced Stuart's creations for the Painted Room and great room at Spencer House. The gilded suite of seat furniture Vardy originated for the Palm Room (about 1758) is an adaptation of French rococo furniture (fig. 10-16).[20] The suite's serpentine outlines, carved with scrolling acanthus, the cartouche-shaped backs of the chairs with central foliate motif, their cabriole legs and setback, and open, scrolled arm support, all point to French sources or prototypes. The production of the suite has been attributed to John Gordon, who later executed furniture for Stuart at Spencer House.[21] A Vardy drawing of a writing table and *cartonnier* from about 1745 reveals that despite his Palladian and Greco-Roman sources, he also studied French rococo furniture early in his career (fig. 10-17). The drawing is of Richard Arundale's *bureau plat* by Bernard von Riesenberg, which was at Temple Newsham, Yorkshire, by 1746.[22]

Before Stuart embarked on the Spencer House proj-

ect, he had created neoclassical furniture for Earl Spencer's country villa, Wimbledon House, Surrey, in about 1757. These, Stuart's earliest executed designs, were in the same neoclassical style as his Kedleston proposals. Unfortunately, Wimbledon House was gutted by fire in 1785, and all that remains of Stuart's furniture designs are two drawings for the decoration of the hall and great dining room (see figs. 6-41, 6-42), and a further two for Lady Spencer's small painted closet with a coved ceiling and putti holding garlands above the frieze (see fig. 6-44).

One drawing shows an architectural-style cabinet (see fig. 6-44), with long bottom drawers, a middle storage section, and half the compartment for books. It has a carved cornice with Corinthian columns at the ends and a plinth base. The Greek scroll frieze matched the surbase and the frieze of the room's decoration, and the plinth base complemented the molded skirting board of the wall. This cabinet was essentially horizontal, its low proportions offset by the display of a series of classical-style vases on

Fig. 10-16. John Vardy. Armchair for the Palm Room, Spencer House, ca. 1758. Probably made by John Gordon of Gordon and Taitt. Carved and gilt wood. Private collection.

Fig. 10-17. John Vardy. Drawing of a *bureau plat* and *cartonnier* (designed by Bernard von Riesenberg), ca. 1745. Pen and ink. RIBA Library Drawings Collection, London, SD 41/5(1).

its cornice. About three years later Stuart reused this formula for an architectural cabinet at Spencer House (see fig. 10-60).

A second drawing from this same commission reveals that a large hallway settee was part of the same scheme (see fig. 6-1). It stood in front of an arched recess with a semicircular window above an oil painting. An ancient couch with a scrolled-over arm and turned legs was the prototype for Stuart's design. Such couches had been developed just before 400 B.C. and were part of many Roman bas-reliefs.[23] A backless couch with curved arms and heavily turned legs, for example, can be seen in a Roman relief from Constantinople from the second or third century A.D. and on the cover of a sarcophagus now in the Vatican Museum (fig. 10-18).[24] Seventeenth- and eighteenth-century antiquaries, such as the painter Pietro Santi Bartoli and the Benedictine monk Bernard de Montfaucon, illustrated such couches in publications that were reprinted all through the eighteenth century. Stuart owned a copy of Santi Bartoli's *Admiranda Romanarum*

antiquitatium of 1693,[25] which includes an engraving of an ancient couch with roll-over arms that was probably the prototype for Stuart's settee (fig. 10-19). The Stuart settee differs from its ancient prototypes, however, in that it is upholstered with a pink fabric tacked to the frame, whereas loose covers, hangings, and pillows were used on Roman specimens.[26]

Two contemporary descriptions shed light on the surviving drawings. In 1759 Thomas Hollis recorded in his diary entry for September 3 that he "dined at Wimbleton. Saw Mrs. Spencer's closet painted in grotesque by Stuart; With the Figures of The Allegro and Penser[oso] after the divine Milton. Stuart's ideas very fine, his execution indifferent."[27] Horace Walpole also found Stuart's closet unremarkable when he visited Wimbledon in about 1758, commenting on "a closet ornamented and painted by Mr Stewart, the ornaments in a good antique taste. Hymen, the Allegro & Penseroso, on the ceiling and in compartments, villainously painted."[28]

Lord Spencer's continuing taste for neoclassical dec-

426

oration and furnishings was evident in Stuart's most important interior commission, the main rooms for Spencer's new London town house, Spencer House on St. James's Place, overlooking Green Park (see fig. 5-3). The interiors reflected the advanced taste of its owner as well as its architect. In a letter to noted collector Sir William Hamilton in 1765, Lord Spencer described himself as not having lost the "taste he had acquired in Italy for vertu" during visits to the great ancient sites and collections of Italy.[29] The house was begun in 1755 to the designs of John Vardy, and Stuart was hired in 1758 to decorate the first-floor apartments, a task that took eight years to complete.

In order to give his interiors at Spencer House a neoclassical flavor, Stuart designed a number of tripod pedestals. This form, one of Stuart's most overtly antique adaptations, became a most popular element of neoclassical interiors in both England and France, and Stuart played a part in its popularization. Both Robert Adam and James Wyatt adopted the form in their work—Adam by 1767, Wyatt by 1775.[30] However, such tripods had been a feature of French interior design since the reign of Louis XIV. By 1709, for example, the sculptor François Girardon had published an engraving that included an antique-style, gilt-wood and bronze tripod, similar to those designed by Stuart. (see fig 11-9).[31] Stuart designed a pair of seven-foot gilt-wood tripod pedestals, or torchères (fig. 10-20, now in the Saloon at Althorp), to stand between the Corin-

Fig. 10-18. A backless couch on the cover of a sarcophagus, part of the monument of the Haterii, 2nd to 3rd century A.D. Marble. The Vatican Museum, Helbig, F.3 no. 1192, Helbig F.4-Speier no. 1075.

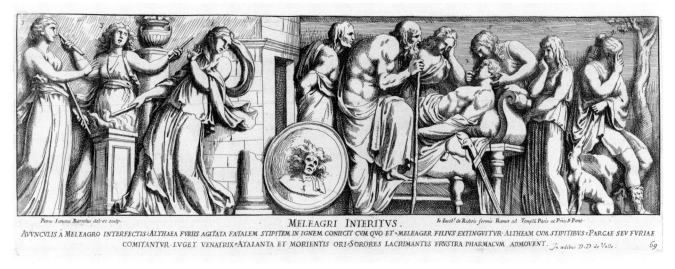

Fig. 10-19. A backless couch on a Roman relief depicting the burial of Meleager. Engraving. From Pietro Santi Bartoli, *Admiranda Romanarum antiquitatum . . .* (1693): pl. 69. Courtesy of the Trustees of The Victoria and Albert Museum, London, National Art Library, 86.J.25.

Fig. 10-20. James Stuart. Torchère (one of a pair) from the Painted Room, Spencer House, 1759–66. Carved and gilt-wood pedestal, painted sides, ormolu candlestand with marble base. Now in the saloon at Althorp, Northampton. Photographed in 2006. The Althorp Collection.

Fig. 10-21. James Stuart. The Painted Room, Spencer House, 1759–66, with the torchères standing between columns and side walls. Photographed in 1926. ©Country Life Picture Library.

NVPTIALE FESTVM
FRONDE VIRENT POSTES ET FERVENT COMPITA FLAMMIS SERTA FERVNT Statius Epit Stella, In Nuptijs ac festis diebus serta
arborumq, rami præ foribus affigebantur.   Martian. Capella. Claudian.'   Petrus Sanc.' Bartol.' del. Sculp.   Io. Iacobi de Rubeis Romæ ad Temp. Pacis cü Priu. S. Pont .   BACCHA   64
In Hortis Burghesiis

Fig. 10-22. "Nupitale Festum" with dancers to either side of a Roman candelabrum. Engraving after the Borghese bas relief (now in the Musée du Louvre, Paris). From Pietro Santi Bartoli, *Admiranda Romanarum antiquitatum . . .* (1693): pl. 64. Courtesy of the Trustees of The Victoria and Albert Museum, London, National Art Library, 86.J.25.

Roman candelabrum, such as one illustrated in Santi Bartoli's *Admiranda Romanarum* (fig. 10-22). The pedestals are painted with winged figures of Victory on a maroon background, depicted in the same colors as the background panels of the room's ceiling. The ancient painted figures were derived from late Roman wall frescoes, such as those from the House of the Dancing Faun at Herculaneum, which Stuart may have seen on his visit to the ruins or in one of the illustrated books available at that time.[32] At the time of Stuart's death, *Pictures of Herculaneum* was listed among the volumes in his library.[33] Griffins were associated with fire in classical mythology and thus were a particularly fitting subject for torchères.[34] Anthemion ornaments and other motifs derived from ancient architectural ornament are seen on the tripods. In a departure, however, Stuart incorporated three inward-turned scrolls of baroque form to support the base of the torchère. The incorporation of these scrolls lightened the ancient tripod form by lifting it off the ground and endowing it with a more graceful, less stony appearance. The torchères were probably executed by the bronze caster Diederich Nicolaus Anderson, who worked on other bronze commissions with Stuart (see chap. 11).

Stuart designed another pair of gilt-wood tripods for Spencer House in 1760. A photograph of 1926 indicates that at that time they each supported a candelabrum and stood on the intermediate and first-floor landings of the staircase hall (fig. 10-23).[35] An earlier photograph indicates that a third example stood in Lady Spencer's dressing room (fig. 10-24).[36] Today they are at Althorp, divided between the picture gallery (fig. 10-25), a room on the second floor, and the chapel. These were based on a marble Roman altar stand from Hadrian's Villa that was in the Church of Santa Maria della Stella in Albano in the eighteenth century (later moved to the Vatican Museum).[37] Piranesi illustrated the ancient tripod in 1764 in *Antichità d'Albano et di Castel Gondolfo* (fig. 10-26).[38] A comparison with the original altar stand indicates a great many similarities: lion's-paw feet, the drums on top with Greek-key motif, bead-and-reel moldings, and incurvate form.

These tripods corresponded to the classical ornament of the walls of the staircase, which Stuart decorated with Greek Ionic pilasters surmounted by a palmette frieze (see fig. 5-14). The frieze derived from the Temple on the Ilissus River illustrated in Stuart and Revett's *Antiquities of Athens* (fig. 10-27).[39] Stuart also inserted a palmette on top of the pilaster leg of the tripod to match the palmette

Fig. 10-23. James Stuart. A gilt-wood tripod, 1759–66, on the intermediate landing of the staircase hall at Spencer House. Photographed in 1926. ©Country Life Picture Library.

thian columns and the side walls of the Painted Room in 1759 (fig. 10-21). Stuart had already experimented with the tripod form in his designs for metal stands (see figs. 11-1, 6-30, 6-31) and wall treatments at Kedleston Hall in 1756 (see figs. 6-32, 6-33).

The Painted Room torchères are composed of three archaeologically inspired elements: the bronze candelabra of nine lights derived from Stuart's conjectural reconstruction of the tripod on the summit of the Choragic Monument of Lysicrates in Athens (see fig. 10-29); a tripod of griffins with a white marble top (also triangular) based on a Roman marble tripod with the three griffins in the Capitoline Museum, Rome (see fig. 10-6); and an incurved triangular pedestal derived from the bases of

Fig. 10-24. James Stuart. Lady Spencer's dressing room, Spencer House, 1758–66, with a gilt-wood tripod on one side of the doorway and carved and gilt-wood chairs from the great room on the other. Photographed ca. 1890. English Heritage / National Monuments Record, Newton 1012 DD54/275.

frieze of the staircase hall, and he added a lantern in classical taste. Today, this hexagonal lantern hangs in the Wooton Hall at Althorp (fig. 10-28). Its triangular wooden capital was adapted from the central capital atop the roof of the ancient Choragic Monument of Lysicrates (fig. 10-29). This selection of ornament was fitting because in ancient times the capital supported a flaming torch; its use by Stuart was a play on the idea of fire and light.[40] The lantern's uprights are composed of foliage and fruit, identical to the gilt-wood strips that Stuart used instead of braid or cord to conceal the ends of the damask and the nails in the drawing rooms of the first floor.[41] The uprights terminate in large scrolls supporting the six uprights on

both the hexagonal cover and the base of the lantern. A frieze of open arabesques sets off the cover and base, and a five-branch candelabra sits within its center.

Marble thrones of antiquity with their winged-animal side terminals provided the starting point for Stuart's gilt-wood sofas and matching armchairs for the Painted Room at Spencer House from about 1764. The classically inspired rich carving and monumental lion supports add a touch of drama, if not the theatrical. Contemporary traveler Arthur Young described the room as a "phoenix" in his account of it in 1769.[42] Almost a century and a half later, another visitor, the Edwardian topographer Edwin Beresford Chancellor, felt that he had stepped back two

Fig. 10-25. James Stuart. Tripod stand from Spencer House, 1759–66, with an ormolu tripod candelabra also designed by Stuart. Gilt wood. Now in the Picture Gallery at Althorp, Northampton. Photographed in 2006. The Althorp Collection.

Fig. 10-26. Roman marble altar stand from Hadrian's Villa (now in the Vatican Museum). Engraving. From Giovanni Battista Piranesi, *Antichita d'Albano e di Castel Gondolfo . . .* , vol. 11 of [Opere / di Giambattista Piranesi] (1764; reprint 1835–37): pl. 8. Courtesy of the Trustees of The Victoria and Albert Museum, London, National Art Library, 110.M.15.

432

Fig. 10-27. The anthemion frieze from the Temple on the Ilissus River. Engraving. From *Antiquities of Athens*, vol. 1 (1762): chap. 2, pl. VIII (detail). Courtesy of the Library, The Bard Graduate Center for Studies in the Decorative Arts, Design, and Culture, New York. *Checklist no. 36.*

Fig. 10-28. James Stuart. Staircase lantern from Spencer House, 1759–66. Ormolu frame with gilt-wood capital. Now in Wooton Hall at Althorp, Northampton. Photographed in 2006. The Althorp Collection.

Fig. 10-29. "The flower on top of the Tholus or cupola, Choragic Monument of Lysicrates." Engraving. From *Antiquities of Athens*, vol. 1 (1762): chap. 4, pl. IX. Courtesy of the Library, The Bard Graduate Center for Studies in the Decorative Arts, Design, and Culture, New York. *Checklist no. 36.*

433

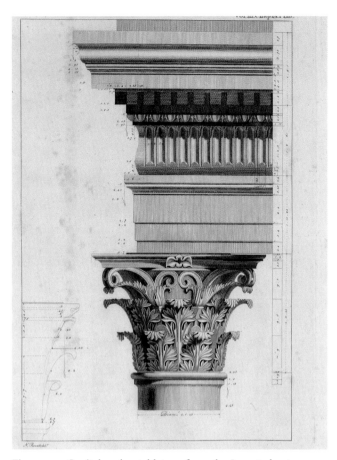

Fig. 10-30. Capital and entablature from the Incantada at Salonica. Engraving. From *Antiquities of Athens,* vol. 3 (1794) chap. 9, pl. III. Courtesy of the Library, The Bard Graduate Center for Studies in the Decorative Arts, Design, and Culture, New York. *Checklist no. 90.*

thousand years when he entered the room in 1908, commenting that "we are no longer in a London reception-room; we are in the *tablinium* in the house of Marcus Lucretius, or in one of the remarkable painted chambers in the dwelling of Meleager; that red light in the sky is not the sun setting over the trees of the Green Park, but the afterglow of some great eruption of Vesuvius! If a door open, surely Glaucus or Diomed or the blind Nydia will appear! It is truly a room in which to dream of the past."[43]

For the six massive gilt-wood armchairs (see fig. 10-1), Stuart employed a large-scale, carved guilloche border and a heavily fluted seat frame derived from ancient architectural motifs. The flutes on the seat rail correspond to those on the door architraves, which derived from the architrave of the frieze of a ruin at Salonica called the Incantada. Stuart studied this monument in the early 1750s, when he was preparing drawings for *Antiquities of Athens* (fig. 10-30). The armrest supports are carved with husks and are in the form of a foliated scroll, like the volute of an Ionic capital found in the same frieze at Salonica. The frames are mounted on lion's legs in a cornerstone position that turn out to complement their serpentine outline.

Animal-leg supports were a basic element of ancient seating forms starting with the Egyptians. Both the Greeks and Romans used them, particularly lion's legs.[44] The massive muscled lion's-leg supports adapted by Stuart are naturalistic in treatment, with furry locks at their upper legs.

Fig. 10-31. Domenico Cunego, after Gavin Hamilton. *Andromache Bewailing the Death of Hector,* 1764. Engraving (Hamilton original, ca. 1761). Fine Arts Museums of San Francisco, Achenbach Foundation for Graphic Arts, 1963.30.37579.

Fig. 10-32. James Stuart. Settee (with curved back) from the Painted Room, Spencer House, 1759–66. Probably carved by Thomas Vardy. Carved and gilt limewood, silk damask upholstery (not original). Courtesy of Spencer House and the Trustees of The Victoria and Albert Museum, London, W.3-1977. *Checklist no. 121.*

Fig. 10-33. James Stuart. Settee (with straight back) from the Painted Room, Spencer House, 1759–66. Probably carved by Thomas Vardy. Carved and gilt limewood, silk damask upholstery (not original). Courtesy of Spencer House and the Trustees of The Victoria and Albert Museum, London, W.1-1977.

Fig. 10-34. Vignette of a lion-flanked throne. Engraving. From *Antiquities of Athens*, vol. 1 (1762): viii, preface tailpiece. Courtesy of the Library, The Bard Graduate Center for Studies in the Decorative Arts, Design, and Culture, New York. *Checklist no. 36.*

Fig. 10-35. James Stuart "Ancient Chair . . . in the Church and Monastery of Mons Kalogeia," ca. 1751–53. Pen and ink. By permission of The British Library, London, Add. Ms. 22,153, fol. 100.

It is believed that this suite is similar to pieces used as props by Gavin Hamilton, Stuart's intimate in Rome, in paintings such as *Andromache Bewailing the Death of Hector,* which was exhibited at the Society of Arts in 1762 but probably had been created a few years earlier (fig. 10-31).[45] They also appear in *Sweet Melancholy (La Douce Melancolie)* of 1756 by Joseph-Marie Vien, one of the Académie de France *pensionnaires* in Rome.[46] A closer prototype, however, is Vardy's sideboard for the dining room with its seated winged-lion supports (see fig. 10-14).

The classical elements of these seating forms are counterbalanced by French Louis XV elements. Their basic shape is French rococo, with a cartouche-shaped splat, serpentine seat rail, square decoration at the angles of the seat rail, and set-back curvilinear armrest support that does not rest on the front legs. Another French feature is the removable padded back that is released from the frame by means of a plunger at the bottom of the back.[47] The back *à chassis* was definitely a French invention. English chairmakers preferred two small catch-plates, which swing into fitted slots at the top of the splat. John Gordon was probably responsible for the frames of the chairs.[48] The original upholstery was green silk damask with brass tacks to match the walls of the room, but in 1772 the firm of Gordon and Taitt provided loose, crimson covers.[49]

The four sofas that accompany the chairs were designed to fit the contours of the Painted Room. Two settees had curved backs that echoed the curved window bays in the apsed bay where they stood (fig. 10-32). The other two, larger in scale, were designed to fit on either side of the window opposite the chimneypiece (fig. 10-33) and under the gilded pier glasses. Rococo in outline, they are reminiscent in form of a Louis XV *canapé.*[50] This arrangement of sofas ensured that the heavily carved lions on the sides of each of the four sofas were seen to best advantage when a visitor entered the room. The winged lions have been attributed to the carver Thomas Vardy, who worked at Spencer House for his brother John Vardy as well as for Stuart.[51] They were probably derived from a type of ancient marble throne,[52] such as that in the Arundel Collection of marbles at Oxford (see fig. 10-4), or one of the many lion-flanked marble thrones that Stuart probably saw during his trip to Italy, including some in Roman collections and churches. While in Greece Stuart had recorded a large-scale lion from the frieze of the Choragic Monument of Lysicrates (see fig. 5-39). Another one

Fig. 10-36. Roman copy of a lion-flanked throne from the Acropolis, Athens, ca. 1st to 2nd century A.D. Marble. Photographed in 2006. Church of San Gregorio Magno, Rome.

served as a vignette in the same volume of *Antiquities of Athens* (fig. 10-34). Although the throne in the vignette has been identified as a front view of one that stood in the proneos of the Parthenon, a Stuart sketch of a chair identifies it as an "ancient chair in church and monastery of Mons Kasozeya" (fig. 10-35).[53] A Roman copy, one of three known, was in the Church of San Gregorio Magno in Rome (fig. 10-36). Another source, particularly for the head of the lion is traceable to Santi Bartoli's engraving of a relief of Bacchantes on a Roman sarcophagus in the Temple of Peace, Rome (fig. 10-37).

Like the armchairs, the seat rails of the sofas are heavily fluted in neoclassical style to correspond to those on the dado rail, and guilloche ornament runs around the backs of the sofas. The smaller curved settee has six legs, while the larger models have eight. The outer legs of the lion, which has outstretched wing and curling tail, form the curving arm support and thus provide the lion with a neck, meeting the frame with a mélange of locks of fur and an egg-and-dart molding that merges into an acanthus scroll. The seat rail meets the central lion leg with a square cube inset with a rosette in the French manner, as do the legs on the armchairs. This neoclassical suite is one of the first attempts to revive classical seat furniture in Western Europe and is so archaeologically correct that it

Fig. 10-37. Horn players and lion, detail from a relief of Bacchantes on a Roman sarcophagus in the Temple of Peace, Rome. Engraving. From Pietro Santi Bartoli, *Admiranda Romanarum antiquitatum . . .* (1693): pl. 47. Courtesy of the Trustees of The Victoria and Albert Museum, London, National Art Library, 86.J.25

Fig. 10-38. A lyre and tilted ewer flanking a bas relief of Bacchanalian dancers, after marble fragments on a wall in the ruins of the Theater of Bacchus. Engraving. From *Antiquities of Athens,* vol. 2 (ca. 1790): chap. 3, p. 23. Courtesy of the Library, The Bard Graduate Center for Studies in the Decorative Arts, Design, and Culture, New York. *Checklist no. 129.*

Fig. 10-39. James Stuart. Pier mirror with dentilled friezes in the Painted Room, Spencer House, 1759–66. Carved and gilt wood, glass. ©Spencer House Limited.

Fig. 10-40. James Stuart. The Music Room with pier table and mirror (right), Spencer House, 1758–66. Photographed in 1926. ©Country Life Picture Library. *Checklist no. 109.*

heralds what has been labeled "proto-Regency."[54]

The Painted Room's strongly neoclassical tables were also an important part of what Arthur Young called the room's "rich but elegant" tone and the unity of effect achieved therein. After a visit in 1769, he commented that "the frames of the tables, sofas, stands, etc. are all carved and gilt in the same taste as the other ornaments of the room."[55] Stuart probably designed guardian lions for the two marble-topped tables, which are only known from a drawing for one of the pair. They were to be placed on either side of the entrance door (the north wall). One of these tables, shown in a 1759 watercolor, now in the British Museum (see fig. 5-2), has tapered, fluted legs that end in paw feet with a band of three bosses above and below. They were derived from a type of marble table such

as the one at Delphi,[56] while the bosses refer to the metal ones used on ancient tables to connect the legs to the tops. Stuart sketched similar tapered lags from the sarcophagus at Scopolo (see fig. 9-7). A second drawing in the RIBA shows a similar table (see fig. 11-8). The stretcher was carved with a Greek fret design, and a ribboned wreath of vine leaves hung from in the center of the table, framing a round plaque in which a tilted ewer hung. The conceit of the tilted ewer was inspired by a relief embedded in a wall near the Theater of Bacchus that Stuart discovered during his visit to Athens and illustrated in *Antiquities* (fig. 10-38).[57] To complete the "antique" effect, a classical tripod stood on the table. Four gilded pier mirrors, with dentilled friezes to match the doorways, provided the room with increased light and the illusion of space. Two were

Fig. 10-41. James Stuart. Pier table from the Music Room, Spencer House, 1758–66. Gilt wood with marble top. Now separated from its mirror and in the Spencer Gallery at Althorp, Northampton. Photographed in 2006. The Althorp Collection.

placed on either side of the windows facing the chimney-piece, and two above the larger settees (fig. 10-39).

The great semicircular pier table with matching mirror, originally placed between the windows in the Music Room at Spencer House, was more of a synthesis of ancient, French rococo, neoclassical, and English Palladian sources (fig. 10-40). Stuart revived the Palladian practice of designing a pier table, with a long mirror of similar width that extended almost to the cornice, for the space between the windows.[58] This elegant white-and-gold pier table with its matching gilt-wood mirror is today at Althorp, the mirror in the Princess of Wales bedroom, the table in its anteroom (fig. 10-41). The wide rectangular lugged frame of the mirror glass has heavy cresting with oversized scrolling acanthus framed by addorsed cornucopia (fig. 10-42). This thematic arrangement of double-branching anthemia and addorsed cornucopia was derived

from a fragment of an ancient Roman architrave preserved at the Palazzo Mattei in Rome and illustrated in Piranesi's *Della Magnificenza ed Architecttura de Romani* (1761; fig. 10-43).[59] A heavy festoon hangs across the surface of the mirror, echoing the garlands strung across the width of the console table. The Greek wave carving on the table frieze matched the surbase of the dado of the room. The console has four square, fluted legs surmounted with square block capitals similar to those Stuart used on the gilded tripods on the staircase landing (see fig. 10-25). Instead of ending in paw feet, however, they tapered down to French peg feet.

Stuart probably borrowed the idea of the semicircular table from antique models. Although there are no actual Greek or Roman specimens, a well-known sarcophagus from Simpelveld in the Netherlands, now in the Rijksmuseum van Oudheden, Leiden, has a semicircular side table supported by three lion monopodia (fig. 10-44).[60] In addition, two silver cups from Berthouville in the Cabinet des Medailles of the Hellenistic period show a pier table supported by figures of a dancing nymph and satyr.[61] Greek and Roman side tables, such as that displayed on this cup, often held silver and gold plate.[62] The Stuart pier table for Spencer House was one of the first semicircular models to appear in the eighteenth century,[63] but the form soon became popular, as did the broader generic type of semicircular table that has remained an icon of refined taste of the second half of the eighteenth century.

Stuart used the same semicircular formula for a pair of pier tables he designed for the great hall at Hornby Castle, Yorkshire, for the fourth Earl of Holdernesse (see fig. 6-46) in the 1760s. The present location of these tables, last photographed in 1906, is not known.[64] Placed on either side of the central door, they were embellished with a heavily fluted frieze to match the fluted band of the chimneypiece and cornice. They were heavier in proportion and more archaeological in character than Stuart's other pier tables. Although they share triple fluted legs and a fluted frieze surmounted by a marble top, they also have lion's-paw feet, and a large-scale triple rosette on the apron sets off the leg forms. The state apartments at Holdernesse House, the London town house of the Earl of Holdernesse at 24 Hertford Street, had similar Stuart tables that appear in photographs of the 1930s and 1940s (fig. 10-45). These were en suite with a pair of massive gilt-wood tables decorated with a key-pattern frieze with acanthus moldings. Twelve fluted and tapered supports ended in paw feet, and the top was fitted with a white, grained marble slab (fig. 10-46).[65]

Fig. 10-42. James Stuart. Cornucopia mirror from the Music Room, Spencer House, 1758–66. Carved and gilt wood, mirror glass. Now in the Princess of Wales Bedroom at Althorp, Northampton. Photographed in 2006. The Althorp Collection.

Fig. 10-43. Roman architrave of cornucopia. Engraving (detail). From Giovanni Battista Piranesi, *Della Magnificenza ed Architecttura de Romani* (1761): pl. xvii. Courtesy of the Trustees of The Victoria and Albert Museum, London, National Art Library, 110.M.2.

Fig. 10-44. Semicircular table on three lion monopodia on the interior wall of a Roman sarcophagus (detail), ca. A.D. 175–225. Marble. Courtesy of the Rijksmuseum van Oudheden, Leiden, Netherlands, No. e1930/12.8.

Fig. 10-45. James Stuart. Pier table in the drawing room at Holdernesse House (later Londonderry House), Hertford Street, London, ca. 1765. Carved and gilt wood, marble top. Photographed in 1962. English Heritage / National Monuments Record AA62/7590.

Fig. 10-46. "End of the Ball Room," with Stuart's pier table, at Holdernesse House. From H. Montgomery Hyde, *Londonderry House and Its Pictures* (1937): pl. IX. Courtesy of the Library, The Bard Graduate Center for Studies in the Decorative Arts, Design, and Culture, New York.

Fig. 10-47. James Stuart. The great room at Spencer House, 1758–64. Photographed in 1895. English Heritage / National Monuments Record BL13187; BB91/660.

Stuart designed two additional gilt-wood console tables with matching mirrors for the great room at Spencer House (fig. 10-47), now both in the great room at Althorp (figs. 10-48, 10-49). The friezes were heavily fluted to match the surbase molding of the great room. Each table has six, square tapering legs, triply fluted, with square block capitals carved with rosettes. The legs terminate in shaped peg feet, and the stretchers are carved with a guilloche enclosing flowers. Heavy floral garlands composed of roses, berries, and pinecones hung from rosettes on the frieze, and a large female mask decorated the cen-

ter of the table. Although the floral garlands and mask have been seen as reverting to Palladian decorative forms,[66] they are in fact derived from ancient sources, while the heavy swags centered by masks can be found in a Piranesi drawing of the marble tripod altar in the Vatican. The verde antique marble slab tops ordered by Stuart's former associate Gavin Hamilton from Domenico de Angelis shop in the Piazza di Spagna took four years to arrive.[67] They have since been replaced.

The large matching mirrors, rectangular in outline, are framed by a fluted surround that relates to the table's

Fig. 10-48. James Stuart. Pier table from the great room, Spencer House, 1759–66. Carved and gilt wood with verd antique marble. Now in the great room at Althorp, Northampton. Photographed in 2006. The Althorp Collection.

Fig. 10-49. James Stuart. Pier table and mirror from the great room, Spencer House, 1759–66. Carved and gilt wood, marble top. Now in the great room at Althorp, Northampton. Photographed in 2006. The Althorp Collection.

fluted frieze (fig. 10-50). Stuart had used a similar frame format, with eared ends with fleurons in his design for the great dining room, Wimbledon House, Surrey (see fig. 6-42). Two putti standing in a chariot drawn by a griffin surmount the frame. The theme of putti charioteers derives from Roman art and literature. Stuart's pier glass cresting may also have an ancient source: a Roman relief sarcophagus, formerly in the Palazzo Giustiniani, Rome, and illustrated in *Dal Pozzo-Albani Collection of Drawings After the Antique* (fig. 10-51).[68] Contemporary traveler Arthur Young described the console tables and mirrors as sitting between the windows with "two slabs very large, of the finest Siena marble, the frames carved in the most exquisite taste and richly gilt. The pier-glasses of a large size, single plates and the frames of the lightest workmanship."[69]

Young also remarked upon the fine carving and gilding of the sofa frames for the suite of white-and-gold seat furniture attributed to Stuart, in the great room at Spencer House.[70] Twenty-six framed armchairs (see fig. 10-47), eighteen side chairs, and four sofas of similar form complemented the room's architectural features and its white and gold scheme (fig. 10-52). Part of a related suite of chairs with a sofa and stools is today at Althorp.[71] These chairs with their distinctive cupid's-bow seat rails were supplied by John Gordon, who is believed to have been responsible for the suite in the Painted Room.[72] Gordon also supplied similar armchairs to the Duke of Atholl at Blair Castle in Perthshire, Scotland, in the late 1740s or 1750s.[73] This same model was designed by Stuart for the first Earl Harcourt for Nuneham Park in about 1760 (see fig. 6-19).[74] In the French rococo taste, with serpentine outline, waisted splats, outward-turned whorl feet, and set-back armrests, the chairs also have removable seat pads, like the monumental chairs from the Painted Room. Their rococo form is tempered with neoclassical details, such as the

Fig. 10-50. James Stuart. Mirror from the great room, Spencer House, 1759–66. Carved and gilt wood, mirror glass. Now in the great room at Althorp, Northampton. Photographed in 2006. The Althorp Collection.

Fig. 10-51. Drawing of a Roman sarcophagus with a relief of putti charioteers. From *The Dal Pozzo-Albani Collection of Drawings after the Antique*, vol. 8 [A47/162]. Courtesy of the Royal Library, Windsor Castle, RL8766.

Fig. 10-52. James Stuart. Chairs from the great room, Spencer House, 1759–66. Probably made by John Gordon of Gordon and Taitt. Carved and gilt limewood and Honduran mahogany, silk upholstery (not original). Private collection.

Fig. 10-53. James Stuart. Chest, from Spencer House, 1759–66. Mahogany, satinwood inlay, gilt-bronze moldings. Now in private rooms at Althorp, Northampton. Photographed in 2006. The Althorp Collection.

Fig. 10-54. Asteas from Paestum. Red-figure kalyx krater, ca. 345 B.C. Terracotta. Staatliche Museen zu Berlin, F3044.

Fig. 10-55. James Stuart. Bedside night cupboard of pedestal form from Spencer House, 1759–66. Mahogany, boxwood patera. Now in storage at Althorp, Northampton. Photographed in 2006. The Althorp Collection.

Fig. 10-56. James Stuart. Bedside cupboard from Spencer House, 1759–66. Mahogany, satinwood inlay, gilt bronze fittings. Now in the Princess of Wales Bedroom at Althorp, Northampton. Photographed in 2006. The Althorp Collection.

Fig. 10-57. Detail of the roof cresting of the Choragic Monument of Lysicrates. From *Antiquities of Athens*, vol. 1. (1762): chap. 4, pl. VIII. Courtesy of the Library, The Bard Graduate Center for Studies in the Decorative Arts, Design, and Culture, New York. *Checklist no. 36.*

fluting on the rail, the carved palmette decoration and acanthus leaves on the arms, and husk on the splat, that relate to the general decorative scheme of the great room.

A photograph of about 1890 (see fig. 10-24) shows two related white-and-gold painted chairs on either side of the doorway in Lady Spencer's dressing room, which adjoined the great room and served as an extension during large gatherings.[75] The figured crimson silk damask that was used on the chairs also covered the walls. A carved decoration of palmettes matched the dressing room frieze which had been inspired by the Erectheion in Athens illustrated in *Antiquities of Athens* (see fig. 5-62).[76]

Other pieces of furniture designed by Stuart for Lady Spencer's bedroom survive today in the private chambers of Lord Spencer at Althorp. There is an oblong mahogany chest (fig. 10-53) with flat hinged top inlaid with a Greek-key pattern and rosette designs in satinwood. It also has ormolu beaded moldings and gilt-bronze side handles with masks. An ancient chest, or *cista,* derived from representations on Greek vases or architectural reliefs, probably provided the model.[77] The chest depicted on a kalyx krater of about 345 B.C. signed by Asteas from Paestum (fig. 10-54), or the chest upon which two figures are seated from the relief on the east pediment of the Parthenon, are but two examples.[78]

Stuart chose to use materials that were fashionable at the time, but when it came to the structure of the pieces

there was less compromise. He could have adapted the chest form to a more conventional contemporary mode of garment storage, particularly the chest of drawers. He chose instead to adhere to the ancient prototype, and it is this that marks the piece as more archaeologically correct than other contemporary cabinet pieces in the neoclassical style. The chest also served to evoke a strong sense of the ancient world through its composition. The circular feet with fluted decoration were a French neoclassical addition that raised the rectangular form above the ground and gave some height to what otherwise would have been a very low model of furniture.

Another component of this suite, the small mahogany bedside cupboard of pedestal form with hidden door and boxwood paterae (now also in the private chambers of Lord Spencer at Althorp) is designed in a sober architectural style (fig. 10-55). For this columned piece Stuart adopted the round form of a temple. This cupboard was the prototype for a series of night tables of pedestal form over the next forty years. A second mahogany bedside cupboard from this suite is not as successful aesthetically nor as evocative of the ancient world because Stuart added neoclassical motifs to what was basically a Georgian cabinet (fig. 10-56). Those motifs—the small acroteria at the corners of the cupboard, illustrated on the cornice of the Choragic Monument of Lysicrates shown in *Antiquities of Athens* (fig. 10-57)—and the fact that the cupboard is part

Fig. 10-58. James Stuart. Washstand table from Lady Spencer's bedroom, Spencer House, 1759–66. Mahogany, inlaid with padouk and boxwood. Courtesy of Spencer House and the Trustees of The Victoria and Albert Museum, London, W.31-1979. *Checklist no. 115.*

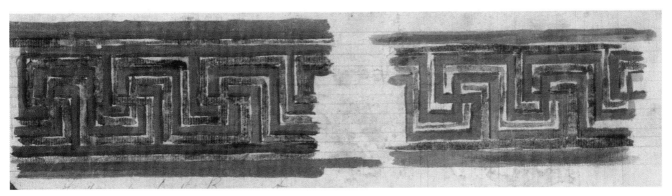

Fig. 10-59. James Stuart. Sketch of a Greek key band for a ceiling beam, ca. 1760. Color wash, pencil. RIBA Library Drawings Collection, London, SD 62/18. *Checklist no. 116.*

of a suite are the only justifications for it being considered neoclassical.

This suite also included a pair of mahogany washstand tables, one of which is now in the Victoria and Albert Museum, London (fig. 10-58). The tops of these are inlaid with the same Greek-key pattern in satinwood. The frieze is carved with fluting, rosettes, beading, and a leaf molding. This combination of running motifs was derived from the entablature of the Temple of Concord, Rome (see fig. 5-37). Stuart sketched a similar design for decoration of

a ceiling beam (fig. 10-59). The washstand's circular, fluted tapering legs are carved with egg-and-dart pattern.

Not all of Stuart's designs for furniture derived their features from ancient decoration. His cabinet furniture was often closer to earlier Georgian examples, such as the Palladian works of William Kent or the sober cabinetwork of the later Georgians. In several instances Stuart grafted Greek-derived ornament onto Georgian forms. For example, a large mahogany wardrobe from the private apartment of Lady Spencer at Spencer House (fig. 10-60)

Fig. 10-60. James Stuart. Wardrobe from Spencer House, 1759–66. Mahogany, inlaid with padouk and boxwood, gilt bronze handles. Now in private rooms at Althorp, Northampton. Photographed in 2006. The Althorp Collection.

is close to the architectural style of William Kent of about 1730. Designed with a long drawer below, it is inlaid with Greek key ornament in satinwood and has fluted Corinthian colonettes at the angles. Comparison with a carved and painted pinewood bookcase designed in the style of Kent (fig. 10-61) reveals that its basic form is quite similar except for the arched heads and broken pediment.[79] Carved architectural ornament is abundant on both models, but the Stuart ornament is smaller in detail. The Stuart cabinet's frieze is carved with rosettes and ribbons, with honeysuckle decoration between them. The cornice is carved with classical architectural running motifs such as egg-and-dart pattern, flutes, and honeysuckle.

Fig. 10-61. After William Kent. Bookcase, ca. 1730–40. Carved and painted pine. Courtesy of the Trustees of The Victoria and Albert Museum, London, W2-1923.

Fig. 10-62. James Stuart. Wardrobe from Spencer House, 1759–66. Mahogany. Now in the Princess of Wales Bedroom at Althorp, Northampton. Photographed in 2006. The Althorp Collection.

A second mahogany wardrobe from this suite is close to a type of mahogany bookcase—with center section projecting forward of two wings—that was popular in mid-eighteenth-century England (fig. 10-62). Stuart simply added Grecian architectural ornament to make the piece part of the neoclassical trend. A prominent Vitruvian scroll band becomes a cornice on the central section and a Greek-key pattern forms the cresting of the side wings of the cupboard. A fluted frieze adorns the midsection and the band beneath the cornice. An egg-and-dart running motif enriches the lower panel doors.

Fig. 10-63. The Saloon, Buckingham House, London. Hand-colored aquatint by W. J. Bennett, after a drawing by J. P. Stephanoff. From W. H. Pyne, *The History of Royal Residences . . .* , vol. 2 (1819): opp. p. 13. By Permission of the British Library, London, 747.f.3.74.

Royal Commissions

Stuart probably had some royal commissions in the 1760s that kept him in the public eye. In addition to the coved ceiling of the Saloon at Buckingham House (see fig. 5-99), he designed a new throne chair for Queen Charlotte at St. James's Palace. In a diary entry, the Duchess of Northumberland described seeing it at the palace on the day before Charlotte's wedding to George III on September 27, 1761: "To see the Queen's chair which is equally fine and beautiful, the Design of it was given by Stewart Architect. It is of scarlet Velvet. Almost cover'd with Gilt Ornaments in an Exquisite taste."[80] Thomas Hollis also wrote about the Stuart throne in his

diary on September 17, 1761. He recollected seeing it the week before the wedding at the workplace of the metal-chaser Diederich Nicolaus Anderson, who completed many of Stuart's finest commissions: "At Mr Anderson's, caster in brass, to see a curious State Chair for the Queen after a design of Mr Stuart's. Met Mr Stuart at Mr Anderson's and was greatly pleased with the chair."[81]

The exact chair to which the Duchess of Northumberland and Hollis were referring is not known, but it has been suggested that this was the same chair transferred from St. James's Palace to the Saloon at Buckingham House for Queen Charlotte's use at the start

Fig. 10-64. James Stuart. Organ case, Newby Hall, Yorkshire, ca. 1767. Mahogany case, oil gilt lead and tin pipes. Photographed in 2006. Courtesy of Mr. Richard Compton, Newby Hall Estate. *Checklist no. 71.*

of the Regency in 1811.[82] This elaborate chair with its scrolled legs and lion finials no longer survives, but it is reproduced under a canopy in W. H. Pyne's *History of Royal Residences* (fig. 10-63).[83] A red morocco sedan chair with elaborate neoclassical metal ornaments made for Queen Charlotte in 1763 and worked on by Anderson may also be by Stuart's hand (see fig. 4-7).[84]

Newby Hall, Yorkshire

Stuart gained few commissions for interiors in the 1760s comparable in size and importance to that for Spencer House and no further royal commissions. For William Weddell, for example, he designed an elaborate mahogany organ case (fig. 10-64), with massive Ionic columns and a gilded apsidal central panel in the form of an inverted shell, for the Doric Hall of Newby Hall, Yorkshire.[85] Organs were prominent features of luxurious high-style interiors in eighteenth-century England. That Thomas Chippendale, John Linnell, James Wyatt, and Robert Adam all designed them indicates the increasing status of an instrument that owed its popularity to the sensation of Handel's organ concertos beginning in the 1730s.[86] Although Adam designed the majority of the furnishings for Newby Hall, the organ is attributed to Stuart because its strong architectural flavor, Greek-key band, and tripod ornaments are typical of his design vocabulary.[87] The paired pilasters flanking free-standing Ionic columns are also indicative; they are the same as those in a Stuart design for a chimneypiece, now in the RIBA Library Drawings Collection (fig. 10-65).[88] The triumphal-arch motif on the

Fig. 10-65. James Stuart. Design for a chimneypiece, ca. 1766. Pencil, pen and ink, gray wash. RIBA Library Drawings Collection, London, SD 62/17. *Checklist no. 72.*

Fig. 10-66. James Stuart. Medallion on the Newby Hall organ case (top right). Photographed in 2006. Courtesy of Mr. Richard Compton, Newby Hall Estate. *Checklist no. 71.*

Fig. 10-67. James Stuart. Medallion in the staircase anteroom, Rathfarnham Castle, County Dublin, Eire, ca. 1769. Plaster. Courtesy of OPW, Dublin, and Rathfarnham Castle.

Fig. 10-68. James Stuart. Medallion on the Newby Hall organ case (top left). Photographed in 2006. Courtesy of Mr. Richard Compton, Newby Hall Estate. *Checklist no. 71.*

Fig. 10-69. James Stuart. Medallion in the staircase anteroom, Rathfarnham Castle, ca. 1769. Plaster. Courtesy of OPW, Dublin, and Rathfarnham Castle.

Fig. 10-70. Giovanni Battista Piranesi. Tripod now in the sculpture gallery at Newby Hall, ca. 1765. Marble. Courtesy of Mr. Richard Compton, Newby Hall Estate.

organ's top half is reminiscent of Stuart's screens at Holdernesse House and Montague House,[89] and the medallion (top right, fig. 10-66) is virtually identical to that above the door to the great room in Spencer House (see fig. 5-34) and another in the staircase landing at Rathfarnam Castle (figs. 10-67).[90] The other medallion on the organ (top left, fig. 10-68) is also in the Rathfarnam staircase landing (fig. 10-69) and is nearly identical to the plaque at the center of a marble mantelpiece designed by Stuart for Lady Spencer's bedroom in Spencer House (see fig. 5-26). The swags and garlands of foliage on the mantelpiece also appear on the organ. The ornamental tripods between the pilasters on the bottom half of the organ are derived from a marble tripod that Weddell bought from Piranesi and which is still in the sculpture gallery at Newby Hall (fig. 10-70).[91] The central raised plinth at the top of the organ once had a classical grouping of "a lion with a cupid seated on his back, playing upon a lyre; the harmony of which seems to divest the royal beast of his natural ferocity."[92] The organ's lack of a base may be accounted for by the need to accommodate this large-scale grouping.

Shugborough, Staffordshire

Stuart also designed neoclassical interiors and furnishings for Shugborough, Staffordshire, for Thomas Anson in about 1763. A record of payment among the Lichfield papers indicates that two tables and two gilt tripod stands were designed by Stuart.[93] These pieces are now in the Red Drawing Room designed by architect Samuel Wyatt in 1794 (fig. 10-71).[94] The white-and-gold rectangular console tables located against the pier walls have a bold fluted frieze and straight triple-fluted legs with block capitals, rosettes, and round ball feet (fig. 10-72). A guilloche-patterned stretcher enclosing a floral ornament, joins the six legs. An egg-and-dart molding rims the table's top and bottom edges. The top is covered with rare green marble acquired from Scarpellino in the Campo Vaccino by the sculptor Joseph Nollekens.[95] These French-style tables are similar to those Stuart designed earlier for the great room of Spencer House in about 1759, but here he abandoned the baroque conceits of a central female mask and heavy swags of flowers that featured in the earlier version (see fig. 10-47).

Stuart designed two gilt tripod stands with ram's-head masks and feet to stand before the mantelpiece of the library (fig. 10-73). Each has an incurvate pedestal on castors edged with egg-and-dart molding, while a central stand is made of a honeysuckle stalk. A guilloche band surmounted by an egg-and-dart molding is topped by a marble inset with a brass rail. Garlands connect the ram's-head masks. The use of the ram's head was particularly fitting for this commission since Thomas Anson raised a herd of Corsican goats on the property. Sir Joseph Banks observed them on his visit to Shugborough in 1768, and they were later painted by Thomas Weaver.[96] Stuart used a similar composition of rams' heads and garlands for the Cat's Monument (see fig. 7-38) in the grounds of the estate, and the outside parapet of the main house sported goat's heads and anthemia (see fig. 6-13).

The finely modeled rams' heads of the tripod stands

Fig. 10-71. Samuel Wyatt. The Red Drawing Room, Shugborough, Staffordshire, 1794, with Stuart's pier tables against the window wall. Photographed ca. 1990s. Courtesy of Shugborough (The National Trust, UK).

Fig. 10-72. James Stuart. Pier table from the Red Drawing Room, Shugborough, ca. 1760s. Gilt and painted wood, ca. 1763–65; green Cippolino marble top. Courtesy of Shugborough, The Anson Collection (The National Trust, UK). *Checklist no. 44.*

were probably derived from one of the many Piranesi plates that illustrated rams' heads; one from the Villa Baronia in Rome shows similar rams' heads emerging from the capital column (fig. 10-74). The overall form is derived from one of the Roman bronze tripods that survived from the ancient world. Stuart painted a tripod with rams' heads in the Painted Room at Spencer House (fig. 10-75) similar to that unearthed at the Temple of Isis at Pompeii but with ram monopodia instead of addorsed sphinxes.[97] Indeed, Stuart was probably responsible for the direct copy that stood in the central hall at Shugsborough

(fig. 10-76). One at Spencer House occupied the Painted Room and is known through a photograph of 1926 (fig. 10-77).[98]

Final Commissions

Furniture design did not play a significant role in the last decade of Stuart's career. Commissions for funerary sculptures and designs for Greenwich Hospital occupied most of his working time. The triple-decker pulpit with reader's desk in Greenwich Chapel of about 1789 represents Stuart's last commission for furniture and his only

Fig. 10-73. James Stuart. Pair of tripod stands, Shugborough, ca. 1760s. Gilt wood, gilt brass surround, marble inserts. Courtesy of Shugborough, The Anson Collection (The National Trust, UK). *Checklist no. 45.*

Fig. 10-74. Rams' heads on capitals of columns at the Villa Boronia near the Porta Salaria, Rome. Engraving (detail). From Giovanni Battista Piranesi, *Della Magnificenza ed Architecttura de Romani* (1761): pl. xvii. By permission of The British Library, London, 1899.d.6.

458

Fig. 10-75. James Stuart. Painted tripod with rams' heads, detail of the wall decoration of the Painted Room, Spencer House, 1764–65. ©Spencer House Limited.

Fig. 10-76. Attributed to James Stuart. Tripod in the central hall at Shugborough, ca. 1764. Gilt wood. Copied from a tripod in the Temple of Isis, Pompeii. Photographed in 1961. English Heritage/National Monuments Record AA62/2239.

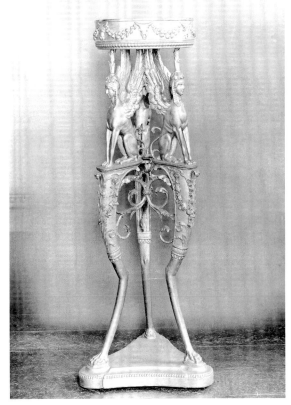

Fig. 10-77. Attributed to James Stuart. Tripod in the Painted Room at Spencer House, ca. 1764. Gilt wood. Copied from a tripod in the Temple of Isis, Pompeii. Photographed in 1926. ©Country Life Picture Library.

Fig. 10-78. James Stuart. Pulpit in the Chapel of the Royal Hospital for Seamen, Greenwich, ca. 1786–89. Joinery by James Arrow with George Seddons; carved by Richard Lawrence. Limewood with gilt details; Coade stone medallions sculpted by John Bacon, ca. 1789, after designs by Benjamin West. Photographed in 2006. Courtesy of the Greenwich Foundation. *Checklist no. 157.*

Fig. 10-79. James Stuart, assisted by Robert Mylne and William Newton. Interior of the chapel of the Royal Hospital for Seamen, 1779–89. Albumen print (detail), ca. 1890. The reader's desk has been separated from the pulpit and is on the left. Courtesy of the Library, The Bard Graduate Center for Studies in the Decorative Arts, Design, and Culture, New York. *Checklist no. 154.*

Fig. 10-80. James Stuart. Panel from the remains of the reader's desk for the chapel of the Royal Hospital for Seamen, ca. 1786–89. Limewood, Coade stone plaques sculpted by John Bacon, ca. 1789, after designs by Benjamin West. Photographed in 2006. Courtesy of the Greenwich Foundation.

surviving nondomestic furniture design. Made of lime-wood with six slender Corinthian columns and an elaborately carved entablature, the pulpit is of a cylindrical form (fig. 10-78), like the bedside cupboard he had designed twenty years earlier for Spencer House (see fig. 10-55). Once again, the design derived from the Choragic Monument of Lysicrates in Athens. Six large-scale coade-stone medallions, based on the Acts of the Apostles and designed by Benjamin West, were placed between the columns in the fix after Stuart's death.[99] The reader's desk (figs. 10-79, 10-80), originally part of the triple pulpit, was square in plan with Corinthian columns at the four corners, its entablature richly carved like that of the pulpit. Similar coade-stone reliefs were placed between the columns after Stuart's death. These were of four prophets, also designed by Benjamin West.[100] Executed by the joiner James Arrow, the pulpit still stands today in the chapel while the reader's desk is no longer there.[101]

461

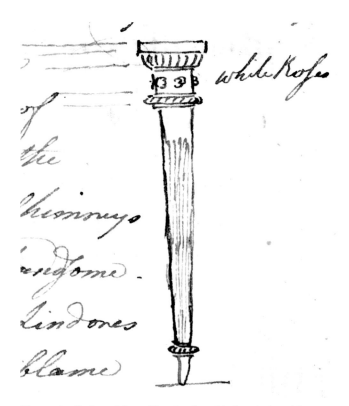

white Rofes

Fig. 10-81. Robert Adam. Sketch of a table leg designed by James Stuart for Spencer House. Pen and ink. From Adam to James Adam, 5 September 1758, National Archives of Scotland, Edinburgh, with kind permission of Sir Robert Clerk of Penicuik, Mss. ref. GD18/4852. *Checklist no. 114.*

★ ★ ★

Stuart's designs reverberated throughout the English design world of his day and eventually had a long-lasting impact on contemporary English taste. His rival Robert Adam continued to study Stuart's work closely, as is reflected in his sketch of a table leg designed by James Stuart for Spencer House, from a letter now preserved in the National Archive of Scotland (fig. 10-81).[102] Even so, Adam's was a very light and delicate neoclassicism, based primarily on ornament, while Stuart's was closer to the archaeological sources he had studied firsthand. Although Stuart still must be considered "transitional," his was a unique hybrid style, combining elements of the rococo and neoclassicism. Stuart's impact, however, was not immediate. Unlike Sheraton and Hepplewhite, whose designs quickly reached the popular market through their publications, Stuart never intended his work to be for the general population, but rather for the upper echelons of English society. The archaeological detail and the strong sculptural elements he incorporated into individual items had a great influence on the furniture developed by Thomas Hope and Charles Heathcote Tatham in the Regency period (1800–30) and by Charles Percier and Pierre-François Fontaine during the Napoleonic Empire (1804–15).

1. David Watkin, *James Athenian Stuart: Pioneer of the Greek Revival* (London: George Allen and Unwin, 1982).

2. Robin Middleton and David Watkin, *Neoclassical and Nineteenth-Century Architecture* (New York: Abrams, 1980): 89–90.

3. Robert Adam and James Adam, *The Works in Architecture of Robert and James Adam Esquires,* vol. 1 (London: the authors, 1778): 5.

4. *Ackermann's Repository of Arts, Literature, Fashions, Manufactures, etc.,* 2nd series (14 December 1822): 314; cited in Dora Wiebenson, *Sources of Greek Revival Architecture* (University Park: Pennsylvania State University Press, 1969): 66.

5. Gisela M. Richter, *Furniture of the Greeks, Etruscans and Romans* (London: Phaidon Press, 1966): 3.

6. John Morley, *The History of Furniture: Twenty-Five Centuries of Style and Design in the Western Tradition* (Boston, New York, and London: Little Brown, 1999): 163.

7. *Antiquities,* vol. 1 (1762): v.

8. D. [E.] L. Haynes, *The Arundel Marbles* (Oxford: Ashmolean Museum, 1975): pl. 21.

9. *Catalogue of Pictures . . . and other effects of the Late James Stuart . . . ,* sale cat., Greenwoods, London, 27 June 1791. Copy in the Courtauld Institute Library, London, B.A. 5059 1791/06/27.

10. John Hardy and Helena Hayward, "Kedleston Hall, Derbyshire," *Country Life* 163 (2 February 1978): 263. The design is now in the RIBA Library Drawings Collection, SD104/31.

11. Clifford Musgrave, *Adam and Hepplewhite and Other Neo-Classical Furniture* (New York: Taplinger, 1966): 181–82.

12. Hardy and Hayward, "Kedleston Hall" (1978): 263.

13. Robert Adam to James Adam, 11 December 1758, Clerk of Penicuik Mss. GD 18 4854, National Archives of Scotland, Edinburgh; see also Leslie Harris, *Robert Adam and Kedleston,* exh. cat., Kedleston, Derbyshire; Cooper-Hewitt Museum, New York (London: National Trust, 1987): 28.

14. Adam vol. 54, pt. 1, nos. 93 (sketch for a table) and 59 (sketch from Stuart's design), Sir John Soane's Museum, Archive; see also Eileen Harris, *The Genius of Robert Adam: His Interiors* (New Haven and London: Paul Mellon Centre for Studies in British Art and Yale University Press, 2001): 14, 23, 34–35.

15. John Harris, "Early Neo-Classical Furniture," *Furniture History* 2 (1966): 2.

16. Ibid.

17. Svend Eriksen, "Lalive de Jully's Furniture 'à la grecque'," Burlington Magazine 103 (July 1961): 340–47.

18. Nicholas Goodison, *Matthew Boulton: Ormolu,* rev. ed. (London: Christies, 2002): 47.

19. Joseph Friedman, *Spencer House: Chronicle of a Great London Mansion* (London: Zwemmer, 1993): 112, figs. 76–77.

20. "The Spencer House Palm Room Seat Furniture," in *Important English Furniture,* sale cat., Sotheby's, London, 29 November 2002, 158–66, lots 154–55.

21. Ibid., 160–62.

22. Alexandre Pradère, *French Furniture Makers: The Art of the Ébéniste from Louis XIV to the Revolution,* trans. Perran Wood (Malibu, CA: J. Paul Getty Museum, 1989): 23.

23. Morley, *History of Furniture* (1999): 22.

24. Richter, *Furniture of the Greeks* (1966): 109; Walther Amelung, *Die Scupturen des Vaticanischen Museums* (Berlin: George Reimer, 1908): cat. II, no. 404, pl. 58.

25. *Catalogue of Pictures . . . and other effects of the late James Stuart . . .* (1791).

26. Richter, *Furniture of the Greeks* (1966): 117.

27. Diary of Thomas Hollis, 3 September 1759, Ms. Eng 1191, Houghton Library, Harvard University; cited in Kerry Bristol, "The Painted Rooms of Athenian Stuart," *Georgian Group Journal* 10 (2000): 166.

28. Paget Toynbee, ed., "Walpole's Journals of Visits to Country Seats," Walpole Society annual, vol. 16 (1928): 15, 43a; cited in John Harris, *The Architect and the British Country House, 1620–1920* (Washington, DC: AIA Press, 1985): 161.

29. Spencer to Hamilton, 25 December 1765, Add. Ms. 75,686, BL; see also Margaret Jourdain, "Furniture Designed by James Stuart at Althorp," *Country Life* 78 (24 August 1935): 205.

30. For the first tripod pedestal designed by Robert Adam in 1767, see Eileen Harris, *Furniture of Robert Adam* (London: Tiranti, 1963): 100, fig 134. For the tripods designed by James Wyatt, see John Cornforth, "On His Own Legs," *Country Life* 187 (28 September 1993): 70–73.

31. Watkin, *James Athenian Stuart* (1982): 35.

32. Musgrave, *Adam and Hepplewhite Furniture* (1966): 182–83.

33. *Catalogue of Pictures . . . and other effects of the Late James Stuart . . .* (1791): 4, no. 39.

34. *The Age of Neoclassicism,* exh. cat., Royal Academy of Art and Victoria and Albert Museum (London: Council of Great Britain, 1972): 780, cat. no. 1657.

35. Friedman, *Spencer House* (1993): 96–97, fig. 53.

36. Ibid., 139 n. 5.

37. Ibid., 139; Amelung, *Scupturen des Vaticanischen Museum* (1908): cat. III, no. 236; 46, pl. 26.

38. Friedman, *Spencer House* (1993): 139.

39. Ibid., 134.

40. Ibid., 137.

41. H. Avray Tipping, "Eighteenth-Century Staircase Lanterns," *Country Life* 63 (14 April 1928): [50].

42. Arthur Young, *A Six Weeks Tour Through the Southern Counties of England and Wales,* 2nd ed. (London: W. Strahan, 1769): 359–60; quoted in Friedman, *Spencer House* (1993): 191.

43. E. Beresford Chancellor, *The Private Palaces of London, Past and Present* (London: Kegan Paul, Trench, Trübner, 1908): 342.

44. Morley, *History of Furniture* (1999): 23.

45. J. Harris, "Early Neoclassical Furniture" (1966): 3–4. The original painting by Hamilton has been lost for many years, but copies by other

artists survive, such as fig. 10-31 by Cunego.

46. Vien's *Sweet Melancholy* is now in the Cleveland Museum of Art, inv. 1996.1.

47. Peter Thornton and John Hardy, "The Spencer Furniture at Althorp—I," *Apollo* (June 1968): 448.

48. Ibid., 450.

49. Transcript of Gordon and Taitt records by N. Truelove, Red Box file on Gordon and Taitt, Department of Furniture and Woodwork, Victoria and Albert Museum, London, cites "Gordon and Taitt. The 1772 bills from the Althorp archive" which consists of some two thousand volumes of papers in the British Library. Trueloves transcript quotes from Gordon and Taitt's London bill, 27 February 1772: "To 2 sets of Crimson Erminet Check Cases lined with linen for the 2 sofas in the Bow Room £6.69/.—To 6 Do for the 6 Elbow Chairs in do.... £8-8/-." Peter Thornton read this as checked loose covers; see Thornton:, "A Very Special Year: The Victoria and Albert Museum's Furniture Acquisitions in 1977," *Connoisseur* 198 (June 1978): 139.

50. Christopher Payne, ed., *Sotheby's Concise Encyclopedia of Furniture* (New York: Harper and Row, 1989): 92.

51. Thornton and Hardy attributed the carving to the sculptor Joseph Wilton, who worked on the Royal State Coach under the direction of Sir William Chambers in the early 1760s. The authors believed that the heads of the lions and the armrests formed of Ionic volutes relate to those parts on the coach; see Thornton and Hardy, "Spencer Furniture at Althorp," (1968): 450. More recent research at the Victoria and Albert attributes the carving to Thomas Vardy of Park Street, Grosvenor Square; see Christopher Wilk, ed., *Western Furniture: 1350 to the Present Day in the Victoria and Albert Museum* (New York: Cross River, 1996): 114. For more information on Thomas Vardy, see Friedman, *Spencer House* (1993): 74–75; David Udy, "The Classical Sources of English Neoclassical Furniture," *Arte Illustrate* 6 (February 1973): 103 n. 4.

52. Morley, *History of Furniture* (1999): 23.

53. Udy, "Classical Sources" (1973): 97.

54. J. Harris, "Early Neoclassical Furniture" (1966): 3.

55. Young, *Six Week's Tour*, 3rd ed. (1772): 114.

56. Udy, "Classical Sources" (1973): 98.

57. Friedman, *Spencer House* (1993): 136.

58. Michael Wilson, *William Kent Architect, Designer, Painter, Gardener, 1685–1748* (London: Routledge, Kegan, Paul, 1984): 110–11.

59. Friedman, *Spencer House* (1993):139.

60. Udy, "Classical Sources" (1973): 98.

61. Richter, *Furniture of the Greeks* (1966): 82.

62. Morley, *History of Furniture* (1999): 15.

63. Udy, "Classical Sources" (1973): 98.

64. Giles Worsley, "Hornby Castle, Yorkshire," *Country Life* 183 (29 June 1989): 193.

65. H. Clifford Smith, "A Catalogue and Valued Inventory of the Furniture and Works of Art . . . of Londonderry House Park Lane W. The Property of the Most Honble. The Marquess of Londonderry,"

typescript, 1939, p. 39. Copy in the National Art Library, Victoria and Albert Museum, 86.W.142.

66. Watkin, *James Athenian Stuart* (1982): 39.

67. Friedman, *Spencer House* (1993): 146.

68. Ibid., 147.

69. Young, *A Six Weeks Tour*, 3rd ed. (1772): 113.

70. Thornton and Hardy, "Spencer Furniture at Althorp" (1968): 444–46.

71. Ibid., 446.

72. Ibid., 448.

73. Ibid., 446.

74. Ibid. There were also two bracket tables designed by Stuart for Nuneham, known from a bill from John Adair: "The Rt Honble Earl Harcourt in 1763 and 1764. For 4 August 1764: To 2 Rich Oval Burnish gold Glass frames, Newnham 11 14 – To 2 Bracket Tables under Do: by Mr Stuart – 16-," in Ms. D.D. Harcourt, Harcourt Estate Papers, c.174, Bodleian Library, Oxford; cited in *Sotheby's Important English Furniture*, sale cat., 3 July 2003, p. 162. The same tables are also described as "after Mr Stuart's design" (Harcourt Estate Papers, c.175).

75. W. 51A&B.1984, Victoria and Albert Museum, London. Another six chairs from the same suite were acquired by Partridge Fine Arts, London, in 1986. Two of these were advertised in 2004; see Lucy Morton and Michelle Stroube, comps., *Furniture, Silver and Works of Art, 2004* (London: Partridge Fine Arts PLC, 2004), no. 24: 58–61.

76. Friedman, *Spencer House* (1993): 142.

77. Richter, *Furniture of the Greeks* (1966): 73.

78. Ibid., 75.

79. Wilson, *William Kent* (1984): 122, fig. 45.

80. Victoria Percy and Gervase Jackson-Stops, "Esquisite Taste and Tawdry Ornament: The Travel Journals of the 1st Duchess of Northumberland—II," *Country Life* 155 (7 February 1974): 251.

81. Diary of Thomas Hollis, 17 April 1761, Ms. Eng 1191, Houghton Library, Harvard University.

82. Sir Hugh Roberts, personal communication, 12 February 2004: "This chair was transferred to Holyrood House for the use of George IV on his visit to Scotland in the 1820s and survived there until the reign of Edward VII. It no longer survives."

83. Pyne, *History of the Royal Residences of Windsor Castle, St. James's Palace . . .*, vol. 2 (London: [L. Harrison] for A. Dry, 1819): opp. p. 13.

84. John Harris puts forward the idea that Stuart contributed to the design of this sedan chair (Royal Collection inv. no. 31182). Jane Roberts, ed., *George III and Queen Charlotte: Patronage, Collecting and Court Taste* (London: Royal Collection Publications, 2004): 268-69; David Watkin, *The Architect King: George III and the Culture of the Enlightenment* (London: Royal Collection Publications, 2004): 91-92.

85. The mechanism of the organ has been attributed to Thomas Haxby, local Yorkshire-based organ builder and musician; see Richard Compton, *Newby Hall* (Derby: Heritage House Group, 2004): 15.

86. Margaret Jourdain, *The Work of William Kent, Artist, Painter, Designer and Landscape Gardener* (London: Country Life, 1948):116.

87. Watkin, *James Athenian Stuart* (1982): 41.

88. John Cornforth, "Newby Hall, North Yorkshire—I," *Country Life* 165 (7 June 1979):1804; Cornforth, "Correspondence: Designs for Newby," *Country Life* 165 (21 June 1979): 2016.

89. Watkin, *James Athenian Stuart* (1982): 41.

90. Friedman, *Spencer House* (1993): 146.

91. John Cornforth, "Newby Hall, North Yorkshire—II," *Country Life* 165 (14 June 1979): 1918.

92. Ely Hargrove, *History of the Castle, Town, and Forest of Knaresborough with Harrowgate*, 4th ed., (York: n.p., 1789): 261; Eileen Harris points out that the figural grouping is not mentioned in the 1792 inventory list; see E. Harris, *Genius of Robert Adam* (2001): 357 n. 71; J. Low, "Newby Hall: Two Late Eighteenth Century Inventories," *Furniture History* 22 (1984): 154.

93. The payment was £200; Expenses in 1763, Lichfield Ms. D615/E (F), Staffordshire Record Office, Stafford; cited in Bristol, "Stuart and the Genesis of the Greek Revival" (1997): 274.

94. John Martin Robinson, *Shugborough* (London: National Trust, 1989): 61.

95. Ibid., 62; Bristol, "Stuart and the Genesis of the Greek Revival" (1997): 274.

96. Robinson, *Shugborough* (1989): 50.

97. Richter, *Furniture of the Greeks* (1966): 112; National Museum inv. 72995; illustrated in Vittorio Spinazzola, *Le Arti decorative in Pompei e nel Museo Nazionale di Napoli*, (Milan: Bestetti and Tumminelli, 1928): pls. 257–59.

98. Friedman, *Spencer House* (1993): 180–81.

99. Eleanor Coade provided them in 1789; see John Bold, *Greenwich: An Architectural History* (New Haven and London: Yale University Press for the Paul Mellon Centre for Studies in British Art in association with English Heritage, 2000): 176. The six medallions represent the conversion of Saint Paul; Cornelius's vision; Peter released from prison by the angel; Elymas struck blind; Saint Paul preaching at Athens and converting Dionysus the Areopagite; and Paul pleading before Felix. See John Cooke and John Maule, *An Historical Account of the Royal Hospital for Seamen at Greenwich . . .* (London: published by the authors, 1789): 105. Coade stone was a synthetic stone, probably made of ground stone and clay and produced from 1760 to about 1840. It was named after Eleanor Coade, founder of the Coade Stone Manufactory.

100. The prophets in the medallions on the reader's desk are Daniel, Micah, Zachariah, and Malachi. Ibid., 106.

101. The reader's desk and pulpit were still together and in one piece in the late nineteenth century (see fig. 10-79), but at some time after that, they were separated, and the reader's desk is stored in the dome.

102. Robert Adam to James Adam, 5 September 1758, Clerk of Penicuik Mss. GD 18,4852, National Archives of Scotland, Edinburgh.

Fig. 11-1. James Stuart. Tripod perfume burner with candle branches, ca. 1760. Probably made by Diederich Nicolaus Anderson. Cast and chased gilt bronze, marble base. Courtesy of Kedleston Hall, The Scarsdale Collection, Ked/Med/17 (The National Trust, UK). *Checklist no. 57.*

JAMES "ATHENIAN" STUART'S

METALWORK

MICHAEL SNODIN

Metalwork, often high in status and usually small in size, is a sensitive barometer of changes in style. This was especially so with neoclassicism, as it was applied to every aspect of design. For the first time, keeping up to date involved more than simply a change in ornament, as designers not only sought to replicate ancient forms in the fixed decoration of their interiors, but also to furnish these interiors with metalwork and other objects that echoed ancient vessels and utensils. In this way, James Stuart, Robert Adam, Sir William Chambers, James Wyatt, and other architects came to play an unprecedented role in the design of metalwork for both private clients and fashion-conscious manufacturers.[1] Stuart's metalwork creations, although few in number, largely predate those of his architectural rivals and served as exemplars in the development of the neoclassical style on the Continent as well as Britain. Whether documented or attributed, they show a consistently individual design idiom, which is very different from that of his contemporaries who used more standardized ornament and forms. The metalwork can be divided into two phases. The first began in the late 1750s when Stuart established two ancient types, the vase and the tripod (fig. 11-1).

These two forms would become the basis of most neoclassical metalwork. The second phase began in the late 1760s when Stuart designed another group of metalwork, made by Matthew Boulton, one of the most celebrated metalsmiths of the eighteenth century. Stuart's later designs belong to the more established phase of neoclassicism, in which the style was applied to a wide range of metalwork, including, as in his case, tureens and hot water urns.

Stuart's earlier metalwork is linked to interior schemes for three clients: Sir Nathaniel Curzon at Kedleston Hall in 1758, John Spencer (from 1765, first Earl Spencer) at Spencer House in 1759, and the Marquess of Rockingham at Wentworth Woodhouse, where Stuart worked from about 1755 to about 1764.[2] While all three schemes included ormolu tripod perfume burners designed by Stuart, the key project, in terms of the range of objects, attributions, and secure dating, is that at Kedleston.[3] There, Stuart (and Matthew Brettingham) were replaced by James Paine and Robert Adam in 1759. The existing metalwork for use at Kedleston was recorded for Robert Adam, no doubt in preparation for Adam's scheme for the dining room, which was put down on paper in 1762 and carried out, with modifications, in 1765.[4] In addition to four pieces of baroque silver and the ormolu tripod, the drawings record one of the two "chestnut" vases and a

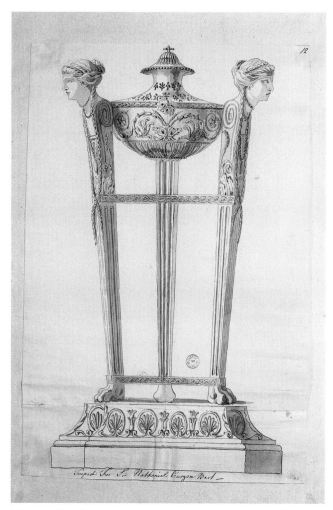

Fig. 11-2. Draftsman unknown. Record drawing of a tripod perfume burner for the dining room at Kedleston Hall, Derbyshire, ca. 1760–62. Pen and ink, gray wash, pencil. By courtesy of the Trustees of Sir John Soane's Museum, London, Adam Ms., vol. 25, no. 90. *Checklist no. 55.*

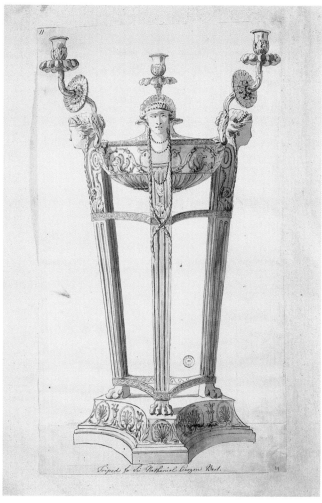

Fig. 11-3. Draftsman unknown. Record drawing of a tripod perfume burner with candelabra for the dining room at Kedleston Hall, Derbyshire, ca. 1760–62. Pen and ink, gray wash, pencil. By courtesy of the Trustees of Sir John Soane's Museum, London, Adam Ms., vol. 25, no. 89. *Checklist no. 56.*

vase-shaped plate warmer, both made of copper and ormolu (figs. 11-2 to 11-5). These drawings, made between 1760 and 1762, may well date from the start of the period, as their inscriptions record Curzon as a baronet (Sir Nathaniel Curzon) rather than a baron (Lord Scarsdale), an elevation he achieved in April 1761. This early date, along with other evidence, suggests very strongly that Stuart also designed the Kedleston vases and the plate warmer, which was made in 1760.

The Tripod

The tripods from the Scarsdale, Spencer, and Rockingham collections are all constructed in the same way and are identical in design, but for the candle branches and cameos used for the hanging medallions (figs. 11-6, 11-7 and see fig. 11-1). The three legs of the ormolu tripod support a removable bowl with a cover, pierced to allow smoke to issue. The legs have lions' feet and terminate with young female heads, whose carefully modeled hair falls in plaits down the fluted legs. Around their necks are three-strand necklaces, from one of which hangs a medallion taken from a cast of an ancient gem. The curved candle branches, which are screwed to the edge of the bowl, pass through flowers halfway along their stems. Under the bowl is a satyr's mask surrounded by fluting (see fig. 11-15), while the bowl is decorated with a border frieze of scrolling acanthus and flowers. The tripod is highly finished, with matte and polished areas, and the classical decorative detail extends into parts that are largely hidden. The white marble base is carved with a delicate frieze of palmettes and anthemions.

The tripod has been firmly established as being designed by Stuart.[5] Even without the evidence of design drawings, his authorship is clear. In 1766 the tripod on Adam's sideboard arrangement at Kedleston was identified by the Countess of Northumberland as "Mr Stewart's tripod."[6] Guidebooks to the house, beginning in about 1769, ascribe both the Sicilian jasper cistern and the tripod to Stuart.[7] Finally, there is the record of a tripod exhibited by "Mr Anderson" at the Free Society of Artists in 1761: "a tripod, from an original design of Mr Stuart's."[8] "Mr Anderson" was almost certainly Diederich Nicolaus

Fig. 11-4. Draftsman unknown. Record drawing of a "chestnut" vase for the dining room at Kedleston Hall, Derbyshire, ca. 1760–62. Pen and ink. By courtesy of the Trustees of Sir John Soane's Museum, London, Adam Ms., vol. 25, nos. 81-83. *Checklist no. 58.*

Fig. 11-5. Draftsman unknown. Record drawing of a plate warmer for the dining room at Kedleston Hall, Derbyshire, ca. 1760–62. Pen and ink, gray wash, pencil. By courtesy of the Trustees of Sir John Soane's Museum, London, Adam Ms., vol. 25, no. 93.

Fig. 11-6. James Stuart. Tripod perfume burner from the Painted Room, Spencer House, London, 1758–66. Cast and chased gilt bronze, marble base. Now in the staircase hall at Althorp. Photographed in 2006. The Althorp Collection.

Anderson, a modeler and chaser of Danish origin, who made the Kedleston plate warmer in 1760 (see fig. 11-23).[9] Given the present tripod's artistic design and high finish it is very likely that it was the one shown in 1761.

The first datable design for this type of tripod appears in Stuart's 1758 drawings of a hall/gallery for the old house of Kedleston (see figs. 6-30, 6-31).[10] They show gilt tripods on marble bases, of very similar design and in two sizes. Although the drawings are too small to include much detail, they are identical in general conception to the tripods as made. They are not placed on the sideboard but on the mantel and on two small pier tables against the room's window wall. The larger tripods on the tables have candle branches. Stuart's design for the Painted Room at Spencer House, dated 1759 (see fig. 5-2), also includes a tripod of the same type with candle branches, again shown on a pier table, although the two tripods that were made were ultimately placed on their own tall tripodic painted wood stands (see fig. 10-20). A final drawing is undated and may relate to Kedleston, Spencer House, or Wimbledon House. It shows the same type of tripod with candle branches but on a larger scale (fig. 11-8). Although there are pencil indications of anthemion ornament on the base, as in the executed examples, the lack of detail on this drawing and the missing upper bracing suggest that it comes from an early stage in the design process. Designed by 1758 and first made about 1760, Stuart's tripods are not only among the earliest of the neoclassical movement, but also seem to be the earliest examples in the classical style to be made in metal since ancient times.

The tripod form was a surprisingly late arrival in the classical revivalist's armory of ancient vessels and utensils.[11] From the late fifteenth century onwards, two ancient forms, the vase and the candelabrum, had been the main focus for transformation into useful and ornamental contemporary objects. The tripod, however, received little attention, perhaps because of its complexity and the difficulties of adaptation, as well as its close association with pagan ritual. Only one sixteenth-century ornament print shows a tripod,[12] and the form did not fully emerge as a practical or even ornamental object until the advent of neoclassicism. These mid-eighteenth-century developments had been preceded by an increased interest in ancient forms, including tripods, associated with the monumental antique style of the French baroque. While most examples appear in paintings, at least some seem to have

Fig. 11-7. James Stuart. Tripod perfume burner for Wentworth Woodhouse, Yorkshire, 1760. Probably made by Diederich Nicolaus Anderson. Cast and chased gilt bronze, marble base. Courtesy of the Trustees of The Victoria and Albert Museum, London, M.46-1948. *Checklist no. 40.*

Fig. 11-8. James Stuart. Design for a side table with tripod perfume burner and a pair of antique-style urns, 1760. Pen and ink, pencil, and yellow washes. RIBA Library Drawings Collection, SD 62/2. *Checklist no. 53.*

been actually made: in a print of about 1709, two tripods, made of gilt wood, are shown in the imaginary Louvre gallery of the sculptor François Girardon (fig. 11-9). Although they stand on a three-legged baroque base, their form is close to that of an antique tripodic altar (usually made of stone), entwined with the snake of Apollo (or Aesculapius), its sacrificial function indicated in the flame-shaped finial. It was only appropriate that this type of tripod, in which the three legs support a vaselike container, should be used later as a design for perfume burners.

The study drawings made in the 1740s and 50s by the *pensionnaires* of the Académie de France in Rome, as well

as those of their foreign followers, clearly show how significant the tripod form had become to these pioneers of neoclassicism. Part of a more a more or less standard repertoire of ancient decorative objects and motifs,[13] the tripods studied went beyond the small handful of surviving ancient examples to those illustrated by Bernard de Montfaucon and others, as well as tripods of ancient form shown in seventeenth-century paintings. The group of such drawings in the Franco-Italian album of Sir William Chambers, assembled in Rome in the early 1750s, includes an ancient stone tripodic altar in the Villa Albani, as well as a study of a more fanciful tripod in a fresco of 1613 – 14

471

by Domenichino in San Luigi dei Francesi. Both recur in a drawing that shows almost the whole repertoire of tripod subjects (fig. 11-10). It most likely dates from the 1770s and is by Pierre-Adrien Pâris, who entered the Académie in 1769.[14]

Antique tripods had by then become an established model for fashionable furniture, such as the small multipurpose piece of furniture marketed as an Athénienne by Jean-Henri Eberts in 1773.[15] These polite confections were very different from the vigorously original compositions of the earliest neoclassicists, such as the combination of a vase and monumental tripod designed by an unknown Frenchman and copied by Chambers in the early 1750s (fig. 11-11). Although broadly derived from

ancient combinations of vases and tripods, it is an assemblage of typically mixed origins, its legs being inspired by a group of terminal figures with winged angels' heads on Francesco Borromini's campanile for S. Andrea delle Fratte, designed about 1653.[16] Stuart had certainly come into contact with the *pensionnaires'* repertoire of forms, as is shown by the vases of standard Académie type shown alongside one of his tripod designs (see fig. 11-8).[17] His tripod, however, although of rather more complex parentage than at first appears, takes a completely different approach, founded, as it is, on a conscious striving to create a convincing modern version of an antique object.

The overall form of Stuart's tripod was probably prompted by another exercise in historical re-creation,

Fig. 11-9. Roy Charpantier. View of the end wall of a "Gallerie du Sr Girardon Sculpteur ordinaire du Roi," ca. 1707. Engraving by Nicolas Chevallier. By permission of The British Library, London, 649.a.6.

472

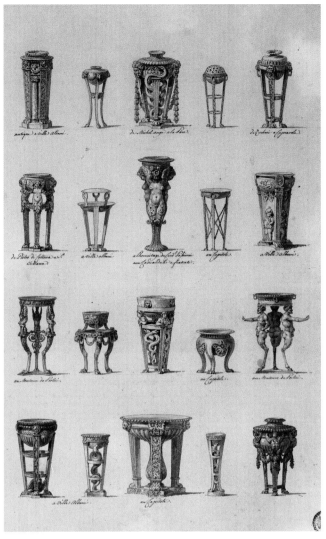

Fig 11-10. Attributed to Pierre-Adrien de Pâris. Study of antique and other tripod forms, ca. 1770s. Pen and ink. Bibliothèque Municipale de Besançon, Coll. Pâris, B.M.B., vol. 476, no. 184.

Fig. 11-11. William Chambers. Sketch of a crater vase and tripod, early 1750s. Pen and ink, gray wash. From Chambers, Franco-Italian album, p. 124, no. 511. Courtesy of the Trustees of The Victoria and Albert Museum, London, 5712.511

namely Stuart's conjectural design for a tripod that may once have stood on top of the Choragic Monument of Lysicrates, published in the first volume of *Antiquities of Athens* (1762; fig. 11-12).[18] The Lysicrates tripod, a prize in a choral competition, would have been made of bronze. Stuart's reconstruction, although provided with the looped carrying handles characteristic of ancient bronze tripods, has thick legs and a central column derived from stone examples. Stuart's metal tripod for manufacture likewise bears very little resemblance to surviving ancient bronze examples, which are generally of much lighter design and construction.[19] It dispenses with the central

column (which was in any case prompted by an indentation on the roof of the monument), and could have been derived from any one of a number of vase-bearing open-legged prototypes in the Académie repertoire (see fig. 11-10). The candle branches, with their curious pierced flowers, which are perhaps intended to suggest the looped handles of metal tripods, seem to be taken from the supporting arms of a famous bronze tripod from the Temple of Isis in Pompeii (see figs. 10-76, 10-77), which also appears among the tripod studies made by Pâris.[20]

The Stuart tripod's most distinctive feature, the female heads, surprisingly has no basis in ancient stone

473

Fig. 11-12. Reconstruction of the
metal tripod surmounting the
Choragic Monument of Lysicrates.
Engraving. From *Antiquities of
Athens,* vol. 1 (1762): chap. 4, p. 36.
Courtesy of the Library, The Bard
Graduate Center for Studies in the
Decorative Arts, Design, and
Culture, New York.
Checklist no. 36.

tripods but may well reflect the contemporary fascination
with tripods incorporating female busts or demi-figures
as shown in the Académie drawings. Stuart, however,
rejects such imaginative inventions, choosing to treat the
whole leg as a female term, as is confirmed by the volute
at the figure's shoulder. Such female terms were unusual
in ancient times, but they are found in French baroque
sculpture, notably in the set of terms made in the 1660s
for the gardens at Versailles, eighteen of which were
engraved by Jean Lepautre in 1674.[21] A Versailles term such
as that of Venus, with its voluted shoulders and hanging
locks, may perhaps have suggested the overall treatment of
Stuart's terms but does not account for their elaborate
coiffeurs with a plaited chignon and long braids. The treatment of the hair, except for the hanging plaits, seems to
have been derived from the elaborate styles shown on

female portrait busts of the Trajanic period, but lacks their
usually very high frontal hair. However, a bust now in the
Metropolitan Museum, traditionally described as that of
Matidia, Trajan's niece, has hair very similar to that
shown by Stuart.[22] Turning to the braids, similar long and
prominent strands of hair occur in archaic Greek Kore
figures and in archaic (and neo-Attic) relief sculpture, but
they are usually twisted rather than plaited, and the rest of
the hair is treated differently.[23] A later relief of a flute-
playing maenad in the so-called Incantada in Salonica,
illustrated in *Antiquities of Athens* in 1794, has similar hair
with a short plait (fig. 11-13). The paintings of classicizing
sixteenth- and seventeenth-century artists, in a tradition
going back to Raphael and Michelangelo and their pupils,
often depicted elaborately plaited hair in a manner that
may well have prompted Stuart to add long plaits to the

Vol. III. Chap.IX. Pl.XIII.

J. Stuart del.

Pub.d as the Act directs April 3. 1792.

Fig. 11-13. Figure of a sculpted flute player from the Incantada at Salonica. Engraving. From *Antiquities of Athens*, vol. 3 (1762): chap. 9, p. XIII. Courtesy of the Library, The Bard Graduate Center for Studies in the Decorative Arts, Design, and Culture, New York. *Checklist no. 90.*

Fig. 11-14. Augustin Pajou, after Daniele da Volterra. Sketch of a caryatid, ca. 1750s. Pencil. École nationale supérieure des beaux-arts, Paris, Pajou vol. 2, no. 66.

475

Fig. 11-15. James Stuart. Satyr on the bowl of the tripod perfume burner in fig. 11-7. Courtesy of the Trustees of The Victoria and Albert Museum, London M.46-1948. *Checklist no. 40.*

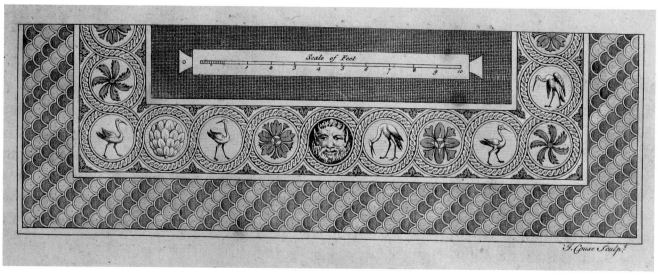

Fig. 11-16. Mosaic pavement with satyr mask. Engraving. From *Antiquities of Athens,* vol. 1 (1762): chap. 2, p. 7. Courtesy of the Library, The Bard Graduate Center for Studies in the Decorative Arts, Design, and Culture, New York. *Checklist no. 36.*

476

Fig. 11-17. Female mask and capital. Engraving. From *Antiquities of Athens,* vol. 1 (1762): chap. 2, p. 11. Courtesy of the Library, The Bard Graduate Center for Studies in the Decorative Arts, Design, and Culture, New York. *Checklist no. 36.*

Trajanic style. Poussin, for example, made many studies of complex plaited hair, some of them derived from Giulio Romano.[24] An especially telling parallel with Stuart's hair treatment occurs in a caryatid figure of the 1540s in a fresco by Daniele da Volterra in Santa Trinità dei Monti, sketched by the sculptor Augustin Pajou, who was at the Académie between 1752 and 1756 (fig. 11-14).

In addition to the maenad of the Incantada, there are other links between the tripod and the illustrations in *Antiquities of Athens.* The satyr mask at the base of the bowl (fig. 11-15) is very similar to one taken from a mosaic pavement in Athens (fig. 11-16), while the floral scrolling above it, with its distinctive joining strap, is probably adapted from a frieze on the Temple of Rome and Augustus at Pola, which was perhaps also used for the decoration of the great room at Spencer House.[25] To these can be added a tailpiece in which an Ionic capital is described as a long plait of hair, at the bottom of which is a female mask with entwined plaits (fig. 11-17). It is possible that Stuart intended the tripod, with its maenads and satyr, to have a Bacchic theme. This can perhaps be linked to his observation in *Antiquites of Athens* that the musical and theatrical contests, such as that won by Lysicrates's choir, took place during the Dionysia, or festival in honor of

477

Fig. 11-18. Robert Adam. "Design of the West End of the Dining Room with the Nich & Sideboard," 1762. Pen and ink, watercolor, pencil additions. Courtesy of Kedleston Hall, The Scarsdale Collection, KED.3.7.7 (The National Trust, UK). *Checklist no. 54.*

Bacchus.[26] Such a theme would of course also have been appropriate for the tripod's use in a room for dining and entertainment, incense being burned in it while dessert was being served, as a way to dispel the lingering odors of cooked meat.

The contemporary impact of the tripod is suggested by George Montagu's account to Horace Walpole of a visit to Kedleston in 1766, where "Adam and Stewart have showed all their Roman and Palmyra skill," and "there is an eating parlour, the prettiest you ever saw, and set out for sacrifice with numberless tripods, vases of crystal, lamps, et cetera, which has been fetched up from Herculanaeum."[27] Allowing for Montagu's exaggerated style, it is clear that Stuart's centrally placed tripod appeared to be an actual ancient object that carried the messages of pagan religion, turning the whole sideboard into an altar (figs.

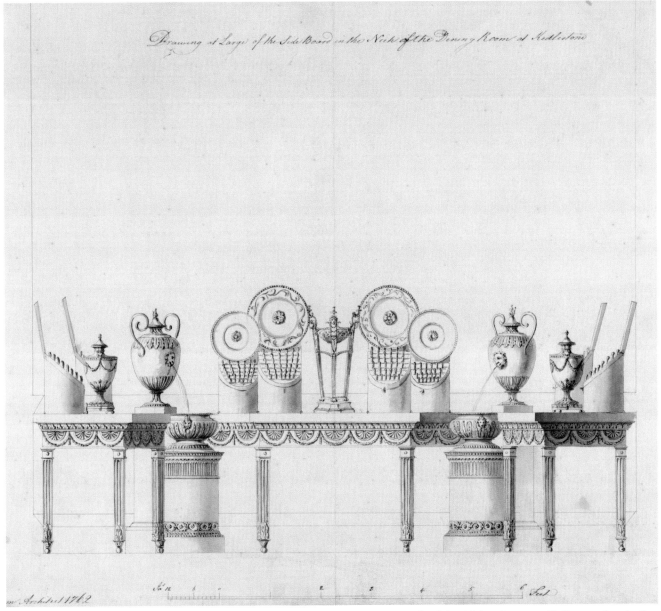

Fig. 11-19. Office of Robert Adam. "Drawing at Large of the Side Board in the Nich of the Dining Room at Kedlestone," 1762. Pen and ink, gray wash, pencil. Courtesy of Kedleston Hall, The Scarsdale Collection (The National Trust, UK).

11-18, 11-19).[28] Its pioneering design is also acknowledged by a rapid sketch by Chambers in his Franco-Italian album probably from memory, of a branched example (fig. 11-20).[29] In the context of the album, this sketch should be set alongside his careful recording in the mid-1750s of useful neo-Palladian details.[30] It is, however, the only Chambers drawing of an object designed by one of his rivals. Where he might have seen the tripod is unclear,

although it is perhaps significant that Diederich Nicolaus Anderson also made metalwork to Chambers's designs.

Anderson, the probable maker of Stuart's tripod, died in 1767, but tripods to the same design continued in production, as a number of surviving examples show. In 1771 three tripods "for incense in or-molu, lined with silver, with three branches for candles, after a design of Mr Stuart's" appeared in the sale of Matthew Boulton's manu-

Fig. 11-20. William Chambers. Sketch of a tripod by James Stuart, after ca. 1758. Pencil. From Chambers, Franco-Italian album, facing p. 2. Courtesy of the Trustees of The Victoria and Albert Museum, London, 5712.

factures at Christies.[31] The only securely documented Stuart-designed Boulton-made tripods to have survived for inspection are four made for Earl Gower in 1774.[32] Their technical details show that Boulton was working from casts or models of the Anderson version. He may have obtained these directly from Anderson's widow, from Sir William Chambers, or most probably from Stuart himself. In 1770–71 Boulton was making the metal tripod for the top of Stuart's replica at Shugborough of the Choragic Monument of Lysicrates.

The "Chestnut" Vases

The two metal vases used by Robert Adam on the sideboard display at Kedleston and shown in his designs of 1762 are now described as "chestnut" vases, because of the presumed function of one as a chestnut warmer (figs. 11-21, 11-22). Their stems, bodies, and lids are made of copper finely patinated to a bronze color. The sides of the square bases carry applied ormolu scrollwork. Their stems rise from a bound-reed molding, the bindings being made of applied ormolu. The stems are fluted and decorated with applied ormolu leaf ornament of two different types. The bodies rise from an ormolu calyx of acanthus and flowers, with a band of pearls at the base. The top rim is decorated with an ormolu running-scroll rim and two goats' heads. From the heads and two ribbons hang vine garlands. The lid is decorated with an open-work Greek key band in ormolu. The top section carries ormolu gadrooning and pearls and a pinecone finial. On the sides of the bodies are medallions of various classical subjects. The spouted vase carries one medallion of a reclining river god (on the side which once had the spout) and another of a youth struggling with a goat. The other vase carries a medallion of a woman holding a bearded mask and another of a faun and nymph. The medallions, which are 6 centimeters in diameter and appear to be cast from squeezes of others, are more finely modeled than the other mounts.

In addition to the medallions, the two vases also differ in significant details and function. One vase has a removable lid and a tinned base metal liner. The knob on the lid is removable, forming the handle of a pair of short copper tongs. This vase probably functioned as an urn for the serving of hot chestnuts at dessert, the tongs perhaps being provided for that purpose. The other vase could once be used as an urn for the service of hot liquid.[33] The spout, now lost, projected from a hole cast in one of the

Fig. 11-21. Attributed to James Stuart. "Chestnut" vase, one of pair, ca. 1757–58. Probably made by Diederich Nicolaus Anderson. Patinated copper, applied ormolu ornament, tinned base metal liner, copper tongs, stained wood base added 1765. Courtesy of Kedleston Hall, The Scarsdale Collection, KED.M.19a (The National Trust, UK).

Fig. 11-22. Attributed to James Stuart. The other "chestnut" vase, ca. 1757–58. Probably made by Diederich Nicolaus Anderson. Patinated copper, applied ormolu ornament, stained wood base added 1765. Courtesy of Kedleston Hall, The Scarsdale Collection, KED.M.19b (The National Trust, UK). *Checklist no. 59.*

flowers in the calyx. The lid is fixed; its knob removes to form the handle of a long pair of copper tongs, which fit inside a tube. The bottom of the body of the vase is pierced with holes, and in the square base is a small removable tray. The drinks would likely have been kept warm by coals or charcoal being put down the tube with the tongs, the ash being removed in the tray. Because of the need to accommodate the tray, the base of the spouted vase is bigger and thicker than that of the other. This may explain the presence of molded corner elements, missing on the other vase.[34] Both vases now stand on shallow wooden bases, resting atop bigger decorated wooden stands. The latter are almost certainly those billed in the accounts in 1765, along with a base that was made for the central tripod. All three bases were evidently provided to give height to these elements following a reassessment of the sideboard scheme when it finally came to be put together.[35] The small wooden base has four holes at the corners, suggesting that it was once fitted with the four ball feet shown in Adam's drawings.

Vases of this form, with bowl-shaped bodies and spool-shaped lids and bases deriving from ancient stone models, were the basic vase type of the Renaissance and later became characteristic of neoclassicism. The Kedleston vases, with their simple outlines and controlled use of ancient elements strikingly contrasted with plain areas, are the earliest datable metal vases of this type in the neoclassical style. They were once even more remarkable, for, as Adam's 1762 drawings and the stand bill of 1765 show, the copper elements of the body and lid and perhaps also the foot were once colored blue rather than the present brown. This coloring, perhaps achieved through patination or lacquering, may have been intended to create the effect of mounted hardstone, lacquer, or porcelain.[36] When the color was changed, or perhaps turned to brown, is unknown.[37]

The vases' early date is evident in the naturalistic lushness of some of the details, most notably the acanthus and flower molding at the bottom of the body and the hanging vine garlands.[38] Such treatment, perhaps due to the individual styles of the modelers employed, is in marked contrast to the tighter and more finely drawn details of the silver vases designed some three to four years later by Robert and James Adam, which were to become the norm for later neoclassicism. This contrast may explain why drawings in the Adam office of the Kedleston vases, made between 1760 and 1762, do not quite match their actual appearance. While the drawings show some parts accurately — the base with its scrolled corners, the ram's heads and cover finial, the beading and medallion subject — there are differences in all other areas. The draftsman shows the bound reed at the foot as a more conventional cushionlike torus, with the grooving in the base above filled with rising acanthus. In the same way, the garland in the drawing is a more conventional leaf garland, without the bow. One possible explanation for these differences is that that the draftsman was following a preliminary design by Adam himself, the vase details being changed in manufacture, but this is unlikely given the vases's inclusion on a sheet of drawings showing the existing silver wine fountain and basin. A more likely explanation is that the draftsman had a tendency towards inaccuracy in detail, coupled with a leaning toward correct and conventional ornament. As the only other person, besides Adam, capable of designing such a ground-breaking object at this early date, it is reasonable to ascribe the design of the vases to Stuart. The existence of a third vase of this type, with the same medallions and base treatment as the spoutless Kedleston example but with some decoration added to the foot, makes it possible that more than two were made for the scheme for the dining room.[39] The close similarity between the finish of the cast elements of the vases and the plate warmer suggests that they were also made by Anderson.

The Plate Warmer
The plate warmer (fig. 11–23) is boldly engraved in script under the top: "Diederich Nicolaus Anderson made this Plate-Warmer in the year 1760." By this time Anderson was one of a small group of modelers and metal chasers whose work at the fringes of the fine arts was becoming increasingly recognized through public exhibitions. Most of these metalworkers were gold chasers. Anderson's position as a worker in bronze and other base metals made him unusual.[40] As the inscription shows, Anderson was evidently proud of his work on this object, which is one of the most ambitious ormolu and base metal objects of its time in England. It demonstrates, as do the handful of other documented Anderson pieces, the maker's extremely high level of workmanship and skill in modeling and chasing.

Of less conventional design than the "chestnut" vases, the plate warmer is shaped as a tall, covered, tapering vase on a small foot, supported by four sphinxes on a

Fig. 11-23. Attributed to James Stuart. Plate warmer, 1760.
Copper gilt, wood base. Made by Diederich Nicolaus
Anderson. Courtesy of Kedleston Hall, The Scarsdale
Collection, KED.M.18 (The National Trust, UK).
Checklist no. 61.

plain base. Most of the back of the vase is open, presumably so that the plates could be placed inside to be warmed in front of the fire, in order to compensate for the food's long and chilly journey from the kitchen. The opening could probably once have been closed with a back plate, now lost (fig. 11-24).[41] The body of the vase and the upper parts of the fixed cover are of patinated copper, of a blacker tone than the bodies of the "chestnut" vases. The body may once have been a different color, as the plate warmer is described in the printed catalogue of about 1769 as "copper gilt after an Antique Bas rilievo."[42] The early record drawing, however, already shows a tonal contrast between the vase's body and its ornaments. The main decoration of the body is formed from a series of male herms holding hands, which appear to support the upper rim molding that is formed as a band of palmettes. Between the herms are individual acanthus leaves. At the base is a calyx of acanthus leaves, surmounted by a band of egg- and-dart – like ornament, strongly modeled to show its overlapping elements. The cover is bordered by a heavy band of egg-and-dart and terminates in an acorn, springing from swirling gadrooning and radiating water leaves. The vase's loop handes, which illogically link the

Fig. 11-24. Back of the plate warmer.

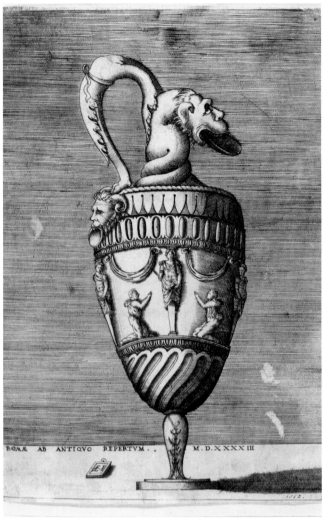

Fig. 11-25. Attributed to James Stuart. Design for a plate warmer for Kedleston Hall, ca. 1757. Pen and ink and wash. Courtesy of Kedleston Hall, The Scarsdale Collection, KED/4/23 (The National Trust, UK). *Checklist no. 60.*

Fig. 11-26. After Agostino Veneziano. One in a set of vase prints, 1543. Engraving. Courtesy of the Trustees of The Victoria and Albert Museum, London, Box EO 129, no. 16852.

cover to the body, are shaped as twisted rope or cloth and issue from bearded satyrs' heads on the edge of the cover.

A design for the plate warmer survives in the records at Kedleston (fig. 11-25). The drawing has lost its original context, having been cut around the drawn edges and stuck to another sheet, and is consequently hard to assess as a drawing, especially in terms of its creator. With that caveat, it is nevertheless possible to attribute it to Stuart. It is certainly not by Robert Adam, as is made clear by a comparison to an Adam design for a straight-sided covered vase for Sir Nathaniel Curzon surrounded by dancing figures and perhaps also intended for a plate-warmer.[43] While there is a lack of comparable Stuart drawings in both subject and type, it is possible to link the crude rendering of the hands and the treatment of the features with known Stuart designs.[44]

The drawing shows an early scheme. The herm figures are joined by draped cloths, and the palmette, lower bands, and acanthus leaves are of different proportions from those on the object as it was made. The cover above the egg-and-dart border is completely plain but for a finial, which is formed as a flaming urn. The record drawing (see fig. 11-4) is identical to the executed plate warmer, except for a more fully realized flaming urn finial, suggesting that the present pinecone finial is a replacement. The loss of the hanging cloths between the herms, presumably

484

Fig. 11-27. James Stuart. Candelabrum and stand, 1760. Probably made by Diederich Nicolaus Anderson. Gilt bronze body, cast bronze ornament, chased and gilt. Courtesy of the Trustees of The Victoria and Albert Museum, London, M.279-1975. *Checklist no. 122.*

because of technical difficulties in their making, has not improved the design, tending to turn the herms into isolated elements. It may have been to compensate for this loss of visual power that the cover ornament was elaborated in the final version.

The plate warmer was probably meant to stand directly in front of the dining room fire, as it still does at Kedleston. Both drawings include sketches of cloths either hanging from or tied to the handles. These may have had some practical role in handling the hot plates. It is probably not by chance that the vase is supported on sphinxes, which occur on the mantels of a number of Stuart's chimneypiece designs, including his scheme for Kedleston (see fig. 6-31). In that scheme the fire opening would have been about 54 inches (137 cm) high, in good proportion to the plate-warmer's approximately 34 inches (86 cm). The plate warmer now stands higher, on a wooden base matching those of the "chestnut" vases and tripod that were supplied in 1765. While the herm form itself may have been taken from an ancient relief, its use to decorate a vase shape, as well as the plate-warmer's overall form and other details may well have been inspired by a set of vase prints by Agostino Veneziano of 1543 (fig. 11-26).[45] One of the vases in the set has herm figures on its side, linked by drapery, while another not only carries herms, with drapes above, but also has a bearded satyr's head at the shoulder with a band of ornament like that at the base of the plate warmer. The precise form of the satyr's head is more closely echoed by one shown in *Antiquities of Athens*, while the curiously isolated acanthus leaves are perhaps taken from the ornamental repertoire of the Académie de France.[46]

The Tripod Candle Vase
Also attributable to Stuart is a type of ormolu candle vase which has long been recognized as one of the earliest expressions of neoclassicism in English design (fig. 11-27). Of the six known pairs, two come respectively from Hagley Hall and Spencer House (see fig. 10-25),[47] at which Stuart designed interiors. In its freely conceived design and combination of baroque and classical elements, the vase recalls the "compositions" of Sir William Chambers, drawn in Rome in the 1750s.[48] At the center of the design is a vase of the same type as the "chestnut" vases, decorated with anthemions in applied openwork. The foot of the vase, with its twisted fluting and guilloche molding, is probably taken from a baroque original,[49] while the tri-

pod legs are also of baroque form. The vase's attribution to Stuart lies in the way it stands on the three legs, much as his plate warmer rests on the four sphinxes. In addition, its candle branches rise from its shoulders in a way similar to the branches on the tripod perfume burner. The attribution is also strengthened by the early date of the candle vase, confirmed by the manner in which some of its elements appear in a design of about 1759 – 62 for a silver sauceboat by Robert Adam for Kedleston.[50] Perhaps most significantly, a comparable vase with curving legs appears as part of the decoration of an early Stuart scheme for the decoration surrounding the sideboard niche of an unknown house (see fig. 6-45).[51] The very high quality of these vases, with their carefully contrasted overlaid elements and use of gilt and matte surfaces, points to Anderson as their likely maker. The vases directly inspired a type of candle vase designed by Robert Adam as well as being copied for elements in ormolu made by Matthew Boulton.[52]

The Later Metalwork
Matthew Boulton's direct copies of the Stuart tripod and parts of the candle vase were not his only link with the architect. In fact, all of Stuart's later metalwork was made by this ambitious and revolutionary Birmingham manufacturer. It was natural that Boulton should have a link with Stuart for the design of his metalwork, just as he had with Sir William Chambers and James Wyatt. Stuart's designs, however, were made for the architect's own clients, although that did not stop Boulton from using them for other clients once he had them in production. Boulton's first work to Stuart's design, made in 1769, was the tripod that surmounted the replica of the Choragic Monument of Lysicrates at Shugborough, built for Thomas Anson.[53] For its manufacture Stuart recommended "my friend Mr Boulton," indicating that the result would be "better and cheaper far than it can be in London."[54] The tripod no longer survives, but it is safe to assume that it followed Stuart's reconstructed design in *Antiquities of Athens* (see fig. 11-12). It was a collaboration between Boulton, who made the frame, and Josiah Wedgwood, who created the ceramic bowl, in 1771.[55] This was not the only such working arrangement. In 1770 Stuart ordered from Boulton an ormolu "Tea Kitchen" (or hot water urn) for his client Mrs. Montagu, the body of which was to be of Wedgwood's "etruscan ware."[56] Boulton also made the ormolu door furniture for Mrs. Montagu's

Fig. 11-28. Attributed to James Stuart. Tripodic tea kitchen, or tea urn, ca. 1770–72. Made by Matthew Boulton. Gilt copper body, tinned copper lining, ivory tap handles, wood base veneered with tortoiseshell. Courtesy of His Grace the Duke of Northumberland, Syon House, Middlesex.

Fig. 11-29. Attributed to James Stuart. Tripodic tea kitchen, or tea urn, ca. 1770. Made by Mathew Boulton. Gilt copper body, tinned copper lining, mother-of-pearl tap handle, ebonized fruitwood base, ormolu ornaments. The Royal Collection, London, RCINH 55429. *Checklist no. 143.*

house in Portman Square (see figs. 5-86, 5-92), which was designed by Stuart beginning in 1775.[57] As the Shugborough tripod was being completed, Stuart was discussing with Boulton the design of "the border of a tea-table" and a "tripodic tea kitchen," both possibly intended for Thomas Anson.[58] The tea table border, perhaps of ormolu, has not survived, if it was ever made. The tripodic tea kitchen, however, can reasonably be identified with two surviving examples in ormolu, one at Syon House and the other in the Royal Collection (figs. 11-28, 11-29).[59] The royal example was acquired in 1938, although Boulton did supply a "tripodic tea kitchen" for royal use in 1770.[60] The surviving tea kitchens (which differ slightly in detail) can be seen as developed versions of the tripod perfume burner first made some ten years earlier. They share the tripod leg, the stretcher, form, and ornament of the base, and methods of construction, as well as a sculptural complexity of design and sense of scale and weight. The candle branch design is very close to those on the candle vases attributed to Stuart (see fig. 11-27). Both forms were linked by Boulton in a blue-john and ormolu candle vase of 1769 – 70, which combined the tea-kitchen candle branches with a foot copied from the earlier candles vases.[61]

The final Boulton products linked to Stuart are two large silver tureens of the same design, made for the commissioners of the Admiralty in 1771 and 1781. Their drawn-out and troublesome manufacture is revealed in an extensive correspondence between Stuart and the Birmingham firm.[62] The tureens have not survived but a record drawing of the example made in 1781 is in the Boulton papers (fig. 11-30). The tureens are of conventional vase-shaped form but are unusual in detail. On the cover is a triton leaning on a cornucopia and blowing a conch. The frieze is formed of shells and addorsed dolphins. The handles are leaf-shaped rather than of the usual neoclassical form. In addition to the trumpet-shaped foot, the bowl is supported on dolphins, the clay models for which were supplied by Wedgwood.[63] Stuart acted as go-between for Boulton and the Admiralty and is very likely to have designed the tureen as well. This is suggested in part by their idiosyncratic design, but mostly by the dolphins, which are echoes of those on the roof of the Choragic Monument of Lysicrates, bringing his metalwork full circle.

James Stuart's designs, although small in number, played a key role in the history of neoclassical metalwork.

Fig. 11-30. Possibly by Matthew Boulton. Record drawing of Stuart's "Soup Tureen made for the Admiralty–1781." Pen and ink, pasted into album. From Boulton and Fothergill, Pattern Book no. 1, p. 111. Birmingham City Archives, Matthew Boulton Papers MS 3782/21/2. *Checklist no. 147.*

His schemes for Kedleston and for Spencer House were the first in Europe to integrate metalwork into the neoclassical interior. For them he created what were probably the earliest metal tripods since ancient times, as well as, in all probability, designing the pieces that established the standard form of neoclassical metal vase. Like his rivals Robert Adam and Sir William Chambers, he was seeking to create objects of ancient form that would fit into a modern setting, both functionally and in terms of style, but in doing so he took a completely different approach. Adam, who crucially started a year or so after Stuart, worked out in the 1760s a way of designing neoclassical metalwork applicable to vessels and utensils of all types. By the early 1770s his easily adaptable vocabulary of forms and ornament had spread from pieces for his clients to the general market. Sir William Chambers, less the conscious innovator, combined his own distinctive repertoire of ornament, fully developed by 1760, with object forms often borrowed from France, to pioneer a more sculptural treatment that ran alongside that inspired by Adam. In both cases their design approaches paralleled those of their broader architectural practice. The same could be said of Stuart, whose metalwork designs, both documented and attributed, show little consistency in terms either of form or ornament, each piece being a unique solution to a particular demand. That this did not prevent his ideas being widely influential is mainly due to Robert Adam, who was able to study the pioneering Kedleston pieces closely and to use the ideas in his own metalwork. In a similar way, Matthew Boulton, adopted elements for his ormolu from Stuart's oeuvre, not only in the form of complete tripods, but also as individual details. Perhaps most significant is the presence of a sketch of the tripod among the drawings of Sir William Chambers (see fig. 11-20), demonstrating very clearly the impact of Stuart's most important metalwork design during the dawn of neoclassicism.

Acknowledgments: In the preparation of this chapter I am greatly indebted to Jill Banks, Richard Edgcumbe, Sir Nicholas Goodison, John Hardy, Simon McCormack, Christopher Payne, Christopher Rowell, Frank Salmon, and Marjorie Trusted. — M.S.

1. See Robert Rowe, *Adam Silver, 1765 – 1795* (London: Faber and Faber, 1965); Frances Fergusson, "Wyatt Silver," *Burlington Magazine* 116 (December 1974): 750 – 55; Kenneth Quickenden, "Boulton and Fothergill Silver: An Épergne Designed by James Wyatt," *Burlington Magazine* 128 (June 1986): 417 – 21; Hilary Young, "Silver Ormolu and Ceramics," in John Harris and Michael Snodin, eds., *Sir William Chambers, Architect to George III*, exh. cat. Courtauld Institute of Art Gallery, London (New Haven and London: Yale University Press with the Gallery, 1996): 149 – 61; Michael Snodin, "Adam Silver Reassessed," *Burlington Magazine* 139 (January 1997): 17 – 25; Nicholas Goodison, *Matthew Boulton: Ormolu*, rev. ed. (London: Christie's, 2002).

2. For Kedleston Hall see Leslie Harris, *Robert Adam and Kedleston: The Making of a Neo-Classical Masterpiece,* ed. Gervase Jackson-Stops, exh. cat., Cooper-Hewitt Museum, New York (London: National Trust, 1987); Eileen Harris, *The Genius of Robert Adam: His Interiors* (London and New Haven: Paul Mellon Centre for Studies in British Art and Yale University Press, 2001). For Spencer House see Joseph Friedman, *Spencer House: Chronicle of a Great London Mansion* (London: Zwemmer, 1993).

3. The Kedleston tripod is in the house, the Spencer House tripods are at Althorp, a tripod from Wentworth Woodhouse is at the Victoria and Albert Museum (M.46-1948). The candle branches on the Althorp examples carry three nozzles, the Kedleston example one only. The Victoria and Albert Museum example was once fitted with branches, now not present. See Goodison, *Matthew Boulton* (2002): 71 – 75.

4. Snodin, "Adam Silver Reassessed," (1997): 17 – 18; E. Harris, *Genius of Robert Adam* (2001): 33 – 37; L. Harris, *Robert Adam and Kedleston* (1987): 30 – 33. Some of the drawings have tentatively been attributed to Diederich Nicolaus Anderson or workshop by Stephen Astley of Sir John Soane's Museum, London.

5. Nicholas Goodison, "Mr Stuart's Tripod," *Burlington Magazine* 114 (October 1972): 695 – 704; and Goodison, *Matthew Boulton* (2002): 71 – 75.

6. Ms. No.121, Alnwick Castle, Northumberland, quoted in Goodison, "Mr Stuart's Tripod" (1972): 696.

7. For example, "Side-board cistern, Solid Sicilian Jasper.-Stuart. Plate-Warmer, copper-gilt after an Antique Bas. rilievo. Antique Tripod, finely chased on the Side-board. – Stuart" in *Catalogue of the pictures, statues &c at Kedleston, with some account of the Architecture* (ca. 1769): 21.

8. Free Society exhibition catalogue (London: William Griffin, 1761): no. 102, catalogued under "Sculptures and Models."

9. For Anderson see Rupert Gunnis, *Dictionary of British Sculptors, 1660 – 1851*, rev. ed. (London: Murrays Book Sales, 1968): 17; Goodison, "Mr Stuart's Tripod" (1972): 730; Goodison, *Matthew Boulton* (2002): passim. In 1767 his brother and sister were living in Flensburg. "Nicolaus Anderson" of Garrard Street, Soho, is described as a "modeller and chaser" in Thomas Mortimer, *The Universal Director . . .* (London: J. Coote, 1763). In the same year he was given a premium of forty guineas by the Society of Arts for a casting in bronze of "a flora,"

see Robert Dossie, *Memoirs of Agriculture, and other Oeconomical Arts,* vol. 3 (London: C. Nourse; Society for the Encouragment of Arts, Manfactures and Commerce, 1782): 442. I am indebted to Richard Edgcumbe for this reference. Anderson's business was carried on for a time after his death (20 July 1767) by his widow, assisted by at least one "man." In addition to the plate warmer, Anderson is recorded as having made (in bronze and ormolu) some "triton" candlesticks, girandoles, and the mounts of a medal cabinet for Lord Charlemont in 1767, to the design of Sir William Chambers. In the same year he made gilt brass borders and a table frame for the Duke of Northumberland at Syon House. Objects attributed to him include a type of griffin-shaped candlestick of about 1760 – 65, designed by Chambers. That he was well-known is suggested by the contact made by Matthew Boulton with his widow, in search of models to copy.

10. A likely terminus post-quem for the drawings is given by the presence of Stuart's marble wine cooler, supplied by Richard Hayward in January 1758. If the wine cooler shows a design rather than the actual object, the drawings can be no earlier than February 1757, when Curzon bought two paintings by Benedetto Luti shown in the drawing of an end wall. They were in existence by December 1758, when one of the group was criticized in Robert Adam to James Adam, Clerk of Penicuick Mss. GD 4854, National Archives of Scotland, Edinburgh, cited in E. Harris, *Genius of Robert Adam* (2001): 19.

11. Jean-Pierre Cuzin, Jean-René Gaborit, and Alain Pasquier, *D'Après l'antique*, exh. cat., Musée du Louvre, Paris (Réunion des musées nationaux, 2000): 336 – 53.

12. A vase and tripod, ca. 1515, attributed to Giovanni Antonio da Brescia. See Elizabeth Miller, *Sixteenth-Century Italian Ornament Prints in the Victoria and Albert Museum* (London: V&A Publications, 1999): 228, cat. no. 65.

13. See James David Draper and Guilhem Scherf, *Augustin Pajou, dessinateur en Italie, 1752 – 1756,* Archives de l'Art français, n.s. vol. 33 (1997); J.-F. Méjanès, "La Traverse et Pajou," in Scherf, ed., *Augustin Pajou et ses contemporains* Louvre conférences et colloques. (Paris, la Documentation française, 1999): 309 – 97; Muriel de l'Epine, *Autour de Pierre-Adrien de Pâris: Un Album des calques* (Paris: Imprimerie Reich, 2001); Janine Barrier, "Chambers in France and Italy," in J. Harris and Snodin, eds., *Sir William Chambers, Architect* (1996): 19 – 33; Barrier, "William Chambers, Augustin Pajou and their Colleagues in Rome," *Apollo* 147 (January 1998): 25 – 31; Michael Snodin, ed., *Sir William Chambers, Catalogues of Architectural Drawings in the Victoria and Albert Museum* (London: V&A Publications, 1996).

14. Snodin, ed., *Sir William Chambers* (1996): cat. nos. 335 (57812.272), 264 (5712.337); de l'Epine, *Autour de Pierre-Adrien de Pâris* (2001): 85.

15. Svend Eriksen and Francis J. B. Watson, "The Athénienne and the Revival of the Classical Tripod," *Burlington Magazine* 105 (March 1963): 108 – 12; Cuzin, Gaborit, and Pasquier, *D'Après l'antique* (2000): 342 – 45.

16. Snodin, ed., *Sir William Chambers* (1996): cat. 55, (5712.326), appendix cat. 17 (5712.511).

17. For vases of this type by Chambers, J. M. Peyre, and an anonymous printmaker, ca. 1770, see Snodin, ed., *Sir William Chambers* (1996): cat. no. 430, (5712.189); Barrier, "William Chambers" (1998): fig. 3; Werner

Oechslin and Oskar Bätschmann, eds., *Die Vase,* exh. cat. (Zurich: Kunstgewerbemuseum der Stadt, Museum für Gestaltung, 1982): cat. no. 190.

18. Goodison, "Mr Stuart's Tripod" (1972); Goodison, *Matthew Boulton* (2002): 74 – 75.

19. See Mark Wilson Jones, "Tripods, Triglyphs, and the Origin of the Doric Frieze," *American Journal of Archaeology* 106 (July 2002): 353 – 90. I am indebted to Frank Salmon for this reference.

20. Cuzin, Gaborit, and Pasquier, *D'Après l'antique* (2000): 339 – 40, cat. no. 154. For Stuart's probable knowledge of the tripod, see chap. 10, by Susan Weber Soros, in this volume.

21. Maxime Préaud, *Antoine Lepautre, Jacques Lepautre et Jean Lepautre (première partie)*, vol 11 of *Inventaire du fonds français, Graveurs du XVIIe siècle* (Paris: Bibliothèque Nationale, 1999): 191, no. 368.

22. Metropolitan Museum of Art, New York, inv. no. 13.229.3. It, or a very similar head, was the basis of a sketch in the Fossombrone Codex, made after 1523. See Arnold Nesselrath, *Das Fossombroner Skizzenbuch* (London: University of London, Warburg Institute, 1993): 188, figs. 64, 65, 192 – 94.

23. See, e.g., a fragment of a choragic ex-voto relief of two bacchantes in the British Museum, which also exists in numerous replicas. The relief also shows a tripod; Salomon Reinach, *Répertoire des statuaire grecque et romaine,* vol. 2, *Sept mille statues antiques* (Paris: E. Leroux, 1912): 499.

24. See, e.g., Louis-Antoine Prat and Pierre Rosenberg, *Nicolas Poussin (1594 – 1665): Catalogue raisonné des dessins,* vol. 1 (Milan: Leonardo, 1994): 428, no. 218, and 484, no. 246.

25. *Antiquities,* vol. 1 (1762): 7; vol. 4 (1816): 11; Friedman, *Spencer House* (1993): 148, 151.

26. *Antiquities,* vol. 1 (1762): 31.

27. Montagu to Horace Walpole, 12 October 1766, in Horace Walpole, *The Yale Edition of Horace Walpole's Correspondence,* vol. 10, ed. W. S. Lewis (New Haven: Yale University Press, 1941): 230.

28. L. Harris, *Robert Adam and Kedleston* (1987): 30 – 33; E. Harris, *Genius of Robert Adam* (2001): 33 – 34.

29. Snodin, ed., *Sir William Chambers* (1996): 63, cat.179; Goodison, *Matthew Boulton* (2002): 76, fig.32.

30. Snodin, ed., *Sir William Chambers* (1996): 58 – 62.

31. *The Superb and Elegant Produce, of Mess. Boulton and Fothergill's Or Moulu Manufactory, at Soho, in Staffordshire,* sale cat., Christie's, London, 11 – 13 April 1771, first day lot 87; second day lots 69, 92; third day, lot 83; catalogue reproduced in Goodison, *Matthew Boulton* (2002): beginning p. 440.

32. Goodison, *Matthew Boulton* (2002): 276.

33. Until the vase can be more fully inspected, it is not possible to be sure how it functioned. The central tube is 15 cm long and 3 cm wide, the removable tray 13.6 by 13.2 cm, and 2.3 cm deep.

34. The Adam record drawing shows the reverse side of the vase with the spout.

35. Account Books: Carpenters and Joiners, November 1765 – September 1766, Family Pavilion, p. 10, Kedleston Papers, Kedleston Hall, "For 22¼ days work of Wm Johnson making pedestal for Tripod and pedestals for blue vases of pear tree stain'd black at 2'6" pr day £2-16-17½"; ibid., p. 12, "Carvers work brt over," "To carving mouldings and ornaments of pedestals; for the Tripod and 2 small pedestals for the Blue vases." I am indebted to Jill Banks for bringing these accounts to my attention. The design drawings of 1762, which lack the stands, misrepresent the relative proportions of the objects on the sideboard.

36. Such as Matthew Boulton's many vases made of ormolu-mounted blue-john (Goodison, *Matthew Boulton* [2002]: passim).

37. The lacquer on the Boulton vases at Syon has discolored (ibid., 296 and pl. 258).

38. The treatment may have sprung from a desire to match Curzon's baroque silver.

39. Exhibited by Hotspur Ltd. at the Grosvenor House Antiques Fair, 1999.

40. For the special position of gold chasers see Richard Edgcumbe, *The Art of the Gold Chaser in Eighteenth-Century London* (Oxford: Oxford University Press, 2000).

41. The means of holding the plates is also missing.

42. *Catalogue of the pictures, statues &c at Kedleston* (ca. 1769): 21; see also, e.g., a circular funerary urn of Servilia, in the British Museum, carved in relief with draped bearded male terms, linked by hanging garlands, in Reinach, *Répertoire des Reliefs* (1912): 514.

43. Adam Drawings, vol. 25, no. 88, Soane Museum.

44. For example, a design for a medal for the Catch Club (RIBA Library Drawings Collection SD 62/33.1; see fig. 12-17, in this volume.

45. Miller, *Sixteenth-century Italian Ornament Prints* (1999): 239, cat. no. 68a, pl. XII, and cat. no. 68b, pl. V. See also a print of a vase by Jean Lepautre with caryatid figures linked by drapes and satyr heads on the body, in Préaud, *Antoine Lepautre, Jacques Lepautre et Jean Lepautre (deuxième partie)*, vol 12 of *Inventaire du fonds français, Graveurs du XVIIe siècle* (Paris: Bibliothèque Nationale, 1999): 35, no. 1116.

46. *Antiquities,* vol. 1 (1762): 11. For the acanthus leaves see very similar sketches by Chambers and Pajou of acanthus leaves on the throne of St Peter in St Peter's; Barrier, "William Chambers" (1998), figs 8, 9.

47. Goodison, *Matthew Boulton* (2002): 76.

48. Snodin, ed., *Sir William Chambers* (1996): cat. 9, 5712.338, p. 36; for an interpretation of its role in early neoclassical metalwork design see David Udy, "Neo-Classicism and the Evolution of Adam's Vase Designs in Silver," *Antique Collector* 43 (August 1972): 192 – 97.

49. See, e.g., a vase from a set of six engravings by Jean le Pautre, illus. in Préaud, *Antoine Lepautre . . . (deuxième partie)* (1999): 267, no. 1950.

50. Adam Drawings, vol. 25, nos. 76, 78, Soane Museum. It was not executed. The sketch design (no. 76) has curving legs similar to the tripod; both designs have a large palmette on the side. See Snodin, "Adam Silver Reassessed" (January 1997): 19.

51. RIBA Library Drawings Collection SD 62/1.

52. Adam's design was made in ormolu for Sir Lawrence Dundas (before 1763) and the Duke of Bolton; see E. Harris, *Genius of Robert*

Adam (2001): 48. For Boulton see Goodison, *Matthew Boulton* (2002): 76.

53. Goodison, *Matthew Boulton* (2002): 72.

54. James Stuart to Thomas Anson, 23 September 1769, Lichfield Ms. D615/P(5)1/6, Staffordshire County Record Office.

55. James Stuart to Josiah Wedgwood, 24 January 1771, Wedgwood to Stuart 29 January 1771, Wedgwood Mss., Keele University Library (on loan from the Wedgwood Museum, Barlaston, Stoke-on-Trent Staffordshire); Wedgwood to Thomas Bentley, 24 – 26 December 1770 etc., Rylands Manuscripts, Rylands Library.

56. Goodison, *Matthew Boulton* (2002): 271.

57. Ibid., 242.

58. "I have some sketches of the subjects we talked of at Soho, the border of the tea table, and the tripodic tea kitchen," in James Stuart to Matthew Boulton, 26 December 1769, Matthew Boulton Papers, Birmingham Central Library.

59. Goodison, *Matthew Boulton* (2002): 271 – 75.

60. Ibid., 271.

61. Ibid., 285, fig. 241.

62. Set out in Rowe, *Adam Silver* (1965): 81 – 84.

63. Josiah Wedgwood to Matthew Boulton, 19 February 1771, Matthew Boulton Papers, Birmingham Central Library.

Fig. 12-1, obverse. Thomas Pingo, after a design by James Stuart. Royal Society of Arts Medal, 1759. Silver. This example was awarded to Miss Sarah Moore for drawing. *Checklist no. 167.*

STUART AND THE DESIGN AND

MAKING OF MEDALS

CHRISTOPHER EIMER

Stuart's return from Italy in 1755 coincided with proposals being made by the Society for the Promotion of Arts, Manufactures and Commerce (now the Royal Society of Arts, or RSA) for the making of a medal, to be offered as a means of encouragement and reward. The society had been founded only two years earlier, in 1753, and this represented the first medal with which they were to be associated. Its design and production were to draw Stuart into an unfamiliar world of die engravers and the associated elements of technical expertise. At the time, Stuart was already beginning to receive commissions for large-scale architectural work from a number of clients with classical interests, most of them members of the Society of Dilettanti (see chap. 4). The miniature format of the medal could not hope to compete with the prestige provided by these building commissions, but the designs and decorative devices with which he was to become most closely associated were to be perfectly adapted from one form of work to the other.

In the promotion of arts, manufactures, and commerce, the original proposals for the RSA, as shaped by its founder, William Shipley, included the distribution of monetary premiums. The prize medal under discussion was complementary to these financial disbursements, but it was not without precedent. In 1737 the Royal Society

of London had introduced the Copley gold medal, which was awarded for work in the sciences.[1] In addition to their prize medal, however, the RSA also wished to encourage the art of medal making, and as a consequence, they introduced a series of premiums for this purpose. It was this extended commitment toward medallic art and design that brought Stuart into the arcane world of medalists and medal making.

The story of the manufacture of the RSA's inaugural medal illustrates how Stuart came to prepare the draft designs for his first medallic commission and to oversee its production (fig. 12-1). It also provides a background for how other medals came to be designed by Stuart, some of which were sponsored by the RSA, some by other societies, and some privately. The first full-blown plan for the offering of medals by the RSA, enlarging upon Shipley's ideas, was made to the society in March 1756 by Henry Baker, a scientist and inventor. Baker proposed that a "dye be made for striking Medals of Gold, Silver and Copper," which was "to be occasionally bestowed by the Society."[2] A committee, which included the jeweler and pottery manufacturer Nicholas Crisp, sculptor Henry Cheere, and artist William Hogarth, concurred with this proposal. Baker will have well understood the effect of such an award, having been the recipient of the Royal Society of London's Copley Medal in 1744. A Medal

Committee of the RSA was formed in April 1756, and among its first members were Stuart and Thomas Hollis, an antiquary who also played an influential role in the direction of the committee.[3]

Crisp developed Baker's ideas for a medal design, which, at its most simplistic, carried a figure representing the arts on one side, and on the other, various symbols of industry and invention, including a watermill.[4] The Medal Committee deemed Crisp's proposals appropriate and ordered them to be chased on two gold plates, the work to be carried out by George Michael Moser, a watch-chaser. Only the principal elements of Crisp's original and somewhat convoluted ideas had been incorporated, and Moser was entrusted "with the care of cutting the Die, by appointing such artist in England, as he shall think proper to cut the same."[5]

In April 1757 Moser attended a meeting of the committee with Richard Yeo, a coin and medal engraver who had been at the Mint since 1749. Both Moser and Yeo had also been members of Saint Martin's Academy of Arts. Yeo was reported to have estimated the engraving work at one hundred guineas and the medal itself as requiring fifteen guineas of gold.[6] The Medal Committee had budgeted only five guineas of gold for the medal and were obliged to form a new device, with the reverse carrying a simple wreath, the recipient's name to be engraved within and around it.

Yeo clarified his position in a letter to the RSA in April 1757. This document provides a rare glimpse of the practices of a die engraver in the middle of the eighteenth century and, in particular, gives a firsthand account of the technical challenges of medal making:

> I had the honour to attend your Committee last week, when questions were proposed to me concerning a medal for your Society. I shew'd the Gentlemen some Medals I have made, among which . . . [one] was the nearest in size to the pattern propos'd, I was ask'd how much would be the value of gold necessary to make a Medal of that size, after the chasing of Mr Mosers. I told the Gentlemen . . . it cou'd not be less than fifteen guineas; but I did not imagine I was understood to mean, that a Medal cou'd not be made after that design, of a lesser size, & consequently of less value in Gold, for it may be equally well executed, in a size of ten guineas value, or even five, if required,

& the expence of engraving the dies, will be less, nearly in the same proportion.

> In all dies that are to be harden'd, & struck there is great hazard of their breaking, cracking or sinking, & that such accidents are seldom in any other manner to be remedied, than by making a new one & that such hazard is proportionately greater, as the Die is larger. I broke two Dies in making the Cambridge Medal & tho' I had a hundred guineas, & five guineas which his Grace sent me as a present it prov'd very unprofitable. But if the hazard be suppos'd less than I have represented it, I wou'd propose to engrave the Dies, of that size for four score guineas, & bear only half of the loss occasion'd by such accidents, & so in proportion as the size agreed on is lesser.[7]

The "hazards" referred to largely centered on matters of purity and grain of steel, which could change character while being heated. This procedure, which the dies underwent for hardening, called for an instinctive judgment as to when the metal had reached the right color, as too much or too little heat could cause them to crack or to sink unduly in use. This meant that the die would collapse into the collar into which it was being held, which could result in a burr of metal running around the edge of the medal or produce some other flaw on its surface. Yeo's fees clearly included a premium of insurance, and one which he was quite prepared to reduce by a proportion equal to the increased risk that the client was prepared to bear.

Despite the various cost-saving measures, the RSA decided to abandon Crisp's designs altogether in favor of a new composition, which was based on a drawing that had been prepared by Stuart. The design for the draft, which has not survived, was presented to the Medal Committee by Hollis and found to be satisfactory to the purpose. Stuart was asked "to get a model in wax made of the said device and to give Mr Yeo Directions to cut the Die for the said Medal."[8] A legend for the new medal was agreed upon, and it was to have a diameter of 51mm and an agreed limit of eight guineas gold. By January 1758 Yeo had still not finished the work, and the society was becoming anxious for the medal, given that mention of it had been made in the premium lists for that year.

The process of making the medal had been fraught with technical difficulties, as Yeo's letter had intimated, but the society was not prepared to shoulder any of the risks mentioned therein. Indeed, they considered that examples of the medal presented by Yeo in May 1758 to be substandard in both expense and execution, and his services were dispensed with.[9]

The society now authorized new dies and puncheons, or punches, to be cut, still using Stuart's design, but its diameter would be 44 mm instead of the 51 mm, thereby further reducing the cost of the gold. Stuart was authorized to appoint another artist for the cutting of new dies and puncheons, using his same designs, and he recommended Thomas Pingo, an engraver of punches at the assay office.[10] Pingo was a member of an established family of engravers, and it is likely that Stuart knew him, whether at first hand or by reputation. Unlike Yeo, Pingo worked as a private engraver and medalist, independent of the mint, and is believed to have set up the first private medal manufactory in Britain, where two of his sons, John and Lewis, were also to work.[11]

In November 1758 Thomas Pingo secured the contract to execute the RSA's prize medal. The experience of having to abort their first medal and the forewarning of the hazards associated with the striking of dies had proved a costly but valuable lesson. Pingo's contract obliged him "to run the hazard of the breaking or cracking of the Dies" until fifty of the medals had been struck and, when needed, to supply puncheons at his own expense. It also stipulated that the work was to be "executed to the satisfaction of Mr Stuart."[12] The punch, a steel tool with the design in relief, enabled further dies to be made. It provided a safeguard in the event of failure, a single master die sometimes taking weeks to make.

The society's first medal (fig. 12-1), designed by Stuart and engraved and manufactured by the Pingos, was ready for presentation in early December 1758. The medal shows a seated Britannia with spear and shield, being honored by figures of Mercury (representing commerce) and Minerva (the arts). On the reverse side is a wreath for the recipient's name, the date, and other details. An honorary presentation of an example in gold was made to Stuart, who received the thanks of the society "for the care and trouble he had taken in forming and drawing the device."[13] Stuart's role was clearly greater than this note of thanks suggests. Understandably frustrated by the time and expense in having to abort their first medal, the society had empowered him to see the medal all the way through to production.

The first recipients of the society's medal were Philip Carteret Webb, for the sowing of acorns, and Lady Louisa Greville, for a drawing. Such was the durability of the medal that it was used for the next fifty years, and among the more eminent recipients were the sculptor John Bacon and the painter James Barry. A progressively deteriorating die necessitated an entirely new medal in 1807, which was designed by the sculptor and draftsman John Flaxman.

Thomas Hollis, Stuart's colleague on the RSA's Medal Committee, was a bachelor of considerable wealth, who combined Whig sympathies with antiquarian interests.[14] One way in which this bore fruit was a scheme for disseminating medals, books, and prints stamped with various devices. An association with the Pingos and Stuart enabled Hollis to indulge his various interests. As is clear from a diary that Hollis started in 1759, Stuart's work on medals extended well beyond the formal structure of the RSA.[15] The diary provides an insight into these activities and reveals the pivotal role that Hollis played in the promotion of medals and support of medalists, not just the Pingos, but also John Kirk. In addition it details the part that Stuart played in the realization of Hollis's schemes.

For the RSA, as no doubt for Hollis, a succession of British victories in the Seven Years' War provided admirable subject matter for the making of commemorative medals. These constitute the first medal premiums to be offered by the society; they were awarded between 1758 and 1763 (Nos. 2, 3, 5, 7, 8, 11, 13, 15, 19). Their designs were prepared by Stuart, who based the principal elements of composition on Roman imperial coinage. Those for the taking of Louisburg and Goree carry the head of Britannia on one side and the figure of Victory standing on the prow of a galley on the other (Nos. 2, 3). This design may be found on the silver coinage of Emperor Augustus, as well as on that of his successors.[16] Another version of that composition survives on one of Stuart's draft designs for the action at Lagos (No. 14), for which no medal appears to have been struck. A variation of it can also be seen on the medal commemorating the taking of Quebec (No. 5).

Perhaps the most celebrated image adapted by Stuart, and certainly the most emotive, was that of the bound captive seated in front of a palm tree. This design finds its genesis in the "Judea Capta" coins of the emperors Titus and Vespasian, which were made after the suppression of the Jewish rebellion in the first century A.D. It was used by Stuart for medals commemorating the subjugation of Canada (No. 7) and the taking of Montreal in 1760 (No. 8), on which he has replaced the palm tree with a Canada fir.

The raised figure of Victory standing on a globe and supported by two figures, on Stuart's medal for the battle of Minden in 1759 (No. 15), recalls the reverses of some third-century Roman coinage, struck for the German campaigns.[17] Similarly, the medal commemorating military action in 1759 at Guadeloupe also pursues the theme of a figure being raised (No. 13), common to second-century Roman coinage. The degree to which Stuart had been influenced and directed by Hollis is unclear, but the latter's diary entries certainly suggest close cooperation. On an evening visit from Stuart, Hollis recalled having "settled the plan of a medal on the taking of Guadeloupe to be prepared at the Society promoting Arts & Commerce."[18] Few of Stuart's medallic drawings survive, but an extant Guadeloupe sketch may be the one mentioned by Hollis (No. 12).

In addition to appearing on the premium medals of the RSA, these medallic designs were adapted for use on a series of plaster medallions that decorated the Temple of Concord and Victory at Stowe (see figs. 4-27, 4-28, 7-11).[19] The adaptation and use of this imagery is hardly surprising, as it represented popular and analogous themes, comparing British achievements in the Seven Years' War with those of the Roman Empire. The coins on which the designs are based were to be found on the engraved plates of published works on numismatics, as well as in the collector's cabinets of travelers who had taken the Grand Tour.[20] They provided Stuart with a topical and readily available source of material for use on the medals. Alongside the coins, there were cabinets of gems and intaglios, all of which constituted the requisite parts of an antiquary's library.

Antiquaries were certainly among the clients from whom Stuart would be receiving commissions, and one of the most prominent of these was Thomas Anson, a founder-member of the Society of Dilettanti. Stuart worked on the building and grounds of Anson's Shugborough Hall (see fig. 7-3), but he also designed a medal for Anson, which was to serve as a memorial to Anson's late brother and great benefactor, Admiral George, Lord Anson (No. 22). The medal, engraved by Thomas Pingo, carries the familiar figure of Victory on a ship's prow. Correspondence with Anson makes clear that Stuart not only designed the medal and organized its manufacture,

but also played a part in its distribution.[21] Admiral Anson had been the subject of books and engraved prints, which were published shortly after his circumnavigation of the world in 1744 (see chap. 4). It probably took little to convince Thomas Anson that a medal would represent an appropriate and distinctive memorial to his illustrious brother.

Another medal collector was the Marquess of Rockingham, who was also one of Stuart's clients. On hearing of William Hunter's acquisition in 1771 of the collection of John Montagu, fourth Earl of Sandwich, Rockingham is said to have written to Hunter, "begging for a sight of the catalogue."[22] Many of these medals were being executed by Thomas Pingo, and the Rockingham papers reveal the direct purchase in 1773 of medals from Pingo, as well as from Stuart.[23] King George III, who was said to have been "fond of ingenious curiosities," also acquired medals, as did other members of the royal family, including Princess Augusta.[24] This royal patronage made medal collecting increasingly fashionable. Thomas Snelling, for example, one of the suppliers to the royal family, was among the most prominent and respected numismatists of his time, with a large retail outlet.[25]

Although the Pingos were responsible for the majority of Stuart-designed medals, John Kirk engraved the dies for a small number of Stuart's medallic compositions (Nos. 6, 8, 11). Kirk's role in the actual striking of his medals is unclear, however, and there is nothing to suggest that, like the Pingos, he operated his own die-sinking manufactory. Indeed, certain elements of technique and design on his medallic work, such as a beaded border, are common to those engraved by the Pingos and suggest that the medals themselves were struck on the same machinery and with the same technical expertise.[26] For Stuart, this would not have affected the preparation of medallic designs, but being able to deal directly with the die engraver responsible for reproducing the draft design would ultimately save both parties a great deal of time and inconvenience.

Stuart's medal of General James Wolfe (No. 6), engraved by Kirk, seems to stand apart stylistically from others by this medalist. A wax model of Wolfe was made by Isaac Gossett, a prolific modeler, and was advertised for subscription in 1760.[27] Models such as this were relatively easy to produce and provided a marketing test for the popularity of a particular image, no doubt resulting in the making of some medals. These models clearly had a commercial value in their own right, which may explain why the medal of Wolfe is signed by both Kirk and Gossett. The signature of Stuart, however, as a designer of medals, is not to be found on any medallic work, whether by Kirk or the Pingos.

Stuart's design for the reverse of the Royal Military Academy medal (No. 20) incorporates the figure of Minerva standing between an owl and a gorgon's head. The influence of Hollis, for whom Athens was the political embodiment of liberty, is all too clear. Indeed, many of the engravings and books owned by Hollis, and which he distributed, are stamped with symbolic legends and devices designed by Stuart. Typically, these incorporate a figure of Athena or Minerva, as well as an owl and a cap of liberty. The tools for their stamping were cut by the Pingos.

A medal of Frederick the Great (No. 4) has Stuart's familiar figure of Victory on the reverse side and was almost certainly sponsored privately by Hollis. As an ally of Britain, the German emperor was a popular figure, whose image appeared on a variety of commemorative ware. Hollis also commissioned Giovanni Cipriani, an Italian artist living in London, to produce drafts for medals. One was for an intended medal of Frederick the Great, but this did not come to fruition, although a design does survive.[28] Another of Cipriani's designs was for a medal commemorating the capture of Louisburg by the British in 1758, the dies for which were engraved by Kirk.[29] This design is clearly based on Stuart's version of the medal (No. 2), and was no doubt thus directed by Hollis.

A classical education enabled Hollis to couple Stuart's medallic compositions with inscriptions taken from suitable texts, Virgil and Milton being particular favorites (see No. 16). In this way Hollis was able to make a practical contribution to Stuart's designs, illustrating the teamwork that was required for successful medal making. This demanded skills of composition, draftsmanship, and steel engraving and knowledge of the mechanical sciences, which were rarely to be found in the hands of one individual.

In addition to his work on medallic design, Stuart has been credited with the making of cast and chased copies, or fantasies consisting of contrived or invented compositions, of sixteenth- and seventeenth-century British medals.[30] However, there is no evidence to suggest that he was directly involved in the mechanics of medal making in any of its manifestations, over and above the preparation of draft designs. Were that to have been the case, there

can be little doubt that Hollis would have given some hint of it in his diary, which is full of anecdote and detail relative to medal making. Indeed, the diary paints a rare and invaluable picture of numismatic life in London between 1759 and 1770.

Stuart's draft designs for medals were frequently adapted in other contexts: on the sketch of an urn (see checklist no. 39), where elements of its central device have been taken from the medal for the capture of Quebec in 1759 (No. 5); on the engraved headpiece to the first volume of *Antiquities of Athens*, which carries a medallic device of George III; and, most conspicuously, on the aforementioned plaster medallions that decorate the walls of the Temple of Concord and Victory at Stowe (see figs. 4-27, 4-28, 7-11).

Given the ephemeral nature of medal making, it is not altogether surprising that so few of Stuart's medal designs have survived. Those that do, however, not only demonstrate versatility, but also reveal the hand of a skilled draftsman. The medals bearing his designs constitute a group that admirably addresses the issue, raised by the Royal Society of Arts in its original proposals, that the nation's medallic art was "capable of great improvement."[31] The indictment had been as much about fabric and production as about design, and the obvious improvements reflect the contributions not only of Stuart, but also of the Pingos, as associate die engravers and medalists for most of Stuart's medal designs.

The first medallic composition with which Stuart can be associated, for the RSA premium medal in 1758, suggests an original hand and one unfettered by outside influence. In general, however, his work in the field of medal design largely reflects ideas that were not wholly his own, essentially reproducing, albeit with modern adaptation, a group of devices of classical origin. Without these restraints and conventions, his medallic work might have evolved along a different and more original line. His close association with the RSA and Thomas Hollis, however, clearly prevented him from establishing any real independence of thought in the medium. Certainly, there is nothing to suggest that he was any less suited to the miniature requirements of the medal than to larger scale architectural composition, and indeed, as his work demonstrates, he was adept at being able to combine the two with considerable harmony.

Fig. 12-1. Obverse   Fig. 12-1. Reverse   Fig. 12-2. Obverse   Fig. 12-2. Reverse

1. **Royal Society of Arts Prize Medal, 1758**

Thomas Pingo, after a design by James Stuart
Gold, scarce; silver, common; copper, rare; 44 mm

Obverse: Britannia, seated left with spear and shield, is conferred with honors by the standing figures of Mercury (Commerce), and Minerva (Arts). ARTS. AND. COMMERCE. PROMOTED. Exergue: SOCIETY INST. LONDON MDCCLIIII. Continuous beaded border. Signed PINGO below the figure of Britannia. Reverse: wreath (space within and around for the recipient's name, subject, and date of award). Continuous beaded border.

Example illustrated in fig. 12-1: 1759. Silver. Awarded to Miss Sarah Moore for drawing. By courtesy of the Trustees of the British Museum, London. *Checklist no. 167*

This is the first premium medal of the Royal Society of Arts. It was awarded in gold and silver for work in arts, manufactures, and commerce; examples in copper are specimen strikings. It was exhibited by Thomas Pingo in 1760.[32]

References: see checklist no. 167.

2. **Louisburg Taken, 1758**

John Pingo, after a design by James Stuart
Gold, very rare; Silver, rare; Copper, scarce; 40 mm

Obverse: bust of Britannia left, a trident projecting from behind her neck. O. FAIR. BRITANNIA. HAIL. Continuous beaded border.
Reverse: Victory standing right, on the prow of a galley, a wreath in her outstretched right hand. LOVISBOVRG TAKEN MDCCLVIII. Continuous beaded border.

Example illustrated in fig. 12-2: Copper. By courtesy of the Trustees of the British Museum, London.

In April 1758 the RSA announced its first premium in the class of die engraving, offering twenty guineas for "a copper medal the size of an English crown," which was to be "executed the best in point of workmanship and boldness of relief, by persons under the age of twenty-five."[33] In October 1758 John Pingo's model was approved, and in March 1759 the completed medal was delivered to the society. The "face" of the die was reported as being cracked, however, and other objections were made regarding the inscription on the reverse. John Pingo was therefore directed to make new dies, keeping the same design but changing the inscription to "Goree Taken MDCCLVIII" (see No. 3).[34]

The head of Britannia, as noted by Thomas Hollis, was based on an antique paste, which almost certainly took the form of a small cameo, in his possession.[35] The obverse legend is taken from "On Leaving Holland" (1744), a poem by Mark Akenside, whose work Hollis frequently quoted.[36]

References: Hawkins, *Medallic Illustrations* (1885/1969): George II, 405, var. 406; Eimer, *British Commemorative Medals* (1987): 658; Betts, *American Colonial History* (1894/1972): 413; Eimer, *Pingo Family* (1998): 11.

This list comprises all the known medal designs by James "Athenian" Stuart, as well as the medals with which he can be associated. They are presented chronologically, according to the presumed sequence of production. This does not always agree with the date of the event commemorated by the medal or the date of the medal's institution, which is given in the first line of each medal entry, but the text, notes, and references include as much evidence of production as is known. A key to abbreviated references will be found at the end of the list.

Fig. 12-3. Obverse   Fig. 12-3. Reverse   Fig. 12-4. Obverse   Fig. 12-4. Reverse

3. Goree Taken, 1758

John Pingo, after a design by James Stuart
Silver, scarce; copper, common; 40 mm

Obverse: bust of Britannia left, trident projecting from
behind her neck. O. FAIR. BRITANNIA. HAIL.
Continuous beaded border.
Reverse: Victory standing right, on the prow of a galley, a
wreath in her outstretched right hand. GOREE. TAKEN.
MDCCLVIII. Continuous beaded border.

Example illustrated in fig. 12-3: Silver. By courtesy of the
Trustees of the British Museum, London. *Checklist no. 168.*

On May 14, 1759, John Pingo was given the RSA premium of twenty guineas for the die engraving of this
medal. He assured the medal committee "that he had cut
the dies and made the puncheons without any assistance,"
and he received an additional ten guineas for his "extraordinary trouble in making a new die" (see No. 2).[37]

Thomas Hollis noted having sent copper medals for
the taking of Goree to "Mr Pitt," and on the edge of one
of these was inscribed "William Pitt Administring."[38]
Examples of other medals are also occasionally found
with their edges thus inscribed (Nos. 5, 9, 13, 19).

References: see checklist no. 168.

4. Frederick the Great, Defeat of the French and
    Austrians, 1757

Thomas Pingo, after a design by James Stuart
Gold, very rare; silver, common; copper, scarce; 42 mm

Obverse: bust right, armored and draped, sash over
left shoulder, hair tied in bow falling over shoulder.
FREDERICVS MAGNVS BOR. REX [Frederick the
Great, King of Prussia]. Signed PINGO on the
truncation.
Reverse: Victory, holding palm frond in left hand and
laurel wreath in outstretched right hand, advancing left
towards a trophy of captured arms; above, an eagle; TE
DVCE FREDERICE SEQVOR. [With you as leader
Frederick, I follow]. Exergue: GALLIS ET AVSTRIACIS
DEVICTIS MDCCLVII [The defeat of the French and
Austrians, 1757].

Example illustrated in fig. 12-4: Gold. By courtesy of the
Trustees of the British Museum, London. *Checklist no. 169.*

It is not clear precisely when this medal was struck, but an
example was exhibited by Thomas Pingo in 1760 at the
RSA.[39] Frederick the Great was a close ally of England,
and the alliance formed between Britain and Prussia in
1756 marks the beginning of the Seven Years' War.

References: see checklist no. 169.

Fig. 12-5. Obverse   Fig. 12-5. Reverse   Fig. 12-1. Obverse   Fig. 12-1. Reverse

5. Quebec Taken, 1759

John Pingo, after a design by James Stuart
Gold, very rare; silver, scarce; copper, scarce; 40 mm

Obverse: bust of BRITANNIA left; below, a naval and
a military trophy of trident and standard, marked
SAVNDERS and WOLFE, crossed and decorated with
a wreath. Continuous beaded border.
Reverse: a captive chained to the base of a trophy of
French arms, which Victory crowns with a wreath.
QVEBEC. TAKEN. MDCCLIX Exergue: SOC.P.A.C.
Continuous beaded border.

Example illustrated in fig. 12-5: Silver. By courtesy of the
Trustees of the British Museum, London.

In November 1759 the RSA offered a premium for a
medal commemorating the capture of Quebec by Major-
General James Wolfe and Vice-Admiral Sir Charles
Saunders. A wax model had already been approved, for
which John Pingo cut the dies and received twenty
guineas.[40] In its early years the Royal Society of Arts was
sometimes referred to as the Society Promoting Arts and
Commerce, which was abbreviated "Soc. P. A. C." on this
and on other medals (Nos. 7, 11, 19). The bust of Britannia
appears in this form on an urn.[41] Some examples of this
medal occur with their edges having been inscribed
"William Pitt Administring" (see No. 3).

References: Hawkins, *Medallic Illustrations* (1885/1969):
George II, 439; Eimer, *British Commemorative Medals*
(1987): 673; Betts, *American Colonial History* (1894/1972):
421; Eimer, *Pingo Family* (1998): 14.

6. Death of General James Wolfe, 1759

John Kirk (engraver), Isaac Gossett (modeler), after a
design by James Stuart
Silver, rare; copper, scarce; 37 mm

Obverse: Bust left, armored and draped. IACOBUS
WOLFE ANGLUS. Below the bust: GOSSET.M.KIRK.F.
Reverse: funerary urn, its base inscribed PRO PATRIA,
amidst arms and standards. IN VICTORIA CAESVS.
Exergue: QVEBECAE SEPT. XIII. MDCCLIX.

Example illustrated in fig. 12-6: Copper. By courtesy of
the Trustees of the British Museum, London. *Checklist no.
170.*

The medal was engraved by John Kirk and modeled by
Isaac Gossett, who advertised waxes of Wolfe's head on
subscription in 1760.[42] Many years later, Stuart exhibited
his designs for the medal at the Society of Artists (1775).[43]

References: see checklist no. 170.

Fig. 12-7. Obverse   Fig. 12-7. Reverse

7. Canada Subdued, 1760

John Pingo, after a design by James Stuart
Silver, scarce; copper, scarce; 39 mm

Obverse: bust left, laureate, hair long, falling over nape of
the neck. GEORGE. II. KING. Continuous beaded
border.
Reverse: female beneath a Canada fir tree, behind which,
a beaver. CANADA SUBDUED Exergue: MDCCLX

S.P.A.C. Continuous beaded border.

Example illustrated in fig. 12-7: Silver. By courtesy of the Trustees of the British Museum, London. *Checklist no. 171.*

A drawing of "the head of his late majesty" was approved for use on a medal, which was the subject of a premium offered by the RSA. For the reverse, it desired "Mr Pingo" to make a "drawing representing a captive woman, after the manner of the antique" and based on the first-century "Judea Capta" coinage of imperial Rome.[44] John Pingo gained a premium of thirteen guineas for the medal in May 1761.[45]

References: see checklist no. 171.

Fig. 12-8. Obverse   Fig. 12-8. Reverse

8. Montreal Taken and the Conquest of Canada Completed, 1760

John Kirk, after a design by James Stuart
Silver, scarce; copper, scarce; 41 mm

Obverse: A female figure seated to right, beneath a Canada fir tree and beside a French shield. MONTREAL TAKEN MDCCLX. Exergue: SOC. PROMOTING ARTS AND COMMERCE.
Reverse: River god of the St. Lawrence reclining against the prow of a galley, a beaver walking on his leg; beyond, a standard decorated with a wreath inscribed AMHERST and surmounted by a lion. THE CONQVEST OF CANADA COMPLETED. Exergue: captured French and native American arms.

Example illustrated in fig. 12-8: Silver. By courtesy of the Trustees of the British Museum, London. *Checklist no. 172.*

In June 1761 John Kirk received the premium of 17 guineas from the Royal Society of Arts for his work on this medal.[46] Thomas Hollis wrote that in August 1760 Kirk showed him "a very fine Model, the design of which was made by Stuart, to be put before the SPAC."[47]

References: see checklist no. 172.

Fig. 12-9. Obverse   Fig. 12-9. Reverse

9. Capture of Pondicherry, 1761

Thomas Pingo, after a design by James Stuart
Silver, scarce; copper, scarce; 39 mm

Obverse: bust right, head laureate and hair tied with ribbon, within a beaded border. GEORGE. THE. THIRD. Below, crossed branches. Continuous beaded border. Signed T.P.F. below the bust.
Reverse: Victory standing right, her left foot on a ball, inscribing a shield COOTE STEEVENS between palms, rudders and two spilt urns running with waters of the INDVS and GANGES rivers. TOTAL. EXPVLSION. OF. THE. FRENCH. FROM. INDIA. Exergue: PONDICHERRY TAKEN MDCCLXI. Continuous beaded border.

Example illustrated in fig. 12-9: Copper. By courtesy of the Trustees of the British Museum, London. *Checklist no. 173.*

In September 1761 Thomas Hollis refers to having visited "Mr Pingo's to see the Medal on the taking of Pondicherry, the Invention of which is Mr Stuart's," and having "bespoke one for my own cabinet in bronze, & 9 in silver for the setts of Medals intended for abroad."[48] A flaw on some examples of this medal occurs as a burr of metal running around the border on the reverse. It suggests the disruption of metal flow during striking, possibly due to a cracked or broken die. The action commemorated by this medal was fought under Sir General Eyre Coote and Rear-Admiral Charles Steevens. Some examples of this medal occur with their edges having been inscribed "William Pitt Adminstring" (see No. 3).

References: see checklist no. 173.

503

Fig. 12-10

Fig. 12-11. Obverse

Fig. 12-11. Reverse

10. Sketch for a proposed medal commemorating the Victory at Belleisle (1759), ca. 1761

James Stuart
Pen and ink, gray wash, pencil; 7⅝ x 6¼ in. (19.5 x 16 cm)

RIBA Library Drawings Collection, London, SD 62/31

This rough sketch (fig. 12-10), depicting Stuart's representation of Britannia or Victory standing on the prow of a galley, closely resembles the composition found on the reverse of John Kirk's medal for the action at Belleisle (No. 11). A drawing for the "design of a medal for Sir Edward Hawke's victory in Quiberon Bay" was exhibited at the Free Society of Artists in 1768 by Stuart.[49] It is unclear whether it is this sketch or a more finished version.

References: see checklist no. 174.

11. Battle of Belleisle, 1759

John Kirk, after a design by James Stuart
Silver, common; copper, scarce; 40 mm

Obverse: Britannia, armed with a trident, is seated upon a sea-horse and crowned by Victory. BRITAIN. TRIVMPHED. HAWKE. COMMANDED Exergue: OFF. BELLEISLE NOV. XX. MDCCLIX Continuous beaded border.
Reverse: Figures of NIGHT and TEMPEST shield FRANCE from the thunder of BRITAIN. Exergue: FRANCE RELINQVISHES THE SEA S.P.A.C. Continuous beaded border.

Example illustrated in fig. 12-11: Silver. By courtesy of the Trustees of the British Museum, London.

In March 1761 the RSA decided to award a premium for the making of a medal for the action at Belleisle, or Quiberon Bay, as it was also known, which had been fought under the command of Admiral Edward Hawke.[50] In April 1762 John Kirk received 30 guineas for his work on this medal.[51]

References: Hawkins, *Medallic Illustrations* (1885/1969): George II, 441; Eimer, *British Commemorative Medals* (1987): 676.

Fig. 12-12

Fig. 12-13. Obverse   Fig. 12-13. Reverse

12. Sketch for a proposed medal commemorating the taking of Guadeloupe, 1759

James Stuart
Pen and ink, color wash, pencil; 7 15/16 x 6 3/4 in. (20 x 17 cm)

RIBA Library Drawings Collection, London, SD 62/30

Having received a visit from Stuart, Thomas Hollis refers to having "settled the plan of a medal on the taking of Guadaloupe."[52]

References: see checklist no. 175.

13. Guadeloupe Taken, 1759

Lewis Pingo, after a design by James Stuart
Silver, rare; copper, scarce; 40 mm

Obverse: Pallas standing to left, one foot on a galley's prow, holding a trident and military standard: MOORE left; BARRINGTON right. Exergue: SOC. PROM. ARTS AND. COMMERCE. Continuous beaded border.
Reverse: Britannia, standing left, raises a female figure holding sugar-canes. GVADALVPE. SVRRENDERS Exergue: MAY. 1. MDCCLIX. Continuous beaded border.

Example illustrated in fig. 12–13: Copper. By courtesy of the Trustees of the British Museum, London. *Checklist no. 176.*

Actions at Guadeloupe and Lagos were the two subjects offered by the Royal Society of Arts in 1761 for the best copper medal the size of an English crown. Lewis Pingo received the premium of twenty guineas for this medal, and it was exhibited in 1762 by Thomas Pingo at the Royal Society of Arts.[53] The action was fought under Admirals Sir John Moore and Samuel Barrington. Some examples of this medal occur with their edges having been inscribed "William Pitt Administring" (see No. 3).

References: see checklist no. 176.

Fig. 12-14

Fig. 12-15. Obverse   Fig. 12-15. Reverse

14. **Sketch for a proposed medal for the taking of Lagos, ca. 1761**

James Stuart
Pen and ink, pencil; 7⅛ x 7½ in. (18 x 19 cm)

RIBA Library Drawings Collection, London,
SD 62/29 (1).

In May 1761 Stuart's drawing, in an advanced form, was considered by the RSA "a proper design for a medal," although a medal commemorating this action never came to fruition.[54] The drawing features a version of Stuart's figure of Britannia or Victory standing on the prow of a galley, a fitting symbol for a naval battle at which Admiral Boscowen burned a number of French ships. In Stuart's other extant drawing for a medal commemorating the taking of Lagos, he shows the prows of the galleys burning (see chronology fig. C6).

References: see checklist no. 178.

15. **Battle of Minden, 1759**

John Pingo, after a design by James Stuart
Silver, scarce; copper, scarce; 40 mm

Obverse: Two soldiers, British and German, support Victory on a globe, who crowns each with a wreath. CONCORD. OF THE. ALLIES Exergue: AVG. I. MDCCLIX. Continuous beaded border. Reverse: Victory seated right, with captured French shields, supports a shield inscribed MINDEN Exergue: SOCIETY. PROM. ARTS AND. COMMERCE. Continuous beaded border.

Example illustrated in fig. 12-15: Silver. By courtesy of the Trustees of the British Museum, London. *Checklist no. 179.*

In April 1762 John Pingo received a premium of twenty guineas from the RSA for this medal.[55] He exhibited it in 1762 at the RSA.[56] The obverse design was adapted by Stuart from a type found on late imperial Roman coinage.

References: see checklist no. 179.

Fig. 12-16. Obverse   Fig. 12-16. Reverse

16. Birth of George, Prince of Wales, 1762

Thomas Pingo, after a design by James Stuart
Gold, very rare; silver, scarce; copper, scarce; 40 mm

Obverse: busts, facing one another, of George III, right,
hair long and tied with ribbon, and Queen Charlotte,
left, her hair braided. A star below. GEORGIVS. III.
REX. CHARLOTTA. REGINA. Signed T. PINGO. F
below the busts.
Reverse: Britannia seated left receives an infant, a star
over its head, from Mercury, standing right, a cornucopia
in his right arm. PACATVMQVE. REGET. PATRIIS.
VIRTVTIBVS. ORBEM [And he will rule a peaceful
world with the virtues of his father]. Exergue: XII. AVG.
MDCCLXII.

Example illustrated in fig. 12-16: Gold. By courtesy of
the Trustees of the British Museum, London. *Checklist no.
180.*

In September 1762 Thomas Hollis recorded an evening
visit from "Pingo" to bring one of his medals struck to
commemorate the birth of the Prince of Wales, its design
"given by Mr Stuart."[57] The medal was exhibited in 1763
by Thomas Pingo at the Royal Society of Arts.[58] The
legend on the reverse side quotes Virgil (Ecl. 4, 17).

References: see checklist no. 180.

Fig. 12-17

17. Preparatory sketches for the proposed Catch Club medal, ca. 1764

James Stuart
Pen and ink, gray wash, pencil; 8⅝ x 6⅛ in. (22 x
15.5 cm)

RIBA Library Drawings Collection, London,
SD 62/33 (1).

References: see checklist no. 181.

Fig. 12-18. Obverse   Fig. 12-18. Reverse   Fig. 12-19. Obverse   Fig. 12-19. Reverse

18. Catch Club, 1764

Thomas Pingo, after a design by James Stuart
Gold, very rare; silver, rare; copper, scarce; 44 mm

Obverse: two male figures seated either side of a tripod, to the left playing a lyre, to the right holding a jug and ewer. LET'S. DRINK. AND. LET'S. SING. TOGETHER Exergue: CATCH CLVB INSTITVTED LONDON MDCCLXII. Continuous beaded border. Signed T. PINGO. F at the bottom edge.
Reverse: a tied wreath (space within and around for an engraved inscription). Continuous beaded border.

Example illustrated in fig. 12-18: Copper. Hunterian Museum and Art Gallery, University of Glasgow, Hunter Collection, Catch Club medal. *Checklist no. 182.*

The Catch Club was an a cappella singing club devoted to round-singing. It offered a ten-guinea premium, or a gold medal to the same value, to the composers of the best catch, canon, and glee, set to words either in English, Latin, Italian, Spanish, or French. In May 1764, Thomas Hollis noted a visit by "Pingo the father," in order "to bring two proof-medals, one in silver for the D. Devonshire, & one in copper for me, from the dyes which he engraved for the Catch Club, after an elegant design of Mr Stuart's. Gave him half a guinea for my own medal."[59]

References: see checklist no. 182.

19. Victory at Plassy, 1758

John Pingo, after a design by James Stuart
Silver, scarce; copper, scarce; 40 mm

Obverse: Victory seated upon an elephant. VICTORY. AT. PLASSY. CLIVE. COMMANDER. Exergue: MDCCLVIII SOC.P.A.C. Continuous beaded border.
Reverse: Robert, Lord Clive, as a Roman general, holds a standard surmounted by the British lion and presents another, surmounted by a dolphin, to Soobah Meer Jaafar. INIVRIES. ATTONED. PRIVILEGE. AVGMENTED. TERRITORY. ACQVIRED. Exergue: A. SOVBAH. GIVEN. TO. BENGAL. MDCCLVIII. Continuous beaded border.

Example illustrated in fig. 12-19: Copper. By courtesy of the Trustees of the British Museum, London.

In 1765 John Pingo gained the premium of thirty guineas for this medal from the Royal Society of Arts.[60] The medal was exhibited in 1765 by John Pingo.[61] Some examples of this medal occur with their edges having been inscribed "William Pitt Administring" (see No. 3).

References: Hawkins, *Medallic Illustrations* (1885/1969): George II, 400; Eimer, *British Commemorative Medals* (1987): 655; Eimer, *Pingo Family* (1998): 30.

Fig. 12-20. Obverse   Fig. 12-20. Reverse   Fig. 12-21. Obverse   Fig. 12-21. Reverse

20. Royal Military Academy, 1765

Thomas Pingo, after a design by James Stuart
Gold, rare; silver, scarce; copper, common; 36 mm

Obverse: bust right of George III, head laureate, hair short, in
curls. AVSPICIIS GEORG. III OPT. PRINC. P.P. [Under
the patronage of George III, the best of rulers and father of
his country]. Signed T. PINGO. F on the truncation.
Reverse: Minerva standing left, between an owl and a
gorgon's shield, an upright spear in her left hand and
palm frond in her right hand. PRAEMIA LAVDI
[Rewards for merit]. Exergue: D. M. GRANBY MAG.
GEN. ORD. MDCCLXV [The Lord Marquis of
Granby, Master-General of the Ordnance, 1765].

Example illustrated in fig. 12-20: Copper. By courtesy of the
Trustees of the British Museum, London. *Checklist no. 183.*

In February 1765 Thomas Hollis refers to having shown the
Pingos many medals prior to the engraving of the
dies for this one, "principally to see & open the mind of Lewis
the Son" and form "the model of the Head of the King."[62]
When Hollis was shown drafts of Stuart's drawing and inscriptions for the medal, he considered that it was "likely to turn
out a poor one, as well for device as inscriptions."[63]

On February 26, 1765, the Marquess of Granby,
master general of the ordnance, approved the design of
the medal and requested the board of ordnance to order
dies. Twenty medals were struck in gold, twenty in silver,
and forty in copper, the gold to be worth £5 5s each and
the silver to weigh about one ounce. Two gold and two
silver medals were awarded at the first public examination of cadets in June 1765, but their presentation was
discontinued in 1770.[64]

No record of payment to Thomas Pingo for the dies
or the medals can be traced in the treasurer's ledgers.[65]
The bill, which can be calculated at about £200, may
have been met privately by Granby, with whom the
medal can be closely associated. The reverse is based on a
design by Stuart, which was used by Hollis for stamping
on bindings and engraved prints. The medal was exhibited in 1766 by Thomas Pingo at the Body of Artists.[66]

References: see checklist no. 183.

21. Lord Camden, Lord Chancellor of Britain, 1766

Thomas Pingo, after a design by James Stuart
Silver, scarce; copper, common; 40 mm

Obverse: bust right, draped with robes and wig of office.
CHARLES LORD CAMDEN CHANCELLOR OF
BRITAIN; signed T. PINGO F. below the bust.
Reverse: standing figures, facing one another, of
LIBERTY, holding staff and cap, and EQVITY, holding
cornucopia and scales. Exergue: MDCCLXVI.

Example illustrated in fig. 12-21: Silver. By courtesy of
the Trustees of the British Museum, London. *Checklist
no. 184.*

In April 1767 Thomas Hollis drafted an advertisement for
this medal at the request of Thomas Pingo.[67] The text
read: "A New Medal [of Lord Camden] sold by
Christopher Pinchbeck, Toyman, at the bottom of the
Haymarket; Samuel Rush, toyman, on Ludgate Hill; John
Kentish Toyman, opposite the Royal Exchange; and
Thomas Pingo, Ingraver, at the Golden head, on the
paved stones, Grays Inn Lane. It was designed by Mr
Stuart."[68]

The medal was exhibited in 1767 by Thomas Pingo
at the Free Society of Artists.[69] Some examples display
flaws on the right-hand edge of the reverse, which were
almost certainly the result of a defective or ill-fitting collar used in the striking of the medal.

References: see checklist no. 184.

Fig. 12-22. Obverse　　Fig. 12-22. Reverse　　　　Fig. 12-23. Obverse　　Fig. 12-23. Reverse

22. **Admiral George, Lord Anson, Defeat of the French off Cape Finisterre, 1747**

Thomas Pingo, after a design by James Stuart
Gold, rare; silver, scarce; copper, rare; 43 mm

Obverse: bust of Anson left, hair short, no drapery, crowned with a laurel wreath by Victory, her left foot on the prow of a galley. GEORGE LORD ANSON VICT. MAY III MDCCXLVII. Signed T. PINGO F. below the bust.
Reverse: Victory, holding wreath in right hand and trophy of arms in left hand, stands upon the back of a sea monster, a small globe below; around, CIRCVMNAVI-GATION within a central beaded circle. In a broad outer border, six laurel wreaths enclosing the names of BRETT, DENNIS, CAMPHEL, KEPPEL, SAVMAREZ and SAVNDERS. Below MDCCXL MDCCXLIV.

Example illustrated in fig. 12-22: 1768. Silver. By courtesy of the Trustees of the British Museum, London. *Checklist no. 185.*

This medal commemorates Admiral George Anson's circumnavigation of the world between 1740 and 1744, as well as his defeat of the French fleet off Cape Finisterre in 1747. His fellow officers, whose names are on the medal, were Admiral Sir Percy Brett, Vice-Admiral Sir Peter Dennis, Vice-Admiral John Campbell, Admiral Viscount Augustus Keppel, Captain Philip Saumarez, and Admiral Sir Charles Saunders.
　　The medal was commissioned in the 1760s by Thomas Anson, the admiral's older brother, a bachelor and Whig member of parliament, who was among the founders of the Society of Dilettanti. A variant of this medal has the spelling of "Campbel" on the reverse. Accounts for payment of this medal include the charge of £80 for the dies, and the supply of fifty gold and eighty silver medals, the cost of each being £6 13s. and 9s. 10d., respectively.[70] Voltaire may have received one of the gold medals.[71] The medal was exhibited in 1769 by Thomas Pingo at the Free Society of Artists.[72]

References: see checklist no. 185.

23. **Nottinghamshire and West Riding of Yorkshire Agricultural Society Prize Medal, 1765**

Thomas Pingo, after a design by James Stuart
Gold, very rare (location unknown); copper, rare; 40 mm

Obverse: Ceres standing left, holding a cornucopia and plough. SOCIETY FOR IMPROVEMENT OF AGRICVLTVRE Exergue: INST. NOTTS. & W.R. YORKS. MDCCLXV. Signed T.P.F. at the bottom edge. Reverse: tied wreath of corn (space within, for an engraved inscription).

Example illustrated in fig. 12-23: Copper. By courtesy of the Trustees of the British Museum, London.

This medal was exhibited in 1770 by Thomas Pingo at the Society of Artists, where it is described as having been designed by Stuart and awarded in gold.[73] Examples in copper are specimen strikings.

References: Eimer, *British Commemorative Medals* (1987): 712; Eimer, *Pingo Family* (1998): 40.

KEY TO ABBREVIATED REFERENCES

Betts, *American Colonial History* (1894/1972)

Charles Wyllys Betts, *American Colonial History Illustrated by Contemporary Medals,* ed. William T. R. Marvin and Lyman Haynes Low (1894; reprint, Boston: Quarterman Publications, 1972).

Eimer, *British Commemorative Medals* (1987)

Christopher Eimer, *British Commemorative Medals and Their Values* (London: Seaby, 1987).

Eimer, *Pingo Family* (1998)

Christopher Eimer, *The Pingo Family and Medal Making in Eighteenth-Century Britain* (London: British Art Medal Trust, 1998).

Hawkins, *Medallic Illustrations* (1969)

Edward Hawkins, comp., *Medallic Illustrations of the History of Great Britain and Ireland to the Death of George II,* ed. Augustus W. Franks and Herbert A. Grueber, vol. 1 (1885; reprint, London: Spink and Son, 1969).

1. Edward Hawkins, comp., *Medallic Illustrations of the History of Great Britain and Ireland to the Death of George II,* ed. Augustus Wollaston Franks and Herbert A. Grueber, vol. 1 (1885; reprint, London: Spink and Son, 1969): George II, 81; Christopher Eimer, *British Commemorative Medals and Their Values* (London: Seaby, 1987): 540.

2. Guard Book, vol. 1, 24 March 1756, RSA. For a general discussion of the medals of the Royal Society of Arts in its early years, see Christopher Eimer, "The Society's Concern with 'The Medallic Art' in the Eighteenth Century," *RSA Journal* 139 (November 1991): 753–62.

3. Eimer, "Society's Concern with 'The Medallic Art'," (1991): 753–62.

4. Written description by Crisp, L.A. A1/9, RSA.

5. Minutes of the Society, vol. 2, p. 13, 16 March 1757, RSA. Moser was also a coppersmith and enamel painter and later the first Keeper of the Royal Academy.

6. Ibid., 30, 6 April 1757, RSA.

7. Yeo to the Society, 13 April 1757, L.A. E1/26, RSA.

8. Minutes of the Society, vol. 2, p. 63, 18 May 1757, RSA.

9. Ibid., 72–73, 7 June 1758, RSA.

10. Ibid., vol. 3, p. 76, 5 July 1758, RSA.

11. For details of the Pingos, see Christopher Eimer, *The Pingo Family and Medal Making in Eighteenth-Century Britain* (London: British Art Medal Trust, 1998).

12. Minutes of the Society, vol. 3, p. 108, 29 November 1758, RSA. Pingo received £84 for his work.

13. Ibid.

14. William Henry Bond, *Thomas Hollis of Lincoln's Inn: A Whig and his Books* (Cambridge University Press, 1990).

15. Diary of Thomas Hollis, 14 April 1759 to 3 July 1770, MS Eng 1191, Houghton Library, Harvard University. Hereafter referred to as "Hollis diary." A microfilm copy is in the library of the Society of Antiquaries of London.

16. Augustus, denarius, (30–27 B.C.), British Museum, Department of Coins and Medals. Edward Mattingly and Harold Sydenham, *Roman Imperial Coinage,* vol. 1 (London: Spink, 1984): 263.

17. Maximianus, Antoninianus, "Concordia Militum" (286–305 A.D.), British Museum, Department of Coins and Medals. Carol Humphrey Vivian Sutherland and Robert Andrew Glendinning Carson, *Roman Imperial Coinage,* vol. 6 (London: Spink and Sons, 1967): 595.

18. Hollis diary, 8 October 1759.

19. George Clarke, "The Medallions of Concord: An Association between the Society of Arts and Stowe," *RSA Journal* 129 (August 1981): 611–16.

20. Ibid., 613.

21. 27 and 31 May, 17 June, 23 September 1769, Lichfield MS D615/P(S)/1/6/24-27, Staffordshire Record Office.

22. George Macdonald, *Catalogue of the Greek Coins in the Hunterian Collection, University of Glasgow* (Glasgow: James Maclehose and Sons, 1899): xv.

23. "To Stewart for 18 silver and 18 brass medals £13 10s," 11 June 1762; "a silver and a copper medal bought from Thomas Pingo," Vouchers for Works of Art, No. 17 (1773), Wentworth Woodhouse Muniments A1000, Sheffield Archives.

24. John Taylor, *Records of My Life,* vol. 2 (London: E. Bull, 1832): 181–82. The collection of George III and its manuscript register are in the Department of Coins and Medals, British Museum.

25. "Thomas Snelling Bookseller, for medals, £32. 0. 6.," 9 October 1764, account book, RA 17122, Royal Archives.

26. See, e.g., Eimer, *Pingo Family* (1998): Nos. 11, 12, 14, 15.

27. *Daily Advertiser* (3 April 1760): 3122.

28. Eimer, *Pingo Family* (1998): No. 219.

29. Hawkins, *Medallic Illustrations* (1885/1969): George II, 407; Hollis diary, 1 June 1759, 26 July 1761, 8 May 1762.

30. See, e.g., Leonard Forrer, comp., *Biographical Dictionary of Medallists . . . ,* vol. 5 (1912; reprint, London: A. H. Baldwin; Maastricht: A. G. van der Dussen, 1980): 702. For several of these copies and fan-

CHAPTER 12

tasies (misattributed to "Athenian" Stuart), see *A Collection of British Historical Medals*, sale cat., Glendining's, London, part 1, 16 March 1989, lots 139–53 (illus.).

31. Minutes of the Society, vol. 3, p. 32, 5 April 1758, RSA.

32. Royal Society of Arts, The Strand, London, 1760, No. 85.1, in Algernon Graves, *The Society of Artists of Great Britain, 1760–1791; The Free Society of Artists, 1761–1783: A Complete Dictionary of Contributors and Their Work from the Foundation of the Society to 1791* (London: George Bell and Sons, 1907).

33. Minutes of the Society, vol. 3, p. 5, 5 April 1758, RSA.

34. Minutes of the Society, 4 October 1758, 21 March 1759, RSA.

35. Hollis diary, 1 June 1759.

36. Odes Book 1, viii., in *The Cambridge History of English Literature 1660–1780*, ed. John Richetti (Cambridge and New York: Cambridge University Press, 2005): 310.

37. Minutes, Committee of Polite Arts, 14 May 1759, RSA.

38. Hollis diary, 24 May 1759.

39. Royal Society of Arts, The Strand, London, 1760, No. 85.3, in Graves, *Society of Artists* (1907).

40. Minutes of the Society, 7 November 1759, 6 and 20 February 1760, RSA.

41. For an illustration, see David Watkin, *Athenian Stuart: Pioneer of the Greek Revival* (London: George Allen and Unwin, 1982): pl. 78.

42. *Daily Advertiser* (3 April 1760): 3122.

43. Society of Artists, Mr Christie's New Great Room, London, 1775, No. 251, in Graves, *Society of Artists* (1907).

44. Minutes, Committee of Polite Arts, 15 and 26 November 1760, RSA.

45. Ibid., 1 and 29 May 1761.

46. Minutes, Committee of Polite Arts, 3 June 1761, RSA.

47. Hollis diary, 30 August 1760.

48. Hollis diary, 17 and 26 September 1761.

49. Free Society of Artists, Pall Mall, London, 1768, in Graves, *Society of Artists* (1907).

50. Minutes of the Society, 31 March 1761, and 23 April 1762, RSA.

51. Ibid., 23 April 1762.

52. Hollis diary, 8 October 1759.

53. Royal Society of Arts, The Strand, London, 1762, No. 136, in Graves, *Society of Artists* (1907).

54. Minutes, Committee of Polite Arts, 29 May 1761 and 23 April 1762, RSA.

55. Minutes, Committee of Polite Arts, 23 April 1762, RSA.

56. Royal Society of Arts, The Strand, London, 1762, No. 185, in Graves, *Society of Artists* (1907).

57. Hollis diary, 24 September 1762.

58. Royal Society of Arts, The Strand, London, 1763, No. 163, in Graves, *Society of Artists* (1907).

59. Hollis diary, 25 May 1764.

60. Minutes, Committee of Polite Arts, 12 August 1763 and 17 May 1765, RSA.

61. Body of Artists, Mr Moreing's Great Room, Maiden Lane, London, 1765, No. 146, in Graves, *Society of Artists* (1907).

62. Hollis diary, 17 February 1765.

63. Ibid., 3 March 1765.

64. Board of Ordnance, Surveyor-General's Minutes, NA (PRO) WO 47/65: 126–27, 165, 345.

65. NA (PRO) WO 47/107: 256.

66. Body of Artists, Mr Moreing's Great Room, Maiden Lane, Covent Garden, 1766, No. 137, in Graves, *Society of Artists* (1907).

67. Hollis diary, 15 April 1767.

68. *London Chronicle* (16–18 April 1767): 376.

69. Free Society of Artists, Pall Mall, 1767, No. 246, in Graves, *Society of Artists* (1907).

70. Anson Manuscript MS D615/P(S)/1/6/22, 23A–C, Staffordshire Record Office.

71. Extracts from two letters from Voltaire (14 June and 7 July 1769) are quoted in Spink, *Numismatic Circular* (July 1912), cols. 13730–32.

72. Free Society of Artists, Pall Mall, London, 1769, No. 172, in Graves, *Society of Artists* (1907).

73. Society of Artists, Mr Christie's New Great Room, London, 1770, No. 201, in Graves, *Society of Artists* (1907).

512

Fig. 13-1. James Stuart. Front elevation of Lichfield House, St. James's Square, London, 1764–66. Photographed in the early 20th century. English Heritage / National Monuments Record CC38/412.

CHAPTER 13

EPILOGUE: THE IMPACT OF STUART OVER TWO CENTURIES

DAVID WATKIN

S tuart and Revett's *Antiquities of Athens* might be seen as a small stone thrown into a very large English pond which nonetheless produced ripples that moved in ever-widening circles throughout Europe and North America for up to two centuries. They can have had no conception of the impact their work would have on Western architecture, culture, and politics, from Glasgow to Munich, from Paris to Philadelphia. For architects and interior designers, for sculptors and artists, as well as for those politically inspired by the notion of ancient Greece as the birthplace of liberty, the plates and text of *Antiquities of Athens* were an unrivaled source of information. This chapter is the unexpected story of a visionary ideal that spread across the world from its beginnings in the Society of Dilettanti in Georgian England.

England and Nineteenth-Century Greek Revival
By 1816, when the fourth volume of Stuart and Revett's *Antiquities of Athens* was published, Sir William Chambers, whose anti-Grecian stance had been attacked so violently in the third volume, had been dead for twenty years. The Greek Revival was about to dominate British architecture, particularly its public buildings, for a quarter of a century. Joseph Woods, editor of the fourth volume, thus adopted

a triumphalist note in his preface, claiming that "on the publication of the first volume, the knowledge of Grecian art burst upon the public in all its splendour"; that "the Grecian architecture was quite unknown: the genius of Stuart first pointed towards it"; and that Stuart's Lichfield House, 15 St. James's Square (1764–66; fig. 13-1; see fig. 5-59), was "the first building erected in England of real Grecian Architecture."[1] His last claim, though enthusiastic, was untrue, but with it began the formulation of the myth about Stuart. The composition of the façade of Lichfield House was wholly Palladian: nothing about it was Greek except its Erechtheion Ionic capitals, and even the associated architrave and frieze were severely truncated.

British architects and artists were the first to appreciate the decorative potential of the Parthenon frieze. They had been familiar with such sculpture from the publication of the second volume of *Antiquities of Athens*, but it was not until the early nineteenth century that knowledge of the Parthenon reached a wider audience. From the moment the Elgin marbles were put on view in London, they had a profound impact. They were shown first to a limited audience in 1807 and then to the general public at the British Museum in 1816.[2] Their fame spread further after casts of them were manufactured

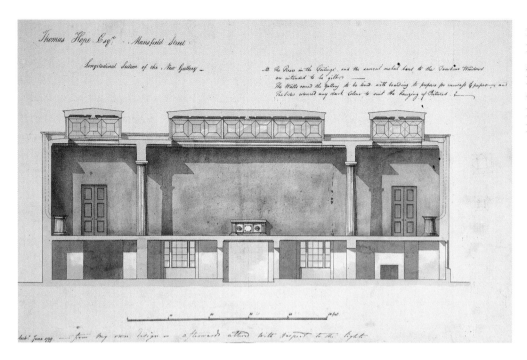

Fig. 13-2. Thomas Hope. Design for the picture gallery, Duchess Street, London, 1799. Drawn by Charles Heathcote Tatham. Ink and colored wash. Private collection.

beginning in 1818. Ambitious examples of Parthenon-influenced design in London include the Ionic screen at Hyde Park Corner (1824–25) and the Athenaeum Club (1827–30). Both were by the architect Decimus Burton (1800–81) and were decorated by fine sculpture inspired by the Parthenon, designed and executed by the Scottish sculptor, John Henning, working with his sons, John and Samuel. Henning had first seen the Elgin marbles in 1811.

Thomas Hope (1769–1831), an early and important patron of the sculptor John Flaxman, studied Greek architecture in detail in Athens in 1799. In the same year, he acquired a large mansion by Robert Adam in Duchess Street, London, and made designs for adding a sizable picture gallery to it (fig. 13-2), with details drawn from the Hephaesteion (Theseum) and the Tower of the Winds. Executed for him by Charles Heathcote Tatham, this pioneering Grecian gallery was ready to be shown to the public in 1804, while Hope published it with the other principal interiors at Duchess Street in *Household Furniture and Interior Decoration* (1807).[3] The bibliography that Hope provided in his book began emphatically with a reference to "Stuart's Athens." A new Picturesque aesthetic, however, also led Hope to complain of engravings of ancient buildings that "from these the least unfaithful, the least inaccurate even, such as Stuart's Athens, Revett's Ionia, no adequate idea can be obtained of that variety of effect produced by particular site, by perspective, a change of aspect, and a change of light."[4]

Sir John Soane (1753–1837) wrote in the margin of his copy of the pamphlet in which Hope had made this observation, "true, and worthy of the most serious consideration of him who wishes to distinguish himself in the higher beauties of architecture."[5] Soane was, nonetheless, a lifelong admirer of Stuart. Indeed, Soane's earliest commonplace book, dating from about 1776,[6] included quo-

Fig. 13-3. John Soane. Design for the state bed at Fonthill House, for William Beckford, 1788. Pen and ink. Sir John Soane's Museum, London, Drawer 8 set 5 no. 8 Fonthill Splendens (Wilts).

Fig. 13-4. William Wilkins.
Grange Park, Northington,
Hampshire, 1809.
Photographed in 1972.
English Heritage / National
Monuments Record
BB72/5352.

tations from the first volume of *Antiquities of Athens*, as well as from Robert Morris's *Lectures on Architecture* (1734), Sir William Chambers's *Treatise on Civil Architecture* (1759), and Stephen Riou's *Grecian Orders of Architecture* (1768), which was dedicated to Stuart.[7] As early as 1788, Soane had designed a sumptuous state bed for William Beckford's palatial house, Fonthill Splendens (fig. 13-3).[8] The bed was surmounted by a large domical structure inspired by Stuart's re-creation of the crowning feature of the Choragic Monument of Lysicrates (see fig. 11-12).

Soane's preparations from 1806 for lectures that he delivered between 1810 and 1820 as professor of architecture at the Royal Academy led him to study, and subsequently to hail, Stuart's achievement. It is interesting that, in the course of condemning the fashion for rococo decoration in English interiors, Soane reminded his students that "at the very time when these miserable apologies for decoration seemed to have become general, fortunately for art, Stuart and Revett, those great luminaries, returned from Athens, and began to overturn the dreadful taste in decoration, which was spreading a baneful influence in every direction."[9] In his lectures he referred to Stuart and Revett by name on eight occasions for their work as archaeologists, praising, for example, Stuart's solution to the placement of mutules and triglyphs "in delineations . . . [where] mutules of equal breadths are placed over, and between, each triglyph."[10]

A new Romantic sensibility, however, led Soane to remark that, because Stuart's Lichfield House in St. James's Square (see fig. 5-59) faced northeast, it "appears flat and uninteresting. But let it be placed in a different situation, the effect would be then as pleasing as it is now uninteresting: all the parts are beautiful."[11] Soane's deep consciousness of the importance of light in architecture had been bolstered by his reading of the important treatise by Nicholas Le Camus de Mézières, *Le génie de l'architecture* (1780), in which, for example, Le Camus complained that the Paris Mint (1768–75) by Jacques-Denis Antoine "seems monotonous . . . of which its northerly exposure is the sole cause."[12]

In unpublished notes, moreover, Soane cited Stuart's temple at Shugborough (see fig. 7-13) as supporting the opinion of the Picturesque theorist, Richard Payne Knight, that Greek temples were unsuitable as models for garden buildings.[13] Soane, who had seen Greek temples in grandiose natural landscapes such as that at Segesta in Sicily, felt that versions of such temples in the modest parks and gardens of England were unacceptable. For similar reasons, he disapproved of William Wilkins's Grange Park, Hampshire (1809; fig. 13-4), the most complete templar house ever erected in Britain, combining on an heroic scale elements of the Hephaesteion (Theseum) and the Choragic Monument of Thrasyllus in Athens.

Soane himself, however, more than any British architect of his generation, used the baseless, fluted or unfluted, Greek Doric order to powerful effect in his buildings and

Fig. 13-5. William and Henry William Inwood. The south vestry, Saint Pancras New Church, Euston Road, London. 1819. Photographed in 1966. English Heritage / National Monuments Record AA 77/6321.

designs. It was appropriate that the editors of the supplementary fifth volume of *Antiquities of Athens* (1830), C. R. Cockerell, Thomas Leverton Donaldson, William Jenkins, William Kinnard, and William Railton, should dedicate it to Soane, "in admiration of his munificence in promoting the Fine Arts and the science of Antiquity."[14]

In common with Wilkins, many early nineteenth-century architects, such as Robert Smirke, John Foster, Henry Goodridge, and William and Henry William Inwood, incorporated into their buildings replicas of works such as the Choragic Monument of Lysicrates, based on plates in *Antiquities of Athens*. The Inwoods even included doorways taken from molds of those on the Erechtheion at their St. Pancras New Church (1819). The caryatid portico at the same church (fig. 13-5) was a sensational re-creation of the entire Porch of the Caryatids at the Erechtheion, as illustrated in *Antiquities of Athens* (fig. 13-6), though the caryatids were far from exact copies. The octagonal tower combined elements from the Tower of the Winds and the Choragic Monument of Lysicrates (see figs. 7-23, 7-32), as did the striking Lansdown Tower at Bath (1824–27; fig. 13-7), designed by Goodridge for William Beckford. Such a combination strangely ignores the great disparity in size between the

Fig. 13-6. Porch of the Caryatids at the Erechtheion, Athens. Engraving. From *Antiquities of Athens,* vol. 2 (ca. 1790): chap. 2, pl. II. Courtesy of the Library, The Bard Graduate Center for Studies in the Decorative Arts, Design, and Culture, New York.

two Athenian buildings, the Tower of the Winds which is monumental in scale, and the Choragic Monument which is diminutive.

Like St. Pancras New Church, Belsay Hall in Northumberland (fig. 13-8) was an inventive and highly sophisticated application of Greek forms to a non-Greek function. It was built in 1807–17 from designs by its owner, Sir Charles Monck (1779–1867). Having visited Athens on his honeymoon in 1805, where he studied the monuments with Sir William Gell (1777–1836), Monck created this stark Greco-Roman villa built round a peristyle and approached through a giant portico in antis. It was based on the Hephaesteion (Theseum) in Athens, with details of the Doric order as well as the Erechtheion Ionic order in the peristyle and in the bookcases in the library, derived from the engravings in *Antiquities of Athens.*[15] In the peristyle, Monck characteristically omitted the most succulent feature of this order, the anthemion necking band, while the bookcases are even more austere.

Another powerful Greek Revivalist was the architect, Edward Haycock (1790–1870), a pupil of Sir Jeffrey Wyatville. His Clytha Park, Monmouthshire (1824–28; fig. 13-9), has an exquisite giant portico in the Erechtheion Ionic order, while his Millichope Park, Shropshire (1835–40), features a six-column Ionic portico above a novel and dramatic basement entrance flanked by two

Fig. 13-7. Henry Goodridge. Lansdown Tower, Bath, 1824–27. Photographed ca. 1960. English Heritage / National Monuments Record D39/287.

Fig. 13-8. Sir Charles Monck. Belsay Hall, Northumberland, 1807–17. Photographed in 1973. English Heritage / National Monuments Record BB78/6768.

Fig. 13-9. Edward Haycock. Clytha Park, Monmouthshire, 1824–28. Photographed in the mid-20th century. ©Crown copyright: Royal Commission on the Ancient and Historical Monuments of Wales. ©Hawlfraint y Goron: Comisiwn Brenhinol Henebion Cymru.

primitivist columns in an unfluted stripped Doric (fig. 13-10).[16] With something of the flavor of funereal architecture, this may be indebted to the arrangement of ancient tombs, such as that at Mylasa, Turkey, with its basement entrance. This was illustrated in *Antiquities of Ionia* from material supplied by Nicholas Revett and Richard Chandler (fig. 13-11).[17]

Meanwhile, Wilkins had employed the Erechtheion Ionic order at Downing College, Cambridge (1806–21), where he also designed an ambitious porter's lodge (fig. 13-12), inspired by the Propylaea. His first book, *Antiquities of Magna Graecia* (1807), a pioneering study of the Greek antiquities in Sicily and Italy, was modeled on the first three volumes of *Antiquities of Athens*.[18] This was followed by his *Atheniensia* (1816),[19] while in his United University Club, Pall Mall East, London (1816–17), Wilkins incorporated porticos with Greek Doric and Erechtheion Ionic orders, and a staircase hall adorned with casts of the Parthenon frieze. This model was to be followed in three other London clubs that sported casts of Greek friezes, whether inside or out: Decimus Burton's Athenaeum (1827–30), Charles Barry's Travellers' Club and his

Fig. 13-10. Edward Haycock. Basement entrance of Millichope Park, Shropshire, 1835–40. Photographed ca. 1977. ©Country Life Picture Library.

Fig. 13-11. "Sepulchral monument at Mylasa," Engraving. From Richard Chandler, William Pars, and Nicholas Revett, *Ionian Antiquities*, vol. 2 (1797): pl. XXIV. By permission of the British Library, London, 745.e.11.

Fig. 13-12. William Wilkins. Perspective view of the Porters Lodge, Downing College, Cambridge, ca. 1806. Engraving. Courtesy of David Watkin.

Reform Club, both of the 1830s. Wilkins's University College, London (1826; fig. 13-13), boasted a gigantic ten-columned Corinthian portico, based on the Temple of Jupiter Olympius in Athens. Stuart had devoted much attention to this unfinished temple, partly as a way of attacking Le Roy who had identified its remains incorrectly in 1758.[20]

When Wilkins published *The Civil Architecture of Vitruvius* (1813, 1817), he included a substantial introduction of seventy-six pages, called "An Historical View of the Rise and Progress of Architecture among the Greeks," which had been written anonymously by the Earl of Aberdeen, to whom the book was dedicated.[21] In 1809 Wilkins had provided a saloon for Aberdeen's London house, with columns in the Erechtheion Ionic order and a frieze inspired by the Elgin marbles. Aberdeen later expanded his introduction into a sympathetic book about the aesthetics of Greek architecture, citing Stuart's *Antiquities of Athens* frequently and arguing that the celebrated definition of beauty by the writer and statesman

Fig. 13-13. William Wilkins. Front elevation of University College, Gower Street, Camden, London, 1826. Undated photograph. English Heritage / National Monuments Record BB77/6568.

Edmund Burke had been displaced by the discovery of the arts of Greece. He noted that the sixth of Burke's seven defining qualities of beauty—that colors should not be "very strong and glaring"[22]—was contradicted by the Parthenon where "the colour, although now somewhat softened by the effects of time and weather, was formerly the most bright and glaring which it is possible to imagine, viz. the dazzling whiteness of the marble of Pentelicus."[23] Despite his admiration for the Parthenon, Aberdeen believed that Greek models should not be copied, but rather translated to suit English needs. In his opinion, "any architect who should slavishly regulate his practice by a strict adherence to the models of antiquity, without fully consulting our peculiar habits and customs, and considering the nature of our climate would probably meet with the neglect he deserved."[24]

Sir William Gell, a friend of Sir Charles Monck, published books on Troy, Greece, and Italy, including *The Itinerary of Greece* (1810) and *Itinerary of the Morea* (1817).[25] He followed Stuart's rather improbable association of the modern inhabitants of Greece with the ancient Athenians, arguing that "notwithstanding the lapse of twenty centuries . . . in Greece the same physical causes which produced the original distinction between the inhabitants of neighbouring districts, still operate with such force, that

no other country affords so many traces of ancient manners, or recalls so frequently the recollection of its former inhabitants."[26] In the second edition of *Itinerary of Greece* (1827), when the Greek Revival was in full swing, Gell introduced a more polemical note by hailing Stuart's achievement in linking archaeology and modern design. He now claimed that this was "of most essential service of the arts by first showing to the world, how very unlike the architecture of the Greeks is that which has disfigured the cities of northern Europe under the name of Grecian."[27] In a mood of optimism, he added that "it is probable that in time the science will be gradually diffused, and that in another century the grandeur and unity of Grecian architecture may reappear."[28]

Further support came from Joseph Gwilt (1784–1863) in his *Encyclopaedia of Architecture* (1842), which contains his awkwardly expressed praise of "the chasteness and purity which . . . [Stuart and Revett] had, with some success, endeavoured to introduce into the buildings of England, and in which their zeal had enlisted many artists, had to contend against the opposite and vicious taste of Robert Adam . . . [and] his depraved compositions."[29] Gwilt's monumental work ran into many subsequent editions so that his opinions of the relative merits of Stuart and Adam were still being published in 1891.

Five years after Gwilt had penned these words, the architect James Elmes (1782–1862) went so far as to claim that in 1847 "no event that ever occurred in the history of architecture in England, and thence throughout all Europe, produced so sudden, decided, and beneficial effect as did the works of James Stuart."[30] Certainly, one of the most striking aspects of Stuart's influence was on a whole generation of practicing architects who felt the need to publish archaeological works on Greek architecture and for whom he was a role model. After William Wilkins, these included: Francis Bedford who published *The Unedited Antiquities of Attica* (1817) with Sir William Gell; John Peter Gandy (later, Deering); and C. R. Cockerell, who contributed to the additional volume of Stuart and Revett's *Antiquities of Athens* (1830) and published a ground-breaking study, *The Temples of Jupiter Panhellenius at Aegina and of Apollo Epicurius at Bassae* (1860; fig. 13-14).[31] Henry William Inwood produced a monograph, *The Erechtheion at Athens* (1827), that became the standard work on this temple.[32] Thomas Leverton Donaldson contributed to *Antiquities of Athens* (1830). Francis Cranmer Penrose specialized in the so-called optical refinements in Greek architecture and published the monumental *Investigation of the Principles of Athenian Architecture* (1851), a book recently described as "the best work ever printed on the Parthenon: it is a monument of scientific method, consistency and unparalleled human skill."[33]

Preliminary remarks in the fourth volume of Revett's *Antiquities of Ionia*, published by the Society of Dilettanti in 1881 noted that before Stuart, "it was Roman taste and magnificence that was admired, and Roman forms and details that were copied."[34] The author, probably James Fergusson, went on to claim:

> It was not until the publication of the first volumes of Stuart's *Antiquities of Athens*, in 1761 and 1787, that the learned practically became aware that Greece possessed a separate style of her own, more elegant and refined than anything that Rome had ever produced, and, though probably less flexible for modern purposes, far more worthy of study than the style that had so long exclusively occupied the attention of Europe.[35]

Contemplation of the inadequacies of Greek Revival buildings had already led the architect C. R. Cockerell

Fig. 13-14. "The painted members of the orders of the temple of Jupiter at Aegina." Colored engraving by Edmund Turrell. From C. R. Cockerell, *The Temples of Jupiter Panhellenius at Aegina, and of Apollo Epicurius at Bassae near Phigaleia in Arcadia . . .* (1860): pl. 9. By permission of the British Library, London, 650.c.24.

(1788–1863) to believe that too rigid an application of Greek forms was unsuitable for modern buildings, even though he was a passionate admirer of Greece. After Soane, Cockerell is generally agreed to have been the most distinguished classical architect at work in England in the first half of the nineteenth century.[36] He had early been familiar with Stuart for, as a boy at Westminster School, he undoubtedly had seen the remarkable backdrop depicting Athens, which Stuart had painted in 1758 for the annual Latin play and which was used for long afterward (see fig. 4-13).[37] Cockerell rushed to see the Elgin Marbles in their shed in Park Lane as early as February 1807, mak-

Fig. 13-15. C. R. Cockerell. Ashmolean Museum and Taylorian Institution, Oxford, 1841–44. Photographed in 1880. English Heritage / National Monuments Record CC50/336.

ing a sketch of a section of the north frieze.[38] On his long Grand Tour (1810–17), he made significant archaeological discoveries, notably at Bassae and Agrigentum, which overthrew many previous assumptions about Greek architecture. He broke with tradition in several areas. His awareness that Greek architects used molded wall-mass and engaged columns questioned the traditional notion of the "honesty" of Greek structure. He understood the role of Greek sculpture as "the voice of architecture." He discovered polychromy at the temple of Aphaia on the island of Aegina and identified the entasis of the columns of the Parthenon. Writing excitedly about entasis to his former master, the architect Smirke, in 1811, he described it as "a most curious fact, which has hitherto escaped Stuart & our most accurate observers—indeed, it is so delicate that unless one measures it, the eye alone cannot perceive it."[39]

Like Leo von Klenze in Bavaria, but unlike Schinkel in Prussia, Cockerell was so distinguished as an archaeologist that he had no need to draw on Stuart for sources and in fact contributed to the additional volume of *Antiquities* (1830). In an early commission at Oakly Park, Shropshire, begun in 1819, he incorporated two porticos of the Doric order of the Temple of Apollo on Delos, as illustrated in *Antiquities of Athens*, but in mature works such as the Ashmolean Museum and Taylorian Institution, Oxford (1841–44; fig. 13-15), he went quite beyond the

world of Stuart to create a rich synthesis of Greek, Roman, and Mannerist architecture.

Scotland as the "Athens of the North": Edinburgh and Glasgow

The plates of *Antiquities of Athens* were used extensively for numerous Greek Revival buildings that established Edinburgh as the "Athens of the North," notably the Royal High School (1825–29; fig. 13-16) by Thomas Hamilton and the National Monument, an uncompleted replica of the Parthenon of 1824–29, by C. R. Cockerell and W. H. Playfair. It is not always noted, however, that Glasgow became an equally Grecian city. The great Glaswegian architect, Alexander "Greek" Thomson (1817–75), a Grecian enthusiast himself, felt that the Greek Revival had been limited by being based on a small number of structures on or near the Acropolis in Athens. These, of course, were known principally through Stuart and Revett's engravings of them. He complained that "this was surely scant material from which to furnish the world with architecture. Yet that was what the promoters of the Greek Revival proposed to do, and they failed not because of the scantiness of the material, but because they could not see through the material into the laws upon which that architecture rested. They failed to master their style, and so became its slaves."[40]

Fig. 13-16. Thomas Hamilton. Royal High School, Edinburgh, 1825–29. Photographed ca. 1950s. Courtesy of A. F. Kersting.

Thomson observed, somewhat ironically, of these monuments that "like the Muses they are nine," seven of which he said appeared in Glasgow. He noted these Glaswegian examples as the Court House (1807) by William Stark, inspired by the Parthenon; the Wellington Street Church (1825) by John Baird, with the Ionic order of the temple on the Ilissus River; the Royal Bank of Scotland (1827) by Archibald Elliot, featuring the Erechtheion Ionic order; Clarendon Place (1839–41) by Alexander Taylor, with the Tower of the Winds order; the Custom House (1839–40; fig. 13-17) by John Taylor, with the Theseion Doric order below an attic from the Choragic Monument of Thrasyllus; and the County Buildings (1842) by Clarke and Bell, with the order and frieze of the Choragic Monument of Lysicrates.

Incomparably greater than the architects of any of these buildings, Thomson was one of the most distinguished heirs to "Athenian" Stuart, acquiring, like him, a

Fig. 13-17. John Taylor. Custom House, Glasgow, 1839–40. Photographed in the mid–late 20th century. RIBA Library Photographs Collection, London.

Fig. 13-18. Alexander "Greek" Thomson. St. Vincent Street Church, Glasgow, 1859. Undated photograph. Conway Library, Courtauld Institute, London, B77/4154.

Hellenistic name tag. He produced a timeless trabeated architecture with Egyptian and Greek elements in Glasgow, such as Moray Place (1857–59) and St. Vincent Street Church (1859; fig. 13-18).[41] He was powerfully influenced by the Choragic Monument of Thrasyllus (319 B.C.), which he praised perceptively as "an example of the freedom with which a master may accommodate familiar forms to an entirely novel combination."[42] The fact that he always described it as though it were still in existence, presumably unaware that it had been destroyed in 1826, shows the extent to which he must have relied on the engravings in *Antiquities of Athens* (vol. 2, ca. 1790; see fig. 10-5).[43] Because use of this monument became a hallmark of the Greek Revival, Stuart and Revett's plates of it were among their most valuable. The only other records of it, by Wheler (see fig. 1-5), Pococke (see fig. 1-11), and Le Roy, were far inferior, Le Roy providing only a perspective view that lacked precise architectural details.[44]

The Choragic Monument of Thrasyllus broke the conventional rules of classical architecture by introducing various peculiarities. It had a solid placed in the middle of the façade, and this pier was narrower than those at either end of the façade. The expected triglyphs and metopes in the frieze were replaced by a continuous row of eleven laurel wreaths. Moreover, its open, trabeated, or

Fig. 13-19. Harvey Lonsdale Elmes. St. George's Hall, Liverpool, 1839–54. Photographed ca. 1959. Courtesy of A. F. Kersting.

Fig. 13-20. Carl Langhans. Brandenburg Gate, Berlin, 1788–89. Photographed in the mid-20th century. RIBA Library Photographs Collection, London.

mullioned frame had a functional flavor that exercised an appeal to modern architects as being more adaptable to a variety of contemporary uses than the full panoply of the orders. It also featured in the only nineteenth-century building in England of comparable quality to Thomson's work in Scotland: St. George's Hall, Liverpool (1839–54; fig. 13-19) by Harvey Lonsdale Elmes, Robert Rawlinson, and C. R. Cockerell, which had monumental side elevations of an ultimately Thrasyllan articulation.

German Idealism and the Classical Ideal

In no country did Philhellenism come to dominate so completely as Germany, where it lasted throughout the nineteenth century.[45] Winckelmann's call for the imitation of Greek art, especially sculpture, became part of a program of new state-funded cultural institutions in which, for example, scholars and politicians united in grand archaeological projects such as the acquisition of the Pergamum Altar.[46] The key monument of early neoclassical architecture in Germany had been the Brandenburg Gate in Berlin (1788–89; fig. 13-20) by Carl Gotthard Langhans (1732–1808). Inspired by the Propylaea in Athens, which Stuart and Revett had not yet published,

it must have been based on Le Roy's engravings, for Langhans had not been to Athens. Demonstrating his belief that the moderns had no need to copy Greek buildings, Le Roy showed the Propylaea as a symmetrical building in the only full-scale restoration study in his book.[47] Stuart is known to have given copies of *Antiquities of Athens* to the library of University of Göttingen.[48] Together with information from Stuart and Revett, the Brandenburg Gate became the model for subsequent monumental Grecian gateways, such as that by Thomas Harrison at Chester Castle, in Chester, England (1810–22), and another by Leo von Klenze in the Propylaea at Munich (1846–60). All these buildings were on flat terrain, however, and thus fail to capture the power of the Athenian Propylaea which towers dramatically above the visitor on a rocky, precipitous site. Stuart's account of the Propylaea in volume two of *Antiquities* was inadequate because circumstances had forced him to leave Athens without investigating it.[49]

The model provided by the Brandenburg Gate was taken up in a starker and more dramatic form by the brilliant young architect, Friedrich Gilly (1772–1800). Dying young, he built little, but his powerful Doric designs,

Fig. 13-21. Wilhelm Julius Ahlborn, after Karl Friedrich Schinkel. *Blick in Griechenlands Blüte* (A Glance at the Golden Age of Greece), 1836. Oil on canvas. Nationalgalerie, Staatliche Museen zu Berlin, NG2/54.

Fig. 13-22. Karl Friedrich Schinkel. Schauspielhaus, Berlin, 1818–21. Undated photograph. Conway Library, Courtauld Institute, London, A90/560.

Fig. 13-23. Karl Friedrich Schinkel.
Perspective view of the main court, Palace
for the King of Greece on the Acropolis,
1834. Watercolor, pen and ink.
Kupferstichkabinett, Staatliche
Museen zu Berlin, SM 35b.44.

notably his monument to Frederick the Great (1796), were widely known to contemporaries in Berlin.[50] These included Karl Friedrich Schinkel (1781–1841), the greatest architect of the first half of the nineteenth century in Germany. He was probably also the architect who put the work of Stuart and Revett to the greatest and most sophisticated use. Schinkel studied with Friedrich Gilly and Gilly's father David and had access to books in the elder Gilly's library, including *Antiquities of Athens*, Le Roy's *Ruines des plus beaux monuments de la Grèce*, and Alois Hirt's lectures on antique sculpture.[51]

A translation into German of *Antiquities of Athens* was published in 1829–33, but before then Schinkel drew on Stuart for details of his visionary painting of 1825, *Blick in Griechensland Blüte* (A Glance at the Golden Age of Greece; fig. 13-21).[52] Though a nostalgic fantasy, the paint-

ing also had the real purpose of urging the Berlin of King Friedrich Wilhelm III of Prussia to regenerate itself, taking as a model the struggle of the Greeks for liberation in the Persian Wars. The painting contains a quotation from Aristotle's hymn referring to Arete, wife of the king of the Phaeacians in the *Odyssey*, praising the self-sacrifice of warriors. Showing the construction of a temple with a vast landscape in the background containing a fabulous classical city, Schinkel's enormous painting made a powerful popular impact. It depicted handsome sun-browned craftsmen, protected by an awning, at work on a curiously formed temple or public building with a great figured frieze, which Schinkel based not on the actual remains of the Parthenon frieze but on Stuart and Revett's plates of it.[53]

Like Alexander Thomson, Schinkel frequently relied on a trabeated architectural language, a key feature of which

529

Fig. 13-24. Karl Friedrich Schinkel. Perspective view of the Palace for the King of Greece on the Acropolis, 1834. Chromolithograph. From Schinkel, *Werke der höheren Baukunst* (1840): pls. 5 and 6. By permission of the British Library, London, Cup.652.c.31.

was taken from the Choragic Monument of Thrasyllus in Athens, as illustrated in *Antiquities of Athens*. In Schinkel's *Sammlung*, he explained of his Schauspielhaus (Play House) in Berlin (1818–21; fig. 13-22) that he had "tried to emulate Greek forms and methods of construction insofar as this is possible in such a complex work."[54] He went on to praise the Thrasyllan model on functional grounds since it allowed window openings of the maximum size. He was also one of the many architects who used the bas-reliefs of the wind gods on the Tower of the Winds, as illustrated in the first volume of *Antiquities of Athens*. He placed these strikingly on the four corner towers of his Schloss Tegel, Berlin, in 1821–24.

More inventively, when he learned from Stuart and Revett that a Roman temple of Augustus had once stood on the Acropolis in axis with the Parthenon, he chose this location for the main court of the palace for the King of Greece, which he planned for the Acropolis in 1834 (figs. 13-23, 13-24).[55] In the grounds of Schloss Glienicke, he built the startling Grosse Neugierde (Great Curiosity) in 1835–37, a belvedere containing a large circular colonnade of columns of the Corinthian order of the Choragic Monument of Lysicrates. This is surmounted by a cupola inspired by the same monument, crowned with a cast bronze reconstruction of the tripod, like Stuart's creation more than sixty years earlier at Shugborough.

Christian Grosch (1801–65) was a Danish architect of German descent whose numerous works in Oslo included

the Greek Doric Exchange (1826–52) and the university (1838; fig. 13-25), the plans for which were submitted to Schinkel for his comment. With their trabeated façades they are strikingly Schinkelesque and form a major urban composition which is also indebted to Schinkel's ideal of civic planning.

While Schinkel dominated architecture in Prussia, Leo von Klenze (1784–1864), with his grandiose and, indeed, largely realized vision, was the leading figure in Bavaria.[56] As he was a Greek archaeologist of some distinction, he did not need to rely on the publications of others, as did architects such as Schinkel. However, he studied the works of Stuart and Revett[57] as well as of Le Roy in conceiving his Grecian masterpieces, notably the Walhalla outside Regensburg and the Propylaea in Munich. The Walhalla, initiated in 1814 and built in 1830–42 (fig. 13-26), was modeled on the Parthenon and was dedicated to the memory of the greatest Germans of all periods. On its stunning site above the Danube, it was the climax of the Greek Revival, though its rich polychromy went beyond the vision of Stuart like so many nineteenth-century revival buildings.

Klenze's Propylaea in Munich (fig. 13-27), which had been projected in 1817, was built in 1846–60 in the Königsplatz as the western entrance to the city, which Klenze had rebuilt as a royal, governmental, and cultural center. Commemorating the Greek War of Independence, the pediments and friezes of the Propylaea were carved by

Fig. 13-25. Christian Grosch. Oslo University, 1838. Photographed ca. 1970s. RIBA Library Photographs Collection, London.

Ludwig von Schwanthaler with scenes from the war. Architecturally, the central gateway made reference to the Athenian Propylaea but was flanked by much higher pavilions or pylons that had an almost Egyptian flavor, their trabeated upper stories featuring Thrasyllan piers.

The Impact of Polychromy

The alarm which has sometimes been aroused by poly-

chromy in Greek architecture and sculpture seems related to a fear of color in Western art. No small matter, this long predates Winckelmann, lying deep and unacknowledged in many attitudes. Thus it has recently been boldly claimed that "chromophobia manifests itself in the many and varied attempts to purge colour from culture, to devalue colour, to diminish its significance, to deny its complexity . . . colour is made to be the property of some 'foreign'

Fig. 13-26. Leo von Klenze. Walhalla, near Regensburg, 1830–42. Undated photograph. Conway Library, Courtauld Institute, London, B73/2311.

Fig. 13-27. Leo von Klenze. The Propylaea, Munich, 1846–60. Undated photograph. Conway Library, Courtauld Institute, London, B74/957.

body, usually the feminine, the oriental the primitive, the infantile, the vulgar, the queer, or the pathological . . . [or] colour is relegated to the realm of the superficial, the supplementary, the inessential or the cosmetic . . . Colour is dangerous, or it is trivial, or it is both."[58]

The notion of Greek polychromatic sculpture was introduced to an astonished French audience by Antoine-Chrysostôme Quatremère de Quincy (1755–1849) in *Le Jupiter olympien* (1814; fig. 13-28).[59] The influential permanent secretary to the Académie des Beaux-Arts from 1816 to 1839, Quatremère de Quincy was the leading architectural theorist and heir to Winckelmann in the promotion

Fig. 13-28. "Le Jupiter Olympien, vu dans son trône et dans l'interieur de son temple." Hand-colored engraving. From Antoine-Chrysostôme Quatremère de Quincy, *Le Jupiter olympien, ou L'art de la sculpture antique . . .* (1815): frontispiece. By permission of the British Library, London, 558*.g.3.

Fig. 13-29. View of the temple portico. Colored engraving. From Jacques-Ignace Hittorff, *Restitution du temple d'Empédocle à Sélinonte, ou l'Architecture polychrôme chez les Grecs* (1851): pl. II. By permission of the British Library, London, 650.c.29.

of Greek idealism in France. The first French translation of *Antiquities of Athens* had appeared in four volumes in 1808–24.[60]

Sir William Gell defended Greek polychromy in his book, *Pompeiana*, written with J. P. Gandy, in which he noted that "the taste of the Romans in preferring the coloured marbles has been censured, and the works of the Greeks referred to as purer models for imitation. The fact however, is, that no nation ever exhibited a greater passion for gaudy colours, with which, in the absence of the rarer marbles, they covered the surfaces of the beautiful pentelic."[61] Pointing as evidence to the Erechtheion and to Greek sculpture, Gell wrote that "Blue marble is mixed with white in one of their best examples, the temple of Minerva Polias, at Athens; while even their statues were seldom left colourless."[62] Gell acknowledged the help he had received from C. R. Cockerell who provided draw-

ings of Pompeiian wall paintings and the plan of the House of Pansa.[63]

Another central figure in relating archaeology to current architecture was the architect and scholar Jacques-Ignace Hittorff (1792–1867) who was a friend of C. R. Cockerell and, a rarity among French architects, an Anglophile. With a high regard for British classical archaeology, in 1827 he published a translation of Gell and Gandy's *Pompeiana*, and in 1832, a translation of Gandy, Bedford, and Gell's *Unedited Antiquities of Attica*. He issued this to be in conformity with Stuart and Revett's *Antiquities of Athens*, of which his translation appeared posthumously in 1881.[64]

In 1822 Hittorff traveled to Italy where he met Thomas Leverton Donaldson, who fired him with the notion that Greek architecture had been colored. Hittorff now established color as the basis of life in Greek architecture in his books, *Architecture antique de la Sicile* (1827) and *Restitution du temple d'Empédocle à Selinunte, ou l'architecture polychrome chez les Grecs* (1845–51; fig. 13-29). His colored plates have a vibrancy that can still shock today.[65] His architectural masterpiece as an architect was the Church of St.Vincent-de-Paul in Paris (1830–46), its mullioned towers owing something to the Choragic Monument of Thrasyllus. Its façade was enlivened with colored enameled panels, while there was rich coloring within, including frescoes by followers of Ingres echoing a procession like that on the Parthenon frieze.[66] The new emphasis on color was seen as dethroning Greek architecture from the divine plateau where, burning in a white light, it had been elevated by Fréart de Chambray, Winckelmann, and Stuart. Students at the École des Beaux-Arts who had won scholarships to the Académie de France à Rome studied Stuart avidly for information about colored ornament for their *envoi,* sets of architectural drawings of an ancient Roman monument in Italy that they were obliged to submit to Paris in their fourth year.[67] The application of painted ornament, because it was essentially temporary, seemed to speak the popular language of the marketplace, almost of the funfair. The academy was shocked by an *envoi* on the temples at Paestum, sent in 1828 by Pierre-François Labrouste (1801–75). Not only he had chosen a Greek, rather than Roman subject, but he also suggested that one of the monuments was not a temple but a civil assembly hall for the people, which he showed in use with trophies, inscriptions, and graffiti.[68] The myth of Greece seemed at an end.

Polychromy became the central issue of architectural enquiry and debate in Europe from the 1830s, and French and German scholars carefully searched *Antiquities of Athens* for evidence about the use of color. In Germany, Gottfried Semper (1803–79), perhaps the greatest architectural theorist of the nineteenth century,[69] published *Preliminary Remarks on Polychrome Architecture and Sculpture in Antiquity* (1834), citing Stuart as part of the archaeological documentation for color.[70] This forty-nine-page pamphlet was the first expression of Semper's lifelong belief that color was paramount to Greek artistic thinking. Complaining that Winckelmann had seen sculpture as white, he pointed out that "Stuart's work, admirable for its time, appeared soon after him, and permitted a more correct view of Greek antiquity."[71] Significantly, he noted of *Antiquities of Athens* that "the indications of antique wall painting that it contained went almost

unnoticed, since they were presented without enthusiasm—as though with disbelief and resistance. They were too foreign to the time."[72]

The views of the Scottish architect Thomson, born in 1817, benefited from two discoveries about Greek architecture made after Stuart's time: the existence of extensive polychromatic decoration and knowledge of entasis, or optical refinements, both discovered by Cockerell and later investigated in detail by Hittorff and Penrose respectively. By 1874 Thomson could thus point to "the exquisite refinement of detail" of the Parthenon, which included some details "so extremely delicate that they escaped the very keen observation of Stuart and Revett, who were the first to delineate the buildings with any degree of accuracy."[73] Of the shimmering color on the Acropolis, Thomson exclaimed: "Fancy all these beautiful forms composed of marble of pearly whiteness, and the azure crimson, and gold with which they were partially tinted, seen from a distance. The colors, blending with white, would yield a chaste irradescence resembling that of an opal."[74] This is a vision which would have appealed to Schinkel but not to Stuart.

Greek Democracy for the United States

English emigrant architects, notably Latrobe, Hadfield, and Haviland, brought the achievement of Stuart and Revett to America. Thomas Jefferson, an amateur architect who served two terms as president from 1801 to 1809, promoted Greek architecture as the expression of the democratic ideals of the new republic. He was able to fulfill a long-held ambition of acquiring *Antiquities of Athens*, buying the first volume when he was in Paris as American ambassador from 1784 to 1789.[75] He was aware that, since the forms of Greek architecture had not been in use between the ancient world and the late-eighteenth century, they had not become overly associated with monarchs, princes, and popes, as had Roman architecture. Grecian forms, therefore, seemed ideal for building a new democracy.

This appropriateness had been hinted at in *Antiquities of Athens,* which suggested that Greek art and architecture flourished at a time of political freedom.[76] Eighteenth-century England, however, still saw itself as the heir to Augustan and imperial Rome, so that it was open to America to adopt the role of heir to republican Greece. This process was initiated for Jefferson by Benjamin Henry Latrobe, who had been a pupil in England of C. R.

Fig. 13-30. Benjamin Henry Latrobe. Roman Catholic Cathedral, Baltimore, 1805–20. Photographed ca. 1902. Library of Congress Prints and Photographs Division, Washington D.C., LC-D4-14266.

Cockerell's father, Samuel Pepys Cockerell. In 1796 Latrobe immigrated to America where he became the father of American Grecian architecture and, indeed, of the architectural profession itself.

Though several copies of *Antiquities of Athens* were circulating in America before the Revolution,[77] it was not until Latrobe that the quality of Greek details and forms began to echo in new buildings, such as his Bank of Pennsylvania, Philadelphia (designed 1798, built 1799–1801, demolished 1867). Built of local marble, this building featured two six-columned porticos of the Ilissus Ionic order and contained an elegant domed rotunda. Latrobe's Harvie-Gamble House, Richmond, Virginia (1798), incorporated a porch with columns of the Delian Doric order, illustrated by Stuart and Revett, with fluting at only the top and bottom of the shafts.

Arguing that "Greece was free" and that this was "the source of her eminence," Latrobe claimed that "in Greece every citizen felt himself important . . . [so] the path of glory was equally open to all."[78] He pointed out that "Greece was free when the arts flourished, and that freedom derived from them much of her support and permanence," and drew attention to his Bank of the United States as the first building in America "in which marble was employed as the principal material of its front," implying a fruitful association of freedom with prosperity and with banking in particular.[79]

Latrobe also wrote uncompromisingly to Jefferson that "principles of good taste are rigid in Grecian architecture. I am a bigoted Greek in the domination of the Roman architecture of Baalbec, Palmyra, and Spalatro."[80] In practice he was far more accommodating, happy to

535

Fig. 13-31. John Haviland. Franklin Institute Building, Philadelphia, 1825–26. Photographed in 1972. Library of Congress Prints and Photographs Division, Washington D.C., HAB5 Pa 51 PHILA, 153.

Fig. 13-32. Robert Mills. Monumental Church, Richmond, Virginia, 1812–17. Photographed ca. 1903. Library of Congress Prints and Photographs Division, Washington D.C., LC-D4 16194.

incorporate features such as the Roman dome in his beautiful Roman Catholic Cathedral, Baltimore, Maryland (1805–20; fig. 13-30). Its grace and lightness owed something to the work in London of John Soane. Despite Latrobe's start in the 1790s, it was not for some years that his Grecian mode was followed, notably by his pupils, Robert Mills and William Strickland.

The two principal English immigrants after Latrobe, were George Hadfield (1763–1826) and John Haviland (1792–1852). Hadfield, a pupil of James Wyatt and an enthusiastic student of Greek architecture, immigrated to America in 1795. His knowledge of *Antiquities of Athens* was evident in his designs for the executive office for the first U.S. Treasury Building (1796–97), as well as his City Hall (1820–26) and Second Bank of the United States (1824), all in Washington.

Haviland, who studied from 1811 to 1814 with James Elmes, a passionate admirer of Stuart, supervised the construction of Elmes's design for St. John's Chapel, Chichester, England (1812–13). This has a polygonal

Fig. 13-33. William Strickland. Merchants Exchange, Philadelphia, 1823–24. Photographed in 1915. Library of Congress Prints and Photographs Division, Washington D.C., LC-USZ62-68494 Lot 6648.

Fig. 13-34. William Strickland. State Capitol, Nashville, Tennessee, 1845–59. Photographed ca. 1863–64. Library of Congress Prints and Photographs Division, Washington D.C., LC-UXZ62-4697.

form echoing the Tower of the Winds and also a cupola that is a miniature version of the Choragic Monument of Lysicrates. Haviland immigrated to America in 1816 and published *The Builder's Assistant*, the first textbook for an American audience to illustrate the Greek orders.[81] His Franklin Institute Building, Philadelphia (1825–26; fig. 13-31), featured a starkly impressive Thrasyllan façade, with four piers rather than the three of the original.

Robert Mills, promoted by Jefferson as a young man, was a pupil of Latrobe until 1808. His Monumental

Church, Richmond, Virginia (1812–17; fig. 13-32), one of the most powerful and inventive buildings of the Greek Revival in America, has many imaginative features and a portico with columns of the Delian Doric order.

William Strickland (1788–1854), another pupil of Latrobe beginning in 1804, studied the volumes on Greek monuments in Latrobe's library, including *Antiquities of Athens*. Strickland made his career with the design of the Second Bank of the United States, Philadelphia (1818–24), its two octastyle Greek Doric porticos

537

Fig. 13-35. Front and side elevations of a Greek Revival church. Engraving. From Asher Benjamin, *The Builder's Guide, or Complete System of Architecture* . . . (1838): pl. LIX. Courtesy of the Art and Architecture Collection, Miriam and Ira D. Wallach Division of Art, Prints and Photographs, The New York Public Library, Astor, Lenox and Tilden Foundations.

based on the measured drawings of the Parthenon by Stuart and Revett. In his Merchants' Exchange, Philadelphia (1832–34; fig. 13-33), Strickland deployed the Greek Corinthian order of the Choragic Monument of Lysicrates, the first use of this form in American architecture. He based it on the measured drawings in *Antiquities of Athens*, while he took inspiration for the unusual curved portico below it from C. R. Cockerell's Literary and Philosophical Institution, Bristol (1821–23), which he had studied on a visit to England in 1825. Strickland's United States Naval Asylum, Philadelphia (1826–33), included a portico in the Ilissus Ionic order, while his magnificent State Capitol, Nashville, Tennessee (1845–59; fig. 13-34), combined an Erechtheion Ionic portico with a Lysicratean tower. Strickland supposedly told his assistants that a successful architect need look no further for models than the plates of *Antiquities of Athens*. One fine product of this practice was the Custom House, Wall Street, New York (1833–42), by Ithiel Town and Alexander Jackson Davis, its side elevations powerfully articulated with rows of giant Thrasyllus piers dividing the windows.

Minard Lafever (1798–1854) was a successful New York architect and author whose books, containing plates inspired by *Antiquities of Athens*, influenced the design and decoration of current domestic architecture, though his own work was more often in the Gothic, Italianate, and Egyptian styles. His *Young Builder's General Instructor* (1829) had plates copied from *Metropolitan Improvements*

Fig. 13-36. Replica of the Parthenon, Nashville, Tennessee, 1897. Stereograph made ca. 1897. Library of Congress Prints and Photographs Division, Washington D.C., LC-USZ62 68137 Lot 7018.

(1827–29) by James Elmes. Other titles by Lafever included *The Modern Builder's Guide* (1833) and *The Beauties of Modern Architecture* (1835).[82]

Another key figure in the spread of information derived from Stuart and Revett was Asher Benjamin (1771–1845), prolific both as an architect and as an author of pattern books, such as *Practice of Architecture* (fig. 13-35) and *The Architect, or Complete Builder's Guide*.[83] Practical and beautiful, they were among the most influential of all Greek Revival handbooks, especially in the American South, Midwest, and New England.

It is an extraordinary tribute to a movement that may be said to have been begun by Stuart and Revett that "by the mid-nineteenth century there was hardly a sizeable town in Europe or North America that did not somewhere possess the cast of at least one of Elgin's marbles."[84] A climax was reached in America when a full-size replica of the Parthenon was built for the Tennessee Centennial and International Exposition, Nashville, in 1897 (fig. 13-36).[85]

Reactions Against Stuart in the Nineteenth Century

The numerous Greek Revival buildings in Britain, Germany, and North America were nourished by the black-and-white engravings of Stuart and Revett and whitened casts of sculptural friezes. Their character reflected the eighteenth-century Enlightenment, "modern, international, sceptical, forward-looking, scientific, and exact."[86] This is what was still wanted in the early nineteenth century, but by the 1830s forces were at work that would undermine this world by a growing emphasis on nationalist ideals. Lord Elgin himself had the misfortune of being confronted with this when, despite his forceful campaign in favor of adopting the Grecian style for the new Houses of Parliament,[87] it was decided that they should be "Gothic or Elizabethan." Criticizing what he called "Gothomania," Elgin's private secretary, William Hamilton, urged that the new buildings should "remind us not of those dark ages . . . but of those brighter days, when under the banner of freedom the human intellect attained its highest eminence."[88] The choice of "Gothic or Elizabethan" which was a romantic gesture intended to express the historic continuity of the British parliamentary system, had also been encouraged by the theory of the Picturesque with its stress on the importance of attending to the genius loci: for example, the Houses of

Parliament occupied an historic medieval site and the new building was to incorporate the fourteenth-century Westminster Hall.

Writers such as James Elmes and Joseph Gwilt, who praised Stuart in the 1840s, were born in the 1780s and were a living part of the early Greek Revival from which they could hardly escape. Color, in particular colored ornament, seemed the way out of the contemporary architectural malaise, whether in the rich polychromy of Pugin's Gothic or of Hittorff's Greek. A central figure in this world was Owen Jones (1809–74), who was responsible in 1851 for the red, blue, and yellow color scheme of the Crystal Palace in which he designed the controversial Greek Court. He published a defiant defense of his design in *An Apology for the Colouring of the Greek Court* (1854).[89] Acknowledging the pioneering work of Stuart and Revett in making known the presence of "painted ornaments," Jones regretted that some of them had been "engraved in their work as if in relief," adding, "but artists were for long after unwilling to accept these fragments as evidence that an entire system of ornamentation prevailed in the Greek buildings."[90] He answered his own question about whether temples were "painted and ornamented" by stating, "*entirely so*, so that neither the colour of the marble nor even its surface was preserved." This extreme view has never been widely held, but Jones referred to his discussions about polychromy with Hittorff and concluded his essay with a translation of Semper's section on polychromy in his *Vier Elemente der Baukunst* (1851).[91]

Jones complained in 1853 that "when Stuart and Revett published their work on Greece it generated a mania for Greek architecture, from which we have barely recovered,"[92] yet in his influential *Grammar of Ornament* (1864) he showed dazzling examples of decoration, including Greek, Roman, Gothic, and Islamic. In his text he expressed characteristically Victorian moralizing modes of thought when he complained that "Greek ornament was wanting, however, in one of the great charms which should always accompany ornament,—viz. Symbolism. It was meaningless, purely decorative, never representative, and can hardly be said to be constructive"; Pompeiian decoration "oftentimes approaches vulgarity"; while the aim of Roman temples was "self-glorification," so that "every part is overloaded with ornament."[93]

In Scotland, Alexander Thomson was, in many ways, an anachronism in maintaining Greek Revival language into the 1870s, for in England it had been overtaken, first by the Italianate Revival and then by the Gothic Revival. The critic W. H. Leeds preceded his monograph on Charles Barry's Travellers' Club, Pall Mall (1830–32), a landmark in the Italianate Revival, with an essay that was a distinguished but devastating attack on the Greek Revival. Associating this with Stuart, he claimed that "the Grecian style is deficient in variety; yet, as if it was not sufficiently monotonous of itself, our practice has been to render it more so by stereotyping columns and capitals— contrary to the practice of the Greeks themselves, who allowed a considerable latitude in regard to matters of detail."[94] He believed that "piece-meal copying of the separate parts is, most assuredly, a very different thing from entering into the spirit of Grecian architecture," though he admitted of Doric and Ionic columns that they cannot "be *attacked* or censured, seeing they are fac-similes of warranted examples, as may at once be attested by our turning to Stuart's 'Athens'."[95]

James Fergusson (1806–86), in his popular study, *History of the Modern Styles in Architecture* (1862), condemned the Greek Revival totally, complaining that "the Grecian Doric is singularly untractable and ill-suited to modern purposes."[96] He was unimpressed by Stuart, writing that "though Stuart practised as an architect after his return from Greece, he does not seem to have met with much patronage, nor did he then succeed in introducing his favourite style practically to his countrymen." Rightly observing that the revival occurred later, he noted that "once the fashion was introduced it became a mania . . . an easily detected sham."[97]

Fergusson set his comments in the context of the fascinating links which he drew between poetry and architecture in the eighteenth and nineteenth centuries. He suggested that Joseph Addison was a parallel to William Chambers, and James Thomson to Robert Adam, but regretted that this harmony had since been broken. He welcomed the simplification in the language of poetry at the beginning of the nineteenth century, when "the poets had exhausted every form of imitation" and therefore "wholly freed themselves from the chains their predecessors had prided themselves in wearing."[98] He lamented, however, that "just when the architects might have done the same, Stuart practically discovered and revealed to his countrymen the beauties of Greek Art," pointing out tartly that "the poets had had the distemper; the architects had still to pass through it."[99] He rejoiced that "at last a reaction set in against this absurdity," but deplored that this

led architecture to a further bondage: this time, to Gothic architecture, but still not to sense.

George Wightwick (1802–72), an unhappy amanuensis of John Soane in 1826–27, published *The Palace of Architecture* (1840), a tribute to Romantic eclecticism in which, though criticizing Greek Revival architecture, he urged the reader to do "homage" to ancient Greek architecture itself as "palpable Truth."[100] The notion of architecture as truth lay behind the doctrines of the Gothic Revivalist, A. W. N. Pugin, and, to some extent, those of John Ruskin (1819–1900). It is intriguing to find that Ruskin had a high regard for certain aspects of Stuart's work. He included engravings of the Parthenon and Erechtheion from *Antiquities of Athens* in the great collection of images of works of art which he began assembling on his appointment as Slade Professor at the University of Oxford in 1870. He subsequently gave these to the university.

In explaining Stuart's engravings to his pupils, Ruskin admitted that "they by no means well express" the quality of their subject but nonetheless commended them for "their modesty, earnestness and honesty."[101] Seeing them as anticipating the kind of honest workmanship associated with the Arts and Crafts movement, he pointed out that "they are not works of genius (either in draughtsman or engraver) . . . but they are absolutely sincere and simple in aim; industrious and faithful work." As a result, he told them that "I wish you, every one, to draw the curve of the Parthenon capital as a first lesson in purity and precision."[102]

In Germany the Grecian legacy of Schinkel and Klenze became a state-organized Philhellenism that prevailed throughout the nineteenth century. It was not so easily challenged on grounds of nationalism as in England, because it had been more firmly rooted from the start as an expression of German values. After unification in 1870, it was also used to bolster the self-conception of the Reich as a European *Kulturnation*.[103] Archaeological excavation which, by moving farther east to Assyria, Egypt, and Axum, left the Greek colonies far behind, releasing Germans from what Edith Butler famously identified as "the Tyranny of Greece over Germany."[104]

In Italy, where there had been much late neoclassical architecture in the early nineteenth century, often with a stern Greek flavor, the growing move to unite the separate states of which the country was composed led to unification in 1861. The need to provide a sense of nation-

Fig. 13-37. A. E. Richardson. New Theatre, or Opera House, Manchester, 1912. Photographed in 1973. English Heritage / National Monuments Record.

hood and of pride in the past not surprisingly now encouraged a Renaissance Revival.[105]

Influence and Appraisals in the Twentieth Century

Just when it might have been supposed that interest in Stuart had run its course, a remarkable tribute to him came from the architect Sir Albert Richardson (1880–1964) in his *Monumental Classic Architecture in Great Britain and Ireland* (1914).[106] This book was part of a program of overthrowing the Gothic Revival and the Arts and Crafts movement, which Richardson saw as having a narrow nationalist base. It had thus stifled the international classical tradition as represented in the work of Stuart, Soane, Cockerell, Elmes, Pennethorne, and Thomson. These architects had upheld the torch of classicism, which had been kept alight on the Continent by architects such as Hittorff and Labrouste in France, Schinkel in Germany, and, in Richardson's day, by the firm of McKim, Mead and White in North America.

Richardson proclaimed unexpectedly that Stuart's Lichfield House in St James's Square "demonstrated how the spirit of the Hellenic art could be interpreted without having recourse to mere reproduction, an important achievement which many of Stuart's successors failed to accomplish" (see fig. 13-1).[107] Richardson went so far as to claim that, even including Chambers and Gandon, "there is not one whose influence was destined to be felt so strongly, at a later period, than that of this shrewd Scotsman." He complained that "Chambers fought shy of the newer teaching, and Gandon, while professing great curiosity as to why Greek architecture should be so much extolled, continued with his opinions concerning that of Rome. Stuart, however, was an energetic persistent man who . . . practised the doctrines he advocated."[108]

Richardson even suggested that Stuart's "pioneer labours instantly acted as a check to the prevalent style . . . [and] by reason of their sequence and iron restraint . . . they imposed the cult of the academic on all having recourse to the principles expounded."[109] For Richardson, Stuart's work had a "formality which is the very life of refinement; and while standing out in clear definition amidst other works of his period, although intimately related to the latter, they, not withstanding, bear an air of unrivalled distinction."[110]

In this remarkable essay in wishful thinking, in which Stuart was cast in an improbable role as an "energetic persistent man" characterized by "iron restraint,"

541

Fig. 13-38. Arthur Beresford Pite. Offices of the London, Edinburgh and Glasgow Assurance Company, Euston Square, London, 1906–08. Undated photograph. Conway Library, Courtauld Institute B82/1937.

Richardson reconstructed Stuart as a man in his own image who could be recruited in the effort to reform early-twentieth-century British architecture along grand classical lines. Richardson's own contribution to this movement can be seen in his New Theatre, Manchester (1912; fig. 13-37), which intelligently combined Grecian elements from Cockerell and Hittorff. His ambitions were paralleled by those of Geoffrey Scott in *The Architecture of Humanism* (1914).[111] The First World War brought an end to these hopes, but a few years before, the works of architects such as Arthur Beresford Pite (1861–1934) had encouraged Richardson to believe that the revival he sought might be at hand.

An Arts and Crafts architect, Pite had been impressed by the Grecian richness of Cockerell, lamenting the 1896 demolition of his Hanover Chapel, Regent Street (1823–25), and the imminent destruction of Nash's Regent Street. He was impressed by the restoration of the ancient Greek city of Selinunte in Sicily by the Beaux-Arts student, Jean Hulot, which had been exhibited in London in 1908. This, Pite felt, was in harmony with the urban and stylistic qualities of his own London, Edinburgh and Glasgow Assurance Company premises in Euston Square (1906–8; fig. 13-38), with a sculptural richness in which he had adopted many of Cockerell's discoveries about Greek

architecture including the unique Bassae Ionic order.[112]

Between the wars, a new, if very localized, interest in Stuart was kindled by the seventh Earl Spencer, who took the unusual step in 1924 of moving back into his London mansion, Spencer House, which the family had been obliged to let for much of the time since 1889. A civilized and learned figure, Lord Spencer restored the house to its eighteenth-century appearance insofar as was possible and published three articles on it and its furniture in 1926.[113]

A new level of scholarship in the study of Stuart arrived with Lesley Lewis, one of the first non-architects to be concerned with him. In 1938 she published a groundbreaking article on Stuart and Revett in the *Journal of the Warburg Institute*.[114] The Warburg Institute, founded in Hamburg, Germany, by Aby Warburg in 1925, was (and happily still is), a center for the academic investigation of the survival, or afterlife, of the classical tradition (*das Nachleben der Antike*).[115] In 1933 with the threat of Nazi persecution, it relocated with its library in London, where it continues to exercise profound influence on the development of the study of the history of art. One unusual early product of the Warburg Institute was the traveling exhibition of photographs of British art, organized in 1941 by the art historians Fritz Saxl and Rudolf Wittkower. They explained that "at a time when the Mediterranean

Fig. 13-39. Page spread entitled "The Greek Revival." From Fritz Saxl and Rudolf Wittkower, *British Art and the Mediterranean* (1948): pl. 76. Courtesy of the Trustees of The Victoria and Albert Museum, National Art Library, London, 51.D.67.

had become a battleground" and "inter-European relations were disrupted by the war, it was stimulating to observe in the arts of this country the agelong impact of the Mediterranean tradition on the British mind" (fig. 13-39).[116]

The exhibition included Stuart and Revett's *Antiquities of Athens*. Although Saxl and Wittkower found that "the statement in the preface to the fourth volume (1816) that 'on the publication of the first volume, the knowledge of Grecian art burst upon the public in all its splendour,' may be an exaggeration," they nonetheless proclaimed that the work "certainly appears in historic retrospect as the corner-stone of the whole movement."[117]

Interestingly, this war-time exhibition chose to emphasize the links of England with the Continent at a time when new books were generally stressing quite the opposite. This was because it had been decided to promote the British war effort by frequent visual and written emphasis on the appeal of the English countryside, the farms and hamlets, and the country ways and crafts of an indigenous, pre-industrial and localized economy.

Sir John Summerson, in his highly regarded *Architecture in Britain*, first published in 1953, was impatient with the Greek Revival, perhaps partly because his earlier promotion of the Modern Movement in architecture gave him an initial lack of sympathy with any revivals.[118] Referring to William Wilkins, he wrote of the "priggish loyalty to Neo-classical ideals . . . servile reproduction of Erechtheum detail . . . [in buildings] as doctrinaire as they could be . . . [marked by] restraint and pedantry."[119] He asked in despair, "What did the reproduction of Greek Doric ever do for English architecture?"[120]

A 1994 attempt at a comprehensive history of architectural theory by a German scholar also adopted a surprisingly sour tone, the author complaining that "*Antiquities of Athens* is unsystematic and at the same time pedantic in its attention to detail. Its manner is doctrinaire and it paints a lifeless, anaemic picture of Greece which largely prevailed in the nineteenth century and was not replaced by anything better. Like Desgodetz, Stuart aimed at providing a definitive theory of architecture but he was quite inadequate to the task."[121]

In 1991 the architect Jan van Pelt observed somewhat obscurely that "when in 1762 the initial volume of the first reliable description of the architectural remains of the Acropolis appeared (Stuart and Revett's *Antiquities of Athens*), ancient Greece had already been assigned its proper historicist designation within a general context of realist resignation."[122] He went on to join in the process of dethroning the myth of Greece, a process begun in the nineteenth century. He did this by criticizing, understandably, the romantic but pretentious reaction to the Acropolis by the American architectural historian Vincent Scully, who wrote, "There is only being and light. Time lies dead in the white and silver light of the outdoor room between the Parthenon and the Erechtheion."[123] Van Pelt's response to this was, "I have never been able to avoid the crowds up there. And so I learned to understand the Acropolis as a place designed for crowds, today and twenty-five centuries ago. It was, after all, nothing but a tasteful version of Disneyland's Main Street USA."[124]

By contrast, J. Mordaunt Crook's *Greek Revival* (1972) which had been partly written at the Warburg Institute with the support of its director, Ernst Gombrich, continued the sympathetic approach of Saxl and Wittkower. Adopting their claim that Stuart and Revett were "the corner-stone of the whole movement," Crook argued that "from the 1760s onwards, Greek Revivalism is a continuous and expanding theme in British architecture and decoration."[125] Change came in 1995 with the publication

of Giles Worsley's *Classical Architecture in Britain*, a major work which has largely superseded Summerson's *Architecture in Britain* as the standard history of British eighteenth-century architecture.[126] Worsley criticized the picture of Stuart presented in Crook's book, questioning in particular the reference to "Greek Revivalism" which we have just quoted. Worsley showed, rightly, that Stuart had himself no wish to replace entirely Roman orders with Greek, but to increase the range available.

In my own monograph on Stuart in 1982, I concluded that "despite Stuart's undoubted role as a pioneer if patchy Greek Revivalist," we should remember that interiors like his Painted Room at Spencer House, "enlivened with painted decoration and plasterwork based on classical models," belonged to "a tradition which went back to Italy in the golden years of the Renaissance in the fifteenth and sixteenth centuries."[27] I thus pointed out that "Kent, Stuart, Chambers, Adam, Mylne, Dance, Wyatt and Soane, all spent formative years in Rome," and their work might be considered "for a moment as simply a late stage in the acclimatisation of England to the ideals of the Italian Renaissance."[128]

Support for such an interpretation can be found in an earlier time, in the decision of Walter Pater (1839–94) to include his celebrated essay on Winckelmann of 1867 in his later volume of essays on Renaissance art, because, he explained, Winckelmann "really belongs in spirit to an earlier age. By his enthusiasm for the things of the intellect and the imagination for their own sake, by his Hellenism, his life-long struggle to attain the Greek spirit, he is in sympathy with the humanists of a previous century. He is the last fruit of the Renaissance, and explains in a striking way its motive and tendencies."[129]

Pater also quoted the erudite French writer Madame de Staël, who had perceived the significance of the pull to the south in Winckelmann's life and affections. She wrote that "he felt in himself an ardent attraction towards the south. In German imaginations even now traces are often to be found of that love of the sun, that weariness of the north (*cette fatigue du nord*) which carried the northern peoples away into the countries of the south."[130] The pull of the warm and colorful south was also strong among writers from the north, writers as varied as Ruskin, Burckhardt, and, of course, James "Athenian" Stuart.

1. *Antiquities*, vol. 4 (1816): xxiii, xxvii, xxviii.

2. William St. Clair, *Lord Elgin and the Marbles,* 3rd rev. ed. (Oxford University Press, 1998), chap. 15.

3. See David Watkin, "Thomas Hope's House in Duchess Street," *Apollo* 159 (March 2004): 31–39. Hope, *Household Furniture and Interior Decoration Executed from Designs by Thomas Hope* (London: Longman, Hurst, Rees and Orme, 1807).

4. Thomas Hope, *Observations on the Plans . . . By James Wyatt, Architect, for Downing College* (London: D. N. Shury, 1804): 9.

5. Cited in David Watkin, *Sir John Soane: Enlightenment Thought and the Royal Academy Lectures* (Cambridge University Press, 1996): 404.

6. Ibid., 6. Soane's favorite edition of Vitruvius was that by Stuart's collaborator, William Newton.

7. Morris, *Lectures on Architecture: Consisting of Rules Founded upon Harmonick and Arithmetical Proportions in Building* (London: Printed for J. Brindley, 1734); Chambers, *Treatise on Civil Architecture* (London: Printed for the author by J. Haberkorn, 1759), widely consulted as *Treatise on the Decorative Part of Civil Architecture*, 3rd ed., (London: Joseph Smeeton, 1791); Riou, *The Grecian Orders of Architecture, Delineated and Explained from the Antiquities of Athens. Also The Parallels Of The Orders of Palladio Scamozzi and Vignola, To Which Are Added Remarks Concerning Publick and Private Edifices With Designs* (London: the author, 1768).

8. This was built but is now lost. See David Watkin, "Beckford, Soane and Hope," in *William Beckford, 1760–1844: An Eye for the Magnificent*, ed. Derek Ostergard, exh. cat, Bard Graduate Center, New York (New Haven and London: Yale University Press, 2001): 38.

9. Watkin, *Soane* (1996): 642.

10. Ibid., 505.

11. Ibid., 316.

12. Le Camus de Mézières, *Le génie de l'architecture, ou l'analogie de cet art avec nos sensations* (Paris: Benoit Morin, 1780): 271. Author's translation. See also Le Camus de Mézières, *The Genius of Architecture, or, The Analogy of that Art with our Sensations,* trans. David Britt (Santa Monica, CA: Getty Center for the History of Art and the Humanities; Chicago: University of Chicago Press, 1992).

13. Watkin, *Soane* (1996): 243.

14. *Antiquities*, vol. 5 (1830): n.p.

15. According to Monck's grandson; see Richard Hewlings, "Belsay Hall and the Personality of Sir Charles Monck," in *Late Georgian Classicism*, ed. Roger White and Caroline Lightburn, Georgian Group Symposium (1987; London: Georgian Group, 1988): 10.

16. John Cornforth, "Millichope Park, Shropshire—I," *Country Life* 161 (10 February 1977): 312, fig. 5.

17. Richard Chandler, Nicholas Revett, and William Pars, *Antiquities of Ionia*, vol. 2 (London: W. Bulmer and W. Nicol, 1797): 25–26 and pls. XXIV–XXVI and XXVIII–XXX.

18. Wilkins, *Antiquities of Magna Graecia* (London: Longman, Hurst, Orme and Rees: 1807). For the connection to *Antiquities of Athens,* see Rhodri Liscombe, *William Wilkins, 1778–1839* (Cambridge University Press, 1980): 34.

19. Wilkins, *Atheniensia or Remarks on the Topography and Buildings of Athens* (London: John Murray, 1816).

20. *Antiquities,* vol. 1 (1762): 44–52; vol. 3 (1794): [11]–18.

21. Vitruvius, *The Civil Architecture of Vitruvius: Comprising those Books of the Author which relate to the Public and Private Edifices of Ancients,* trans. William Wilkins (London: Longman, Hurst, Rees, Orme, and Brown, 1812–17).

22. Edmund Burke, *A Philosophical Enquiry into the Origin of our Ideas of the Sublime and the Beautiful,* 5th ed. (London: J. Dodsley, 1767): 222.

23. George Hamilton-Gordon, Earl of Aberdeen, *Inquiry into the Principles of Beauty in Grecian Architecture; With an Historical View of the Rise and Progress of the Art in Greece* (London: John Murray, 1822): 15.

24. Ibid., 44.

25. Gell, *The Itinerary of Greece* (London: T. Payne, 1810); Gell, *Itinerary of the Morea* (London: Rodwell and Martin, 1817). For Gell see Edith Clay, *Sir William Gell in Italy: Letters to the Society of Dilettanti, 1831–1835* (London: Hamish Hamilton, 1976).

26. Gell, *Itinerary of Greece* (1810): ii.

27. Ibid., 2nd ed. (1827): 46.

28. Ibid.

29. Gwilt, *Encyclopaedia of Architecture, Historical, Theoretical, and Practical,* 1842, new ed. by Wyatt Papworth (London: Longmans, Green, 1891): 226.

30. James Elmes, "Historical Architecture in Great Britain," *Civil Engineer and Architect's Journal* 10 (1847): 339.

31. Gandy, Bedford, and Gell, *The Unedited Antiquities of Attica, comprising the Architectural Ramains of Attica, Megara, and Epirus* (London: Longman, Hurst, Rees, Orme, and Brown, and John Murray, 1817), reprinted as vol. 3 of *Antiquities of Ionia* by Chandler, Revett, and Pars (London: Murray, Rodwell, Weale, 1840); Cockerell, *The Temples of Jupiter Panhellenius at Aegina and of Apollo Epicurius at Bassae near Phigaleia in Arcadia* (London: John Weale, 1860).

32. Inwood, *The Erechtheion at Athens: Fragments of Athenian Architecture and A Few Remains in Attica Megara and Epirus* (London: James Carpenter and Son, Josiah Taylor, Priestly and Weale, 1827).

33. Penrose, *Investigation of the Principles of Athenian Architecture, or, The Results of a Survey Conducted Chiefly with Reference to the Optical Refinements Exhibited in the Construction of the Ancient Buildings at Athens* (1851; 2nd ed., London and New York: Macmillan, 1888). In the second edition, Penrose acknowledged the study of curvature by John Pennethorne, *The Geometry and Optics of Ancient Architecture, Illustrated by Examples from Thebes, Athens and Rome* (London and Edinburgh: Williams and Norgate, 1878). The quotation is from Panayotis Tournikiotis, ed. *The Parthenon and Its Impact in Modern Times,* trans. Cox and Solman (Athens: Melissa, 1994): 79.

34. Revett, *Antiquities of Ionia*, vol. 4 (London: Society of Dilettanti / Macmillan, 1881): [1].

35. Ibid.

36. See David Watkin, *The Life and Work of C. R. Cockerell* (London: Zwemmer, 1974).

37. The backdrop was commissioned from Stuart by Dr. Markham in 1758 and replaced with an identical copy in 1808. This survived until 1858, when Cockerell designed new scenery. See Admiral John Markham, *A Naval Career During the Old War: Being a Narrative of the Life of Admiral John Markham* (London: Sampson Low, Marston, Searle, and Rivington, 1883): 14.

38. Frederick Cummings, "Phidias in Bloomsbury: B. R. Haydon's Drawings of the Elgin Marbles," *Burlington Magazine* 106 (July 1964): 327, fig. 12. The drawing by Cockerell may be a mid-twentieth-century fake.

39. Ibid., p. 17. Entasis is a convex curve, especially in the shaft of a column, sometimes supposed to have been adopted to correct a possible impression of concavity.

40. Alexander Thomson, "Art and Architecture," *British Architect* 2 (1874): 51. See David Watkin, "The German Connection," in *"Greek" Thomson*, ed. Gavin Stamp and Sam McKinstry (Edinburgh University Press, 1994): 189–97.

41. See Gavin Stamp, *Alexander "Greek" Thomson* (London: Laurence King, 1999): 70–73 and 140–49.

42. Gavin Stamp, ed., *The Light of Truth and Beauty: The Lectures of Alexander "Greek" Thomson Architect, 1817–1875* (Glasgow: Alexander Thomson Society, 1999): 33.

43. This point has been made by Gavin Stamp; see ibid., 162.

44. Le Roy, *Les Ruines des plus beaux monuments de la Grèce* (Paris: Guerin and Delatour, Nyon; Amsterdam: Neaulme, 1758), pt. 1: pl. VIII. He based such vedute on the work of Piranesi.

45. For a brilliant survey of Philhellenism, see Suzanne Marchand, *Down from Olympus: Archaeology and Philhellenism in Germany, 1750–1970* (Princeton University Press: 1996).

46. The Pergamum Altar, or Altar of Zeus, dates to the second century B.C. In the 1870s it was removed from the Greek town of Pergamum in Asia Minor (now Turkey), by the German archaeologist Carl Humann, and taken to Berlin, where it was reassembled as part of a new Pergamum Museum.

47. Le Roy, *Ruines* (1758), pt. 2: pl. XIII. Describing this plate as "a potent image," Robin Middleton traced its influence on buildings that were not gateways or propylaea, such as: the Cour du Mai, Palais de Justice, Paris (ca. 1780) by Pierre Desmaisons and Jacques-Denis Antoine, the British Museum, London (1823–47) by Robert Smirke, and the Royal High School, Edinburgh (1825–29) by Thomas Hamilton; see Middleton's introduction to *The Ruins of the Most Beautiful Monuments of Greece* by Julien-David Le Roy, trans. David Britt (Los Angeles: Getty Research Institute, 2004): 143.

48. Stuart's relations with Göttingen are revealed a letter sent from London by Georg Christoph Lichtenberg to Christian Gottlieb Heyne, 16 March 1775, cited in *Georg Christoph Lichtenberg: Schriften und Briefe*, ed. Franz Mautner, vol. 4 (Frankfurt-am-Main, Insel Verlag, 1983): 179. I am indebted to Marcus Köhler for this reference.

49. *Antiquities,* vol. 2 (ca. 1790): 37–38. In the descriptive text (p. 40) to the plan of the Propylaea (chap. 5, pl. II), and in the lettering on the plan, Stuart confused "The Temple of Victory without Wings" with "The edifice anciently adorned with the paintings of Polygnotus."

50. Rolf Bothe et al., *Friedrich Gilly, 1772–1800, und die Privatgesellshaft junger Architekten*, exh. cat., Internationalen Bauausstellung, Berlin, and Berlin Museum (Berlin: Verlag Willmuth Arenhövel, 1984): figs. 34–36.

51. For the contents of the library, see Friedrich Gilly, *Essays on Architecture, 1796–1799*, intro. by Fritz Neumayer (Santa Monica: Getty Center, 1994): 181–82, and Alste Oncken, *Friedrich Gilly, 1772–1800* (Berlin: Deutscher Verein für Kunstwissenschaft, 1935): 30.

52. The original painting was destroyed in 1945 but is known from an excellent copy of 1836 by Wilhelm Ahlborn (Berlin: National Gallery).

53. *Antiquities*, vol. 2 (ca. 1790): pls. XVIII, XXI–XXIV. See Stelios Lydakis, "The Impact of the Parthenon Sculptures on 19th and 20th Century Sculpture and Painting," in Tournikiotis, *Parthenon* (1994): 238–39. As evidence that Schinkel's source was Stuart's engravings, see Jenifer Neils's suggestion to "note in particular the inclusion of part of the Nike parapet and the reversal of direction on the slab with Zeus and Hera" (Neils, *The Parthenon Frieze* [Cambridge and New York: Cambridge University Press, 2001]: 232).

54. Karl Friedrich Schinkel, "Das neue Schauspielhaus in Berlin," in *Sammlung architektonischer Entwürfe* (Berlin, 1819–40).

55. A point made by Barry Bergdoll, *Karl Friedrich Schinkel: An Architecture for Prussia* (New York: Rizzoli, 1994): 217.

56. See Adrian von Buttlar, *Leo von Klenze: Leben, Werk, Vision* (Munich: C. H. Beck, 1999).

57. Winfried Nerdinger, ed., *Leo von Klenze: Architekt zwischen Kunst und Hof* (Munich: Prestel, 2000): 149.

58. David Batchelor, *Chromophobia* (London: Reaktion, 2000): 22–23.

59. Quatremère de Quincy, *Le Jupiter olympien, ou l'art de la sculpture antique considéré sous un nouveau point de vue: ouvrage que comprend un essai sur le goût de la sculpture polychrome . . . et l'histoire de la statuaire en or et ivoire chez les grecs et les romains* (Paris: Firmin Didot, 1814).

60. There were also abridged translations in French and German. For publication details of some of the translations of Stuart and Revett, see Eileen Harris, *British Architectural Books and Writers, 1556–1785*, assisted by Nicholas Savage (Cambridge and New York: Cambridge University Press, 1990): 449–50; and *Early Printed Books, 1478–1840, Catalogue of the British Architectural Library*, vol. 4 (Munich: Saur, 2001): 2012–22.

61. William Gell and J. P. Gandy, *Pompeiana. The Topography, Edifices and Ornaments of Pompeii* (1817–19; 2nd ed., London: Rodwell and Martin, 1821): 160.

62. Ibid.

63. Ibid., p. xvi, pls. XXXIV, XLII–XLIII.

64. Stuart and Revett, *Les antiquités d'Athènes et de l'Attique*, trans. Jackques Ignace Hittorf, 5 vols. (Paris: Librairie Centrale d'Architecture, 1881).

65. For Hittorff, see Robin Middleton, "Perfezione e colore: la policromia nell'architettura francese del XVIII e XIX secolo," *Rassegna* 23 (1985): 55–67.

66. See *Hittorff (1792–1867): un architecte du XIXe siècle*, exh. cat., Musée Carnavalet, Paris, and Wallraf-Richartz-Museum, Cologne (Paris: Musée Carnavalet, 1986): 111–52, 297–305.

67. See Marie-Louise Cazalas et al., *Paris, Rome, Athènes: Le voyage en Grèce des architectes français aux XIXe et XXe siècles,* exh. cat., École nationale supérieure des Beaux-Arts, Paris, et al. (Paris: École nationale supérieure des Beaux-Arts, 1982): 25–48.

68. Neil Levene, "The Romantic Idea of Architectural Legibility: Henri Labrouste and the Neo-Grec," in Arthur Drexler, ed., *The Architecture of the École des Beaux-Arts* (London: Secker and Warburg, 1977): 325–416.

69. See Harry Francis Mallgrave, *Gottfried Semper: Architect of the Nineteenth Century* (New Haven and London: Yale University Press, 1996).

70. Gottfried Semper, *Vorläufige Bemerkungen über bemalte Architectur und Plastik bei den Alten* (Altona: Johann Hammerich, 1834); trans. by Harry Francis Mallgrave and Wolfgang Herrmann as *The Four Elements of Architecture and Other Writings* (Cambridge University Press, 1989).

71. Semper, *Four Elements* (1989): 57.

72. Ibid.

73. Stamp, *Light of Truth and Beauty,* (1999): 159.

74. Ibid., 161.

75. William Howard Adams, ed., *The Eye of Thomas Jefferson,* exh. cat. (Washington: National Gallery of Art, 1976): 99.

76. *Antiquities,* vol. 1 (1762): iv.

77. Talbot Hamlin, *Greek Revival Architecture in America* (Oxford University Press, 1944): 36, 64.

78. Latrobe, "Anniversary Oration to the Society of Artists," Philadelphia, 1811, in Latrobe, *The Journals of Benjamin Henry Latrobe, 1799–1820: From Philadelphia to New Orleans,* ed. Edward C. Carter II, John C. Van Horne, and Lee W. Formwalt, vol. 3 of Series 1, Journals, The Papers of Benjamin Henry Latrobe (New Haven: Maryland Historical Society and Yale University Press, 1980): 67–91.

79. Ibid.

80. Ibid.

81. Haviland, *The Builder's Assistant,* 3 vols. (1818–21; 2nd ed., 4 vols., Baltimore: F. Lucas, 1830).

82. Lafever, *The Young Builder's General Instructor; containing the Five Orders of Architecture . . .* (Newark: W. Tuttle, 1829); Elmes, *Metropolitan Improvements, or London in the Nineteenth Century . . .* (London: Jones, 1827–29); Lafever, *The Modern Builder's Guide* (New York: Henry C. Sleight, Collins and Hannay, 1833) and Lafever, *The Beauties of Modern Architecture* (New York: D. Appleton, 1835).

83. Benjamin, *Practice of Architecture, Containing the Five Orders of Architecture, and An Additional Column and Entablature* (1833; 4th ed., Boston: Benjamin B. Mussey, 1839), reprinted as *Practice of Architecture and The Builder's Guide: Two Pattern Books of American Classical Architecture* (New York: Da Capo Press, 1994).

84. Mary Beard, *The Parthenon* (London: Profile Books, 2002): 18.

85. Wilbur F. Creighton and Leland R. Johnson, *The Parthenon in Nashville: Pearl of the Tennessee Centennial Exposition* (Brentwood, TN, J. M. Press, 1989).

86. William St. Clair, "Rivals for the Ruined Piles," review of *The Ruins of the Most Beautiful Monuments of Greece,* by Julien-David Le Roy, trans. David Britt, intro. by Robin Middleton, *Times Literary Supplement* (12 November 2004): 12–13.

87. William St. Clair, *Lord Elgin and the Marbles,* 3rd rev. ed. (Oxford University Press, 1998): 276.

88. Hamilton, *Second Letter from W. R. Hamilton., Esq. to the Earl of Elgin on the propriety of adopting the Greek style of architecture in the construction of the new Houses of Parliament* (London: John Weale, 1836): [3] and 23. A substantial booklet of 65 pages, the *Second Letter* is well documented with source references from Winckelmann to Wilkins. It is an important if neglected document in the history of the Greek Revival.

89. Jones, *An Apology for the Colouring of the Greek Court in the Crystal Palace . . . with a Fragment on the Origin of Polychromy, by Professor Semper* (London: Crystal Palace Library and Bradbury and Evans, 1854).

90. Ibid., 6–7.

91. Ibid., 47–56.

92. Jones, "An attempt to define the principles which should determine form in the decorative arts," in Owen Jones, et al., *Lectures on the Results of the Great Exhibition of 1851, Delivered before the Society of Arts, Manufacture and Commerce, at the Suggestion of H.R.H. Prince Albert,* 2nd series (London: David Bogue, 1853): 290.

93. Jones, *The Grammar of Ornament* (London: Day and Son, 1856): 33, 40, 44.

94. W. H. Leeds, "An Essay on the Present State of Architectural Study and the Revival of the Italian Style," in *The Travellers' Club House,* ed. Charles Barry (London: John Weale, 1839): 14–15.

95. Ibid.

96. Fergusson, *History of the Modern Styles in Architecture,* vol. 2 (1862; 3rd ed., London: John Murray, 1891): 71–72. Also in 1862 the popular novelist Anthony Trollope, always sensitive to the architectural settings of his characters, published *Orley Farm,* in which he described "Groby House," near Leeds. Clearly in the style of Wilkins or Smirke, this bleak country house found no favor with Trollope, who observed drily that "the house is Greek in its style of architecture—at least so the owner says; and if a portico with a pediment and seven Ionic columns makes a house Greek, the house in Groby Park undoubtedly is Greek" (chap. 7, para. 10.). Wilkins would doubtless have regarded a portico with an uneven number of columns as a solecism, though a colonnade of this kind appeared at the Temple of Hera I (Basilica) at Paestum. The austerity of the house at Groby Park even seems to have affected the kind of food eaten in it, for Trollope gives an entertaining account of a horrendously inadequate luncheon.

97. Fergusson, *History of the Modern Styles,* vol. 2 (1891):71–72.

98. Ibid., 3.

99. Ibid.

100. Wightwick, *The Palace of Architecture: A Romance of Art and History* (London: James Fraser, 1840): 70.

101. "The Ruskin Art Collection at Oxford," in *The Works of John Ruskin,* ed. Edward Tyas Cook and Alexander Wedderburn, vol. 21 (London: George Allen; New York: Longmans, Green, 1906): 117.

102. Ibid.

103. See Marchand, *Down from Olympus* (1996).

104. Butler, *The Tyranny of Greece over Germany: A Study of the Influence Exercised by Greek Art and Poetry over the Great German Writers of the 18th, 19th and 20th Centuries* (Cambridge University Press: 1935).

105. See Rosanna Pavoni, ed., *Reviving the Renaissance: The Use and Abuse of the Past in Nineteenth-century Italian Art and Decoration*, trans. Adrian Belton (Cambridge University Press: 1997).

106. Richardson, *Monumental Classic Architecture in Great Britain and Ireland During the Eighteenth and Nineteenth Centuries* (London: Batsford, 1914).

107. Ibid., 32.

108. Ibid., 33.

109. Ibid.

110. Ibid.

111. Scott, *The Architecture of Humanism: A Study in the History of Taste* (London: Constable, 1914).

112. David Watkin, "Cockerell Redivivus," in *The Golden City: Essays on the Architecture and Imagination of Beresford Pite,* ed. Brian Hanson (London: Prince of Wales's Institute of Architecture, 1993): 1–11.

113. Earl Spencer, "Spencer House, St James's Place—I," *Country Life* (30 October 1926): 660–67; pt. 2, (6 November 1926): 698–704; pt. 3, (13 November 1926): 757–59). See Joseph Friedman, *Spencer House: Chronicle of a Great London Mansion* (London: Zwemmer, 1993): 266–73.

114. Lewis, "Stuart and Revett: Their Literary and Architectural Careers," *Journal of the Warburg Institute* 2 (1938–39): 128–46.

115. Ernst Gombrich, *Aby Warburg: An Intellectual Biography* (1970; 2nd ed., Oxford: Phaidon, 1986).

116. Saxl and Wittkower, *British Art and the Mediterranean* (Oxford University Press, 1948): preface.

117. Ibid., 76.

118. Summerson, *Architecture in Britain, 1530–1830* (1953; 4th ed., Harmondsworth: Penguin Books, 1965): 303.

119. Ibid.

120. Cited in J. Mordaunt Crook, *The Greek Revival: Neo-Classical Attitudes in British Architecture, 1760–1870* (London: John Murray, 1972): 138.

121. Hanno-Walter Kruft, *A History of Architectural Theory from Vitruvius to the Present* (London: Zwemmer, 1994): 212.

122. Robert Jan van Pelt and Carroll William Westfall, *Architectural Principles in the Age of Historicism* (New Haven and London: Yale University Press, 1991): 197.

123. Vincent Scully, *The Earth, the Temple, and the Gods: Greek Sacred Architecture* (New Haven and London: Yale University Press, 1962): 185.

124. Van Pelt and Westfall, *Architectural Principles* (1991): 197.

125. Crook, *Greek Revival* (1972): 77.

126. Worsley, *Classical Architecture in Britain: The Heroic Age* (New Haven and London: Yale University Press, 1995).

127. Watkin, *Athenian Stuart: Pioneer of the Greek Revival* (London: George Allen and Unwin, 1982): 57.

128. Ibid.

129. Pater, "Winckelmann," in *The Renaissance: Studies in Art and Poetry* (1873; 4th ed, London: Macmillan, 1893): xvi.

130. Ibid., p. 189, trans. from Madame de Staël, "Lessing et Winckelmann" (1813); see also Staël, *De L'Allemagne*, ed. Comtesse Jean de Pange, vol. 2 (Paris: Hachette, 1958–60): 66.

APPENDIX:
STUART AND HIS CRAFTSMEN

CHRONOLOGY

CHECKLIST

BIBLIOGRAPHY

549

APPENDIX:

JAMES STUART AND

HIS CRAFTSMEN

GEOFFREY BEARD

While Stuart, like his architect contemporaries, used a wide and tested range of craftsmen to carry out his designs, he was no mean hand at doing them himself. Among his many talents, learned early as a painter of fans, he was good at depicting decorative schemes in paint. He carried out several commissions, including: a "closet, ornamented and painted by Mr. Stewart" at Wimbledon Park, Surrey for John, first Earl Spencer (ca. 1758, dest. 1785)[1]; a "Flora and four pretty little Zephyrs"[2] and the "Four Seasons" on the Tapestry Room ceiling, Hagley Hall, Worcestershire (ca. 1758–59); the amazing and significant Painted Room at Spencer House, London (1759–66), for his patron, John Spencer; and the "Zephirs and Zephirettes" in a bedroom for Elizabeth Montagu in her house at 23 Hill Street, London (1767).[3] He was also responsible for at least fifteen funerary monuments, chiefly executed by Peter Scheemakers and his son Thomas[4]; fifteen bas-reliefs, mainly in the great hall or saloon at Wentworth Woodhouse, Yorkshire (ca. 1755)[5]; and several chimneypieces, such as that originally at Spencer House, London, before its removal to the Spencer family seat, Althorp, Northampton.[6] In addition there were many medals in gold, silver, and bronze,[7] designs for furniture and the allied arts, including the tripod perfume burner and plate warmer at

Kedleston, Derbyshire, settees and chairs for the Painted Room at Spencer House, London, the organ case at Newby Hall, Yorkshire, and the proposed altar and rose-window of St. George's Chapel, Windsor,[8] as well as numerous landscape buildings, such as the Temple of the Winds at Mount Stewart, County Down, and Rathfarnham Castle, County Dublin.[9]

Stuart was at times indolent—Elizabeth Montagu complained of his "disinterestedness and contempt of money" and of his failure to deliver designs and proper accounts.[10] While his architectural practice was "in consequence very limited, and he owed his principal commissions almost entirely to members of the Dilettanti Society and their friends,"[11] he has an important place in the history of architectural achievements. Nevertheless, the catholic nature of his duties causes the following list to bump along—from carver to engraver, metal-chaser to sculptor, and mason to stuccoist. Stuart knew many craftsmen, some of them involved in other aspects of jobs on which he was also working, but only when there is documentary evidence (or the strongest circumstantial evidence) of involvement is the name included in the following list. This has an alphabetical arrangement by surname, which perhaps eases the transition.

550

Abbreviations

dest.   destroyed

fol.   folio

fl.   *floruit* (flourished, or active)

q.v.   *quod vide* (used herein for cross references whether before or after the entry)

RSA   Royal Society of Arts

RHS   Royal Hospital for Seamen, Greenwich

SPAC   Society for Promotion of Arts, Manufactures and Commerce

Name is in brackets when the first name is not known.

ADAIR, John (*fl.* 1749–80), Carver, Gilder

Had premises in St. Ann's Court, Covent Garden, from 1749, but by 1763 was located in Wardour Street, Soho.[12] One of the craftsmen most consistently employed by Stuart. Partnered (1769–77) with William Adair, who was described in 1773 as a joiner to His Majesty's Privy Chamber.[13]

ca. 1756–64: NUNEHAM COURTENAY, Oxfordshire
Initially met Stuart at Nuneham Courtenay, Oxfordshire (ca. 1756),[14] where Stuart was responsible for a number of chimneypieces and other decorative details. Supplied two bracket tables designed by Stuart on August 4, 1764.[15]

1763–69: SHUGBOROUGH, Staffordshire, and ca. 1764–66: LONDON, 15 ST. JAMES'S SQUARE (Lichfield House)
Adair submitted a bill for £65.16.6 for work done from June 1763 to September 1766, which Stuart approved in 1767, and included carving and gilding numerous window frames, gluing a wooden crest, and carving two models based on Stuart's designs.[16] Adair charged £4.10.0 for drawing and preparing a wooden model of Stuart's Ionic capitals for the front elevation of St. James's Square between June 1763 and September 1764.[17] The second model was for the *aplustre* (trophy with naval emblems and ornaments), to be affixed to Stuart's Triumphal Arch at Shugborough.[18]

1765–68: LONDON, 24 HERTFORD STREET (Holdernesse House)
According to Lord Holdernesse's account book, received £698 between 1765 and 1768 for miscellaneous work probably carried out at Holdernesse House.[19]

ca. 1766–72: LONDON, 23 HILL STREET
Did carving and gilding, but annoyed Elizabeth Montagu, the owner, by billing what she considered an "exorbitant" rate for carving.[20]

1774–80: LONDON, 22 PORTMAN SQUARE
Received a first payment of £60 on October 17, 1774, for work done most likely at Portman Square (dest. 1941).[21] Adair received his final payment of £55.18.0 on May 1, 1780.[22]

ca. 1775: SHELBURNE HOUSE, London, or BOWOOD, Wiltshire
Received a payment between February and July 1775 for goods supplied and work carried out "by order of Mr. Stuart."[23]

ANDERSON, Diederich Nicolaus (*fl.* from 1760, d. 1767), Bronze Modeler, Chaser

Of Danish extraction, as proved in 1779 by his wife Penelope's will. Supplier of metalwork to Stuart, Sir William Chambers, and Robert Adam. Anderson was one of twenty-four appointed by SPAC (RSA), to judge the premium medal designed by Stuart in 1757. In 1763 he embellished in gilt metal a sedan chair (in the Royal Collection), which was made by Samuel Vaughan, after a design attributed to Stuart. Anderson died on July 20, 1767, leaving his effects to his wife.[24]

ca. 1757–60: KEDLESTON, Derbyshire
Probably responsible for the two "chestnut" vases in the dining room, the design of which is attributed to Stuart.[25] In 1760, after a design attributed to Stuart, made a plate warmer with his name and the date engraved on the concealed rim.[26] In about the same year, probably executed an ormolu tripod perfume burner with candle branches, which was described in 1766 in the travel diary of the Duchess of Northumberland as "Mr Stewart's tripod."[27]

ca. 1759–66: SPENCER HOUSE, London
May have been the bronze worker responsible for the hexagonal lantern Stuart designed for Earl Spencer's staircase and the tripod pedestals and candlestands for the Painted Room (all now at Althorp, Northampton).[28] Executed a pair of three-light, gilt-bronze candle vases for the great room, also based on Stuart's designs,[29] as well as the gilt-brass, S-shaped escutcheons Stuart designed for the doors of all the principal first-floor rooms.

ca. 1760: WENTWORTH WOODHOUSE, Yorkshire
Working from Stuart's designs, probably executed a tripod perfume burner (now in the Victoria and Albert Museum, London), of similar form to those made for Kedleston and Spencer House, as well as a pair of candle vases.[30]

1761: FREE SOCIETY OF ARTISTS
A "Mr Anderson" exhibited a tripod here "from an original design of Mr Stuart's."[31]

ca. 1763: ASHBURNHAM PLACE, Sussex
Stuart may have contributed to the interior decorations, including the designs for two tripods probably executed by Anderson (now in the Metropolitan Museum of Art, New York).[32]

ARROW, James (*fl.* from 1750, d. 1791), Carpenter, Joiner

First mentioned in 1750 in the bank account of the architect, Henry Flitcroft (London, Drummond's Bank). Worked for Sir William Chambers and Stuart. Held the post of Surveyor to the Victualling Office and Inspector of Repairs to the Admiralty (1774–85).[33]

1781–: RHS, Greenwich, CHAPEL
One of a team of craftsmen who had worked under Sir William Chambers at Somerset House and were recommended by Stuart for the chapel.[34] Supervised by the architect Newton (q.v.), who took over the direction of the chapel from Stuart in 1788, and was assisted by furniture-maker Seddon (q.v.).[35] Submitted a bill for gallery, font, and pews,[36] and executed the reader's desk and pulpit for the chapel.[37]

BACON, John (1740–1799), Sculptor

The son of a cloth-worker, he was apprenticed in 1755 to Crisp (q.v), who owned a porcelain factory at Vauxhall where Bacon learned to model figures. Was employed as a modeler and stone-carver in Spitalfields (ca.

1764–66). In 1769 became a modeler at the Coade Artificial Stone Manufactory (q.v.) and was made Chief Designer in 1771, a position he held until his death. Also ran a large workshop of between fifteen and twenty men who produced busts, chimney-pieces, and wall memorials.[38]

1785–ca. 1790: RHS, Greenwich, CHAPEL
Became associated with the hospital from 1785 onward through his employment at the Coade Artificial Stone Manufactory from which Newton (q.v.) commissioned statues of Faith, Hope, Charity, and Meekness. Bacon carved these figures in Coade stone to the designs of West (q.v.), and in ca. 1790 installed them in the niches of the octagonal entrance vestibule beneath the dome.[39] Also executed a marble door-case for the portal leading from the vestibule into the chapel, including an architrave frieze of two angels with fes-toons, supporting the Sacred Writings (finished 1789). At the east end of the chapel, carved marble angels in the spandrels over the altarpiece by West.[40] May have been the sculptor who worked on the organ loft at the west end, executing designs, which Newton probably created and Stuart altered.[41]

[BANISTER] (fl. 1763–69), Carpenter
1763–69: SHUGBOROUGH, Staffordshire
In February 1765 or 1766, owner Thomas Anson paid him for carpentry work, proba-bly at Shugborough rather than Lichfield House, making another payment of £45.11 on October 28, 1768.[42]

BARNEY, Joseph (1751–1827), Painter, Engraver
Of Wolverhampton. Came to London ca. 1767 where he studied under Antonio Zucchi and Kauffman (q.v.). Employed most often by Boulton (q.v.), 1778–ca.1781, to touch up by hand Boulton's "mechanical paintings."[43]

ca. 1776: LONDON, 22 PORTMAN SQUARE
Finished by hand the original paintings Rebecca (q.v.) and Cipriani (q.v.) supplied to Boulton for the ceilings of Mrs. Montagu's dressing room and other rooms (dest. 1940).[44]

BARRY, James (1741–1806), Painter
Born in Cork. Began his career by copying prints and studying with the landscape painter John Butts and history painter Jacob Ennis. Came to London in 1764, and through the influence of Edmund Burke, went to work for Stuart, copying watercolors of Athens into oil paintings and possibly preparing material for Antiquities of Athens. After Stuart's death, considered applying for the post of Serjeant-Painter, but decided against it, after learning the annuity was only £18.[45]

1771: THE FREE SOCIETY
In 1771 Stuart exhibited a "lanthorn of Demosthenese" at the Free Society, which was in all likelihood executed by Barry.[46]

BASIRE, James (1730–1802), Engraver
Came from an English family of engravers, including his London-based father, Isaac Basire (1704–68). Frequently engraved Stuart's designs but also worked for William Hogarth, West (q.v.), and Robert Adam. Adam hired Basire to engrave plates for his Spalatro but complained in 1758 of Basire's slow progress and suggested that Stuart had bribed him to produce inferior work. About 1760 became engraver to the Society of Antiquaries, a post he held until his death, and in 1770 was appointed to engraver to the Royal Society.[47]

1754: ANTIQUITIES OF ATHENS
Engraved the finished drawings for the first volume of Antiquities of Athens (1762) by Stuart and Nicholas Revett.[48]

ca. 1764: ADMIRALTY
Engraved the two Mediterranean Passes designed for the Admiralty by Stuart.[49]

1764, 1766, and 1775: FREE SOCIETY OF ARTISTS
Exhibited engravings at the Free Society of Artists, after designs by Stuart.[50] Commissioned in 1773 to engrave Edwards's (q.v.) drawing of "Le Champ de Drap d'or. The Interview of Henry VIII, King of England, and the French King, Francis I . . . ," for which he received 200 guineas.[51]

1765: HERMES
Basire engraved a plate after a design by Stuart for the second edition of James Harris's Hermes.[52]

BASTARD, John, the Younger (1722–78), Mason
From Blandford, from a family of masons and architects. Worked at Stoneleigh Abbey in 1764 and for James Paine in the rebuild-ing of Middlesex Hospital, London (1755–78).[53]

1769–ca. 1773: RHS, Greenwich, INFIRMARY and KING CHARLES BLOCK
Under Robinson's (q.v.) supervision, with Jelfe (q.v.) rebuilt the southwest pavilion of Wren's King Charles Block in Portland stone, for which he received £1,081 between 1771 and 1772.[54] In 1770 made 126 banisters and in 1773 received £686 for a cornice and other projects.[55]

BENT, William (fl. 1767–ca.1806), Ironmonger
Lived in St. Martin's Lane, London, and provided door furniture, under the supervi-sion of Robert Adam, in 1767 for Sir Rowland Winn at Nostell Priory, Yorkshire, and in 1773 for Sir Watkin Williams Wynn at 20 St. James's Square, London.[56]

1781–: RHS, Greenwich, CHAPEL
One of the Somerset House team of crafts-men recommended by Stuart in 1781 and approved by the directors for "reinstating the Chapel and Cupola in a Style of ele-gance equal at least to what they were in before the Fire."[57]

BOULTON, Matthew (1728–1809), Engineer, Manufacturer
BOULTON AND FOTHERGILL
Born in Birmingham. In 1759 inherited his father's buckle and toy-making business. Partnered with John Fothergill (d. 1782), and in 1762 opened a toy factory in Soho, eventually expanding the production to Sheffield plate, silver, and ormolu.[58] His ormolu production in particular brought Boulton in touch with Stuart, especially through his use of the architect's designs for silver and tripods and orders for furniture mounts. Boulton produced tripods after Stuart's designs, including four for the sec-ond Earl Gower in 1774, the models of which probably came from Stuart, Anderson's (q.v.) widow, or Sir William Chambers.[58A] In 1776 Boulton formed a short-lived partnership with Jee, Eginton & Co. (q.v.) to produce "mechanical paint-

ings," and shortly thereafter, began to focus his efforts on various engineering enterprises.[59]

1769–71: SHUGBOROUGH, Staffordshire, LANTHORN OF DEMOTHENES
Stuart designed a copy of the Choragic Monument of Lysicrates, Athens, known to eighteenth-century British travelers as the "Lanthorn of Demosthenes," for which Boulton made the tripod surmounting the building.[60] The tripod and black basalt bowl by Wedgwood (q.v.) no longer survive, but were replaced by a fiberglass model in 1965.[61] In 1769 Stuart and Boulton also corresponded about a "tripodic Tea-Kitchen" and tea-table border for Anson.[62]

1770–71: MRS. MONTAGU
Stuart ordered a tripodic tea kitchen (tea urn) for Mrs. Montagu from Boulton and Wedgwood, requesting that the body and neck be made of "Etruscan painted ware" mounted in ormolu.[63] In February 1771 Wedgwood sent a sample vase and neck made of black basalt to Soho,[64] but the order does not seem to have been completed.[65]

1771 and 1781: ADMIRALTY
With Stuart acting as agent and possible designer, Boulton supplied the Admiralty with a large silver soup tureen in 1771[68] and 1781.[69]

1776–82: LONDON, 22 PORTMAN SQUARE
Due to Mrs. Montagu's frustrations with Stuart, she hired Boulton, her relative by marriage, to counsel her on decorating her house and to order ornaments directly from various tradesmen.[70] In 1776 Cipriani (q.v.) and Rebecca (q.v.) designed originals for Boulton's new "mechanical paintings" for use on Mrs. Montagu's dressing-room ceiling.[71] Two years later, the mechanical paintings were incorporated into the design of the great room as well.[72] In 1779 Boulton supplied gilt ornaments for the doors of the new house, including patterned borders for the panels and escutcheons.[73] He received his final payment of £56.0.0 in March 1782.[74]

ca. 1777: BELVEDERE, Erith, Kent
Stuart ordered die-stamped pewter decoration for walls, doors, and chimneypieces

from Boulton and Fothergill,[66] and Lord Eardley, the owner, purchased "mechanical paintings" from the Birmingham manufacturer as well. These may have been the thirteen inset paintings by Kauffman (q.v.), which decorated the dining room walls.[67]

BROMWICH, Thomas K. (fl. 1740–87), Paper-stainer, Paper-hanger, Upholsterer
Flourished as a linen draper and upholsterer "At the Golden Lyon," Ludgate Hill, London (1740–48); "Thomas Bromwich & Leonard Leigh, Paper-Stainers" (1758–65); Bromwich & Isherwood (1766); and "Bromwich, Isherwood & Bradley, Paper-hangers, 35 Ludgate Hill" (1770–88). In 1761 became Master of the Painter-Stainers' Company, and in 1763 was appointed "Paper Hanging Maker in Ordinary to the Great Wardrobe." Supplied upholstery to many of the leading designers and patrons of the era.[75]

ca. 1764–66: LONDON, 15 ST. JAMES'S SQUARE (Lichfield House)
After Anson's death, his executors listed "Birimwich [Bromwich] paper Hanger" as in receipt of an outstanding bill for £6.14.0.[76]

1769: RHS, Greenwich, DINING ROOM
Stuart probably designed the dining-room ceiling. This may have been one of the ceilings with papier-mâché ornaments by Bromwich mentioned in the minutes of the Court of Directors in November 1769.[77]

ca. 1782: LONDON, 22 PORTMAN SQUARE
Was paid £39.18.0 for work that was carried out under either Stuart or Joseph Bonomi.[78]

CATTON, Charles (1728–98), Painter
Born at Norwich and trained as a painter to a coach-builder in London, becoming the most prominent craftsman specializing in this art. Served as coach-painter to George III during which time he collaborated with the coach-builder, Samuel Butler and the cabinetmaker, John Linnell for painting the panels on a state coach. May have worked as a scene painter at Covent Garden Theatre in 1767, and became a Master of the Paper-Stainers' Co. in 1784.[79]

ca. 1779–: RHS, Greenwich, CHAPEL
With de Bruyn (q.v.), Milbourne (q.v.), and

Rebecca (q.v.), painted sixteen monochrome roundels in chiaroscuro placed over the lower windows of the chapel. Painted the second four of the series in oil on canvas at the west end of the south side of the chapel: *St. John Baptizing, Calling of Peter and Andrew, Our Lord Preaching from a Ship,* and *The Stilling of the Tempest.*[80] One of the artisans brought over from Somerset House who signed a contract on June 6, 1781, to work on the chapel.[81]

CHAPMAN, John (fl. 1766–68), Painter
1766–68: RHS, Greenwich, INFIRMARY
Contracted as a painter in 1766.[82]

CIPRIANI, Giovanni Battista (1727–85), Decorative painter
Born in Florence and studied at the Accademia del Disegno in Florence. Went to Rome in 1750 where he met Sir William Chambers and Wilton (q.v.). Accompanied them back to England in 1756. In the 1770s, designed scenery for the Theatre Royal, Drury Lane, and Covent Garden, working with, among others, Kauffman (q.v.). As a decorative painter, was employed primarily by Chambers, including at Somerset House in 1776, but worked for Robert Adam as well.[83]

1766: LONDON, 23 HILL STREET
Decorated the doors and walls of the Silver Room (dressing room) or "Room of Cupidons" (dest.).[84]

ca. 1776–: LONDON, 22 PORTMAN SQUARE
With Rebecca (q.v.), was hired in July 1776 by Boulton to design and paint "mechanical paintings" for Mrs. Montagu's dressing room.[85] In November 1779 ceiling pictures and an invoice for £39.7.6 were delivered to Mrs. Montagu.[86] In 1782 painted four muses on the commode in Mrs. Montagu's dressing room, for which he was paid £22.1.0.[87] With Rebecca, painted the semicircular overdoors and elliptical vault of the antechamber (later small drawing room) on the second floor.

CLARK, Thomas (fl. from 1742, d. 1782), Plasterer
A well-known plasterer based at Westminster; in 1752 became Master Plasterer to the Office of the Works, a position he held until his death. In 1770

partnered with another plasterer, Charles Clarke (*fl.* 1770–83).[88]

1759–64: SPENCER HOUSE, London
Seems to have worked with Rose (q.v.) on plastering Lady Spencer's dressing room as well as the other first-floor state rooms. Received compensation on May 25, 1759, for plasterwork, which was completed by 1764.[89]

1766–68: RHS, Greenwich, INFIRMARY
Contracted to do plaster work on the new building.[90]

COADE, Eleanor (1733–1821), Artificial Stone Maker
COADE ARTIFICIAL STONE MANUFACTORY
Born in Exeter. By 1766 Eleanor had established herself in London as a linen-draper, and in 1769 founded a manufactory of artificial ceramic stone with her mother, Eleanor Enchmarch, at Lambeth in London.[91] The firm hired the best modelers, sculptors, and designers, including Bacon (q.v.), who worked as the factory's chief designer from 1771. Was well connected with the architectural community and employed by many of that profession, including Robert Adam, the Wyatts, Yenn (q.v.), and Stuart.[92]

1785–89: RHS, Greenwich, CHAPEL
Contributed significantly to the interior decoration of the chapel, including thirty-two pilaster capitals and bases,[93] thirty-two cherubs' heads,[94] and two panels of hospital arms in front of the galleries.[95] Newton (q.v.) commissioned the four colossal statues of Faith, Hope, Charity, and Meekness, designed by West (q.v.), from the Coade manufactory, which Bacon installed in the octagonal vestibule. On May 4, 1787, submitted an estimate for six angels at £7.7 each and a pencil sketch for a "Communion Table like an Altar in Artif. Stone Greek Caryatids as Angels."[96] In 1789 inserted six Coade-stone alto-relievos of scenes from the Acts of the Apostles into the pulpit, as well as four medallions of the prophets Daniel, Micah, Zechariah, and Malachi into the reader's desk, all designed by West.[97]

COLLINS, John (*fl.* 1766–68), Joiner
1766–68: RHS, Greenwich, INFIRMARY
Worked as a joiner on this project.[98]

CRISP, Nicholas (ca. 1704–74), Jewelry, Pottery Manufacturer
From 1751 co-owned a porcelain factory at Vauxhall. Went bankrupt in 1763 and later operated a pottery at Bovey Tracey.

1756: SPAC (RSA)
Appointed to the RSA's Medal Committee in April 1756. Proposed a design for a medal in 1756, the model of which was executed on two gold plates by Moser (q.v.). Crisp's composition called for more gold than the society had allocated for, and it was abandoned in favor of a design by Stuart, who joined the committee in 1757.[99]

DALL, Nicholas Thomas (*fl.* before 1748, d. 1777), Painter
Of Scandinavian origin, studied in Italy beginning in the 1740s. In London by November 1756, perhaps at the encouraging of Thomas Anson. Worked as a scene painter at Covent Garden between 1757 and 1776. Known for his landscapes and scenes of ruins.[100]

ca.1768, 1770, 1775: SHUGBOROUGH, Staffordshire
Stuart commissioned Dall to paint a large oil on canvas of the Temple of Minerva Polias for the orangery (dest. 1855). The designs for this and other paintings for the library were shown to Stuart in 1770.[101] Did a series of landscapes of Shugborough, including the view of "Shugborough and the Park from the East," a large watercolor in the Swallow Passage (ca. 1768), and most of the west front (1768). Dall also painted two tempera panels for the Bust Parlour, which are signed and dated 1775. One depicts the ruins opposite the west front of the house, and the other shows Oakedge, a nearby house Anson bought for his sisters in 1768. There are finished studies in watercolor by Dall for his oil paintings of 1768 and 1775.[102]

DANIEL, William (*fl.* 1767), Tiler
1767: SHUGBOROUGH, Staffordshire, or LONDON, 15 ST. JAMES'S SQUARE (Lichfield House)

Supplied tiles and was paid on November 12, 1767.[103]

DEAVIL, Isaac (*fl.* 1767)
1767: SHUGBOROUGH, Staffordshire, or LONDON, 15 ST. JAMES'S SQUARE (Lichfield House)
Was paid £40.0.0 for unspecified work on December 26, 1767.[104]

DE BRUYN (LE BRUN), Theodore (1730–1804), Painter
Born in Amsterdam, but trained with Nicholas van den Bergh in Antwerp. Belonged to a school of *grisaille* painting under the influence of Jacob de Wit and Martin Joseph Geeraerts. Was probably in England by 1760. Like Rebecca (q.v.), was famed for his bas-reliefs.[105]

ca. 1779 –: RHS, Greenwich, CHAPEL
With Milbourne (q.v.), Rebecca (q.v.), and Catton (q.v.), painted sixteen monochrome roundels in chiaroscuro placed over the lower windows of the chapel. Bruyn painted the first four paintings of the series on copper at the east end of the south side of the chapel: *The Nativity, The Angel Appearing to the Shepherds, The Adoration of the Magi,* and *The Flight into Egypt.*[106]

DEVALL, Jeremiah (*fl.* 1776–83), Plumber
Probably connected with the important Devall family of master-masons. Worked for Sir William Chambers at Somerset House (1776–83).[107]

1781–: RHS, Greenwich, CHAPEL
One of the craftsmen from Somerset House approved by the board to work on the chapel in 1781.[108]

DEVALL SR., John (1701–74), DEVALL JR., John (1728–94), Masons
Worked at many commissions together. Devall Jr. admitted to the Masons' Company in 1777 and became Master of the Masons' Company in 1784, a post his father had occupied in 1760.[109] Began working in 1788, after the death of Stuart, for Samuel Wyatt (q.v.) at Shugborough, Staffordshire.[110]

1756–64: SPENCER HOUSE, London
Devall Sr. was the chief mason here, execut-

ing marble chimneypieces for Vardy in 1756 and ornament in the first-floor state rooms, such as Lady Spencer's dressing room.[111]

1755: SION HILL, Kew
Devall Sr. received payment from Holdernesse in 1755 for masonry work here,[112] which may have included the execution of Stuart's design for a dark gray marble chimneypiece with yellow marble columns.[113]

ca. 1761–65: LONDON, 24 HERTFORD STREET (Holdernesse House)
Devall Jr. was one of the craftsmen who received payment from Holdernesse between 1761 and 1765. This may have been for masonry work done at Holdernesse under Stuart's direction.[114]

1781–ca. 1789: RHS, Greenwich, CHAPEL
One of the craftsmen from Somerset House to sign an agreement on June 6, 1781, to do restoration work at Greenwich.[115] Supplied a Corinthian base to Stuart's design in 1782.[116] In 1783 began masonry work on the dome,[117] and the following year, was commissioned to build statuary bases for the columns to the organ loft.[118] Between 1784 and 1789 was the mason contracted to rebuild the Queen Mary Block after the fire.[119] Executed all the marble work for the chapel in 1788, for which he was paid £1,897.[120]

DEVIS, Arthur (1712–87), Painter
A painter of conversation pieces with sitters in outdoor settings. As his work became less fashionable in the second half of the eighteenth century, he experimented with painting on glass, and in 1762 began to repair paintings for Sir Roger Newdigate and others, including Stuart at the RHS, Greenwich, in 1777.[121]

1777: RHS, Greenwich, PAINTED HALL
A "Mr. Devis," most likely Arthur rather than his half-brother, landscape painter Anthony Devis (1729–1816), cleaned and repaired Sir James Thornhill's paintings for £1,000 at Stuart's suggestion.[122]

DONALDSON, James (ca. 1756–1843), Architect
Studied under Thomas Leverton and exhibited at the Royal Academy in 1777 through Leverton's offices. Lived at Hart Street, Bloomsbury.[123]

ca. 1779–: RHS, Greenwich, CHAPEL
Served as Mylne's clerk. Signed a letter to Mrs. Palmer (q.v.), dated September 5, 1781.[124] May also have been responsible for a drawing of the "Section of the West End in the Chapel."[125]

EDWARDS, Edward (1738–1805), Draftsman
Served his apprenticeship under an upholsterer, for whom he drew designs for furniture. Between 1771 and 1806, was a frequent exhibitor of primarily biblical and literary subjects at the RSA, the Free Society of Artists, and the Royal Academy.[126]

1771: SOCIETY OF ANTIQUARIES
On behalf of the Society of Antiquaries, Stuart commissioned Edwards to make a drawing of "Le Champ de Drap d'or. The Interview of Henry VIII, King of England, and the French King, Francis I . . . ," an anonymous painting in the Royal Apartments at Windsor, for which he was eventually paid 110 guineas.[127] Basire (q.v.) engraved the drawing.

EGINTON, Francis (1737–1805), Painter on glass, Japanner, Modeler, Figure-Caster
JEE, EGINTON & CO.
Lived in Birmingham and was at first in charge of the japanned-ware department at Boulton's (q.v.) Soho manufactory, but also cast figures for the firm from vases and ornaments and designed silver plate and ormolu. May have joined his brother John Eginton and Edward Jee in Jee, Eginton & Co., a firm that manufactured gilt frames. In 1776 this company partnered with Boulton & Fothergill to produce "mechanical paintings," but after an altercation in June 1780, Eginton left the firm.[128] He applied the mechanical process in his work as a popular glass-painter, often on ecclesiastical buildings.[129]

1778–79: LONDON, 22 PORTMAN SQUARE
Boulton commissioned Jee, Eginton, & Co. to produce gilt frames for Cipriani's (q.v.) and Rebecca's (q.v.) "mechanical paintings" decorating Mrs. Montagu's dressing room.[130] In July 1778 Mrs. Montagu wrote to Boulton about the "mechanical paintings" that Francis Eginton was producing

either for the gallery ceiling or for the mahogany doors with gilt ornaments for the reception suite.[131]

EVANS, Charles (fl. 1774–85), Carpenter
Based in London. A carpenter by trade, but also acted as an architect. His projects included supervising the internal alterations to 30 Upper Grosvenor St., London, for Sir Thomas Cave of Stanford Hall, Leicestershire in 1777 and designing Badminton Church, Gloucestershire, for the Duke of Beaufort in 1785.[132]

ca. 1764–66: LONDON, 15 ST. JAMES'S SQUARE (Lichfield House)
May have been the Evans known to have worked on this house and who was paid £300 in June 1764.[133] After Anson's death, Anson's executors list a "Mr. Evans Carpenter" in 1773 as being owed an outstanding bill of £27.6.0. This may be Charles Evans or William Evans (q.v.) who did work at Shugborough.[134]

1774–80: LONDON, 22 PORTMAN SQUARE
Mrs. Montagu paid Evans £104.19.0 pounds on November 28, 1774, and made regular payments to him until March 1778 for carpentry work all done probably at Portman Square.[135] In 1780 Evans was still employed at Portman Square, as Mrs. Montagu questioned in a letter to Leonard Smelt whether Stuart had given Evans' head workman sufficient directions to finish the pillars in the house.[136] When, out of frustration with Stuart, Mrs. Montagu brought in Boulton (q.v.) and architect James Wyatt as consultants, Evans and his glazier helped them put glass into her sashes.[137]

EVANS, William (fl. 1768–80), Carpenter
Probably a local Staffordshire man who came to work for Stuart as part of a team of craftsmen.[138]

1768: SHUGBOROUGH, Staffordshire
Was paid £8.3.9 on May 2nd £22.7.0 on December 31, 1768, for carpenter's work.[139] Sent Anson a receipt for £500 in June 1769 via Stuart.[140]

FERGUSON, John (*fl.* 1782–85), Carpenter
1782–85: RATHFARNHAM CASTLE, Co. Dublin, TEMPLE OF THE WINDS
Did the marquetry floor on the upper room of the Temple of the Winds.[141]

GANDON, James (1742–1823), Architect
Born in London. Studied with Sir William Chambers, from whom he developed an appreciation of academic, conservative classicism. Opened his own practice in 1765. After winning second prize in the competition for the Royal Exchange at Dublin, was much employed in Ireland.[142]

ca. 1780: RHS, Greenwich, CHAPEL
Probably assisted Stuart with the design of the altar end.[143]

ca. 1780: LONDON, 22 PORTMAN SQUARE
After Norris's (q.v.) death in 1779, Stuart formed a loose and short-lived partnership with Gandon. Worked at 22 Portman Square as either Stuart's assistant or partner. Responsible for at least one drawing, for the roof,[144] for which he was paid £50.[145]

GILLERT, Richard (*fl.* 1766), Mason
1766: SHUGBOROUGH, Staffordshire, TRIUMPHAL ARCH
Signed the capping on the top of the arch, "Richard Gillert 1766."[146]

GLODE, Richard (*fl.* 1760s), Bricklayer
1764–68: RHS, Greenwich, INFIRMARY
One of the principal contractors for the construction of the building.[147]

GORDON AND TAITT, Cabinetmakers, Upholsterers
GORDON, John (*fl.* from 1748, d. 1777/78), TAITT, John (*fl.* from 1767, d. 1800), and TAITT, Richard (*fl.* 1767–96)
From 1748 Gordon seems to have operated from a complex of buildings situated in the vicinity of Swallow St., Little Argyle St., and King St., Golden Square, where Gordon offered cabinetmaking, upholstery, and joinery services. Provided furniture and ulphostery (1747–53) for the London houses of the Duke of Gordon. Supplied at least two suites of seating furniture (ca. 1748–56) for the second Duke of Atholl at Blair Castle, Perthshire. By 1767 had

formed a partnership with Taitt, providing a suite of furniture for Croome Court that year.[148]

ca. 1758–74: SPENCER HOUSE, London
Probably responsible for the gilded suite of seat furniture desgined by Vardy for the Palm Room in ca. 1758.[149] In ca. 1764 may have executed the six armchairs and four sofas designed by Stuart to complement the Painted Room.[150] Supplied a white and gold suite of furniture for Stuart's great room.[151]

ca. 1760: NUNEHAM COURTENAY, Oxfordshire
Executed a suite of seating furniture for the first Earl Harcourt in ca. 1760, based on Stuart's design and similar to that provided for the great room at Spencer House.[152]

GOSSET, Isaac (1713–99), Carver, Wax-Modeler
From a Huguenot family of carvers. Learned frame-carving and wax-modeling from his uncle Matthew Gosset (1683–1744) of Poland Street, Soho. Worked sometimes as a carver, but was more famous for his profiles in wax, which were copied and reproduced by James Tassie and Wedgwood (q.v.).[153]

ca. 1759–64: LONDON, 15 ST. JAMES'S SQUARE (Lichfield House), or SHUGBOROUGH, Staffordshire
Received a payment from Stuart in 1764.[154] In ca. 1760 Stuart designed a medal of General James Wolfe, which was engraved by Kirk (q.v.) and modeled by Gosset.[155] The payment may have been for this, or Stuart may have been acting as an agent for Anson for another commission.

GOUPY, Louis (ca. 1674–1747), Painter
A French Huguenot who came to London by 1710 where his brother worked as a fan-painter in the Covent Garden area. Went to Italy in 1719 with Lord Burlington but was replaced by William Kent. After his return to his London, unsuccessfully attempted to switch from working as a fan-painter to a history and portrait painter. Eventually forced to earn a living as a drawing and painting tutor.[156]

GOUPY, Joseph (ca. 1689–before 1782), Painter
Nephew and pupil of the painter, Louis Goupy (q.v.). Went to Italy around 1700, where he may have studied with Marco Ricci, the Italian painter and caricaturist. Returned to London by 1711. Although trained as an etcher and printmaker, became known principally as a painter in gouache and commanded large sums for his copies of old master paintings.[157] Stuart's early biographers state that as a young boy he designed and painted fans for "Goupee of the Strand."[158] It is unclear whether this was Louis Goupy, Joseph Goupy, or a combination of the two. Stuart left his employment as a fan painter, ca. 1735.[159]

GREEN, Samuel (*fl.* ca. 1781–89), Organ Maker
ca. 1781–89: RHS, Greenwich, CHAPEL
Commissioned to supply a new organ for the chapel.[160]

GROVES, John (*fl.* 1781), Bricklayer
1781–: RHS, Greenwich, CHAPEL
One of the craftsmen at Somerset House recommended by Stuart in 1781.[161]

HALL, Humphrey (*fl.* 1767), Bricklayer
1767: SHUGBOROUGH, Staffordshire, or LONDON, 15 ST. JAMES'S SQUARE (Lichfield House)
Was paid £1.6 for "Bricklayers Work" on October 4, 1767.[162]

HALL, John (*fl.* 1756–73), Engraver
Received a premium from SPAC in 1756. Exhibited an engraving after a 1758 painting by Gavin Hamilton at the Free Society in 1773. Engraved plates of the Incantada at Salonika for Stuart.

1773: AN ACCOUNT OF THE VOYAGES . . .
Engraved the plate, "Interview of the Princess Oberhea and Capt. Wallis in Otaheitee," probably after Stuart's designs, that appeared in the first volume of John Hawkesworth's *Account of the Voyages* . . . (1773).[163]

HARRISON, Thomas (1744–1829), Architect
The son of a carpenter, was born in Richmond, North Yorkshire. Through the

patronage of Sir Lawrence Dundas of Aske, went to Rome in 1769 with George Cuitt, a landscape painter, to study Roman antiquities. Returned to England in 1776 and became well-known in England for working in the Greek Revival style.[164]

1768: SHUGBOROUGH, Staffordshire, or LONDON, 15 ST. JAMES'S SQUARE (Lichfield House)
A "Harrison" was paid £2.12.2 on May 24, 1768, for unidentified work.[165]

HARTLEY, David (1732–1813), British Stateman, Scientist, Political Pamphleteer
Born in Bath, son of the philosopher David Hartley. Became a doctor, inventor, and scientist. In 1773 patented fireplates, thin wrought-iron sheets nailed to ceiling joists and placed below the floor boards. They were intended to slow the spread of fire and seal the rooms to eliminate the circulation of air. The sheets could be riveted together to protect large areas and were broadly used by Henry Holland, James Wyatt, and Chambers.[166]

1778: LONDON, 22 PORTMAN SQUARE
By October 1778 had added fireplates to Mrs. Montagu's new house.[167]

HAXBY, Thomas (1729–96), Instrument Maker
A York craftsman famed for his skillful work making musical instruments, particularly keyboard instruments. Son of a carpenter, Robert Haxby (b. 1704), from whom he may have acquired woodworking skills. In 1756 opened a shop advertising the repair of various instruments. By 1758 was a freeman listed as a musical instrument maker.[168]

ca. 1766: NEWBY HALL, Yorkshire
Stuart designed a mahogany organ case for the owner, William Weddell. Haxby is thought to have been responsible for the mechanism.[169]

HAYWARD, Richard (1728–1800), Sculptor
Born at Bulkington, Warwickshire. Apprenticed to Christopher Horsnaile (fl. 1700–42), and in 1749 became free of the Masons' Company. In 1753 traveled to Rome. Executed a number of monuments

at Westminster Abbey and worked under architects such as Adam and Chambers.[170]

1757–58: KEDLESTON, Derbyshire
Working from a design by Stuart, supplied the marble wine cooler for under the dining room sideboard in January 1758.[171]

HIMS, John (fl. 1767), Tiler
1767: SHUGBOROUGH, Staffordshire, or LONDON, 15 ST. JAMES'S SQUARE (Lichfield House)
Supplied tiles and was paid £2.12.2 on October 17, 1767.[172]

[HITCHCOX] (fl. ca. 1758–62), Mason
Son of William Hitchcox, a mason employed particularly by Miller (q.v.), the "gentleman architect."[173]

1759–ca. 1762: HAGLEY, Worcestershire, TEMPLE OF THESEUS
Stuart received £25 from Sir Thomas Lyttelton for the design, but construction was overseen by Miller and his patron, George, first Lord Lyttelton.[174] By March 17, 1759, Hitchcox had been commissioned as the mason for the project, but in February 1761, he was nearly replaced for his slow progress. The structure was not complete before March 1761, and possibly not before September 1762, but definitely was finished in 1764.[175]

HOLMES, John (1727–97), Clockmaker, Mechanical Engineer
Born in York, the son of an ironmonger and grandson of the well-known watchmaker, John Smeaton (b. ca. 1624), possibly from Whitkirk. Arrived in London in 1750 and became known particularly for his high quality domestic clocks.[176]

1777–85: RHS, Greenwich, COUNCIL ROOM
In February 1777 was paid £1.15 for repairing and cleaning the Council Room's long case double pendulum clock made by Daniel Quare in 1716. After fire destroyed the main turret clock in 1779, Holmes was commissioned to advise on and supply a replacement,[177] for which he was paid £120. The finished piece was installed ca. 1781.[178] Officially contracted to maintain all the hospital's clocks in June 1781,[179] and in 1784 was hired to replace Quare's clock with a new one.[180] In May 1785 produced

to Stuart's design a spring clock with a case carved and gilt with the signs of the Zodiac (present location unknown).[181]

HOLROYD, George (fl. 1781), Plumber
1781: RHS, Greenwich, CHAPEL
One of the craftsmen from Somerset House recommended by Stuart in 1781 to repair the chapel.[182]

HOOPER, John (fl. 1756–68), Mason
Lived at Woodstock, Oxfordshire. Employed at Audley End (1761–64), where he did masonry work and carved stone in the Gothic style.[183]

1761: SHUGBOROUGH, Staffordshire, TRIUMPHAL ARCH
Submitted estimate of £282.14.1 to erect the monument.[184]

1762–64: NUNEHAM COURTENAY, Oxfordshire
The Church of All Saints was taken down in October, and a new church, probably designed by Stuart and the first Earl Harcourt, was erected by 1764. The contracting mason was Hooper, who was perhaps employed from ca. 1756 to work on the villa there, by Stiff Leadbetter, the executant architect. Hooper's final bill to Lord Harcourt was for 552 12s 0¼d.[185]

HOROBIN, John (fl. ca. 1764–68), Mason
Based in Yorkshire, but after earning his freedom from the Masons' Company in June 1764, founded a masonry firm in Windmill Street, Piccadilly.[186]

1764: WENTWORTH WOODHOUSE, Yorkshire
Submitted a bill for £219.14.6 authorized by Stuart for masonry work and for "superintend[ing] the performance of the Masons work to the several Chimneys" in various rooms, including those in the lady's dressing room, drawing room, "supping" room, and marquess's dressing room.[187]

1768: LONDON, 24 HERTFORD STREET (Holdernesse House)
Designed by Stuart, ca. 1760–65. Was paid £41 in January 1768, but some of the payment due to Horobin may, however, have been for work at Holdernesse's Yorkshire seat, Hornby Castle.[188]

[JACKSON] (*fl.* 1764–68), **Smith**
1764–68: RHS, Greenwich, INFIRMARY
Was the smith for the project.[189]

JEE, EGINTON & CO., see Eginton, Francis.

JELFE, William (*fl.* from 1739, d. 1771), **Mason**
In 1739 was apprenticed to his uncle, Andrews Jelfe (d. 1758) and teamed up with him for masonry work at the Horse Guards (1750–58). The following year became a member of the Masons' Company. Served as stonemason to George III.[190]

1769–71: RHS, Greenwich, INFIRMARY and KING CHARLES BLOCK
Under Robinson's (q.v.) supervision, worked until his death in 1771 with Bastard (q.v.) on rebuilding the southwest pavilion of Wren's King Charles Block in Portland stone. The work was done for an estimated cost of £5,664.[191]

KAUFFMAN [KAUFFMANN, KAUFMANN], (Maria Anna) Angelica (1741–1807), **Decorative painter, Engraver**
Born in Switzerland. Early on, established herself in Florence, Rome, and Naples, creating portraits and works in the neoclassical style, before coming to England in 1766. Became a successful portrait artist, and was one of two women elected to be a Foundation Member of the Royal Academy, where she exhibited (1769–97). In 1781 moved to Italy with her second husband, Antonio Zucchi, and eventually settled in Rome, where she continued to produce paintings and became the most famous and successful painter in that city.[192]

1769–71: RATHFARNAM CASTLE, Dublin County
May have painted the ten ceiling panels in the Long Gallery (replaced in the twentieth century), after designs by Stuart.[193] These works may have also been "mechanical paintings" provided by Boulton and Fothergill (q.v.), to whom Kauffman sold a number of original designs in 1776, in which case, she probably had no direct involvement in the decoration of the house.[194]

After 1776: BELVEDERE, Kent
Dining room walls, thirteen inset paintings of unspecified subjects, only six of which were remaining in 1938.[195] These may have been "mechanical paintings" provided by Boulton.[196]

Before 1781: LONDON, 22 PORTMAN SQUARE
Traditionally thought to have been responsible for the paintings on the great room ceiling,[197] but these works were almost certainly reproduced through Boulton's mechanical processes.[198]

KIRK, John (*fl.* from ca. 1740, d. 1776), **Engraver**
Was a student of Swiss medalist Jacques-Antoine Dassier, who served as assistant engraver at the Royal Mint in London (1741–45). Engraved the dies for a few of the medals designed by Stuart. In ca. 1760 worked with modeler Isaac Gosset to produce Stuart's medal commemorating the death of General James Wolfe. When Stuart and Hollis collaborated on a series of victory medals proclaiming Britain's triumphs during the Seven Years' War for the RSA, Kirk was awarded two premiums for the Montreal Taken medal in 1761 and the Battle of Belleisle medal in 1762.[199]

LAWRENCE, Richard (*fl.* 1732–95), **Carver**
Apprenticed in 1746 to the talented carver, Sefferin Alken (*fl.* 1744–82), and by 1760 was working for the Royal Palaces as the Surveyor and Repairer of Carved Work. Did carving at Horace Walpole's house, Strawberry Hill, at Inveraray Castle, and at Somerset House (1777–91) under Sir William Chambers.

1770–ca. 1789: RHS, Greenwich, KING CHARLES BLOCK and CHAPEL
Carved large medallions and lions' heads in the King Charles Block in 1770. In 1773 was paid £101 for carving faces of Corinthian capitals and pilasters in the same building.[200] After the fire in the Queen Mary Block, was one of the Somerset House craftsmen to sign the agreement on June 6, 1781, to rebuild the chapel.[201] Carved and gilded a frame with ornament deriving from the Erechtheion capitals for West's (q.v.) twenty-five-foot-high altar-

piece (commissioned 1781, installed 1789).[202] Was contracted in 1784 to execute most of the stone-carving for the chapel.[203] In 1786 submitted an estimate of about £100 for carving the pulpit,[204] and another for turning, carving, and bronzing eight candelabra.[205] The same year executed twenty-four faces of Ionic capitals in marble for the six columns of the organ gallery. In 1787 carved thirty-two cantilivers on the north side of the chapel, for which he was paid £528.[206] Also carved 462 balusters for the galleries and two marble angels, and did carving over the gallery doors and for the soffits of the windows.[207] His name appears on a drawing for "the 2 pannels on the returns of the Organ gallery."[208] May have carved the lectern and font (ca. 1789).

LOVELL, James (*fl.* 1750–80), **Plasterer**
1758: HAGLEY HALL, Worcestershire
Worked extensively in plaster and stone. Probably known to Stuart through his work at Croome Court, Worcestershire, where he assisted William Linnell (ca. 1703–63) with thirteen chimneypieces, and at Hagley, Worcestershire where he supplied a chimneypiece surmounted by a stucco relief of Pan courting Diana, signed by Vassalli (q.v.).[209] Lovell worked on ceiling paintings at Hagley for George, first Lord Lyttelton, cousin of Earl Temple at Stowe, and designed stucco decoration for Vassalli to carry out at Croome Court.

ca. 1758: STOWE, Buckinghamshire, TEMPLE OF CONCORD AND VICTORY
Lovell, was the author, in the late 1750s, of the Stowe medallions—sixteen plaster roundels, based on medals, in the main designed by Stuart and executed by Pingo Jr. (q.v.)—which are in the Temple of Concord and Victory at Stowe, Buckinghamshire. Lovell's name appears on two of the medallions in the ante-temple.[210]

MASON, William (1725–97), **Clergyman, Writer, Garden Designer**
Born in Hull and educated at St. John's College, Cambridge. Was ordained in 1754, becoming chaplain to Lord Holdernesse, whom he advised on the restoration of Hornby Castle in 1760.[211]

1764–ca. 1772: NUNEHAM COURTENAY,

Oxfordshire, CHAPEL and TEMPLE OF FLORA
Painted the altarpiece representing the
parable of the Good Samaritan in the
Church of All Saints, designed by the first
Earl Harcourt and Stuart.[212] Beginning in
1772, worked with George Simon
Harcourt, Viscount Nuneham, who would
become the second Earl Harcourt in 1777,
to design a much-admired flower-garden
between the chapel and the Palladian
house. The architectural highlight of the
gardens, the Temple of Flora, is a structure
with a Doric portico similar to the Portico
of Philip on Delos shown in volume 3 of
Antiquities of Athens and featured in a drawing by Stuart now in the RIBA.[213]

[MERRY] (*fl.* 1765–66), **Carpenter**
1765 or 1766: SHUGBOROUGH,
Staffordshire, or LONDON, 15 ST. JAMES'S
SQUARE (Lichfield House)
Received payment for carpenter's work.[214]

**[MILBOURNE, MELBOURNE,
MELBOURN, MILBURNE]** (*fl.* late
18th century), **Painter**
English. May be the John Milbourn who
studied under Francis Cotes and was
awarded a Society of Arts premium in 1764.
Exhibited portraits at the Royal Academy
in 1772–74. Covent Garden employed a
scene-painter (1785–89) called at various
times Melbourne, Melbourn, and
Milbourne, and the Old Theatre at
Portsmouth had a "Mr. Milbourn" working
for them in 1783.[215]

ca. 1779: RHS, Greenwich, CHAPEL
With Catton (q.v.), de Bruyn (q.v.), and
Rebecca (q.v.), painted sixteen mono-
chrome roundels in chiaroscuro placed over
the lower windows of the chapel. Painted
four of the series at the west end of the
north side of the Chapel: *Our Saviour
Walking on the Sea and Saving Peter from
Sinking, Healing the Blind, The Raising of
Lazarus*, and *The Transfiguration*.[216]

MILLER, Sanderson (1716–80),
Architect
Born at Edgehill, son of Sanderson Miller, a
wealthy merchant. Was an amateur architect
who employed professional assistants to
implement construction. Hitchcox (q.v.)
most frequently served in this capacity.[217]

1754–61: HAGLEY HALL, Worcestershire
Stuart would encounter Miller as the architect of Hagley Hall, Worcestershire, which
was erected 1754–60 for George, first Lord
Lyttelton. Stuart first worked as a decorative
painter at Hagley Hall, painting the ceiling
of the Tapestry Room with "Flora and the
Zephyrs" and the Four Seasons, and
designed the famous Doric Temple of
Theseus in the park (ca. 1758–59).[218]

[MOREHOUSE] (*fl.* 1764––68), **Mason**
1764–68: RHS, Greenwich, INFIRMARY
One of the principal contractors for the
project.[219]

MOSER, George Michael (1703–83),
Engraver, Chaser, Enameler
Born in Switzerland, and trained in Geneva
as a coppersmith, chaser, and engraver. Was
probably in London by 1726, but definitely
by 1729–30. Chief promoter in the 1730s of
a school for painting and drawing, which
met at Salisbury Court, and in this capacity,
was assisted by Stuart, Sir Joshua Reynolds
(1723–92), and Marcus Tuscher (1705–51).
Worked primarily in the French Rococo
style, creating gold and silver boxes, watch-
cases, candlesticks, and other objects in this
mode.[220]

SPAC (RSA)
Crisp (q.v.), who was a member of SPAC,
presented proposals in 1756 for a premium
medal. His ideas and models were executed
on two gold plates by Moser. The society
found the design to be too costly and abandoned it in favor of a design by Stuart, which
was executed as a medal by Pingo Jr. (q.v.).[221]

MYLNE, Robert (1733–1811), **Architect**
Descended from a long line of Scottish
master-masons who had their beginnings in
contruction in the fifteenth century. First
apprenticed as a carpenter, but persuaded
his father to let him train as an architect.
Traveled to Paris in 1754 and then to Italy
in 1755, where he spent the next four years
primarily in Rome. Became Surveyor to St.
Paul's Cathedral and to Canterbury
Cathedral in 1767. Worked on a number of
public and domestic buildings, but never
achieved the eminence of contemporary
architects Robert Adam and James Wyatt.[222]

1775–81: RHS, Greenwich
Was clerk of works, assisting Stuart on a
number of projects, such as constructing a
wharf for the Queen Mary Block in
1777.[223] Several drawings for the chapel
survive in the RIBA, including contract,
working, and four survey drawings of the
interior of the west end of the chapel,
which all originated in Mylne's office.[224]
Mylne complained in 1781 to the Board of
Governors of Stuart's inadequacies as an
architect.[225] Stuart counter-charged that
Mylne was trying to usurp him and was
guilty of altering Stuart's drawings and substituting his own.[226] In September 1782 the
Admiralty and Board of Directors dismissed
Mylne, but did pay him an additional
£310.10 compensation two years later for
work that fell outside the duties of his
office. Newton (q.v.) was hired as his
replacement.[227]

NEWTON, William (1735–90),
Architect
Born to a cabinetmaker in Holborn. Was
apprenticed in 1750 to William Jones in
Covent Garden, London, and after his
training went to work for Matthew
Brettingham, but was on his own by 1764.
Went to Rome in 1766, returning to
London the following year. Was a talented
draftsman who designed in the Adam style,
but seems to have had a more successful
career as a decorator than architect. In 1787
he helped edit and prepare the second volume of Stuart and Revett's *Antiquities of
Athens* for publication.[228]

1781–90: RHS, Greenwich, CHAPEL and
BOY'S SCHOOL
The board officially authorized Newton to
begin assisting Stuart in rebuilding the
chapel on February 9, 1782, but he may
have made his first designs for Stuart at the
end of 1781.[229] Was appointed clerk of
works in December 1782. Seems to have
been entirely responsible for the Boy's
School, beginning work there ca. 1783.[230]
After Stuart's death, applied for the
Surveyorship, but first Sir Robert Taylor
then Yenn (q.v.) were instead appointed to
succeed Stuart.[231] Newton put forth a
grievance to the board arguing his claims to
the Surveyorship and asserting that he had
fulfilled many of the duties of the post for

Stuart, including executing most of the working drawings and some of the general ones as well.[232] As a concession, the board put the completion of the chapel under his direction.[233] In *The Architecture of M. Vitruvius Pollio*, published posthumously in 1791, Newton claimed primary authorship of the chapel,[234] and after his death in 1790, his executors, including his brother and Smirke (q.v.), unsuccessfully sought compensation for Newton's alleged role as designer and architect of the chapel.[235]

NOLLEKENS, Joseph (1737–1823), Sculptor

Born in London into a family of painters originally from Antwerp. In 1750 became a pupil of Scheemakers (q.v.). Was awarded premiums by the RSA (1759–62), after which he traveled to Rome where he acted as a dealer, copier, and restorer of antiquities. Returned to England in 1770 and established a successful contemporary sculpture business in Mortimer Street, working in marble, stone, and plaster.[236]

1761–70: RSA and FREE SOCIETY OF ARTS
Nollekens sent several sculptural works from Rome for Stuart to display at RSA exhibitions in London. After the establishment of the Royal Academy, however, Stuart chose to exhibit Nollekens's works at the Free Society of Artists instead of the more prestigious Royal Academy, a decision which Nollekens greatly resented.[237]

ca. 1764: SPENCER HOUSE, London
In Rome Spencer commissioned Nollekens to create the marble sculpture, *Boy on a Dolphin*, which may have stood in the Painted Room.[238]

1765–68: SHUGBOROUGH, Staffordshire, and LONDON, 15 ST. JAMES'S SQUARE (Lichfield House)
While in Italy, Nollekens dealt in and copied antiquities for Thomas Anson, with Stuart acting as his agent. He corresponded with both Stuart and Anson.[239] In 1765 Nollekens sent Stuart a plaster cast of *Castor and Pollux*, intended for Anson, and in 1768 he won a gold medal at the Academy of St. Luke for his reproduction of the group in marble (now in the Victoria and Albert Museum, London).[240] The statues he made and collected for Anson were displayed not only in the main house at Shugborough, but in the greenhouse and the lower room of the Tower of the Winds.[241] In addition to sculpture, Nollekens acquired rare green Cippolino marble slabs from Scarpellino in the Campo Viccino, which were used as tops for a pair of white and gold pier tables designed by Stuart for Shugborough.[242]

1773–76: LORD ROCKINGHAM
Stuart's association with Lord Rockingham probably led to a commission for Nollekens to provide a group of the *Judgment of Paris* for his London townhouse (Rockingham House).[243]

NORRIS SR., Richard (ca. 1719–79), Architect, Bricklayer
NORRIS JR., Richard (1750–92), Architect

Norris Sr. lived at Hampstead, but had premises in Holburn. His son was probably Stuart's pupil, in that he exhibited a design of a Triumphal Arch "from a design of Mr. Stuart" at the Free Society exhibiton of 1766. Became surveyor to a number of institutions, including Christ's Hospital and the London Assurance Corporation. Appears to only have done minor architectural projects.[244]

1764: LONDON, 15 ST. JAMES'S SQUARE (Lichfield House)
Norris Sr. was employed as a bricklayer but may have acted as the executant architect.[245] Was paid £500 in June 1764. His responsibilities also seem to have included keeping the accountbook and handling payments to the master craftsmen.[246] Norris, a trained architect, prepared designs for the house as well, but these no longer survive.[247] Received a payment for cabinetwork, perhaps in 1765.[248] In 1773 when Anson's executors compiled their list of tradesmen with outstanding bill, they noted that "Norris Brick laier" was owed £4.16.0.[249]

1774–79: LONDON, 22 PORTMAN SQUARE
Was probably employed at Portman Square primarily as a bricklayer, but may have assisted Stuart in his architectural capacity as well. After his death in May 1779, was replaced by Gandon (q.v.).[250] Norris Jr. seems to have also done some work for Mrs. Montagu, having received a payment for £49.19.0 on 3 June 1784.[251]

ca. 1779–80: CAMDEN PLACE, Kent
In 1780 Norris Jr. collaborated with Stuart, and at Pratt's request they moved a version of the Choragic Monument of Lysicrates, or Lanthorn of Demosthenes, to a new location on the grounds and consulted with Pratt's daughter Elizabeth about the construction of a Cold Bath.[252]

[NOTTERSHAW] (fl. 1768), Upholsterer

1768: SHUGBOROUGH, Staffordshire, or LONDON, 15 ST. JAMES'S SQUARE (Lichfield House)
Was paid £24.14.0 on December 31, 1768, for upholstery work.[253]

PALMER, James (fl. 1766), Smith

Smith/brassfounder to George III, but also did work for Adam, Chambers, and Paine. Resided at Air Street, Piccadilly.[254]

1776: LONDON, 22 PORTMAN SQUARE
£13.0.0 was paid on July 3, 1776, to Palmer & Co. for work done on the new house.[255]

PALMER, Mrs. Martha (fl. 1781), Smith

Possibly the widow of Palmer (q.v.).

1781: RHS, Greenwich, CHAPEL
One of the craftsmen from Somerset House to sign the agreement on June 6, 1781, to begin work on the chapel was a "William Clark for Mrs. Palmer."[256] Mylne's clerk Donaldson (q.v.), sent Mrs. Palmer a letter in September 1781 with a drawing of "Patterns or Modells of the intended Iron work for the Roof of the Chapel."[257]

PAPWORTH, John, (1750–99), Plasterer

Apprenticed to Rose (q.v.), and became a leading plasterer in the second half of the eighteenth century. Based at Wells Street, Oxford Road, London. Was joined in the business by his eldest son, Thomas (1773–1814), who took over the firm after his father's death.[258]

1781: RHS, Greenwich, CHAPEL
One of the Somerset House craftsmen recommended by Stuart in 1781 to restore the chapel.[259] Papworth is mentioned on a pencil sketch for the center of the staircase

ceiling,[260] and by December 1784 the board had approved his estimate for £1,350 for work on the chapel ceiling,[261] which had been presented with an ornamental panel to demonstrate the proposed work.[262] In 1787 and 1788 submitted bills for ceiling decoration, including a central ornament, foliage, shells, and cherubim, all of which were modeled by hand and covered in consecutive coats of oil and color.[263]

PHILLIPS AND SHAKESPEAR,
Carpenters, Architects
PHILLIPS, John (ca. 1709–75), and SHAKESPEAR, George (fl. from 1758, d. 1797)
John Phillips was from an English family of masons and carpenters, including his uncle, Thomas Phillips (ca. 1689–1736), who was a respected London master carpenter. Took over his uncle's business and partnered with George Shakespear. Phillips occasionally drafted his own designs, but he and Shakespear were particularly known for their work as master builders.[264] Lord Holdernesse hired them to work on his house at Arlington St. (1758–66), his wine vaults in Bolton Row (1765), and at Sion Hill (1760–69).[265]

1764–68: RHS, Greenwich, INFIRMARY
Did the carpentry work during the construction of the new building.[266]

ca. 1768: LONDON, 24 HERTFORD STREET (Holdernesse House)
Received a payment from Lord Holdernesse in September 1768 for carpenter's work at Mr. Merry's stables in Park Lane,[267] which were probably near Holdernesse House. Phillips and Shakespear may have built and/or designed the latter structure, in which case Stuart would have been responsible then for the ornament.

PINCHBECK, Richard (fl. 1762), Toy maker
In 1762 Stuart designed a medal to commemorate the birth of George, Prince of Wales. This was executed by Pingo Jr. (q.v.), whose signature appears on the obverse, below the facing busts of King George III and Queen Charlotte. It was sold through the auspices of the Pinchbeck family, particularly Richard Pinchbeck.[268]

PINGO JR., Thomas (1714–76), Medalist
Born in Italy, Pingo came to England about 1742, and soon established a family home in Gray's Inn Lane, London, and a good business—drawing, modeling, and engraving medals. He became engraver of punches at the Assay Office in 1756. Sons John (1740–1827) and Lewis (1743–1830) were also engravers of dies and punches. Pingo was the die engraver and medalist of Stuart's choice to realize his designs. In 1771 Pingo, with Stuart's support, was the successful appointee as third engraver at the Mint, under the chief engraver, Yeo (q.v.). At his death, his son, Lewis, succeeded him in this post and his other son, John, succeeded him at the Assay Office. Both sons submitted medals to committees, of which Stuart was a member.[269]

1758: THOMAS HOLLIS and SPAC (RSA)
In 1757 Stuart joined the Medal Committee of SPAC (RSA), and after the society aborted the first medal executed by Yeo in November 1758, Stuart recommended Pingo to execute his design for a premium medal. The Pingo family also executed most of the other medals Stuart and Hollis designed for the society, including Louisburg Taken (1758), Goree Taken (1759), Frederick the Great, Defeat of the French and Austrians (ca. 1757 or later), Quebec Taken (1759–60), Canada Subdued (1761), Capture of Pondicherry (1761), Guadeloupe Taken (ca. 1761), Battle of Minden (ca. 1762), Birth of George, Prince of Wales (1762), Catch Club Medal (1764), and Victory at Plassy (ca. 1763).[270]

REBECCA, Biagio (1735–1808), Decorative painter
Born at Osimo, Italy. Studied in Rome at the Accademia di San Luca, where he met West (q.v.) and portraitist George James (d. 1795), with whom he traveled to England in 1761 and briefly partnered. Was one of the foremost and most active painters of the period, working for Robert Adam, Sir William Chambers, James and Samuel Wyatt (q.v.), and Henry Holland, as well as Stuart.[271]

ca. 1776–: LONDON, 22 PORTMAN SQUARE
With Cipriani (q.v.), designed and painted "mechanical paintings" for Mrs. Montagu's

dressing room, which were put into gilt frames made by Jee, Eginton, and Co. The artists, who were hired in 1776 by Boulton (q.v.) via the architect James Wyatt and John Wyatt,[272] may have been paid £39.7.6 in November 1779 for this work.[273] Cipriani and Rebecca supplied the originals to be reproduced by Boulton's mechanical process, and Barney (q.v.) finished the paintings by hand.[274] With Cipriani, painted the semicircular overdoors and elliptical vault of the antechamber (later small drawing room) on the second floor and executed overdoor panels with Shakespearean themes for the morning room.[275]

ca. 1779: RHS, Greenwich, CHAPEL
With Catton (q.v.), de Bruyn (q.v.), and Milbourne (q.v.), painted sixteen monochrome roundels in chiaroscuro placed over the lower windows of the chapel. Painted the last four of the series at the west end of the north side of the chapel: The Last Supper, The Trial before Pilate, The Crucifixion, and The Resurrection. Series terminates with a painting of the Ascension above the altarpiece between the cornice and ceiling, designed by West (q.v.) and executed in chiaroscuro by Rebecca.[276] Also painted in grisaille after designs by West: fourteen life-size figures of the Apostles and Evangelists in the recesses between the upper windows and the four Prophets in the circles above the gallery-doors.[277]

RICHTER, John Augustus (fl. late 18th century), Scagliola worker
Richter and his partner, Domenico Bartoli (fl. ca. 1765–94), were the leading scagliola workers in the late eighteenth century, having premises in Great Newport Street, London (1767–96). They worked for Robert Adam and Sir William Chambers, among others. In 1770 Richter patented his process of inlaying scagliola and plaster in marble and metals to imitate various ornaments, including flowers and birds.[278] Bartoli supplied verd antique scagliola columns and pilasters in 1790 (after Stuart's death), for Mrs. Montagu's house at 22 Portman Square, London.[279]

1782: RHS, Greenwich, CHAPEL
On March 23, 1782, submitted an estimate of £486.12.0 for eight scagliola columns 23

feet, 6 inches high and 2 feet 8 inches in diameter and for thirty-two pilasters 9 feet 9 inches high.[280] The columns were raised in 1784, and the following year the pilasters were fixed on the gallery level,[281] with Richter cleaning, oiling, and repolishing them before the opening of the chapel in 1789.[282]

ROBINSON, William (ca. 1720–75), Architect

Born at Keyper, Durham. Appointed clerk of works at Greenwich in 1746 and trained under Stuart's predecessor, Thomas Ripley. Was chiefly an official architect, occupying the post of clerk of works at Whitehall, Westminster, and St. James's (1754–66) followed by that of secretary to the Board of Works and clerk itinerant.[283]

ca. 1764–ca. 1774: RHS, Greenwich, INFIRMARY and KING CHARLES BLOCK
In 1760 Stuart was asked by the board of directors to build the hospital's Infirmary. Robinson acted as clerk of works (1764–68), supervising the execution of Stuart's designs for the Infirmary.[284] Also under Stuart's surveyorship, oversaw the rebuilding of the southwest pavilion of Wren's King Charles Block (1769–74) in Portland stone by the masons Jelfe (q.v.) and Bastard (q.v.). The work was done for an estimated cost of £5,664.[285] In 1772 refitted the dining hall in this building to increase the number of pensioners who could be accommodated and constructed an underground corridor to link the dining halls and kitchens in the King Charles and King William Blocks.[286]

ROOKER, Edward (d. 1774), Architectural Engraver, Pantomime Actor

1760: RSA
Stuart was on the organizational committee for the February 1760 exhibition in the society's great room, where Rooker showed engravings from *Antiquities of Athens*.[287]

1773: *AN ACCOUNT OF THE VOYAGES . . .*
The plate, "Byron and the Patagonians," from the first volume of John Hawkesworth's *Account of the Voyages . . .* (1773), appears to have been engraved by Rooker. Like Hall's (q.v.), it was probably based on a design Stuart exhibited at the Free Society in 1773.[288]

ROSE, Joseph and Co (*fl.* 1740–1800), Plasterers

The best-known firm of eighteenth-century plasterers, working extensively for Robert Adam.

The firm consisted of descendants of seventeenth-century Yorkshire plasterers settled at Norton, near Sheffield. Joseph Rose Sr. (ca. 1723–80), the head of the firm, served a seven-year York apprenticeship beginning in 1738 and developed into a well-known rococo plasterer. He collaborated with his brother, Jonathan Sr. and after 1760, with Jonathan's sons, Joseph Jr. (1745–99) and Jonathan Jr. Joseph Jr. went to Rome in 1768, where he gained a classical education, which he used to help steer the firm toward neoclassicism. The careers of Joseph Sr. and Joseph Jr. are hard to separate, and at Joseph Sr.'s death in 1780, Joseph Jr. took over the company. Stuart would have encountered the Roses' work (1751–63) at Wentworth Woodhouse, Yorkshire.[289]

ca. 1755–ca. 1768: WENTWORTH WOODHOUSE, Yorkshire
Stuart was responsible for some of the interior decoration here, and Jonathan Sr. and Joseph Sr. executed plasterwork under his direction in the dining, drawing, "supping," and writing rooms and on the ceiling and walls of the Great Hall.[290]

ca. 1758–ca. 1764: SPENCER HOUSE, London
Was employed by both Vardy (q.v.) and Stuart as a plasterer. Joseph Rose received payments on December 23, 1758, and February 17, 1759, for plasterwork in Lady Spencer's dressing room and the other first-floor state-rooms.[291]

ca. 1764–66: LONDON, 15 ST. JAMES'S SQUARE (Lichfield House)
In a letter of September 17, 1766, Stuart wrote Anson: "Rose returns his sincerest thanks you for the money you have been pleased to remit him. . . ."[292] In 1773 when Anson's executors drew up a list of outstanding creditors, "Rose plasters," was in receipt of an outstanding bill for £2.19.6.[293] Rose Jr. also worked for Samuel Wyatt (q.v.) at Shugborough in 1794, six years after Stuart's death.[294]

1765–66: LONDON, 24 HERTFORD ST.

(Holdernesse House)
According to Lord Holdernesse's account book, Joseph Rose received a payment of £200 in 1765 and £625 on May 7 and December 5, 1766. The plasterwork was in all probability done at Holdernesse House.[295]

ROUCHEAD [ROVEHEAD, ROUCHARD OR RONCHART], Alexander, Sr. (*fl.* from 1713, d. 1776), Mason

Perhaps of French extraction. Became free of the Masons' Company in 1728. Lived in North Audley Street, London, in a house of his own building. Was the "Alexander Rovehead" who oversaw the construction of the Naval Hospital at Stonehouse, Plymouth (1758–64), and probably was also responsible for the structure's design.[296]

1764–70: LONDON, 15 ST. JAMES'S SQUARE (Lichfield House)
In addition to providing designs, Stuart oversaw construction here. Rouchead, who was the chief mason and built the entire front elevation, received his initial payment of £400 in June 1764.[297] In April 1770 submitted a final invoice to Anson in which he claimed a total of £2,682.2.9 for all work done since 1764, £282.2.9 of which was outstanding.[298]

RUSSELL, Henry (*fl.* 1764–72), Painter

Was a painter at Bagshot Park under James Paine in 1770–72.

1764–ca. 1768: SHUGBOROUGH, Staffordshire, or LONDON, 15 ST. JAMES'S SQUARE (Lichfield House)
Painted a portrait of Lord Hardwicke, and Stuart acted as a liaison.[299] In 1773 Anson's executors listed "Russel painter" as in receipt of outstanding bill for £0.19.0, which may have been for this commission.[300]

SAUNDERS, John (*fl.* 1762–64), Mason

1762–64: NUNEHAM COURTENAY, Oxfordshire
Did masonry work on the Church of All Saints and may have designed the "highly ornamented Seat of the Corinthian Order" in the garden.[301]

SAYER, Thomas (fl. 1772)

1772: SHUGBOROUGH, Staffordshire, or LONDON, 15 ST. JAMES'S SQUARE (Lichfield House)
Billed £15.3.11 on October 3, 1772, for primarily putting up latticework and fencing.[302]

SCHEEMAKERS, Peter (1691–1781), and SCHEEMAKERS, Thomas (1740–1808), Sculptors

Son of a sculptor from Antwerp, Peter came to London via Rome in 1720, where he subsequently ran a workshop with his fellow Fleming Laurent Delvaux (1695–1778). The two went to Rome to study the antique in 1728, returning to London two years later. Scheemakers became one of the most successful English sculptors in the eighteenth century. In 1755/56 his workshop entered into a mutually beneficial partnership with Stuart. After Peter Scheemakers returned to Antwerp in 1771, his son Thomas, who had trained in the family workshop and studied at the Royal Academy schools in 1772, took over the firm. He collaborated with Stuart until 1781.[303] Exhibited a "model of a monument from a design of Mr Stuart" at the Royal Academy in 1782.[304]

1759–63: WESTMINSTER ABBEY, London
Peter Scheemakers's first collaboration with Stuart (1759–62) was a bust of George Augustus, third Viscout Howe, General of the British Forces in America, for which the Court of the Province of Massachusetts Bay paid £250.[305] They also collaborated on a sculpture of Rear-Admiral Watson (1760–63; partly dismantled in 1957). The East India Company hired Stuart in 1760 to design the monument and oversee its execution and installation by Scheemakers, for which Stuart paid him £1,000.[306]

1761–62, 1764–66: WIMPOLE, Cambridgeshire, CHICHELEY CHAPEL, St. Andrew's Church
In 1761 Philip Yorke, first Earl of Hardwicke, commissioned Stuart and Scheemakers to design and execute a monument to Catharine Yorke, née Freman, the first wife of Hon. Charles Yorke, for which the sculptor received £221 from Lord Hardwicke in March 1762.[307] In 1764 Stuart and Peter Scheemakers (assisted by his son) began to work on a monument to Lord Hardwicke and his wife, Margaret Yorke (d. 1761).[308] While the second Earl of Hardwicke's accounts show that Scheemakers received £1,100 between 1764 and 1766 for sculpting the work and overseeing its installation on the north wall of the chapel,[309] Stuart's compensation is not recorded.[310]

ca. 1758–66: SPENCER HOUSE, London
A number of chimneypieces here have been attributed to the Scheemakers workshop, including one in the Palm Room and another in Lady Spencer's closet, both of which may have been designed by Stuart.[311] In the great room, executed a white marble chimneypiece (now at Althorp) with a frieze derived from the one on the Choragic Monument of Lysicrates.[312] May have carved three plaster panels over the chimneypiece in the Painted Room.[313] Seems to also have produced the chimneypieces in the music room and Lady Spencer's dressing room, after designs by Stuart.[314]

1763–69: SHUGBOROUGH, Staffordshire
Peter Scheemakers first worked at Shugborough under Thomas Wright's direction, carving a drawing room chimneypiece (before 1748) and a bas-relief after Poussin's "Et in Arcadia Ego" for the Shepherd's Monument (ca. 1755–56),[315] to which Stuart may have later added an aedicule.[316] By September 1764 Scheemakers had begun to carve two sarcophagi, busts of Admiral and Lady Anson, and an *aplustre,* or naval trophy, for Stuart's Triumphal Arch, for which Scheemakers asked £800.[317] The monument seems to have been mostly finished in 1766, with Scheemakers adding his final contributions, medallions of Neptune and Minerva establishing naval discipline, in 1769.[318]

1764–ca. 1766: LONDON, 15 ST. JAMES'S SQUARE (Lichfield House)
In September 1764 asked for Scheemaker's assistance with two of the volutes for his beloved Ionic capitals for the front elevation.[319] The Scheemakers workshop was probably also responsible for the carved chimneypiece in the drawing room with panels of reliefs adapted from the Choragic Monument of Lysicrates.[320]

1765–83: RSA and FREE SOCIETY OF ARTISTS
Perhaps at Stuart's encouragement, Thomas Scheemakers exhibited two bas-reliefs executed from the architect's designs at the Free Society of Artists exhibition in 1765. He continued to exhibit models "designed by Stuart" at this venue, including in 1766, 1770, 1782, and 1783.[321-22]

1771: ST. GILES'S CHURCH, WIMBORNE ST. GILES, Dorset
Stuart and Thomas Scheemakers created a wall monument to Anthony Ashley Cooper, fourth Earl of Shaftesbury (d. 1771) on the south side of the chancel (damaged 1908).[323]

ca. 1773: CHURCH OF ST. MARY THE VIRGIN, Preston-on-Stour, Warwickshire
Thomas Scheemakers created a monument to Thomas Steavens, signed "J. Stuart inv."[324]

ca. 1773: CHURCH OF ST. MARY THE VIRGIN, Braughing, Hertfordshire
Thomas Scheemakers and Stuart worked together on three monuments in Hertfordshire, all of which featured sarcophagi and double portrait medallions. The first was erected ca. 1773 to Ralph (brother of Catharine Yorke, née Freman) and Agnes Freman of Hames in Hertfordshire.

1778 and ca. 1779: CHURCH OF ST. JOHN THE BAPTIST, Eastnor, Hertfordshire
In 1778 Thomas Scheemakers and Stuart were commissioned to execute the second Hertfordshire monument to Joseph Cocks, a cousin of the Yorke family. About a year later Scheemakers erected a wall-monument to Mary Cocks (d. 1779), which was signed "J. Stuart inv."[325]

1781: CHURCH OF ST. NICHOLAS OF MYRA, Chiswick, London
At Wedgwood's (q.v.) request, Thomas Scheemakers and Stuart collaborated on a wall monument to Wedgwood's partner, Thomas Bentley (d. 1780).[326]

1783: MOUNT STEWART, Co. Down, TEMPLE OF THE WINDS
Robert Stewart, first Marquess of Londonderry, paid Stuart in June 1783 about £54 for architectural and interior elements, including a chimneypiece executed by Thomas Scheemakers.[327]

[SCOTT] (*fl.* 1755–70)
1755 WENTWORTH WOODHOUSE, Yorkshire
In September 1755 took measure of the panels over the doors in the saloon possibly for "Views on the Thames."[328]

1770: LONDON, 15 ST. JAMES'S SQUARE (Lichfield House)
May have been the "Mr. Scot" who measured and signed Rouchead's (q.v.) final bill in 1770.[329]

SEDDON, George (ca. 1727–1801), Furniture-maker
GEORGE SEDDON AND SONS
Founder of the largest firm of furniture-makers in London in the late eighteenth-century. Was from Lancashire. Came to London to be a furniture-maker and by 1753 had established a shop in Aldersgate Street. His sons Thomas (1761–1804) and George (1765–1815) joined him in the business around 1785, and by 1786 George Seddon and Sons was employing 400 cabinetmakers, upholsterers, carvers, and gilders.[330]

ca. 1781–89: RHS, Greenwich, CHAPEL
Assisted Arrow (q.v.) with the pulpit, reader's desk, and presses.[331]

ca. 1782: LONDON, 22 PORTMAN SQUARE
Received a payment of £200.0.0 for unspecified work.[332] This may have been a piece of furniture decorated with paintings by Boulton and Fothergill (q.v.), as in 1782 Boulton responded to Seddon's inquiry about paintings for Mrs. Montagu, informing him that they could be adjusted to fit the object they were to ornament.[333]

[SHIRLEY] (*fl.* 1780), Ironworker
Was based in Birmingham.

ca. 1780: LONDON, 22 PORTMAN SQUARE
Received payment for ironwork in 1780. Was commissioned through Boulton (q.v.), but Stuart, as Mrs. Montagu's architect, would probably have been somewhat involved in choosing craftsmen to realize his designs.[334]

[SKETCHLEY] (*fl.* 1768)
1768: SHUGBOROUGH, Staffordshire, or LONDON, 15 ST. JAMES'S SQUARE (Lichfield House)

Was paid £10.8.0 on October 24, 1768, for deal.[335]

[SLEEFORD] (*fl.* 1764–66)
1764–66: SHUGBOROUGH, Staffordshire, and LONDON, 15 ST. JAMES'S SQUARE (Lichfield House)
Stuart hired Sleeford in June 1764 for work at Shugborough.[336] Two years later Sleeford made a model for a spindle and sent it to London, only to have Anson's servants refuse to receive it.[337]

SMELT, Leonard (1719–1800), Clerk of works
Supervised the erection of Mrs. Montagu's house, 22 Portman Square, London, during her absence at Bath and elsewhere.[338]

SMIRKE, Robert (1752–1845), Painter, Book Illustrator
Born at Wigton, near Carlisle. In 1766 moved to London and studied with a coach painter. Became a pupil of the Royal Academy in 1772, where he exhibited primarily small-scale works with literary subjects from 1786 onward. Was frequently employed illustrating books. His son, the architect Sir Robert Smirke (1780–1867), was one of the main proponents of the Greek Revival style in the nineteenth century.[339]

1782: LONDON, 22 PORTMAN SQUARE
In 1782 received a payment of £63.0.0 for unidentified work, which may have been done under either Stuart or Bonomi.[340]

SPANG, Michael Henry (*fl.* from ca. 1756, d. 1762), Sculptor
Of Danish extraction. Came to England ca. 1756. Protégé of Sir William Chambers and worked for Robert Adam at Kedleston in 1759.[341]

ca. 1759–66: SPENCER HOUSE, London
Executed the statues and urns over the west front of the house. Contributed to the first-floor state rooms.[342]

STRINGER, John (*fl.* 1764), Mason
1764: SHUGBOROUGH, Staffordshire, or LONDON, 15 ST. JAMES'S SQUARE (Lichfield House)
Was paid £8.2.6 on November 1, 1764, for bricks.[343]

[SWANN] (*fl.* ca. 1765-66), Upholsterer
1765 or 1766: SHUGBOROUGH, Staffordshire, or LONDON, 15 ST. JAMES'S SQUARE (Lichfield House)
Received payment for blue damask.[344]

THOMPSON, Thomas (*fl.* 1767), Bricklayer
1767: SHUGBOROUGH, Staffordshire, or LONDON, 15 ST. JAMES'S SQUARE (Lichfield House)
Was paid £4.9.8 for bricklayer's work on November 24, 1767.[345]

TRUBSHAW, Charles Cope (1715–72), Architect
Came of an extensive Staffordshire family of builder/masons and learned carving under Peter Scheemakers (q.v.) in London. Set up business as a sculptor and master mason, executing monuments, carving chimneypieces, and supplying decorative carving to various clients, including Sir William Bagot of Blithfield and Viscount Chetwynd of Ingestre.[346]

1765–68: SHUGBOROUGH, Staffordshire, TOWER OF THE WINDS and STABLES
Executed Stuart's designs. Was probably completed by 1765. May also have been the architect responsible for erecting the stables in ca. 1767.[347] Was paid £31.16.0 on May 19, 1768, and £13.10.6 on December 31, 1768.[348]

VARDY, John (1718–1765), Architect, Engraver, Furniture Designer
Born in Durham. Received a number of appointments through the Georgian Office of Works. Became a disciple of William Kent, and his public and private commissions show a strong Palladian influence.[349]

1755–65: SPENCER HOUSE, London
Designed the exterior and ground-floor state rooms, to which Stuart may have made some minor contributions, including designing a chimneypiece in the Palm Room.[350] Stuart may have adapted elements of Vardy's designs for use in first-floor state rooms. After Stuart was hired, Vardy continued to produce designs for the house,[351] and until his death seems to have been responsible for supervising and paying the craftsmen.[352]

VARDY, Thomas (b. 1724), Carver
Of Park Street, Grosvenor Square. Came to London ca. 1740. In 1750 became a freeman of the Joiners' Company of London. Was a leading carver, much used by patrons and architects. Worked with his brother John Vardy (q.v.) on many commissions.[353]

ca. 1755–ca. 1766: SPENCER HOUSE, London
Possibly carved a pair of console tables for the dining room (ca. 1755–58) based on John Vardy's designs.[354] Is believed to have been responsible for carving the winged lions on the four gilt-wood sofas that Stuart designed for the Painted Room at Spencer House in ca. 1759–66.[355] Did carving in the first-floor state rooms.[356]

VASSALLI, Francesco (fl. 1724–63), Stuccoist
One of a family long seated at Riva St. Vitale, near Lugano. Although little is known of him, he was in England by 1724. A "John Vassalli" worked at Croome Court, Worcestershire, in 1758–59 and may have been a relative, or the same as Francesco. Stuart also worked there as a painter. Late in life Vassalli resided in Staffordshire, where he carried out stuccowork in Shugborough's dining room and library under Thomas Wright ca. 1748.[357]

1758: HAGLEY HALL, Worcestershire
Executed Rococo plasterwork to the interiors, including a panel signed at bottom left, over the White Hall chimneypiece by Lovell (q.v.), and flowers, swags, and trophies on the ceiling and walls of the drawing room. Stuart was hired in 1758 to add paintings of "a Flora and four pretty little Zephyrs" to Vassalli's ceiling, and the payments he received from Lord Lyttelton of £35 on November 3, 1758, and £20 on July 30, 1759, were probably for this decorative work.[358]

1759: CROOME COURT, Worcestershire
Stuart's work at Hagley may have led to his employment at Croome Court in 1759, where he designed a ceiling for an unidentified room.[359] Vassalli, who was in charge of the stuccowork there, submitted a bill in March 1761 for £47.15.0 for the "Ceiling in ye Salon according to My designe" and £22.5.0 for "That done before according to Mr. Stuard designe."[360]

VILE AND COBB, Cabinetmakers, Upholsterers
VILE, William (1715–67), and COBB, John (ca. 1715–88)
Vile and Cobb formed a partnership in 1751 and established premises at the corner of St. Martin's Lane and Long Acre. The firm received royal commissions and called themselves "Cabinetmakers and Upholsterers to His Majesty." Although they were known for their high prices, they were much patronized by the aristocracy. Vile retired in ca. 1764, and Cobb continued to work with his foreman, Samuel Reynolds (fl. 1751–85).[361]

ca. 1761–65: LONDON, 24 HERTFORD ST. (Holdernesse House)
Like John Devall (q.v.), Rose (q.v.), and Adair (q.v.), received payment from Lord Holdernesse for work done in all likelihood at Holdernesse House between 1761 and 1765.[362]

WARRELEY, James, and WARRELEY, Thomas (fl. ca. 1765), Plumbers
ca. 1765: SHUGBOROUGH, Staffordshire, TOWER OF THE WINDS
Inscibed their names on the leadwork of the roof of this structure in 1765. Were paid £4.0.0 for unspecified work on December 26, 1767.[363]

WEBB, John (fl. 1764–65), Mason
Was a local Staffordshire man.

1764: SHUGBOROUGH, Staffordshire
In July 1764 Webb began to work on Stuart's Triumphal Arch, first adding commemorative vases that he had wrought and gilt to the outer ends of the entablature.[364] Made suggestions regarding the placement of the sarcophagi, portrait busts, and *apulstre* (large naval trophy) by Scheemakers (q.v.), hoisted them into position, and carried out any necessary modifications.[365] In the summer of 1764 Webb added vases of artificial stone to the ridgeline of the greenhouse according to a drawing Stuart had sent him.[366] Also carried out renovations to the Attic floor of the manor house. In a September 1764 letter to Thomas Anson, Stuart stated: "I wrote to Webb about the bearings for his Chimneys. . . . Bearings are made very securely in the manner I men

tioned to him last post."[367] On December 11, 1767, received £12.16.10 for bricks and tiles.[368]

WEDGWOOD, Josiah (1730–95), Potter
WEDGWOOD AND BENTLEY
Born in Burslem to a family of potters, in business since 1656. Established his own highly successful factory and became known for his experiments with techniques and methods of ceramic production. In 1768–69 partnered with the merchant Thomas Bentley (1730–80). On June 13, 1769, opened the Etruria Works near Burslem, where he developed new wares, including black basalt and his famous Jasper.[369]

Well-acquainted with Stuart, Boulton (q.v.) and others. In 1770 traveled with Stuart, who advised him about establishing showrooms next to Boulton's in the Adelphi, an area developed (1768–74) by the Adam brothers.[370] Wedgwood produced a series of portrait medallions of Fellows of the Royal Society, including two depicting Stuart, which are listed in the firm's 1773 and 1779 catalogues.[371]

1769: BLITHFIELD HALL, Staffordshire
In September 1769 Wedgwood wrote to Bentley that he was to supply vases for the large drawing room, which may have been designed by Stuart.[372]

1770–71: SHUGBOROUGH, Staffordshire, LANTHORN OF DEMOSTHENES
The monument was completed at the end of 1770, when considerable difficulties were experienced in providing a bowl that would not crush the masonry of the tripodic support. Wedgwood suggested that he fire a black basalt bowl that could later be gilt, and Stuart agreed.[373] Based on a wooden prototype sent from Soho, it was finished in April 1771, but it is not clear whether the bowl and tripod were put in position. Neither object survives, and in 1965 the National Trust, restored the monument and reproduced the pieces in fiberglass.[374]

1770–71: MRS. MONTAGU
In 1770 Stuart commissioned a "tripodic tea kitchen" (tea urn) for Mrs. Montagu from Boulton and Wedgwood.[375] Wedgwood made a sample of the black

basalt vase and neck and sent it to Boulton, who was to mount it in ormolu.[376] There is no evidence, however, that the piece was ever finished.[377]

1771–72: ASHLEY CHURCH, Staffordshire
In 1770 Deborah Chetwynd commissioned Stuart and Wedgwood to codesign a funerary monument to her recently deceased father Sir William Chetwynd of Ingestre, neighbor of Thomas Anson.[378] The sculptor of the piece is unknown, but possibly Trubshaw (q.v.).[379]

1778: LONDON, 22 PORTMAN SQUARE
Stuart ordered Jasper tablets depicting the Muses for a chimneypiece frieze.[380]

ca. 1780s: BELVEDERE HOUSE, Erith, Kent
Stuart incorporated green and lilac Jasper plaques provided by Wedgwood in a painted pine chimneypiece in the anteroom to the dining room (removed in 1961, now in a private collection).[381]

WEST, Benjamin (1738–1820), Painter, Draftsman
Born in Springfield [now Swarthmore], Pennsylvania; moved to Philadelphia in 1756. Studied in Italy (1760–63) where he was exposed to the neoclassical ideals of Anton Raphael Mengs, Gavin Hamilton, and others. Moved to London in 1763, where he initially painted portraits but soon earned a reputation for paintings of a historical nature, eventually becoming history painter to George III. On Joshua Reynold's death, succeeded him as the Royal Academy's second president.[382]

ca. 1779–89: RHS, Greenwich, CHAPEL
Designed a number of the interior ornaments for the chapel, including paintings of the Apostles, Evangelists, and Prophets executed in grisaille by Rebecca (q.v.), and in ca. 1779 a series of roundels installed beneath the galleries, depicting events in the life of Jesus, and painted in chiaroscuro by Catton (q.v.), Rebecca, Milbourne (q.v.), and de Bruyn (q.v.).[383] In November 1781 the General Court hired West to paint the altarpiece, *The Preservation of St. Paul from Shipwreck on the Island of Melita (Malta)*, for which he was paid £1,200. Was set into a gilt frame made by Lawrence (q.v.).[384] Above it is the terminus to the subgallery roundels, a painting of the Ascension,

which West designed and Rebecca executed in chiaroscuro. Designed the four oval medallions depicting the prophets and six circular ones showing scenes from the Acts of the Apostles, which Bacon (q.v.), as an employee of the Coade Artificial Stone Manufactory (q.v.), executed and set into the reader's desk and pulpit in 1789.[385] In ca. 1785, also designed the statues of Charity, Faith, Meekness, and Hope, carved by Bacon in Coade stone and installed in the entrance vestibule.[386]

WHITE, Charles (fl. 1765–84), Architect
Employed by the Board of Ordnance. First exhibited at the RSA in 1765 and exhibited at the Free Society of Artists (1768–83) primarily works of a topographical nature.[387]

–1784: RHS, Greenwich, CHAPEL
Had known Stuart for about twenty years when Stuart offered him Mylne's position of clerk of works in 1782. The board, however, favored Newton for this appointment, and Stuart convinced White to take a subordinate position with the understanding "that he meant to Resign, as soon as the Chapel should be finished, & added that Mr Newton would succeed him, and [White] of course should succeed Mr Newton."[388] Acted at times as an intermediary between Newton and the craftsmen, including Samuel Wyatt (q.v.),[389] but there was friction between Newton and White, resulting in the latter's dismissal in 1784.[390]

WILTON, Joseph (1722–1803), Sculptor
Born in London. Trained on the Continent with the Flemish artist Laurent Delvaux and from 1744 at the Academy in Paris under Jean-Baptiste Pigalle, where he learned to work in marble. Went to Rome, and in 1750 received the Jubilee gold medal from Pope Benedict XIV. After copying antique statues in Florence (1751–55), he returned to England with Sir William Chambers, the sculptor G. B. Capezzuoli, and Cipriani (q.v.). In 1760 Wilton was appointed Carver of State Coaches to George III, and with Chambers, Capezzuoli, and Cipriani, designed and carved a new state coach, which was completed in 1762. In 1761 was named Statuary to His Majesty, which led to a number of public and private statuary commissions. In

1760 he may have met Stuart at Croome Court, where he was commissioned to carve a frieze of lapis lazuli in the center of a chimneypiece in the Tapestry Room.[391]

ca. 1756–64: NUNEHAM COURTENAY, Oxfordshire
Executed a chimneypiece designed by Stuart in the great drawing room.

ca. 1758–64: SPENCER HOUSE, London
Did decorative carving in the first-floor state rooms.[392]

WOOLLETT, William (1735–1785), Printmaker
Apprenticed to John Tinney (fl. 1729–61) in London. Made a name for himself with his bestselling print, *The Destruction of the Children of Niobe* (1761), after Richard Wilson's painting (ca. 1759–60). In 1776 was appointed Engraver in Ordinary to George III.[393]

1764: THOMAS ANSON
Stuart handled the negotiations for Anson when Woollett wanted to engrave a painting by Gaspard Dughet [Poussin] in Anson's collection.[394]

WYATT, Samuel (1737–1807), Carpenter, Architect, Engineer
Born in Weeford, Staffordshire. In 1760 Adam hired him first as a carpenter at Kedleston Hall, Derbyshire, then promoted him to clerk of works. Collaborated (1768–74) with his brother, James Wyatt (1746–1813) on a number of projects, after which he struck out on his own, setting up a practice in London that specialized in neoclassical country houses and model farm buildings.[395]

1767–68: SHUGBOROUGH, Staffordshire
While working at Blithfield, received payment on November 12, 1767, for "Deals" and was paid another £10.0.0 on December 31, 1768.[396] Samuel Wyatt was hired after Stuart's death to make changes at Shugborough in 1790, most notably in 1794 to the Red Drawing Room.[397]

1769: BLITHFIELD HALL, Staffordshire, ORANGERY
Carried out most of the construction work at Blithfield, including building new family rooms and a drawing room for Sir William

Bagot.[398] Stuart may have designed the new entrance façade and other alterations to the manor house, which were not implemented,[399] and an orangery with baseless Doric pilasters, which was built by Samuel and Joseph Wyatt in 1769.[400]

1781: RHS, Greenwich, CHAPEL
One of the craftsmen employed at Somerset House who Stuart recommended in 1781 to work at Greenwich after the fire.[401] In December 1782 sent White (q.v.) pieces of fir timber for the beams for the chapel.[402]

YENN, John (1750–1821), Architect
Was a pupil of Sir William Chambers, with whom he maintained a close business and personal relationship until Chambers's

death in 1796. From 1780 served as clerk of works at Richmond New Park Lodge and from 1782 at Kensington Palace, the Queen's House, and the Royal Mews.[403] When Stuart's successor Sir Robert Taylor died in 1788, the Board of Works appointed Yenn as Surveyor of the RHS, Greenwich.[404]

1780–82: LONDON, 22 PORTMAN SQUARE
Jee, Eginton, and Co. submitted a bill in 1780 for doors, which contained errors, but Stuart failed to identify them and approved the invoice.[405] At Smelt's (q.v.) suggestion, Mrs. Montagu hired a measurer to survey the work independently. Yenn was paid £21.0.0 in June 1782 for his survey.[406]

YEO, Richard (ca. 1720–79), Medalist
In 1746 produced the official medal commemorating the Battle of Coulloden. Appointed assistant engraver at the Royal Mint in 1749 and Chief Engraver in 1775.[407]

1757–58: SPAC (RSA)
Was much involved with the early medal designs of Stuart, including the cutting of dies and puncheons for the RSA medal commissioned in 1757. Yeo encountered numerous technical difficulties when making the medal. The finished work was finally produced in May 1758, but the society was unhappy with the cost of the medal and the quality of the work. Yeo was dismissed in June 1758 and replaced by Pingo Jr. (q.v.).[408]

Editor's note: Some of the information herein has been drawn from the essays in this volume. We are especially grateful to Kerry Bristol for sharing her original research conducted while preparing her Ph.D. dissertation on James Stuart. This includes many of the citations from the Lichfield Manuscripts which are located in the Staffordshire Country Record Office, Stafford, and are cited below as "Lichfield Ms." Matthew Boulton Papers, Birmingham City Archive, Central Library, are cited as "Boulton Papers." All other references are given in short form; the full citation will be found in the bibliography. We are also grateful to Michelle Hargrave for her many contributions to this appendix.

1. Toynbee, ed., "Walpole's Journals of Visits to Country Seats" (1927–28): 15.

2. Lord Lyttelton to Mrs. Montagu, 21 October 1758, Montagu Papers MO 1280, as cited in Bristol, "22 Portman Square" (2001): 72; also quoted in Bolton, "Hagley Park" (16 October 1915): 526.

3. Elizabeth Montagu to Leonard Smelt, 3 November 1767, Montagu Papers MO 4994, Henry E. Huntington Library, cited in Bristol, "The Painted Rooms of 'Athenian' Stuart," (2000): 165–74; Croft-Murray, *Decorative Painting in England*, vol. 2 (1970): 284; Stuart to Thomas Anson, 17 June 1769, Lichfield Ms. D615/P(S)/1/6/26; Blunt, ed., *Mrs. Montagu, "Queen of the Blues,"* vol. 1 (1923): 164.

4. Roscoe, "James 'Athenian' Stuart and the Scheemakers Family" (September 1987): 178–84. See also chap. 9 in this volume.

5. Young, *Six Months Tour,* vol. 1 (1770): 281; Stuart to Marquess of Rockingham, 28 September 1755, Wentworth Woodhouse Muniments R1-70, Sheffield Archives; Hussey, *English Country Houses, Early Georgian 1715–1760* (1955): 153; Binney, "Wentworth Woodhouse Revisited—II" (24 March 1983): 710.

6. Webb, "Chimney-Pieces by Scheemakers" (14 March 1957): 491–93.

7. Eimer, "James 'Athenian' Stuart" (1994): 131–37. See also chap. 12 in this volume.

8. See, for example, Register of Chapter Acts 1748–1773, 12 June 1771 and 12 July 1771, Windsor, St. George's Chapel Archives VI.B.7, 483 (447) and 485 (449). A signed design for the east end of St. George's Chapel is preserved in ibid., F.212; Robinson, *Windsor Castle* (2001). For the organ at Newby, see Cornforth, "Newby Hall, North Yorkshire—I" (7 June 1979): 1802–6.

9. Bence-Jones, *Burke's Guide to Country Houses,* vol. 1 (1978): 216–17; McParland, "Rathfarnham Castle Co., Dublin" (9 September 1982): 735–37.

10. Mrs. Elizabeth Montagu to Leonard Smelt, 24 April, 1780, Montagu Papers MO 5026, Henry E. Huntington Library, as cited in Bristol, "22 Portman Square" (2001): 79–80.

11. Colvin, *A Biographical Dictionary of British Architects* (1995): 939–40.

12. Mortimer, *The Universal Director* (1763); Beard, *Craftsmen and Interior Decoration* (1981): 241.

13. Bristol, "Stuart and the London Building Trades" (2003): 3; Beard and Gilbert, *Dictionary of English Furniture Makers* (1986): 2.

14. Lee MS D/LE/D4/14, Buckinghamshire Records and Local Studies Service, Aylesbury.

15. MS. D.D. Harcourt, Harcourt Estate Papers, c.174, and c. 175, Bodleian Library, Oxford; Sotheby's London, *Important English Furniture* (3 July 2003): lot 104.

16. Bill John Adair to Thomas Anson, for work 4 June 1763 to 2 September 1766, Lichfield Ms. D615/E(H)/1/1.

17. Bristol, "Stuart and the Genesis of the Greek Revival" (1997): 289–91; Sheppard, ed., *Survey of London,* vols. 29–30 (1960): 143.

18. Bill John Adair to Thomas Anson, for work 4 June 1763 to 2 September 1766, Lichfield Ms. D615/E(H)/1/1; Bristol, "Stuart and the Genesis of the Greek Revival" (1997): 283.

19. Bristol, "Stuart and the London Building Trades" (2003): 2–3; Egerton Ms. 3497, fol. 64 (Stuart), and 66, 67, 73 (Adair), BL.

20. Elizabeth Montagu to Leonard Smelt, 2 April, 1780, Montagu Papers MO 23, Henry E. Huntington Library, as cited in Bristol, "Stuart and the Genesis of the Greek Revival" (1997): 321.

21. C. Hoare & Co. Ledger 92 (1774–1775), fol. 87, as cited in Bristol, "22 Portman Square" (2001): 74.

22. C. Hoare & Co. Ledger 7 (1780–1781), fol. 65, as cited in Bristol, "22 Portman Square" (2001): 84 n. 31.

23. Beard and Gilbert, *Dictionary of English Furniture Makers* (1986): 2.

24. *Wills,* Anderson, PRO, Prob. 11/379/331; wife, Penelope (1769), 11/1053/230; Mortimer, *Universal Director . . .* (1763); Gunnis, *Dictionary of British Sculptors, 1660–1851* (1968): 17; Goodison, *Matthew Boulton: Ormolu* (2002): 38; Beard, *Craftsmen and Interior Decoration* (1981): 242.

25. Knox, "Acquisitions for National Trust Properties" (April 1997): 50, fig. 1; Snodin, "Putting Adam into Context" (1995): 13–14.

26. L. Harris, *Robert Adam and Kedleston* (1987): 26–31, 34, cat. nos. 11–14, 18.

27. Ms. No.121, Alnwick Castle, Northumberland, quoted in Goodison, "Mr Stuarts's Tripod" (October 1972): 696. See also Goodison, *Matthew Boulton: Ormolu* (2002): 38, 71–76, and Goodison, "Mr Stuarts's Tripod" (October 1972): 695–705.

28. Goodison, "Mr Stuart's Tripod" (October 1972): 696; Friedman, *Spencer House* (1993): 179; Thornton and Hardy, "Spencer Furniture at Althorp" (June 1968): 440–57.

29. Robinson, *Spencer House* (2002): 32; Goodison, *Matthew Boulton: Ormolu* (2002): 76, 377, nn. 48, 49. See also Snodin, "Adam Silver Reassessed" (January 1997): 19–20.

30. E. Harris, *Furniture of Robert Adam* (1963): 105, no. 152; Watkin, *Athenian Stuart* (1982): 32.

31. Free Society exhibition catalogue (London William Griffin, 1761): no. 102, catalogued under "Sculptures and Models."

32. Sotheby's, *Ashburnham Collection: Part II,* 26 June 1953, cat. no. 71; Goodison, *Matthew Boulton: Ormolu* (2002): 76, 377 n. 47.

33. Beard, *Craftsmen and Interior Decoration* (1981): 242; Colvin, *Biographical Dictionary of British Architects* (1995): 79.

34. James Stuart to [?], n.d., Letters from Surveyors, Architects, and others as to Works, ADM 65/106, NA; L. Lewis, "Architects of the Chapel" (1947): 260–61, and Bold, *Greenwich* (2000): 173. See also ADM 67/12, Minutes of General Court Meetings, entry for 4 July 1781, 7–8, 11–12, NA.

35. Ms. New/1/1/6, RIBA Library; Beard, *Craftsmen and Interior Decoration* (1981): 242.

36. Papworth, "William Newton and the Chapel of Greenwich Hospital" (27 August 1891): 420.

37. Cooke and Maule, *Royal Hospital for Seamen* (1789): 105–6; ADM 68/823 and 68/824, NA; Bold, *Greenwich* (2000): 176.

38. Gunnis, *Dictionary of British Sculptors* (1968): 24–25; Whinney, *Sculpture in Britain* (1988): 303–21; Clifford: "John Bacon and the Manufacturers" (1985): 288–304.

39. Whinney, *Sculpture in Britain* (1988): 303–4; Bristol, "Stuart and the Genesis of the Greek Revival" (1997): 348; Cooke and Maule, *Royal Hospital for Seamen* (1789): 100; Bold, *Greenwich* (2000): 176, 260 n. 226.

40. "Greenwich Hospital," English Heritage, NMR Red Box File—London, unidentified clipping, n.p.

41. L. Lawrence, "Greece and Rome at Greenwich" (January 1951): 23; Bristol, "Stuart and the Genesis of the Greek Revival" (1997): 353; Watkin, *Athenian Stuart* (1982): 53.

42. Fragments of payments, February 1765 or 1766, Lichfield Ms. D615/E(H)1/2, and 1768, Lichfield Ms. D615/E(H)1/2; Bristol, "Stuart and the Genesis of the Greek Revival" (1997): 271 n. 824.

43. Croft-Murray, *Decorative Painting in England,* vol. 2 (1970): 167–68.

44. Ibid., and 188–89; Robinson and Thompson, "Matthew Boulton's Mechanical Paintings" (1970): 501–2.

45. Pressly, *Life and Art of James Barry* (1981); Barry, *Works of James Barry, Esq.* (1809).

46. Barry, *Works of James Barry, Esq.* vol. 1. (1809); 22–23; Bristol, "Stuart and the Genesis of the Greek Revival" (1997): 192–93 n. 572.

47. Robert Adam to James Adam, 25 June 1758, Clerk of Penicuik Ms. GD 18 4850, National Archives of Scotland, Edinburgh; Nichols, *Minor Lives* (1971): 289–90; Bristol, "Stuart and the Genesis of the Greek Revival" (1997): 132.

48. E. Harris, *Books and Writers* (1990): 441.

49. Stuart to Thomas Anson, 18 September 1764, Lichfield Ms. D615/P(S)/1/6/14, and 6 October 1764, Lichfield Ms. D615/P(S)/1/6/15.

50. Goodison, *Matthew Boulton: Ormolu* (2002): 376 n. 29.

51. Sweet, *Antiquaries* (2004): 96.

52. James Harris, *Hermes* (1765): 325–26.

53. Gunnis, *Dictionary of British Sculptors* (1968): 41; Colvin, *Biographical Dictionary of British Architects* (1995): 108–10; Leach, *James Paine* (1988): 195.

54. ADM 68/876 and 67/11, NA; NMM ART/3, fol. 39; Bold, *Greenwich* (2000): 167.

55. ADM 68/876, NA; Gunnis, *Dictionary of British Sculptors* (1968): 41; Colvin, "Bastards of Blandford" (1948): 192–93.

56. Beard, *Craftsmen and Interior Decoration* (1981): 245–46.

57. ADM 67/12, Minutes of General Court Meetings, entry for 4 July 1781, 7–8, 11–12, NA. See also James Stuart to [?], n.d., Letters from Surveyors, Architects, and others as to Works, ADM 65/106, NA; L. Lewis, "Architects of the Chapel" (1947): 260–61; and Bold, *Greenwich* (2000): 173.

58. Goodison, *Matthew Boulton: Ormolu* (2002).

58a. Ibid., 76, 276, 440–42.

59. Ibid., 76, 276; Robinson, "Eighteenth-Century Commerce and Fashion" (1963): 39–60; Robinson and Thompson, "Matthew Boulton's Mechanical Paintings" (1970): 497–507.

60. Stuart to Thomas Anson, 23 September 1769, Lichfield Ms. D615/P(S)/1/6/27.

61. Josiah Wedgwood to Thomas Bentley, 24 December 1770, E25-18334, Keele University Library; Robinson, *Shugborough* (1989): 26–27, 90; Goodison, *Matthew Boulton: Ormolu* (2002): 53, 71–72, 75–76, 101, 276.

62. James Stuart to Matthew Boulton, 26 December 1769, Boulton Papers, S3, no.

274; Goodison, *Matthew Boulton: Ormolu* (2002): 76, 247, 271, 286, 346.

63. Josiah Wedgwood to Thomas Bentley, 24 December 1770, E25-18334, Keele University Library; Reilly, *Wedgwood,* vol. 1 (1989): 397–99, 446.

64. Josiah Wedgwood to Matthew Boulton, 19 February 1771, Boulton Papers, as cited in Goodison, *Matthew Boulton: Ormolu* (2002): 49, 101.

65. John Wyatt to Josiah Wedgwood, 19 March 1771, Boulton Papers, Ms. 3782/1/9, p. 73; Goodison, *Matthew Boulton: Ormolu* (2002): 271.

66. Kelly, *Decorative Wedgwood* (1965): 65–66.

67. Robinson and Thompson, "Matthew Boulton's Mechanical Paintings" (1970): 504; Bristol, "Stuart and the Genesis of the Greek Revival" (1997): 319; Croft-Murray, *Decorative Painting in England,* vol. 2 (1970): 248.

68. Boulton and Fothergill to James Stuart, 5 October 1771, Boulton Papers, Ms. 3782/1/9, p. 212–13; Boulton and Fothergill to James Stuart, [1771], Boulton Papers, Ms. 3782/1/9, pp. 161–62; Rowe, *Adam Silver* (1965): 83; Goodison, *Matthew Boulton: Ormolu* (2002): 377 n. 52.

69. John Hodges to James Stuart, 1 April 1781, Boulton Papers, Ms. 3782/1/11 as cited in Goodison, *Matthew Boulton: Ormolu* (2002): 377 n. 52; John Hodges to James Stuart, 23 July 1781, Boulton Papers, Ms. 3782/1/11, p. 808; John Hodges to James Stuart, 10 October 1781, Boulton Papers, Ms. 3782/1/11, p. 856; John Hodges to James Stuart, 29 December 1781, Boulton Papers, Ms. 3782/1/11, pp. 908–9; Boulton and Fothergill Pattern Book, no. 1, (1762–70), Boulton Papers, Ms. 3782/21/2, p. 111; Rowe, *Adam Silver* (1965): 83–84.

70. Watkin, *Athenian Stuart* (1982): 49; Bristol, "22 Portman Square" (2001): 74–78.

71. John Hodges to John Wyatt, 18 July 1776, Boulton Papers, old number Ms. No. 140, Letter Book G, p. 664, as cited in Bristol, "22 Portman Square" (2001): 78.

72. Robinson and Thompson, "Matthew Boulton's Mechanical Paintings" (1970): 504.

73. Goodison, "Matthew Boulton's Ormolu Door Furniture" (November 1969): 688.

74. C. Hoare & Co., Ledger 11 (1781–1782), fol. 441, 25 May 1782, as cited in Kerry Bristol, "22 Portman Square" (2001): 80.

75. Beard and Gilbert, *Dictionary of English Furniture Makers* (1986): 110; Heal, *London Furniture Makers* (1953): 25; Entwisle, "Eighteenth-century London Paperstainers" (November 1952): 106–10.

76. "Mr. Goodals Acct of Bills paid by Him: Bills of the Late Tho. Anson Esqe.," [1773], Lichfield Ms. D615/P(S)/1/6/54; Beard, *Craftsmen and Interior Decoration* (1981): 248.

77. Worsley, "Out from Adam's Shadow" (14 May 1992): 100–3.

78. C. Hoare & Co. Ledger 11 (1781–1782), fol. 441, 3 April 1782, as cited in Bristol, "22 Portman Square" (2001): 81.

79. Croft-Murray, *Decorative Painting in England*, vol. 2 (1970): 54, 183–84.

80. Cooke and Maule, *Royal Hospital for Seamen* (1789): 106; ADM 68/823, NA; Bold, *Greenwich* (2000): 176–77.

81. Copy of a letter to John Ibbetson, Ms. New/1/1/1, RIBA Library. See also ADM 67/12, Minutes of General Court Meetings, entry for 4 July 1781, 7–8, 11–12; James Stuart to [?], n.d., Letters from Surveyors, Architects, and others as to Works, ADM 65/106, NA; L. Lewis, "Architects of the Chapel" (1947): 260–61; and Bold, *Greenwich* (2000): 173.

82. ADM 67/21, NA; Bold, *Greenwich* (2000): 209 n. 43.

83. Croft-Murray, *Decorative Painting in England*, vol. 2 (1970): 185–86.

84. Delany, *Autobiography and Correspondence*, 2nd series, vol. 1 (1862): 508; Blunt, ed., *Mrs Montagu, "Queen of the Blues,"* vol. 1 (1923): 152; Croft-Murray, *Decorative Painting in England*, vol. 2 (1970): 188.

85. John Hodges to John Wyatt, 18 July 1776, Boulton Papers, old number Ms. No. 140, Letter Book G, p. 664, as cited in Bristol, "22 Portman Square" (2001): 78; Robinson and Thompson, "Matthew Boulton's Mechanical Paintings" (1970): 504.

86. Boulton and Fothergill to Mrs. Montagu, 18 November 1779, Boulton Papers, Ms. 3782/1/11, p. 498, and Mrs. Montagu to Matthew Boulton, 22 November 1779, Boulton Papers, old number Box 330, No. 18, as cited in Bristol, "22 Portman Square" (2001): 78; Croft-Murray, *Decorative Painting in England*, vol. 2 (1970): 188.

87. C. Hoare & Co. Ledger 13 (1782–1784), fol. 412, 27 January 1783, as cited in Bristol, "22 Portman Square" (2001): 81, 85, n. 84; Blunt, ed., *Mrs Montagu, "Queen of the Blues,"* vol. 2 (1923): 119.

88. Beard, *Craftsmen and Interior Decoration* (1981): 250.

89. Friedman, *Spencer House* (1993): 186–87, 344–45.

90. ADM 67/21, NA; Bold, *Greenwich* (2000): 209 n. 43.

91. Kelly, *Mrs Coade's Stone* (1990); Gunnis, *Dictionary of British Sculptors* (1968): 105–9.

92. Beard, *Craftsmen and Interior Decoration* (1981): 252.

93. ADM 68/813, NA; Bold, *Greenwich* (2000): 176.

94. ADM 68/815, NA; Bold, *Greenwich* (2000): 176.

95. Cooke and Maule, *Royal Hospital for Seamen* (1789): 107.

96. Estimate by Eleanor Coade, 4 May 1787, Ms. New/1/1/13, RIBA Library; L. Lewis, "Architects of the Chapel" (1947): 264; ADM 68/821, NA; Bold, *Greenwich* (2000): 176.

97. Cooke and Maule, *Royal Hospital for Seamen* (1789): 106–7; ADM 68/823 and 6/824, NA; Bold, *Greenwich* (2000): 176.

98. ADM 67/21, NA; Bold, *Greenwich* (2000): 209 n. 43.

99. Written description by Crisp, L.A. A1/9, RSA; Minutes of the Society, vol. 2, pp. 13, 16 March 1757, RSA; See also 30, 6 April 1757, RSA; Eimer, "James 'Athenian' Stuart" (1994): 131.

100. Croft-Murray, *Decorative Painting in England*, vol. 2 (1970): 196–97.

101. Stuart to Thomas Anson, 25 September 1770, Lichfield Ms. D615/P(S)/1/6/28; Bristol, "Society of Dilettanti" (July 2000): 48–49.

102. Croft-Murray, *Decorative Painting in England*, vol. 2 (1970): 196–97; Robinson, *Shugborough* (1989): 19–20, 22, 67; *Shugborough, Staffordshire* (1980): 8–9.

103. 1767, Lichfield Ms. D615/E(H)1/2.

104. Ibid.

105. Croft-Murray, *Decorative Painting in England*, vol. 2 (1970): 54, 177–78.

106. Cooke and Maule, *Royal Hospital for Seamen* (1789): 106; ADM 68/820, NA; Bold, *Greenwich* (2000): 176–77.

107. Beard, *Craftsmen and Interior Decoration* (1981): 256.

108. James Stuart to [?], n.d., Letters from Surveyors, Architects, and others as to Works, ADM 65/106, NA; ADM 67/12, Minutes of General Court Meetings, entry for 4 July 1781, 7–8, 11–12, NA; Copy of a letter to John Ibbetson, Ms. New/1/1/1, RIBA Library; L. Lewis, "Architects of the Chapel" (1947): 260–61; and Bold, *Greenwich* (2000): 173.

109. Beard, *Craftsmen and Interior Decoration* (1981): 256; Gunnis, *Dictionary of British Sculptors* (1968): 129.

110. Robinson, *Shugborough* (1989): 61.

111. Robinson, *Spencer House* (2002): 1; Jackson-Stops, "Spencer House, London" (29 November 1990): 42–47; Friedman, *Spencer House* (1993): 186–87, 344–45.

112. Worsley, "Hornby Castle" (29 June 1989): 189.

113. John Harris, "Newly Acquired Designs by James Stuart" (1979): 77.

114. Egerton Ms. 3497, fol. 64, *passim*, BL.

115. James Stuart to [?], n.d., Letters from Surveyors, Architects, and others as to Works, ADM 65/106, NA; ADM 67/12, Minutes of General Court Meetings, entry for 4 July 1781, 7–8, 11–12, NA; Copy of a letter to John Ibbetson, Ms. New/1/1/1, RIBA Library; L. Lewis, "Architects of the Chapel" (1947): 260–61; and Bold, *Greenwich* (2000): 173.

116. Ms. E5/24/5, RIBA Library; L. Lewis, "Architects of the Chapel" (1947): 261; Bristol, "Stuart and the Genesis of the Greek Revival" (1997): 340–41.

117. ADM 68/881, NA; Bold, *Greenwich* (2000): 173.

118. Ms. E5/28/4 RIBA Library; L. Lewis, "Architects of the Chapel" (1947): 263; Bristol, "Stuart and the Genesis of the Greek Revival" (1997): 349 n. 1066.

119. ADM 68/813, NA; Gunnis, *Dictionary of British Sculptors* (1968): 129.

120. Gunnis, *Dictionary of British Sculptors* (1968): 129.

121. Waterhouse, *Painting in Britain* (1978): 192–95; Belsey, "Arthur Devis," *Grove Art Online.* Oxford University Press, http://www.groveart.com/, accessed 22 November 2005.

122. Minutes of General Court Meetings, 27 January 1777, 218, ADM 67/11, NA; Bold, *Greenwich* (2000): 153.

123. Colvin, *Biographical Dictionary of British Architects* (1996): 315–16.

124. L. Lewis, "Architects of the Chapel" (1947): 260–67.

125. ADM 65/106, NA; L. Lewis, "Architects of the Chapel" (1947): 261.

126. Edwards, "Edward Edwards" (June 1930): 840–50.

127. Joseph Ayloffe to Philip Yorke, second Earl of Hardwicke, 1 February 1771, Add. Ms. 35,609: 304, and Edward Edwards to Hardwicke, 2 February 1771, Add. Ms. 35,609: 305, BL.

128. Kerry Bristol, "22 Portman Square" (2001): 78; Robinson and Thompson, "Matthew Boulton's Mechanical Paintings" (1970): 503–5.

129. "Glass Painters of Birmingham" (1927): 63.

130. Robinson and Thompson, "Matthew Boulton's Mechanical Paintings" (1970): 504.

131. Mrs. Montagu to Matthew Boulton, 25 July 1778, Boulton Papers, old number Ms. Box 330, No. 13, as cited in Bristol, "22 Portman Square" (2001): 78.

132. Colvin, *Biographical Dictionary of British Architects* (1995): 355.

133. Stuart to Thomas Anson, 19 June 1764, Lichfield Ms. D615/P(S)/1/6/7; Sheppard, ed., *Survey of London,* vols. 29–30. (1960): 142–43.

134. Mr. Goodals Acct of Bills paid by him: Bills of the Late Tho. Anson Esqe., Lichfield Ms. D615/P(S)/1/6/54; Bristol, "Stuart and the Genesis of the Greek Revival" (1997): 297.

135. C. Hoare & Co. Ledger 93 (1775–1776), fol. 99, 26 June 1775, payment of £41.0.0; ledger 95 (1775–1777), fol. 38, 15 March 1776, payment of £54.0.0 and 18 June 1776, payment of £101.13.6; Ledger 96 (1776–1778), fol. 451, 14 April 1777, payment of £31.10.0 and 28 April 1777, payment of £23.8.7; Ledger 99 (1778–1779), fol. 46, 31 May 1777, payment of £50.0.0, fol. 47, 28 October 1777, payment of £135.16.6 and fol. 48, 19 March 1778, payment of £100.0.0, all as cited in Bristol, "22 Portman Square" (2001): 74.

136. Mrs. Montagu to Leonard Smelt, 25 April 1780, Montagu Papers MO 2025, Henry E. Huntington Library, as cited in Bristol, "22 Portman Square" (2001): 79.

137. Mrs. Montagu to Matthew Boulton, 5 September [1780], Boulton Papers, old number Ms. Box 330, No. 30, as cited in Bristol, "22 Portman Square" (2001): 77.

138. Bristol, "Stuart and the Genesis of the Greek Revival" (1997): 271 n. 824.

139. 1768, Lichfield Ms. D615/E(H)1/2.

140. Stuart to Thomas Anson, 31 June 1769, Lichfield Ms. D615/P(S)/1/6/26.

141. Reeves-Smyth, *Irish Country Houses* (1994): 29–32; Jackson-Stops, "Mount Stewart—I" (6 March 1980): 648.

142. Colvin, *Biographical Dictionary of British Architects* (1995): 385–87; Duffy, *James Gandon* (1999): 86; Mulvany, *Life of James Gandon.* (1969).

143. Duffy, *James Gandon* (1999): 100, 263–64.

144. National Library of Ireland MS. 20016, as cited in McParland, *James Gandon* (1985): 206; Bristol, "22 Portman Square" (2001): 78–80.

145. C. Hoare & Co. Ledger 7 (1780–1781), fol. 65, 3 March 1780, as cited in Bristol, "22 Portman Square" (2001): 80.

146. Robinson, *Shugborough* (1989): 90.

147. Bold, *Greenwich* (2000): 209.

148. Beard and Gilbert, *Dictionary of English Furniture Makers* (1986): 355–57; Heal, *London Furniture Makers* (1953): 64–65.

149. Sotheby's, London, "The Spencer House Palm Room Seat Furniture," *Important English Furniture,* sale cat. (29 November 2002): 158–66, lots 154–55.

150. Thornton and Hardy, "Spencer Furniture at Althorp—I" (June 1968): 448.

151. Ibid, 446; Coleridge, "Chippendale" (December 1960): 252–56; Thornton, "A Very Special Year" (June 1978): 138–43.

152. Thornton and Hardy, "Spencer Furniture at Althorp—I" (June 1968): 44; Warren, "Nuneham Courtney, Oxfordshire" (29 November 1913): 755.

153. Gunnis, *Dictionary of British Sculptors* (1968): 175–76; Beard, *Craftsmen and Interior Decoration* (1981): 261; "Courtiers and Classics: The Gosset Family," (9 May 1985): 1282–83.

154. Stuart to Thomas Anson, [June or July 1764], Lichfield Ms. D615/P(S)/1/6/8A.

155. *Daily Advertiser,* 3 April 1760, p. 3122.

156. Croft-Murray, *Decorative Painting in England,* vol. 2 (1970): 212–13.

157. Ibid., 211–13; Bristol, "Stuart and the Genesis of the Greek Revival" (1997): 30–31, 34–35; Graves, *Society of Artists* (1907): 308; Robertson and Dance, "Joseph Goupy" (December 1988): 356.

158. H.A., "Traits for the Life of the Late Athenian Stuart" (February 1788): 95; Smith, *Nollekens and His Times* (1949): 10; Copy letter, Taylor to James Gandon, 19 August 1809, Add. Ms. 22,152: 29, BL; Stuart and Revett, *Antiquities of Athens,* vol. 4 (1816): xxi–xxii; Oppé, "Memoirs of Thomas Jones" (1946–48): 74; Bristol, "Stuart and the Genesis of the Greek Revival" (1997): 30–31; Croft-Murray, *Decorative Painting in England,* vol. 2 (1970): 211–13.

159. Robertson and Dance, "Joseph Goupy" (December 1988): 356; Bristol, "Stuart and the Genesis of the Greek Revival" (1997): 34–37.

160. Cooke and Maule, *Royal Hospital for Seaman* (1789): 102; Bold, *Greenwich* (2000): 173.

161. James Stuart to [?], n.d., Letters from Surveyors, Architects, and others as to Works, ADM 65/106, NA; ADM 67/12, Minutes of General Court Meetings, entry for 4 July 1781, 7–8, 11–12, NA; Copy of a letter to John Ibbetson, Ms. New/1/1/1, RIBA Library; L. Lewis, "Architects of the Chapel" (1947): 260–61; and Bold, *Greenwich* (2000): 173.

162. 1767, Lichfield Ms. D615/E(H)1/2.

163. Graves, *Society of Artists* (1907): 248. See *Minutes*, vol. 3 (6 February 1774), archive of the Society of Dilettanti, London; Martelli, *Jemmy Twitcher* (1962): 94; Abbott, *John Hawkesworth* (1982): 121; Smith, *European Vision* (1985): 13.

164. Colvin, *Biographical Dictionary of British Architects* (1995): 466–70.

165. 1768, Lichfield Ms. D615/E(H)1/2.

166. [Holland], *Resolutions of the Associated Architects* [1793]: 19–20; Hartley, *Account of the Method of Securing Buildings* (1774).

167. Mrs Montagu to Matthew Boulton, 1 October 1778, Boulton Papers, old number Ms. Box 330, No. 15, as cited in Bristol, "22 Portman Square" (2001): 80. See also Mrs. Montagu to Mrs. Robinson, 29 December 1779, Add. Ms. 40,663, fols. 96–98, BL; Blunt, ed., *Mrs Montagu, "Queen of the Blues,"* vol. 2 (1923): 64–65; Bristol, "22 Portman Square" (2001): 74.

168. Haxby and Malden, "Thomas Haxby of York" (1983): 59–73.

169. Compton, *Newby Hall* (2004): 15.

170. Gunnis, *Dictionary of British Sculptors* (1968): 194–95.

171. L. Harris, *Robert Adam and Kedleston* (1987): 27, nos. 11–14.

172. 1767, Lichfield Ms. D615/E(H)1/2; Bristol, "Stuart and the Genesis of the Greek Revival" (1997): 271.

173. Colvin, *Biographical Dictionary of British Architects* (1995): 653.

174. Bristol, "Stuart and the Genesis of the Greek Revival" (1997): 303–4; Cousins, "Athenian Stuart's Doric Porticoes" (2004): 50.

175. Cousins, "Athenian Stuart's Doric Porticoes" (2004): 50–52.

176. Watson, "John Holmes" (March 2003): 289–301; Watson, "John Holmes" (December 2003): 643–53.

177. O. Harris, "Greenwich Hospital Clock" (Summer 1998): 172.

178. Watson, "John Holmes" (March 2003): 295.

179. O. Harris, "Greenwich Hospital Clock" (Summer 1998): 172.

180. L. Lewis, "Architects of the Chapel" (1947): 263.

181. Cooke and Maule, *Royal Hospital for Seamen* (1789): 109; O. Harris, "Greenwich Hospital Clock" (Summer 1998): 172.

182. James Stuart to [?], n.d., Letters from Surveyors, Architects, and others as to Works, ADM 65/106, NA; Copy of a letter to John Ibbetson, Ms. New/1/1/1, RIBA Library; L. Lewis, "Architects of the Chapel" (1947): 260–61; and Bold, *Greenwich* (2000): 173.

183. Gunnis, *Dictionary of British Sculptors* (1968): 208.

184. John Hooper to Thomas Anson, 1 November 1761, Lichfield Ms. D615/P(S)/1/6/30.

185. Worsley, "Nuneham Park Revisited—II" (10 January 1985): 65.

186. Mortimer, *Universal Director* (1763): 49; Masons' Company List of Freemen 1677–1795, Ms. 5308: 31, Guildhall Library.

187. John Horobin to Marquess of Rockingham, 12 September to 24 December 1763, Wentworth Woodhouse Muniments R1-32, Sheffield Archives; Paget, ed., "Walpole's Journals of Visits to Country Seats" (1927–28): 71; Bristol, "Stuart and the Genesis of the Greek Revival" (1997): 240–41.

188. Egerton Ms. 3497, fol. 72, BL; Bristol, "James Stuart and the London Building Trades" (2003): 3.

189. Bold, *Greenwich* (2000): 209.

190. Gunnis, *Dictionary of British Sculptors* (1968): 218.

191. ADM 68/876 and 67/11, NA; ART/3, fol. 39, NMM; Bold, *Greenwich* (2000): 167.

192. Croft-Murray, *Decorative Painting in England,* vol. 2 (1970): 53, 55–56, 67–68, 227–28; Roworth, *Angelica Kauffman* (1992).

193. McParland, "Rathfarnham Castle" (9 September 1982): 737.

194. Robinson and Thompson, "Matthew Boulton's Mechanical Paintings" (August 1970): 497–507.

195. Croft-Murray, *Decorative Painting in England,* vol. 2 (1970): 211–13, 228; L. Lawrence, "Stuart and Revett" (1938–39): 142.

196. Bristol, "Stuart and the Genesis of the Greek Revival" (1997): 319; Robinson and Thompson, "Matthew Boulton's Mechanical Paintings" (August 1970): 497–507.

197. See for example, Croft-Murray, *Decorative Painting in England,* vol. 2 (1970): 229; Blunt, ed., *Mrs. Montagu, "Queen of the Blues,"* vol. 2 (1923): 241; Waagen, *Galleries and Cabinets of Art* (1857): 282.

198. Robinson and Thompson, "Matthew Boulton's Mechanical Paintings" (August 1970): 504, 506.

199. Hawkins, *Medallic Illustrations* (1969): 440–41, 447; Eimer, *British Commemorative Medals* (1987): 674, 676, 679; Betts, et al., *American Colonial History* (1972): 422, 429. Eimer, *Pingo Family* (1998): 236.

200. ADM 68/876, NA; Gunnis, *Dictionary of British Sculptors* (1968): 236.

201. James Stuart to [?], n.d., Letters from Surveyors, Architects, and others as to Works, ADM 65/106, NA; ADM 67/12, Minutes of General Court Meetings, entry for 4 July 1781, 7–8, 11–12, NA; Ms. New/1/1/1, RIBA Library; L. Lewis, "Architects of the Chapel" (1947): 260–61; and Bold, *Greenwich* (2000): 173.

202. Bold, *Greenwich* (2000): 173.

203. Gunnis, *Dictionary of British Sculptors* (1968): 236; ADM 68/813, NA.

204. Richard Lawrence to John Ibbetson, 19 August 1786. Ms. New/1/1/9, RIBA Library, London; Bristol, "Stuart and the Genesis of the Greek Revival" (1997): 352. On this Lewis says the estimate was 200 pounds; L. Lewis, "Architects of the Chapel" (1947): 263–64.

205. Richard Lawrence to John Ibbetson, 10 November 1786. Ms. New/1/1/10, RIBA Library, London; L. Lewis, "Architects of the Chapel" (1947): 263.

206. ADM 68/819, NA; Gunnis, *Dictionary of British Sculptors* (1968): 236.

207. Bold, *Greenwich* (2000): 176; ADM 68/813, 68/816, and 68/818, NA.

208. L. Lewis, "Architects of the Chapel" (1947): 261.

209. Gunnis, *Dictionary of British Sculptors* (1968): 244; Beard, *Craftsmen and Interior Decoration* (1981): 269; Hussey, *English Country Houses: Early Georgian 1715–1760* (1955): 198.

210. Clarke, "Medallions of Concord" (August 1981): 611–16.

211. Batey, "William Mason" (1973): 11–25; Worsley, "Hornby Castle" (29 June 1989): 188–93.

212. "Nuneham Courtenay Chapel" (22 April 1931); Burney, *Diary and Letters of Madame D'Arblay,* vol. 1 (1892): 385; Batey, "Nuneham Park—I" (5 September 1968): 542.

213. Worsley, "Nuneham Park Revisited—II" (10 January 1985): 64–67.

214. February 1765 or 1766, Lichfield Ms. D615/E(H)1/2.

215. Croft-Murray, *Decorative Painting in England,* vol. 2 (1970): 244–45; Graves, *Society of Artists* (1907): 165.

216. Cooke and Maule, *Royal Hospital for Seamen* (1789): 107; *Pictorial Handbook of London* (1854): 728.

217. Colvin, *Biographical Dictionary of British Architects* (1995): 653–55.

218. Croft-Murray, *Decorative Painting in England,* vol. 2 (1970): 284; Cousins, "Athenian Stuart's Doric Porticoes" (2004): 48–54.

219. Bold, *Greenwich* (2000): 209.

220. Whitley, *Artists and Their Friends,* vol. 1 (1928): 27; Bristol, "Stuart and the Genesis of the Greek Revival" (1997): 37; Artnet, "George Michael Moser" (2000/2005).

221. Eimer, "James 'Athenian' Stuart" (1994): 131; Mallett, "Nicholas Crisp" (1973): 28–32, 92–96, 170–74.

222. Colvin, *Biographical Dictionary of British Architects* (1996): 678–85; Richardson, *Robert Mylne Architect and Engineer* (1955).

223. ADM 67/11, NA; Bold, *Greenwich* (2000): 167.

224. Richardson, ed., *Catalogue of the Drawings Collection of the Royal Institute of British Architects,* vol. *S* (1976): 126.

225. Robert Mylne to John Ibbetson, 15 December 1781, Letters from Surveyors, Architects, and others as to Works, ADM 65/106, NA; Richardson, ed., *Catalogue of the Drawings Collection of the Royal Institute of British Architects,* vol. *S* (1976): 126; L. Lewis, "Architects of the Chapel" (1947): 261–62. See also Robert Mylne to James Stuart, 6 July 1782, Letters from Surveyors, Architects, and others as to Works, ADM 65/106, NA.

226. Minutes of General Court Meetings, 3 September 1782, 46–48, ADM 67/12, NA; Lewis, "The Architects of the Chapel at Greenwich Hospital" (1947): 260–67; Bold, *Greenwich* (2000): 175.

227. Minutes of General Court Meetings, 10 September 1782, 49–50, ADM 67/12, and 7 April 1784, 82–83, ADM 67/12, NA; Bristol, "Stuart and the Genesis of the Greek Revival" (1997): 340–43.

228. Watkin, *Athenian Stuart* (1982): 52–54; Colvin, *Biographical Dictionary of British Architects* (1995): 701–4.

229. Manuscripts New/1/8/2(i) and New/1/8/8(i), RIBA Library, London; ADM 65/106, NA; L. Lewis, "Architects of the Chapel" (1947): 262.

230. L. Lewis, "Architects of the Chapel" (1947): 263.

231. Manuscript ADM 67/12, Minutes of General Court Meetings, entries for 22 February and 30 October 1788, 162–63, NA; L. Lewis, "Architects of the Chapel" (1947): 263–64.

232. William Newton to Benjamin West, 23 October 1788, Ms. New/1/1/19, RIBA British Architectural Library, London; Bristol, "Stuart and the Genesis of the Greek Revival" (1997): 343–46; L. Lewis, "Architects of the Chapel" (1947): 264–65.

233. Ms. New/1/8/8(i), RIBA British Architectural Library, London; L. Lewis, "Architects of the Chapel" (1947): 264.

234. Pollio, *Architecture of M. Vitruvius Pollio* (1791): note to advertisement; Watkin, *Athenian Stuart* (1982): 52–53.

235. "Obituary of Considerable Persons" (August 1790): 766; Ms. New/1/8/8(ii), RIBA British Architectural Library, London; Bristol, "Stuart and the Genesis of the Greek Revival" (1997): 347–50.

236. Gunnis, *Dictionary of British Sculptors* (1968): 276–79; Whinney, *Sculpture in Britain* (1988): 287; Bristol, "Stuart and the Genesis of the Greek Revival" (1997): 274; Kenworthy-Browne, "Establishing a Reputation" (7 June 1979): 1844–48; Kenworthy-Browne, "Genius Recognised" (14 June 1979): 1930–31.

237. Smith, *Nollekens and His Times* (1949): 5, 10, 19–20; Kenworthy-Browne, "Genius Recognised" (14 June 1979): 1930–31.

238. Howard, "Boy on a Dolphin" (June 1964): 177–89; Friedman, *Spencer House* (1993): 156.

239. Nollekens' letters to Anson are Joseph Nollekens to Thomas Anson, 26 July 1765–19 April 1768, Lichfield Ms. D615/P(S)/1/6/1 through 6; Bristol, "Stuart and the Genesis of the Greek Revival" (1997): 274. See also Stuart to Thomas Anson, [before 23 August 1764], Lichfield Ms. D615/P(S)/1/6/10, and Stuart to Thomas Anson, 23 September 1769, Lichfield Ms. D615/P(S)/1/6/27.

240. Joseph Nollekens to Thomas Anson, 9 December 1767, Lichfield Ms. D615/P(S)/1/6/5, and 19 April 1768, Lichfield Ms. D615/P(S)/1/6/6; Kenworthy-Browne, "Establishing a Reputation" (7 June 1979): 1844–48; (14 June 1979): 1930–31. V&A, acc. no. A.59–1940.

241. Lichfield Ms. D615/P(S)/1/6/1; Bristol, "Society of Dilettanti" (July 2000): 46–54; Lees-Milne, "Shugborough—I" (April 1967): 212.

242. John Dick to Thomas Anson, 14 October 1765, Lichfield Ms. D615/P(A)/2; Bristol, "Stuart and the Genesis of the Greek Revival" (1997): 274; Robinson, *Shugborough* (1989): 62.

243. Penny, "Lord Rockingham's Sculpture Collection" (1991): 21–34.

244. Colvin, *Biographical Dictionary of British Architects* (1995): 708–9.

245. Stuart to Thomas Anson, 6 October 1764, Lichfield Ms. D615/P(S)/1/6/15.

246. Stuart to Thomas Anson, 19 June 1764, Lichfield Ms. D615/P(S)/1/6/7; Stuart to Thomas Anson, [before 23 August 1764], Lichfield Ms. D615/P(S)/1/6/10; Stuart to Thomas Anson, [September 1764], Lichfield Ms. D615/P(S)/1/6/13; Bristol, "Stuart and the London Building Trades" (2003): 7. See also Stuart to Thomas Anson, [October or November 1764], Lichfield Ms. D615/P(S)/1/6/16; and Stuart to Thomas Anson, [1 December 1764], Lichfield Ms. D615/P(S)/1/6/19.

247. Stuart to Thomas Anson, [October or November 1764], Lichfield Ms. D615/P(S)/1/6/16; Bristol, "Stuart and the London Building Trades" (2003): 7–8.

248. Undated, Lichfield Ms. D615/E(H)1/2.

249. "Mr. Goodals Acct of Bills paid by Him: Bills of the Late Tho. Anson Esqe.," [1773], Lichfield Ms. D615/P(S)/1/6/54; Bristol, "Stuart and the Genesis of the Greek Revival" (1997): 297–98.

250. Bristol, "Stuart and the London Building Trades" (2003): 10.

251. C. Hoare & Co., Ledger 16 (1783–1784), fol. 244, as cited in Bristol, "22 Portman Square" (2001): 82.

252. Charles Pratt to Elizabeth Pratt, 20 September 1780, MS U840 C7/8, Centre for Kentish Studies, Maidstone. See also Charles Pratt to Frances Stewart [1779], MS U840 C3/2.

253. 1768, Lichfield Ms. D615/E(H)1/2.

254. Beard, Craftsmen and Interior Decoration (1981): 274.

255. C. Hoare & Co. Ledger 95 (1775–1777), fol. 38, 3 July 1776, as cited in Bristol, "22 Portman Square" (2001): 74, 84 n. 20..

256. James Stuart to [?], n.d., Letters from Surveyors, Architects, and others as to Works, ADM 65/106, NA; ADM 67/12, Minutes of General Court Meetings, entry for 4 July 1781, 7–8, 11–12, NA; Copy of a letter to John Ibbetson, Ms. New/1/1/1, RIBA Library; L. Lewis, "Architects of the Chapel" (1947): 260–61; and Bold, Greenwich (2000): 173.

257. As quoted in L. Lewis, "Architects of the Chapel" (1947): 260–67.

258. Beard, Craftsmen and Interior Decoration (1981): 274; Jourdain, English Decorative Plasterwork (1933): xii; Beard, Decorative Plasterwork (1975): 231–32.

259. James Stuart to [?], n.d., Letters from Surveyors, Architects, and others as to Works, ADM 65/106, NA; ADM 67/12, Minutes of General Court Meetings, entry for 4 July 1781, 7–8, 11–12, NA; Copy of a letter to John Ibbetson, Ms. New/1/1/1, RIBA Library; L. Lewis, "Architects of the Chapel" (1947): 260–61; and Bold, Greenwich (2000): 173.

260. L. Lewis, "Architects of the Chapel" (1947): 261.

261. Stuart to the Board, 24 December 1784, ADM 67/12, p. 102, NA; Bristol, "Stuart and the Genesis of the Greek Revival" (1997): 351 n. 1074.

262. Bold, Greenwich (2000): 176; ADM 67/615, NA.

263. Bold, Greenwich (2000): 176; ADM 67/818 and 67/821, NA.

264. Colvin, Biographical Dictionary of British Architects (1995): 751, 859–60.

265. MD 6610/3, MD 6610/6, and MD 6610/1, Sheffield Archives.

266. Bold, Greenwich (2000): 209.

267. MD 6610/5, Sheffield Archives.

268. Bristol, "Stuart and the Genesis of the Greek Revival" (1997): 230.

269. Eimer, Pingo Family (1998). For letters to Anson regarding Pingo's appointment at the Mint, see Stuart to Thomas Anson, 27 May 1769, Lichfield Ms. D615/P (S)1/6/24, and 17 June 1769, Lichfield Ms. D615/P(S)/1/6/26.

270. Eimer, "James 'Athenian' Stuart" (1994); Eimer, "Society's Concern with 'The Medallic Art'" (1991): 753–62; Eimer, Pingo Family (1998); Bristol, "Stuart and the Genesis of the Greek Revival" (1997): 214–26.

271. Croft-Murray, Decorative Painting in England, vol. 2 (1970): 54, 258–62.

272. John Hodges to John Wyatt, 18 July 1776, Boulton Papers, old number Ms., No. 140, Letter Book G, p. 664, as cited in Bristol, "22 Portman Square" (2001): 78; Robinson and Thompson, "Matthew Boulton's Mechanical Paintings" (1970): 504.

273. Boulton and Fothergill to Mrs. Montagu, 18 November 1779, Boulton Papers, Ms. 3782/1/11, p. 498, and Mrs. Montagu to Matthew Boulton, 22 November 1779, Boulton Papers, old number Ms., Box 330, No. 18, as cited in Bristol, "22 Portman Square" (2001): 78.

274. Beard, Craftsmen and Interior Decoration (1981): 215; Croft-Murray, Decorative Painting in England, vol. 2 (1970): 188.

275. Watkin, Athenian Stuart (1982): 49.

276. Cooke and Maule, Royal Hospital for Seamen (1789): 105–7; Pictorial Handbook of London (1854): 728.

277. Papworth, "William Newton and the Chapel" (27 August 1891): 418; Bold, Greenwich (2000): 176.

278. Beard, Craftsmen and Interior Decoration (1981): 277–78.

279. Bristol, "Stuart and the Genesis of the Greek Revival" (1997): 328.

280. John Augustus Richter, 23 March 1782, Ms. New/1/1/3, RIBA Library, London.

281. L. Lewis, "Architects of the Chapel" (1947): 261–63; Bristol, "Stuart and the Genesis of the Greek Revival" (1997): 350 n. 1072.

282. ADM 67/820 and 67/823, NA; Bold, Greenwich (2000): 176. Bold gives the date of the installation of the pilasters and columns as 1788.

283. Colvin, Biographical Dictionary of British Architects (1995): 832; Bristol, "Stuart and the Genesis of the Greek Revival" (1997): 331–32.

284. Cooke and Maule, Royal Hospital for Seamen (1789): 117; Bold, Greenwich (2000): 208–9.

285. ADM 68/876 and 67/11, NA; ART/3, fol. 39, NMM; Bold, Greenwich (2000): 167.

286. ADM 67/11, NA; Bold, Greenwich (2000): 167–68.

287. Minutes of the Society, vol. 4, 27 February 1760, and vol. 5, 5 March 1760, RSA; Wood, History of the Royal Society of Arts (1913): 228–29.

288. Graves, *Society of Artists* (1907): 248. See *Minutes*, vol. 3 (6 February 1774), archive of the Society of Dilettanti, London; Martelli, *Jemmy Twitcher* (1962): 94; Abbott, *John Hawkesworth* (1982): 121, 151; Smith, *European Vision* (1985): 13; Sandwich to David Garrick, 16 April 1773, Ms. SAN/F/36/10, National Maritime Museum.

289. Beard, *Craftsmen and Interior Decoration* (1981): 279–83.

290. Wentworth Woodhouse Muniments A-1201, A-1000 (1761), and A-1098, 2, 42, Sheffield Archive; Bristol, "Stuart and the London Building Trades" (2003): 3; Binney, "Wentworth Woodhouse Revisited—II" (24 March 1983): 710.

291. Friedman, "Spencer House" (August 1987): 87; Friedman, *Spencer House* (1993): 186–87, 344–45

292. Stuart to Thomas Anson, 17 September, 1766, Lichfield Ms. D615/P(S)/1/6/21; Survey of London, *Parish of St. James Westminster*, vol. 29–30 (1960): 143.

293. "Mr. Goodals Acct of Bills paid by Him: Bills of the Late Tho. Anson Esqe.," [1773], Lichfield Ms. D615/P(S)/1/6/54; Bristol, "Stuart and the Genesis of the Greek Revival" (1997): 297.

294. Robinson, *Shugborough* (1989): 61.

295. Egerton Ms. 3497, fol. 64, 67, 69, BL; Bristol, "Stuart and the London Building Trades" (2003): 3; Sykes, *Private Palaces* (1989): 185.

296. Colvin, *Biographical Dictionary of British Architects* (1995): 835–36; Survey of London, *Parish of St. James Westminster*, vol. 29–30 (1960): 90–91, 142–43, 192.

297. Stuart to Thomas Anson, 19 June 1764, Lichfield Ms. D615/P(S)/1/6/7; see also Stuart to Thomas Anson, [September 1764], Lichfield Ms. D615/P(S)/1/6/13; 6 October 1764, Lichfield Ms. D615/P(S)/1/6/15; [October or November 1764], Lichfield Ms. D615/P(S)/1/6/17; [4 November 1764], Lichfield Ms. D615/P(S)/1/6/18. Bristol, "Stuart and the London Building Trades" (2003): 8.

298. Alexander Rouchead to Thomas Anson, 7 April 1770, Lichfield Ms. D615/P(S)/1/6/31.

299. Stuart to Thomas Anson, [before 23 August 1764], Lichfield Ms. D615/P (S)/1/6/10.

300. "Mr. Goodals Acct of Bills paid by Him," [1773], Lichfield Ms. D615/P(S)/1/6/54.

301. Worsley, "Nuneham Park Revisited—II" (10 January 1985): 66.

302. Stuart to Thomas Anson, 3 October 1772, Lichfield Ms. D615/P(S)/1/6/29.

303. E. Harris, "Cracking the Poussin Code" (May 2006): 30–31; Roscoe, "Peter Scheemakers" (2 October 1996–5 January 1997): 1–12; Roscoe, "Stuart and the Scheemakers Family" (September 1987): 178–84; Roscoe, "Peter Scheemakers" (1999): 163–304.

304. Graves, *Royal Academy of Arts*, vol. 7 (1905–6): 42.

305. Court Records, the Province of Massachusetts Bay, 1 February 1759, 495, as cited in Roscoe, "Stuart and the Scheemakers Family" (September 1987): 178.

306. Stuart to the Directors of the East India Company, 29 June 1763, India Office Records, Miscellaneous Letters Received, E/1/45, No. 150, as cited in Roscoe, "Stuart and the Scheemakers Family" (September 1987): 179; Bristol, "Stuart and the Genesis of the Greek Revival" (1997): 360–62.

307. Roscoe, "Stuart and the Scheemakers Family" (September 1987): 181.

308. James Stuart to Thomas Anson, 19 June 1764, Lichfield Ms. D615/P(S)/1/6/7; [June or July 1764], /1/6/8A and 8B; [before 23 August 1764], /1/6/10; 4 September 1764, /1/6/12. See also Roscoe, "Stuart and the Scheemakers Family" (September 1987): 182.

309. Daniel Wray to Philip Yorke, second Earl of Hardwicke, 30 August 1766, Add. Ms. 35,401, fol. 308, BL; Roscoe, "Stuart and the Scheemakers Family" (September 1987): 182.

310. John Yorke to Philip Yorke, second Earl of Hardwicke, 10 September 1778, Add. Ms. 35,375, fol. 219, BL; Bristol, "Stuart and the Genesis of the Greek Revival" (1997): 364–69.

311. Dibdin, *Bibliotheca Spenceriana*, vol. 3 (1814–15): 509, as cited in Friedman, *Spencer House* (1993): 134; Spencer, "Spencer House—I" (30 October 1926): 663.

312. Webb, "Chimney-Pieces by Scheemakers" (14 March 1957): 491–93; Jackson-Stops, "Spencer House" (29 November 1990): 42–47; Bradley and Pevsner, *London*, vol. 6 (2003): 623.

313. Robinson, *Spencer House* (2002): 26, 32.

314. Typescript notes for the restoration of Spencer House [by Joseph Friedman], V&A Furniture department, Red Box file Spencer House, n.p., n.d.

315. E. Harris, "Flair for the Grandiose" (2 September 1971): 548; Robinson, *Shugborough* (1989): 31; Yorke, *Travel Journal of Philip Yorke* (1968): 161; Bristol, "Stuart and the Genesis of the Greek Revival" (1997): 358–59.

316. Watkin, *Athenian Stuart* (1982): 28; For Stuart's drawing of the columns, see British Library, Add. Mss. 22,153, fol. 177; E. Harris, "Cracking the Poussin Code" (May 2006): 26–31.

317. Stuart to Thomas Anson, 10 July 1764, Lichfield Ms. D615/P(S)/1/6/9; [before 23 August 1764], Lichfield Ms. D615/P(S)/1/6/10; 1 September 1764, Lichfield Ms. D615/P(S)/1/6/11; 18 September 1764, Lichfield Ms. D615/P(S)/1/6/14; [October or November 1764], Lichfield Ms. D615/P(S)/1/6/17. See also Philip, Viscount Royston, to Philip Yorke, 1st Earl of Hardwicke, 22 August 1763, Hardwicke Papers, Add. Ms. 35,352, fol. 406 (verso), BL.

318. Robinson, *Shugborough* (1989): 25, 90; Stuart to Thomas Anson, 17 June 1769, Lichfield Ms. D615/P(S)/1/6/26.

319. Stuart to Thomas Anson, [September 1764], Lichfield Ms. D615/P(S)/1/6/13. Roscoe, "Stuart and the Scheemakers Family" (September 1987): 181; Survey of London, *Parish of St. James Westminster*, vol. 29–30 (1960): 142–43. See also Stuart to Thomas Anson, 6 October 1764, Lichfield Ms. D615/P(S)/1/6/15; Bristol, "Stuart and the Genesis of the Greek Revival (1997): 288.

320. Webb, "Chimney-Pieces by Scheemakers" (14 March 1957): 493; Friedman, *Spencer House* (1993): 186.

321-22. Graves, *Society of Artists* (1907): 227; Bristol, "Stuart and the Genesis of the Greek Revival" (1997): 369 n. 1123.

323. Bristol, "Society of Dilettanti" (July 2000): 53; Roscoe, "James 'Athenian' Stuart" (September 1987): 184.

324. Roscoe "Peter Scheemakers and Classical Sculpture" (1990): 169; Bristol, "Stuart and the Genesis of the Greek Revival" (1997): 370.

325. Roscoe, "Stuart and the Scheemakers Family" (September 1987): 184; Bristol, "Society of Dilettanti" (July 2000): 53; Whinney, *Sculpture in Britain* (1988): 238.

326. Stuart to 2nd Earl of Hardwicke, Add. Ms. 35.607, BL; Roscoe, "Stuart and the Scheemakers Family" (September 1987): 184;V&A 8458-1878.

327. Fitz-Gerald, "Temple of the Winds" (April 1968): 206–9; and Jackson-Stops, "Temple of the Winds" (1997): 25–29.

328. Stuart to Marquess of Rockingham, 28 September 1755,Wentworth Woodhouse Muniments R 1-70, Sheffield Archives.

329. Alexander Rouchead to Thomas Anson, 7 April 1770, Lichfield Ms. D615/P(S)/1/6/31.

330. Beard and Gilbert, eds: *Dictionary of English Furniture Makers* (1986): 793–98.

331. Ms. New/1/1/1, RIBA Library; Beard, *Craftsmen and Interior Decoration* (1981): 242; Papworth, "William Newton and the Chapel" (27 August 1891): 420.

332. C. Hoare & Co., Ledger 16 (1783–1784), fol. 239, as cited in Bristol, "22 Portman Square" (2001): 81.

333. Matthew Boulton to George Seddon, 10 January 1782, old number Letter Book I, p. 912, as cited in Beard and Gilbert, eds: *Dictionary of English Furniture Makers* (1986): 796.

334. Mrs. Montagu to Leonard Smelt, 25 April 1780, Montagu Papers MO 5025, Henry E. Huntington Library, San Marino, as cited in Bristol, "Stuart and the Genesis of the Greek Revival" (1997): 322.

335. 1768, Lichfield Ms. D615/E(H)1/2.

336. Stuart to Thomas Anson, 19 June 1764, Lichfield Ms. D615/P(S)/1/6/7; Stuart to Thomas Anson, [June or July 1764], Lichfield Ms. D615/P(S)/1/6/8A.

337. Stuart to Thomas Anson, 17 September 1766, Lichfield Ms. D615/P(S)/1/6/21.

338. Bristol, "Stuart and the Genesis of the Greek Revival" (1997): 321–22.

339. Croft-Murray, *Decorative Painting in England*, vol. 2 (1970): 279–80; Houfe, *Dictionary of British Illustrators* (1978): 458.

340. C. Hoare & Co. Ledger 11 (1781–1782), fol. 441, 30 March 1782, as cited in Bristol, "22 Portman Square" (2001): 81, 85 n. 84.

341. Gunnis, *Dictionary of British Sculptors* (1968): 361.

342. Friedman, "Spencer House" (August 1987): 83; Friedman, *Spencer House* (1993): 186–87, 344–45.

343. 1764, Lichfield Ms. D615/E(H)1/2.

344. February 1765 or 1766, ibid.

345. 1767, ibid.

346. Colvin, *Biographical Dictionary of British Architects* (1995): 990–92; Oswald, "Blithfield," pts. II and III (4 November 1954): 1576–79; (11 November 1954): 1664–67.

347. Robinson, *Shugborough* (1989): 85.

348. 1768, Lichfield Ms. D615/E(H)1/2.

349. Colvin, *Biographical Dictionary of British Architects* (1995): 1009–10.

350. Friedman, *Spencer House* (1993): 19–20, 67–68, 86, 89, 99, 107, 122, 134–39.

351. Ibid., 67–68, 76, 81, 84, 88–89, 99, 102, 107, 122, 160–63, 189, 344–45.

352.Vardy received £3,636.6.10 for his own compensation and £12,701.11. 6 to cover the bills of various tradesmen; Friedman, *Spencer House* (1993): 344–45.

353. Colvin, *Biographical Dictionary of British Architects* (1995): 1010; Friedman, *Spencer House* (1993): 74–75.

354. Friedman, *Spencer House* (1993): 19–20; Robinson, *Spencer House* (2002): 1, 3, 7–16.

355.Wilk, ed., *Western Furniture* (1996): 114.

356. Friedman, *Spencer House* (1993): 186–87, 344–45.

357. Beard, *Craftsmen and Interior Decoration* (1981): 288–89; Philip,Viscount Royston, to Philip Yorke, 1st Earl of Hardwicke, 22 August 1763, Hardwicke Papers, Add. Ms. 35,352, fol. 407 (verso) (Yorke), BL; E. Harris, "Flair for the Grandiose" (2 September 1971): 546–50; Bristol, "Stuart and the Genesis of the Greek Revival"

(1997): 269; Godber, "Marchioness Grey of West Park," (1968): 161; Robinson, *Shugborough* (1990): 29.

358. George, Lord Lyttelton to Mrs. Montagu, October 1758, Montagu Papers MO 1280 21, Henry E. Huntington Library, San Marino, as cited in Bristol, "Stuart and the Genesis of the Greek Revival" (1997): 301; McCarthy, "Documents on the Greek Revival in Architecture" (November 1972): 765.

359. Beard, "Decorators and Furniture Makers" (1993): 88, 92; E. Harris, *Genius of Robert Adam* (2001): 42.

360. Building bills no. 18, March 1761, Croome Archives, Croome Estate Office, Worcestershire.

361. Beard and Gilbert, eds., *Dictionary of English Furniture Makers* (1986): 923–28; Heal, *London Furniture Makers* (1953): 189; Beard, "Vile and Cobb" (June 1990): 1394–1405.

362. Egerton Ms. 3497, fol. 64, *passim,* BL.

363. 1767, Lichfield Ms. D615/E(H)1/2; Robinson, *Shugborough* (1989): 85.

364. Stuart to Thomas Anson, 10 July 1764, Lichfield Ms. D615/P(S)/1/6/9; Bristol, "Stuart and the Genesis of the Greek Revival" (1997): 282; Lees-Milne, "Shugborough—I" (April 1967): 212.

365. Stuart to Thomas Anson, [before 23 August 1764], Lichfield Ms. D615/P(S)/1/6/10; 1 September 1764, Lichfield Ms. D615/P(S)/1/6/11; 18 September 1764, Lichfield Ms. D615/P(S)/1/6/14; Roscoe, "Stuart and the Scheemakers Family" (September 1987): 180.

366. Stuart to Thomas Anson, 19 June 1764, Lichfield Ms. D615/P(S)/1/6/7; [June or July 1764], Lichfield Ms. D615/P(S)/1/6/8A; 10 July 1764, Lichfield Ms. D615/P(S)/1/6/9.

367. Stuart to Thomas Anson, 18 September 1764, Lichfield Ms. D615/P(S)/1/6/14.

368. 1767, Lichfield Ms. D615/E(H)1/2.

369. Meteyard, *Life of Josiah Wedgwood* (1980); Reilly, *Josiah Wedgwood* (1992).

370. Josiah Wedgwood to Thomas Bentley, 24–26 December 1770, Keele University Library E25-18335), reprinted in Meteyard, *Life of Josiah Wedgwood,* vol. 2 (1980): 221–23; Reilly, *Wedgwood,* vol. 1 (1989): 446.

371. Reilly and Savage, *Wedgwood Portrait Medallions* (1973): 10–12, 315; Thomas, "Josiah Wedgwood's Portrait Medallions" (June 1963): 51.

372. Oswald, "Blithfield—III" (11 November 1954): 1664–67.

373. Josiah Wedgwood to Thomas Bentley, 24 December 1770 (Keele University Library E25-18334), cited in Goodison, *Matthew Boulton: Ormolu* (2002): 101, reprinted in Meteyard, *Life of Josiah Wedgwood,* vol. 2 (1980): 221–23.

374. Boulton and Fothergill to Josiah Wedgwood, 9 January 1771, Boulton Papers, Ms. 3782/1/9, no. 7; James Stuart to Josiah Wedgwood, 24 January 1771, Leith Hill Place Collection; Josiah Wedgwood to James Stuart, February 1771, E25-18339, Keele University Library; Josiah Wedgwood to Thomas Bentley, 3 April 1771, Leith Hill Place Collection; as cited in Reilly, *Wedgwood,* vol. 1 (1989): 446–47; Josiah Wedgwood to James Stuart, 29 January 1771, E25-18337-25, Keele University Library, as reprinted in Finer and Savage, *Selected Letters of Josiah Wedgwood* (1965): 102–3.

375. Wedgwood to Bentley, 24 December 1770, E25-18334, Keele University Library; Goodison, *Matthew Boulton: Ormolu* (2002): 101, 271; Reilly, *Wedgwood,* vol. 1 (1989): 397–99, 446.

376. Wedgwood to Matthew Boulton, 19 February 1771; cited in Goodison, *Matthew Boulton: Ormolu* (2002): 49, 101.

377. Goodison, *Matthew Boulton: Ormolu* (2002): 271.

378. Wedgwood to Bentley, 13 July 1772, as reprinted in Meteyard, *Life of Josiah Wedgwood,* vol. 2 (1980): 225–26.

379. Bristol, "Stuart and the Genesis of the Greek Revival" (1997): 372.

380. C. Hoare & Co. Ledger 95 (1775–1777), fol. 38, 13 March 1776, payment of £22.8.6, and Ledger 99 (1778–1779), fol. 46, 19 August 1777, payment of £14.13.0, as cited in Bristol, "22 Portman Square" (2001): 72, 84 n. 21; Kelly, *Decorative Wedgwood* (1965): 74–75; Young, ed., "Genius of Wedgwood," (1995): cat. no. C31.

381. Kelly, *Decorative Wedgwood* (1965): 65–66, 69, 75, figs. 25–26.

382. Staley, *Benjamin West* (1989); Croft-Murray, *Decorative Painting in England,* vol. 2 (1970): 290–92; Wood, *History of the Royal Society of Arts* (1913): 45.

383. ADM 68/823 and ADM 68/820, NA; Bold, *Greenwich* (2000): 176–77.

384. Minutes of General Court Meetings, 16 November 1781, 14–15, ADM 67/12, NA; Bold, *Greenwich* (2000): 173.

385. Cooke and Maule, *Royal Hospital for Seamen* (1789): 105–7; John Cooke and John Maule to John Ibbetson, 27 February 1788, Ms. New/1/1/15, RIBA Library, London; Bristol, "Stuart and the Genesis of the Greek Revival" (1997): 352.

386. Cooke and Maule, *Royal Hospital for Seamen* (1789): 100.

387. Colvin, *Biographical Dictionary of British Architects* (1995): 1041.

388. Memorial of Charles White to the Governors and Directors of the Royal Hospital at Greenwich, 17 February 1784, Manuscript ADM 65/106, Letters from Surveyors, Architects, and others as to Works, NA; Bristol, "Stuart and the Genesis of the Greek Revival" (1997): 343 n. 1049.

389. L. Lewis, "Architects of the Chapel at Greenwich Hospital" (1947): 263.

390. Bristol, "Stuart and the Genesis of the Greek Revival" (1997): 343 n. 1049.

391. Gunnis, *Dictionary of British Sculptors* (1968): 434–37; Whinney, *Sculpture in Britain* (1988): 261–69; Parker, "Tapestry Room from Croome Court" (March 1961): 110–11.

392. Friedman, *Spencer House* (1993): 186–87, 344–45.

393. Fagan, *Catalogue Raisonné of the Engraved Works of William Woollett* (1885).

394. Stuart to Anson, 10 July 1764, Lichfield Ms. D615/P(S)/1/6/9; [before 23 August 1764], D615/P(S)/1/6/10.

395. Skempton, "Samuel Wyatt and the Albion Mill" (1971): 53–73; Robinson, *Wyatts* (1979); Colvin, *Biographical Dictionary of British Architects* (1995): 1124–28.

396. 1767, Lichfield Ms. D615/E(H)1/2; 1768, Lichfield Ms. D615/E(H)1/2.

397. Robinson, *Shugborough* (1989): 34–38, 61.

398. Bristol, "Stuart and the Genesis of the Greek Revival" (1997): 299; Pennant, *Journey from Chester to London* (1782): 82; Bagot, *Memorials of the Bagot Family* (1824): 97, 144–46.

399. Cornforth, "On His Own Legs" (28 September 1993): 70–73; Bagot, *Memorials of the Bagot Family* (1824): 146.

400. Bristol, "Society of Dilettanti" (July 2000): 51.

401. James Stuart to [?], n.d., Letters from Surveyors, Architects, and others as to Works, ADM 65/106, NA; ADM 67/12, Minutes of General Court Meetings, entry for 4 July 1781, 7–8, 11–12, NA; Copy of a letter to John Ibbetson, Ms. New/1/1/1, RIBA Library; Bold, *Greenwich* (2000): 173.

402. L. Lewis, "Architects of the Chapel" (1947): 263.

403. Colvin, *Biographical Dictionary of British Architects* (1995): 1134–36.

404. Minutes of General Court Meetings, 22 February and 30 October 1788, 162–63, ADM 67/12, NA.

405. Mrs. Montagu to Leonard Smelt, 3 May [1780], Montagu Papers, MO 5027, Henry E. Huntington Library, San Marino, as cited in Bristol, "22 Portman Square" (2001): 80, 84 n. 60.

406. Mrs. Montagu to Leonard Smelt, 16 December 1780, Montagu Papers, MO 5033, Henry E. Huntington Library, San Marino; C. Hoare & Co., Ledger 13 (1782–1784), fol. 396, 7 June 1782, all as cited in Bristol, "22 Portman Square" (2001): 80–81, 85 n. 90.

407. Eimer, "James 'Athenian' Stuart" (1994): 131.

408. Minutes of the Society, vol. 2, p. 63, 18 May 1757, and p. 72–73, 7 June 1758, RSA; Eimer, "James 'Athenian' Stuart" (1994): 131.

Fig. C1. Title page illustration depicting James Stuart at work. Engraving by James Basire. From *The Rudiments of Ancient Architecture* . . . (1789). By permission of The British Library, London, 7822.cc.38.

CHRONOLOGY OF THE LIFE AND WORK OF JAMES ATHENIAN STUART

COMPILED BY SUSAN WEBER SOROS

ca. 1713
James Stuart born in Creed Lane, London

mid-1720s
Apprentices as a fan painter to "Goupee of the Strand," probably Louis Goupy or his nephew Joseph.

ca. 1734
Joins (or perhaps helps found) an artists' school or academy run by George Michael Moser, in Greyhound Court, Arundel Street, London, and later in Salisbury Court, London.

n.d., ca. 1730s
Creates his earliest known surviving work: a self portrait in charcoal and wash, depicting himself with stylus in hand.

ca. 1741
Travels to Paris, briefly earning a living there as a fan painter before continuing on to Italy.

1744
Shares a house in the Salita di San Giuseppe, Rome, with James Paston.

1745
Travels by ship off the coast of Tuscany, possibly from Rome to Florence. Captain George Edgcumbe characterized him as a "friend of the Pretender."

1746
Commissioned by the second Earl of Ashburnham to produce two paintings, probably narrative or allegorical in subject matter. March: Resides in Florence; plans a trip to Bologna.

1748
Travels to Naples with Gavin Hamilton, Matthew Brettingham, and Nicholas Revett. Issues first "Proposal" with Nicholas Revett for "a new and accurate description of the Antiquities &c. in the Province of Attica." Revised proposals issued 1750, 1752, 1753, 1755.

1748–50
Resides in the Villa Tomati on the Via Felice, Rome, with Gavin Hamilton and Nicholas Revett.

ca. 1750
Designs a twenty-five bay Country House (not executed).

1750
One of his sisters dies in Holland. Provides an essay and etchings (etchings, dated 1749, and research by Stuart, text in Latin and Italian) for Abbate Angelo Bandini, *De Obelisco Caesaris Augusti*, a treatise on the Obelisk of Pharoah Psammetichus II excavated in the Campus Martius, Rome. This essay is reprinted by Stuart in the form of an open letter to Count Malton, later second Marquess of Rockingham, in the same year. Visits Venice with Nicholas Revett. July to November: Makes drawings at Pola in the Venetian Republic.

579

Fig. C2. James Stuart. Design for painted decoration, n.d. Pencil. Courtesy of Lowell Libson Limited.

1751
January: Embarks for Greece. March 18: arrives in Athens. March: Elected Member of the Society of Dilettanti, London, with Nicholas Revett, proposed by Sir James Gray. May: Visited in Athens by Dawkins and Wood.

ca. 1753
One of his sisters, possibly Sarah Teresia Stuart, dies.

1753–54
September: Leaves Revett in Athens and travels toward Constantinople, surviving an assassination attempt by his escort and escaping to Salonica, where Revett joins him in January 1754. They travel onward to Smyrna. Paints portraits of Smyrna and Salonica merchants, two brothers, James and Nicholson Lee (one painting now lost).

ca. 1754–55
Returns to England with Nicholas Revett, after a period of quarantine in Marseilles. Arrives in London January 1755. Resides at James Dawkins's house in London until ca. 1757.

ca. 1755–63, n.d.
Designs chimneypiece for the drawing

room at Sion Hill, Isleworth, Middlesex, for Robert D'Arcy, fourth Earl of Holdernesse, and a Choragic Monument for the park at Sion Hill (n.d.).

ca. 1755–64
Makes designs for Wentworth Woodhouse, Yorkshire, for the second Marquess of Rockingham (house now privately owned):

Fig. C3. James Stuart. View of the Temples of Rome and Augustus, Pola, 1750s–60s. Gouache. RIBA Library Drawings Collection, London, SD 146/6. *Checklist no. 15.*

painted panels for the dining room (not executed); minor alterations to the back of the house and link corridors; interior of the Marble Saloon including fifteen bas-reliefs; two, possibly three chimneypieces, and panels over the niches in the hall. Installs Antinous relief (a copy of a second-century Roman portrait).

1755
Paints portraits of King William III and of George II for the second Marquess of Rockingham to hang in the Whig Club, York (later the Rockingham Club). Both now lost.

ca. 1756, 1765
Designs a Doric portico at The Grove, Watford, Hertfordshire, and undated minor decorative additions to the house (chimneypiece, medallions, doorcases). Designs cold bath (1765), for Thomas Villiers, first Lord Hyde.

ca. 1756–64, 1771
Designs interiors and chimneypieces for Nuneham Park, Nuneham Courtenay, Oxfordshire for the first Earl Harcourt (extensively altered). Exterior windows were adapted from drawings later published in *Antiquities of Athens.* Co-designs, with Earl Harcourt, All Saint's Church (1764), a church/temple in Nuneham Park. Probably

designs Temple of Flora in Nuneham Park (1771).

1756
Elected member of the Society for the Promotion of Arts, Manufactures and Commerce, London (SPAC; later the Royal Society of Arts). First recorded act in the society is to propose Sir Joshua Reynolds for membership. August: Delivers an account of silk production on the island of Andros to SPAC.

1756–69
Makes designs for Shugborough, Stafford-shire, for Thomas Anson: alterations, including second-story addition to the cor-ridors that linked the wings to the central portion of the house (altered); interior work, including bedroom and small painted dressing room (now lost) and designs of furniture; the greenhouse or orangery (1756–64, demolished 1855), Doric Temple (ca. 1760), Triumphal Arch (1761–69), Tower of the Winds (ca. 1764–65), and Lanthorn of Demosthenes (1764–69). Makes alterations to the Shepherd's Monument, designs riverside colonnade, designs a stone slab of addorsed griffins on the Cat's Monument, and designs almshouses (attributed).

1757–58
Prepares preliminary drawings for the Great Saloon and other interiors at Kedleston Hall for Sir Nathaniel Curzon, later Lord Scarsdale (unexecuted). Designs "chestnut" vases, vase-shaped plate warmer, ormolu tripods, and Sicilian jasper cistern for the dining room of Kedleston Hall for Nathaniel Curzon. Tripods exhibited by metalworker Diederich Nicolaus Anderson at the Free Society of Artists (1761). Design of prize medals for the Royal Society of Arts, London (RSA; medals used from 1758–1805).

Fig. C4. James Stuart. Pier table, one of a pair, from the Red Drawing Room, Shugborough, ca. 1763–65. Gilt and painted wood, green Cippolino marble top. For the other pier table, see fig. 10-72. Courtesy of Shugborough, The Anson Collection (The National Trust, UK).

ca. 1758
Designs decoration for Lady Spencer's closet, the hall, and dining room of Wimbledon House, Surrey, for John Spencer, later first Earl Spencer (destroyed by fire in 1785). Designs medal to com-memorate Frederick the Great, Defeat of the French and Austrians, for the RSA.

1758
Moves to 7 Grosvenor Street, Mayfair, London. Designs scenery for the Latin play at Westminster School, London (last used 1808). Designs two medals, commemorat-ing the capture of Louisburg and capture of Goree (design revised in 1759). Elected Fellow of the Royal Society, London, and of the Society of Antiquaries, London. Designs an interior, probably for Harcourt House, 1 Cavendish Square, London, for George Simon, Viscount Newnham. Appointed surveyor to the Royal Hospital for Seamen, Greenwich (retains post until his death).

1758–59
Designs a Greek Doric temple for the park at Hagley Hall near Stourbridge, West Midlands, for the first Lord Lyttelton, and designs ceiling of the Tapestry Room,

including ceiling paintings. (*Flora*, executed by Cipriani, damaged by fire 1925, *Seasons*, executed by Stuart.)

1758–66
Designs interiors and furnishings for Spencer House, St. James's Place, London, for the first Earl Spencer. Furniture includes mahogany inlaid chest of drawers with ormolu moldings, mahogany cup-board, pair of mirrors and console tables for the great room, lantern for the main stairs, gilded suite of furniture and torchères for the Painted Room, and pair of mahogany tables and wardrobe for Lady Spencer's bedchamber.

ca. 1759, before 1761
Designs ceiling for Croome Court, Worces-tershire, for George William, sixth earl of Coventry (executed by Francesco Vassalli).

1759
Paints a scene from Shakespeare's *Tempest* for Mrs. Elizabeth Montagu for 23 Hill Street, London. Designs medals commemo-rating capture of Guadeloupe, capture of Quebec (1759–60), and battle of Minden (after 1759; exhibited by John Pingo at the Society of Arts, 1762).

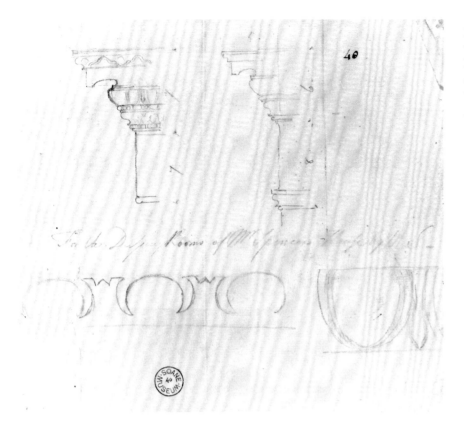

Fig. C5. Robert Adam. Drawing of the dressing room cornice, Spencer House, designed by James Stuart, ca. 1760. Pencil. By courtesy of the Trustees of Sir John Soane's Museum, London, Adam Ms., vol. 54, series 3, no. 40. *Checklist no. 111.*

1759–62
Designs monument to Brigadier-General George Augustus, third Viscount Howe, General of the British Forces in America, executed by Peter Scheemakers, in the northwest tower of Westminster Abbey, London, for the Court of the Province of Massachusetts Bay. (Monument altered and removed to floor in nineteenth century).

ca. 1760
Designs medal commemorating death of General James Wolfe (exhibited by Thomas Pingo at the Society of Artists, London, 1775).

ca. 1760–65
Remodels interior of the Great Hall, possibly including furniture, at Hornby Castle, North Yorkshire, for Robert d'Arcy, fourth Earl of Holdernesse (interior gutted 1930s, most of castle demolished).

1760
Designs medals to commemorate capture of Montreal and conquest of Canada. June 9: marries his housekeeper, Ann Taylor, in the church of St. James the Less, Piccadilly, London. Date of Ann's death is not known.

1760–63
Designs monument to Admiral Charles Watson, executed by Peter Scheemakers, for the north entrance of Westminster Abbey, London, for the East India Company (partially dismantled in 1957).

Fig. C6. James Stuart. Sketch, one of two, for a proposed medal commemorating the taking of Lagos, ca. 1761. Pen and ink, gray wash, pencil. For the other sketch, see fig. 12-14. RIBA Library Drawings Collection, London, SD 62/29 (2).

1760–68
Designs the Infirmary, Greenwich Hospital (damaged by fire 1811, altered 1840, bomb damaged 1940, 1941, converted 1998–99 to the Dreadnought Library, University of Greenwich). Appointed Portrait Painter to the Society of Dilettanti, London. May: First Dilettanti portrait commission, to paint his deceased patron James Dawkins.

ca. 1761

Makes preliminary designs for a medal commemorating sea battles at Lagos (unexecuted). Designs medal commemorating the battle of Belleisle.

ca. 1761–66

Designs interiors for Holdernesse House, No. 24 Hertford Street. Park Lane, London (later Londonderry House) for Robert d'Arcy, fourth Earl of Holdernesse (major alterations 1825–28; demolished 1964).

1761

March: Becomes co-chairman of the Committee of Polite Arts of the RSA. Designs State Chair for Queen Charlotte for St. James's Palace, London. Designs medal to commemorate the capture of Pondicherry.

1761–62

Designs monument to Mrs. Charles Yorke (Catharine Freman), executed by Peter Scheemakers, for Chicheley Chapel, St. Andrew's Church, Wimpole, Cambridgeshire.

1762

Designs medal to celebrate the birth of the Prince of Wales (exhibited by Thomas Pingo at the RSA, 1763). Designs medal for the Catch Club, London (1762–64). Publishes volume 1 of *Antiquities of Athens* with Nicholas Revett (book was not available until January 1763).

ca. 1763, n.d.

Designs medal commemorating the victory at Plassy. Possibly designs the coved ceiling for the Saloon, Buckingham House, for George III, and a chimneypiece (n.d.) for the King's Audience Chamber at Windsor Castle for George III.

1763

Moves to Hollis Street, Westminster, London. First recorded mention of Stuart's chronic gout; suffers debilitating attacks for the rest of his life.

Fig. C7. James Stuart. View of the gate of Athene Archegetis, Athens, 1750s–60s. Gouache. The engraved version appears in vol. 1 of *Antiquities* (1762). RIBA Library Drawings Collection, London, SD 145/1. *Checklist no. 21.*

1763–64

Medal designs adapted to make plaster medallions on the walls of the Temple of Concord and Victory, Stowe, belonging to Richard Grenville, Earl Temple.

ca. 1764–ca. 1780

Rebuilds Belvedere, near Erith, Kent, for Sir Sampson Gideon (demolished 1959).

1764

Designs interiors for a house in Spring Gardens, London, for Sir Charles Saunders. Designs Admiralty passes for the Admiralty, engraving by James Basire. Proposes a design for a "Lazaretto," or quarantine hospital, at Chetney Hill, Stangate Creek, near Chatham for the Admiralty (unexecuted). December 28: Birth of Stuart's son, John Francis Stuart (christened February 9, 1765; dies ca. 1768–69).

1764–65

Employs artist James Barry to make oil paintings of drawings and watercolor views of Athens.

1764–66

Designs 15 St. James's Square, London (renamed Lichfield House, 1831), for Thomas Anson (minor work continues to 1771; alterations by Samuel Wyatt, 1791–94). Designs monument to the Lord Chancellor Philip, first Earl of Hardwicke, and his wife the Countess of Hardwicke, executed by Peter Scheemakers, with Thomas Scheemakers, for the east wall of Chichley Chapel, St. Andrew's Church, Wimpole, Cambridgeshire.

1764–82

Succeeds William Hogarth as Serjeant-Painter in the Office of Works (post abolished in 1782).

ca. 1765

Designs premium medal given by the Society for the Improvement of Agriculture in Nottinghamshire and the West Riding of Yorkshire (exhibited 1770 by Thomas Pingo at the Society of Arts). Designs medal for the Royal Military Academy (exhibited at the Body of Artists, 1766).

Fig. C8. James Stuart. View of the amphitheater at Pola from the west, 1750s–60s. Gouache. Exhibited by Stuart in 1766. RIBA Library Drawings Collection, London, SD 146/4. *Checklist no. 17.*

1765
Exhibits four watercolors of architectural views of ancient buildings in Athens at the Free Society of Artists, London.

1765–66
Spends the winter in Bath, Avon, for health reasons.

1766
Consulted by Provost Sumner of King's College, Cambridge, asked to review the design of an altarpiece for the chapel. Exhibits four watercolors (gouaches) of views of ancient sites in Athens, a drawing of the story of Cyrus, Eleazer, and Nebuchadnezzar from the travels of Cyrus written by Ramsey, and a sketch of the story of Ulysses and Nausica from Homer's *Odyssey*. Models from Stuart designs executed by Thomas Scheemakers—a nymph supplying Bacchus with wine, cupid presenting the ensigns of victory to Venus after she has gained the golden apple, and Cupid unveiling Modesty—are shown at the Free Society of Artists, London. Designs medal to mark Earl Camden's appointment as Lord Chancellor of Britain (exhibited at the Free Society of Artists, London, 1767).

1766–72
Designs and paints decoration at 23 Hill Street, London for Mrs. Elizabeth Montagu: four medallions in the ceiling of the great room and the decoration of a bedroom including chimneypiece, door frames, and painted ceiling with a scheme of Aurora surrounded by eight roundels containing putti.

ca. 1767
Designs organ case for Newby Hall, Yorkshire for William Weddell.

1767
Buys the lease of a substantial house at 35 Leicester Fields, London (now demolished); makes alterations and additions, including a workroom or painting studio at the rear of the house. Lives here for the remainder of his life. Exhibits three architectural views of ancient sites at Athens at the Free Society of Artists, London. Designs monument to Elizabeth Mason, wife of poet William Mason, executed by John Bacon, for Bristol Cathedral.

1768
Joseph Nollekens entrusts two portraits and a terracotta to Stuart, to place at best advantage in London exhibitions; Stuart offends Nollekens by showing them at the Free Society, London. Exhibits the design for a medal commemorating Sir Edward Hawke's victory in Quiberon Bay, drawing of a Medusa head from an antique cameo, and three mythological subjects—the Judgment of Paris, Choice of Hercules, and Judgment of Midas—at the Free Society of Artists, London.

ca. 1769
Designs new entrance façade (attributed) and orangery for Blithfield House, Staffordshire, for William Bagot, first Lord Bagot (built by Samuel Wyatt from Stuart's design).

1769
Exhibits *Sappho Writing an Ode which Cupid Dictates* at the Free Society of Artists, London. Designs a border for a tea table and a "tripodic tea kitchen" (tea urn), executed by Boulton and Fothergill, for Thomas Anson of Shugborough. Presents a paper on Egyptian hieroglyphics to the Royal Society, London. Advises on the design of a house in Fulham, possibly Ranelagh House, for Sir Philip Stevens. Designs ground-floor saloon, morning room, and suite of first-floor rooms, also possibly a Doric entrance portico with zodiac ceiling, at Rathfarnham Castle, County Dublin, for Henry Loftus, first Earl of Ely.

1769–74
Refits the Governor's apartments, possibly including two new chimneypieces and a ceiling design, within King Charles Block, Royal Hospital for Seamen, Greenwich. Extension and reconstruction of the southwest pavilion of the King Charles Block, creation of underground passageway linking King Charles Block with King William Block, Royal Hospital for Seamen, Greenwich.

Fig. C9. James Stuart. View of the Arch of Hadrian, Athens, with the ruin of the Temple of Jupiter Olympius in the background, 1750s–60s. Gouache. Exhibited by Stuart in 1767. RIBA Library Drawings Collection, London, SD 145/9. *Checklist no. 25.*

1760s
Designs medal to commemorate Admiral George, Lord Anson's defeat of the French off Cape Finisterre and his circumnavigation, commissioned by Thomas Anson, the admiral's older brother (exhibited Free Society of Artists, London, 1769).

n.d., possibly 1760s
Designs a bridge for Kenwood House, Hampstead, for William Murray, first Earl of Mansfield.

1769–71
Designs tripod, executed by Boulton and Fothergill, ca. 1769–70, with ceramic bowl executed by Wedgwood, for placement on the replica of the Choragic Monument of Lysicrates at Shugborough for Thomas Anson.

ca. 1770
Designs Etruscan painted-ware tea urns, made by Wedgwood and mounted in ormolu, for Mrs. Elizabeth Montagu.

1770
Designs "two seahorses . . . executed by Thomas Scheemakers," at the Free Society of Artists exhibition, London.

1771
January: Commissions Wedgwood to make twelve small pots for the palette of his paint box with tray. Designs Gothic altarpiece and east window for St. George's Chapel, Windsor (removed 1786). Designs monument to William, Viscount Chetwynd, with a black basalt urn, made by Wedgwood, for the Church of St. John the Baptist, Ashley, Shropshire, Staffs. Designs monument to Anthony Ashley Cooper, fourth Earl of Shaftesbury, executed by Thomas Scheemakers, at south side of the chancel at St. Giles Church, Wimborne St. Giles, Dorset. Designs silver tureen for the Admiralty, Greenwich, executed by Boulton and Fothergill. A view of the Lanthorn of Demosthenes exhibited by one of his pupils at the Free Society of Artists, London. Exhibits four architectural views of ancient sites in Athens, and the *Reconciliation of Cupid and Psyche,* at the Free Society of Artists, London.

ca. 1773
Designs monument to Dr. Ralph Freman, executed by Thomas Scheemakers, for St. Mary the Virgin church, Braughing, Hertfordshire, for Philip Yorke, nephew. Designs monument to Thomas Steavens, executed by Thomas Scheemakers, for St. Mary the Virgin church, Preston-on-Stour, Warwickshire.

Fig. C10. James Stuart. View of the bridge over the Ilissus connecting the Panathenaic stadium with the city of Athens, 1750s–60s. Gouache. Exhibited by Stuart in 1774. RIBA Library Drawings Collection, London, SD 146/1. *Checklist no. 24.*

Fig. C11. James Stuart. View of the Temple of Apollo at Corinth, 1750s–60s. Gouache. Exhibited by Stuart in 1782. RIBA Library Drawings Collection, London, SD 146/2. *Checklist no. 19.*

1773
Exhibits thirteen views, plans, and elevations from the unpublished portion of the *Antiquities of Athens,* and four views from John Hawkesworth's unpublished *Account of the Voyages undertaken by the Order of his Present Majesty for making Discoveries in the Southern Hemisphere and successively performed by Commodore Byron, Captain Wallis, Captain Carteret, and Captain Cook in the Dolphin, the Swallows, and the Endeavour,* at the Free Society of Artists, London.

1773–81
Designs Prospect House (early, probably unexecuted designs were 1766), also called Hill House, Wimpole Hall, Cambridgeshire, for Philip Yorke, second Earl of Hardwicke (altered by Humphrey Repton, ca. 1802; demolished mid-nineteenth century).

1774
Exhibits twelve views, plans, and elevations from the unpublished portion of the *Antiquities of Athens;* also a view of a ruin in Italy, and two watercolor views of an amphitheater and ruin in Thessalonica, at the Free Society of Artists, London. Conducts a detailed survey with fellow director Thomas Hicks of the Derwentwater estate, for the board of the Royal Hospital for Seamen, Greenwich. Refits the dining hall to increase accommodation in the King Charles Block, Royal Hospital for Seamen, Greenwich.

ca. 1775–80
Makes alterations at Warfield Park, Bracknell, Berkshire, for John Walsh.

1775
Designs frontispiece to James Hermes's *Philosophical Arrangements.* Exhibits designs for the General Wolfe medal, Admiral Hawke medal, and Catch Club medal at the Free Society of Artists, London. Designs monument to Catharine Venables Vernon for Sudbury Church, Derbyshire.

1775–81
Designs Montagu House, Portman Square, London, for Mrs. Elizabeth Montagu (bombed 1941 and later demolished).

1777–81
Extension of terrace and Thames river wall, construction of a new wharf, and enlargement of the embankment, Greenwich Hospital.

1778
Exhibits three portraits, a sketch entitled *Parental Amusement,* print from a Raphael drawing, and two architectural views from Athens at the Free Society of Artists, London. August 21: Marries Elizabeth Blacland of Sittingbourne in Kent.

1778–79
Designs monuments to Joseph Cocks and Mary Cocks, executed by Thomas Scheemakers, for St. John the Baptist Church, Eastnor, Herefordshire.

ca. 1779–80
Designs interiors for Camden Place, Chislehurst, Kent, for Charles Pratt, Earl Camden, Choragic Monument of Lysicrates, and cold bath for the grounds.

1779
Daughter Frances Charlotte Stuart born (christened November 5). Exhibits drawing of Montagu House at the Royal Academy, London. Exhibits two unfinished proofs of a basso relievo in the Temple of Minerva, and an etching from a drawing by Il Pomarancio at the Free Society of Artists, London.

1779–88
Designs chapel at Royal Hospital for Seamen, Greenwich, with the assistance of Robert Mylne (to 1782), followed by William Newton (to 1790).

ca. 1780
Designs 45 Harley Street, London, for an unidentified patron (demolished). Designs a "Grecian Ruin," or amphitheater, at Park Place, Remenham, Berkshire, for General Henry Seymour Conway (upper story destroyed, lower story survives).

1780

Exhibits five architectural views of ancient sites in Athens, a portrait of a dog, two landscape subjects, three mythological subjects, and four medallions in plaster at the Free Society of Artists, London.

1780–81

Designs the Temple of the Winds for Mount Stewart, County Down Ireland, for Robert Stewart, first Marquis of Londonderry.

1781

Second Stuart silver tureen ordered for the Admiralty. Designs monument to Thomas Bentley, partner of Wedgwood, executed by Thomas Scheemakers, for St. Nicholas Church, Chiswick, Middlesex. Son John George Hardinge Stuart born (christened August 25).

1781–82

Extension of the southwestern pavilion of the King Charles block, Royal Hospital for Seamen, Greenwich.

1782

"Model of a monument from a design of Mr. Stuart" by Thomas Scheemaker exhibited at the Royal Academy, London. Exhibits twenty architectural drawings of ancient sites, including two of reliefs from the Choragic Monument of Lysicrates and eight of the Tower of the Winds, made for the first volume of *Antiquities of Athens*, and three of the great Temple at Minerva, made for the second volume of *Antiquities,* as well as *Harmony and Design* and *Rural Happiness,* at the Free Society of Artists, London.

1783

Daughter Elizabeth Ann Stuart born (christened July 24). Exhibits eight architectural engravings from *Antiquities of Athens* (including the headpieces for several chapters), a drawing of a Leda, a drawing from a basso relievo at Athens, and a drawing for the frontispiece in James Harris's "Philological Disquisitions," probably referring to *Philological Inquiries* (1781), at the Free Society of Artists, London.

1783–84

Designs the Boys' School, Royal Hospital for Seamen, Greenwich, with William Newton.

1785

Son James Stevens Stuart born (christened December 15; dies of smallpox, 1787).

1788

February 2: Dies at his house in Leicester Square, London, and is buried in the crypt of the Church of St. Martin in the Fields, London. March: Birth of posthumous son, James Stuart (christened May 8).

ca. 1790

Posthumous publication of volume 2 of *Antiquities of Athens.* Although the title page is dated 1787, several plates are dated 1789, and the first review of the book appeared in February 1790.

1791

June 27: Public auction of his effects by Greenwoods auctioneers, London.

1795

Posthumous publication of volume 3 of *Antiquities of Athens,* under the editorship of Willey Reveley.

1816

Posthumous publication of volume 4 of *Antiquities of Athens,* issued by Josiah Taylor.

CHECKLIST OF THE EXHIBITION

1. **Self-portrait**

   James Stuart
   ca. 1730–35
   Charcoal and wash on tinted paper
   18½ x 15 ¹⁵⁄₁₆ in.(47 x 40.5 cm)

   RIBA Library Drawings Collection,
   London, POR/STUA/1

   References: *RIBA Journal*, 3rd series, 42
   (25 May 1935): 798; Croft–Murray,
   Decorative Painting in England, vol. 2
   (1970): 284; Richardson, ed., *Catalogue
   of the Drawings Collection of the RIBA,*
   vol. S (1976): no. [6], 126; Watkin,
   Athenian Stuart (1982): 14, fig. 1;
   Colvin, *Biographical Dictionary* (1995):
   795.

   Illustrated: fig. 2-6.

2. **Portrait of James Stuart**

   William Camden Edwards, after
   Samuel Provan
   1827 (Provan original ca. 1748)
   Engraving
   12⅞ x 11⁹⁄₁₆ in. (32.7 x 29.4 cm)

   Inscribed: "James Stuart, F. R.S. & F.
   S.A."; "Proven [sic] Pinx.t Rome"; W.
   C. Edwards sculpt."; "Dedicated (by
   Permission) to John Soane. Esqr,,
   Architect to the Bank of England.

   Professor of Architecture in the Royal
   Academy. F. R.S. F. S.A. Member of the
   Academies for Painting, Sculpture and
   Architecture, in Parma and Florence.
   From a Picture in the possession of
   Richard Brettingham, Esqr,, Shotford
   Hall, Norfolk. Published by Priestly
   and Weale, High Street, Bloomsbury,
   1827"

   By courtesy of the Trustees of Sir John
   Soane's Museum, London, 69/3/4

   References: Colvin, *Biographical
   Dictionary* (1995): 795; Duffy, *James
   Gandon* (1999): 99 illus. (right top);
   Forrest, *St. James's Square* (2001): fig. 31.

   Illustrated: fig. 2-8.

3. **Souvenir fan leaf (unmounted)**
   With views of Rome: from left, Arch of
   Titus, Arch of Constantine, and the
   Forum

   Italian
   Mid- to late eighteenth century
   Watercolor on skin
   11 ¹⁄₁₆ x 22⅞₁₆ in. (28 x 57 cm)

   Inscribed (signature probably a forgery): "Jose Goupy: 1738 NA."

   By courtesy of the Trustees of The
   British Museum, London, Lady
   Charlotte Schreiber Collection 335;

   1891-7-13-719

   References: Cust, comp., *Catalogue of
   the Collection of Fans* (1893): 52, no. 251;
   Staniland, *Fans* (1985): 4, fig. 7; Hart and
   Taylor, *Fans* (1998): 57, 62–63, fig. 30.

   Illustrated: fig. 2-5.

4. **Saint Andrew on the Way to
   Martyrdom**

   James Stuart, after a painting by
   Niccolò Circignani, known as Il
   Pomerancio
   20 March 1746
   Etching, with pen and ink inscriptions
   15 x 9¼₁₆ in. (38 x 23 cm)

   Inscribed: "Pomarancio Inv."; "J. Stuart
   Sculp." The margins are inscribed with
   a letter from Stuart to Jacob Hinde, 20
   March 1746.

   Courtesy of the Beineke Rare Book
   and Manuscript Library, Yale University,
   New Haven, OSB fc 144

   References: Bristol, "Stuart and the
   Genesis of the Greek Revival" (1997):
   49–50, fig. 1; Marciari, "Athenian
   Stuart in Florence" (September 1998):
   612–14.

   Illustrated: fig. 3-2.

5. **Measured study of a first-floor window of the Palazzo Pandolfini, Florence**

James Stuart
ca. 1746–50
Pen and ink, pencil
9 x 6⁵⁄₁₆ in. (22.8 x 16 cm)

Inscribed: "Raphael. Pandolfini" and other inscriptions

RIBA Library Drawings Collection, London, SD 62/21

Illustrated: fig. 3-3.

6. **Sketch elevation of the Villa Farnesina, Rome**

James Stuart
ca. 1742–50
Pen and ink
10¾ x 16⅝ in. (27.4 x 42.2 cm)

Inscribed: "By little Farnese." (pencil); "Little farnesi" (ink); and a scale (ink)

RIBA Library Drawings Collection, London, SD 62/23

7. **Sketchbook**
Open to fol. 195v, a design of a Tuscan temple, after Vitruvius's description; pen and ink

James Stuart
ca. 1750

Book (closed): 11⅝ x 8¹¹⁄₁₆ x 1³⁄₁₆ in. (29.5 x 22 x 3 cm)

Edinburgh University Library, Laing Mss., La.III.581

Illustrated: fig. 3-21; see also fig. 3-20.

8. **Sketchbook**
Open to pages 75 verso and 76 recto, "Laws of Opake objects," study of the effects of light on columns; pen and ink, pencil

James Stuart
ca. 1748–50
7¹¹⁄₁₆ x 5⁵⁄₁₆ in. (19.5 x 13.5 cm)

Inscribed: Signed "Stuart" on first and last pages

RIBA Library Drawings Collection, London, SKB/336/2 [L3/4]

References: Richardson, ed., *Catalogue of the Drawings Collection of the RIBA*, vol. S (1976): no. 2, 123; Watkin, *Athenian Stuart* (1982): 20; Colvin, *Biographical Dictionary* (1995): 796.

Illustrated: fig. 3-16; see also figs. 2-28, 6-2, 6-4, 6-5, 7-22, 10-2.

9. *De Obelisco Caesaris Augusti e Campo Martio nuperrime effosso epistola Jacobi Stuart Angli ad Carolum Wentworth Comitem de Malton . . .*

Open to tab. 1, elevations of the Obelisk of Psammetichus II, 1749; etching. Inscribed: descriptive letterpress, and "J. Stuart delin. & Sculp. Romae 1749"

James Stuart
Rome: Niccolò and Marco Pagliarini, 1750
Book (closed): 17⅛ x 11¾ x ⅝ in. (43.5 x 30 x 4.1 cm); foldout plate: 41¾ x 26¾ in. (106 x 68 cm)

By permission of The British Library, London, 140.h.18

References: Lawrence, "Stuart and Revett" (1938–39): 129–30; Crook, *Greek Revival* (1968): 259; Mulvany, *Life of James Gandon* (1969): 195–96; Wiebenson, *Sources of Greek Revival Architecture* (1969): 4; Watkin, *Athenian Stuart* (1982): 14–15, fig. 2; Colvin, *Biographical Dictionary* (1995): 794; Bristol, "Stuart and the Genesis of the Greek Revival" (1997): 24, 63; Ingamells, ed., *Dictionary of British and Irish Travellers in Italy* (1997): 910; Bristol, "Newly-Discovered Drawing" (2001): 43.

Illustrated: fig. 3-1; see also figs. 3-10, 3-11, 3-12.

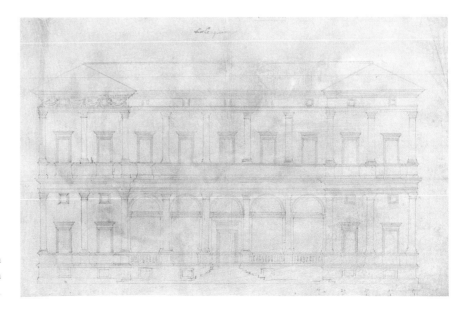

No. 6. James Stuart. Sketch elevation of the Villa Farnesina, Rome.

No. 10. Page 1 of *De obelisco Caesaris Augusti e Campi Martii* (1750).

10. *De obelisco Caesaris Augusti e Campi Martii ruderibus nuper eruto commentarius auctore Angelo Maria Bandinio accedunt CLL. Virorum epistolae atque opuscula.*
Open to p. 1, with engraved vignette of the Campus Martius and capital letter designs by James Stuart

Angelo Maria Bandini
Rome: Pallade, 1750
Book (closed): 16⅜ x 11¹³⁄₁₆ x 2 in. (42 x 30 x 5 cm)

By permission of The British Library, London, 138.h.5

Illustrated: herein; see also figs. 3–9, 3–13.

11. *Antiquities of Athens*, volume 4
Open to frontispiece, portrait of Nicholas Revett; engraving by Isaac Taylor. Inscribed: "Nicholas Revett, Esqr."; "Engraved by Isaac Taylor."; "London. Published Jan 1, 1810, by J. Taylor"

James Stuart and Nicholas Revett; ed. by Joseph Woods
London: J. Taylor, 1816
Book (closed): 21⁵⁄₁₆ x 15 x 2 in. (54.1 x 38.1 x 5.1 cm)

Courtesy of the Library, The Bard Graduate Center for Studies in the Decorative Arts, Design, and Culture, New York

Reference: Jupp, *Descriptive List of Original Drawings*, vol. 3 (1871): 5.

Illustrated: fig. 4–6; see also figs. 5–21, 9–7.

12. *A Journey into Greece . . .*
Open to pp. 396–97, with text regarding the Tower of the Winds, and an illustration of the Lanthorn of Demosthenes. Inscribed: "It is not a Charger; / but a Shield, / from which he Shaketh / down hail and Tempest."; "he holdeth a Conch / shell in his Hand"; "is the driest of all / Winds at Athens"; "a Vase curiously / wrought, perhaps it / is designed to represent / a fire Pot of Brass / Τωεάυγου, Pollux, & [illegible]"; "[Gar]bino & Libeccio"

George Wheler
London: William Cademan, Robert

Kettlewell, and Awnsham Churchill, 1682
Book (closed): 12¹⁄₁₆ x 8¹⁄₁₆ x 1⅛ in. (30.6 x 20.5 x 2.9 cm)

Inscribed: on the title page, "James Stuart 1755"; extensive handwritten notes by Stuart throughout the volume

Durham University Library, Routh 60.c.19

References: Wiebenson, *Sources of Greek Revival Architecture* (1969): 20; Middleton and Watkin, *Neoclassical and Nineteenth Century Architecture* (1980): 68; Watkin, *Athenian Stuart* (1982): 15; Constantine, "Question of Authenticity," in Clarke, ed., *Rediscovering Hellenism* (1989): 19–20; Kaufman, "Architecture and Travel in the Age of British Ecelecticism" in Blau and Kaufman (eds.), *Architecture and Its Image* (1989): 72; E. Harris, *British Architectural Books and Writers* (1990): 290, 440–43, 448; Crook, *Greek Revival* (1995): 4–6, 13, 18, 30; Scott, *Pleasures of Antiquity* (2003): 89.

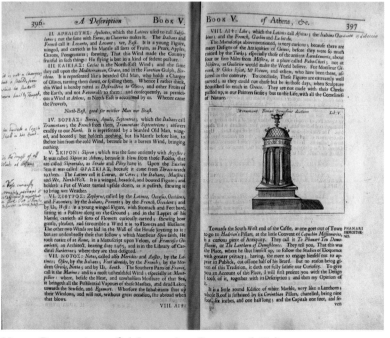

No. 12. Pages 396–97 of *A Journey into Greece . . .* (1682).

13. **Album**

Once belonging to the naturalist and botanist Sir Joseph Banks. Open to p. 21, no. 301, "Ternofaco a fish caught in the sea near Syra . . ." by James Stuart (ca. 1751–54); gouache, heightened with white; pen and ink. Inscribed: with lengthy descriptive note; signed "J. Stuart."

Plate: 5⅜ x 7¾ in. (13.6 x 19.7 cm)

By courtesy of the Trustees of The British Museum, London, 197*d.4

Reference: Bristol, "Stuart and the Genesis of the Greek Revival" (1997): 92, fig. 13.

Illustrated: fig. 2-15.

14. **View of the Arch of the Sergii (Porta Aurata) at Pola (now Pula), Istria, Croatia**

James Stuart
1750s–60s
Gouache
10 x 15⅜ in. (25.5 x 39 cm)

RIBA Library Drawings Collection, London, SD 146/8

View published in *Antiquities of Athens,* vol. 4 (1816): chap. 3, pl. I

References: Graves, *Society of Artists* (1907): 247–49; Richardson, ed., *Catalogue of the Drawings Collection of the RIBA,* vol. S (1976): no. [4] 20, 126; Watkin, *Athenian Stuart* (1982): 20; Lever and Richardson, *Art of the Architect* (1984): 31; Colvin, *Biographical Dictionary* (1995): 795–96.

Illustrated: fig. 2-9.

15. **View of the Temples of Rome and Augustus, Pola**

James Stuart
1750s–60s
Gouache
10 x 15³⁄₁₆ in. (25.5 x 38.5 cm)

RIBA Library Drawings Collection, London, SD 146/6

No. 16. James Stuart. View of the back of the Temples of Rome and Augustus, Pola.

View published in *Antiquities of Athens,* vol. 4 (1816): chap. 2, pl. I

References: Graves, *Society of Artists* (1907): 247–49; Richardson, ed., *Catalogue of the Drawings Collection of the RIBA,* vol. S (1976): [4] 18, 125; Watkin, *Athenian Stuart* (1982): 18; Lever and Richardson, *Art of the Architect* (1984): 31; Colvin, *Biographical Dictionary* (1995): 795–96.

Illustrated: chronology, fig. C3.

16. **View of the back of the Temples of Rome and Augustus, Pola**
With the Temple of Poseidon on the left

James Stuart
1750s–60s
Gouache
11⅝ x 18½ in. (29.5 x 47 cm)

RIBA Library Drawings Collection, London, SD 146/7

View published in *Antiquities of Athens,* vol. 4 (1816): chap. 2, pl. II

References: Graves, *Society of Artists* (1907): 247–49; Richardson, ed., *Catalogue of the Drawings Collection of the RIBA* (1976): [4] 18, 125; Watkin,

Athenian Stuart (1982): 20; Lever and Richardson, *Art of the Architect* (1984): 31; Colvin, *Biographical Dictionary* (1995): 795–96.

17. **View of the Amphitheatre at Pola from the west**

James Stuart
1750s–60s
Gouache
11⅝ x 18½ in. (29.5 x 47 cm)

RIBA Library Drawings Collection, London, SD 146/4

View published in *Antiquities of Athens,* vol. 4 (1816): chap. 1, pl. I

References: Graves, *Society of Artists* (1907): 247–49; Dircks, "Library and Collections of the Royal Institute of British Architects—II" (18 December 1920): 81 illus.; Richardson, ed., *Catalogue of the Drawings Collection of the RIBA,* vol. S (1976): [4] 16, 125; Watkin, *Athenian Stuart* (1982): 20; Lever and Richardson, *Art of the Architect* (1984): 31; Colvin, *Biographical Dictionary* (1995): 795–96.

Illustrated: chronology, fig. C8.

591

No. 18. James Stuart. View of the interior of the Amphitheatre at Pola.

18. **View of the interior of the Amphitheatre at Pola**

James Stuart
1750s–60s
Gouache
11 7⁄16 x 18¼ in. (29 x 46.5 cm)

RIBA Library Drawings Collection, London, SD 146/5

View published in *Antiquities of Athens*, vol. 4 (1816): chap. 1, pl. II

References: Graves, *Society of Artists* (1907): 247–49; Dircks, "Library and Collections of the Royal Institute of British Architects—II" (18 December 1920): 81; Richardson, ed., *Catalogue of the Drawings Collection of the RIBA*, vol. S (1976): [4] 17, 125; Watkin, *Athenian Stuart* (1982): 20; Lever and Richardson, *Art of the Architect* (1984): 31; Colvin, *Biographical Dictionary* (1995): 795–96.

19. **View of the Temple of Apollo at Corinth**

James Stuart
1750s–60s
Gouache
11 7⁄16 x 18¼ in. (29 x 46.5 cm)

RIBA Library Drawings Collection, London, SD 146/2

View published in *Antiquities of Athens*, vol. 3 (1794): chap. 6, pl. I

References: Graves, *Society of Artists* (1907): 247–49; Richardson, ed., *Catalogue of the Drawings Collection of the RIBA*, vol. S (1976): [4] 13, 125; Watkin, *Athenian Stuart* (1982): 20; Lever and Richardson, *Art of the Architect* (1984): 31; Colvin, *Biographical Dictionary* (1995): 795–96.

Illustrated: chronology, fig. C11.

20. **View of a Stoa or Portico**
Identified by Stuart as the Poikile portico

James Stuart
1750s–60s
Gouache
10 7⁄16 x 15 3⁄16 in. (26.5 x 38.5 cm)

RIBA Library Drawings Collection, London, SD 145/5

View published in *Antiquities of Athens*, vol. 1 (1762): chap. 5, pl. I

References: Graves, *Society of Artists* (1907): 247–49; Richardson, ed., *Catalogue of the Drawings Collection of the*

RIBA, vol. S (1976): [4] 6, 125; Watkin, *Athenian Stuart* (1982): 20; Lever and Richardson, *Art of the Architect* (1984): 31; Colvin, *Biographical Dictionary* (1995): 795–96.

21. **View of the Gate of Athene Archegetis, Athens**

James Stuart
1750s–60s
Gouache
12 x 18 5⁄16 in. (30.5 x 46.5 cm)

RIBA Library Drawings Collection, London, SD 145/1

View published in *Antiquities of Athens*, vol. 1 (1762): chap. 1, pl. I

References: Graves, *Society of Artists* (1907): 247–49; Richardson, ed., *Catalogue of the Drawings Collection of the RIBA*, vol. S (1976): [4] 2, 125; Watkin, *Athenian Stuart* (1982): 20; Lever and Richardson, *Art of the Architect* (1984): 31; *Architecture and Its Image* (1989), 75–76, fig. 68 (etching plate); Colvin, *Biographical Dictionary* (1995): 795–96.

Illustrated: chronology, fig. C7.

22. **View of the Temple of Theseus, Athens from the southwest**

James Stuart
1750s–60s
Gouache
12 x 18 5⁄16 in. (30.5 x 46.5 cm)

RIBA Library Drawings Collection, London, SD 145/8

View published in *Antiquities of Athens*, vol. 3 (1794): chap. 1, pl. I

References: Graves, *Society of Artists* (1907): 247–49; Richardson, ed., *Catalogue of the Drawings Collection of the RIBA*, vol. S (1976): [4] 10, 125; Watkin, *Athenian Stuart* (1982): 20; Lever and Richardson, *Art of the Architect* (1984): 31; Colvin, *Biographical Dictionary* (1995): 795–96.

Illustrated: fig. 1-1.

23. **View of the Ionic Temple on the River Ilissus near Athens**

James Stuart
1750s–60s
Gouache
12 x 18⅜₆ in. (30.5 x 46.5 cm)

RIBA Library Drawings Collection, London, SD 145/2

View published in *Antiquities of Athens,* vol. 1 (1762): chap. 2, pl. I

References: Graves, *Society of Artists* (1907): 247–49; Landy, "Stuart and Revett Pioneer Archaeologists" (December 1956): 252–54, fig. 1 (engraving); Richardson, ed., *Catalogue of the Drawings Collection of the RIBA,* vol. S (1976): [4] 3, 125; Watkin, *Athenian Stuart* (1982): 20; Lever and Richardson, *Art of the Architect* (1984): 31; Colvin, *Biographical Dictionary* (1995): 795–96; McCarthy, *Classical and Gothic* (2005): 88–89, pl. 3.

Illustrated: fig. 3-25.

24. **View of the Bridge over the Ilissus River Connecting the Panathenaic Stadium with the city of Athens**
James Stuart
1750s–60s
Gouache
11⅞₆ x 18⅛ in. (29 x 46 cm)

View published in *Antiquities of Athens,*

vol. 3 (1794): chap. 7, pl. I

RIBA Library Drawings Collection, London, SD 146/1

References: Graves, *Society of Artists* (1907): 247–49; Richardson, ed., *Catalogue of the Drawings Collection of the RIBA,* vol. S (1976): [4] 14, 125; Watkin, *Athenian Stuart* (1982): 20; Lever and Richardson, *Art of the Architect* (1984): 31; Colvin, *Biographical Dictionary* (1995): 795–96.

Illustrated: chronology, fig. C10.

25. **View of the Arch of Hadrian, Athens** With the ruin of the Temple of Jupiter Olympius in the background

James Stuart
1750s–60s
Gouache
11¼ x 15⅛ in. (28.5 x 38.5 cm)

View published in *Antiquities of Athens,* vol. 3 (1794): chap. 3, pl. I

RIBA Library Drawings Collection, London, SD 145/9

References: Lawrence, "Stuart and Revett" (1938–39): figs. 22a–22b (engraving); Richardson, ed., *Catalogue of the Drawings Collection of the RIBA,* vol. S (1976): [4] 11, 125; Watkin, *Athenian Stuart* (1982): 25, fig. 8 (engraving); Lever and Richardson, *Art*

of the Architect (1984): 31; Robinson, *Shugborough* (1989): 25 (engraving); Colvin, *Biographical Dictionary* (1995): 795–96.

Illustrated: chronology, fig. C9.

26. **View of the Theater of Bacchus** With Nicholas Revett sketching in the foreground.

James Stuart
1750s–60s
Gouache
10⅝ x 15⅛ in. (27 x 38.5 cm)

RIBA Library Drawings Collection, London, SD 145/7

View published in *Antiquities of Athens,* vol. 2 (ca. 1790): chap. 3, pl. I

References: Graves, *Society of Artists* (1907): 247–49; Richardson, ed., *Catalogue of the Drawings Collection of the RIBA,* vol. S (1976): [4] 9, 125; Watkin, *Athenian Stuart* (1982): 26, fig. 11; Lever and Richardson, *Art of the Architect* (1984): 31; *Architecture and Its Image* (1989): 65, fig. 59 (engraving); Friedman, *Spencer House* (1993): 136; Colvin, *Biographical Dictionary* (1995): 795–96.

Illustrated: fig. 2-12.

No. 20. James Stuart. View of a
Stoa or Portico.

No. 26A. James Stuart. View of the Choragic Monument of Lysicrates.

26A. View of the Choragic Monument of Lysicrates or "Lanthorn of Demosthenes"
Walled into the garden end of the Hospitum of the Capuchins

James Stuart
1750s–60s
Facsimile of gouache original
10⅝ x 15⅛ in. (27 x 38.5 cm)

RIBA Library Drawings Collection, London, SD 145/4

View published in *Antiquities of Athens*, vol. 1 (1762): chap. 4, pl. 1

References: *Royal Institute of British Architects Journal*, 3rd series, 38 (6 December 1930): frontispiece; Richardson, ed., *Catalogue of the Drawings Collection of the RIBA*, vol. S (1976): [4] 5, 125; Watkin, *Athenian Stuart* (1982): 26, fig. 11; Robinson, *Shugborough* (1989): 26 illus.; Friedman, *Spencer House* (1993): 137, fig. 109 (engraving); Colvin, *Biographical Dictionary* (1995): 795–96.

27. View of the Tower of the Winds, Athens
Also known as the Horologium of Andronikos Cyrrhestes

James Stuart
1750s–60s
Gouache
12⅜ x 16¹⁵⁄₁₆ in. (31.5 x 43 cm)

RIBA Library Drawings Collection, London, SD 145/3

View published in *Antiquities of Athens*, vol. 1 (1762): chap. 3, pl. 1

References: Graves, *Society of Artists* (1907): 247–49; Richardson, ed., *Catalogue of the Drawings Collection of the RIBA*, vol. S (1976): [4] no. 4, 125; Crook, *Greek Revival* (1972): pl. 5; Watkin, *Athenian Stuart* (1982): 20, 26; Lever and Richardson, *Great Drawings from the Collection of the Royal Institute of British Architects* (1983): 12, pl. 5, 59, fig. 4, no. 23; Lever and Richardson, *Art of the Architect* (1984): 31; *Architecture and Its Image* (1989): 76–77, fig. 69 (engraving); Colvin, *Biographical Dictionary* (1995): 795–96.

Illustrated: introduction, p. 12.

28. View of the Monument of Philopappus, Athens

James Stuart
1750s–60s
Gouache
11⅜ x 17¹⁵⁄₁₆ in. (29.5 x 45.5 cm)

RIBA Library Drawings Collection, London, SD 145/10

View published in *Antiquities of Athens*, vol. 3 (1794): chap. 5, pl. I

References: Graves, *The Society of Artists* (1907): 247–49; Richardson, ed., *Catalogue of the Drawings Collection of the RIBA*, vol. S (1976): [4] no. 12, 125; Watkin, *Athenian Stuart* (1982): 20; Lever and Richardson, *The Art of the Architect* (1984): 31; McCarthy, *Classical and Gothic* (2005): pl. 2, fig. 5.2.

Illustrated: fig. 2–11.

29. **View of the Caryatid Porch, the Erechtheion, the west end of the Temple of Minerva Polias, and the Pandrosium on the Acropolis, Athens**

James Stuart
1750s–60s
Gouache
10 7/16 x 15 1/8 in. (26.5 x 38.5 cm)

RIBA Library Drawings Collection, London, SD 145/6

View published in *Antiquities of Athens*, vol. 2 (ca. 1790): chap. 2, pl. II

References: Graves, *Society of Artists* (1907): 247–49; Clarke, "English Discovery of Greece" (March 1941): 72 illus. (engraving); Landy, "Stuart and Revett" (December 1956): 255–57, fig. 5; Richardson, ed., *Catalogue of the Drawings Collection of the RIBA,* vol. S (1976): [4] no. 4, 125; Crook, *Greek Revival* (1972): pl. 5; Watkin, *Athenian Stuart* (1982): 19; Lever and Richardson, *Great Drawings from the Collection of the Royal Institute of British Architects* (1983): 23, 58–59; Lever and Richardson, *Art of the Architect* (1984): 31; Friedman, *Spencer House* (1993): 128–29 illus.; Colvin, *Biographical Dictionary* (1995): 795–96.

Illustrated: fig. 2-10.

30. **View of the Incantada or Propylaea of the Hippodrome, Salonica**

James Stuart
1750s–60s
Gouache
12 3/8 x 18 1/8 in. (31.5 x 46 cm)

RIBA Library Drawings Collection, London, SD 146/3

View published in *Antiquities of Athens*, vol. 3 (ca. 1794): chap. 9, pl. I

References: Graves, *Society of Artists* (1907): 247–49; Richardson, ed., *Catalogue of the Drawings Collection of the RIBA,* vol. S (1976): [4] 14, 125; Watkin, *Athenian Stuart* (1982): 20, 29, fig. 27 (detail); Lever and Richardson, *Art of the Architect* (1984): 31; Colvin, *Biographical Dictionary* (1995): 795–96.

Illustrated: fig. 1-16.

31. **Portrait of James Lee**

James Stuart
ca. 1753–54
Oil on canvas
25 5/16 x 21 9/16 in. (64.3 x 54.7 cm)

The Hunterian Museum and Art Gallery, University of Glasgow, GLAHA 44250

References: Hopkinson, "Portrait by James Athenian Stuart" (November 1990): 794–95, fig. 48; Bristol, "Stuart and the Genesis of the Greek Revival" (1997): 95–96, fig. 14.

Illustrated: fig. 4-2.

32. **Portrait of James Dawkins**

James Stuart; engraving by James McArdell
ca. 1768
Mezzotint
12 13/16 x 8 13/16 in. (32.5 x 22.4 cm)

Inscribed: printed recto, "J. Stuart Delin:"; "Js McArdell fecit"; "James Dawkins, junr,, Esqr,,"; in pen and ink in the hand of Horace Walpole, "he travelled to Palmyra & Balbec with Mr Wood."

By courtesy of the Trustees of The British Museum, London, McArdell C.S. 51, II; a.154.Port.o.15

Reference: Bristol, "Stuart and the Genesis of the Greek Revival" (1997): 199, fig. 26.

Illustrated: fig. 2-7.

33. **"The five orders of PERRIWIGS"**

William Hogarth
1761
Engraving
11 7/8 x 8 3/4 in. (30.2 x 22.2 cm)

Inscribed: "The five orders of PERRI-WIGS, as they were worn at the late CORONATION, measured Architectonically"; extensive printed letterpress

Guildhall Library, City of London, Hogarth Collection, loc. 64, p543527x

Reference: Bristol, "Stuart and the Genesis of the Greek Revival" (1997): 146–47, fig. 20.

Illustrated: fig. 2-14.

34. **Box used to store measuring instruments**

Once belonging to James Stuart
n.d.
Stained pine, green felt lining
1 1/8 x 25 x 2 9/16 in. (2.9 x 63.4 x 6.5 cm)

Inscribed: inside lid, "Formerly belonged / To Poor Stuart / B [onomi] copied from catal. [ogue]."

By courtesy of the Trustees of Sir John Soane's Museum, London, X1232

Reference: Greenwood, "Catalogue of Pictures . . . and Other Effects of the Late James Stuart" (27 June 1791): lot 26.

Illustrated: fig. 2-22.

35. *Les Ruines des plus beaux monuments de la Grèce . . .*
Open to pl. VI, View of the Propylaeum, Athens; engraving by Jacques Philippe Le Bas

Julien-David Le Roy. Inscribed: "Le Roy Arch. del. in Græciâ"; "Vüe des ruines des Propylées où de la Porte de la Citadelle d'Athene"; "Le Bas Sculp"
Paris: H. L. Guerin & L.F. Delatour, Jean-Luc Nyon; Amsterdam: Jean Neaulme, 1758
Book (closed): 22⁷⁄₁₆ x 17¾ x 2 in. (57 x 45 x 5 cm)

By permission of The British Library, London, 1899.g.30

References: Wiebenson, *Sources of Greek Revival Architecture* (1969): 33–34; Crook, *Greek Revival* (1972): 18; Pevsner, *Outline of European Architecture* (1973): 356; Middleton and Watkin, *Neoclassical and Nineteenth Century Architecture* (1980): 69; Watkin, *Athenian Stuart* (1982): 14; E. Harris, "Stuart and Revett" in *British Architectural Books and Writers* (1990): 43–44; Curl, *Classical Architecture* (2001): 147; Scott, *Pleasures of Antiquity* (2003): 89.

Illustrated: fig. 1-6.

36. *Antiquities of Athens*, volume 1
Open to title page. Inscribed: title and "James Basire Sculp"

James Stuart and Nicholas Revett
London: John Haberkorn, 1762
Book (closed): 21⁵⁄₁₆ x 15 x 1⅝ in. (54.1 x 38.1 x 4.1 cm)

Courtesy of the Library, The Bard Graduate Center for Studies in the Decorative Arts, Design, and Culture, New York

References: Nichols, *Literary Anecdotes*, vol. 9 (1815): 143–50; Ellis, *Original Letters of Eminent Literary Men* (1843): 379–89; Hamilton, *Historical Notes of the Society of Dilettanti* (1855): 42–45; Clarke, "English Discovery of Greece" (March 1941): 72; Landy, "Stuart and Revett" (December 1956): 252–59;

Wiebenson, *Sources of Greek Revival Architecture* (1969): 1–18; Crook, *Greek Revival* (1972): 13–17; Pevsner, *Outline of European Architecture* (1973): 356; Middleton and Watkin, *Neoclassical and Nineteenth Century Architecture* (1980): 88–90; Watkin, *Athenian Stuart* (1982): 15–22; Lever and Richardson, *Great Drawings from the Collection of the Royal Institute of British Architects* (1983): no. 23; *Architecture and Its Image* (1989): 63, 67, 70, 73–80; E. Harris, "Stuart and Revett" in *British Architectural Books and Writers* (1990): 439–50; Eisner, *Travelers to an Antique Land* (1991): 71–72; Jenkyns, *Dignity and Decadence* (1992): 50–52; Curl, *Georgian Architecture* (1993): 77–82; Friedman, *Spencer House* (1993): 128, 130; Colvin, *Biographical Dictionary* (1995): 794; Worsley, *Classical Architecture in Britain* (1995): 258–60; Curl, *Classical Architecture* (2001): 147; Scott, *Pleasures of Antiquity* (2003): 89; McCarthy, *Classical and Gothic* (2005): 83–92.

Illustrated: see bibliography; see also figs. 1-29, 3-26, 3-33, 3-36, 3-37, 5-39, 7-23, 7-32, 10-27, 10-29, 10-34, 10-57, 11-12, 11-16, 11-17.

37. *Antiquities of Athens*, volume 1
Once owned by the second Marquess of Rockingham.

James Stuart and Nicholas Revett
London: John Haberkorn, 1762.
Gold tooled red morocco; binding designed by Stuart
Book (closed): 21¼ x 15⅜ x 1¹³⁄₁₆ in. (54 x 39 x 4.5 cm)

By permission of The British Library, London, c.160.ee.2

References: Nixon, *Five Centuries* (1978): no. 69; Bond, *Thomas Hollis* (1990): 56–57, fig. 19; Nixon and Foot, *History of Decorated Bookbinding* (1992): 88, pl. 93 (similar binding on a similar set).

Illustrated: fig. 4-1.

38. *The Latin Play at Westminster School*
Depicting the 1808 copy of a backdrop designed by James Stuart in 1758

George Reid Sarjent
1840
Watercolor
21½ x 18¼ in. (56.6 x 46.4 cm)
(framed)

By permission of the Governing Body of Westminster School, London

References: Markham, *Naval Career* (1883): 14; Colvin, *Biographical Dictionary* (1995): 796.

Illustrated: fig. 4-13.

39. **Design for ornament, with a vase on a pedestal flanked by griffins**

James Stuart
ca. 1759
Pen and ink and gray wash
10⁹⁄₁₆ x 12¼ in. (26.8 x 31.1 cm)

Inscribed: verso, "Athenian – Jas. Stewart. J.B. Papworth"

The Pierpont Morgan Library, New York. Bequest of Junius S. Morgan and Gift of Henry S. Morgan, 1966.10:39

References: *Exhibition of Drawings of Architectural Subjects* (1884): no. 303; J. Harris, *Catalogue of British Drawings for Architecture* (1971): 228, 231, fig. 34; Watkin, *Athenian Stuart* (1982): 54, fig. 78; Bristol, "Stuart and the Genesis of the Greek Revival" (1997): 242, fig. 34.

40. **Tripod perfume burner for Wentworth Woodhouse, Yorkshire, for the second Marquess of Rockingham**

James Stuart ; probably made by Diederich Nicolaus Anderson
1760
Cast and chased gilt bronze, marble base
21³⁄₁₆ x 10⅝ x 7⁵⁄₁₆ in. (53.97 x 27 x 18.6 cm)

Courtesy of the Trustees of The Victoria and Albert Museum, London, M.46a-1948

No. 39. James Stuart. Design for ornament.

References: E. Harris, *Furniture of Robert Adam* (1963): 64–65, fig. 6; Udy, "Neo-Classicism and the Evolution of Adam's Vase Designs" (August 1972): 194, 196, fig. 6; Goodison, "Mr. Stuart's Tripod" (October 1972): 695–96, 701, figs. 65–66; Middleton and Watkin, *Neoclassical and Nineteenth Century Architecture* (1980): 90; Ottomeyer and Pröschel, *Vergoldete Bronzen,* vol. 1 (1986): 270, pl. 4.10.2; Snodin and Styles, *Design and the Decorative Arts: Britain* (2001): 201, fig. 35; Goodison, *Matthew Boulton: Ormolu* (2002): 38, 74, figs. 28–29, 276; Christie's London, *Out of the Ordinary* (10 May 2006): 358.

Illustrated (other tripod in pair): figs. 11-7 and 11-15 (detail).

41. **The great hall, Wentworth Woodhouse**
Also called the Grand Saloon or Marble Saloon, viewed from the southeast

Ornament designed by James Stuart
ca. 1755–68
Photographed in 1987

English Heritage / National Monuments Record, Swindon BB93/2854

References: Young, *Six Months Tour,* vol. 1 (1770): 281; O. B., "Wentworth Woodhouse, Yorkshire" (31 March 1906): 451 illus., 455 illus.; Tipping, "Wentworth Woodhouse—III" (4 October 1924): 513–14, fig. 2; Lawrence, "Stuart and Revett" (1938–39): 141; Pevsner, *Yorkshire: The West Riding* (1967): 60 illus., 542; Hussey, *English Country Houses,* vol. 1, *Early Georgian* (1984): 149, fig. 246, 153; Colvin, *Biographical Dictionary* (1995): 796; Scott, *Pleasures of Antiquity* (2003): 117–18, fig. 74.

Illustrated: fig. 6-7a.

42. **Chimneypiece on the south wall of the long gallery, Wentworth Woodhouse**

Attributed to James Stuart
Late 1750s–early 1760s
Photographed in 1987

English Heritage / National

Monuments Record, Swindon BB93/2931

References: Tipping, "Wentworth Woodhouse," parts I and III (20 September 1924): 410 (bottom); (4 October 1924): 515, fig. 5; Lawrence, "Stuart and Revett" (1938–39): 141; Binney, "Wentworth Woodhouse Revisited—II" (24 March 1983): 710, fig. 8; Colvin, *Biographical Dictionary* (1995): 796.

Illustrated: fig. 6-11.

43. *The West Front of Shugborough, Staffordshire*

Moses Griffith
1769
Watercolor
11⅜ x 19¼ in. (29 x 49 cm)

Courtesy of Shugborough, Staffordshire, The Anson Collection, SHUG.P.66
(The National Trust, UK)

Illustrated: fig. 6-12.

44. Pier table from the Red Drawing Room, Shugborough, Staffordshire (one of a pair), for Thomas Anson

James Stuart
ca. 1763–65
Gilt and painted wood, green Cippolino marble top
34⁷⁄₁₆ x 72¼ x 27³⁄₁₆ in. (87.5 x 183.3 x 69 cm)

Courtesy of Shugborough, Staffordshire, The Anson Collection, SHUG.F.34a (The National Trust, UK)

References: *Shugborough* (1973): 17; *Shugborough* (1980): 19; Robinson, *Shugborough* (1989): 37 illus., 62 illus.; Bristol, "Stuart and the Genesis of the Greek Revival" (1997): 274.

Illustrated: fig. 10-72; see also chronology fig. C4.

45. Gilt tripod stand from Shugborough (one of a pair), for Thomas Anson

James Stuart
ca. 1760s
Gilt wood, gilt brass surround, marble inserts
36 x 17 in. (91.5 x 43.2 cm)

Courtesy of Shugborough, Staffordshire, The Anson Collection, SHUG.F.37 (The National Trust, UK)

References: *Shugborough* (National Trust, 1973): 17; *Shugborough* (National Trust, 1980): 19; Robinson, *Shugborough* (1989): 62–63 illus.; Bristol, "Stuart and the Genesis of the Greek Revival" (1997): 274; *Shugborough Estate* (1999): 10.

Illustrated: fig. 10-73.

46. The dining room, Nuneham Park, Oxfordshire, for Simon, first Earl Harcourt

Attributed to James Stuart,
ca. 1756–64
Photographed in 2006

References: Warren, "Nuneham Courtney" (29 November 1913): 752 illus.; Worsley, "Nuneham Park Revisited—I" (3 January 1985): 19, fig. 8; Stillman, *English Neo-Classical Architecture,* vol. 1 (1988): 130.

Illustrated: fig. 6-22.

47. Chimneypiece in the dining room at Nuneham Park

James Stuart
ca. 1756–64
Photographed in 2006

References: Worsley, "Nuneham Park Revisited—I" (3 January 1985): 19, figs. 3–5; Stillman, *English Neo-Classical Architecture*, vol. 1 (1988): 130, fig. 75; Bristol, "Stuart and the Genesis of the Greek Revival" (1997): 247, fig. 35b.

Illustrated: fig. 6-24.

48. Design for a chimneypiece at Nuneham Park

James Stuart
ca. 1756
Pen and ink, watercolor
9¹¹⁄₁₆ x 12¹³⁄₁₆ in. (24.6 x 32.5 cm)

Inscribed: "At Newnham by Mr Stewart"

RIBA Library Drawings Collection, London, SD 104/31

References: Warren, "Nuneham Courtney" (29 November 1913): 752; Richardson, ed., *Catalogue of the Drawings Collection of the RIBA,* vol. S (1976): [1]: 123.

Illustrated: fig. 6-27.

49. Design for the decoration of the window wall of a state room, Kedleston Hall, Derbyshire, for Nathaniel Curzon

James Stuart
1757–58
Pen and ink, color wash, pencil inscriptions
13⅞ x 20½ in. (35.2 x 52.1 cm)

Inscribed: written in 4th window from the left, "these upper windows are in length twice their breadth, the Lower ones are not near so high. Whether that was intended to be so?"; scale at bottom.

Courtesy of Kedleston Hall, Derbyshire, The Scarsdale Collection, KED/231/10/3 (The National Trust, UK)

References: J. Harris, "Early Neo-Classical Furniture" (1966): 3; Musgrave, *Adam and Hepplewhite* (1966): 41, 182, fig. 6; Goodison, "Mr. Stuart's Tripod" (October 1972): 695–66, fig. 62; Hardy and Hayward, "Kedleston Hall—II" (2 February 1978): 262–63, fig. 4; Watkin, *Athenian Stuart* (1982): 33, fig. 20; L. Harris, *Robert Adam and Kedleston* (1987): 27–29, fig. 14; E. Harris, "Stuart and Revett" in *British Architectural Books and Writers* (1990): fig. 12; Bristol, "Stuart and the Genesis of the Greek Revival" (1997): 251, fig. 38; Banham, *Interior Decoration,* vol. 2 (1997): 1244; E. Harris, *Genius of Robert Adam* (2001): 19–20, fig. 13.

Illustrated: fig. 6-30.

50. Design for the decoration of the chimneypiece wall of a state room, Kedleston Hall

James Stuart
1757–58
Pen and ink, watercolor, pencil
15 x 21¾ in. (38.1 x 55.2 cm)

Courtesy of Kedleston Hall, Derbyshire, The Scarsdale Collection, KED/1/10-4 (The National Trust, UK)

References: J. Harris, "Early Neo-

Classical Furniture" (1966): 3; Goodison, "Mr. Stuart's Tripod" (October 1972): 696, fig. 71; Hardy and Hayward, "Kedleston Hall—II" (2 February 1978): 262–64, fig. 6; Watkin, *Athenian Stuart* (1982): fig. 21; L. Harris, *Robert Adam and Kedleston* (1987): 27–28, fig. 11; Stillman, *English Neo-Classical Architecture,* vol. 1 (1988): 112, 114, fig. 62; E. Harris, "Stuart and Revett" in *British Architectural Books and Writers* (1990): fig. 12; Banham, *Interior Decoration,* vol. 2 (1997): 1244; Bristol, "Stuart and the Genesis of the Greek Revival" (1997): 251, fig. 38.

Illustrated: fig. 6-31.

51. **Design for the decoration of the end wall of a state room, Kedleston Hall**

James Stuart
1757–58
Pen and ink, watercolor, pencil
14¾ x 12¾ in. (37.5 x 32.4 cm)

Courtesy of Kedleston Hall, Derbyshire, The Scarsdale Collection, KED/1/10-2 (The National Trust, UK)

References: J. Harris, "Early Neo-Classical Furniture" (1966): 3; Goodison, "Mr. Stuart's Tripod" (October 1972): 696, fig. 70; Hardy and Hayward, "Kedleston Hall—II" (2 February 1978): 262–64, fig. 7; Watkin, *Athenian Stuart* (1982): 34, fig. 22; L. Harris, *Robert Adam and Kedleston* (1987): 27–28, fig. 12; Stillman, *English Neo-Classical Architecture,* vol. 1 (1988): 115, fig. 63; Banham, *Interior Decoration,* vol. 2 (1997): 1244; Bristol, "Stuart and the Genesis of the Greek Revival" (1997): 252–53, fig. 41; E. Harris, *Genius of Robert Adam* (2001): 20, fig. 15.

Illustrated: fig. 6-33.

52. **Design for the decoration of the end wall of a state room, Kedleston Hall**

James Stuart
1757–58
Pen and ink, watercolor, gray wash
14¹⁄₁₆ x 12⁷⁄₈ in. (35.7 x 32.7 cm)

Courtesy of Kedleston Hall,

Derbyshire, The Scarsdale Collection, KED/1/10-1 (The National Trust, UK)

References: J. Harris, "Early Neo-Classical Furniture" (1966): 3; Goodison, "Mr. Stuart's Tripod" (October 1972): 696, fig. 69; Hardy and Hayward," Kedleston Hall—II" (2 February 1978): 262–64, fig. 5; Watkin, *Athenian Stuart* (1982): 33–34, fig. 23; L. Harris, *Robert Adam and Kedleston* (1987): 27–28, fig. 13; Stillman, *English Neo-Classical Architecture,* vol. 1 (1988): 115, fig. 63; Banham, *Interior Decoration,* vol. 2 (1997): 1244; Bristol, "Stuart and the Genesis of the Greek Revival" (1997): 252, fig. 39; E. Harris, *Genius of Robert Adam* (2001): 20, 23, figs. 13–14; Snodin and Styles, *Design and the Decorative Arts: Britain* (2001): 232, fig. 33.

Illustrated: fig. 6-32.

53. **Design for a side table**
With tripod perfume burner and a pair of antique-style urns

James Stuart
1760
Pen and ink, pencil, and yellow wash
10⁵⁄₈ x 7⅛ in. (27 x 18 cm)

RIBA Library Drawings Collection, London, SD 62/2

References: Musgrave, *Adam and Hepplewhite and Other Neo-Classical Furniture* (1966): 41, fig. 6; J. Harris, "Newly Acquired Designs" (1979): 73–74, fig. 16b; Lever, *Architects' Designs for Furniture* (1982): 46–47, fig. 14; Friedman, *Spencer House* (1993): 156, fig. 138.

Illustrated: fig. 11-8.

54. **"Design of the West End of the Dining Room," Kedleston Hall**

Robert Adam
1762
Pen and ink, watercolor, pencil additions
13½ x 17¾ in. (34.3 x 45.1 cm)

Inscribed: recto, "Design of the West End of the Dining Room with the

Nich & Sideboard"; "Robt Adam Architect 1762"; with scale

Courtesy of Kedleston Hall, Derbyshire, The Scarsdale Collection, KED.3.7.7 (The National Trust, UK)

References: E. Harris, *Furniture of Robert Adam* (1963): 63–64, fig. 3; Musgrave, *Adam and Hepplewhite* (1966): 181, fig. 2; Goodison, "Mr. Stuart's Tripod" (October 1972): fig. 61; Wilson, "Kedleston Fountain" (1983): 6, figs. 12–13; L. Harris, *Robert Adam and Kedleston* (1987): 30–31, figs. 15–16; Stillman, *English Neo-Classical Architecture,* vol. 1 (1988): 115, fig. 63; Snodin, "Adam Silver Reassessed" (January 1997): 18, fig. 27; E. Harris, *Genius of Robert Adam* (2001): 33, fig. 143; Snodin and Styles, *Design and the Decorative Arts: Britain* (2001): 232, fig. 33.

Illustrated: fig. 11-18.

55. **Record drawing of a tripod perfume burner for the dining room, Kedleston Hall**

Draftsman unknown
ca. 1760–62
Pen and ink, gray wash, pencil
17⅛ x 11½ in. (43.6 x 29.2 cm)

Inscribed: "Tripod for Sir Nathaniel Curzon Bart."

By courtesy of the Trustees of Sir John Soane's Museum, London, Adam Ms., vol. 25, no. 90

References: Goodison, "Mr. Stuart's Tripod" (October 1972): 695, fig. 59; Goodison, *Matthew Boulton: Ormolu* (2002): 71–74, fig. 24; Christie's London, *Out of the Ordinary* (10 May 2006): 358.

Illustrated: fig. 11-2.

56. **Record drawing of a tripod perfume burner for the dining room, Kedleston Hall**

Draftsman unknown
ca. 1760–62
Pen and ink, gray wash, pencil
20½ x 11⅜₆ in. (52 x 29.3 cm)

Inscribed: "Tripod for Sir Nathaniel Curzon Bart."

By courtesy of the Trustees of Sir John Soane's Museum, London, Adam Ms., vol. 25, no. 89

References: Goodison, "Mr. Stuart's Tripod" (October 1972): 695, fig. 57; Ottomeyer and Pröschel, *Vergoldete Bronzen,* vol. 1 (1986): 270, pl. 4.10.1; Goodison, *Matthew Boulton: Ormolu* (2002): 71–74, fig. 23; Christie's London, *Out of the Ordinary* (10 May 2006): 358.

Illustrated: fig. 11-3.

57. **Tripod perfume burner, Kedleston Hall**

James Stuart; probably made by Diederich Nicolaus Anderson
ca. 1760
Cast and chased gilt bronze, marble base
35¹³⁄₁₆ x 15⅜ in. (91 x 39 cm) (with base)

Courtesy of Kedleston Hall, Derbyshire, The Scarsdale Collection, Ked/Med/17 (The National Trust, UK)

References: E. Harris, *Furniture of Robert Adam* (1963): 64–65; Goodison, "Mr. Stuart's Tripod" (October 1972): 696–99, fig. 56; Middleton and Watkin, *Neoclassical and Nineteenth Century Architecture* (1980): 90; Ottomeyer and Pröschel, *Vergoldete Bronzen,* vol. 1 (1986): 270, pl. 4.10.2; Reilly, *Wedgwood,* vol. 2 (1989): 489, fig. 817; Knox, "Acquisitions for National Trust Properties" (April 1997): 50, fig. 1; E. Harris, *Genius of Robert Adam* (2001): 34, fig. 44; Goodison, *Matthew Boulton: Ormolu* (2002): 38, 71–75, 276, figs. 25–27; Bristol, "James Stuart and the London Building Trades" (2003): 2;

Christie's London, *Out of the Ordinary* (10 May 2006): 358.

Illustrated: fig. 11-1.

58. **Record drawing of a "chestnut" vase for the dining room at Kedleston Hall**

Draftsman unknown
ca. 1760–62
Pen and ink
11⅞₆ x 16⅜₆ in. (29 x 41.1 cm)

Inscribed: "For Nathaniel Curzon Baronet"; with scale

By courtesy of the Trustees of Sir John Soane's Museum, London, Adam Ms., vol. 25, nos. 81–83

References: Wilson, "Kedleston Fountain" (1983): 6, 10–11, fig. 14; Snodin, "Putting Adam into Context" (1995): 13–14, fig. 1.

Illustrated: fig. 11-4.

59. **"Chestnut" vase at Kedleston Hall (one of a pair)**

Attributed to James Stuart; probably made by Diederich Nicolaus Anderson
ca. 1757–58
Patinated copper, applied ormolu ornament, shallow stained base, further stained wood base added 1765
21 x 9½ in. (53.3 x 24.1 cm) (with base)

Courtesy of Kedleston Hall, Derbyshire, The Scarsdale Collection, KED.M.19b (The National Trust, UK)

Reference: Knox, "Acquisitions for National Trust Properties" (April 1997): 50, fig. 1.

Illustrated: fig. 11-22.

60. **Design for a plate warmer, for Kedleston Hall**

Attributed to James Stuart
ca. 1757
Pen and ink and wash
18 x 11⅜₆ in. (45.7 x 28.7 cm)

Courtesy of Kedleston Hall,

Derbyshire, The Scarsdale Collection, KED/4/23 (K.4.22.1) (The National Trust, UK)

References: L. Harris, *Robert Adam and Kedleston* (1987): 34, fig. 18; Goodison, *Matthew Boulton: Ormolu* (2002): 38, 371 n. 38.

Illustrated: fig. 11-25.

61. **Plate warmer, Kedleston Hall**

Attributed to James Stuart; made by Diederich Nicolaus Anderson
1760
Patinated copper, applied ormolu ornament, stained wood base
45¼ x 20½ (114.9 x 52.1 cm) (with base)

Marks: engraving on the rim, "Diedrich Nicolaus Anderson made this Plate-Warmer in the year 1760"

Courtesy of Kedleston Hall, The Scarsdale Collection, KED.M.18 (The National Trust, UK)

References: L. Harris, *Robert Adam and Kedleston* (1987): 34 illus.; E. Harris, *Genius of Robert Adam* (2001): 34; Goodison, *Matthew Boulton: Ormolu* (2002): 35–38, fig. 7.

Illustrated: figs. 11-23 and 11-24 (back).

62. **Design for the wall of a painted room with coved recess**

James Stuart
ca. 1757–58
Pencil, pen, and yellow-gray washes
14 x 7¼ in. (35.5 x 18.5 cm)

RIBA Library Drawings Collection, London, SD 62/1

References: Hardy and Hayward, "Kedleston Hall—II" (2 February 1978): 264, fig. 7; J. Harris, "Newly Acquired Designs" (1979): 73, fig. 16a.

Illustrated: fig. 6-45.

63. **Painted ceiling of the Tapestry Room, Hagley Hall, Worcestershire, for George, first Lord Lyttelton**

Corner vignettes of "zephyrs" by James Stuart; central panel attributed to Giovanni Battista Cipriani
1758–59
Photographed in 2006

References: Young, *Six Months Tour*, vol. 2 (1770): 349; Neale, *Views of the Seats of Noblemen and Gentlemen*, series 1, vol. 1 (1822): n.p. ("Hagley Park"); Bolton, "Hagley Park—I" (16 October 1915): 523 illus., 526; Lawrence, "Stuart and Revett" (1938–39) 138; Nares, "Hagley Hall—II" (26 September 1957): 609–10, fig. 4; Croft-Murray, *Decorative Painting in England*, vol. 2 (1970): no. 1, 284; Hussey, *English Country Houses*, vol. 1, *Early Georgian* (1984): 199, fig. 355; Banham, *Interior Decoration*, vol. 2 (1997): 1243–44; Bristol, "Stuart and the Genesis of the Greek Revival" (1997): 301–2, fig. 75; Bristol, "Society of Dilettanti" (July 2000): 50; Bristol, "Painted Rooms of 'Athenian' Stuart" (2000): 169–70, fig. 4.

Illustrated: fig. 6-37.

64. **One of the four "zephyrs," detail of the painted ceiling, Tapestry Room, Hagley Hall**

James Stuart
1758–59
Photographed in 2006

References: Bristol, "Stuart and the Genesis of the Greek Revival" (1997): 301–2, fig. 76; Bristol, "Society of Dilettanti" (July 2000): 49–50, fig. 8; Bristol, "22 Portman Square" (Summer 2001): 72, fig. 1.

Illustrated: fig. 6-38.

65. **Design for the decoration of the chimney wall in the hall, Wimbledon Park, Surrey, for John, later first Earl Spencer**

James Stuart
ca. 1758
Pen and ink, pencil, gray wash

7⅞ x 11 1/16 in. (20 x 28 cm)

Inscribed: in the borders of the roundels, "Bacchus"; "Mercury Fortune"; "Ceres"

RIBA Library Drawings Collection, London, SD 62/5 (1)

References: J. Harris, "Newly Acquired Designs" (1979): 74, pl. 18a; Watkin, *Athenian Stuart* (1982): 40, fig. 41; Friedman, *Spencer House* (1993): 131, fig. 101; Bristol, "Stuart and the Genesis of the Greek Revival" (1997): 256–57; fig. 43.

Illustrated: fig. 6-41.

66. **Design for the decoration of the chimney wall of the great dining room, Wimbledon Park**

James Stuart
ca. 1758
Pen and ink, color wash
7⅛ x 11 7/16 in. (18 x 29 cm)

RIBA Library Drawings Collection, London, SD 62/5 (2)

References: J. Harris, "Newly Acquired Designs" (1979): 74–75, pl. 18b; Lever, *Architects' Designs for Furniture* (1982): 46–47, figs. 13a–b, pl. III; Watkin, *Athenian Stuart* (1982): 40, fig. 41; J. Harris, *Architect and the British Country House* (1985): 160–61, fig. 43; Bristol, "Stuart and the Genesis of the Greek Revival" (1997): 256–57, fig. 43.

Illustrated: fig. 6-42.

67. **Design for the decoration of a closet, Wimbledon Park**

James Stuart
ca. 1758
Pen and ink, color wash
7⅞ x 5 15/16 in. (20 x 15 cm)

Inscribed: On frame of right hand picture, "VENUS VICTRIX"

RIBA Library Drawings Collection, London, SD 62/6 (1)

References: J. Harris, "Newly Acquired Designs" (1979): 75, pl. 19; Lever,

Architects' Designs for Furniture (1982): 46, fig. 13b; J. Harris, *Architect and the British Country House* (1985): fig. 160; Bristol, "Stuart and the Genesis of the Greek Revival" (1997): 256, fig. 42b; Bristol, "Painted Rooms of 'Athenian' Stuart" (2000): 165–66, fig. 2.

Illustrated: fig. 6-1.

68. **Design for the decoration of a closet with bookcase, Wimbledon Park**

James Stuart
ca. 1758
Pen and ink, color wash
7 13/16 x 5 15/16 in. (19.8 x 15.1 cm)

Inscribed: on picture frame, "ALLEGRO" and "PENSOROSO"

RIBA Library Drawings Collection, London, SD 62/6 (2)

References: J. Harris, "Newly Acquired Designs" (1979): 75, pl. 20; Lever, *Architects' Designs for Furniture* (1982): 46, fig. 13; Bristol, "Stuart and the Genesis of the Greek Revival" (1997): 256, fig. 42a; Bristol, "Painted Rooms of 'Athenian' Stuart" (2000): 165–66, fig. 2.

Illustrated: fig. 6-44.

69. **Design for a chimneypiece, overmantel, and fire grate**

James Stuart
Late 1750s–early 1760s
Pen and ink, graphite, gray wash
13 7/16 x 8 5/16 in. (34.2 x 21.2 cm)

The Pierpont Morgan Library, New York. Bequest of Junius S. Morgan and Gift of Henry S. Morgan, 1966.10:37

References: J. Harris, "Early Neo-Classical Furniture" (1966): 1–6, pl. vA; J. Harris, *Catalogue of British Drawings for Architecture* (1971): 228–29, pl. 171; Stillman, *English Neo-Classical Architecture*, vol. 1 (1988): 130–31, fig. 76.

Illustrated: fig. 6-26.

70. **The great hall, Hornby Castle, Yorkshire, for Robert Darcy, fourth Earl of Holdernesse**

Attributed to James Stuart
ca. 1760s
Photographed in 1906

© Country Life Picture Library

References: "Hornby Castle" (14 July 1906): 57 illus.; Worsley, "Hornby Castle—I" (29 June 1989) 190–91, fig. 7; Worsley, "Out from Adam's Shadow" (14 May 1992): 102; Worsley, *England's Lost Houses* (2002): 72–73.

Illustrated: fig. 6-46.

71. **The Organ Case at Newby Hall, Yorkshire, for William Weddell**

James Stuart
ca. 1767
Mahogany case, oil gilt lead and tin pipes
Photographed in 2006

Courtesy of Mr. Richard Compton, Newby Hall Estate, Yorkshire

References: *Newby Hall* (1968): 11 illus., 21; Cornforth, "Newby Hall—I" (7 June 1979): 1804–6, fig. 9; Watkin, *Athenian Stuart* (1982): 41, fig. 42; Middleton, "Sculpture Gallery at Newby Hall" (August 1986): 53; Friedman, *Spencer House* (1993): 146; Bristol, "Stuart and the Genesis of the Greek Revival" (1997): 154, fig. 21; *Welcome to Newby* (2004): 15 illus.

Illustrated: figs. 10-64, 10-66 (detail), 10-68 (detail).

72. **Design for a chimneypiece**

James Stuart
ca. 1766
Pencil, pen and ink, gray wash
8⅜ x 11¹⁄₁₆ in. (21.2 x 28 cm)

Inscribed: "4 feet"

RIBA Library Drawings Collection, London, SD 62/17

References: Cornforth, "Correspondence, Designs for Newby"

(21 June 1979): 2016 illus.; J. Harris, "Newly Acquired Designs" (1979): 77, pl. 27b; Watkin, *Athenian Stuart* (1982): 43, fig. 41.

Illustrated: fig. 10-65.

73. **Belvedere, the Seat of Sir Sampson Gideon**

Engraving by R. Godfrey
Published by F. Blyth, 1777
Hand-colored engraving
6⅞ x 8³⁄₁₆ in. (17.5 x 20.7 cm)

Inscribed: "BELVEDERE The Seat of Sr SAMPSON GIDEON BART."; "Godfrey Sc"; "Pubd. By F. Blyth Septr 1. 1777"

Courtesy of Bexley Local Studies and Archive Centre, Bexleyheath

Illustrated: fig. 6-57.

74. **Front elevation of Belvedere House, Erith, Kent, for Sir Sampson Gideon**

James Stuart
ca. 1764–80
Photographed in 1937

English Heritage / National Monuments Record, Swindon
C37/756

References: *London And Its Environs* (1761): 271; Strickland, "Belvedere As It Was" (26 January 1912), *Belvedere House, 1947–60*, Erith Borough Council Correspondence LAER/DA 4/4/23; Lawrence, "Stuart and Revett" (1938–39): 142, fig. 24b; "Has Mansion Any Merit?" (6 March 1953): frontispiece; "Princess Alexandra Visits Belvedere" (3 July 1959): 1; "Gilded Ceiling in the Gold Room" (9 October 1959): 12; McMillan, *Royal Alfred Story* (1965): 66–67 illus.; Croft-Murray, *Decorative Painting*, vol. 2 (1970): no. 2, 228; Kelly, *Decorative Wedgwood* (1965): 75; Watkin, *Athenian Stuart* (1982): 51, fig. 64; Worsley, "First Greek Revival Architecture" (April 1985): 229; Brunton and Godfrey, "Royal Alfred Institution for Old Seamen" (April 1992): 191–92; Worsley,

"Out from Adam's Shadow" (14 May 1992): 101; Colvin, *Biographical Dictionary* (1995): 796–97; Bristol, "Stuart and the Genesis of the Greek Revival" (1997): 318, fig. 83; Bristol, "Society of Dilettanti" (July 2000): 54, fig. 16.

Illustrated: fig. 6-58.

75. **Chimneypiece formerly in the anteroom to the dining room, Belvedere House**

James Stuart; plaques by Josiah Wedgwood
ca. 1780s
Photographed in 2005

Private collection

References: Kelly, *Decorative Wedgwood* (1965): 65–66, 75, fig. 26; Wakin, *Athenian Stuart* (1982): 51, fig. 66; Bristol, "Stuart and the Genesis of the Greek Revival" (1997): 319; Wooler, *Great Estates: Six Country Houses* (2000): 80–81.

Illustrated: fig. 6-60.

76. **The dining room, Belvedere House**

James Stuart
ca. 1764–80
Photographed in 1937

English Heritage / National Monuments Record, Swindon
BB99/06823

References: Watkin, *Athenian Stuart* (1982): 51; Bristol, "Stuart and the Genesis of the Greek Revival" (1997): 319, fig. 86; Bristol, "Society of Dilettanti" (July 2000): 54, fig. 16.

Illustrated: fig. 6-61.

77. **Ceiling of an unidentified room, Belvedere House, possibly later the billiard room**

James Stuart
ca. 1764–80
Photographed in 1943

English Heritage / National Monuments Record, Swindon A43/7147

References: Watkin, *Athenian Stuart* (1982): 51; Bristol, "Stuart and the Genesis of the Greek Revival" (1997): 318.

Illustrated: fig. 6-64.

78. **Coved ceiling cornice in an unidentified room, Belvedere House**

James Stuart
ca. 1764–80
Photographed in 1937

English Heritage / National Monuments Record, Swindon C37/752

References: Lawrence, "Stuart and Revett" (1938–39): fig. 24a; Watkin, *Athenian Stuart* (1982): 51; Bristol, "Stuart and the Genesis of the Greek Revival" (1997): 318.

Illustrated: fig. 6-62.

79. **Drawing Room, or saloon, on the principal floor, Rathfarnham Castle, County Dublin, Eire, for Henry Loftus, first Earl of Ely**

James Stuart
ca. 1769
Photographed in 2006

Courtesy of OPW, Dublin, and Rathfarnham Castle

References: Georgian Society, *Records of Eighteenth-Century Domestic Architecture,* vol. 5 (1913): figs. LXXXIV, LXXXV (right), LXXXVI (top); McParland, "Rathfarnham Castle" (9 September 1982): 737; Worsley, "Out from Adam's Shadow" (14 May 1992): 101; Smyth, "Castle Restoration to Be a Classical Pay-Off" (14 May 1992): 7;

Bristol, "Stuart and the Genesis of the Greek Revival" (1997): 328–29, 351, fig. 91.

Illustrated: fig. 6-50.

80. **Ceiling in the Gilt Room, Rathfarnham Castle**

James Stuart
ca. 1769
Photographed in 2006

Courtesy of OPW, Dublin, and Rathfarnham Castle

References: Georgian Society, *Records of Eighteenth-Century Domestic Architecture,* vol. 5 (1913): figs. LXXXVII (bottom); Scantlebury, "Rathfarnham Castle" (February 1951): 29; McParland, "Rathfarnham Castle" (9 September 1982): 735–37, fig. 4; Madden, "Rathfarnham Castle" (1987): 25–26 illus.; Worsley, "Out from Adam's Shadow" (14 May 1992): 101; Bristol, "Society of Dilettanti" (July 2000): 50–51, fig. 9; Bristol, "James Stuart and the London Building Trades" (2003): 2–4, fig. 4.

Illustrated: fig. 6-54.

81. **Ceiling of the breakfast room, or boudoir, Rathfarnham Castle**

James Stuart
ca. 1769
Photographed in 2006

Courtesy of OPW, Dublin, and Rathfarnham Castle

References: Georgian Society, *Records of Eighteenth-Century Domestic Architecture,* vol. 5 (1913): figs. LXXXVII (top); Scantlebury, "Rathfarnham Castle" (February 1951): 29; Madden, "Rathfarnham Castle" (1987): 25–26 illus.; Worsley, "Out from Adam's Shadow" (14 May 1992): 101.

Illustrated: fig. 6-53.

82. **Ceiling in a room, probably a morning room, on the prinicipal floor, Rathfarnham Castle**

James Stuart
ca. 1769
Photographed in 2006

Courtesy of OPW, Dublin, and Rathfarnham Castle

Illustrated: fig. 6-52.

83. **Ceiling in the little dining room, Camden Place, Kent, for Charles Pratt, Baron Camden, later first Earl Camden**

James Stuart
ca. 1779–80
Photographed in 2006

Courtesy of The Chislehurst Golf Club, Kent

Reference: Worsley, "Out from Adam's Shadow" (14 May 1992): 101–2, fig. 6.

Illustrated: fig. 6-66.

84. **The Doric Temple at Hagley, Worcestershire, for George, first Lord Lyttelton**

James Stuart
1758–59
Photographed in 2006

Courtesy of the Viscount Cobham

References: Bolton, "Hagley Park—I" (16 October 1915): 526–28; Wyndham, *Chronicles of the Eighteenth Century* (1924): 296; Lawrence, "Stuart and Revett" (1938–39): 138, 141; Nares, "Hagley Hall—I" (19 September 1957): 548–49, fig. 6; J. Harris, "Early Neo-classical Furniture" (1966): 4; Pevsner, *Studies in Art, Architecture and Design* (1968): 197–211; Crook, *Greek Revival* (1972): 50, fig. 48, 77, 96; Pevsner, *Outline of European Architecture* (1973): 357; Richards, *Who's Who in Architecture* (1977): 311; Watkin, *Athenian Stuart* (1982): 27; Hussey, *English Country Houses,* vol. 1, *Early Georgian* (1984): 196, fig. 351; Worsley, "First Greek Revival Architecture" (April 1985): 226; Stillman, *English Neo-Classical Architecture,* vol. 1 (1988):101–3, fig. 51; Worsley, "Out from Adam's Shadow"

(14 May 1992): 102; Curl, *Classical Architecture* (2001): 148, fig. 6.1; Colvin, *Biographical Dictionary* (1995): 758; Bristol, "Stuart and the Genesis of the Greek Revival" (1997): 302–5, fig. 77; Bristol, "Society of Dilettanti" (July 2000): 50–51, fig. 2; Cousins, "Athenian Stuart's Doric Porticoes" (2004): 48–54, fig. 1.

Illustrated: fig. 7-2.

85. *Shugborough and the Park from the East*

Nicholas Thomas Dall
ca. 1768–69
Oil on canvas
60¼ x 99¾ in. (153 x 253.5 cm) (framed)

Courtesy of Shugborough, Staffordshire, The Anson Collection, SHU.P.16 (The National Trust, UK)

References: Hussey, "Shugborough" (25 February 1954): 510–13, fig. 1; Hussey, *English Country Houses,* vol. 2, *Mid Georgian* (1984): 79, fig. 143; Robinson, *Shugborough* (1989): no. 16, 19 illus., 64.

Illustrated: fig. 7-3.

86. Covered dish depicting garden buildings at Shugborough, Staffordshire

Joseph Wedgwood and Thomas Bentley
1774
Glazed earthenware (Queensware)
7⅛ x 8 1/16 in. (18 x 20.5 cm)

Courtesy of Shugborough, Staffordshire, The Anson Collection (The National Trust, UK)

References: Raeburn et al., eds., *Green Frog Service* (1995): Cat. View, 124, 139–41; Young, ed., *Genius of Wedgwood* (1995): 16–17.

Illustrated: fig. 7-35.

87. *The Orangery and Ruins, Shugborough*

Nicholas Thomas Dall
ca. 1768–75
Watercolor
21⅞ x 43¼ in. (55.5 x 110 cm) (framed)

Courtesy of Shugborough, Staffordshire, The Anson Collection, SHUG.P.68 (The National Trust, UK)

References: *Shugborough* (1980): 51; Robinson, *Shugborough* (1989): 20; Young, ed., *Genius of Wedgwood* (1995): G276, p. 194; *Shugborough* (1999): 27.

Illustrated: fig. 7-15.

87A. *The West Front of Shugborough, Staffordshire*

Nicholas Thomas Dall
1768
Watercolor
27 3/16 x 46⅛ in. (69 x 117.5 cm) (framed)

Courtesy of Shugborough, Staffordshire, The Anson Collection (The National Trust, UK).

References: Hussey, "Shugborough" (25 February 1954): 510–13, fig. 5; *Shugborough* (1973): cover illus., 10, 22; *Shugborough* (1980): cover illus., 29, 35, 50.

Illustrated: fig. 7-40.

88. The Doric Temple in the park at Shugborough

James Stuart
1760
Photographed in 2006

Courtesy of Shugborough, Staffordshire (The National Trust, UK)

References: Lawrence, "Stuart and Revett" (1938–39): 141; Hussey, "Classical Landscape Park—I" (15 April 1954): 1128, fig. 9; Lees-Milne, "Shugborough—II" (May 1967): 212 illus.; Crook, *Greek Revival* (1972): 76–77; *Shugborough* (1973): 32; Middleton and Watkin, *Neoclassical and Nineteenth Century Architecture* (1980): 88; Watkin, *Athenian Stuart* (1982): 27; Stillman, *English Neo-Classical Architecture,* vol. 1 (1988): 100; Jenkyns, *Dignity and Decadence* (1992): 50; Worsley, *Classical Architecture in Britain* (1995): 258–60; Bristol, "Stuart and the Genesis of the Greek Revival" (1997):

279–81; figs. 57a–b; *Shugborough* (1999): 26, 28 illus.; Bristol, "Society of Dilettanti" (July 2000): 47–51, fig. 2.

Illustrated: fig. 7-13.

89. The Triumphal Arch (facing east) in the park at Shugborough

James Stuart
ca. 1764
Photographed in 2006

Courtesy of Shugborough, Staffordshire (The National Trust, UK)

References: Lawrence, "Stuart and Revett" (1938–39): 22 illus., 141; Hussey, "Classical Landscape—II" (22 April 1954): 1120–21, figs. 2 and 4; Crook, *Greek Revival* (1972): 50; *Shugborough* (1973): 33; Middleton and Watkin, *Neoclassical and Nineteenth Century Architecture* (1980): 88; Watkin, *Athenian Stuart* (1982): 25, fig. 7; Roscoe, "James 'Athenian' Stuart and the Sheemakers Family" (September 1987): 180, fig. 4; Stillman, *English Neo-Classical Architecture,* vol. 1 (1988): 103; Robinson, *Shugborough* (1989), 23 illus., 25, 90 illus.; Jenkyns, *Dignity and Decadence* (1992): 50; Colvin, *Biographical Dictionary* (1995): 796; Worsley, *Classical Architecture in Britain* (1995): 258–60; Bristol, "Stuart and the Genesis of the Greek Revival" (1997): 281–84; fig. 58; *Shugborough* (1999): 27–28 illus.; Bristol, "Society of Dilettanti" (July 2000): 47, fig. 4, 49.

Illustrated: figs. 7-6.

90. *Antiquities of Athens,* **volume 3**
Open to chap. 3, pl. IV, the southeast elevation of the Arch of Hadrian; James Stuart; engraving by W. Lowry. Inscribed: with measurements and "Stuart delt."; "W. Lowry sculpt."; "Published as the Act directs"

James Stuart and Nicholas Revett; ed. by Willey Reveley
London: John Nichols, 1794
Book (closed): 21 5/16 x 15 x 1 15/16 in. (54.1 x 38.1 x 4.9 cm)

Courtesy of the Library, The Bard Graduate Center for Studies in the Decorative Arts, Design, and Culture, New York

Reference: Crook, *Greek Revival* (1972): fig. 56.

Illustrated: fig. 7-7; also see figs. 1-24, 3-23, 3-27, 5-25, 6-18, 6-43, 10-30, 11-13.

91. *The Journey from Chester to London*
Open to pl. V, facing p. 68, "The Temple of the Winds at Shugborough"; engraving by James Fittler, after a watercolor by Moses Griffith. Inscribed: title and "Ms. Griffith Del . . ."; "J. Fittler Sculp."

Thomas Pennant
London: B. White, 1782
Book (closed): 10 x 8 x 2 in. (25.4 x 20.3 x 5.1 cm)

Courtesy of the Library, The Bard Graduate Center for Studies in the Decorative Arts, Design, and Culture, New York

References: *Shugborough* (1973): 32–33; Robinson, *Shugborough* (1989): 24–25, 24 illus. (top).

Illustrated: fig. 7-25.

92. **The Tower of the Winds at Shugborough**

James Stuart
1764–65
Photographed in 2006

Courtesy of Shugborough, Staffordshire (The National Trust, UK)

References: Yorke, "Travel Journal of Philip Yorke" (1768): 161; "Mr. Stuart the Architect" (1 March 1788): 3; Lawrence, "Stuart and Revett" (1938–39): 141, fig. 25b; Hussey, "Classical Landscape—II" (22 April 1954): 1222–23, fig. 9; Honour, "Adaptations from Athens" (22 May 1958): 1120; Lees-Milne, "Shugborough," parts I and II (April 1967): 215, fig. 7; (May 1967): 212; Crook, *Greek Revival* (1972): 50; *Shugborough* (1973): 32–33; Middleton

and Watkin, *Neoclassical and Nineteenth Century Architecture* (1980): 88; Watkin, *Athenian Stuart* (1982): 26–27, fig. 9; Stillman, *English Neo-Classical Architecture,* vol. 1 (1988): 83, 102–10, fig. 52; *Architecture and Its Image* (1989): 79, fig. 75, 80; Robinson, *Shugborough* (1989), 25, 85–86 illus.; Jenkyns, *Dignity and Decadence* (1992): 50; Curl, *Georgian Architecture* (1993): 79, fig. 83; Colvin, *Biographical Dictionary* (1995): 796; Worsley, *Classical Architecture in Britain* (1995): 258–60; Bristol, "Stuart and the Genesis of the Greek Revival" (1997): 284–85; fig. 60; *Shugborough* (1999): 25–26 illus.; Bristol, "Society of Dilettanti" (July 2000): 47, fig. 3, 49–50.

Illustrated: Fig. 7-1.

93. **Choragic Monument of Lysicrates at Shugborough**
Also known as the Lanthorn of Demosthenes

James Stuart
1764–69
Undated photograph

Courtesy of Shugborough, Staffordshire (The National Trust, UK)

References: "Mr. Stuart the Architect" (1 March 1788): 3; Lawrence, "Stuart and Revett" (1938–39): fig. 22d, 141; Hussey, "Classical Landscape—II" (22 April 1954): 1121–22, fig. 6; Honour, "Adaptations from Athens" (22 May 1958): 1120; Kelly, *Decorative Wedgwood* (1965): 104–5; Lees-Milne, "Shugborough," parts I and II (April 1967): 214–15, fig. 6; (May 1967): 212; Crook, *Greek Revival* (1968): 11; *Shugborough* (1973): 18, fig. 8; Middleton and Watkin, *Neoclassical and Nineteenth Century Architecture* (1980): 88; Watkin, *Athenian Stuart* (1982): 26–27, fig. 10; Roscoe, "James 'Athenian' Stuart and the Sheemakers Family" (September 1987): 180, fig. 4; Stillman, *English Neo-Classical Architecture,* vol. 1 (1988): 83, 101–3, fig. 53; Robinson, *Shugborough* (1989): 25–27, 90; Jenkyns, *Dignity and Decadence* (1992): 50; Colvin, *Biographical Dictionary* (1995): 796; Worsley, *Classical Architecture in Britain* (1995): 258–60;

Young, ed., *Genius of Wedgwood* (1995): C30, 68; Bristol, "Stuart and the Genesis of the Greek Revival" (1997): 286–88; fig. 63; *Shugborough* (1999): 27–28 illus.; Bristol, "Society of Dilettanti" (July 2000): 48–50, fig. 5.

Illustrated: fig. 7-9.

94. *Détails des nouveaux Jardins à la mode et Jardins Anglo-Chinois . . . , volume* 1
Open to book 2, pl. 3, "Tour de Diogene à Kew," or The Choragic Monument of Lysicrates, probably in the garden of Sion Hill, Kew, for Robert Darcy, fourth Earl of Holdernesse; engraving. Inscribed: "Temple de la Victoire à Kew / Mosquée Executée à Kew / Tour de Diogene à Kew"

Georges-Louis Le Rouge
Paris, 1776
Book (closed): 11 13/16 x 11 13/16 x 3 1/8 in. (30 x 30 x 8 cm)

By permission of The British Library, London, 34.f.11

References: Percy and Jackson-Stops, "Exquisite Taste and Tawdry Ornament" (7 February 1974): 250; Worsley, "Out from Adam's Shadow" (14 May 1992): 102; J. Harris, "Le Rouge's Sion Hill: A Garden by Brown" (1999–2000): 26–28, fig. 13.

Illustrated: fig. 7-34.

95. **Elevation and section for a church**
Possibly a preliminary design for the Church of All Saints at Nuneham Park, Oxfordshire, for Simon, first Earl Harcourt

James Stuart
ca. 1764
Pen and ink, gray wash
13 13/16 x 9 7/16 in. (35 x 24 cm)

RIBA Library Drawings Collection, London, SD 62/4

References: J. Harris, "Newly Acquired Designs" (1979): 74, pl. 17b; Watkin, *Athenian Stuart* (1982): 29, fig. 18.

Illustrated: fig. 7-42.

96. **The Church of All Saints at Nuneham Park, Oxfordshire**

Simon, first Earl Harcourt, with James Stuart
1764
Photographed in 2006

Courtesy of Brahma Kumaris: The Global Retreat Centre

References: *New Pocket Companion for Oxford* (1783): 136; *Diary and Letters of Madame D'Arblay*, vol. 1 (1892): 385; "Nuneham Courtenay Chapel" (18 March 1931), (1 April 1931), (22 April 1931); Hussey, "Nuneham Courtenay—I" (7 November 1941): 868–69, fig. 11; Batey, "Nuneham Park—I", "Creation of a Landscape" (5 September 1968): 541–42, fig. 5; Batey, "Nuneham Courtenay" (1968): 113–14; Worsley, "Nuneham Park Revisited—II" (January 1985): 64–65, figs. 3–4, 6; Worsley, "Out from Adam's Shadow" (14 May 1992): 102; Bristol, "Stuart and the Genesis of the Greek Revival" (1997): 247–49, fig. 37a.

Illustrated: fig. 7-5.

97. **Two designs for an orangery for Blithfield Hall, Staffordshire, for Sir William Bagot**

James Stuart
ca. 1769
Pen and ink, pencil
7⅞ x 12¾ in. (20 x 32.4 cm)

Courtesy of Nancy, Lady Bagot

References: Oswald, "Blithfield—I" (28 October 1954): 1491–92; Nancy, Lady Bagot, *Blithfield Hall* (1973): cover illus., 26; Bristol, "Stuart and the Genesis of the Greek Revival" (1997): 299–300, fig. 74; Bristol, "Society of Dilettanti" (July 2000): 51; Bristol, "Painted Rooms of 'Athenian' Stuart" (2000): 171.

Illustrated: fig. 7-19.

98. **The Orangery at Blithfield Hall**

James Stuart; executed by Samuel and Joseph Wyatt
1769

Photographed in 2006

Courtesy of Nancy, Lady Bagot

References: Oswald, "Blithfield—I" (28 October 1954): 1489, 1491–92, fig. 3; Nancy, Lady Bagot, *Blithfield Hall* (1973): cover illus., 26, fig. 26; Bristol, "Stuart and the Genesis of the Greek Revival" (1997): 299–300; Bristol, "Society of Dilettanti" (July 2000): 51; Bristol, "Painted Rooms of 'Athenian' Stuart" (2000): 171.

Illustrated: fig. 7-17.

99. **Elevation of the south front of Prospect House, or Hill House, Wimpole Hall, Cambridgeshire, for Philip Yorke, second Earl of Hardwicke**

James Stuart
ca. 1775
Pen and ink, gray wash
9⅜ x 11¹³⁄₁₆ in. (23.8 x 30 cm)

Inscribed: "South front"

RIBA Library Drawings Collection, London, SD 62/7 (1)

References: J. Harris, "Newly Acquired Designs" (1979): 75, fig. 21a; Bristol, "Society of Dilettanti" (July 2000): 52; Adshead, "*Modern Italian Loggia* at Wimpole" (2000): 154–55, fig. 5; Bristol, "Painted Rooms of 'Athenian' Stuart" (2000): 170–71.

Illustrated: fig. 7-46.

100. **North-to-south section of Prospect House**

James Stuart
ca. 1775
Pen and ink, gray wash
9¼ x 10⅝ in. (23.5 x 27 cm)

Inscribed: "the Room 20 feet square / 15 high 1½ feet to an Inch / Section thro' both fronts / Roof / 20 feet / 15 feet / Pannel / 20 feet / 14 feet / 3 x 4"

RIBA Library Drawings Collection, London, SD 62/7 (2)

References: J. Harris, "Newly

Acquired Designs" (1979): 75, fig. 21b; Bristol, "Society of Dilettanti" (July 2000): 52; Adshead, "*Modern Italian Loggia* at Wimpole" (2000): 154–55, fig. 4; Bristol, "Painted Rooms of 'Athenian' Stuart" (2000): 170–71.

Illustrated: fig. 7-47.

101. **"The Park Building at Wimpole"**

Daniel Lerpiniere
1778
Engraving
17¼ x 23¼ in. (43.8 x 59.1 cm)

Inscribed: "At secura quies, et nescia fallere Vita / Dives opum variarum; at latis otia fundis / Mugistusq. boum, mollesq. sub arbore somni / Non absunt." (Yet peace they have and a life of innocence / Rich in variety; they have for leisure / Their ample acres . . . cattle low, and sleep is soft / Under a tree.); "The Park Building at Wimple, Cambridge-Shire, the Seat of the Earl of Hardwicke. Stuart Architect. Lerpinier sculp. 1778."

By permission of The British Library, London, King George III Topographical Collection, K. Top, vol. 8, pl. 83A

References: Trevilyn and Plumtree, *Journal of a Tour to the Sources of the River Cam* (1800): 2; Lawrence, "Stuart and Revett" (1938–39): 138, 142; *Inventory of Historical Monuments*, vol. 1, *West Cambridgeshire* (1968): 217; Stroud, "Charms of Natural Landscape" (13 September 1979): 759–60, figs. 6–7; *Wimpole Hall* (1979): 39, 54; Worsley, "First Greek Revival Architecture" (April 1985): 229; Parry, "Wimpole Hall" (26 March 1986): 23; Stillman, *English Neo-Classical Architecture*, vol. 1 (1988): 112, 114, 126–27, figs. 61 and 70; Jackson-Stops, *English Arcadia* (1991): 88–89; Souden, *Wimpole Hall* (1991): 28; Colvin, *Biographical Dictionary* (1995): 797; Bristol, "Society of Dilettanti" (July 2000): 51–52, fig. 10; Adshead, "*Modern Italian Loggia* at Wimpole" (2000): 152–53, fig. 3; Bristol, "Painted Rooms of 'Athenian' Stuart" (2000): 170–71.

Illustrated: fig. 7-4.

No. 106. James Stuart. Design for
a three-bay loggia.

**102. The Choragic Monument at
Camden Place, Kent**

James Stuart
1779–80
Photographed in 2006

Courtesy of the Chislehurst Golf
Club, Kent

References: "Camden Place" (8
October 1870): 386; Worsley, "Out
from Adam's Shadow" (14 May 1992):
101; Mitchell, *Chislehurst Golf Club*
(1994): 95–98.

Illustrated: fig. 7-33.

**103. The Temple of the Winds, Mount
Stewart, County Down, for Robert
Stewart, later first Marquess of
Londonderry**

James Stuart
ca. 1782–83
Photographed ca. 1980

Courtesy of Mount Stewart, County
Down (The National Trust, UK)

References: Lewis, *Topographical
Dictionary of Ireland*, vol. 1 (1837): 674;
Crook, *Greek Revival* (1972): 50, fig. 6,
79–80, fig. 75, 102; Bence-Jones,

Burke's Guide to Country Houses, vol. 1,
Ireland (1978): 216–17; Watkin,
Athenian Stuart (1982): 27, 62;
Stillman, *English Neo-Classical
Architecture,* vol. 1 (1988): 103; Reeves-
Smyth, *Irish Country Houses* (1994): 29;
fig. 6; Colvin, *Biographical Dictionary*
(1995): 797; Bristol, "Stuart and the
Genesis of the Greek Revival" (1997):
285, figs. 62a–62b; Curl, *Classical
Architecture* (2001): 33–34, fig. 2.32;
Bristol, "James Stuart and the London
Building Trades" (2003): 2.

Illustrated: fig. 7-26.

**104. Upper room of the Temple of the
Winds, Mount Stewart**

James Stuart; plasterwork by William
Fitzgerald; marquetry floor by John
Ferguson
ca. 1782–83
Photographed ca. 1980

Courtesy of Mount Stewart, County
Down (The National Trust, UK)

Reference: Jackson-Stops, "Mount
Stewart—I" (6 March 1980): 647–49,
fig. 8.

Illustrated: fig. 7-28.

**105. Stairwell and coffered dome in the
Temple of the Winds, Mount
Stewart**

James Stuart
ca. 1782–83
Photographed ca. 1980

Courtesy of Mount Stewart, County
Down (The National Trust, UK)

Reference: Jackson-Stops, "Mount
Stewart—I" (6 March 1980): 647–49,
fig. 9.

Illustrated: fig. 7-27.

106. Design for a three-bay loggia

James Stuart
ca. 1755–88
Pen and ink, wash
7¼ x 9¹³⁄₁₆ in. (18.5 x 24.9 cm)

RIBA Library Drawings Collection,
London, SD 62/12

Reference: J. Harris, "Newly Acquired
Designs" (1979): 76, pl. 25a; Stillman,
English Neo-Classical Architecture, vol. 1
(1988): 87.

607

107. Design for a sculpture gallery

James Stuart
ca. 1755–88
Pen and ink, color wash, pencil
9⁹⁄₁₆ x 15³⁄₁₆ in. (24.3 x 38.6 cm)

Inscribed: "J Stuart"; "width of the Gallery 14 feet"

RIBA Library Drawings Collection, London, SD 62/13

Reference: J. Harris," Newly Acquired Designs" (1979): 76–77, pl. 25b.

Illustrated: fig. 6-35.

108. View of Spencer House, St. James's Place, London, from Green Park

Artist unknown
ca. 1780
Watercolor
7⅞ x 6⅞ in. (20 x 17.5 cm)

City of London, London Metropolitan Archives, SC/PZ/WE/01/1473

References: Weale, *Pictorial Handbook of London* (1854): 769; Chancellor, *Private Palaces* (1908): 337–41; Chancellor, *Memorials of St. James's Street* (1922): 109–10; Pearce, *London's Mansions* (1986): 80–81; Sykes, *Private Palaces* (1986): 173–74; Friedman, "Spencer House" (August 1987): 81–83; Summerson, *Georgian London* (1988): 93–94; Jackson-Stops, "Spencer House, London" (29 November 1990): 43; Lambert, "Rebirth of Spencer House" (February 1991): 134; Jones, "Roman Taste and Greek Gusto" (June 1992): 970–72; Worsley, "Spencer House" (24/31 December 1992): 38–39; Friedman, *Spencer House* (1993): 76–88, pl. viii; Bristol, "Stuart and the Genesis of the Greek Revival" (1997): 257–58; Banham, *Interior Decoration,* vol. 2 (1997): 1243–44; *Spencer House* [n.d.]: [1].

Illustrated: fig. 5-3.

109. The Music Room, Spencer House, for John, later first Earl Spencer

James Stuart
1758–66
Photographed in 1926

© Country Life Picture Library

References: Young, *Six Weeks Tour* (1772): 112; Earl Spencer, "London Houses: Spencer House—II" (6 November 1926): 701, fig. 4; Lawrence, "Stuart and Revett" (1938–39): 139; Friedman, "Spencer House" (August 1987): 90; Robinson, *Spencer House* (1991; rev. ed. 2002): 20–21 illus.; Lambert, "Rebirth of Spencer House" (February 1991): 139 illus.; Jones, "Roman Taste and Greek Gusto" (June 1992): 976; Bristol, "Stuart and the Genesis of the Greek Revival" (1997): fig. 46; Bradley and Pevsner, *London,* vol. 6, *Westminster* (2003): 623; *Spencer House* [n.d.]: [2].

Illustrated: fig. 10-40.

110. Lady Spencer's dressing room, Spencer House

James Stuart
1758–66
Photographed in 1996

© Spencer House Limited

References: Young, *Six Weeks Tour* (1772): 111–12; Lawrence, "Stuart and Revett" (1938–39): 139; Sykes, *Private Palaces* (1985): 175–76; Jackson-Stops, "Spencer House" (29 November 1990): 46, fig. 10; Robinson, *Spencer House* (1991; rev. ed. 2002): 22–23 illus.; Jones, "Roman Taste and Greek Gusto" (June 1992): 976 illus.; Bradley and Pevsner, *London,* vol. 6, *Westminster* (2003): 623; *Spencer House* [n.d.]: [2].

Illustrated: fig. 5-30.

111. Drawing of the dressing room cornice, Spencer House, designed by James Stuart

Robert Adam
ca. 1760
Pencil
7⅜ x 9¹⁄₁₆ in. (18.8 x 23 cm)

Inscribed: "For the Dressing Rooms of Mr Spencer House by Mr S."

By courtesy of the Trustees of Sir John Soane's Museum, London, Adam Ms., vol. 54, series 3, no. 40

References: Earl Spencer, "Spencer House—II" (16 November 1926): 700; Lawrence, "Stuart and Revett" (1938–39): 139.

Illustrated: chronology fig. C5.

112. The "mosaic ceiling" of Lady Spencer's dressing room, Spencer House

James Stuart
1765–66
Photographed in 2006

© Spencer House Limited

References: Young, *Six Weeks Tour* (1772): 111–12; Friedman, "Spencer House" (August 1987): 90; Jones, "Roman Taste and Greek Gusto" (June 1992): 976, pl. xv; Friedman, *Spencer House* (1993): 141, fig. 117; Bristol, "James Stuart and the London Building Trades" (2003): 2, 4, fig. 3.

Illustrated: fig. 5-32.

113. *L'Antiquité expliquée et représentée en figures*, volume 3, Supplement
Open to plate LVIII, a ceiling of the Baths of Augustus, Rome; engraving. Inscribed: "PEINTURE A FRESQUE DE LA VOUTE D'UNE CHAMBRE / DES BAINS DES AUGUSTES A ROME"

Bernard de Montfaucon
Paris: Delaulne [et al.], 1719
Book (closed): 17½ x 11¹³⁄₁₆ x 2⅝ in. (44.5 x 30 x 60 cm)

By permission of The British Library,

London, G11130

Reference: Friedman, *Spencer House* (1993): 141, fig. 118.

Illustrated: fig. 5-33.

114. Sketch of a table leg designed by James Stuart for Spencer House

Robert Adam
5 September 1758
Pen and ink
14 ⅜ x 18 ⅝ in. (36.6 x 47.4 cm)

From Adam to James Adam, 5 September 1758, National Archives of Scotland, Edinburgh, with kind permission of Sir Robert Clerk of Penicuik, Mss. ref. GD 18/4852

Reference: Bristol, "Stuart and the Genesis of the Greek Revival" (1997): 237, fig. 44.

Illustrated: fig. 10-81.

115. Washstand table from Lady Spencer's bedroom, Spencer House (one of a pair)

James Stuart
1759–66
Mahogany, inlaid with padouk and boxwood
34 ⅝ x 42 ⅛ x 24 in. (88 x 107 x 61 cm)

Courtesy of Spencer House and the Trustees of The Victoria and Albert Museum, London, W.31-1979

References: Young, *Six Weeks Tour* (1772): 110–15; Thornton and Hardy, "Spencer Furniture at Althorp—III" (October 1968): 267, fig. 2; Tomlin, *Catalogue of Adam Period Furniture* (1972): 9, A6; Yorke, *English Furniture* (1990): 79, fig. 79; Friedman, *Spencer House* (1993): 154–55, 185 n. 38.

Illustrated: fig. 10-58.

116. Sketch of a Greek key band for a ceiling beam

James Stuart
ca. 1760
Color wash, pencil
1 ¼ x 2 ¹⁵⁄₁₆ in. (3.2 x 7.4 cm)

Inscribed: "Frett work for the Beams of"

RIBA Library Drawings Collection, London, SD 62/18

Reference: J. Harris, "Newly Acquired Designs" (1979): 77, fig. 28a.

Illustrated: fig. 10-59.

117. The great room, Spencer House

James Stuart
1758–64
Photographed in 1996

©Spencer House Limited

References: Young, *Six Weeks Tour* (1772): 113–14; Leygon, *Decoration in England* (1914): 202, fig. 210; Earl Spencer, "Spencer House—II" (16 November 1926): 698–704; figs. 1–3; Lawrence, "Stuart and Revett" (1938–39): 139; Crook, *Greek Revival* (1972): 75, fig. 58; Watkin, *Athenian Stuart* (1982): 38–39, fig. 31; Pearce, *London's Mansions* (1986): 82–83, fig. 57; Friedman, "Spencer House" (August 1987): 90; Stillman, *English Neo-Classical Architecture,* vol. 1 (1988): 117–18, pl. 61; Jackson-Stops, "Spencer House" (29 November 1990): 46, fig. 9; Lambert, "Rebirth of Spencer House" (February 1991): 139, 142 illus.; Jones, "Roman Taste and Greek Gusto" (June 1992): 972, fig. 8, 975–76; Worlsey, "Spencer House" (24/31 December 1992): 40–41; Friedman, *Spencer House* (1993): 143, fig. 121, 142–54, fig. 227, 278, fig. 253, 320–21, fig. 273, 272, fig. 241, 324, pl. 37; Banham, *Interior Decoration,* vol. 2 (1997): 1244; Bristol, "Stuart and the Genesis of the Greek Revival" (1997): fig. 48; Bradley and Pevsner, *London,* vol. 6, *Westminster* (2003): 623; *Spencer House* [n.d.]: [2].

Illustrated: fig. 5-35.

118. Design for wall decoration of the Painted Room, Spencer House

James Stuart
1759
Pen and ink, gray wash, watercolor
11 ¼ x 16 in. (28.5 x 40.5 cm)

Inscribed: with measurements and "MDCCLVIIII"

By courtesy of the Trustees of The British Museum, London, 1955-4-16-13, British Reg PIIIb

References: Croft-Murray, "Drawing by Athenian Stuart" (1957): 14–15 illus.; Eriksen and Watson, "'Athénienne' and the Revival of the Classical Tripod" (March 1963): fig. 19, 110, 112; E. Harris, *Furniture of Robert Adam* (1963): 62–63, fig. 2; Rowe, *Adam Silver* (1965): 38; Musgrave, *Adam and Hepplewhite and Other Neo-Classical Furniture* (1966): 31, 40, 41, 181, fig. 3, 226; Thornton and Hardy, "Spencer Furniture at Althorp—II" (June 1968): 448–49, fig. 16; Croft-Murray, *Decorative Painting in England,* vol. 2 (1970): 50, 116, fig. 73; Goodison, "Mr. Stuart's Tripod" (October 1972): 695, fig. 63; Watkin, *Athenian Stuart* (1982): 37, fig. 28; Sykes, *Private Palaces* (1986): fig. 9, opp. 256; Wilton-Ely, "Pompeian and Etruscan Tastes" (1989): 53, fig. 3; Jones, "Roman Taste and Greek Gusto" (June 1992): 975; Friedman, *Spencer House* (1993): 68, fig. 8, 133; Bristow, *Architectural Colour in British Interiors* (1996): 81, fig. 81.

Illustrated: fig. 5-2.

119. The Painted Room, Spencer
House, looking toward the bow

James Stuart
1759–66
Photographed in 2006

©Spencer House Limited

References: Young, *Six Weeks Tour*
(1772): 110–15; Chancellor, *Private
Palaces* (1908): 342–43 illus.; Leygon,
Decoration in England (1914): 178–79,
figs. 180–81; Bolton, "James Stuart at
Portman House and Spencer House"
(1 May 1915): 10★–12★ illus.; "Spencer
House" (1 May 1915): Alcove Room;
Lawrence, "Stuart and Revett"
(1938–39): 132, 139; Croft-Murray,
Decorative Painting in England, vol. 2
(1970): 116, fig. 74; Richards, *Who's Who
in Architecture* (1977): 311; Middleton and
Watkin, *Neoclassical and Nineteenth
Century Architecture* (1980): 89–90 illus.;
Pearce, *London's Mansions* (1986): 83,
fig. 58; Sykes, *Private Palaces* (1986): 176,
181–82 illus.; Friedman, "Spencer
House" (August 1987): 90; Stillman,
English Neo-Classical Architecture, vol. 1
(1988): 82, pl. 69; Wilton-Ely, "Pompeian
and Etruscan Tastes" (1989): 51–54, figs.
1–2; Jackson-Stops, "Spencer House"
(29 November 1990): 44–47, pls. 6–8;
Robinson, *Spencer House* (1991): 30–32
illus.; Lambert, "Rebirth of Spencer
House" (February 1991): 139, 144 illus.;
Jones, "Roman Taste and Greek Gusto"
(June 1992): 973–76, figs. 9, 11, 13;
Worsley, "Out from Adam's Shadow"
(14 May 1992): 103; Friedman, *Spencer
House* (1993): 132–33, 155, fig. 137; 261,
273, fig. 242, 321–22, fig. 274; 324–29,
pl. 38, 154–83; Worsley, *Classical
Architecture in Britain* (1995): 260–61,
fig. 297; Banham, *Interior Decoration,*
vol. 2 (1997) 1244; Bristol, "Stuart and
the Genesis of the Greek Revival"
(1997): figs. 50–51; Morley, *History of
Furniture* (1999): 19, fig. 367; Bristol,
"Painted Rooms of 'Athenian' Stuart"
(2000): 166–67, fig. 3; Cornforth,
London Interiors (2000): 46–47 illus.;
Bradley and Pevsner, *London*, vol. 6,
Westminster (2003): 623; *Spencer House*
[n.d.]: [2], [4].

Illustrated: fig. 5-1.

120. Armchair for the Painted Room,
Spencer House

James Stuart; probably carved by
Thomas Vardy
1759–66
Carved and gilt limewood, silk
damask upholstery (not original)
37 x 25⅝ x 25⅝ in. (94 x 65 x 65 cm)

Courtesy of Spencer House and the
Trustees of The Victoria and Albert
Museum, London, W.8-1977

References: Chancellor, *Private Palaces
of London* (1908): fig. between 342–43;
Tipping, "Furniture at Althorp—I"
(11 June 1921): 759; Lawrence "Stuart
and Revett" (1938–39): 139; Thornton
and Hardy, "Spencer Furniture at
Althorp—II" (June 1968): 450–51,
fig. 19; *Age of Neo-Classicism* (1972):
no. 1658, 780–81; Tomlin, *Catalogue of
Adam Period Furniture* (1972): A4, 8
illus.; Thornton, "Very Special Year"
(June 1978): 138–39, illus.; Norman,
"Scheme to Restore Spencer House"
(24 November 1981): 12; Watkin,
Athenian Stuart (1982): 37; Sykes,
Private Palaces (1986), 176; Pearce,
London's Mansions (1986): 83, fig. 58;
Friedman, "Spencer House" (August
1987): 90, 93, fig. 15; Wilton-Ely,
"Pompeian and Etruscan Tastes"
(1989): 54, figs. 1–2; Amery, "Where
the Gods Must Dance at Night" (12
November 1990): 13; Robinson,
Spencer House (1991; rev. ed. 2002):
31–32 illus.; Lambert, "Rebirth of
Spencer House" (February 1991): 243
illus.; Jones, "Roman Taste and Greek
Gusto" (June 1992): 973, fig. 9,
975–76, fig. 15; Worsley, "Spencer
House" (24/31 December 1992):
39–40; Friedman, *Spencer House*
(1993): 179; Worsley, *Classical
Architecture in Britain* (1995): 261, fig.
297; Wilk, *Western Furniture* (1996):
114 illus.; Morley, *History of Furniture*
(1999): 166, fig. 300, fig. 367.

Illustrated: fig. 10-1.

121. Settee from the Painted Room,
Spencer House

James Stuart; probably carved by
Thomas Vardy
1759–66
Carved and gilt limewood, silk
damask upholstery (not original)
30¾ x 66⅛ x 28⅜ in. (78 x 168 x
72 cm)

Courtesy of Spencer House and the
Trustees of The Victoria and Albert
Museum, London, W.3-1977

References: Young, *Six Weeks Tour*
(1772): 114–15; Chancellor, *Private
Palaces* (1908): fig. between 342–43;
Earl Spencer, "Spencer House—II"
(13 November 1926): 758, fig. 6;
Lawrence, "Stuart and Revett"
(1938–39): 139; Musgrave, *Adam and
Hepplewhite* (1966): 197, fig. 80;
Thornton and Hardy, "Spencer
Furniture at Althorp—II" (June
1968): 450–51, fig. 19; Watkin, *Thomas
Hope* (1968): 206; *Age of Neo-Classicism*
(1972): no. 1658, 780, fig. 131; Tomlin,
Catalogue of Adam Period Furniture
(1972): A/5, p. 9 illus.; Udy, "Classical
Sources of English Neo-Classical
Furniture" (February 1973): 100, fig. 2;
Thornton, "Very Special Year" (June
1978): 138–39 illus.; Norman,
"Scheme to Restore Spencer House"
(24 November 1981): 12; Watkin,
Athenian Stuart (1982): 37, figs. 25–26,
30; Jackson-Stops, ed., *Treasure Houses
of Britain* (1985): no. 185, 269; Pearce,
London's Mansions (1986): 83, fig. 58;
Sykes, *Private Palaces* (1986): 176, fig.
182; Friedman, "Spencer House"
(August 1987): 90, 92, fig. 15; Wilton-
Ely, "Pompeian and Etruscan Tastes"
(1989): 54, figs. 1–2; Jackson-Stops,
"Spencer House, London"
(29 November 1990): 45–46 illus., 47;
Lambert, "Rebirth of Spencer House"
(February 1991): 243 illus.; Worsley,
"Spencer House" (24/31 December
1992): 39–40; Jones, "Roman Taste
and Greek Gusto" (June 1992): 973,
fig. 9; 975–76, fig. 15; Friedman,
Spencer House (1993): 179; Worsley,
Classical Architecture in Britain (1995):
261, fig. 297; Wilk, *Western Furniture*

(1996): 114 illus.; Morley, *History of Furniture* (1999): 166, fig. 367; Robinson, *Spencer House* (2002): 30–32 illus.

Illustrated: fig. 10-32.

122. Candelabrum and stand (one of a pair)

James Stuart; probably made by Diederich Nicolaus Anderson
1760
Gilt-bronze body, cast-bronze ornament, chased and gilt
18 9/16 x 12 1/2 x 11 3/8 in. (47.2 x 31.7 x 28.8 cm)

Courtesy of the Trustees of The Victoria and Albert Museum, London, M.279-1975

References: Earl Spencer, "Furniture at Spencer House" (13 November 1926): 757, fig. 2; Udy, "Neo-Classicism and the Evolution of Adam's Vase Designs" (August 1972): 193, fig. 4, 195; Watkin, *Athenian Stuart* (1982): 39, fig. 34; Friedman, *Spencer House* (1993): 156, 179, fig. 172; Robinson, "New Light from the Nursery" (28 September 1995): 80 illus.; Goodison, *Matthew Boulton: Ormolu* (2002): 76–77, figs. 33–34; Robinson, *Spencer House* (2002): 32 illus.

Illustrated: fig. 11-27.

123. Exterior of Holdernesse House, Hertford Street, London

ca. 1761–66
Photographed ca. 1937

©Country Life Picture Library

References: Oswald, "Londonderry House" (10 July 1937): 38–39, fig. 1; Hyde, *Londonderry House* (1937): fig. I; Lawrence, "Stuart and Revett" (1938–39): 39; Watkin, *Athenian Stuart* (1982): 41–42; Pearce, *London's Mansions* (1986): 86; Sykes, *Private Palaces* (1986): 242–43; Worsley, "Out from Adam's Shadow" (14 May 1992): 102; Colvin, *Biographical Dictionary*

(1995): 796; Banham, *Interior Decoration*, vol. 2 (1997): 1244; Bristol, "Stuart and the Genesis of the Greek Revival" (1997): 307–8; J. Harris, "Le Rouge's Sion Hill" (1999–2000): 27–28; Cornforth, *London Interiors* (2000): 117 illus.

Illustrated: fig. 5-48.

124. North end of the drawing room, Holdernesse House, for Robert D'Arcy, fourth Earl of Holdernesse

James Stuart; altered by Philip and Benjamin Dean Wyatt, 1825–28
ca. 1761–66
Photographed ca. 1937

©Country Life Picture Library

References: Oswald, "Londonderry House" (10 July 1937): 39, fig. 2, 42–43; Watkin, *Athenian Stuart* (1982): 42, fig. 44; Sykes, *Private Palaces* (1986): 184–85 illus.; Bristol, "Stuart and the Genesis of the Greek Revival" (1997): 308–9, fig. 79; Bristol, "James Stuart and the London Building Trades" (2003): 2, 5, fig. 5.

Illustrated: fig. 5-49.

125. Central section of the drawing room, Holdernesse House

James Stuart; altered by Philip and Benjamin Dean Wyatt, 1825–28
ca. 1761–66
Photographed ca. 1937

©Country Life Picture Library

References: Oswald, "Londonderry House" (10 July 1937): 39, fig. 2, 42–43; Hyde, *Londonderry House* (1937): fig. XIV; Watkin, *Athenian Stuart* (1982): 42, fig. 44; Bristol, "Stuart and the Genesis of the Greek Revival" (1997): 308–9, fig. 81; Cornforth, *London Interiors* (2000): 120–21 illus.

Illustrated: fig. 5-50.

126. The boudoir, Holdernesse House

James Stuart
ca. 1761–66
Photographed ca. 1937

©Country Life Picture Library

References: Oswald, "Londonderry House" (10 July 1937): 41, fig. 9, 42–43; Hyde, *Londonderry House* (1937): fig. XII; Watkin, *Athenian Stuart* (1982): 42, fig. 46; Bristol, "Stuart and the Genesis of the Greek Revival" (1997): 309.

Illustrated: fig. 5-52.

127. "Drawings, made from designs of Flowers & Pateras for Ceilings. Vases. Cornices. Frizes's. [*sic*] Architraves. Bases, of Columns. Imposts and their Bases. Picture frames. Trophies. Ornaments in. Pannells. and parts of different Cielings [*sic*]. Collected cheifly [*sic*] from Noble-mens Houses."
Open to p. 98, "Ornaments, in a Cieling [*sic*] at Lord Holdernesses"; pen and ink, ink wash. Inscribed: with scale and "Stewart Archt"

John Carter
1766
Sketchbook (closed): 8 9/16 x 6 7/8 in. (21.8 x 17.6 cm)

Inscribed: on the cover, "J. Carter – Architectural Details 1766"; on the title page, "J. Carter / Vol. II"

Courtesy of the Trustees of The Victoria and Albert Museum, London, D.386-1890

References: Oswald, "Londonderry House" (10 July 1937): 42; Lawrence, "Stuart and Revett" (1938–39): 139; Watkin, *Athenian Stuart* (1982): 42, fig. 47; Bristol, "Stuart and the Genesis of the Greek Revival" (1997): 155, 308, fig. 78a.

Illustrations: fig. 5-55; see also 5-53, 5-56, 5-57, 5-60, 5-61, 5-93.

128. **Front elevation of Lichfield House, 15 St. James's Square, London, for Thomas Anson**

James Stuart
1764–66
Photographed in 2006

References: Halley, "Lichfield House" (May 1910): 274–75 illus.; Bolton, "James Stuart and Portman House and Spencer House" (1 May 1915): 6★ illus.; Lawrence, "Stuart and Revett" (1938–39): 140; Sheppard, ed., *Survey of London,* vol. 30, *Parish of St. James* (1960): 151–52, 168–69 illus.; Crook, *Greek Revival* (1972): 5, fig. 114; Watkin, *Athenian Stuart* (1982): 43–44, fig. 52; Corley, *Lichfield House* (1983): 52, 56; Sykes, *Private Palaces* (1986): 185 illus.; Stillman, *English Neo-Classical Architecture,* vol. 1 (1988):130, figs. 65 and 78; Bristol, "Stuart and the Genesis of the Greek Revival" (1997): 296–97, figs. 69–70; Bristol, "James Stuart and the London Building Trades" (2003): 2, 7, fig. 7; Pevsner and Bradley, *London,* vol. 6, *Westminster* (2003): 630, fig. 55.

Illustrated: fig. 5-59.

129. *Antiquities of Athens*, volume 2
Open to ch. 2, pl. VIII, "Base, capital and entablature of the portico of Minerva Polias"; engraving. Inscribed: with measurements and "Publish'd Octr.27.th 1787 According to Act of Parliament"

James Stuart and Nicholas Revett; ed. by William Newton
London: John Nichols, ca. 1790
Book (closed): 21 5/16 x 15 x 1 3/4 in. (54.1 x 38.1 x 4.4 cm)

Courtesy of the Library, The Bard Graduate Center for Studies in the Decorative Arts, Design, and Culture, New York

Illustrated: fig. 5-62 and 6-21; see also figs. 2-2, 3-22, 3-34, 10-5, 10-38, 13-6.

130. **Main drawing room, principal floor, Lichfield House**

James Stuart; ceiling panels painted by Biagio Rebecca, 1794
1764–66
Photographed in 1958

City of London, London Metropolitan Archives, 58/0438

References: "Mr. Stuart the Architect" (1 March 1788): 3; Halley, "Lichfield House" (May 1910): 276–77 illus.; Richardson and Gill, *London Town Houses* (1911): frontispiece, 64; Bolton, "James Stuart at Portman House and Spencer House" (1 May 1915): 6★ illus., 12★; Bolton, "Town Houses . . . Lichfield House" (12 May 1917): 2★, fig. 1, 4★–6★; Lawrence, "Stuart and Revett" (1938–39): 140; Summerson, "Society's House" (15 October 1954): 926–27, fig. 4; Sheppard, ed., *Survey of London,* vol. 30, *Parish of St. James* (1960): 142–48, 165 illus.; Richards, *Who's Who in Architecture* (1977): 311; Watkin, *Athenian Stuart* (1982): 42–45, 61, fig. 51; Corley, *Lichfield House* (1983): 2 illus., 5–7, 38, 42; Pearce, *London's Mansions* (1986): 86–87; Sykes, *Private Palaces* (1986): 115, 186 illus.; Stillman, *English Neo-Classical Architecture,* vol. 1 (1988): 83, 87, 89, fig. 42, 112; Worsley, "Out from Adam's Shadow" (14 May 1992): 103; Jenkyns, *Dignity and Decadence* (1992): 51, 53, fig. 30; Colvin, *Biographical Dictionary* (1995): 796; Banham, *Interior Decoration,* vol. 2 (1997): 1244; Bristol, "Stuart and the Genesis of the Greek Revival" (1997): 288–94, fig. 64; Bristol, "Society of Dilettanti" (July 2000): 48, fig. 6, 50; Forrest, *St. James's Square* (2001): 42, 49–50; Bristol, "Newly-Discovered Drawing" (2001): 42; Bristol, "James Stuart and the London Building Trades" (2003): 6, 8–9; Pevsner and Bradley, *London,* vol. 6, *Westminster* (2003): 629; Wratten, *History and Architecture of No. 15 St James's Square* [n.d.]: 5, 38, 42–43 illus.

Illustrated: fig. 5-71.

131. **Chimneypiece in the main drawing room, principal floor, Lichfield House**

James Stuart; carving attributed to the Scheemakers workshop
1764–66
Photographed in 1958

City of London, London Metropolitan Archives, 96.0 St Jam 76/11997

References: Halley, "Lichfield House" (May 1910): 277 illus., 23; Bolton, "Town Houses . . . Lichfield House" (12 May 1917): 6★ illus. (left bottom figure); Lawrence, "Stuart and Revett" (1938–39): 140; Sheppard, ed., *Survey of London,* vol. 30, *Parish of St. James* (1960): 170 illus.; Bristol, "Stuart and the Genesis of the Greek Revival" (1997): 296–97, figs. 69–70; Bristol, "James Stuart and the London Building Trades" (2003): 2, 7, fig. 7; Pevsner and Bradley, *London,* vol. 6, *Westminster* (2003): 630.

Illustrated: fig. 5-69.

132. **The music room, Lichfield House**

James Stuart; alterations by Samuel Wyatt, 1791–94
1764–66
Photographed in 1958

City of London, London Metropolitan Archives, 58/0441

References: Bolton, "Town Houses . . . : Lichfield House" (12 May 1917): 4★ illus. (middle figure); Lawrence, "Stuart and Revett" (1938–39): 140; Sheppard, ed., *Survey of London,* vol. 30, *Parish of St. James* (1960): 152, 167 illus. (a); Corley, *Lichfield House* (1983): 57; Sykes, *Private Palaces* (1986): 185, 187 illus.; Pearce, *London's Mansions* (1986): 86–87, fig. 59 (detail); Bristol, "Stuart and the Genesis of the Greek Revival" (1997): 59; Bristol, "Society of Dilettanti" (July 2000): 50; Pevsner and Bradley, *London,* vol. 6, *Westminster* (2003): 630.

Illustrated: fig. 5-72.

133. **Design for a garden loggia, possibly for Lichfield House**

James Stuart
n.d.
Pencil, pen and ink, color wash
12½ x 10⅛ in. (31.8 x 25.7 cm)

Inscribed: with scale and "Mowles" [?Bowles]

RIBA Library Drawings Collection, London, SD 62/3

Reference: J. Harris, "Newly Acquired Designs by James Stuart in the British Architectural Library Collection" (1979): 74, pl. 17a.

Illustrated: fig. 5-75.

134. **Ceiling of the bedchamber, 23 Hill Street, London, for Mrs. Elizabeth Montagu**

James Stuart
1766–72
Photographed in 2003

By kind permission of Rosemary Baird

References: Croft-Murray, *Decorative Painting in England,* vol. 2 (1970): no. 18, 188; Bristol, "Painted Rooms of 'Athenian' Stuart"(2000): 167–68; Bristol, "22 Portman Square" (Summer 2001): 72; Baird, "'Queen of the Bluestockings,'" (August 2003): 43–49, figs. 5–6, 8; Bristol, "James Stuart and the London Building Trades" (2003): 9–10.

Illustrated: fig. 5-79.

135. **Panel, detail of the great room ceiling, 23 Hill Street**

Painted by James Stuart
1766–72
Photographed in 2003

By kind permission of Rosemary Baird

References: Croft-Murray, *Decorative Painting in England,* vol. 2 (1970): no. 18, 188; Baird, "'Queen of the

Bluestockings,'" (August 2003): 49, fig. 11.

Illustrated: fig. 5-78.

136. **Chimneypiece in the bedchamber, 23 Hill Street**

James Stuart
1766–72
Photographed in 2003

By kind permission of Rosemary Baird

Reference: Baird, "'Queen of the Bluestockings,'" (August 2003): 48, fig. 10.

Illustrated: fig. 5-83.

137. **Montagu House, 22 Portman Square, London, for Mrs. Elizabeth Montagu**

James Stuart
ca. 1775–81
Photographed in 1894

English Heritage / National Monuments Record, Swindon 12691A

References: Chancellor, *Private Palaces* (1908): 323–24 illus.; Bolton, "James Stuart at Portman House and Spencer House" (1 May 1915): 6★–12★, figs. 1★–6★; Crook, *Greek Revival* (1972): 75; Watkin, *Athenian Stuart* (1982): 47, 50–51, fig. 54; Worsley, "First Greek Revival Architecture"(April 1985): 323–24 illus.; Colvin, *Biographical Dictionary* (1995): 795–97; Bristol, "Stuart and the Genesis of the Greek Revival" (1997): 320–27, fig. 87; Bristol, "Society of Dilettanti" (July 2000): 51; Bristol, "22 Portman Square" (Summer 2001): 72–83.

Illustrated: fig. 5-87.

138. **Entrance hall, Montagu House**

James Stuart
ca. 1775–81
Photographed in 1894

English Heritage / National

Monuments Record, Swindon BB80/3470

References: "Mr. Stuart the Architect" (1 March 1788): 3; Shanhagan, *Exhibition* (1779): 69–70; Leygon, *Decoration in England* (1914): 152, fig. 156; Blunt, *Mrs. Montagu,* vol. 2 (1923): 13, 18, 73 illus., 82–83, 101; Lawrence, "Stuart and Revett" (1938–39): 132–33, 142–43; Kelly, *Decorative Wedgwood* (1965): 74–75; Croft-Murray, *Decorative Painting in England,* vol. 2 (1970): no. 19, 178, no. 3, 167, 188–89, no. 9, 229; Hobhouse, *Lost London* (1971): 47–48, fig. 47; Richards, *Who's Who in Architecture* (1977): 311; Watkin, *Athenian Stuart* (1982): 47–48, fig. 58; Pearce, *London's Mansions* (1986):100–4, fig. 75; Sykes, *Private Palaces* (1986): 185, 218–21; Worsley, "Out from Adam's Shadow" (14 May 1992): 101; Colvin, *Biographical Dictionary* (1995): 795–97; Duffy, *James Gandon* (1999): 98–100; Bristol, "Painted Rooms of 'Athenian' Stuart" (2000): 169; Bristol, "James Stuart and the London Building Trades" (2003): 10.

Illustrated: fig. 5-90.

139. **Reception room or gallery, Montagu House**

James Stuart and Joseph Bonomi
1775–83
Photographed ca. 1915

© Country Life Picture Library

References: Bolton, "James Stuart at Portman House and Spencer House" (1 May 1915): 8★ (upper right); Watkin, *Athenian Stuart* (1982): 49–50, fig. 62; Bristol, "Stuart and the Genesis of the Greek Revival" (1997): 327, fig. 89; Bristol, "22 Portman Square" (Summer 2001): 75, fig. 3.

Illustrated: fig. 5-96.

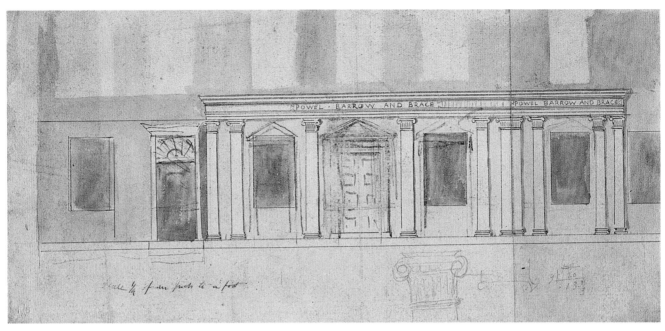

No. 142. James Stuart. Elevation of a shop front.

140. **The morning room, Montagu House**

James Stuart
ca. 1775–81
Photographed ca. 1915

© Country Life Picture Library

References: Bolton, "James Stuart at Portman House and Spencer House" (1 May 1915): 8★ (middle figure); Watkin, *Athenian Stuart* (1982): 48, fig. 59; Bristol, "Stuart and the Genesis of the Greek Revival" (1997): 327, fig. 88; Bristol, "22 Portman Square" (Summer 2001): 77, fig. 6, 81–82.

Illustrated: fig. 5-95.

141. **The drawing room (formerly the dining room), Montagu House**

James Stuart
ca. 1775–81
Photographed in 1894

English Heritage / National Monuments Record, Swindon
BB96/754D (BL12696)

References: Bolton, "James Stuart at Portman House and Spencer House" (1 May 1915): 10★, 8★ (bottom figure); Pearce, *London's Mansions* (1986): 100–4, fig. 77; Bristol, "Stuart and the Genesis of the Greek Revival" (1997): fig. 90; Bristol, "22 Portman Square" (Summer 2001): 79, fig. 8, 82–83.

Illustrated: fig. 5-94.

142. **Elevation of a shop front for Powel, Barrow and Brace**

James Stuart
ca. 1755–88
Pencil, pen and ink, pink and gray wash
6¹¹⁄₁₆ x 13¹⁵⁄₁₆ in. (17 x 35.4 cm)

Inscribed: with scale and "POWEL BARROW AND BRACE"

RIBA Library Drawings Collection, London, SD 62/14

Reference: J. Harris, "Newly Acquired Designs" (1979): 77, pl. 26a.

143. **Tripodic tea kitchen, or tea urn**

Attributed to James Stuart; made by Matthew Boulton
ca. 1770
Gilt-copper body, tinned copper lining, mother-of-pearl tap handle, ebonized fruitwood base, ormolu ornaments
21⅝ x 20¹⁄₁₆ x 20¹⁄₁₆ in. (55 x 51 x 51 cm)

The Royal Collection, London, RCINH 55429

References: [Queen Mary], *Catalogue of Bibelots,* vol. 4 (1938–45): 6, no. 10; Goodison, *Matthew Boulton: Ormolu* (2002): 271–75, pl. 231; Roberts, ed., *George III and Queen Charlotte* (2004): cat. no. 279, 272–73.

Illustrated: fig. 11-29.

144. "A Design for/The East End of St. Georges Chapel," Windsor Castle, for the Dean and Canons of St. George's Chapel

James Stuart
1771
Gouache, pen and ink inscriptions
27 1/16 x 16 15/16 in. (68.7 x 43 cm) (visible drawing)

Inscribed: with measurements and title; signed "J. Stuart."

St. George's Chapel Archives and Chapter Library, Windsor, F.21. By permission of the Dean and Canons of Windsor

References: Hope, *Windsor Castle,* vol. 2 (1913): 426; Watkin, *Athenian Stuart* (1982): 55–56, fig. 80; Stillman, *English Neo-Classical Architecture,* vol. 1 (1988): 81; Worsley, "Out from Adam's Shadow" (14 May 1992): 102; Colvin, *Biographical Dictionary* (1995): 796; Bristol, "Stuart and the Genesis of the Greek Revival" (1997): 169–70; Bristol, "Society of Dilettanti" (July 2000): 53–54, fig. 15; Watkin, *Architect King* (2004): 146, fig. 90.

Illustrated: fig. 2-29.

145. Admiralty Pass

James Stuart; engraving by James Basire
ca. 1764
Engraving
19 1/2 x 12 3/4 in. (49.6 x 32.4 cm)

Inscribed: recto, with lengthy printed text and, in pencil, "1780"; verso, "Com sa / a Mediterranean Pass"

By courtesy of the Trustees of The British Museum, London, M.m. 3:-62

References: Lawrence, "Stuart and Revett" (1938–39): 133; Bristol, "Stuart and the Genesis of the Greek Revival" (1997): 355, fig. 102a.

Illustrated: fig. 2-19.

146. Admiralty Pass

James Stuart; engraving by James Basire,
ca. 1764
Engraving
20 3/4 x 13 1/2 in. (52.8 x 34.3 cm)

Inscribed: recto, with lengthy printed text and "Stuart del / Basires Sculp"; verso, in pencil, "a Mediterranean pass"

By courtesy of the Trustees of The British Museum, London, M.m. 3:-63

References: Lawrence, "Stuart and Revett" (1938–39): 133; Bristol, "Stuart and the Genesis of the Greek Revival" (1997): 355, fig. 102b.

Illustrated: fig. 2-20.

147. Boulton and Fothergill Pattern Book, no. 1 (1762–90)
Open to p. 111, a record drawing of Stuart's "Soup Tureen made for the Admiralty – 1781"; possibly drawn by Matthew Boulton; pen and ink

1781
19 1/8 x 12 1/2 in. (48.5 x 31.8 cm)

Inscribed: "Soup Tureen made for the Admiralty – 1781"

Birmingham City Archives, Matthew Boulton Papers, MS 3782/21/2

Reference: Goodison, *Matthew Boulton: Ormolu* (2002): 122–24, fig. 96.

Illustrated: fig. 11-30.

No. 148. "A Perspective View of the Royal Hospital for Seamen," foldout plate in *An Historical Account of the Royal Hospital for Seamen at Greenwich* (1789).

148. *An Historical Account of the Royal Hospital for Seamen at Greenwich* Open to foldout plate, "A Perspective View of the Royal Hospital for Seamen at Greenwich, taken from the River Thames."; engraving by James Newton; drawn by Thomas Lancey. Inscribed: with title and "Thos. Lancey, Greenwich delt. et Script."; "Engraved by James Newton"; "Publish'd September 22d: 1789, by the"; "Revnd. John Cooke and John Maule A.M. Chaplains. at Mr. Shentons. No. 5 Cornhill, as the Act directs."

John Cooke and John Maule
London: published by the authors, 1789
Book (closed): 11⁵⁄₁₆ x 9 x 11/16 in. (28.7 x 22.9 x 1.8 cm); plate, 27⁵⁄₈ x 11¹⁄₁₆ in. (70.1 x 28.1 cm)

Courtesy of the Library, The Bard Graduate Center for Studies in the Decorative Arts, Design, and Culture, New York

149. "Elevation of the East-front of the Infirmary," Royal Hospital for Seaman at Greenwich, London

J. Newton
Engraving removed from John Cooke and John Maule, *An Historical Account of the Royal Hospital for Seamen at Greenwich* (London: published by the authors, 1789)
8³⁄₁₆ x 10¹⁵⁄₁₆ in. (20.8 x 27.8 cm)

Inscribed: with title and "Engrav'd by J. Newton."; "Published Septr. 22d. 1789 by the Revd. John Cooke and John Maule A.M."

Courtesy of the Library of The Bard Graduate Center for Studies in the Decorative Arts, Design, and Culture, New York

References: *Inventory of the Historical Monuments*, vol. 5, *East London* (1930): 21; Bold, *Greenwich* (2000): 209–11, fig. 271.

Illustrated: fig. 8-8.

150. Chimneypiece in the Admiral's Study (formerly the council room of the Governor's apartment) in the northeast part of the King Charles Block, the Royal Hospital for Seaman at Greenwich

Attributed to James Stuart
ca. 1769–74
Photographed in 2006

Courtesy of the Greenwich Foundation

Reference: Worsley, "Out from Adam's Shadow" (14 May 1992): fig. 7.

Illustrated: fig. 8-4.

151. The southwest pavilion of the King Charles Block, the Royal Hospital for Seaman at Greenwich

As rebuilt by James Stuart
1769-74
Photographed in 2006

Courtesy of the Greenwich Foundation

References: *Inventory of the Historical Monuments*, vol. 5, *East London* (1930): 21, 23, fig. 58; Worsley, "Out from Adam's Shadow" (14 May 1992): 101; Bold, *Greenwich* (2000): 167–71.

Illustrated: fig. 8-3.

152. Contract drawing, with flap closed to show the interior decoration of the east end of the chapel of the Royal Hospital for Seamen at Greenwich
Flap opens to show the west end of the chapel

James Stuart, probably assisted by William Newton
1782
Pen and ink, color wash
16⅛ x 24 in. (41 x 61 cm); flier, 11⅝ x 4¾ in. (29.5 x 12 cm)

Inscribed: recto, "Chapel. sketch of East & West End."; "The capitals & bases of the columns, & the principal Door case, to be / of white marble. The Columns to be of Scagliola in

imitation / of Giallo antico.";
"Approved by the Commissioners and / Governors of Greenwich Hospital / at a General Court / 14 March 1782 / [s.] Jno Ibbetson / Secy / James Stuart Surveyor Received 20 May 1782 R Mylne." On flier, "Approved by the Commissioners / & Governors of Greenwich Hospital / at a General Court / 14 March 1782 / [s.] James Stuart / Jno Ibbeston"; "Received at the Clerk of the Cheque's Office 18 May 1782 / and in the Clerk of the Work's Office 20 May 1782 [s.] . . . Mylne"

RIBA Library Drawings Collection, London, SB 62/4 (1)

Reference: Lewis, "Architects of the Chapel" (1947): 262-63, fig. 3.

Illustrated: fig. 8-36 (with flap closed); fig. 8-37 (with flap open).

153. Contract drawing for the interior elevation of the south wall (not as built) of the chapel, the Royal Hospital for Seamen at Greenwich

James Stuart, probably assisted by William Newton
1782
Pencil and watercolor, ink inscriptions
16¹⁄₁₆ x 28³⁄₁₆ in. (40.8 x 71.6 cm)

Inscribed: "Chapel sketch of side"; [s] "James Stuart Surveyor"; "Approved by the Commissioners and / Governors of Greenwich Hospital at / a General Court 19 March 1782" [s] "Jno Ibberton secy"; "the Clerk of the Cheques office / 1782 and delivered the same / [illegible] the works office"; [s] "Received 29 May 1782 R. Mylne"

RIBA Library Drawings Collection, SB 62/4 (2)

References: Lewis, "Architects of the Chapel" (1947): 262-63, fig. 5; Richardson, ed., *Catalogue of the Drawings Collection of the RIBA*, vol. S (1976): 127.

Illustrated: fig. 8-13.

154. Interior of the chapel of the Royal Hospital for Seamen at Greenwich

James Stuart, assisted by Robert Mylne and William Newton
ca. 1890
Albumen print
6⅟₁₆ x 7¹³⁄₁₆ in. (15.5 x 19.8 cm)

Courtesy of the Library, The Bard Graduate Center for Studies in the Decorative Arts, Design, and Culture, New York

References: *London and Its Environs,* vol. 1 (1761): 127; Mulvany, *Life of James Gandon* (1846): 197; *Pictorial Handbook of London* (1854): 180–81; 400–1; Cooke and Maule, *Historical Account of the Royal Hospital for Seamen* (1789): 100–7; Dallaway, *Anecdotes of the Arts of England* (1800): 154–55; Papworth, "William Newton and the Chapel of Greenwich Hospital" (1891): 417–20; Lawrence, "Stuart and Revett" (1938–39): 142–43, fig. d; Lewis, "Architects of the Chapel" (1947): 260–67; "Greenwich Chapel Restored"(13 June 1955): 10; Lewis, "Greece and Rome at Greenwich" (January 1951): 17–24; *Inventory of the Historical Monuments,* vol. 5, *East London* (1968): 21; Croft-Murray, *Decorative Painting in England,* vol. 2 (1970) no 3, 291; Crook, *Greek Revival* (1972): 75, fig. 17; Watkin, *Athenian Stuart* (1982): 52–54; Harwood and Saint, *Exploring England's Heritage* (1991): 153; Worsley, "Out from Adam's Shadow" (14 May 1992): 100–1 illus.; Colvin, *Biographical Dictionary* (1995): 797; Worsley, *Classical Architecture in Britain* (1995): 290–91, 293, fig. 329; Bold, *Greenwich* (2000): 174–76.

Illustrated: fig. 10-79 (detail).

155. Interior of the chapel of the Royal Hospital for Seamen at Greenwich, looking toward the altar

James Stuart, assisted by Robert Mylne and William Newton
1779–89
Photographed in 2006

Courtesy of the Greenwich Foundation

Illustrated: fig. 8-1.

156. Interior of the chapel of the Royal Hospital for Seamen at Greenwich, looking toward the organ

James Stuart, assisted by Robert Mylne and William Newton
1779–89
Photographed in 2006

Courtesy of the Greenwich Foundation

Illustrated: fig. 8-11.

157. Pulpit in the chapel of the Royal Hospital for Seamen at Greenwich

James Stuart; joinery by James Arrow with George Seddons; carved by Richard Lawrence

1786–89

Limewood with gilt details; Coade-stone medallions sculpted by John Bacon, ca. 1789, after designs by Benjamin West

Photographed in 2006

Courtesy of the Greenwich Foundation

References: Watkin, *Athenian Stuart* (1982): 53–54, fig. 75; Bold, *Greenwich* (2000): 176.

Illustrated: fig. 10-78.

158. Interior of the chapel of the Royal Hospital for Seamen at Greenwich, showing the original triple-decker pulpit

Edward Hopley, after Mrs. R. B. B. Hopley
Facsimile of an engraving

Inscribed: "Edward Hopley. Aqua Fortis."; "From a drawing by Mrs. R. R. B. Hopley." "THE CHAPEL ROYAL GREENWICH."; pencil "London"

National Maritime Museum, London, Greenwich PAH 3281

Illustrated: fig. 8-28.

159. "Elevation of the East-front of the Boys School and Dormitory"

James Newton
Engraving removed from John Cooke and John Maule, *An Historical Account of the Royal Hospital for Seamen at Greenwich* (London: published by the authors, 1789)
8¼ x 11 in. (21 x 27.9 cm)

Inscribed: with title and "Engrav'd by J. Newton."; "Published Septr. 22 1789. by the Revd. John Cooke and John Maule A.M."

Courtesy of the Library, The Bard Graduate Center for Studies in the Decorative Arts, Design, and Culture, New York

References: Worsley, "Out from Adam's Shadow" (14 May 1992): 101; Bold, *Greenwich* (2000): 226–27, fig. 287.

Illustrated: fig. 8-38.

160. *Hermes, or, A Philosophical Inquiry Concerning Universal Grammar*
Open to frontispiece showing a Herm; after James Stuart; engraving by James Basire. Inscribed: "see Herm. p. 324-325."; "Engrav'd by Basire."

James Harris
2nd ed. London: John Nourse and Paul Valliant, 1765
Book (closed): 8⅜ x 5¾ x 1⁹⁄₁₆ in. (21.3 x 14.5 x 4 cm)

By permission of The British Library, London, 1086.d.4

References: Watkin, *Athenian Stuart* (1982): 48; Colvin, *Biographical Dictionary* (1995): 795 n. 1; Bristol, "Stuart and the Genesis of the Greek Revival" (1997): 165.

Illustrated: fig. 4-33.

161. *Philosophical Arrangements*
Open to frontispiece showing the portico of a temple to Ceres; after James Stuart; engraving by Isaac Taylor. Inscribed: "See p. 460.461"; "Engrav'd by Isaac Taylor."

James Harris
London: John Nourse, 1775
Book (closed): 8⅞ x 5½ x 1⁹⁄₁₆ in. (22.5 x 14 x 4 cm)

By permission of The British Library, London, 673.e.23

References: Watkin, *Athenian Stuart* (1982): 48; Colvin, *Biographical Dictionary* (1995): 795 n. 1; Bristol, "Stuart and the Genesis of the Greek Revival" (1997): 166.

Illustrated: fig. 4-34.

162. *Philological Inquiries*
Open to frontispiece showing a philosopher and scholars; after James Stuart; engraving by William Sharp. Inscribed: "Jas. Stuart Esqr. del."; Wm. Sharp Sculpt."

James Harris
London: John Nourse, 1781
Book (closed): 8⅞ x 5½ x 1⁹⁄₁₆ in. (22.5 x 14 x 4 cm)

By permission of The British Library, London, 673.e.25

Illustrated: fig. 4-35.

163. *An Account of the Voyages Undertaken by order of the Present Majesty for Making Discoveries in the Southern Hemisphere and Successively Performed by Commodore Byron, Captain Wallis, Captain Carteret, and Captain Cook . . .*, volume 1
Open to pl. 23, facing p. 27, "A representation of the interview between Commodore Byron and the Patagonians"; engraving after a design attributed to James Stuart

John Hawkesworth
London: W. Strahan and T. Cadell in the Strand, 1773
Book (closed): 11½ x 9½ x 2⅜ in. (29 x 24 x 6 cm)

By permission of The British Library, London, 455.a.21

References: Graves, *Society of Artists* (1907): 248; Bristol, "Stuart and the Genesis of the Greek Revival" (1997): 193-98, fig. 23.

Illustrated: fig. 4-40.

164. "A representation of the attack of Captain Wallis in the Dolphin by the natives of Otaheite"

After James Stuart; engraving by Edward Rooker
1773
Proof engraving, pl. 21 removed from an album of prints published in John Hawkesworth's *Account of the Voyages . . .*, vol. 1 (1773)
20³⁄₁₆ x 24³⁄₁₆ in. (51.2 x 61.4 cm) (framed)

Inscribed: "E. Rooker sculp."

By permission of The British Library, London, Add. Ms. 23,921, fol. 5

References: Hawkesworth, *Account of the Voyages,* vol. 1 (1773): pl. 21 facing p. 442; Graves, *Society of Artists* (1907): 248; Bristol, "Stuart and the Genesis of the Greek Revival" (1997): 193-98, figs. 24-25.

Illustrated: fig. 4-41.

165. "A representation of the surrender of the island of Otaheite to Captain Wallis by the supposed Queen Oberea"

After James Stuart; engraving by John Hall
1773
Proof engraving, pl. 22 removed from an album of prints published in John Hawkesworth's *Account of the Voyages . . .*, vol. 1 (1773)
20³⁄₁₆ x 24³⁄₁₆ in. (51.2 x 61.4 cm) (framed)

Inscribed: "J. Hall sculp."

By permission of The British Library, London, Add. Ms. 23,921, fol. 3a

References: Hawkesworth, *Account of the Voyages,* vol. 1 (1773): pl. 22 facing 462; Graves, *Society of Artists* (1907): 248; Bristol, "Stuart and the Genesis of the Greek Revival" (1997): 193-98, figs. 24-25.

Illustrated: fig. 4-42.

166. Sketchbook
Open to fol. 11, sketches of Athenian coins; pen and ink, pencil. Inscribed: with lengthy descriptive note

James Stuart
1751-52
Book (closed): 12⅝ x 9¹⁄₁₆ x 7¹⁄₁₆ in. (32 x 23 x 1 cm)

By permission of The British Library, London, Add. Ms. 62,088

Illustrated: fig. 2-16.

167. Royal Society of Arts medal

James Stuart; made by Thomas Pingo
Designed, 1757; this example struck,
1759
Silver
1 ¾ in. (4.4 cm)

Inscribed: obverse, ARTS. AND.
COMMERCE. PROMOTED; exergue, SOCIETY INST. LONDON
MDCCLIIII. Signed PINGO below
the figure of Britannia

By courtesy of the Trustees of
The British Museum, London,
Reg. # 1901-11-10-9

References: Hawkins, comp., *Medallic Illustrations,* vol. 2 (1885): no. 401, 684;
Wood, *History of the Royal Society of Arts* (1913): 316; Watkin, *Athenian Stuart* (1982): 54; Allan, "Early Medals of the Royal Society of Arts" (July 1983): 1, fig. 2; Eimer, *British Commemorative Medals* (1987): no. 648;
Bond, *Thomas Hollis* (1990): 91; Eimer, "Society's Concern with the Medallic Art" (November 1991): 753-62; Eimer, "James 'Athenian' Stuart: Medallic Design" (1994): 131-33, fig. 4; Syson, "Designs on Posterity" (1994): 235, no. 8c; Colvin, *Biographical Dictionary* (1995): 795 n. 1; Bristol, "Stuart and the Genesis of the Greek Revival" (1997): 209-10, fig. 27; Eimer, *Pingo Family* (1998): no. 9, 46-47 illus.

Illustrated: fig. 12-1.

168. Goree Taken medal

James Stuart; made by John Pingo
Designed, 1759 (variation on a design of 1758)
Silver
1 ⁹⁄₁₆ in. (4 cm)

Inscribed: obverse, O. FAIR.
BRITANNIA. HAIL. Reverse,
GOREE. TAKEN. MDCCLVIII.

By courtesy of the Trustees of
The British Museum, London,
Reg. # M 8639 (Cat. no. MI 691/415)

References: Hawkins, comp., *Medallic Illustrations,* vol. 2 (1885): no. 415, 691;

Allan, "The Early Medals of the Royal Society of Arts" (July 1983): 1, fig. 3; Eimer, *British Commemorative Medals* (1987): no. 661; Bond, *Thomas Hollis* (1990): 52-53, fig. 17; Eimer, "James 'Athenian' Stuart: Medallic Design and Procedure" (1994): 132-33, fig. 5; Eimer, *The Pingo Family* (1998): no. 12, 48-49 illus.

Illustrated: fig. 12-3.

169. Frederick the Great, Defeat of the French and Austrians medal

James Stuart; made by Thomas Pingo
Designed, ca. 1758–60, exhibited, 1760
Gold
1 ¹¹⁄₁₆ in. (4.2 cm)

Inscribed: obverse, FREDERICUS
MAGNUS BOR. REX [Frederick
the Great, King of Prussia]. Signed
PINGO on the truncation. Reverse,
TE DUCE FREDERICK SEQUOR
[With you as leader Frederick, I follow]; exergue, GALLIS ET
AUSTRIACIS DEVICTIS MDC-
CLVII [The defeat of the French and
Austrians, 1757].

By courtesy of the Trustees of
The British Museum, London,
Reg. # GIII Brand.M.69

References: Friedensburg and Seger,
Schlesiens Münzen und Medaillen
(1901): 4379; Eimer, *Pingo Family*
(1998): no. 8, 46-47 illus.

Illustrated: fig. 12-4.

170. Death of General James Wolfe medal

James Stuart; engraved by John Kirk;
modeled by Isaac Gossett
Designed, ca. 1760; exhibited, 1775
Copper / bronze
1 ⁷⁄₁₆ in. (3.7 cm)

Inscribed: obverse, IACOBUS
WOLFE ANGLUS; below the bust,
GOSSET.M.KIRK.F. Reverse, PRO
PATRIA and IN VICTORIA
CAESUS; exergue, QUEBECAE
SEPT. XIII. MDCCLIX.

By courtesy of the Trustees of
The British Museum, London,
Reg. # M 8649 (Cat. no. MI 706/440)

References: Hawkins, comp., *Medallic Illustrations,* vol. 2 (1885): no. 440, 706;
Betts, *American Colonial History Illustrated by Contemporary Medals*
(1972): no. 422; Eimer, *British Commemorative Medals* (1987): no. 674;
Eimer, "James 'Athenian' Stuart: Medallic Design" (1994): 135-36, fig. 15.

Illustrated: fig. 12-6.

171. Canada Subdued medal

James Stuart; made by John Pingo
Designed, 1760; earliest example
struck, 1761
Silver
1 ⁹⁄₁₆ in. (3.9 cm)

Inscribed: obverse, GEORGE. II.
KING. Reverse, CANADA SUB-
DUED; exergue, MDCCLX S.P.A.C.

By courtesy of the Trustees of
The British Museum, London,
Reg. # M 8670 (Cat. no. MI 711/448)

References: Hawkins, comp., *Medallic Illustrations,* vol. 2 (1885): no. 448, 711;
Betts, *American Colonial History Illustrated by Contemporary Medals*
(1972): no. 430; Allan, "Early Medals of the Royal Society of Arts" (July 1983): 1-2, fig. 5; Eimer, *British Commemorative Medals* (1987): no. 680;
Eimer, "James 'Athenian' Stuart: Medallic Design" (1994): 132-33, fig. 8; Syson, "Designs on Posterity" (1994): 232-33, fig. 8; Bristol, "Stuart and the Genesis of the Greek Revival" (1997): 219, fig. 30; Eimer, *Pingo Family* (1998): no. 15, 48-49 illus.; O'Connell, *London 1753* (2003): 190, fig. 4.9.

Illustrated: fig. 12-7.

172. **Montreal Taken and the Conquest of Canada Completed medal**

James Stuart; made by John Kirk
Designed, 1760; earliest example
struck, 1761
Silver
1⅝ in. (4.1 cm)

Inscribed: obverse, MONTREAL
TAKEN MDCCLX; exergue, SOC.
PROMOTING ARTS AND COM-
MERCE. Reverse, THE
CONQUEST OF CANADA COM-
PLETED; wreath inscribed,
AMHERST.

By courtesy of the Trustees of
The British Museum, London,
Reg. #: M 8668 (Cat. no. MI 711/447)

References: Hawkins, comp., *Medallic
Illustrations*, vol. 2 (1885): no. 447, 697;
Betts, *American Colonial History
Illustrated by Contemporary Medals*
(1972): no. 429, 191-92; Eimer, *British
Commemorative Medals* (1987): no. 679;
Bristol, "Stuart and the Genesis of the
Greek Revival" (1997): 219; Eimer,
Pingo Family (1998): no. 236, 90-91
illus.

Illustrated: fig. 12-8.

173. **Capture of Pondicherry medal**

James Stuart; made by Thomas Pingo
Designed, 1761; earliest example
struck, 1761
Copper/bronze
1⅟₆ in. (3.9 cm)

Inscribed: obverse, GEORGE. THE.
THIRD.; signed T.P.F. below the bust.
Reverse, COOTE STEEVENS;
INDUS and GANGES; TOTAL.
EXPULSION. OF. THE. FRENCH.
FROM. INDIA; exergue,
PONDICHERRY TAKEN
MDCCLXI.

By courtesy of the Trustees of
The British Museum, London,
Reg. # M 4656 (Cat. no. Brown 72)

References: Brown, *British Historical
Medals, 1760-1837*, vol. 1 (1980): no. 72,
p. 3; Eimer, *Commemorative Medals*

(1987): no. 686; Bristol, "Stuart and the
Genesis of the Greek Revival" (1997):
220, 224-25; Eimer, *Pingo Family*
(1998): no. 20, 50-51 illus.; O'Connell,
London 1753: (2003): 191, no. 4.10.

Illustrated: fig. 12-9.

174. **Sketch for a proposed medal
commemorating the Victory at
Belleisle**

James Stuart
ca. 1761
Pen and ink, gray wash, pencil
inscription
7¹¹⁄₁₆ x 6⁵⁄₁₆ in. (19.5 x 16 cm)

Inscribed: "There present thy
Thunder"

RIBA Library Drawings Collection,
London, SD 62/31

References: Bristol, "Stuart and the
Genesis of the Greek Revival" (1997):
221; Eimer, *Pingo Family* (1998): no.
221, 87 illus.

Illustrated: fig. 12-10.

175. **Sketch for a proposed medal
commemorating the taking of
Guadeloupe**

James Stuart
1759
Pen and ink, color wash, pencil
7⅞ x 6¹¹⁄₁₆ in. (20 x 17 cm)

Inscribed: "[…] taken"; "CONI-
UNCT. EXPEDITION.";
"MOORE/
BARRINGTON"; "SOC. PROM.
ARTS AND. COMMERCE"

RIBA Library Drawings Collection,
London, SD 62/30

References: Eimer, "James 'Athenian'
Stuart: Medallic Design" (1994): 133-
34, fig. 9, no. 8d, 235, Bristol, "Stuart
and the Genesis of the Greek
Revival" (1997): 220, 222-23; Eimer,
Pingo Family (1998): 87, fig. 222.

Illustrated: fig. 12-12.

176. **Guadeloupe Taken medal**

James Stuart; made by Lewis Pingo
Designed, 1759; earliest examples
struck, ca. 1761; exhibited, 1762
Copper/bronze
1⁹⁄₁₆ in. (4 cm)

Inscribed: obverse, MOORE; BAR-
RINGTON; exergue, SOC. PROM.
ARTS AND. COMMERCE.
Reverse: GUADALUPE. SURREN-
DERS; exergue, MAY. 1. MDCCLIX.

By courtesy of the Trustees of
The British Museum, London,
Reg. # M 8644 (Cat. no. MI 697/427)

References: Hawkins, comp., *Medallic
Illustrations* (1885): no. 427, 697; Betts,
*American Colonial History Illustrated by
Contemporary Medals* (1972): no. 417, 186;
Eimer, *British Commemorative Medals*
(1987): no. 665; Eimer, "James 'Athenian'
Stuart: Medallic Design" (1994): 133-34,
fig. 10; Syson, "Designs on Posterity"
(1994): 235, no. 8e; Bristol, "Stuart and
the Genesis of the Greek Revival"
(1997): 220, 222-23; Eimer, *Pingo Family*
(1998): no. 22, 50-51 illus.; O'Connell,
London 1753 (2003): 190, fig. 4.6.

Illustrated: fig. 12-13.

177. **Medallion in the Temple of
Concord and Victory at Stowe,
Buckinghamshire**

James Stuart; executed by James Lovell
1763
Terracotta, plaster, lead inscription and
ribbon, wood
Photographed in 2006

Inscribed: "MARTINIQUE &C."

Courtesy of Stowe Landscape
Gardens, Buckinghamshire (The
National Trust, UK)

References: Clarke, "Medallions of
Concord" (August 1981): 616; Watkin,
Athenian Stuart, (1982): 54; Coutu,
"Eighteenth-Century British Monu-
ments" (1993): 70-84, fig. 136; Eimer,
"James 'Athenian' Stuart: Medallic
Design" (1994): 136; Bristol, "Stuart
and the Genesis of the Greek

Revival" (1997): 226-28; Eyres, "Celebration and Dissent" (Spring 2001): 31-50.

Illustrated: fig. 7-11.

178. Sketch for a proposed medal for the taking of Lagos

James Stuart
ca. 1761
Pen and ink, pencil
7⅛ x 7½ in. (18 x 19 cm)

Inscribed: "[…] off Lagos"; "NAVAL. VICTORY. OFF. LAGOS. AVG. XVIII. MDCCLIX."; "SOC. P.A.C."

RIBA Library Drawings Collection, London, SD 62/29 (1)

References: Eimer, "James 'Athenian' Stuart: Medallic Design" (1994): 132-33, fig. 6; Bristol, "Stuart and the Genesis of the Greek Revival" (1997): 221; Eimer, *Pingo Family* (1998): no. 224, p. 89 illus.

Illustrated: fig. 12-14.

179. Battle of Minden medal

James Stuart; made by John Pingo
Designed: n.d.; earliest examples struck, ca. 1762; exhibited, 1762
Silver
1 9⁄16 in. (4 cm)

Inscribed: obverse, CONCORD. OF. THE. ALLIES; exergue, AUG. I. MDCCLIX. Reverse, shield inscribed MINDEN; exergue, SOCIETY. PROM. ARTS AND. COMMERCE.

By courtesy of the Trustees of The British Museum, London, Reg, # M 8654 (Cat. no. MI 700/431)

References: Hawkins, comp., *Medallic Illustrations*, vol. 2 (1885): no. 431, 700 illus.; Eimer, *British Commemorative Medals* (1987): no. 669; Eimer, "James 'Athenian' Stuart: Medallic Design" (1994): 133; Bristol, "Stuart and the Genesis of the Greek Revival" (1997): 223, fig. 32; Eimer, *Pingo Family* (1998): no. 23, 50-51 illus.

Illustrated: fig. 12-15.

180. Birth of George, Prince of Wales medal

James Stuart; made by Thomas Pingo
Designed, 1762; earliest example struck, 1762; exhibited, 1763
Gold
1 9⁄16 in. (4 cm)

Inscribed: obverse, GEORGIUS. III. REX. CHARLOTTA. REGINA; signed T. PINGO. F below the busts. Reverse, PACATUMQUE. REGET. PATRIIS.VIRTUTIBUS.ORBEM [And he will rule a peaceful world with the virtues of his father]; exergue, XII. AUG. MDCCLXII.

By courtesy of the Trustees of The British Museum, London, Reg. # GIII Eng.M.49 (Cat. no. B77)

References: Walpole, *Anecdotes of Painting*, vol. 5 (1937): 109; Brown, *British Historical Medals,* vol. 1 (1980): 17, no. 77; Eimer, *Commemorative Medals* (1987): no. 699; Eimer, "James 'Athenian' Stuart: Medallic Design" (1994): 133; Colvin, *Biographical Dictionary* (1995): 795 n. 1; Bristol, "Stuart and the Genesis of the Greek Revival" (1997): 230; Eimer, *Pingo Family* (1998): no. 26, 52-53 illus.; Roberts, (ed.), *George III and Queen Charlotte* (2004): 365, no. 465.

Illustrated: fig. 12-16.

181. Preparatory sketches for the proposed Catch Club medal

James Stuart
ca. 1764
Pen and ink, gray wash, pencil
8⅝ x 6⅛ in. (22 x 15.5 cm)

Inscribed: "LET US DRINK AND LET US SING TOGETHER"; "ET CANTARE PARES ET RESPONDERE" [Equal in the song and ready in the response]

RIBA Library Drawings Collection, London, SD 62/33 (1)

References: Eimer, "James 'Athenian' Stuart: Medallic Design" (1994): 133, 135, fig. 14; Syson, "Designs on

Posterity" (1994): no. 8f, 235-36; Eimer, *Pingo Family* (1998): no. 224, 88 illus.

Illustrated: fig. 12-17.

182. Catch Club medal

James Stuart; made by Thomas Pingo
Designed, 1762-64; proof medals struck, 1764
Copper
1 ¾ in. (4.4 cm)

Inscribed: obverse, LET'S DRINK. AND. LET'S. SING. TOGETHER; exergue, CATCH CLUB INSTITUTED LONDON MDCCLXII; signed T. PINGO. F at the bottom edge

The Hunterian Museum and Art Gallery, Univeristy of Glasgow, Hunter Collection, Catch Club medal

References: Davis and Waters, *Tickets and Passes* (1922): 152, figs. 397-98; Viscount Gladstone, *Story of the Noblemen and Gentlemen's Catch Club* (1930): 10-12; Brown, *British Historical Medals, 1760-1837,* vol. 1 (1980): no. 83, 18-19; Eimer, "James 'Athenian' Stuart: Medallic Design" (1994): 133, 135, fig. 13; Syson, "Designs on Posterity" (1994): 235-36, fig. 8g; Bristol, "Stuart and the Genesis of the Greek Revival" (1997): 230-31; Eimer, *Pingo Family* (1998): no. 28, 52-53 illus.

Illustrated: fig. 12-18.

183. **Royal Military Academy medal**

James Stuart; made by Thomas Pingo
Designed, ca.1765; medals struck,
1765–70; exhibited 1766
Bronze
1 7/16 in. (3.6 cm)

Inscribed: obverse, AUSPICIIS
GEORG. III OPT. PRINC. PP.
[Under the patronage of George III,
the best of rulers and father of his
country]; signed T. PINGO. F. on the
truncation. Reverse, PRAEMIA
LAUDI [Rewards for merit]; exergue,
D. M. GRANBY MAG. GEN. ORD.
MDCCLXV [The Lord Marquis of
Granby, Master-General of the
Ordinance, 1765].

By courtesy of the Trustees of
The British Museum, London,
Reg. #: 1981-9-17-8 (Cat. no. Brown
93)

References: Brown, *British Historical
Medals 1760-183*, vol. 1 (1980): no. 93,
22; Eimer, *Commemorative Medals*
(1987): no. 710; Eimer, "James
'Athenian' Stuart: Medallic Design"
(1994): 133–34, fig. 12; Eimer, *Pingo
Family* (1998): no. 33, 54.

Illustrated: fig. 12-20.

184. **Lord Camden, Lord Chancellor of
Britain medal**

James Stuart; made by Thomas Pingo
Designed, 1766–67; exhibited, 1767
Silver
1 9/16 in. (4 cm)

Inscribed: obverse, CHARLES
LORD CAMDEN CHANCELLOR
OF BRITAIN; signed T. PINGO F.
below the bust. Reverse, LIBERTY
and EQUITY; exergue, MDCCLXVI.

By courtesy of the Trustees of
The British Museum, London,
Reg. #: M 9242 (Cat. no. Brown 97)

References: "A New Medal . . ."
[Advertisement] (16-18 April 1767):
376; Brown, *British Historical Medals,
1760-1837*, vol. 1 (1980): no. 97, 23;
Eimer, "James 'Athenian' Stuart:

Medallic Design" (1994): 133; Bristol,
"Stuart and the Genesis of the Greek
Revival" (1997): 231–32; Eimer, *Pingo
Family* (1998): no. 35, 54-55 illus.

Illustrated: fig. 12-21.

185. **Admiral George, Lord Anson,
Defeat of the French off Cape
Finisterre medal**

James Stuart; made by Thomas Pingo
Designed, ca. 1760s; exhibited, 1769
Silver
1 11/16 in. (4.3 cm)

Inscribed: obverse, GEORGE
LORD ANSON VICT. MAY III
MDCCXLVII; signed T. PINGO F.
below the bust. Reverse, CIRCUM-
NAVIGATION; BRETT, DENNIS,
CAMPHEL, KEPPEL, SAUMAREZ
and SAUNDERS; below, MDCCXL
MDCCXLIV.

By courtesy of the Trustees of
The British Museum, London,
Reg. # M 8573 (Cat. no. MI 634/325)

References: Hawkins, comp., *Medallic
Illustrations,* vol. 2 (1885): no. 325, 634;
Betts, *American Colonial History
Illustrated by Contemporary Medals*
(1972): no. 345; Wedgwood, *Letters*, vol.
2 (1973): 26 November 1772 [E. 1823-
25]; Eimer, *British Commemorative
Medals* (1987): no. 616; Eimer, "James
'Athenian' Stuart: Medallic Design"
(1994): 133-34, fig. 10; Syson, "Designs
on Posterity" (1994): 235, no. 8e;
Bristol, "Stuart and the Genesis of the
Greek Revival" (1997): 157; Eimer,
Pingo Family (1998): 23, no. 38, 56-57,
illus.

Illustrated: fig. 12-22.

186. **Monument to Brigadier-General
George Augustus, third Viscount
Howe, Westminster Abbey, London**

James Stuart; sculpted by Peter
Scheemakers
1759-62
Photographed in 2006

Courtesy of the Dean and Chapter of
Westminster

References: Brayley and Neale, *History
and Antiquities of the Abbey Church of
St. Peter,* vol. 2 (1823): 237; Webb,
"Chimney-Pieces by Scheemakers"
(14 March 1957): 493; Wilson et al.,
*New Bell's Cathedral Guides: Westminster
Abbey* (1986): 165, fig. 5; Roscoe, "James
'Athenian' Stuart and the Scheemakers
Family" (September 1987): 179, fig. 2;
Bristol, "Stuart and the Genesis of the
Greek Revival" (1997): 162, 359-60,
fig. 103; Bristol, "Society of Dilettanti"
(July 2000): 52, fig. 11; Bradley and
Pevsner, *London,* vol. 6, *Westminster*
(2003): 177; Bristol, "James Stuart and
the London Building Trades" (2003):
3, 6.

Illustrated: fig. 9-3.

187. **Monument to Admiral Charles
Watson, Westminster Abbey,
London**

James Stuart; sculpted by Peter
Scheemakers
1760-63 (partly dismantled and reinstalled in 1957)
Photographed in 2006

Courtesy of the Dean and Chapter of
Westminster

References: Brayley and Neale, *History
and Antiquities of the Abbey Church of
St. Peter, Westminster,* vol. 2 (1823):
214; Webb, "Chimney-Pieces by
Scheemakers" (14 March 1957): 493;
Wilson et al., *New Bell's Cathedral
Guides: Westminster Abbey* (1986): fig. 30;
Roscoe, "James 'Athenian' Stuart and
the Scheemakers Family" (September
1987): 179, fig. 3; Blundell, *Westminster
Abbey* (1989): 117, fig. 18; Colvin,
Biographical Dictionary (1995): 797;

Bristol, "Stuart and the Genesis of the Greek Revival" (1997): 360–64; Bristol, "Society of Dilettanti" (July 2000): 52–53, fig. 12; Bradley and Pevsner, *London*, vol. 6, *Westminster* (2003): 145; Bristol, "James Stuart and the London Building Trades" (2003): 5–6.

Illustrated: figs. 9-1 (detail) and 9-4.

188. **Monument to Catharine Yorke (née Freman), Chicheley Chapel, St. Andrew's Church, Wimpole, Cambridgeshire**

James Stuart; sculpted by Peter Scheemakers
1761–62
Photographed in 2006

References: *Inventory of Historical Monuments in the County of Cambridge*, vol. 1, *West Cambridgeshire* (1968): 213; Roscoe, "James 'Athenian' Stuart and the Scheemakers Family" (September 1987): 181–82, fig. 8; Souden, *Wimpole Hall* (1991): 86; Bristol, "Stuart and the Genesis of the Greek Revival" (1997): 364; Bristol, "Society of Dilettanti" (July 2000): 53, fig. 13.

Illustrated: fig. 9-5.

189. **Preliminary designs for the monument to Philip, first Earl Hardwicke**

James Stuart; sketched by Peter Scheemakers
1764
Pen and ink
4¾ x 12¾ in. (12.2 x 32.5 cm)

Inscribed: with measurements and "this window / stopt"; "first"; "second"

The late Earl of Lichfield and Staffordshire Record Office, D615/P(S)/1/6/8b.

Reference: Roscoe, "James 'Athenian' Stuart and the Scheemakers Family" (September 1987): 181–83, fig. 9.

Illustrated: fig. 9-8.

190. **Monument to the first Earl and Countess of Hardwicke, Chicheley Chapel, St. Andrew's Church, Wimpole, Cambridgeshire**

James Stuart; sculpted by Peter Scheemakers with Thomas Scheemakers
1764–66
Photographed in 2006

References: *Inventory of Historical Monuments in the County of Cambridge*, vol. 1, *West Cambridgeshire* (1968): 213, pl. 127; Watkin, *Athenian Stuart* (1982): 55, fig. 79; Roscoe, "James 'Athenian' Stuart and the Scheemakers Family" (September 1987): 182, fig. 10; Souden, *Wimpole Hall* (1991): 86, fig. 26; Colvin, *Biographical Dictionary* (1995): 797; Bristol, "Stuart and the Genesis of the Greek Revival" (1997): 365–69, fig. 104; Bristol, "Society of Dilettanti" (July 2000): 53, fig. 14; Bradley and Pevsner, *London*, vol. 6, *Westminster* (2003): 145; Bristol, "James Stuart and the London Building Trades" (2003): 6.

Illustrated: fig. 9-6.

191. **Monument to Mary Mason, Bristol Cathedral**

James Stuart; sculpted by J. F. Moore
ca. 1767
Photographed in 2006

Courtesy of the Dean and Chapter of Bristol Cathedral

References: Colvin, *Biographical Dictionary* (1995): 797; Bristol, "Stuart and the Genesis of the Greek Revival" (1997): 154, 369, fig. 106.

Illustrated: fig. 4-17.

192. **Monument to William, Lord Chetwynd, Church of St. John the Baptist, Ashley, Staffordshire**

James Stuart; urn by Wedgwood and Bentley, 1772
1771–72
Photographed in 2006

References: Meteyard, *Life of Wedgwood*, vol. 2 (1866): 225; Colvin, *Biographical Dictionary* (1995): 797; Bristol, "Stuart and the Genesis of the Greek Revival" (1997): 371–72.

Illustrated: fig. 4-24.

193. **Monument to Anthony Ashley Cooper, fourth Earl of Shaftsbury, St Giles's Church, Wimbourne St. Giles, Dorset**

James Stuart; sculpted by Thomas Scheemakers
1771; damaged by fire, 1908; repaired under the direction of Sir Ninian Comper
Photographed in 2006

Reference: Bristol, "Stuart and the Genesis of the Greek Revival" (1997): 370–71, fig. 107.

Illustrated: fig. 9-9.

194. **Monument to Ralph Freman, Church of St. Mary the Virgin, Braughing, Hertfordshire**

James Stuart; sculpted by Thomas Scheemakers
ca. 1773
Photographed in 2006

References: Roscoe, "James 'Athenian' Stuart and the Scheemakers Family" (September 1987): 184, fig. 11; Whinney, *Sculpture in Britain* (1988): 238; Bristol, "Stuart and the Genesis of the Greek Revival" (1997): 370–71; Bristol, "Society of Dilettanti" (July 2000): 53.

Illustrated: fig. 9-10.

195. **Drawing of a variant of the monument to Thomas Steavens**

James Stuart; drawn by Thomas Scheemakers
ca. 1773
Pen and ink, watercolor wash
11½ x 8¼ in. (29.2 x 21 cm) (visible)

Inscribed: "Scheemakers, Thomas /
monument to Jerry Pierce, M.D.
(d. 1762) / in St. Swithin's Church,
Walcot (near Bath)."

By courtesy of the Trustees of The
Victoria and Albert Museum, London,
8408.14 (Box H. 13)

Illustrated: fig. 9-11.

196. **Monument to Thomas Steavens, Church of St. Mary the Virgin, Preston-on-Stour, Warwickshire**

James Stuart; sculpted by Thomas Scheemakers
ca. 1773
Photographed in 2006

References: Physick, *Designs for English Sculpture* (1969): fig. 99; Colvin, *Biographical Dictionary* (1995): 797; Bristol, "Stuart and the Genesis of the Greek Revival" (1997): 370.

Illustrated: fig. 9-12.

197. **Monument to the Hon. Catharine Venables Vernon, Church of All Saints, Sudbury, Derbyshire**

James Stuart
1776
Photographed in 2006

Reference: Colvin, *Biographical Dictionary* (1995): 797.

Illustrated: fig. 4-20.

198. **Monument to Joseph Cocks, Church of St. John the Baptist, Eastnor, Herefordshire**

James Stuart; sculpted by Thomas Scheemakers
1778
Photographed in 2006

References: Meteyard, *Life of Wedgwood,* vol. 2 (1866): 460; Colvin, *Biographical Dictionary* (1995): 797; Bristol, "Stuart and the Genesis of the Greek Revival" (1997): 164.

Illustrated: fig. 9-15.

199. **Monument to Mary Cocks, Church of St. John the Baptist, Eastnor, Herefordshire**

James Stuart; sculpted by Thomas Scheemakers
ca. 1779
Photographed in 2006

References: Meteyard, *Life of Wedgwood,* vol. 2 (1866): 460; Colvin, *Biographical Dictionary* (1995): 797; Bristol, "Stuart and the Genesis of the Greek Revival" (1997): 164.

Illustrated: fig. 9-16.

200. **Monument to Thomas Bentley, Church of St. Nicholas of Myra, Chiswick, London**

James Stuart; sculpted by Thomas Scheemakers
1781
Photographed in 2006

References: Colvin, *Biographical Dictionary* (1995): 797; Bristol, "Stuart and the Genesis of the Greek Revival" (1997): 364-65, 370-71, figs. 105a-b.

Illustrated: fig. 9-13.

201. **Drawing of the monument to Thomas Bentley**

James Stuart; drawn by Thomas Scheemakers
ca. 1780
Pen and ink, watercolor wash
Visible, 12⅞ x 9 in. (32.6 x 22.9 cm)

By courtesy of the Trustees of The Victoria and Albert Museum, London, 8408.9a (Box H.10, formerly in album 93.B.23)

Illustrated: fig. 9-14.

202. **Portrait Medallion of James Stuart**

Designer unknown; made by Wedgwood and Bentley
After 1777
Jasper with green dip and white relief
4⅛ x 3⅛ in. (10.5 x 8 cm)

Marks: "WEDGWOOD" impressed below truncation; "7-9" inscribed

The Wedgwood Museum Trust, Barlaston, Staffordshire, no. 4094

References: Meteyard, *Life of Josiah Wedgwood,* vol. 2 (1866): 220, fig. 43 (this example destroyed 1941); Jonas, *Notes of An Art Collector* (1907), opp. 43 (similar example); Lawrence, "Stuart and Revett" (1938-39): 132; Scheidemantel, *Josiah Wedgwood's "Heads of Illustrious Moderns"* (1958): fig. no. 146, 25; *American Wedgwoodian* (February 1969): no. 146, 45; Reilly and Savage, *Wedgwood: The Portrait Medallions* (1973): 315 illus.; Reilly and Savage, *Dictionary of Wedgwood* (1980): 328 illus.; Sotheby's New York, *English Pottery* (24 April 1982): lot no. 487; Reilly, *Wedgwood,* vol. 1 (1989): fig. 786; Reilly, *Wedgwood Jasper* (1994): 106, fig. 70; Colvin, *Biographical Dictionary* (1995): 795; Reilly, *Wedgwood* (1995): 406; Young, ed., *Genius of Wedgwood* (1995): 18, fig. 10, cat. no. 31, 68-69.

Illustrated: fig. 2-1.

203. **Portrait miniature of James Stuart**

Attributed to Philip Jean
ca. 1778
Watercolor and body color on ivory
2⅛ x 1¾ in. (5.4 x 4.4 cm)

The National Portrait Gallery,
London, NPG 55a

References: James Stuart Jr., *Memoir of His Father,* British Library Add. Ms. 27,576 (ca. 1856-60): 10; Lawrence, "Stuart and Revett" (1938-39): 132; Croft-Murray, *Decorative Painting in England,* vol. 2 (1970): 284; Robinson, *Shugborough* (1989): 25 illus.; Friedman, *Spencer House* (1993): 125, fig. 98; Colvin, *Biographical Dictionary* (1995): 795.

Illustrated: frontispiece.

204. **Portrait miniature of Elizabeth Stuart, second wife of James Stuart**

Attributed to Philip Jean
ca. 1778
Watercolor and body color on ivory
2¼ x 1⅞ in. (5.7 x 4.8 cm)

The National Portrait Gallery,
London, NPG 55b

References: James Stuart Jr., *Memoir of His Father,* British Library Add. Ms. 27,576 (ca. 1856-60): 10; Lawrence, "Stuart and Revett" (1938-39) 132; Croft-Murray, *Decorative Painting in England,* vol. 2 (1970): 284; Robinson, *Shugborough* (1989): 25, illus.; Friedman, *Spencer House* (1993): 125, fig. 98; Colvin, *Biographical Dictionary* (1995): 795.

Illustrated: fig. 2-30.

THE·ANTIQVITIES·OF
ATHENS·

MEASVRED · AND · DELINEATED
BY · JAMES · STVART . F·R·S· AND · F·S·A·
AND · NICHOLAS · REVETT·
PAINTERS · AND · ARCHITECTS·

VOLVME · THE · FIRST·

LONDON
PRINTED · BY · JOHN · HABERKORN · MDCCLXII.

BIBLIOGRAPHY

Key: Archive abbreviations and short forms of bibliographic references used in the endnotes and picture captions are given in **boldface.** *Relevant archival holdings are in parentheses.*

ARCHIVES AND REPOSITORIES

Archivio Storico del Vicaraiato, Rome (Regisro delle Anime).

Bedfordshire and Luton Archives and Records Services (Lucas Papers).

Beinecke Rare Book and Manuscript Library, Yale University, New Haven (Stuart letter to Jacob Hinde).

Bexley Public Libraries, Local Studies and Archive Centre (Erith Borough Council Correspondence, Belvedere House 1947–1960; sales catalogues; Declaration of Trust, 1851; Prints, drawings, and photographs).

Birmingham City Archives (Matthew Boulton Papers).

Bodleian Library, Oxford (Gough Manuscripts; Harcourt Estate Papers; Stuart drawing for a country house).

Brinsley Ford Archive, Paul Mellon Centre for Studies in British Art, London (Stato dell'Anime [Regisro delle Anime], transcriptions by Edward Corp; Registers of the parishes of the S. Andrea delle Fratte in the Strada Felice and S. Lorenzo in Lucina in the Strada Carozze).

RIBA Library Drawings Collection— British Architectural Library, Royal Institute of British Architects, at The Victoria and Albert Museum, London: Drawings Collection (Stuart gouaches; designs and drawings; and Italian sketchbook containing preliminary designs; plans, elevations, and details of buildings in N. Italy; topographical views and notes on painting); British Architectural Library Archive (William Newton Papers; William Chambers Papers); Photographic Collection.

BL—British Library, London, Department of Manuscripts (Album of Buckler views, vol. 1; Album of topographical views, including drawing by Thomas Baskerville; Althorp Papers; Anson Correspondence; Athenian Notebook by Stuart; William Chambers's Letter-Books; Egerton Manuscripts, Minutes of the Royal Society and of the Society of Antiquaries; Egerton Manuscripts, Leeds Papers, including Robert Darcy, fourth Earl of Holdernesse, Correspondence and Papers; Harcourt Papers; Hardwicke Papers; James Harris Autograph Papers; printed copy of "Essay upon the Rise and Progress of Criticism," by James Harris; Thomas Pelham Holles, Duke of Newcastle, Official Correspondence; Liverpool Papers; Horace Mann Papers; Mrs. Elizabeth Montagu Correspondence; Rev. Richard Pococke Travel Journals; copies of the James Russel Correspondence; Memoir of James Stuart by his son, James Stuart Jr.; Josiah Taylor Papers relating to the publication of the fourth volume of *Antiquities of Athens*; Sketches, plan and proof plates for *Antiquities of Athens;* George Vertue Commonplace Books; John Wilkes, M.P., Correspondence and Papers).

British Museum, London: Department of Greek and Roman Antiquities; Department of Coins and Medals; Department of Prints and Drawings; Museum Archives (General Meeting Minutes, Standing Committee Minutes, 1759).

Buckinghamshire Records and Local Studies Service, Aylesbury (Lee Papers).

Cambridge Central Library, Cambridgeshire Collection (Wimpole Photos; W. B. Trevilyan and James Plumtree, "A Journal of a Tour to the Source of the River Cam," typescript).

Cambridge University Library (William Palmer Collection, Reverend A. C. Yorke, "Studiuncula Winepolana," and "Wimpole as I Knew It."; W. B. Trevilyan and James Plumtree, "A Journal of a Tour to the Source of the River Cam").

Centre for Kentish Studies, Maidstone (Pratt Manuscripts).

Chatsworth Archives (Lady Burlington's vouchers).

City of Westminster Archives Centre (Poor Rate Books; Hanover Square Parish Records; St. James Piccadilly Parish Records; Saint Martin-in-the-Fields Parish Records; Hinde Papers).

Croome Archives, Croome Estate Office (Builders' bills).

East Sussex Record Office (Ashburnham Papers).

Edinburgh University Library (Stuart sketchbook in Laing Manuscripts).

English Heritage / National Monuments Record Office, Swindon (Red Box Files; Buildings Records; *Country Life* photo archive).

Family Record Centre, Islington (Josiah Harman will; Elizabeth Stuart will; Josiah Taylor will).

Greenwich Heritage Centre (Prints, drawings, and photographs of the Royal Hospital for Seamen, Greenwich).

Guildhall Library, London (Prints and Drawings, including Hogarth series; Lysons' *Environs of London* series; Mason's Company List of Freemen; Parish Records).

Hammersmith and Fulham Archives and Local History Centre (Folder, Sir Philip Stephens' House in Fulham).

Henry E. Huntington Library, San Marino, CA (Montagu Papers).

Hertfordshire Archives and Local Studies (Eardley Papers).

Holkham Hall Archives, Holkham Hall, Norfolk (Brettingham Correspondence).

Houghton Library, Harvard University, Cambridge, MA (Diary of Thomas Hollis).

House of Lords, London (Original Acts, Parliamentary Archives).

Irish Architectural Archive, Dublin (Irish Georgian Society photographs).

Istituto Nazionale per la Grafica, Rome (Stuart engravings).

Joint Library of the Hellenic and Roman Societies, London (Wood donation).

Kedleston Hall, Derbyshire (Kedleston Papers, account books).

Keele University Library, Staffordshire (Wedgwood Manuscripts, on loan from The Wedgwood Museum, Barlaston, Stoke-on-Trent, Staffordshire).

King's College, Cambridge, UK (Muniment Room: Manuscript "Altarpiece 1742–75").

London Metropolitan Archives, City of London (Photographs of buildings; John Vardy drawings; engravings and paintings of Spencer House; John Nost will).

Marylebone Public Library, London (John Henning Correspondence).

Morgan Library, New York (Angelica Kauffman Album).

NA—The National Archive, Kew, formerly Public Record Office (Admiralty Papers; Royal Greenwich Hospital for Seamen In-Letters, Minutes of General Court Meetings, Various Accounts and Ledgers, 1696–1865; Office of Works Papers; Wills and Administrations; Solicitor's Letters, 1780–85 inclusive; Surveyor-General's Minutes; journal of the proceedings of James Stuart and Thomas Hicks Esqrs.; Letters from Surveyors, Architects, and others as to Works; State Papers Foreign, Tuscany).

National Archives of Scotland, Edinburgh, formerly Scottish Record Office (Clerk of Penicuik Manuscripts, Robert Adam and Family Correspondence).

National Library of Ireland, Dublin (Ely Papers).

National Maritime Museum Library, London (Stuart designs for buildings at the Royal Hospital for Seamen, Greenwich, and Sandwich Manuscripts).

Royal Academy of Arts, London (William Chambers lecture notes).

Royal Archives, Windsor Castle (Account book).

Royal Society, London (Minutes; Journal Copy Books; Raymond and Beverly Sackler Archive Resource [Biographies of Fellows], Certificates of Election and Candidature, Available online at http://www.royalsoc.ac.uk/library).

RSA—Royal Society of Arts, London, formerly the Society for the Promotion of Arts, Manufactures, and Commerce (Stuart Correspondence; Stuart proposals; Committee Minutes; Minutes of the Society; Guard Book; subscription book).

John Rylands University of Manchester Library (Rylands Manuscripts).

St. George's Chapel Archives and Chapter Library, Windsor (Register of Chapter Acts, 1748–73; Audit Book, "Account of all the great Works which have been executed in St George's Chapel Windsor since the year 1782"; Stuart drawing).

Sheffield Archives, Sheffield City Libraries (Wentworth Woodhouse Muniments, Marquess of Rockingham Papers and Personal Account Books; Vouchers for Works of Art; Account Book; Journal of Payments; Furniture Inventory; Malton Correspondence).

Sir John Soane's Museum, London (Robert Adam and Office Papers and Drawings; John Vardy Spencer House designs; Lichfield House designs for alterations; George Basevi Correspondence, ed. Arthur Bolton, typescript).

Society of Antiquaries, London (Minute Books; microfilm copy of the Diary of Thomas Hollis).

Society of Dilettanti, Library of the Society of Antiquaries, London (Minutes of the Society; portraits of members).

Staffordshire and Stoke-on-Trent Archive Service: Staffordshire County Record Office (Bagot Manuscripts; Lichfield Manuscripts).

University of London (Diary of Sir John Parnell).

Vatican Library (Codex Barberini and Biblioteca Apostolica Vaticana, Dipartimento dei Manoscritti, Cod. Vat. 9024).

V&A—The Victoria and Albert Museum, London: Department of Prints and Drawings (John Carter sketches from Holdernesse House and Lichfield House; John Vardy drawings; William Chambers Franco-Italian album; Joseph Goupy engraving); Department of Furniture and Woodwork (Red Box Files).

Warwickshire County Record Office, Warwick (Newdigate Papers; Diary of Sanderson Miller; Deeds of Lease and Release).

West Yorkshire Archive Service, Leeds (Osborne family, Duke of Leeds Collection; Diaries of Lady Amabel Polwarth née Yorke, Vyner Manuscripts).

William Salt Library, Staffordshire (Topographical prints and drawings).

BOOKS AND PERIODICALS

A. H. [Anthony Highmore]. "Further Particulars of the late Athenian Stuart." *Gentleman's Magazine* 58 (March 1788): 216–18.

Abbott, John Lawrence. *John Hawkesworth: Eighteenth-Century Man of Letters.* Madison: University of Wisconsin Press, 1982.

———. "Thomas Hollis and the Society, 1756–1774 (i–iii)." *RSA Journal* 119 (September–November 1971): 711–15, 803–7, 874–78.

Aberdeen, George Hamilton-Gordon, Earl of. *Inquiry into the Principles of Beauty in Grecian Architecture; With an Historical View of the Rise and Progress of the Art in Greece.* London: John Murray, 1822.

"Access Visits Rathfarnham Castle." *Access* 4, no. 1 (February 1994): n.p. Copy in the Guides Office, Office of Public Works, Dublin.

"Account of Joseph Nollikins." *European Magazine, and London Review* 13 (June 1788): 387.

Ackermann's Repository of Arts, Literature, Fashions, Manufactures, etc., 2nd series, 14 (December 1822): 314.

Adam Loftus and the Ely Family, Rathfarnham Castle and the Loftus Family. London: privately printed, [after 1905].

Adam, Robert. *The Ruins of the Palace of the Emperor Diocletian at Spalatro in Dalmatia, by R. Adam.* London: printed for the author, 1764.

Adam, Robert, and James Adam. *The Works in Architecture of Robert and James Adam. . . .* Vol. 1, pt. 1. London: the authors, 1773.

Adams, William Howard, ed. *The Eye of Thomas Jefferson.* Exh. cat. Washington, D.C.: National Gallery of Art, 1976.

Addison, Joseph. "Pleasures of the Imagination." *Spectator,* no. 412 (23 June 1712); no. 413 (24 June 1712); no. 415 (26 June 1712); no. 417 (28 June 1712); no. 420 (2 July 1712).

Adshead, David. "*A Modern Italian Loggia* at Wimpole." *Georgian Group Journal* 10 (2000): 150–63.

The Age of Neo-Classicism: [catalogue of] *the Fourteenth Exhibition of the Council of Europe* [held at] *the Royal Academy and the Victoria and Albert Museum, London, 9 September–19 November, 1972.* London: Arts Council of Great Britain, 1972.

Alberts, Robert C. *Benjamin West: A Biography.* Boston: Houghton Mifflin, 1978.

Allason, Thomas. *Picturesque Views of the Antiquities of Pola in Istria.* London: John Murray, 1819.

Allan, D. G. C. "The Early Medals of the Royal Society of Arts." *Medal* 3 (July 1983): 1–3.

Allan, D. G. C., and John Lawrence Abbott, eds. *The Virtuoso Tribe of Arts and Sciences: Studies in the Eighteenth-Century Work and Membership of the London Society of Arts.* Athens and London: University of Georgia Press, 1992.

llen, Brian. *Towards a Modern Art World.* New Haven and London: Yale University Press, for the Paul Mellon Centre for Studies in British Art, Yale Center for British Art, 1995.

Amateur [pseud.]. "Mr. Lyde Browne." *British Society of Dilettanti. Notes and Queries,* 2nd series, 9 (18 February 1860): 124–25.

Amelung, Walther. *Die Sculpturen des Vaticanischen Museums.* Vol. 2. Berlin: George Reimer, 1908.

Amery, Colin. "Where the Gods Must Dance at Night." *Financial Times* (12 November 1990): 13.

Ancient and Historical Monuments in the City of Salisbury. London: H.M.S.O., 1980.

Andrews, Malcolm. *The Search for the Picturesque: Landscape Aesthetics and Tourism in Britain, 1760–1800.* Stanford University Press, 1989.

The Annual Register, or a View of the History, Politics, and Literature for the Year 1773. London: J. Dodsley, 1775.

Antiquities. See Stuart, James, and Nicholas Revett. *The Antiquities of Athens.*

Antram, Nicholas, Gervase Jackson-Stops, and Alastair Laing. *Kedleston Hall.* London: National Trust, 1988.

Arbiter. "Spencer House as a Club?" *Country Life* 60 (11 December 1926): 946.

Archer, John. "The Beginnings of Association in British Architectural Esthetics." *Eighteenth Century Studies* 16 (Spring 1983): 241–64.

Aristotole. *Aristotle Poetics.* Trans. by Stephen Halliwell. 2nd ed. Loeb Classical Library. Cambridge, MA, and London: Harvard University Press, 1995.

Arnason, H. Harvard. *The Sculptures of Houdon.* London: Phaidon, 1975.

Arnold, Dana. "Count Gazola and the Temples at Paestum: An Influential Grand Tour Guide." *Apollo* 136 (August 1992): 95–99.

———, ed. *The Georgian Villa.* Strand: Alan Sutton Publishing Ltd., 1996.

Artnet. "George Michael Moser." Excerpted from *The Grove Dictionary of Art.* London: Macmillan, 2000. http://www.art-net.com/library/05/0598/T059830.asp. Accessed 26 July 2004 and 10 November 2005.

"Athens Stuart, unexpectedly. . . ." [Obituary.] *World,* no. 359 (22 February 1788): 3.

Ayres, James. *Building the Georgian City.* New Haven and London: Yale University Press for the Paul Mellon Centre for Studies in British Art, 1998.

Bagget, Maury, ed. "Blithfield Hall and its Estate." *Baggett/Bagot Family History.* http://baggethistory.com/blithfield.html. Accessed 1 September 2004.

Bagot, Nancy, Lady. *Blithfield Hall: A Descriptive Survey and History*. Derby: English Life Productions, 1973. Copy in the National Monuments Record Office, Swindon.

Bagot, Mrs. Charles [Sophia Louisa]. *Links with the Past*. 3rd ed. London: Edward Arnold, 1902.

Bagot, William, 2nd Baron. *Memorials of the Bagot Family*. Blithfield: William Hodgetts, 1824.

Baillie, Thomas. *The Case of the Royal Hospital for Seamen, at Greenwich: Containing a Comprehensive View of the Internal Government; in Which are Stated the Several Abuses that Have Been Introduced into the Great National Establishment. . . .* London: n.p., 1778.

Baird, Rosemary. *Mistress of the House: Great Ladies and Grand Houses, 1670–1830*. London: Weidenfeld and Nicolson, 2003.

———. "'The Queen of the Bluestockings.' Mrs. Montagu's House at 23 Hill Street Rediscovered." *Apollo* 158 (August 2003): 43–49.

Baker, Malcolm. *Figured in Marble: The Making and Viewing of Eighteenth-Century Sculpture*. London: Victoria and Albert Publications, 2000.

[Baker, Robert]. *Observations on the Pictures Now in Exhibition at the Royal Academy, Spring Gardens, and Mr. Christie's*. London: John Bell and G. Riley, 1780.

Ball, Francis Elrington. *A History of the County of Dublin: The People, Parishes and Antiquities from the Earliest Times to the Close of the Eighteenth Century*. 6 vols. Dublin: Alex. Thom and Co., 1902–20.

Bandini, Angelo Maria, et al. *De Obelisco Caesaris Augusti e Campi Martii ruderibus nuper eruto commentarius auctore Angelo Maria Bandinio accedunt CLL. Virorum epistolae atque opuscula / Dell'obelisco di Cesare Augusto: scavato dalle rovine del Campo Marzo*. Rome: Pallade, 1750.

Banham, Joanna, ed. *Encyclopedia of Interior Design*. Vol. 2. London and Chicago: Fitzroy Dearborn Publishers, 1997.

Barker, Godfrey. "The Spencer Line." *Connoisseur* 207 (July 1981): 179–83.

Barnes, G. R., and J. H. Owen, eds. *The Private Papers of John, Earl of Sandwich, First Lord of the Admiralty, 1771–1782*. London: Navy Records Society, 1932–38.

Barr, Bernard, and John Ingamells, comps. *A Candidate for Praise: William Mason, 1725–97, Precentor of York*. Exh. cat. York Art Gallery; York Minster Library, *1973*.

Barrier, Janine. "William Chambers, Augustin Pajou and Their Colleagues in Rome." *Apollo* 147 (January 1998): 25–31.

Barry, Charles, ed. *The Travellers' Club House. . . . Studies and Examples of the Modern School of English Architecture*. London: John Weale, 1839.

Barry, James. *The Works of James Barry, Esq*. 2 vols. London: T. Cadell and W. Davies, 1809.

Bartoli, Pietro Santi. *Admiranda romanarum antiquitatum ac veteris sculpturae vestigia: anaglyphico opere elaborata, ex marmories exemplaribus quae Romanae adhuc extant, in Capitolio, aedibus, hortisque virorum principum ad antiquam elegantiam*. 2nd ed. Rome: Rubeis, 1693.

Batchelor, David. *Chromophobia*. London: Reaktion, 2000.

Batey, Mavis. "Nuneham Park, Oxfordshire." Parts I and II. *Country Life* 144 (5 September 1968): 540–42; (12 September 1968): 640–42.

———. "Nuneham Courtenay: An Oxfordshire Eighteenth-Century Deserted Village." *Oxoniensia* 33 (1968): 108–24.

———. "William Mason: English Gardener." *Garden History* 1, no. 2 (1973): 11–25.

Battle, Arthur. *Edwardian Chislehurst: Memories of the Village Baker*. Rainham, Kent: Meresborough, 1988.

Baugh, Daniel A. *British Naval Administration in the Age of Walpole*. Princeton University Press, 1965.

Bayne, Robert. *Moor Park*. London: Longmans, Green and Co., 1871.

Beaglehole, John Cawte. *The Life of Captain James Cook*. Stanford University Press, 1974.

Beard, Geoffrey W. *Georgian Craftsmen and Their Work*. London: Country Life, 1966.

———. *Decorative Plasterwork in Great Britain*. London: Phaidon, 1975.

———. *Craftsmen and Interior Decoration in England, 1660–1820*. Edinburgh: J. Bartholomew and Sons; New York: Holmes and Meier, 1981.

———. "Vile and Cobb: Eighteenth-century London Furniture Makers." *Antiques* 137 (June 1990): 1394–405.

———. "Decorators and Furniture Makers at Croome Court." *Furniture History* 29 (1993): 88–113.

Beard, Geoffrey, and J. Homery Folkes. "John Chute and Hagley Hall." *Architectural Review* 3 (March 1952): 199–200.

Beard, Geoffrey, and Christopher Gilbert, eds. *Dictionary of English Furniture Makers, 1660–1840*. Leeds: Furniture History Society: W. S. Maney and Son, 1986.

Beard, Mary. *The Parthenon*. London: Profile Books, 2002.

Beckett, Alison. "Getty Plan for Spencer House." *Daily Telegraph* (12 April 1983): 8.

Bedford, Francis, Sir William Gell, and John Peter Gandy. *The Unedited Antiquities of Attica, comprising the Architectural Remains of Eleusis, Rhamnus, Sunium, and Thoricus*. London: Longman, Hurst, Rees, Orme, and Brown, and John Murray, 1817.

Belanger, Terry. "A Directory of the London Book Trades, 1766." *Publishing History* 1 (1977): 7–48.

Bell, Charles Francis, ed. *Annals of Thomas Banks, Sculptor, Royal Academician, with Some Letters from Sir Thomas Lawrence, P. B. A., to Banks's Daughter*. Cambridge University Press, 1938.

Belsey, Hugh. "Arthur Devis." Grove Art Online. Oxford University Press. http://www.groveart.com/. Accessed 22 November 2005.

Beltramini, Guido, et al. *Palladio and Northern Europe: Books, Travellers, Architects*. Milan: Skira Editore, 1999.

Bence-Jones, Mark. *Burke's Guide to Country Houses*. Vol. 1, *Ireland*. London: Burke's Peerage Ltd., 1978.

Benjamin, Asher. *The Builder's Guide, or Complete System of Architecture. . . .* Boston: Bazin and Ellsworth, 1838.

———. *Practice of Architecture, Containing the Five Orders of Architecture, and An Additional Column and Entablature. . . .* 4th ed. Boston: Benjamin B. Mussey, 1839.

———. *Practice of Architecture and The Builder's Guide: Two Pattern Books of American Classical Architecture*. New York: Da Capo Press, 1994.

Bergdoll, Barry. *Karl Friedrich Schinkel: An Architecture for Prussia*. New York: Rizzoli, 1994.

Berkeley, George. *The Works of George Berkeley, Bishop of Cloyne*. Ed. by Arthur Aston Luce and Thomas Edmund Jessop. 9 vols. [London]: Nelson, [1948–57].

Betts, Charles Wyllys. *American Colonial History Illustrated by Contemporary Medals*. Ed. by William T. R. Marvin and Lyman Haynes Low. New York: Scott Stamp and Coin Company, 1894. Reprint, Boston: Quarterman Publications, 1972.

Bevington, Michael. "The Development of the Classical Revival at Stowe." *Architectura* 21, no. 2 (1991): 136–63.

Bewley, Christina, and David Bewley. *Gentleman Radical: A Life of John Horne Tooke, 1736–1812*. London: Tauris Academic Studies, 1998.

Biddulph, Elizabeth Philippa Yorke, Baroness. *Charles Philip Yorke, Fourth Earl of Hardwicke, Vice-Admiral, R.N., A Memoir by his Daughter, The Lady Biddulph of Ledbury*. London: Smith, Elder and Co., 1910.

Bignamini, Ilaria. "George Vertue, Art Historian, and Art Institutions in London, 1689–1768: A Study of Clubs and Academies." Walpole Society annual, vol. 54 (1988): 1–148.

Bindman, David. *Hogarth and his Times: Serious Comedy*. Berkeley: University of California Press, 1997.

Bindman, David, and Malcolm Baker. *Roubiliac and the Eighteenth-Century Monument: Sculpture as Theatre*. New Haven: Yale University Press for the Paul Mellon Centre for Studies in British Art, 1995.

Binney, Marcus. "Wentworth Woodhouse Revisited." Parts I and II. *Country Life* 173 (17 March 1983): 624–27; (24 March 1983): 708–11.

———. *Sir Robert Taylor: From Rococo to Neoclassicism*. London: Allen and Unwin, 1984.

———. "Wentworth Woodhouse, Yorkshire." *Country Life* 185 (24 January 1991): 60–62.

Black, Jeremy. *The British Abroad: The Grand Tour in the Eighteenth Century*. New York and London: Alan Sutton Publishing Ltd., 1992.

Black, Jeremy, and Philip Woodfine, eds. *The British Navy and the Use of Naval Power in the Eighteenth Century*. Atlantic Highlands, NJ: Humanities Press International, 1989.

Blackburne, Francis. *Memoirs of Thomas Hollis*. 2 vols. London: n.p., 1780.

Blane, Gilbert, Sir. *A Short Account of the Most Effectual Means of Preserving the Health of Seamen, Particularly in the Royal Navy*. London: n.p., 1780.

Blau, Eve, and Edward Kaufman, eds. *Architecture and Its Image: Four Centuries of Architectural Representation, Works From the Collection of The Canadian Centre for Architecture*. Exh. cat. Canadian Centre for Architecture, Montreal; the Dallas Museum of Art; the École nationale supérieure des beaux-arts, Paris. Montreal: Canadian Centre for Architecture; Cambridge, MA: Distributed by the MIT Press, 1989.

Blondel, Jacques–François. *Cours d'architecture, ou, Traité de la décoration, distribution and construction des bâtiments: contenant les leçons données en 1750, and les années suivantes*. 9 vols. Paris: Chez Desaint, Librairie, 1771–77.

Bloy, Marjie. "The Age of George III: John Wilkes (1725–1798)." *A Web of English History*. http://ds.dial.pipex.com/town/terrace/adw03/c-eight/people/wilkes.htm. Accessed 17 September 2004. Site to be moved to http://www.historyhome.co.uk/.

Blundell, Joe Whitlock. *Westminster Abbey: The Monuments*. London: John Murray, 1989.

Blunt, Reginald, ed. *Mrs Montagu, "Queen of the Blues," Her Letters and Friendships from 1762 to 1800*. 2 vols. London: Constable and Co.; Boston and New York: Houghton Mifflin, 1923.

Bodnar, Edward W. *Collection Latomus*. Vol. 43, *Cyriacus of Ancona and Athens*. Bruxelles-Berchem: Latomus Revue d'Études Latines, 1960.

Bold, John. *Greenwich: An Architectural History of the Royal Hospital for Seamen and the Queen's House*. New Haven and London: Yale University Press for the Paul Mellon Centre for Studies in British Art in association with English Heritage, 2000.

Bold, John, and Edward Chaney, eds. *English Architecture Public and Private: Essays for Kerry Downes*. Lincoln: Hambledon Press, 1993.

Bolton, Arthur T. "Croome Court, Worcestershire." *Country Life* 13 (25 April 1903): 536–42.

———. "Newby Hall, Ripon." *Country Life* 35 (13 June 1914): 878–95.

———. "Croome Court, Worcestershire." *Country Life* 37 (10 April 1915): 482–89.

———. "James Stuart at Portman House and Spencer House." *Country Life* 37, no. 956 Suppl. (1 May 1915): 6★–12★.

———. "Hagley Park, Worcestshire." Part I. *Country Life* 38 (16 October 1915): 520–28.

———. "West Wycombe, Buckinghamshire." Parts I and II. *Country Life* 39 (1 January 1916): 16–24; (8 January 1916): 48–55.

———. "Town Houses of the XVIII Century: Lichfield House, No. 15 St. James's Square." *Country Life* 41 (12 May 1917): 2★–6★.

———. *The Architecture of Robert and James Adam*. London: Country Life, 1922.

Bond, William Henry. *Thomas Hollis of Lincoln's Inn: A Whig and His Books*. Cambridge and New York: Cambridge University Press, 1990.

Borroni Salvadori, Fabia. "Ignazio Enrico Hugford, collezionista con la vocazione del mercante." *Annali della Scuola Normale Superiore di Pisa*. 3rd series, 13, no. 4 (1983): 1025–56.

———. "Artisti e viaggiatori agli Uffizi nel Settecento, part 1." *Labyrinthos* 4, nos. 7–8 (1985): 3–72.

Boswell, James. *The Life of Samuel Johnson*. Ed. by Henry Morley. London: George Routledge and Sons, 1885.

Bothe, Rolf, et al. *Friedrich Gilly, 1772–1800, und die Privatgesellschaft junger Architekten*. Exh. cat., Internationalen Bauausstellung, Berlin and Berlin Museum. Berlin: Verlag Willmuth Arenhövel, 1984.

Bottari, Giovanni Gaetano. *Raccolta di Lettere sulla Pittura, Scultura ed Architettura*. Vol. 5. Milan: Giovanni Silvestri, 1822.

Boutry, Philippe, [et al.], eds. *Le Grecia Antica: mito e simbolo per l'età della grande rivoluzione: genesi e crisi di un modello nella cultura del Settecento*. Milano: Guarini, 1991.

Bowen, H.V. *War and British Society, 1688–1815*. Cambridge University Press, 1998.

Bowie, Theodore, and Diether Thimme, eds. *The Carrey Drawings of the Parthenon Sculptures*. Bloomington and London: Indiana University Press, 1971.

Bowron, Edgar Peters, and Joseph J. Rishel. *Art in Rome in the Eighteenth Century*. Exh. cat. Philadelphia Museum of Art and Museum of Fine Arts, Houston. London: Merrell; Philadelphia: the Museum; New York: St. Martins' Press, 2000.

Bradley, Simon, and Nikolaus Pevsner. *London*. Vol. 6, *Westminster*. Buildings of England. New Haven and London: Yale University Press, 2003.

Brayley, Edward Wedlake, and John Preston Neale. *The History and Antiquities of the Abbey Church of St. Peter, Westminster*. 2 vols. London: Hurst, Robinson, and Co., 1818–23.

Breman, Paul, and Denise Addis. *Guide to Vitruvius Britannicus*. New York: Benjamin Blom, Inc., 1972.

Brewer, James Norris. *The Beauties of Ireland: Being Original Delineations, Topographical, Historical, and Biographical, of Each County*. London: Sherwood, Jones, and Co., 1825–26.

Brewer, John. *The Sinews of Power: War, Money and the English State, 1688–1783*. New York: Alfred A. Knopf, 1989.

———. *The Pleasures of the Imagination: English Culture in the Eighteenth Century*. London: Harper Colllins, 1997.

Breval, John. *Remarks on Several Parts of Europe: Relating Chiefly to their Antiquities and History. Collected upon the Spot in Several Tours Since the Year 1723 . . . 1723–28*. 2 vols. Rev. ed., London: Lintot, 1738.

Bristol, Kerry. "James 'Athenian' Stuart and the Society." *RSA Journal* 144 (November 1996): 29.

Bristol, "Stuart and the Genesis of the Greek Revival" (1997)
———. "James 'Athenian' Stuart (1713–1788) and the Genesis of the Greek Revival in British Architecture." Ph.D. diss., University of London, at the Courtauld Institute of Art, 1997.

———. "The Society of Dilettanti. James 'Athenian' Stuart and the Anson Family." *Apollo* 152 (July 2000): 46–54.

———. "The Painted Rooms of 'Athenian' Stuart." *Georgian Group Journal* 10 (2000): 164–74.

———. "A Newly-Discovered Drawing by James Stuart." *Architectural History* 44 (2001): 39–44.

———. "22 Portman Square: Mrs Montagu and her 'Palais de la vieillesse'." *British Art Journal* 2 (Summer 2001): 72–85.

———. "James Stuart and the London Building Trades." *Georgian Group Journal* 13 (2003): 1–11.

Bristow, Ian C. *Architectural Colour in British Interiors, 1615–1840*. New Haven and London: Yale University Press, 1996.

Broad, Violet, et al. *Rathfarnham, Gateway to the Hills: The Story of Rathfarnham Past and Present from the Dodder to Kilmashogue*. Dublin: Irish Countrywomen's Association, 1990.

Broomfield, J. H. "Lord Sandwich at the Admiralty Board: Politics and the British Navy, 1771–1778." *The Mariner's Mirror: The Journal of the Society for Nautical Research* 51 (1965): 7–17.

Brown, Beverly, and Diana Kleiner. "Giuliano da Sangallo's Drawings after Ciriaco d'Ancona: Transformations of Greek and Roman Antiquities in Athens." *Journal of the Society of Architectural Historians* (USA) 43 (December 1983): 321–35.

Brown, Iain Gordon. "The Picturesque Vision: Fact and Fancy in the Capriccio Plates of Robert Adam's Spalatro." *Apollo* 136 (August 1992): 76–82.

———. *Monumental Reputation: Robert Adam and the Emperor's Palace*. Edinburgh: National Library of Scotland, 1992.

———. "'With an Uncommon Splendour': The Bindings of Robert Adam's Ruins at Spalatro." *Apollo* 137 (January 1993): 6–11.

Brown, Laurence A. *A Catalogue of British Historical Medals, 1760–1960*. Vol. 1, *The Accession of George III to the Death of William IV, 1760–1837*. London: Seaby Publications; Beverly Hills, CA: Distributed by Numismatic Fine Arts, 1980.

Brown, Lesley, ed. *New Shorter Oxford English Dictionary on Historical Principles*. 2 vols. 4th rev. ed., Oxford: Clarendon Press; New York: Oxford University Press, 1993.

Brown, Roderick, ed. *The Architectural Outsiders*. London: Waterstone, 1985.

Browning, Iain. *Palmyra*. London: Chatto and Windus, 1979.

Brunton, Anne, and Barbara Godfrey. "Royal Alfred Institution for Old Seamen, Belvedere." *North West Kent Family History Society* 6 (April 1992): 191–92.

Bryant, Julius. *Mrs. Howard, A Woman of Reason (1688–1767)*. Exh. cat. Marble Hill House, Twickenham. London: English Heritage, 1988.

———. *Marble Hill, Twickenham*. London: English Heritage, 2002.

———. *Kenwood: Paintings in the Iveagh Bequest*. New Haven and London: Yale University Press, 2003.

———. *Thomas Banks (1735–1805): Britain's First Modern Sculptor*. Exh. cat. London: Sir John Soane's Museum, 2005.

Bryant, Margaret E. *The London Experience of Secondary Education*. London and Atlantic Highlands, N.J.: Athlone Press, 1986.

Buchner, Edmund. *Die Sonnenuhr des Augustus: Nachdruck aus RM 1976 und 1980 und Nachtrag über die Ausgrabung 1980/1981*. Mainz am Rhein: Zabern, 1982.

Burke, Edmund. *A Philosophical Enquiry into the Origin of our Ideas of the Sublime and the Beautiful*. 5th ed. London: J. Dodsley, 1767.

———. *The Correspondence of Edmund Burke*. Vol. 1, *April 1744–June 1768*. Ed. by Thomas W. Copeland. Vol. 2, *July 1768–June 1774*. Ed. by Lucy S. Sutherland. Cambridge University Press, 1958, 1960.

Burke, Joseph. *English Art, 1714–1800*. Oxford: Clarendon Press, 1976.

Burney, Fanny. *The Early Diary of Frances Burney, 1768–1778*. Ed. by Anne Raine Ellis. 2 vols. London: George Bell and Sons, 1889.

———. *The Diary and Letters of Madame D'Arblay (Frances Burney)*. Ed. by W. C. Ward. Vol. 1. London and New York: Frederick Warne and Co., 1892.

Busco, Marie. *Sir Richard Westmacott, Sculptor*. Cambridge and New York: Cambridge University Press, 1994.

Bushell, Thomas Alexander. *Imperial Chislehurst*. Buckingham: The Barracuda Collection, 1997.

Butler, Eliza Marian. *The Tyranny of Greece over Germany: A Study of the Influence Exercised by Greek Art and Poetry over the Great German Writers of the 18th, 19th and 20th Centuries*. Cambridge University Press, 1935.

Byron, John. *Byron's Journal of His Circumnavigation, 1764–1766*. Ed. by Robert Emmett Gallagher. Hakluyt Society, 2nd series, pt. 2, no. 122. Cambridge University Press, published for the Society, 1964.

Caldwell, Andrew. "An Account of the Extraordinary Escape of James Stewart, from being Put to Death by Some Turks in Whose Company He Happened to be Travelling." *European Magazine, and London Review* 46 (November 1804): 369–71.

"Camden Place, Chiselhurst [sic]." *Illustrated London News* 57 (October 1870): 386.

Campbell, Colen, continued by James Gandon and John Woolfe. *Vitruvius Britannicus; or, The British Architect, Containing the Plans, Elevations, and Sections of The Regular Buildings, both Publick and Private in Great Britain. . . .* Vols. 4 and 5. London: n.p., 1767 and 1771.

Le Camus de Mézières, Nicholas. *La génie de l'architecture, ou l'analogie de cet art avec nos sensations*. Paris: Benoit Morin, 1780.

———. *The Genius of Architecture, or, The Analogy of that Art with our Sensations*. Trans. by David Britt. Santa Monica, CA: Getty Center for the History of Art and the Humanities; Chicago: University of Chicago Press, 1992.

Carli, Giovanni Rinaldo, Conte. *Delle Antichità Italiche*. 5 vols. Milan: Nell'imperial monistero di S. Ambrogio Maggiore, 1788–91.

Carr, Denis J. *Sydney Parkinson: Artist of Cook's Endeavour Voyage*. Canberra: British Museum (Natural History) and Australian National University Press, 1983.

Carr, J. A. "Historical Sketch of Rathfarnham Castle." Copy in the Guides Office, Office of Public Works, Dublin.

Carter, Harold B. "The Royal Society and the Voyage of HMS *Endeavour* 1768–71." *Notes and Records of the Royal Society of London* 49 (1995): 245–60.

Carteret, Philip. "*A Letter from* Philip Carteret, *Esquire, Captain of the* Swallow Sloop, *to* Mathew Maty, M.D. *Sec.* R. S. *on the Inhabitants of the Coast of Patagonia*." *Philosophical Transactions of the Royal Society* 60 (1771): 20–26.

———. *Carteret's Voyage Round the World, 1766–1769*. Ed. by Helen Wallis. Vol. 2, Hakluyt Society, 2nd series, pt. 2, no. 124. Cambridge University Press for the Society, 1965.

Cash, Derek. *Access to Museum Culture: The British Museum from 1753 to 1836*. London: The British Museum, 2002.

Cassas, Louis-François, and Joseph Lavallée. *Voyage pittoresque et historique de l'Istrie et de la Dalmatie*. Paris: Vilain, 1802.

[Catalogue of Josiah Wedgwood's "Heads of Illustrious Moderns" exhibition.] *American Wedgwoodian* 3 (February 1969): 42–62.

Catalogue of the Pictures, Statues, &c. at Kedleston: with Some Account of the Architecture. n.p., ca. 1769.

A Catalogue of the Paintings, Sculptures, Models, Drawings, Engravings, &C. now Exhibiting in the Great Room Belonging to the Society for the Encouragement of Arts, Manufactures, and Commerce in the Strand. Pt. 1. London: n.p., 1761.

Caylus, Anne Claude Philippe, Comte de. *Recueil d'antiquités égyptiennes, étrusques, greques et romaines*. Paris: Desaint and Saillant, 1752–67.

Cazalas, Marie-Louise, et al. *Paris, Rome, Athènes: Le Voyage en Grèce des architectes français aux XIXe, et XXe siècles*. Exh. cat. École nationale supérieure des beaux-arts, Paris. Paris: the museum, 1982.

Chalkin, Christopher. *English Counties and Public Building, 1650–1830*. London: Hambledon Press, 1998.

Chambers, Neil, ed. *The Letters of Sir Joseph Banks: A Selection*. London: Imperial College Press, 2000.

Chambers, William. *Treatise on Civil Architecture*. London: printed for the author by J. Haberkorn, 1759.

———. *Treatise on the Decorative Part of Civil Architecture. . . .* 3rd ed. London: Joseph Smeeton, 1791.

Chancellor, E. Beresford. *The Private Palaces of London, Past and Present*. London: Kegan Paul, Trench, Trübner, 1908.

———. *Memorials of St. James's Street.* London: Grant Richards, 1922.

Chandler, Richard. *Travels in Asia Minor; or, An Account of a Tour Made at the Expense of the Society of Dilettanti.* Oxford: Clarendon Press, 1775.

———. *Travels in Asia Minor, 1764–1765.* Ed. by Edith Clay. Oxford: Clarendon Press, 1825. New ed., London: British Museum, 1971.

Chandler, Richard, Nicholas Revett, and William Pars. *Antiquities of Ionia.* Vol. 1, *Ionian Antiquities.* 1769; 2nd ed. London: W. Bulmer and W. Nicol, 1821. Vols. 2–5. London: George Nicol, et al., 1797–1815.

Chaney, Edward. *The Evolution of the Grand Tour: Anglo-Italian Cultural Relations since the Renaissance.* London and Portland, OR: Frank Cass, 1998.

Chartier, Roger. *The Order of Books: Readers, Authors and Libraries in Europe between the Fourteenth and the Eighteenth Centuries.* Trans. by Lydia G. Cochrane. Cambridge: Polity Press, 1994.

Cherry, Bridget, Charles O'Brien, and Nikolaus Pevsner. *London.* Vol. 5, *East.* Buildings of England. New Haven and London: Yale University Press, 2005.

Chilvers, Ian, ed. *The Concise Oxford Dictionary of Art and Artists.* Oxford and New York: Oxford University Press, 1996.

Chislehurst and St. Paul's Cray Commons. Chislehurst: Chislehurst and St. Paul's Cray Commons Conservators, 1970.

Chisholm, Kate. *Fanny Burney: Her Life, 1752–1840.* London: Chatto and Windus, 1998.

Choiseul-Gouffier, Marie-Gabriel-Florent-Auguste de, Comte. *Voyage pittoresque de la Grèce.* Vol. 1. Paris: n.p., 1782.

Christie's, London. *The Superb and Elegant Produce, of Mess. Boulton and Fothergill's Or Moulu Manufactory, at Soho, in Staffordshire.* Sale cat. 11–13 April 1771.

———. *A Capital Well-chosen Collection of Italian, French, Flemish and Dutch pictures, Marble Busto's, Valuable Bronzes, Drawings and c.* Sale cat. 28 January 1785.

———. *British Drawings and Watercolours including Architectural Drawings.* Sale cat. 19 December 1989.

———. *British Art on Paper.* Sale cat. 17 November 2004.

———. *Out of the Ordinary: The Discerning and Individual Taste of Christopher Gibbs and Harris Lindsay.* Sale cat. 10 May 2006.

Clark, Martin Lowther "The English Discovery of Greece." *Architectural Review* 89 (March 1941): 71–74.

Clark, Peter. *British Clubs and Societies, 1580–1800: The Origins of an Associational World.* Oxford and New York: Oxford University Press, 2000.

Clarke, Basil F. L. *The Building of the Eighteenth-Century Church.* London: S.P.C.K., 1963.

Clarke, Charles. "An Account of the Very Tall Men. . . ." *Philosophical Transactions of the Royal Society* 57 (1767): 75–79.

Clarke, Edward Daniel. *Critique on the Character and Writings of Sir George Wheler, as a Traveller: In a letter to the Rev. F. Wrangham.* York: Thomas Wilson and Sons, 1820.

Clarke, George. "Grecian Taste and Gothic Virtue: Lord Cobham's Gardening Programme and Its Iconography." *Apollo* 97 (June 1973): 566–71.

———. "The Medallions of Concord: An Association Between the Society of Arts and Stowe." *RSA Journal* 129 (August 1981): 611–16.

Clarke, Graeme Wilber, ed., with the assistance of James Christopher Eade. *Rediscovering Hellenism: The Hellenic Inheritance and the English Imagination.* Cambridge and New York: Cambridge University Press, 1989.

Clay, Edith. *Sir William Gell In Italy: Letters to the Society of Dilettanti, 1831–1835.* London: Hamish Hamilton, 1976.

Clifford, Helen M. "The Richmond Gold Cup, Social, Sporting and Design History." *Apollo* 137 (February 1993): 102–6.

Clifford, James Lowry. *Hester Lynch Piozzi (Mrs. Thrale).* Oxford: Clarendon Press, 1941.

Clifford, Timothy. "'Mr. Stuart's Tripod' and a Candelabrum." *Burlington Magazine* 114 (December 1972): 874.

———. "John Bacon and the Manufacturers." *Apollo* 122 (1985): 288–304.

Clinkscale, Martha Novak. *Makers of the Piano.* 2 vols. Oxford and New York: Oxford University Press, 1993–99.

Cochrane, James Aikman. *Dr. Johnson's Printer; The Life of William Strahan.* London: Routledge and Kegan Paul, 1964.

Cockerell, Charles Robert. *The Temples of Jupiter Panhellenius at Aegina, and of Apollo Epicurius at Bassae near Phigaleia in Arcadia. . . .* London: John Weale, 1860.

Coke, Mary, Lady. *The Letters and Journals of Lady Mary Coke.* Ed by the Hon. James Archibald Home. 4 vols. Edinburgh: David Douglas, 1889–96.

Coleridge, Anthony. "Chippendale, The Director and some Cabinet-makers at Blair Castle." *Connoisseur* 46 (December 1960): 252–56.

———. "English Furniture Supplied for Croome Court: Robert Adam and the 6th Earl of Coventry." *Apollo* 151 (February 2000): 8–19.

Colvin, Howard Montagu. "The Bastards of Blanford." *Archaeological Journal* 104 (1948): 192–93.

———. *A Biographical Dictionary of British Architects, 1600–1840.* 3rd ed. New Haven and London: Yale University Press, 1995.

———, et al., eds. *The History of the King's Works.* Vol. 5, *1660–1782.* London: H.M.S.O., 1976.

A Companion to the Kraus Reprint of Reports I to IX of the Historical Manuscripts Commissions. Nendeln: Kraus-Thomson Organization Press, 1977.

Compton, Richard. *Newby Hall.* Derby: Heritage House Group, 2004.

Conan, Michel. *Bourgeois and Aristocratic Cultural Encounters in Garden Art, 1550–1850.* Washington, D.C.: Dumbarton Oaks Research Library and Collection, 2002.

Conder, Edward, Jr. *Records of the Hole Crafte and Fellowship of Masons: With a Chronicle of the History of the Worshipful Company of Masons of the City of London.* London: Swan, Sonnenschein and Co.; New York: Macmillan, 1894.

Constantine, David. *Early Greek Travellers and the Hellenic Ideal.* Cambridge University Press, 1984.

———. *Fields of Fire: A Life of Sir William Hamilton.* London: Phoenix Press, 2002.

Cook, James. *The Journals of Captain James Cook on His Voyages of Discovery.* Vol. 1, *The Voyage of the Endeavor 1768–1771.* Ed. by John Cawte Beaglehole. Hakluyt Society [Works] Extra series, no. 34a. Cambridge University Press for the Society, 1955.

Cooke, John, and John Maule. *An Historical Account of the Royal Hospital for Seamen at Greenwich.* London: the authors, 1789.

Corley, Brigitte. *Lichfield House, 15 St. James's Square.* London: Clerical, Medical and General Life Assurance Society, 1983.

Cornforth, John. "Millichope Park, Shropshire." Parts I and II. *Country Life* 161 (10 February 1977): 310–13; (17 February 1977): 370–73.

———. "Newby Hall, North Yorkshire." Parts I–III. *Country Life* 165 (7 June 1979): 1802–6; (14 June 1979): 1918–21; (21 June 1979): 2006–9.

———. "Correspondence. Designs for Newby." *Country Life* 165 (21 June 1979): 2016.

———. "Newby in the 19th Century." *Country Life* 168 (25 December 1980): 2406–9.

———. "On His Own Legs." *Country Life* 187 (28 September 1993): 70–73.

———. *London Interiors from the Archives of Country Life.* London: Aurum, 2000.

———. *Early Georgian Interiors.* New Haven and London: Yale University Press, 2004.

"Courtiers and Classics: The Gosset Family." *Country Life* 177 (9 May 1985): 1282–83.

Cousins, Michael. "Athenian Stuart's Doric Porticoes." *Georgian Group Journal* 14 (2004): 48–54.

Coutu, Joan Michele. "Eighteenth-Century British Monuments and the Politics of Empire." Ph.D. diss., University College, London, 1993.

Cox-Johnson, Ann. *John Bacon R. A., 1740–1799.* St. Marylebone Society publication, no. 4. London: St. Marylebone Society Publications Group: distributed by Strathmore Bookshop, 1961.

Cradock, Joseph. *Literary and Miscellaneous Memoirs.* 4 vols. London: J. B. Nichols, 1826–28.

Craik, George L., and Charles MacFarlane. *The Pictorial History of England: Being a History of the People, as well as a History of the Kingdom.* London: C. Knight, 1838–41.

Craske, Matthew Julian. "The London Trade in Monumental Sculpture and the Development of the Imagery of the Family in Funerary Monuments of the Period 1720–1760." Ph.D. diss., Queen Mary and Westfield College, London, 1992.

Craven, Maxwell. *John Whitehurst of Derby: Clockmaker and Scientist, 1713–88.* Ashbourne: Mayfield Books, 1996.

Creighton, Wilbur F., and Leland R. Johnson. *The Parthenon in Nashville: Pearl of the Tennessee Centennial Exposition.* Brentwood, TN: J. M. Press, 1989.

Crinson, Mark, and Jules Lubbock. *Architecture—Art or Profession? Three Hundred Years of Architectural Education in Britain.* Manchester and New York: Manchester University Press, 1994.

Croft-Murray, Edward. "A Drawing by Athenian Stuart for the Painted Room at Spencer House." *British Museum Quarterly* 21 (1957): 14–15.

———. "The Hôtel Grimod de La Reynière: The Salon Decorations." *Apollo* 78 (November 1963): 377–83.

———. *Decorative Painting in England, 1537–1837.* Vol. 2. Feltham, Middlesex: Country Life Books, 1970.

Crook, Joseph Mordaunt. *The Greek Revival.* RIBA Drawings series. Feltham: Country Life Books, 1968.

———. *The Greek Revival: Neo-classical Attitudes in British Architecture, 1760–1870.* 1972. Rev. ed., London: John Murray 1995.

Cruickshank, Dan. "Adapt and Survive." *Architects' Journal Renovations Supplement* 29 (June 1988): 22–29.

Cruickshank, Dan, and Peter Wyld. *London, the Art of Georgian Building.* London: Architectural Press; New York: Architectural Book Publishing Co., 1975.

Cullen, J. B. "The Associations of Rathfarnham Castle, County Dublin, Now a Jesuit Residence." *Irish Ecclesiastical Record* 20 (October 1922): 369–80.

Cummings, Frederick. "Phidias in Bloomsbury: B. R. Haydon's Drawings of the Elgin Marbles." *Burlington Magazine* 106 (July 1964): 323–28.

Cunningham, Allan. *The Lives of the Most Eminent British Painters, Sculptors and Architects.* 6 vols. London: John Murray, 1829–33.

Curl, James Stevens. *Classical Architecture: An Introduction to Its Vocabulary and Essentials, with a Select Glossary of Terms.* 1992. 2nd ed. London: B. T. Batsford, 2001.

———. *Georgian Architecture.* 1993. 2nd ed. Newton Abbot: David and Charles, 2002.

Cust, Lionel, comp. *Catalogue of the Collection of Fans and Fan-Leaves Presented to the Trustees of the British Museum by the Lady Charlotte Schreiber.* London: Longmans and Co., 1893.

Cust, Lionel, and Sir Sidney Colvin. *History of the Society of Dilettanti.* 1898. Reprint, London and New York: Macmillan, 1914.

Cuzin, Jean-Pierre, Jean-René Gaborit, and Alain Pasquier. *D'après l'antique.* Exh. cat. Musée du Louvre. Paris: Réunion des musées nationaux, 2000.

Daily Advertiser (3 April 1760): 3122.

Dallaway, James. *Anecdotes of the Arts in England; or, Comparative Remarks on Architecture, Sculpture, and Painting, Chiefly Illustrated by Specimens at Oxford*. London: Cadell and Davies, 1800.

Dalrymple, Alexander. *A Letter from Mr. Dalrymple to Dr. Hawkesworth, Occasioned by Some Groundless and Illiberal Imputations in His Account of the Late Voyages to the South*. London: J. Nourse, et al., 1773.

D'Alton, John. *The History of County Dublin*. London: Tower Books of Cork, 1976.

Dalton, Richard. [A collection of fifty-two engraved plates from drawings by Richard Dalton of antiquities in Sicily, Greece, Asia Minor and Egypt.] London: [n.p., 1751–1752].

———. *Remarks on XII Historical Designs of Raphael, and the Musaeum Graecum et Aegyptiacum*. London: M. Cooper, 1752.

Danish Institute at Rome. "Danmark og Italien. 'T.'" http://www.dkinst-rom.dk/dansk/homepage.htm. Accessed 7 June 2004.

Darnton, Robert. "What is the History of Books." *Daedalus* 3 (Summer 1982): 65–83.

Daunton, M. J. "House-ownership from Rate Books." *Urban History Yearbook, 1976* (1976): 21–27.

Davidson, Bernice F. *Raphael's Bible: A Study of the Vatican Logge*. University Park: Pennsylvania State University Press for the College Art Association of America, 1985.

Davis, Rose Mary. *The Good Lord Lyttelton; A Study in Eighteenth-Century Politics and Culture*. Bethleham, PA: Times Publishing Co., 1939.

Davis, William John, and Arthur William Waters. *Tickets and Passes of Great Britain and Ireland*. Leamington Spa: privately printed, 1922.

Delany, Mary Granville. *The Autobiography and Correspondence of Mary Granville, Mrs. Delaney*. Ed. by Lady Llanover. 3 vols. London: Richard Bentley, 1861.

———. *The Autobiography and Correspondence of Mary Granville, Mrs. Delaney*. Ed. by Lady Llanover. 2nd series. 3 vols. London: Richard Bentley, 1862.

Deleuze, Gilles, and Félix Guattari. *A Thousand Plateaus: Capitalism and Schizophrenia*. Trans. by Brian Massumi. London: Athlone Press, 1988.

Desgodetz, Antoine. *Les Édifices antiques de Rome, dessinés et mesurés très exactement. . . .* Paris: J. B. Coignard, 1682.

Diario Ordinario (6 April 1748): 3–4; (4 May 1748): 11; (11 July 1750): 16; (3 August 1750): 9–10; (21 February 1750): 8–9.

Dibdin, Thomas Frognall. *Bibliotheca Spenceriana; or, A Descriptive Catalogue of the Books Printed in the Fifteenth Century, and of Many Valuable First Editions, in the Library of George John, Earl Spencer, K. G. . . .* Vol. 3. London: Longman, Hurst, Rees and Co., 1814–15.

Dickins, Lilian, and Mary Stanton, eds. *An Eighteenth Century Correspondence*. London: John Murray, 1910.

Dickson, David, and Cormac Ó'Gráda, eds. *Refiguring Ireland: Essays in Honor of L. M. Cullen*. Dublin: Lilliput Press, 2003.

Dircks, Rudolf. "The Library and Collections of the Royal Institute of British Architects—II." *Royal Institute of British Architects Journal*, 3rd series, 28 (18 December 1920): 81–92.

Dizionario biografico degli Italiani. Vol. 61. Ed. by Mario Caravale and Giuseppe Pignatelli. Rome: Istituto della Enciclopedia Italiana, 2003.

Doig, Allan. "James Adam, James Essex and an Altar-Piece for King's College Chapel, Cambridge." *Architectural History* 21 (1978): 79–82.

D'Onofrio, Cesare. *Gli obelischi di Roma*. [1965]. 3rd ed. Rome: Romana società editrice, 1992.

Dossie, Robert. *Memoirs of Agriculture, and Other Oeconomical Arts*. Vol. 3. London: C. Nourse; The Society for the Encouragement of Arts, Manufactures, and Commerce, 1782.

Downes, Kerry. *Sir John Vanbrugh, A Biography*. London: Sidgwick and Jackson, 1987.

Draper, James David, and Guilhem Scherf. *Augustin Pajou, dessinateur en Italie 1752–1756*. Archives de l'Art français, n.s., vol. 33. Nogent-Le-Roi: Librarie des arts et métiers-Éditions Jacques Laget, 1997.

Draper, Marie P. G. "When Marlborough's Duchess Built." *Country Life* 132 (2 August 1962): 248–50.

Drexler, Arthur, ed. *The Architecture of the École des Beaux-Arts*. London: Secker and Warburg, 1977.

Duffy, Hugo. *James Gandon and His Times*. Kinsale, County Cork: Gandon Editions, 1999.

Dunhill, Rosemary. *Handel and the Harris Circle*. Hampshire Papers, 8. Hampshire County Council, 1995.

Dunmore, John. *French Explorers in the Pacific*. Vol. 1, *The Eighteenth Century*. Oxford: Clarendon Press, 1965.

Edgcumbe, Richard. *The Art of the Gold Chaser in Eighteenth-Century London*. Oxford University Press, 2000.

Edwards, R. "Edward Edwards, ARA (1738–1806) and the Furniture of an Earlier Age." *Country Life* 67 (June 1930): 840–50.

Edwards, Ralph. "Letters to the Editor: Neoclassic Furniture, 'The Battle of the Styles'." *Apollo* 87 (January 1968): 66–67.

Edwards, Ralph, and Margaret Jourdain. *Georgian Cabinet Makers, c. 1700–1800*. 1944. Rev. 3rd ed. London: Country Life, 1955.

Ehrhardt, Wolfgang. "Der Fries des Lysikratesmonuments." *Antike Plastik* 22 (1993): 7–67.

Eimer, Christopher. *British Commemorative Medals and Their Values*. London: Seaby, 1987.

———. "The Society's Concern with 'The Medallic Art' in the Eighteenth Century." *RSA Journal* 139 (November 1991): 753–62.

———. "James 'Athenian' Stuart: Medallic Design and Procedure." In *Designs on Posterity: Drawings for Medals*. Ed. by Mark Jones. Exh. cat. The British Museum. London: British Art Medal Trust, 1994, pp. 131–37.

———. *The Pingo Family and Medal Making in Eighteenth-Century Britain*. London: British Art Medal Trust, 1998.

Eisner, Robert. *Travelers to an Antique Land: The History and Literature of Travel to Greece*. Ann Arbor: University of Michigan Press, 1991.

Ellis, Sir Henry. *Original Letters of Eminent Literary Men of the Sixteenth, Seventeenth and Eighteenth Centuries*. London: Printed for the Camden Society by J. B. Nichols and Son, 1843.

Elmes, James. *Lectures on Architecture, Comprising the History of the Art from the Earliest Times to the Present Day*. Vol. 1. 2nd ed. London: Priestley and Weale, 1823.

———. *Metropolitan Improvements, or London in the Nineteenth Century. . . .* London: Jones, 1827–29.

———. "History of Architecture in Great Britain: A Brief Sketch or Epitome of the Rise and Progress of Architecture in Great Britain." *Civil Engineer and Architects' Journal* 10 (1847): 338–41.

Elofson, Warren M. *The Rockingham Connection and the Second Founding of the Whig Party, 1768–1773*. Montreal: McGill-Queens University Press, 1996.

Elsner, John, and Roger Cardinal, eds. *The Cultures of Collecting*. London: Reaktion Books, 1994.

Enciclopedia dei Papi. 3 vols. Rome: Istituto della Enciclopedia Italiana, 2000.

Entwisle, E. A. "Eighteenth Century London Paperstainers: Thomas Bromwich at the Golden Lyon on Ludgate Hill." *Connoisseur* 130 (November 1952): 106–10.

Eriksen, Svend. "Lalive de Jully's Furniture 'à la grecque.'" *Burlington Magazine* 103 (August 1961): 340–47.

———. "Marigny and Le Goût Grec." *Burlington Magazine* 104 (March 1962): 96–101.

Eriksen, Svend, and Francis John Bagott Watson. "The 'Athénienne' and the Revival of the Classical Tripod." *Burlington Magazine* 105 (March 1963): 108–12.

Esdale, Arundell. "Croome D'Abitot Church." *Architect and Building News* 138 (29 June 1934): 387–89.

Eustace, Katharine. *Michael Rysbrack, Sculptor, 1694–1770*. Exh. cat. Bristol Art Gallery. City of Bristol Museum and Art Gallery, 1982.

Evans. Joan. *A History of the Society of Antiquaries*. Oxford University Press, 1956.

Evans, Auctioneer. *Catalogue of the late Joseph Nollekens . . . which will be sold by auction by Mr Evans, 93 Pall Mall, London*. Sale cat. 18–19 December 1823. Copy in British Museum Prints and Drawings Department.

Exhibition of Drawings of Architectural Subjects by Deceased British Artists. London: the Burlington Fine Arts Club, 1884.

Eyres, Patrick. "Celebration and Dissent: Thomas Hollis, The Society of Arts, and Stowe Gardens." *Medal* 38 (Spring 2001): 31–50.

———. "'Patriotizing, Strenuously, The Whole Flower Of His Life.' The Political Agenda of Thomas Hollis's Medallic Programme." *Medal* 36 (Spring 2000): 8–23.

Fagan, Louis. *A Catalogue Raisonné of the Engraved Works of William Woollett*. London: The Fine Art Society, 1885.

Fairclough, Oliver. "Sir Watkin Williams-Wynn and Robert Adam: Commissions for Silver, 1868–80." *Burlington Magazine* 137 (June 1995): 376–86.

Family Search. International Genealogical Index. The Church of Jesus Christ of Latter Day Saints. http://www.familysearch.org. Accessed 3 June 2004.

Farington, Joseph. *The Diary of Joseph Farington*. Vols. 12 and 16. Ed. by Kathryn Cave. New Haven and London: Yale University Press for the Paul Mellon Centre for Studies in British Art, 1983, 1984.

Farquharson, J., and Colin MacDonald. "Greenwich Hospital and Sir Christopher Wren's Designs." *Architectural Review* 29 (January 1911): 3–12.

Faulkner, Thomas. *An Historical and Topographical Account of Fulham; Including the Hamlet of Hammersmith*. London: printed for T. Egerton et al., 1813.

Feather, John. "John Nourse and His Authors." *Studies in Bibliography* 34 (1981): 205–26.

Feret, Charles James. *Fulham Old and New, Being an Exhaustive History of the Ancient Parish of Fulham*. 3 vols. London: Leadenhall Press; New York: Charles Scribner's Sons, 1900.

Fergusson, Frances. "Wyatt Silver." *Burlington Magazine* 116 (December 1974): 750–55.

Fergusson, James. *History of the Modern Styles of Architecture*. 2 vols. 1862. 3rd ed. London: John Murray, 1891.

Ferrey, Benjamin. *Recollections of A. N. Welby Pugin, and His Father, Augustus Pugin; with Notices of their Works*. London: Stanford, 1861.

Ficacci, Luigi. *Giovanni Battista Piranesi: The Complete Etchings*. Koln: Taschen, 2000.

Ficoroni, Francesco de. *Gemmae Antiquae Litteratae aliaequae rariores. . . .* Rome, Sumptibus Venantii Monaldini bibliopolæ, 1757.

Finer, Ann, and George Savage. *The Selected Letters of Josiah Wedgwood*. London: Cory, Adams and Mackay, 1965.

Fischer von Erlach, Johann Bernhard. *Entwurff einer historischen architectur. . . .* 2nd ed. Leipzig: [n.p.], 1725.

Fischer von Erlach, Johann Bernhard. *A Plan of Civil and Historical Architecture. . . .* Trans. by Thomas Lediard. [London], 1730.

Fitz-Gerald, Desmond, Knight of Glin. *The Temple of the Winds, Mount Stewart: A Historical Note*. [Belfast]: Committee for Ireland, The National Trust, Northern Ireland Committee, 1966.

———. "The Temple of the Winds: An Antique Irish Banqueting House." *Connoisseur* 167 (April 1968): 206–9.

Flaxman, John. *Lectures on Sculpture*. 1829. New ed., London: Bell and Sons, 1889.

Fleming, James. "Historic Irish Mansions: No. 41, Rathfarnham Castle, Co. Dublin, Occupied by the Jesuit Fathers." *Weekly Irish Times* (13 February 1937): 7.

Fleming, John. "The Hugfords of Florence—II, with a Provisional Catalogue of the Collection of Ignazio Enrico Hugford." *Connoisseur* 136 (November 1955): 197–206.

———. *Robert Adam and his Circle in Edinburgh and Rome*. London: John Murray, 1962.

Ford, Boris, ed. *The Cambridge Guide to the Arts in Britain*. Vol. 5, *The Augustan Age*. Cambridge University Press, 1991.

Ford, Brinsley. "The Grand Tour." *Apollo* 114 (December 1981): 390–400.

Forrer, Leonard, comp. *Biographical Dictionary of Medallists: Coin, Gem, and Seal-Engravers, Mint-Masters, and C., Ancient and Modern, with References to Their Works B.C. 500–A.D. 1900*. Vol. 5. 1912. Reprint, London: A. H. Baldwin; Maastricht: A. G. Van Der Dussen, 1980.

Forrest, Denys. *St. James's Square: People, Houses, Happenings*. 1986. 2nd rev. ed., London: Quiller Press, 2001.

Forster, Georg, and Johann Reinhold Forster. *A Voyage Round The World, in His Britannic Majesty's Sloop, Resolution, Commanded by Capt. James Cook during the Years 1772, 3, 4 and 5*. Vol. 1. London: B. White, et al., 1777.

Fowler, John, and John Cornforth. *English Decoration in the 18th Century*. 2nd ed. London: Barrie and Jenkins, 1978.

Fréart, Roland, sieur de Chambray. *Parallèle de l'architecture antique et de la moderne. . . .* Paris: Edmé Martin, 1650. Trans. and ed. by John Evelyn. London: John Place, [1664].

Friedensburg, Ferdinand, and Hans Seger. *Schlesiens Münzen und Medaillen der neuren Zeit*. Breslau: Verein für das Museum Schlesischer Altertümer, 1901.

Friedman, Joseph. "Spencer House." *Apollo* 126 (August 1987): 81–99.

———. *Spencer House: Chronicle of a Great London Mansion*. London: A. Zwemmer, 1993.

Friedman, Terry. *James Gibbs*. New Haven and London: Yale University Press for the Paul Mellon Centre for Studies in British Art, 1984.

Friel, Ian. *Maritime History of Britain and Ireland, c. 400–2001*. London: British Museum Press, 2003.

Frommel, Christopher Luitpold, Stefano Ray, and Manfredo Tafuri, eds. *Raffaello Architetto*. Exh. cat. Campidoglio, Palazzo dei Conservatori, Rome. Milan: Electa, 1984.

Gage, John. *Colour and Culture: Practice and Meaning from Antiquity to Abstraction*. London: Thames and Hudson, 1993.

Gallet, Michel. *Paris Domestic Architecture of the 18th Century*. Trans. by James C. Palmes. London: Barrie and Jenkins, 1972.

Gandy, Michael. *Catholic Missions and Registers, 1700–1880*. Vol. 1, *London and the Home Counties*. London: M. Gandy, 1993.

Gell, Sir William. *The Itinerary of Greece*. London: T. Payne, 1810.

———. *Itinerary of the Morea*. London: Rodwell and Martin, 1817.

Gell, Sir William, and John P. Gandy. *Pompeiana: The Topography, Edifices and Ornaments of Pompeii*. 2 vols. 1817–19. 2nd ed., London: Rodwell and Martin, 1821.

George, M. Dorothy. *London Life in the XVIIIth Century*. London: K. Paul, Trench, Trubner, 1925.

Georgian Society. *Records of Eighteenth-Century Domestic Architecture and Decoration in Dublin*. Vol. 5. Dublin: Irish Georgian Society, 1913.

Gibbon, Michael. "The First Neoclassical Building? Temple of Concord, Stowe, Buckinghamshire." *Country Life* 155 (11 April 1974): 852–53.

———. "Stowe, Buckinghamshire: The House and Garden Buildings and Their Designers." *Architectural History* 20 (1977): 31–44.

Gilboy, Elizabeth Waterman. "Wages in Eighteenth-Century England." *Harvard Economics Studies*. Vol. 45. Cambridge, MA: Harvard University Press, 1934.

"A Gilded Ceiling in the. . . ." *Daily Telegraph* (9 October 1959): 12.

Gilly, Friedrich. *Essays on Architecture, 1796–1799*. Santa Monica, CA: Getty Center for the History of Art and Humanities, 1994.

Giornale de' Letterati (1753): 366–68.

Gilpin, William. *Observations, Relative Chiefly to Picturesque Beauty Made in . . . 1772 on Several Parts of England. . . .* 2 vols. London: R. Blamire, 1786.

Girardon, François. [*A Collection of Engravings from Designs by F. G. by Various Engravers.*] Paris, [1707]. Copy in the British Library, London.

Girouard, Mark. "44 Berkeley Square, London." *Country Life* 132 (27 December 1962): 1648–51.

———. *Life in the English Country House: A Social and Architectural History*. New Haven and London: Yale University Press, 1978.

Gladstone, Herbert John Gladstone, 1st Viscount, Guy Boas. *The Story of the Noblemen and Gentlemen's Catch Club*. London: privately printed, 1930.

Gladstone, Herbert John Gladstone, 1st Viscount, Guy Boas, and Harald Christophersen. *The Nobleman and Gentleman's Catch Club: Three Essays Towards Its History*. London: Noblemen and Gentlemen's Catch Club, 1996.

"Glass painters of Birmingham: Francis Eginton, 1737–1805." *Journal of the British Society of Master Glass Painters* 2, no. 2 (1927): 63.

Glencross, Alan. *The Buildings of Greenwich*. London: London Borough of Greenwich, 1974.

Glendinging's, London. *A Collection of British Historical Medals*. Sale cat. Part 1, 16 March 1989.

Godber, Joyce. "The Life of the Marchioness Grey of Wrest Park, 1722–97." Bedfordshire Historical Record Society annual, vol. 47 (1968).

Gombrich, Ernst. *Aby Warburg: An Intellectual Biography*. 1970. 2nd ed. Oxford: Phaidon, 1986.

Goodison, Nicholas. "Matthew Boulton's Ormolu Door Furniture." *Burlington Magazine* 111 (November 1969): 687–88.

———. "Mr Stuart's Tripod." *Burlington Magazine* 114 (October 1972): 695–705.

———. "William Chamber's Furniture Designs." *Furniture History* 26 (1990): 67–90.

———. *Ormolu: The Work of Matthew Boulton*. 1974. Rev. ed. as *Matthew Boulton: Ormolu*. London: Christie's, 2002.

Gorbunova, Xenia. "Classical Sculpture from the Lyde Browne Collection." *Apollo* 100 (December 1974): 460–67.

Gore, St. John, comp. *English Taste in the Eighteenth Century from Baroque to Neo-classic*, Exh. cat. The Royal Academy of Arts. 2nd ed. London: The Academy, 1955.

Gould, John, comp. *A Dictionary of Painters, Sculptors, Architects and Engravers: Containing Biographical Sketches of the Most Celebrated Artists, from the Earliest Ages to the Present Time, to Which is Added an Appendix Comprising the Substance of Walpole's Anecdotes of Painting in England, from Vertue, Forming a Complete English School*. London: Gale and Curtis, 1810.

"Grand Military And Musical Festival. . . ." *Lady's Newspaper* (26 July 1851): frontispiece.

Graves, Algernon. *The Royal Academy Of Arts: A Complete Dictionary of Contributors and Their Work from Its Foundation in 1769 to 1904*. 8 vols. London: H. Graves, 1905–6.

———. *The Society of Artists of Great Britain, 1760–1791; The Free Society of Artists, 1761–1783: A Complete Dictionary of Contributors and Their Work from the Foundation of the Societies to 1791*. London: George Bell and Sons, 1907.

———. *A Dictionary of Artists Who Have Exhibited Works in the Principal London Exhibitions from 1700 to 1893*. 1884/1901. 3rd ed. Reprint, Weston-Super-Mare: Kingsmead Press, 1984.

Gray, Thomas. *Correspondence of Thomas Gray*. Ed. by Paget Toynbee and Leonard Whibley. Vol. 3. Oxford: Clarendon Press, 1935.

Green, Tim. *100 Years in the Wilderness: The Story of An Uncommon Road*. Harrow: Wilderness Publishing, 1997.

Greenslade, Michael W., and Sambrooke Arthur Higgins Burne, eds. *Essays in Staffordshire History: Presented to S. A. H. Burne*. Collections for a History of Staffordshire, vol. 6, 4th series. Staffordshire Record Society, 1970.

Greenwich Hospital: Its Painted Hall and Chapel: A Hand-book Guide for Visitors. London: H. G. Clarke, [1857].

Greenwood's London. *A Catalogue of Pictures, by Moreland, Prints and Drawings, A Few Lots of Household Furniture, A Grand Piano Forte, by Pether, Books, and Books of Prints, Drawing Paper, and other Effects of the Late James Stuart, Esq.–Deceased. . . .* Sale cat. London, 27 June 1791. Copy in the Library, Courtauld Institute of Art, London.

Griggs, Tamara. "Drawn from Nature: Text and Image in *The Antiquities of Athens* (1762–1816)." (Forthcoming).

Grose, Francis, Thomas Astle, and Edward Jeffrey, comps. *Antiquarian Repertory: A Miscellany, Intended to Preserve and Illustrate Several Valuable Remains of Old Times*. Vol. 2. London: F. Blyth, J. Sewell, and T. Evans, 1779.

Grosley, Pierre Jean. *A Tour to London, or, New Observations on England and Its Inhabitants*. Trans. by Thomas Nugent. London: Lockyer Davis, 1772.

Gross, Hanns. *Rome in the Age of the Enlightenment: The Post-Tridentine Syndrome and the Ancien Régime*. Cambridge Studies in Early Modern History. Cambridge and New York: Cambridge University Press, 1990.

The Grove Dictionary of Art. Ed. by Jane Shoaf Turner. New York: St. Martin's Press, 2000.

Grueber, Herbert A., ed. [Plates to] *Medallic Illustrations of the History of Great Britain and Ireland to the Death of George II*. 1904–11. Reprint, Lawrence, MA: Quarterman Publications; London: British Museum Publications, 1979.

Grundy, C. Reginald. "Documents Relating to an Action Brought against Joseph Goupy in 1738." Walpole Society annual, vol. 9 (1920–21): 77–87.

Guilding, Ruth. "Classical Sculpture and the English Interior, 1640–1840. Purpose and Meaning." Ph.D. diss., University of Bristol, 2000.

Gunnis, Rupert. *Dictionary of British Sculptors, 1660–1851*. 1953. Rev. ed. London: Murray's Book Sales, 1968.

Gunnis, Rupert, and Margaret Dickens Whinney. *The Collection of Models by John Flaxman, R. A., at University College London*. London: Athlone, 1967.

Gwilt, Joseph. *An Encyclopaedia of Architecture, Historical, Theoretical, and Practical*. 1842. Rev. ed. by Wyatt Papworth. London: Longmans, Green, and Co., 1891.

Guys, Pierre Augustin. *Voyage litteraire de la Grèce, ou Lettres sur les Grecs anciens et modernes, avec un Parallèle de leur Moeurs*. 4 vols. 1771. 3rd ed. Paris: Veuve Duchesne, 1783.

Haas, James M. "The Pursuit of Political Success in Eighteenth-Century England: Sandwich, 1740–1771." *Bulletin of the Institute of Historical Research* 43 (1970): 56–77.

H. A. "Traits for the Life of the Late Athenian Stuart." *Gentleman's Magazine* 58 (February 1788): 95–96.

Hager, Hellmut, and Susan S. Munshower. *Architectural Fantasy and Reality: Drawings from the Accademia nazionale di San Luca in Rome, Concorsi Elementi, 1700–1750*. Exh. cat. Museum of Art, Pennsylvania State University and Cooper-Hewitt, New York. Museum University Park, PA: Museum of Art, Pennsylvania State University, 1981.

Hakewill, James. *The History of Windsor, and Its Neighbourhood*. London: E. Lloyd, 1813.

Halley, J. M. W. "Historical Town Houses: Lichfield House, No. 15 St. James's Square." *Architectural Review* 28 (May 1910): 273–78.

Hamilton, Gavin. *Letters of Gavin Hamilton, Edited from the Mss. at Landsdowne House*. Reprinted from the *Academy*. Ed. by Lord Edmond Fitzmaurice. Devizes, Wiltshire: n.p., 1879.

Hamilton, William Richard. *Second Letter from W. R. Hamilton., Esq. to the Earl of Elgin on the Propriety of Adopting the Greek Style of Architecture in the Construction of the New Houses of Parliament*. London: John Weale, 1836.

———. *Historical Notices of the Society of Dilettanti*. London: printed for priv. circ., 1855.

Hamlin, Talbot. *Greek Revival Architecture in America*. London and New York: Oxford University Press, 1944.

Hanson, Brian, ed. *The Golden City: Essays on the Architecture and Imagination of Beresford Pite*. London: Prince of Wales's Institute of Architecture, 1993.

Harcourt, Edward William, ed. *The Harcourt Papers*. 14 vols. Oxford: James Parker and Co., 1880–1905.

Harcourt-Smith, Sir Cecil. *The Society of Dilettanti; Its Regalia and Pictures*. London and New York: Macmillan and Co., 1932.

Hardy, Emma, and M. G. Sullivan. *The Biographical Dictionary of Sculptors in Britain, 1660–1851*. Ed. by Ingrid Roscoe. New Haven and London: Yale University Press, 2006.

Hardy, John, and Helena Howard. "Kedleston Hall, Derbyshire." Part II. *Country Life* 163 (2 February 1978): 262–66.

Hargrove, Ely. *History of the Castle, Town, and Forest of Knaresborough: with Harrowgate, and Its Medicinal Waters*. 4th ed. York: n.p., 1789.

Harris, Eileen. *The Furniture of Robert Adam*. London: Tiranti, 1963.

———. "A Flair for the Grandiose: The Architecture of Thomas Wright." Part II. *Country Life* 150 (2 September 1971): 546–50.

———. *British Architectural Books and Writers, 1556–1785*. Assisted by Nicholas Savage. Cambridge and New York; Cambridge University Press, 1990.

———. *The Genius of Robert Adam: His Interiors*. New Haven and London: Paul Mellon Centre for Studies in British Art and Yale University Press, 2001.

———. "Cracking the Poussin Code." *Apollo* 163 (May 2006): 26–31.

Harris, Eileen, and John Martin Robinson. "New Light on Wyatt at Fawley." *Architectural History* 27 (1984): 263–67.

Harris, Frances. *A Passion for Government: The Life of Sarah, Duchess of Marlborough*. Oxford: Clarendon Press, 1991.

Harris, James. *Hermes, or, A Philosophical Inquiry Concerning Universal Grammar*. 2nd ed. London: John Nourse and Paul Vaillant, 1765.

———. *Philosophical Arrangements*. London: John Nourse, 1775.

———. *Philological Inquiries*. London: John Nourse, 1781.

———. *The Works of James Harris, Esq., with an Account of His Life and Character by His Son, the Earl of Malmesbury*. London: F. Wingrave, 1801.

Harris, John. "Early Neo-Classical Furniture." *Journal of the Furniture History Society* 2 (1966): 1–6.

———. "The Dundas Empire." *Apollo* 86 (September 1967): 170–79.

———. *Sir William Chambers, Knight of the Polar Star*. With contributions by J. Mordaunt Crook and Eileen Harris. Studies in Architecture, vol. 9. London: A. Zwemmer, 1970.

———. *A Catalogue of British Drawings for Architecture, Decoration, Sculpture and Landscape Gardening, 1550–1900, in American Collections*. Upper Saddle River, NJ: Gregg Press, 1971.

———. "Newly Acquired Designs by James Stuart in the British Architectural Library Drawings Collection." *Architectural History* 22 (1979): 72–77.

———. *The Architect and the British Country House, 1620–1920*. Washington, D.C.: AIA Press, 1985.

———. "The Neo-Palladians and Mid-Century Landscape." *The Glory of Venice: Art in the Eighteenth Century*. Ed. by Jane Martineau and Andrew Robinson. New Haven and London: Yale University Press, 1994.

———. *The Palladian Revival: Lord Burlington, His Villa and Garden at Chiswick*. Exh. cat. Canadian Centre for Architecture, Montreal, et al. London: Royal Academy of Arts; New Haven and London: Yale University Press, 1994.

———. "Le Rouge's Sion Hill: A Garden by Brown." *London Gardener, or Gardener's Intelligencer* 5 (1999–2000): 24–28.

———. "Sion Hill: A Postscript." *London Gardener, or Gardener's Intelligencer* 6 (2000–2001): 81.

Harris, John, and Michael Snodin, eds. *Sir William Chambers: Architect to George III*. Exh. cat. Courtauld Institute of Art Gallery, London. New Haven and London: Yale University Press with the Institute, 1996.

Harris, Leslie. *Robert Adam and Kedleston: The Making of a Neo-Classical Masterpiece*. Ed. by Gervase Jackson-Stops. Exh. cat. Kedleston, Derbyshire; Cooper-Hewitt Museum, New York. London: National Trust, 1987.

———. "The Picture Collection at Kedleston Hall." *Connoisseur* 198 (July 1978): 208–17.

Harris, Oliver. "The Greenwich Hospital Clock by Daniel Quare." *Art Journal* 24 (Summer 1998): 172.

Harris, Philip Rowland. *A History of the British Museum Library, 1753–1973*. London: British Library, 1998.

Harrison, Walter. *A New and Universal History, Description and Survey of the Cities of London and Westminster, the Borough of Southwark, and Their Adjacent Parts.* London: J. Cooke, 1775.

Hart, Avril, and Emma Taylor. *Fans.* London: Victoria and Albert Publications, 1998.

Hartley, David. *An Account of the Method of Securing Buildings (and Ships) against Fire, as Presented to His Majesty.* London, n.p., 1774.

Hartop, Christopher. "Robert Adam's Tureens for Sir Watkyn Williams-Wynn." *Christie's International Magazine* (April 1996): 28.

Harwood, Elain, and Andrew Saint. *London. Exploring England's Heritage* Series. London: H.M.S.O. in association with English Heritage, 1991.

"Has Mansion Any Merit?" *The Erith Observer and Kentish Times,* no. 4474 (3 July 1959): frontis.

Haskell, Francis. *Patrons and Painters: A Study in the Relations between Italian Art and Society in the Age of the Baroque.* 2nd ed. New Haven and London: Yale University Press, 1980.

Haskell, Francis, and Nicholas Penny. *Taste and the Antique: The Lure of Classical Sculpture, 1500–1900.* 1981. Rev. ed. New Haven and London: Yale University Press, 1982.

Hasted, Edward. *The History and Topographical Survey of the County of Kent.* Vol. 2. 2nd ed. Canterbury: n.p., 1797.

Haviland, John. *The Builder's Assistant.* 3 vols. 1818–21; 2nd ed., 4 vols., Baltimore: F. Lucas, 1830.

Hawkesworth, John, et al. *An Account of the Voyages Undertaken by the Order of His Present Majesty for Making Discoveries in the Southern Hemisphere and Successively Performed by Commodore Byron, Captain Wallis, Captain Carteret, and Captain Cook. . . .* Vol. 1. London: W. Strahan and T. Cadell, 1773.

Hawkins, Edward, comp. *Medallic Illustrations of the History of Great Britain and Ireland to the Death of George II.* Ed. by Augustus Wollaston Franks and Herbert A. Grueber. Vol. 2. 1885. Reprint, London: Spink and Son, 1969.

Haxby, David, and John Malden. "Thomas Haxby of York (1729–1796): An Extraordinary Musician and Musical Instrument Maker." *The British Institute of Organ Studies* 7 (1983): 59–73.

Hay, C. S. *The History of Sandleford Priory.* Thatcham Printers, Transactions of the Newbury District Field Club, 1981.

Haynes, Denys Eyre Lankester. *An Historical Guide to the Sculptures of the Parthenon.* London: British Museum, 1971.

———. *The Arundel Marbles.* Oxford: Ashmolean Museum, 1975.

Heal, Sir Ambrose. *The London Furniture Makers, from the Restoration to the Victorian Era, 1660–1840.* 1953. Reprint, New York: Dover Publications, 1972. Rev. ed., London: Portman Books, 1988.

Heely, Joseph. *Letters on the Beauties of Hagley, Envil, and the Leasowes.* Vol. 1. London: R. Baldwin, 1777.

Heller, Deborah. "Bluestocking Salons and the Public Sphere." *Eighteenth-Century Life* 22 (May 1998): 59–82.

Hellyer, Arthur George Lee. "A Garden on a Grand Scale: Developments at Newby Hall, Yorkshire." *Country Life* 125 (12 March 1959): 510–12.

Hermann, Luke. *Paul and Thomas Sandby.* London: B. T. Batsford in association with the Victoria and Albert Museum, 1986.

Herrmann, Wolfgang. *The Theory of Claude Perrault.* Studies in Architecture, vol. 12. London: A. Zwemmer, 1973.

———. *Laugier and Eighteenth Century French Theory.* London: A. Zwemmer, 1962.

Hewlings, Richard. "The Link Room at Chiswick House: Lord Burlington as Antiquarian." *Apollo* 141 (January 1995): 28–29.

Hicks, Carola. *Improper Pursuits: The Scandalous Life of Lady Di Beauclerk.* London: Pan Books, 2002.

Higham, Charles Strachan Sanders. *Wimbledon Manor House under the Cecils.* London: Longmans, 1962.

Highmore, Anthony. See A. H.

Hilles, Frederick Whiley. *The Literary Career of Sir Joshua Reynolds.* Cambridge University Press, 1936.

Hirschfeld, Christian. *Théorie der Gartenkunst.* 5 vols. Leipzig: M. G. Weidmanns Erben and Reich, 1779–85.

Hittorff, Jacques-Ignace. *Restitution du temple d'Empédocle à Sélinonte, ou l'Architecture polychrôme chez les Grecs.* Paris: n.p., 1845.

Hittorff (1792–1867): Un architecte du XIXème. Exh. cat. Musée Carnavalet, Paris and Wallraf-Richartz-Museum, Cologne. Paris: the Museum, 1986.

Hobhouse, Hermione. *Lost London: A Century of Demolition and Decay.* London: Macmillan, 1971.

Hodnett, Edward. *Five Centuries of English Book Illustration.* Aldershot, England: Scolar Press, 1988.

Hoff, Michael C., and Susan I. Rotroff, eds. *The Romantization of Athens: Proceedings of an International Conference Held at Lincoln, Nebraska, April 1996.* Oxford: Oxbow Books, 1997.

[Holland, Henry]. *Resolutions of the Associated Architects; with the Report of a Committee by Them Appointed to Consider the Causes of the Frequent Fires, and the Best Means of Preventing the Like in Future.* [England: n.p., 1793].

Homer. *The Iliad of Homer.* Translated by Mr. Pope. Ed. by Alexander Pope. 4 vols. London: Bernard Lintot, 1715–18.

Honig, Elizabeth. "The Beholder as Work of Art: A Study in the Location of Value in Seventeenth-Century Flemish Painting." *Nederlands Kunsthistorisch Jaarboek* 46 (1995): 252–97.

Honour, Hugh. "Adaptations from Athens." *Country Life* 123 (22 May 1958): 1120–21.

Hope, Thomas. *Observations on the Plans and Elevations Designed by James Wyatt, Architect, for Downing College, Cambridge, in a Letter to Francis Annesley, Esq, M. P.* London: D. N. Shury, 1804.

———. *Household Furniture and Interior Decoration Executed from Designs by Thomas Hope.* London: Longman, Hurst, Rees and Orme, 1807.

Hope, William Henry St. John. *Windsor Castle: An Architectural History.* Vol 2. London: Country Life, 1913.

Hopkinson, Martin. "A Portrait by James 'Athenian' Stuart." *Burlington Magazine* 132 (November 1990): 794–95.

Hopper, R. J. "The Second Marquis of Rockingham as a Coin Collector." *Antiquary's Journal* 62 (1992): 316–46.

Horn, David Bayne. *British Diplomatic Representatives, 1689–1789.* London: Royal Historical Society, 1932.

"Hornby Castle, Yorkshire, The Seat of the Duke of Leeds." *Country Life* 20 (14 July 1906): 54–64.

"The House where Diana's Great Aunt Grew up." *Standard* (16 December 1982): 7.

Houfe, Simon. *Dictionary of British Illustrators and Caricaturists, 1800–1914.* Woodbridge, Eng.: Antique Collectors' Club, 1978.

Howard, Elizabeth. "Fragments of Family History." 21 November 1862. *Lord Meade's Budget.* http://www.lordsmeade.freeserve.co.uk/elizhoward-fragments.rtf. Accessed 29 August 2004.

Howard, Seymour. "Boy on a Dolphin: Nollekens and Cavaceppi." *Art Bulletin* 46 (June 1964): 177–89.

———. *Bartolomeo Cavaceppi, Eighteenth-Century Restorer.* New York: Garland Publishing, 1982.

Howe, Ellic. *A List of London Bookbinders, 1648–1815.* London: Bibliographical Society, 1950.

Hudson, Derek B. *Sir Joshua Reynolds, A Personal Study, With Reynolds' Journey from London to Brentford, now first published.* London: G. Bles, 1958.

Hunting, Penelope. "The Empress at Chislehurst." *Country Life* 165 (29 March 1979): 934–36.

Hussey, Christopher. "Wimpole Hall, Cambridgeshire." Parts I and II. *Country Life* 61 (21 May 1927): 806–13; (28 May 1927): 844–51.

———. "Nuneham Courtenay, Oxon." Parts I and II. *Country Life* 90 (7 November 1941): 866–70; (14 November 1941): 910–13.

———. "Ashburnham of Ashburnham." Parts I–III. *Country Life* 113 (16 April 1953): 1158–60; (23 April 1953): 1246–50; (30 April 1953): 1334–38.

———. "Shugborough, Staffordshire." Parts I and II. *Country Life* 115 (25 February 1954): 510–13; (4 March 1954): 590–93.

———. "Shugborough, Staffordshire: A Classical Landscape Park." Parts I and II. *Country Life* 115 (15 April 1954): 1126–29; (22 April 1954): 1220–23.

———. *English Country Houses.* Vol. 1, *Early Georgian, 1715–1760.* London: Country Life, 1955. Reprint, Woodbridge: Antique Collector's Club, 1984.

———. *English Country Houses.* Vol. 2, *Mid Georgian, 1760–1800.* London: Country Life, 1956. Reprint, Woodbridge: Antique Collector's Club, 1984.

———. "Wimpole Hall, Cambridgeshire." Part II. *Country Life* 142 (7 December 1967): 1466–71.

Hyde, H. Montgomery. *Londonderry House and Its Pictures.* London: Cresset Press, 1937.

Ingamells, John, ed. *A Dictionary of British and Irish Travellers in Italy, 1701–1800.* New Haven and London: Yale University Press for the Paul Mellon Centre for Studies in British Art, 1997.

An Inventory of the Historical Monuments in London. Vol. 5, *East London.* London: H.M.S.O., 1930.

An Inventory of Historical Monuments in the County of Cambridge. Vol. 1, *West Cambridgeshire.* London: H.M.S.O., 1968.

"In Hospital Environment." *The Architects' Journal* 199 (6 April 1994): 6.

Inwood, Henry William. *The Erechtheion at Athens: Fragments of Athenian Architecture, and a Few Remains in Attica, Megara, and Epirus.* London: James Carpenter and Son, Josiah Taylor, Priestly and Weale, 1827.

Ireland, John, and John Nichols. *Hogarth's Works: With Life and Anecdotal Descriptions of His Pictures.* London: Chatto and Windus, 1874.

Irwin, David. "Gavin Hamilton: Archaeologist, Painter, and Dealer." *Art Bulletin* 44 (June 1962): 87–102.

———. "English Neo-Classicism and Some Patrons." *Apollo* 78 (November 1963): 360–67.

———. *English Neoclassical Art: Studies in Inspiration and Taste.* London: Faber and Faber, 1966.

———. "Neo-classical Design: Industry Plunders Antiquity." *Apollo* 174 (October 1972): 288–97.

———. *John Flaxman, 1755–1826: Sculptor, Illustrator, Designer.* New York: Rizzoli; [London]: Christie's, 1979.

Irwin, David, and Francina Irwin. *Scottish Painters at Home and Abroad, 1700–1900.* London: Faber and Faber, 1975.

Iversen, Erik. *Obelisks in Exile.* Vol. 1, *The Obelisks of Rome.* Copenhagen: Gad, 1968.

J. R. B. "Ashburnham Place." *Sussex County Magazine* 27 (December 1953): 566–75.

Jackson–Stops, Gervase. "Exquisite Contrivances. The Park and Gardens at Wimpole." Part I. *Country Life* 166 (6 September 1979): 658–61.

———. *Wimpole Hall, Cambridgeshire.* London: The National Trust, 1979.

———. "Mount Stewart, Co. Down: A Property of the National Trust." Part I. *Country Life* 167 (6 March 1980): 646–69.

———. Review of *Athenian Stuart: Pioneer of the Greek Revival*, by David Watkin. *Country Life* 172 (11 November 1982): 1524–25.

———. *Robert Adam and Kedleston.* London: National Trust, 1987.

———. "Spencer House, London." *Country Life* 184 (29 November 1990): 42–47.

———. "The Orient and the Antique: The Shugborough Landscape." *Country Life* 185 (11 July 1991): 72–75.

———. *An English Arcadia, 1600–1990: Designs for Gardens and Garden Buildings in the Care of the National Trust.* London: The National Trust, 1991.

———. "The Temple of the Winds." *Mount Stewart, County Down.* London: The National Trust, 1997.

———, et al., eds. *The Fashioning and Functioning of the British Country House.* Studies in the History of Art, vol. 25. Washington, D.C.: National Gallery of Art; Hanover [NH]: University Press of New England, 1989.

Jenkins, Ian, and Kim Sloan. *Vases and Volcanoes: Sir William Hamilton and His Collection.* London: British Museum Press, 1996.

Jenkyns, Richard. *The Victorians and Ancient Greece.* Cambridge, MA: Harvard University Press, 1980.

———. *Dignity and Decadence: Victorian Art and the Classical Inheritance.* Cambridge, MA: Harvard University Press, 1992.

Jervis, Simon. "Two Unknown Suites of Early Neo-Classical Designs." *Burlington Magazine* 126 (1984): 343–47.

Johns, Christopher M. S. "Papal Patronage and Cultural Bureaucracy in Eighteenth-Century Rome: Clement XI and the Accademia di San Luca." *Eighteenth-Century Studies* 22 (Autumn 1988): 7–23.

Johnson, R. Brimley. *Bluestocking Letters.* London: John Lane, 1926.

Jonas, Maurice. *Notes of an Art Collector.* London: Routledge, 1907.

Jones, E. A. "Adam Silver." *Apollo* 29 (1939): 55–59.

Jones, Mark, ed. *Designs on Posterity: Drawings for Medals.* Exh. cat. The British Museum. London: British Art Medal Trust, 1994.

Jones, Mark Wilson. "Doric Measure and Architectural Design 2: A Modular Reading of the Classical Temple." *American Journal of Archaeology* 105 (October 2001): 675–713.

———. "Tripods, Triglyphs, and the Origin of the Doric Frieze," *American Journal of Archaeology* 106 (July 2002): 353–90.

Jones, Mary Gwladys. *Charity School Movement.* Cambridge University Press, 1938.

Jones, Owen, et al. *Lectures on the Results of the Great Exhibition of 1851, Delivered before the Society of Arts, Manufacture and Commerce, at the Suggestion of H.R.H. Prince Albert.* 2nd series. London: David Bogue, 1853.

———. *An Apology for the Colouring of the Greek Court in the Crystal Palace.* London: Crystal Palace Library and Bradbury and Evans, 1854.

———. *The Grammar of Ornament.* London: Day and Son, 1856.

Jones, Stephen. "The Spencer House Question." *Design Bazaar,* supplement to *Harpers and Queen* (February 1988): 16–17, 72.

———. "Roman Taste and Greek Gusto: The Society of Dilettanti and the Building of Spencer House, London." *Antiques* 141 (June 1992): 968–77.

Joppien, Rüdiger, and Bernard Smith. *The Art of Captain Cook's Voyages.* Vol. 1, *The Voyage of the Endeavour, 1768–1771. . . .* New Haven and London: Yale University Press and Australian Acadamy of the Humanities, for the Paul Mellon Centre for Studies in British Art, 1985.

Jordan, Gerald, and Nicholas Rogers. "Admirals as Heroes: Patriotism and Liberty in Hanoverian England." *Journal of British Studies* 28 (July 1989): 201–24.

Jourdain, Margaret. *English Decorative Plasterwork of the Renaissance.* 1926. Reprint, London: B. T. Batsford, 1933.

———. "Furniture Designed by James Stuart at Althorp." *Country Life* 78 (24 August 1935): 204–5.

———. *The Work of William Kent, Artist, Painter, Designer and Landscape Gardener.* London: Country Life, 1948.

Jupp, Edward Basil. *A Descriptive List of Original Drawings, Engravings, Autograph Letters and Portraits, Illustrating the Catalogues of the Society of Artists of Great Britain: from Its Commencement, in the Year 1760, to Its Close, in the Year 1791.* 6 vols. London: n.p., 1871.

Kelly, Alison. *Decorative Wedgwood in Architecture and Furniture.* London: Country Life, 1965.

———. *Mrs. Coade's Stone.* Upton-upon-Severn: Self Publishing Association, 1990.

Kelly, Jason. *Archaeology and Identity in the British Enlightenment: The Society of Dilettanti, 1732–1808.* (Forthcoming).

Kelsall, Frank. "Liardet versus Adam." *Architectural History* 27 (1984): 118–26.

Kenworthy-Browne, John. "Monument to Three Captains (in Westminster Abbey)." *Country Life* 161 (27 January 1977): 180–82.

———. "Establishing a Reputation. Joseph Nollekens: The Years in Rome." Part I. *Country Life* 165 (7 June 1979): 1844–48.

———. "Genius Recognised. Joseph Nollekens: The Years in Rome." Part II. *Country Life* 165 (14 June 1979): 1930–31.

———. "Matthew Brettingham's Rome Account Book, 1747–1754." Walpole Society annual, vol. 49 (1983): 37–132.

———. "Designing Around the Statues: Matthew Brettingham's Casts at Kedleston." *Apollo* 137 (April 1993): 248–52.

King, Gregory. *Two Tracts.* Ed. by G. E. Barnett. Baltimore: The John Hopkins Press, 1936. Available at King, Gregory. "Gregory King's Estimate of Population and Wealth, England and Wales, 1688." University of York, Department of Mathematics. www.york.ac.uk/depts/maths/histstat/king.htm. Accessed 27 May 2004.

Knox, Tim. "Acquisitions for National Trust Properties." *Apollo* 145 (April 1997): 50.

———. "'A Mortifying Lesson to Human Vanity.' Ralph Willett's Library at Merly House, Dorset." *Apollo* 152 (July 2000): 38–45.

643

Krafft, Jean-Charles. *Recueil des plus jolies maisons de Paris et de ses environs.* Paris: J. L. Scherff, 1809.

Kruft, Hanno-Walter. *A History of Architectural Theory from Vitruvius to the Present.* London: A. Zwemmer, 1994.

Laborde, Alexandre, comte de. *Description des nouveaux jardins de la France et de ses anciens châteaux. . . .* Paris: Delance, 1808.

Lafever, Minard. *The Young Builder's General Instructor; Containing the Five Orders of Architecture. . . .* Newark: W. Tuttle, 1829.

———. *The Modern Builder's Guide.* New York: Henry C. Sleight, Collins and Hannay, 1833.

———. *The Beauties of Modern Architecture.* New York: D. Appleton, 1835.

Laing, Alastair. "O tempera, o Mores! The Ruin Paintings in the Dining Room at Shugborough." *Apollo* 137 (April 1993): 227–32.

Lambert, Elizabeth. "The Rebirth of Spencer House." *Architectural Digest* 48 (February 1991): 134–43, 200, 202.

Landy, Jason. "Stuart and Revett and their Interpretation of Greek Architecture." M. A. thesis, Institute of Fine Arts, New York University, 1953.

———. "Stuart and Revett: Pioneer Archaeologists." *Archaeology* 9 (December 1956): 252–59.

Lang, Andrew. *Pickle the Spy, or the Incognito of Prince Charles.* 3rd ed. London: Longmans, Green and Co., 1897.

Langford, Paul. *The First Rockingham Administration.* Oxford University Press, 1973.

———. *A Polite and Commercial People, England, 1727–1783.* Oxford University Press, 1992.

Latrobe, Benjamin. *The Journals of Benjamin Henry Latrobe, 1799–1820: From Philadelphia to New Orleans.* Ed. by Edward C. Carter II, John C. Van Horne, and Lee W. Formwalt. Vol. 3 of Series 1, Journals, The Papers of Benjamin Henry Latrobe. New Haven: Maryland Historical Society and Yale University Press, 1980.

Laugier, Marc-Antoine. *Essai sur l'architecture.* Paris: Chez Duchesne, 1753

Lawrence, Arnold Walter. *Greek Architecture.* Harmondsworth: Penguin Books, 1957.

Lawrence, Lesley. "Stuart and Revett: Their Literary and Architectural Careers." *Journal of the Warburg Institute* 2 (1938–39): 128–46. See also Lesley Lewis.

Leach, Peter. "The Life and Work of James Paine." Ph.D. diss., University of Oxford, 1975.

———. *James Paine.* London: A. Zwemmer, 1988.

Lees-Milne, James. *The Age of Adam.* London: B. T. Batsford, 1947.

———. "Shugborough, Staffordshire." Parts I and II. *Connoisseur* 164 (April 1967): 211–15; 165 (May 1967): 4–11.

Legrand, Jacques Guillaume, and Charles Paul Landon. *Description de Paris, et de ses édifices, avec un précis historique et des observations sur le caractère de leur architecture, et sur les principaux objets d'art et de curiosité qu'ils renferment.* 2 vols. Paris: C. P. Landon, 1806–9.

Legyon, Francis. *Decoration in England, 1660–1770.* London: B. T. Batsford, 1914.

L'Épine, Muriel de. *Autour de Pierre-Adrien de Pâris: Un Album des calques.* Paris: Imprimerie Reich, 2001.

LeRoy, Julien-David. *Les Ruines des plus beaux monuments de la Grèce.* 1758. 2nd ed. 2 vols. Paris: Guerin and Delatour, 1770. Trans. by David Britt as *The Ruins of the Most Beautiful Monuments of Greece.* Los Angeles: Getty Research Institute, 2004.

Leslie, Charles Robert, and Tom Taylor. *Life and Times of Sir Joshua Reynolds.* Vol. 1. London: John Murray, 1865.

Lever, Jill. *Architect's Designs for Furniture.* London: Rizzoli, 1982.

———, ed. *Catalogue of the Drawings Collection of the Royal Institute of British Architects.* Vol. O-R. [Farnborough, Eng.]: Gregg International, 1976.

Lever, Jill, and Margaret Richardson. *Great Drawings from the Collection of the Royal Institute of British Architects.* Exh. cat., Drawing Center, New York. London: Trefoil Books, 1983.

———. *The Art of the Architect: Treasures from the RIBA's Collections.* London: Trefoil Books, 1984.

Lewis, H., and Son. [Advertisement]. *British Society of Dilettanti, Notes and Queries,* series 4, 3 (2 January 1869): [between 24 and 25].

Lewis, Lesley. "The Architects of the Chapel at Greenwich Hospital." *Art Bulletin* 29 (1947): 260–67.

———. "Greece and Rome at Greenwich." *Architectural Review* 119 (January 1951): 17–24.

———. *Connoisseurs and Secret Agents in Eighteenth-Century Rome.* London: Chatto and Windus, 1961.

———. "Elizabeth, Countess of Home, and Her House in Portman Square." *Burlington Magazine* 109 (August 1967): 443–53.

Lewis, Michael. *The Navy of Britain. A Historical Portrait.* London: George Allen and Unwin Ltd., 1948.

Lewis, Samuel. *A Topographical Dictionary of Ireland. . . .* Vol. 2. London: S. Lewis and Co., 1837.

Lichtenberg, Georg Christoph. *Schriften und Briefe.* Ed. by Franz Mautner. 4 vols. in 6. Frankfurt-am-Main: Insel Verlag, 1983.

Lincoln, Margarette. *Representing the Royal Navy: British Sea Power, 1750–1815.* Aldershot: Ashgate in association with the National Maritime Museum, 2002.

Lippincott, Louise. *Selling Art in Georgian London: The Rise of Arthur Pond.* New Haven and London: Yale University Press, 1983.

Liscombe, Rhodri. *William Wilkins, 1778–1839.* Cambridge University Press, 1980.

Lithgow, William. *The Totall Discourse of the Rare Adventures and Painefull Peregrinations . . . in Europe, Asia and Affrica.* 1632. Reprint, Glasgow: James MacLehose and Sons, 1906.

Loftus, John Henry, Marquis of Ely. *A Famous Castle: Reminiscences of the Lovely Dolly Munro*. Manchester, England: privately printed, 1893.

London and Its Environs Described. Vol. 1. London: R. and J. Dodsley, 1761.

London Chronicle (16–18 April 1767): 376.

Londonderry, Marquess of. *The Londonderry Album. Portraits from a Great House in the 1890s*. London: Blond and Briggs, 1978.

"Lord Anson." *Spink & Son's Monthly Numismatic Circular* 20 (July 1912): 13730–32.

Lord, John. "Richard Hayward: An Early and Some Later Commisions." *Church Monuments* 12 (1997): 67–76.

Lovejoy, Arthur Oncken, and George Boas. *Primitivism and Related Ideas in Antiquity: Contributions to the History of Primitivism*. 1935. Reprint, New York: Octagon Books, 1965.

Low, Jill. "The Art and Architectural Patronage of William Weddell (1736–1792) of Newby Hall and His Circle." Ph.D. diss., University of Leeds, 1981.

———. "Newby Hall: Two Late Eighteenth Century Inventories." *Furniture History* 22 (1984): 135–65.

Lysaght, Averil. "Captain Cook's Kangaroo." *New Scientist* 1 (14 March 1957): 17–19.

Lysons, Daniel and Samuel. *Magna Britannia; Being a Concise Topographical Account of the Several Counties of Great Britain*. Vol. 1, *Bedfordshire, Berkshire, Buckinghamshire*. London: T. Cadell and W. Davies, 1806.

Lyttelton, George, Baron. *Memoirs and Correspondence of George, Lord Lyttelton, from 1734 to 1773*. Ed. by Sir Robert Phillimore. Vol. 2. London: James Ridgway, 1845.

Macdonald, Colin. "Greenwich Hospital." *Architectural Review* 29 (February 1911): 77–83.

Macdonald, George. *Catalogue of the Greek Coins in the Hunterian Collection, University of Glasgow*. Glasgow: James Maclehose and Sons, 1899.

Mackley, Alan. "Clerks of the Works." *Georgian Group Journal* 8 (1998): 157–66.

MacMahon, Rev. T. "Rathfarnham Castle." *Dublin Historical Record* 41 (1987): 21–23.

Macmillan, Duncan. *Painting in Scotland: The Golden Age*. Oxford: Phaidon Press, 1986.

Macquoid, Percy. "Furniture of the XVII and XVIII Centuries: Furniture at Hornby Castle." *Country Life* 31 (30 March 1912): 475–79.

———. "Furniture At Hornby Castle and Holdenby." *Country Life* 33 (19 April 1913): 13*–16*.

———. "XVIII Century Furniture at Hornby Castle." *Country Life* 34 (27 September 1913): 13*–19.*

Madden, Gráinne. "Rathfarnham Castle." *Irish Arts Review* 4, no. 1 (1987): 22–27.

Major, Thomas. *The Ruins of Paestum, otherwise Posidonia, in Magna Graecia*. London: T. Major, 1768.

Malden, John. *John Henning, 1771–1851– "... A Very Ingenious Modeller. . . ."* Paisley: Renfrew District Council Museum and Art Galleries, 1977.

Mallett, J. V. G. "Nicholas Crisp, Founding Member of the Society of Arts." Parts I–III. *RSA Journal* 121 (1973): 28–32, 92–96, 170–74.

Mallgrave, Harry Frances. *Gottfried Semper: Architect of the Nineteenth Century*. New Haven and London: Yale University Press, 1996.

Malton, Thomas, the Younger. *A Picturesque Tour through the Cities of London and Westminster, Illustrated with the Most Interesting Views Executed in Aquatints*. 2 vols. London: T. Malton, 1792.

Marchand, Suzanne. *Down from Olympus: Archaeology and Philhellenism in Germany, 1750–1970*. Princeton University Press, 1996.

Marciari, John. "Athenian Stuart in Florence." *Burlington Magazine* 140 (September 1998): 612–14.

Marcus, Geoffrey Jules. *Heart of Oak. A Survey of British Sea Power in the Georgian Era*. London, New York and Toronto: Oxford University Press, 1975.

Markham, John. *A Naval Career During the Old War: Being a Narrative of the Life of Admiral John Markham*. Ed. by Sir Clements R. Markham. London: Sampson Low, Marston, Searle and Rivington, 1883.

Marriott, J. W. *A Short History of Chislehurst*. Chislehurst, Kent: E. C. Waters and Son, 1912.

Martelli, George. *Jemmy Twitcher: A Life of the Fourth Earl of Sandwich, 1718–1792*. London: Jonathan Cape, 1962.

Martineau, Jane, and Andrew Robison. *The Glory of Venice: Art in the Eighteenth Century*. New Haven and London: Yale University Press, 1994.

Mason, William. *The English Garden: A Poem*. York: A. Ward, J. Todd; London: T. Cadell, H. Denoyer, 1777.

Matthew, Henry Colin Gray, and Harrison, Brian, eds. *Oxford Dictionary of National Biography in Association with the British Academy, from the Earliest Times to the Year 2000*. 61 vols. Oxford University Press, 2004.

Mattingly, Edward, and Harold Sydenham. *Royal Imperial Coinage*. Vol. 1, *Augustus to Vitellius*. London: Spink, 1984.

Mau, August. *Pompeii, Its Life and Art*. Trans. by Francis W. Kelsey. New York: Macmillan, 1907.

Maxted, Ian. "The London Book Trades 1735–1775: A Checklist of Members." Exeter Working Papers in British Book Trade History; EWP03. Devon Library Services, 2001. http://www.devon.gov.uk/etched?_IXP_=1&_IXR=100158. Accessed 1 March 2006.

McCall, Dorothy. *Patchwork of the History of Chislehurst*. N.p., 1963.

McCarthy, Michael. "Documents on the Greek Revival in Architecture." *Burlington Magazine* 114 (November 1972): 760–69.

———. "James Lovell and His Sculptures at Stowe." *Burlington Magazine* 115 (April 1973): 220–32.

———. "Sir Roger Newdigate and John Breval: Drawings of the Grand Tour." *Apollo* 136 (August 1992): 100–104.

———. "'The Dullest Man that Ever Travelled?' A Re-Assessment of Richard Pococke and of his portrait by J.-E. Liotard." *Apollo* 143 (May 1996): 22–29.

———, ed. *Lord Charlemont And His Circle.* Dublin and Portland, OR: Four Courts Press, 2001.

———. *Classical and Gothic: Studies in the History of Art.* Dublin and Portland, OR: Four Courts, 2005.

McCormick, Thomas J., and John Fleming. "A Ruin Room by Clérisseau." *Connoisseur* 149 (April 1962): 239–43.

McIntyre, Ian. *Joshua Reynolds: The Life and Times of the First President of the Royal Academy.* London: Allen Lane, 2003.

McMillan, Anthony Stewart. *The Royal Alfred Story.* Ed. by Joan F. Lafferty. London: The Royal Alfred Merchant Seamen's Society, 1967.

McParland, Edward. "Rathfarnham Castle, Co. Dublin." *Country Life* 172 (9 September 1982): 734–37.

———. *James Gandon, Vitruvius Hibernicus.* London: A. Zwemmer, 1985.

———. Review of *Lord Charlemont and His Circle,* ed. by Michael McCarthy. *Apollo* 157 (January 2003): 56.

Mead, Williams Edward. *The Grand Tour in the Eighteenth Century.* Boston and New York: Houghton Mifflin Company, 1914.

"Memoirs of the Late Sir Philip Stephens, Bart." *European Magazine, and London Review* 56 (December 1809): 407–9.

Meteyard, Elizabeth. *The Life of Josiah Wedgwood.* 2 vols. 1866. 1st reprint, London: Cornmarket Press, 1970. 2nd reprint, Barlaston, Staffordshire: Josiah Wedgwood and Sons, 1980.

Michel, Christian. *Charles-Nicholas Cochin et l'art des Lumières.* Rome: École Française de Rome, 1993.

Middleton, Richard. "Pitt, Anson and the Admiralty, 1756–1761." *History* 55 (1970): 189–98.

Middleton, Robin, ed. *The Beaux-Arts and Nineteenth-century French Architecture.* London: Thames and Hudson, 1982.

———. "Perfezione e colore: la policromia nell'architettura francese del XVIII e XIX secolo." *Rassegna* 23 (1985): 55–67.

———. "The Sculpture Gallery at Newby Hall." *Architectural Association Files* 13 (Autumn 1986): 48–60.

Middleton, Robin, et al. *The Mark J. Millard Architectural Collection.* Vol. 2, *British Books: Seventeenth through Nineteenth Centuries.* Washington D.C.: National Gallery of Art; New York: George Braziller, 1998.

Middleton, Robin, and David Watkin. *Neoclassical and Nineteenth Century Architecture.* New York: Abrams, 1980.

Miller, Corrine, ed. *Drawing from the Past: William Weddell and the Transformation of Newby Hall.* Leeds Museums and Galleries (City Art Gallery), 2004.

Miller, Elizabeth. *Sixteenth-Century Italian Ornament Prints in the Victoria and Albert Museum.* London: V&A Publications, 1999.

Miller, Hugh. *First Impressions of England and its People.* London: John Johnstone, 1847.

Milward, Richard. *Historic Wimbledon.* Gloucestershire: The World Press, 1989.

Mingay, Gordon E. *English Landed Society in the Eighteenth Century.* London: Routledge and Kegan Paul Ltd., 1963.

Miscellaneous. "Notes on Books, etc." *Society of British Dilettanti, Notes and Queries,* 2nd series, 2, no. 30 (26 July 1856): 80.

Mitchell, T. C., ed. *Captain Cook and the South Pacific.* British Museum Yearbook, vol. 3. London: British Museum, 1979.

Mitchell, William M. *Chislehurst Golf Club: 100 Years of Golf at Camden Place.* Droitwich, England: Grant Books for Chislehurst Golf Club, 1994.

Monks, Sarah. "National Heretopia: Greenwich as Spectacle, 1694–1869." *Rising East: The Journal of East London Studies* 2, no. 1 (1998): 156–66.

Montfaucon, Bernard de, *L'Antiquité éxpliquée et représentée en figures.* 5 vols. Paris: Delaulne et al., 1719.

Moore, Andrew, ed. *Houghton Hall: The Prime Minister, the Empress and the Heritage.* Exh. cat. Castle Museum and the Iveagh Bequest, Kenwood. London: Philip Wilson; Wappingers Falls, NY: Antique Collectors' Club, 1996.

Morley, John. *Regency Design, 1790–1840: Gardens, Buildings, Interiors, Furniture.* London: A. Zwemmer, 1993.

———. *Furniture: the Western Tradition; History, Style, Design.* London: Thames and Hudson, 1999.

———. *The History of Furniture: Twenty-Five Centuries of Style and Design in the Western Tradition.* Boston, New York, and London: Little Brown, 1999.

Morelli, Emilia. *Le Lettere di Benedetto XIV al Card. De Tencin.* 3 vols. Rome: Edizioni de storia e letteratura, 1955–84.

———. *Tre Profili, Benedetto XIV, Pasquale Stanislao Mancini, Pietro Roselli.* Quaderni del Risorgimento series, vol. 9. Rome: Edizioni dell'Ateneo, 1955.

Morris, Neal. "Royal Naval College Campus Work Begins." *Building Design: A Weekly Newspaper* 1336 (30 January 1998): 2.

Morris, Robert. *Lectures on Architecture: Consisting of Rules Founded upon Harmonick and Arithmetical Proportions in Building.* London: J. Brindley, 1734.

Morris, Roger. *Naval Power and British Culture, 1760–1850. Public Trust and Government Ideology.* Aldershot: Ashgate, 2004.

Morris, Susan. "The Midas Touch." *Antique Collector* 62 (March 1991): 38–43.

Morselli, Raffaella, and Rossella Vodret, ed. *Ritratto di una Collezione: Pannini e la Galleria del Cardinale Silvio Valenti Gonzaga.* Milan: Skira, 2005.

Mortimer, Thomas. *The Universal Director, or, The Nobleman and Gentleman's True Guide to the Masters and Professors of the Liberal and Polite Arts and Sciences, and of the Mechanic Arts, Manufactures, and Trades. . . .* London: J. Coote, 1763.

Morton, Lucy, and Michelle Stroube, comps. *Furniture, Silver and Works of Art, 2004.* London: Partridge Fine Arts PLC, 2004.

Mosser, Monique, and Daniel Rabreau. *Charles de Wailly: peintre architecte dans l'Europe des Lumières.* Exh. cat. Hôtel de Béthune-Sully. Paris: Caisse nationale des monuments historiques et des sites, 1979.

"Mr. Stuart the Architect. . . ." [Obituary.] *Times* [London] (1 March 1788): 3.

Mulvany, Thomas. *The Life of James Gandon.* Dublin: Hodges and Smith, 1846.

———. *The Life of James Gandon.* 1846. Rev. ed., ed. by Maurice Craig. London: Cornmarket Press, 1969.

Museum of London. *Ivory, Feathers, and Lace.* Exh. cat. Museum of London, 1985.

Musgrave, Clifford. *Adam and Hepplewhite and Other Neo-Classical Furniture.* London: Faber and Faber; New York, Taplinger, 1966.

Nares, Gordon. "Hagley Hall, Worcestershire." Parts I and II. *Country Life* 122 (19 September 1957): 546–49; (26 September 1957): 608–11.

Nash, Paul W., et al. *Early Printed Books, 1478–1840: Catalogue of the British Architectural Library Early Imprints Collection.* Vol. 4. Munich:-Saur, 2001.

Neale, John Preston. *Views of the Seats of Noblemen and Gentlemen in England, Wales, Scotland and Ireland.* Vol. 3. London: Sherwood, Neely, and Jones, and Thomas Moule, 1820.

Neils, Jenifer. *The Parthenon Frieze.* Cambridge and New York: Cambridge University Press, 2001.

Nerdinger, Winifried, ed. *Leo von Klenze: Architekt zwischen Kunst und Hof.* Munich: Prestel, 2000.

Nesselrath, Arnold. *Das Fossombroner Skizzenbuch.* London: University of London, Warburg Institute, 1993.

Neufforge, Jean François de. *Recueil élementaire d'architecture, contenant plusieurs études des ordres d'architecture. . . .* Vols. 1 and 5. Paris: the author, 1757–68.

Neverov, O. "The Lyde Browne Collection and the History of Ancient Sculpture in the Hermitage Museum." *American Journal of Archaeology* 88 (1984): 33–42.

"A New Medal. . . ." [Advertisement] *London Chronicle* (16–18 April 1767): 376.

A New Pocket Companion for Oxford: or, Guide through the University. Rev. ed. Oxford: D. Prince and J. Cooke, 1783.

Newby Hall: An Illustrated Survey of the Yorkshire Home of the Compton Family. Derby: English Life Publications, [1968].

"Newby Hall, Yorkshire." *Country Life* 19 (20 January 1906): 90–99.

Newman, John. *Somerset House.* London: Scala Books, 1990.

Nichols, John. *Literary Anecdotes of the Eighteenth Century. . . .* Vol. 9. 1782. New ed., London: Nichols, Son and Bentley, 1816.

———. *Minor Lives: A Collection of Biographies.* Ed. by Edward LeRoy Hart. Cambridge, MA: Harvard University Press, 1971.

Nixon, Howard M. *Five Centuries of English Bookbinding.* London: Scolar Press, 1978.

Nixon, Howard M., and Mirjan M. Foot. *The History of Decorated Bookbinding in England.* Oxford: Clarendon Press, 1992.

Noble, Joseph Veach, and Derek de la Solla Price. "The Water Clock in the Tower of the Winds." *American Journal of Archaeology* 72 (1968): 345–55.

Noble, Percy. *Park Place, Berkshire: A Short History of the Place and an Account of the Owners and Their Guests.* London: F. Calder Turner, 1905.

Norman, Geraldine. "Scheme to Restore Spencer House." *Times* [London] (24 November 1981): 12.

———. "Trust Hopes to Take over Spencer House." *Times* [London] (20 December 1982): 2.

Notizia delle Accademie erette in Roma per Ordine della Santita di N. Sig. Papa Benedetto Decimoquarto. Rome: [Giuseppe Collini], 1740.

"Nuneham Courtenay Chapel, Oxon." Supplement to *Architect's Journal* (18 March 1931; 1 April 1931; 22 April 1931).

O. B. "Wentworth Woodhouse, Yorkshire." *Country Life* 19 (31 March 1906): 450–62.

"Obituary of Considerable Persons [James Stuart]." *Gentleman's Magazine* 60, part 2 (August 1790): 766.

[Obituary, James Stuart]. *Morning Herald,* no. 2275 (6 February 1788): 3.

Observations on Two Trials at Law, Respecting Messieurs Adam's New-Invented Patent-Stucco. London: Fielding and Walker, 1778.

"On Saturday morning. . . .". [Obituary, James Stuart]. *Times* [London] (12 February 1788): 3.

O'Connell, Sheila. *London 1753.* London: British Museum Press, 2003.

Oechslin, Werner, and Oskar Bätschmann, eds. *Die Vase.* Exh. cat. Zurich: Kunstgewerbemuseum der Stadt, Museum für Gestaltung, 1982.

Old Bailey Proceedings Online. www.oldbaileyonline.org. Accessed 1 February 2006.

Oncken, Alste. *Friedrich Gilly 1772–1800.* Berlin: Deutcher Verein für Kunstwissenschaft, 1935.

Oppé, A. P., ed. "Memoirs of Thomas Jones." Walpole Society annual, vol. 32 (1946–48).

Osborne, Edgar, ed. *Newby Hall: An Illustrated Survey of the Yorkshire Home of the Compton Family.* Derby: English Life Publications, n.d.

Ostergard, Derek, ed. *William Beckford 1760–1844: An Eye for the Magnificent.* Exh. cat. The Bard Graduate Center, New York. New Haven and London: Yale University Press and the Bard Graduate Center, 2001.

Oswald, Arthur. "West Wycombe Park, Bucks." Parts I and II. *Country Life* 73 (6 May 1933): 466–71; (13 May 1933): 494–99.

———. "Londonderry House, Park Lane." *County Life* 82 (10 July 1937): 38–44.

————. "Blithfield, Staffordshire." Parts I–III. *Country Life* 116 (28 October 1954): 1488–92; (4 November 1954): 1576–79; (11 November 1954): 1664–67.

Ottomeyer, Hans, and Peter Pröschel. *Vergoldete Bronzen: die Bronzearbeiten des Spätbarock und Klassizismus.* Vol. 1. Munich: Klinkhardt and Beirmann, 1986.

Oxoniensis [pseud]. "Queries with Answers, John Tweddell: Athenian Stuart." *British Society of Dilettanti, Notes and Queries,* 3rd series, 2 (4 October 1862): 274–75.

P. W. "Memorandum Book on Art." *British Society of Dilettanti, Notes and Queries,* 2nd series, 9 (14 April 1860): 294.

P. W. "Architectural Societies." *British Society of Dilettanti, Notes and Queries,* 3rd series, 3 (21 February 1863): 157.

Page, W., ed. *Victorian History of the County of Sussex.* Vol. 9. London: A. Constable and Co., 1905.

Le Panthéon: Symbole des révolutions de l'église de la nation au temps des grands hommes. Exh. cat. Hôtel de Sully, Paris, and the Centre canadien d'architecture, Montreal. Paris: Caisse nationale des monuments historiques et des sites, Picard; Montreal: Centre canadien d'architecture, 1989.

"The Papers of the Society of Artists of Great Britain." Walpole Society annual, vol. 6 (1917–18): 113–30.

Papworth, Wyatt. "William Newton and the Chapel of Greenwich Hospital." *R.I.B.A. Journal* 27–28 (27 August 1891): 417–20.

Parker, James. "The Tapestry Room from Croome Court." *Connoisseur* 147 (April 1961): 109–13.

Parry, Eric. "Wimpole Hall." *Architects' Journal* 183 (26 March 1986): 36–58.

Parslow, Christopher Charles. *Rediscovering Antiquity: Karl Weber and the Excavation of Herculaneum, Pompeii, and Stabiae.* Cambridge University Press, 1995.

Pastor, Ludwig, Freiherr von. *The History of the Popes from the Close of the Middle Ages.* Vol. 8. Ed. by R. F. Kerr. London: Kegan, Paul, Trench, Trübner, and Co., 1908. Vols. 35–36. Ed. by E. F. Peeler. London: Routledge and Kegan Paul, 1961.

Pater, Walter. *Renaissance Studies in Art and Poetry.* 1873. 4th ed., London: Macmillan, 1893.

Patterson, Allen. "Edwardian Terraces Brought to Life." *Country Life* 90 (10 October 1941): 1024–28.

Paulson, Ronald. *Hogarth: His Life, Art, and Times.* New Haven and London: Yale University Press, 1971.

Pausanias. *Guide to Greece.* 2 vols. Trans. by Peter Levi. Rev. ed. Harmondsworth: Penguin, 1979.

Pavoni, Rosanna, ed. *Reviving the Renaissance: The Use and Abuse of the Past in Nineteenth-Century Italian Art and Decoration.* Trans. by Adrian Belton. Cambridge University Press, 1997.

Payne, Christoper, ed. *Sotheby's Concise Encyclopedia of Furniture.* New York: Harper and Row, 1989.

Pearce, David. *London's Mansions: The Palatial Houses of the Nobility.* London: B. T. Batsford, 1986.

Pearson, W. H. "Hawkesworth's Alterations." *Journal of Pacific History* 7 (1972): 45–72.

Pennant, Thomas. *The Journey from Chester to London.* London: B. White, 1782.

Pennethorne, John. *The Geometry and Optics of Ancient Architecture, Illustrated by Examples from Thebes, Athens and Rome.* London and Edinburgh: Williams and Norgate, 1878.

Penny, Nicholas. "Lord Rockingham's Sculpture Collection and The Judgment of Paris by Nollekens." *John Paul Getty Museum Journal* 19 (1991): 5–34.

Penrose, Francis Cranmer. *Investigation of the Principles of Athenian Architecture: or, The Results of a Survey Conducted Chiefly with Reference to the Optical Refinements Exhibited in the Construction of the Ancient Buildings at Athens.* 1851. 2nd ed., London and New York: Macmillan, 1888.

Percy, Victoria, and Gervase Jackson-Stops. "Exquisite Taste and Tawdry Ornament: The Travel Journals of the 1st Duchess of Northumberland." Part II. *Country Life* 155 (7 February 1974): 250–52.

Perrault, Claude. *Ordonnance des cinq espèces de colonnes selon la méthode des anciens.* Paris: Jean Baptiste Coignard, 1683.

Pevsner, Nikolaus. *London.* Vol. 1. *The Cities of London and Westminster.* Vol. 2, *South.* 3rd ed. rev. by Bridget Cherry. Buildings of England. Harmondsworth, England, and New York: Penguin Books, 1973–99.

————. *Yorkshire: The West Riding.* Buildings of England. 2nd rev. ed. by Enid Radcliffe. Harmondsworth, Middlesex, England: Penguin, 1967.

————. *An Outline of European Architecture.* London: Allen Lane, 1973.

Phillips, Son, and Neale, London. *Catalogue of A Collection of Antient and Modern Pictures, The Genuine Property of Mr. Stuart Artist and Collector, Deceased. . . .* Sale cat. 4 February 1799. Copy in the Library, Courtauld Institute of Art, London, and in the Getty Research Institute.

Physick, John. *Designs for English Sculpture, 1680–1860.* London: H.M.S.O., 1969.

Picard, Liza. *Dr. Johnson's London.* London: Phoenix Press, 2001.

Picturesque Tour of the River Thames, Illustrated by Twenty-Four Coloured Views, A Map and Vignettes, from Original Drawings Taken on the Spot by William Westall and Samuel Owen. London: R. Ackermann, 1828.

Piganiol de la Force, Jean-Aimar. *Nouvelle description de la France.* 7 vols. 2nd ed. Paris: F. Delaulne, 1722.

Piranesi, Giovanni Battista. *Della Magnificenza ed Architettura de' Romani.* Rome: n.p., 1761.

————. *Diverse manière d'adornare i cammini. . . .* Rome: Generoso Salomoni, 1769.

————. *Différentes vues de quelques restes de trois grands édifices: qui subsistent encore dans le milieu de l'ancienne ville de Pesto, autrement Possidonia qui est située dans la Lucanie.* [Rome: n. p., 1778].

————. *I Vasi, Candelabri, Cippi, Sarcofagi, Tripodi, Lucerne ed Ornamenti antichi disegn.* Vol. 2. Rome: n.p., 1778.

———. [*Opere / di Giambattista Paranesi*]. Vol. 11, *Antichita d'Albano e di Castel Gondolfo. . . .* 1764. Reprint. Paris: Firmin Didot, 1835–37.

———. *Piranesi: The Complete Etchings.* Ed. by Luigi Ficacci. Cologne and New York: Taschen, 2000.

Plomer, H. R., G. H. Bushnell, and E. R. Mc. Dix. *A Dictionary of the Printers and Booksellers Who Were at Work in England, Scotland and Ireland from 1726 to 1775.* Oxford University Press, 1932.

Plutarch. *Plutarch's Lives.* Loeb Classical Library. 11 vols. Trans. by Bernadotte Perrin. London: Heinemann; New York: Macmillan, 1914–26.

———. *Life of Antony.* Ed. by Christopher Pelling. Cambridge University Press, 1988.

Pococke, Richard. *A Description of the East, and Some Other Countries.* 2 vols. London: W Bowyer, 1743–45.

———. *The Travels through England of Dr. Richard Pococke, Successively Bishop of Meath and Ossory during 1750, 1751, and Later Years.* Ed. by James Joel Cartwright. 2 vols. Westminster: the Camden Society, 1888.

Pool, Bernard. *Navy Board Contracts, 1660–1832.* London: Longmans, 1966.

Potts, Alex. *Flesh and the Ideal: Winckelmann and the Origins of Art History.* New Haven and London: Yale University Press, 1994.

Powys, Ursula. "Recreations of A Georgian Family." *Country Life* 127 (24 March 1960): 640–42.

Pradère, Alexandre. "Madame du Pompadour et le goût grec." *Connaissance des arts* 454 (December 1989): 106–9.

———. *French Furniture Makers: The Art of the Ébéniste from Louis XIV to the Revolution.* Trans. by Perran Wood. Malibu, CA: J. Paul Getty Museum, 1989.

Prat, Louis-Antoine, and Pierre Rosenberg. *Nicolas Poussin (1594–1665): Catalogue raisonné des dessins.* Vol. 1. Milan: Leonardo, 1994.

Préaud, Maxime. *Antoine Lepautre, Jacques Lepautre et Jean Lepautre (Première and Deuxième Parties).* Inventaire du fonds français, Graveurs du XVIIe siècle, vols. 11 and 12. Paris: Bibliothèque nationale, 1999.

Pressly, William J. *The Life and Art of James Barry.* New Haven and London: Yale University Press, 1981.

Prest, Wilfrid. *Albion Ascendant: English History, 1660–1815.* Oxford University Press, 1998.

Price, Liam, ed. *An Eighteenth-Century Antiquary: The Sketches, Notes and Diaries of Austin Cooper (1759–1830).* Dublin: John Falconer, 1942.

"Princess Alexandra Visits Belvedere." *Erith Observer and Kentish Times* (3 July 1959): 1.

Pritchard, John A. *A History of Erith.* Part 5, *Belvedere and Bostall.* 2nd ed. London: Borough of Bexley Libraries and Museums Department, 1994.

Probyn, Clive T. *The Sociable Humanist. The Life and Works of James Harris, 1709–1780: Provincial and Metropolitan Culture in Eighteenth-Century England.* Oxford: Clarendon Press, 1991.

Project Gutenberg Literary Archive Foundation. "Pickle the Spy; or, The Incognito of Prince Charles by Andrew Lang." http://www.gutenberg.org/etext/6807. Accessed 3 July 2004.

Pyne, W. H. *The History of Royal Residences of Windsor Castle, St. Jame's Palace, Carlton House, and Frogmore.* Vols. 1 and 2. London, A. Dry, 1819.

Quatremère de Quincy, Antoine-Chrysos-tôme. *Le Jupiter olympien: ou, L'art de la sculpture antique considéré sous un nouveau point de vue; ouvrage qui comprend un essai sur le goût de la sculpture polychrome. . . .* Paris: Firmin Didot, 1814.

Queen Mary. *Catalogue of Bibelots, Miniatures and Other Valuables: The Property of H.M. Queen Mary, 1920–.* Vol. 4. Privately printed, 1938–45.

Quickenden, Kenneth. "Boulton and Fothergill Silver: An Épergne Designed by James Wyatt." *Burlington Magazine* 128 (June 1986): 417–21.

Quickenden, Kenneth, and Neal Adrian Quickenden, eds. *Silver and Jewellery: Production and Consumption since 1750.* Proceedings of the Conference for the Association of Art Historians, University of Central England in Birmingham, April 1994. Birmingham, England: Article Press, 1995.

Quilley, Geoff, and John Bonehill, eds. *William Hodges, 1744–1797: The Art of Exploration.* Exh. cat., National Maritime Museum, Greenwich, and the Yale Center for British Art, New Haven. New Haven; London: Yale University Press for the National Maritime Museum, Greenwich, 2004.

R. R. [Review of vol. 2 of *Antiquities of Athens*]. *Analytical Review* (8 October 1790): 121–30.

Racinet, Auguste. *Le Costume Historique.* Vol. 6. Paris: Librarie du Firmin-Didot et Cie, 1888.

"The Racing Cups." *Christie's Magazine* (July/August 1998): 3.

Raeburn, Michael, Ludmilla Voronikhina, and Andrew Nurnberg, eds. *The Green Frog Service.* London: Cacklegoose Press in association with the State Hermitage, St. Petersburg, 1995.

Ramsay, Andrew Michael. *The Travels of Cyrus, To which is Annexed, A Discourse upon the Theology and Mythology of the Pagans.* Vol. 2. London: T. Woodward and J. Peele, 1727.

Ramsey, Allan. *A Dialogue on Taste.* 2nd ed. London: n.p., 1762. First published in *The Investigator*, no. 332 (1755).

Raspi Serra, Joselita, ed. *La Fortuna di Paestum e la memoria moderna del dorico, 1750–1830.* Exh. cat. Certosa di S. Lorenzo, Padula, Salerno; Palazzo Braschi, Rome; National Academy of Design, New York. 2 vols. New York: National Academy of Design, 1986.

Raspi Serra, Joselita, ed. *Paestum and the Doric Revival, 1750–1830: Essential Outlines of an Approach.* New York: National Academy of Design; Florence: Centro Di, 1986.

"Rathfarnham Castle and Some of Its Former Owners." Pamphlet. Copy in the Guides Office, Dublin Office of Public Works, Rathfarnham file.

Read, Benedict. *Victorian Sculpture*. New Haven and London: Yale University Press, 1982.

Read, Brian. *General Conway and His Jersey Temple*. Henley-on-Thames: Archaeological and Historical Group, 1985.

Redford, Bruce. "The Measure of Ruins: Dilettanti in the Levant, 1750–1770." *Harvard Library Bulletin* 13 (Spring 2002): 5–6.

Redgrave, Samuel. *A Dictionary of Artists of the English School: Painters, Sculptors, Architects Engravers and Ornamentists: with Notices of Their Lives and Works.* London: Longmans, Green, and Co., 1874. 2nd ed. London: G. Bell, 1878.

Reeves-Smyth, Terence. *Irish Country Houses.* Appletree Guide. Belfast: Appletree Press, 1994.

Reid, Thomas. *Treatise on Clock and Watch Making 1826: Theoretical and Practical.* Edinburgh: John Fairbairn, 1826.

Reilly, Robin. *Wedgwood Jasper.* London: Charles Letts, 1972.

———. *Wedgwood Portrait Medallions. An Introduction.* Exh. cat. National Portrait Gallery, London. London: Barrie and Jenkins, 1973.

———. *Wedgwood.* 2 vols. New York: Stockton Press, 1989.

———. *Josiah Wedgwood, 1730–1795.* London: MacMillan, 1992.

———. *Wedgwood Jasper.* Rev. ed. London: Thames & Hudson, 1994.

———. *Wedgwood: The New Illustrated Dictionary.* Woodbridge, Suffolk: Antique Collectors' Club, 1995.

Reilly, Robin, and George Savage, eds. *Wedgwood: The Portrait Medallions.* London: Barrie and Jenkins, 1973.

———. *The Dictionary of Wedgwood.* Woodbridge, Suffolk: Antique Collectors' Club, 1980.

Reinach, Salomon. *Répertoire de la statuaire grecque et romaine.* Vol. 2, *Sept mille statues antiques.* Paris: E. Leroux, 1912.

A Reply to Observations on Two Trials at Law, Respecting Messieurs Adams's New-Invented Stucco; containing Mr. Wallace's reply to Mr. Dunning with the Summary of the Evidence and Charge to the Jury, as Taken down in Court. London: J. Bew, 1778.

"Report from Europe: 'Spencer House.'" *Antiques* 158 (September 2000): 268.

Reynolds, Sir Joshua. *Discourses on Art.* Ed. by Robert W. Wark. New Haven and London: Yale University Press for the Paul Mellon Centre for Studies in British Art, 1975.

Richards, James Maude, ed. *Who's Who in Architecture.* London: Weidenfeld and Nicolson, 1977.

Richardson, Albert Edward Sir. *Monumental Classic Architecture in Great Britain and Ireland During the Eighteenth and Nineteenth Centuries.* London: B. T. Batsford, 1914.

———. *Robert Mylne Architect and Engineer, 1733 to 1811.* London: B. T. Batsford, 1955.

Richardson, Albert Edward, and C. Lovett Gill. *London Houses from 1660–1820: A Consideration Of Their Architecture and Detail.* London: B. T. Batsford, [1911].

Richardson, Lawrence. *A New Topographical Dictionary of Ancient Rome.* Baltimore and London: John Hopkins University Press, 1992.

Richardson, Margaret, ed. *Catalogue of the Drawings Collection of the Royal Institute of British Architects.* Vol. S. Farnborough, Eng.: Gregg International, 1976.

Richetti, John, ed. *The Cambridge History of English Literature, 1660–1780.* Cambridge (Eng.) and New York: Cambridge University Press, 2005.

Richter, Gisela M. A. *The Furniture of the Greeks, Etruscans and Romans.* London: Phaidon Press, 1966.

Ridley, Ronald T. "To Protect the Monuments: the Papal Antiquarian (1534–1870)." *Xenia Antiqua* 1 (1992): 117–54.

Rimbault, Edward F. "Critical Observations on London Buildings." *Notes and Queries,* 3rd series, 6 (23 July 1864): 71–72.

Riou, Stephen. *The Grecian Orders of Architecture. Delineated and Explained from the Antiquities of Athens. Also the Parallels of the Orders of Palladio Scamezzi, and Vignola, to which are Added Remarks Concerning Publick and Private Edifices with Designs. . . .* London: the author, 1768.

Roberts, Hugh. "A Postscript on Lalive de Jully's Furniture 'à la grecque'." *Burlington Magazine* 131 (May 1989): 350–53.

Roberts, Jane, ed. *George III and Queen Charlotte: Patronage, Collecting and Court Taste.* London; Royal Collection Publications, 2004.

Roberts, Lynette. *The Endeavour: Captain Cook's First Voyage to Australia.* London: Peter Owen Ltd., 1954.

Robertson, Bruce, and Robert Dance. "Joseph Goupy and the Art of the Copy." *Bulletin of the Cleveland Museum of Art* 75 (December 1988): 355–82.

Robins, [Auctioneer], London. *"Catalogue of the Splendid Collection of Sculpture and Works of Art of Charles Rossi, Esq. R. A. At his Gallery in Grove Place, Lisson Grove, North . . . which will be Sold by Auction, by Mr. George Robins on the Premises on Tuesday, March 3, 1835, and Following Day."* Sale cat. 3–4 March 1835. Copy in the National Art Library, The Victoria and Albert Musuem, London.

Robinson, Eric. "R. E. Raspe, 'Franklin's Club of Thirteen,' and the Lunar Society." *Annals of Science* 11 (June 1955): 142–44.

———. "Eighteenth-Century Commerce and Fashion: Matthew Boulton's Marketing Techniques." *Economic History Review,* n. s. 16, no. 1 (1963): 39–60.

Robinson, Eric, and Keith Thompson. "Matthew Boulton's Mechanical Paintings." *Burlington Magazine* 112 (August 1970): 497–507.

Robinson, Henry. "The Tower of the Winds and the Roman Market-Place." *American Journal of Archaeology* 47 (July 1943): 291–305.

Robinson, John Martin. *The Wyatts: An Architectural Dynasty*. Oxford University Press, 1979.

———. *Shugborough*. London: The National Trust, 1989.

———. *Temples of Delight: Stowe Landscape Gardens*. London: The National Trust, 1994.

———. "New Light from the Nursery." *Country Life* 189 (28 September 1995): 80.

———. *Windsor Castle. The Official Illustrated History*. London: The Royal Collection, 2001.

———. *Spencer House: A Short History*. 1991. Rev. ed. by Jane Rick. London: Spencer House, Ltd., 2002.

Rodger, Nicholas A. M. *The Insatiable Earl: A Life of John Montagu, Fourth Earl of Sandwich, 1718–1792*. London: Harper-Collins, 1993.

Rollin, Charles. *Histoire ancienne des Égyptiens, des Carthaginois, des Assyriens, des Babyloniens, des Medes et des Perses, des Macedoniens, des Grecs*. Vol. 11. Paris: Veuve Estienne, 1737.

Roscoe, Ingrid. "James 'Athenian' Stuart and the Scheemakers Family: A Lucrative Partnership between Architect and Sculptors." *Apollo* 126 (September 1987): 178–84.

———. "Peter Scheemakers, and Classical Sculpture in Early Georgian England." Ph.D. diss., University of Leeds, 1990.

———. *Peter Scheemakers: "The Famous Statuary," 1691–1781*. Exh. cat. Centre for the Study of Sculpture, Henry Moore Institute, Leeds. Leeds City Art Gallery, 1996.

———. "Peter Scheemakers, Business Conduct and Workshop Practice with Catalogue Raisonné." Walpole Society annual, vol. 61 (1999): 163–304.

Le Rouge, Georges-Louis. *Détails des nouveaux Jardins à la mode et Jardins Anglo-Chinois. . . .* Vol. 1, book 2. Paris: n.p., 1776–87.

Rouquet, Jean André. *The Present State of the Arts in England*. London: J. Nourse, 1755.

Rousseau, Jean-Jacques. *Émile, ou, de l'éducation*. Paris: Duchesne, 1762.

Rowe, Robert. *Adam Silver, 1765–1795*. London: Faber and Faber, 1965.

Roworth, Wendy Wassyng, ed. *Angelica Kauffman: A Continental Artist in Georgian London*. London: Reaktion Books, 1992.

Royal Institute of British Architects Journal, 3rd series, 38 (6 December 1930): frontis.; 42 (25 May 1935): frontis.

"Royal Naval College: Greenwich Chapel Restored." *Times* [London] (13 June 1955): 10.

The Royal Society. Library and Archive catalogue. http://www.royalsoc.ac.uk/library. Accessed 14 July 2004.

Rudé, George. *Hanoverian London: 1714–1808*. Stroud, Gloucestershire: Sutton Publishing, 2003.

The Rudiments of Ancient Architecture, in two parts, Containing an historical account of the five orders, with their proportions and examples of each from the antique, also Vitruvius on the temples and intercolumniations. . . . London: I. and J. Taylor, 1789.

Ruskin, John. *The Works of John Ruskin*. Ed. by Edward Tyas Cook and Alexander Wedderburn. 39 vols. London: George Allen; New York: Longmans, Green, 1903–12.

Russel, James. *Letters from a Young Painter Abroad to His friends in England*. Vol. 1. 2nd ed. London: W. Russel, 1750.

Russell, Francis. "Securing the Future." *Country Life* 171 (23 July 1987): 96–99.

Ryskamp, Charles, and Frederick A. Pottle, eds. *Boswell: The Ominous Years, 1774–1776*. Melbourne, London, and Toronto: William Heinemann Ltd., 1963.

Sala, George Augustus, ed. *Gaslight and Daylight, with Some London Scenes They Shine Upon*. London: Chapman and Hall, 1859.

Salmon, Edward. *Life of Admiral Sir Charles Saunders, K. B.* London: Pitman and Sons, 1914.

Salmon, Frank. "British Architects and the Florentine Academy, 1753–1794." *Mitteilungen des Kunsthistorischen Institutes in Florenz* 34, no. 1–2 (1990): 199–214.

———. "Charles Cameron and Nero's Domus Aurea: 'una piccolo esplorazione'." *Architectural History* 36 (1993): 69–93.

———. *Building on Ruins: The Rediscovery of Rome and English Architecture*. Aldershot; Burlington, VT: Ashgate Press, 2000.

———. "Perspectival Restoration Drawings in Roman Archaeology and Architectural History." *Antiquaries Journal* 83 (2003): 397–424.

Sandby, Paul. *A Collection of One Hundred and Fifty Select Views, in England, Scotland and Ireland*. Vol. 1. London: Boydell, 1783.

Saumarez, Philip. *Log of the Centurion, Based on the Original Papers of Captain Philip Saumarez . . . 1740–44*. Ed. by Leo Heaps. London: Hart-Davis, MacGibbon, 1973.

Saussure, César de. *A Foreign View of England in the Reigns of George I and George II: The Letters of Monsieur César de Saussure to his Family*. Trans. and ed. by Madame van Muyden. London: John Murray, 1902.

Saxl, Fritz, and Rudolf Wittkower. *British Art and the Mediterranean*. London and New York: Oxford University Press, 1948.

Sayer, Robert. *Ruinen und Ueberbleibsel von Athen nebst andern merkwürdigen Altherthümern Griechenlands*. Trans. by Georg Christoph Kilian. Augspurg: Gedruckt bey Johann Lotter, 1764.

Scantlebury, Rev. C. "Rathfarnham Castle." *Dublin Historical Record* 12 (February 1951): 21–30.

Scheidemantel, Vivian J. *Josiah Wedgwood's "Heads of Illustrious Moderns."* Exh. cat. Art Institute of Chicago. Chicago: n.p., 1958.

Scherf, Guilhem, ed., *Augustin Pajou et ses contemporains*. Louvre conférences et colloques. Paris: la Documentation française, 1999.

Schinkel, Karl Friedrich. *Sammlung architektonischer Entwürfe*. Berlin: n.p., 1819–40.

———. *Werke der höheren Baukunst*. 2 parts. Potsdam: Verlag von Ferdinand Riegel, 1840.

———. *Collection of Architectural Designs, including Designs which Have Been Executed and Objects Whose Execution Was Intended.* 1886. Reprint, New York: Princeton Architectural Press, 1989.

Scott, Geoffrey. *The Architecture of Humanism: A Study in the History of Taste.* London: Constable, 1914.

Scott, Jonathan. *The Pleasures of Antiquity: British Collectors of Greece and Rome.* New Haven and London: Yale University Press, 2003.

Scott, Mick. *A View from the River.* Bexley Libraries and Museums Department, 1984.

Scully, Vincent. *The Earth, The Temple and the Gods: Greek Sacred Architecture.* New Haven and London: Yale University Press, 1962.

"Sculpture in England." *Builder* (7 January 1871): 1–3.

Searle, Muriel. *Chislehurst in Old Picture Postcards.* Zaltbommel, Netherlands: European Library, 1989.

Second Report of the Royal Commission on Historical Manuscripts (1871): Papers of the Rt. Hon. the Earl of Mount Edgcumbe. London: H.M.S.O., 1874.

Sedgwick, Romney, ed. *The House of Commons, 1715–1754.* 2 vols. London: published for the History of Parliament Trust by H.M.S.O., 1970.

Semper, Gottfried. *Vorläufige Bemerkungen über bemalte Architectur und Plastik bei den Alten.* Altona: J. F. Hammerich, 1834.

———. *The Four Elements of Architecture and Other Writings.* Trans. by Harry Francis Mallgrave and Wolfgang Hermann. Cambridge and New York: Cambridge University Press, 1989.

Serlio, Sebastiano. *Tutte l'Opere d'Architettura. . . .* Venice: Francesco de Franceschi Senese, 1634.

———. *Sebastiano Serlio on Architecture.* Vol. 1, *Books I–V of Tutte l'Opere d'Architettura et Prospetiva* [1737]. Trans. and ed. by Vaughan Hart and Peter Hicks. New Haven and London: Yale University Press, 1996.

Shanhagan, Roger [Robert Smirke and William Porden]. *The Exhibition, or a Second Anticipation, being Remarks on the Principal Works to be Exhibited Next Month at the Royal Academy. . . .* London: Richardson and Urquhart under the Royal Exchange, 1779.

Shaw, William Francis. *The Parish of Erith in Ancient and Modern Times.* London: Mitchell and Hughes, 1885.

Shelagh, M. Bond. "A Craftsman of Skill and Invention Emlyn's Work at St. George's Chapel, Windsor." *Country Life* 132 (13 September 1962): 607–9.

Sheppard, F. H. W., ed. *Survey of London.* Vols. 29–30, *The Parish of St. James Westminster. Part 1. South of Piccadilly.* Vols. 39–40, *The Grosvenor Estate in Mayfair. Part 1: General History* and *Part 2: The Buildings.* London: Athlone Press for the Greater London Council, 1960 and 1977–80.

Sherwood, Jennifer, and Nikolaus Pevsner. *Oxfordshire.* Buildings of England. Harmondsworth: Penguin, 1974.

The Shugborough Estate, A Souvenir Estate Guide. Pamphlet. Privately printed, 1999.

Shugborough, Staffordshire. Pamphlet. Rev. eds. London: National Trust, 1973, 1980.

Sicca, Cinzia, and Alison Yarrington, eds. *The Lustrous Trade: Material Culture and the History of Sculpture in England and Italy, c. 1700–c. 1860.* London and New York: Leicester University Press, 2000.

Skempton, A. W. "Samuel Wyatt and the Albion Mill." *Architectural History* 14 (1971): 53–73.

Skinner, Basil. *Scots in Italy in the 18th Century.* Edinburgh: Board of Trustees of the National Galleries of Scotland, 1966.

Smith, Arthur Hamilton, ed. *A Catalogue of the Ancient Marbles at Lansdowne House, based upon the work of Adolf Michaelis.* London: privately printed, 1889.

———. "Recent Additions to the Sculptures of the Parthenon." *Journal of Hellenic Studies* 13 (1892–93): 88–100.

Smith, [Auctioneer]. *A Catalogue of the Genuine Stock in Trade of Mr. Richard Hayward, Statuary, Deceased: Consisting of Elegant Marble Chimney Pieces, . . . Monuments, . . . Portland Stone Obelisk . . . : Which Will Be Sold by Auction by Mr. Smith on the Premises . . . on Tuesday, the 4th of November, 1800, and Two Following Days, at Eleven O'clock, (by Order of the Executors).* Sale cat. 4–6 November 1800. Copy in the Library, Courtauld Institute of Art, London, and the Getty Research Institute.

Smith, Bernard. *European Vision and the South Pacific.* 2nd ed. New Haven and London: Yale University Press, 1985.

Smith, H. Clifford. "A Catalogue and Valued Inventory of the Furniture and Works of Art . . . of Londonderry House Park Lane, W., The Property of the Most Honble. The Marquess of Londonderry." Typescript, 1939. Copy in the National Art Library, The Victoria and Albert Museum, London.

———. "Henry Keene: A Georgian Architect." *Country Life* 97 (30 March 1945): 556–57.

Smith, John Thomas. *Nollekens and His Times.* 1828. Rev. ed., London: Turnstile Press, 1949.

———. *A Book for a Rainy Day: or, Recollections of the Events of the Last Sixty-Six Years.* London: Richard Bentley, 1845.

Smyth, Anne-Marie. "Castle Restored to Be a Classical Pay-Off." *Evening Press* [Dublin] (14 May 1992): 7.

Snodin, Michael, ed. *Rococo: Art and Design in Hogarth's England.* Exh. cat. Victoria and Albert Museum. London: Trefoil Books and the Museum, 1984.

———. "Putting Adam into Context." Paper presented at the Association of Art Historians Conference, University of Central England in Birmingham, April 1994. In *Silver and Jewellery: Production and Consumption Since 1750.* Ed. by Kenneth Quickenden and Neal Adrian Quickenden. Birmingham, Article Press, 1995, pp. 13–20.

———. *Sir William Chambers*. Catalogues of Architectural Drawings in The Victoria and Albert Museum. London: V&A Publications, 1996.

———. "Adam Silver Reassessed." *Burlington Magazine* 139 (January 1997): 17–25.

Snodin, Michael, and John Styles. *Design and the Decorative Arts: Britain, 1500–1900.* London: V&A Publications, Distributed by Harry N. Abrams, 2001.

Solkin, David H. *Art on the Line. The Royal Academy Exhibitions at Somerset House, 1780–1836.* New Haven and London: Yale University Press, 2001.

Sotheby's London. *The Ashburnham Collection: Part II, Catalogue of Important French and English Furniture, Porcelain and Works of Art.* Sale cat. 26 June 1953.

———. *Property from the estate of Alfred J. Moran.* Sale cat. 2–3 November 1989, lot 358.

———. *Important English Furniture.* Sale cat. 29 November 2002.

———. *Important English Furniture.* Sale cat. 3 July 2003.

Sotheby's New York. *English Pottery.* Sale cat. 24 April 1982.

Souden, David. *Wimpole Hall, Cambridgeshire.* London: The National Trust, 1991.

Soufflot et l'architecture des lumières, colloquium proceedings, [Paris]: Ministère de l'environnement et du cadre de vie, Direction de l'architecture: Centre national de la recherche scientifique, 1980. 2nd ed. Paris: École Nationale Supérieure des Beaux-Arts, 1986.

Spencer House: A Brief History. [n.p., n.d.] Copy in the V&A Red Box Files, Furniture Department, Victoria and Albert Museum, London, Buildings File: London: Spencer House box 153 and at The Bard Graduate Center, New York.

Spencer, John, 7th Earl. "Spencer House. St. James's Place." Parts I and II. *Country Life* 60 (30 October 1926): 660–67; (6 November 1926): 698–704.

———. "Furniture at Spencer House." *Country Life* 60 (13 November 1926): 757–59.

Spencer, Terence John Bew. *Fair Greece! Sad Relic; Literary Philhellenism from Shakespeare to Byron.* London: Weidenfeld and Nicolson, 1954.

Spinazzola, Vittorio. *Le Arti decorative in Pompei e nel Museo nazionale di Napoli.* Milan: Bestetti and Tumminelli, 1928.

Squibb and Son, London. *An Extensive Collection Of Paintings; Fine Bronzes, Valuable Effects.* Sale cat. 12–21 May 1823.

Σ. Σ. [pseud.]. *British Society of Dilettanti Notes and Queries,* 2nd series, 9 (28 January 1860): 64–65.

St. Clair, William. *Lord Elgin and the Marbles.* 3rd rev. ed. Oxford and New York: Oxford University Press, 1998.

———. *That Greece Might Still be Free: The Philhellenes in the War of Independence.* New York and London: Oxford University Press, 1972.

———. "Rivals for the Ruined Piles." Review of *The Ruins of the Most Beautiful Monuments of Greece* by Julien-David Le Roy, trans. by David Britt, intro. by Robin Middleton. *Times Literary Supplement* (12 November 2004): 12–13.

Staël, Madame de [Anne-Louise-Germaine de]. *De l'Allemagne.* Ed. by Pauline la comtesse Jean de Pange. 5 vols. New ed. Paris: Hachette, 1958–60.

Staley, Allen. *Benjamin West: American Painter at the English Court.* Exh. cat. Baltimore Museum of Art, 1989.

Stamp, Gavin. *Alexander "Greek" Thomson.* London: Laurence King, 1999.

———, ed. *The Light of Truth and Beauty: The Lectures of Alexander "Greek" Thomson Architect 1817–1875.* Glasgow: Alexander Thomson Society, 1999.

Stamp, Gavin, and Sam McKinstry, eds. *"Greek" Thomson.* Edinburgh University Press, 1994.

State of Facts Relative to Greenwich Hospital. [London]: n.p., [1779].

Steegman, John. *The Rule of Taste from George I to George IV.* London: Macmillan and Co., 1936.

Stevenson, Christine. *Medicine and Magnificence: British Hospital and Asylum Architecture, 1660–1815.* New Haven and London: Yale University Press for the Paul Mellon Centre for Studies in British Art, 2000.

Stillman, Damie. *English Neo-Classical Architecture.* Vol. 1. London: A. Zwemmer; New York: Distributed in the USA by Sotheby's Publications: Harper and Row, 1988.

Stone, Lawrence, ed. *An Imperial State at War. Britain from 1689 to 1815.* London and New York: Routledge, 1994.

Stowe Landscape Gardens. London: National Trust, 1997.

Strabo. *Geography.* Trans. by Horace Leonard Jones. 8 vols. Loeb Classical Library. Cambridge, MA: Harvard University Press, 1988–2000.

Strickland, H. "Belvedere as It Was." *Erith Times, Belvedere and Abbey Wood Chronicle* (26 January 1912). Extract in "Erith Borough Council Correspondence: Belvedere House, 1947–1960," Bexley Libraries and Archives service.

Stroud, Dorothy. *Henry Holland: His Life and Architecture.* London: Country Life, 1966.

———. "The Charms of Natural Landscape. The Park and Gardens at Wimpole." Part II. *Country Life* 166 (13 September 1979): 758–62.

Strutt, Joseph. *Biographical Dictionary of Engravers.* 2 vols. London: Robert Faulder, 1785–86.

Stuart, James. *De Obelisco Caesaris Augusti e Campo Martio nuperrime effosso epistola Jacobi Stuart Angli ad Carolam Wentworth Comitem de Malton. . . .* Rome: Niccolò and Marco Pagliarini, 1750.

———. *A Discourse Delivered to the Students of the Royal Academy, on the Distribution of Prizes, December 10, 1772.* London: W. Griffin and T. Davies, 1773.

653

Antiquities

Stuart, James, and Nicholas Revett. *The Antiquities of Athens.* Vol. 1. London: printed by J. Haberkorn, 1762. Vol. 2, ed. by William Newton. London: printed by John Nichols, [ca. 1790]. [Although the title page is dated 1787, several plates are dated 1789, and the first review of the book appeared in February 1790.] Vol. 3. ed. by Willey Reveley. London: printed by J. Nichols, 1794. Vol. 4, ed. by Joseph Woods. London: printed by T. Bensley, for J. Taylor, 1816.

———. *The Antiquities of Athens, and Other Places in Greece, Sicily, etc.,: Supplementary to the Antiquites of Athens by James Stuart . . . and Nicholas Revett. . . .* Vol. 5. London: Priestley and Weale, 1830.

———. *Les antiquités d'Athènes et de l'Attique.* Trans. by Jacques Ignace Hittorff. 5 vols. Paris: Librairie Centrale d'Architecture, 1881.

Stuart [no relation to James Stuart]. *Critical Observations on the Buildings and Improvements of London.* 2nd ed. London: J. Dodsley, 1771. Reprint, ed. by Dianne S. Ames. Augustan Reprint Society, publication no. 189–90. Los Angeles: William Andrews Clark Memorial Library, University of California, 1978.

Sulivan, Richard Joseph. *A Tour Through Parts of England, Scotland and Wales in 1778.* 2nd rev. ed. London: T. Becket, 1785.

Sullivan, M. G. "Rapin, Hume and the Identity of the Historian in Eighteenth Century England." *History of European Ideas* 28 (2002): 145–62.

———. "Female Inheritance, Workshop Collboration and Strategies for Survival: The Nost Family Workshop (1676–1780)." Forthcoming.

Summerson, John. "The Society's House: An Architectural Study." *Journal of the Royal Society of Arts* 102 (15 October 1954): 920–33.

———. *Architecture in Britain, 1530–1830.* 1953. Rev. ed., Harmondsworth: Penguin Books, 1965.

———. *Georgian London.* London: Barrie and Jenkins, 1988.

Sumner, Ann, and Greg Smith, eds. *Thomas Jones (1742–1803): An Artist Rediscovered.* Yale University Press in association with National Museums and Galleries of Wales, 2003.

The Susan Burney Letters Project. "Letter Extract 2: The Gordon Riots, St. Martin's Lane, London, 8 June 1780." Humanities Research Centre, University of Nottingham. http://www.nottingham.ac.uk/hrc/projects/burney/letters/gordon.phtml. Accessed 15 July 2004.

Sutherland, Carol Humphrey Vivian, and Robert Andrew Glindinning Carson. *Roman Imperial Coinage.* Vol. 6, *From Diocletian's reform (A.D. 294) to the death of Maximinus (A.D. 313).* London: Spink and Son, 1967.

Sweet, Rosemary. *Antiquaries: The Discovery of the Past in Eighteenth-Century Britain.* London and New York: Hambledon and London, 2004.

Sykes, Christopher Simon. *Private Palaces: Life in the Great London Houses.* London: Chatto and Windus, 1985; New York: Viking Press, 1986.

Syson, Luke. "Designs on Posterity: Drawings for Medals. The British Museum, 11 September–25 October 1992." In *Designs on Posterity: Drawings for Medals.* Ed. by Mark Jones. Exh. cat. The British Museum, London. Collection of essays first presented at the 1992 Congress of the Fédération Internationale de la Médaille (London). London: British Art Medal Trust, 1994, pp. 233–75.

Szambien, Werner. *Jean-Nicolas-Louis Durand, 1760–1834: De l'imitation à la norme.* Paris: Picard, 1984.

T. "Wimpole Hall, Cambridgeshire, a Seat of Viscount Clifden." *Country Life* 23 (15 February 1908): 234–41.

Tanoulas, Tasos. "Through the Broken Looking Glass: The Acciaiuoli Palace in the Propylaea Reflected in the Villa of Lorenzo il Magnifico at Poggio a Caiano." *Bollettino d'arte* 82 (April/June 1997): 1–32.

Taylor, George Crosbie. "Nuneham Courtenay, Oxon." Part II. *Country Life* 90 (14 November 1941): 910–13.

Taylor, John. *Records of My Life.* 2 vols. London: E. Bull, 1832.

The Topographer for the Year 1790, Containing a Variety of Original Articles Illustrative of the Local History and Antiquities of England. Vol. 3. London: J. Robson, J. Walker, C. Stalker, 1791.

Thomas, John. "Josiah Wedgwood's Portrait Medallions of Fellows of the Royal Society." *Notes and Records of the Royal Society of London* 18 (June 1963): 45–63.

Thomson, Alexander. "Art and Architecture: A Course of Four Lectures." Part 3. *British Architect* 2 (1874): 50–52, 82–84.

Thornton, Peter. "Letter to the Editor: Proto-neo-Classicism: The Battle of the Giants." *Apollo* 87 (April 1968): 310–11.

———. "A Very Special Year. The Victoria and Albert Museum's Furniture Acquisitions in 1977." *Connoisseur* 198 (June 1978): 138–45.

———. *Form and Decoration: Innovation in the Decorative Arts, 1470–1870.* New York: Abrams, 1998.

Thornton, Peter, and John Hardy. "The Spencer Furniture at Althorp." Parts I–III. *Apollo* n.s. 87 (March 1968): 179–89; n.s. 87 (June 1968): 440–51; n.s. 88 (October 1968): 266–77.

Tiernan, John. "The Triumphal Arch, Shugborough Park, Staffordshire: Repair Works, 1988–93." *Transactions of the Association for Studies in the Conservation of Historic Buildings* 19 (1994): 3–15.

Tipping, H. Avray. "Furniture at Althorp." Parts I and II. *Country Life* 49 (11 June 1921): 721–23; 49 (18 June 1921): 771–73.

———. "Wentworth Woodhouse, Yorkshire." Part III. *Country Life* 56 (4 October 1924): 512–19.

———. "Eighteenth-Century Staircase Lanterns." *Country Life* 63 (14 April 1928): xlviii–iii.

"To Select One of the Many. . . ." *Art Quarterly* 10 (Summer 1992): 20.

Tomalin, Claire. *Samuel Pepys: The Unequalled Self.* London: Viking, 2002.

Tomlin, Maurice. *Catalogue of Adam Period Furniture, Victoria and Albert Museum.* London, South Kensington: Victoria and Albert Museum, 1972.

Tournikiotis, Panayotis, ed. *The Parthenon and Its Impact in Modern Times.* Trans. by Cox and Solman. Athens: Melissa, 1994.

Toynbee, Paget, ed. "Walpole's Journals of Visits to Country Seats." Walpole Society annual, vol. 16 (1927–28): 9–80.

Traversari, Gustavo. *L'Arco dei Sergi. Rilievi e riconstruzioni di I. Gismondi.* Podova: CEDAM, 1971.

Treasures from Althorp. Exh. cat. London: Victoria and Albert Museum, 1970.

Trevilyan, W. B., and James Plumtree. "Journal of a Tour to the Source of the River Cam Made in July 1800." Typescript in Cambridge Central Library, Cambridgeshire Collection.

Trotter, Thomas. *Medicina Nautica: An Essay on the Diseases of Seaman.* 3 vols. London: T. Cadell, Jr., and W. Davies, 1797–1803.

Turberville, Arthur Stanley, ed. *Johnson's England: An Account of the Life and Manners of His Age.* Vol. 1. Oxford: Clarendon Press, 1933.

Turner, Nicholas. "John Bouverie as a Collector of Drawings." *Burlington Magazine* 136 (February 1994): 90–99.

Twelfth Report of the Royal Commission on Historical Manuscripts. Vol. 1. London: H.M.S.O., 1890.

Udy, David. "Neo-Classicism and the Evolution of Adam's Vase Design in Silver." *Antique Collector* 43 (August 1972): 192–97.

———. "The Classical Sources of English Neoclassical Furniture." *Arte Illustrata* 6, no. 52 (February 1973): 96–104.

———. "New Light on the Sources of English Neo-Classical Design." *Apollo* 103 (March 1976): 202–7.

———. "The Furniture of James Stuart and Robert Adam." *Discovering Antiques: The Story of World Antiques,* no. 42 (1971): 994–98.

Uglow, Jenny. *Hogarth: A Life and a World.* New York: Farrar, Straus and Giroux, 1997.

———. *The Lunar Men: The Friends who Made the Future, 1730–1810.* London: Faber and Faber, 2002.

Van Pelt, Robert Jan, and Carroll William Westfall. *Architectural Principles in the Age of Historicism.* New Haven and London: Yale University Press, 1991.

Vasari, Giorgio. *Lives of the Painters, Sculptors and Architects.* 2 vols. Trans. by Gaston du C. de Vere. Ed. by David Ekserdjian. Every man's Library. London: David Campbell; Distributed by Random House, 1996.

Vasi, Giuseppe. *Delle magnificenze di Roma antica e moderna: libro secondo che contiene le piazza principali di Roma con obelischi colone, ed altri ornamenti . . . da Guiseppe Vasi da Corleone . . . e dal medesimo fidelissimamente disegnate, ed inscise in rame, secondo lo stato presente, a' quail si aggiunge una breve spiegazione di tutti le cose notabili in dette piazza. . . .* Vol. 2. Rome: Stamperia di Apollo, Presso gli Eredi Barbiellini, 1752.

Veale, Elspeth. "The Marquess of Rockingham's House in Wimbledon." *Georgian Group Journal* 14 (2004): 243–60.

Walter Veit, ed. *Captain James Cook: Image and Impact, South Seas Discoveries and the World of Letters.* Melbourne: Hawthorn Press, 1972.

Vertue, George. "Vertue—III." Walpole Society annual, vol. 22 (1933–34).

Vitruvius Pollio. *Les dix livres d'architecture de Vitruve.* Ed. and trans. by Claude Perrault. 1673; 2nd ed. Paris: Jean Baptiste Coignard, 1684.

Vitruvius Pollio. *The Architecture of M. Vitruvius Pollio.* Trans. by William Newton. Ed. by James Newton. Vol. 2. London: James Newton, 1791.

———. *The Civil Architecture of Vitruvius: Comprising those Books of the Author which relate to the Public and Private Edifices of Ancients.* Trans. by William Wilkins. London: Longman, Hurst, Rees, Orme, and Brown, 1812–17.

———. *On Architecture.* 2 vols. Trans. by Frank Stephen Granger. Loeb Classical Library. 1931–34. London: Heinemann; Cambridge: Harvard University Press, 1983–99.

———. *Vitruvius: Ten Books of Architecture.* Trans. and ed. by Ingrid D. Rowland and Thomas Noble Howe. Cambridge and New York: Cambridge University Press, 1999.

Vivian, Frances. *The Consul Smith Collection.* Munich: Hirmer Verleg, 1989.

Von Buttlar, Adrian. *Leo von Klenze: Leben, Werk, Vision.* Munich: C. H. Beck, 1999.

A Voyage Round the World, in His Majesty's Ship the Dolphin, Commanded by the Honourable Commodore Byron . . . By an Officer on Board the Said Ship. London: J. Newbery and F. Newbery, 1767.

W. W. W. "The Statue of Niobe." *British Society of Dilettanti, Notes and Queries,* 4th series, 4 (28 August 1869): 170–71.

Waagen, Dr. Gustav Friedrich. *Galleries and Cabinets of Art in Great Britain Being an Account of More Than Forty Collections of Paintings, Drawings, Sculptures, MSS., and C. Visited in 1854 and 1856, and Now for the First Time Described. . . .* London: John Murray, 1857.

Waddell, Gene. "The Principal Design Methods for Greek Doric Temples and Their Modification for the Parthenon." *Architectural History* 45 (2002): 1–31.

Walker, Stephanie, ed. *Vasemania: Neoclassical Form and Ornament in Europe: Selections from the Metropolitan Museum of Art.* Exh. cat. The Bard Graduate Center, New York. London and New Haven: Yale University Press for the Bard Graduate Center and the Metropolitan Museum of Art, 2004.

Wallace, Richard W. "Joseph Goupy's Satire of George Frederic Handel." *Apollo* 117 (February 1983): 104–5.

Waller, Maureen A. *1700: Scenes from London Life.* New York: Four Walls Eight Windows, 2000.

Walpole, Horace. *Anecdotes of Painting in England; [1760–1795]. . . .* Ed. by Ralph N. Wornum. 3 vols, Rev. ed. London: Swan, Sonnenschein, Lowrey and Co., 1888.

———. *Anecdotes of Painting in England; [1760–1795], with some Account of the Principal Artists; and Incidental Notes on Other Arts.* Vol 5. Ed. by Frederick Whiley Hilles and Philip B. Daghlian. London: H. Milford, Oxford University Press; New Haven and London: Yale University Press, 1937.

———. *The Yale Edition of Horace Walpole's Correspondence.* Vol. 10, *Horace Walpole's Correspondence with George Montagu,* ed. by W. S. Lewis, and Ralph S. Brown, Jr. New Haven and London: Yale University Press; London: H. Milford, Oxford University Press, 1941.

———. *The Yale Edition of Horace Walpole's Correspondence.* Vol. 29, *Horace Walpole's Correspondence with William Mason,* ed. by W. S. Lewis, Grover Cronin, Jr., and Charles H. Bennett. New Haven and London: Yale University Press, 1955.

———. *The Yale Edition of Horace Walpole's Correspondence.* Vol. 35, *Horace Walpole's Correspondence with John Chute, Richard Bentley, the Earl of Strafford, Sir William Hamilton, the Earl and Countess Harcourt [and] George Hardinge,* ed. by W. S. Lewis, A. Dayle Wallace, and Robert A. Smith. New Haven and London: Yale University Press, 1973.

The Walpole Society Online. "The Memoirs of Thomas Jones, Pencerrig." Transcribed from NLW MS 23812D. http://www.llgc.org.uk/pencerrig/ thjones_s_001.htm. Accessed 1 July 2004.

Walpoole, George Augustus, ed. *The New British Traveller.* London: Alexander Hogg, 1784.

Ward-Jackson, Peter. *English Furniture Designs of the 18th Century.* London: Victoria and Albert Museum, 1958.

———. *Italian Drawings.* Vol. 1, *14th–16th Century.* Victoria and Albert Museum Catalogues. London: H.M.S.O., 1979.

Ware, Isaac. *A Complete Body of Architecture: Adorned with Plans and Elevations.* London: T. Osborne and J. Shipton, 1756.

Warren, T. Herbert. "Nuneham Courtney, Oxfordshire." *Country Life* 34 (29 November 1913): 746–55.

Waterhouse, Ellis. *Painting in Britain, 1530–1790.* Pelican History of Art. London: Penguin Books, 1953.

———. *Painting in Britain, 1530 to 1790.* The Pelican History of Art. 1953. 4th ed., London: Penguin Books, 1978.

Watkin, David. *The Life and Work of C. R. Cockerell.* London: A. Zwemmer, 1974.

———. *The Triumph of the Classical: Cambridge Architecture, 1804–1834.* Exh. cat. Cambridge University Press for the Fitzwilliam Museum, 1977.

Watkin, *Athenian Stuart* **(1982)**
———. *Athenian Stuart: Pioneer of the Greek Revival.* London: George Allen and Unwin, 1982.

———. *The English Vision: The Picturesque in Architecture, Landscape and Garden Design.* New York: Harper and Row, 1982.

———. *Sir John Soane, Enlightenment Thought and the Royal Academy Lectures.* Cambridge and New York: Cambridge University Press, 1996.

———. *The Architect King: George III and the Culture of the Enlightenment.* London: Royal Collection Publications, 2004.

———. "Thomas Hope's House in Duchess Street [Newly Discovered Drawings by Adam, Tatham, and Hope]." *Apollo* 159 (March 2004): 31–39.

Watkin, David, et al. *A House in Town: 22 Arlington Street, Its Owners and Builders.* Ed. by Peter Campbell. London: B. T. Batsford in association with Eagle Star Holdings PLC, 1984.

Watson, Chris. "John Holmes: A View on his Life and Work." *Antiquarian Horology* 27 (March 2003): 289–301.

———. "John Holmes: Time for a Further Look." *Antiquarian Horology* 27 (December 2003): 643–53.

Weale, John. *The Pictorial Handbook of London: Comprising Its Antiquities, Architecture, Arts. . . .* Bohn's Illustrated Library. London: Henry G. Bohn, 1854.

Webb, Daniel Carless. *Observations and Remarks during Four Excursions Made to Various Parts of Great Britain. . . .* London: Allen and Co., 1812.

Webb, E. A., G. W. Miller and J. Beckwith, comps. *The History of Chislehurst, Its Church, Manors, and Parish.* 1899. Reprint, Baron Books Buckingham for the Chislehurst Society, 1999.

Webb, Margaret. "Chimney-Pieces by Scheemakers." *Country Life* 121 (14 March 1957): 491–93.

Webb, Marjorie Isabel. *Michael Rysbrack: Sculptor.* London: Country Life: 1954.

Wedgwood, Josiah. *Letters of Josiah Wedgwood.* Ed. by Katherine Euphemia, Lady Farrer. 3 vols. Manchester: E. J. Morten in association with the Trustees of the Wedgwood Museum, [1973].

Weinreb, Ben, and Christopher Hibbert, eds. *The London Encyclopaedia.* London: Macmillan, 1983.

Weiss, Roberto. *The Renaissance Discovery of Classical Antiquity.* 2nd ed. Oxford and New York: B. Blackwell, 1988.

Welcome to Newby, Home of the Compton Family. Heritage House Group Ltd., 2004.

Westmacott, Richard. "An Address to British Sculptors." *Builder* 19 (29 June 1861): 438.

Wheler, George. *A Journey into Greece, by George Wheler, Esq; In Company of Dr Spon of Lyons. In Six Books . . . with Variety of Sculptures.* London: Cademan, Kettlewell and Churchill, 1682.

Whinney, Margaret. *Sculpture in Britain, 1530–1830.* Harmondsworth, Eng.: Penguin Books, 1964. 2nd ed. Revised by John Physick. London and New York: Penguin Books, 1988.

White, Roger, and Caroline Lightburn, eds. *Late Georgian Classicism: Pages Given at Georgian Group Symposium, 1987.* London: Georgian Group, 1988.

Whitehurst, John. "Experiments on Ignited Substances. By Mr John Whitehurst, in a Letter to James Stuart, Esquire, F. R. S." *Philosophical Transactions of the Royal Society* 66, part 2 (1776): 575–77.

Whitley, William Thomas. *Artists and Their Friends in England, 1700–1799.* 2 vols. London and Boston: The Medici Society, 1928.

Whitney, Lois. "English Primitivistic Themes of Epic Origins." *Modern Philology* 21 (May 1924): 337–78.

Wiebenson, Dora. *Sources of Greek Revival Architecture.* London: A. Zwemmer; University Park: Pennsylvania State University Press, 1969.

Wiebenson, Dora, and Claire Baines. *The Mark J. Millard Architectural Collection.* Vol. 1, *French Books: Sixteenth through Nineteenth Centuries.* Washington D.C.: National Gallery of Art; New York: Braziller, 1993.

Wightwick, George. *The Palace of Architecture: A Romance of Art and History.* London: James Fraser, 1840.

Wilk, Christopher, ed. *Western Furniture, 1350 to the Present Day in the Victoria and Albert Museum.* New York: Cross River, 1996.

Wilkins, William. *The Antiquities of Magna Graecia.* London: Longman, Hurst, Orme, and Rees, 1807.

———. *Atheniensia, or, Remarks on the Topography and Buildings of Athens.* London: John Murray, 1816.

Wilkinson, Clive. *The British Navy and the State in the 18th Century.* Woodbridge: The Boydell Press in Association with the National Maritime Museum, 2004.

Willett, Ralph. *A Description of the Library at Merly in the County of Dorset.* London: printed for the author by John Nichols, 1785.

Williams, A. F. Basil. *The Whig Supremacy, 1714–1760.* Oxford: Clarendon Press, 1962.

Williams, Glyndwr, ed. *Documents Relating to Anson's Voyage Round the World, 1740–1744.* London: Navy Records Society, 1967.

Wills, Geoffrey. "Early Signs of Neo-Classicism, and the Goût Grec." *Apollo* 96 (October 1972): 318–21.

Wilson, Christopher, et al. *The New Bell's Cathedral Guides: Westminster Abbey.* London: Bell and Hyman, 1986.

Wilson, Gillian. "The Kedleston Fountain." *Journal of the J. Paul Getty Museum* 11 (1983): 1–12.

Wilson, Ken. *Camden Place, Chislehurst: The Story of a Country House in Words and Drawings.* Bromley Library Service, 1981.

Wilson, Michael. *William Kent: Architect, Designer, Painter, Gardener, 1685–1748.* London: Routledge, Kegan, Paul, 1984.

Wilson, Richard, and Alan Mackley. *Creating Paradise. The Building of the English Country House, 1660–1880.* London and New York: Hambledon and London, 2000.

Wilton, Andrew, and Ilaria Bignamini, eds. *The Lure of Italy in the Eighteenth Century.* Exh. cat. London: Tate Gallery, 1996.

Wilton-Ely, John. "Pompeian and Etruscan Tastes in the Neo-Classical Country House Interior." In *The Fashioning and Functioning of the British Country House.* Ed. by Gervase Jackson-Stops, et al. Studies in the History of Art, vol. 25. Washington, D.C.: National Gallery of Art; Hanover [NH]: Distributed by the University Press of New England, 1989.

Wimpole Hall The Park. London: The National Trust, 1983.

Winckelmann, Johann Joachim *Anmerkungen über die Baukunst der Alten.* Leipzig: J. G. Dyck, 1762.

———. *Anmerkungen über die Geschichte der Kunst des Alterthums.* Dresden: Waltherischen Hof Buchhandlung, 1767.

———. *Briefe.* Ed. by Hans Diepolder and Walther Rehm. 4 vols. Berlin: De Gruyter, 1952–57.

———. *Winckelmann: Writings on Art.* Ed. by David Irwin. London: Phaidon, 1972.

———. *The History of Ancient Art.* 2 vols. Trans. by Giles Henry Lodge. 1849–73; London: Sampson Low, Marston, Searle and Rivington, 1881.

Withers, Robert. *Survey of Estates Belonging to the Right Honorable Philip, Earl of Hardwicke K. G. Situate in the Parishes of Wimpole and Arrington on the County of Cambridge.* Cambridge: privately printed, 1815; rev. ed. 1828.

Wolseley, Viscountess. "Historic Houses of Sussex, No. 69 Ashburnham Place." *Sussex County Magazine* 7 (January 1933): 6–13.

Wood, Henry Trueman. *A History of the Royal Society of Arts.* London: John Murray, 1913.

Wood, Robert. *The Ruins of Palmyra, otherwise Tedmor, in the Desart.* London: [Robert Wood], 1753.

———. *The Ruins of Balbec, otherwise Heliopolis in Coelosyria.* London: n.p., 1757.

Woodley, Roger. "Robert Mylne (1733–1811): The Bridge between Architecture and Engineering." Ph.D. dissertation. Courtauld Institute of Art, University of London, 1998.

Wooler, Oliver. *The Great Estates: Six Country Houses in the London Borough of Bexley.* London: Bexley Council Directorate of Education and Leisure Services, 2000.

The Worshipful Company of Fan Makers. "Company History." http://www.fanmakers.com/history.htm. Accessed 4 July 2004.

Worsley, Giles. "The First Greek Revival Architecture." *Burlington Magazine* 127 (April 1985): 226–29.

———. "Nuneham Park Revisited—I and II." *Country Life* 177 (3 January 1985): 16–19; (10 January 1985): 64–67.

———. "Hornby Castle, Yorkshire." *Country Life* 183 (29 June 1989): 188–93.

———. "Stuart at Sion." *Country Life* 184 (4 October 1990): 187.

———. "Out from Adam's Shadow." *Country Life* 186 (14 May 1992): 100–103.

———. "Attribution Re-Inforced." *Country Life* 186 (30 July 1992): 66

———. "Spencer House, London." *Country Life* 186 (24/31 December 1992): 38–41.

———. *Classical Architecture in Britain: The Heroic Age.* New Haven and London: Yale University Press, 1995.

———. *England's Lost Houses: From the Archives of Country Life.* London: Aurum, 2002.

Worsley, Richard. *Museum Worsleyanum; or,*

A Collection of Antique Basso Relievos Bustos, Statues and Gems. . . . 2 vols. London: [The Shakespeare Press, 1798–1803].

Wragg, Brian. *The Life and Works of John Carr of York*. Ed. by Giles Worsley. New York: Oblong, 2000.

Wratten, Nigel. *The History and Architecture of No. 15 St. James's Square*. N.p., n.d.

Wyndham, Maud. *Chronicles of the Eighteenth Century, Founded on the Correspondence of Sir Thomas Lyttelton and His Family*. Vol. 2. London: Hodder and Stoughton, 1924.

Wynne, Michael. "Members from Great Britain and Ireland of the Florentine Accademia del Disegno 1700–1865." *Burlington Magazine* 132 (August 1990): 536.

Yeomans, David. *The Architect and the Carpenter*. Exh. cat. London: RIBA Heinz Gallery, 1992.

Yorke, James. *English Furniture*. New York: Gallery Books, 1990.

Yorke, Philip. "The Travel Journal of Philip Yorke, 1744–63." Ed. by Joyce Godber. The Bedfordshire Historical Record Society annual, vol. 47 (1968).

Young, Arthur. *A Six Weeks Tour through the Southern Counties of England and Wales*. London: W. Nicoll, 1768. 2nd ed. London: W. Strahan, 1769. 3rd ed., London: W. Strahan, W. Nicholl, T. Cadell; Salisbury: B. Collins; Edinburgh: J. Balfour, 1772.

———. *A Six Months Tour through the North of England*. . . . 2 vols. London: W. Strahan, et al., 1770.

Young, Hilary, ed. *The Genius of Wedgwood*. Exh. cat. London: Victoria and Albert Museum, 1995.

Zabaglia, Niccola. *Castelli e Ponti di Maestro Niccola Zabaglia con alcune ingegnose pratiche e con la descrizione del trasporto dell' Obelisco Vaticano e di altri del Cavaliere Domenico Fontana*. Ed. by Filippo Maria Renazzi. 2nd ed. Rome: Crispino Puccinelli, 1824.

Index

Illustrations are indicated by italic page numbers.

Ornaments

The ornaments used throughout the book are engravings selected from the four volumes of *Antiquities of Athens* (Courtesy of the Library, The Bard Graduate Center for Studies in the Decorative Arts, Design, and Culture, New York):

Endpapers: Foldout map of Greece Archipelago, vol. 3 (1794).
Half title page: detail of fig. 10-38.
Preface (p. 10): vol. 8 (1794): chap. 5, p. 35.
Chap. 1 (p. 19): vol. 2 (ca. 1790): chap. 5, p. 37.
Chap. 2 (p. 59): vol. 1 (1762): preface, p. 1.
Chap. 2 (p. 90): vol. 1 (1762): chap. 1, p. 6.
Chap. 3 (p. 103): vol. 1 (1762): chap. 1, p. 1.
Chap. 4 (p. 147): vol. 1 (1762): chap. 3, p. 13.
Chap. 5 (p. 195): vol. 1 (1762): chap. 5, p. 37.
Chap. 5 (p. 258): vol. 4 (1816): chap 9, p. 53.
Chap. 6 (p. 265): vol. 4 (1816): chap. 1, p. 5.
Chap. 7 (p. 317): vol. 1 (1762): chap. 4, p. 27.
Chap. 8 (p. 355): vol. 4 (1816): chap. 4, p. 19.
Chap. 9 (p. 385): vol. 3 (1794): chap. 9, p. 53.
Chap. 10 (p. 413): vol. 4 (1816): chap. 2, p. 11.
Chap. 11 (p. 467): vol. 4 (1816): chap. 6, p. 33.
Chap. 11 (p. 490): vol. 3 (1794): chap. 6, p. 43.
Chap. 12 (p. 495): vol. 1 (1762): dedication page.
Chap. 13 (p. 515): vol. 3 (1794): after p. xviii.
Part title (p. 549): detail from fig. 10-38.
Appendix (p. 550): vol. 4 (1816): preface p. 4.
Chronology (p. 579): vol. 4 (1816): chap. 1, p. 9.
Checklist (p. 588): vol. 3 (1794): chap. 6, p. 41.
Bibliography (p. 626): vol. 1 (1762), title page.

Photocredits

Unless listed below, photographs were taken or supplied by the lending institutions, organizations, or individuals credited in the picture captions and are protected by © (copyright). Most names are not repeated here.

Dirk Bakker: fig. 6-60.

©Bildarchiv Preussischer Kulturbesitz, Berlin: Antikensammlung, SMB / Ingrid Geske, fig. 10-54; Kupferstichkabinett, SMB / Jörg P. Anders, fig. 13-23; Nationalgalerie, SMB / Jörg P. Anders, fig. 13-21.

©Clive Boursnell: figs. 5-76 through 5-85.

By kind permission of Sir Robert Clerk of Penicuik Bt.: fig. 10-81.

Courtauld Institute of Art, London: Conway Library, figs. 9-18, 9-20; Photographic Survey, figs. 4-22, 5-4, 9-22.

©Country Life Picture Library, London: fig. 9-2.

English Heritage – National Monuments Record, Swindon: / Hallam Ashley, fig. 13-8; / G. Barnes, fig. 13-5; / © Nicholas Cooper, fig. 1-23; / Bill Drummond, fig. 7-12; / L. Herbert-Felton, figs. 5-51, 5-67, 5-68; / M. A. Keeling, fig. 1-26; / H. Bedford Lemere, figs. 5-87, 5-90, 5-92, 5-94, 5-97, 10-47; / Eric de Mare, fig. 1-28; / G. B. Mason, fig. 1-32.

Michael Erwee: figs. 3-15, 10-36.

©Sir Nicholas Goodison: figs. 11-28.

©Hunterian Museum and Art Gallery, University of Glasgow: figs. 4-2, 12-18.

Istituto Nazionale per la Grafica, Rome, By kind permission of the Ministero per i Beni e le Attività Culturali: figs. 3-4, 3-5.

©Leeds Museums and Art Galleries (Temple Newsam House), UK / Bridgeman Art Library, London: fig. 4-18.

The late Earl of Lichfield and Staffordshire Record Office, Reproduced by courtesy of the late Earl of Lichfield: figs. 2-27, 9-8.

Library of Congress Prints and Photographs Division, Washington, DC: / George N. Barnard, fig. 13-34; / Jack Boucher, fig. 13-31; / William Henry Jackson, Detroit Publishing Co., figs. 13-30, 13-32; / B. L. Singley, Keystone View Co., fig. 13-36; / B. Wallace: fig. 13-33.

©National Museum of Antiquities, Leiden, The Netherlands: fig. 10-44.

©Neumeister Münchener Kunstauktionshaus, Munich: fig. 4-3 (Auction 138–Lot 1679).

The National Trust Photo Library, Swindon, ©NTPL: figs. 4-23, 7-15; / Peter Aprahamian, figs. 7-26, 7-28, 7-29, 7-30; / John Blake, fig. 7-13; / Christopher Hill, figs. 4-37, 7-27; / John Hammond, figs. 4-9, 6-30, 6-31, 6-32, 6-33, 11-18, 11-19, 11-25; / Nadia Mackenzie, fig. 11-24; / Peter Rogers Ltd., fig. 10-71; / Bruce White, figs. 4-27, 4-28, 6-12, 6-13, 6-34, 6-36, 7-1, 7-2, 7-6, 7-11, 7-20, 7-21, 7-24, 7-31, 7-35, 7-36, 7-38, 7-39, 7-40, 7-48, 10-8, 10-72, 10-73, 11-1, 11-21, 11-22, 11-23, chronology fig. C4; / Mike Williams, figs. 7-3, 7-9.

©Partridge Fine Arts Plc, London: fig. 10-52.

Prudence Cuming Associates Ltd. / Simon Robertson, figs. 9-1, 9-3, 9-4

The Royal Collection © 2006 Her Majesty Queen Elizabeth II: figs. 4-7, 10-51, 11-29.

Réunion des Musées Nationaux, Paris, ©Photo RMN / Réne-Gabriel Ojéda, fig. 10-9.

Sheffield Archives, Reproduced by permission of the Head of Libraries, Archives and Information, Sheffield City Council, The Wentworth Woodhouse Muniments have been accepted in lieu of Inheritance Tax by Her Majesty's Government and allocated to Sheffield City Council: fig. 2-13.

©Sotheby's Picture Library, London: fig. 10-16.

©Spencer House Limited: / Mark Fiennes, fig. 5-9, 5-12, 5-13, 5-16, 5-30, 5-34, 5-35, 5-36, 5-40; / Bruce White, figs. 5-1, 5-8, 5-14, 5-18, 5-19, 5-20, 5-22, 5-23, 5-24, 5-29, 5-32, 5-41, 5-42, 5-43, 5-44, 5-45, 5-46, 5-47, 10-39, 10-75.

V&A Images / The Victoria and Albert Museum, London: figs. 1-5, 1-8, 3-6, 4-31, 5-5, 5-15, 5-17, 5-53, 5-55, 5-56, 5-57, 5-60, 5-61, 5-93, 7-41, 9-11, 9-14, 10-1, 10-14, 10-19, 10-22, 10-26, 10-32, 10-33, 10-37, 10-43, 10-58, 10-61, 11-7, 11-11, 11-15, 11-20, 11-26, 11-27, 13-39.

Courtesy of Robert Weighton: fig. 4-15.

Bruce White: ornaments listed above and figs. 1-24, 1-29, 2-2, 3-22, 3-23, 3-26, 3-27, 3-33, 3-34, 3-36, 3-37, 4-6, 4-13, 4-17, 4-20, 4-24, 5-21, 5-25, 5-31, 5-38, 5-39, 5-59, 5-62, 6-15, 6-16, 6-17, 6-18, 6-21, 6-22, 6-24, 6-25, 6-37, 6-38, 6-43, 6-48, 6-50, 6-52, 6-53, 6-54, 6-55, 6-66, 7-5, 7-7, 7-8, 7-10, 7-17, 7-18, 7-19, 7-23, 7-25, 7-32, 7-33, 7-43, 8-1, 8-2, 8-3, 8-4, 8-8, 8-11, 8-18, 8-19, 8-22, 8-23, 8-24, 8-38, 9-5, 9-6, 9-7, 9-9, 9-10, 9-12, 9-13, 9-15, 9-16, 10-5, 10-20, 10-25, 10-27, 10-28, 10-29, 10-30, 10-34, 10-38, 10-41, 10-42, 10-46, 10-48, 10-49, 10-50, 10-53, 10-55, 10-56, 10-57, 10-60, 10-62, 10-64, 10-66, 10-67, 10-68, 10-69, 10-70, 10-78, 10-79, 10-80, 11-6, 11-12, 11-13, 11-16, 11-17, 13-2, 13-6, 13-12, checklist no. 148.